W9-CTW-416

FOR REFERENCE

Do Not Take From This Room

Contemporary
Literary Criticism

Guide to Gale Literary Criticism Series

For criticism on	You need these Gale series
Authors now living or who died after December 31, 1959	*CONTEMPORARY LITERARY CRITICISM (CLC)*
Authors who died between 1900 and 1959	*TWENTIETH-CENTURY LITERARY CRITICISM (TCLC)*
Authors who died between 1800 and 1899	*NINETEENTH-CENTURY LITERATURE CRITICISM (NCLC)*
Authors who died between 1400 and 1799	*LITERATURE CRITICISM FROM 1400 TO 1800 (LC)* *SHAKESPEAREAN CRITICISM (SC)*
Authors who died before 1400	*CLASSICAL AND MEDIEVAL LITERATURE CRITICISM (CMLC)*
Authors of books for children and young adults	*CHILDREN'S LITERATURE REVIEW (CLR)*
Black writers of the past two hundred years	*BLACK LITERATURE CRITICISM (BLC)*
Short story writers	*SHORT STORY CRITICISM (SSC)*
Poets	*POETRY CRITICISM (PC)*
Dramatists	*DRAMA CRITICISM (DC)*
Major authors from the Renaissance to the present	*WORLD LITERATURE CRITICISM, 1500 TO THE PRESENT (WLC)*

For criticism on visual artists since 1850, see

MODERN ARTS CRITICISM (MAC)

ISSN 0091-3421

Volume 75

Contemporary Literary Criticism

Excerpts from Criticism of the Works
of Today's Novelists, Poets, Playwrights,
Short Story Writers, Scriptwriters, and
Other Creative Writers

Thomas Votteler
EDITOR

Christopher Giroux
Elizabeth P. Henry
Drew Kalasky
Marie Lazzari
Thomas Ligotti
Kyung-Sun Lim
Sean René Pollock
David Segal
Bridget Travers
Janet Witalec
ASSOCIATE EDITORS

Gale Research Inc. • DETROIT • WASHINGTON, D.C. • LONDON

Riverside Community College
Library
4800 Magnolia Avenue
Riverside, California 92506

STAFF

Thomas Votteler, *Editor*

Christopher Giroux, Elizabeth P. Henry, Drew Kalasky, Marie Lazzari, Thomas Ligotti, Kyung-Sun Lim, Sean René Pollock, David Segal, Bridget Travers, Janet Witalec, *Associate Editors*

Jennifer Brostrom, Jeffery Chapman, Jennifer Gariepy, Ian A. Goodhall, Margaret Haerens, Dale R. Miller, Brigham Narins, Mali Purkayastha, Lynn M. Spampinato, *Assistant Editors*

Jeanne A. Gough, *Permissions & Production Manager*
Linda M. Pugliese, *Production Supervisor*
Donna Craft, Paul Lewon, Maureen Puhl, Camille Robinson, Jennifer VanSickle, Sheila Walencewicz, *Editorial Associates*

Sandra C. Davis, *Permissions Supervisor (Text)*
Maria L. Franklin, Josephine M. Keene, Michele Lonoconus, Denise M. Singleton, Kimberly F. Smilay, *Permissions Associates*
Jennifer A. Arnold, Brandy C. Merritt, Shalice Shah, *Permissions Assistants*

Margaret A. Chamberlain, *Permissions Supervisor (Pictures)*
Pamela A. Hayes, Keith Reed, *Permissions Associates*
Arlene Johnson, Barbara Wallace, *Permissions Assistants*

Victoria B. Cariappa, *Research Manager*
Maureen Richards, *Research Supervisor*
Robert S. Lazich, Mary Beth McElmeel, Tamara C. Nott, *Editorial Associates*
Daniel Jankowski, Julie Karmazin, Donna Melnychenko, *Editorial Assistants*

Mary Beth Trimper, *Production Director*
Shanna Heilveil, *Production Assistant*

Cynthia Baldwin, *Art Director*
Nick Jakubiak, C. J. Jonik, *Desktop Publishers*

Since this page cannot legibly accommodate all copyright notices, the acknowledgments constitute an extension of the copyright notice.

While every effort has been made to ensure the reliability of the information presented in this publication, Gale Research Inc. neither guarantees the accuracy of the data contained herein nor assumes any responsibility for errors, omissions or discrepancies. Gale accepts no payment for listing; and inclusion in the publication of any organization, agency, institution, publication, service, or individual does not imply endorsement of the editors or publisher. Errors brought to the attention of the publisher and verified to the satisfaction of the publisher will be corrected in future editions.

The paper used in this publication meets the minimum requirements of American National Standard for Information Sciences—Permanence Paper for Printed Library Materials, ANSI Z39.48-1984. ∞™

This publication is a creative work copyrighted by Gale Research Inc. and fully protected by all applicable copyright laws, as well as by misappropriation, trade secret, unfair competition, and other applicable laws. The authors and editors of this work have added value to the underlying factual information herein through one or more of the following: unique and original selection, coordination, expression, arrangement, and classification of the information.

Gale Research Inc. will vigorously defend all of its rights in this publication.

Copyright © 1993
Gale Research Inc.
835 Penobscot Building
Detroit, MI 48226-4094

All rights reserved including the right of reproduction in whole or in part in any form.

Library of Congress Catalog Card Number 91-118494
ISBN 0-8103-4981-7
ISSN 0091-3421

Printed in the United States of America
Published simultaneously in the United Kingdom
by Gale Research International Limited
(An affiliated company of Gale Research Inc.)
10 9 8 7 6 5 4 3 2 1

I(T)P™

The trademark **ITP** is used under license.

Contents

Preface vii

Acknowledgments xi

Preface

A Comprehensive Information Source
on Contemporary Literature

Named "one of the twenty-five most distinguished reference titles published during the past twenty-five years" by *Reference Quarterly*, the *Contemporary Literary Criticism (CLC)* series provides readers with critical commentary and general information on more than 2,000 authors now living or who died after December 31, 1959. Previous to the publication of the first volume of *CLC* in 1973, there was no ongoing digest monitoring scholarly and popular sources of critical opinion and explication of modern literature. *CLC*, therefore, has fulfilled an essential need, particularly since the complexity and variety of contemporary literature makes the function of criticism especially important to today's reader.

Scope of the Series

CLC presents significant passages from published criticism of works by creative writers. Since many of the authors covered by *CLC* inspire continual critical commentary, writers are often represented in more than one volume. There is, of course, no duplication of reprinted criticism.

Authors are selected for inclusion for a variety of reasons, among them the publication or dramatic production of a critically acclaimed new work, the reception of a major literary award, revival of interest in past writings, or the adaptation of a literary work to film or television.

Attention is also given to several other groups of writers—authors of considerable public interest—about whose work criticism is often difficult to locate. These include mystery and science fiction writers, literary and social critics, foreign writers, and authors who represent particular ethnic groups within the United States.

Format of the Book

Each *CLC* volume contains about 500 individual excerpts taken from hundreds of book review periodicals, general magazines, scholarly journals, monographs, and books. Entries include critical evaluations spanning from the beginning of an author's career to the most current commentary. Interviews, feature articles, and other published writings that offer insight into the author's works are also presented. Students, teachers, librarians, and researchers will find that the generous excerpts and supplementary material in *CLC* provide them with vital information required to write a term paper, analyze a poem, or lead a book discussion group. In addition, complete bibliographical citations note the original source and all of the information necessary for a term paper footnote or bibliography.

Features

A *CLC* author entry consists of the following elements:

- The **Author Heading** cites the form under which the author has most commonly published, followed by birth date, and death date when applicable. Uncertainty as to a birth or death date is indicated by a question mark.

- A **Portrait** of the author is included when available.

- A brief **Biographical and Critical Introduction** to the author and his or her work precedes the excerpted criticism. The first line of the introduction provides the author's full name, pseudonyms (if applicable), nationality, and a listing of genres in which the author has written. Previous volumes of *CLC* in which the author has been featured are also listed in the introduction.

- A list of **Principal Works** notes the most important works by the author.

- The **Excerpted Criticism** represents various kinds of critical writing, ranging in form from the brief review to the scholarly exegesis. Essays are selected by the editors to reflect the spectrum of opinion about a specific work or about an author's literary career in general. The excerpts are presented chronologically, adding a useful perspective to the entry. All titles by the author featured in the entry are printed in boldface type, which enables the reader to easily identify the works being discussed. Publication information (such as publisher names and book prices) and parenthetical numerical references (such as footnotes or page and line references to specific editions of a work) have been deleted at the editor's discretion to provide smoother reading of the text.

- Critical essays are prefaced by **Explanatory Notes** as an additional aid to readers. These notes may provide several types of valuable information, including: the reputation of the critic, the importance of the work of criticism, the commentator's approach to the author's work, the purpose of the criticism, and changes in critical trends regarding the author.

- A complete **Bibliographical Citation** designed to help the user find the original essay or book follows each excerpt.

- A concise **Further Reading** section appears at the end of entries on authors for whom a significant amount of criticism exists in addition to the pieces reprinted in *CLC*. Cross-references to other useful sources published by Gale Research in which the author has appeared are also included: *Children's Literature Review, Contemporary Authors, Something about the Author, Dictionary of Literary Biography, Drama Criticism, Poetry Criticism, Short Story Criticism, Contemporary Authors Autobiography Series*, and *Something about the Author Autobiography Series*.

Other Features

CLC also includes the following features:

- An **Acknowledgments** section lists the copyright holders who have granted permission to reprint material in this volume of *CLC*. It does not, however, list every book or periodical reprinted or consulted during the preparation of the volume.

- A **Cumulative Author Index** lists all the authors who have appeared in the various literary criticism series published by Gale Research, with cross-references to Gale's biographical and autobiographical series. A full listing of the series referenced there appears on the first page of the indexes of this volume. Readers will welcome this cumulated author index as a useful tool for locating an author within the various series. The index, which lists birth and death dates when available, will be particularly valuable for those authors who are identified with a certain period but whose death dates cause them to be placed in another, or for those authors whose careers span two periods. For example, Ernest Hemingway is found in *CLC,* yet a writer often associated with him, F. Scott Fitzgerald, is found in *Twentieth-Century Literary Criticism.*

● A **Cumulative Nationality Index** alphabetically lists all authors featured in *CLC* by nationality, followed by numbers corresponding to the volumes in which the authors appear.

● A **Title Index** alphabetically lists all titles reviewed in the current volume of *CLC.* Listings are followed by the author's name and the corresponding page numbers where the titles are discussed. English translations of foreign titles and variations of titles are cross-referenced to the title under which a work was originally published. Titles of novels, novellas, dramas, films, record albums, and poetry, short story, and essay collections are printed in italics, while all individual poems, short stories, essays, and songs are printed in roman type within quotation marks; when published separately (e.g., T. S. Eliot's poem *The Waste Land*), the titles of long poems are printed in italics.

● In response to numerous suggestions from librarians, Gale has also produced a **Special Paperbound Edition** of the *CLC* title index. This annual cumulation, which alphabetically lists all titles reviewed in the series, is available to all customers and is published with the first volume of *CLC* issued in each calendar year. Additional copies of the index are available upon request. Librarians and patrons will welcome this separate index: it saves shelf space, is easy to use, and is recyclable upon receipt of the following year's cumulation.

Citing *Contemporary Literary Criticism*

When writing papers, students who quote directly from any volume in the Literary Criticism Series may use the following general forms to footnote reprinted criticism. The first example pertains to material drawn from periodicals, the second to material reprinted in books:

[1]Anne Tyler, "Manic Monologue," *The New Republic* 200 (April 17, 1989), 44-6; excerpted and reprinted in *Contemporary Literary Criticism,* Vol. 58, ed. Roger Matuz (Detroit: Gale Research Inc., 1990), p. 325.

[2]Patrick Reilly, *The Literature of Guilt: From 'Gulliver' to Golding* (University of Iowa Press, 1988); excerpted and reprinted in *Contemporary Literary Criticism,* Vol. 58, ed. Roger Matuz (Detroit: Gale Research Inc., 1990), pp. 206-12.

Suggestions Are Welcome

The editor hopes that readers will find *CLC* a useful reference tool and welcomes comments about the work. Send comments and suggestions to: Editor, *Contemporary Literary Criticism,* Gale Research Inc., Penobscot Building, Detroit, MI 48226-4094.

Acknowledgments

The editors wish to thank the copyright holders of the excerpted criticism included in this volume, the permissions managers of many book and magazine publishing companies for assisting us in securing reprint rights, and Anthony Bogucki for assistance with copyright research. We are also grateful to the staffs of the Detroit Public Library, the Library of Congress, the University of Detroit Library, Wayne State University Purdy/Kresge Library Complex, and the University of Michigan Libraries for making their resources available to us. Following is a list of the copyright holders who have granted us permission to reprint material in this volume of *CLC*. Every effort has been made to trace copyright, but if omissions have been made, please let us know.

COPYRIGHTED EXCERPTS IN *CLC*, VOLUME 75, WERE REPRINTED FROM THE FOLLOWING PERIODICALS:

African Arts, v. XXI, August, 1988 for a review of "Anthills of the Savannah" by John Povey. © 1988 by the Regents of the University of California. Reprinted by permission of the publisher and The Literary Estate of John Povey.—*American Film,* v. XIV, September, 1989 for an interview with John Patrick Shanley by *American Film.* Copyright 1989 by *American Film.* Reprinted by permission of the William Morris Agency, Inc. for the author.—*The American Spectator,* v. 22, May, 1989. Copyright © *The American Spectator* 1989. Reprinted by permission of the publisher.—*The Antigonish Review,* n. 80, Winter, 1990 for "Robertson Davies and the Not-So-Comic Realities of Art Fraud" by Wilfred Cude. Copyright 1990 by the author. Reprinted by permission of the publisher and the author.—*The Atlantic Monthly,* v. 189, May, 1952 for "Men Fighting" by Charles J. Rolo. Copyright 1952, renewed 1979 by The Atlantic Monthly Company, Boston, MA. Reprinted by permission of the author.—*Book World—The Washington Post,* July 20, 1986; January 12, 1992. © 1986, 1992, *The Washington Post.* Both reprinted with permission of the publisher.—*Boston Review,* v. XII, October, 1987 for "The Language of Film" by John Gianvito. Copyright © 1987 by the Boston Critic, Inc. Reprinted by permission of the author.—*CALYX, A Journal of Art & Literature by Women,* v. 8, Fall, 1983 for a review of "Flowers from the Volcano" by Ingrid Wendt. Copyright © 1983 by CALYX, Inc. Reprinted by permission of the publisher and the author.—*Canadian Literature,* n. 126, Autumn, 1990 for "A Cycle Completed: The Nine Novels of Robertson Davies" by George Woodcock; n. 127, Winter, 1990 for "Satire & Romance" by Muriel Whitaker. Both reprinted by permission of the respective authors.—*The Chariton Review,* v. 10, Spring, 1984. Copyright © 1984 by Northeast Missouri State University. Reprinted by permission of the publisher.—*Chicago Reader,* 1990. © 1990, Chicago Reader, Inc. Reprinted by permission of the publisher.—*Choice,* v. 27, March, 1990. Copyright © 1990 by American Library Association. Reprinted by permission of the publisher.—*The Christian Science Monitor,* June 18, 1984 for a review of "Danny and the Deep Blue Sea" by John Beaufort; March 31, 1988 for "Essays on Life in Central America Today" by Marjorie Agosin. © 1984, 1988 The Christian Science Publishing Society. All rights reserved. Both reprinted by permission of the respective authors.—*Civil War History,* v. XXII, June, 1975. Copyright © 1975 by The Kent State University Press. Reprinted by permission of the publisher.—*Commonweal,* v. CXII, December 20, 1985. Copyright © 1985 Commonweal Foundation. Reprinted by permission of Commonweal Foundation./ v. LXIX, January 9, 1959. Copyright © 1959, renewed 1987, Commonweal Publishing Co., Inc. Reprinted by permission of Commonweal Foundation.—*Comparative Drama,* v. 10, Winter, 1976-77. © Copyright 1977, by the Editors of *Comparative Drama.* Reprinted by permission of the publisher.—*Critique: Studies in Contemporary Fiction,* v. XXXII, Fall, 1990. Copyright © 1990 Helen Reid Educational Foundation. Reprinted with permission of the Helen Dwight Reid Educational Foundation, published by Heldref Publications, 1319 18th Street, N. W., Washington, DC 20036-1802.—*Discourse: A Review of the Liberal Arts,* v. XII, Spring, 1969 for "Experimentation as Technique: The Protest Novels of John Steinbeck" by Bryant N. Wyatt. © 1969 by the author. Reprinted by permission of the author.—*Encounter,* v. LXV, November, 1985 for "Andrei Tarkovsky" by Mark Le Fanu. © 1985 by the author. Reprinted by permission of the author.—*English Studies in Canada,* v. XIII, June, 1987 for "'The Rebel Angels': Robertson Davies and the Novel of Ideas" by James Mulvihill. © Association of Canadian University Teachers of English 1987. Reprinted by permission of the publisher and the author.—*Essays on Canadian Writing,* n. 39, Fall, 1989. © 1989 Essays on Canadian Writing Ltd. Reprinted by permission of the publisher.—*Evergreen Review,* v. 6, January-February, 1962 for "The Cannibal Feast" by E. S. Seldon. Copyright © 1962, by Evergreen Review, Inc. Renewed 1990 by Grove Weidenfeld. Reprinted by permission of Grove Weidenfeld.—*Extrapolation,* v. 19, May, 1978. Copyright 1978 by Thomas D. and Alice S. Clareson. Reprinted by permission of Kent State University Press.—*Feminist Studies,* v. 7, Spring, 1981. Copyright © 1981 by Feminist Studies, Inc. Reprinted by permission of the publisher, c/o Women's Studies Program, University of Maryland, College Park, MD 20742.—*The Film Journal,* v. 2, 1974. © 1974 *The Film Journal.* All rights reserved. Reprinted by permission of the publisher.—*Film Quarterly,* v. XVIII, Fall, 1964 for "Ivan's Childhood" by Lee Atwell; v. XXIX, Spring, 1976 for "Solaris" by Timothy Hyman; v. XXXV, Fall, 1981 for "Lost Harmony" by Michael Dempsey. © 1964, 1976, 1981 by The Regents of the University of California. All reprinted by permission of The Regents and the respective authors.—*German Life & Letters,* v. XXVI, October, 1972. Reprinted by permission of the publisher.—*Latin American Literary Review,* v. XX, January-June, 1992. Reprinted by permission of the publisher.—*The Literary Criterion,* v. 23, 1988. Reprinted by permission of the publisher.—*The Literary Review,* Fairleigh Dickinson University, v. 24, Summer, 1981 for "Lacan, Language, and Literary Criticism" by Ellie Ragland-Sullivan. Copyright © 1981 by Fairleigh Dickinson University. Reprinted by permission of the author.—*London Review of Books,* v. 10, November 10, 1988 for "Magnanimous Cuckolds" by Jack Matthews; v. 12, December 6, 1990 for "Serious Dr Sonne" by Philip Purser; v. 14, March 26, 1992 for "Above the Consulting-Room" by John Sturrock. All appear here by permission of the *London Review of Books* and the respective authors.—*Los Angeles Times,* February 5, 1986; March 5, 1988; February 9, 1989. Copyright, 1986, 1988, 1989, *Los Angeles Times.* All reprinted by permission of the publisher.—*Los Angeles Times Book Review,* November 15, 1987; December 17, 1989. Copyright, 1987, 1989, *Los Angeles Times.* Both reprinted by permission of the publisher.—*Maclean's Magazine,* v. 102, January 23, 1989 for "The Living Dead: A Master's Ghost Story Spans Generations" by John Bemrose. © 1989 by *Maclean's Magazine.* Reprinted by permission of the publisher and the author./ v. 103, March 19, 1990; v. 104, September 23, 1991. © 1990, 1991 by *Maclean's Magazine.* Both reprinted by permission of the publisher.—*The Massachusetts Review,* v. VIII, Autumn, 1967. © 1967. Reprinted from *The Massachusetts Review,* The Massachusetts Review, Inc. by permission.—*Massachusetts Studies in English,* v. VII, 1978 for "Lacan and the Play of Desire in Poetry" by William Shullenberger. Copyright © 1978 by the author. Reprinted by permission of the author.—*The Mississippi Quarterly,* v. XXIV, Fall, 1971; v. XXVIII, Winter, 1974-75. Copyright 1971, 1975 Mississippi State University. Both reprinted by permission of the publisher.—*The Missouri Review,* v. XII, 1989 for an interview with Chinua Achebe by Kay Bonetti. Copyright © 1989 by American Audio Prose Library, Inc. Reprinted by permission of Chinua Achebe and AAPL, Inc.—*MLN,* v. 98, December, 1983. © Copyright 1983 by The Johns Hopkins University Press. All rights reserved. Reprinted by permission of the publisher.—*Modern Age,* v. 27, Summer-Fall, 1983. Copyright © 1983 by the Intercollegiate Studies Institute, Inc. Reprinted by permission of the publisher.—*Modern Fiction Studies,* v. 37, Autumn, 1991. Copyright © 1991 by Purdue Research Foundation, West Lafayette, IN 47907. All rights reserved. Reprinted with permission.—*The Month,* v. CCLVIII, August-September, 1987. © The Editor 1987. Reprinted by permission of the editor of *The Month* magazine.—*National Review,* New York, v. XXVII, February 14, 1975. © 1975 by National Review, Inc., 150 East 35th Street, New York, NY 10016. Reprinted with permission of the publisher.—*The New Criterion,* v. V, September, 1986 for "Becoming Elias Canetti" by Roger Kimball. Copyright © 1986 by The Foundation for Cultural Review. Reprinted by permission of the author.—*New Directions for Women,* v. 18, January, 1989; v. 21, January-February, 1992. © Copyright 1989, 1992 New Directions for Women, Inc., 108 West Palisade Ave., Englewood, NJ 07631. Both reprinted by permission of the publisher.—*The New Leader,* v. LXXII, January 23, 1989. © 1989 by The American Labor Conference on International Affairs, Inc. Reprinted by permission of the publisher.—*New Left Review,* n. 55, May-June, 1969. Reprinted by permission of the publisher.—*The New Republic,* v. 171, November 30, 1974. © 1974 The New Republic, Inc. Reprinted by permission of *The New Republic.*—*New Statesman,* v. 111, May 16, 1986; v. 113, April 24, 1987. © 1986, 1987 The Statesman & Nation Publishing Co. Ltd. Both reprinted by permission of the publisher.—*New York* Magazine, v. 19, October 20, 1986; v. 21, November 14, 1988; v. 24, January 7, 1991. Copyright © 1993 K-III Magazine Corporation. All rights reserved. All reprinted with permission of *New York* Magazine.—*The New York Review of Books,* v. 1, February, 1963. Copyright © 1963 Nyrev, Inc. Renewed 1991 by James Raymond West. Reprinted with permission from *The New York Review of Books.*/ v. XXII, March 6, 1975; v. XXV, January 25, 1979; v. XXXVI, April 13, 1989; Copyright © 1975, 1979, 1989 Nyrev, Inc. All reprinted with permission from *The New*

York Review of Books.—The New York Times, October 14, 1982; November 24, 1982. Copyright © 1982 by The New York Times Company. Both reprinted by permission of the publisher.—*The New York Times Book Review,* August 3, 1986, November 5, 1989. Copyright © 1986, 1989 by The New York Times Company. Both reprinted by permission of the publisher.—*The New Yorker,* v. LXI, October 7, 1985 for "Noise in the Bronx" by Edith Oliver; v. LXII, October 20, 1986 for a review of "The Dreamer Examines His Pillow" by Edith Oliver; v. LXIV, November 14, 1988 for "Divorce Italian Style" by Mimi Kramer; v. LXIV, March 26, 1990 for a review of "Joe Versus the Volcano" by Terrence Rafferty; v. LXVI, December 24, 1990 for "The Big Tease" by Mimi Kramer. © 1985, 1986, 1988, 1990 by the respective authors. All reprinted by permission of the publisher.—*Newsweek,* v. CX, December 21, 1987; v. CXI, January 25, 1988. Copyright 1987, 1988, by Newsweek, Inc. All rights reserved. Both reprinted by permission of the publisher.—*Notes on Mississippi Writers,* v. VIII, Fall, 1975. Reprinted by permission of the publisher.—*The Observer,* July 21, 1991. Reprinted by permission of The Observer Limited, London—*Parnassus: Poetry in Review,* vs. 12-13, 1985. Copyright © 1985 Poetry in Review Foundation, NY. Reprinted by permission of the publisher.—*Queen's Quarterly,* v. 93, Spring, 1986 for "Keeping the Good Wine Until Now" by D. O. Spettigue. Copyright © 1986 by the author. Reprinted by permission of the author.—*Quill and Quire,* v. 57, August, 1991 for "Atwood's Dark Parables, Davies's Ballad of Bankruptcy" by George Woodcock. Reprinted by permission of *Quill and Quire* and the author.—*The Review of Contemporary Fiction,* v. 4, Spring, 1984. Copyright, 1984, by John O'Brien. Both reprinted by permission of the publisher.—*Romanian Review,* v. XXIV, 1970. All reprinted by permission of the publisher.—*Science-Fiction Studies,* v. 14, November, 1987; v. 19, March, 1992. Copyright © 1987, 1992 by SFS Publications. Both reprinted by permission of the publisher.—*Sight and Sound,* v. 42, Spring, 1973; v. 55, Summer, 1986; v. 56, Spring, 1987. Copyright © 1973, 1986, 1987 by The British Film Institute. All reprinted by permission of the publisher.—*Slavic Review,* v. 48, Summer, 1989 for a review of "Sculpting in Time: Reflections on the Cinema" by Valerie Z. Nollan. Copyright © 1989 by the American Association for the Advancement of Slavic Studies, Inc. Reprinted by permission of the publisher and the author.—*South Atlantic Quarterly,* v. 88, Fall, 1989. Copyright © 1989 by Duke University Press, Durham, NC. Reprinted with permission of the publisher.—*The Southern Humanities Review,* v. 13, Fall, 1979 for a review of "September September" by Jan Nordby Gretlund. Copyright 1979 by Auburn University. Reprinted by permission of the author.—*The Southern Review,* Louisiana State University, v. 21, Spring, 1985 for "Shelby Foote's Civil War" by James M. Cox. Copyright, 1985, by the author. Reprinted by permission of the author.—*The Spectator,* v. 212, January 24, 1964; v. 258, May 9, 1987; v. 267, July 27, 1991. © 1964, 1987, 1991 by *The Spectator.* All reprinted by permission of *The Spectator.*—*Steinbeck Quarterly,* v. XV, Winter-Spring, 1982. All rights reserved. Reprinted by permission of the editor-in-chief.—*The Times Literary Supplement,* n. 4617, September 27, 1991; n. 4618, October 4, 1991. © The Times Supplements Limited 1991. Both reproduced from *The Times Literary Supplement* by permission.—*Twentieth Century Literature,* v. 11, October, 1965. Copyright 1965, Hofstra University Press. Reprinted by permission of the publisher.—*The Village Voice,* v. XXXIII, February 2, 1988 for "Witness to the Persecution" by Suzanne Ruta; v. XXXIV, April 25, 1989 for "Mind Set" by Sally Eckhoff; Copyright © News Group Publications, Inc., 1988, 1989. Both reprinted by permission of *The Village Voice* and the respective authors.—*VLS,* n. 73, April, 1989 for a review of "Woman of the River" by Dan Bellm. Copyright © 1989 News Group Publications, Inc. Reprinted by permission of *The Village Voice* and the author.—*The Virginia Quarterly Review,* v. 55, Spring, 1979. Copyright, 1979, by *The Virginia Quarterly Review,* The University of Virginia. Reprinted by permission of the publisher.—*The Women's Review of Books,* v. II, October, 1984 for "American in the Singular" by Jan Clausen. Copyright © 1984. All rights reserved. Reprinted by permission of the author.—*World Literature Today,* v. 62, Spring, 1988. Copyright 1988 by the University of Oklahoma Press. Reprinted by permission of the publisher.—*Yale French Studies,* ns. 55-56, 1977. Copyright © Yale French Studies 1977. Reprinted by permission of the publisher.

COPYRIGHTED EXCERPTS IN *CLC*, VOLUME 75, WERE REPRINTED FROM THE FOLLOWING BOOKS:

Alegría, Claribel. From "The Writer's Commitment," in *Lives on the Line: The Testimony of Contemporary Latin American Authors.* Edited by Doris Meyer. University of California Press, 1988. Copyright © by The Regents of the University of California. Reprinted by permission of the publisher.—Bayley, John. From *Selected Essays.*

Cambridge University Press, 1984. © Cambridge University Press 1984. Reprinted with the permission of the publisher and the author.—Beatty, Sandra. From "Steinbeck's Play-Women: A Study of the Female Presence in 'Of Mice and Men', 'Burning Bright', 'The Moon Is Down', and 'Viva Zapata!'"in *Steinbeck's Women: Essays in Criticism.* Edited by Tetsumaro Hayashi. The Steinbeck Society of America, 1979. © 1979 Tetsumaro Hayashi. All rights reserved. Reprinted by permission of the publisher.—Burroughs, William S. From *Naked Lunch.* Grove Press, Inc., 1959. Copyright © 1959 by William Burroughs. All rights reserved.—Cameron, Donald. From an interview in *Conversations with Canadian Novelists.* Macmillan of Canada, 1973. © Donald Cameron 1973. All rights reserved. Reprinted by permission of Robertson Davies and Donald Cameron.—Ciopraga, Const. From a preface to *Poems of Light.* by Lucian Blaga. Burcuresti: Minerva, 1975. Reprinted by permission of the publisher.—Codrescu, Andrei. From an introduction to *At the Court of Yearning: Poems.* By Lucian Blaga, translated by Andrei Codrescu. Ohio State University Press, 1989. © 1989 by the Ohio State University Press. All rights reserved. Reprinted with permission of the publisher.—Cornis-Pop, Marcel. From an afterword to *At the Court of Yearning: Poems.* By Lucian Blaga, translated by Andrei Codrescu. Ohio State University Press, 1989. © 1989 by the Ohio State University Press. All rights reserved. Reprinted with permission of the publisher.—Davies, Robertson. From *One Half of Robertson Davies.* The Viking Press, 1977. Copyright © Robertson Davies, 1977. All rights reserved. Used by permission of Viking Penguin, a division of Penguin Books USA Inc. In Canada by Macmillan of Canada.—Forché, Carolyn. From a preface of *Flowers from the Volcano.* By Claribel Alegría, translated by Carolyn Forché. University of Pittsburgh Press, 1982. Copyright © 1982, Claribel Alegría and Carolyn Forché. All rights reserved. Reprinted by permission of the publisher.—French, Warren. From *John Steinbeck.* Twayne, 1961. Copyright © 1961, by Twayne Publishers, Inc. Renewed 1984 by Warren French. All rights reserved. Reprinted with the permission of Twayne Publishers, Inc., an imprint of Macmillan Publishing Company.—Gikandi, Simon. From *Reading Chinua Achebe: Language & Ideology in Fiction.* James Currey, 1991. © Simon Gikandi 1991. Reprinted by permission of the publisher.—Grossvogel, David I. From *The Self-Conscious Stage in Modern French Drama.* Columbia University Press, 1958. Copyright © 1958 Columbia University Press, New York. Renewed 1986 by David I. Grossvogel. Used by permission of the publisher.—Hitchins, Keith. From "'Gindirea': Nationalism in Spiritual Guise," in *Social Change in Romania: Debate on Development in a European Nation.* Edited by Kenneth Jowitt. University of California Press, 1978. © 1978 by the Regents of the University of California, 1978. Reprinted by permission of the publisher.—Innes, C. L. From *Chinua Achebe.* Cambridge University Press, 1990. © Cambridge University Press 1990. Reprinted with permission of the publisher and the author.—Kael, Pauline. From "Looney Fugue" in *Hooked.* Dutton, 1989. Copyright © 1985, 1988, 1989 by Pauline Kael. All rights reserved. Used by permission of Dutton, an imprint of New American Library, a division of Penguin Books USA Inc.—Kazin, Alfred. From *Bright Book of Life: American Novelists & Storytellers from Hemingway to Mailer.* Atlantic-Little, Brown, 1973. Copyright © 1971, 1973 by Alfred Kazin. Reprinted by permission of the author.—Knapp, Bettina L. From *Fernand Crommelynck.* Twayne, 1978. Copyright © 1978 by G. K. Hall & Co. All rights reserved. Reprinted with the permission of Twayne Publishers, an imprint of Macmillan Publishing Company.—Levant, Howard. From *The Novels of John Steinbeck: A Critical Study.* University of Missouri Press, 1974. Copyright © 1974 by The Curators of the University of Missouri. All rights reserved. Reprinted by permission of the publisher.—Marks, Lester Jay. From *Thematic Design in the Novels of John Steinbeck.* Mouton, 1969. © copyright 1969 Mouton & Co., Publishers. Reprinted by permission of Mouton de Gruyter, a Division of Walter de Gruyter & Co.—Nemoianu, Virgil. From *A Theory of the Secondary: Literature, Progress, and Reaction.* Johns Hopkins University Press, 1989. © 1989 The Johns Hopkins University Press. All rights reserved. Reprinted by permission of the publisher.—Pearce, Richard. From *Stages of the Clown: Perspectives on Modern Fiction from Dostoyevsky to Beckett.* Southern Illinois University Press, 1970. Copyright © 1970, by Southern Illinois University Press. All rights reserved. Reprinted by permission of the publisher.—Sheridan, Alan. From translator's note to *Ecrits.* By Jacques Lacan. Norton, 1977. Copyright © 1977 by Tavistock Publications Limited. All rights reserved. Reprinted by permission of W. W. Norton & Company, Inc.—Skerl, Jennie. From an introduction to *Naked Lunch.* By William S. Burroughs. Grove Press, 1984. Copyright © 1959 by William Burroughs. All rights reserved. Reprinted by permission of Grove Press, Inc.—Swann, Joseph. From "From 'Things Fall Apart' to 'Anthills of the Savannah': The Changing Face of History in Achebe's Novels," in *Crisis and Creativity in the New Literature in English.* Edited by Geoffrey V. Davis and Hena Maes-Jelinek. Rodopi, 1990. © Editions Rodopi B. V. Amsterdam 1990. Reprinted by permission of the

xiv

publisher.—Tarkovsky, Andrey. From *Sculpting in Time: Reflections on the Cinema.* Translated by Kitty Hunter-Blair. The Bodley Head, 1986. Translation © Kitty Hunter-Blair, 1986.—Turner, David. From "Elias Canetti: The Intellectual as King Canute," in *Modern Austrian Writing: Literature and Society after 1945.* Edited by Alan Best and Hans Wolfschütz. Wolff, 1980. © 1980 Oswald Wolff (Publishers) Ltd. Reprinted by permission of Berg Publishers Ltd.

PHOTOGRAPHS AND ILLUSTRATIONS APPEARING IN *CLC*, VOLUME 75, WERE RECEIVED FROM THE FOLLOWING SOURCES:

Photograph by Stephen Long: **p. 1;** Photograph by Layle Silbert: **p. 32;** Copyright 1982 Chris Felver: **p. 83;** Dust jacket of *The Naked Lunch*, by William Burroughs. Reprinted by permission of Grove Press: **p. 111;** Bildarchiv der Österreichischen Nationalbibliothek: **p. 118;** Photo property of Raphael Sorin, Paris: **p. 138;** Consulate General of Belgium: **pp. 149, 157;** © Alicia Johnson: **p. 171;** Dust jacket of *The Papers of Samuel Marchbanks*, by Robertson Davies. Copyright © 1986 by Robertson Davies. Used by permission of Viking Penguin, a division of Penguin Books USA Inc.: **p. 179;** Dust jacket of *Rebel Angels*, by Robertson Davies. Copyright © 1981 by Robertson Davies. Used by permission of Viking Penguin, a division of Penguin Books USA Inc.: **p. 194;** Dust jacket of *What's Bred in the Bone*, by Robertson Davies. Copyright © 1985 by Robertson Davies. Used by permission of Viking Penguin, a division of Penguin Books USA Inc.: **p. 207;** Dust jacket of *The Lyre of Orpheus*, by Robertson Davies. Copyright © 1988 by Robertson Davies. Used by permission of Viking Penguin, a division of Penguin Books USA Inc.: **p. 223;** Photograph by Rollin A. Riggs: **p. 228;** © Jerry Bauer: **p. 273;** Susan Shacter/Onyx: **p. 318;** The Granger Collection, New York: **p. 334;** © 1983 Richard L. Allman: **p. 359.**

Chinua Achebe

1930-

(Born Albert Chinualumogu Achebe) Nigerian novelist, short story writer, poet, and essayist.

The following entry presents criticism of Achebe's works published between 1987 and 1992. For further discussion of Achebe's life and works, see *CLC*, Volumes 1, 3, 5, 7, 11, 26, and 51.

INTRODUCTION

Achebe is one of the most important figures in contemporary African literature. His novels, which chronicle the colonization and independence of Nigeria, are among the first works in English to present an intimate and authentic rendering of African culture.

The son of Igbo (or Ibo) missionary teachers, Achebe was born in Nigeria in 1930. He attended Church Mission Society School in Ogidi and Government College in Umuahia before obtaining a bachelor's degree from Ibadan University in 1953. He began working for the Nigerian Broadcasting Company a year later and in 1958 began his literary career with the publication of his most famous novel, *Things Fall Apart*. Since the 1970s Achebe has taught literature at both American and Nigerian universities.

Things Fall Apart is considered a classic of contemporary African fiction for its realistic and anthropologically informative portrait of Igbo society. Set in the village of Umuofia during the initial stages of colonization in the late 1880s, this book traces the conflict between Igbo and Western customs through Okonkwo, a proud village leader whose refusal to adapt to European influence leads him to murder and suicide. *No Longer at Ease*, set in the Nigerian city of Lagos during the late 1950s, details the failure of Obi Okonkwo, the grandson of the protagonist of *Things Fall Apart*, to successfully combine his traditional Igbo upbringing with his English education and affluent life-style. While *No Longer at Ease* was less universally praised than *Things Fall Apart*, some critics defend such stylistic weaknesses of the second novel as slack language and weak character development as a deliberate attempt to demonstrate the consequences of one culture's dilution by another.

Arrow of God describes Igbo village life during the 1920s. This novel centers on Ezeulu, a spiritual leader, who sends his son Oduche to a missionary school to learn about Western culture and technology. Upon his return Oduche attempts to destroy a sacred python, setting in motion a chain of events in which Ezeulu is stripped of his position as high priest and imprisoned by the English colonial leaders. Achebe's next novel, *A Man of the People*, focuses on the tribulations of a Nigerian teacher who joins a political

organization endeavoring to remove a corrupt bureaucrat from office. In this novel Achebe condemns the widespread abuse of power by Nigeria's leadership once the country was granted its independence from Great Britain.

Anthills of the Savannah, published in 1987, is Achebe's first novel since the publication of *A Man of the People* in 1966. Set in Kangan, an imaginary West African nation, the novel concerns three childhood friends who as adults become government leaders. When one of the men fails in his attempt to be elected President-for-Life, he begins to suppress his opposition. He eventually has one of his friends killed and is killed himself in a military coup; the third friend dies in a street riot. In *Anthills of the Savannah* Achebe examines the ways in which individual responsibility and power are often exploited to the detriment of an entire society. He also devotes greater attention to female characters, who in this novel are more completely developed than those in his previous work and exhibit strength and composure as the bearers of traditional morals and precepts.

Achebe is also the author of several volumes of poetry, short stories, and essays. *Christmas in Biafra, and Other Poems* is highly regarded for its ironic depiction of the Nigerian civil war. The short stories in *Girls at War, and Other Stories* reflect his concern with individual fulfillment and disillusion with war and nationalism. In the essay collection *Morning Yet on Creation Day* he commented on literary and political topics, particularly language and the writer's role in society. *Hopes and Impediments: Selected Essays* is a collection of fourteen essays and speeches that includes a controversial essay attacking

Joseph Conrad's *Heart of Darkness* as racist as well as a tribute to James Baldwin and several commentaries on post-colonial Africa and the social forces that have shaped it.

Achebe is credited with helping establish the field of modern African literature. His novels are praised as historically insightful presentations of the African past as well as balanced examinations of contemporary Africa. In addition, his successful fusion of Igbo folklore, proverbs, and idioms with Western political ideologies and Christian doctrines is considered highly innovative. Critics note, however, that Achebe's writing has relevance beyond the borders of Nigeria and beyond the arenas of anthropology, sociology, and political science. As Douglas Killam observed: "Achebe's novels offer a vision of life which is essentially tragic, compounded of success and failure, informed by knowledge and understanding, relieved by humor and tempered by sympathy, embued with an awareness of human suffering and the human capacity to endure."

PRINCIPAL WORKS

Things Fall Apart (novel) 1958
No Longer at Ease (novel) 1960
The Sacrificial Egg, and Other Stories (short stories) 1962
Arrow of God (novel) 1964
A Man of the People (novel) 1966
Beware, Soul Brother, and Other Poems (poetry) 1971
Christmas in Biafra, and Other Poems (poetry) 1973
Girls at War, and Other Stories (short stories) 1973
Morning Yet on Creation Day (essays) 1975
The Trouble with Nigeria (essays) 1983
Anthills of the Savannah (novel) 1987
Hopes and Impediments: Selected Essays (essays) 1988

CRITICISM

Joseph Swann   (essay date 1988)

[*In the following essay, originally presented at the XIth Annual Conference on Commonwealth Literature and Language Studies in German-speaking Countries in June 1988, Swann comments on the relationship between Achebe's novels and history.*]

Two statements from Chinua Achebe's essay on **"Colonialist Criticism"** throw an interesting light on his novels. In the first he takes issue with those critics who have found his writing too earnest:

> I hold, however, and have held from the very moment that I began to write that earnestness *is*

appropriate to my situation. Why? I suppose because I have a deep-seated need to alter things within that situation, to find for myself a little more room than has been allowed me in the world.

In the second he suggests a relation between the service the artist renders to society and the social roots of his creative work:

> And so our world stands in just as much need of change today as it ever did in the past. Our writers responding to something in themselves and acting also within the traditional concept of an artist's role in society—using his art to control his environment—have addressed themselves to some of these matters in their art.

The tension between these two statements, the one political, or in our current terminology 'committed', the other what we would call aesthetic, accounts for a lot that is specifically African, and specifically modern, in Chinua Achebe's writing.

It is present, for instance, in the changing relation Achebe's novels have to history. For if, as C. L. Innes and Bernth Lindfors have remarked [in *Critical Perspectives on Chinua Achebe*], the novels "can be seen as a tetralogy, documenting Nigerian history between 1890 and 1965"— and *Anthills of the Savannah* brings the quintet in this respect simply more up to date—the approach the five novels take to history is quite different. They are, to borrow Achebe's own metaphor, a family, all of them portraying, criticizing, interpreting the matter of history, and all of them concerned with the living word in which history, for the creative writer, is made. But if, like the photographer, we look at them from a certain angle, we see in them characteristic emphases; and if we look further from the oldest to the youngest of these novels we can trace in their features a development from contemplation to action that exactly mirrors the commitment to society and to art which engendered it.

Things Fall Apart, Achebe's now famous first novel, is a picture of Ibo village life at the turn of the century, when the white man first came up the Niger. It is the story, perhaps even the tragedy, of Okonkwo, the great man of Umuofia who is brought down by anger and by the ambition which is fear of failure. Abiola Irele speaks of the "tragic conflict" in his character, but points out at the same time that Achebe's purpose in this novel is to show the "living structure" of Ibo society, to show it "as an organism animated with the life and movement of its members" ["The Tragic Conflict in the Novels of Chinua Achebe," in *Critical Perspectives on Chinua Achebe*], and it is this purpose which takes precedence in the story:

> 'Ekwefi!' a voice called from one of the other huts. It was Nwoye's mother, Okonkwo's first wife.
> 'Is that me?' Ekwefi called back. That was the way people answered calls from outside. They never answered yes for fear it might be an evil spirit calling.
> 'Will you give Ezinma some fire to bring to me?' Her own children and Ikemefuna had gone to the stream.

Ekwefi put a few live coals into a piece of broken pot and Ezinma carried it across the clean-swept compound to Nwoje's mother.
'Thank you, Nma,' she said. She was peeling new yams, and in a basket beside her were green vegetables and beans.
'Let me make the fire for you,' Ezinma offered.
'Thank you, Ezigbo,' she said. She often called her Ezigbo, which means 'the good one.'

The author's tone is instructive, explanatory: this, he says, is the way it was, and he as a story-teller stands outside both the picture and the action he describes. The details contribute to the sense of integrity which this picture conveys, a sense of life before the fall, although it is a life fraught with the inconsistencies which will help bring that fall about. Okonkwo passes through this tableau like a sleep-walker. He is there, with all his weaknesses, but he seems hardly to touch the picture, nor it him. He too is pictured from the outside, and his personal drama is related to that of his people only inasmuch as it happens to take place at the same time. There is no foreground or background here: all is equally foreground. But in this detached objectivity lies the commitment of the teacher—Achebe has made quite a point of this—reconstructing the dignity and humanity of his past for a disillusioned world. Happening, meaning and message are one, and they are presented as the material of history.

In *Arrow of God* this is not the case. Ezeulu, the central figure in the novel, is the instrument which in its obstinacy brings about his people's defection. His tragedy is integral with that of the clan, but, being so, it raises the question far more forcibly than does Okonkwo's, as to whether this is unmitigated tragedy at all. In *Things Fall Apart* Okonkwo's father and his son both represent another side of Ibo culture, the gentler, less ambitious characteristic which Okonkwo learns to call *agbala*. And we are told

That is how Okonkwo first came to know that agbala was not only another name for woman, it could also mean a man who had taken no title.

The values which lead his son to embrace Christianity are rooted here in the very speech of the tribe; for these are, among other things, the values which forced Okonkwo's father to an ignominious death and led Okonkwo himself to slay the child from the neighbouring clan who called him in his turn father. Achebe, who never gives easy answers, suggests in these passages that the transition to Christianity, which preluded, of course, the whole colonial enterprise, might have brought gain as well as loss. But now, in *Arrow of God* there is no such clarity. The reader is left to interpret; and one valid interpretation would seem to be that Ulu himself willed the defection of his people: willed it, not for any reason of cultural dissatisfaction, but as a simple historical necessity, to safeguard the bare existence of the clan.

Paradoxically, where Okonkwo is seen from the outside, and therefore clearly known, Ezeulu, with the inner workings of whose psyche we are far more acquainted, remains "known and at the same time Unknowable." In him we see the watchful leader and judge of the affairs of the village; but in him too we explore the emotional and intellec-

tual darkness with which the white man's law and religion confront him. There is far more dynamic range in his character than there is to Okonkwo's, and this is reflected in the language of the novels. Speaking of the fears of the two men, we read in Ezeulu's case:

He was now an old man but the fear of the new moon which he had felt as a little boy still hovered round him. It was true that when he became Chief Priest of Ulu the fear was often overpowered by the joy of his high office; but it was not killed. It lay on the ground in the grip of the joy.

In contrast to this, the passage on Okonkwo seems impersonal, essayistic:

. . . his whole life was dominated by fear, the fear of failure and of weakness. It was deeper and more intimate than the fear of evil and capricious gods and of magic, the fear of the forest and the forces of nature . . . It was not external but lay deep within himself. It was the fear of himself, lest he should be found to resemble his father.

Where *Things Fall Apart* is a depiction, *Arrow of God* is a conscious interpretation of history, a multi-layered exploration of the thoughts, feelings and deeds which make it up, and of the culture in which these thoughts, feelings and deeds inhere. Very little, in this exploration, is given; for it is an exploration, not of the facts, but of the why's and wherefore's of history. What *is* given, however, is the same picture of village life as in *Things Fall Apart;* only this time it is given as background and counterbalance to the drama of Ezeulu. It is no longer there for its own sake, but incidentally.

Where *Things Fall Apart* is immediate and direct, the meaning of *Arrow of God* is indirect. The matter of history is immersed in the dialectic between the world we observe and our attempts to penetrate it with our minds. If *Things Fall Apart* claims truth to history, it does so for the sake of a present historical purpose: to enlighten and instruct. And the concept of history which it serves is, as one would expect, known, clear and ready-made. In *Arrow of God* this concept has radically changed. History now is process and act: the creative act of writing, the experience of reading and never quite finding out. In this perspective *No Longer at Ease,* Achebe's second novel, and *A Man of the People,* his fourth, are closer to the first novel than to *Arrow of God.* In both of them the meaning is direct, in both it is now ironical; in the earlier novel the irony is moral, and rather obvious; in the later it is a more subtly satirical one.

History now has moved closer to the present. *No Longer at Ease* is set just before independence, *A Man of the People* in the troubled years of the mid-sixties when the first Nigerian republic gave way to military rule. Ngugi [in "Chinua Achebe: A Man of the People," in *Critical Perspectives on Chinua Achebe*] has praised the increasing involvement of the novel in its history: "The teacher no longer stands apart to contemplate. He has moved with a whip among his pupils, flagellating himself as well as them"; but he criticizes Achebe for still keeping to the bounds of individual morality—or immorality, for several writers have pointed out that the hero of this novel is dangerously close to the corrupt system of values he criticizes. But this again is Achebe's complexity. If the novelist as critic intervenes in the historical process, he does so for the sake of his own truth, not the historian's. And that truth is something whose vitality is intimately connected with its lack of a clear edge. As Douglas Killam points out, [in *The Writings of Chinua Achebe*], Odili Samalu, whose story this is, is not a stereotype, and if he seems to be the young man who knows all the answers, those answers betray themselves by their glibness, as well as by the questionable consequences Odili draws from them. Doing so, they betray Odili, however, as being fully human. Gareth Griffiths [in "Language and Action in the Novels of Chinua Achebe," in *Critical Perspectives on Chinua Achebe*] has compellingly shown how the words of this first person narrator weave a pattern both of mistrust and of trust. His clichés, which "undermine the confidence which the reader has in Odili's reliability as a narrator," at the same time force the reader to make the only sort of judgement which in a real world is possible: a judgement based on the cohesive force of language as it acts in the mental and emotional complex of our lives. For Griffiths,

> *A Man of the People* is Achebe's first attempt completely to dissociate himself from the solutions and figures he creates. But it is a logical technique for a man whose work as a whole shows the finest kind of objectivity.

The objectivity of depiction in *Things Fall Apart* and of the exploratory act of language forced upon the reader in *Arrow of God* has taken a further step towards immediacy. Vision, and then reflection, have shifted into the play of language out of which our world is made. "Achebe's writings," Wolfgang Klooß has said, "are more than mere explanations of the African, i.e. Nigerian, reality. They form an integral part of this reality . . ." The degree of integration in Achebe's writing, the degree of its intervention in history, is increasing.

Twenty-two years have elapsed since *A Man of the People*: years that have seen worse things in Africa than that book prophesied. And then, in 1987, Achebe published *Anthills of the Savannah.* Set in an African country whose young, recently established military ruler has just sought confirmation from the people in his aim to become President-for-Life, it seems to take up just where *A Man of the People* left off. Technically, too, it pursues the development already evident in the other books: it is as different from them, that is to say, as they are from each other. Indeed in this difference lies its continuity.

Its form is very mixed, very relaxed. The narrative is shared by three first person speakers, each of whom, in other chapters, becomes the vehicle of a third person discourse; and this discourse blossoms out at times into essay and prose poem, as well as into full-blooded thriller. In addition there are passages where the narrator is an omniscient being above the action, and these merge into yet other moments of distant, philosophical reflection. It is not difficult to follow these changes (although at one moment the author himself forgets who is supposed to be

speaking), but it is difficult to follow the time-sequence in the novel. There are indications; and one can spend some interesting hours piecing the jigsaw together, but the conclusion forced upon one is that it does not matter: history here has finally broken with time. Not the material but the telling of the history is the substance of the novel. *Anthills of the Savannah* reports, to a lesser extent it interprets, and it certainly criticizes; but doing these things it above all constitutes its world.

It is the story of two women, the highly educated Beatrice, administrator in one of the offices of state, and Elewa, the shop-girl. And it is the story of three men, Chris, Sam and Ikem: three boys groomed in the best schools and universities—or in Sam's case at the Royal Military Academy at Sandhurst—who find themselves, after the coup, in leading positions in the West African Republic of Kangan. Sam, now a colonel, is His-Excellency-the-Head-of-State, a reincarnation, as Chris observes, of medieval tyranny. Chris, in the early days of the coup his closest advisor, is now a disaffected Minister of Information, the last man, as he says, ever to find out what is going on—for that is the prerogative of 'Major Samsonite', the odious director of the State Research Council who has his nickname from the paper-stapling device that is his favourite instrument of torture. Ikem, poet and intellectual, has taken over Chris's old chair at the *National Gazette,* in whose columns he wages a single-handed fight against the regime. *Anthills* is the story of Chris and Beatrice, of Ikem and Elewa, and of their attempts to form a common front against the encroaching tyranny.

The attempt fails of course, because of the different temper, as well as the particular situation, of the individuals concerned; but its failure becomes the drama of those individuals, and into that drama people from all walks of life are drawn. Beginning with a cabinet meeting, we are taken to a public execution, an expatriate party and a gathering of elders and their metropolitan kinsmen from the province of Abazon. This is Ikem's province as well as Beatrice's, and the refusal of this area to endorse the new ruler's ambitions is in fact the main trigger of the plot; for it is in connection with this refusal that first Ikem and then Chris are impeached and sacrificed. Equally important, however, is the light thrown by one of the elders at this meeting on the relation between story and world:

> 'So why do I say that the story is chief among his fellows? The same reason I think that our people sometimes will give the name Nkolika to their daughters—Recalling-Is-Greatest . . . The story is our escort; without it we are blind. Does the blind man own his escort? No, neither do we the story; rather it is the story that owns and directs us. It is the thing that makes us different from cattle; it is the mark on the face that sets one people apart from their neighbours.

The dignified speech of *Things Fall Apart* and *Arrow of God* reaches here into the present, and what it tells us is that the story we hear is continuous with our world. This is the specifically African aesthetic of *Anthills*—although it is an aesthetic shared by any people for whom meaning is, as it is not in the West, inherent in language, in myth. And it is this that governs, to an ever-increasing degree,

Achebe's history. For, as in the example of *mbari* which Achebe quotes in an earlier essay [from ***Morning Yet on Creation Day***]—*mbari* is the shrine of the Earth Goddess, a work of art created, not by a single craftsman, but by the common people under his guidance—so too in his own Nigerian history, the language which interprets, which makes meaning, is indivisible from the language which it interprets. This oneness of world and language is a condition visible throughout Achebe's writing. It is the reason why his seriousness was such an obstacle to critics whose one aesthetic was still moulded by the romantic separation of meaning and thing. That a writer should want to perform an action in the world, that he should speak of changing it, was for them anathema. To a West which is gradually leaving behind this aesthetic, however, Achebe's latest novel comes as a work of considerable relevance and maturity. It has, sure enough, been criticized for its mixture of forms. But precisely here lies its modernity. ***Anthills*** is serious, but it does not have to take itself seriously any more. The language of the novel plays in and out of the language of its African world: its hotch-potch is its radical strength.

Achebe's commitment here is to a history made vital and actual in language, and aware of itself as such. History is not, as it was in ***Things Fall Apart,*** there in the past to be known and told about: it comes into being in the minds and feelings of those involved in it. It is the product of the words which form it. That, I think, is why there is no fixed standpoint in ***Anthills,*** no single story teller and no single story: the face of history has become a crowd snapshot, with its own very real claim to objectivity. And this takes us back to ***Things Fall Apart.*** For if there is an important linear development in Achebe's attitude to history, a movement from involved detachment to detached involvement, the more important development is circular. ***Things Fall Apart*** was also, it will be remembered, a mixed, imbalanced form.

Anthills of the Savannah is involved in the genesis of history. What takes place here does so inside the characters who tell their story. They, mentally and emotionally, are struggling to find guidelines through the morass of violence and fear which has taken the place of corruption in their society. Ikem especially grasps the importance in this enterprise of the common people:

> he had always felt a yearning, without very clear definition, to connect his essence with earth and earth's people;

and

> It is the failure of our rulers to re-establish vital inner links with the poor and dispossessed of this country, with the bruised heart that throbs painfully at the core of the nation's being.

There is something *déjà vu* about this—and Ikem is a convicted reformist, not a revolutionary. But he is passionate in his conviction. And it is this passion, this sense of going somewhere, that also shines through the clichés of Chris and his sophisticated girlfriend. These people are real, they constitute history because of, not despite, their inadequacies. They are dispensable, and they—the two men at least—are dispensed with: Ikem at the hands of the State Research Council, and Chris at the hands of a half drunken policeman whom he tries to stop raping a girl on his flight up-country from the capital. But it is in this flight itself that the real language of history is spoken. Chris is being smuggled out of Bassa by a taxi-driver and his mates; at a road-block one of the men thrusts him out of the car because it will be safer to go through on foot. Chris almost gives himself away; his fear makes him totally inarticulate, and it is left to his companion to talk the pair of them through. As they come out across the bridge they discuss their experience:

> 'You think you no go forget your job again?' his companion asked teasingly. 'When you no fit talk again that time, fear come catch me proper and I begin pray make this man no go introduce himself as Commissioner of Information!'
> 'Me Commissioner? At all. Na small small motor part na him I de sell. Original and Taiwan.'
> 'Ehe! Talkam like that. No shaky-shaky mouth again. But oga you see now, to be big man no hard but to be poor man no be small thing. Na proper wahala. No be so?'
>
> . . . . .
>
> They walked along merrily discussing in confidential tones their recent success. Chris wondered why the soldier had stopped them in the first place. Had he noticed them get down from the taxi?
> 'At all!' said his companion. 'Make I tell you why he stop us? Na because of how you de walk as to say you fear to kill ant for road. And then you come again take corner-corner eye de look the man at the same time. Nex time make you march for ground with bold face as if to say your father na him get main road.'

This is not *déjà vu*, although it *is* the translation into a modern idiom of the sentiments and even the perspective which inspired ***Things Fall Apart.*** For it is the right of the children to inherit the tongue of their fathers, and it is their duty to use it. Achebe uses it here to create the objectivity of a history that comes into being on the page: these words are simply there. The net which caught the random life of the Ibo village is the same which catches now the speech patterns in which the life of a community is formed. For language of such vitality is not only the matter but the moving force of history. It is Beatrice who, after the common death, diagnoses her people's plight as that of "an alienated history." The novel's language shows a way out of it.

For the anthills of Ikem's vision are symbols, things which speak and, speaking, link past and future: " . . . like anthills surviving to tell the new grass of the savannah about last year's brush fires." And the novel itself is now symbol, not discourse. It is not about anything, nor does it have any purpose, beyond itself: it *is,* it has become, history. A history neither reported now, nor interpreted, but presented as the thing-in-language of a high objectivity. And when Beatrice and Elewa, the survivors, name Ikem's daughter 'AMAECHINA: May-the-path-never-close' they express the hope that may arise out of this objectivity.

History, we are told in this novel, is learning a language; it is learning that one is not alone. For in it we assimilate the events that made and make us. History and myth have been deconstructed: they have once again been liberated into language. (pp. 191-203)

> Joseph Swann, "From 'Things Fall Apart' to 'Anthills of the Savannah': The Changing Face of History in Achebe's Novels," in Crisis and Creativity in the New Literature in English, edited by Geoffrey V. Davis and Hena Maes-Jelinek, Rodopi, 1990, pp. 191-203.

John Povey   (review date August 1988)

[*Povey is an English educator. In the following review, he assesses the significance of* Anthills of the Savannah *to Achebe's career and examines the political themes in the novel.*]

Chinua Achebe completed his classic tetralogy in 1966 with the publication of **Man of the People,** his pessimistic yet prescient description of the corrupt years just before the military coup. Then there was a gap. He eschewed writing. The Civil War preoccupied him, first in his dedicated allegiance to the Biafran cause, later as he tried to assimilate the horrors that conflict brought to the Igbo people. A couple of short stories and a selection of poems were all he essayed in the immediate post-war years, during which the partial healing of the Nigerian body politic attended Achebe's own spiritual reconciliation. Recently there was a curious publication, **The Trouble with Nigeria,** in which, with an intriguing mixture of exasperation and affection, Achebe tried to speculate why Nigeria, in many ways so lively and exciting, was so intrinsically ungovernable, seeming to relish, or at least tolerate, chaos above order. Achebe likened local politics to the defiant habits of daredevil drivers along the roads: selfish and belligerent attitudes are cheerfully transferred into the political arena. Now, unexpectedly, there is at last a fifth novel. Its appearance had been awaited with eagerness balanced with anxiety, for expectation was so unreasonably high. Achebe's reputation now erected a possible barrier to dispassionate critical reception, because it is inevitably against the impressive distinction of his previous novels that his latest effort will be measured.

Anthills of the Savannah cannot repeat the heroic dignity of **Things Fall Apart** or **Arrow of God.** It does not match the profound ironies of **No Longer at Ease** or **Man of the People.** This is deliberate. Achebe has determined some different intention in his latest work. One could even suggest that it is almost a fictional development of his vigorous polemic **The Trouble with Nigeria** since it asks precisely the same question through the personal experiences of four carefully contrived and balanced characters whom Achebe sets into a fictional West African country, Kangan. Kangan suffers under a regime markedly like Idi Amin's Uganda—certainly worse than anything yet perpetrated in Nigeria. The book is structured around three men who were at school together and as childhood friends rose to power together. Ikem Osodi is the journalist-intellectual who very soon learns that his view of the inde-

pendence of thought and press brings him into direct conflict with the president. Chris Oriko becomes the politician who still believes honesty and truth have some place in the new society and that his service can moderate the extremes of dangerous authority. The president, having achieved power by a military coup, almost pathologically moves from a genuine determination to improve his country into a state of power lust and paranoia fed by the gossip of treasons whispered to him by sly and self-serving cronies. The degeneration of an otherwise decent person intoxicated by power is impressively delineated. Chris Oriko is the pivot of the events. He begins as an idealistic man whose humane tolerance and honor remain, in spite of the evidence that the president has become a dictatorial monster who no longer functions within the ambit of rational decency.

The story is a bitter and, sadly enough, too accurate statement of the circumstances of modern Africa. Yet this book has moved beyond the expectations of the genre. It has been designed as a means of exploring, and protesting, the tragic circumstances that result from the corrupt administrations imposed upon that continent. In the earlier novels Achebe, with great literary skill, was supreme in making action convey to the reader the terrifying truths he exposed. Okonkwo's killing of the messenger and Ezeulu's determined refusal to eat the sacred yam are single acts that persuade one of the inevitability of his historical interpretation. Here Achebe falls into a pattern of writing in which he explains and discusses rather than represents. In exchange for the sharply observed event, there are numerous pages of dialogue and long passages of anxious introspection. The author's personal presence is continuous and extended. In some measure his characters have become puppets to be manipulated so that the horrendous circumstances of this time are exposed. Perhaps Achebe's own vision has become swamped with the terrible situations in Africa. They may seem to scream so urgently for condemnation that the literary characteristics of detachment or irony seem an evasive method of proclaiming the real accusation that has to be made.

Perhaps Achebe is foreseeing a further role for the novel as a political device. Just as he used his earlier novels to challenge the misapprehensions of the colonial decades, now he speaks as both prophet and doomsayer. There is some potential optimism in the fourth figure, Beatrice Okoh, who becomes one of the most effectively developed female characters in Achebe's work. That at the end she gives birth suggests the prospect of some ultimate survival of the human spirit in spite of the deaths of the honorable people with whom she was lovingly involved. The dust jacket blurb talks of this novel being "filled with hope." One characteristic of Achebe's distinction as a novelist has been his powerfully ironic last lines, which have become almost a signature of his work. In this novel the last lines are in pidgin: "What kind trouble you wan begin cause now? I beg-o. Hmm!" The "hmm" suggests a curious final irresolution both in the character and the author. Perhaps Achebe is in a state where he feels that his judgment of events is "hmm." But then again, perhaps he is contemplating what trouble he can begin to cause!

This novel does succeed, to the extent that its argument is vigorous and convincing, though this is not normally considered the ultimate justification of such a work. Yet, as one reviews the events presented and the interplay of character so deftly designed, one recognizes a major writer at work. If by some miracle the writer's block has broken away, one looks forward with renewed optimism and confidence to the publication of Achebe's sixth book, which will continue and sustain the reputation of this distinguished humanist and man of letters. (pp. 21-3)

> *John Povey, in a review of "Anthills of the Savannah," in* African Arts, *Vol. XXI, No. 4, August, 1988, pp. 21-3.*

A. Ravenscroft (essay date 1988)

[*A South African-born educator, Ravenscroft has written extensively on Achebe and Nigerian literature. He identifies as his major concern the effects of colonialism on the Third World. In the following excerpt, he discusses technical and thematic aspects of* Anthills of the Savannah.]

In Chapter Nine of **Anthills of the Savannah,** the village elder from a distant province declares: 'To some of us the Owner of the World has apportioned the gift to tell their fellows that the time to get up has finally come.' And later: '. . . . it is only the story can continue beyond the war and the warrior.' With an emphasis, both thematic and technical, upon 'the story', **Anthills of the Savannah** is a novel that not only chronicles the ill times but peers, uncertainly, beyond them.

Even before Independence in the 1960s African writers like Soyinka (e.g. *A Dance of the Forests*) and Achebe (e.g. *No Longer At Ease*) were telling their people that the time to get up had come, and for two decades since then have been displaying for them the reasons why they are not yet fully erect. In his satirically entitled drama *A Play of Giants* (1984), Soyinka created three monstrous tyrants, based quite obviously upon Bokassa of the Central African Republic, Mobutu of Zaire, and Amin of Uganda, and showed how their bloated arrogance, greed, savagery, and lawlessness had nothing to do with genuine African concepts of power and humane government.

Achebe's fifth novel (the first for twenty-one years) is not as direct as Soyinka's iron-fisted satirical farce. It deals with a trio of friends adventitiously at the apex of power after a military coup in the fictional West African state of Kangan. These are, however, no monsters, but decent, warm-hearted, though self-centred, educated men: the Sandhurst-trained army officer who becomes President, the London-graduate journalist his Commissioner for Information, and the poet, also a London graduate, who is editor of the official Government newspaper. Although the latter (Ikem Osodi) has from the beginning a true though vague, uninformed sympathy with the poor majority of ordinary people, the trio belong to the tiny minority of the educated elite who imitate the manners and, in varying degrees, the values of their former British colonial masters. Culturally a little pretentious (he plays his 45 r.p.m. Mozart record at 33 r.p.m,), the President is athlet-

ic, courteous, urbane, but very consciously plays the part of his notion (gained at his British-type high school) of an English gentleman—'Not very bright, but not wicked', as Ikem observes. That is, until he attends his first Organization of African Unity Conference and is there patronized by an African Emperor and an African President-for-Life. On his return home he starts dramatizing his role as Head of State ever more imperiously and imperially, seeing every public gathering or demonstration as a major threat to State security and thus to his personal position as Head of State. He gradually turns away from his former friend and confidant, Chris Oriko, the Information Commissioner, and relies increasingly on his sinister Head of Security.

Neither Chris nor Ikem clearly perceives this change, Chris because he is too close to the President and is blinded by the elation of playing politics, Ikem because he is too busy investigating public abuses and writing his 'Crusading Editorials' which do produce a few social reforms. Ikem has published poems, a play, and a novel, but though he possesses both poetic fervour and social conscience, he believes that there is an 'ultimate enmity between art and orthodoxy'. The novel seems to imply that the fate that overwhelms him owes as much to his own individualistic impetuosity (a courageous refusal to be silenced) as it does to chance circumstances concatenated by the Security Police. Yet the barrier that his elitist education has erected between his individuality and his perception of the stubborn sense of rural African community that still exists among ordinary people is beginning to crumble before the end, and the mother of his posthumous child is not an intellectual but very much an urban 'woman of the people'.

Of the three friends, Chris is nearest the centre of the novel; chiefly because he is allowed an opportunity to grope through the veil of his own moral blindness, to learn that power doesn't so much corrupt, as deaden sense and intuition, and turn energy into lethargy. But late as it is, he does find a sticking point, and once he defies the President and has to go underground, he learns, Gloucester-like through journeying, the obverse of power-wielding. The blasted health on which he gains unaccustomed insights is a long-distance bus journey through the kingdom he had been part-ruler of, right into the drought-stricken, disaffected province, where only anthills are to be discerned in the desolate landscape.

If **Anthills of the Savannah** had ended here, it would have meant that in the twenty-one years since **A Man of the People,** Achebe had learned only to confirm the rather bleak, intellectually cynical vision of political Africa that the earlier novel tends to project. Now, however, the urban masses comprise people with individual lineaments. And the final chapter, even with its acrid question: 'What must a people do to appease an embittered history?' is about the unorthodox, strangely ecumenical naming ceremony for Ikem's child, performed by Chris's woman-friend Beatrice (with her Anglican enclave upbringing and a London Honours degree in English) who has emerged in the course of the novel as a latter-day analogue of a traditional village priestess of Idemili, daughter of the Almighty, who was sent to clothe naked Power in 'a loincloth of peace and modesty'. In naming the daughter of the poet, she is joined by the a-religious, semi-literate mother, by the newly politicized student, by the ordinary, family-man taxidriver, by the devotee of the Yahwe Evangelical Sabbath Mission, by a 'proper grade-one Moslem', and even by a highly ambivalent Security captain of cloudy loyalties.

Despite the transparent clarity with which dictatorship and the grinding down of the masses are shown to be the aims of both inhuman and merely incomplete men, Achebe catches the tunes of hope for African people, even if in ambivalent or partly muffled tones. His faith in the precolonial humanity of African society (a faith he celebrated in *Things Fall Apart* and *Arrow of God*) points him to the still viable though much modified rural village culture expressed through the wisdom, tolerance, and humour of the Abazon elder in the Harmony Hotel scene in Chapter Nine. But Achebe also implies that the modern urban proletariat have in some way inherited snatches of this African communality: instances of Pidgin homespun seem repeatedly to carry populist wisdom analogous to the proverbs of pre-literate village speech—linguistic attempts, in other words, to make sense of buffeting experience.

In *A Man of the People* Achebe used Pidgin chiefly to indicate informality in the relationship between speaker and person addressed, but in *Anthills of the Savannah* Pidgin occurs much more extensively in the characters' speeches and at the same time assumes the characteristics of a living vernacular. Even more than with Achebe's previous novels, the reader has to listen with a very sensitive ear indeed to the kinds of language characters and narrators use. With political orthodoxies side-stepped, the sounds of

hope come through across a range of diverse language levels—the sophisticated English of the educated elite, the demotic Pidgin of the people, the proverbial and parable-like cadences of the Abazon elder, the liturgical incantation of Ikem's 'Hymn to the Sun', the lyricism of Beatrice's temple-priestess lovemaking with Chris, the transformation of traditional kolanut ritual into litany for blessings not only upon the infant being named but upon all the life of Kangan. Technically, therefore, **Anthills of the Savannah** is more adventurous than Achebe's earlier novels, with transitions (usually, but not invariably, well contrived) from omniscient narrator to one of four character-narrators and back, across a wider variety than before of language usage, with a sharper sniffing out of injustice and corruption, yet with a stronger faith in African self-reliance, however ambivalently the signals of its reality might flash upon the novelist. (pp. 172-75)

> *A. Ravenscroft, "Recent Fiction From Africa: Chinua Achebe's 'Anthills of the Savannah'—A Note," in* The Literary Criterion, *Vol. 23, Nos. 1-2, 1988, pp. 172-75.*

Chinua Achebe with Kay Bonetti (interview date 1989)

[*In the following interview, Achebe discusses his novels and comments on Nigerian culture and his reasons for becoming a writer.*]

[*Bonetti*]: *When people speak of African literature, they say African literature, as opposed to Nigerian literature, South African literature, Somalian literature. Is there a reason for that?*

[Achebe]: We generally talk of Africa as one because that's the way Europe looks at Africa, and many people in Europe and America who have not travelled, or who are perhaps not well educated, probably think that Africa is one small state or something somewhere. Another reason is that the quantity of the literature is not overwhelming yet, so one can put them all together. But it is growing. Suddenly Nigerian literature is a substantial body of literature. Somalian literature is not enough yet to form a body by itself, but it can fit into the general name of African literature. We ourselves do not have any difficulty at all in recognizing regional differences, but there are distinctive qualities—even within Nigeria. The literature which is beginning, just beginning, to come out of the Moslem part of Nigeria is very different from the literature which is coming out of the south. Very few people know of this yet, outside of Nigeria. As time goes on, I think there will be greater and greater and greater emphasis on the differences.

Can you tell us about the political and cultural makeup of Nigeria?

One quarter of the entire population of Africa is in Nigeria, so we say that every fourth African is a Nigerian. During the European scramble for Africa, Nigeria fell to the British. It wasn't one nation at that point; it was a large number of independent political entities. The British brought this rather complex association into being as one

---

Achebe on Joseph Conrad's *Heart of Darkness*:

Students of *Heart of Darkness* will often tell you that Conrad is concerned not so much with Africa as with the deterioration of one European mind caused by solitude and sickness. They will point out to you that Conrad is, if anything, less charitable to the Europeans in the story than he is to the natives, that the point of the story is to ridicule Europe's civilizing mission in Africa. A Conrad student informed me in Scotland that Africa is merely a setting for the disintegration of the mind of Mr. Kurtz.

Which is partly the point. Africa as setting and backdrop which eliminates the African as human factor. Africa as a metaphysical battlefield devoid of all recognizable humanity, into which the wandering European enters at his peril. Can nobody see the preposterous and perverse arrogance in thus reducing Africa to the role of props for the break-up of one petty European mind? But that is not even the point. The real question is the dehumanization of Africa and Africans which this age-long attitude has fostered and continues to foster in the world. And the question is whether a novel which celebrates this dehumanization, which depersonalizes a portion of the human race, can be called a great work of art. My answer is: No, it cannot.

Chinua Achebe, in his Hopes and Impediments: Selected Essays, *Doubleday, 1988.*

nation and ruled it until 1960 when Nigeria achieved independence. Christian missionaries from Europe were active in the southern part of Nigeria, so today there's Christianity in the south and Islam in the north. The three major groups in the nation are the Yoruba in the southwest, the Ibo in the southeast, and the Hausa, finally, in the north. This is simplifying it, but that's roughly the picture.

The differences, as I understand it, between the Yoruba and the Ibo was that the Yoruba had a system of royalty, and the Ibo were more egalitarian.

Yes, yes. The Ibos did not approve of kings. They may have had kings in the past, and I suspect they did because they seem to know a lot about kings. They had five titles and the fifth and the highest title was that of king. For every title there is something you do for the community, you feast the community, you entertain the community, you produce so much money, you produce so many yams. The title for king fell out of use because its final requirement was that the man who aspires to be king would first pay all the debt owed by every single man and every single woman in the community!

Is it because of the more pragmatic and egalitarian government of the Ibos that the Christians seemed to take hold there more easily?

What you say is probably one of the answers. The other, I think, is the openness of the Ibo system. The Ibo world view is basically a world view of change. Nothing is permanent, everything is in motion. Ibo art is full of drama, of activity, of tension. The Ibo saw the Europeans and the power they had and listened to what they preached; they put two and two together, and said, you know, these people are so powerful, there must be something in what they believe. The Ibo respect power, and they respect success. A man who succeeds as a farmer, who succeeds as a householder—these things are highly regarded. In Ibo belief, every man and woman is created separately by a unique god-agent called a *chi,* and this *chi* is virtually responsible for success in life. Your *chi* is the representative of the supreme god, of the almighty. So the two of you sit over there, before you come into the world, and agree on what kind of life you are going to have, and make a pact. The trouble begins, of course, when you come here and halfway through your life you want to change. Your *chi* says, "Well, you know, a deal is a deal. We agreed that you are going to be a poor man, a poor woman. We agreed that you will suffer, we agreed to this. Why do you want to change now?"

How do you come to know the nature of your chi?

You learn it from your success in life. If you are a failure, if everything you touch crumbles into dust and ashes, then you know after a while, "Well, I have a bad *chi.*" But it's not just a bad *chi,* it's a metaphor "I have a bad life." And when you have a bad life, the Ibo say "It's because you wanted it that way." This is where this idea of the pact comes in—it puts some of the blame back onto you. It's nearly permanent, but if you strive, if you say "No!" strongly enough, you might begin to shift it a bit.

Isn't it a paradox that you can rebargain with the forces and change your chi?

The Ibo never accept anything which is rigid and final and absolute: "wherever one thing stands, another thing will stand beside it." The duality, you see. So when they say you've made a bargain, they say, "Yes, it's a bargain, it will hold, it's binding." But, in the final extremity, if you really desire strongly enough to change it, there are ways in which you might set about doing it. Nothing is final and absolute.

As when Okonkwo's father [in **Things Fall Apart**], *who is a bit of a wastrel, asks Chielo, the oracle of the hills for better luck with his harvest and she tells him, "If you want better yam harvests, go work."*

Yes. She tells him off because he hasn't been working very hard. He's a nice fellow, he's good on the flute and he's a good, decent man. The world needs people like him. But if you are constantly drinking and borrowing money and never paying back, your children are going to be in difficulty. The society frowns on this kind of thriftlessness but the society doesn't want you to swing to the other extreme. It is really a question of balance.

And this is Okonkwo's flaw?

That is Okonkwo's flaw. One can see how it comes about. Okonkwo is brought up in the shadow of his father, who hasn't made it, and this is a very materialistic society, but materialistic in a particular way. You have to be able to feed your family, and if you don't, it's a matter of shame. So Okonkwo's whole life is an attempt to make up for what his father didn't achieve. This is a great mistake. It is a metaphor for what we have all observed, that a very weak father will generally produce a very strong son. And a very strong father will generally produce a weak son. This is cause and effect, and bringing up a child then becomes a balancing between strength and weakness to show the child that there is value in both. The Ibo society is full of sayings that draw your attention to that, because this is a culture that on the surface, believes very much in strength.

Are we to infer that Nwoye is weak?

That is how he would appear to a man like Okonkwo, who would misread Nwoye, as he misread his father. But that's not really true. These are people who reflect the other half of human reality, the music side, the story side, as opposed to the war side. And one is as valid as the other. The flaw of Okonkwo—not only Okonkwo but to some extent of Ezeulu, is that they would not give way ultimately. But the whole meaning of this kind of story is that people come to a critical moment in their history where something has to give, and that there are people among them who will make themselves available to stand fast. Without that, the history of people would become very trite, very trivial. It would simply become no history at all. The story of **Things Fall Apart** is told because Okonkwo did not shift, so we are talking about him today.

It seems like standing fast is a two-edged sword. In **Arrow of God** *it becomes an extremely complicated issue.*

Dealing with humans is complex enough. When you bring the divinities into a story, it becomes impossible to unravel. One is not really sure, for instance, when Ezeulu says, "My god tells me to do this," what exactly he is saying. Is there any way of disputing when a priest, any priest, says, "This is my conviction, this is what the god I serve thinks about this." Have we any right to doubt? And when the priest says this, how much is his own wish and will and how much of it is the will of the gods, or is it the will of the community? These are very difficult questions, and they probably don't have an answer. We must take things as they are. A priest is somebody who abides by the ritual.

How do we fit Obika's death into this? The community clearly sees Obika's death as proof that Ezeulu was not being straight with them about the wish of Ulu in the matter of the yam festival.

That's what the community thinks, but they don't really know. Obika's death complicates the matter even further, because it gives a handle to the community. But if it is not really so, then the conclusion to the story asks this very question: Is Ulu actually punishing Ezeulu in this way, by taking his son and then by destroying his priesthood? Ezeulu is destroying himself, as well. So is there a bigger necessity in the universe? Has the time come for these local divinities to give way to perhaps a bigger concept of deity, a bigger concept of religion? Who knows?

The irony is even further compounded by the fact that while every people must have those who say, "Here I stand," the fact is Okonkwo loses a child to the forces of Christianity, and Ezeulu loses his community to Christianity.

But what are the options? There are no options, this is it. We are at a juncture in history when the options are finished. The people are going to accept the Europeans, they are going to accept Christianity, or some of them are, and they are going to send their children to school. They can do nothing to stop this. But there is one saving grace, that they had a priest, a chief priest, who said, "No" at some point. That stands like a pillar in the course of their history, a place from which they can take bearing.

People have commented that **Things Fall Apart** *reads like a Greek tragedy, even down to the end where the suicide takes place off-stage. Are there traceable associations between traditional African belief structure and that of ancient Greece?*

This has to be handled with caution because there's a lot of emotion and a lot of prejudice to break through, to push aside. It would seem, quite clearly, that ancient Egypt was the first major civilization we know and that the civilization of ancient Egypt derived a lot of its origins from farther south, from Ethiopia and perhaps even from west Africa. But the history of Europe which Europe prefers to situate in Greece—and not beyond—would probably need to be looked at again. Some people are beginning to look at the debt of European civilization to Africa and the Middle East. This is something which has apparently been deliberately overlooked. Encyclopedias, for instance, tell you that ancient Egypt was originally called Kemet. This word Kemet means black, but they deliberately tell you that this "black" comes from the black soil of Egypt, from the soil brought from the Nile. So this blackness has nothing to do, in case you think so, with people who are black, yet if you look at the pictures of the Pharoahs, they are negroid. I have no doubt in my mind that lots of the words, the language, and the thoughts, the religion, and the customs of the Mediterranean derived extensively from Egypt, and this in turn derived from further south in Africa.

Were you thinking of a classical structure when you wrote **Things Fall Apart** *and* **Arrow of God**?

No, that was exactly the way I thought the story should be told. It could be told in many ways, I think, but there was one way which I could tell it to my greater satisfaction. It had to be lean, not convoluted, direct and even simple. The opposite of the grandeur of an epic is the simplicity of its telling.

Did you have to educate yourself about traditional culture and mythology or did you grow up with that?

It was around me, because—even though my father, who was a teacher, and my mother were both Christian converts from their childhood, there were other people around who were not Christians. The community was half Christian and half not Christian, even within my father's family. My father tried very hard to make his younger brother a Christian, and he was constantly becoming a Christian, falling off again, and coming back. There were others, there were uncles who did not accept the Christian faith, and the village still had its festivals, had its ceremonies, and so on. I could see all that, and my father, who was a very devout Christian, had enough knowledge of the traditional society that he would tell about it, the history of that town, of that people. I was fascinated by it, so I listened.

I read that you started thinking about becoming a writer in response to your colonial education in the university. Is this true?

You can't explain why you become a writer, actually, in one word. But you can certainly show strands of the story, and that certainly was one. The moment I realized in reading *Heart of Darkness* that I was not supposed to be part of Marlowe's crew sailing down the Congo to a bend in the river, but I was one of those on the shore, jumping and clapping and making faces and so on, then I realized that was not me, and that that story had to be told again. Now, I didn't realize this automatically. I read some of the colonial novels as a child without seeing anything happening, even identifying with the invading European. Literature can put you on the wrong side if you are not very careful, if you are too young. If the heroes are these people from abroad, and the natives are the enemy, then as a young reader you take sides with invaders of your country. The moment you realize the trick that has been played on you, that's the moment that I think that you decide "This is not my story." It happened with Conrad, it happened with Joyce Cary. Joyce Cary was even closer because in *Mr. Johnson,* the chief character is from the south which is rather like Nigeria. I could not visualize this character. This was the first English Department class at the University of Ibadan, which had just been founded. Every single student there had difficulty with *Mr. Johnson.* The staff, which was all white, you know, English, Oxford and so on—they thought this was marvelous. They told us this is the image of a poet, you're not supposed to see an ordinary African here. So you have this buffoon, really, and he's supposed to be a very great African character; this book is supposed to be the great African novel. Our teachers meant well, they wanted us to read something which related to us. This is why they included Joyce Cary's book in the syllabus, but it did do something for us because we said "Oh, this is Nigeria? What happened to the Nigeria I would recognize? What has been written about that?" This is one course of my inspiration. My Christian background was another, but going even further back, I think the traditional attitude of Ibo people, of African peoples, to storytelling was part of it.

Everything you have just said would imply that you felt at the time a necessity for written literature in Africa, even though the oral tradition was strong. Why?

Because writing had come to Africa and writing is a very powerful thing indeed. There was no running away from it, even if one wanted to. Colonialism itself needed a literature to justify what it was doing. It was really saying, "If we are going to take over these people and their land and their lives and their history, we've got to find a good story to justify it. If we're going to cart away their diamonds and gold, we've got to be able to say that they didn't have any need or use or understanding of these things. They don't really own them, you see, they just happened to be lying around in the same place as these things." This is colonial ideology and to counter colonialism, you need your own ideology. This is really putting it very, very crudely. (pp. 63-72)

Was writing in English a conscious choice for you?

My literary education was in English, though I read Ibo. There wasn't really a literature yet in written Ibo. I read the Bible, the hymnbook, the Book of Common Prayer, a few translations like *Pilgrim's Progress,* which was one of the things that the missionaries translated into Ibo. But the bulk of Ibo literature was oral. It was only later that I made the decision that I must write certain things in the Ibo language, as well. I've done some things, mostly poetry.

Is the choice to write in European languages controversial?

There are now people who say, "Oh, anything you write in a European language is not African literature, it is European literature. So we must all forget English or French or Portuguese." My position is this is too doctrinaire, and there is a case for writing in these languages in Africa today because these languages are spoken in Africa. We work with them, they are the languages in which we transact a good deal of our busines as nations. If we do that, we must also write in them. But I think there is also the need for developing African literature in African languages. So it's not just a question of one or the other, but both, in my case.

How difficult is it to transmute traditional elements— mythology and idioms—into English?

Writing itself is a translation, if you think of it properly— you are translating what you feel or hear in your mind into language. You are translating ideas into language. But there are certain things you cannot convey as well from one language to another as others, and you know that, you deal with it, you go as far as you can. Because I have written in the two languages, I know it's not simply easier to write in the Ibo language. Sometimes it's much more difficult.

Aren't there cases where there simply are no words in English, or no phrases or no existing idioms that will convey a certain thought and vice-versa?

Yes. There, you go back and use the words in the inner language. This is why you find some Ibo words in my novels. Even a word like *chi,* which occasionally I have tried to translate as "personal god" or "guardian angel" or whatever—this is not a good, an adequate translation. So you go back to *chi.*

When did you actually start writing stories?

I played around with short stories in school and university, but I didn't really think of myself as a writer until after I left the university. I was very, very busy in broadcasting at that time, because Nigeria was visited by Queen Elizabeth II and her husband. In the night, I would go back to my novel, to this thing I was scribbling. This was around '55, '56.

Was that **Things Fall Apart?**

Actually, ***Things Fall Apart*** and ***No Longer At Ease.*** My original intention was to write a saga covering three generations of the Okonkwo family in one book. The first draft was that way, but as soon as I finished it, I felt it was not quite right, I was trying to cover too much time, and it tended to be rather light and superficial. So my decision was that I should do three separate books, one on each generation.

What happened to the middle one?

The middle generation—when I got to it, I got stuck. It's very interesting, it's very strange. That is my father's generation. That was Isaac's—Okonkwo's son's—story. It just didn't have the way, the image—and later on I began to suspect that I did not know enough about this very, very strange generation, my father's generation, to be able to do justice to it in the novel. I didn't know enough about my father—why did he become a Christian? Why did people of the generation decide to abandon their religion and their faith? What was it? It's a good story, but I think that it probably isn't as simple as I imagined originally. (pp. 73-6)

You've said that the writer's role is to explain society to itself. Do you see yourself as a writer who presents answers in his books, or one who poses questions?

The latter, one who poses questions, is a more congenial role for me, and more meaningful, because once you ask the right questions, I think that the answers will be easier. If you go back into my culture, we did not have a written literature. But we had art, and this art had a way in which it interpreted the world. It had values, it had things it wanted to do, it had positions it took on such things as the relationship between the artist and the rest of the community. For instance, in the Mbari ceremony, ordinary men and women in the community would be selected and secluded with professional artists. Together they would create an artwork for the community to celebrate. Anybody can become an artist, provided he works in the proper environment with those who have special talent. Everybody has some art in them, art is made for the community, the community is involved. During the period when this group is working, which might be days, weeks, and even years, the community feeds them. They are not supposed to do any other thing but to create the art. This is some of the background that I bring to my own creative process, this is one source of my inspiration. Art which is closely lined with the people who make it, or from whom it is made. Art which celebrates the entire life of the community—not praising them, because that's not what I'm talking about, not about adulation.

So in the art of the Mbari, everything is presented, warts and all, as in your books. You show medicine men who take the sacrifices home to make a pot of chicken stew instead of burying them. But you portray it all to celebrate and not to denigrate?

That's right. You criticize as harshly as you like, you fight with people, but that's not denigrating them. You are not questioning their humanity, you are not making them look like animals. Art has to be in the service of people. If I see an artist who says, "I don't care about society, I don't care what happens to people," that's not an artist. You may as well have a priest who says, "I don't care about religion." Art makes our passage through life easier. All kinds of things come into the art, even those which are threatening, like the white District Officer. Why do you put him there? To channel his energy, like a lightening conductor, you see.

You mentioned the need of the artist and the right of the artist to withdraw—and yet you have lived consistently a public life.

You can't write a novel in the marketplace. You must snatch your moments of privacy, your moments of introspection out of this rather chaotic world.

It's been twenty-two years since the publication of **Man of the People,** *and now* **Anthills of the Savannah.** *Has your public life, your work as a citizen of Nigeria during the Biafran War, especially, taken you away from writing?*

If it has, then it's a dreadful price to pay, but I'm not afraid to pay that price. It would be very easy for the artist to say, "I withdraw, you see, to my contemplation." That would be very simple. What do you do, then, about these people that you are supposed to be working for? How do you understand them? How do you know them? It's a very, very fine balance between involvement and withdrawal.

Was the work on **Anthills of the Savannah** *another reason for this relative silence from you in the last twenty-two years?*

It took a long time, yes. I began it fifteen, sixteen years ago. I wasn't working on it consistently. I began and it didn't make itself available, so I put it aside. I was writing poetry, short stories, children's books, essays. It just wasn't there, and I never push my work. I never write very much, I write slowly. But this time, there was the block, and it could very well have been the Biafran war, it could very well be that I was too involved in society, but that's the price I have to pay for my views. If I had a different view, then perhaps I would write more novels, but I wouldn't care to write more novels that were founded on what I regard as a wrong kind of relationship with the world.

How would you describe the humor in your work?

Our humor is founded on very close observation, very, very close observation of reality. You find some humorous proverbs, for instance, and the humor is that whoever made these proverbs was not going around the world with his eyes closed. For example, the dog says that those who have buttocks do not know how to sit. This proverb deals with someone who has all the opportunities but blows everything, you know, blows it all away. Then you think of the dog sitting—obviously, a dog has no buttocks, but it sits immaculately. A dog sitting, you know, is a perfect form. The proverb brings what we see in nature, the way the dog sits, into relationship with something which is totally different, far more serious. One of the worst things is a very pompous person who has no sense of his own ridiculousness. Anybody who can laugh at himself, at his condition, has some hope.

Anthills of the Savannah *is cautionary in light of history. It is so easy to pass off as a buffoon somebody who is ultimately extremely dangerous.*

Those are not jokers and we laugh at our own peril. The glint of the weapon is in the voluminous folds of the laughter. The problem isn't simply going to go away because people are laughing. They've got ultimately to do something about it themselves.

How do you relate **Anthills of the Savannah** *to the books that precede it?*

It is part of the rest. What I've tried to do is retell modern African history in fictional terms. I pick what I think are crucial moments in that history and focus my attention on them—sort of the junctions, the crossroads of that history. *Things Fall Apart* was the first coming of the white man to Iboland; *A Man of the People* the first military coup in this African country. And *Anthills of the Savannah* situates itself in an Africa of military rule, in an Africa in which the woman is now stepping out of her role as the woman in reserve.

In **Anthills of the Savannah** *the reader realizes in chapter seven that Beatrice is talking, and at the end that she's talking about events that are to come in the novel. How did you determine that narrative structure?*

I think that was commandeered, actually, by the story. This difficulty probably had something to do with it: my reflection on the role of the artist, the role of the half-mad divinity who possesses diviners, artists, and decides who should be a storyteller. In the end, it came down to two real voices, one of the voice of the person chosen to tell the story, and the third person voice, the one that is not ascribed to anybody. We might call it the authorial voice, but it isn't really, it is this third force, and the rest are really contributions as witnesses.

Sam, Chris, and Ikem are all killed. Their flaw has been, as Beatrice pointed out to them, that they think they are Kangan, that they embody its history. The lesson that's learned is that they aren't Kangan; Kangan is everybody, as represented by the people gathered in Beatrice's apartment at the end of the novel.

That's right. But, of course, having said that, the hope is that at least now we know. This little group is not just a group of survivors, they are people who know, who have seen, and who have learned something. The tragedy of somebody like Chris is that he died just as he was beginning to see.

Why does the figure of balance transfer from the male to the female?

Traditionally when the men have tried and failed, then they have called in the women. The women have the insights for survival. They are creators of life, and for some reason or other, they have not been allowed much say in the affairs of the world. We find all kinds of excuses for keeping them away, and we can't go on with that kind of pretense. We've got to try something else. But it's not a guarantee. It's only a conditional source of hope.

At the end Ikem's female baby is given a male name that means "May the path never close." And the Moslem elements of the culture, the Christian people, and the traditional, all dance together. You have this vision of what is possible for this country.

Yes, yes. That is the hope, that is the hope. It's the only one that I can see. That child you mentioned, "May the path never close"—there is nothing that guarantees that she will survive. A lot still depends on how the survivors handle their history from now on. This is really where the hope lies, that we will perform better, and if we do, then there is hope. If we don't then god help us. (pp. 77-83)

Chinua Achebe and Kay Bonetti, in an interview in The Missouri Review, *Vol. XII, No. 1, 1989, pp. 61-83.*

C. L. Innes   (essay date 1990)

[*An American educator, Innes has commented that "Achebe's novels are particularly interesting to me not only for their concern with the relationship between individual, national, and European identities and traditions, but also because they develop a new kind of fiction, blending these traditions in a complex literary form that is nevertheless accessible to a wide readership." In the following excerpt, Innes remarks on the relationship of Achebe's short fiction to his novels.*]

Between the publication of *Things Fall Apart* and *No Longer At Ease,* Achebe published two shorter pieces of fiction, **'The Sacrificial Egg'** in 1959 and **'Chike's School Days'** in 1960. The latter at first sight may seem to be in

part an elaboration of some of the autobiographical reminiscences in the essay, **'Named for Victoria, Queen of England'**, but most of the details given about Chike's family differ from Achebe's. The sketch also includes some of the details which will later be either elaborated or alluded to in the novel which was to be written twenty-five years later, *Anthills of the Savannah.* One such detail is the amused memory of the half-understood counting rhyme, 'Ten Green Bottles', which Chike and his fellow primary school pupils sing with great vigour; another is the English proverb so much loved by Chike's teacher and by Beatrice's schoolmaster father, 'Procrastination is a lazy man's apology'. Like many of the stories, it provides the opportunity for a variation or another perspective on a theme or story which Achebe will deal with elsewhere. Thus, the conflict and consequences created by marriage to an *osu*, given a contemporary setting in *No Longer At Ease,* is here, in a two-page flashback within the six-page sketch, placed in the first decades of the century, and focused on Chike's parents, two early Christian converts supported by the missionary, Mr. Brown. In this case the marriage is also bitterly opposed by the mother of the young man, but Chike's father neither wavers (as Obi does in the face of this opposition) nor effects a reconciliation through the next generation (as Nnaemeka does in **'Marriage Is A Private Affair'**). Here the mother reacts by renouncing Christianity and returning to 'the faith of her people'. The whole episode concerning the marriage of Chike's parents is told in the voice and from the perspective of non-Christian villagers, and acts as a counterpoint to the rigid certainty of the Christian father and schoolteacher as well as the innocent pleasure which Chike experiences in his discovery of English language and storytelling—those 'jaw-breaking words from [the] *Chambers Etymological Dictionary*'; his delight in the sound of English words often conveying 'no meaning at all'; the first sentences in his *New Africa Reader* 'like a window through which he saw in the distance a strange, magical new world'. Those seemingly innocent first sentences have from the adult reader's perspective particularly ironic implications: 'Once there was a wizard. He lived in Africa. He went to China to get a lamp.' The tale for European children, plucked from its Arabic origins, takes for granted the exoticism of both Africa and China, and the unreality and unsavouriness of wizards. For Chike, these European cultural assumptions and perspectives mingle happily with the fantasy and magic evoked by what to the English reader are 'homely' words such as 'periwinkle' and more literary and latinate ones such as 'constellation'.

These final sentences and Chike's delight in half-understood English words have a peculiar impact on the reader because the sketch has already introduced us to two 'wizards'. One is the missionary Mr. Brown, chiefly respected by the villagers 'not because of his sermons, but because of the dispensary he ran in one of his rooms' from which Amos, Chike's father, had emerged 'greatly fortified'; the other is the diviner, consulted by Elizabeth, Chike's grandmother, whom the villagers knew to be 'a man of great power and wisdom'. Her visit to the diviner who, like Mr. Brown, combines spiritual concern and the knowledge of healing, is described in considerable detail, which subverts the assumptions by which such men have been dismissively termed 'witch-doctors' and 'wizards' in European myth and colonial discourse.

'Chike's School Days' is deceptively simple in appearance, seemingly a rambling sketch, to whose random nature even the narrator draws attention when he declares after that two page 'digression' about the marriage of Chike's parents that 'we have wandered from our main story'. The fact that it has been ignored by most critics, even when discussing the other stories in the same collection, suggests that it has been taken at face value. But with the first two novels in mind, readers should by now have learned to look twice at such declarations by the fictive narrator. Second and third readings reveal that this is a carefully constructed and closely packed piece which explores and sets off reverberations in the reader's mind from a multiplicity of conflicts and contrasts, from the suggested but unforeseen consequences concerning the colonial encounter, and from the innocent youngster's delighted discovery of an exotic English language and literature, whose cultural assumptions he is not yet able to question, although the reader has already seen the power with which the teacher, notorious for his floggings, and the father, unwavering in his Christian certitude, will impose them.

'The Sacrifical Egg' is one of the many stories in [*Girls at War, and Other Stories*] which focus on people, periods and perspectives which are more marginal in the four novels published by 1966. Whereas the novels have told the stories of those who aspired to be central to their communities or their nation, these stories dwell on the perspectives and situations of those who have never seen themselves as holders of power—for the most part they are concerned with physical and psychological survival, a struggle in which they generally see themselves as more or less lucky rather than good or clever. Instead of the titled men, priests, university graduates and politicians who are the focal characters in the novels, these short stories concentrate on women who become outcasts such as Akueke of the story of that name and Gladys in **'Girls At War'**, clerks such as Julius and Uncle Ben in rural towns like Onitsha, taxi-drivers and ex-bicycle repairers such as Jonathan Iwegbu and Rufus Okeke, eager school children such as Chike and Veronica. It is appropriate, therefore, that the story placed first in the collection, **'The Madman'**, should be about a character who is the greatest outsider of all, and about the movement of a man who complacently believes in his centrality to the position of being an outcast. Indeed, displacement from centre to periphery might well be seen as *the* Achebe plot, the structure which informs almost all of his fiction. His primary interest is not so much in what happens when 'things fall part' as in establishing that 'the centre cannot hold'.

And like many of the other stories, **'The Sacrifical Egg'** establishes an ironic tension between the reader's assumption of the desirability of a central and consistent faith or philosophy and the main character's acceptance of contradictions and inconsistencies. Unlike Okonkwo and Ezeulu, Obi and Odili, who are so concerned with distinguishing between old and new, good and bad beliefs and customs, characters like Julius Obi and Uncle Ben find no difficulty in accommodating Igbo beliefs and attitudes as well as Christian ones. Though Julius sings in the CMS Choir and is therefore approved as a suitable husband by Janet's devoutly Christian mother, all three of them accept the dreadful reality of Kitikpa, the evil god of smallpox, and of the nightmasks which swirl past Julius in the dark. Like Uncle Ben, they also accept the reality of Mami Wota, the legendary seductress who brings untold wealth but no children. Appropriately, both stories are set in Umuru, a thinly disguised Onitsha, which gathers to its market not only Igbos from the inland villages, but also different kinds of peoples from along the Niger and Anambara rivers. The traditional market place has had grafted on to it the European Palm Oil trading company 'which bought palm-kernels at its own price and sold cloth and metalware, also at its own price', and it is here that young men like Julius and Ben, with their Standard Six certificates, find work as clerks. In the case of Julius Obi, the tragic reality of Kitikpa and the abyss created first by quarantine and then death overwhelms all other divisions. For the cheerfully garrulous Uncle Ben, however, the jumble of beliefs in the baleful power of Mami Wota and the supremacy of White House Whisky have a happier outcome.

Like *A Man of the People,* published in the same year (1966), **'Uncle Ben's Choice'** gains its effect from its use of a first-person narrator who is also the central character in his own story. Both, as young men, are charmingly irresponsible lovers of life and women and dangerously complacent. Odili's attempt to reconcile the traditional and 'modern' at the end of the novel is a conscious one; for Uncle Ben the question of reconciliation does not arise, since he has, despite his elevation to Senior Clerk in the Niger Trading Company, always remained 'a true son of our land' who never regrets following his kinsman's reminder: 'Our fathers never told us that a man should prefer wealth instead of wives and children.'

'The Voter', first published in the important African cultural journal *Black Orpheus* in 1965, was also written about the same time as *A Man of the People,* and belongs to the same world, for it concerns the electoral proceedings of the Minister for Culture, holder of many honorary titles and doctorates, in his home village. This time the story is told from the point of view of a narrator sympathetic to one of the Minister's vote gatherers, one Rufus Okeke—Roof for short. Except perhaps for Roof's energy and lack of malice (he is just doing his job), there are no redeeming features in this election campaign—no idealistic young Odilis, no wider concern for the welfare of the nation. For the elders and the younger members of the village alike, the issue is money, and votes are sold to the highest bidder. Having committed his vote twice, Rufus has no qualms about dividing his vote, tearing the ballot paper in half and posting one half in each candidate's box. The futility of this exercise escapes him, but is for the reader merely the final example of the whole travesty of democracy which the story has unveiled, the emptiness of: 'Election morning. The great day every five years when the voters exercise their power.'

As young men, Rufus and Uncle Ben have in common certain character traits: a cheerful energy and pride in 'know-

> **Indeed, displacement from centre to periphery might well be seen as *the* Achebe plot, the structure which informs almost all of his fiction. His primary interest is not so much in what happens when 'things fall part' as in establishing that 'the centre cannot hold'.**
>
> **—C. L. Innes**

ing their way around', a desire for and enjoyment of the good things of life, and admiration for those who have them. But the older Uncle Ben has learned what Rufus has yet to learn and may never learn, that there are things more important than wealth, and these include above all wives and children. That lesson is learned and reiterated even more forcefully by yet another cheerfully energetic survivor, Jonathan Iwegbu, whose story is told in **'Civil Peace'**, which was first published in *Okike* in 1971. The reader might well view the wit, energy, compassion and muted optimism of this story in the aftermath of the civil war with something of the admiring incredulity with which he or she responds to Jonathan Iwegbu's unfailing optimism as he counts his blessings after the devastation of the war. Chief among those blessings is the survival of himself, his wife, and three of his four children. But as Jonathan reiterates, 'Nothing puzzles God' and he is delighted to recover his bicycle and then find his house still standing and only partly damaged in Enugu—and anyway, there are plenty of old bits of zinc and cardboard with which to repair it. For Jonathan, every small act of recovery—even the money earned by the hard work of his wife and himself—is *ex gratia*, an act of grace bestowed upon the lucky by the unfathomable gods. Hence when he is robbed of what he and his friends termed an *egg-rasher* (*ex gratia*) payment of twenty pounds from the federal government (in return for his hard-earned but worthless Biafran money), Jonathan does not complain:

> 'I count it as nothing,' he told his sympathizers, his eyes on the rope he was tying. 'What is *egg-rasher*? Did I depend on it last week? Or is it greater than other things that went with the war? I say, let *egg-rasher* perish in the flames! Let it go where everything else has gone. Nothing puzzles God.'

The second half of this story, the account of the robbery, suggests that Achebe might well, if he so wished, prove a dramatist. The episode mingles fear, suspense and hilariously grim comedy as the off-stage robber leader and his chorus of thugs introduce themselves, satirically join in the cries for assistance, offer to call for the 'soja' when neither neighbours nor police respond, and reassure the frightened family:

> 'Awrighto. Now make we talk business. We no be bad tief. We no like for make trouble. Trouble done finish. War done finish and all the katakata

wey de for inside. No Civil War again. This time na Civil Peace. No be so?'

'Na so!' answered the horrible chorus.

Three of the stories in this collection, including the two longest, **'Vengeful Creditor'** and the volume's title story, focus on women and their aspirations, blighted in each case by the society and the circumstances that surround them. The earliest published of the three is **'Akueke'**, which was first printed in 1962. Set in traditional Igbo society, this story powerfully establishes the isolation of Akueke, surrounded by her well-meaning but uncomprehending brothers:

> Akueke lay on her sick-bed on one side of the wall of enmity that had suddenly risen between her and her brothers. She heard their muttering with fear. They had not yet told her what must be done, but she knew . . . Last night Ofodile who was the eldest had wanted to speak but had only stood and looked at her with tears in his eyes. Who was he crying for? Let him go and eat shit.

Neither Akueke nor her brothers consciously question the laws of a society which dictates that young girls must marry an approved suitor, and that those struck with 'the swelling disease' must be carried out and left in the bush. Yet in each case, Akueke's response is one of passive resistance. Akueke longs for her mother and her mother's people in whose presence, she believes, 'This would not have happened to her', although her illness is seen by her brothers as punishment for her pride and unwillingness to conform to accepted patterns of female behaviour, a judgement she has at least partially internalized. The first half of the story ends with an appalling image of Akueke's isolation as her sorrowing brothers follow the conventions of society and abandon her in the bush, too exhausted to resist any longer.

The second half of the story extends the enigma of Akueke and her situation. Incredibly, she survives and reappears at the house of her mother's father. How, we are not told. Are we to believe, as the brothers at first do, that this is the ghost of Akueke? Or perhaps the 'swelling' was not the dreaded fatal disease at all, as the grandfather implies when he demands of the shocked brothers, 'If you don't know what the swelling disease is why did you not ask those who do?' Was this a psychosomatic illness, like the illnesses suffered by so many European women in the nineteenth century, as a means of resisting the intolerable demands of a patriarchal society? Can Akueke find psychological sustenance only so long as she is seen and respected as 'mother', and not as younger sister and predestined wife? Does the story reveal above all the conflicting attitudes to women in Igbo culture, both in myth and practice, so that women are on the one hand denigrated and isolated, denied control over their own lives, and on the other hand elevated as mother figures and carriers of spiritual meaning? The questions are unresolved, and we are left to contemplate the figure of Akueke, 'unsmiling and implacable', readopted as Matefi and about to begin again the path of daughter and future bride, for 'When she marries', the old man concludes, 'her bride price will be mine not yours.'

There could scarcely be a sharper contrast with the traditional setting and mode of **'Akueke'** than **'The Vengeful Creditor'**, published almost a decade later in the first issue of *Okike*. Opening not in a small rural village hut but in a busy urban supermarket, and characterizing a confident, wealthy working woman who is also a wife and mother, we seem to have moved a long distance from the world of Akueke and the psychological isolation that was her lot. Nor is there the compassion and suspended judgement which hovers over the dilemma of all the characters in the earlier story, male and female alike; here the satire and judgement is directed sharply against Mrs. Emenike, along with her husband and others of their class who are so willing to sacrifice the poor and relatively helpless so that their own lives may not be discomforted. The difference between the two stories marks a more general change in Achebe's fiction from concern with those such as Unoka, Nwoye and Akueke for whom the cultural and psychological conventions and norms of their society do not allow adequate fulfilment, to an increasing recognition (seen in *A Man of the People*) of the importance of class interest as a factor in the denial of individual fulfilment.

As a means of focusing on the ways in which private and public concerns converge, Achebe uses the issue of free primary education and its abortive introduction by the Western and Eastern Regional Governments in 1955-57. Mrs. Emenike, a social worker, and her civil servant husband, are quickly disillusioned with its introduction when their servants begin deserting them in order to attend school. On one of their brief and infrequent visits to Mr. Emenike's home village, they secure the services of ten-year-old Veronica for a wage of £5 a year and, more importantly as far as Veronica is concerned, the vague promise of schooling for her when their youngest child no longer needs a 'baby-nurse'. As Veronica watches the Emenike children escape each day from the world of her household duties and the moment of her own return to schooling seems ever more distant, she tries to eliminate the baby whom she sees as the obstacle to her own education, by giving him red ink to drink. Her choice of ink has been made credible by a previous warning from Mrs. Emenike, who has found her playing with it, that red ink is poisonous, but the ink is also a symbol of the education she so avidly desires. Veronica is no passive resister like Akueke, or like her tired and harassed mother, and the red ink spilt over the baby's front is a potent image of the bloody vengeance that the poor may take upon the middle classes who blindly and selfishly exploit them and frustrate their aspirations to share in those things the Emenikes so complacently take for granted as their right— bountiful food, work and good wages, and education for their children. As David Carroll points out in his discussion of this story [in *Chinua Achebe*], Mrs. Emenike's response, 'Perhaps it's from me she learnt', when Veronica's horrified mother protests that she could not have learned such things from home, is doubly ironic. For Veronica *has* learned by example from the Emenikes that the welfare and rights of others can be dispensed with if they stand in the way of her getting what she wants. And the remark

also epitomizes Mrs. Emenike's smug certainty that she is blameless, a blind complacency which suggests little hope of change from the top.

Although he has written a number of poems about the Civil War, **'Girls at War'** is Achebe's only work of fiction which covers the Civil War period (**'Civil Peace'** refers back to it, but is essentially about its aftermath). Written mainly from the point of view of Reginald Nwankwo, a Biafran official from the Ministry of Justice, it records a series of meetings with a young woman called Gladys, whose changing appearance and responses to the war become for Reginald 'just a mirror reflecting a society that had gone completely rotten and maggoty at the centre.' But here, as so frequently in the story, Reginald's own stance is called into question by the violence of his dismissal of a society from which he considers himself detached. Nor is the reader allowed to see Gladys as 'just a mirror', and insofar as she *does* reflect her society, it is Reginald's image that stares back at us. Although Achebe here uses free indirect speech rather than first person narration, in some ways this story shares the technique so effectively used in *A Man of the People,* where the complacent young man who prides himself on his relative idealism gradually reveals the confusion and corruptibility of his own motives, especially in relation to his attitudes to women. In this short story, the circumstances and the consequences are much grimmer, and the judgement passed on Reginald is much harsher, although his attitudes and behaviour are likely to be neither more nor less damnable than those of the average male reader of a story such as this.

Reginald has encountered Gladys three times: the first is at the very beginning of the Civil War 'in the first heady days of warlike preparation when thousand of young men (and sometimes women too) were daily turned away from enlistment centres because far too many of them were coming forward burning with readiness to bear arms in defence of the exciting new nation.' The parenthetical 'and sometimes women too' subtly suggests the marginal role of women in the narrator's consciousness, as well as the contrast between the role some of them would wish to play as opposed to that which they will be permitted in the war effort. Accordingly, Reginald has forgotten their first encounter, when Gladys as a schoolgirl had obtained a lift with him to go to Enugu to enrol in the militia only to be told by Reginald to go back to school and join the Red Cross.

In the beginning, Reginald has questioned neither his attitudes nor his advice, nor even his amusement at 'the girls and the women who took themselves seriously' as warriors, just like 'the kids who marched up and down the streets at the time drilling with sticks and wearing their mothers' soup bowls for steel helmets'. However his second encounter with Gladys appears to chasten him as, despite his manifest annoyance, her businesslike and uncorruptible devotion to duty dampens his 'suppressed rage' at her treating him just like anybody else and awakens his 'intellectual approval' of her thoroughness. The possibility that his 'intellectual approval' and sudden new belief 'in this talk about revolution' has anything to do with his 'first real look at her, startlingly from behind . . . a beautiful girl in a breasty blue jersey, khaki jeans and canvas shoes', is not entertained by Reginald.

The third and final meeting takes up the major portion of the story, when 'things had got very bad'. As an official with the right connections, Reginald Nwankwo and his family are able to survive much more comfortably than the average Biafran citizen, and again and again, Reginald deflects his guilt and unease on to those like Gladys whom he sees as worthless goodtime girls. Nor is Gladys presented as a passive receptacle of Reginald's desires; she angrily points out the contradictions between his actions and the attitudes he expresses, contradictions which Reginald himself sometimes recognizes and rather guiltily indulges. So he collects a carload of charity food for his wife and children (and some for his driver) trying to avoid the eyes of the 'scarecrow crowd of rags and floating ribs' hanging around the depot, offers a ride to 'a very attractive girl by the roadside' and roughly dismisses a despairing old woman who is also seeking a lift. His means of avoiding embarrassment is to bury himself in a book. Yet he immediately condemns Gladys for what he assumes to be her connection with 'some well-placed gentleman' and for wearing the wig and clothing which attracted him to 'save her life' and give her a lift, and to call her 'a beauty queen'. While condemning her as a loose girl, whose ideals are lost, he plots to take her to his own house, where he lives as 'a gay bachelor'. At the 'real swinging party' to which he takes her, he silently condones the outburst of a drunken Red Cross pilot:

> 'These girls who come here all dolled up and smiling, what are they worth? Don't I know? A head of stockfish, that's all, or one American dollar and they are ready to tumble into bed.'

Though rejoicing as freely as his fellow party goers in the food, liquor and the luxury of 'real bread', Nwankwo salvages his conscience by priggishly refusing to dance 'as long as this war lasts', ostentatiously watching with disapproval while Gladys and others set out to enjoy themselves.

Reginald is shocked by Gladys's refusal to use euphemisms and her directness of language which fuses imagery of war and male sexual intercourse:

> 'You want to shell?' she asked. And without waiting for an answer said, 'Go ahead but don't pour in troops!'

A paragraph follows, describing the much-used rubber condom which Reginald has ready to prevent 'pouring in troops'. The protective device, 'the real British thing', could well be an image of Reginald's own consciousness and language, ever capable of avoiding direct physical and emotional contact, and the responsibilities that might ensue. One way of avoiding such responsibility is to dismiss Gladys, and indeed all the girls of her generation, as worthless:

> He had his pleasure but wrote the girl off. He might just as well have slept with a prostitute, he thought. It was clear as daylight that she was kept by some army officer. What a terrible transformation in the short period of less than two

years! . . . What a terrible fate to befall a whole generation! The mothers of tomorrow!

The next morning, Reginald is 'feeling a little better and more generous in his judgements', Nevertheless Gladys remains not an individual with whom he has made physical and emotional contact, but a symbol of society, and Reginald sees himself as the saviour of that society in the person of the symbolic Gladys. The ending of the story is swift and terrible, with a denouement which reveals not Reginald but Gladys as the true saviour who, as Reginald runs to save his own skin, sacrifices her own life in an attempt to rescue a crippled soldier.

Although the themes and techniques of Achebe's short stories are often closely related to those found in the novels, the characters are those who appear only in the background or in the margins of his major works. Here, in ***Girls At War and Other Stories*** he brings those marginalized characters into the foreground—the women, the children, the clerks, the poor traders and craftsmen—and also focuses a much harsher light on those who exploit or ignore them, the complacent middle-class professionals like Mrs. Emenike and Reginald Nwankwo. With the writing of ***Anthills of the Savannah*** fifteen years later, Achebe will create a novel which gives space and voice to these characters and to his concern with their fate at the hands of the privileged elite. It is a concern which he will also voice in his 1983 political tract, ***The Trouble With Nigeria.*** (pp. 121-33)

> *C. L. Innes, in her* Chinua Achebe, *Cambridge University Press, 1990, 199 p.*

Achebe on writing in English:

For an African, writing in English is not without its serious set-backs. He often finds himself describing situations or modes of thought which have no direct equivalent in the English way of life. Caught in that situation he can do one of two things. He can try and contain what he wants to say within the limits of conventional English or he can try to push back those limits to accommodate his ideas. The first method produced competent, uninspired and rather flat work. The second method can produce something new and valuable to the English language as well as to the material he is trying to put over. *But* it can also get out of hand. It can lead to *bad* English being accepted and defended as African or Nigerian. I submit that those who can do the work of extending the frontiers of English so as to accommodate African thought-patterns must do it through their mastery of English and not out of innocence.

> *Chinua Achebe, in his "The Role of the Writer in a New Nation," in* African Writers on African Writing, *edited by G. D. Killam, Northwestern University Press, 1964.*

Onyemaechi Udumukwu (essay date Autumn 1991)

[*In the following excerpt, Udumukwu examines the two novels* A Man of the People *and* Anthills of the Savannah, *in which Achebe explores the conditions of Nigerian life after independence.*]

The significance of Achebe's creativity manifests itself in his revelation of lived experience in Nigeria in its harrowing verities. Specifically, he has revealed the lack of contact between the leaders and the ordinary people. He has also shown that this lack of contact has precipitated a condition of contrasts and an unevenness in development. In addition he has portrayed the nature of the security apparatus in Nigeria and has enabled us to re-examine the gains of military leadership.

The aim of this [essay] is to illuminate the nature of Achebe's reaction against the negation of the expectations of national independence from colonial rule. In order to do this our attention will be focused on his two novels that reveal the nature of existence in postindependence Nigeria—*A Man of the People* and *Anthills of the Savannah.*

The promise of national independence from colonial rule has not materialized for the majority of the people in Nigeria. Hence, freedom from colonial domination and the desire for prosperity have been translated into a nightmare of needs. It is strictly in this sense—the failure to fulfill the goals of independence—that we use the term *negation.* This negation of the hopes of independence, it is widely agreed, has been precipitated partly by the continued domination of the Nigerian economy by Western imperialists and other foreign interests. This condition of existence in postindependence, it is argued, constitutes a state of neocolonialism. Although Nigeria has gained state power in the form of political independence, this is essentially a "flag independence." State power, understood as the embodiment of the power of the dominant social group which supervises existence, was merely handed over to an elite social group. It is followed by a multilateral, but new form of colonial domination, whereby Western nations compete to control the Nigerian economy. (p. 472)

To say that Chinua Achebe's contribution to the emergence and survival of the Nigerian novel has been formidable and crucial is to indicate an important line of continuity in this novelistic tradition. Achebe's creative endeavors in postindependence reveal a specific consciousness oriented toward an attempt to inspire a genuine form of leadership and political activism for his country. Consequently, the problem of leadership and its correlative abuse of power constitute a major thematic preoccupation in Achebe's postindependence writing. As we will show in this discussion, Achebe has revealed that the negation of independence in Nigeria has been occasioned by the failure of the leaders to rise up to the challenge of leadership. This, indeed, is the very distortion of what Achebe has conceived as the quality of a true leader. He says that the true leader "must put the people and country first before his own interest" ["**The Writer's Role in Society,**" *African Concord,* 1987].

Two cardinal points can be made about this assertion by Achebe. First, it implies that one of the causes of the present impasse in postindependence Nigeria is the failure of the leaders to have a plan, a blueprint, or a direction for the new nation at independence. Thus, having led the peo-

ple out from under the colonial yoke, the leaders seem to be baffled by the problem of what to do with their freedom. The second point is that Achebe's statement opens our insight into a major thematic preoccupation of the Nigerian novel (and his novels in particular) in the postindependence period: the leaders' lack of contact with the ordinary people. (pp. 473-74)

In the two novels *A Man of the People* and *Anthills of the Savannah,* Achebe reveals a picture of opportunistic politicians—both civilian and military—who appropriate state power and divert it into a lucrative means of acquiring material wealth. In *A Man of the People* the career of Nanga and his corrupt ilk is terminated provisionally with the intervention of a military rule that promises to correct the ills of the previous regime and to maintain sanity in the nation. Note that Max, one of the figures of opposition who is killed by the civilian regime, is declared a hero of the "revolution." In *Anthills of the Savannah* the military is already in power. Sam, the military head of Kanga, perpetuates the same ills as the civilian politicians before him. By the end of the novel he is overthrown by another military regime. In a sense then, the two types of leadership—military and civilian—in these two novels enable us to x-ray the overall leadership crisis in the nation in postindependence.

In *Anthills of the Savannah* the leaders' lack of contact with the aspirations of the ordinary people manifests itself in the attempt of the leaders to reduce national interests to their personal interests. This is evident in the indiscriminate scramble among the leaders to appropriate political and state power as a means of attaining financial profit. The relationship between the military head of government in Kangan, Sam, and the civilian Commissioner for Information, Chris, illustrates, from the first page of the novel, such a scramble:

> "But me no buts, Mr. Oriko! The matter is closed, I said. How many times, for God's sake, am I expected to repeat it? Why do *you* find it so difficult to swallow my ruling? On anything?"
>
> "I am sorry, Your Excellency. But I have no difficulty swallowing *and* digesting your rulings."
>
> For a full minute or so the fury of his eyes lay on me. Briefly our eyes had been locked in combat. Then I had lowered mine to the shiny table-top in ceremonial capitulation. Long silence. But he was not appeased. Rather he was making the silence itself grow rapidly into its own kind of contest, like the eyewink duel of children. I conceded victory there as well. Without raising my eyes I said again: "I am very sorry, Your Excellency."

The passage is typical of the historical situation and the political circumstances in Nigeria, particularly in the second half of the 1980s. Since the country's political independence in 1960, the control of state power in the country has oscillated between the military and the civilians. As power changes hands between the high echelon of the military and a small group of the educated section of the civilian population, thereby becoming some sort of duel, the expectations of nationhood, of rising to the challenge of rulership, dissipate. In the passage above the scramble for power that exists between Chris and Sam blurs issues of national survival. The confrontation between them becomes too personal. About Sam, we are told that "for a full minute or so, the fury of his eyes lay on me [Chris]." The source of Sam's fury seems to be connected with a past that he and Chris had shared. The two characters, with Ikem, had been mates in the secondary school, and later they had travelled abroad for their tertiary education. But in the secondary school Sam was the less brilliant. Both Chris and Ikem, his academic betters, are aware of the deficiency of their friend.

We noted earlier that the passage we are discussing here is *typical* of the historical situation in Nigeria. We can note that Sam does not refer to a specific military head of government whom we know. In her thirty years in existence as an independent political entity, Nigeria has had six military heads of government. It will be futile to say that Sam is this or that head of government. Yet, he reminds us of these men. Northrop Frye has recognized that a distinctive feature of the novel is that it "deals . . . with characters wearing their *personae* or social masks" ["The Four Forms of Fiction," in *The Theory of the Novel*, edited by Philip Stevick]. Sam, then, is a *mask* that Achebe has created and has imbued with human proportion with the purpose of reminding us of what social existence is.

There are two senses in which we use the term *mask* here. The first use refers to the individuality of Sam as distinct from other characters, say Chris, or Ikem. There is a second use of the term that connects Sam with the other characters and with history. The first use refers to the man per se. The second use by contrast connects the man with his setting and history. The second use is more profound and determines the first because it serves as an index to the character's milieu.

From this second use of the term, Sam can be perceived as the traditional Igbo mask, *agaba*. Unlike the other Igbo masks such as the *ijele* mask, and *mmau* mask, the *agaba* is wild in action and weird in appearance. The person who carries this mask wields a matchet, an indication of its destructive character. Thus, in order to avert a possible damage by this mask, a rope is tied around its waist and held by an attendant as a safety device. The *agaba* is played by adults, and in terms of character it is aggressive without being sadistic. Inasmuch as the *agaba* asserts its presence by causing a stampede in his audience, frightening the dancers and percussionists, and occasionally charging at the attendant who restrains it, it does not engage in cruelty for its own sake. In *A Man of the People* Achebe gives us an account of a "tame" *agaba* in performance. Unlike the classical *agaba* played by adults, the tame version in *A Man of the People* is played by children:

> The last, its wooden mask-face a little askew and its stuffed pot-belly looking really stuffed, was held in restraint by his attendant tugging at a rope tied round his waist as adult attendants do to a real, dangerous Mask. . . .

> While the Mask danced here and there brandishing an outsize matchet the restraining rope round his waist came undone. One might have expected this sudden access to freedom to be followed by a wild rampage and loss of life and property. But the Mask tamely put his matchet down, helped his disciples retie the rope, picked up his weapon again and resumed his dance.

In *Anthills of the Savannah* Sam is depicted as an *agaba*. His actions are described from the perspectives of the other characters, particularly Chris and Ikem whom Achebe represents as the first and the second witnesses respectively. Chris is the attendent who restrains the *agaba*, and he recognizes his crucial role. His account begins in medias res, at the stage when the masquerade has turned dangerous. He says, "I have thought of all this as a game that began innocently enough and then went suddenly strange and poisonous." The other members of the Executive Council constitute the dancers and percussionists in the masquerade. The ordinary people of Kangan are the audience. The first scene in the novel offers us a symmetry of Sam as *agaba*. In this scene his temperament is cacophonous, varying from a fiery annoyance to friendly reconciliation.

The significance of the *agaba* motif in *Anthills of the Savannah* is that it enables us to perceive the immense power wielded by Sam. The short story writer and novelist I. N. C. Aniebo has agreed that this power is so enormous that the man at the center becomes oblivious of the need to exploit this power in order to deal with social needs. Aniebo is optimistic that the military can mobilize the population to action. But Achebe does not idolize the military, and this contradicts Aniebo's opinion. It seems that what Achebe is doing here is to bring the *agaba*, the restrainer, the dancers, and the audience within a capsule for close inspection. As an active performer, like any other mask, the *agaba* is not stationary. Hence, this demands that his audience must keep pace with his active efforts. In order to depict this swirl of action that binds both the *agaba* and his companions, Achebe uses the multiple narrators, namely teller-characters and reflector-characters as narrative transmitters. [In his *A Theory of Narrative*] Franz Stanzel has distinguished between teller-characters and reflector-characters as agents of narrative transmission. This distinction has enabled him to achieve a more synthetic approach that integrates the theoretical approaches of his principal predecessors such as Norman Friedman, Wayne Booth, and Gérard Genette. The synthetic method of Stanzel manifests itself in his reduction of the traditional ideal types of narrative point of view to two main types.

Nevertheless, the confrontation between Chris and Sam, noted earlier, opens up to a more ruthless political strategem adopted by members of the dominant social group. The question to ask, however, is: how does this reveal the lack of contact with the ordinary people? First, it is important to note that the opening scene cited earlier is foregrounded against the background of the Abazon question. The Abazon question represents a major conflict in the novel. Thus, it is introduced in the second sentence in the novel. Sam says, "I will not go to Abazon."

Abazon is one of the four provinces in Kangan. But the more interesting point about this province is that it is affected by severe drought. We can note that the head of government has adopted this natural catastrophe for his own personal political games and ruses. The story of the Abazon province goes back to the early years of the regime. The Elder tells us that his people had refused to vote in a referendum so that Sam can become a president for life. He says, "When we were told two years ago that we should vote for the Big Chief to rule for ever and all kinds of people we had never seen before came running in and out of our villages asking us to say yes . . . we knew that cunning had entered that talk" (*Anthills*). According to the Elder, his people had suspected that the whole plan was a mere contrivance because Ikem had not advised them to pledge their support—Ikem is from the Abazon province.

As a result of their refusal to give their mandate to Sam, he has ordered that the amenities provided by the central government to that province be withdrawn: "Because you said no to the Big Chief, he is very angry and has ordered all the water bore-holes they are digging in your area to be closed so that you will know what it means to offend the sun." So there are subtle indications that Sam's refusal to visit the drought-affected province is linked with the inhabitants' refusal to give him the mandate for life-presidency. It is very important that the novel opens with this revealing circumstance. It immediately calls our attention to a basic doubt in the leadership.

The dilemma that is suffered by the Abazon inhabitants and the ruthless game played with the amenities provided by the state is earlier revealed in *A Man of the People.* In that context, Nanga orders the Public Works Department to cart away the water-pipes they had deposited earlier in Odili's village: "The culmination came at the weekend when seven Public Works lorries arrived in the village and began to cart away the pipes they had deposited several months earlier for our projected Rural Water Scheme."

The Abazon question, as we have noted earlier, has a more profound political implication that connects this novel with history. In spite of the political instability in the nation since independence, none of the leaders in the country has demanded a referendum to facilitate his stay in office for a lifetime as we see in the Abazon case. The military rulers have usually rationalized their intervention in civilian politics on the grounds of assuring a corruption-free regime, ready, as it were, to hand over the state power to the civilians. But apart from Nigerian politics, there are cases in Africa whereby the leaders have converted their provisional position in office to last for a lifetime. Countries like Zaire, Malawi, and the Ivory Coast, to mention but a few, are not too far removed from this type of politics. And this extends the historical implication of Achebe's novel. In other words, the account we receive in the novel does not limit the setting of the novel to a specific geographical and historical boundary (say Nigeria in the 1980s), but it extends to what is possible.

But apart from the question of life-presidency, Nigerian party-politics in both the First and Second Republics were not entirely democratic per se. The realization of democratic freedom has been marred by primordial cleavages that are both ethnic and economic in nature. In the light

of this, the provision of basic amenities is usually tied to political gains. The people have also believed that politics is a means of deriving some sense of security from the state. Thus, it is believed that a vote for the party in power or one that has a strong-hold in one's ethnic background, is an assurance of a chunk from the "national cake." Even as the nation prepares for the Third Republic, many citizens do not seem to share the high optimism of the government for a new political order. Many, it seems, still believe that politics in the Third Republic will create the avenue to new advantages. The *Newswatch* magazine reports on the enthusiasm of a party member: "I need a party card because you never can tell if government will not ask for it tomorrow before it does anything for you." Such cynicism has close links with the dilemma of the fictional characters from Abazon.

Perhaps the more engaging aspect of Achebe's *Anthills of the Savannah* is that it is the culmination of the narrative subtlety that has characterized his craft. This manifests itself in the deliberate ease with which he withholds very vital information that smooths his narrative traffic, and, when he finally releases such a piece of information, the reader is ultimately rewarded with a deep poetic insight. Note that even though the Abazon question is introduced in the second sentence of the novel, and casually mentioned on page fifty-two, the reader only gains an understanding of the complete picture on pages 116-117 in the text [1988 Doubleday Anchor edition].

The question may be asked: how do we ascertain that the Abazon question constitutes a vital piece of information and is therefore central to the conflict in the novel? The Abazon problem constitutes a central segment in the overall conflict in the novel because in each of the three moments when it is mentioned and discussed, it is presented in the form of a scene. Phyllis Bentley has argued [in "Use of Summary" and "Use of Scene," in *The Theory of the Novel,* edited by Philip Sterick] that the scene, as distinct from the summary, has a specific use in the overall action of a novel. Whereas the summary enables the novelist to "traverse rapidly large tracks of the world of the novel which are necessary to the story, but not worth dwelling upon," the scene gives the reader the "feeling of participating in the action very intensely." Put in another sense, the summary enables the writer to create the proper background for the account he gives to the reader, whereas the scene serves to foreground the specific aspects of the action that demand intense attention. Thus, the use of scene projects the Abazon issue to prominence.

This subtle means of withholding information is present in *Things Fall Apart.* As the action of the novel opens, we are told of Okonkwo's fame. But the action shifts in order to foreground this fame within the framework of his struggle to overcome his personal fears of failure and his father's failure and effeminate nature.

This lack of solicitude for the needs of the people manifests itself, also, in the existence of contrasts in the form of an uneven distribution of basic social amenities between the members of the dominant social group on the one hand and members of the dominated social group on the other hand. This inequitable distribution of amenities whereby a section of the population enjoys a better life and other sections live in misery is a negation of the expectations of independence. Thus in *A Man of the People* Odili is amused and surprised that in the capital city, Bori, the urban-poor can afford only to live in shacks, or sleep in the streets, and can only afford pails for the disposal of human waste. In the same city he finds out that the members of the ruling social group, such as Nanga, live in mansions with the basic amenities. He says: "Here was I in our capital city, reading about pails of excrement from the cosy comfort of a princely seven bathroom mansion with its seven gleaming, silent action water-closets." Acebe's subtle contrast between the seven gleaming water closets and the pail system of human waste disposal is an index to our failure in postindependence to deal with the more elementary and basic problem of everyday existence such as the disposal of human waste. We ought to pay attention to the underlying satire in this contrast. Achebe seems to confront us with a very fundamental question: isn't it quite interesting that the Nangas of Nigerian independence lack the ability to even handle mere waste? Ngũgĩ wa Thiong'o thinks that this failure in the leaders is a consequence of their "lack of creativity" ["Chinua Achebe: A Man of the People," in his *Homecoming: Essays on African and Carribean Litterature, Culture, and Politics*]. But this lack of creativity is central even in the leaders' failure to recognize the value of life for the people and the need to organize life.

Bori as a microcosm of the society at large is full of contrasts and unevenness in development. Affluence exists alongside poverty. Achebe presents these images in order to reveal what independence means to Nigerians. As Odili walks along the well-lit main streets of Bori in the early hours of the morning, he sees: "a nightsoil man carrying his bucket of ordure on top of a battered felt hat . . . [and] beggars sleeping under the eaves of luxurious department stores and a lunatic sitting wide awake by the basket of garbage he called his possession."

There is also the contrast between the town and the rural areas. In both *Anthills of the Savannah* and *A Man of the People,* the image of the rural area is a wasteland. In fact, in *Anthills of the Savannah,* Abazon is stricken by drought. And whereas Bori has good roads, electricity, and a water supply, the provision of these needs for the people of Urua and Anata has been turned into a political game. Anata, as we see in the novel, comes to life in the wake of electioneering campaigns when Nanga goes *home* to solicit for votes. This reminds us of a similar condition in Ngũgĩ's *Petals of Blood*. In that novel, Ngũgĩ emphasizes that one indicator to the negation of independence in Kenya is the existence of contrasts in living conditions. Thus the old Ilmorog is depicted as a social backwater that is trapped in a desert condition. Nderi wa Riera, the MP from Ilmorog, like Nanga, goes *home* in order to beg for votes and disappears shortly after the elections.

Apart from revealing the nature of the loss of vital link between the people and the rulers in Nigeria, Achebe's novels enable us to see the nature of the security apparatus within the social totality that circumscribes his novels. The security apparatus as distinct from the educational system or the arts is an aspect of what Althusser [in his *Lenin and Philosophy and Other Essays*] has identified as the Repressive State Apparatus (RSA). The RSAs serve to secure the political conditions under which the other instances of the social totality function.

The security apparatus in *Anthills of the Savannah* is represented by the police, the army, and the security intelligence (the secret police). It is used, as we see, for the purpose of *hegemony,* of maintaining the predominance of the individual military man or a tiny section of the military. Hegemony is a crucial political concept in Marxist scholarship. Antonio Gramsci [in his *Selections from the Prison Notebooks*] has two meanings of hegemony. First, it is a process in society whereby a fraction of the dominant social group exercises control through its morality and intellectual leadership over other allied fractions of the dominant social group. Secondly, it is an interconnection between the dominant and the dominated social groups. In this second meaning of the concept [as elaborated by Martin Carnoy in his *The State and Political Theory*], it manifests itself in the attempts of the dominant social group to use its political and intellectual leadership in order to establish its view of the world as all-inclusive and to shape the needs of the subordinate social group, or, as Althusser would put it, to interpolate the dominated into the capacious world view of the dominant group. In this section we are using hegemony in Gramsci's second meaning above, that is to say, as a relationship between the dominant and dominated social groups in Nigeria in postindependence.

We can see then that the security apparatus, more often than not, serves to carry out the personal intentions of the man at the head as such, at the expense of the nation and its people. Major (later colonel) Ossai, the Chief Security boss of Kanga, is the main character used to dramatize this role. The crucial role of the security in maintaining hegemony is demonstrated by the unwavering faith Sam invests in Ossai. For Sam, Ossai is far more competent than the members of the executive council. Thus we are told that the anxiety occasioned in the president by the untimely arrival of the Abazon delegation has been "swiftly assuaged by his young, brilliant and aggressive Director of State Research Council" (*Anthills*). Apparently, Ossai has proven to be more competent and swift than the civilian members of the executive council and is thus a source of joy to his boss (Sam). But the choice of words ascribed to Ossai—"young," "brilliant," and "aggressive"— reveals the characteristicly brusque nature of the security personnel. The celebration of raw force is obvious in the rude approach in which the Orderly ("of the quivering hand") relates to Prof. Okong, and also the traffic policeman to Ikem. In addition, Ossai embodies the brutality that is common in the security system. We are told that his hands are "enormous" and "oversize" even for a man "as big as he." Thus, there is an eerie beastly nature associated with Ossai. This animalistic character is demonstrated in the manner in which Ossai executes torture on his victims. He "invented the simplest of tortures for preliminary interrogations. No messy or cumbersome machinery but a tiny piece of office equipment anyone could pick up in a stationery store and put in his pocket—a paper stapler in short, preferably the Samsonite brand."

The image of Ossai has revealed much to us about the nature of the security apparatus in Nigeria. In free societies, the security intelligence primarily functions to help the nation to defend itself against aggressors and to restore confidence in itself. But in the context of an undeveloped economy such as Nigeria, the security apparatus serves through coercion to sustain the predominance of a ruler.

Nevertheless, the image of Ossai also reveals the thin line of demarcation between sanity and insanity or between rational man and the beast. Apart from this, Achebe uses the image of Ossai in order to reveal the ineluctable tragic consequence that lurks in the abuse of power. The individual who arrogates power to himself at the expense of problems that are man-centred, runs the risk of not only destroying himself but also the entire society.

The security in Achebe's novels speaks a monolithic language. In this regard the one-eyed Dogo in *A Man of the People* is a cousin to Ossai. Ossai, perhaps, is sophisticated to a degree. He has a uniform and carries arms; that is, his force is aided by technology. But one-eyed Dogo is a lesser being. He rushes for the whole hulk with his bare hands. In order to understand Dogo in his act, we need to suspend our belief in technology.

Now, if Ossai is instrumental to Sam, Dogo worships Nanga. There are four occasions in which we meet this human machine in *A Man of the People.* And in each of these occasions, he never stops short of "killing and eating." First, he is casually mentioned in the opening scene as Nanga meets the people of Anata during his "family reunion." Secondly, we meet him in action as Odili goes to Nanga's place at Bori. Note the tone of Dogo in this exchange:

> "Who you want?" he scowled.
> "Chief Nanga."
> "He give you appointment?"

Note, also, the brusqueness and the monotone that characterize his language. In all the occasions where we have that grisly encounter with Dogo, one basic fact recurs. He is one-eyed, and, hence, he fails to see clearly. In other words, as a cousin to Ossai, his perception is blunt. He is only propelled by brute and raw energy except when he is restrained by his political master.

This discussion on the image of the security apparatus can open up to another crucial aspect in Achebe's account of the negation of independence. This is his re-examination of military leadership and the needs of contemporary Nigeria. The question is whether the military is an effective alternative of leadership in postindependence Nigeria. (pp. 474-82)

In *A Man of the People,* the military is portrayed as a corrective regime. Toward the end of the novel we are told that the military takes over the government in order to end the excesses of the old civilian regime: "The rampaging bands of election thugs had caused so much unrest and dislocation that our young Army officers seized the opportunity to take over." There are two angles from which we can view this piece of information. From the point of view of Odili, it is good news for him because he can get married to Edna without any more harrassment from Nanga and Dogo, nor objection from Edna's greedy father. Nanga we are told has been arrested in the wake of the military takeover. From the broader social angle, the military takeover serves to quell the violence that erupted after the elections. And in order to gain credibility, the military releases Eunice from prison and "pronounces Max a hero of the revolution." In these examples, the military seems to receive a rather subtle applause.

However, by the time we get to *Anthills of the Savannah* Achebe seems to have developed a sense of doubt about the military intervention in politics. In fact the novel unfolds an important lesson on military leadership. That is that national development and national survival do not lie in the hands of the military because its dictatorial form of governance distances it from the ordinary people; they neither lie, he seems to say, with the elite, the workers, nor students, because these groups of people are liable to divert political power in order to satisfy their individual greed. This is eloquently stated by Elewa's uncle: "We have seen too much trouble in Kangan since the white man left because those who make plans make plans for themselves only and their families." This sheer greed and selfishness, as we see in the novel, has provoked national instability. The insight Achebe has offered us, then, is that the government should realize the needs of the ordinary people and the important role they can play in national development: "This world belongs to the people of the world not to any little caucus, no matter how talented."

In the foregoing discussion we have pointed out that the relation of difference between Achebe's novels and existence in postindependence manifests itself in his ability to reveal the negation of social existence in terms of the lack of contact between the members of the dominant social group and the ordinary people, the existence of contrast in society, the nature of the security apparatus, and Achebe's reconsideration of military leadership in the country. In all these cases we have been preoccupied with Achebe's revelation of social totality from the perspective of the dominant social group. In other words, we have been preoccupied with Achebe's revelation of social totality from the perspective of the dominant social group. In other words, we have been preoccupied with the insight Achebe gives us into the nature of leadership in postindependence and how it has proven ineffective in dealing with the more immediate problems that threaten happiness at the grassroots level. But a question needs to be asked. How do the ordinary people receive this negation of independence? How, do they see their own frustration after independence? A study of *A Man of the People* and *Anthills of the Savannah* does reveal that the reaction of the people to the negative character of their existence has been dynamic. Consequently, we will now shift our attention to a consideration of the people's reaction to their own existence.

Let us begin with the question: who are the people? From the point of view of ideology, the concept of the people can be understood within the ambit of action, and in terms of the separation between the subject, that is, those who know and act, and the object of action, that is, those who are known and acted upon. In postindependence Nigeria, the organization of society can be perceived from the perspective of the dominant social group that is the subject, and the ruled, the object who are made up of the rural peasants and workers and urban workers and urban poor. The term people, as distinct from the leaders, becomes an umbrella word for all the other members of the society who are integrated through hegemony into the political and intellectual leadership of the rulers (or the subject). Gramsci has argued that the nature of this integration of the object into the morality of the subject is stabilized by a situation of consent. But it is more crucial to note that the people are alienated in that their need for nationhood and the meaning of this national consciousness have become alien or an illusion to them. As a result, this condition of alienation makes it impossible for them to realize their own essence, that is, their own condition of being. Having said this, our definition will have to surmount another hurdle. Do the people recognize or have the historical knowledge of their relation to action as object? Do they also realize the limit imposed by their historical position in connection with their needs. Or, to recall Paulo Freire, are they conscientized? Conscientization, as his translator says, is a condition of "learning to perceive social, political, and economic contradictions, and to take action against the oppressive elements of reality" [*Pedagogy of the Oppressed*].

In *A Man of the People* the people are portrayed as disillusioned with the prevailing violence in their context. But they seem to be unaware of the condition of their jaded existence. In other words they have a distorted perception of their condition. For them this distortion and life in postindependence are one and the same. Thus, they seem to perceive independence as their leaders do, in terms of a huge national cake. They do not see any evil in engaging in a scramble for chunks from this cake. The people of Anata have rallied around Nanga for they believe that he will bring their share of the cake. We are told: "Tell them that this man had used his position to enrich himself and they would ask you—as my father did—if you thought that a sensible man would spit out the juicy morsel that good fortune placed in his mouth." But the ex-policeman puts it more directly: "We know they are eating . . . but we are eating too. They are bringing us water and they promise to bring us electricity. We did not have those things before; that is why I say we are eating too." Here the people of Anata and Urua are immersed in the decadence and corruption that have characterized the leadership in the nation. Thus the language of Nanga has been accepted as the all-inclusive language. Note that Nanga urges Odili to come to the capital in order to take up a "strategic post in the civil service." In his view, "we shouldn't leave everything to the highland tribes . . . our people must press for their fair share of the national cake." In a point that is akin to the one we are pursuing here, M. J. C. Echeruo has argued ["Chinua Achebe," in *A Celebration of Black and African Writing,* edited by Bruce King and Kolawole Ogungbesan] that a factor that distinguishes *A Man of the People* from Achebe's earlier novels is the lack of a system of value in which the characters of

Odili and Nanga can be judged in isolation from society. But crucially, the value that animates the people's consciousness of independence as a huge cake is in fact secreted not by the people, but by the Nangas who project it as the all-inclusive value. What is happening here is that the people have been entangled in the false notion that such consciousness is the norm.

In a sense then, we can argue that the people of Anata and Urua suffer from a condition of false consciousness. They are neither dejected by nor indifferent to the prevailing asphyxiating morality secreted by the Nangas. These states—that is, of indifference and dejection—are implicated in a condition of awareness. At least to be indifferent toward a condition, one has to know what has precipitated one's indifference; indifference is in itself a reaction against what one recognizes as being in existence whether it has negative or positive implications. But the people of Urua and Anata are not aware; hence they lack a true knowledge of the essence of their condition. They live in the world and fail to recognize the truth of this world. Thus, they are not only ignorant, but they suffer from the worst kind of ideological blindness. Note that there is a contrast between them and the people of Umuofia and Umuaro. In *Things Fall Part* Umuofians recognize manliness and the need for one to struggle, but they also recognize that there is a limit to one's struggle. When Okonkwo stretches this need beyond the limit, Umuofia abandons him.

It might be objected that the people of Anata and Urua still have a modicum of value. They reacted violently against Josiah's greed as he appropriates Azoge's stick in order to "make medicine" with it and turn the population into blind buyers. As they say: "Josiah has taken away enough for the owner to notice." In the event, they stage a boycott of Josiah's store. But ironically, the same Josiah who has been ostracized by the village triumphs later in his new alliance with Nanga. It seems that what the village rejects Nanga has accepted. And in the new political setup, Nanga's ideal triumphs over that of the village and, in fact, encapsulates the village within its own values: " . . . I saw Josiah the outlawed trader, mount the few steps to the dais and whisper to Chief Nanga who sprang up immediately searching the crowd." The people turn into a faceless crowd that is roped into this new alliance between Josiah and Nanga.

We have pointed out earlier that one of the causes of the frustration at independence is that the leaders were ideologically unprepared for independence. They fought for political freedom, but confusion does exist concerning what to make out of independence in terms of a defined direction. And the people seem to have shared in this confusion.

By the time we get to *Anthills of the Savannah,* however, the civil war, the oil boom, and the economic depression of the 1980s seem to have provided enough evidence to the people on the nature of the leadership they have had. In the later novel Achebe portrays the people as still disillusioned with the discrepancy between actual existence and what they expect from life, but they no longer suffer from a condition of false consciousness. They have recognized their historical position. As cited above, this recognition is more eloquently articulated by Elewa's uncle in spite of his rustic and rather simple ways: "We have seen too much trouble in Kangan since the whiteman left because those who make plans make plans for themselves and their families." The more fundamental aspect of this character's recognition is the existence of two social groups—"those who make plans" (the subject) and "we" who have "suffered too much trouble" (the object). This recognition establishes a basic contrast between the people in *Anthills of the Savannah* and the people of Anata. Note that the ex-policeman in *A Man of the People* says "they are eating and we are eating too," thereby recognizing no distinction between the Nangas and the people. Ikem also recognizes that "The prime failure of this government . . . is the failure of our rulers to re-establish vital inner links with the poor and dispossessed of this country with the bruised heart that throbs painfully at the core of the nation's being."

Nevertheless, the people in *Anthills of the Savannah,* represented by Elewa's uncle, and the Abazon delegation, have not launched themselves into a program in order to shake the status quo. Put in another way, their needs in postindependence have not been articulated within the compass of motives and ends in order to attain a possible order of existence. But they are not complacent; they have hope and do not revel, as it were, in their own jaded existence. In this regard, Arthur Ravenscroft is right to have acknowledged that "*Anthills of the Savannah* is a novel that not only chronicles the ill times but peers uncertainly beyond them" ["Recent Fiction From Africa: Chinua Achebe's *Anthills of the Savannah*—A Note," *The Literary Criterion* (1988)]. Based on this evidence, we can identify another crucial lesson in Achebe's *Anthills of the Savannah.* In this novel Achebe seems to believe that Nigeria can be a better place to live because providence has endowed her with natural resources and intellect. But all these have to be managed by a responsible leadership. The author seems to believe that human life is meaningful to the extent that man recognizes a basic communalism, that egalitarian nature of man: that is, no matter his satisfaction or achievement, man must recognize the need to interact with his kind, with other people. Perhaps it is within this context that we can appreciate Lindfors' observation ["Achebe's African Parable," in *Critical Perspectives on Chinua Achebe,* edited by C. L. Innes and Bernth Lindfors] that Achebe's creative talent reveals a fundamental African parable. This is true because what Achebe reveals of his society has a wider continental application. Furthermore, Achebe's creative vision is imbued with a sympathy with the overall welfare of the people. He has stated this fact more pointedly in a different context: "When Nigeria learns to deal fairly with all its citizens . . . the defenders of its policies will have an easier time in court. . . . And its prospects for progress and stability will be infinitely brighter" (*Trouble With Nigeria*).

Finally, we will now consider the image of the anthill in *Anthills of the Savannah.* The significance of this image to Achebe's reaction against the negation of the expectations of independence is that it offers the reader deep insight into the ideological content of the novel. The image of the anthill is revealed in the title of the novel. But it is repeated with refrain in three other instances in the text:

> anthills surviving to tell the new grass of the savannah about last year's brush fires
>
> anthills in the scorched landscape . . .
>
> gazing out into the empty landscape, [he] had become aware of the anthills.

In each of these instances we notice the longevity and imposing stature of the anthills. Note also the poetic qualities with which they are imbued. In the first instance, the anthills are personified and endowed with the ability to talk. It is also interesting that two of the instances above are derived from Ikem's poem fragments.

In any case, the anthills we are referring to here are the nests or mounds of the termites of the *macrotermes* species that are found in savannah and rain forest habitats. Apart from their symmetrical grandeur, there are two aspects of the anthill that can incite the creative imagination. The first is the hierachical order that prevails in the nest. Within this order, the queen occupies the center, and life in the nest revolves around her. The second aspect is that when the individual members of the three-caste system in the nest—reproductive, workers, and soldiers—migrate to form other colonies due to unfavorable environmental factors, the anthills remain uninhabited. The order that existed earlier is transferred to another habitat.

Achebe's use of the image of the anthill seems to have been based on this second stage of the nest. Note that in the first quotation above the anthill is said to have survived an earlier harsh weather condition. The question then is this: how does this empty structure with its internal chambers and labyrinthine paths serve to shed light on Achebe's message? It seems that Achebe makes an analogy between the structure of the state and the internal structure of the anthill. Like the anthill, the state is imbued with a complex internal structure that is animated by a central morality in the same way life in the anthill revolves around the queen. But the more compelling importance of this analogy is that Achebe seems to tell us that there is a need to evolve a more enduring idea and permanent form of national consciousness; and a need to rigorously define and allow this morality to activate our motives and our plans. The validity of this point will be appreciated when we recognize that our existence and political strategies in postindependence have been characterized by the lack of a defined direction. Thus, after thirty years of independence Nigeria has continued to grope about in search of a direction. The country has moved from Westminster Parliamentary system, to military dictatorship, to the American-styled presidential system. At present we are working hard on a clean slate in order to construct a two-party state. Moreover, it is now the norm for each government to cancel the projects that the preceding government had initiated. Is this not the dilemma of Operation Feed the Nation, The Green Revolution, The Ethical Revolution, and now MAMSER (Mass Mobilization for Social Justice, Economic Recovery, and Self-Reliance), and Rural Development? Achebe seems to call our attention to the inherent lesson from the structure of the anthill that withstands the harsh condition. Within this framework, also, we can appreciate the significance of the "last grin," the joke shared by Chris and Ikem. The joke reminds leaders that the nation survives beyond the private whims of a few individuals. The individuals who control the state will be changed in the wake of a new regime in the same way the termites abandon their nest in the wake of unfavorable weather conditions.

To sum up: our principal purpose in this essay has been to clarify the nature of Achebe's reaction against the negation of the ideals of independence from colonial rule. We began, therefore, by identifying the condition of existence in postindependence as neocolonial. Achebe, we have argued, has enabled us to see its inherent truth. Specifically, he has revealed the lack of contact between the leaders and the ordinary people. Apart from this, he has shown that this lack of contact has led to the condition of contrasts and an unevenness in development. Achebe has enabled us to see the nature of the security apparatus and to re-examine the gains of military leadership. We have also shown that the people's reaction to their condition of existence has varied from resignation to critical assessment.

From a dialectical point of view these contradictions are materials that must be negated for society to evolve a new order. But Achebe has not set out to articulate the means of attaining social change. He is optimistic that sanity will be restored. This optimism is expressed in a marriage and a birth in the two novels respectively. Odili begins to make arrangement for his marriage to Edna in **A Man of the People,** and Elewa is delivered of a baby who is christened Amaechina in **Anthills of the Savannah.** (pp. 483-89)

> *Onyemaechi Udumukwu, "Achebe and the Negation of Independence," in* Modern Fiction Studies, *Vol. 37, No. 3, Autumn, 1991, pp. 471-91.*

Simon Gikandi   (essay date 1991)

[*In the following excerpt from his book-length study* Reading Chinua Achebe: Language & Ideology in Fiction, *Gikandi identifies the role of the storyteller in modern Africa as Achebe's chief concern.*]

> . . . you also have the storyteller who recounts the event—and this is one who survives, who outlives all the others. It is the storyteller, in fact, who makes us what we are, who creates history. The storyteller creates the memory that the survivors must have—otherwise their surviving would have no meaning.
>
> [Chinua Achebe, in an interview with Bill Moyers, *A World of Ideas*]

Achebe's concern with the power and authority of storytelling, of the function of the storyteller in the contemporary African situation, and the relationship of writers and intellectuals to the men of power in the postcolonial state, acquires its most urgent resonance in **Anthills of the Savannah.** For this novel, published after a gap of almost twenty years—during which the politics of Nigeria had unfolded through several military coups, a civil war, and endemic corruption—centres not so much on historical

events and those who perform in the theatre of post-colonial politics, but on the form which the story of the nation takes and the interpretative problems its polis presents for those seeking concrete meanings to some of the most turbulent events on the African scene. In privileging the position of the storyteller, in comparison to 'the man who agitates, the man who drums up the people' and 'the warrior, who goes forward and fights', Achebe is also calling attention to the need for his readers to look beyond the narrated events, which are grim and pessimistic, toward the future of renewal and rebirth suggested at the end of the novel.

The power of the storyteller, Achebe suggests in the epigraph that opens this [essay], does not lie simply in his or her mastery of the narrated event; rather, the narrator outlives the events he or she narrates and becomes the avatar of those memories which are crucial to the reinvention of our lives. In talking about the current political and socio-economic crisis in Africa, Achebe is not sure whether the journey we have taken since independence has been toward life or death. However, writing about this 'bad patch' as a 'segment of history' allows us to see beyond the limitations of the postcolonial moment:

> if you take the wide view of things, then you begin to see [the present crisis] as history, as human history over a long period of time, and that we are passing through a bad patch. It is not death. We are passing through a bad patch, and if we succeed, then even this experience of the bad patch will turn out to be an enrichment.

The way narrative recreates history and memory, and how this recreation gives meaning to moments of crisis and then transcends them to point out new vistas for the future, is a crucial theme in **Anthills.** In this novel, says Achebe, 'there is more of looking into the future, not just for women but for society generally; how, for example, we can use our past creatively'.

In many ways, this concern with meanings and their realization in a future utopian moment is not new in Achebe's works; nor is his preoccupation with the ways in which the past can be made, through narration, to speak to the present. As we have seen in the previous chapters, all his novels can be read as one continuous quest for the meaning of the Nigerian nation in particular and the African experience in general. Achebe adopts different, and often experimental, narrative strategies, to explicate and dramatize the real and symbolic organization of the African world and to trace the evolution of certain discourses which determine the way we speak about the continent and its people. Nowhere can we find a better summary of Achebe's mission and vision as a writer as in his powerful introduction to the journal *African Commentary,* of which he is the publisher:

> We are . . . committed to reclaiming the rich heritage of Africa, every inch of it, and redrawing the contours of African history which in the hands of others has been drawn, and is drawn, with great malice and lurid falsehood . . . The perspectives will be many, reflecting the complexity of the problem but out of the welter will emerge a sound, clear vision of the way forward.

What makes Achebe's ideological concerns and strategies of representation in **Anthills** so different from those in **No Longer at Ease** and **A Man of the People,** novels which basically deal with similar themes of political corruption, the absence of a national ethos, the pitfalls of national consciousness, and oppression and domination, is the simple fact that it is written twenty five years after independence in a postcolonial situation whose character and identity, in both the positive and negative sense, are no longer in doubt. For even when they appear to be dealing with the problems of the new or emerging nation, **No Longer** and **A Man** are narratives which use the postcolonial moment as what Edward Said calls [in 'Intellectuals in the Post-Colonial World,' *Salmagundi,* 1986] the occasion 'for a retrospective reflection on colonialism, the better to understand the difficulties of the present in newly independent states'. Such a retrospective examination of colonialism is not a priority in Achebe's writing agenda in **Anthills**: he does not dismiss our colonial past as a significant cause of our present problems, but he is fully aware of the interpretative and ideological limitations of positing colonialism as the sole origin of our present crisis.

True, Achebe still believes that the problems which all African countries face are, in an institutional and constitutive sense, traceable to colonialism and its systems: 'The withdrawal of the colonial powers was in many ways merely a tactical move to get out of the limelight, but to retain the control in all practical ways. In fact it turned out to have been even a better idea than running these colonies, because now you could get what you were getting before without the responsibility for admininstering it. You handed responsibility back to the natives, but continued to control the economy in all kinds of ways'. But this kind of diagnosis raises several important questions which will come to determine, in crucial ways, the narrative strategies in Achebe's novel: what responsibility do Africans themselves bear for this crisis? Why have the ideologies and discourses of national consciousness, which provided clarity and vision in the nationalist period, failed to enlighten us about the postcolonial situation? Is it possible to redefine the contours of the African experience and how do we explicate those meanings that define the African world?

For narrative to dramatize and provide imaginary answers and resolutions to such questions and problems, for narrative to map a terrain in which diverse groups of Africans can speak about their condition and its problematics, it must clearly go beyond what Said calls a politics and rhetoric of blame, to come to grips and hence rethink the process of decolonization as the condition that has established the postcolonial society Achebe deals with in **Anthills.** Although Achebe's narrative looks toward the future, it is also retrospective: most of the stories within it are told by narrators (Chris and Ikem) who are already dead by the time we read the novel; furthermore, these narrators are as obsessed with the past as they are concerned about the future. Indeed, the temporal conjunction between past and future allows Achebe to deal with two of his primary ideological concerns—the need to reinterpret the past to understand the present and his determination to break out-

side the vicious cycle of history to seek new possibilities beyond what he would call 'frozen time'.

Achebe's diagnostic engagement with the past, and his quest for an unknown terrain beyond neocolonial reification, is part of a continuing effort to reinscribe and reinterpret Africa as 'the terrain contested with Europe'. In this process of reinterpretation, as Said has forcefully argued, the present moment is 'a holding and crossing-over' between 'colonialism and its genealogical offspring'; it is a gap between a past which the writer must engage and transcend at the same time. As a result, says Said, many postcolonial writers:

> . . . bear their past within them—as scars of humiliating wounds, as instigation for different practices, as potentially revised visions of the past tending toward a future, as urgently reinterpretable and re-deployable experiences in which the formerly silent native speaks and acts on territory taken back from the colonialist.

Indeed, in trying to map out new spaces for the nation, Achebe's main characters—Sam, Chris, Ikem and Beatrice—have to interrogate the past they shared, must often revise the meaning of that past in order to explain the choices they have made in the present. And in using different narrative voices, Achebe questions the three men's claim to speak for the African; the narrative redeploys the African space as heterogenous and multiple, defined by differences and contradictions, not homogenized into a singular national voice.

Achebe's rejection of a monological narrative voice, which I will explore in greater detail below, has important implications for the way he reconceives the postcolonial situation and for the way he posits narrative as a means of liberation and consciousness. This is particularly the case within the context of the independent African nation and the function of the new state as an instrument that represses rather than succours human freedom. In Fanon's theories of narrative, whose influence on Achebe's latter works cannot be underestimated, the function of narration in a colonial situation is to realize human freedom through the liberation of the nation. For Fanon, '[T]o fight for national culture means in the first place to fight for the liberation of the nation, that material keystone which makes the building of a culture possible' [*The Wretched of the Earth*]. In Fanon's later work, as Patrick Taylor has noted [in *The Narrative of Liberation: Perspective on Afro-Caribbean Literature, Popular Culture, and Politics*], 'the liberated nation is the symbol of the totality of freedom in a temporal and spatial dimension . . . Decolonization, as the entry into time and challenge to the colonizer's domination over history, transforms the lost space of the colony into the space, reconquered, of the new nation'.

But the subsequent history of the postcolonial state has put Fanon's sanguine views on liberation and human freedom into question: the new nation does not always enable the constitution of a national culture or the transformation of history into a realm of freedom; on the contrary, the new nation has become an instrument of repressing cultural identity and of promoting, in one way or the other, the cultural values of the colonizer. In this sense, the new nation has betrayed its mandate and the desires and expectations of its populace. The African world, rather than follow the trajectory suggested by earlier narratives of liberation, has been turned upside down. Thus, Achebe looks at the world—'the way it is organized'—and finds it 'inadequate': 'When you look at the possibility and then at what has been achieved, you can feel very, very bitter indeed'. How can narrative liberate us from this grim, and—within the context of previous nationalist discourse—unexpected history?

Within the complexities and reversals of the postcolonial situation, Achebe's novel is plagued by doubts about its own relevance. This may appear strange, especially in view of Achebe's affirmative delcarations on the power of art to rewrite history and to evacuate the self from the events that entrap it in frozen time. Nevertheless, as several reviewers have observed, **Anthills** is a novel which is haunted by (ostensibly) authorial digressions on the function of narration and writing in the postcolonial moment. Such digressions often take the form of metacommentaries—commentaries on either the ideological environment in which the narrative is produced, or on the ways in which the work should be read, or even a discussion on the capacity of stories to conceal meanings. In Frederic Jameson's view, metacommentary is the process by which an act of interpretation engages itself with the strangeness of its situation; 'every individual interpretation must include an interpretation of its own existence, must show its own credentials and justify itself' ['Metacommentary,' in *The Ideologies of Theory: Essays 1971-1986*].

And so the initial question to pose here, as a form of entry into Achebe's text, is this: why does the author need to justify the function of his narrative and its concern with hermeneutics, the art of interpretation and critical reflection? We can possibly approach this problem by taking up Achebe's central premise about narrative, a premise articulated by the old Abazon elder in the middle of the novel:

> The story is our escort; without it, we are blind. Does the blind man own his escort? No, neither do we the story; rather it is the story that owns and directs us. It is the thing that makes us different from cattle; it is the mark on the face that sets one people apart from their neighbours.

Here, narrative is presented as a form of insight (without it we are blind) and an agency with immense constitutive powers (it determines our movement, character, and identity). But this metacommentary on how narratives should be read and used already points to the crisis of meaning Achebe faces as a writer in a postcolonial situation; simply put, the old narratives of liberation, which assumed that the nation would be the fulfillment of human freedom, no longer have legitimacy. However, Achebe will not succumb to the postmodernist seduction which expresses its disappointment with the politics of liberation; he will not share the now common belief that narrative is 'no longer an adequate figure for plotting the human trajectory in society. There is nothing to look forward to: we are struck within our circle. The line is now enclosed within a circle'.

On the contrary, Achebe is seeking ways of establishing new forms of narration that might have the power to liberate us from the circle of our postcolonial moment; he seeks a narrative that speaks about, but also transcends its historical imperatives. In the discourse on the story which is presented to us by the elder from Abazon, then, the power of narrative is that of an utterance, of a voice which carries within it compelling power and magic. Moreover, the old man isolates three functions of narrative which are clear indicators of the way Achebe would prefer to see his own postcolonial intellectual project: stories have dispersed (or plural) meanings, they are avatars of collective memories, and they have an erratic character.

In the first instance, the old man argues that all stories and the ideologies they support have a dialogic character; 'for what is true comes in different robes'. If earlier nationalist narratives had assumed that the nation spoke one truth in one voice, in the postcolonial moment we are told to come to terms with the different voices and functions we play in our societies. Secondly, the power of the story is tied to its function as a depository of memories and its capacity for recall: recalling, says the old man, is greatest, because it allows the story to 'continue beyond the war and the warrior. It is the story that outlives the sound of war-drums and the exploits of brave fighters. It is the story, not the others, that saves our progeny from blundering like blind beggars into the spikes of the cactus fence'. Clearly, the story seems to perpetuate historical events so that their meaning and significance will not be lost to future generations which might then be condemned to repeat the sins of their ancestors. At the same time, however, the story, in the process of recall, frees the subjects from the contigencies of the historical event; by abdicating the historical imperatives that evoked it in the first place, the story becomes timeless and hence acquires the power to direct our actions beyond the conditions that generated it. For Achebe, 'The storyteller appeals to the mind, and appeals ultimately to generations and generations and generations'.

Third, the story has power precisely because of its complex, and even erratic character; the narrative threatens those in control because its agenda allows for different meanings. In his discourse on the power of stories, the old man evokes the name of the god Agwu, the patron saint of narrators who appears, unlike his brother Madness, to be a person of logic and control: 'Madness unleashes and rides his man roughly into the Wild savannah. Agwu possesses his own just as securely but has him corralled to serve the compound'. However, the logic that propels Agwu to corral the storyteller to serve the community conceals the record and imperative of struggle that informs every narrative as it seeks to establish an oppositional stance vis-à-vis the dominant structures. As Ikem will later assert, 'storytellers are a threat. They threaten all champions of control, they frighten usurpers of the right-to-freedom of the human spirit—in state, in church or mosque, in party congress, in the university or wherever. That's why'.

Indeed, the story by rewriting history (by creating a timeless and autonomous version of events so that they can speak to future generations) contests the constant attempt, by powerful institutions, to repress those collective memories that threaten control, memories that are obliterated when official history is textualized. Achebe's concern with the character and functions of stories (he tells Rutherford that 'the very nature of the story is one of the key issues in this novel') arises from his need to valorize the capacity of narrative to resist power. The struggle between power and narrative establishes the terrain in which the function of the story as the escort of the people can be explored: 'You have the story, you have the story-teller, so it is an exploration of the story and the story-teller and the way in which those who commandeer power would wish to commandeer history and so would be afraid of story-tellers' [Chinua Achebe, in an interview with Anna Rutherford, *Kunapipi* (1987)].

But my initial question still remains: why does Achebe find it necessary to make the story an issue in the text, and why does he take great pains to underscore the relevance and legitimacy of narratives of liberation? The possible answer to this question is suggested by a general problematic in interpretation—the fact that works need commentaries on the way they should be read because their meanings are often censored by the other historical factors that accompany the invention of narratives. In Jameson's words, metacommentary 'aims at tracing the logic of the censorship itself and of the situations from which it springs: a language that hides what it displays beneath its own reality as language, a glance that designates, through the very process of avoiding, the object forbidden'. In a world which has been turned upside down, Achebe believes that reality itself is a forbidden object; thus, narrative must be geared toward the institution of an African hermeneutics that might help us recover the hidden objects of our contemporary history. (pp. 125-31)

> *Simon Gikandi, in his* Reading Chinua Achebe: Language & Ideology in Fiction, *James Currey, 1991, 165 p.*

FURTHER READING

Bibliography

Baldwin, Claudia. "Chinua Achebe." In her *Nigerian Literature: A Bibliography of Criticism, 1952-1976*, pp. 21-45. Boston: G. K. Hall & Co., 1980.
> Bibliography of reviews, essays, and books on Achebe's fiction and poetry from 1958 through 1976.

Lindfors, Bernth. "Chinua Achebe." In his *Black African Literature in English: A Guide to Information Sources*. American Literature, English Literature, and World Literatures in English Information Guide Series, edited by Theodore Grieder, vol. 23, pp. 247-62. Detroit: Gale Research Co., 1979.
> Lists bibliographies, biographies, autobiographies, interviews, and criticism on Achebe's works.

Criticism

Babalola, C. A. "A Reconsideration of Achebe's *No Longer At Ease*." *Phylon* XLVII, No. 2 (June 1986): 139-47.

Identifies *No Longer At Ease* as a vigorous topical satire and examines the novel's themes of social and moral decadence, cultural conflict, antipathy between youth and old age, and human fallibility.

Balogun, F. Odun. "Achebe's 'The Madman': A Poetic Realisation of Irony." *Okike*, No. 23 (February 1983): 72-9.
> Explores Achebe's use of irony in his short story "The Madman."

———. "Chekhov's 'Sleepy' and Achebe's 'Vengeful Creditor': Thematic Similarities and Differences." *Comparative Literature Studies* 21, No. 4 (Winter 1984): 487-96.
> Assesses the two stories cited as responses to conditions of social inequity.

———. "Nigerian Folktales and Children's Stories by Chinua Achebe." *Journal of Black Studies* 20, No. 4 (June 1990): 426-42.
> Commends Achebe as a pioneer of Afrocentric children's stories in English and notes that these stories are stylistically similar to Achebe's other fiction.

———. "Tradition and Modernity in the African Short Story: Achebe and Io Liyong," "*Girls at War and Other Stories*: A Study of the Failure of the Elites in Moral Leadership," and "The Poetry of Irony in *Girls at War and Other Stories*." In his *Tradition and Modernity in the African Short Story: An Introduction to a Literature in Search of Critics*, pp. 57-63; 65-80; 81-96. New York: Greenwood Press, 1991.
> Contends that Achebe's short stories are a case study of Nigeria's moral health from its colonial past to its present neocolonial reality and identifies irony as the principal element of Achebe's style.

Beckmann, Susan. "Language as Cultural Identity in Achebe, Ihimaera, Laurence and Atwood." *World Literature Written in English* 20, No. 1 (Spring 1981): 117-34.
> Examines how the loss of an ancestral language is reflected in the style and thematic concerns of the Nigerian, New Zealander, and Canadian writers cited.

Cham, Mbye B. "Language as Index of Character, Humor and Conflict in *Arrow of God* and *A Man of the People* by Chinua Achebe." *A Current Bibliography on African Affairs* 17, No. 3 (1984-85): 243-65.
> Discussion of Achebe's methods for dealing with the limitations of standard English in the representation of non-English characters, moods, and situations.

Cott, Jonathan. "Chinua Achebe: At the Crossroads." *Parabola* VI, No. 2 (May 1981): 30-9.
> Interview in which Achebe discusses his children's stories and comments on his novels.

Dailly, Christophe. "The Novelist as a Cultural Policy-Maker." *Presence Africaine* 125 (1983): 202-13.
> Includes discussion of *Things Fall Apart* in an assessment of modern African novels that both exemplify and explore the synthesis of traditional African and Western cultures.

Diamond, Larry. "Fiction as Political Thought." *African Affairs* 88, No. 352 (July 1989): 435-45.
> Contends that Achebe established himself as a political philosopher, commentator, and prophet in *Anthills of the Savannah*.

Egudu, R. N. "Achebe and the Igbo Narrative Tradition."

Research in African Literatures 12, No. 1 (Spring 1981): 43-54.

Observes that Achebe's use of anecdotes from Igbo folklore and social experience firmly place him in the Igbo storytelling tradition.

Fleming, Bruce. "Brothers under the Skin: Achebe on *Heart of Darkness.*" *College Literature, Double Issue: Teaching Postcolonial and Commonwealth Literatures* 19-20, Nos. 3-1 (October 1992-February 1993): 90-9.

Explores the basis of Achebe's charge that *Heart of Darkness* reflects Conrad's racism.

Gakwandi, Shatto Arthur. "The Illusion of Progress: Achebe's *No Longer at Ease* and Beti's *Mission to Kala*" and "Disenchantment: Soyinka's *The Interpreters* and Achebe's *A Man of the People.*" In his *The Novel and Contemporary Experience in Africa,* pp. 27-42; 66-86. London: Heinemann, 1977.

Argues that *No Longer at Ease* portrays the alienating effect of foreign education while *A Man of the People* indicts post-independence African society for its "greed, violence and ignorance from which there is no apparent way to escape."

Gikandi, Simon. *Reading Chinua Achebe: Language and Ideology in Fiction.* London: James Currey, 1991, 165 p.

Analysis of Achebe's novels. The chapter on *Anthills of the Savannah* is excerpted in the entry above.

Gillard, G. M. "Centre and Periphery in Achebe's Novels." *The Literary Half-Yearly* XXI, No. 1 (January 1980): 146-54.

Asserts that each of Achebe's novels is organized around an opposition of centrality and periphery.

Ikegami, Robin. "Knowledge and Power, the Story and the Storyteller: Achebe's *Anthills of the Savannah.*" *Modern Fiction Studies, Special Issue: Postcolonial African Fiction* 37, No. 3 (Autumn 1991): 493-507.

Examines "both Achebe's storytelling and his view of the act of storytelling as manifested in [*Anthills of the Savannah*] to determine the ways in which power and knowledge impinge upon stories and their tellers."

Innes, C. L. *Chinua Achebe.* Cambridge: Cambridge University Press, 1990, 199 p.

Study of Achebe's novels, essays, poetry, and short stories, characterizing them as a response to events in Nigerian history. A chapter on Achebe's short stories is excerpted in the entry above.

Killam, G. D. *The Novels of Chinua Achebe.* New York: Africana Publishing Corp., 1969, 106 p.

Analysis of *Things Fall Apart, No Longer at Ease, Arrow of God,* and *A Man of the People.* Killam concludes that the vision of life expressed in Achebe's novels is essentially tragic.

Lawson, William. "Chinua Achebe in New England." *Yardbird Reader* 4 (1975): 99-118.

Interview in which Achebe discusses the effects of Western culture on African writers who have lived in the West.

Lindfors, Bernth. "Chinua Achebe's Undergraduate Writings." In his *Early Nigerian Literature,* pp. 91-106. New York: Africana Publishing Co., 1982.

Argues that Achebe's writings while at University College Ibadan reveal his incipient literary ability.

Macdonald, Bruce F. "Chinua Achebe and the Structure of Colonial Tragedy." *The Literary Half-Yearly* XXI, No. 1 (January 1980): 50-63.

Contends that the complexity of *Things Fall Apart* derives from the interaction of two major levels of tragic conflict: historic confrontation and the individual's fear of annihilation.

MacDougall, Russell. "Okonkwo's Walk: The Choreography of Things Falling Apart." *World Literature Written in English* 26, No. 1 (Spring 1986): 24-33.

Explores Achebe's method of characterizing Okonkwo through recurrent stylized descriptions of his gestures, posture, and walk.

——. "The 'Problem of Locomotion' in *No Longer at Ease.*" *World Literature Written in English* 29, No. 1 (Spring 1989): 19-25.

Argues that action in *No Longer at Ease* progresses in the same manner as the action in *Things Fall Apart:* a stylized "rhythm of inevitability" established through patterns of posture, gesture, and motion.

Maduka, Chidi T. "African Religious Beliefs in Literary Imagination: *Ogbanje* and *Abiku* in Chinua Achebe, J. P. Clark and Wole Soyinka." *The Journal of Commonwealth Literature* XXII, No. 1 (1987): 17-30.

Includes discussion of Achebe's use of the traditional African religious concept of *Ogbanje,* which involves reincarnation and predestination, in *Things Fall Apart.*

McCarthy, B. Eugene. "Rhythm and Narrative Method in Achebe's *Things Fall Apart.*" *Novel* 18, No. 3 (Spring 1985): 243-56.

Discerns the rhythms and repetition of oral tradition in Achebe's narrative.

McEwan, Neil. "Colonial Africa: Achebe, Oyono, Camara Laye" and "Independence: Soyinka, Achebe, Armah." In his *Africa and the Novel,* pp. 20-60, 61-101. Atlantic Highlands, N. J.: Humanities Press, 1983.

Discusses the style and themes of Achebe's first four novels with emphasis on *Things Fall Apart* and *A Man of the People.*

Nnolim, Charles E. "The Form and Function of the Folk Tradition in Achebe's Novels." *Ariel* 14, No. 1 (January 1983): 35-47.

Investigates Achebe's use of Igbo folkways to enrich and give form, structure, and meaning to his narratives.

Nwachukwu-Agbada, J. O. J. "An Interview with Chinua Achebe." *The Massachusetts Review* 18, No. 2 (Summer 1987): 273-85.

Wide-ranging discussion covering Achebe's novels, essays, and his thoughts on trends in criticism on African literature.

Nwoga, D. Ibe. "The Igbo World of Achebe's *Arrow of God.*" *The Literary Half-Yearly* XXVII, No. 1 (January 1986): 11-42.

Commends Achebe's ability to select atypical features of Igbo experience to create a fictional though not fictitious Igbo world for his novels.

Ogbaa, Kalu. "Death in African Literature: The Example of Chinua Achebe." *World Literature Written in English* 20, No. 2 (Autumn 1981): 201-13.

Explores the Igbo concept of unnatural death through

an examination of the protagonist Ezeulu's death in *Arrow of God.*

———. *Gods, Oracles and Divination: Folkways in Chinua Achebe's Novels.* Trenton, N.J.: Africa World Press, 1992, 269 p.

Explores Achebe's successful fusion of traditional Igbo culture with the European form of the novel.

Ogu, Julius N. "The Concept of Madness in Chinua Achebe's Writings." *The Journal of Commonwealth Literature* 18, No. 1 (1983): 48-54.

Notes that in many works, most notably the short story "The Madman," Achebe examines the Igbo conception of the causes and cures of madness.

Okafor, Clement A. "Chinua Achebe: His Novels and the Environment." *CLA Journal* XXXII, No. 4 (June 1989): 433-42.

Argues that Achebe has successfully combined the English tradition of the novel with Igbo oral tradition.

Okoye, Emmanuel Meziemadu. *The Traditional Religion and Its Encounter with Christianity in Achebe's Novels.* Bern: Peter Lang, 1987, 370 p.

Compares the descriptions given in Achebe's first four novels of the interaction between traditional Igbo religion and Christianity with ethnographic and historical sources on the subject. Okoye concludes that "Achebe has shown a generally true and critical picture of the past."

Ola, Virginia U. "Pessimism and Commitment in the Works of Achebe and Armah: A Comment." In *Literature of Africa and the African Continuum,* edited by Jonathan A. Peters, Mildred P. Mortimer, and Russell V. Linnemann, pp. 129-36. Washington, D.C.: Three Continents Press, 1989.

Asserts that the novels of Achebe have been mistakenly labeled pessimistic when they are in fact predominately analytic and satiric.

Olagoke, D. Olu. "Varieties in the English of Achebe." *The Literary Half-Yearly* XXIII, No. 2 (July 1982): 18-37.

Examines the ways in which Achebe "has effectively bent the English language . . . to describe cultures, traditions, experiences and situations that have no direct equivalents in [a] native English environment."

Olorounto, Samuel B. "The Notion of Conflict in Chinua Achebe's Novels." *Obsidian II* I, No. 3 (Winter 1986): 17-36.

Focuses on Achebe's depiction in *Things Fall Apart* and *Arrow of God* of the ways in which domestic, personal, communal, and intercultural conflicts are traditionally addressed in African culture.

Opata, Damian U. "Eternal Sacred Order Versus Conventional Wisdom: A Consideration of Moral Culpability in the Killing of Ikemefuna in *Things Fall Apart.*" *Research in African Literature* 18, No. 1 (Spring 1987): 71-9.

Argues that both textual and extratextual evidence suggest that "although Okonkwo felt some temporal sense of moral revulsion after he had killed Ikemefuna, he cannot thereby be said to have committed any offense against Earth."

Owusu, Kofi. "The Politics of Interpretation: The Novels of Chinua Achebe." *Modern Fiction Studies, Special Issue: Postcolonial African Fiction* 37, No. 3 (Autumn 1991): 459-70.

Addresses the theme of the use and abuse of power in

Things Fall Apart, No Longer at Ease, A Man of the People, and *Anthills of the Savannah.*

Palmer, Eustace. "Chinua Achebe: *Things Fall Apart, No Longer at Ease, A Man of the People, Arrow of God.*" In his *The Growth of the African Novel,* pp. 63-101. London: Heinemann, 1979.

Contends that in each of his novels Achebe "gives a powerful presentation of the beauty, strength and validity of traditional life and values and the disruptiveness of change."

Povey, John. "Achebe's War Poetry." *The Literary Half-Yearly* XXI, No. 1 (January 1980): 78-90.

Interprets Achebe's poetry in *Christmas in Biafra* as his attempt to find a more effective and powerful vehicle than the novel for precise emotional statement.

Shankar, D. A. "Chinua Achebe as Critic: A Note." In *The Colonial and the Neo-Colonial Encounters in Commonwealth Literature,* edited by H. H. Anniah Gowda, pp. 229-34. Mysore, India: University of Mysore, 1983.

Discussion of Achebe's literary criticism.

Shelton, Austin J. "Failures and Individualism in Achebe's Stories." *Studies in Black Literature* II, No. 1 (Spring 1971): 5-9.

Addresses the theme of tragic reversal in Achebe's first four novels.

Singh, Satyanarain. "The Spiritual in Terms of the Secular: Achebe's Social Vision in *Arrow of God.*" In *The Colonial and the Neo-Colonial Encounters in Commonwealth Literature,* edited by H. H. Anniah Gowda, pp. 121-34. Mysore, India: University of Mysore, 1983.

Explores Achebe's portrayal of traditional African religion in *Arrow of God.*

Sinha, A. K. "The Satire in Chinua Achebe's *A Man of the People.*" In *Modern Studies, and Other Essays,* edited by R. C. Prasad and A. K. Sharma, pp. 252-60. New Delhi: Vikas Publishing House Ltd., 1987.

Examines the irony and humor that contribute to the satiric presentation of post-independence Africa in *A Man of the People.*

Winters, Marjorie. "An Objective Approach to Achebe's Style." *Research in African Literature* 12, No. 1 (Spring 1981): 55-68.

Calls for an objective assessment of the literary style of Achebe's novels.

Wren, Robert M. *Achebe's World: The Historical and Cultural Context of the Novels of Chinua Achebe.* Washington, D.C.: Three Continents Press, 1980, 221 p.

Examines *Things Fall Apart, No Longer at Ease, Arrow of God,* and *A Man of the People* in relation to Igbo culture and Nigerian history. Wren includes a selected primary and secondary bibliography.

Additional coverage of Achebe's life and career is contained in the following sources published by Gale Research: *Black Literature Criticism,* Vol. 1; *Black Writers; Children's Literature Review,* Vol. 20; *Contemporary Authors,* Vols. 1-4; *Contemporary Authors New Revision Series,* Vols. 6, 26; *Contemporary Literary Criticism,* Vols. 1, 3, 5, 7, 11, 26, 51; *Dictionary of Literary Biography,* Vol. 117; *Major 20th-Century Writers; Something about the Author,* Vols. 38, 40; and *World Literature Criticism.* For related criticism, see the entry on Nigerian literature in *Twentieth-Century Literary Criticism,* Vol. 30.

Claribel Alegría

1924-

Nicaraguan-born Salvadoran poet, novelist, short fiction writer, biographer, essayist, editor, nonfiction writer, translator, and author of children's books.

The following entry covers Alegría's career through 1992.

INTRODUCTION

Alegría is best known for writings in which she depicts the concerns, histories, and traditions of the peoples of Nicaragua and El Salvador. Mixing geographical, historical, political, and cultural references in her poetry and prose, Alegría attempts to create a literature of social and political awareness from a Latin American perspective.

Born in Estelí, Nicaragua, in 1924, Alegría lived there until she was nine months old. Due to her father's support of Nicaraguan guerrilla leader Augusto César Sandino, Alegría's family was forced into exile by Anastasio Somoza, a Nicaraguan politician who later became commander-in-chief of the Nicaraguan army and eventually the nation's president. The family settled in Santa Ana, a small town in El Salvador that became the setting for much of Alegría's writing. In 1943 she traveled to the United States to study at George Washington University. While in America, Alegría married Darwin J. Flakoll, who became her frequent collaborator and later translated many of her works into English. Beginning with the 1948 publication of her first volume of poetry, *Anillo de silencio,* Alegría produced diverse works of poetry, fiction, biography, and history, yet her work remained untranslated until 1978, when she was awarded the Casa de las Americas poetry prize for *Sobrevivo.* Alegría returned to Nicaragua for the first time in 1979 after the Sandinista Front for National Liberation overthrew the Somoza government. She remains an outspoken critic of the Salvadoran government and lives in exile from El Salvador, residing alternately in Managua, Nicaragua and Mallorca, Spain.

Alegría has stated that her aim as a writer is to illuminate the political situation in Central America. Consequently, Latin American history pervades her writings. In the bilingual poetry collection *Flores del volcán/Flowers from the Volcano,* Alegría dramatizes the imperialistic forces that have ruled Latin America: "Gold disappeared and continues / to disappear on *yanqui* ships, / the golden coffee mixed with blood." War and its consequences are also an integral feature of Alegría's poetry. In "Estelí," a poem appearing in *Sobrevivo,* Alegría addresses the effects of civil war on El Salvador, focusing on the image of the river that runs through the small town of her birth: "your channel has been filled. / With mud and blood / it has been filled / with empty cartridges / with shirts / pants / and corpses / sticking like algae / to the rocks." In her nonfic-

tion, Alegría repeatedly affirms her commitment to insurgency. Works such as *No me agarran viva: La mujer salvadoreña en lucha* (*They Won't Take Me Alive*), the biography of Salvadoran rebel Ana María Castillo Rivas, have garnered praise for their descriptions of guerrilla warfare and evocations of life within resistance circles.

Alegría's first novel, *Cenizas de Izalco* (*Ashes of Izalco*), is a love story, cowritten with Flakoll, which recounts the repressive aspects of small-town life in El Salvador. Although set in the 1980s, the narrative focuses on events that occurred in 1932, the year the Salvadoran government massacred hundreds of political dissidents in Alegría's adopted hometown of Santa Ana. A Salvadoran native who resides in the United States, Carmen Rojas returns to the village of her youth and discovers a diary that was written around the time of the massacre recounting her mother's love affair with Frank Wolff, a smug and self-absorbed American writer. Because Alegría provides little direct discourse about the massacre itself, critics often characterize *Ashes of Izalco* as a commentary on the United States' involvement in the war-torn countries of El Salvador and Nicaragua; as residents and symbols of the

United States, Carmen and Frank are as removed from the violence of Central America as are many Westerners.

Albúm familiar (Family Album) and *Luisa en el país de la realidad (Luisa in Realityland)* emphasize Latin America's cultural heritage and milieu rather than specific historical events. Both works have been cited as examples of magic realism in which fantastic incidents are presented in an objective style to obscure distinctions between illusion and reality. In *The Talisman* and *Village of God and the Devil,* which are included in the short fiction collection *Family Album,* Alegría examines the role that religion, spirituality, and magic play in her homeland's culture. *Luisa in Realityland,* a series of poems and prose vignettes in which history and dreams are juxtaposed, similarly demonstrates the importance of mysticism in a political environment in which brutal reality seems to many Latin Americans more fantastic than myth. As the document of a young girl's upbringing in a family of "fabulous liars" who are able to convince themselves and others of the validity of their invented stories, *Luisa in Realityland* has been praised by Sinda Gregory as a "completely textured piece of literature which is as concerned with modes of perception as with that which is perceived and just as dependent on the resonance between images as on the images themselves."

PRINCIPAL WORKS

Anillo de silencio (poetry) 1948
Suite (poetry) 1951
Vigilias (poetry) 1953
Acuario (poetry) 1955
Tres cuentos (juvenilia) 1958
Huésped de mi tiempo (poetry) 1961
New Voices of Hispanic America [editor and translator with Darwin J. Flakoll] (poetry) 1962
*Vía única (poetry) 1965
Cenizas de Izalco [with Flakoll] (novel) 1966
　　[*Ashes of Izalco,* 1989]
†*Aprendizaje* (poetry) 1970
Pagaré a cobrar y otros poemas (poetry) 1973
El detén (novel) 1977
Sobrevivo (poetry) 1978
La encrucijada salvadoreña [with Flakoll] (essays) 1980
Suma y sigue (poetry) 1981
Flores del volcán/Flowers from the Volcano (poetry) 1982
Nicaragua: La revolución sandinista; Una crónica política, 1855-1979 [with Flakoll] (history) 1982
No me agarran viva: La mujer salvadoreña en lucha [with Flakoll] (biography) 1983
　　[*They Won't Take Me Alive,* 1987]
Albúm familiar (novellas) 1984
　　[*Family Album: Three Novellas,* 1991]
Despierta, mi bien, despierta (novel) 1986
Luisa en el país de la realidad (novel) 1987
　　[*Luisa in Realityland,* 1987]

Mujer del río/Woman of the River (poetry) 1989

*This volume contains *Auto de fé* and *Communicacíon a larga distancia.*

†This volume incorporates selections from *Anillo de silencio, Vigilias, Acuario, Huésped de mi tiempo,* and *Vía única.*

CRITICISM

Electa Arenal　(essay date Spring 1981)

[*Arenal has written extensively about Central American literature. In the excerpt below, she examines how the poetry collection* Sobrevivo *reflects Alegría's Nicaraguan origins and political views.*]

In 1978, the poetry prize of the prestigious Casa de las Americas of Havana, Cuba, was awarded to *Sobrevivo/I Survive,* by Claribel Alegría, and *Línea de fuego/Firing Line,* by Gioconda Belli. Thus, Cuba and Casa's Latin American jury reflected their passionate identification with the imminent triumph of national liberation forces in Nicaragua, and at the same time responded to the call of the international women's movement for women's voices to be more fully heard. Both *I Survive* and *Firing Line* are books on love and revolution. Both Alegría and Belli span, through their lives and their work, half a century of dynastic *caudillismo*—imperialism's last mask in Nicaragua—against which a painfully long and costly people's war was waged. Their poems recapture and record the elements of that often tragic resistance, the sacrifices and determination to prevail that characterized those forty-seven years of the Somozas' dictatorship. The women's poetry summarizes, intensifies, and recalls what vanished with the experience, what is depersonalized in statistics about Latin America. In the capture of the very breath of detail, in the all-encompassing view of events and strategies, and in the intertwining of the personal and the political, Alegría's and Belli's roles as poets and as women converge.

Alegría and Belli represent two modes of being for women writers in Latin America. These two modes can be traced far back in the history of Spanish American literature, but also reflect the generations of the two poets, and their life histories. Alegría and Belli have a similar intellectual and poetic heritage. Both were privileged enough to have been educated—in an area of the world where illiteracy rates for women reach 90 percent. Both learned English. Both traveled. Both belonged to a milieu that included writers and artists from the entire continent, an ambience in which the art of the Mexican Revolution (1910-20) and the poetry of the Spanish Civil War (1936-39) were significant points of reference and departure. Both women, in exile, were active witnesses to the end of *Somocismo,* the era of rule by Somoza and his two sons. Each in her own way is a contributor to the new period of revolutionary effervescence and national reconstruction that began in July of 1979. Central to both is the ethical aesthetic in which the writer is viewed as a "spokespoet" whose deeds must eventually fulfill her words. Few women have been called upon to fulfill this role, and few have been remembered when they have actually done so.

But as poets of different generations, their relations to exile, to activism, and to specific literary influences diverge. For Alegría, dedication to writing incorporates political commitment. For over twelve years, she has lived a literary life in Mallorca, expressing her solidarity with Latin American revolution primarily through her work. For Belli, after a period of literary initiation, poetry became a fertile offshoot of dedicated militancy. How Alegría and Belli came into the struggle, and how it found expression in their work can be gleaned from their books. . . . (pp. 19-20)

Alegría's poetic and political consciousness, which did not find its way into print until the 1950s, emerged from the experience of exile in her childhood. When she was nine months old, her father was forced into exile. The family moved to El Salvador, her mother's birthplace, where she grew and took up citizenship. Her Nicaraguan origin, nevertheless, shaped her identity. The times through which she has lived, her travels, and her literary work have led her to an internationalism of a revolutionary Hispanic cast. After the triumph of the Sandinistas, she and her husband, Darwin Flakoll, spent six months traveling throughout Nicaragua, gathering information and seeing and hearing from people firsthand, for a five-hundred-page book they are now writing.

Alegría's exile and return runs parallel to the history of *Sandinismo,* that is, the Sandinist resistance movement. One of the short poems entitled **"Time,"** in *I Survive* can be seen in that light:

> I walked around
> my past
> my future
> and suddenly my present
> took fire.

This almost lifelong exile taught perseverance and gave perspective. From her experience, Alegría fashioned an epic vision whose sweep encompasses pre-Columbian myths and finds in geography and landscape sources for interpreting the grotesque reality of contemporary Latin America. In **"Estelí,"** she describes the harshness and bitterness of this reality in a poem about Estelí, the town where she was born, and its river:

> . . . .
> your channel has been filled.
> With mud and blood
> it has been filled
> with empty cartridges
> with shirts
> pants
> and corpses
> sticking like algae
> to the rocks.

An encompassing mythic and social vision characterizes **"Flowers of the Volcano."** Like the political poetry of Pablo Neruda and César Vallejo, of León Felipe and Ernesto Cardenal, and like the murals of José Clemente

Orozco and David Alfaro Siqueiros, **"Flowers of the Volcano"** is eclectic and panoramic, ethical and impure. It conjoins the pre-Columbian past and our postindustrial epoch of Toyotas and televisions; the masses of men, women, and children who descend in a red wave assert the continuity of humanity and its primacy. Specific historical and geographical references both serve as backdrop and stand in high relief: Central American history has been dramatically affected by its geography, and geography becomes a metaphor for historical events.

From the craters of the volcanos fiery lavas have erupted as have social upheavals. Alegría's description of the children sent from their hideout homes in the volcano to sell flowers and deliver messages to clandestine workers in towns and cities reveals the tenacious spirit of resistance inspired by Sandino which the Somozas never succeeded in crushing. Alegría sketches Latin America's history of imperialist devastation. She tempers the drama with ironically humorous treatment of the hurricanes and earthquakes that make Central America tremble.

The deaths caused by the Somoza carnage are made bearable and comprehensible only by analogy. Alegría explains the price of the inevitable victory of a long-suffering people through the myth of Chac and Tlaloc. In the myth, the yearly ripening of crops and the renewed lease on the planet depended on the sacrifice of human blood. (The lunar calendar carved in stone reflects the cyclical concept of time held by many indigenous groups. Each one hundred years, the earth was to come to an end; permission for another cycle had to be assured through human sacrifices.)

I Survive, the collection that includes **"Flowers of the Volcano,"** asserts the strength of human life and mourns human suffering. The title refers both to the daily act of surviving and to the miracle and the guilt of surviving in our times. Alegría has felt in her flesh and in her verse the death of more than forty thousand of her compatriots. When writing her earlier books, her anguish about Central America was perhaps too close; she turned to Auschwitz and Hiroshima as symbols and intimations of present horrors and those to come.

"Flowers of the Volcano" and six other poems in *I Survive* draw directly on Spanish American politics, reminiscences of family, exile, and death. **"Sorrow,"** the longest poem—dedicated to guerrilla-poet Roque Dalton—evokes with chilling immediacy the murdered, the imprisoned, the tortured, and the "disappeared." These themes are underscored by quotations from García Lorca, Antonio Machado, Miguel Hernández, Pablo Neruda, and a popular Argentine tango.

Alegría's earlier poetry established an approach to personal themes still visible in her work, a distilled and abstracted simplicity, as in **"I Expected to Spend my Time."** This simplicity now allows her to interweave powerfully complex historical and personal themes. Nine of the twenty-three poems in the book are composed of fewer than eight lines:

> I expected to spend my time
> loving

and being loved.
I began to realize
that I spent it shattering
while I in turn was
sh
at
ter
ed.

Through her poetry, Alegría demonstrates how hard survival is, how enmeshed her life has been with the lives of those who must persevere removed from the immediate ongoing struggle. (pp. 20-3)

> *Electa Arenal, "Two Poets of the Sandinista Struggle," in* Feminist Studies, *Vol. 7, No. 1, Spring, 1981, pp. 19-27.*

Carolyn Forché   (essay date 1982)

[*Forché is an American poet, journalist, and editor who translated Alegría's* Flores del volcán/Flowers from the Volcano *into English. In the following excerpt from her preface to that volume, Forché offers a personal reminiscence of Alegría and examines the themes of violence and death in Alegría's poetry.*]

"I have no *fusil* [rifle] in my hand, but only my testimony." [Claribel Alegría's] hands sculpt her language as she speaks. The late sun dissolves in the Mediterranean, the hour's bells drop down the terraces of Mallorca. She moves into another of her memories.

> I was attending a conference of writers and intellectuals. We Latin Americans were sitting around our table and it seems that there was a package addressed to us. It was casually tossed from one mailboy to another. The one who caught it was killed. The other was injured in the explosion. Months later, in another part of the world, I was asked what I would have done if we had been issued rifles. I explained that I could not take up the gun, that I would not be good with a gun. I would have asked for bandages and medicines instead—this is one thing I know how to use. The other is the word.

The ink of memory washed in blood, clouds that are wrapped around the open wounds of the *Cordillera.* Claribel Alegría is a poet who has called herself a cemetery, willing to provide herself as a resting place for those whose bodies have never been recovered, the friends whose flesh has been mutilated beyond recognition. They are the dead who have become "too many to bury," who do not cease to exist and who seem to besiege surviving poets with pleas to witness on their behalf, to add their names to a litany and, in so doing, illuminate a senseless brutality.

[The poems in *Flores del volcán/Flowers from the Volcano*] are testimonies to the value of a single human memory, political in the sense that there is no life apart from our common destiny. They are poems of passionate witness and confrontation. Responding to those who would state that politics has no place in poetry, that expressions of the human spirit in art should be isolated in aesthetics, she would add her voice to that of Neruda's: *we do not wish to please them.*

In her poems, we listen to the stark cry of the human spirit, stripped by necessity of its natural lyricism, deprived of the luxuries of cleverness and virtuosity enjoyed by poets of the north. It is enough that the poet succeed in denying herself any justifiable indulgence.

In translating the work of contemporary Latin Americans, it is marginally possible to reproduce essential content, but in altering substance, there are always precipitates: those of music and atmosphere, specificities of tone. The unique characteristics are lost—in the case of Spanish, which has been called "the verbal medium of the spirit" (Castelar), its onomatopoeic and emphatic qualities, its syntactical freedom and a subtlety that survives abbreviation.

But in these we are not talking about the real difficulty— that of translating the human condition, the reality of one world, so that it may be intelligible to those of a world which has been spared its harshness.

Claribel Alegría's memory is suffused with death, the recurring vision of a young poet whose waterlogged body never washed ashore. She echoes the primitive wisdom: *there are lies more believable than the truth.* The cries of those who vanish assail her with accounts of torture and disappearance, the "blue theater" where a close friend witnessed the methodic dismemberment of a young man, whose flesh was sliced from him until his death. It is a world of live wires touched to genitals, of beatings, ice-water plunges, the parrot's perch, and of food, water, and sleep deprivation. The techniques of torture have been so refined that victims are forgiven their indiscretions. Few talk. The rest seem to have an almost yogic ability to sever mind from body. I was told of the "helmet," a sound chamber affixed to the skull that intensifies the screams of the victim until he can no longer bear the sound of his own voice.

That voice, after death, continues to cry out in the poetry of the impassioned. It becomes one of the "rosary of names" that must be whispered, both because they have become prayers and because their very mention can, at times, endanger the living.

Due to the social and familial circumstances of her life, Claribel Alegría has not lived in her native El Salvador for many years. Her residencies in Mexico, Chile, and Uruguay have broadened her sense of geopolitical identity to embrace the continent. Her years in North America and Europe have necessitated an integration of identities—a truce between a consciousness that is distinctly and essentially Latin American and one that is globally aware of human fragility and mutual dependencies, social, political, economic, and cultural—that has moved many Latin Americans living abroad to question the validity of the term "exile" in the modern world.

She is nostalgic for the music of her own language, for the fraternity of dipping a warm tortilla into a common pot of beans and meat. Her poetry fills with verdant jungles, volcanos, the glow of their craters, the spillage of black rock; with olive trees twisted by time, trees that are wisely neglected to assure that their fruit will be moist and firm. We are immersed in memories of crumbling aristocratic elegance: French wines, leather-spined books, English roses that have since been supplanted for her by flowers splashing down the volcanos in the arms of *campesino* children.

She carries within her the heavy, ancient blood of the Pipiles and laces her language with a mestizo richness, words like the stones of a land where mystery is still palpable. She is attentive to her dreams, trusting them for news of her homeland, and she is comfortable with the deceased, with the powers of amulets and herbs and the gift of understanding the language of coincidence and omen.

Had she realized her dream to become a painter, she would have applied her pigments with a palette knife, with the decisive strokes of a poet not afraid to speak plainly. Like Chagall, whom she loves, her canvases would have reflected a private reality, unique in its perceptions. In my days with her, I have grown to understand that I have been in the presence of a woman whose imagination was nurtured by a culture that persists to encourage wonder in the twentieth century, where the sixth sense is an empirical one.

In [*Flowers from the Volcano*], we have her account of her search for the grave of Garcia Lorca in Andalusia, undertaken while Franco was still alive. An impossible search. We are invited to explore the candlelit village of Santa Ana where she spent her childhood, a place stripped of hope now, strafed by DDT and altered by the calm history of disintegration. We glimpse condors, tangos, the smoke of *copal*, a particular kind of light, *izote*, the constant presence of death, the face of an assassin transformed by traffic lights until he is seen as one of the many faces of his kind.

The poet is finally silenced herself, taking on the persona of the imprisoned, where she continues her poem "with tears, with fingernails and coal—the poem we are all writing." (pp. xi-xiv)

> Carolyn Forché, in a preface to Flowers from the Volcano *by Claribel Alegría, translated by Carolyn Forché, University of Pittsburgh Press, 1982, pp. xi-xiv.*

Ingrid Wendt   (review date Fall 1983)

[*Wendt is an American poet, critic, and educator. In the following review of* Flowers from the Volcano, *she praises Alegría's depiction of human courage in the face of destruction.*]

Refusing to accept theories of impending global disaster—asserting instead that humanity "will not merely endure" but "prevail"—in his Nobel Prize acceptance speech William Faulkner stated the poet's duty: to remind us "of the courage and honor and hope and pride and compassion and pity and sacrifice" of those before us and around us, whose heritage we live, and must live up to. More than twenty years later the voice of Salvadoran poet Claribel Alegría, in her latest volume *Flowers from the Volcano,* bears courageous witness to this same resolve.

"I am alone," she writes in the poem **"We Were Three."**

> My dead stand watch
> and send signals to me,
> they assail me
> in the radio and paper.

> . . .

> My dead arise, they rage.
> The streets are empty
> but my dead wink at me.
> I am a cemetery,
> I have no country
> and they are too many to bury.

Suffering in exile the daily news of political repression in her homeland—the news of torture, death and disappearances of friends and compatriots, more than 40,000 in the last five years—Alegría expresses in these nine, long poems, a personal as well as a collective grief. Unable to visit the graves of the dead, indeed at her distance unable even to receive clear accounts of already-hazy facts, Alegría uses the tools of her language in a way common to all poetry but uniquely personal, too: to "name," to "define," to make visible the essence of what she knows has happened, to make it *real*—and by so doing, to allow the grief to happen, the healing and renewal to begin.

In this way each poem becomes its own kind of service, its resting place for memories wrenched out of context, for the names of the dead (a "rosary of names") which reappear in these poems like litanies, insubstantial as spirits among surreal landscape imagery: "Shadows of faces / that no longer exist," "Voices that rise and are gone."

In these poems we often see a blending of fact and allegory, history and myth. In **"Toward the Jurassic Age,"** for example, Alegría describes a new breed of animal "the size of an iguana," brought into Palma, that has grown so big it devours plantations and "can only be killed / by rockets dropped from planes." **"Santa Ana in the Dark"** is more than an account of a village deprived by its local dictator of electricity; it is an account of civilization's gradual return to the "Dark Ages"—where religion runs by the powers of revenge, and God metes out punishment through members of an impotent church. In **"Sorrow"** Alegría searches for the lost grave of Federico García Lorca—the poet killed during the Spanish Civil War—identifying herself more and more with a variety of political prisoners until she is the one in jail, meeting the memories/spirits of dead poets and martyrs—in particular, the Salvadoran poet Roque Dalton, and the Chileans Victor Jara, Violetta Parra, and Pablo Neruda.

We are also given some glimpses into the early life of the poet: helping, and learning from, her father, the village doctor; and with him climbing the volcano:

> mist licking our legs,
> the branches with orchids and moss.
> We climbed to the sun;
> the very peak
> once more to the sun of Central America.

And in another poem:

> We grew up without knowing
> of light in other places
> and we marveled when someone

carried a lamp.
Sun and moon were enough,
the curtain of fireflies opening,
closing in the night.

. . .

All of this to tell you
I am desperate to go back.

For all their intensity, however, these poems are not without a certain amount of irony that sometimes borders on wit. **"Letter to Time"** begins:

Dear Sir:
I write this letter on my birthday.
I received your gift. I don't like it.
It is always the same.

These and other lines exemplify what W. S. Merwin once said about the greatest function of irony: to give us enough poise to approach what would otherwise be unbearable truth. Reading these lines we may smile; but we do not laugh.

In her introduction to *Flowers from the Volcano,* translator and poet Carolyn Forché remarks that here "we listen to the stark cry of the human spirit, stripped by necessity of its natural lyricism, deprived of the luxuries of cleverness and virtuosity enjoyed by poets of the north." For the most part, I agree. The style of these poems is consistently urgent, insistent. The poet has no time, no heart—as these short, clipped lines emphasize—for dancing with language or sound.

Forché's translations are accurate, always, and literal. But comparing the Spanish with the English translation, I wonder at her decision to lengthen Alegría's poetic lines: to compress three, four, sometimes more short lines from the Spanish into one long one in the English, and also to eliminate most of the "and's"—to sever syntactical (and to my ears, lyrical) connections present in the original text. Perhaps this is necessary. Readers (myself included, although my own father is Chilean) unaccustomed to the nuances of foreign tones may need additional harshness to better comprehend the harsh realities being shown.

Flowers from the Volcano is a painful book to read, but an important one. It moves us to confront the issue of our North American presence in El Salvador (and Nicaragua, and Lebanon, and Grenada), and the erosion of what we call civilization in the name of democracy.

Reading the title poem, in which Alegría announces repeatedly "the cycle is closing," we have also a vision not totally void of hope. Just as "Cuscatlecan flowers / thrive in volcanic ash," the children (whose families live in the bowl of the extinct volcano) will stream down the mountainside "with their bouquets of flowers. . . . They are only children in rags / with flowers from the volcano . . . but the wave is swelling."

If, in one sense, the poet sees herself as a cemetery—and her poems as resting places for the dead—we could perhaps say also that each poem here is a new kind of flower "from the volcano": a transformation of life from molten stone, of growth from the force of destruction. These poems are a testimony to human courage and endurance.

They give us the hope that the values and the lives they bespeak will "not merely endure" but "prevail." (pp. 75-8)

Ingrid Wendt, in a review of "Flowers from the Volcano," in CALYX: A Journal of Art and Literature by Women, *Vol. 8, No. 1, Fall, 1983, pp. 75-8.*

Michael Korson   (review date Spring 1984)

[*In the following excerpt, Korson examines Alegría's treatment of such themes as loss, persecution, and suffering in* Flowers from the Volcano.]

As a Latin American (though she was born in Nicaragua, her family moved to Salvador when she was a child, and she considers herself to be Salvadoran), Alegria finds it impossible to escape the suffering of the faceless and nameless throughout that area's history. [Carolyn Forché, in her preface to *Flowers from the Volcano*], tells us that Alegría makes of herself a "cemetery willing to provide herself as a resting place for those whose bodies have never been recovered . . . They are the dead who have become 'too many too bury,' who do not cease to exist and who seem to besiege surviving poets with pleas to witness on their behalf . . . "

In **"We Were Three"** (where Alegría uses the metaphor of the cemetery to describe herself) the "persecuted voices" of two mysteriously dead or missing friends ("no one can say / how they died") assail her as if "one voice / dying by torture in prison." However, the poem does not remain a dirge for these friends (whom the poet refers to as "my dead"), but moves from their memory to an embrace of all faceless victims of repression. At the end of the poem, Alegria has no country—she abandons the idea of separatism due to nationality—and is thus able to empathize with all those suffering, either deceased or still alive.

Throughout these poems, we hear the same voices of the persecuted that follow and speak to the poet. Even while seeking "refuge in the arms of Mother Culture" (in a museum while "pretending to study / a Corot, a Cezanne") she is haunted by a vision of slaves "trying to escape the stones that imprison them." In this poem (**"Sorrow"**) Alegria is also visited by the words of dead Latin American poets—Roque Dalton, a Salvadoran; Victor Jara, a Chilean folksinger; the Peruvian Cesar Vallejo; and the Spanish poets Miguel Hernandez, Federico Garcia Lorca, and Antonio Machado. Here, Forché includes within her translations the original Spanish of these poets, and the effect is very powerful. As we are reading along and encounter the Spanish, we are reminded of where this poetry comes from, and are presented, as well, with a rich musical blend of languages.

As if to escape the constant reminder of suffering and inhuman conditions that these voices force upon her, Alegría attempts (in **"Sorrow"**) to find refuge in her own loneliness: "with a chip of coal I begin to write: / my loneliness, my—" However, she is unable to withdraw into herself, and again the voices return as if being screamed from inside a prison:

this backdrop of cries
punctuated by a scream

a sudden, a terrified silence
they start up again more loudly
shut up! the turnkey shouts
clanking his keys on the bars. . . .

We must imagine this prison to be like the ones Forché describes from her own stay in El Salvador that are too small for the prisoner to stand or sit in and eventually cause one to lose the ability to walk.

Because she is so conscious of widespread suffering, Alegría can never have her own solitude:

I am not alone
they are here
the transient guests . . .

In fact, her identity merges with that of the oppressed, so that she can say she is "again the tortured one / his howl and silence. . . ." The history of repression and victimization in Latin America is very long and thus there are many names—the poet's "rosary of names"—for her to count and remember. Alegría is aware of the suffering of others to the extent that she can feel the torment of the dead: "they are more alone than we are."

In **"Santa Ana In The Dark"** the poet returns, through her memory, to the village of her childhood. Even under the control of tyranny ("Let there be darkness / declared Don Raimundo"), this is still a place of special significance:

And the morning star, Sirius
and Seven Little Sisters
brighter in the darkness of Santa Ana
than anywhere else in this world.

Forché says that Alegría succeeds "in denying herself any justifiable indulgence," and in this poem we can see in what soil these roots of humility, and power to restrain from complaint, are grown:

We grew up without knowing
of light in other places
and we marveled when someone
carried a lamp.
Sun and moon were enough;
the curtain of fireflies opening,
closing in the night.

Even from her exile, she is aware of the pain that the people and town still undergo: "Our house in Santa Ana crumbles . . . " "The garden once filled with birds is empty." The lives that she remembers—the women who for the last forty years "dress up on Sundays / for High Mass in the cathedral"; Don Santiago, who once had a pharmacy and "sold everything cheap or on credit"—are remembered for their dignity through suffering adversity. When she revisits the village in her dreams, it seems to her to be "the open country of death." Yet, she concludes the poem: "I am desperate to go back."

In her preface, Forché comments on the difficulty of translating Latin American poetry into English. She admits that in the process much of the character of the Spanish—such as its musical quality—is lost. I admire her frankness. Auden says in his introduction to the collected work of the Greek poet Cavafy that one can only hope to capture in translation a particular tone of voice unique to the poet.

Forché's translations are forceful, and convey the rich texture of language implicit with the original work.

In **"My Good-Byes"** Claribel Alegría bids farewell to those she is leaving behind as she enters exile. She remembers again her native village: "My valley is a burial ground of races. . . . " "My America is spilled blood. . . . " At the end of the poem, she shares with us these words a friend writes to her: "for our America a destiny / that would not fill us with shame." To this wish we all should lend our voices. (pp. 91-3)

Michael Korson, "Voices of Persecution," in The Chariton Review, *Vol. 10, No. 1, Spring, 1984, pp. 90-3.*

Jan Clausen   (review date October 1984)

[*In the following excerpt, Clausen praises Alegría for creating "a poetry of witness" in* Flowers from the Volcano, *but faults Carolyn Forché for numerous errors in translation.*]

According to the jacket copy, **Flowers from the Volcano** "brings to the American [sic] reader for the first time a substantial selection of poems by a writer who has become a courageous and major force in Latin American poetry." Given that this volume will constitute a great many *North American* readers' introduction to Claribel Alegría's work, it's particularly unfortunate that it suffers from some serious editing and translation problems, the responsibility for which must be shared by Carolyn Forché and the University of Pittsburgh Press.

Most immediately apparent of these is the fact that no attempt has been made to indicate when the nine selections were written or where they first appeared; Forché's preface is silent as to her criteria for inclusion, and she neglects to situate the pieces thematically or stylistically within the larger body of Alegría's poetry. (In fact, the poems are drawn from collections published over more than two decades, as I was finally able to learn by consulting *Suma y sigue,* a volume of Alegría's selected poetry published by Visor, Madrid in 1981 with a useful critical overview by Mario Benedetti.) Instead, Forché writes of the Central American context of political violence and torture in such a way as to attach to Alegría the emergent stereotype of the tormented Latin writer: "In her poems, we listen to the stark cry of the human spirit; stripped by necessity of its natural lyricism." This is a much less complex account than the work deserves, for it certainly displays a great deal of "natural lyricism," and is capable besides of humor, whimsy, irony, and exquisite moments of private tenderness.

"Toward the Jurassic Age," the opening poem, finds Alegría countering tyranny with an almost light-hearted surrealism. She writes of an unnamed "they" who started out iguana-sized and have grown large enough to menace the population:

there are herbivores
and carnivores among them
the carnivores know one another
by the military caps that crown

their crests
but both are harmful

Herbivores and carnivores, both harmful: one thinks of the "moderate" Duarte and outright-fascist D'Aubuisson in El Salvador.

"Letter to Time" is equally fanciful, its sinister undertones more metaphysical than political in nature. Written on the poet's birthday, the letter requests Time to lay off, cease his inexorable visits. As in **"Toward the Jurassic Age,"** much of the effectiveness rests on the dry, flat tone and the selection of the perfect image for a menacing figure; Time becomes an older man with an "unchanging face," whose "greeting tastes of musty rooms" and who has about him a definite suggestion of the child molester: "a friend of my father's / with one eye on me."

The long, eight-part **"Sorrow"** and the book's title poem are the two most explicitly political pieces, if one means by this that they confront head-on the themes of repression and resistance which loom so large in Central American experience. **"Sorrow"** is unified by a series of invocations of poets and other artists who have been sacrificed in the liberation struggle, notably the Salvadorean poet Roque Dalton, killed in 1975. In one section Alegría describes a pilgrimage in search of the site of the murder of Federico García Lorca. In others, she merges her own identity with that of furtive, impoverished exiles who must seek refuge in museums or public baths; or she speaks in the voice of the imprisoned, listens to the screams of the tortured, inscribes on the prison wall with a piece of charcoal the unanswerable question, "Who raised up this prison's bars?"

Perhaps in part because I know the poet's sharing of the most extreme suffering she describes is merely imaginative, in part because her descriptions lack their usual sharpness and freshness ("a gray light filters from outside / there is no sun / there are no birds, no foliage"), I was less moved by this poem than by the more personal expression of loss in **"We Were Three"**:

> I am alone.
> My dead stand watch
> and send signals to me,
> they assail me
> in the radio and the paper.
> The wall of my dead
> rises and reaches from Aconcagua to Izalco.

"Flowers from the Volcano" describes a legacy of seemingly unredeemed bloodshed stretching back to pre-Columbian times ("Who said that my country was green? / It is more red, more grey, more violent"). The poet is clearly more distant from "the dead *guerrillero* / and the thousand betrayed faces," the "children in rags / with flowers from the volcano," than she is from the victims of **"Sorrow"** and **"We Were Three."** She closes with the grimly ambiguous prediction that "the cycle is closing," "today's Chacmol still wants blood"; it's unclear whether she expects anything hopeful to emerge from the carnage.

My favorites are two poems which combine political insight with the exquisite skill in communicating private experience which seems to be one of Alegría's hallmarks. In

"Santa Ana in the Dark" she sketches a portrait of the Salvadorean city in which she grew up; she achieves both a loving tribute and a devastating sketch of the conditions and consequences of Central American "underdevelopment." Santa Ana is run by Don Raimundo, "accustomed to command," who has defied the God of Genesis by decreeing darkness in the city, as a result of which children fail to learn "their 40-watt history"; meanwhile, unmarried aunts live on in a stupefying yet charming miasma of conservative Catholicism, vanilla sweets, and gossip; everyone halfway promising is felled by disease or silenced by repression; DDT kills off the birds. Nevertheless,

> It didn't matter
> when we were young.
> Everything was green.
> We grew up without knowing
> of light in other places
> and we marveled when someone
> carried a lamp.

The poem closes with the abrupt admission that "at times I'm assailed / by a violent desire / to go back" [my translation].

"My Goodbyes," the closing poem, makes the equally dangerous admission that at times the poet desires intensely to leave behind not only Santa Ana, which she once more evokes, but the entire "somber, green, difficult" continent whose vastness and particularity, physical beauty and political torment she masterfully renders. She begins with the line, "The afternoon jet plucks me from Ezeiza." The distance the airplane gives to her consideration of the continent and the haste of the overflight provide the appropriate framework for an expression of alienation:

> My America is spilled blood,
> the theater of Cain and Abel,
> a struggle with no quarter given
> against starvation, rage or impotence.

Yet Latin America's unity is also suggested in her snatched views of the pampas, of Santiago; her recollections of the Guatemala she swallows "without tasting," and of "the phosphorescent streets of Mérida." And the poem, itself unified by repeated words and phrases, circles back from its opening among the "faces of the Rio de la Plata" to a close in which Alegría quotes from her friend Roa's wistful letter (written while tanks roll toward Buenos Aires) in which he recalls their shared desire for a better destiny for their America "in the singular."

The English version of **"My Goodbyes"** illustrates some of the problems presented by Forché's translations. (While my own Spanish leaves much to be desired, it has sufficed for me to be able to identify omissions and alterations in a great many cases.) The repeated words and phrases noted above, for example, are lost in the English, with "la mancha morada de las pampas" ("the purple stain of the pampas") rendered by Forché as a "violet glimpse of the pampas," while "la mancha morada de Atitlán" becomes "the cobalt [!] stain of Atitlán." The repetition of the verbs "arrancar" (to pull out, uproot) and "recorrer" (to go over, travel over) is likewise lost. The phrase "nuestra América / así en singular" ("Our America / like that in the singular") is translated simply as "our America," thus omitting the poet's crucial emphasis on America's unity. Santiago in the "crepúsculo" ("dusk") turns into Santiago in the "dust." When Alegría writes of pressing her good-byes "between the pages of a book / I don't read" ("entre las hojas de un libro / que no leo"), Forché injects a small note of melodrama, "pressing them in a book / I will never read." (pp. 7-8)

All of this is to say that *Flowers from the Volcano* falls far short of being the ideal introduction to Alegría's work. Nevertheless, it's well worth reading. More translations will no doubt follow, as commercial and university presses, their interest sparked by blood-spattered headlines, display increasing enthusiasm for Central American literature.

However ironic this enthusiasm may seem, however symptomatic of the sickness of an empire that habitually "discovers" the cultures it is attempting to destroy, the fact is that North Americans need this literature, which is both historically rich and, thanks largely to Nicaragua, particularly lively at the present moment. Its life can give us life, its agonized awareness of death sensitize us to our own monumental task—which is not, after all, primarily literary, but a very prosaic, pedestrian matter of organizing, of stopping appropriations and troop maneuvers. (p. 8)

> *Jan Clausen, "America in the Singular," in* The Women's Review of Books, *Vol. II, No. 1, October, 1984, pp. 7-8.*

Alegría's best poems are her most personal, ones in which she recalls the squalor of her native village, for example, and the domestic tyrannies of her father, the local doctor. In revealing a genuine nostalgia for these things, the Salvadorean poet dramatizes the bittersweet passions felt by everyone, but especially exiles, for that paradox we call home.

—David Kirby, in Library Journal, **November 15, 1982.**

Helene J. F. De Aguilar   (review date 1985)

[*In the following excerpt, De Aguilar faults* Flowers from the Volcano *as derivative and unaffecting.*]

The Nicaraguan-born, Salvadorean-raised Claribel Alegría is introduced to the reader [in *Flowers from the Volcano*] with what seems appalling accuracy in Carolyn Forché's "Preface: With Tears, with Fingernails and Coal":

> Responding to those who would state that politics has no place in poetry, that expression of the human spirit in art should be isolated in aesthetics, she would add her voice to that of Neruda's: *we do not wish to please them.*

In her poems, we listen to the stark cry of the human spirit, stripped by necessity of its natural lyricism, deprived of the luxuries of cleverness and virtuosity enjoyed by poets of the north. It is enough that the poet succeeds in denying herself any justifiable indulgence.

All things being equal, of course, a translator's preface can hardly be cited in evidence against a poet. But in this case Forché's remarks are hard to overlook, so assiduously does Alegría seem to labor to corroborate them. From the paranoid challenge to those Unmoved Readers whose hosts would banish politics from art and—God forbid!—preserve aesthetics, Forché, and it does seem Alegría as well, proceed to the obligatory banishment of "natural lyricism": the immediate result of this policy is the commemoration of some terrible times in equally terrible verse:

> From Roa,
> "I write these lines
> while the tanks roll by to Buenos Aires.
> I do not watch, but I hear their screeching.
> Remember what we talked about
> with Bud and you
> attentive to our thoughts:
> for our America a destiny
> that would not fill us with shame?"
> Good-bye Roa
> and Zoraida
> and Sebastián
> and Manolo
> and Lucho
> and Pueyrredón.
>
>   (**"My Good-Byes"**)

Anything less lyrical can scarcely be imagined. The Preface's rancor about "poets of the north" and their shameless wallowing in "cleverness and virtuosity"—a privilege they enjoy presumably because they have not suffered—does not find direct support in Alegría's poetry which, while cramped and turgid, is not insulting or, for that matter, ridiculous. But the grudge is indirectly implied. Axiomatic for her is the self-sufficiency of pain for artistic achievement. In **"My Good-Byes"** she tells us "My America is spilled blood, / the theater of Cain and Abel," for all the world as though this state of affairs were unique and—worse still—intrinsically poetic. Unadorned misery is *not* synonymous with virtue or with racial superiority. That "cleverness" or "virtuosity" might be *attributes* in a poet whose subject is suffering never crosses Alegría's mind.

Nor does the poet find it incongruous that having jettisoned literary considerations she has effectively and of her own free will invested the demented villains of the piece, the torturers, oppressors, and murderers, with full creative and imaginative responsibility for her poetry. The victims need but scream.

For neither Alegría nor [Gloria] Fuertes is "inspiration" relevant. Poetry as beauty, metamorphosis, or transcendence is not within their range of interest or ability. But the forfeiture of art-as-transformation, above and beyond whatever other troublesome consequences it entails, immediately imposes upon the poet different and severe hardships of which Alegría, at least, remains unaware.

True, she strips away that hateful lyricism with no qualms—and for that matter, precious little difficulty. But what on earth replaces it? Personal charisma, distinguished intellect, and—most definitely—a sense of humor must replace delphic frenzy for a poet estranged from divine possession. But neither special insight nor arresting poignancy nor—most definitely—any sense of humor can be detected in Alegría's writing. The longest poem in *Flowers from the Volcano,* "Sorrow," exhibits with irritating insistence Alegría's dearth of creative flair:

> it is better to have itching fungi
> leaving our feet bloody
> leaving a shriek within us
> *me moriré en París con aquacero*
> *un día del cual tengo ya el recuerdo*
> (I will die in Paris with a heavy rain shower
> on a day of which I still have memory)
>
> . . .
>
> that is how your death arrived, Roque Dalton
> the implacable news of your death
> in the smudged headlines
> your death in the bloodless voice of the radio
> it arrived without precision
> in broken images
> you were a lookout
> a beacon slicing through fog
> it is dangerous, Roque
> to go about proclaiming Che
> Jesus and Sandino
> to ignore the real boss
> to open your eyes
> to feel that your own memory
> opens wounds, each wound
> a small flame rising
> the echoes are still coming back
> the false accusations
> I'll never know who killed you
> but you are dead, Roque Dalton,
> and they wrap your death in fog.

The affectation of apostrophe ("it is dangerous, Roque . . . ") is perhaps inevitable in a poem composed from the outset of assembled quotations, sometimes bizarrely or wrongly identified, from dead poets. (Vallejo, for instance, was Peruvian, not Guatemalan as the Notes state. Moreover he said he *already* remembered the day of his death, that is to say, *before* its occurrence. In Forché's translation he *still* remembers it and thus appears to be writing from beyond the grave. Another quotation "ascribed to Machado" is not by Machado.) Similarly predictable, and embarrassing, is the poet's vainglorious and obviously unjustifiable self-inclusion among the martyrs whom she invokes by Christian name, suggesting at once her own intimacy and the reader's alienation; the tie that binds is clearly private property:

> I ask and the answer is clear:
> I am Georgina
> I am Nelson
> I am Raúl
> again the tortured one
> his howl and silence
> I stretch out on my cot
> with my eyes open
> and not so much as a fissure of light

> the screams are cut
> I begin counting the names
> my rosary of names

"Sorrow" is a completely disjointed statement held together by Alegría's ubiquitous and obviously well-intentioned ego: it is not, in fact, a poem at all but rather a catalogue of favorite texts and remembered losses.

Even at her least derivative Alegría is boring. The fault lies not in her topic but in her abilities. The title poem of her anthology, "Flowers from the Volcano" strains over ninety-two lines after an effect accomplished in seven by her compatriot Alfonso Quijada Urías. Here is Urías' "Post Card" ("Postal"):

> So then you see this country
> which might be the size of a wood-shaving,
> and next a train like a toy which goes by every
>   evening filled with little soldiers
> who although they seem pretend are actually
>   real,
> and you see, too, the volcanoes like small
>   smudges of blue ink,
> and you cannot find a reason (although one does
>   exist)
> why there are so many little soldiers in a country
>   the size of a wood-shaving.

Urías is a master at the sort of artistry so alien to Alegría. No spoiled, sheltered gringo, he has nonetheless retained his interest in aesthetics and is at pains to prepare a delicate canvas. On this canvas he evokes a small, innocent, *paradoxically* tormented land. We stumble into this country as if by accident, tripping over a casual connective adverb ("*entonces,*" "so then") which constitutes a fairy-tale-like border. The effect of this strategy is wonder: the reader *looks up, looks around,* and *sees* the landscape new, uncoerced because he is discovering an unknown world, not taking notes on the known.

This is hardly possible for Alegría's public, who are being whacked over the head from the opening declamation. Her "fourteen volcanos" rise initially like Roman arches, our reaction to which is pretty well determined by past exposure. After three scant lines of more tropical intent we reach a rhetorical question of paralyzing dullness:

> Fourteen volcanos rise
> in my remembered country
> in my mythical country.
> Fourteen volcanos of foliage and stone
> where strange clouds hold back
> the screech of a homeless bird.
> Who said that my country was green?
> It is more red, more gray, more violent:
> Izalco roars,
> taking more lives.
> Eternal Chacmol collects blood,
> the gray orphans
> the volcano spitting bright lava
> and the dead *guerrillero*
> and the thousand betrayed faces,
> the children who are watching
> so they can tell of it.
> Not one kingdom was left us.
> One by one they fell
> through all the Americas.

Note that Urías' question—he, too, is perplexed by the irrational scale of human woe—is silent, taken for granted. It is the inborn question of mankind; this doomed search for the answer we cannot find "although one does exist" makes us brothers and fixes our complicity in the poem's diminutive, desolate conclusion. The childlike prettiness and delicacy of Urías' landscape prove far more affecting, not to mention more accurate, than do Alegría's "betrayed faces" and hovering children, for Alegría *lectures* her readers, and in a surly manner at that, on topics which require no sermonizing:

> Gold disappeared and continues
> to disappear on *yanqui* ships,
> the golden coffee mixed with blood.
>
> . . .
>
> The golden coffee is unloaded
> in New York where
> they roast it, grind it
> can it and give it a price.
> *Siete de Junio*
> *noche fatal*
> *bailando el tango*
> *la capital.*
> From the shadowed terraces
> San Salvador's volcano rises.

If the *"yanqui ships"* and "golden coffee mixed with blood" business sounds tiresomely familiar, it is because such wording was already non-poetry years ago when Neruda patented the formulation. For Neruda, however, the implacably unrefined imagery, devoid of wordplay, melody, or innovative vision was a deliberate strategem, deriving shock value—its sole poetic value—from its very *contrast* with surrounding poetic norms, including his own. Shock value being short-lived, Alegría fails to capture anything of artistic worth when she borrows from "United Fruit Company." She simply incorporates Neruda's most dated diction into her own rough tone.

Flowers from the Volcano contains nine poems. Two or three are not "political" and one of these, **"Letter to Time,"** turns out to be a most appealing protest. A saucy Adina is better than a choking Kundry; in **"Letter to Time"** Alegría forgoes the apocalyptic agonies whose demands overwhelm her talents and confines herself to the more negotiable tribulations of a woman's aging:

> Dear Sir:
> I write this letter on my birthday.
> I received your gift. I don't like it.
> It is always the same.

The futility of human opposition to Time's visitations possesses innate pathos but limited shock value, so Alegría is not tempted to essay any ill-advised Horror and Pity. Instead, she is dry and direct:

> I forbid you to come back.
> Each time I see you my spine stiffens.
> Stop following me.
> I beg you.
> It has been years since I loved another
> and your gifts are no longer of interest.

The reader's spine stiffens in solidarity despite some less-than-ideal translation, for we too have loved others for years. ("It has been years since I loved another" suggests, on the contrary, a longstanding and exclusive devotion precisely *to* time.) We can guess as well the outcome of Alegría's petition:

> You will win.
> I knew it when I began.

Why Forché translates "when I began" rather than "when I began my letter" (*al comenzar mi carta*) is her secret. I suspect she found the heightened solemnity of the former, á la *Four Quartets,* irresistible.

In any event, Alegría *could* write with charm if she would. But she scorns such frivolities and will not relinquish the Grand Vision to which her skills are so manifestly inadequate. Her intransigence is her loss. (pp. 369-77)

> *Helene J. F. De Aguilar, "Distressing Land-scapes," in* Parnassus: Poetry in Review, *Vol. 12, No. 2 & Vol. 13, No. 1, 1985, pp. 369-85.*

Jane Dibblin   (review date 24 April 1987)

[*In the following essay, Dibblin offers a mixed assessment of Alegría's biography* No me agarran viva: La mujer salvadoreña en lucha (They Won't Take Me Alive).]

It is hard to talk of the freshly dead with anything but reverence. Harder still not to deify someone who has died young and was killed for the sake of their beliefs.

On 17 January 1981 Ana María Castillo Rivas was gunned down by plainclothes Salvadorean security forces as she tried to make a crucial arms drop. She was 31 years old and had a daughter of 13 months. Born into a comfortable, liberal family, she left them to join the guerillas of the Farabundo Marti Popular Liberation Forces (FPL), becoming *Companera* Eugenia, in the high command of the San Salvador front, head of the supply section during the general offensive of 1981. To write *They Won't Take Me Alive* Claribel Alegría interviewed Eugenia's friends, sisters and husband. The result is at times stiff with political jargon, often exasperating, nevertheless deeply moving.

Through the interviews Eugenia emerges as near perfect; tireless, never complaining, a woman whose political commitment and human understanding went from strength to strength. There's no doubt that she was a remarkable woman, impassioned yet meticulous. But that can't be her whole story. I want to know more. How did she cope with living underground, with carrying on an intensely caring relationship with her husband Javier when they were often separated and always anticipating the death of the other? How did she resolve what must have been an acute dilemma when she decided to have a baby and raise her with the guerillas in hiding?

I need to know not out of voyeurism but because otherwise Eugenia and her *companeros* become sanctified heroes, out of reach of mere mortal readers. Eugenia's story could be an inspiration but only if it builds a bridge with the reader, passing on some of her hard-won wisdom. *I . . . Rigo-*

berta Menchu [edited by Elizabeth Burgos-Debray], and [Domitila Barrios de Chungara's] *Let Me Speak,* the first the story of an Indian woman in Guatemala, the second that of a woman from a Bolivian tin mine, are more successful in this: their humour, their fears and sadnesses make their personal sacrifices seem more possible.

The difference is that these women were still alive to tell their own histories and those of their communities. Could Alegría have written a different book only a year after Eugenia's death? I attended the funeral in Managua of an *internationalista,* a young doctor killed by the Contras. The Europeans and Americans were visibly shocked and shaken. His Nicaraguan friends, including his wife, stood, tears streaming down their faces, fists raised, shouting their defiance in cracked voices, *patria libre o morir! no pasaran!* On every other page of *They Won't Take Me Alive* Eugenia loses another *companera,* another friend is captured and tortured. How else can the surviving Salvadoreans meet those deaths but by militancy, by translating their grief into new determination?

As it is, we get tantalising glimpses into what Eugenia might have had to say for herself.

> She started carrying out a large number of armed operations with an extraordinary serenity. Serenity doesn't imply a lack of fear. We talked this over together and she told me: 'Anyone who tells you he isn't afraid is telling lies. How could you not live in fear? The point is to overcome it.'

And, at the end, quite suddenly, there are three letters from Eugenia to Javier which she wrote just before she died, and some insights which breathe life into the memory of her: that she sang constantly to keep up everyone's spirits—completely out of tune—and that she was so preoccupied she wrote off countless cars out of absentmindedness.

There is also an excellent historical preface by Amanda Hopkinson and, after the recent spate of films mediating the war in Central America through the eyes of American journalists (*Under Fire, Salvador . . .*), it's a relief to see the struggle documented from the inside. For all its lapses into stiffness [*They Won't Take Me Alive*] is a book which challenges and which lingers in the mind. (pp. 28-9)

> *Jane Dibblin, "Too Little, Too Soon," in* New Statesman, *Vol. 113, No. 2926, April 24, 1987, pp. 28-9.*

Carolyn Forché   (review date 15 November 1987)

[*In the following excerpt, Forché favorably assesses Alegría's autobiographical novel* Luisa en el país del realidad (Luisa in Realityland).]

In 1977, I began translating the poetry of Claribel Alegria into English. As a neophyte, I expected to find such work difficult, but Alegria's eluded me for extra-linguistic reasons. It reflected the severity of life under military dictatorships in the Nicaragua of her birth (still ruled by Somoza) and the El Salvador of her girlhood and upbringing. In matters regarding torture, disappearance, imprison-

ment and the struggle for social justice, dictionaries and grammars were of little help. I found it difficult to distinguish the literal from the metaphorical: Were a prisoner's fingers actually cut off, or did the poet mean to suggest that the imprisoned musician no longer felt moved to play his guitar? The answer was yes, the musician's hands had, in fact, been mutilated.

So as to assure that my translations would do some justice to the poems, I traveled to Deya, Mallorca, where Claribel Alegria lived, after having spent more than 30 years in self-imposed exile. Her house was frequented then by writers of the "Boom," many of them her dearest friends, including Gabriel Garcia Marquez and Julio Cortazar. Its terrace faced the sacred mountain, Teix, and it was here that she held an informal salon for travelers and exiles; here that glasses were filled with Mallorquin wine as the sun dropped into the Teix and goat bells rang on its slopes, while in low voices the harshest stories were told, and in ringing tones, the magical tales of Claribel Alegria's childhood recounted. It was Cortazar who first urged her to write them down, but it was years before she did so—only now do we have *Luisa in Realityland,* an autobiographical novel alternately written in verse and anecdotal prose vignettes.

"In Luisa's family there were many fabulous liars," one such passage of prose begins, "including herself of course." By way of such an admission do we enter Luisa's "Realityland" of myth-making uncles, prescient animals, ancestral chambers and the sexual secrets of Catholic childhood. In the prose vignettes, a family in mourning gives burial to a stranger's corpse at the very hour their own son is buried far away; a man who has never left his village so convincingly invents his own memories of Paris that he can reminisce with Parisians; a ghost's bedroom slippers are heard in a house for 60 years. We are in the realm of magic realism, or rather as Alejo Carpentier and Garcia Marquez have suggested, in the realm of ordinary Latin American life.

Like Claribel, Luisa spends part of her dream life painting "cabbages with eyes, noses or ears lurking in the leaves, plazas filled with empty chairs; black-frocked pastors preaching to starving dogs and two-legged cows." She fills more than seventy canvases and longs to find a gallery to exhibit her work in the dream world "for friends she kept meeting in that other dimension." Then she begins a canvas impossible to finish: red dots on a gray field, mysteriously red, dripping and running like blood, and as the actual world of politics and struggle intrude upon the world of her dreams, she turns away from painting and devotes herself to poetry.

The poems throughout this work are by turns incantatory and elegiac, as if the past were somehow haunted by the present. The poet harshly admonishes her younger self for attempting to create an oasis of art and motherhood in a world of violence and injustice. By turns she addresses a lover still alive and perhaps a love who preceded her into death, whose identity remains mysterious, but whose absence brings special poignancy to these remembrances, as if the life they evoke were larger than themselves, and transcended the narrowly personal to become the collective memory of Central Americans in this decade.

The prose vignettes recall for me the stories Claribel Alegría told on her terrace that balmy summer 10 years ago, including the most horrific: her Chilean friend's encounter with "the blue theater," where she was made to witness the death by slow dismemberment of a university schoolmate. The details are here, as vivid as those burned into my memory at the first telling. Now that such stories are committed to paper there is less risk that they will ever be viewed as apocryphal.

Luisa in Realityland closes with a long poem in parts, which is actually a repetition of earlier poems out of sequence, as if the work were an echo chamber and yet, by such repetition, further meaning accrues to the poems, so that they become a more complete utterance of one woman's struggle to preserve her past and redeem her present. (pp. 3, 10)

> Carolyn Forché, "The Ghosts of a Central American Girlhood," in Los Angeles Times Book Review, *November 15, 1987, pp. 3, 10.*

Suzanne Ruta   (review date 2 February 1988)

[*Ruta is an American journalist, fiction writer, and editor. In the review below, she examines anecdotal aspects of* Luisa in Realityland *and relates the novel to Alegría's previous works.*]

The time, the 1930s. The place, a small town in western El Salvador. A 10-year-old girl gets out of bed at night and steals into her moribund grandmother's bedroom.

> "You're a saint and you're going to die. I want you to ask the Virgin to grant me three wishes."
>
> "What are they?"
>
> "I want to leave this place; I want to love my husband very much and I want to be a writer."
>
> "I'll ask for the first two but not for the last. I don't like the way those poetesses live."

The scene is from *Album familiar* (1982), a novella by Claribel Alegría, who grew up to see all three wishes granted in abundance. Her parents sent her to college in the United States. She married an American and moved to Paris, where her close friends were Carlos Fuentes, Mario Benedetti, Julio Cortázar, the Latin "Cosa Nostra" of '50s exiles. She later lived for 20 years on the paradisiacal island of Mallorca with her husband and collaborator Darwin Flakoll, to whom she still dedicates love poems, and even without her grandmother's blessing she has produced more than 20 books in Spanish, including poetry, novels, and oral history.

Told another way, Alegría's life, like those of many Central Americans, is a recurring horror story. When she was born, in Estelí, Nicaragua in 1924, the U.S. Marines "made life impossible for my father," she recalled when I interviewed her recently by phone. Her father, a doctor, had been a revolutionary since his teens and was an ardent supporter of Sandino. Obliged to leave Nicaragua for good

when the Somozas put a price on his head, he spent the rest of his life as a restless exile in El Salvador. The marines were stationed off the coast of El Salvador in 1932, when the Martinez regime, at the start of a long period of military rule, massacred 30,000 Pipíl Indian peasants. Claribel was seven at the time and living in Santa Ana, the heart of the coffee-growing district, scene of the rebellion and its brutal repression. Her bedroom window faced the National Guard headquarters across the street. Peering out, she could see the colonel mistreating peasants who were rounded up with their thumbs tied behind their backs (a practice still followed by Salvadoran security forces). At night she lay in bed listening to the guns.

For years after she left El Salvador, political disagreement with conservative family members cast a shadow on her visits home. Many of her friends, colleagues, and contemporaries fighting dictatorship in Latin America have been imprisoned, tortured, disappeared, and killed, and since 1980 her own conspicuous criticism of the regime has kept her in exile from El Salvador. Although—or perhaps because—her cousin is currently Salvadoran Minister of Defense, she cannot return home.

Luisa in Realityland charts Alegría's ambiguous attachment to Santa Ana, the sleepy Salvadoran town she couldn't wait to leave but has always returned to in her writings. A town whose name she pronounces lovingly, even while condemning it as "the most reactionary city in El Salvador," home of the coffee growers, the oligarchs whose final departure from her country she hopes she will live to see. Luisa, like Lewis Carroll's Alice, is a little girl with a mind of her own, trying to make sense of a world where surrealism is not a writer's whimsical invention but a given of local history. The book consists of a series of vignettes, anecdotes, and incidents, told as they might have been to friends in Paris or Deya. They're tinged with an exile's nostalgia and with blood.

The anecdotes alternate with incantatory lyric poems which, like a Greek chorus, deepen the reach of the prose chapters. This is a poet's novel: brief, fragmentary, condensed, understated, oblique. Details and juxtapositions are more important than storylines. Early on, for example, Luisa recalls, in the storybook tone that marks the beginning chapters, the day she visited the room of a local prostitute. The incident itself could be bittersweet, even maudlin: innocent child visits angry whore and by her innocence softens the whore's anger. But Alegría has managed to charge the narrative with the tensions of class relations in a small Central American town 50 years ago. The little girl plays tennis three days a week with a pimple-faced boy. One day, tired and sweaty after the game, she stops in front of the whore's beaded curtain and wangles an invitation to look beyond it. The confident upper-class girl, comfortable in her healthy sweat, rejection unimaginable to her, enters a room where "a pungent odor of disinfectant filled her lungs." The rich sweat for pleasure; the poor bathe in disinfectant.

Many anecdotes are transmitted verbatim as they were told to the young Luisa by loving aunts, uncles, teachers, priests, nursemaids. Yet almost every story meant to entertain or edify the child has a disturbing underside, as when an uncle tells her about her Nicaraguan great grandfather, a man so capricious and tyrannical that after a fight with his neighbors he moved his entire house, each adobe brick and beam and even the trees in the courtyard, to another place, and founded his own city. This is a wonderful tale, reminiscent of Carpentier or García Marquez, from the new-world continent of empire builders. The uncle repeats himself for emphasis: "Tata Pedro had every single thing carried on the backs of mules or people from San Rafael del Norte to La Concordia. That's the name of the town your great grandfather founded." Along with family legend, the child is introduced to a time when people—peasants, Indians—were regarded as slightly less efficient beasts of burden than the quadruped variety the Spanish brought over. Here again the nasty truth shows in the details.

Some anecdotes stand on their own. In the three short paragraphs that constitute "Aunt Filiberta and her Cretonnes," we learn the whole story of Luisa's aunt and her *machista* husband. Every time he beats her, she loads her brood of kids into the ox cart and drives away to town. He comes from the country to woo her back again with a serenade, and before they return home together, she buys enough flowered fabric to recover all her furniture. Other anecdotes are well matched with companion poems, to illuminate a common theme. Exile is one of these. Alegría gives a prose sketch of a myth-making uncle who spent his whole life in Santa Ana dreaming so vividly of Paris that he manages to convince a visiting French consul that he studied at the Sorbonne. The poem **"Not Yet,"** which follows this sketch, presents the adult Luisa longing for a return to her country, from which she's exiled by "a heavy boot with foreign hobnails." The two brief texts play off each other: an earlier generation of educated Salvadorans lived in their own country as if in exile from the real, European world, while the current generation has come to pin its hopes on home, with equal frustration in the end.

Sometimes a motif is repeated through a series of anecdotes to make a point by accumulation. In the vignettes of life in the ruling class, the motif is emptiness, absence. Little Luisa goes with her nurse to visit the museum-size house of a former Salvadoran president's family. The family is away in Europe, where they own two mansions and a castle, and their domestic staff works full time to preserve the furniture and clothes from decay in the empty house. A rich woman, godmother to a poor Santa Ana girl, sends her goddaughter an eagerly awaited birthday present; it turns out to be an empty cookie tin. An oligarch's estate, empty because the family is away, is protected by barbed wire and 30 Great Danes. The moral vacuum at the top in El Salvador is what Alegría has in mind here, but perhaps she's also alluding to her belief that someday the oligarchy will have to give up and leave the country for good.

"The dead need to be remembered and to be named so they don't fall into limbo," Luisa's mother warns her, and the girl finds her bedtime prayers for deceased family, friends, and favorite authors an increasing chore. The list grows longer, "and if accidentally, or out of sheer fatigue, she forgot someone, she would wake up later with her

heart pounding." A child saying "God bless Miguel de Cervantes y Saavedra" is merely cute, but in the context of Santa Ana, where a terrible massacre has occurred and been hushed up, Luisa's preoccupation with the naming of the dead takes on a sinister meaning. In its second half, the book moves from reminiscences of a time of "somnolence and peace" to the contemporary narration of war in Central America. Luisa's childhood obsession with memory, her dread of limbo, foreshadows her vocation as a writer—to speak for those who have been silenced.

This sense of purpose led Alegría and her husband to collaborate on an earlier novel, ***Cenizas de Izalco*** (1966), set in Santa Ana at the time of the 1932 massacre. The work of rescuing souls from limbo was complicated by the zeal of the Martínez dictatorship, which set out to destroy every trace of the *matanza,* sacking private libraries and public archives. All Alegría had to go on were recollections of childhood conversations with her Pipíl Indian nurse, who was from brutalized Izalco; three yellow newspaper clippings her father had managed to preserve; and a brief mention in a book by historian William Krehm. Again in collaboration with her husband, Alegría has written a history of Nicaragua from Walker to the Sandinistas and compiled three books of oral history—"testimony" from Salvadoran women guerrillas and political prisoners. Miserable to be living in comfortable exile during the Nicaraguan civil war, she explains, Alegría and her husband packed up and arrived in Managua six weeks after the fall of Samosa, and in 1982 they moved to Managua for good, just as another civil war was getting under way.

In the midst of so much death, Alegría represents herself in her poems as a ghoul or carrion-eating buzzard surrounded by corpses. Throughout ***Luisa in Realityland,*** the buzzard, a black pariah bird, is played off against the Gypsy. These are a pair of almost Jungian archetypes, the nay- and yea-saying elements in the poet's soul. The Gypsy, who first appears to Luisa in a dream, is cast sometimes as a brightly colored jungle bird, sometimes as a soap bubble or rainbow. The novel can be read—especially the second half, when Alegría's storytellers are Chilean torture victims and Nicaraguan prisoners of war—as a kind of diary of self-analysis. How, she asks herself, when so many have died, do we continue to live? The answer seems to lie with the Gypsy, a feminist, scamp, thief, liar, and poet. Sometimes her lies come true and sometimes they are merely, like hope itself, a form of necessary self-delusion.

Is Alegría's optimism a matter of temperament, the birthright of a favorite child of a large, loving, and comfortable family? Or is it historically grounded? Whatever its source, the poet's optimism leaps across all obstacles. Despite Reagan's request for another $270 million for the contras, the $2.5 million per day in U.S. military aid that keeps Duarte in power, the last words in this remarkable little book are "the future."

Suzanne Ruta, "Witness to the Persecution," in The Village Voice, *Vol. XXXIII, No. 5, February 2, 1988, p. 61.*

Marjorie Agosin (review date 31 March 1988)

[*Agosin is a Chilean-born poet, critic, editor, and educator. In the following essay, she characterizes* Luisa in Realityland *as "a collective history of a people" and an indication of Alegría's desire for peace in her homeland.*]

Claribel Alegría, born in 1924 in Nicaragua but raised from early childhood in El Salvador, is one of the richest literary voices of Central America. She is a poet, essayist, journalist, and novelist, but above all a writer deeply committed to the restoration of peace in her region.

While living in the United States in the early '60s, she published *New Voices of Hispanic America,* an anthology that included early work of some writers who have since become major figures in contemporary Latin American literature.

In 1982, North American readers became reacquainted with Alegría with the publication of *Flowers from the Volcano,* translated by the poet Carolyn Forche. In this collection of poems, the realities of political upheaval in Central America are revealed in language of great poetical intensity.

Luisa in Realityland is an eclectic collection of personal essays, vignettes, and poems portraying life today in Central America, life dominated by violence, fear, and a loss of innocence: "In my country / sometime ago / the soldiers / began killing children." Although sometimes uneven in its literary quality and tone, this book is sustained by the nostalgic voice of the child narrator. Her vision and story of her own life become a collective history of a people surrounded by "a broken mirror of war," a lost land, and a landscape of seemingly forbidden childhood.

The style of the book is neither bitter, nor propagandistic, nor a political statement regarding the region's turmoil. It is a book by a writer driven by a vision of peace and committed to peace and justice for all people, not just her own, the composition of a poet moved by an obsessive desire for a better tomorrow. Here are a few lines from her poem **"Epitaph"**: "I don't want a gravestone over my body / only fresh grass / and a flowering jasmine."

Luisa in Realityland intertwines real events with fables from Central American lore. The fantastic and the real, hope and despair, are neither heightened nor disguised; they are simply accepted as what is. Yet a vision of peace pervades this personal memoir of Luisa in Realityland, if not yet Wonderland:

> The sky splits open
> rolls up like a scroll
> of shadows
> inviting us to enter and be dazzled
> come, love
> let's return to the future.

> *Marjorie Agosin, "Essays on Life in Central America Today," in* The Christian Science Monitor, *March 31, 1988, p. 20.*

Seymour Menton (review date Spring 1988)

[*Menton is an American critic and educator who special-*izes *in Spanish and Portuguese literature. In the following excerpt, he offers a mixed review of* Despierta, mi bien despierta.]

[The title of Claribel Alegría's novel **Despierta, mi bien, despierta**], derived from the Hispanic happy-birthday song "Las mañanitas," refers to the political awakening of the protagonist Lorena. However, the main theme is her unhappy marriage in the tradition of [Gustave] Flaubert's *Madame Bovary* and [Maria Luisa] Bombal's *Ultima niebla.* Although her millionaire husband is too absorbed in his business ventures to pay much attention to her, the forty-year-old Lorena attends a university class in creative writing, where she meets and falls in love with a young revolutionary. He makes her feel sexually and psychologically fulfilled for the first time in her life. The brief idyllic love affair comes to an abrupt end when he has to leave for an indefinite period of time, presumably on a revolutionary mission. An anonymous letter informs her husband of her infidelity, he reacts violently, she leaves home, and the novel ends melodramatically with Lorena's discovering her lover's severed head on her car seat.

The narrator's thoughts and sentiments, effectively expressed in first- and second-person point of view, constitute the major part of the brief novel, which, in spite of its brevity, also captures the life-style and attitudes of upperclass Salvadorans and their resentment against Archbishop Romero for sympathizing with the guerrillas' goals. On the other hand, the guerrilla lover's revolutionary activities are never described. The technique of the self-conscious novel—the protagonist is writing a novel for her creative-writing class, which is the novel we are reading—detracts from the work's basic sincerity and is not sufficiently developed. (pp. 256-57)

> *Seymour Menton, in a review of "Despierta, mi bien, despierta," in* World Literature Today, *Vol. 62, No. 2, Spring, 1988, pp. 256-57.*

Claribel Alegría (essay date 1988)

[*In the following essay, Alegría outlines her political views and her aims as a writer.*]

Political commitment, in my view, is seldom a calculated intellectual strategy. It seems to me more like a contagious disease—athlete's foot, let's say, or typhoid fever—and if you happen to live in a plague area, the chances are excellent that you will come down with it. Commitment is a visceral reaction to the corner of the world we live in and what it has done to us and to the people we know. Albert Camus penned a phrase in "The Myth of Sisyphus" that impressed me profoundly. "If a man believes something to be true yet does not live in accordance with that truth," he said, "that man is a hypocrite."

Each of us writers, I have found, is obsessed with the personal equation and, however successfully he or she camouflages it, is surreptitiously pushing a world view.

"What am I doing here? Where am I going?"

These are the eternal existential—and profoundly political—questions, and the creative writer dedicates his life to communicating the answers he has stumbled across while negotiating the booby traps and barbed wire barricades of this twentieth-century obstacle course.

Let me be unashamedly personal, then. I spent the greater part of my life writing poetry, without the slightest notion that I had an obligation to commit myself literarily or politically to what was happening in my country—El Salvador—or my region—Central America.

There were political antecedents that marked me, of course. Thirty thousand peasants were slaughtered in El Salvador when I was seven years old. I remember with hard-edged clarity when groups of them, their crossed thumbs tied behind their backs, were herded into the National Guard fortress just across the street from my house, and I remember the *coup de grace* shots startling me awake at night. Two years later, I remember just as clearly my father, a Nicaraguan exile, telling me how Anastasio Somoza, with the benediction of the Yankee minister, had assassinated Sandino the night before.

I left El Salvador to attend a U.S. University; I married, had children, and wrote poetry, convinced that Central American dictators—Martínez, Ubico, Carías, Somoza— were as inevitable and irremediable as the earthquakes and electrical storms that scourge my homeland.

The Cuban revolution demonstrated that social and political change was possible in Latin America, but surely the Yankees with their helicopter gunships and Green Berets would never permit such a thing to happen again. Nevertheless Fidel and Che sensitized me to the currents of militant unrest just below the surface of the American *mare nostrum* in the Caribbean. We watched the eddies and whirlpools from Paris and later from Mallorca while I nourished my growing burden of middle-class guilt. What was I doing sitting on the sidelines while my people silently suffered the implacable repression of the Somoza dynasty in Nicaragua and the rotating colonel-presidents in El Salvador? Some of my poems took on an edge of protest, and my husband and I wrote a novel [*Ashes of Izalco*] about my childhood nightmare: the 1932 peasant massacre.

Central American reality is incandescent, and if there be no place there for "pure art" and "pure literature" today, then I say so much the worse for pure art and pure literature.

—*Claribel Alegría*

I caught the political sickness from the Sandinista revolution. Shortly after Somoza's overthrow in 1979, my husband and I went to Nicaragua for six months to research a book about the historical epic of Sandino and his successors of the FSLN. We were in Paris, on our way home to Mallorca, when we heard of the assassination of Archbish-op Oscar Arnulfo Romero, the only Salvadoran figure of international prestige who had served as the voice of the millions of voiceless in my country. In response to that brutal and tragic event, all but two or three of El Salvador's artists and intellectuals made the quiet decision, without so much as consulting each other, to do what we could to try to fill the enormous vacuum left by his death.

Since then, I have found myself writing more and more poems and prose texts that reflect the misery, the injustice, and the repression that reign in my country. I am fully aware of the pitfalls of attempting to defend a transient political cause in what presumes to be a literary work, and I have tried to resolve that dilemma in a roughshod way by dividing my writing into two compartments: the "literary-poetic," if you will, and what I have come to think of as my "crisis journalism."

Political concerns do have a way of creeping into my poetry, however—simply because the Central American political situation is my major obsession, and I have always written poetry under obsession's spur. When I think back, though, I can truly say that my "commitment" to literature has always been, and remains, a simple attempt to make my next poem less imperfect than the last.

But there is something further: in Central America today, crude reality inundates and submerges the ivory tower of "art for art's sake." What avant-garde novelist would dare write a work of imagination in which the Salvadoran people, in supposedly free elections, could only choose between Robert D'Aubuisson, the intellectual author of Monseigneur Romero's assassination and the recognized mentor of the infamous "Squadrons of Death" and José Napoleón Duarte, who, as the nation's highest authority for the greater part of the last four years, has systematically failed to bring the known perpetrators and executors of that sacrilegious deed to justice?

What Hollywood writer four short years ago could have envisioned a script in which all the horrors of Vietnam are being reenacted on the Central American isthmus?

> America, America, God shed his grace on thee,
> and crowned thy good with brotherhood,
> from sea to shining sea.

Can this be the America that sends Huey helicopter gunships, A-37 Dragonflies, and "Puff, the magic dragon" to rain napalm and high explosives on the women, children, and old people in El Salvador's liberated zones, to convert the village of Tenancingo among others into a second Guernica? Is this the nation that christens Somoza's former assassins of the National Guard as "freedom fighters" and "the moral equivalent of the Founding Fathers" and sends them across the Nicaraguan border night after night to spread their message of democracy by slaughtering peasants, raping their women, and mowing down defenseless children while blowing up the cooperatives and health clinics and schools the Nicaraguans have so painfully constructed over the past six years?

How has America become entrapped in this morass of blood and death?

An American President, John F. Kennedy, made a prophetic statement twenty-five years ago. His words were: "Those who make peaceful evolution impossible, make violent revolution inevitable."

Anastasio Somoza, Jr., made peaceful evolution impossible in Nicaragua, so the Nicaraguan people had no choice but to overthrow him. Again today, as it has so often in the past, the U.S. government has allied itself with the forces in El Salvador who make peaceful evolution impossible: the forces that have put an abrupt end to the limping agrarian reform program, have encouraged a recrudescence of the Squadrons of Death—and have forced a suspension of peace negotiations with the FMLN-FDR.

The burning question for all of us today is: how will America find its way out of this bloody swamp?

Central American reality is incandescent, and if there be no place there for "pure art" and "pure literature" today, then I say so much the worse for pure art and pure literature. I do not know a single Central American writer who is so careful of his literary image that he sidesteps political commitment at this crucial moment in our history, and were I to meet one, I would refuse to shake his hand.

It matters little whether our efforts are admitted into the sacrosanct precincts of literature. Call them newspapering, call them pamphleteering, call them a shrill cry of defiance. My people, sixty percent of whom earn less than eleven dollars per month, know that only through their efforts today will it be possible for their children and grandchildren to eventually have equal opportunity to learn the alphabet and thus gain access to the great literature of the world: a basic human right that has been denied most of their elders. (pp. 308-11)

> Claribel Alegría, "The Writer's Commitment," in Lives on the Line: The Testimony of Contemporary Latin American Authors, edited by Doris Meyer, University of California Press, 1988, pp. 308-11.

Electa Arenal   (review date January 1989)

[In the following essay, Arenal considers Luisa in Realityland a fictionalized autobiography.]

"Solo me quedan fragmentos" (all I have left are fragments) wrote Claribel Alegria in a poem some 30 years ago. In **Luisa in Realityland,** her fictionalized self-portrait, she picks up those shards through the looking glass, humorously, luminously, darkly. Death and exile, survival and struggle characterize Alegria's journey through life.

A doctor's daughter, the protagonist experiences a childhood and youth in some respects similar to that of her North American counterparts: she enjoys middle-class comforts provided by car, maids, college away from home, international travel and friendships. But the differences are startling. Political conflicts and violence pattern the fabric of everyday life. Death weaves in and out of every memory. Exile and the longing for homelands (her father's for Nicaragua, hers for El Salvador, her friends' for Chile, Argentina, Uruguay) flow from past to present,

from present back to the past. Indigenous legends, customs, foods and beliefs color Luisa's nostalgia.

Luisa in Realityland is made up of 89 titled passages, 52 in prose and 37 in verse. Most of the prose pieces are one or two pages long. The longest, "Granny and the Golden Bridge," retells in a little over three pages, an anecdote about a friend's "crazy grandmother," a spunky, selfless, cunning guerrilla collaborator. Guerrillas, we learn, are born of love and tenderness, of curiosity and conscience.

Five of the chapter-fragments have sequels. Wilf, who opens the book, is a shadowy character, a haunting representation of several recurring motifs: internationalism, clandestine activity, the disappeared. The Nicaraguan great-grandfather, subject of three fragments, is a character out of which Latin American magical realism is made. Maniacal, stubborn, hot-headed, he founds a town named La Concordia (Harmony). Two friends, two famous writers, each tender a "prophecy." One is personal, another political. Julio [Cortazar] predicts that Luisa will find a way to get to Paris for the birth of her grandchild. It is his own death that leads to the fulfillment of the prediction, echoing the eternal cycle of death and rebirth, so prominent a theme in all of Alegria's poetry. Jose Coronel Urtecho passes her "a sheet of paper on which he had written: 'You will live to see the liberation of Central America.' "

In some sense, **Luisa in Realityland** tells the life of a person who lives in, out and through the expectation, doing her part by observing, recording and accompanying those who die and live at many fronts. It is a woman's text, attending to daily matters and domestic routines, made up of patches, connections, attachments between and among people. Moments of chit-chat hyphenate the drama of social strife. Through a girl-child's eyes we view domestic violence, the separations and relations between servants and their employers, children and their parents, relatives and friends, and the hypocrisy of patriarchal imperatives.

"There are women who accept and others who don't." Those who do are treated with understanding, because "it's not that they were useless / it's that their husbands / their fathers / their brothers / wanted them like that." But most of them don't. Early on, Luisa decides to seek motherhood but shun matrimony. Her secret First Communion wish is that on the heels of marriage and pregnancy God grant her widowhood.

In the prose sections the myth-making storyteller turns family anecdote into fabulous truth. Unfortunately, many verse sections of this autobiographical work do not meld stylistically with the passages of prose. Some seem too translucent, lacking in creative transformation. Others are weighed down with jarring juxtapositions of personal and cosmic themes. At its best, however, the melange of prose and verse, narrative and impressionistic portrayal, dream and history, serves well to convey Alegria's magical and tragic sense of life. Hovering around 10 years of age, she slides from birth to death and back again, using experience and reminiscence to make time a matter of consequence.

> Electa Arenal, "Alegria's Life Mixes Tragedy and Magic," in New Directions for Women, Vol. 18, No. 1, January, 1989, p. 16.

Dan Bellm   (review date April 1989)

[*In the review below, Bellm notes that Alegría is most successful in* Mujer del rio/Woman of the River *when writing "outside her own history."*]

Like more than half a million of her compatriots, Claribel Alegría can't go home again. At 65, this gracious, diminutive woman may not look dangerous, but her 20-odd books of poetry, fiction, and political history have been forceful enough to scare the government of El Salvador. Alegría's own family is in some ways a microcosm of the civil war: her cousin is the Salvadoran minister of defense. In a recent poem, **"Farewells,"** she recalled her last visit home in 1979 to see her dying mother, and a relative named Alberto "lecturing me / to stop sowing hatred / with my writings" as he drove, unfazed, through rural scenes of misery completely unchanged since their childhood. When her mother died in 1982, her brother warned her not to go back; there could be two funerals instead of one.

Alegría's verse is plainspoken, not at all given to elusive metaphor or dense language, as though her mission were too urgent for such roadblocks. Her tools are a keen visual memory (or as she says, "anaconda eyes"), an ear for a good story, and a knack for building to a flourish. In **"And I Dreamt I Was a Tree,"** for instance, she shakes off an unwanted profusion of green, only to find that

> Scarcely any leaves
> were left me:
> four or five at most
> maybe fewer
> and I shook myself again
> more furiously
> and they didn't fall:
> like steel propellers
> they held fast.

Her invariably short lines make these slender poems look inviting, even cozy, on the page, but the best of them are anguished and fierce.

Woman of the River, skillfully translated by Alegría's collaborator on nine books, her husband D. J. Flakoll, is the second bilingual collection of her poetry to appear from the University of Pittsburgh Press; ***Flowers From the Volcano*** came out in 1982. In ***Woman of the River,*** Alegría centers as ever on the personal themes of home and homeland, longing and disillusion, memory and hope. But the two strongest poems, tellingly, are located outside her own history. **"The Woman of the Sumpul River"** describes, largely through the eyes of a victim who lost her husband and three of her four children, a May 1980 massacre in which some 600 refugees trying to cross into Honduras were shot to death or drowned. Hiding from the soldiers, the woman covers her baby's face with soft leaves to console him, to keep him from crying out and giving them away; "mingling with the earth," they thus become invisible, impossible to kill. **"Documentary"** is conceived as a film of the Salvadoran coffee harvest, a social spectacle rich in visual ironies:

> A chorus of children
> and women

> with the small white coffin
> move politely aside
> as the harvest passes by. . . .
> a peasant
> with hands bound behind him
> by the thumbs
> and his escort of soldiers
> blinks at the airplane:
> a huge bee
> bulging with coffee growers
> and tourists.

But Alegría unaccountably ends the vivid "film" on a weary note. A Third World ABCs lesson ("A for alcoholism . . .") peters out after the letter F: "F for the feudal power / of fourteen families / and etcetera, etcetera, etcetera. / My etcetera country, / my wounded country, / my child, / my tears, / my obsession."

The self-deprecating word "obsession" crops up three times in this book, and it's a key to the strength and the weakness of Alegría's verse. "If a dream exasperates you," she writes elsewhere, "you'll become obsessed, / a sleepwalker / a poet." Like many exiles torn from their roots, she can hardly turn her attention elsewhere, but exasperated nostalgia leads to some monotonous ruts: the ever-recurring shade tree in her parents' yard, or abstract laments for "the poor children of my country." The static, complaining **"Not Yet"** admits the problem: "It is difficult to sing you / from exile / difficult to celebrate / your nebulous / jagged map. / I can't do it yet / a dry sob / sticks in my throat."

Alegría's work is indeed nourished by difficult dreams of home, but she breaks past the dry sob when she tells stories, as in **"Deadly Leap,"** a fanciful memoir of Salvadoran poet Roque Dalton, a man she hardly knew, who was killed in 1975: "almost everyday you sent me / butterfly wings / scribbled with signs / I couldn't understand. / I stumbled into you / everywhere / I began collecting myths / things that really happened to you." Ever the mythmaker, Dalton even told a friend that Alegría had once taught him a dizzying soar-and-drop ballroom dance step, the "mortal leap." True story or not ("Did I dream it / did you dream me?"), ***Woman of the River*** shows that Claribel Alegría has the grace to take new risks and land on her feet. (pp. 3-4)

> *Dan Bellm, in a review of "Woman of the River," in* VLS, *No. 73, April, 1989, pp. 3-4.*

Fran Handman   (review date 5 November 1989)

[*In the following review, Handman praises Alegría and Flakoll's subtle incorporation of political commentary in* Cenizas de Izalco (Ashes of Izalco).]

A political polemic presented in the form of a novel is a tricky hybrid. To be persuasive while balancing the message with the medium is no mean feat. ***Ashes of Izalco,*** which was originally published in Spanish in 1966 and is now appearing in a workmanlike translation by Darwin J. Flakoll, accomplishes this with varying degrees of success. The story focuses on two central characters: Carmen Rojas, an upper-class Salvadoran who returns in the mid-

1960's to her native village, Santa Ana, for her mother's funeral; and Frank Wolff, an emotionally bankrupt American alcoholic who comes to Santa Ana in 1931. The connection between them is revealed when Carmen reads an old diary and discovers that her mother, Isabel, had an affair with Frank. Carmen is the observer, seeing and commenting on everything: the smug, materialistic American, the frivolousness of the Salvadoran upper class and the inhuman abuse suffered by the exploited peasants. Frank, on the other hand, is the self-absorbed American who, while desperately trying to grasp happiness through Isabel, isn't even aware of the revolutionary turmoil that is taking place around him—until he witnesses the massacre of thousands of peasants in the town of Izalco. The story, whose violent climax is based on actual historical events, is rich with the sights and sounds of a Salvadoran village, with energetic, sometimes humorous insights into the lives and attitudes of the stratified population, even as the Salvadoran writer Claribel Alegría and her husband, Mr. Flakoll, make points, from their perspective, about the behavior and attitudes of North Americans in Latin America. Cinematic-style fast cuts, employed by the authors to move the reader through rapid transitions, although occasionally confusing, are generally deftly handled in this selectively enlightening novel.

> *Fran Handman, in a review of "Ashes of Izalco," in* The New York Times Book Review, *November 5, 1989, p. 25.*

Jack Miles   (review date 17 December 1989)

[*In the following essay, Miles offers a mixed assessment of* Ashes of Izalco.]

Born in Nicaragua but reared in El Salvador, Claribel Alegría is the author of the prose poem, *Luisa in Realityland,* about the intrusion of war into the life of the Salvadoran upper class, and the co-editor of the bilingual poetry collection, *On the Front Line: Guerrilla Poems of El Salvador.* If she is something less than the poetess laureate of the FMLN rebels, her sympathies are clear from her bibliography.

They would seem to be equally clear from the title of [*Ashes of Izalco*], co-authored in 1966 with her husband, Darwin J. Flakoll, but only now released in English. Izalco is a Salvadoran town near the Guatemala border, named for a nearby volcano. It was there in 1932 that the most infamous mass murder of *la matanza,* the decade-long Salvadoran slaughter of the 1930s, took place. Hundreds of disarmed Indians, their thumbs bound together, were herded into the central plaza to hear an address by Gen. Maximiliano Hernández Martínez. But the truck that was to have brought the general brought, instead, an army death squad. The captives were machine-gunned to the last man and boy.

Against this background, the title, *Ashes of Izalco,* would seem to announce a phoenix, the guerrillas of yesterday arising as today's *Frente Farabundo Martí de Liberación Nacional.* The epigraph to the book, from Francisco de Quevedo, only reinforces the initial impression. Translated, it reads:

> They will be dust,
> but the dust will have feeling.
> Ash, but the ash
> will be in love.

Quevedo was a satirist, however, and there is something inverted, if scarcely satirical, about *Ashes of Izalco.* Which is to say that, quite deliberately, it does not keep its opening promise. Though it is set during the Salvadoran civil war of the 1930s, and though all its characters know that a war is under way, no major character ever speaks a line for either of the contending sides. Neither the rebels nor those who are beating them back are granted much personal or ideological space in its pages. Here are no Marxist guerrilla voices, no North American imperialist voices, and only rarely, even in a culturally conservative, upper-class setting, anything approaching a foursquare authoritarian or militaristic voice.

The novella is, instead, a visit to Graham Greeneland in which the usual roles of observer and observed have been exchanged. There are, in the Greene manner: a dissolute American writer, fleeing his past; an earnest Seventh-Day-Adventist missionary whom he knew as a boy and has sought out in his extremity; a hot, dusty, isolated tropical town, its ancient upper class smug, its primeval lower class numb; and one beautiful, restless woman, reading French novels and yearning for someone to talk to, the wife of the chess-playing, patriarchal, conventionally *macho* town physician. What makes the result decidedly un-Greene-like is that the observing, interpreting, organizing intelligence is local and often female rather than foreign and male.

The novella opens just after the death of Isabel, the doctor's wife. Carmen, her daughter, having returned home for the funeral, has found, among her mother's papers, the diary of Frank, the American writer, whom she remembers only vaguely. What she learns from the diary is that Frank and her mother had a brief, passionate affair—they slept together just once—and then parted. To Frank, the Salvadoran beauty was a last chance at a new beginning. To Isabel, the American was a beginning that could only entail a dozen cruel endings. He had already cut all his ties. After her night with him, she discovered the power of hers—and chose them over him.

As Carmen's thoughts interrupt and interpret her reading of Frank's diary, the novella becomes, for all its brevity, two kinds of story: the love story of Isabel and Frank; and a middle passage for Carmen, who, married to a passionless American and living in the United States, measures her distance both from Santa Ana and from her husband by the depth of her mother's unsuspected pain.

Why then the title and the epigraph? What has this intensely personal melodrama to do with the ashes of Izalco?

The answer is not at all obvious, but what the book has to do with Izalco may be what America has to do with El Salvador. The United States as a political power is absent from this novella: No diplomat or soldier ever makes an appearance. American culture, people and products, however, are omnipresent. Virgil, the missionary, exhorts his peasants to reform their agriculture as they reform their lives (he dies with them at Izalco). Frank implores Isabel to abandon her life in Santa Ana and share his. A Santa Ana dowager, gossiping about a recent wedding, notes approvingly that all the gifts were imported from the United States. Finally, the narrator herself—reading a stranger's diary and discovering her own mother—is married to an American and residing in Washington, D.C. Like so many of her countrymen, she has made our country hers.

It is this cultural traffic, the novella hints, that has made it possible for the ruling class of El Salvador to regard that country's civil war rather as Beverly Hills might regard the drug wars of South Central Los Angeles; that is, as trouble in a remote neighborhood. (El Salvador is no larger in area than Los Angeles, Orange and San Diego Counties combined.) Mulholland Drive doesn't know and isn't eager to learn what the LAPD or the FBI or the DEA is doing on Martin Luther King Boulevard. Whatever it is, it's probably necessary. In *Ashes of Izalco,* the upper class of Santa Ana regards most of El Salvador just that way. In innumerable ways, the United States is far more vividly present to the upper-class mind (as Manhattan might be to Mulholland) than the local rebels are.

The Izalco massacre, as described in Frank's penultimate letter to Isabel, comes thus as a late and monstrous intrusion rather than a true climax. Frank Wolff does not interpret the atrocity. Neither does Carmen Rojas as she reads his diary, decades later. If the reader is invited to interpret it, the invitation is severely muted.

Not least for that muting, *Ashes for Izalco* is an unsatisfying book. Isabel, provocatively personal with Frank without departing from the propriety of her station, is an intriguing character. Frank, whose debauched past is attributed rather than evoked, is a good deal less intriguing; and unfortunately, Frank, through his diary and letters, does most of the talking. For its brevity, moreover, the novella is overcrowded with minor characters.

And yet it is often interesting and always alive. Farabundo Martí, an offstage presence, is described as Augusto Sandino's secretary. Other details offered in passing provide—against the authors' transparent determination not to write a conventional political novel—background information on the long-running civil war. More important, the central subject—Isabel's refusal to escape and Frank's ensuing despair (chronicled in his last letters to her)—grows in power when joined to the memory of the Izalco massacre. Alegría and Flakoll may decline every opporunity to draw parallels. We are left wondering, nonetheless, whether the ashes of Izalco are not of at least two kinds. (pp. 3, 11)

> *Jack Miles, "Murder in a Remote Neighborhood," in* Los Angeles Times Book Review, *December 17, 1989, pp. 3,11.*

Y. Jehenson   (review date March 1990)

[*In the following review, Jehenson questions Alegría and Flakoll's intent in writing* Ashes of Izalco.]

[*Ashes of Izalco* is a] collaborative novel written in two

voices. It relates the events of 1932 experienced by one of the authors (Alegría) when 30,000 Indians and peasants were massacred in Izalco, El Salvador, in the name of anti-communism. It is difficult, however, to determine what the authors' objective is. Is it a novelistic depiction of life in a small Latin American village, its failed love relationships, its parochialism, its stifling atmosphere? Or is it a historical novel, a testimonial based on real events as Alegría announces on the book's jacket? The depiction of the insularity of Santa Ana, especially as concerning the women, is well done, if somewhat redundant. There is the woman who escapes into books; there is the humiliated Mama Juana, whose youngest child has been fathered by her son-in law; there is the resigned Carmen "dying a little more each day" in her marriage; there are women who choose duty over love, who stay in loveless marriages and take their husband's infidelities in stride. Yet the novel seems dated. It also lacks the depth of similar testimonial literature. Its events, characters, and style are not so vivid and vital as those of Elena Poniatowska's *Massacre in Mexico,* which relates a similar experience. It lacks the commitment, the passion of either Domitila Barrios de Chungara's *Let Me Speak* (1978) or Rigoberta Menchú's *I, Rigoberta Menchu* (1984), which also derive from personal experiences.

> *Y. Jehenson, in a review of "Ashes of Izalco: A Novel," in* Choice, *Vol. 27, No. 7, March, 1990, p. 1150.*

Alan West   (review date 12 January 1992)

[*In the following essay, West asserts that* Albúm familiar (Family Album) *examines how an individual's beliefs are manifested in interpersonal relationships.*]

Claribel Alegría's writing is a tree with many branches: poetry, testimony, fiction, essay, historical research. Sometimes all genres are encompassed in one work, as in *Luisa in Realityland* (1987). *Family Album* is more straightforward fiction, in the form of three novellas, written over a period of eight years: *The Talisman* (1977), *Family Album* (1982) and *Village of God and the Devil* (1985).

All three works focus on a family or a nucleus of close personal relationships that reveals crucial features of people's beliefs. In *The Talisman,* Karen, a young Guatemalan woman of 15, is in a strict Catholic school in California, seeking refuge from a turbulent and violent recent past. The product of a broken home, she lived seven years with her mother and her mother's boyfriend, who was physically, emotionally and sexually abusive. Karen's milieu and past are revealed to us in a kaleidescope of voices and memories that visit her constantly. Apparitions, dreams, the present, reminiscences, admonitions glide effortlessly by as Alegria weaves a tale of longing, rebellion and desire. Karen searches for some moral and emotional stability and one of the nuns, Sister Mary Ann, earnestly tries to provide it—as well as to improve her academic performance.

But the sister inhabits a different world. She gives Karen a talisman to ward off evil, but it is unclear, at best, whether this object will help the adolescent against destructive forces (at one point Karen wants to crush the talisman). Her relationship with Sister Mary Ann is symptomatic: It is an odd mix of Christian abnegation, genuine caring and helping, morbid fascination, voyeurism and tortured sexuality.

The second novella, *Family Album,* is set in Paris and recounts the journey of Ximena, a Nicaraguan woman and her transformation during the latter part of the insurrection that overthrew the U.S.-backed Somoza dynasty. Alegria entwines personal/family history with the political urgency of a revolution in the making, dramatically bringing up issues of commitment and struggle. Ximena's cousin is Armando, Sandinista representative in France. Another family member, Mario, is among the guerrillas who stage the assault on the National Palace.

The most compelling parts, however, are the memories of her family, especially Uncle Sergio, who every year during the Feast of St. Anthony of Padua would celebrate his own funeral, with coffin, pall bearers and solemn procession to the cemetery. Armando's departure creates a major change in Ximena's life and here is where the story falters. The shifts are perhaps too abrupt, Ximena's transformation is sudden and unconvincing (even though we are rooting for her) and some of the political conversations that lead up to her big decision are wooden and lack daring.

Deya is a small town in Mallorca where ghosts, spirits and supernatural forces are as common as morning coffee. It is the setting for the third novella, *Village of God and the Devil,* which is dedicated to the British poet Robert Graves and his wife Beryl, who lived on the island for many decades and are characters in the work. Slim and Marcia, a writer and anthropologist respectively, have bought a house and settled into their busy work schedules. But quickly enough the world of the uncanny intrudes: Marcia sees an old villager, Don Antonio, who has been dead for three months; she communes with a spirit, Sea Eagle; the village claims a blood victim each year, a poltergeist wanders from one house to another; stories abound of dreams that turn true (a woman, Janice, dreams of a doll without limbs and months later gives birth to a girl without arms); a hedonist, Ben, who was to celebrate a Black Mass on Good Friday, is decapitated in a car accident.

When Marcia and Slim stumble onto the philosopher's stone of Ramon Lull (1232-1316), which according to one character, is nothing other than a miniature black hole, then the narrative shifts gears (and time zones). Moreover, the black hole is in a bird cage in Graves's magic garden, where it has been abandoned for 40 years. If all of this sounds far-fetched, it is. But Alegria handles it without batting an eyelash and with considerable good humor. One wishes, though, that the Lull-black hole sequence had been placed earlier in the story—it would have made the piece more taut and focused.

Most of Alegria's work published in English has been of a social/political nature, understandable given what her native El Salvador has lived through for the last decade. It's rewarding to read work of hers that is more leisurely paced and fantastic. This new collection deepens our knowledge of one of the region's finest writers.

Alan West, "Alegria in Fantasyland," in Book World—The Washington Post, *January 12, 1992, p. 5.*

Bessy Reyna (review date January-February 1992)

[*In the following excerpt, Reyna offers a positive review of* Family Album.]

In Claribel Alegria's *Family Album* . . . three novellas flow from one another because of her simple yet elegant language. The similarity of the structure in which the narrative is developed and the imaginative stories that each of her characters recounts to keep each other enchanted make readers want to read more.

In the first, *The Talisman,* fifteen-year-old Karen is able to both survive and control her environment by bringing to life cartoon characters and summoning the presence of family members who live in another city. Faced with expulsion from her Catholic school, Karen chooses Sister Mary Ann, a mean-spirited nun "with eyes sharp as broken glass and a voice like a flute out of tune," to be her spiritual advisor. What ensues is a story of survival and emotional conflict, a sensual story where Karen's tales, told with a veneer of innocence, intrigue and excite the nun so much that she starts breaking the convent's rules by sneaking Karen into her bedroom. By the end, Sister Mary Ann is under Karen's spell, and the girl reaffirms the power of sexuality that had just been awakened in her by her stepfather.

In *Family Album,* the second story, Alegria blends a historic event—a daring guerrilla attack against Nicaraguan dictator Anastasio Somoza—with the political awakening of Ximena. She is an upper-class Salvadoran woman living in Paris whose Nicaraguan cousin, also in exile there, confronts her with the political reality in Central America to the point where she can no longer remain aloof. She is compelled to become involved in the struggle against oppression in Nicaragua. The family album, from which the story and the book take their name, is filled not only with pictures of Ximena's relatives, but also with snapshots of many of their friends who joined the guerrillas—whose faces mysteriously disappear from the album upon their deaths. In spite of its somber political tone, Alegria balances the story through Ximena's humorous remembrances of family members. Some are quite unusual, like her uncle Sergio, a madman who stages his own funeral once a year.

The last novella, *Village of God and the Devil,* is the longest and the most complex of the three. It takes us for a wonderful and intriguing summer voyage to the village of Deya on the island of Mallorca where the locals and the tourists fight for space. The most magical and unbelievable events can become reality because of "the amount of ferrous oxide . . . which caused a polarization in the electromagnetic forces to sharpen people's sensibilities." In this town, poltergeists move from one house to another, and the spirit of Lulio, an alchemist who in 1237 fabricated a philosopher's stone "which swallows everything in its path," now shows up to find it. Alegria's village is full of interesting people and unusual, ghostly and, at times, very humorous stories.

Family Album [enables] English-speaking audiences to have another opportunity to read the work of one of Latin America's most outstanding women writers.

> *Bessy Reyna, "Sisters Writing South of the Border," in* New Directions for Women, *Vol. 21, No. 1, January-February, 1992, p. 21.*

Teresa Longo   (essay date January-June 1992)

[*In the essay below, Longo examines how in the poem "Sorrow" Alegría alludes to the lives and works of such Latin American writers as Roque Dalton, Federico García Lorca, and Pablo Neruda to reflect the repressive aspects of Latin American culture and to transform the poem into "a labour of resistance."*]

In a 1984 essay on writing and commitment the Salvadoran poet [Claribel Alegría] maintains that she finds herself writing more and more about the "misery, the injustice, and the repression" that reign in her country (**"The Writer's Commitment"**). In the same essay, Alegría adds that "in Central America today, crude reality inundates and submerges the ivory tower of 'art for art's sake'." "It matters little whether our efforts are admitted into the sacrosanct precincts of literature. Call them newspapering, call them pamphleteering, call them a shrill cry of defiance." To write is to resist repression.

The poem **"Sorrow"** from the collection *Flores del volcán* [**Flowers from the Volcano**] (1982) is one of Alegría's many efforts to respond to contemporary society's "crude reality." As Electa Arenal has aptly noted [in "Two Poets of the Sandinista Struggle," *Feminist Studies* (Spring 1981)], " 'Sorrow' . . . evokes with chilling immediacy the murdered, the imprisoned, the tortured, and the 'disappeared.' These themes are underscored [in the poem] by quotations from García Lorca, Antonio Machado, Miguel Hernández, Pablo Neruda, and a popular Argentine tango." To Electa Arenal's remarks I would add that the evocation of the imprisoned, the tortured and the disappeared—especially of Alegría's fellow Salvadoran, Roque Dalton—goes beyond an underscoring of the work's thematic content. Indeed, to use Berger's terminology, the "labour" of Alegría's poetry consists of [what John Berger has termed] a reassembling of "what has been scattered": like Alegría herself, the poets whose works are quoted in **"Sorrow"** all suffered forced separations—exile, imprisonment or death—from their native countries. When Alegría incorporates their work into her poetry, she defies that separation. At the same time, she draws attention to the very significant role which intertextuality plays in her work. In my analysis of **"Sorrow,"** I argue that for Alegría, intertextuality serves a dual purpose: **"Sorrow"** 's intertext initially reveals the extremely repressive, negative situation which frames the context of contemporary writing; the same intertext ultimately becomes the force which converts poetry into a labour of resistance.

Alegría begins **"Sorrow"** with a declaration of the poem's intertextual composition: "Voces que vienen / que van / que se confunden" ["Voices that rise and are gone"]. Among the poems which constitute **"Sorrow"** 's intertext, poetry by Roque Dalton—to whom Alegría's dedicates **"Sorrow"**—is of exceptional significance. Alegría introduces her fellow Salvadoran's contribution early in the text: the lines, "cuando sepas que he muerto / no pronuncies mi nombre" ["when you learn that I am dead / don't utter my name" (my translation)] appear in the poem's first section immediately after Alegría's declaration of **"Sorrow"** 's intertextual make-up. As the poem progresses, these lines from the Revolutionary poet's "Alta hora de la noche" ["At the Peak of Night"] echo throughout each of **"Sorrow"** 's eight sections.

In section one, Alegría evokes the presence not only of Roque Dalton but also of Victor Jara—"¿eres tú Victor Jara?" ["Is that you, Victor Jara?"], Federico García Lorca—"verde que" ["green, I want you green"] and Pablo Neruda—"puedo escribir los versos más tristes esta noche" ["Tonight I can write the saddest verses"]. As we know, Lorca was executed and his body thrown into an unmarked grave while the Falangists were occupying Granada in 1936; Neruda was forced into exile in 1949; Chilean security forces assassinated Victor Jara in 1973; and Roque Dalton was killed in El Salvador in 1975. In **"Sorrow,"** these poets' lives, together with fragments of their poetry reemerge as "un enjambre de sombras / rostros que ya no existen" ["these shadows of faces / that no longer exist"]. Here in the negative, "no existen" ["no longer exist"], the "no" reminiscent of Dalton's "no pronuncies" ["don't utter"] surfaces as a sign of the life-negating, silencing powers which dominate modern society.

In the second section of **"Sorrow,"** as Alegría recounts her search for García Lorca's unmarked grave, she appropriates an intertextual fragment by Antonio Machado: "el crimen fue en Granada" ["the crime was in Granada"]. The poetry which Alegría quotes here is, in its own right, a model of writing as an act of resistance: Machado had said, "Que fue en Granada el crimen / *sabed*—¡pobre Granada!—¡en su Granada!" ["The crime was in Granada know this—¡poor Granada!—¡in his Grandada" (my translation)]. The poet's "sabed," ["know this"] suggests that Machado envisioned his writing as a means of *making known* the truth. Alegría's appropriation of the Machado poem stresses her own poetic convictions concerning the labour of contemporary poetry: for the Salvadoran writer, poetry attempts to make known the truth—to counter the silence which stems from repression. At the same time, Alegría's **"Sorrow,"** also reveals the overwhelming difficulties against which modern poetry struggles: "y *no entiendo* / los ademanes vagos / las señales / el crimen fue en Granada / en su Granada / todo el mundo lo sabe / pero *nadie es capaz* de un detalle preciso / de decir por ejemplo / allí mismo lo echaron / al borde de ese olivo" ["*I do not understand* / vague gestures and directions / the crime was in Granada / in his Granada / everyone knows that / but *no one is capable* / of the precise detail / of saying for example / they flung his body down / at the foot of that olive tree"]. Again, the "no" of Dalton's "no pronuncies" echoes throughout the text in order to underscore the silence characteristic of a repressive social order. In addition, Alegría's use of the present tense in "pero nadie *es* capaz / de un detalle preciso" [but no one *is* capable / of the precise detail"] suggests that the kind of events—which in 1936 resulted in Lorca's death, and in Machado's exile—continue to define the context of modern writing.

The poem's third and fifth sections reveal the uncertain, extremely negative situation of contemporary Hispanic poets who, like Alegría herself, have lived in exile. [The critic adds in a footnote: In this section of the poem, Alegría suggests that the plight of the expatriated writer is shared by many. Her repetition of the pronoun, "nosotros" ["we"] is significant in this respect.] Dalton's poetry again resonates throughout the text: "Un tatuaje en la frente / nos señala / . . . nos olfateamos en el metro / . . . y *no sabemos* si es nuestro sudor / o la carroña de la patria" ["This mark on our foreheads / betrays us / . . . we sense one another in the Metro / . . .*we don't know* if it is our sweat / or the rotten taint of our land"]. Alegría defines the expatriated writer as one whose life is marked by "helplessness," "stagnant dreams" and "shame." She summarizes the exiled poet's bleak existance in the lines "a *no tener* un cinco en el bolsillo / . . . y *nadie tiene* un cinco" ["*not having* even small change . . . and *no one has* even small change"]. Here, echoes of Dalton's work resurface in the negatives, "a no tener" ["not having"] and "nadie tiene ["no on has"]. In addition, Alegría's "no sabemos" ["we don't know"], "nadie tiene" ["no one has"] and Roque's "no pronuncies" ["don't utter"] ultimately merge in this section of the poem with an intertextual fragment from an Argentine tango: "al mundo *nada le importa* / yira yira" ["*nothing matters* to the world / yira, yira"]. Again, as in the "Lorca section," the poem communicates a certain hopelessness: "salgo a la calle / a caminar *sin rumbo*" ["I return to the street to wander"]. Faced with the negativity of world indifference, poetry's labour of resistance emerges as a near-to-impossible task.

The poet's hopelessness reaches its climax in sections four and six of **"Sorrow"** when she writes of Roque Dalton's death. In the following lines, Alegría recalls hearing the news of the assassination: "Obstinadas / confusas / me llegan las noticias / hechos truncados / fríos / frases contradictorias / que me acosan / así llegó tu muerte / Roque Dalton / . . . en los signos borrosos / de un periódico . . . / en imágenes rotas / imprecisas" ["Stubborn / confused / the news comes to me / truncated facts / cold, contradictory sentences / that pursue me / that is how your death arrived, Roque Dalton / . . . in the smudged headlines . . . in broken images"]. Here, the adjectives, "confusas" ["confused"], "truncados" ["truncated"], "contradictorias" ["contradictory"] and "borrosos" ["smudged"] emphasize Alegría's suffering as she reacts to Dalton's murder. At the same time, this focus on the indefinite reveals the poet's frustration—her difficulty in uncovering (and making known) the truth, and thus fulfilling her labour as a poet. The language which begins, here, as an uncertainty—an imprecise understanding of Roque's assassination—is significant because, like much of **"Sorrow,"** it reveals the vacuousness of the present

world situation. Indeed, the "no" in Dalton's own "no pronuncies" is a sign of this contemporary emptiness; it also stresses the life-negating, silencing powers of repression.

In addition, in sections four and six of **"Sorrow"** the negatives reminiscent of Dalton's "no pronuncies" become exceptionally prominent: "siguen llegando ecos / acusaciones falsas / y *nunca sabré* quién te mató pero estás muerto / Roque Dalton / y envolvieron tu muerte / en la neblina" ["the echoes are still coming back / the false accusations / *I'll never know* who killed you / but you are dead, Roque Dalton, and they wrap your death in fog"]. Previously in the poem, Alegría suggested that, even today, no one can offer precise information concerning events like Lorca's death. Her lament serves, above all, as a criticism of contemporary civilization—as an insinuation that, especially today—"nadie *es* capaz" ["no one *is* capable"], society suffers from violations of basic human rights. Now, Alegría's references to "false accusations" and to the unclear or unknown events surrounding Dalton's death fulfill a similar function. The lines, "y envolvieron tu muerte / en la neblina" ["and they wrap your death in fog"] in reference to the death of a prominent Salvadoran revolutionary, emphasize the political repression against which the poet labours. Historians inform us that at the time of **"Sorrow"** 's publication, government repression in El Salvador was strong: the killing of Salvadorans who opposed the military order in the late 1970s occurred at the rate of 1000 per month. The "neblina" ["fog"] about which Alegría writes is a sign not only of the stifling of information about Roque Dalton, but also of the overwhelming repression—the stifling of human rights—which prevailed in her country.

As we have seen, a great deal of **"Sorrow"** is devoted to the unveiling of the contemporary threat to human dignity. And **"Sorrow"** 's intertext, due to its incorporation of Dalton's "cuando sepas que he muerto / no pronuncies mi nombre" ["when you learn that I am dead / don't utter my name"], reveals the negative, repressive situation which frames the context of contemporary writing. Yet in Dalton's "Alta hora de la noche," from which Alegría appropriates this intertextual fragment, there are, of course, additional lines which the poet does not quote. Among these is the positive declaration: "Pronuncia flor, abeja, lágrima, pan, tormenta" ["Say flower, bee, tear, bread, storm"]. This line from "Alta hora de la noche" is of particular significance because the same kind of life-affirming language also resonates throughout much of **"Sorrow."** Therefore, in spite of its repressive context, in spite of what appears to be an impossible task, **"Sorrow"** also reveals poetry's strength as a force of resistance.

In the Lorca section, for example, in addition to the negatives, "y no entiendo" ["and I don't understand"], "nadie es capaz" ["no one is capable"] and "te negaron la lápida" ["there is no tombstone"], we also hear, "pero alguien dejó un árbol / un olivo / alguien que supo / lo dejó" ["but someone left a tree, an olive / someone knew and left it standing"]. Thus, in response to the repression surrounding Lorca's death, the poem offers a declaration of life. Alegría's incorporation of a fragment from Miguel Hernández's "Aceituneros" ["Olive Workers"] later reinforces this declaration: "andaluces de Jaén / aceituneros altivos / decidme en el alma ¿quién? / quién levantó los olivos?" ["Andalucians of Jaén / proud olive workers / tell me in you heart, who? / who raised the olive trees?" (my translation)]. The intertextualization of Hernández's poem reveals **"Sorrow"**'s own declaration of the positive: Hernández's "olivos" ["olive trees"], like Dalton's "flor" ["flower"] and "abeja" ["bee"], are signs of a natural inclination toward the affirmation of life. At the same time, in "Aceituneros," Hernández choice of the adjective, "altivos" ["proud"]—in order to describe the olive workers—implies that their's is a dignified labour. It is also a labour which defies and resists repression. According to Alegría, poetry's labour of resistance is also a dignified and life-affirming act.

Yet as we have seen, resistance often emerges as a near to impossible task. This is the case in Alegría's portrayal of the seemingly aimless existence of the exiled writer. Nevertheless, even in her portrayal of exile, Alegría ultimately succeeds in countering the negative—"no sabemos" ["we don't know"] and "nada le importa" ["nothing matters"]—with positive statements from "Alta hora de la noche." Alegría responds to Dalton's life-affirming, "Pronuncia . . . *lágrima*" ["Say . . . *tear*"], with the images, "un *llanto* endurecido" ["*calloused tears*"] and "*mirada húmeda*" ["*damp eyes*"], which like "shame" and "hopelessness," also define the life of the exiled writer. But in opposition to "shame" and "hopelessness," the poet's "tears" primarily suggest that beyond repression, there are also signs of life. Furthermore, in "Alta hora de la noche," the life-affirming, "Pronuncia . . . lágrima" ["Say . . . tear"] is folllwed by an even stronger statement: "Pronunica . . . *tormenta*" ["Say . . . *storm*"]. This second statement—which Alegría communicates via an intertextual fragment from César Vallejo—concludes the exile section: "me moriré in París con *aguacero*" / un día del cual tengo ya el recuerdo" ["I will die in Paris with a *heavy rain shower* / on a day of which I still have memory"]. As Dalton's work becomes more pronounced, its implications also become more forceful: the response to the denial of human dignity and life is an inevitable storm of resistance.

Echoes of Roque's work continue to penetrate the last two sections of **"Sorrow"**: sections seven and eight offer a commentary on repression from the point of view of the writer as a political prisoner. As it has in the previous sections of the poem, Dalton's "no pronuncies" reemerges as a sign of the repressive social context which defines modern writing: "¿Quién sembró los barrotes? / sólo una luz palúdica / me llega desde afuera / *no hay* sol / *no hay* pájaros / *no hay* verdes" ["Who raised the bars? / a gray light filters from outside / *there is no* sun / *there are no* birds, *no* foliage"]. In section seven, however, the poet ultimately appropriates the negative in order to convert it into a life-affirming sign of resistance: "vuelvo a mi rosario / *no estoy sola* / están ellos / los huéspedes de paso" ["I return to my rosary / *I am not alone* / they are here / the transient guests"]. The poet's "no estoy sola" ["I am not alone"] conveys **"Sorrow"**'s most fundamental message: the labour of poetry "is to bring together what life has separated

or violence has torn apart." Again, **"Sorrow"** unites the voices of the exiled, the tortured and the murdered: "están Victor / Violeta / el poeta pastor / salto alegre del catre / y tropiezo con Roque" ["there are Victor and Violeta / the shepherd poet / I leap from my cot / and stumble into Roque"]. The poem thus resists repression by defying the space which separates. And as the poet assumes a collective voice, she empowers her work as an act of resistance: " . . . grabo en el muro: / más solos están ellos / que nosotros" ["I scratch on the wall: / they are more alone than we are"].

As we know, Roque Dalton's poetry is an essential empowering component in **"Sorrow"**'s collective voice. In addition to the "no" of Dalton's "no pronuncies"—and Alegría's "no hay . . ." ["there is no . . ."]—the affirmative "Pronuncia flor, abeja, lágrima, pan, tormenta" ["Say flower, bee, tear, bread, storm"] resurfaces in the poem's final sections: in response to imprisonment, we hear "no estoy sola / están ellos / y hay vino / y guitarras / y hay tabaco" ["I am not alone / they are here / there is wine / there are guitars, tobacco"]. Like Dalton's "flower" or "bee," Alegría's "wine," "guitars" and "tobacco" confront repression by affirming life. As the poem draws to a close, the poet offers the following declaration: "existen los barrotes / nos rodean / también existe el catre / y sus ángulos duros / y el poema río / que nos sostiene a todos / y es tan substantivo / como el catre / el poema que todos escribimos / con lágrimas / y uñas y carbon" ["the bars do exist / they surround us / the cot also exists / with its hard sides / the river poem / that sustains us all / and is as substantial as the cot / the poem we are all writing / with tears, with fingernails and coal"]. Here, the poet's "existen" ["they exist"] serves, above all, as a declaration of survival. Repression does exist, and the role or "labour" of poetry is to counter its destructive force so that people can survive.

In this final section of **"Sorrow,"** Alegría reiterates the message that poetry derives its power through its collective voice. In this "poem we are all writing" the intertext plays an essential role in countering the forces of repression. And in **"Sorrow"**'s final lines, Roque Dalton's intertextual voice continues to contribute significantly to the poem's collective labour. Indeed, when Alegría writes about the "poema *río* / . . . el poema que todos escribimos / con *lágrimas* / y uñas y carbón" ["the *river* poem / . . . the poem we are all writing / with *tears*, with fingernails and coal"], **"Sorrow"** once again echoes Dalton's "Alta hora de la noche." As we know, Dalton had said, "Cuando sepas que he muerto no pronuncies mi nombre / . . . Pronuncia flor, abeja, lágrima, pan, *tormenta*" ["When you learn that I am dead don't utter my name / . . . Say flower, bee, tear, bread, *storm*."] For this Salvadoran poet, "tormenta" ["storm"] of course refers to the Revolution in his country. As Dalton's imagery is transformed in **"Sorrow"** from a "storm" into a "river" and "tears," Alegría acknowledges the painful situation in which her country finds itself. At the same time, she affirms the revolutionary struggle to which her fellow Salvadoran dedicated his poetry and his life. For both Roque Dalton and Claribel Alegría, writing is a revolutionary force—a labour of active resistance. In **"Sorrow,"** Alegría defies the repres-

sion which reigns in her country. And she gives new life
to the revolutionary voices of the "river poem." (pp. 18-
24)

*Teresa Longo, "Claribel Alegría's 'Sorrow': In
Defiance of the Space Which Separates," in*
Latin American Literary Review, *Vol. XX,
No. 39, January-June, 1992, pp. 18-26.*

**Additional coverage of Alegría's life and career is contained in the following sources
published by Gale Research:** *Contemporary Authors,* **Vol. 131 and** *Hispanic Writers.*

Lucian Blaga

1895-1961

Rumanian poet, philosopher, playwright, and journalist.

The following entry presents an overview of Blaga's career.

INTRODUCTION

One of the preeminent Rumanian authors of the interwar period, Blaga was well known as both a poet and a philosopher. Believing mystery to be an integral part of human life, he used his poetry to illuminate its significance to individuals and society. Blaga is also recognized for his philosophy, a type of pantheism dominated by the search for an elusive metaphysical principle that he called the "Great Anonymous."

The son of a Rumanian Orthodox priest, Blaga was born in the village of Lancrăm, Transylvania. As Transylvania was still part of the Austro-Hungarian empire at the time, Blaga received a predominantly German education and was particularly influenced by the philosophical writings of Gotthold Lessing, Friedrich Nietzsche, and Henri Bergson. After graduating from the Sibiu Orthodox Seminary, Blaga went on to study philosophy and biology at the University of Vienna, writing a dissertation entitled "Culture and Cognition." Following the 1919 publication of his first collection of poems, *Poemele luminii* (*Poems of Light*), Blaga and a group of leading Rumanian authors founded the journal *Gîndirea* ("Thought"), which was dedicated to exploring Rumanian national identity and later became the most influential literary periodical of its time. Blaga began his careers as a journalist and diplomat when he was appointed press attaché to Vienna in 1932. He returned to Rumania in 1939 to take up a professorship in philosophy at the University of Cluj. After the Communist takeover of Rumania in 1949, he was forced to relinquish his post and forbidden to publish his writings; in 1956, when awarded the Nobel Prize for Literature, he was prevented by the Rumanian government from accepting it. Until his death in 1961, Blaga worked as a librarian and translated works by such German authors as Johann Wolfgang von Goethe and Friedrich Schelling.

Blaga's poetry is often viewed in relation to his philosophy. In his philosophical writings Blaga asserted that mystery is the principle behind all creation. He called this principle the "Great Anonymous," as it could not be ascertained directly but only seen residually in nature. The "Great Anonymous" also represented for Blaga the cultural soul of the Rumanian people, forming the collective ethnic consciousness that was the cornerstone for his theory of "style." Blaga used the term "style" to refer to the characteristics that distinguish one culture from another, including differences in landscape and environment. In his

poetry Blaga reworks Rumanian folklore to depict the relation between the individual and his or her cultural environment. In addition, his poetry frequently describes the perpetual search for the "Great Anonymous." As Virgil Nemoianu explains, "Blaga's [philosophy] is a neo-Platonism in reverse: the creation is indeed trying to rush back to its source and to be reunited with it, but the 'Great Anonymous,' full of dark suspicions and sly jealousy, set obstacles against this yearning and built brakes in nature against the emergence of truly integrative Types or Ideas. At times, indeed, it seems more interested in thwarting than in generating." While some critics have seen Blaga as a nature poet concerned only with the physical world and present experience, others have seen him as expressing a profound melancholy and nostalgia for a lost paradise. Most critics, however, concur that the connection between Blaga's poetry and philosophy reveals the ways in which his theory of culture is to some extent inseparable from his literary works.

PRINCIPAL WORKS

Poemele luminii   (poetry)   1919
  [*Poems of Light,* 1975]
Pasii profetului   (poetry)   1921
  [*In the Footsteps of the Prophet* published in *Poems of Light* (partial translation), 1975]
Zamolxe   (drama)   1921
Tulberarea apelor   (drama)   [first publication]   1923
În marea trecere   (poetry)   1924
  [*In the Great Passage* published in *Poems of Light* (partial translation), 1975]
Daria   (drama)   1925
Meşterul Manole   (drama)   1927
Lauda somnului   (poetry)   1929
  [*In Praise of Sleep* published in *Poems of Light* (partial translation), 1975]
La cumpăna apelor   (poetry)   1933
  [*At the Watershed* published in *Poems of Light* (partial translation), 1975]
Avram Iancu   (drama)   [first publication] 1934
*Orizont şi stil   (philosophy)   1935
*Spaţiul mioritic   (philosophy)   1936
*Geneza metaforei şi sensul culturii   (philosophy)   1937
La curţile dorului   (poetry)   1938
  [*In the Courtyard of Yearning* published in *Poems of Light* (partial translation), 1975]
Nebănuitele trepte   (poetry)   1943
Trilogia cunoaşterii   (philosophy)   1943
Trilogia culturii   (philosophy)   1944
Trilogia valorilor   (philosophy)   1946
Opere. 5 vols.   (poetry, dramas, essays, and philosophy) 1974-77
At the Court of Yearning   (poetry)   1989

*These works were later published in *Trilogia culturii.*

CRITICISM

Edgar Papu   (essay date 1970)

[*In the following essay, Papu considers Blaga's importance to modern Rumanian culture.*]

A poet, an essayist, a philosopher, a consummate translator of art, Lucian Blaga belongs to the family of the great modern creators, destined to have a manysided commanding influence over the culture they belong to. [These types] of scholars, heralded already by Nietzsche, and who cannot be absent from a privileged place neither in the history of poetry nor in the history of thinking, have appeared in orderly succession from [Miguel de] Unamuno to [Jean-Paul] Sartre. Their fecund polyvalence cannot be separated from the unity of their own personality which, from all sides, radiates the same vivid originality and the same message. Lucian Blaga is in no way inferior to the most illustrious representatives of this family.

That is why he marks a unique moment in Romanian culture. Very keen on penetrating deep into the essence of his native land and, at the same time, a real polypode of universal cognizance of ideas, Blaga carried the resources of the Romanian spirit to a culminating convergency. He makes his own inner horizon, connected with the spiritual profile of his people, coincide with the reflexes of the great horizons of the circuit. Unamuno surprised an "essence" of Spain and established its place in the world, and Blaga did exactly the same for Romania. No doubt that investigated from a scientific angle today, the fact that Romanian culture was made to know itself, to define itself, to set off its specific characters and its right to existence, constituted an older tendency, expressed by many, from Nicolae Bălcescu down to Nicolae Iorga. However, with them, this tendency was of a historicist nature, and rhetorical in manner. It is Blaga who first included the search for final traits in the philosophic register, by applying the concepts and categories of the philosophy of culture especially to the Romanian "sub-history," to the unrecorded strata of the visible, known history. He did not derive his ideas from documents or charters, but from the investigation of the life and mythical traditions of the village, i.e. from where there results an original intuitive philosophy of the genuine folk art, an analysis of the *dor* (longing), the determining of the mental horizon of the pastoral transhumance. All is integrated within that unity of organicist vision—the millenary reconcilliation with the "secret" core of nature which Blaga attributes to his people and to his soil.

That is why, of his three trilogies [*Trilogia cunoaşterii, Trilogia valorilor,* and *Trilogia culturii*], the latter—less affected by the agnostic metaphysics of Blaga the philosopher—seems to be the most consistent. Perhaps in it the spirit of Blaga—to a great extent subjective and metaphysical—draws nearer to the objective essence of things. With exceptionally subtle intuition, he applies to the Romanian people an original philosophy of culture, as Unamuno did to the Spanish people, Okakura Kakuro to the Japanese people, Martinez Estrada to the Argentinean pomp and to the "gaucho" type.

Blaga would certainly not have reached, in the plane of thinking, such intuitive keenness, if he had not been, at the same time, a poet. Attempts have often been made to establish a parallelism between his philosophy and his poetry. However, greater stress was laid on the thread of cognition connected in both registers with a sense of mystery. We think, however, that the parallelism is equally fruitful in culture too, a domain to which Blaga makes the most substantial contribution. Thus, it is precisely his poetry which to a great extent adhered to expressionism, that shows how with Blaga a foreign trend can become a Romanian phenomenon in the sense of applying it to the philosophy of culture. No doubt that in his poetry, the element of anxious searching, accompanied by the violence of the emotional shock, is no less intense even than in the greatest lyrical achievements of expressionism. Still the tumult is spent mostly in the depths while to the surface rises a horizon of peace where there is none of the despair, the alarm and dread which spring from the poetry of the German expressionists. Here, to follow Blaga's line of thinking, we can surprise the same transformation which, centuries before, in architecture, the Gothic had undergone when entering Romanian soil. In the monasteries of Stephen the Great or in the wooden churches in Maramureş, the transcendent élan of that style, its cry towards the heights, all of a sudden accepted an integration within the order of immanence, a reconcilliation with nature and its objects. In the same way, Blaga's profoundly problematic sensitiveness as anxious as that of expressionism is decanted in a behaviourist manner into the calm rounding off of a harmonious vocabulary. Thus Blaga finds in himself, too, not only without, the Romanian vision of life which aroused such an echo.

Perhaps this loud echo is not due only to the written work of Lucian Blaga, but to his great personality as teacher and cultural guide. He was, for a time, a professor of the theory of culture at the university of Sibiu and set up in that town, around his periodical *Saeculum,* a strong spiritual nucleus the fruits of which are being turned to account in Romanian culture today too. A number of poets, essayists, men possessing a vast and thorough culture were formed there, and through them, the germ sown by Lucian Blaga developed into a beautiful arborescence. If one of his most brilliant spiritual descendants, poet and dramatist Radu Stanca, died prematurely, even before the master, a number of critics, essayists and poets of his posterity are in full activity; they possess a remarkable personality with a special note of originality ensured by their effort to turn to account the views of Blaga, whose justness and fecundity are confirmed in contact with the predominant ideas of the present.

The presence of Blaga marked one of the richest moments of Romanian culture from which there resulted a strong force of radiation which imparted to contemporary Romanian culture one of its powerfully pronounced directions. (pp. 52-3)

> *Edgar Papu, "A Multilateral Personality," in* Romanian Review, *Vol. XXIV, No. 4, 1970, pp. 52-3.*

Dumitru Ghişe   (essay date 1970)

[*In the following essay, Ghişe questions Blaga's reliance on myth, folklore, and mysticism in his* Trilogia culturii.]

Blaga, the poet, has become an integral part of Romanian consciousness, less so Blaga, the philosopher. Part of the explanation for this seems to lie in the fact that Blaga's philosophy appears to us inescapably remote both because of the years that separate it from us and because of its metaphysical-spiritualist bias; all this, despite its monumentality and harmony, the result of a thorough knowledge of conceptual architecture emerging from an uncommon inherent energy, with *The Trilogy of Culture* holding pride of place. Trained at the German idealist-irrationalist school of the turn of the century, as far as the broad implications of his system are concerned, Blaga is indebted to *Lebensphilosophie* in general and to the morphology of culture postulated by Riegl, Frobenius and Spengler in particular. However, it should be stressed that the Roma-

nian thinker tried hard to go beyond his model and that there are very real differences between Blaga and his predecessors, which the former took special pride in pointing out on several occasions, and considered that thereby his philosophy was offered almost unprecedented opportunities.

Under the impact of the source that shaped his thinking, in Blaga the concept of culture is divorced from and opposed to that of civilization, free from any causal explanation or objective determination, floating as it were mythically in a self-contained world whose scope can only be described by means of abysmal categories. Hence the ups and downs of Blaga's philosophy of culture despite its lyrical grandeur. For his whole theoretical structure which he took admirable pains to place on the category of style as on an Archimedean term of reference—considering style as a salient defining feature of human culture, an inherent dimension of any creative human endeavour—is an echo, on yet another level, of the main idea inspiring the German philosophy mentioned at the beginning of this study, that life is unpredictable, indeterminate, which is as much as saying that life cannot be translated into rational terms.

In this general frame of reference, opposed to the fruitful principles of scientific determinism and rationalism, explanation is supplanted by description, vague and obscure speculation replaces genuine knowledge of man, his life and the universe. Turning to "abysmal noology," a new subject that Blaga wanted to set up in the hope that it might help him to get over the limitations of the morphological method and reveal the stylistic matrix peculiar to every culture, he failed however to go beyond his predecessors and impelled by the demiurgic force of his poetic imagination, contriving a mythical and metaphorical terminology, Blaga immersed himself deeply in the mysterious areas beyond the bright zones of consciousness. In an effort to bring to us his message from the realm of "superlight," the rich ancestral world of the subconscious, Blaga has only managed to create the magical, quivering and frail image of the stylistic matrix.

That is why following Blaga through the maze of his speculative constructions, among the many hidden factors whose operation gives rise to the varied constellation of styles, the reader is bound to get often baffled to the point of annoyance.

George Călinescu very early expressed his reservations about Blaga's philosophy and moreover, unequivocally disapproved of him, describing him as a "true mystic" who accepted delirium as an instrument of investigation and who overstepped the bounds in search of novel expressions. Blaga—as he himself confesses in **"The Appearance of the Metaphor and the Meaning of Culture"**—was fully aware that his attempt to create a philosophical vision and thereby to explain the ultimate significance of style and culture, of man's creative destiny, had failed to find a language that would meet his scientific requirements. To drive home his ideas he often had to resort to "strange images," mythical not philosophical images, that is to go beyond philosophy proper into the obscure realm of mythosophy. I think it would be fair to say that the inherent shortcomings of Blaga's philosophic vision have had their revenge leaving their imprint on form.

It is precisely these drawbacks, stemming from its speculative-metaphysical ideas, that make *The Trilogy of Culture* appear remote in time and ideas to the contemporary reader holding a Marxist conception of culture. Moreover, carried away by his idealistic assumptions, Blaga failed to understand the dialectical and historical character of culture. He oversimplified and, thereby, distorted Marxist theory, reducing it to something it has never been, that is to rigid economic determinism or mere philosophic naturalism. One of the most obvious proofs that this view was wrong, seems to the present writer to be the noble, generous and vastly fruitful quality of Marxist philosophy to assess and take up a critical but discriminating stand toward various non-Marxist theories including Lucian Blaga's own theory. Moreover, Marxist philosophy critically takes over from these theories—despite their repudiable surface—everything that is truly valuable, any fruitful embryo apt to provide a constructive starting point. Dialectical negation—as Hegel himself argues—is not mere rejection. Dialectical negation contains of necessity as its constituent elements both rejection and preservation.

This is also true of Blaga, the philosopher of culture. For, his idealistic system, the "Northern mist" enwrapping his thinking, are alive with a rich core of observations and analyses deriving from an intensive examination of vast areas of culture.

The wide background of a hesitating philosophy, dubious like the uncertainty hidden by the shade, is lighted by the tantalizing fireworks of a supple thinking with a very fine and acute intellectual calligraphy whose analyses and individual observations acquire an autonomy and value entirely their own. The critical dissociations and analyses that Blaga makes with regard to Freudianism, the revelation of the one-sidedness and inefficiency of Spengler's morphology of culture, Blaga's deep insights throwing light on the differences between the condition of man as he really is and the way he is presented by Christian spirituality, his profound ideas on the stylistic grounds of the diversification of the Christian spirit, his criticism of Nietzscheanism whose criteria he describes as a "hysterical grimace of a decadent," his emphasis on the limitations of Heidegger's existentialist theory—are as many individual elements worthy of special consideration. The number of these elements, many of them constructive, could be multiplied, if discriminatingly abstracted from Blaga's general system they can provide valuable "substance" for another philosophical structure at a different ideological level.

What seems to be of paramount importance about Blaga is that he was a great humanist. Blaga did not share Spengler's view that culture is the parasitical product of a soul detached from man and subjugating him. On the contrary, Blaga argues that culture is closely linked to man's creative destiny, it is his fulfilment, his particular fine manner of being Man, of transgressing his caducity, of surviving the moment.

Man's thirst for transcendence, the organic need for im-

provement and self-improvement every human being feels, led Blaga to emphatically investigate the relation of the relative to the absolute. The absolute he always spelled with a capital letter or else he called it the Great Anonymous. This is all true, but as remarked by other Blaga scholars, his spiritualism was in unequivocal disagreement with the idea of "divine revelation" and with any "theological supernaturalism." Blaga would not accept the description that he was an irrationalist. He conceived the unconscious as having a cosmos-like rather than a chaotic character. He happily described his philosophy as "ecstatic rationalism." We do not propose to examine the fine differences and distinctions of Blaga's philosophy nor the extent this sui-generis rationalism is warranted by his work but we think it is in place to mention here that Blaga significantly described himself as "neither catholic, nor orthodox, but simply a philosopher." That is to say his idealims should be confused neither with religious mysticism in general nor with orthodox mysticism in particular as shown by a closer examination of his philosophy. This is further borne out by the fact that some of his contemporaries representing rightwing ideology and politics saw in Blaga's thinking and intellectualism a threat to "heaven," a downright rejection of God himself, that is a threat to their own orthodox ideology. Viewed in retrospect, the violent opposition of such critics can only place Blaga's philosophy in a favourable light as its aim is noble and dignified, trying to discover the "mysteries" of the universe.

Consequently, a fruitful dialogue with Blaga, the philosopher of culture, appears not only possible but even necessary. The dialectics of development is impossible outside confrontation of ideas. Lucian Blaga's *Trilogy of Culture* provides the opportunity of such a confrontation, for its intellectual substance, no matter what form it assumed, prompts to reflection, arouses questions and calls for answers.

In full agreement with Blaga, we admit that there is no stylistic void, that style lends a culture its distinctive stamp. This truth is obvious and need not be demonstrated. However, it must be stated—in order to round off the idea put forward by Blaga and also unlike him—that human spirituality viewed in its constant features and extreme generality contains the distinctions of particularity. Or, to be more accurate, the general exists only in the particular. The culture of any people, its spiritual matrix or peculiar make-up, is an undeniable reality, the result of its historical and social development different from other peoples but occurring within the same broad context. The spiritual physiognomy, the peculiar moral and cultural features of a people do not spring accidentally from an unfathomable abyss, they are not nor can they be the mythical expression of ineffable irrationalism, the outcome of a series of hidden factors that grow into an a-historical stylistic matrix. This stand alone makes possible the scientific explanation and the genuine philosophical analysis of the cultural phenomenon. This is precisely the prospect opened up by Marxism as regards the birth, the structure and finality of culture. Philosophy alone will not do to explain this phenomenon that has to be progressively assessed. Philosophy can only proceed from the facts provided by all sciences about man. Archaeology turns out to be just as necessary in this case as cybernetics or psychology. The elaboration and gradual development of a general theory of culture is undoubtedly as complex as it is difficult. That is why in embarking upon the elaboration of *The Trilogy of Culture,* Blaga set himself an unenviable and discouraging task. Given the scope of the work under examination it is fairly easy to see that his attempt, on the whole, necessarily ran certain risks. All the more valuable is then the significance of his daring gesture and partial success. Incidentally, he is the first great explorer in the history of Romanian thinking who, attempting to formulate a coherent theory of the cultural phenomenon, erected a systematic, monumental philosophical structure.

His aspiration is all the nobler since his basic impulse constantly rested on the wish to find the clue that would explain as many features of the Romanian entity as possible. It was Blaga's strong conviction, which he constantly emphasized, that culture is not something superposed on man's existence, a decorative arabesque, a superfluous embellishment. For him culture was closely linked to man's mode of being. And this is certainly true. However, the way he conceived this mode of being estranged him from fact. That is why, while understanding his protest against the mechanism of capitalist urban civilization one can hardly share his idea of a romantic refuge into the mythical and metaphysical world of the village.

In his work light and shade, wisdom and naive candour constantly crisscross. Like Siamese twins, with the same blood running in their veins, the poet and the philosopher are constantly joined together helping each other or disturbing each other. They coexist and share the same dreams entertaining the same illusions. However, there is passion and beauty on the generous hymn of praise that he sings—far from any exclusivism or obscure passion—to the creative spirit of the people, there is thrill and humility in his description of yearning, and spontaneousness, wistful self-restraint, moderation and balance, in his artistic taste and stylistic bias, etc., all of which he views as distinct peculiarities of the spiritual make-up of the Romanian people. Romanian folk art and folk ornamentation can be given prominence in the historical studies of philosophy—Blaga says with moderate pride—and the lyrical substance of folk poetry he considered so profusely vital and replete with possibilities that he likened it to the vegetation of the whole earth.

"The careful, unremitting examination of our folk culture," Blaga writes, "has led us to the invigorating conclusion about the existence of a Romanian stylistic matrix. Its latent powers, that we have got a glimpse of, entitle us to state that we are possessed of a high cultural potential. All we can say beyond any doubt is that we are the fortunate bearers of exceptional possibilities. All we can be sure of, without fear of exaggeration, is that we have been destined to cast light on a stretch of land by the flower we shall grow tomorrow. All we can hope for, without indulging in illusions, is the pride of some spiritual, historical initiatives that will time and again spark off and arrest the interest of other peoples." This statement contains in a nutshell the crystal-clear expression of all the potentialities of a

thinking whose discriminating investigation holds every promise to be fully rewarding. (pp. 62-4)

Dumitru Ghişe, "The Trilogy of Culture," in Romanian Review, *Vol. XXIV, No. 4, 1970, pp. 62-4.*

Ştefan A. Doinaş (essay date 1970)

[*In the following essay, Doinaş analyzes Blaga's view of the nature and function of language.*]

In Lucian Blaga's lyrical poetry, the dialectics of Silence and of Words transcends the explanatory biographical detail (we refer to the pages in *The Chronicle and the Chant of the Ages,* which mentions that Blaga when a child was "shy of words" until an advanced threshold of this age) and crystalizes into genuine poetics, implied in the lyrical act. Besides, the relation between Silence and Words cannot be explained without involving, in a way, Blaga's metaphysics. As has already been observed (Nicolae Balotă in *Euphorion,* Bucharest, 1969), Silence and Words mark two different ontological regions: the former corresponds to a realm of the non-created, an area of the undetermined pre-existence, a paradisiacal space (how often the word "paradise" recurs in Blaga's poetry!) in which man lives in a state of ineffable grace; the latter signifies man's entrance into temporality and determination, his "fall" into "sin," that is to say subjection to his own mortal condition. Let us see how this divorce between dumbness and utterance appears lyrically, this threshold of extreme precariousness on which is established the special status of the Poet as a preeminently talking creature.

The non-created is, first of all, a sort of lost age of our being: "a nameless land" which the poet bitterly regrets having deserted ("But I remember the time when I still was not / as a distant childhood, / And I am so sorry I did not stay on / in the nameless land" (**"Quietness among Old Things"**); it then implies, as childhood does, a certain *innocence* of the creature, a candour which man having entered the age of utterance, achieves in moments when he is silent, symbolized by the purity of the swan ("Lucian Blaga is as dumb as a swan. / In his land / the snow of the creature takes the place of the word" (**"Selfportrait"**); at other times, this realm forces itself on him through its most significant quality, through "its extinguished light" ("I search, I don't know what I am searching for. Under yesterday's stars, / under the past ones, I am searching / the extinguished light I keep praising." (**"Yesterday's Light"**); finally, this realm which, being pure virtuality resembles childhood, which implying the state of paradisiacal bliss recalls "the first light," this realm of the essential innocence is at the same time—due to its complete indefiniteness—a realm of the "immaculate." Nothing, in front of which the creature feels the supreme existential thrill as if facing the sacred, as if facing death: "Mother—nothingness—the great! The fear of the great / makes, night after night, my garden shudder" (**"From the Depth"**). The poet admits that this silence constitutes the very core of his being: "Silence is my spirit" (**"The Stalactite"**) his heirloom from an age of grace, previous to his "entrance in the world."

On the contrary Words are the expression of our existence amid suffering and death. They are seen once, under the shape of *tears* ("But words are the tears of those who would have liked / so much to weep and could not. / How bitter are all the words, / therefore—let me / go about among you, dumb / and come to meet you with closed eyes" (**"To the Readers"**); at other times, under the shape of tombs ("Princess, our words are tombs, don't you think so? / Tombs in which time has enclosed its sufferings / in front of the beauty that comes to meet it / wounding it with its bitter charm. / Under these vaults, under the sacred, / well, you know, one should speak less / and more seldom. We should not play with tombs" (**"The Princesses"**). For Blaga to speak seems to be an enormous vanity, an act which the very spectacle of Nature itself continually calls man away from: "Man, I'd like to tell you more, / but it would be in vain, / and besides, the stars are coming out / motioning to me to be silent" (**"The Mystery of the Initiate"**). How can the position of the poet be accounted for, he who is a creature destined to give expression to all he feels by means of *words?* What is the hidden reason of this conspiracy of silence which all things around the creature endowed with speech plot in order to dissuade it from the "sin" of utterance? And first of all why is utterance a "sin"? The replies to these questions imply a metaphysics underlying Blaga's lyrical act, derived from his philosophic conception of the phenomenon of culture, in general.

A short piece of poetry, **"Holding the Great Blind Man by the Hand"**, which is included in the volume [*In the Great Passage*] with the modest subtitle of "variant" gives us the key to this attitude. Leading the "great blind man"—no doubt a hypostasis of the Creator—about the world, the poet praises to him the cosmic order: "I say, Father the course of the suns is good." But instead of rejoicing, the old man keeps silent: "He is silent—because he is frightened at words. / He is silent—because with him every word changes into fact." The significance of these two lines is enough to explain Blaga's position to the Word and to Words. Uttering itself, the Word first created the world, compelled it *to be;* but obliging it to be in *time* and in *space* it forces on it a status of limitation. In other words, the creation is a degraded state of the non-created: it is its part "fallen" when coming under the condition of evolution and death which every "individualization" implies. That such is the state of things is proved by the act of bitter tenderness which the Creator commits on the seventh day, when all the creatures have been left to their own fate: to comfort them the Lord "kisses them with His lips," to express his love and compassion for them in a gesture identical with the one which condemned them: "For the apparitions and all the creatures / that knew of death, He wished / to comfort, kissing them with the lips" (**"The First Sunday"**). The action of "the great Blind Man" avoiding to utter a word, signifies the Creator's refusal—aware of the first determination which the utterance of the first Word brought into existence—to compel, once again, through one more word uttered by Him. Thus the word means compulsion, determination, that is "doom"; the fact of *being in the world,* established by the first Word, is a verdict pronounced by the divine lips, that all creatures obey; when the Creator uttered His Word he sentenced us *to be,* that is *to suffer and to die.* But by dooming

us through His Word, the Creator left us at the same time the doom of the word, that is to say the possibility of dooming, in our turn, the things of this world, of limiting them and circumscribing them by uttering their name; of forcing upon them a status of evolution and death. This situation should not surprise us at all: if the first Word, the Creator of all things, could be pronounced only by introducing into the world—the very fact of its determination—suffering and death, attributes that are necessarily connected with every principle of individualization, the human word, our everyday speech is so much the more the cause of the arbitrary separation from the great Whole, therefore the cause of limitation and death. By dooming us to be, the first Word endowed every word—uttered in the same way as the first Word was—with its primary property, with its sad privilege of dooming. By speaking man proves he has been doomed and that, at the same time, he dooms—by naming—all that is around him. The poet feels this thing to be a "sin" that lies heavy on his house: "I understood the sin that lies heavy on my house / like ancestral moss. / Oh, why did I explain time and the stars / otherwise than the old woman who lays her hemp to rot in the swamp?" (**"I Understood the Sin . . ."**). Hence a genuine mystic system of inaction, a genuine veneration of silence, for words like facts limit and sentence; the man that Blaga acknowledges is a "friend of the depth," a "companion of stillness" who "dances over facts," knowing that "the mystic fruit" shaded by his hands "becomes rounded off somewhere else," knowing that the brother's question and the sister's surprise are compensated by the obedience and comprehension of the serpent "whose eyes are eternally open / to the wisdom of beyond" (**"I Am No Son of the Fact"**).

Still the Word did not bring about only the creature's frail and woebegone fate, but its entire existential mystery: despite its conditioning in space and time, the creation continues to be, qualitatively, an immense, inexhaustible Mystery whose profound, impenetrable sense has not been cleared up in any way by the divine Word. The things around us certify it: "Has dew fallen on the things / or is it just a delusion? / Maybe their faces are weeping / because of some inner woe. Does a heart throb in things? / Taking up all the room around / have they thoughts, passions? / Without eyes they look at the world / those carriers of senses / those bearers of passions" (**"De rerum natura"**). In the same way, human speech—faithful to its kinship with the first Word is, on the one hand, an instrument that "connects step and thought with destruction"; but on the other, it offers—in an ideal hypostasis—the possibility of restoring almost wholly the mystery of existence, the intimate mystery of the creature or to use the poet's expression—to take shape in an utterance "equal with nature's essential combustion." "You creature—shall I ever find the proper / fiery silver sound, and the rite / of an utterance equal / for ever to your combustion? / . . . / Incomprehensible by the hearths / but understood by gods and stones / where is the word which like a halo / will raise you above time?" (**"Combustion"**). No doubt that this speech which can suspend the creature's temporal status, is not our everyday speech. To surprise significances, it must rise above the contingent, it must take shape in a "tale" (so, it must be a creator); and in order to take shape in a tale, it must be stimulated by the virtue of love ("Invention is more vivid / when love prompts it," says Blaga); "by completing beyond nature" the things, it makes their sense and innermost law "blossom," due to its property of "added magic," of "word uttered"; in other words, it distinguishes itself through its character of verbal "rite," of "magic charm." Consequently, besides our common speech, the agent of our introduction into suffering and death, which by naming things, individualizes them, submits them to an inexorable principle of evolution and annihilation, there is another speech able to "raise things above time," to restore to the world its entire wealth of significances, to "save" the creature from its eternal gliding away. This special speech is the poet's speech. But *how* and *when* is such a miracle possible? What is the inner condition of such a speech, a "redeeming" speech, redeeming the things it names and, at the same time, redeeming its own essence?

We think it proper to point out the similitude between Blaga's conception of speech and Hölderlin's as set off by Heidegger in his famous exegesis *Hölderlin und das Wesen der Dichtung*. The German poet considers speech the "most innocent of all pursuits" but at the same time man's most dangerous possession since—as his exegete explains—through speech "one can express all that is purest and most abstruse, but also all that is intricate and common. Nay, in order that essential speech should be understood and thus become the property of the community, it must also become common." And further: "What is pure and what is common form together a single utterance. Speech as such never appears directly as an essential speech or, on the contrary, as a mere sonorous void. On the contrary, essential speech is often so simple that it has the air of being unessential speech. And, on the other hand, what appears at first sight essential, is often nothing but prattle and narrations. Thus speech is always obliged to wear the appearance it generates itself, and in this way it compromises all that is absolutely its own, genuine utterance." It is not difficult to identify in these Heideggerian explanations the poetical theses contained implicitly in Blaga's lyrical poetry.

The practical consequences of this position are clearly revealed in Lucian Blaga's theoretical works, especially in **"On Magical Thinking"** and **"The Genesis of the Metaphor and the Sense of Culture."** If the essence of the human being consists in "to set the mystery and try to reveal it" then genuine poetry—one of the forms of this attempt, invariably doomed to failure, to emphasize the cosmic mystery—is that which connects them to two modalities proper to human thinking: the mythical thinking and the magic thinking. The former "endeavours to reveal a mystery with the means of imagination," converting the mystery of existence "if not adequately, in a positive manner through figures that satisfy through themselves"; in the latter "the mystery itself as such acquires consistency like in a lucid appendix of its own." Genuine poetry should therefore have a certain mythical and magic "content" at the various levels of the verbal material into which it is incorporated: at the lexical level it will grant preference to the words with a "magic content" (the skies, hillock, fountain, flower, yearning etc.) or to those with a

"mythical content" (high up, low down, deep etc.), the content meaning in this case a sort of force, a sort of irradiating energy; at the level of the images, it will rely mostly on "revealing" metaphors (which represent an axiological addition as compared to the "suggestive" ones, as they set off a "hidden side" of the object); finally, at the level of the verbal discourse, it will practise exorcizing forms or those of the mythical ritual. Why such a preference for the mythical and the magic? Because in this way, the poet's word sends the spoken speech back to its own origins, to the initial innocence and efficiency in which the original virtues of the first Word are divulged: the poet's song means essential waste which bestows upon the listener the quality of lasting beyond time: "Where there is a song, there is loss too / a godlike, sweet loss of self. / But he who listens acquires a living contour, / in the gradually complete harmonies / a temple, a menhir, or becomes a lily" (**"Where There is a Song"**).

Now the double acceptation of the term "to save" can be fully grasped, when Blaga asserts that the Poet is called upon "to save the words." On the one hand, the Poet has the role of saving them from their condition of instruments of individual determination, of saving them from the sin they have fallen into, at the same time as man; restoring them to their origin, he returns to them their essential virtue, re-building "a speech long since lost." But by restoring them to their origin, the Poet returns them to the first Silence, that is he "saves them" in the sense that he makes them come to a close, he makes them end in the silence in which they were once conceived: he compels them to find their end in their own beginning. That is why the Poet's words are "extinguished," they have an essential edge of Silence, the same as a plant uprooted from its natural soil preserves, clinging to its still unconsoled roots, a part of the soil that nourished it. "With extinguished words on my lips," says Blaga, "I have sung and still sing the great passing, the sleep of the world, the wax angels" (**"Biography"**). When in the poem **"The Rhymer,"** he says he only "translates" into the Romanian language a "song which his heart (. . .) is telling him sweetly murmured in its own tongue," this speech of the heart, does not mean the dumb speech of pure sentiments, but the speech of dumbness itself, of the first great Silence. This idea is, in fact, resumed more explicitly in **"The Poets."** "While speaking, they are dumb. Through the ages that are born and die, / with their song, they serve a speech long since lost. / Deep, through the nations that rise and set / they come and pass on the heart's road. / Through sound and word they differ, they compete. / They are alike through what they do not say. . . . "

Doomed to use words, and doomed to doom through words, the Poet is for Lucian Blaga the man who, par excellence, saves himself in his hypostasis as Creator and—due to his verbal rite—he saves the words, returning them to "the nameless land" of Silence, their native land. (pp. 81-3)

Ştefan A. Doinaş, "Silence and Words," in Romanian Review, *Vol. XXIV, No. 4, 1970, pp. 81-3.*

A. Paleologu   (essay date 1970)

[In the following essay, Paleologu discusses Blaga's dramas.]

Lucian Blaga's theatre is a modern theatre linked to the vast anti-naturalistic and poetic trend which from W. B. Yeats to F. Werfel and Paul Claudel, from J. M. Synge to Garcia Lorca, Ramón del Valle Inclán and Michel de Ghelderode and up to now, to Beckett and Eugen Ionescu, has dominated the great lines of the dramaturgy of this century, in accordance with the theories and action of a great number of innovators in the field of the drama from Gordon Craig to Antonin Artaud. But Lucian Blaga's theatre is, as revealed in his main works, a tragic theatre, evincing genuine tragic elements and embracing, as we shall see, all the constitutive elements of the genre. It brings about that deep regenerative commotion, characteristic of the tragedy, and which is the effect known by the name of *catharsis*. Thanks to I. L. Caragiale's comic genius and to the tragic genius of Blaga's dramaturgy, Romanian literature achieves in the highest possible degree this polarity always evinced by a culture reaching the classical stage.

Blaga's theatre has been considered to be a "Christian theatre." It is quite true that three of Blaga's plays (*The Troubling of the Waters, Master-Builder Manole* and *The Children's Crusade,* the pantomime *Resurrection* only resorting to a symbolical Christian image) deal with Christian themes, constituting that communal sacred background against which the tragical breaking off takes place. But Blaga's theatre cannot possibly be essentially Christian, first of all because we cannot think of a purely religious or irreligious tragedy. The tragic element arises when a confrontation takes place, a confrontation between the cosmic and sacred conceptions of a community on the one hand and the individual conscience, on the other hand, the latter evincing "profane" aspirations, convinced either of the imperative of a crude life or of a free spirit, creating its own values and hence a superior stage of the human being when, both revolt and order are forceful and their opposition is expressed in a dispute of supreme tension. Tragedy and its terms are ambiguous, there is antithesis between the evil and good in it; evil and good coexist in each of its terms, in variable proportions. The forces of evil are set going in a destructive way when the hero's passion or even *justice* go beyond certain limits, where the hero is sure to meet with calamity. And this calamity has an implacably necessary character, assumed by the hero. All this takes place in Blaga's theatre (and particularly in *Zamolxes,* the *Troubling of the Waters, Master-Builder Manole, The Children's Crusade* and *Avram Iancu*). In the second place, Blaga's theatre cannot be Christian, not only because of the fact that the writer's philosophical views are allegedly unchristian (which eventually led him to a noisy breaking off with the orthodox group of writers contributing to *Gindirea,* a review for which he had written for two decades, being one of its main founders), but because what is fundamental in Lucian Blaga's whole work, constituting its original kernel, are its very "heathen" elements, its heresies. Blaga considered the popular heresies an organic modality of the Romanian people of integrating the heathen reminiscences into orthodoxy and

of thus maintaining themselves outside ecumenicity, using those points of least resistance through which the framework of the "ecclesia," not completely overlapping the primitive, ancestral ethos, incorporates—preserving them—the latter's persistent elements. This phenomenon of "christianizing heathenism" is classical, even in the more vigilantly dogmatic field of catholicism. But we find it difficult to admit, as it was asserted, that Blaga's own stand would be at least one of affinity with orthodoxy, and that one might find a eulogy of the organic structure of orthodoxy in *The Troubling of the Waters* and *The Children's Crusade.* The writer showed a particular attention to the revealing character of heresies as symptoms of some pagan vestiges poetically convertible, but the spiritual level of his experiences was a "heathenism" similar to that of Goethe, constituting the background of a philosophical pantheism analogous (not identical) to Goethe's.

Lucian Blaga's predilection for the heathen substratum of the traditional forms of a communal life providing him with poetical material, his pronounced sense of ritualism and myth, associated with his keen intellectual acuity and dialectical aptitude, explain why he has so far been the only Romanian poet capable of a tragical creation. Eminescu alone, if he had had the time necessary to accomplish his project in the field of the theatre, would have perhaps succeeded in achieving it before. Lucian Blaga's philosophical work, a vast theoretical variant of his poetry, postulating those "abysmal categories" of the unconscious mind, considers existence in "the horizon of mystery" to be the very essence of the human being. A poet's philosophy! In fact, despite his power of systematically organizing ideas, despite his rich scientific information and theoretical ingenuity in handling it, Lucian Blaga didn't create philosophy in his "trilogies" proper. In any case he did not create a scientifically grounded philosophy. We consider it worth mentioning, however, that Blaga's training and début under the sign of German expressionism somehow represents his siding with the "left"; the very movement was later on to suffer, through some of its leaders, the rigours of the Nazi régime (Werfel was exiled, Kasimir Edschmid persecuted, etc). In Romania, Blaga proved to have taken, alongside the painters Marcel Iancu and M. H. Maxy, an advanced stand, also implying a protest against bourgeois civilization. In fact, expressionism as well as the philosophical conceptions which influenced Blaga (Klages, Spengler) arose from such a protest, but the horror they were inspired with by the reality of the capitalist world and man's alienation under the conditions of exploitation found expression in a refusal of reality in general and of technical civilization in particular. Hence the lack of confidence in the idea of progress and even disgust at the social as against the "cosmic" and the metaphysical, an evasive attitude, implying backward consequences. Our dialectical materialist stand makes us reject Lucian Blaga's philosophy, but it forbids us to deny the whole of it. It is not only a work of rare beauty in itself, offering a great number of most fruitful suggestions for the studies of art and ethnography, but also a monumental theoretical effort, marking a date in the history of Romanian thinking. Lucian Blaga's later adhesion to Romania's revolutionary transformation was undoubtedly the result of a long and deep debate of conscience. And when it took place it assumed the form of a kind of Dionysiac exaltation. Maybe the triumph of the socialist revolution was for him, besides an ideal of social justice which had never been alien to him, a triumph of the Faustian man, a vast and irresistible devilry of history, an assertion of the inherent, "chthonic" forces and of a "logos of nature."

This notion of the demoniacal brings us back to our theme. The demoniacal, the key of Blaga's whole vision and creation, plays an overwhelming part in his theatre, standing for everything that is frenzy of the feelings, exaggerated vitality but creative passion at the same time, in other words a form of that appetite of the absolute, characteristic of the human being, tragical by either its disastrous implications or by the impossiblity of being fulfilled. Anyhow, the pathos of the absolute or of the transcendental—in order to use Blaga's own terms—lends the dramatic edifice—and the artistic work taken as a whole as well—a humanistic accent, a Promethean dimension, in spite of its religious language.

Except for the play **Daria** (1925) and the witty biblical comedy **Noah's Ark** (1944), drawing on a folk legend in which the devil, taken in at last, appears under a Bogomilic name, all Blaga's plays have a "demoniacal" overtone, being supported by such characters as Zamolxes, in the dramatic poem bearing the same name, Miss Nona in **The Troubling of the Waters,** the father in **Ivanca,** masterbuilder Manole in the play with the same name, monk Teodul in **The Children's Crusade, Avram Iancu** and less so **Anton Pan** in the corresponding plays. **Zamolxes,** a play considered to be rather a mere lyrical poem, using dialogue, which should have been better incorporated in the volume of poems **The Prophet's Steps** (simultaneously published) has, in fact, a particular, theatrical value. **Zamolxes,** [subtitled] "*A Pagan Mystery*," is a perfect tragedy, in which the elementary liberty of an iconoclastic humanity, of a cosmic eagerness represented by Zamolxes, faces the order of the citadel and of the law, represented in its turn by Magus and all his pantheon. In order to arrest the progress of and make Zamolxes' teaching inoffensive, the Magus turns him into a god, erecting his statue in the pantheon. Zamolxes, the smasher of idols, breaks his own statue to pieces and is killed by the crowd of his own adorers, who do not recognize him. The inherent pantheism which is also dealt with in the theme "Christ—the earth" in **The Troubling of the Waters,** may be here noticed from the very beginning. Zamolxes' soliloquy starts by asserting "the thirst for the cosmos," for whatever belongs to germination and becoming. "So lonely was I that I had long forgotten to tell my own being from the surrounding things. You are but one man to one man: you and I. / Loneliness washes out these limits, / and getting mixed with their secret, you get lost into the rock / You trickle away into the waves and into the earth." At a certain moment, while in his cave Zamolxes has the successive vision of three men—"messengers of liberty"—an old man drinking hemlock, a young man with a crown of thorns on his head and a man fastened to a stake. Without bearing a name, we recognize in them Socrates, Jesus and Giordano Bruno; they are somehow Zamolxes' "demons" and they urge him to carry through his mission. The third makes a short apology as to how the thought must be

made to come true—*Zamolxes:* Who has put you to the Stake? / *The man put to the stake:* The ever watchful sober man / *Zamolxes:* I don't know him / *The man put to the stake:* The sober man is the one who prevents you / From exhausting a thought / When you are half-way he clasps you in his arms / and cries out to you: "Enough, you fool!" / For, see, a whole thought is a calamity. / But I, I ask you: Is it a calamity? So be it (Act 2, II). In "the ever watchful sober man" the spirit is accused of prudence and authority, of constant watchfulness. The first man had likewise urged him: "When a spring, you can't help running to the sea! / What are you awaiting, Zamolxes?" When Zamolxes is fêted, an orgiastic dance of bacchantes breaks loose, in the exultant yells of the vintagers who throw clusters of grapes all around them. Lucian Blaga changes Zamolxes, the uranic divinity of the Getae, whose religion is ascetic and abstinent as maintained by the Romanian historian Vasile Pârvan, into a human hero, with an earthly philosophy, who, when turning into a god, is adored with a "chthonic" and Dionysiac worship. This euhemerism is not only natural with a playwright for whom a tragical hero, doomed to die, cannot be a divinity, but it also expresses Blaga's preference for the earthly and demoniacal. His permanent tendency is to draw as much as possible what is cultural towards what is pagan and orgiastic, what is divinity to what is "chthonic." Unlike Pârvan, Blaga places Zamolxes within the field of "Thracian-Phrygian insanity" and he defends this frenzy in an article written under the sign of "revolt," published in the year when **Zamolxes** came out.

The closeness with the saps of the earth is also expressed by a crude, but at the same time refined sensuality pervading Lucian Blaga's whole dramatic (as well as lyrical) work, getting rounded off in such images as the following: "And in the river we catch sheat fishes, plump as the thighs of young maids" (**Zamolxes,** Act 1, II). This voluptuousness of bare legs, often sung by Blaga, seems to get the sense of a "chthonic" ritual, very much like magic. Nona, the "daughter of the earth" in **The Troubling of the Waters** also exclaims: "If you were a dusty Bible / I should leave my footprints on you" (scene II), or: "Tomorrow I shall walk barefoot / through the ashes of a burnt God." (Scene V) and the Parson says to Nona: "and all the same if green grass were here around us / I could dance before you, a mad, barefooted man" (scene II), or "I feel as if you passed your toes through my blood" (scene V).

The Troubling of the Waters, which was considered by G. Călinescu to be a mixture of "a Faustian poem and drama in the manner of Ibsen," brings upon the stage a Transylvanian orthodox parson, at the time of the Reformation, who is in love with Nona, a young Transylvanian Saxon girl who lures the young priests so as to make them join Lutheranism, that is the faith for which, unlike for orthodoxism or catholicism, God is everybody's and everywhere. Besides, the hero is also tempted by an old man who, just like Zamolxes, has the theory of the existence of Christ—the Earth. Though the old man, who has set the church on fire, is killed by the crowd, the priest becomes converted to the reformed faith, letting us however learn that he will be baptized with earth, that is in the spirit of the earthly religion, theoretically condemned. **The Trou-**

bling of the Waters is a Faustian poem indeed, but grafted on a South-Eastern ancestral background. The originality of this magnificent dramatic poem of a treble, interfering tragic character (Nona, the Old Man, and the Priest between the two as a "broken conscience") arises from this very dialectical fusion of two contrasting modalities of the demoniacal (in fact this is also the fusion of Blaga's German cultural moulding and his Danube-Carpathian hereditary cultural heritage.) Two years later, in 1925, Blaga gave a replica to *The Troubling of the Waters,* by writing a "dramatic play," against a modern urban background. We refer to *There Are Facts,* which later on got the title of *Ivanca,* according to the name of the main woman character. Obviously drawing on Freud's theories, much in fashion at the time, literary criticism has set it side by side with the play *Daria,* published in the same year, also inspired by Freudism. If *Daria* is, in our opinion, deprived of any value, *Ivanca* is unjustly set on the same level with it. The play is, maybe, artful, as the main hero appears as old and far from being true to life (a painter, Luca, haunted by the idea of the crime he is going to commit, is helped to get rid of it by a doctor who incites him to "action," to commit murder, a murder which has fortunately no consequences, as the bullet shot by Luca hits nothing else but the painter's self-pride). But the text is of a great literary value. The character of the Father, a priest unfrocked because of his disgraceful adventures, a kind of elderly satyr, cynical and intellectualized, has a demoniacal overtone, lending him a certain dramatic intensity. Ivanca, the red-haired girl, is likewise a minor replica to Nona. The shortcoming of the play does not lie in the fact that it has Freud's theory as a starting point, but in that it comes back to it, it reconstitutes Freud's theory in a close circuit, with a demonstrative clinical air. Young Luca [gets] rid of his obsessions and repressions through "action" (probably aware of this shortcoming Blaga tried to diminish the impression produced by changing the title of the play). In *Ivanca* the obscure instinctual force is only half transfigured, in what might have been dramatic fatality. But that "greenish light of subterraneous phosphorescences" as Tudor Vianu called it and which is characteristic of the play, is not devoid of genuine poesy.

As regards the character of human rebellion, the Promethean character of the vital frenzy in Blaga's dramaturgy, it was once remarked that all Blaga's Prometheuses are bound: to a woman, to earth, etc. The poet makes woman—mother or wife, lunatic or sweetheart—the embodiment of the principle of defending life against divinity. Any tragical action is after all such a rebellion against divinity. That is why the tragic element needs a means of expression which should be similar to that of the sacred element, and namely *ritualism.* The ritual gesture has the symbolical function of recreating the cosmic order; it is the repetition of an original, archetypical gesture and hence it stands for a suspension of time, of the lapse of time, for a return to "the time at the beginning of the time." The "ritual time" is an "anti-time," it is "always." The tragic element uses the ritual as a Promethean rape of one of the god's secrets. Hence that effect of *catharsis* of the tragic element. *Catharsis* is not only the final effect of tragedy; there is also an initial *catharsis,* that suspense,

that going out of everyday life and of diversity, that vacuum brought about and claimed by the apprehension of a supreme act. The most ritualized of Lucian Blaga's tragedies is *Master-Builder Manole.* Taking place in a "Romanian mythical period," as called by the author himself, it takes over one of the most impressive folk myths, changing but little the initial narrative scheme. Just like in the well-known Romanian legend, master-builder Manole builds up, seven times running, a monastery whose walls fall down as soon as it is erected. The interpretation of the data is personal, however. The explanation, suggested through the medium of abbot Bogumil, is that the edifice will fall to the ground as long as it is the exclusive enterprise of Satanail, that is of the devil, and as long as it is not in favour with the spirit, with divinity. A divine miracle is needed so that this condition may be fulfilled and the divine miracle, in its turn, can take place only through a sacrifice, that is the sacrifice of Mira, the master-builder's wife. The condition is fulfilled by Manole who builds in the woman. The denouement of the play also raises the problem of the likewise dramatic relations between the man and the artist, as after having made the sacrifice Manole has remorses and wants to pull down his work. But the crowds prevent him from doing it, which suggests the fact that the work of art has an existence independent of its creator. As one can see, the theme of the play is the consumption of a sacrifice, a "ritual of building," a theme that is well known and well located within specialized literature. In order that a building may resist, may last, it must integrate a soul, in the name of a conviction of Bogomilic origin that the demoniac and the spirit must become united. *The Children's Crusade* was considered to be either an apology of spirituality, directed to eternity, being wise and tolerant with the worldly life which is known to be but an illusion, or, on the contrary, an apology of the crusade spirit of catholicism, in any case a mystical Christian play. In fact, these two types of Christian spirituality are only set in contrast and confronted with an equal and objective justification. Everybody is right: both abbot Ghenadie and monk Teodul and the Princess, as sovereign and as mother. The teacher, the image of a humanistic scholar, gets the adhesion of our minds and of course that of the author. But the characters enjoying his true and obscure sympathy are two: Teodul, not as a Christian clergyman and perhaps a saint, but as a demoniacal being, of a mysterious and ambiguous force (we don't know if he is an emissary of good or evil, if he is inspired by the Holy Spirit or by Satan, and the author himself doesn't seem to be quite sure of it) and Ioana, the lunatic, the spirit of the woods, the wild mother of a wolf cub, the one who kills Teodul. Beyond the opposition between catholicism and orthodoxism, a mere ineffectual antithesis, these two demoniacal creatures express the deep conflict of the drama in which the Princess is involved. Crazy Ioana is the former's "Doppelgängerin" reduced to the elementary, again "chthonic" principle of maternal instinct. These two demoniacal creatures are the real protagonists of the drama. The symbolical background of the drama is created by the myth of the "child" and of the "orphan" representing original purity and the principle of the mythical hero or divinity (Dionysos, Moses, Jesus, etc.). The child and particularly the orphan child has the symbolic, mythical function of "the beginning, of the primordiality on which a new life is founded." The same, significant function is that of the "not yet born" young man, prodigious appearance, the result of an "ontological mutation" in man from a legendary bird: Avram Iancu, the leader of the Romanians in Transylvania during the 1848 revolution. The ambiguity of this genesis in **Avram Iancu,** creating—in the people's consciousness—such a being from a man with a legal status, lends the hero invested with the demon of revolt and struggle, a historic and even "transhistoric" mission.

Blaga's theatre cannot be acted in a "naturalist" way, with the theatrical routine of the bourgeois alcove dramas; neither can it be acted in a "heroic" spectacular way. There are some directives as to how this theatre should be staged in two articles written by Blaga himself: "We are sure that children would accept a simplified, abstract, symbolical theatre even sooner than grown-up people, who are too accustomed to the laziness of their imagination. Such a theatre is quite natural for children, a revolution for grown-up people." A few lines above: "Children will always live in Elizabethan times, so to say, and they would perfectly understand Shakespeare's theatre, whose scenery is often reduced to mere indications." In the other article:

> It goes without saying that the new theatre also requires a new staging. And a new acting. Lines reduced, just like the soul, to the essential. It requires a style and a framework which should support the inner drama, through its successive variations. The acting no longer imitates the people in the street. It interprets, becoming more musical than it is natural or more geometrical than it is natural, according to circumstances and spiritual content.

In a theatre of this kind a most important and difficult problem is that of how to utter the words. The word acquires an importance and a share exceeding the mere function of conveyance, and a value of incantation which does not mean, of course, that the literal meaning may be altered or ignored. In a theatre of this kind both the voice and the body, as well as the whole material on the stage, must be expressive, graphical. The rhythm of gesticulation and the verb must have a ceremonial gravity. The recitation of such a poetic text, written in verses like those of Claudel, requires an extreme practice of breathing, of a breath capable of what Antonin Artaud called "an affective athletics." The same Artaud underlined the extreme importance of breath, which, he said, was in inverse ratio with outward acting: "the more temperate and introspective the acting, the wider and the denser the breath will be, as well as more substantial and overloaded with reflexes." This is also the case of Lucian Blaga's theatre. (pp. 83-7)

> *A. Paleologu, "Symbols on the Stage," in* Romanian Review, *Vol. XXIV, No. 4, 1970, pp. 83-7.*

Const. Ciopraga   (essay date 1975)

[*In the following excerpt, Ciopraga examines the dominant themes of Blaga's poetry.*]

Through the insistence with which he dwells upon his fundamental questions relating to *mystery, transience, eros* and the rest, Blaga is a creator of the problematic kind, with moments of tension and of relaxation, steeped in contemporary philosophy and seduced by age-old mythical resonances, by *the forest of symbols.* Both modern and archaic (not old-fashioned) in expression, a seeker of analogies between self and cosmos, apologist of white light yet savoring moonlike penumbras, the effigy of the writer is captivating and imposes respect. One cannot penetrate the inmost nature of this poet, one of the greatest in Romanian literature, without a feeling of affective participation, albeit theoretically one may not agree with his philosophy. What holds one's interest is the picture of a complex spirit. In the case of other writers, contact with a few representative works can be amply instructive. Blaga has to be known *in toto,* in his monumental aspects and in his disconcerting, eyebrow-raising ramblings. Structurally, he is a romantic of a dual nature, at the beginning of a Dionysiac frenzy ("Do you not feel my madness when you hear / life murmuring within me? . . . Do you not feel my radiance?"), touched at the same time by metaphysical sadness. Over the years, the graph of vital frenzy drops. Sadness, in ebb-and-flow rhythms, is maintained in varied nuances. Eminescu's philosophical ideas were usually implied in his work, poetical or prose (his prose-writings are in a way *demonstrations,* as with Sartre and Camus). Blaga rises to a personal philosophical system in its own right, with learned weaponry (**The Trilogy of Knowledge, The Trilogy of Culture, The Trilogy of Values**), anti-intellectualist and agnostic in attitude, open to psycho-spiritual revelations. That skepticism, lack of faith in the possibilities of reason (among other interests, Bergsonian irrationalism) should invade his poetry and drama, is obvious—the one sphere (philosophy) incapable of separation from the other (creation). Blaga's poetry is essentially a sequence of reachings-out towards the transcendent, a mode of expansion in the miraculous grandeur of the cosmos, and of inner exile, bespeaking a dilemmatical personality. From **Poems of Light** in 1919, followed by **The Prophet's Footsteps, In the Great Passage, In Praise of Sleep, In the Courtyard of Yearning** and **Unsuspected Steps,** down to the posthumous publications of 1962, there come unceasingly into his system of spiritual experiences advances and withdrawals, presumption and resignation, a self-centred Titanism and indulgence in a particular kind of deliberate anonymity. His efforts to reconcile eternity with transience proving vain, sundry discontinuities are betrayed in his outlook. It is rather the thin film of a fatalism under which perhaps the human condition itself is manifested.

Does the rejection of contemporary intellectualism on the one hand, and the eulogy of the village (an ideal village, non-historical) on the other, have any touching-point with the clamorous turn-of-the-century dispute between *urbanitas* and *rusticitas*? In Blaga's "mythologies" we can see, in a special way, the effect of the age-long forces of accumulation, forces which to assert themselves in the most striking possible manner require an *écart*, a distancing from the present. The legendary and the mythical inevitably come into opposition with exact history, because the latter sterilizes, reduces, cools the flight of imagination. As the exponent of a nation with Daco-Thracian antecedents lost in the mist of antiquity (we should not forget, among the writer's dramas, a "Zamolxis," "pagan myth"), a Blaga, laden with mythology, is not an isolated case. On the contrary, he stands—with peculiarities of his own—alongside Eminescu and Sadoveanu. For any great creation implies a basic mythology, that is, an instrument for transfiguration. Long ago it was remarked that the Greeks did not transpose reality into art, they introduced it through the intermediary of fiction into myths. We are aware that the modern novel is likewise, despite diverse formulas, the expression of personal *mythologies,* different from writer to writer. In the case of the most realistic of Romanian novelists of a few decades ago, Rebreanu, a critic (E. Lovinescu) observed that the protagonist in *Ion* "transcends reality", being conceived "larger than life, a typical expression of what Nietzsche called 'will power' the will of the instinct to dominate, and consequently a symbolical creation" (*The History of Modern Romanian Civilisation,* II). Sadoveanu's protagonist in *The Hatchet* is also a symbolic figure, connected affectively with the store of ancestral memories. The paradox of Blaga, a spirit consumed with a longing for certainty, is his parallel involvement in the imprecisions of mystery, in a misty zone of the subconscious, in a sleeping-time of thought. The word no longer denotes precisely: delights in the unclear and the enigmatic. **"The Holy Bird"** (a poem inspired by a sculpture by Brâncusi), "listening to wordless revelations guessing at the mysteries in the depths" symbolizes a particular form of knowing. Something unreal, inexplicable, accompanies the flight of this consciousness—bird. Because knowledge can do irreparable harm, the appeal to a revelation through *non-speech,* which will not radically distort the mystery, intervenes:

> Rise up, endlessly
> but never disclose to us what you see . . .

Always leaving one eye open to the mirage, with Blaga *show yourself* and *hide yourself* express the oscillation between a *daemonium meridiani* and the uncertainties of *the noon of sleep.* The workings of consciousness accordingly permanently, tragically, manifest the drama of the divided self.

The fundamental reason for existential dissatisfaction remains the dualism between the self and the world. The *non-self* proves cramped for the *self* constructed on a different scale. The poet has a feeling of cosmic unity, but only up to a point, beyond which follows crisis. Nostalgia for paradise lost, metaphysical longing for the unseen and unheard, the ritual game of ascending *unsuspected steps* towards the sublime, function within a spiritual decor of tension and agitation, under the fatidical sign of unfulfillment. After a brief devastating upsurge, after high-temperature combustions, with Blaga anxiety arises in an atmosphere of "disintegration" (one poem bears the title **"Fraying paradise"**), with vast horizons of "ashes". Eminescu's unrest concerning existence was finally overcome to a certain extent in detached contemplation, in a healing *beyond good and evil;* the *Titan* in Eminescu's poetic myth, feverish, irreconcilable, possessed by fabulous aspirations, finally turns into a figure with an *Olympian* mask, at any rate more serene than not. Blaga, a solitary,

hurls himself into the light or dares the darkness: initially, he tries to be a Titan himself. Presumptuous, he measures himself against the gods and rejects them through the role of the *demon* that gives him wings. Troubled, obsessed, he turns to the mountain, the place where one can reach for the absolute. The interval of apparent calm in **"Pax magna"** makes only more pregnant the contrast with his restless mask:

> Maybe, after their eternal war,
> God and Satan thought it wiser to clasp hands
> that each might thus be greater . . . So they've
> made peace
> in me; together they have dripped into my soul
> faith and love, doubts and lies.

What is expressionistic in Blaga is equally related to the paroxysmal practices of the romantics; through the uninterrupted questioning, through the obsessive monologue, through the striving to see miracles, he wants to attain to the very essence of things. And this essence seems, after long distillation, to be sometimes found in the primary zones, *ab originem,* or in the simple, elementary forms of contemporary life. By "baptism in the earth", that is, by a return to primordial meanings, to Goethe's stratum of *names,* revelation occurs not by way of complexity, but of simplicity. The answer [that] such a baptism offers does not amount to a clarification, but rather to an act of resignation. The age-old gesticulating alluded to in another poem ("I understand the sin that weighs upon my house") advances in opposition to the tortures of consciousness the same lesson of integration into the elementary:

> Oh, why did I interpret the weather and the stars
> otherwise than the old woman who wets her
> hemp in the pool?
> Why did I wish for another smile than the stone-
> mason's
> who scatters sparks at the roadside?

But the super-individualized poetic self, which does not accept the common measure, reappears. Facing the universe, Eminescu declaims Olympian monologues, detached, at a distance of thousands of centuries: "The moon pours her voluptuous glowing light over everything . . . ". The word that characterizes Eminescu, as he contemplates the spaces, is *forever,* a forever as a philosophical equivalent of eternity. Blaga, imbued with the new *mal du siècle* that is modern anxiety, is more involved in the present, a more *committed* figure. The defining word for him, in his role of explorer of the universe, is yearning. Eminescu's Olympianism was the expression of a painful victory, by rising from the terrestrial to the astral. With Blaga, a relative "Apollinization" takes place towards the end of his life. Apart from this, he "writhes about", listening to subconscious voices of the original self, dramatizing, breaking out into exclamations.

The verbal signs with which the poet operates at the beginning (in ***Poems of Light***) are "boundlessness", "the too serene blue", "the clear eaves of eternity", "the unknown seas", "the high", "the incandescent" or fire. Cosmic perspectives, common to the romantics but also to Romanian folk-poetry, alternate in ***Footsteps of the Prophet*** with involvement in an intimate, personal Nature, with mythical undertones. An astral Blaga, consumed with aspiration to the transcendent, coexists with another, a "telluric" Blaga, imbued with a feeling for matter, stirred by the spectacle of immediate Nature. Spiritual moments of minimum and maximum succeed one another in perpetual undulation: thus, after depression and decline, an image of summer crops (**"In the Wheatfield"**) triggers off reserves of vitality. In the yellow wheatfield a young woman "gathers with her gaze the sky's sheaves of blue / and sings". The observer among the poppies, "only *body*, only *clay*", feels himself being reborn, spiritualized through a naturistic influx: "She sings / and I listen / On her warm lips my soul is born". The tumult of reiterated questions has calmed. Time itself slumbers, symbolically, amongst the poppies: "A cricket chirps in his ear" (**"Summer"**). Unstable armistice, exposed to mutations. The poet's ultrasensitive hearing is on the alert for voices, mysteries bound up with a *mundus subterraneus,* the heartbeats of the earth, signs coming from labyrinthine depths:

> Was the earth to tell me
> nothing? All this mercilessly broad
> and murderously dumb earth,
> nothing?

Putting an ear to the ground to "hear better" should be understood as a possibility of reconciling with the terrestrial, beginning with the decyphering of an alphabet of mystery. But matter too undergoes inexorable erosion, while the mythological Pan, "blind and old" symbol of unconscious physiological life, lives out an excruciating agony. In Blaga's system of analogies, the demigod represents inevitable degradation, cause of sorrow and universal apprehension. The panic is not inescapable, however, because in the eternal circuit death and germination tend towards equilibrium "The dew-drops are big and warm", says Pan, "the little horns crop up, the buds are full". All the kingdoms of nature are invoked in a mythological-magical vision, so that between Nature and *Pannism* there is interference, even confusion. Sun, earth, stones, snakes, grapes ("breasts of milk"), grass and the rest make up an infinity of *twins.* As one of the cogenerate elements, alloy of earth and heaven, the poet picks up "the thoughts of a dead man" who has become a tree ("some tree grown out of myself ?"), or talks to the earth, seen as a fulcrum for his great escapes into the astral. The expressionistic outcry in **"I want to play"** ("Earth, give me wings: / an arrow I would be, to cleave / the boundlessness") reappears in a poem in *The Prophet's Footsteps.* For the "formidable soul" that differentiates him from the rest of the universe, the "passing body" is too confined, and thus his fascination for the grandiose:

> Give me a body
> you mountains,
> you oceans
> give me another body to pour my madness in
> totally!
> Big earth, be my trunk,
> be the chest for this tremendous heart
> be shelter of the storms that crush me,
> be the amphora for my stubborn ego.
>   (**"Give me a body you mountains"**)

Losing point in the face of death, stubbornness dons a sar-castic mask, preserving a final vanity. Terrorized by Fate's immanence, the Greek tragedians burst forth in lofty laments, purged of individual significance, concerned with man's fate in general. Sorrows, says Blaga in a gnomic-type formulation, "are deep only when they laugh". Which is a way of defying with dignity the absurdity of *passing.* Only "passing animals" look "without fear", with "quiet eyes", at their shadows projected in the waters, while the law of dying arches mythically, menacingly, "over a long, long story". Revived by the existentialists a few decades ago (**"The Myth of Sisyphus"** dates from 1943), the absurd appears to them as the refusal of existence to conform to human reason. Confronted with the *absurd walls*—obstacles which Blaga too takes into consideration, in another way—the answer on the plane of consciousness, proposed by Camus, is a revolt, a creative revolt, which alone can attenuate the feeling of bitterness. Blaga perceives the contradictions between eternity and transience with bitterness rather than revolt: "So let bitterness laugh in me today" (**"Follow me, comrades"**). There is no hint of outright pessimism, in the current connotation of the term. Beginning with *In the Great Passage,* the drama of ideas feeds the sorrow felt by the lucid spirit, split between totality and fragment. Neutralization of anxiety is not possible for man, whose very *blood* carries in it, fatal datum, the seed of death. The questions bearing upon *the great passage* oscillate unceasingly between depths and heights, under the sign of Heraclites' *flowing.* "Which way should one go?"; "Whom should I worship?"; "Who calls me, who drives me away?" . . . *Above* and *below,* comparable in their philosophic, existential meaning with Camus' *absurd walls,* give rise to stereotyped monologues, as in **"Heraclitus by the Lake"** or in **"A Swan's Song Came from the Sky."** In the first of the two, we read:

> Any lifting of the hand
> Is nothing but another doubt.
> Pain requests
> the low mystery of the dust.

But these lines could quite simply be transferred into the second monologue, whose argument is as follows:

> Futile you look for something to believe in.
> The dust is full with the hum of mysteries,
> but it is too close to the heels
> and too far from the brow . . .

Because the motion of the heavenly bodies continues unperturbed, anxiety swells, becoming tyrannic. Is there any antidote to this feeling of ephemeralness, that "has poisoned man's wells?" Blaga advances no solutions. This is not the role of poetry. Through the medium of the poetic myth, Blaga puts forward experiences. One method of defence, in *Poems of Light,* was the erotic; a method of *forgetting,* in fact: first biological fusion, tension, burning, then the melting together of the ashes with the earth. Another method, in a monologue from *In the Great Passage,* might be the "shaking free" of oneself, absence in consciousness, akin to the state of unspeaking animals: "All the herds of the earth have holy aureoles / above their heads" (**"I Understand the Sin . . . "**). The God of childhood having been "lost forever / in the dust, in fire, in the air and on the waters", in other words, in the four elements, an archaic pantheism takes his place. Instead of contestation and opposition, the individual "poring over the questions of the world" might be able to accept the transcendental censure represented by The Great Blind Man, a symbolic figure that lays stumbling-blocks in man's condition. One might tell the tyrannical Blind Man that "the movement of the suns is right . . . ", but nearness to these suns does not assure revelation. Another possibility might be silence, fusion with Earth, the "baptism in the earth" referred to above. . . . All these are hypotheses, working variants. Nearer certainty is the idea in **"The Soul of the Village,"** a poem-manifesto exalting the place where "eternity was born" and where the "thirst for salvation is healed" through attunement to universal rhythms. It is of course an abstract village, an illusion-village, symbolization of elementariness and tranquility. But no escapade can halt the tumble towards death.

The dramatism of the poet of *In the Great Passage* is impressive through pathetic tension, through the plurality of its searchings, which in their contradictory succession display an explosive awareness, doubled by an enormous capacity for metaphorical representation. If the ostentatious vitalism of *Poems of Light* ("My heart is not in my head, / nor have I brains in my heart / I am drunk with the world, heathen that I am.") becomes moderated with age, *the heart,* the poet's sensibility, gives the imagination ever greater weight, causing poetical discourse to hold sway over cold *argument.* The world-weariness in **"Signs,"** at the extreme limit, fails through a total negation, in which industrial civilization is seen as a catastrophe. The remedy remains in the undefiled realms of the state of nature; the innocence of wild creatures incorporated in Nature has the last word: "From the distant wilderness with huge stars / only deer will venture into the towns, / to graze the scant grass of the ashes". Here it can be seen that *passing* is not a personal problem. After so many tormenting, nightmarish visions, as of some Georg Trakl, ending in a sensation of nothingness, a tense profile, **"The Worker"** in his blue leather apron, switches the perspectives for a moment. Sure of himself, he demonstrates that "only things born of man's powers are beautiful". The joy of action, breathing light, represents it would seem, the sole efficient riposte to nothingness, to *passage* in general. The conclusion appears to be that the miracle of salvation resides in man himself.

An attitude of short duration. A tone of acute sadness in the face of unsolved mystery marks the strange world of *In Praise of Sleep.* The romantics cultivated sleeptherapy, Hölderlin, Novalis, Eminescu preferring the dream-state to waking. Does Blaga believe in sleeptherapy or in glowing dream-worlds? To him, sleep is tormented by anxieties and forebodings, peopled by strange mythical apparitions: "Under the gates the creatures of sleep / come in—red dogs and cares" (**"Old Town"**). Whispered words have, as in **"Biography,"** fearful, occult reverberations. With "muted" words, the poet has sung and still sings of "the great passage, the sleep of the world", "of wax angels" thus "tempting himself" into thinking that "the world is a song". Orphism, pure song, relieved of contingencies, is not, however, the style characteristic of Blaga, who, between sleep and waking, peregrinates: "now guilty on the roofs of hell, / now sinless on

the lily-mountain". A term with divers connotations for Blaga, sleep means a way of escape, postponement, suspension in the void, self-deception, a tempo that overturns logic, but also a prefiguration of death. In the "sleep of the world", "mysteries of my ancestors" file past, or "tales of long-forgotten blood" are elucidated. Unable to project himself on a fantastic voyage into the future, at the level of the subconscious man practices an *éternel retour,* wordlessly reconstructs his origins: "In sleep my blood wave-like draws back from me into my parents". . . . (pp. 37-48)

A sort of *captatio* is exercised upon the reader of Blaga's poems, an arcane initiatory ritual; the currency of words, their connotations, semantic mutations are amplified, combine unexpectedly, giving substance to symbolic metaphors. Can the poet's myths be related to archaic prototypes, as is the case with the French classics, for instance? Blaga proceeds in another manner, placing himself, autonomous, in a limitless mythical time. In the absence of a "great uniting myth", he quenches his thirst "fragmentarily", with "splinters" of myths, rather as Yeats (whom he translated) does. The Irishman was enthralled from an early age by the Celtic myths, which inclined him towards a world of "fables, figures and feelings" that preserves a Celtic imprint. "I searched for a symbolical language (says Yeats in his *Essays*), which would pierce the boundaries of the past, being associated with familiar denotations and widely known ideals".

To the accusation that his poetry "is mythical, metaphysical", Blaga admits not only frequent mythical, but "even theological" themes: free, though, as with Yeats, of the rigours of dogma. He is preoccupied not so much with *returning* within the perimeter of stock symbols, some of them generalized over a wide area in the Balkans, as with a personal *analogical stylization,* to the extent to which a modern writer can revitalize the functions of symbolic metaphor. He consequently invents in the *spirit,* not the *letter* of his collective folk models. He employs mythical elements "in the freest manner, as a means of poetic expression". And along the same line of thought: "My motifs are not treated dogmatically. I always use them in a creative way: I freely modify and amplify them as the need arises. I think up mythical motifs at every step, because without a mythical thinking, fortunately or otherwise, no poem can come into being". The mythical vision consists essentially in transfiguration, progressive reincarnation, naturally in support of knowing. Three broad categories of symbolic metaphors should be noted. The earlier volumes abound in symbols denoting the elements: earth (mountain, stalactite, stone), water (sea, wells, springs), fire (and as a corollary, ashes), air (wind, wafted aromas). After *In the Great Passage,* these become less frequent or pass into the shadows, while symbols of a zoomorphic type multiply, representations based upon folkmythology: "prophet-doves", "the firebird", "flaming birds", "sick birds", "grey owls", "apocalyptic cockerels", vultures, nightingales, swans, but also fawns, stags, "the fabled boar", "yellow horses", enigmatic serpents, gigantic butterflies. The later years are characterized by vegetable-symbols, starting with "the wondrous seed", productive of fruits, ore tokening the ears of grain, wine "crowned with fragrance", trees, woods. Greek and Nordic mythical reminiscences combine with modern landscapes, likewise possessed of a mythical aura:

> The strength of wing descends from air
> into a reedy happiness.
>
> And the water's vegetation
> bursts into emerald.
> The seed of the divine swan
> sings everywhere in the evening,
> sings in the bodies of Karins,
> Marys, Floras, Margarets.
>
> ("April")

In Blaga's thinking, as well as in his poetry, *to look at* and *to see* are actions with different connotations. A philosopher with systematic studies, doctor at the University of Vienna, the author of *The Unsuspected Steps* hopes to penetrate the complex *ordo rerum* by an inner illumination, by revelation. His system of symbolic metaphors is only apparently that of a visual person.

Impressionism reduced man to his retina. Van Gogh changed all that by making things partake of his inner life. He ran from impression rendered from the outside, seeking instead the expression charged with the inner soul.

—*Lucian Blaga*

What follows from this? Mystery has to be explored, pierced, made palpable through a multiple approach, felt in its totality. Projected upon the screen of a consciousness in darkness (the typical "I wait for my dusk" . . .), certainty is awaited not only in the form of *mystical sight,* but as a penetration, to things and into phenomena, in the Truth that (as an aphorism from **"Stones for my Temple"** puts it) "our entire self creates, with its passions and its creative bursts". The world which "syllogistic deduction mediates" for us is situated at a lower level than the other, subjectivized one, that the senses perceive:

> My eyes washed by the starred dome,
> I know that I too carry
> in my soul, many many stars
> and milky ways,
> wonders of darkness.
> But I can't see them,
> there's too much sun in me,
> that's why I can't see them.

Here the sun doubtlessly symbolizes lucid, noon-day awareness. But the technique of mythical revelation involves the eyes being "turned" inwards, not to see precisely, but to encourage immersion into the unfathomable depths:

> I wait for my day to set,
> for my horizon to close its eyelids,
> I wait for my dusk, my night and pain,

> the darkening of my sky
> so the stars in me might rise,
> my stars
> which I have not
> yet seen.

Heavenly bodies, mountains, waters, subterranean wells hide multiple, sorrowful mysteries; mystery obsesses the animals too, but in another manner. A "dragon with eyes turned towards the Pole Star" (thus outwards) "dreams of blue milk filched from sheepfolds". The poet's obstacles are on the inside, so not *visible* mountains and stars, inscribed upon maps, interest him:

> But the mountains—where are they? The mountains
> I am to move with faith out of my way?
> I can't see them,
> I want them, I shout for them, and—they are not!

Mountains of this sort are related in their symbolic significance to Ion Barbu's abstract "mountains in the spirit".

Over and over again the inadequacy of speech is emphasized: no one answers the *shout* adressed to the mountain. Between *signs* and *significations* a split has occurred, which for a seeker of the absolute acquires tragic dimensions: "Sometimes I say things that do not encompass me, / sometimes I love things that do not respond". Symbols, signs, metaphors sometimes have the virtue of a *cypher* for opening mysteries, at other times translate the tension, the curse of not knowing. A wanderer across waters, like some Biblical character, the poet sends out his *pigeons* (symbols of the alert mind) "to try the grasses of the sky", but the way through to the absolute is inaccessible. So long as the capacity to transcend is limited, it would seem that installation alongside *earth* and *water* might guarantee a minimum of inner calm, if not adjustment to the ashen *story* of existence. But here too, terrible mysteries interpenetrate one another, in all manner of ways, like *runes,* indecypherable signs of an overall mystery that is the cosmic mystery. If "the soul does not orient itself to nature, but nature to the soul" (a thesis from **"The Philosophy of Style"**), it follows that no matter where he might be, man carries with him the burden of inexorable damnation, because mystery is in the first place a drama of consciousness. If the woods teem with owls and wild beasts, if in the mountains "the shepherd heaps earth over his lambs killed by the powers of the forest," and "bells or maybe coffins—sing under the grass in thousands," this expresses an exacerbated unease, transmitted from man to nature. For Blaga a symbolism of light alternates with a symbolism of darkness. Since the instrument for establishing correlations is lacking the world seems one huge cryptograph, as Schopenhauer imagined it, an entity founded upon invisible relations between its parts: "Like runes, for centuries forgotten, / all things bear a signature". (pp. 49-54)

A few general considerations, for an overall picture. The trajectory of Blaga's poetry displays to a large extent *undulation,* outpouring into the world and introspection, see-sawing between the cosmic and the individual as a reaching-out towards the high and to self-contemplation. Poetry as a process of feverish *searching,* not as a *result* or a *game*. An astonishing imaginative vocation encourages staring at the sun and the terror of degradation in darkness, from which results the transition from exultancy ("the world is a song") to falling into ashes ("Come, end, lay ashes over everything . . ."). Highly personal in his vision and his timbre, the author of **Unsuspected Steps** does not stand alone. He approaches Eminescu less by virtue of the dream-state (Eminescu's dreaming tends towards glamour) as by *yearning,* hunger for the absolute, and more than this by a propensity for myth, each with his own personal peculiarities. He approaches his contemporary Ion Barbu, partisan of "the cleanliness of the crystallographic body" that aspires to "dawns of ice", and of the transcendent, in his concentrated manner of expression. But Barbu's tension terminates in the glacial. Blaga's tension is feverish, a trait that explains his series of questions and his fire-hot imagery. The theoretician of **"The Mioritic Space,"** one of the great poets of mankind, could not be placed as an artist within a context of irremediable tragedy. The signs of "Apollinization" towards the end of his life permit his inclusion, after detours, in the national stylistic matrix. Blaga's poetic creation likewise constitutes as a body an exceptional document of the human condition in general. (pp. 57-8)

> *Const. Ciopraga, in a preface to* Poems of Light *by Lucian Blaga,* Bucuresti: Minerva, 1975, pp. 37-58.

Keith Hitchins   (essay date 1978)

[*In the following excerpt, Hitchins examines Blaga's writings on Rumanian culture and national identity in* Trilogia culturii.]

From the beginning of his career, Blaga was involved in the historical controversy over the ethnic makeup of the Romanian people. He set himself against the dominant Latinist view by tracing the origins of Romanian ethnic evolution to the Thracians, who inhabited Dacia before the Roman conquest. This biological absolute appealed to his metaphysical bent of mind, while as a poet he was attracted to the overflowing vitality and cosmic vision of the Thracian world, which he portrayed with force and originality in his "pagan drama" **Zamolxe** (1921). Blaga argued that the Romanians had more than the rationality and balance of the Latins; they possessed a vital Slav/Thracian heritage, which from time to time erupted like a "violent storm from the metaphysical depths of the Romanian soul," upsetting the Latin sense of symmetry and harmony—a storm he characterized as the "revolt of our non-Latin sources." As he always did in matters of ethnicity, Blaga maintained a sense of proportion and shunned artificial restraints on creativity. Thus Thracianism never imposed itself upon his work, and when an aggressive, narrow "Thracomania" gained momentum in the late 1920's and 1930's, he disassociated himself from it.

Blaga's concept of style is fundamental to his understanding of autochthonism. He set forth his concept in a more or less definitive form in **"Orizont si stil"** [**"Horizon and Style"**]. By "style" he meant the sum total of categories that differentiated historical periods, works of art, and ethnic communities from one another. He thought the sources of style were in the unconscious categories of the mind, which he proposed as the primordial determinants of the originality of cultures. The unconscious, moreover, provides the key to Blaga's philosophy of culture, for in his view style grew out of the collective ethnic psychology. Unlike Freud and the psychoanalytic school, Blaga did not regard the unconscious as a "chaos," as merely the source of animal instincts, but endowed it with a host of primary and secondary categories, which, grouped together, he called the "stylistic matrix." He attributed to the unconscious such primary categories as spatial and temporal "horizons," an axiological "accent," "attitudes" of advance or withdrawal, and "aspirations" to form and order, and such secondary categories as preferences for movement or calm, for sobriety or the picturesque, and for the massive or the delicate. The unconscious, then, was the zone of true creative impulses. Although Blaga did not deny the contribution of human reason and will, he insisted that the fundamental stylistic direction was determined by forces beyond the control of the conscious. Despite his criticism of Freud, his debt to psychoanalysis is evident, and it helps to explain why he placed little confidence in rationalism and why "mystery" (or the unknown) became the "supreme angle of vision" from which he viewed the world. He also owed much to the theories of Jung about the collective unconscious, for the stylistic matrix represented the synthesis of thousands of years in the life of the group—a complex fusion of all that was characteristic of the collectivity and of the individuals who composed it. Consequently, the stylistic matrix was continually evolving as new elements were slowly incorporated; in this sense it was a product of history, and its evolution helped to explain the variations in styles from region to region and from period to period. In elaborating his theory of style, Blaga attempted to establish a new foundation for traditionalism in the obscure, archaic, and biological depths of the race.

Blaga's theory of style was greatly influenced by the German exponents of the morphology of culture—notably Leo Frobenius (1873-1938), an ethnologist and authority on prehistoric art, and Spengler. An early admirer of the *Decline of the West,* Blaga described Spengler as a "Copernicus of history" because of his substitution of morphology for chronology in the treatment of human development and his search for the "archetypal phenomena" behind historical facts; he placed Spengler alongside Kant and Einstein as revolutionizers of thought. Blaga borrowed Spengler's technique of the comparative study of civilizations and the antinomy between culture and civilization, but he found Spengler's overall approach essentially deficient. It reduced the phenomena of culture to form, despite the fact that they encompassed many other elements; it was limited to description while the phenomena of culture required explanation; and it made the intuition of space the determining factor of style, treating it as a creative act of the conscious sensibility rather than a product of the unconscious categories as Blaga had proposed.

Blaga attempted to apply his theories on style in **"Spaţiul mioritic,"** the most important philosophical study of Romanian traditionalism in the interwar period. By "mioritic space" Blaga was referring to the *plai,* the ridge or slope of a hill usually covered with meadows, of Romanian folk ballads—especially "Miorita" ["The Little Ewe"]. To Blaga the *plai* represented more: it was the spatial horizon specific to Romanian culture, the "infinitely undulating horizon" of hill and valley which formed the "spiritual substratum of the anonymous creations of Romanian popular culture." From this unconscious horizon of the stylistic matrix, Blaga derived the "massive" preference of Romanian popular poets for the alternation of accented and unaccented syllables and for the unique arrangement of Romanian peasant houses, which were separated from one another by green spaces—the "unaccented syllables between the houses." He pointed out that the Saxons of Transylvania, who had lived side-by-side with the Romanians for seven centuries, built their homes quite differently, in a fashion corresponding to the German unconscious spatial horizon. Blaga emphasized that the landscape did not determine the psychic state of the individual or of the ethnic collectivity. The relationship between psyche and space was more profound and went back to a much earlier era. The Romanian, for example, had the sense of dwelling in the mioritic space even though he might be living on the great Bărăgan plain, while the Saxon, who inhabited the same landscape as the Romanian, was dominated by the spirit of "Gothic space" (*spaţiul gotic*), inherited from remote ancestors in Germany.

In his search for the coordinates of the Romanian cultural style Blaga focused on the rural world, where he thought the constituent elements of Romanian spirituality lay. . . . [To Orthodoxy] he accorded an "organic" place in the national psyche. However, Blaga was not interested in religious dogma; by Orthodoxy he meant an ethnic-geographical area separate from Roman Catholic and Protestant Europe. Moreover, he believed the elements that distinguished the three branches of Christianity came from early "spiritual infiltrations" of the "local genius" into the universal Christian doctrine as it spread over various lands. These infiltrations endowed Roman Catholicism with the categories of "authority" (a "will to power," "a subtle juridical spirit"), Protestantism with those of "liberty" ("independence of judgment," "conceptualization of problems," "duty"), and Orthodoxy with those of the "organic" ("life," "the earth," "nature"). These differences were, then, the results of style rather than doctrine—a point Blaga illustrated with examples of how each religion regarded the church, the nation, and culture. Catholicism conceived of the church as a universal state, Protestantism as a community which embodied liberty, and Orthodoxy as an organism in which each member was responsible for the deeds of others. Toward the nation, Catholicism was almost disdainful, since it pursued international goals; Protestantism considered membership in the nation the result of deliberate choice by the individual, who was responding to a sense of duty; Orthodoxy saw the nation as a destiny which it enthusiastically embraced. Finally, Catholicism promoted multi-dimensional cultural movements which served one idea—for example, Romanesque, the Gothic, and the Baroque; Protestantism favored individual creations of great originality; and Orthodoxy inspired works that were "spontaneous, anonymous,

and folkloric." Blaga thought that Catholicism and Protestantism fostered the growth of cities, while Orthodoxy was peculiarly suited to the development of the village. Consequently, the villages in the West seemed to him to be miniature cities that had lost their rural character and creative originality. Conversely, the city in Eastern Europe resembled an oversized village, while the village had retained its primitive creative power even where it had been touched by outside cultural influences.

Blaga used the term "Orthodox" in a cultural rather than a religious sense. He made it clear that the originality of the Romanian spirit was not to be sought in Orthodox dogma, but in the "derogations" of it brought about by the "spirit of heresy"—that is, in the semi-pagan folklore preserved in sacred legends, *bocete,* and *colinde.* It seemed to him that Orthodox doctrine had had a levelling effect on the peoples of southeastern Europe; consequently, the stylistic elements that differentiated Romanians from their Bulgarian and Serbian coreligionists manifested themselves most strongly in popular poetry and art. Behind the "mask" of Orthodoxy the Romanians had preserved their ancient, pre-Christian beliefs and customs—especially their way of understanding and feeling existence, which in Blaga's view went back to pagan Thracian times. Peculiar to the Romanian was a view of the world that fused nature with the transcendental, or—as Blaga expressed it—the world was perceived as a receptacle of the unseen. In this "sophianic perspective" the earth was suffused by a heavenly light in the same way nature was transformed into a church in the folk ballad "Miorita." Blaga judged the most important stylistic determinant of Orthodoxy to be its way of regarding the transcendental.

For Blaga, Romanian spirituality, which primarily determined the national character, had been preserved best in the rural world. He had been born in a small Transylvanian village, and the memories of his childhood remained a strong influence on his thought throughout his life. He conceived of the Romanian village as the locale of the organic, eminently human mode of existence. Using Spengler's antinomy, he defined the creative life of the village as "culture"; the city was the embodiment of "civilization"—the mechanized, bourgeois world whose imminent doom Blaga, like many of his Romanian and West European contemporaries, foresaw. His early poetry in particular is filled with the expressionist anxiety that European man was living at the end of an age—a sentiment he revealed in stark, apocalyptic visions of the modern city and "machinism." The city was characterized by "non-creative" preoccupations such as the accumulation of positive knowledge and the formulation of rationalist conceptions; it was a place where man lost his "cosmic sentiment," and his attachment to a uniquely human mode of existence. The scientific spirit, one of the hallmarks of modern European civilization, seemed to dissolve the "concrete phenomena" of existence and to isolate the world from man. (Such a view followed naturally from Blaga's conception of the world as essentially anti-rational and therefore intractable to the reasoned structures of science.) The village, on the other hand, was preeminently the region of myth and magic thought, and it assimilated concrete appearances and brought man into a creative relationship with existence. Blaga's praise of magic thought reveals his general tendency to exalt the primitive mentality at the expense of the civilized. Magic thought did not seek to establish universally valid relationships, but rather sought to organize individual human experience in close connection with specific temporal and spatial data. This type of thought, he argued, was truly creative, for it established bold relationships between very different things. Thanks to this "magic perspective," the peasant was endowed with the gift of organizing his experience in accordance with his vital interests.

Blaga's affection for the village led him to extend the antinomy between the rural world and the city into a theory of "minor cultures" and "major cultures" in **"Geneza metaforei și sensul culturii"** [**"The Genesis of Metaphor and the Sense of Culture"**]. Minor cultures, represented by the village, were in no way inferior in their structures to major cultures, represented by the city, nor did they represent a retarded stage in the historical evolution of society. They were independent realities which expressed a different mode of existence, classified by Blaga as "naive" and "childlike." In a later article Blaga likened minor cultures to prehistory, which for him was a form of "permanent life" that did not evolve but maintained itself parallel to history. Blaga used this notion of prehistory in his theory of the evolution of Romanian history. Taking the Roman evacuation of the province of Dacia in the third century as his starting point, he claimed that the beginnings of the Romanian people coincided with their "withdrawal from history" into an ahistorical world where—with one or two brief interruptions—they led an organic existence with a rhythm all its own until the middle of the nineteenth century. During this long "boycott of history," there was a rich development in peasant art, village architecture, and popular poetry and music quite apart from the broader European cultural currents. Thus Blaga offered a metaphysical explanation of Romanian uniqueness so dear to the traditionalists.

Because Blaga was intent upon establishing the permanent values of a culture, historical perspective was generally absent from his writings on style. He offers no examples of change in a culture caused by a modification of the stylistic matrix from which it originated, even though his theory made provision for such modifications. For example, he derives the Buddhist content of ancient Indian thought and of twentieth-century Indian thought from the same sources. His treatment of the Romanian village is similarly ahistorical. However, as Blaga himself pointed out, his village was not a real Romanian village at all. Rather, it was his idea of a village, a hypothetical place where he concentrated the essence of the Romanian character as he saw it. (pp. 158-64)

Keith Hitchins, " 'Gindirea': Nationalism in Spiritual Guise," in Social Change in Romania: Debate on Development in a European Nation, *edited by Kenneth Jowitt, University of California Press, 1978, pp. 140-173.*

Andrei Codrescu (essay date 1989)

[*Codrescu is a Rumanian-born American poet, memoirist, editor, and journalist. His poetry, which reveals the influences of the Dadaist and Surrealist movements, has been likened to the works of Walt Whitman and William Carlos Williams for its replication of American vernacular. In the following excerpt from the introduction to Blaga's* Court of Yearning: Poems, *Codrescu discusses the prominent traits of Blaga's poetry.*]

Poems of Light and *The Footprints of the Prophet* are the work of a fully conscious voice. The sensuality of [Blaga's] images is reminiscent of impressionism, but the images are only outward expressions of a sensibility that seeks to become one with the cosmos, to leave consciousness behind for a total identification with nature. In an essay on art, Blaga says, "Impressionism reduced man to his retina," then adds, "Van Gogh changed all that by making things partake of his inner life. He ran from impression rendered from the outside, seeking instead the expression charged with the inner soul." The act of animating matter with his soul is Blaga's avowed intention, but there is, simultaneously, a wish to disappear in the pure spirit. Death, sleep, and stasis rule the elliptic world of Blaga's sensual projections. Perspective is abolished in favor of a primordial immersion in generative, preverbal energy: "The light that pierces me when I see you, love, / is perhaps the last drop of that light / spun on the first day of creation" (**"The Light"**). The ontological attraction of this light is a constant in Blaga's poetry. Hell's flames illumine paradise in **"The Light of Paradise."** "Between sunrise and sunset / I am only wound and mud" (**"Psalm"**). "We are guests on the porch / of a new light" (**"At the Court of Yearning"**). This is light before images, before distinction and individuation, light from which all proceeds and is generated but not yet made manifest. The poet uses his power to prevent manifestation, to stop time. It is a protean and, in a "real" sense, futile operation. Time stops for no one. The poet is one of time's most resolute enemies and, at the same time, a sensitive and grateful observer of its passing in things and seasons. Blaga is a splendid nature poet, and his numerous poems about the seasons, particularly autumn, are ambiguous idylls possessing both infinite regret and immense pleasure.

The many love lyrics scattered through his work are only casually aimed at the beloved, for their primary purpose is to induce an ecstatic joining with the primal state, a meta-orgasm. Time is of the essence; Blaga's lyrics repair quickly to the garden, where the beginning of the world is always in a state of imminent consummation. The lovers who populate Blaga's woods and villages are constructs for the transport of seeds, quickly unraveling time machines intended to return the world to ecstatic nonbeing. The poet is both demiurge and satyr.

Blaga must have occasionally been stung by criticism of his arrogant disregard for the contemporary world, because he does sometimes introduce the modern world in startling—but stiff—figures, as if doing penance. There is the worker next to his "steel wheels," a figure from the hell of satanic mills, whose "news" the poet spreads willy-nilly. There are "trains" in a particularly chilling poem written on the eve of World War II that prefigures that technological nightmare. Most of the time, however, the "real world" is only the glimmer of distant lights from a horizon, and the poet makes every effort to keep it at a distance. The profound sorrow and wrenching pain of some of his best lyrics come from the knowledge that the contemporary world has already been emptied of spirit, that the poet is pursuing phantoms. The tone of this desolation is a familiar one in European literature, though Blaga's peculiar position at the crossroads of East and West make his accents slightly more profound. His sorrow is for a world *recently* emptied, as if the poet got there only a few moments after the tragic event. The freshness of much of his work comes from the implied nearness of paradise. Paganism has just departed, Christianity has just arrived—but it, too, is being chased away by horrifying machines. The poet, now satyr, now monk, stands in the desert holding the world still. His weapons are silence, sleep, death, stasis, an obliterating sensual excess. There is some kinship here with the atmosphere of Stefan George's poetry, or Miguel de Unamuno's *Tragic Sense of Life,* or even Oswald Spengler's *Decline of the West,* but it is a superficial resemblance only. Their world has already been occupied by reason. In Blaga's world the mythic fertility of the beginnings has left an atmosphere in which the poet has made his home. If Blaga resembles anyone, it would have to be Rilke, to whom he dedicates a touching poem. Expressionism, with its vitalistic and avant-garde offshoots, was the backdrop for these two poets whose sensibilities lay in a great desire to disappear in the mythic collective unconscious. Both felt their condition as one of exile, but where Rilke was in fact an exile, Blaga's exile consisted in an acute yearning for the very place where he was. This place, moreover, retains the imprint of myth in its vacated shell. The poet finds the "footprints of the prophet" everywhere. Every single thing in nature is warm with the bodies of gods. The divine presence flees the poet and expression itself: "Human language, made expressly to trap things existing externally in space, is unable to pinpoint the methodically organized and continuous process woven from the indefinable nuances of consciousness. This process can be caught only with the help of a profound intuition that has freed itself from the mathematical procedures of the intellect, with its categories formed for spatial realities" (**"Faces of an Age"**). (pp. xv-xvii)

> *Andrei Codrescu, in an introduction to* At the Court of Yearning: Poems *by Lucian Blaga, translated by Andrei Codrescu, Ohio State University Press, 1989, pp. xi-xix.*

Marcel Cornis-Pop   (essay date 1989)

[*In the following excerpt, Cornis-Pop examines the development of Blaga's philosophy as reflected in his poetry.*]

Lucian Blaga—poet, philosopher, playright, essayist, translator—holds a singular position in modern Romanian literature, comparable to that of [T. S.] Eliot and [Ezra] Pound in the English-speaking countries. Blaga was a true originator, "the first important Romanian poet who managed to synchronize Romanian poetry effectively

with European art forms." In 1919, when Blaga's first book, *Poemele luminii* [*Poems of Light*], appeared, the first wave of Romanian avant-gardists (Brâncuşi, Tristan Tzara, Marcel Iancu, Victor Brauner, Benjamin Fundoianu) had just emerged on the European scene, contributing their share to a modern "revolution." But this enthusiastic, experimental phase soon ended with the transplantation of Tzara, Brauner, Fundoianu, and others mainly to France; also with the symbolic suicide of Urmuz, "a dadaist before Dada, and a surrealist before surrealism," shortly after his "bizarre pages" were published in magazine form. Blaga, whose innovative work spanned the early half of this century and left its unmistakable imprint on the latter half, is a more central figure in the drama of "mimetic rivalry" between modern Romanian literature and its Western counterparts. In adapting Expressionism to Romanian poetry, Blaga followed from the beginning an original course, reappraising the models, reliving the "will to modernity" in terms specific to Romanian culture. Together with Tudor Arghezi and Ion Barbu, Blaga represents a "constructivist" phase in Romanian modernism. Picking up the scattered pieces of Dadaism, futurism, and Expressionism, and avoiding the excesses of the new French art (surrealism), their work participated, however indirectly, in a reconstruction of European art in a post-Dada age.

The poetry that best suits me, is ultramodern but also, I think, in certain ways more traditional than ordinary traditionalism, because it revives one of the connections with our primitive substratum.

—*Lucian Blaga*

Modernity for Blaga was doubly constituted and in tension. As he speculated in a 1926 interview, "The poetry that best suits me, is ultra-modern but also, I think, in certain ways more traditional than ordinary traditionalism, because it revives one of the connections with our primitive substratum." After Mihai Eminescu, Blaga is the most important link within Romanian culture between tradition and modernity, between a "heroic age" of trial and survival and the modern age of consolidation. Blaga was a poet of double vocation, an innovator (disrupter) and a consolidator. His work had to fill in the gaps and simultaneously provide that dramatic leap that the longer history of Romanian poetry warranted. *Poems of Light* reveals a remarkably mature poet who left no area of traditional poetry unrevised. Formally these poems resort to free prosodic and typographic procedures, attuned—much like William Carlos Williams's poetry—to the flow of poetic thought. Thematically they violate existing conventions, combining several preoccupations: autobiographical, speculative, self-reflexive. Neither simply erotic, nor naturistic, this poetry alternates image and idea, punctuating the tensions between inner and outer reality.

In the "anti-intellectualist adventure" of modern literature, often dissociating experience from intellect (spirit), Blaga's spiritual, reflexive poetry sounded from the beginning a dissenting note. His early poems were conceived in the Expressionistic spirit of German *Lebensphilosophie,* while his later poems illustrate a more skeptical, phenomenological attitude toward reality. These poems are illuminated by (and in turn illuminate) different sides of Blaga's philosophy. At the same time they render the conceptual aspects of Blaga's work problematic, submitting them to a nondialectic, poetic interrogation.

Blaga acquainted himself with Expressionism during his 1916 trip to Vienna and his subsequent studies there (1919-20). In Romania, he was the first to mention Däubler, Trakl, or Heym, and he used his Expressionistic readings as a catalyst for his own poetic work. *Poems of Light* brings together conflicting sides of "the new style" in an original synthesis: Dionysian vitalism and spiritualization, sensual euphoria and metaphysical melancholia, interest in the primitive substratum and abstract transcendentalism. Blaga's Expressionism was from the beginning comprehensive and contradictory: a poetic style rather than a rigid doctrine, it emphasized the passage from sensation to abstraction, from material to spiritual, from fact to its problematization—and back. Blaga felt closer in spirit to the three precursors of Expressionism, Nietzsche, Strindberg, and Van Gogh, than to such later theorizers as W. Worringer. His early poems were often articulated around plastic or abstract visualizations, recalling the visual expressionism of Van Gogh and Brâncuşi:

> Red vines,
> green vines strangle the houses
> with savage and lusty embraces—
> like squid they squeeze their prey.
> The rising sun washes the blood
> off his lancepoints which
> have hunted and killed
> the night.
>
> **["At the Seashore"]**

Blaga could pass both for an imagist, "one of the most original creators of sensory images in [Romanian] literature" [Eugen Lovinescu, *Critice*], and for a cerebral poet, the creator of a mysterious and abstruse Blaga-land.

The motif of light central to *Poems of Light* is handled by Blaga in a way that reinforces the duality of his poetry. Blaga's light "has a double nature: . . .on the one hand there is the kind of light which we could call *solar*— apparently related to the light of reason—and on the other hand there is *lunar* or *stellar* light apparently corresponding to extra-rational lights." The first is a negator of mystery, the second an extension and enhancer of it. These two facets of light, Apollonian and Dionysian, revealing and concealing, are balanced through an act of poetic will:

> I will not crush the world's corolla of wonders
> and I will not kill
> with reason
> the mysteries I meet along my way
> in flowers, eyes, lips, and graves.

> The light of others
> drowns the deep magic hidden
> in the profound darkness.
> I increase the world's enigma
> with my light
> much as the moon with its white beams
> does not diminish but increases
> the shimmering mystery of night—
>
> **["I Will Not Crush the World's Corolla of Wonders"]**

This equilibrium, however, is short-lived and problematic: the poetic self can recapture mystery only through an act of self-assertion whose success threatens mystery with annihilation. Blaga's poetry illustrated from the beginning a paradoxical dialectic of mystery/mastery, with the two conflicting terms locked inescapably together. Each phase in his work explored a new angle of this dialectic, seeking a way out of the ontological and poetic dilemma.

The early poems celebrate individual expression, cosmic vitalism, movement. Many begin with the first-person pronoun (which in Romanian can be omitted), followed by an abundance of verbal forms. The typical tone is hortatory, the gesticulation grandiose. But the verbs often express hypothetical or desired actions, a rhetorical imperative:

> O, I want to dance as I have never danced!
> Let God not feel himself a prisoner in me.
> Earth, give me wings:
> I want to be the arrow
> tearing infinity,
>
> . . . . .
>
> I want to dance
> torn by the lightning of unborn desire
> so God will breathe freely in me
> and will not say:
> "I am a prisoner in his dungeon."
>
> **["I Want to Dance!"]**

These poems are less monological than they seem: they often shift mood, attitude, and verbal modality. The presence of a speaker is conspicuous in them, but he is only seldom the Expressionistic, "*dictatorial* self that commands everything and imposes itself as a decisive factor in the interrelation with the entire cosmos" [Marin Mincu, Introduction to *Poezii: Texte comentate* by Lucian Blaga]. Already in *Poems of Light* Blaga intuited (and exploited dramatically) some of the tensions inherent in the Expressionist stance, that blend of "*cosmic enthusiasm and tragic hysteria,* troubled speech and . . .verbal invention" that he recognized in Nietzsche. Expressionism wanted to affirm subjectivity, but ultimately effaced it through overstatement (Worringer's "expressionistic cry") and excessive spiritualization. The two alternatives offered by Expressionism (cosmic expansion and introversion, empathy and abstraction) dissolved the subject into the suprapersonal.

Blaga's poetry after *Poems of Light* explored the tensions inherent in poetic subjectivity against the background of a larger ontological drama. The change of tone is already evident in *Pasii profetului* [*The Footprints of the Prophet*] (1921). Poems like **"Pan," "Autumn Chill," "Autumnal Sunset," "Lines Written on Dry Grape Leaves,"** and most conspicuously **"The Death of Pan"** suggest a shift in (natural and emotional) seasons with many cultural reverbera- tions. The old, Dionysian fervor is displaced by an ascetic interiority. The mythos of pagan summer is followed by a richly shaded mythos of autumn. The Expressionist self (like Blaga's Pan) is defeated by the sly signs of time and a complex cultural semiotics that it can no longer control. Increasingly aware of the gaps between self and world, signs and their meanings, Blaga's middle-period poems emphasize rupture and discontinuity rather than unity of thought. They begin—according to Marin Mincu—a slow process of de-rhetoricizing and disrupting Expressionism.

Poems of Light was patiently constructed and graded around a core of poetic ideas. The middle poems are less dynamic and layered, bringing to the fore the silent spaces between metaphors and lines. Blaga's images, even when borrowed from a traditional, mythic-pastoral fund, are jarring and distorted:

> Owl-sized butterflies come from the East
> to seek their ashes in the fire.
> At the roots of pines, near the cursed hemlocks,
> the shepherd lays earth on top of his lambs
> killed by the powers of the woods.
> Walking over the narrow ridge
> shepherd girls brush their naked shoulders
> against the moon—
> their daring covers them
> with the golden pollen they shake from it.
>   [**"In the Mountains"**]

As this sample shows, Blaga did not give up his hope of reconnecting a fragmented human world to the cosmic whole. His nocturnal, surrealistic figures move according to an invisible purpose, touched by a lunar "pollen" that, as usual, connotes poetic mystery. In *The Footprints of the Prophet* and *În marea trecere* [*In the Great Passing*] (1924), the transcendent is asserted and denied with the same gesture, called up from its silent fictionality, as in these passages from **"Psalm"**:

> Show yourself in these thorns, Lord,
> so I'll know what you want me to do.
>   . . . . .
> You are the mute, unmoved identity
> (rounded in itself *a* is *a*)—
> you ask nothing. Not even my prayer.

And:

> You locked yourself up in the coffin of the sky.
> O if only you were closer to life
> than to death
> you would speak to me.
> From wherever you are, from earth
> or story, you would speak to me.

The transcendental interests Blaga precisely as mythic (emblematic) *fiction:* the middle-period poems abound in references to myth and its relatives ("story," "legend," "riddle," "the fairy tale of the spoken blood"). Blaga responded to the modern angst of the "great passing" by re- asserting the value of mythic narration.

Beginning with *Lauda somnului* [*In Praise of Sleep*] (1929), Blaga used Expressionist techniques very loosely, subordinating them to an original mythopoesis, a symbol- ic redefinition of Romanian spiritual realities. Like his countryman Mircea Eliade, Blaga pursued a personal syn- thesis between the rationalistic heritage of the West and the untapped magicomythic potential of the East. Myth for him was an important tool for relating two great cul- tural traditions. Blaga's "mythic spiritualism" took a more conservative turn in later poems, but it still managed to steer away from the orthodox, ethnocentric line pro- moted by the journal *Gîndirea,* of which he had been co- founder. Blaga liked to associate his later poems with the "heretical spontaneity of the popular genius." One can find this revisionist spirit at work in **"Holding the Great Blind Man's Hand," "The Saint's Path," "Archangel Re- turning Home," "Carol," "Good Tidings for the Blooming Apple," "Uninvited Guests," "Lark,"** and so on—poems that reactivate the metaphoric potential of biblical myths.

Most of the poems written by Blaga in the twenties my- thologize the relation of self to cosmos. Individual biogra- phy recapitulates cosmic evolution in its succession of ini- tiating phases (a fact underscored in the titles of volumes: *In the Great Passing, On the Great Water Divide, In Praise of Sleep*). At the same time, the cosmos is personal- ized, attuned to the spiritual life of the individual. As a re- cent Blaga critic and editor, George Gană, notes, Blaga's conversion of

> the space of the great passing into one of man's
> participation in the cosmic absolute, is an act of
> mythic thought. . . . Blaga's uniqueness resides
> not in his plastic imagination, his gift of inven-
> tion (on this account his poetry falls short by
> comparison to Eminescu's or Arghezi's), but
> rather in his capacity to alter the ontological sta-
> tus of the real, . . .affecting both our aesthetic
> understanding and our existential feeling. The
> world is transfigured by the poet's eye—
> rendered fluid and musical, or, on the contrary,
> dense and dark, suggestive of death.

Blaga's mythopoetic imagination works ambivalently, dis- closing and enhancing the ontological rupture between self and world.

Like his earlier Expressionist phase, Blaga's mythopoetic stage is troubled by the drama of ontological and cognitive separation. The self it depicts is uprooted, "scattered in the storm of time," estranged from the original horizon of mystery. The insomniac poet of *In Praise of Sleep* wan- ders, "when guiltily, on hell's roofs, / when guileless, on orchid mountain" (**"Biography"**), registering the "signs of leaving," diminution and regress. The whole ontological perspective is reversed, with the transcendent preempted by the terrestrial: "smoke fallen from the hearth" trails on the ground, "domes [have] fallen into water," "naked an- gels / shivering lie down in the hay" or "rot under the sod." In *La cumpăna apelor* [*On the Great Water Divide*] (1933), the entire cosmic world is afflicted by a mysterious "sickness . . .nameless, faceless," that the poet tries to ex- orcise not through words (for "no voice can tame" this sickness), but through silent rituals.

Silence becomes an important topic in the later Blaga poems. In a memorable **"Self-Portrait,"** Lucian Blaga ap- pears

> . . .mute like a swan.

In his country
the snow of being fills the place of the word.
Since the beginning
his soul has been searching,
mutely searching
to the last frontiers of the world.

Blaga's swanlike muteness has little in common with Beckett's nihilistic silence. Even though it questions the "expressionist" optimism of Blaga's early poetry, it does *not* end his poetic exploration. On the contrary, it pushes the orphic quest beyond the given boundaries of discursive reality, teasing new meanings out of the cosmic "runes." *On the Great Water Divide* builds on the orphic theme explicitly. But even the earlier *In Praise of Sleep* gradually moved from the elegiac theme of the great passing to a more hopeful note in **"Closing"**: "Each book seems a cured illness to you, brother," each poem a response to the cosmic "sickness." Like the sick music-makers, the poet carries "an illness in the strings"; for that reason, his music participates in the world's "living mystery," enriching it with its own "riddles."

On the Great Water Divide and *La curţile dorului* [*At the Court of Yearning*] (1938) also envision an alternative that takes us beyond the drama of Expressionist individualism. This alternative, suggested already in poems like **"The Soul of the Village," "I Understood the Sin that Weighs Down My House,"** and **"Native Village,"** but made more explicit in **"The Village of Miracles," "Return,"** and **"With the Old Ones,"** calls for the abandonment of Expressionist subjectivity and a return to the mythic anonymity of the village. *Anonymous,* Blaga cautioned, "does not mean *collective.* The collective is a sum of individuals. The anonymous, however, is the *metaphysical* sum of all. This is where I think I differ from German Expressionism—which is alternatively collectivist and individualist." Blaga's distinction between metaphysical sum and social sum, ontological unity and social conformity, gets somewhat blurred in the poems written by him in the late thirties. These poems oppose ritual integration to individual expression, advocating the return to an idealized, atemporal village, in touch with cosmic existence. This image is played against that of a generic city with its "clock of shadows" and "halo of ash," which in *At the Court of Yearning* becomes the symbolic site of Blaga's diplomatic "exile."

Still, as **"I Am Not a Son of Deed"** suggests, the poet's integration in the larger community is not devoid of tension:

Don't avert your eyes,
don't condemn my laziness.
I grow among you, but shadowed by my hands
the mystical fruit ripens elsewhere.

The poet feels more at home in an idealized village of the mind, conversing with "the snake with eyes eternally open / on the wisdom of the beyond" or with his "kinfolk washed by waters under the rocks." Even this imaginary village occasionally looks like a "crumbling paradise":

Apocalyptic roosters crow—
and crow—keep crowing
from Romanian villages.
Fountains open their eyes

in the night and listen
to the dark news.

. . . . .

From woods of sleep
and other dark places
beasts raised by storms
steal in to drink dead water
from old mill pools.
Draped in fields of grain
the earth is a sea of burning waves.
[**"Transcendental View"**]

By the time Blaga's poetry reached *Nebănuitele trepte* [*The Unsuspected Stair*] (1943), its exuberant or mournful Expressionism had been almost entirely subdued. Blaga himself acknowledged that his Expressionism had become, especially with *In Praise of Sleep,* "so *well organized* and *crystalline,* that it deserved the label *neoclassical.*" European art, he further argued, had entered a phase of consolidation: "There are no more revolutions in the artistic fields, in literature, music, or the plastic arts. . . . Artists now pursue perfection, not innovation. In this sense we can talk about a new classicism, because classicism is interested in perfecting the means that have become part of tradition." Blaga's poetry sought confirmation, not new departures, reworking previous themes (he had always been a poet of intensive rather than extensive thematics) and cultivating the "anonymity" of folk prosody. "The self is no longer cosmic, or anonymous and problematized, but quasi-*domestic,* turned back to the intimate and patriarchal joys of life. . . . The feeling of metaphysical anxiety and estrangement has all but disappeared. The 'ontological rupture' has been sutured" [Mincu].

Blaga's newly won serenity and his continued focus on ontological themes at a time when other poets were exploring more pressing sociohistorical dramas could appear escapist. But his visions of new light were, as always, tentative and problematic. The nostalgic, recuperative mood of these poems is often broken by lucid self-remonstrations:

I told myself often:
it is but memory—of a past hour.
No more dreams for you, poet.
No light no star no power stays.

Forget Arcadia. Forget the hour.
that will not sound, the not-yet rounded
hour, the unfulfilled unborn hour.
In your fog wheat does not ripen,
at your fountain pitchers do not fill.
Barely does word filter from
the world the sun rules.
Others are always holding
the legend.
Miracles are elsewhere,
stars are increasing their distance.
[**"Changing Season"**]

As **"Epitaph"** intimates, the briefly revealed "unsuspected stair" leads now downward, to the earth mothers, not upward toward a problematic transcendent. Blaga's poetry wins back some of its biographical and emotional concreteness, even if at the expense of its previous complexity.

Drama is not absent from Blaga's posthumously published

poetry, written between 1943 and the year of his death. This part of Blaga's work is sufficiently diverse in tone and attitude, revealing a troubled face under its placid and resigned surface. Critics like Constantin Ciopraga have tended to privilege those poems that celebrate late love and the mystery of germination in a cosmos reduced to a "proud garden," praising their "Apollonian" serenity: "The emergence out from the mystical night, the reconversion of the nocturnal into light, through integration into the flux of nature, demonstrates the way in which an exultation, characteristic of the Romanian spirit as a whole, triumphs in Blaga" [Const. Ciopraga, Preface to *Poemele Lununi* by Lucian Blaga]. But equally conspicuous (at least in cycles like **"Ecce Tempus," "The Iron Age," "Ships of Ashes," "The Song of Fire"**) are the poems that focus on the ravages of time and on change—social or cosmic. Occasionally a more personal note of anxiety having to do with Blaga's marginalization after 1946 is cautiously sounded. The formal composure of these poems is disturbed by a somber, nocturnal imagery appropriate for the "iron age" traversed by Romania during and after World War II. Several *artes poeticae* emphasize the subversive, germinative role of poetry: "They are silent like the dew. Like the seed. Like a yearning. / Mute like the waters that plow under the field" (**"The Poets"**).

One could more accurately sum up (as Ciopraga does . . .) Blaga's poetry as an unstilled dialectic movement, affirming and denying simultaneously: "Blaga's poetry is essentially a sequence of reaching-outs towards the transcendent, a mode of expansion in the miraculous grandeur of the cosmos, and of inner exile, bespeaking a dilemmatic personality. . . . An astral Blaga, another, an 'earthy' Blaga suffused with a feeling for matter, stirred by the spectacle of immediate Nature."

Our duty, when faced by a true mystery, is not to explain it, but to deepen it, to transform it into a greater mystery.

—Lucian Blaga

It is for his "dilemmatic" pathos, rather than for his "Apollonian" serenity, that later Romanian poets have returned to Blaga. His poetry epitomized for them the dramatic fate of modern Romanian literature: emerging vigorously in the year of the European peace treaties (1919), disputed by critics in the early thirties when Romanian modernism went through a phase of reconstruction, imitated but also misused in the forties, banned in the Stalinist fifties, reedited in the sixties, analyzed extensively in the seventies and eighties. The "Blaga case" has been reopened periodically, his poetic battles fought several times over. Blaga's final integration began after his death, when his work was "rediscovered" by several generations of poets eager to reconnect the broken circuit of Romanian poetry after a decade of Soviet-inspired "proletarian" art.

Almost every poet coming of age in the mid-sixties followed Blaga's poetic orbit from Expressionist euphoria to introversion and from discursiveness to somber reflexivity. This massive reorientation of Romanian poetry after 1970 was precipitated, as in Blaga's case, by a sense of personal (existential) drama, but also by the more pressing awareness of a collective drama involving a generation of poets born in the "liberalized" sixties and reaching their maturity in the re-Stalinized Romania of the mid-seventies. The early work of these poets found in Blaga's "revelatory metaphor" a powerful exploratory tool. Their recent work has been forced to repeat the drama of Blaga's poetry, fractured midway between light and dark, expressed and silent, visible and censored sides. (pp. 189-200)

> *Marcel Cornis-Pop, in an afterword to* At the Court of Yearning: Poems *by Lucian Blaga, translated by Andrei Codrescu, Ohio State University Press, 1989, pp. 189-202.*

Virgil Nemoianu (essay date 1989)

[*In the following excerpt, Nemoianu presents the central ideas of Blaga's philosophical writings in order to establish their relevance to modern Western thought.*]

Blaga's *oeuvre* is double-centered. Blaga started writing poetry and philosophy almost simultaneously, and he continued to express himself in both media throughout his active career. His dramas are to some extent scenic, but certainly poetic, and they should be seen as an extension of his central poetry. Similarly, Blaga's philosophy is concentric rather than architectonic. His epistemology (1930-1934) is placed in the middle, while his philosophy of culture (essentially 1935-1937) and of values (essentially 1939-1942) as well as other pieces are placed in widening circles around it, mostly unfolding and applying the central tenets. The opening poem in Blaga's first volume proclaimed that the poet's duty was to compound the mysteries of the world, not to explain them away. The central thesis of Blaga's *Trilogy of Knowledge* was closely similar. Blaga's views about paradigms of science or the stylistics of religion are applications of his central theories, much as his dramas (1921-1944) can be seen as full expansions of some of his central poetic statements. A curious kind of self-mirroring pervades Blaga's twin-structured production.

Placing Blaga's prose in the context of the Western philosophical tradition is unquestionably a useful exercise, but in isolation it provides a misleading image of Blaga. He appears to be a neo-Spenglerian who has absorbed the influences of Bergson, Dilthey, and Nietzsche, while reacting somehow against a Platonist background. In a word, from a purely Western point of view Blaga seems an interesting but minor continuator of nineteenth-century theories of value and vitalism and the philosophy of culture. His merit consists of his articulation of some Spenglerian concepts and in his application of them to the generally neglected area of Romanian culture or to minor cultures in general. His epistemological contributions and his ideas on the history of science seem sketchy, and his comments on science and religion somewhat amateurish or perhaps just outlines of what was done later and better by others. Another approach is needed.

A short presentation of the main ideas in the *Trilogy of Knowledge* may be more useful to begin with. In the first of the essays of the book, **"Eonul dogmatic" ["The Age of Dogma"]**, Blaga argued that ancient Greek-Latin rationalism and skepticism had reached a point of exhaustion around A.D. 100 and that a turning point occurred in the history of philosophy when thinkers like Philo of Alexandria and the early Church Fathers began to use dogma as a creative response to the insoluble antinomies of reality. With the advent of scholasticism, the ensuing millenium of dogmatic thinking was finally replaced by a new period of rationalist "local" thinking, similar to the one whose crisis in antiquity had released the "emphatic and monumental spirituality" of the "dogmatic age." Blaga claimed to notice that, as the twentieth century proceeded, a kind of intellectual stalemate set in that was quite similar to the one that had obtained a little under nineteen centuries ago. Hence the need to investigate shapes of thinking that can serve as an alternative to rationalism and that are better adapted to a time of intellectual crisis.

In the **"Age of Dogma,"** Blaga suggested what these modes of creative, irrational, and arbitrary thinking might be. He explained what he meant by "minus-knowledge," a type of knowledge that, far from lessening the area of mystery, tends to deepen and expand it, and by the "ecstatic intellect," which, as opposed to the "enstatic intellect" (i.e., one limited to the logical limits of human normality), tries to escape from itself or to place itself in an adversary position to its own logical bearings. Blaga also declared with enthusiasm that modern physical theories, such as Einstein's theory of relativity or Max Planck's quantum theory, along with the insights of Michelson and Eddington (later Bohr) as well as the entelechial biology of Hans Driesch or Freud's theory of the unconscious, were examples of the "dogmatic" method in science. However, he fully developed these observations only in his book-length essay about "luciferic cognition" (1933). Whereas the "paradisal" knowledge of the rationalists and logicians strives to unify, to limit, and to defuse, luciferic cognition will admit that the central category in human existence is mystery, and it will actually endeavor to expand its domain by further problematizing and fragmenting the usual objects of knowledge. Most of Blaga's book was devoted to a detailed classification of the types of epistemological mystery and of the approaches appropriate to them. He also analyzed the inner articulations of mystery—the "transfigured antinomies" and similar elements—as well as the relationship between the "phanic material" (appearance) and "cryptic material" (the unknowable reality), which cross each other to produce any given object or event.

Blaga contended that rationalism and empiricism are neither a privileged nor a promising way to achieve knowledge or to satisfy human aspirations, whereas an integration of knowledge and mystery is much more appropriate. In the terms used throughout his investigation this means

a concession, that is, a cooperative attitude of the principal towards the secondary.

There is at least a partial analogy here to the strategies of poetic discourse, as Blaga himself pointed out in **Geneza metaforei si sensul culturii [The Emergence of Metaphor and the Meaning of Culture]** and in **Artă si valoare [Art and Value]**, and this is the first sense in which Blaga's philosophy of knowledge might be said to be an extension of metaphorical and aesthetic methods to the whole field of human knowledge and action. However, aestheticism ceases to be an aim in itself, the principal, and regains its natural position: a dissheveled concubine of reality, and resident of its secondary thickets. Blaga's ambitious and broadly systematic approach to epistemological problems as a whole inflated the aestheticist approach to the ironic point where it could join with other areas of nonrational discourse in a viable alternative to human communication with reality. This strategy was fortified by Blaga's resort to a causal explanation of why rationalist readings must be assigned a subordinate role in approaching reality, in **Cenzura transcendenta [Transcendent Censorship]**.

In this book Blaga's purpose was to outline a scenario that would plausibly explain man's relation to the world. He declared himself a full agnostic about the nature of the world's originating factor. However, he did assume that there is a "Great Anonymous," an originating factor of the universe, although we permanently ignore its nature, and can only infer certain facts from the structure of our cognitive strategies. Reality is not only difficult to explain and to understand, but it is positively hostile to our attempts to solve its mysteries. The Great Anonymous, it would appear, in a most ungodlike fashion set up a "transcendent censorship" to defend itself against the growth of and potential competition from its own creation. Human endeavor is a continuous struggle against the barring censorship of the structuring principle of the universe, which is expressed in the active opposition of reality against our cognitive efforts. Problematizing and producing crisis, enhancing mystery, transfiguring antinomies, reckless cultural creativity, dogmatic pronouncements—these are just some of the strategies that humans can use against the retarding agents. Everywhere in the world, imperfection, dispersal, and incoherence hinder and disturb understanding and harmonious growth. Blaga's position is neo-Platonism in reverse. The creation is indeed trying to rush back to its source and to be reunited with it, but the Great Anonymous, darkly jealous and slyly suspicious, set obstacles against this yearning for return and built brakes in nature against the emergence of truly integrative types of ideas, so that it seems at times more interested in thwarting than in generating. According to Blaga, the setup betrays a clear anguish about any possible alternative theogonic processes (the Father's fear of the Son), or even about any generative amplitude. Blaga thought that his theory about the Great Anonymous was placed halfway between theology and demonology. Any human knowledge is degraded; implanted in it is a yearning for transcendent truth, no less than the impossibility of grasping it. Grace is always severely limited, blocked, and censored. The principal (as the appeal to transcendence) and the secondary, as the perpetual return to imperfection, diversity, and digression, hold each other in check.

It should be clear from this cursory account that Blaga's philosophy could fit into the family of thinking of which the writings of Saul Kripke, Thomas Kuhn, Nelson Goodman, and Paul Feyerabend are also a part: paradigmatic, pluralist, and mildly relativist. Blaga differs in some significant ways from the neoskeptical and agnostic orientations that have become powerful in the second half of our century and with which the names of Jacques Derrida and Richard Rorty (as well as, again, Paul Feyerabend, in another side of his work) are associated. For these thinkers, as well as for their followers in modern literary criticism, the limitations or impossibilities of knowledge are reflective of ontological gaps or blurs, of a void or lack in the zone where reality used to reside. For Blaga the explanation of epistemological paralyses and relativities is that mystery (and, we could add, secondariness) is mandated by the structuring principles of reality itself. He speaks explicitly about the dogged resistance and even initiative of objects against attempts to exhaust them by knowledge (to remain imperfect, to stay anchored in the secondary). In a sense, for him reality as such would not be possible without ontological absence—knowledge would somehow consume reality. Conversely, human life would not be the same if devoid of ontological absence—the latter is the indispensable background (and perhaps also the cause) for human creativity and invention as a response to the blankness and failure of cognitive endeavors. Blaga's unexpected twist to modern relativism adds a more constructive and optimistic dimension to it; however, closer parallel analyses are needed to place him among twentieth-century skeptics.

There are other streams feeding into Blaga's thought. I mention two of them very briefly. One is (as noted before) an aesthetic epistemology, that is, a mode of thinking that treats aesthetics as a substitute for all monocentric philosophies and unified methodologies, and as a principle of organization, not a formal effect. Treating philosophy according to an aesthetic principle of organization (in the mode of the symptomatic and the secondary) tends to avoid conclusions and firm alternatives or directions. In the same way that "ironies" and qualifications constitute the texture and coherence of a poem, so in a philosophy of the kind proposed by Blaga, do the conceptual parts relativize each other or keep each other in a state of suspension, interrogation, and mystery. This is a concept of aesthetics that, far from the neo-Classical and even Romantic views of perfection, sees art as the chief constant that incorporates into itself disorder, asymmetry, imperfection, and randomness. This view of art perceives it (no less than the real world) as being dominated by the principle of discreteness, as a *regio dissimilitudinis*.

A second stream is the theological tradition, particularly strong in the Eastern Orthodox branch of Christianity, of "negative theology": an approach to God by the gradual elimination of all affirmative characterization and a stripping away of attributes. This mode of thinking is used in diverse religions, from Zen Buddhism to Judaism and Islam, and it was used in Western Christianity by many mystics, such as Meister Eckhart, and was conceptualized by Nicolaus Cusanus among others. In all cases this kind of theology tries to reach God by saying what He is not, rather than what He is. However, Blaga's main point of reference was the Patristic tradition and, in an exceptional sense, Pseudo-Dionysius the Areopagite (fl. c. A.D. 500), to which he was attracted not merely owing to negative (or apophatic) theology, but also because the Areopagite had well assimilated the neo-Platonic inheritance of the relationship between God and the universe.

Another way in which Blaga's work is relevant to modern thinking in general and to the theory of the secondary in particular is best explained by a parallel to the otherwise entirely different theorizing of his slightly younger countryman, Mircea Eliade. The chief premise of Eliade's philosophy of myth and religion is that while most of the formally structured high religions were shaped within the last 3000 years or so, they are founded on an older religious stratum. This neolithic religiosity was common to Western and Eastern areas of the globe and involved a detection of sacrality in the objects and the phenomena of the natural world, or a coinherence of transcendence and immanence. The systematic religions, from Buddhism and Hinduism to monotheism, are, in a sense, specializations of this broader inchoate fund. All the great religions are somehow rationalistic when compared to the background of vague sacrality against which they stand out, Eliade suggests.

The general direction of Blaga's system is similar. The importance of Western philosophical rationalism is not denied, and when all is said and done, it is preserved as the broad and loose framework least inapt for the functioning of any reflective discourse. However, Blaga states with unabashed emphasis that outside the Western mainstream there are other modes of knowledge and reflection, and other modes of intellectual perception that have their own dignity and usefulness, that are older, and that relate in different ways to the logical system of the last 3000 years. From this vantage point the "primitive" and the heretical have many things in common. Many "Third World" intellectuals and writers have tried to put forward a similar argument in the last twenty or thirty years or even earlier. Among the attempts were those of African intellectuals that tried to define the cultural identity of their religious tradition and their relationship to the world, the "third-way" political philosophies of Islamic and Hindu thinkers or writers, and the various theoretizations of the distance between South America and the West. These attempts can be seen in turn as continuing the powerful and coherent explanatory system for cultural clash provided by the Russian Slavophiles of the second half of the nineteenth century and perhaps even of the distinction between culture and civilization as developed in the nineteenth century by German philosophers of history. The whole trend indicates a definite unease about the process whereby a centralized set of philosophical concepts can establish a uniform dominance over all areas of human activity and knowledge; it also questions a methodology and a conceptual framework that seem indigenous to a very definite and limited historical and geographical environment and that were perhaps determined by this environment and chiefly suitable to it. However, most of the above-mentioned opposition envisages a simple kind of dichotomy: Western modes of reasoning and perception versus the other modes of approaching the universe (more intuitive and perceptive, more involved with and more deeply rooted in the objectual world and in large wholes). This starkly contrasting presentation is, first, almost always likely to be reductive and simplifying. Besides, it plays ironically into the hands of the adversary by confirming the type of antithetical dialectics that is so central to the utilitarian and rational civilization it purports to battle. In more than one case the alternative is neutralized by becoming dependent upon its very antithesis, and it loses its autonomy when it designates itself the victim of the historical process or the target of utopian wishes. The confidence that truth is a unified field is thus preserved, and the opposition must depend upon it.

It is to Blaga's great credit that he largely avoided the trap of self-victimization, by conceding to the Western modes of conceptualization their own dignity and usefulness. His important strategic decision was to regard rationalism and analytical investigation (for example) as legitimate elements of some larger category, or as local specializations in a broader field of cognitive reactions and creative initiatives. Blaga thus gained an added flexibility and a relative indeterminacy in relating the different kinds of human understanding and behavior to each other; instead of competing with each other or excluding each other, they coexist—with some mutual indifference or neglect. However, the neglect is benign and the indifference is relative, because they share common uncertainties and imperfections. The secondary is secondary and insists on remaining secondary with a certain pride of its own. Blaga's portrait of epistemological possibilities thus faithfully mirrors the image of a world in which the paths to absolute and certain knowledge are blocked, and the hegemony of the principal is curtailed.

Blaga is one of the very few philosophers who are genuinely useful in bridging the gap between the Northern and Southern hemispheres of our planet as well as between the heretic, "primitive," and early historical modes of thinking and the mature empiricist or rationalist ones. As the globalization of intellectual discourse proceeds, Blaga's philosophy will grow in importance. (pp. 162-68)

> *Virgil Nemoianu, "The Dialectics of Imperfection: Girard, Blaga, Serres," in his* A Theory of the Secondary: Literature, Progress, and Reaction, *The Johns Hopkins University Press, 1989, pp. 153-70.*

FURTHER READING

Andreescu, Gabriel. "Classification of Poetic Items: The Volumes *Plumb* by Bacovia and *Poemele luminii* by Blaga." *Revue Roumaine de Linguistique* XXVI, No. 2 (March-April 1981): 181-88.
> Empirical analysis of Blaga's *Poems of Light* in which Andreescu uses semantic criteria to assess the poems on a non-subjective scale.

Catanoy, Nicholas. Review of *Poezii/Poems,* by Lucian Blaga. *World Literature Today* 57, No. 4 (Autumn 1983): 625.
> Reviews Michael Taub's translation of Blaga's poems.

Hitchins, Keith. Review of *Opere. 3: Teatru,* by Lucian Blaga. *World Literature Today* 61, No. 1 (Winter 1987): 89.
> Considers Blaga's development as a dramatist as reflected in the third volume of his collected works.

Oprea, Magdalena. "Poetic Means in Investigating Drama." *Poetics* 13, Nos. 1-2 (April 1984): 149-69.
> Asserts that the principle behind artistic creation is an "existential rhythm" that is evident in the alternation between verse and prose found in Blaga's plays.

Papu, Edgar. "Manifold Portrait." *Romanian Review* 40, No. 5 (1986): 46-54.
> A collection of interviews with Blaga's contemporaries in which they describe their first encounters with him and their assessments of his influence on Rumanian culture.

Smock, Frederick. "Increase the Enigma." *American Book Review* 12, No. 3 (July-August 1990): 25.
> A review of *At the Court of Yearning,* a selection of Blaga's poetry translated into English by Andrei Codrescu.

Strenski, Ivan. "Eliade's Theory of Myth and the 'History of Religions'." In his *Four Theories of Myth in Twentieth-Century History: Cassirer, Eliade, Lévi-Strauss and Malinowski,* pp. 104-280. London: Macmillan, 1987.
> Examines the influence of Blaga's philosophy and poetry on [Mircea] Eliade's theory of myth.

William S. Burroughs
Naked Lunch

(Full name William Seward Burroughs; has also published under the pseudonym William Lee) Born in 1914, Burroughs is an American novelist, essayist, critic, and scriptwriter.

The following entry focuses on Burroughs's novel *Naked Lunch,* originally published in 1959 as *The Naked Lunch.* For further discussion of Burroughs's life and works, see *CLC,* Volumes 1, 2, 5, 15, 22, and 42.

INTRODUCTION

Naked Lunch is among the most innovative and controversial works in American literature. Intended, according to Burroughs, to be "necessarily brutal, obscene, and disgusting," the novel is composed of loosely related sections containing graphic descriptions of drug use, murder, and sadomasochistic homosexual acts. First published in France, *Naked Lunch* aroused critical debate in the United States in advance of its 1962 American edition, which appeared following three years of court trials for obscenity. Although some reviewers denounced the book on moral grounds, such writers as Mary McCarthy and Norman Mailer praised Burroughs for his masterful use of lurid subject matter in a work of high literary value.

After graduating from Harvard in 1936 Burroughs engaged in various pursuits, including graduate studies in anthropology, as well as working as an exterminator, a private detective, and a copywriter for an advertising agency. In 1943 he was living in New York City, where he first began using morphine and other narcotics. Burroughs was constantly threatened with arrest for drug offenses, and in 1946 he left New York to seek locales more conducive to buying and using drugs. After brief stays in Texas, Louisiana, Mexico, and South America, he settled in 1953 in Tangier, Morocco, where a number of expatriate American writers and artists had gathered. Drugs were easily acquired in Tangier, and over the next four years Burroughs indulged his habit to a point where his existence became one of aimless inactivity. In 1957 he traveled to England to undergo a controversial treatment for addiction using a nonaddictive drug known as apomorphine. After several relapses he was cured of his addiction to narcotics in 1959.

While Burroughs was in Tangier he compiled a mass of notes based on his experiences and fantasies while under the influence of drugs and during periods of withdrawal. In 1959 these notes were collected and published as *Naked*

Lunch by Maurice Girodias's Olympia Press, which was located in Paris and specialized in pornography. Publication of the book was delayed in the United States due to the threat of censorship. Grove Press, Burroughs's American publisher, successfully defended *Naked Lunch* in obscenity trials in Boston and Los Angeles, and the novel was released in 1962. Since that time no other book has been tried for obscenity in the United States.

Burroughs explained the title of *Naked Lunch* as "the frozen moment when everyone sees what is on the end of every fork." Presenting no consistent narrative or point of view, the novel is structured as an assemblage of "routines," which are self-contained set pieces that take various forms, including monologues, essays, passages of chaotic imagery, and narrative fragments. *Naked Lunch* has been variously interpreted as an allegory satirizing the repressiveness of American society, a literary experiment that attacks language as an instrument of government control, and either a condemnation or a celebration of drugs. Consisting of elements from diverse literary genres, including the detective novel and science fiction, *Naked Lunch* depicts a blackly humorous, sinister world dominated by bizarre sex and violence, fantastic metamorphoses, and cartoonish characters like the County Clerk, a bigoted official who relates gruesome anecdotes in a setting that resembles the American South; Bradley the Buyer, a narcotics cop who becomes an amoebic blob that consumes junkies; and Dr. Benway, an expert in psychological control who placidly manipulates entire societies and engages in grotesque medical experiments. In *Naked Lunch,* as well as his subsequent fiction, Burroughs uses drug addiction as a metaphor for the human condition, postulating a world in which all human beings compulsively and destructively seek gratification for a multitude of needs. As Burroughs has stated, his major concern throughout his work has been "with addiction itself (whether to drugs, or sex, or money, or power) as a model of control, and with the ultimate decadence of humanity's biological potentials."

PRINCIPAL WORKS

Junkie (novel) 1953; also published as *Junky* [uncensored edition], 1977
The Naked Lunch (novel) 1959; also published as *Naked Lunch,* 1962
The Soft Machine (novel) 1961; also published as *The Soft Machine* [revised edition], 1966
The Ticket That Exploded (novel) 1962; also published as *The Ticket That Exploded* [revised edition], 1967
The Yage Letters (letters) 1963
Nova Express (novel) 1964
The Last Words of Dutch Schulz (novel) 1970
The Wild Boys (novel) 1971; also published as *The Wild Boys* [revised edition], 1979
Exterminator! (novel) 1973
Blade Runner: A Movie (novel) 1979
Port of Saints (novel) 1979
Cities of the Red Night (novel) 1981
The Burroughs File (prose and diaries) 1984
The Place of Dead Roads (novel) 1984
The Adding Machine (essays) 1985
Queer (novel) 1986
The Western Lands (novel) 1987

CRITICISM

E. S. Seldon (essay date January-February 1962)

[*In the following essay, Seldon applauds* Naked Lunch *as one of the most imaginative and original works of twentieth-century literature.*]

[*Naked Lunch*] is not the most impressive American literary debut in Paris since 1934, date of [Henry Miller's]

Tropic of Cancer; it's one of the most impressive literary debuts of the past century. At a moment when, I think, we have no lack of talents, Mr. Burroughs comes along and reminds us of what was lacking, all the same: not names to remember, but works. *Naked Lunch* is a finished work of literature, original, mature, challenging. The writer has something unusual and important to say, and he has found the only right way of saying it. This is one contemporary writer who can drop dead tomorrow, confident not in promise, but in fulfillment.

And I should think he might very well drop dead, William Burroughs. Not just from the strain of sustained originality (all traces of labor, of course, have been scrupulously removed), but from nervous exhaustion. This is a strenuous book, in a sense Teddy Roosevelt and Jack London might not have appreciated, a spiritual sense, and its exploration of frontiers beyond statistical mediocrity and institutional culture is hair-raising, both in perils run and alarming discoveries made. This is a case of overcivilization so extreme as to have blown off the top of the thermostat. Not to be mealy-mouthed, this is a book calculated to scare the shit out of anyone old enough to read it, and to set the behavioral scientists to counting over their methodological beads with new urgency. In other words, this is a book to the scale of world literature in an age of flight to outer space.

There are "influences," of course, but they have been fully assimilated. Henry Miller, what we used to call the "surrealist" Miller, he of the Cosmodemonic Telegraph Company and the other genial satires of life in what Rimbaud called the *raw, new metropolises* of the late-modern world. Burroughs has concentrated the old man's gift, boiled it down, writes with a better ear, and fires off salvos of such episodes at a time. Orwell must have provided clues for such divertissements as "technological surgery," and for the unforgettable day "the electronic brain went berserk playing six-dimensional chess with the Technician and released every subject in the R.C." thus precipitating a scene of mass carnage that Burroughs handles with easy mastery in a set piece worthy of Zola. This is the last paragraph:

> Rock and Roll adolescent hoodlums storm the streets of all nations. They rush into the Louvre and throw acid in the Mona Lisa's face. They open zoos, insane asylums, prisons, burst water mains with air hammers, chop the floor out of passenger plane lavatories, shoot out lighthouses, file elevator cables to one thin wire, turn sewers into the water supply, throw sharks and sting rays, electric eels and candiru into swimming pools . . . in nautical costumes ram the *Queen Mary* full speed into New York harbor, play chicken with passenger planes and busses, rush into hospitals in white coats carrying saws and axes and scalpels three feet long, throw paralytics out of iron lungs (mimic their suffocations flopping about on the floor and rolling their eyes up), administer injections with bicycle pumps, disconnect artificial kidneys, saw a woman in half with a two-man surgical saw, they drive herds of squealing pigs into the Curb, they shit on the floor of the United Nations and wipe their ass with treaties, pacts, alliances.

There is no lack of characters or events in *Naked Lunch,* and Mr. Burroughs never lets his knife-edge plain style dull into rhetoric. The nothing-if-not extreme situations and states of consciousness he treats are neither glamorized nor watered down. Intensely readable at whatever point you open it, his book is nonetheless put together in a completely original way which, to describe abstractly, sounds hopelessly confusing. All that really baffles, however, is his awe-inspiring artistry. He takes us on a very lively, scary, broadening journey, not in space and time, but from one particular kind of withdrawal from familiar existence out into what the analysts call the "real" world—way, way out into the social, collective world—and then right back again to where we started, staring fixedly at one shoe, or a crack in the wall.

Somewhere in the background, we are dimly aware of changing locales, just as, in the foreground, we are aware of shifting, splitting, and all but merging characters who might be either facets of a single character never portrayed as such (but presumably the author) or sole remaining fragments of different, individual characters in literal dissolution. What is so extraordinary is that this lack of a central character as such, as well as of a conventional narrative as such, produces nothing like blurriness or lack of coherence. To the contrary, it serves to sharpen the points of what Mr. Burroughs has to say; it leaves no possible *out* for the reader who might wish to pretend that Mr. Burroughs is saying something else than what, by this means, he so unequivocally gets said.

The purpose of all this, I am pretty sure, is not to make a hero, or an anti-hero, of the drug addict. Extreme addiction, which only in its terminal stages resembles the terminal stages of schizophrenia, is in its intermediate stages a cure for schizophrenia. Is this junky logic? I have no idea, but it is quite enough logic—and quite compellingly enough demonstrated in *Naked Lunch*—to create a unique angle of vision. We who are not addicts think of dope as an escape into nothing, an evasion of responsibility, a kind of ultimate selfishness. Well, this may not be the case, or rather, it may leave out an important aspect of the total case, which is betrayed by our ferocious persecution of the addict. After all, why should we care? Is individual self-destruction of such moment in a world of organized collective destruction—worse, of culturally defended *absolute* preconditions for collective destruction? From this point of view—where addiction, not idealized but literalized, is one pole of a conduct of life, the other pole of which is an adequately comprehended "reality" of much more savage scale and much more unmistakably *dangerous* cast—from this point of view, life appears as a choice between methods of arriving at the same disastrous conclution. And there may be a little more dignity (certainly a more nearly traditional *kind* of dignity) in the cool refusal to participate, to go to hell in your own way, patiently running through the pharmacopoeia and using up your own veins, than there is in projecting your inadequacies and dissatisfactions into socio-political and scientific schemes of what Burroughs calls a variously "Liquefactionist" or "Divisionist" character.

If I am not mistaken, this is a completely secular, truly sci-entific, historical *and* psychological restatement of the human predicament mankind once thought of religiously, as a choice between desiccation in the Thebaid or the anchorite's cell, for example, and wallowing in the world-historical brutalities of empire. Only such "extreme" statements, of course, can illuminate the human condition, caught up as we are at any given moment in the illusion that the five or ten degrees of the scale we occupy constitutes the full range of human possibility, from zero to infinity.

Much more unmistakable is the fact that Burroughs is a superb writer, and *Naked Lunch* a novel of revolt in the best late-modern sense. He is a much less genial writer than Henry Miller, and a much more intelligent one than Céline. And I had better insist: for all his spiritual strength, he invokes no fuzzy, subliminal powers, whether of a transcendental or an unconscious variety. He is quite as aware of what he is revolting against as of the individual human predicament he sympathizes with sufficiently not to understate its gravity. On the one hand, he gives a stunning going over to the objective, "scientifically" reinforced madness of institutional culture, while on the other, he shows the doomed individual desperately trying to preserve his own identity, at whatever cost—if necessary, all else failing, within the private world of his own skin:

> The body knows what veins you can hit and conveys this knowledge in the spontaneous movements you make preparing to take a shot. . . . Sometimes the needle points like a dowzer's wand. Sometimes I must wait for the message. But when it comes I always hit blood.

These lines are written with love; and to all, in the months and years to come, who try to tell you *Naked Lunch* is "a nasty book," just reply as I do, "Don't you mean lucid?"

Not too far beneath the hard, glittering, bitter surface of this original work, it is possible to hear a desperate cry not unlike that of the poet Artaud from the madhouse at Rodez. It is the cry of every as yet "uninstitutionalized" man everywhere to the impersonal collective forces which have him in their grip: just let us possess what at least exists, "the actual body of our immediate being in sempiternal time and space." American, more privileged than Artaud, and a generation younger (i.e., older), Burroughs understands also what desperation there is in studied deafness to this cry, as Artaud did not. This is why, like Sade, he deliberately "confuses" the executioners and the victims. *Naked Lunch* is a very worldly-wise, late-modern, nothing-if-not civilized version of the cannibal feast.

If, nonetheless, there should be a twenty-first century, this is one of the few works of our day historians could turn to for a grasp, both imaginative and intelligent, of the strange historical phase of the human condition we are living through: when reason is in official, institutional alliance with brute force, and the individual psyche systematically reduced to a garbage pail for the "negative" contents of life—i.e., whatever science cannot "use." There is no complacency here about "the present state of our knowledge." (pp. 110-13)

E. S. Seldon, "The Cannibal Feast," in Evergreen Review, *Vol. 6, No. 22, January-February, 1962, pp. 110-13.*

Mary McCarthy (essay date February 1963)

[*McCarthy was a respected American novelist, essayist, and critic. During the 1930s, she was a major figure among the New York Intellectuals, a group of writers and thinkers whose leftist social and political beliefs had a major influence on modern critical thought. In the following essay, McCarthy applauds Burroughs for his avant-garde style and places* Naked Lunch *among the most important works of postwar literature.*]

"You can cut into *The Naked Lunch* at any intersection point," says Burroughs, suiting the action to the word, in "an atrophied preface" he appends as a tail-piece. His book, he means, is like a neighborhood movie with continuous showings that you can drop into whenever you please—you don't have to wait for the beginning of the feature picture. Or like a worm that you can chop up into sections each of which wriggles off as an independent worm. Or a nine-lived cat. Or a cancer. He is fond of the word "mosaic," especially in its scientific sense of a plant-mottling caused by a virus, and his Muse (see etymology of "mosaic") is interested in organic processes of multiplication and duplication. The literary notion of time as simultaneous, a montage, is not original with Burroughs; what is original is the scientific bent he gives it and a view of the world that combines biochemistry, anthorpology, and politics. It is as though *Finnegans Wake* were cut loose from history and adapted for a cinerama circus titled "One World." *The Naked Lunch* has no use for history, which is all "ancient history"—sloughed-off skin; from its planetary perspective, there are only geography and customs. Seen in terms of space, history shrivels into a mere wrinkling or furrowing of the surface as in an aerial relief-map or one of those pieced-together aerial photographs known in the trade as mosaics. The oldest memory in *The Naked Lunch* is of jacking-off in boyhood latrines, a memory recaptured through pederasty. This must be the first space novel, the first serious piece of science fiction—the others are entertainment.

BOSTON, Jan. 13 (AP) Superior Court Judge Eugene A. Hudson took under advisement today a suit by the state attorney general asking that the book *Naked Lunch,* by William S. Burroughs, be declared obscene and banned from sale in Massachusetts.

—The New York Times, *1965.*

The action of *The Naked Lunch* takes place in the consciousness of One Man, William Lee, who is taking a drug cure. The principal characters, besides Lee, are his friend, Bill Gains (who seems momentarily to turn into a woman called Jane), various members of the Narcotic Squad, especially one Bradley the Buyer, Dr. Benway, a charlatan medico who is treating Lee, two vaudevillians, Clem and Jody, A. J., a carnival con man, the last of the Big Spenders, a sailor, an Arab called Ahmed, an archetypal Southern druggist, Doc Parker ("a man don't have no secrets from God and his druggist"), and various boys with whining voices. Among the minor characters are a number of automobiles, each with its specific complaint, like the oil-burning Ford V-8, a film executive, the Party Leader, the Vigilante, John and Mary, the sex acrobats, and a puzzled American housewife who is heard complaining because the Mixmaster keeps trying to climb up under her dress. The scene shifts about, shiftily, from New York to Chicago to St. Louis to New Orleans to Mexico to Malmo, Sweden, Venice, and the human identities shift about shiftily too, for all these modern places and modern individuals (if that is the right word) have interchangeable parts. Burroughs is fond too of the word "ectoplasm," and the beings that surround Lee, particularly the inimical ones, seem ectoplasmic phantoms projected on the wide screen of his consciousness from a mass séance. But the haunting is less visual than auditory. These "characters," in the colloquial sense, are ventriloquial voices produced, as it were, against the will of the ventriloquist, who has become their dummy. Passages of dialogue and description keep recurring in different contexts with slight variations, as though they possessed ubiquity.

The best comparison for the book, with its aerial sex acts performed on a high trapeze, its con men and barkers, its arena-like form, is in fact a circus. A circus travels but it is always the same, and this is Burroughs' sardonic image of modern life. The Barnum of the show is the mass-manipulator, who appears in a series of disguises. *Control,* as Burroughs says, underlining it, *can never be a means to anything but more control—like drugs,* and the vicious circle of addiction is reenacted, world-wide, with sideshows in the political and "social" sphere—the social here has vanished, except in quotation marks, like the historical, for everything has become automatized. Everyone is an addict of one kind or another, as people indeed are wont to say of themselves, complacently: "I'm a crossword puzzle addict, a High-Fi addict," etcetera. The South is addicted to lynching and nigger-hating, and the Southern folk-custom of burning a Negro recurs throughout the book as a sort of Fourth-of-July carnival with fireworks. Circuses, with their cages of wild animals, are also dangerous, like Burroughs' human circus; an accident may occur, as when the electronic brain in Dr. Benway's laboratory goes on the rampage, and the freaks escape to mingle with the controlled citizens of Freeland in a general riot, or in the scene where the hogs are let loose in the gourmet restaurant.

On a level usually thought to be "harmless," addiction to platitudes and commonplaces is global. To Burroughs' ear, the Bore, lurking in the hotel lobby, is literally deadly (" 'You look to me like a man of intelligence.' Always ominous opening words, my boy!"). The same for Doc Parker with his captive customer in the back room of his pharmacy (" . . . so long as you got a legitimate condition and an Rx from a certified, bona feedy M.D., I'm honored to serve you"), the professor in the classroom ("Hehe hehe he"), the attorney in court ("Hehe hehe he," likewise). The complacent sound of snickering laughter is an alarm signal, like the suave bell-tones of the psychiatrist and the emphatic drone of the Party Leader ("You see men and women. *Ordinary* men and women going about their ordinary everyday tasks. Leading their ordinary lives. That's what we need . . .").

Cut to ordinary men and women, going about their ordinary everyday tasks. The whine of the put-upon boy hustler: "All kinda awful sex acts." "Why cancha just get physical like a human?" "So I guess he come to some kinda awful climax." "You think I am innarested to hear about your horrible old condition? I am not innarested at all." "But he comes to a climax and turns into some kinda awful crab." This aggrieved tone merges with the malingering sighs of the American housewife, opening a box of Lux: "I got the most awful cold, and my intestines is all constipated." And the clarion of the Salesman: "When the Priority numbers are called up yonder I'll be there." These average folks are addicts of the science page of the Sunday supplements; they like to talk about their diseases and about vile practices that paralyze the practitioner from the waist down or about a worm that gets into your kidney and grows to enormous size or about the "horrible" result of marijuana addiction—it makes you turn black and your legs drop off. The superstitious scientific vocabulary is diffused from the laboratory and the mental hospital into the general population. Overheard at a lynching: "Don't crowd too close, boys. His intestines is subject to explode in the fire." The same diffusion of culture takes place with modern physics. A lieutenant to his general: "But, chief, can't we get them started and they imitate each other like a chained reaction?"

The phenomenon of repetition, of course, gives rise to boredom; many readers complain that they cannot get through *The Naked Lunch.* And/or that they find it disgusting. It *is* disgusting and sometimes tiresome, often in the same places. The prominence of the anus, of faeces, and of all sorts of "horrible" discharges, as the characters would say, from the body's orifices, becomes too much of a bad thing, like the sado-masochistic sex performances— the automatic ejaculation of a hanged man is not everybody's cantharides. A reader whose erogenous zones are more temperate than the author's begins to feel either that he is a square (a guilty sentiment he should not yield to) or that he is the captive of an addict.

In defense, Swift could be cited, and indeed between Burroughs and Swift there are many points of comparison; not only the obsession with excrement and the horror of female genitalia but a disgust with politics and the whole body politic. Like Swift, Burroughs has irritable nerves and something of the crafty temperament of the inventor. There is a great deal of Laputa in the countries Burroughs calls Interzone and Freeland, and Swift's solution for the Irish problem would appeal to the American's dry logic. As Gulliver, Swift posed as an anthropologist (though the study was not known by that name then) among savage people; Burroughs parodies the anthropologist in his descriptions of the American heartland: " . . . the Interior

a vast subdivision, antennae of television to the meaningless sky. . . . Illinois and Missouri, miasma of mound-building peoples, grovelling worship of the Food Source, cruel and ugly festivals." The style here is more emotive than Swift's, but in his deadpan explanatory notes ("This is a rural English custom designed to eliminate aged and bedfast dependents") there is a Swiftian factuality. The "factual" appearance of the whole narrative, with its battery of notes and citations, some straight, some loaded, its extracts from a diary, like a ship's log, its pharmacopeia, has the flavor of eighteenth-century satire. He calls himself a "Factualist" and belongs, all alone, to an Age of Reason, which he locates in the future. In him, as in Swift, there is a kind of soured utopianism.

Yet what saves *The Naked Lunch* is not a literary ancestor but humor. Burroughs' humor is peculiarly American, at once broad and sly. It is the humor of a comedian, a vaudeville performer playing in *One,* in front of the asbestos curtain to some Keith Circuit or Pantages house long since converted to movies. The same jokes reappear, slightly refurbished, to suit the circumstances, the way a vaudeville artist used to change Yonkers to Renton when he was playing Seattle. For example, the Saniflush joke, which is always good for a laugh: somebody is cutting the cocaine/the morphine/the penicillin with Saniflush. Some of the jokes are verbal ("Stop me if you've heard this atomic secret" or Dr. Benway's "A simopath . . . is a citizen convinced he is an ape or other simian. It is a disorder peculiar to the army and discharge cures it"). Some are mimic buffoonery (Dr. Benway, in his last appearance, dreamily, his voice fading out: "Cancer, my first love"). Some are whole vaudeville "numbers," as when the hoofers, Clem and Jody, are hired by the Russians to give Americans a bad name abroad: they appear in Liberia wearing black Stetsons and red galluses and talking loudly about burning niggers back home. A skit like this may rise to a frenzy, as if in a Marx Brothers or a Clayton, Jackson, and Durante act. *E.g.,* the very funny scene in Chez Robert, "where a huge icy gourmet broods over the greatest cuisine in the world": A. J. appears, the last of the Big Spenders, and orders a bottle of ketchup; immediate pandemonium; A. J. gives his hog-call, and the shocked gourmet diners are all devoured by famished hogs. The effect of pandemonium, all hell breaking loose, is one of Burroughs' favorites and an equivalent of the old vaudeville finale, with the acrobats, the jugglers, the magician, the hoofers, the lady-who-was-cut-in-half, the piano player, the comedians, all pushing into the act.

Another favorite effect, with Burroughs, is the metamorphosis. A citizen is turned into animal form, a crab or a huge centipede, or into some unspeakable monstrosity like Bradley the Narcotics Agent who turns into an unidentifiable carnivore. These metamorphoses, of course, are punishments. The Hellzapoppin effect of orgies and riots and the metamorphosis effect, rapid or creeping, are really cancerous onslaughts—matter on the rampage multiplying itself and "building" as a revue scene "builds" to a climax. Growth and deterioration are the same thing: a human being "deteriorates" or "grows" into a one-man jungle. What you think of it depends on your point of view; from the junky's angle, Bradley is better as a carnivore eating the Narcotics Commissioner than he was as "fuzz"—junky slang for the police.

The impression left by this is perplexing. On the one hand, control is evil; on the other, escape from control is mass slaughter or reduction to a state of proliferating cellular matter. The police are the enemy, but as Burroughs shrewdly observes in one passage: "A *functioning* police state needs no police." The policeman is internalized in the citizen. You might say that it would have been better to have no control, no police, in the first place; then there would be no police states, functioning or otherwise. This would seem to be Burroughs' position, but it is not consistent with his picture of sex. The libertarian position usually has as one of its axioms a love of Nature and the natural, that is, of the life-principle itself, commonly identified with sex . . . But there is little overt love of the life-principle in *The Naked Lunch,* and sex, while magnified—a common trait of homosexual literature—is a kind of mechanical mantrap baited with fresh meat. The sexual climax, the jet of sperm, accompanied by a whistling scream, is often a death spasm, and the "perfect" orgasm would seem to be the posthumous orgasm of the hanged man, shooting his jissom into pure space.

It is true that Nature and sex are two-faced and that growth is death-oriented. But if Nature is not seen as far more good than evil, then a need for control is posited. And, strangely, this seems to be Burroughs' position too. *The human virus can now be treated,* he says with emphasis, meaning the species itself. By scientific methods, he implies. Yet the laboratory of *The Naked Lunch* is a musical-comedy inferno, and Dr. Benway's assistant is a female chimpanzee. It is impossible, as Burroughs knows, to have scientific experiment without control. Then what? Self-control? Do-it-yourself? But self-control, again, is an internalized system of authority, a subjection of the impulse to the will, the least "natural" part of the personality. Such a system might suit Marcus Aurelius, but it hardly seems congenial to the author of *The Naked Lunch.* And even if it were (for the author is at once puritan and tolerant), it would not form the basis for scientific experiment on the "human virus." Only for scientific experiment on oneself.

Possibly this is what Burroughs means: in fact his present literary exercises may be stages in such a deliberate experiment. The questions just posed would not arise if *The Naked Lunch* did not contain messages that unluckily are somewhat arcane. Not just messages; prescriptions. That—to answer a pained question that keeps coming up like a refrain—is why the book is taken seriously. Burroughs' remarkable talent is only part of the reason; the other part is that, finally, for the first time in recent years, a talented writer means what he says to be taken and used literally, like an Rx prescription. The literalness of Burroughs is the opposite of "literature." Unsentimental and factual, he writes as though his thoughts had the quality of self-evidence. In short, he has a crankish courage, but all courage nowadays is probably crankish. (pp. 4-5)

Mary McCarthy, "Dejeuner sur l'Herbe," in The New York Review of Books, *Vol. 1, No. 1, February, 1963, pp. 4-5.*

An excerpt from *Naked Lunch*

Dr. Benway had been called in as advisor to the Freeland Republic, a place given over to free love and continual bathing. The citizens are well adjusted, cooperatives, honest, tolerant and above all clean. But the invoking of Benway indicates all is not well behind that hygienic facade: Benway is a manipulator and coordinator of symbol systems, an expert on all phases of interrogation, brainwashing and control. I have not seen Benway since his precipitate departure from Annexia, where his assignment had been T.D.—Total Demoralization. Benway's first act was to abolish concentration camps, mass arrest and, except under certain limited and special circumstances, the use of torture.

"I deplore brutality," he said. "It's not efficient. On the other hand, prolonged mistreatment, short of physical violence, gives rise, when skillfully applied, to anxiety and a feeling of special guilt. A few rules or rather guiding principles are to be borne in mind. The subject must not realize that the mistreatment is a deliberate attack of an anti-human enemy on his personal identity. He must be made to feel that he deserves *any* treatment he receives because there is something (never specified) horribly wrong with him. The naked need of the control addicts must be decently covered by an arbitrary and intricate bureaucracy so that the subject cannot contact his enemy direct."

Every citizen of Annexia was required to apply for and carry on his person at all times a whole portfolio of documents. Citizens were subject to be stopped in the street at any time; and the Examiner, who might be in plain clothes, in various uniforms, often in a bathing suit or pyjamas, sometimes stark naked except for a badge pinned to his left nipple, after checking each paper, would stamp it. On subsequent inspection the citizen was required to show the properly entered stamps of the last inspection. The Examiner, when he stopped a large group, would only examine and stamp the cards of a few. The others were then subject to arrest because their cards were not properly stamped. Arrest meant "provisional detention"; that is, the prisoner would be released if and when his Affidavit of Explanation, properly signed and stamped, was approved by the Assistant Arbiter of Explanations. Since this official hardly ever came to his office, and the Affidavit of Explanation had to be presented in person, the explainers spent weeks and months waiting around in unheated offices with no chairs and no toilet facilities.

Documents issued in vanishing ink faded into old pawn tickets. New documents were constantly required. The citizens rushed from one bureau to another in a frenzied attempt to meet impossible deadlines.

William S. Burroughs, in his Naked Lunch, *Grove Press, 1959.*

Lionel Abel   (essay date Spring 1963)

[*Abel was an American educator and critic. In the following essay, he argues that if* Naked Lunch *is considered literature, then the state of literature has seen a general decline.*]

Mary McCarthy is quite right in comparing Burroughs'

images to a moving picture. For one can begin to read Burroughs' book at any point, the middle, the beginning, or the end. But what she says is misleading if understood to imply that the book has real continuity, as most films have. One can begin to read anywhere in *Naked Lunch* insofar as any part or section of the book is anywhere in the book. I think, too, that Miss McCarthy might have specified the *kind* of movie *Naked Lunch* suggests: it is rather like those pornographic films that give dispirited people a dull pleasure. It is also like another kind of film: the documentaries, shown after the war, of Nazi concentration camp atrocities. Combine the two kinds of film in your imagination and you will have some notion of what is peculiar to Mr. Burroughs' work. His scenes of linked, unlovely bodies are scenes of bodies bitten, beaten, and mangled, bodies in the process of destroying other bodies and of being destroyed by them, with sex, of some horrible form, going on all the while. Now let me say right here that I find pornographic films without interest. And I could never bear the newsreel films of concentration camp horrors. How can anyone enjoy, I wonder, the dullness—amalgamated with horror—in Mr. Burroughs' book?

I think I understand why Norman Mailer likes this sort of thing. But I do not understand his way of formulating his liking. For there is neither "beauty" nor "exquisiteness" in *Naked Lunch,* as he attests. And when Robert Lowell calls the book " . . . completely powerful and serious . . . as good as anything in prose or poetry written by a 'beat' writer . . . " his is fundamentally an aesthetic judgment, a judgment of the book in comparison with other books. For Lowell has not at all faced up to the question of why anyone should want to read, let alone praise, *Naked Lunch.* Miss McCarthy, more aware that the book is problematic, tries to justify it as humorous: " . . . what saves *Naked Lunch* is . . . humor." And she gives some instances of Burroughs' humor, not a single one even vaguely funny to this reader. Miss McCarthy should know better, having far more humor herself.

Should people read *Naked Lunch* to be saddened by it? But there is little sadness in the work, just as there is no humor. Such sadness as I felt came to me not in the course of reading, but afterward, when I reflected on why the book was written, on why it has become part of literature. What need could such a work satisfy? It must have satisfied some need to have achieved its present vogue.

Very probably there is a metaphysical need in many people which cannot nowadays be satisfied by the "high" experiences of ethical decision, speculative wonder, communion with nature or with others; such "high" experiences are not now capable of putting people in touch. And evidently there is a persisting need to be in touch with something—no matter what—that can be felt as ultimately real, decisively so.

A quarter of a century ago in Paris, the philosopher Jean Wahl gave a lecture, now famous, in which he made the point that transcendence—the act of going beyond appearances—may move upward or downward: one may transcend upward toward God, or clear values, or downward toward obscure values, or the "dark gods" of whom Lawrence wrote. And Wahl, in making his point, coined two new words: trans-ascendence and trans-descendence. I remember his saying to me of the second word: "Isn't it beautiful?" But what the word describes is most eminently not beautiful, and not exquisite either, to refer once again to Mailer's two adjectives for Burroughs' effort. For to trans-descend means to get to the real at some point where everything normally valid in experience is forgotten or discarded, notably the beautiful. The goal is to arrive at the conviction that one has touched on something incorrigibly, incontrovertibly extreme, no matter how horrid, no matter how painful, no matter how far outside any moral or aesthetic discrimination. The main thing is utterness: being as utterness. And this utterness, for some reason or other, people hope to experience nowadays in nausea, in dread, in violence, in impotence, or in "total need"—Burroughs' phrase for the situation of the drug addict.

One wonders: if there is a metaphysical impulse, a real need for Being, why is this need not satisfied today in so-called higher experiences? Modern skepticism, no doubt, has destroyed the prestige of God, moral decision, speculative wonder, love or rapture. But why has it not destroyed the metaphysical prestige of crime or drug addiction? There is an interesting saying by a somewhat criminal-minded Sabbatian Cabbalist of the eighteenth century: "When the brave knights are beaten and the wise men want to retreat, a know-nothing will sneak in through a sewer and take the castle by stealth . . . "

Our skepticism is strong when it comes to trans-ascendence, weak when it comes to trans-descendence.

Now it is foolish, I think, to justify *Naked Lunch* as literature. Its descriptions of hallucinatory states under drug addiction are neither beautiful nor exquisite nor brilliant nor informative. I even wonder whether they are true. According to the author himself, the junkie has no sense of sex or sense of shame or interest in his own sexual organs: "It is doubtful if shame can exist in the absence of sexual libido. . . . The junkie's shame disappears with his non-sexual sociability which is also dependent on libido. . . . The addict regards his body impersonally as an instrument to absorb the medium in which he lives, evaluates his tissue with the cold hands of a horse trader." *Naked Lunch* supposedly describes states of consciousness where anything like sex, according to the author himself, could not even be dimly glimpsed. Yet the hallucinations described all involve sex, and the author's prose is constantly sexualized. Is this due to literary influences? The influence of Henry Miller, or perhaps of Lautréamont? But the question remains: why the insistence on sex, however horrible, if a true description of the junkie's state of mind would have to leave out sex altogether?

Apparently Mr. Burroughs' book is no more in the service of the true than it is in the service of the beautiful. In fact, it has only a tiny bit of literary merit. And yet it does satisfy something in the reader. Something not exactly literary, but something from which literature cannot completely separate itself: the need for utterness, utterness in some form, however degraded, painful, spasmodic, or obscene, utterness as a sign, at least, of something more real than the things we are normally in contact with. In an age of crisis literature will trans-ascend or trans-descend, one or the other. That *Naked Lunch* trans-descends is its single claim to be literature.

Trans-descending has recently become a veritable cult: utterness, and the search for it, have served to justify violence in sex, in morals, in extremist politics (Black Muslim or Castroite), and in art. Did not André Breton prophesy during the last war: "Beauty will be convulsive, or not be"? In a much admired play by Edward Albee, *The Zoo Story,* a schizophrenic bum is pitted, with the author's evident support, against a domesticated and conformist intellectual. At the climax of the play the protagonist forces the trivial character he has been denouncing to impale him on a knife. The bum dies: a sacrifice to utterness. Now the values asserted in this work are much the same as those used by Norman Mailer in his essay "The White Negro" to justify hipsters and psychopaths. I should note, too, that Jean Genet first attracted attention to himself in Paris as a person with serious aims by announcing a criminal one: the aim was to kill a young man beautiful enough to be worthy of being killed by Genet. And very recently James Baldwin excited the interest of sophisticated people in this country by threatening the whole white population with black violence. In his *New Yorker* article, "From a Region in My Mind," Baldwin alternately beseeched and bullied white Americans as follows: Help us save you—from us! The electric effect of his article, which did not contain a single clear political idea and was full of abusive threats— of a racist sort, by the way—can be explained only by its extremism, for extremism has now become very modish. Nor is it hard to understand why. We live in a world where trivia have become preponderant; moreover, to complicate matters, ahead of our present-day trivia, in the political future, lies possible catastrophe. Naturally, most of those inclined to support any escape from triviality, are themselves quite incapable of being untrivial, except vicariously. These are the fellow travelers of the cult of utterness and they make up a good part of the audience for Mailer's and Baldwin's books, for Genet's novels and plays, and for William Burroughs' *Naked Lunch.*

I feel sorry for William Burroughs insofar as he had to write his book, but I feel sorry, too, for literature, insofar as it is now in some sense dependent on and cannot be altogether dissociated from an effort such as his. For clearly, literature cannot justify itself solely as literature; it is not independent of life, it needs to be needed for some other purpose than a purely literary one. For what purpose? In this era, the purpose seems to be, perhaps must be, the satisfaction of a metaphysical need not satisfied elsewhere. In which case, however lacking in literary merit *Naked Lunch,* it is going to be considered and judged—and admired—as literature. (pp. 109-12)

Lionel Abel, "Beyond the Fringe," in Partisan Review, *Vol. XXX, No. 1, Spring, 1963, pp. 109-12.*

Richard Kostelanetz (essay date October 1965)

[*Kostelanetz is an American poet, essayist, and critic. In the following essay, he places Burroughs among the best of the Beat writers while asserting that* Naked Lunch *transcends such narrow identification.*]

In the past decade or so, the experience of drugs has replaced sex as the "daring" subject of avant-garde literature. Like so much else in modern literature, this new writing is largely concerned with special states of consciousness; but whereas the former deals with madnesses from more-or-less "natural" causes—varieties of mental derangement from neurosis through perversion to insanity—the latter literature portrays externally induced psychic experience. Authors of drug literature include Aldous Huxley (of the best known and, perhaps, the least convincing), Henri Michaux, Michael McClure, Clarence L. Cooper, Paul Bowles, Alexander Trocchi and even Alexander King, among others; but, to my mind, the most extraordinary work in this drug literature so far is William Burroughs' *Naked Lunch.* Probably the most universally controversial book since Joyce's two masterpieces— indeed, perhaps the sole contemporary work capable of inspiring arguments that dissolve friendships—*Naked Lunch* is a great work precisely because it transcends a concern with narcotics as such to realize a drug experience in an achieved and appropriate literary style. In this respect, *Naked Lunch* does for heroin what Malcolm Lowry's *Under the Volcano* did for alcoholism; by fusing a certain neglected experience to a resonant literary technique, Burroughs takes narcotics out of the realm of reportage and scientific treatise (its prime domain so far) and appropriates it as a viable subject for literature.

In essence, *Naked Lunch* is a report of the hallucinatory madness Burroughs experienced during withdrawal from heroin addiction; and in structure, the book is a collection of scenes, gathered (and perhaps edited and revised) from notes he jotted down while undergoing withdrawal shock, notes whose contents were not remembered afterwards. The narrator is identified as William Lee; but since Burroughs used that name as a *non-deplume* for his earlier, first novel *Junkie,* one assumes that Lee is Burroughs himself, a *persona* in his own dream world.

Subject to wild dreams since youth, the narrator, while in withdrawal, further excites and deranges his mind with a variety of non-addicting hallucinating drugs until he has some of the most extraordinary fantasies ever recorded in print, fantasies which are so wildly original that one suspects they could not possibly be created by a conscious mind. Like all truly unprecedented contemporary creations, these fantasies are simultaneously shocking and comic, managing to evoke at once both horror and humor. "The President is a junky but can't take it direct because of his position. So he gets fixed through me. . . . From time to time we make contact, and I recharge him." Burroughs' ideal male (shades of the American archetype) is possessed of an incredible homosexual competence:

In Tumbucktu I once saw an Arab boy who could play the flute with his ass, and the fairies told me he was really an individual in bed. He could play a tune up and down the organ hitting the most erogenously sensitive spots, which are different on everyone, of course. Every lover had his special theme song which was perfect for him and rose to his climax. The boy was a great artist when it came to improvising new combines and special climaxes . . .

In his apparently chaotic, but basically coherent, style, Burroughs is able to capture the simultaneous impact that many events have upon the relaxed, free-associating mind:

> Minarets, palms, mountains, jungle. . . . A sluggish river jumping with vicious fish, vast weed-grown parks where boys lie in the grass, play cryptic games. Not a locked door in the city. Anyone comes into your room at any time. The Chief of Police is a Chinese who picks his teeth and listens to denunciation presented by a lunatic. Every now and then the Chinese takes the toothpick out of his mouth and looks at the end of it. Hipsters with smooth-copper-colored faces lounge in doorways twisting shrunk heads on gold chains, their faces blank with an insect's unseeing calm.

Furthermore, Burroughs is able to record unerringly that certain movement between immediacy and memory. Emphasis shifts between fact and fancy (the reader is never quite sure where one ends and the other begins) into the nether-region where both converge:

> I can feel the heat closing in, feel them out there making their moves, setting up their devil doll stool pigeons, crooning over my spoon and dropper I throw away at Washington Square Station, vault a turnstile and two flights down the iron stairs, catch an uptown A train. . . . And right on time this narcotics dick in a white trench coat (imagine tailing somebody in a white trench coat—trying to pass as a fag I guess) hit the platform. . . .

Throughout the book, Burroughs confronts social fact with his hallucinatory powers, creating a continuous stream of original, arresting images.

Although much of the book is distinctly beautiful, in the best contemporary mode of unusual, difficult beauty, *Naked Lunch* is still among the most horrifying and terrible books ever written. Admittedly, the disintegration of psyche and environment is among the stock themes of contemporary literature; but no single book I know has presented it with such oppressive intensity and enveloping totality. In contrast to books which depict a sick man in a reasonably healthy world or those which portray a good man pitted against the world's evil, *Naked Lunch* evokes a world of total sickness, without an outpost of purity or even a glimmering hope of cure. To describe this quality, the American critic Kenneth Rexroth, in a masterful impressionist stroke, once quipped, "When you get through with Celine's great classic [*Journey to the End of Night*], you wonder why everybody didn't hang himself. When you finish Burroughs' book you wonder why do don't yourself." The emotion is exaggerated; but the contrast is appropriate; the discrimination, true. No other book evokes the possible horror of a contemporary existence with such thoroughness or such uncompromising images of decay and violence as *Naked Lunch.*

At the center of this deracinated universe is the narrator himself. Though intelligent, educated and independently wealthy, Burroughs has one sole mission in life, to feed his habit. Besides so dominating the addict's attention that he neglects everything else, particularly his bodily needs, heroin functions as a depressant that lifts the addict out of the world of pain into a euphoria that is both painless and timeless. He remarks, in a telling detail, that an addict can contemplate the end of his shoe for eight hours. The addict lives an oppressively isolated existence, never trusting those from whom he gets narcotics, identifying with fellow junkies only in their common servitude. He indirectly evokes his own emotional sterility in the cold, clinician's tones he uses to describe the putridity of those around him:

> Willy has a round, disk mouth lined with sensitive, erectile black hairs. He is blind from shooting in the eyeball, his nose and palate eaten away sniffing H., his body a mass of scar tissue hard and dry as wood.

Many a writer views the misfortune of life with strongly felt indignation; and even Hemingway's stoical stance implies the suppression of emotion. Burroughs, in sharp contrast, is so detached from the plight of himself and those around him that he is incapable of even a minimal involvement. He is, literally, alienated beyond awareness of alienation.

The brief clinical essays on comparative narcotics reveal Burroughs' scholarly flair; yet behind the textbookish tone one perceives a sense of the total and inescapable horror of the heroin addict's life—the constant, ineluctable movement between consciousless euphoria and the overwhelming pain of abstinence:

> Eventual result of junk are—especially true of heroin addiction where large doses are available to the addict—is permanent backbrain depression and a state much like terminal schizophrenia: complete loss of affect, autism, virtual absence of cerebral event.

Continually Burroughs remarks that contrary to popular belief heroin dampens rather than stimulates sexual appetite. "He [the addict] is conscious of his surroundings, but they have no emotional connotation and in consequence no interest." Burroughs also remembers, metaphorically, that during addiction "the days glide by strung on a syringe with a long thread of blood." Despite the icy, distant, objective tones of these passages, the reader knows that Burroughs, who notes in the introduction to *Naked Lunch* that he has used nearly every known narcotic, is always writing from personal experience.

In his fantasies, Burroughs lives in an alien, imaginary city, evoked in stunning images of incomprehensibility and decay:

> All the streets of the City slope down between deepening canyons to a vast, kidney-shaped plaza full of darkness. Walls of street and plaza are perforated by dwelling cubicles and cafes, some a few feet deep, others extending out of sight in a network of rooms and corridors.

In this city, whose people have gone completely berserk, a normal mind and body are non-existent:

> IND's stand around in front of the cafe tables,

long streamers of saliva hanging off their chins, stomachs noisily churning, others ejaculate at the sight of women. A contingent of howling simopaths swing from chandeliers, balconies and trees, shitting and pissing on passers-by. A battalion of rampant bores prowls the streets and hotel lobbies in search of victims.

In contrast to, say, Allen Ginsberg, who screams his disgust, Burroughs' strategy is to present grotesque details and then accent the horror of his materials by employing a completely deadpan rhetoric.

The people of the city fall into two groups—the horrendously evil, usually identified by specific names, and the anonymous dregs. Among the former are Salvador Hassan O'Leary, the mythical international mogul, the Man behind the Man, who "held 23 passports and had been deported 49 times"; Doctor Benway, a scientific man using his knowledge for purposeless, unprecedented evil, who is in charge of "interrogation, brainwashing and control" in Annexia, a totalitarian country. In the middle of a violent riot he runs about sampling the blood of the dead; later, he appears as an expert in the Ministry of Mental Hygiene and Prophylaxis directing experiments to separate man from his nature. Another figure, "A. J." is a devilish prankster who puts pirhana fish into a socialite's swimming pool, a mixture of Yage, Hashish and Yohimbine into the punch used at the Fourth of July celebration at the American Embassy, and a South American vine that turns one's gums too much into the "pure spring water" that the anti-Floride society served as a dinner toast.

The figures in the background of the novel, the second group, are the nameless scum of the addict's world—Middle Eastern homosexuals who cruelly rape and abuse young boys, the incurable addicts impoverished by the expense of their habit, addicts who pose as policemen to steal the junk of others. There are the lonely old opium addicts—"a few old relics from hop-smoking times, spectral panitors, grey as ashes, phantom partners sweeping out dusty halls with a slow old man's hand, coughing and spitting in the junk-sick dawn, retired asthmatic fences in theatrical hotels. . . . " The old junkies so furiously pounce upon junk and remain so hopelessly unaware of anything besides this dominating quest that, "The spit hangs off their chin, and their stomach rumbles. . . . You expect any moment a great blob of protoplasm will flop right out and surround the junk." With none of these characters does the alienated Burroughs have any sympathy or close relations; and no one in the book appears capable of redeeming his world.

To name his city, Burroughs coins "Interzone," along with other imaginative terms, to classify the people who comprise his world of hell. The "Liquificationists" are the constant pleasure-seekers, taking from whoever is willing, "given to every form of perversion, especially sadomasochistic practices. . . . " The "Senders" are the powerful brutes, "the most dangerous and evil men in the world." The "Divisionists" seems to be Burroughs' metaphorical equivalent of the sociologists' "lonely crowd." "They are called Divisionists because they literally divide. They cut off tiny bits of their flesh and grow exact replicas of themselves in embryo jelly. It seems probable, unless the process of division is halted, that eventually there will be only one replica of one sex on the planet." These people give the city the oppressive feel of a crowded box. "The Zone is a single, vast building," Burroughs writes, employing an imaginative metaphor; "The rooms are made of plastic cement that bulges to accommodate people, but when too many crowd into one room, there is a soft plop and someone squeezes through the wall right into the next house." In these resonant images of human insignificance, environmental decay, oppressiveness and madness—images strung on a disjointed but coherent narrative—Burroughs creates one of the most fabulous cities in modern writing, a mythic city which remotely resembles, perhaps as an anti-utopian vision of the possible, the ones we know.

The book is constructed as a report—better, a series of reports—written by a traveller in a foreign land (and published after his return); and like any piece of reportage, it subscribes to the aesthetics of accuracy. "There is only one thing a writer can write about: *What is in front of his senses at the moment of writing. . . .* " "I am a recording instrument," Burroughs says; "I do not impose 'story,' 'plot,' 'continuity' . . . Insofar as I succeed in *direct* recording of certain areas of psychic process I may have a limited function . . . " As a reporter, he succeeds in evoking his singular experience; as an artist, he sustains his vision of life through the entire book. Because his book aims to be more vision than narrative, Burroughs, relying more upon images than plot, *Naked Lunch* achieves the overall spatial form that justifies its author's boast, "You can cut into *Naked Lunch* at any intersection point." (Since heroin experience is the achievement of timelessness, this form is deftly appropriate.) Indeed, Burroughs' plan gives the book the most contemporary of structures, what Marshall McLuhan calls "corporate form. . . . an evening watching television programs is an experience in a corporate form—an endless succession of impressions and snatches of narrative," adding that to render this aesthetic experience "on paper, the method of discontinuous non-story must be employed." As McLuhan pointed out in his brilliant essay on Burroughs, *Naked Lunch* joins Joyce's *Finnegans Wake* in belonging among the few contemporary literary works that successfully emulate the formal revolution of electronic media.

All writers are or once were active readers; and Burroughs, a Harvard alumnus, was surely, at one time at least, influenced by literature. Like most original modern books, *Naked Lunch* joins and still transcends several traditions of modern and American writing. On one hand, as an excursion into hell, somewhat fantasied, of the modern metropolis, *Naked Lunch* reminds us of Nathanael West's *Miss Lonlyhearts,* Edward Dahlberg's *Bottom Dogs,* and Henry Roth's *Call It Sleep;* yet in no great way does Burroughs particularly echo any of these writers. Although his scatological wit, vignette structure or (perhaps) lumpen-Bohemian milieu recall Henry Miller's works, Burroughs' novel lacks the affirmation of an unconventional life and the emotional engagement with his materials that marks Miller's writing. Indeed, whereas Miller's books work to persuade the reader to emulate the author, *Naked Lunch* is totally repelling. As an example of the modern form of autobiographical novel, in which authentic facts and experience are purposely transformed, Burroughs suggests affinities again with Miller and Celine and also with Jean Genet and Curzio Malaparte, yet without ever echoing any of them. In that all but Miller write of a first-person narrator going down, down, down in the course of the book (In Genet's case, the relevant comparison is with *Thief's Journal,* not *Our Lady of the Flowers*), there are similarities; but Celine and Genet and, to a lesser extent, Malaparte are deeply conscious of their alienation, bitterly attacking the enemy world. Burroughs cannot conceive of any war against normal society; for there is no world outside the one he knows; and I suspect that this stance explains why he can so unself-consciously relate in accurate detail an existence that nearly all his readers would find unspeakably filthy and sub-moral—Burroughs, apparently, does not sense that such readers exist!

As an unprecedently imaginative and powerful, rather than flawless work of art, *Naked Lunch* belongs in the major American tradition. In its movement away from normal social life into the realm of metaphysical experience and in opening the reader's mind to untypical individual experience (rather than cutting off and defining a familiar segment), Burroughs' book is what Richard Chase defined as a "romance," the dominant mode of American prose fiction; and it particularly descends from *Moby-Dick* and *Absalom, Absalom* in its penetrating, unfettered exploration of deamonic consciousness. Like all these books, *Naked Lunch* haunts the reader's mind with pregnant hints—it suggests more than it defines, questions more than its answers, opens more than it closes. Furthermore, the ritual of continual quest without fulfillment is peculiar to both our literature and life. This pattern is at the heart of the American novel from Cooper, through Melville, Twain and even James and Bellow; and just as typically American is the sprawling formlessness of *Naked Lunch*'s structure. For these and many other reasons, *Naked Lunch* is a characteristically American masterpiece.

However, the book, it must be said, also succumbs to the pitfalls endemic in this type of novel. Most indicatively, it is wildly uneven—only occasionally is Burroughs able to sustain a successful image for more than one or two sentences, and a completely coherent paragraph is rarer still. As in nearly all works of disjointed narrative, too many flat passages fall between the original and interesting ones. Aside from the narrator, the characters, though extraordinarily exaggerated, mythic creations, never project beyond a two-dimensional frame; for they are largely aspects of Burroughs' psyche, alter-egoes of a many faceted mind. Some of his original metaphors do not quite succeed—in crudest terms, the style is a collection of great hits and appalling misses—and many, many images and allusions are either too foggy or private to have any communicative value. Nonetheless, in all, these deficiencies are very much entwined with the book's special achievement; though not really excusable, they are the characteristic excesses of the kind of fiction that Burroughs writes.

Naked Lunch is by far the best book to come from any of the "beat" writers; and by "beat" I mean any writers who publish primarily in journals like *Evergreen Review, Big Table, Kulcher, City Lights* and in anthologies with "beat" in the title. *Naked Lunch,* in its originality and richness of experience and style, its power and unpretentious authenticity, its vision and integrity, takes its place above all the lengthy works of Jack Kerouac, Lawrence Ferlinghetti and those with whom Burroughs usually publishes; the only other writer in this circle who remotely approaches his is Hubert Selby, Jr.

Although *Naked Lunch* will, I suspect, become a modern classic, Burroughs himself is probably fated to remain a minor writer. His subsequent creative works are distinctly less realized and less affecting—indeed, less significant. They include *The Exterminator, The Soft Machine, The Ticket That Exploded, Dead Fingers Talk* (actually a composite of passages from NL., SM., TTE), and *Nova Express*), as well as unnumerable shorter pieces in various literary magazines. ("All the people starting little magazines write to me asking for material," he once said, "and I always send them something. I have trunks full of unpublished material.") In sum, these later works are evidence of Burroughs' unquenchable faith in the theory that certain composing methods sometimes viable in painting and music are applicable to literature. Some of the books/sections/pages are produced with what Burroughs called the cut-up method. He writes on several pages, cuts them up, scrambles the scraps and sets down the result in a fixed final form. [In that the final version is fixed, the cut-up method differs from other literary experiments in the aesthetics of serendipity, such as Marc Saporta's (in emulation of John Cage's music compositions), in which the fixed pages are shuffled, producing a new combination with each deal.] Other books/pages/sections are written with fold-in principles: "I take a page of text, my own or someone else's, and fold it lengthwise down the middle and place it on another page of text, my own or someone else's, lining up the lines. The composite text is then read across, half one text and half the other." Since all but one of his books do not contain prefatory notes identifying which method was used to compose what (and, in the exception, *Nova Express,* the confused syntax and punctuation obfuscate the preface's intentions), it is hard to discern whether one method provides better results than another. Nonetheless, except for an occasional striking image, surely an achievement that has little to do with the method, these books fail to sustain my interest. The decomposed narrative is certainly challenging for a reader, as well as capable of possibly offering special perceptions and configurations; but my own experience with Burroughs' later works reveals that the more perservering the effort, the most frustrating and soporific the results. Perhaps someone else, I am willing to admit, can make more sense of these books than I can; for the moment, nonetheless, a purely subjective response will be the sole, however inadequate, criterion for judgment. *Nova Express* seems the most successful of these later books—it contains more realized images, as well as an interesting overall conception (perhaps the "hallucinatory interplanetary cops-and-robbers game with the nova police on one side and the nova mob on the other" is a metaphor for the Cold War); but for me, at least, the novel failed to assume any significance.

In contrast, Burroughs without his compositional methods, I would say, can produce better prose than Burroughs-*cum*-paraphernalia; and when he harnesses his rich imagination, his unself-conscious honesty and his succinct style into a conventional form, he can produce excellent writing. For example, his letters of 1953 to Allen Ginsberg (whose replies, however, seem mannered), published as *In Search of Yage,* contain some stunning passages about Burroughs' adventures in and responses to South America.

As someone who is, by long inclination, very sympathetic to experiment in literature, I hesitate to make this final statement; but the evidence inexorably suggests that if Burroughs rejected his relentless obsession with literature-by-chance, he could, quite possibly, produce some excellent, effectively original writing again.

Burroughs' career is changing. He has left North Africa and returned to America, supposedly to assume permanent residence there. Once an uptown New York junkie, hanging around 103rd Street and Broadway, a father figure to way-out Columbia undergraduates (Allen Ginsberg, Alan Ansen, Jack Kerouac, et al), Burroughs is now a public figure, a lecturer-reader at avant-garde occasions, a "name" *Playboy* has commissioned to grace its pages (with a piece on his native St. Louis!), a luminary who tells reporters he wants to instruct the young people of America. In all, this new life seems hardly the appropriate existence for a revolutionary, visionary writer; but who knows, just as Burroughs in the past has transcended the conventions of both beat literature and narcotics report-

---

Burroughs on the writing of *Naked Lunch*:

In 1956 I went to London and took the apomorphine cure with Doctor John Dent. *Naked Lunch* would never have been written without Doctor Dent's treatment. The cure completed, I spent the summer with Alan Ansen in Venice. It was during this summer that A. J.'s Annual Party took shape and the gondola scene was written. Some of the Border City material was also written at this time and the concept of Freelandt evolved. . . .

Back in Tangier in September of 1956, I settled in a room on the garden at the Villa Muniria. For the first time in my life I began writing full-time and the material from which *Naked Lunch* was later abstracted and a good deal of the material that went into *The Soft Machine* and *The Ticket that Exploded* was produced at this time. Often I would take a notebook to dinner with me and make notes while I ate. . . .

Between 1956 and 1958 I saw a number of visitors in Tangier. Jack Kerouac was there in 1957, Allen Ginsberg and Peter Orlovsky in the same year. Alan Ansen made several trips to Tangier and helped me type the manuscript. In 1957 I made a trip to Scandinavia and wrote some of the Freelandt section for *Naked Lunch* in a cubicle room in Copenhagen.

William S. Burroughs, in his The Adding Machine, *Seaver Books, 1985.*

---

age, perhaps, too, he may as a writer transcend the pitfalls of the celebrity life. Nonetheless, behind him, Burroughs has left in *Naked Lunch* an important autobiographical novel, surely among the most original realized fictions, perhaps among the greatest literary works, of our time. (pp. 123-30)

Richard Kostelanetz, "From Nightmare to Serendipity: A Retrospective Look at William Burroughs," in Twentieth Century Literature, *Vol. 11, No. 3, October, 1965, pp. 123-30.*

Frank D. McConnell   (essay date Autumn 1967)

[*McConnell is an American educator and critic. In the following essay, he places* Naked Lunch *among the most important literary works concerned with drug addiction.*]

Although William Burroughs' *Naked Lunch* has existed as a book for nearly eight years, the best commentary on it is still slight enough to be contained as a preface to the Grove Press paperback edition: I mean the testimony of Norman Mailer and Allen Ginsberg given at the Boston obscenity trial in 1966. That testimony, at least, has the merit of restraint imposed by having to translate a living understanding of the book into the ludicrous terms of the Supreme Court's shibboleths for distinguishing "literary merit" from "obscenity"—the final test being whether "the material is *utterly* without redeeming social value." One has the strong feeling that both witnesses—especially Ginsberg—are "camping" to some extent, putting the court on by answering questions in precisely the sort of school-marmish, bad-Arnoldian jargon the court obviously requires; and certainly one of the funniest moments in the trial is Ginsberg's reading of a poem on Burroughs' work from his own volume, *Reality Sandwiches,* followed by defense attorney Edward de Grazia's bathetic one-liner, *"No more questions."*

But camp or not, this testimony remains more useful than almost anything else that has been written about *Naked Lunch.* Even bad Arnoldian criticism is better than what has otherwise normally been done with the book, which is to convert it into either the sacred text or the abomination of desolation for the hippie generation, depending on one's age, education, social status, and opinions about drugs versus liquor as a relaxant. This is partly the fault of the government itself, of course, in forcing underground a book which, in the last analysis, does not belong there: the generation now reacting so viscerally to *Naked Lunch* is the same generation which only a few years ago was handing surreptitious copies of it around with other such high school delights as clandestine beer or pot and photocopied pornographic cartoons. Naturally this has imposed on the book an aroma which persists after it becomes suddenly "legal," and which determines its meaning as a newly public statement: not necessarily, however, an aroma inherent to *Naked Lunch* itself. Miss Susan Sontag (who is rather a more masculine Tom Wolfe in her espousal of the hippie style) has kind words for Burroughs in *Against Interpretation,* but they are the wrong words. To say that what we must grasp in *Naked Lunch* is "not the 'content,' but the principles of (and balance between) variety and redundancy" is simply to perpetuate the image of Burroughs as an ultimately debased Byron which has already done so much harm to the book and many of its readers. The leitmotif of our new youth may or may not be a euphoric celebration of no-content, but this is certainly not the message of *Naked Lunch,* which shouts from every page the horror of vacuity and the terrible necessity for the rebirth of will. Surely it is one of the most ironic perversions of a text in literary history that an author for whom capitalism is a stronger symbol of imaginative death than for anyone since Brecht should become the hero of a cult revelling in the repeatability of the mass-produced artifact, and have his picture immortalized in a pattern for "psychedelic" wallpaper.

Even more disconcerting than the book's adulators, however, have been its detractors—for the most part older academic critics who should really know better. Accepting *Naked Lunch* along with *On the Road, V.,* and other contemporary novels into the syllabus of modern literature classes is scant recognition indeed, coupled as it usually is with the tacit assumption that Burroughs' book is primarily of sociological interest as a deranged apologia for the drug life—an assumption actually taken over from the wild youngsters, and transvalued by a pose less critical or intellectual than parental in the worst, Theobald Pontifex, sense of the word. The most surprising—and most articulate—expositor of this approach is none other than Leslie Fiedler, a critic to conjure with for almost any American novel written before 1955, but strangely homiletic after that date. In *Waiting for the End,* Fiedler devotes a whole chapter to Burroughs, and it is a disappointing moment in a brilliant career. Beginning with the premise that Burroughs, along with Kerouac, Ginsberg, and Norman O. Brown, is primarily a writer *for* adolescents—not simply one read widely *by* adolescents—Fiedler addresses himself not to the problems of the book itself, but to the pseudo-problems with which the adolescents have surrounded the book. The drug problem, according to Fiedler, is simply another permutation of the American myth of westering, out of which he has gotten so much mileage: a retreat into the last undiscovered territory, the inner space of the mind. And, he tells us, the dilemma from which Burroughs and his tribe of young junkies are fleeing is their love-hate relation to the affluent society, the knowledge that in seeking poverty they are seeking "a state costing someone (usually their absentee parents) . . . a sum equal to that demanded for fairly comfortable living in the years of the depression." These are the tones of a post-New Deal Lord Chesterfield, and they do not improve as the essay progresses: we are finally informed that Burroughs is naive in every conceivable respect, hardly a man any human family would want to acknowledge, and redeemed—if at all—by "only a stupidity monumental enough to be called holy."

Waiting for the End was written while *Naked Lunch* was still contraband, and one likes to assume that Fiedler read the book under unfavorable circumstances: the whole essay is very unlike him. At any rate, it is a misuse of the book. Granted that Burroughs' work is intimately related to what is rapidly becoming *the* social problem in the

United States, and that the critic has perhaps less right than anyone to abdicate his involvement in such problems (Fiedler has always been a prime exemplar of this duty), there is little to be gained by also abdicating the prerogatives of criticism itself: and in this case that means allowing even a book as "in" as *Naked Lunch* to articulate its own values, which may not be the values of its enthusiasts. Of contemporary critics only Ihab Hassan in such essays as "The Novel of Outrage" [*The American Scholar* (1965)] has managed to attain this necessary imaginative poise toward Burroughs' work.

We return, then, to the trial testimony of Mailer and Ginsberg, constrained—but refreshingly so—to evaluation rather than polemic. Both men have not only to defend the book, but prior to that, to prove to the court's satisfaction that *Naked Lunch is* a book. Mailer is at his most cogent when he answers de Grazia's questions about the putative "notes" Burroughs is supposed to have made during the most abject stages of his addiction, and which, runs the tale, Ginsberg later collected and edited into *Naked Lunch.* The question of these notes had apparently been brought up earlier by Assistant Attorney General Cowin in his prosecution of the book—and significantly, it is one raised by Fiedler in his very different prosecution of Burroughs. Mailer answers it in a lengthy defense of what used to be called "automatic writing"—the idea that "one's best writing seems to bear no relation to what one is thinking about." He goes on to testify to the strong sense of an underlying structure he has in reading *Naked Lunch,* and to its importance for him as a deeply religious book— "It is Hell precisely." The citation of the book's religious character is important, and we shall return to it later. But in the matter of the book's unity or lack of it—and the folklore that has grown up around the existence of "notes"—the more interesting testimony is given implicitly by Ginsberg, supposedly the *miglior fabbro* of its genesis. In answer to what must be the defense's first question, whether he has read the book entitled *Naked Lunch,* Ginsberg replies "Yes. . . . Yes, a number of times," and proceeds to an immensely useful explication of some of its "ideas having social importance" and of the political parties of Interzone, the mythic territory in which the bulk of *Naked Lunch* takes place. It is a tacit recognition of the autonomy of the book, precisely as *Burroughs'* book, and it should serve as an object lesson in reading *Naked Lunch.* Whether or not Ginsberg did collect and arrange snippets of Burroughs' writing, and whether or not, as Burroughs himself says, even the title of the book was suggested by Jack Kerouac and only later understood by the author, the book's unity is a function not of such information but of something at once more simple and more subtle than this: the final fact of its inclusion between covers or, in the most honest terms, its packaging. For we mistake *Naked Lunch* if we read it as anything other than one of our most packaged, consumer-oriented books, and therefore one of our most insidious: set like a depth-charge within the inmost form of a cash-and-carry culture, an eminent prefabrication to subvert prefabricators and all their works.

This is something very different from the act of faith we make in the unity of allegory like, for example, Blake's or

Swift's: in a radical way, *Naked Lunch* is a stern criticism of allegory. Burroughs is not concerned with objectifying the possible directions of the moral will. He is doing instead something that could not possibly have been done without the precondition of a full-flowered drug traffic: writing a book in which the only alternatives are absolute (and therefore dynamically formless) will or its absolute lack. The question whether Burroughs' talent has been helped or hurt by his long addiction is meaningless: his talent *is,* irreducibly, his addiction and his cure from it, at least at the time of writing the Introduction to *Naked Lunch.* That Introduction, indeed, is an essential and central part of the book, in spite of Grove Press' numbering its pages in small case Roman numerals. It is the act of retrospective packaging which gives the book its peculiar and brilliant satiric form, and the key to the basic economic theme in all its ramifications:

> Junk is the ideal product . . . the ultimate merchandise. No sales talk necessary. The client will crawl through a sewer and beg to buy. . . . The junk merchant does not sell his product to the consumer, he sells the consumer to his product. He does not improve and simplify his merchandise. He degrades and simplifies the client. He pays his staff in junk.

This is the meaning of the title, as Burroughs, always anxious to avoid any allegorizing, tells us: the naked lunch, where everyone really *sees* what is on the end of the fork, where there is no chance left for the allegorical or metaphoric translation (and avoidance) of the alternatives of will and not-will, because the packager—proprietor of *"Bill's Naked Lunch Room"*—has made a commitment to language which involves not less than everything. In a poetic system of this austerity, allegory is a capitulation, metaphor a final temptation to not-will. As Burroughs writes in his later *Nova Express,* "Since junk *is* image the effects of junk can easily be produced and concentrated in a sound and image track. . . . " The presiding genius of *Naked Lunch* is that most anti-metaphoric of writers, the Ludwig Wittgenstein of the *Tractatus:*

> Ludwig Wittgenstein *Tractatus Logico-Philosophicus:* "If a proposition is NOT NECESSARY it is MEANINGLESS and approaching MEANING ZERO."

> And what is More UNNECESSARY than junk if You Don't Need it?

The party of Interzone with which Burroughs obviously identifies, the Factualists, are the logical positivists of the imagination, dedicated to warfare against the Divisionists, Liquefactionists, and Senders, all of them concerned in some way with the translation of one thing or one person into another, by duplication, annihilation, and control (the Factualists become the Nova Police of the later book). This is why readings—some of them highly laudatory—of *Naked Lunch* which take the book as a relatively straightforward use of drug addiction as a *symbol* for all that is wrong with our society do it an injustice. There is no symbolization (past the sheerly verbal level of naming) at all in the book, and Burroughs would not want us to look for any. Junk *is* image, and therefore image *is* junk: the terri-

ble purity of Burroughs' style will not allow us to extrapolate symbolic matrices because it will not allow terms for the problem other than its own. Any second series of correspondences would be, in the book's own terms, a retreat into image-junk and a final betrayal into addiction.

I am saying, of course, that Burroughs' book operates on probably the most severely minimal linguistic principle out of which poetry can be made at all, and that the critic approaching it is faced at the first turn with the book's internal hostility to the act of explication. After such knowledge, what action? *Naked Lunch* is, I think, undeniably a great book. And its greatness constitutes a very serious challenge to criticism—a perfectly just test of the relevance of its techniques not only to the present of literature but, in fact, to the past which is everywhere and always a function of that present. For in spite of the assertions of some theorists that criticism as a craft is normally ten years or so behind the avant-garde of literature itself, the only alternatives to a criticism able to cope intelligently and productively with what is most vital in the contemporary scene seem, in the last analysis, either the autistic examination of an *a priori* unavailable past or the politely sterile non-statement of our Sunday Book Reviews.

The minimal poetry of *Naked Lunch* is not, in fact, without precedent. But the tradition to which it belongs, what I have called "the literature of addiction," is one whose importance for our imaginative heritage has never been fully articulated—could not have been, perhaps, before its stark incarnation in Burroughs' book. It is an approximate form and an approximate tradition, developing slowly and for the most part only in flashes in larger works: but it can be identified as primarily an English-American tradition of literature, and as definitively Romantic in its origins and its imaginative direction.

In the simplest terms, of course, the junky himself is an invention of the Romantic era. The disreputable, shabby, compulsive wanderer carrying his mysterious and holy wound is a figure first incarnated in the alcoholic Burns or in the mad Chatterton who so fascinated Wordsworth, and brought to a nearly final development in Coleridge himself, who really died an imaginative death in his addiction, to be reborn as "S.T.C.," defender of Christianity and architect of Victorianism. Burroughs' strange and disgusting characters called Sollubi are a permutation of this archetype:

> The Sollubi are an untouchable caste in Arabia noted for their abject vileness. De luxe cafés are equipped with Sollubi who rim the guests while they eat—holes in the seating benches being provided for this purpose. Citizens who want to be utterly humiliated and degraded—so many people do, nowadays, hoping to jump the gun—offer themselves up for passive homosexual intercourse to an encampment of Sollubis. . . . Nothing like it, they tell me. . . . In fact, the Sollubi are subject to become wealthy and arrogant and lose their native vileness. What is origin of untouchable? Perhaps a fallen priest caste. In fact, untouchables perform a priestly function in taking on themselves all human vileness.

It is only after the Romantics had taught us, with their

strong radical Protestant bent, the impossibility of a transubstantiation of things from *above,* that the negative eucharist of the outlaw and the sensualist became an aesthetic possibility. And the addict—the nature of the addiction, of course, being of no real importance—was the inevitable celebrant of the new mass, an absolute exile into the world of things in themselves. This is a reaction, finally, neither Byronic nor "Satanic" in the melodramatic sense of Mario Praz' *The Romantic Agony:* it is much closer to the resolute materialism which informs Shelley's finest poems, and to the emotional and intellectual ambivalence about addiction which runs through the first great drug-book, De Quincey's *Confessions of an English Opium-Eater.*

We must distinguish, however, between the literature of addiction proper and the vast number of works in which addiction and the addict serve simply as more or less serious type-cases of sensual exotica or social "problems" in the editorial-writer's sense. Wilde's Dorian Gray in the last stages of his degradation feels "the hideous hunger for opium," but we note the fact only as another minor flourish in that masterpiece of titillation. Even less central to what I am talking about is the kind of treatment given addiction in a book like Nelson Algren's 1949 novel, *The Man with the Golden Arm.* That book, which was not as much debased by its movie version as some critics would like to believe, is finally a study in anti-heroism in the hardboiled vein for which addiction as an imaginative, phenomenological fact is of very little importance, as witness the purple prose describing the anti-hero's first "fix":

> It hit all right. It hit the heart like a runaway locomotive, it hit like a falling wall. Frankie's whole body lifted with that smashing surge, the very heart seemed to lift up-up-up—then rolled over and he slipped into a long warm bath with one long orgasmic sigh of relief.

Whatever the considerable merits of Algren's book, in its treatment of the drug life itself, it is not really much beyond the handling of the "dope fiends" who shuffle around the corners of Dashiell Hammett's mystery novels. In fact, Burroughs' own book, *Junky,* a tough-realistic novel written straightforwardly to make some money, belongs more in this class than in the tradition of Coleridge, De Quincey, Malcolm Lowry and *Naked Lunch.*

What differentiates that tradition from other, more external treatments of the addict is not so much the element of autobiography in the works I have mentioned—although it certainly exists and is important—but rather the strong ambivalence toward the drug which is present from the real beginning of the tradition, the prefatory note to *Kubla Khan.* It is precisely this ambivalence which has proved so dangerous a component of *Naked Lunch,* leading many to suppose the book really is a defense of drugs rather than a work which transcends the poles of approval or disapproval of addiction. Those who are not addicted should really find *Naked Lunch* no less accessible than those who are—in fact, most of those who prize the book as secret cult-knowledge actually belong to a movement toward the non-addictive hallucinogens and marijuana which has less to do with the imaginative energy of *Naked Lunch* than the "straight" attitude toward drugs. The "hallucina-

tions" which make up the bulk of the book are not the futuristic and numinous visions reported by users of LSD, but are rather clarified visions of present reality made more terrible by what we have already described as the addict's absolute dependence on real *things* in their aspect of maximum power. Burroughs, in *Naked Lunch* and more blatantly in *The Soft Machine* and *Nova Express,* is a brilliant writer of science fiction (as, in a very different fashion, are John Barth in *Giles Goat-Boy,* Thomas Pynchon in *V.,* and Kurt Vonnegut in *Cat's Cradle*); and science fiction, as should be obvious by now, is the least futuristic of popular genres, attempting as it does a constant purification of the present through the neo-romance landscape of the future.

The ambivalence at the heart of the prefatory note to *Kubla Khan* is Coleridge's central ambivalence toward the Romantic epistemology: his refusal to accept both the full import of the autonomous imagination and, at the same time, the world of untransfigured phenomena. And so addiction and the drug become an aesthetic necessity for the poem: the sunny pleasuredome, literally what the mind *can do* to the world of things, is transposed into the fictive past of an opium dream and labelled a "fragment." Kubla and the youth with flashing eyes and floating hair are both the new man of the non-numinous universe, and Coleridge fears them both with that orthodox side of his mind which cries "Beware," as much as he identifies with them with another part of his being. So the drug is not the cause of the vision as much as it is, for Coleridge, the inevitable result of vision at all: if the "person from Porlock" had not existed to interrupt the dream (which is probably the case), he would have had to be invented, just as fragmentation is not the actual state but the necessary and sufficient condition for presenting the poem.

Coleridge helps us see the drug life as only the latest permutation of our basic imaginative patrimony, the problem of the sublime, of the world as consumer commodity and poetry as, literally, the packaging of experience. The expansion of consciousness, achieved with the aid of British sensational philosophy until the mid-nineteenth century and increasingly with the aid of pharmacology after that point, was a poetic difficulty long before it became a social one. But from its beginnings, almost, it was intimately bound up with drugs and with economics. Wordsworth, thinking about Coleridge (then abroad and trying to recover from his addiction) writes, in *Resolution and Independence:*

> But how can he expect that others should
> Build for him, sow for him, and at his call
> Love him, who for himself will take no heed at
>   all?

And De Quincey, remembering the mysterious and celestial-seeming druggist who sold him his first tincture of opium, becomes fascinated by the economics of ecstasy:

> Here was the secret of happiness about which philosophers had disputed for so many ages, at once discovered; happiness might now be bought for a penny and carried in the waistcoat pocket; portable ecstasies might be had corked up in a

pint bottle; and peace of mind could be sent down in gallons by the mail coach.

A century later, Malcolm Lowry says of his own addiction: "The real cause of alcoholism is the complete baffling sterility of existence as *sold* to you." And with Burroughs, what had begun as *an* aesthetic necessity becomes *the* necessary aesthetic, the addict is finally sold to the addiction, and **Naked Lunch** comes into being as an attempt to retranslate the "ultimate merchandise" of the chemical sublime into meaningful and thereby surmountable fact.

It is no surprise, then, to find at the heart of **Naked Lunch** Coleridge himself, in the guise of his most important creation, the Ancient Mariner: the first great Romantic junky, addicted to the natural world itself. The Professor's lecture on the Campus of Interzone University is perhaps the stylistic matrix of the whole book:

> Consider the Ancient Mariner without curare, lasso, bulbocapnine or straitjacket, albeit able to capture and hold a live audience. . . . What is his hurmp gimmick? He he he he. . . . He does not, like so-called artists at this time, stop just *anybody* thereby inflicting unsent-for boredom and working random hardship. . . . He stops those who cannot choose but hear owing to already existing relation between The Mariner (however ancient) and the uh Wedding Guest. . . .

It is a remarkable parallel to the moment in that other great modern drug-book, *Under the Volcano,* where the Consul analyzes his alcoholism—and the movement of Lowry's entire novel—under the aspect of another Romantic quester, the poet in Shelley's *Alastor.* But the reference to Coleridge has if anything greater relevance than the invocation of Shelley. For just as the Ancient Mariner's compulsion arises from his never really finding the appropriate language for his experience, so that he must tell his tale again and again *ad infinitum, in exilio,* so the deliberate reduction of linguistic power we have noted in **Naked Lunch** is a desperate attempt to tell the tale truly once for all, and so be rid of it. **Naked Lunch** is, as Mailer implied at the trial, a religious confession: that is, it is not the journal of a cure, but *is* the cure from word-image-junk, a talking cure which makes a striking fictive anticipation of the method used by the organization called Synanon in rehabilitating addicts. The drug, as the option to total not-will, is totally demonic—so totally that possession as a term for it becomes pitifully inadequate. " 'Possession' they call it," writes Burroughs toward the end of the book. "As if I was usually there but subject to goof now and again. . . . *Wrong! I am never here.* . . ." And the cure lies inevitably in possessing the demons—in exerting the narrative control which can describe them as "fragmentary," can place them in past time, and can finally achieve the point toward which the whole book moves, the absolutely denotative language of the Appendix, an article by Burroughs published in *The British Journal of Addiction.* The release is the book, the whole book, which without either Introduction or Appendix would be immeasurably crippled, dull and "unpoetic" as those sections may be in themselves. "I am not," Burroughs writes, "an entertainer."

This is the context in which we must understand the 231 pages of "hallucination." Those hallucinations themselves, however, describe a general movement which is anything but fragmented. Roughly, the first 20 pages are a narrative, "realistic" in flashes, of the problems of obtaining junk and fighting off the police: then with increasing disjunction of narrative time and realistic detail, the story moves toward the central, long vision of "Interzone": the last 20 pages tend again toward "realism," ending with Burroughs' fantasy of killing the narcotics detectives Hauser and O'Brien, only to learn that they do not exist—"Far side of the world's mirror, moving into the past with Hauser and O'Brien." Bracketed between the diminishing realism of the induction and the growing realism of the denouement, the Interzone section is forced inevitably into the *fictive* shape of a withdrawal symptom— whatever Burroughs' actual state at the composition of the episodes. "Interzone" is precisely that—the world between human will and its negation: the point at which, in the absence of the drug, speech at all becomes possible, but correlatively, the point at which the drive toward resumed addiction is at its strongest. The induction ends with the death in Tangier of a girl addict; the denouement concludes with the narrator's first willed act, a killing, however illusive. Between these two deaths, the images of Interzone continually tend toward an allegorization of the drug life (which for Burroughs, the poet, would be, of course, re-addiction), and are continually reduced to the anti-allegorical, minimal visions which are perhaps the single greatest imaginative triumph of **Naked Lunch.**

Interzone is, in fact, a blasted idyll, where the will projects and then destroys its own suspension in a polysexual, universally addicted junky's reverie. And in this respect, the two episodes which account for by far the lion's share of "shock" in **Naked Lunch,** "Hassan's Rumpus Room" and "A. J.'s Annual Party," are both brilliantly managed and unroariously funny subversions of two of our most cherished myths of escape, "party time" and promiscuity— they are the nearest thing we have, in fact, to Petronius' epochal annihilation of the symposium in the Banquet of Trimalchio.

Angus Fletcher, in his superb study, *Allegory,* has indicated how intimately bound up is the allegorical method with the assumptions of primitive demonism. It is only another sign of Burroughs' masterful control of his work, then, that the intense demonisms of Interzone are so consistently thwarted in their movement to become allegories. The key point of control over this technique is Burroughs' revaluation of "possession" which I have already cited. The master addict is *never* there: the body is not a carrier of demonism, but itself demonic. Burroughs tells us that what the addict craves is the presence of an alien substance in his bloodstream, a possession carried to the ultimate metabolic level of physicality. And in **Nova Express** he develops this motif in one of his most striking correlations of image, junk, and what Whitehead called "the witness of the body":

> What scared you all into time? Into body? Into shit? I will tell you: *"the word."* Alien Word *"the."* *"The"* word of Alien Enemy imprisons *"thee"* in Time. In Body. In Shit. Prisoner, come

out. The great skies are open. I Hassan i Sabbah
rub out the word forever.

It is under the sign of corporeality itself seen as addictive that the intensely grotesque sexual episodes of Interzone are generated. The process, in fact, is almost Swiftian in its range, a reverse alchemy transmuting semen into excrement in much the same way *The Mechanical Operation of the Spirit* transmutes pneuma into flatulence. And here, too, the pervasive economic orientation of the book is operating. For it is no distortion of the text to see in it the basic economic equivalences of Jungian psychology, semen as an archetype of gold and divinity, and excrement as an archetype of money (non-valuable currency) and infantilism.

Finally, my reading of **Naked Lunch** leads back, at this level of abstraction, to the Supreme Court's own terms for evaluation: for the last question we can ask about the book *is,* actually, one about its social value (the only substitute for bad Arnoldian criticism being, naturally, better Arnoldian criticism). In one of the finest critical aphorisms of this century, Leslie Fiedler has described America as "a world doomed to play out the imaginary childhood of Europe." It is only appropriate that the literature of addiction, European and Romantic in genesis, should find its fullest articulation in an American novel, just as it is inevitable that America should become the most addicted country in the West, and that only within the last half-century. And the "redeeming social value" of **Naked Lunch,** as a novel written within, and taking advantage of, the predispositions of addicted America, is not anything as simple as an anti-drug temperance tract. The "soft flutes of Ramadan," prime image of temperance in Burroughs' work, are heard only at a distance and faintly, disappearing around the corner. For Burroughs, the will to health and cure is fundamentally the will to look directly and honestly at the terms of his exile, and the problem becomes one of revising our characteristic humanist myth, the archetype of the Central Man inherited from Emerson and Whitman. The illusion that one has become God, achieved by Coleridge and De Quincey through the drug, is a basic datum of the American poetic experience, entering our tradition as the birthright of man himself rather than the gift of nature-*cum*-chemistry. It is the indelible achievement of Burroughs to return this myth to its origins; to give the Whitmanian body which is a part of all that grows and moves its most somber articulation. *Naked Lunch* is the grim and absolutely honest testimony of one who has come back from the last reaches of the Romantic self, the completion, as it were, of one of F. Scott Fitzgerald's most important creations, the monumental alcoholic of "The Lost Decade" ("Jesus. . . . Drunk for ten years"). And miraculously it somehow manages to preserve the fundamental nobility of that vision of the self, even in its revulsion. Burroughs will tell us that it is our duty to will health, but he will also insist that we will it meaningfully, without regression to easy but exhausted versions of the spirit. And as our most seriously Whitmanian novelist, he fittingly gets perhaps his best reading from our most Whitmanian poet, Allen Ginsberg:

> A naked lunch is natural to us,
> we eat reality sandwiches,

But allegories are so much lettuce.
Don't hide the madness.

                                        (pp. 665-80)

Frank D. McConnell, "William Burroughs and the Literature of Addiction," in The Massachusetts Review, *Vol. VIII, No. 4, Autumn, 1967, pp. 665-80.*

Burroughs on the publication of *Naked Lunch:*

In 1958 I moved to Paris and took up residence at no. 9, rue Git-le-coeur on the recommendation of Allen Ginsberg who was living there with Peter Orlovsky. I had a suitcase full of manuscripts with me, but Maurice Girodias of Olympia Press had rejected the first version of *Naked Lunch*. Other rejections from American publishers followed, and I was again losing interest in writing.

It was Allen Ginsberg who insisted that I send some short extracts to *The Chicago Review* which was then edited by Irving Rosenthal. The *Big Table* issue followed. One morning in room 15 at 9 rue Git-le-coeur I received a visit from Sinclair Beiles, whom I had known previously in Tangier. He was working for Girodias, who, after seeing the *Big Table* issue, now wanted to publish *Naked Lunch*. He wanted a complete manuscript in two weeks. With the help of Brion Gysin and Sinclair the manuscript was finished in two weeks and a month later the book was published.

William S. Burroughs, in his The Adding Machine, *Seaver Books, 1985.*

Richard Pearce   (essay date 1970)

[*Pearce is an American educator, essayist, and critic. In the following excerpt, he focuses on the ambiguity resulting from the multiple narrative viewpoints of* Naked Lunch.]

Whether one approves or disapproves of William Burroughs's **Naked Lunch,** there is little danger of its being served up lukewarm. The novel's acclamation at the 1962 Edinburgh Festival by Mary McCarthy and Norman Mailer was followed by a host of reviews that were solely cold or hot, and during the next year a long battle raged among the epistlers of the *Times Literary Supplement.* While readers of **Naked Lunch** are diminishing, the novel has been made a part of America's literary and cultural history by some of our best critics, and for good reason. For Burroughs attacked our society not so much as a satirist with the desire to reform, but, as Tony Tanner has shown in a brilliant discussion of Burroughs's works, to attack and destroy the foundations of Western culture. The power and vitality of **Naked Lunch,** his best novel, are due to its sheer destructiveness.

There is no need to investigate the apocryphal genesis, to decide how much of the book was heroin hallucination and how much was edited by Burroughs and/or Allen Ginsberg. We can take the novel at face value. "The title," Burroughs insists, "means exactly what the words say:

NAKED Lunch—a frozen moment when everyone sees what is on the end of every fork." Straight off, the narrator implies that this dope addict's picture, however obscene and eccentric, is his metaphor for the modern human condition. The implication is developed more explicitly when he describes the "pyramid of junk," where from the highest entrepreneur to the lowest pusher and from the lowest pusher to the most degenerate addict one level feeds on the level below—and "it is no accident that junk higher-ups are always fat and the addict on the street is always thin." The principles upon which this pyramid is built could easily apply to the whole Western and Westernized world's scheme of economic and social values: "1—Never give anything away for nothing. 2—Never give more than you have to give (always catch the buyer hungry and always make him wait). 3—Always take everything back if you possibly can."

But as we read on in the novel two questions arise: Where, in relation to the world he describes, does the narrator stand? What is his attitude toward the naked lunch? For at first we are listening to a man who has escaped from the addict's world, and who is going to describe it with unsparing accuracy; his tone is objective to the point of appearing scientific, and he is clearly didactic. But suddenly we find that the narrator is no longer standing apart from the addict's world but describing what he sees from within. He has shifted into a new gear—his style is jazzy, his diction argot, his posture involved, his attitude quivering between joy and outrage. Throughout the novel we are uncertain whether drug addiction is the living death he claims it to be when he is objective, or whether with all its repulsiveness it is not a vital and creative response to the terrifying emptiness of modern life.

The novel's ambiguity could easily be dismissed as a kind of formless and arrogantly uncritical rebellion of the beatnik tribe. But this novel continues to be disturbing, to coerce us to look again at what is on the end of our forks, and I think this is in great part due to a contradiction not bridged by the fine irony to which we have become accustomed in the modern novel.

The ambiguity of **Naked Lunch** is established in the introduction, which literally splits in two with scant transition when the narrator concludes his "Deposition" and begins "speaking *Personally*." This formal split results from the narrator's schizophrenic point of view. . . . In the first part, Burroughs's narrator is a converted drug addict addressing society—a square addressing squares. But in the second part, he alienates the average reader and excludes the squares just as Genet excludes the white spectators whom he insists be present at performances of *The Blacks*. Now the narrator is an insider addressing insiders, and he ends his introduction with the call "Paregoric Babies of the World Unite" and with a sardonic admonition to the young initiate.

The novel can be said to take off from an initial scene in the Kafkaesque Reconditioning Center, which Dr. Benway has established in Freeland. The doctor learns that the electronic brain has gone berserk playing six-dimensional chess with the technician, and it has released all the inmates. From the rooftop Benway and the narra-

tor view the result—an apocalyptic vision of the most fantastic kinds of perversion and sadism. And the scene is shaped in the form of a tall tale, except that the terrifying and repulsive overtones often obscure the comedy. At one point the narrator stops and turns to us, "Gentle reader, the ugliness of that spectacle buggers description. . . . I fain would spare you this, but my pen hath its will like the Ancient Mariner." This last reference is more than a sly wink at the Great Romantic Junkie, for Burroughs's narrator is the Modern Mariner, and the parallel is important. When the Ancient Mariner is converted he becomes a square; he discovers that the square world is beautiful and valuable, and he laments his earlier "Life-in-Death." The Modern Mariner is converted too, but his lament is ambivalent; the descriptions of his Life-in-Death are too lively.

The style of the whole book is schizophrenic, hovering between mock-scientific reporting and jazzlike improvisation. Burroughs's definitions are ingenious and convincing: the "smother party," which derives from "a rural English custom designed to eliminate aged and bedfast dependents"; "Bang-utot," which is a "condition . . . [occurring] in males of S.E. Asiatic extraction," who die dreaming that the penis has entered the body and killed them; the "Mugwump," a person who "has no liver, maintaining himself exclusive on sweets"; the "Latah," who at the snap of the fingers compulsively imitates one's every motion and has been known to injure himself trying to imitate the motions of several people at once. The small-scale inventiveness is developed to an extreme in the wildly sadistic and obscene improvisations that pervade the novel. And while the improvisations are destructive we must not ignore their creative dimension; they are disarming, in fact, just because they are destructive and creative simultaneously. For while the improvisations are obscene and perhaps the product of narcotic hallucination, the improvisor gathers his vital energy from renewed attacks on the middle-class bringers of death. He shapes his fantasia of sexual perversion from caricatures of the businessman, who is symbolically and literally responsible for the "pyramid of junk." And Burroughs's style, reminiscent of Henry Miller's, can best be described as comic and orgiastic, where new and short-lived forms of life are born out of the continual destruction of the old.

We can push Burroughs's antecedent even further back, to Walt Whitman, who also combined scientific and orgiastic styles, relentless catalogs and life-evoking rhythms. One effect of this combination in both writers is to create a sense of veracity and universality: when we finish **Naked Lunch** we feel that junk is as common as grass, and the feeling is reinforced by current hippie argot.

This comparison with Whitman is not meant to elevate Burroughs's achievements; it might even serve to measure his limitations. But, then, the differences are not only of genius but also of world view. The contradictions that Whitman and his transcendentalist predecessors so proudly embraced were rooted in an underlying order—every separate person, thing, artifact was an individuation of the Eternal Spirit. In Burroughs's world, however, the contradictions result from an essential and universal chaos. It may be a disguised platitude to say that in the last hundred years our sacred symbol has changed from grass to junk, but it is interesting to note how little the sacerdotal attitude has changed with it. Following the theory of Charles Walcutt's *American Literary Naturalism,* we might say that the naturalism and scientism in *Naked Lunch* spring from transcendentalist sources, from a sacred attitude toward the mundane. But when faith in eternal harmony is lost, when the common object is no longer a symbol for the heavenly essence, esthetic and organic order gives way to improvisation. When Burroughs fixes his attention on the lowest stratum of our society and its most repulsive activities, it is in part to protest that this is both the result and image of middle-class living, but it is also to transform it, as Whitman transformed his quotidian detail, into a life-invoking ritual. However, Whitman was prophetic and Burroughs is apocalyptic; Whitman sang about new beginnings, Burroughs shows a world bent on destruction. The ritual in *Naked Lunch* begins with destruction, and the evanescent new life will not be in the form of the old.

The true beginning for the narrator of *Naked Lunch* comes toward the end of the novel, when he shoots Hauser and O'Brien, the Narcotic Cops who had been the first to arrest him fifteen years earlier. After calling the Narcotics Bureau he discovers that there is no Hauser or O'Brien, that in the final step of his addiction he has been "occluded from space-time," "locked out," never again to have "a Key, a Point of Intersection." The implication here is twofold. First, the narrator's tale begins with an act of destruction. Second, the act is imaginative, since he is occluded from objective reality, although nonetheless destructive. The arch destroyer in *Naked Lunch* is the narrator, who destroys our familiar world with his imagination. One way he destroys it is through his schizophrenic point of view, for when he addresses us as a convert he draws us into his world, and when he speaks with the voice of the junkie he quickly sunders all connections with the world we know. The other way he destroys is through an improvisation that abrogates order and depends on building anew with each step. He is like the medieval rebels and demons—Cain and the tormentors of the miracle plays, the fools of the *sottie* drama, the leaders of the Dance of Death—who thrived on destruction and perversely affirmed life by improvising in an orderless world.

Since *Naked Lunch* ritualistically destroys our habitual ways of seeing and judging, we may seem to lack a basis for criticism. Fortunately this is not the case. Burroughs had both courage and ingenuity in presenting us with the devil's view of the world, and his book is far more honest than Mailer's *American Dream,* which reaches toward the same end. Still, Burroughs has let us down. We can think back to the vitality of the Wakefield Cain, we can remember the sportiveness of the York tormentors, we can recall the *sottie* fools who ended their plays by destroying their whole flimsy world, and the innumerable Death figures who were so maliciously alive as they led Society through its dance. Burroughs's improvisations lack the sharpness, the individuality, the variety of his medieval predecessors. And while it would be easy to blame this on the dullness of modern living or of the narcotic's escape, I rather think it is due to his failure to fully live up to his role as destroyer, to fully enjoy the act of destruction, to embrace contra-

diction instead of ambivalence—to accept the enormous strain of improvising in the void. (pp. 88-94)

> *Richard Pearce, "The World Upside Down II: William Burroughs's 'Naked Lunch' and Nabokov's 'Lolita',"* in his Stages of the Clown: Perspectives on Modern Fiction From Dostoyevsky to Beckett, *Southern Illinois University Press, 1970, pp. 84-101.*

Alfred Kazin   (essay date 1973)

[*A highly respected American literary critic, Kazin is best known for his essay collection* On Native Grounds *(1942), a study of American prose writing since the era of William Dean Howells. In the following excerpt from his* Bright Book of Life, *he examines Burroughs's narrative technique.*]

Burroughs is the great autoeroticist of contemporary fiction, the man who writes to stock up his private time machine. The "absurdity," the world-craziness which he claims to reproduce in its comic disorganization, consists in dislodging all the contents of his mind in a spirit of raw kaleidoscopic self-intoxication. These rapid shifts and indiscriminate couplings of scenes take place in Burroughs's books as if they were violently oscillating and exploding in the telescopic eyepiece of an astronomer who just happens to be gloriously soused. He writes scenes as fluently as other people write adjectives, so that he is always inserting one scene into another, *turning* one scene into another. Burroughs's fiction happenings are a wholly self-pleasing version of what D. H. Lawrence called the "pure present." Lawrence meant that the act of creation could renew the world. What Burroughs means by it is reverie, a world forever being reshuffled in the mind, a world that belongs to oneself like the contents of a dream.

Burroughs has written a meditation on the famous last words in pure stream-of-consciousness produced by the gangster Dutch Schultz as he was dying. "Morphine administered to someone who is not an addict produces a rush of pictures in the brain as if seen from a speeding train. The pictures are dim, jerky, grainy, like an old film." Burroughs likes to reproduce that indistinctness as well as the rush. In *The Naked Lunch,* his best book but a prototype of all the rest, you get in addition to the wildly funny indiscriminateness of what Burroughs calls the "cut-up novel" (which arbitrarily splices fragmentized memories, pictures, notes), instructions on the possible use of the drugged subject by outside control. Burroughs is himself a great cutup, and he declaims the supposed death-throes of our totalitarian and doomed society with the wildest possible imitation of solemn manipulation. "The biocontrol apparatus is prototype of one-way telepathic control. The subject could be rendered susceptible to the transmitter by drugs or other processing without installing any apparatus."

Burroughs is a comedian who gets his astral kicks by composing in wild blocks of scenes, in wild fantasies, in the excited mixing of remembered pictures and his own words with the derisive echoes of popular speech. It is impossible to suspect him of base erotic motives in his innumerable scenes of one shadowy stranger servicing another like a piece of plumbing. Nor, since he described at the beginning of *The Naked Lunch* his struggle with drugs and then went off into a beautiful tailspin of fantasy that showed how much he delighted in memories of his addiction, should one expect from *The Soft Machine, Nova Express, The Ticket That Exploded, The Wild Boys,* books different from his others.

The square world is of course "mad." But the closer fact, to the amused appreciative witness of Burroughs's wild gift for *continuous* fantasy, is that he is mad about anything he can get down on paper. To judge from his obsession with "The Job," Burroughs would seem to be the victim of a mad impatience with the dullness of existence. He loves being taken up by the act of writing, filling up paper from the scene immediately present to his mind as he writes. His private memory theater is staggering. He is so evidently consumed by this that he convinces the reader that oddity, drift, spacelessness are the real sensations. The "outside" world, the agreed-upon world, the supposedly constituted world with some logical and/or legal order to it—this is less significant to Burroughs than the delicious bouillabaisse of his internal sensations. We no longer have to trek back and forth between the square world and our own drunkenness. We are at home, where consciousness is king.

The effect of a purely internal, swooshed-up medium is to speed Burroughs up and down, across and every which way, past all the mental countries that do emerge in Burroughs's self-hypnosis. The vividness of the chase is startling even when we don't know how we got from one fold of the inner life to the other—or which one we are in:

> There is only one thing a writer can write about: *what is in front of his senses at the moment of writing* . . . I am a recording instrument . . . I do not presume to impose "story" "plot" "continuity". . . . Insofar as I succeed in *Direct* recording of certain areas of psychic process I may have limited function . . . I am not an entertainer. . . .

> "Possession" they call it . . . Sometimes an entity jumps in the body—outlines waver in yellow orange jelly—and hands move to disembowel the passing whore or strangle the nabor child in hope of alleviating a chronic housing shortage. As if I was usually there but subject to goof now and again . . . *Wrong! I am never here* . . . Never that is *fully* in possession, but somehow in a position to forestall ill-advised moves . . . Patrolling is, in fact, my principle [*sic*] occupation. . . . No matter how tight Security, I am always somewhere *Outside* giving orders and *Inside* this straight jacket of jelly that gives and stretches but always reforms ahead of every movement, thought, impulse, stamped with the seal of alien inspection. . . .

Burroughs gives us an extravaganza version of the noticeable speedup created by literature's relentless documentation of internal consciousness. Generally in twentieth-century literature, the more "advanced" the poet, the more mind space he seems to travel for us. This process, assisted by the endless "circuits" (Burroughs's key word)

created by technology and ubiquitous "communications," encouraged by our idea of life as a continuum of moments, has made this mental speedup—the writer's temptation to think of himself as effecting total coverage of his internal world—very important to our contemporary literary rites. Consciousness has in truth become king, separating itself from the external world that it has learned to treat as flashes of light along the pathways of the mind.

No one has carried this stress on the private movie theater to such lengths as has Burroughs. Self and world become utterly opposed places. The mind has an illusion of infinite freedom, playfulness, caprice, that the body—especially when drugged and subject to the mind—cannot sustain. There develops, as an absolute joke on the "world," the difference between the speed of thought and the slowness of the body. The mind leaps at will through all space and time as naturally—a recurring theme in Burroughs—as a man being hanged leaps through all his memories and has an ejaculation with the total relaxing of his body into death.

This speedup is taken by Burroughs as a criticism of the world: the world becomes a nut place simply because it is the opposite of the private movie theater. Hence the addict, the homosexual, the odd man out still in touch with his feelings is pursued by what Burroughs in *The Wild Boys* calls the "thought-control mob," the narcotics cops and the despots of the communications monopoly who are the villains in *Nova Express.* The "wild boys" who come into the book of that name are not important except as a culmination of the continual fantasy of boys in rainbow-colored jockstraps coldly doffing them and turning their totally impersonal couplings into a piece of American science fiction. But they do express this fantasy of perfect freedom and Burroughs's fond reverie over adolescent sex around the golf course and the locker rooms in his native St. Louis in the 1920s. "Freedom" is mostly freedom from women; the wild boys have such an aversion to women that the boys continue the race by artificial insemination, and thus "a whole generation arose that had never seen a woman's face nor heard a woman's voice." But this idosyncratic sense of freedom reproduces Burroughs's typical "fun"-scene—an undirected daydream, a fusion of *Amazing Stories* and porno-sade thriller that effects a high degree of fiction as personal performance; the different items suddenly get animated with a marvelously unexpectable profusion and disorder. Anything can get into a Burroughs novel, lead its own life for a while, get swooshed around with everything else.

Burroughs became an imaginative force in our self-indulgent literature of disaster with *Naked Lunch.* He was able to turn his addiction to morphine, "junk," into a startling ability to report the contents of his marvelously episodic imagination. His expressed aversion to hallucinogens is significant. He did not want to have *his* mind changed—Burroughs does not need inspiration! He wanted, in the tradition which is really his own—transcribing open sexual fantasy into literary energy—to make the fullest possible inventory and rearrangement of all the stuff natural to him. He wanted to put his own mind on the internal screen that is his idea of a novel.

More than anyone else I can think of in the fiction that is now written as a parody of the "system," Burroughs showed himself absolutely reckless in writing for his own satisfaction only. One recognized a novelist interested in nothing but self-expression. He had gone very far in his own life and had put just about everything into the personal system that is his novels. He was an addict from thirty to forty-five. He had an insatiable sort of mind; he was well educated, made a point of being specially well informed—the intelligent crank in action—obviously had a taste for slumming, yet his mind had some marked resemblance to his inventive grandfather and namesake Burroughs, who did not invent the adding machine but thought up the little gadget that kept it steady, and to his uncle Ivy Lee, the public relations man for old John D. Rockefeller who helped to sweeten that fetid reputation.

Burroughs worked in advertising and, typically, was an exterminator. His descriptions of Latin America and North Africa show an unmistakably upper-class American taste for practicing discomfort (rather like Theodore Roosevelt proving that he was no weakling). He has for all his flights into the ether a great shrewdness about American racketeering, political despotism, police agencies, plus a real insight into how machines work and how the innumerable technical objects, stimuli and drugs in contemporary America affect the organism. He has put himself to some ruthless tests, for his compositions show the natural curiosity of a scientist, a fondness for setting up ordeals, and above all an utterly idosyncratic gift for reliving technical operations, for subjecting himself to anything as an experiment.

"Experiment" of a peculiarly trans-literary, personal, Edison-inventive kind is indeed the big theme in all of Burroughs's work. So it is all a game, even when the material reminds you of Frank Kermode's saying that the counter-logical devices of the modern novel treat time and cause as it is treated by a totalitarian interrogator. Burroughs indeed writes his books as if he were responding to a totalitarian interrogator who, like a nineteenth-century detective, has only one person to investigate. But the self, taken as nothing but itself, its memories, fantasies, random cruelties, is a depressive, even when it rejoices in its unintelligibility.

Like so many American social theorists of fiction, who believe that society is nothing but a swindle, a racket, a "thought-control mob," Burroughs seems to me a victim of solitude. No situation, no line, no joke, lasts very long with him. Everything turns in on itself. Outside, the planets and constellations reel to prove that life has no meaning, that there is not and cannot be anything but our own sacred consciousness. Everything outside is *hell.* And after writing this, I open the Sunday *Times* at random and find an advertisement for the "Capitalist Reporter" that cries out: "Money! Opportunity Is All around You! American treasures are all around you—attic, church bazaar, house-wrecking yards, thrift shops, etc. Old bottles, obsolete fishing lures, prewar comics . . . names and addresses of people who buy *everything,* from old mousetraps to dirigibles to USED ELECTRIC CHAIRS. . . . " (pp. 263-71)

Alfred Kazin, "Absurdity as a Contemporary

Style: Ellison to Pynchon," in his Bright Book of Life: American Novelists & Storytellers from Hemingway to Mailer, *Atlantic-Little, Brown, 1973, pp. 243-82.*

Jennie Skerl   (essay date 1984)

[*In the following excerpt from her introduction to the twenty-fifth anniversary edition of* Naked Lunch, *Skerl examines the themes, structure, style, and cultural background of the novel.*]

Naked Lunch established William S. Burroughs's reputation as a major postwar American writer, and it remains the single work by Burroughs that has received the most critical attention: it is a landmark, constantly reread and reinterpreted. Since the first publication of *Naked Lunch* in Paris twenty-five years ago, Burroughs has created a body of fiction that makes him one of our foremost experimentalist writers. Yet, *Naked Lunch* deserves its pre-eminence as Burroughs's most famous book, for it is a powerful vision whose iconoclastic force has not declined with the passage of time. The vision of *Naked Lunch* is both a critique of present structures of reality and a revision of those structures: the result is a new consciousness that creates its own artistic form through a variety of avant-garde prose techniques.

The source of Burroughs's vision in *Naked Lunch* is hipsterism and its environment—what Burroughs has called "the carny world." Hipsterism is a style of consciousness that derives from the special viewpoint and social condition of the drug addict, an "angle of vision" Burroughs described in his first, more conventional, novel *Junkie.* The addict's "hip" attitude began to influence alienated artists and intellectuals in the late 1940s and 1950s, the period during which Burroughs himself was an addict. The hipster was defined by Norman Mailer in his 1957 essay "The White Negro" as a "philosophical psychopath," and this is an apt definition of Burroughs's stance as an addict-writer. The hipster rejects the larger, bourgeois social order and its demands for conformity and seeks to discover a new self free from social conditioning. He lives in a continual present within a fluid mental universe in which context alone determines action. The self constantly adapts to inner and outer forces, creating itself from moment to moment, guided by the principles of honesty, courage, and spontaneity. The addict-hipster, of course, is responding to the need to maintain his drug habit in a hostile social environment, but Burroughs was one of the first to perceive that the addict's hip viewpoint would become the *Weltanschauung* of post-war America—the "American existentialism" that fueled the "beat" and "hip" rebellions of the 1950s and 1960s.

The addict-hipster of the 1940s was part of an underworld subculture of drug users, petty criminals, hustlers, conmen, sexual deviants, and sideshow entertainers. In a *Paris Review* interview in 1965, Burroughs called this subculture "the carny world" and mentioned the detailed notes he had made on this milieu over the years. *Junkie* was partly an exploration of this world: its inhabitants, customs, territory, and socioeconomic relationships. But, although *Junkie* had recorded the experience of addiction and its world, it had not made hipsterism the basis of its form as does *Naked Lunch*—that took many years of experimentation as Burroughs tried to discover a form adequate to his own consciousness of self and world. As he remarked in a letter to Kerouac in 1954, "I tell you the novel form is completely inadequate to express what I have to say. I don't know if I can find a form." Consciousness and form came together in the final manuscript of *Naked Lunch,* which creates a new kind of fiction: the pop art novel, which is both a technique and a vision of reality.

In the pop art novel Burroughs attacks the reader's conventional perception of reality, creating a new consciousness in which conventional polarities—the forbidden and the permitted—are seen as part of one field of possibilities. Burroughs creates this vision by including within the genre of the novel elements of popular culture that modern urban bourgeois society usually ignores or suppresses: obscene language, description of bodily functions, oral folklore, the manners and mores of "underground" subcultures, and the style of "subliterature." This socially suppressed material is combined with what is usually psychologically repressed: taboo sexual and aggressive desires freely expressed in spontaneous, improvised fantasy. Morally and aesthetically, the pop art novel subverts the norm because it allows forbidden experiences, parodies established social and artistic forms, and breaks all rules of decorum. This reversal also constitutes a new reality in which all cultural possibilities exist within one field of consciousness, and consciousness is a free play with forms. In this world of total possibility, the individual is an autonomous being who can create a self and a world free of external conditioning.

On the literal level, *Naked Lunch* purports to be a record of opiate addiction, treatment, and cure. The untitled first section recapitulates the action of Burroughs's earlier novel *Junkie,* the story of an addict's quest for "the final fix," the ultimate drug that will free him from society, body, and mind as defined by the dominant social order, and thus provide an alternative source of value. As in *Junkie,* the narrator-protagonist tells of his travels from New York City, to the Midwest, to the South, and to Mexico in an attempt to escape the law and to find an environment allowing easy access to drugs. The narrator of *Naked Lunch* ends his journey in Tangier, presumably the location of the fantastic scenes that follow. In contrast to the factual reportage of *Junkie,* however, the opening of *Naked Lunch* establishes a very different voice and style: Burroughs assumes the persona of "Bill Lee," the addict-hustler who with great gusto tells the story of his experiences, interspersing factual observations with satirical fantasy episodes. In the second section ("Benway") and throughout the rest of the book, fantasy takes over, transforming Tangier into the imaginary realm of Interzone, and many voices tell many stories in which the experience of addiction and withdrawal is used as the basis for satire, fantasy, and prophecy. As Burroughs explains in the "Atrophied Preface," placed at the end of the novel, Lee is taking a cure, and the novel represents the disjointed memories and hallucinations of withdrawal, a realistic justification for the fragmentary form and grotesque imagery.

But by the end of the book the hipster has also become "Agent Lee," simultaneously an actor in a mythic battle over the fate of mankind and a visionary writer who attempts to alter the consciousness of the reader. For the preface also says that *Naked Lunch* is "a blueprint, a How-To Book" about "how to extend levels of experience." Agent Lee is the angle of vision through which we the readers see the "naked lunch"—heightened visions of the here and now, the only final fix the addict ever finds. Lee rejects the earlier endless quest of *Junkie* as illusory and hopeless; in *Naked Lunch* all drugs have been tried and all have led to greater bondage rather than freedom from the conditions of physical and social existence. Again and again, the novel explodes into visionary episodes that reveal the permanent alienation of the disillusioned protagonist who opposes the delusions of addiction with his new insight. Thus *Naked Lunch* is a journey the narrator and reader take together through the text which is a world without transcendence, but a world that transforms the reader's consciousness.

The County Clerk sequence in *Naked Lunch* derived from contact with the County Clerk in Cold Springs, Texas. It was in fact an elaboration of his monologue, which seemed merely boring at the time, since I didn't know yet that I was a writer.

—*William S. Burroughs, in his* The Adding Machine, *1985.*

Burroughs thus universalizes the addict experience. The terms "addiction" and "junk" are not to be interpreted only on the literal level in *Naked Lunch;* they are also metaphors for the human condition. The former addict perceives that all of humanity is victimized by some form of addiction. The addiction experience has led to the realization that the body is a biological trap and that society is run by "control addicts" who use the needs of the body to satisfy their obsession with power. The basic metaphor of addiction leads to the creation of an entire metaphorical world, or a mythology, that provides narrative form—that is, characters, plot, and setting. What is innovative about Burroughs's mythology is his reliance upon popular culture for his mythological materials and thus his creation of new form—the pop art novel.

The hustling, amoral lifestyle of the carny world provides the physical, social, and economic environment of *Naked Lunch.* The chief setting is Interzone, a dystopia based on all the places Burroughs has been and all the junk neighborhoods he has seen. Interzone is the modern city as Waste Land in which all the cities, peoples, and governments of the world are combined into one huge beehive of commerce, sex, addiction, political manipulation, and rivalry. In this imaginary world, all sexuality is on the level of pornography. The economic system is based on the "Algebra of Need," Burroughs's analysis of the drug market which he had outlined in "Deposition: Testimony Concerning a Sickness," included as the Introduction to the 1962 Grove Press edition. In his analysis all of politics is a plot in which a secret few conspire to manipulate and control the many. Religion is one of the ways in which the power elite manipulates the masses. The carny relationship of conman and mark is the basis of Burroughs's analysis of power and the social order.

The science and art of this world are drawn from popular culture. The science of *Naked Lunch* is the popularized scientific knowledge of the mass media, the pseudoscience of L. Ronald Hubbard's Scientology, Wilhelm Reich's orgonomy, and Burroughs's own metaphorical analysis of addiction. From the various forms of popular fiction, Burroughs derives his plot, characters, many images, and aspects of his style. *Naked Lunch* draws primarily from the detective story, the Gothic tale, older science fiction of the mad-doctor variety, and pornography. What popular science and popular fiction have in common is a paranoid view of the world that Burroughs accepts as valid. They also offer simple solutions to complex problems—theories and images that provide Burroughs with metaphors with which to build a mythology.

Based on these materials from personal experience and popular culture, *Naked Lunch* introduces the pop mythology that his subsequent novels continue to develop. In *Naked Lunch* Burroughs transforms the body's addictive nature into an entity called the "Human Virus" or the "evil virus." The virus lives upon the human host, satisfying its own needs for drugs, sex, or power (the three basic addictions for Burroughs) through demonic possession which dehumanizes the human being by making him subservient to a physical or psychological need. When addicted/possessed, the human being becomes identical with the virus and regresses downward to a lower form of life. Numerous transformations of characters in the novel from men to sub-human organisms illustrate this descent. The social structure mirrors the individual process of addiction/possession on a larger scale. The social dynamic of addiction is that of predator and victim. The major social institutions (government, business, organized religion) built upon this cannibalistic structure are also viruses, or cancers, which take over the healthy social body and warp it to fill their parasitic needs, eventually leading the human race to destruction. The orgasm-death of the hanged man is a recurrent image in the novel that epitomizes the sadism of social control.

The action of the myth consists of a battle between the forces of good and evil for control of both the individual and all of humanity. The three conspiratorial political parties of Interzone—the Liquefactionists, the Divisionists, and the Senders—seek to rule the world through parasitic possession. The party leaders are "control addicts" who attempt to make all men conform to a single image reflecting the person or force in control. The only force fighting these evil parasites is the Factualist party, the fourth party of Interzone. The Factualists are a radical group that represents individual freedom. Factualist agents attempt to foil the plots of the villains by revealing them. The entire

novel can be seen as such a revelation, and the two Factualists in the book—Lee the Agent and A. J.—are Burroughs's alter egos. The title, *Naked Lunch,* refers to the authorial intention to reveal the facts. There is a flaw in the Factualist program, however. Since all the agents are human, they are all potential addicts who may succumb at any moment. Thus the situation is never resolved; the cosmic battle between good and evil is never-ending, like the plot of a comic strip—a comparison Burroughs himself has made.

Unlike the psychologically developed personalities of the realistic novel, the characters in *Naked Lunch* are the one-dimensional caricatures of popular fiction, the focal points for impersonal forces in a Manichean universe. Good and evil characters are often very much alike, and only the results of their actions reveal whether they represent the forces of control or of liberation. Bill Lee, Burroughs's version of himself as the addict-writer and as a Factualist agent, is as one-dimensional as other characters. He barely exists except for his voice and his actions. Lee's function is to see, to tell what he sees, and thus to expose the system of social control. He does not exist as a person outside of his function as "agent."

Burroughs's vision in *Naked Lunch* is presented in an experimental form derived from painting, film, and music. The basic organizational technique is juxtaposition, called collage in painting, and montage in photography and film. The overall structure of *Naked Lunch* is a montage of "routines" that, theoretically, can be read in any order. The routines are dramatically realized fantasies consisting of monologues, dialogues, plot episodes, scene descriptions, and collage passages of associative imagery. The organization within routines is improvisational, like the technique of jazz music. Typically, Burroughs begins with a person, a conversation, or an event which is factual or credible and improvises on this theme in a fantastic or satiric style. Structure within routines is based on a rhythm of expansion and contraction: statement of theme, improvisation, climax, sometimes return to theme, and then a new improvisation. Routines usually end in one of two ways: either in a climax of violent, chaotic action, or with a meditative passage of juxtaposed images built around a single theme.

The avant-garde structure of *Naked Lunch* accomplishes three purposes. First, it is a way to present the flow of consciousness, and *Naked Lunch* is overtly presented as a record of Lee's consciousness. Second, it is a way to expand the reader's awareness. Juxtaposition creates new mental associations in the mind of the reader. Furthermore, the lack of conventional literary narrative gives a dreamlike power to the images presented. Third, both juxtaposition and improvisational fantasy fulfill a satirical function in *Naked Lunch.* These techniques enable Burroughs to use his popular materials as a weapon for attacking the social order. The combination of avant-garde technique, critical intention, and popular materials is what makes Burroughs a pop artist, not just one who uses popular materials. Burroughs's pop-art novel can be compared to the work of several contemporary visual artists who combine fine art and popular art in order to question accepted cultural norms. Like Andy Warhol, Roy Lichtenstein, Jim Dine, George Segal, and Claes Oldenburg, Burroughs uses powerful pop icons for primary imagery. James Rosenquist, Robert Rauschenberg, and British artist Richard Hamilton are similar to Burroughs in the use of collage to make critical statements about the society that produced these popular images.

Extensive use of montage increases the disorder of a composition, but *Naked Lunch* contains several unifying elements. First, the order of the routines is not wholly arbitrary. There is an overall psychological pattern which repeats the organic and improvisational structure of individual routines, an order of increasing complexity in the use of experimental techniques, and a distinct beginning and ending—an autobiographical frame provided by the opening section and the concluding "preface." Also, the pop mythology ties the routines together by providing an underlying narrative of which each fragment is a part. Finally, the unifying sensibility of William S. Burroughs lies behind the book: *Naked Lunch* is the creation of one man's consciousness even though he calls himself within the novel a "recording instrument" who passively transcribes "areas of psychic process." The vision and voice of *Naked Lunch* are unmistakably the product of one personality called William S. Burroughs.

In many ways, it is the voice of *Naked Lunch* that is the work's most innovative and iconoclastic technique. The voice is oral, colloquial, parodic—and very funny. The informal speech of many groups is imitated, particularly the language of the addict underworld. Burroughs's medley of imitations is exuberant in its virtuosity, and his skill in presenting the spoken word in print is such that the novel's prose often resembles poetry. Imitation of the speech of particular socio-economic groups, however, also has a satiric effect. Parody of a linguistic mode has the effect of calling into question the entire cultural basis for identity and status. The voice of *Naked Lunch* is also funny because of its use of traditional satirical techniques: the parody of social types, the undercutting of intellectual pretentions with physical grossness, the exaggeration of the actual in fantasy, taking metaphors literally, and the humorous incongruity of arbitrarily juxtaposed images or episodes—another kind of undercutting technique. Burroughs's obscenity is a major element in his humor, as it is often an element in traditional satire. In fact, Burroughs has himself referred to Swift's "A Modest Proposal" as a model for the recurrent hanging scenes.

But in spite of all of the parallels with traditional satire, *Naked Lunch* is ultimately a parodic rather than a satiric work. It attacks without implying any positive standard, as traditional satire does. The individual, anarchic freedom that lies behind the destructive satire exists in a vacuum with no moral or social structure to support it or to give satire any function but destruction. The only values upheld by Burroughs's parodic style are the energy and laughter that come from the freedom from external control and the joy in spontaneous response to the impulses of the moment. These are the hipster's values, and *Naked Lunch* is a masterpiece embodying the hipster mentality.

Naked Lunch was a seminal work for Burroughs himself.

In this novel he first achieves the characteristic style that has been the foundation for all his subsequent fiction. Soon after the publication of *Naked Lunch,* he produced three novels that form a closely-knit experimental trilogy: *The Soft Machine* (1961), *The Ticket That Exploded* (1962), and *Nova Express* (1964). Although these novels grew out of *Naked Lunch,* the latter stands alone as a self-contained work and differs significantly in technique. The trilogy introduces the random technique of the cutup and can be seen as an exhaustive exploration of that method of creating non-narrative fiction, whereas *Naked Lunch* does not use cutups. Thus the three later novels contain far less narrative in the form of improvisational fantasy, which is what gives *Naked Lunch* its verve. The trilogy also creates a new science-fiction mythology about the Nova Mob versus the Nova Police, and, although that mythology is related to the Human Virus myth of *Naked Lunch,* the latter is unique to that work. It is the balance between montage and improvisational narrative, and between a suggested mythic world and contemporary American society, that gives *Naked Lunch* its iconoclastic power. Perhaps no other single work by Burroughs has the authority of *Naked Lunch,* although Burroughs has never stopped being an innovator, satirist, and visionary thinker.

Burroughs's novel succeeded in iconoclasm only too well, for his inclusion of taboo subject matter and language resulted in censorship problems upon first publication in the United States by Grove Press in 1962. The publisher defended the novel in a censorship trial in Boston and prepared to defend the book in Los Angeles as well. Although the case in Los Angeles was dropped, the judge at the Boston trial in 1965 declared *Naked Lunch* to be obscene. The decision was reversed by the Massachusetts Supreme Court in 1966. (The 1966 Evergreen Black Cat Edition of *Naked Lunch* contains the court decision and excerpts from the trial testimony as prefatory matter.) The censorship trial of *Naked Lunch* is significant because it was the last major censorship trial of a literary work in the United States, marking the end of an era that began in the 1870s when Anthony Comstock led a crusade for stricter obscenity laws. Thus, the *Naked Lunch* trial was a major step in eliminating censorship of the printed word in the United States, and its importance in this respect should not be forgotten. (pp. v-xv)

> *Jennie Skerl, in her introduction to* Naked Lunch *by William S. Burroughs, Grove Press, Inc., 1984, pp. v-xix.*

Michael Leddy   (essay date Spring 1984)

[*In the following essay, Leddy discusses the ambiguous, sometimes contradictory, narrative perspectives in* Naked Lunch.]

Naked Lunch is often thought of as a book of revelation, a book that makes present to us the "real scene," that shows us "what is on the end of every fork"; its jacket blurbs speak of it as an "absolutely devastating ridicule" of the ills of America; its author is said to "illuminate every level of hell" or is likened to a man knocking on the door to tell us that our house is on fire. Yet the "Deposition" that prefaces the novel suggests by its title both revelation and concealment, presence and absence. As testimony given under oath—here an implicit oath, the presupposition of literary convention that an author will tell his reader the truth, that an author is to be trusted—a deposition is a revelation of knowledge achieved through personal experience; a witness' testimony is valuable because he knows the real scene and can make it present to us. At the same time, to make a deposition is to conceal, to be absent; it is testimony given in writing to substitute for the production of a witness. Burroughs reminds us throughout *Naked Lunch* that all writing is in a sense a deposition: a text is never the author-witness himself but the language he leaves behind for our inspection; as such, a text is a "disembodied voice," whose owner, "The Man In Possession," never shows up, whose owner is ultimately "the Invisible Man," if not "exactly invisible . . . at least difficult to see." If a reading of the "Deposition" cannot produce the witness himself, it can at least help us to see more clearly the structure of the testimony (and the larger testimony that is *Naked Lunch*) that he has left behind.

Burroughs' "Deposition" initially appears to be genuine self-revelation, marked by use of the first-person, blunt syntax, and a recounting of the real scene, life at "the end of the junk line" in the Native Quarter of Tangier. There is a sense of urgency in its voice, a desire to reveal to the audience, like some Ancient Mariner, the truth gained through experience; it speaks the truth in italicized sentences. The "Deposition" reveals not only personal history—"a" sickness—but a category of human experience of which the Burroughs odyssey is representative—The Sickness, an allegorical drama in which the particular reveals the universal, in which every pusher is the Pusher, the Man, in which all addicts buy off the same Monkey. The tendency to reveal is also evident in the abundance of categorical statements (revealing in that they are explicit, "naked") and in the attempts to work out formulae for understanding the junk world (the junk pyramid, the principles of monopoly, and the Algebra of Need).

While the "Deposition" does reveal things about the junk world and Burroughs' own experiences, it also conceals; paradoxically, passages in which Burroughs seems most present suggest absence. The first-person opening paragraph of the "Deposition" suggests the absence from *Naked Lunch* of an authoritative "Author": Burroughs tells us that he "*apparently* took detailed notes" before he "awoke from The Sickness"; he is without "precise memory of writing the notes" published as *Naked Lunch* thus placing the work in the realm of dream and the unconscious. Note too the refusal to speak of a finished text, the implication that a covering title has been applied to a group of fragments. Absence of conscious control of the text is also evident in Burroughs' comment on the novel's title: the invention of Jack Kerouac, its meaning was not clear to Burroughs until his "recent recovery." Taken together, these statements point to an author who is little more than a "recording instrument" who imposes nothing on his material; they also evoke the figure of the Romantic poet in his most extreme incarnations—the Coleridge of "Kubla Khan," presenting (or purporting to present) a dream-fragment (and self-consciously introducing it as

such), the Shelleyan poet-prophet who expresses what he does not understand.

But while Burroughs in effect absents himself from the composition of *Naked Lunch,* he is simultaneously exercising quite conscious control over the circumstances of composition, the "set." Clearly, the "Deposition" indicates that the novel is the product of the addict (the author awoke at forty-five, i.e., in 1959), yet in other contexts Burroughs has indicated that he awoke at an earlier date and that *Naked Lunch* was not written during the period of addiction:

> It was written mainly in Tangier, after I had taken the cure with Dr. Dent in London in 1957. [1956 seems to be the correct date; the letter to the *British Journal of Addiction* describing the cure is dated 1956.] I came back to Tangier and I started working on a lot of notes I had made over a period of years. Most of the book was written at that time. [*Writers at Work: The Paris Review Interviews, Third Series*]

Even this statement is ultimately ambiguous, for Burroughs also says that "from manuscripts collected over a period of years, I *assembled* what became the book" (*Paris Review,* emphasis added). But it seems safe to conclude that there was at least some process of selection; in this sense the novel (not the notes) was written (i.e., made, put together) by the nonaddict. The emphasis on the addict as author seems stranger in light of the fact that Burroughs deliberately sets off those sections of the text said to result from a drug state, as if to distinguish them from the rest of the novel. If the Introduction is indeed a deposition, it seems that the witness has concealed the truth and committed perjury; he has created, in the manner of the con man, his own set. But as Burroughs tells us elsewhere, "everything is illusion" [*The Job,* William S. Burroughs and Daniel Odier] and it follows that "there is no accurate description of the creation of a book, or an event" (*Paris Review*). The problem posed by this opening paragraph ironically confirms the dictum that "the word" can only be indicated "by mosaic of juxtaposition"; the single voice of the "Deposition" is only revealed to be suspect when set against other voices; the truth can only begin to emerge when, as it were, more witnesses are called.

The danger of the opening paragraph for the reader is that it is a genuine con, not a transparent joke to strengthen the sense of community between author and audience (is there anything in the language to suggest that Burroughs is not being completely serious?), but an attempt to deceive the audience (if we assume that there is an objective reality, or at least greater and lesser degrees of accuracy). Burroughs, the recording instrument here, makes and plays back his own recording of the circumstances of composition; while ostensibly revealing his lack of control, he exercises his control under the reader's nose. It is this ability to make "a hole in reality" (*Job*), to create the other's perceptions, that distinguishes the con man, and we should bear in mind that "deposition" can also denote the act of putting down, here the putting down of the authorial con, which is in effect a put-down of the reader, an act of aggression that denies the community of writer and audience. The same con (concealment) is lurking in the testimony concerning (presumably) "Hassan's Rumpus Room" and "A. J.'s Annual Party":

> Certain passages in the book that have been called pornographic were written as a tract against Capital Punishment in the manner of Jonathan Swift's *Modest Proposal*. These sections are intended to reveal capital punishment as the obscene, barbaric and disgusting anachronism that it is. As always the lunch is naked.

Whether the lunch *is* naked, whether there is any connection (in the text or legitimately inferable) between making it " 'all the way' " and execution by the state, is doubtful; indeed, later Burroughs statements seem to contradict this allegorical reading. Daniel Odier's mention of Mary leads not to Burroughs-the-corrector-of-interviewers ("Excuse me, that scene is about capital punishment") but to a diatribe against Woman (*Job*); *Nova Express*'s Inspector Lee says that the "so called pornographic sections" map the Garden of Delights of sexuality. Most likely, the Burroughs-Swift equation is an attempt to make the book respectable, a bid for the "social significance" Burroughs says is "quite beside the point" (*Job*). Of course, there is also social significance in depicting sex "degraded for control purposes" (*Paris Review*), as an "area of terminal sewage" (*Nova*), but perhaps not exactly of the type that the gentle reader would regard as acceptable.

But how *is* the reader, gentle or otherwise, to regard Burroughs' statement of intent? He can accept it as genuine, in which case he will probably view the scene as unsuccessful. Or he might choose to read it as a transparent con; "tract" and the capitals on "Capital Punishment" could suggest irony, and Burroughs must be aware of the contradiction inherent in an allegorical reading (things as other things) of a naked lunch (things as they are). But it is not clear what, then, the statement is to mean—that the passages are in fact merely pornographic? Burroughs' technique is reminiscent of Renaissance apologists who stress the allegorical or moral significance of "questionable" passages in such absurd ways that it becomes clear that there is no such significance, that the passages in question are purely erotic. A third alternative is to dismiss Burroughs' claim as false, which is to call into question the act of reading itself: if an author will not tell his reader the truth, is the reader " 'to take these glib lies like a greased and nameless asshole' "? Each of these readings involves the reader in a "skin game," a situation in which he has no chance of winning: he must play the mark to Burroughs' con man, choose between two unsatisfactory alternatives (capital-punishment allegory or mere pornography: Scylla or Charybdis), or be a "wise guy" who thinks his own perceptions are sufficient.

But while Burroughs is conning the reader, he is also conning himself, becoming entangled in self-contradiction. The recording instrument has again made its own recording; it has acquired intentionality, the ability to impose meaning upon what it records. The junk-sick writer, with no precise memory of writing, here remembers his intent and neatly works it in with the concept of naked lunch, which he claims not to have understood while writing. More importantly, Burroughs is caught in the contradiction of seeking to confine a text that "spill off the page in all directions"; he invokes the authority of the Author in the interests of closure and denotation. The language of the "Deposition" carefully excludes any indication that the capital punishment/orgasm-by-hanging equation is the "meaning" of the rumpus room and blue movie passages, or even *a* meaning (it is only the intention), but Burroughs closes the text to some extent simply by introducing this (alleged) intention: the text no longer speaks for itself. Whether or not the reader accepts the author's explanation, he is obliged to address himself to it; it must be part of any discussion of the passages in question. To Burroughs' revelation/concealment of intent, the reader can only respond with the street boy of "Ordinary Men and Women": " 'Well that's a point of view' " and proceed to the "Post Script." The voice of the "Deposition" is only one of many voices in *Naked Lunch;* it does not have "the word."

We have seen that while the "Deposition" contains much in the way of apparently straightforward self-revelation, it simultaneously moves in the direction of absence and concealment. This movement gathers force in the "Post Script," where we find Burroughs away from the formalities of the courtroom, "speaking *Personally,*" reminding us again that a written statement, no matter how revealing, is not the author himself. Yet the word *"Personally"* (compare the skeptical quotation marks around the word "evil,") and all the words that follow call into question once again the idea of a personal voice, the author as personally present. The blunt, self-contained prose of the "Deposition" (i.e., it needs little to explain its sense) is exploded; first-person narrative is replaced by what Barthes would call "a tissue of citations, resulting from the thousand sources of culture": sprawling sentences filled with slang, allusions, and other voices, most notably that of the Opium "Smoker"; Burroughs' personal account of addiction gives way to an anonymous voice from inside the tent. The personal urgency of the "Deposition" is recalled only to be mocked: "So that's the World Health Problem I was talking about back in The Article"; self-dramatization becomes self-parody. Similarly, the genuine solution of apomorphine treatment is replaced by facile rhetoric: "Paregoric Babies of the World Unite. We have nothing to lose but Our Pushers." The universal drama of Pusher and Monkey is rendered ludicrous: the junkie "wants The Cold like he wants His Junk"; he lives in "The Old Ice House" or in a tent with a "Lamp." (Burroughs' sardonic, scornful tone here seems dangerously close to the "self-righteous position" he condemns in the "Deposition" proper and probably reflects his ambivalent identification with the junk world; he is no longer inside the tent but still writes of the life inside.) Finally, the only "Burroughs" voice that remains is that of the con man. While the con in the "Deposition" lurks below the surface of the text, the con man here is in full view, again involving the reader in a skin game: he must either play the mark to Honest Bill or remain on the side of "Fro-Zen Hydraulic," the dead world of junk. As Anthony Hilfer notes [in his "Mariner and Wedding Guest in William Burroughs' *Naked Lunch,*" *Criticism* (1980)] Burroughs' Charybdis is not a satisfactory alternative to Scylla. Yet if the reader is to continue to the novel itself, he must "shack up with Charybdis," trade wise-guy status for that of mark, succumbing to a con of community ("Treat you right," "You know the type") that is soon to be exploded.

The promised community never materializes; instead, the author-guide, like Lee, "keep[s] slipping away," often appearing only as a director orchestrating fadeouts, "somewhere *Outside* giving orders." As the talking asshole gains control over the body of which it is a part, so other voices take over the body of the book, entering and exiting "like vaudeville skits." Like the "Deposition," the novel proper challenges the idea of a personal voice: the "Atrophied Preface" explains that various characters "are subject to say the same thing in the same words to occupy, at that intersection point, the same position in space-time"; thus, individual character is subsumed within an all-inclusive system of language (the "Word . . . divided into units which be all in one piece") and is defined by the language it employs. Yet Burroughs simultaneously chooses to retain his own voice; unlike a conventional director, he insists upon appearing in his own film, not in momentary, unobtrusive Hitchcock fashion, but repeatedly (in the notes) and, at times, at length (in the longer notes and in the "Atrophied Preface").

Ultimately, Burroughs' oscillation between absence and presence seems to reflect an ambivalence with regard to his audience and the validity of communication through language. Mary McCarthy's comment that *Naked Lunch* is of and for addicts (and ex-addicts) seems only half-right; one wonders how many "Old time, veteran Schmeckers" have access to the productions of Grove Press. Indeed, the parenthetical notes on the junk world destroy the sense of community established at the outset: the reader is not an insider here, and it is difficult to imagine a text that offers less of a common ground for author and audience; Burroughs presents not simply a "subset" of a category of common human experience (e.g., homosexuality as a subset of the shared experience of sexuality), but a completely other category of human experience, of life inside the tent. And coupled with an ambivalence toward the audience is an uncertainty concerning the validity of communication itself. While the Professor's Coleridge lecture suggests that a fruitful author-audience is possible, it is one based upon " 'ESP awareness' "; the Professor stresses that " 'nothing can ever be accomplished on the verbal level'." Furthermore, such communication can take place only with those " 'who cannot choose but hear owing to already existing relation between The Mariner [Burroughs] . . . and the uh Wedding Guest [reader]' "; the sense of the passage is that all communication involves telling someone something he is prepared to hear or already knows. Communication thus becomes a con: Lee telling the subway fruit what he is prepared to hear ("giving the fruit his B production,") or telling the County Clerk what he already knows (" 'Well, Mr. Anker, you know yourself all a Jew wants to do is doodle a Christian girl,' "). The Exterminator interrupts his explanation of his assignment to remind himself that the reader "cannot understand"; Burroughs himself fails in an attempt to wise up a fellow junky:

> I tried to tell him: "Some morning you will wake up with your liver in your lap" and how to process raw opium so it is not plain poison. But his

eyes glaze over and he don't want to know. Junkies are like that most of them they don't want to know . . . and you can't tell them anything.

Burroughs' intention is to communicate, "to make people aware of the true criminality of our times, to wise up the marks," and it is hard to believe that he would continue to write if he did not hold some faith (*most* junkies don't want to know, i.e., some do) in the ability to communicate through language (if only as a way to facilitate ESP awareness), but the difficulties involved lead not to a greater effort, but to a tendency to forsake straightforward communication, to displace the personal voice. Thus, Burroughs presents genuine social commentary in the anonymous form of the Factualist bulletins; criticism of bureaucracy is put in the mouth of Doctor Benway, rendering it suspect. Burroughs' voice, when it surfaces, often takes on an aggressive quality: depicting scenes of violence, he says his pen "hath its will like the Ancient Mariner" (see also the Mariner capturing and holding an audience); when he unlocks his word hoard,

> The Word will leap on you with leopard man iron claws, it will cut off fingers and toes like an opportunist land crab, it will hang you and catch your jissom like a scrutable dog, it will coil round your thighs like a bushmaster and inject a shot glass of rancid ectoplasm.

Burroughs creates a text that not only intends to show the reader that his own perceptions are insufficient, but that seeks to do away with the reader's identity altogether: "*Naked Lunch* demands Silence from The Reader." This tendency reaches its logical extreme in Burroughs' expressed desire to write something that would kill his reader. The Word, complete in itself, needs nothing from its audience; as Susan Sontag observes [in her *The Discontinuous Universe*],

> A landscape doesn't demand from the spectator his "understanding," his imputations of significance . . . ; it demands, rather, his absence, it asks that he not add anything to it. . . . An object worthy of contemplation is one which, in effect, annihilates the perceiving subject.

The complement of reader-annihilation is authorial self-annihilation, the aggression of silence. This tendency achieves its fullest form in the "Atrophied Preface," in which the threat to unlock the word hoard is preceded by the confession "I don't have The Word." Mixed in with Burroughs' digressions and explanations are mosaics of juxtaposition which, like the "Post Script," emerge as tissues of citations, but here the tissue is composed of the text itself, turned over to "Rewrite." The recording instrument begins to talk to itself, foreshadowing the cut-up technique ("the pieces can be had in any order") and the tape-recorder experiments of *The Ticket That Exploded.* In *Ticket* Burroughs postulates that "Communication must be made total. only way to stop it"; he envisions turning over communication to tape recorders as a means toward silence: "get it out of your head and into the machines stop arguing stop complaining stop talking" (*Ticket*). With machines doing the talking, there is no need for either speaker (writer) or audience, and

Since no one is there to listen, why keep running the tape?—Why not shut the whole machine off and go home? Exactly what i intend to do. (*Ticket*)

It is appropriate that *Naked Lunch* ends with the words of the Chinese pushers who "all packed in," who, sharing with Burroughs an ambivalence toward the buyers of their product, make a gesture of emptiness ("I don't have The Word"; " 'No glot . . . C'lom Fliday' "), of concealment (the pushers do have junk; does Burroughs have The Word?). If the reader decides to c'lom Fliday, to return to *Naked Lunch,* he will only be met with the same gesture. The owner of the word hoard finally packs in, Word and all, "Departed have left no address" (*Ticket* by way of *The Waste Land*). (pp. 33-8)

> Michael Leddy, " 'Departed Have Left No Address': Revelation/Concealment Presence/Absence in 'Naked Lunch'," in The Review of Contemporary Fiction, *Vol. 4, No. 1, Spring, 1984, pp. 33-40.*

Robin Lydenberg   (essay date Spring 1984)

[*In the following essay, Lydenberg argues that in* Naked Lunch *Burroughs used the traditional techniques and rhetoric of fiction to render his subject matter literal and scientific rather than figurative and aesthetic.*]

There seems to be an unbridgeable gap between traditional literary criticism and a text like William Burroughs' *Naked Lunch.* Burroughs' project in this novel is to cure the "image addiction" and "morality addiction" of Western thought by producing a text which will defy and destroy these systems. The inability of humanistic literary criticism to account for a novel like *Naked Lunch* stems from the fact that such a criticism is based on the very structures of metaphor and morality which Burroughs attacks. By laying bare the abstract mechanisms by which metaphor and morality insinuate themselves into our thinking, Burroughs throws the reader into a horizontal world of literal meaning and materiality. The grotesque physical literalness of *Naked Lunch,* however, is not the materiality of things as we find them in the world; it is a materiality of absence, a kind of literal mysticism which opens up the possibility of "non-body experience" and the freedom and purity of silence. I will attempt in this essay to explore the gap which separates Burroughs' work from conventional critical analysis, and to open the possibility of an alternative assessment built on an understanding of his radical aesthetics of silence.

Although *Naked Lunch* was brought before the Massachusetts Supreme Court on obscenity charges in the mid-sixties and still arouses dismay and disgust in many highly sophisticated readers, the critical language in which its literary importance was first proclaimed is strikingly moral. John Ciardi [in his "Book Burners and Sweet Sixteen," *Saturday Review* (1959)], describes Burroughs' early novel as a "monumentally moral descent into the hell of narcotics addiction" created by an author "engaged in a profoundly meaningful search for true values." Allen Ginsberg [in the excerpts from the Boston trial reprinted in *Naked Lunch*], similarly judges Burroughs' intentions as "moral . . . defending the good," and he lauds the author himself for the "courage" and "idealism" of his "total confession" of "exactly really what was going on inside his head." Perhaps the most hyperbolic claims appear in Norman Mailer's abstract and allegorical pronouncement [at the trial]: "William Burroughs is in my opinion—whatever his conscious intention may be—a religious writer. There is a sense in *Naked Lunch* of the destruction of soul. . . . It is a vision of how mankind would act if man was totally divorced from eternity."

Of course, Ginsberg and Mailer were defending *Naked Lunch* not just in a literary forum but in a legal one. They felt obliged to adopt the perspective, the values, and the vocabulary of the American systems of law and morality in order to win acquittal for Burroughs' work. However, since the obscenity law requires only that the work in question be proven not "utterly without redeeming social value," the degree of intensity of the moral language of these critics must arise from some source other than simply the legal circumstances surrounding the publication of *Naked Lunch.* I propose that the rhetoric of court and church and the rhetoric of mainstream humanistic literary criticism often overlap, and that the grounds for an aesthetic defense of *Naked Lunch* before the "Academy" are as strictly predetermined as the grounds for its legal defense in the courtroom. The tradition of literary humanism is based on a moral vision of the universe and on the place of art in that universe. Whether *Naked Lunch* is condemned as morally bankrupt or championed as a novel of moral quest, it is being judged within the framework of ethical dualism which dominates Western thought.

The deep irony of Burroughs' legal and literary status is that *Naked Lunch* is invariably translated into the very language and thought systems it challenges. In the "Atrophied Preface," which appears provocatively displaced at the conclusion of *Naked Lunch,* Burroughs himself gives a blunt summary of his novel that calls into question the ethical rhetoric of his defenders and attackers alike: "Abstract concepts, bare as algebra, narrow down to a black turd or a pair of aging cajones." What becomes increasingly explicit in Burroughs' later work is that he is more interested in science and technology than in the "abstract concepts" of ethics, that he is more committed to the obliteration of the author and the "authority" of language than to making a "total confession of what was going on inside his head."

When Burroughs concedes in an interview with Daniel Odier that he is a "great moralist," one feels he is executing a kind of semantic slide, simultaneously approaching and retreating from that ethical stance: "Q: It has been said that you are a great moralist; what do you think? A: Yes, I would say perhaps too much so." From this initial equivocation, Burroughs proceeds to clarify his moral position as the demand for the destruction of three basic formulas: nation, family, and our present methods of birth and reproduction. These social and biological institutions, Burroughs argues, establish "word locks" or "mind locks" which dictate our ways of thinking and feeling, stifling spontaneous life and change. I would argue that the

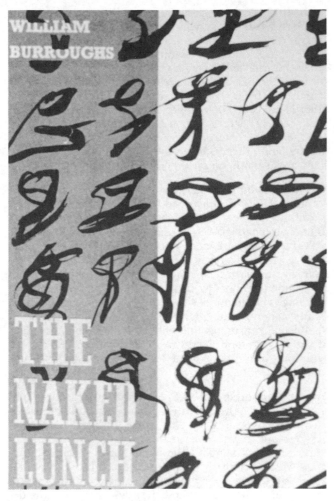

Dust jacket for the 1959 Olympia Press edition of Naked Lunch.

mainstay of the nation/family/birth establishment is, of course, the dualism of Christian morality. In referring to himself as a moralist, therefore, Burroughs is redefining the term itself in the most provocative way. As we shall see, Burroughs' moral position is essentially that he is opposed to moral dualism.

There are very few instances in which Burroughs reverts to the language of moral categories, but they are telling exceptions. In the discussion of heroin addiction that precedes the text of *Naked Lunch,* Burroughs defines evil as the "Algebra of Need": "a basic formula of 'evil' virus . . . The face of 'evil' is always the face of total need. A dope fiend is a man in total need of dope. Beyond a certain frequency need knows absolutely no limit or control. In the words of total need: *'Wouldn't you?'* Yes you would. . . . Because you would be in a state of total sickness, total possession, and not in a position to act in any other way." Again redefining our moral categories, Burroughs condemns as evil the collapse of individual will and identity rather than the possibly illegal or immoral acts the addict-in-need might perpetrate. But even thus redefined, the moral terminology is kept isolated by quotation marks, quarantined like some kind of "evil" virus in its own right, never quite to be trusted.

The "evil" virus of addiction takes many forms—addiction to drugs, sex, religion—but all are variations on a pattern of control and domination of the individual's will. In *The Job,* Burroughs draws an explicit parallel between drug addiction and the "addiction to rightness, to being in the right." We might also diagnose this as the addiction to moral dualism. One of the strongest weapons of mass control is this rhetoric of indignation which manipulates the individual through disgust, shame and guilt: "Senators leap up and bray for the Death Penalty with inflexible authority of virus yen. . . . Death for dope fiends, death for sex queens (I mean fiends) death for the psychopath." The infectious "yen" of his addiction makes the morality junky physically dependent for survival on his righteous destruction of other life. Burroughs sees moral censure itself as both evil and obscene: "An uglier reflection than society's disapproval would be hard to find the mean cold eyes of decent American women tight lips and no thank you from the shop keeper snarling cops pale nigger killing eyes reflecting society's disapproval fucking queers I say shoot them."

Moral indignation, then, is a kind of internal parasite feeding off man's "hate metabolism." In *Naked Lunch,* two Nationalists speak with distrust of an " 'Arty type . . . No principles' " whom they suspect of experimenting with a cure for this "hate metabolism" of conflict. The Nationalists anticipate an attack on the entire "fear hate death syndrome" which maintains their power: " 'Might do almost anything. . . . Turn a massacre into a sex orgy. . . . ' 'Or a joke'." It is the deadly seriousness of moral disapproval and guilt which imprisons offenders and judges alike, and one primitive form of liberation offered by *Naked Lunch* is through the farcical pranks and sexual frenzies of its characters. It would seem that the expulsion of this life-draining virus can only be achieved through a violent undermining of the entire dual system of morality, a system built on antithesis and conflict.

Burroughs' later fiction is far more sober and didactic in its attack on the moral code, and it is also more explicit in identifying the danger of this code in the binary opposition of its structure rather than in its "alleged content." In *Nova Express,* Inspector Lee of the Nova Police explains with scientific detachment that nothing is "right" or "wrong" in an ethical sense, but that these terms merely arise in a biological situation where one life form conflicts with the survival of another. Moral rhetoric is merely a disguise for this biological confrontation. As Lee explains further, to attack the abuses of the manipulative control systems of the Nova Mob (the control addicts) with a vigilante's righteousness would merely "'keep this tired old injustice show on the road,' " and merely reinforce the dualism and hierarchy of the moral code. Thus Lee and the Nova Police offer no morally superior system to replace the Mob's control, but rather propose only a " 'program of total austerity and total resistance'." The battle between the Nova Police and the Nova Mob is not a moral battle of right against wrong, but a biological, a technological conflict. The ultimate solution is the dismantling of the machines of control—the machines of fear, shame, and guilt. At the end of *Nova Express,* the narrator advises: "Shut the whole thing right off—*Silence*—When you answer the machine you provide it with more recordings to be played back to your 'enemies' keep the whole nova machine running—The Chinese character for 'enemy' means to be similar to or to answer—Don't answer the machine—Shut it off—."

While Burroughs attempts to dissolve the Chinese character for enemy, to shut down the enemy machine of moral dualism and conflict, literary critics stubbornly reconstruct that figure in their interpretations of his fiction. Whether they are defending or attacking *Naked Lunch,* critics force the novel to "be similar to or to answer" some abstract concept firmly established in our moral rhetoric. In his book *Chaos in the Novel—The Novel in Chaos,* Alvin Seltzer confesses rather inelegantly that reading *Naked Lunch* makes "our gorges rise right along with our intellects and emotions." He then proceeds to make the novel palatable once again by a typical humanistic sleight of hand: "The validity of the satire does finally justify Burroughs' savage treatment of the human species. Like Swift's, his contempt results from idealism, and finds expression in the most debased aspects of life." Seltzer concludes his explorations of *Naked Lunch*'s Blue Movie of multiple sex acts and hangings with a disturbing understatement of Burroughs' moral intent: "Burroughs will not let us forget that being human is a rather unpleasant business." Such efforts to disguise the foul taste of *Naked Lunch* with a kind of idealistic, moral, and inevitably symbolic dressing are the norm rather than the exception.

David Lodge examines with a more sophisticated and critical eye the possible political and social satire behind Burroughs' novel. Burroughs himself claims in the "Deposition" to *Naked Lunch* that the Blue Movie sequence is "a tract against Capital Punishment in the manner of Jonathan Swift's *Modest Proposal.*" David Lodge [in his "Objections to William Burroughs," *The Novelist at the Crossroads*] challenges this claim on the primary grounds that Burroughs' narrative "suspends rather than activates the reader's moral sense." Lodge argues in a later reexamination of *Naked Lunch* that the elimination of a realistic frame for the satire robs us of our "bearings and empirical reality": the absence of "norms . . . by which its nauseating grotesquerie can be measured and interpreted" makes it impossible for us to "apply the episode . . . to the real world and draw an instructive moral." From within the context of conventional literary humanism, Lodge assumes that "empirical reality" and "norms" form the unquestionable basis of all perception and interpretation of the world. Such notions are, in fact, expressions of a particular pattern of dualistic thought which measures good against evil, reality against fantasy, statement against truth.

I think Lodge is correct in his conclusion that *Naked Lunch* fails as moral satire in the manner of Swift, but he seems to avoid a recognition of the way in which Burroughs' text does succeed. Lodge argues that Burroughs' text is confused, uncontrolled, and at best an interesting failure; from another perspective, however, one might perceive in the ambiguity of *Naked Lunch* the result of Burroughs' determination to undermine those moral norms and conventions which claim the status of reality and

truth. In *S/Z,* Roland Barthes describes the classical or "readerly" text as one which is limited in its plurality by certain "blocks" (Burroughs calls them "mind locks"): "These blocks have names: on the one hand truth, on the other empiricism." The classical text, of course, owes its status to the fact that it shares with conventional literary criticism a belief in these concepts. Burroughs, on the other hand, is trying to approach the limitless plural of an ideal, radical text: "As soon as we say that something is real then immediately things are not permitted" (*Job*). His declared aim, then, is to reverse and explode our assumptions about truth, empiricism and moral norms.

When Burroughs himself draws the comparison between sections of *Naked Lunch* and Swift's *Modest Proposal,* he is "talking to the machine," he is answering the machine in its own language, responding to accusations that parts of *Naked Lunch* are merely pornographic—lacking in artistic merit because they are lacking in moral purpose. We have already seen how much more far-reaching than an opposition to capital punishment are the "moral" reforms Burroughs has in mind: a revolution in our ideas of nation, family and reproduction. He has argued that any such "halfway" measure as the reform or even the destruction of the legal system would be "like trying to abolish the symptoms of a disease while leaving the disease itself untouched" (*Job*).

The obvious difference between Swift's procedures and those of Burroughs is that the *Modest Proposal* is spoken in what Lodge describes as "a tone of calm reasonableness" meant to incite the reader's corrective response, a response which supplies the moral and emotional reactions which the text omits. But the corrective morality which is thus aroused by the satirical text is an early symptom of the righteousness addiction which Burroughs denounces as strongly as he denounces the addictions to drugs, sex and domination. Even in the section of the introduction where he compares himself to Swift, he calls the scene a "naked lunch." "If civilized countries want to return to Druid Hanging Rites," he argues, "let them see what they actually eat and drink. Let them see what is on the end of that long newspaper spoon."

Burroughs' purpose is not to incite reform, to measure inappropriate action against a set of empirical norms, but simply to reveal a more naked truth. As Allen Ginsberg has described Burroughs' method [in his "On Burroughs' Work," *Reality Sandwiches, 1953-60*]:

> The method must be purest meat
> and no symbolic dressing,
> actual visions & actual prisons
> as seen then and now.
>
> . . . . .
>
> A naked lunch is natural to us,
> we eat reality sandwiches.
> But allegories are so much lettuce.
> Don't hide the madness.

Nevertheless, the instinct of the humanistic critic confronted with Burroughs' writing is repeatedly to dress it up as allegory and moral satire, to distance and defuse the novel by making it a mediating or disposable code serving a more abstract and therefore less threatening vision.

The binary opposition which forms the basis of allegory, satire, and metaphor coincides with and supports the comforting dualism of our moral code; good/evil, mind/body, imaginative/real, figurative/literal, meaning/text are all building blocks of the same edifice. We have already seen how Burroughs translates the vertical hierarchy of right over wrong into a horizontal and biological confrontation between different life forms. Similarly, the rhetorical forms which serve as vehicles for the humanist's moral vision—allegory, satire, metaphor—are laid bare or leveled by Burroughs' fictions. The hierarchical structure of interpretation, assuming ascension to a symbolic meaning or moral intention which "justifies" a literary text, is undermined by Burroughs' insistent literalness. Rather than the transcendent "code" language of image or metaphor, Burroughs insists his text merely offers experiments scientifically detached and uncommitted, a horizontal arrangement of shifting and random juxtapositions. Burroughs advises us to learn how to write and read horizontally: " 'Learn to think and write in association blocks which can then be manipulated according to the laws of association and juxtaposition. . . . Read newspapers and magazines for juxtaposition statements rather than alleged content'." This stance is a determined resistance to the evasive transformations worked by image in all its forms, and by its official defender—the literary critic.

In *The Job,* Daniel Odier asks the author to explain the "symbolism" of two passages in his later fiction: one in which two characters are split in half and rejoined to make two new persons, and another in which "lesbian agents with penises grafted onto their faces" drink spinal fluid. These images are so threatening or indigestible that Odier hopes for some deeper or hidden meanings which would justify and detoxify them. Burroughs responds patiently to the first query with a lengthy scientific explanation which concludes, "There is no particular symbolism. It's just a possibility which I imagine in the course of time might be in the reach of medical science." Burroughs seems almost embarrassed by his interviewer's persistence in this line of questioning, and he dismisses the second image quickly with, "Oh, just a bit of science fiction, really."

The critic in this case wants Burroughs to translate his text into the language of "abstract concepts" which, in the process of all abstract or "blind" prose, will suck the life, color, and vividness out of things and leave us with a more comforting blandness of "meaning." Burroughs refuses to feed our desire, our need, for metaphorical explanation, our need to reaffirm our principles, our assumptions about language, literature, and the human condition. Burroughs responds to Odier on this occasion like the reluctant Chinese pushers in *Naked Lunch* who evade the insistent Western junky's demands with " 'No glot . . . C'lom Fliday.' "

There seems to be a need which always brings us to the belief in a primitive or mythical first stage of language, the promise of the transcendence and magical oneness of metaphor. Burroughs sees this symbolic notion of vertical transcendence as the "lie" which keeps us from facing the horizontal facts that we are "dying animals on a doomed planet." So, image itself is an addiction—as Burroughs puts it, "Junk *is* image"—and the only cure for this addiction may be the nauseating visions of Burroughs' prose. His novels provide a kind of literary emetic cure which parallels the apomorphine emetic cure Burroughs credits with his victory over heroine addiction. Inspector Lee prescribes " 'Apomorphine and silence. I order total resistance directed against this conspiracy to pay off peoples of the earth in ersatz bullshit'." In the peculiar economics of Burroughs' fiction, the individual is preyed upon by "brokers of exquisite dreams and memories tested on the sensitized cells of junk sickness and bartered for raw materials of the will." That "raw materials of the will" is the very stuff of life which is parasitically destroyed by the "Algebra of Need." The "pyramid of junk, one level eating the level below" which Burroughs describes in the "Deposition" is precisely the vertical hierarchy of symbolic meaning and ethical dualism which displaces and devours the literal text and the actual world.

Burroughs' distrust of allegory and metaphor stems from his commitment to individual will. Allegory or symbol screens out the literal, the fact, the signifier, to illuminate the idea; nothing happens, life fades and is replaced by abstraction. Frank McConnell [in his "William Burroughs and the Literature of Addiction," *Massachusetts Review* (1967)] has described Burroughs' prose as a "stern criticism" of the "capitulation" to allegory and as a condemnation of "metaphor as a final temptation to not-will." The imposition of authorial will means the refusal to allow "allegorical or metaphorical translation (and avoidance)."

Burroughs' opposition to this moral/metaphorical prose in *Naked Lunch* and beyond may be quite clearly represented in the pointed juxtaposition of two descriptions of the same scene. The narrator is explaining a particular procedure for shooting up heroin:

> Provident junkies, known as squirrels, keep stashes against a bust. Every time I take a shot I let a few drops fall into my vest pocket, the lining is stiff with stuff. I had a plastic dropper in my shoe and a safety-pin stuck in my belt. You know how this pin and drooper routine is put down: "She seized a safety pin caked with blood and rust, gouged a great hole in her leg which seemed to hang open like an obscene, festering mouth waiting for unspeakable congress with the dropper which she now plunged out of sight into the gaping wound. But her hideous galvanized need (hunger of insects in dry places) has broken the dropper off deep in the flesh of her ravaged thigh (looking rather like a poster on soil erosion). But what does she care? She does not even bother to remove the splintered glass. . . . What does she care for the atom bomb, the bed bugs, the cancer rent."

The description is "put down" in quotation marks as a voice to be distinguished from the flat factual delivery which introduces it. This description is full of just the sort of moral rhetoric that demands the reader's disgust and righteous condemnation of the subject. The rhetorical lament of "What does she care for . . . " calls up the popular domestic genres of soap opera and tawdry modern romance adventure—another familiar cultural "addiction." Burroughs counters this excessive and manipulative prose, its exaggerated and parenthetically equivocated metaphors ("Looking rather like a poster on soil erosion"), with a direct, almost scientific prose:

> The real scene you pinch up some leg flesh and make a quick stab hole with a pin. Then fit the dropper *over, not in* the hole and feed the solution slow and careful so it doesn't squirt out the sides. . . . When I grabbed the Rube's thigh the flesh came up like wax and stayed there, and a slow drop of pus oozed out the hole. And I never touched a living body cold as the Rube there in Philly.

Burroughs does not pursue the attack on junk and drug addiction through the whining manipulation of his first version of the scene, but straight ahead, in tactile connection with "the real scene." The hyped-up description that is "put down" in the rhetoric of moral outrage and disgust is part of the addiction itself, part of the attraction of the addiction. In his flattened version of the scene, Burroughs is trying to take the thrill out of junk, just as he tries to take the thrill out of violence and sex orgy in the Blue Movie scene. For it is the thrill which becomes the source of a need strong enough to drive one to barter "raw materials of the will."

I do not mean to argue here that this detached "recording instrument" represents Burroughs' poetic voice (or lack of one). In fact, by the end of the second version of the shoot-up scene, the style slides from detached objectivity to the rather stagey voice of the hard-boiled detective. We cannot locate the author or the "truth" in either of these voices "put down" in the text. We must look to the negative space between them, to the space cleared by the antithetical clash of these two ways of seeing. It is here, as we shall see later, in the "hiatus between thoughts" that Burroughs' new poetry will show itself. This flat prose, then, is not Burroughs' answer to the first version of the scene, but merely one of many guises, one of many technical devices—along with tape recorders, scissors, pirated texts of all varieties—used by the author to undermine the hegemony of moral and metaphorical rhetoric.

One of the most common responses of the critic to *Naked Lunch* is the translation of the world of drug addiction into a metaphor for other more abstract forms of addiction, oppression, and control. Of course, Burroughs himself makes this connection, but he is careful to explain that the relationship between the various types of "evil virus" in the "Algebra of Need" is not metaphorical or allegorical, but logical, literal, mathematical: "If you wish to alter or annihilate a pyramid of numbers in a serial relation, you alter or remove the bottom number. If we wish to annihilate the junk pyramid, we must start with the bottom . . . *the Addict . . . the one irreplaceable factor in the junk equation.*" Burroughs insists further, "I have almost completed a sequel to *Naked Lunch.* A mathematical extension of the Algebra of Need beyond the junk virus." The "evil virus," then, travels from one host to another along mathematical lines of extension or along biological circuits of need itself—it proceeds by literal metonymic juxtaposition and contagion rather than by metaphorical resemblance.

The literalness—mathematical, scientific, naturalistic, supernaturalistic—which pervades Burroughs' prose style is part of his campaign to free literature from morality and symbolic rhetoric, to seize for it the independence of the sciences: " 'A doctor is not criticized for describing the manifestations and symptoms of an illness, even though the symptoms may be disgusting. I feel that a writer has the right to the same freedom. In fact, I think that the time has come for the line between literature and science, a purely arbitrary line, to be erased'."

This scientific or technical voice often intrudes abruptly in *Naked Lunch,* breaking in on the tone of a passage or the development of some farcical and fantastic situation. Very often these intrusions are made literal in their own right by Burroughs' use of parentheses that represent visually the splicing in of a different voice in the text. Once again, it must be stressed that these intrusions do not represent the hierarchical domination of one voice over another, but a surgical attack on all structures of hierarchy, continuity and control:

> "But you wouldn't believe it, certain disgruntled elements chased us right down to our launch."
>
> "Handicapped somewhat by lack of legs."
>
> "And a condition in the head."
>
> (Ergot is a fungus disease grows on bad wheat. During the Middle Ages Europe was periodically decimated by outbreaks of Ergotism, which was called St. Anthony's fire. Gangrene frequently supervenes, the legs turn black and drop off.)

Another scene describes the narrator's plans to get rid of The Rube, a travelling companion whose uncontrollable habit is making him a social liability:

> I decided to lop him off if it meant a smother party. (This is a rural English custom designed to eliminate aged and bedfast dependents. A family so afflicted throws a "smother party" where the guests pile mattresses on the old liability, climb up on top of the mattresses and lush themselves out.) The Rube is a drag on the industry and should be led out into the skid rows of the world. (This is an African practice. Official known as the "Leader Out" has the function of taking old characters out into the jungle and leaving them there.)

As these examples demonstrate, Burroughs does not justify his text, as some critics would do, by pointing to a personal idealism underlying a fierce social satire, but rather by insisting, however spuriously, on the scientific and historical objectivity, on the literalness of his images:

> Carl talked to the doctor outside under the narrow arcade with rain bouncing up from the street against his pant legs, thinking how many people he tell it to, and the stairs, porches, lawns, driveways, corridors and streets of the world there in the doctor's eyes . . . stuffy German alcoves, butterfly trays to the ceiling, silent porten-

tous smell of uremia seeping under the door, suburban lawns to sound of the water sprinkler, in calm jungle night under silent wings of the Anopheles mosquito. (Note: This is not a figure. Anopheles mosquitos *are* silent.)

No matter how nostalgic and evocative a series of images may be, they are almost always weighted down and literalized by death, decay, stagnation.

Burroughs is not merely producing a prose style which proceeds by alternating voices—literal and lyrical—but rather each intrusion forces us to return to what precedes it and reconsider its significance and its effect on us. We are reading, then, by a peculiar kind of looping process which continually revises and begins again. Thus reading *Naked Lunch* proceeds like a tape recording inched and smudged, clearing away conventional sound or meaning and allowing hidden voices to emerge: "Like a moving film the flow of thoughts flow stop change and flow again. At the point where one flow stops there is a split-second hiatus. The new way of thinking grows in this hiatus between thoughts." Roland Barthes has identified a similar process as the "metonymic skid" that takes place imperceptibly in all reading; Burroughs, as usual, exposes these hidden patterns and makes a naked lunch of the reading process itself. Burroughs' metonymic juxtapositions or skids cut up the lubricity of all metaphorical connections. The stern "Note" which asserts the literalness of the mosquito image is far more than an anti-metaphorical affectation. It equates the metaphorical evasion, which would domesticate the mosquito's silent threat of death into a mere "figure," with the evasion of death and disease, which is the very subject of the scene between Carl and the German doctor. The contempt, disinterest, and hypocrisy which characterize the doctor's treatment of Carl's "native" friend are based on the avoidance of truth: "saying without words: 'Alzo for the so stupid peasant we must avoid use of the word is it not? Otherwise he shit himself with fear. Koch and spit they are both nasty words I think?' He said aloud: 'It is a catarro de los pulmones'." Such rhetorical evasion (moral or metaphorical) is designed to distract us from the obscenity, the unthinkableness of human life itself. In response to this evasion, Burroughs returns us always to the hard facts of time, of life in the body: the sequence of the junky's days strung together on the thread of blood which flowers in the needle, the orgiast's days strung together on the thread of semen discharged by a hanged man into a black void, and on what Burroughs describes as the "long lunch thread from mouth to ass all the days of our years."

Nostalgic images and memories of places, objects and actions associated with innocence and youth are punctuated by parenthetical details evoking death, silence, decay. Evocative "train whistles" and adolescent dreams are reduced to images with no personal vibrations, no moral or sentimental impact; nostalgia and sentimentality approach silence, emptiness, coldness, transparency. In that transparent landscape suddenly the evasive veil of sentiment is torn aside and we see clearly the inexorable progress of human mortality: "Time jump like a broken typewriter, the boys are old men, young hips quivering and twitching in boyspasms go slack and flabby, draped over an outhouse seat, a park bench, a stone wall . . . twitching and shivering in dirty underwear, probing for a vein in the junk-sick morning, in an Arab café muttering and slobbering."

Lyricism and symbolic abstraction are the evasive methods of a moral/metaphorical order; Burroughs destroys them with a relentless and often disgusting literalness. There is an accumulation of material objects in *Naked Lunch,* a cluttered mosaic, a chaotic encyclopedia of things, but they whirl by us so quickly that they never acquire the weightiness of materiality as we find it in Balzac or Dickens or Flaubert. The literalness which anchors Burroughs' text is instead the literalness of absence, the materiality of loss: the absence of sound ("silent wings of the Anopheles mosquito"), the absence of transcendent meaning ("TV antennas to the meaningless sky"), the absence of legs lost to gangrene infection, the disappearance of the sick or aged disposed of in jungles or death-dealing sanitariums.

This paradoxical convergence of literalness and absence represents quite accurately the peculiar technological mysticism of Burroughs' fiction, his scientific belief in what he calls "non-body experience." Burroughs suggests, again parenthetically, that some drug intoxications are actually "space time travel": "(It occurs to me that preliminary Yage nausea is motion sickness of transport to Yage state)." Thus, the material reality of the body's response (nausea) corroborates the presence of non-body experience. Later in *The Job,* Burroughs argues that drugs are unnecessary, that the mind can open up space travel simply by leaving "verbal garbage behind." Burroughs clearly sees the three modes of travel—by NASA, by drugs, and by the controlled manipulation of silence—as literally equivalent. For Burroughs, literalness asserts not only the material fact of the body, but the literal possibility of escape from that body: "The way OUT is the way IN."

This negative or mystical literalness leads to a new way of thinking, a way which protects the integrity and will of the individual from the dualistic and hierarchical "mind locks" of Western thought: "It is no oceanic organismal subconscious body thinking. It is precisely delineated by what it is not. . . . There are no considerations here that would force thinking into certain lines of structural or environmental necessities." Free from all conditioning and patterning, words can approach the directness of a random mosaic, " 'like articles abandoned in a hotel drawer, defined by negatives and absence'." Finally we may learn to "stop words to see and touch words to move and use words like objects."

Edward Said [in his *Beginnings*] defines modern writing as containing a materiality which is textual rather than genetic. I take this to mean that in modern works the "thingness of the action," as Aristotle calls it, is not drawn mimetically from the writer's belief in the reality of the world around him, but from his confrontation with the "thingness" of his medium, his recognition that words are objects. Thus language and mind become the very focus of the modern radical text. In Burroughs' radical vision, all materiality stems ultimately from the materiality of language, a materiality which is masked by abstraction, by a "blind prose" of euphemisms which obscures and devours fact and reference.

The threat to individual identity and will, therefore, comes not only from the imposing structures of moral and metaphorical rhetoric, but from language itself. Not only must words become tangible (and thus controllable) objects, but the entire manipulative system of Western language and thought must be made visible. Literalness comes back to the naked seeing that is always Burroughs' goal; to be literal is to make the word an object, a fact, a body. If the word is made external and visible, we can "see the enemy direct."

The mathematical extension of the way drug addiction destroys or controls individual will, establishing an alien "Man Within" whose tapeworm craving is never satisfied, is in fact an extension of the "evil" virus of word and image:

> I have frequently spoken of word and image as viruses or as acting as viruses, and this is not an allegorical comparison. It will be seen that the falsifications in syllabic Western languages are in point of fact actual virus mechanisms. . . . If we can infer purpose from behavior, then the purpose of a virus is TO SURVIVE. To survive at any expense to the host invaded. To be an animal, to be a body. To be an animal body that the virus can invade.

Burroughs argues that the word itself is the body virus, the infection of materiality that keeps us from non-body experience. We only escape the body and language by making them visible, "Gentle reader, we see God through our assholes in the flash bulb of orgasm. . . . The way OUT is the way IN."

Again we see the peculiarly mystical goal of Burroughs' literalness—the word is made object so that we can expel it and escape into silence, the literal absence of words. Just as the drug addict can't survive without heroin or the righteousness addict without indignation, the "compulsive verbalizer," the Word addict, can't survive in silence. And literalness, as Susan Sontag has argued [in her "The Aesthetics of Silence," *Styles of Radical Will*], is one of the ultimate weapons and strategies of silence. Through inventory, catalogue, surface, through verbal patterns which proceed by material accumulation, " 'meaning' is converted into 'use.' " In William Burroughs' fiction, language is used up, the parasite exhausted and starved out, finally leaving no symbolic residue:

> *Naked Lunch* demands Silence from the Reader. Otherwise he is taking his own pulse . . .
>
> (pp. 75-84)

Robin Lydenberg, "Beyond Good and Evil: 'How-To' Read 'Naked Lunch'," in The Review of Contemporary Fiction, Vol. 4, No. 1, Spring, 1984, pp. 75-85.

FURTHER READING

Bibliography

Goodman, Michael B. *William S. Burroughs: An Annotated Bibliography of His Works and Criticism.* New York: Garland Publishing, 1975, 96 p.
    Comprehensive primary and secondary bibliography.

Maynard, Joseph, and Miles, Barry. *William S. Burroughs: A Bibliography, 1953-73.* Charlottesville: University Press of Virginia, 1978, 243 p.
    Comprehensive bibliography of works by and about Burroughs, including entries from obscure European and American literary magazines.

Rushing, Lynda Lee. "William S. Burroughs: A Bibliography." *Bulletin of Bibliography and Magazine Notes* 29, No. 3 (July-September 1972): 87-92.
    Extensive bibliography that includes foreign language editions of Burroughs's works, critical essays, and reviews.

Biography

Bockris, Victor. *With William Burroughs: A Report From the Bunker.* New York: Seaver Books, 1981, 250 p.
    Transcripts of interviews with Burroughs that were conducted between 1974 and 1981.

Morgan, Ted. *Literary Outlaw: The Life and Times of William S. Burroughs.* New York: Avon Books, 1988, 659 p.
    An exhaustive and extensively researched biography of Burroughs's life and career that includes a chapter devoted to the writing, publication, and critical reception of *Naked Lunch.*

Skerl, Jennie. *William S. Burroughs.* Boston: Twayne Publishers, 1985, 127 p.
    Brief overview of Burroughs's life and career with critical interpretations of his major works, including *Naked Lunch.*

Criticism

Adam, Ian W. "Society as Novelist." *Journal of Aesthetics and Art Criticism* XXV, No. 4 (Summer 1967): 375-86.
    A comparative study of *Naked Lunch* and William Makepeace Thackery's *Vanity Fair.*

Elliot, George P. "Destroyers, Defilers, and Confusers of Men." *The Atlantic Monthly* 222, No. 6 (December 1968): 74-80.
    In discussing the "literary nihilism" prevalent in post-World War II fiction, Elliot dismisses *Naked Lunch,* stating: "[It] does not just express disgust and confusion for me; it disgusts and confuses me, to no end."

Estrin, Barbara L. "The Revelatory Connection: Inspired Poetry and *Naked Lunch.*" *Review of Contemporary Fiction* 4, No. 1 (Spring 1984): 58-64.
    Views *Naked Lunch* as a modern variation of divinely or naturally inspired literature, suggesting that it "deals with the writer's dissolution as he expresses not his own personality but the force of the drug which compels him to act."

Fiedler, Leslie A. "The Alteration of Consciousness," and "The End of the Novel." In his *Waiting for the End,* pp. 155-69, 170-78. New York: Stein and Day, 1964.

A derisive summary of Burroughs's early works, asserting that he is "naïve" artistically, ideologically, and philosophically.

Goodman, Michael Barry. *Contemporary Literary Censorship: The Case History of Burroughs'* Naked Lunch. Metuchen, N.J.: The Scarecrow Press, 1981, 330 p.

Detailed examination of the attempts to supress *Naked Lunch,* based primarily on transcripts from the various court cases, administrative hearings, writers' conferences, and the correspondence of Burroughs and others.

Hassan, Ihab. "The Novel of Outrage: A Minority Voice in Postwar American Fiction." *The American Scholar* XXXIV, No. 2 (Spring 1965): 239-53.

Offers a brief discussion of *Naked Lunch* as an expression of disgust and disillusionment with the human condition "which attempts to redeem creation by abolishing it, abolishing both Word and Flesh."

Hoffman, Frederick J. "Conclusion: The Wheel of Self." In his *The Mortal No: Death and the Modern Imagination,* pp. 453-93. Princeton, N.J.: Princeton University Press, 1964.

Argues that *Naked Lunch* "is entirely a destructive expression, without joy in destruction or anxiety over the search for an alternative."

Lydenberg, Robin. *Word Cultures: Radical Theory and Practice in William S. Burroughs' Fiction.* Urbana: University of Illinois Press, 1987, 224 p.

Extensive analytical overview of Burroughs's works.

Mathieson, Kenneth. "The Influence of Science Fiction in the Contemporary American Novel." *Science-Fiction Studies* 12, No. 1 (March 1985): 22-32.

Identifies *Naked Lunch* as a "distinct historical departure in American writing" due to characteristics in the novel's style and theme usually associated with the science fiction genre.

McCarthy, Mary. "Burroughs' *Naked Lunch.*" *Encounter* XX, No. 4 (April 1963): 92-4, 96, 98.

McCarthy restates her opinion, presented in a speech at the 1962 International Writers' Conference in Edinburgh, that *Naked Lunch* exemplifies a "new kind of novel."

Michelson, Peter. "Beardsley, Burroughs, Decadence, and the Poetics of Obscenity." *TriQuarterly,* No. 12 (Spring 1968): 139-55.

Compares the characteristic qualities of literary decadence evinced in the works of Aubrey Beardsley with those found in Burroughs's works, particularly *Naked Lunch.*

Peterson, R. G. "A Picture Is a Fact: Wittgenstein and *The Naked Lunch.*" *Twentieth Century Literature* 12, No. 2 (July 1966): 78-86.

Posits "that the world of the *Naked Lunch* takes its shape from certain views expressed or implied in Ludwig Wittgenstein's *Tractatus Logico-Philosophicus.*"

Skerl, Jennie, and Lydenberg, Robin, eds. *William S. Burroughs at the Front: Critical Reception, 1959-1989.* Carbondale: Southern Illinois University Press, 1991, 274 p.

A collection of major critical essays and reviews of Burroughs's works, arranged chronologically, and a selected bibliography of primary and secondary sources.

"Ugh. . . . " *Times Literary Supplement,* No. 3220 (14 November 1963): 919.

A negative review of *Naked Lunch, The Soft Machine, The Ticket That Exploded,* and *Dead Fingers Talk.* This review initiated a great deal of correspondence in subsequent issues.

Weinstein, Arnold. "Body Control: The Erotic Project in *Les Liaisons dangereuses* and *Naked Lunch.*" In his *The Fiction of Relationship,* pp. 119-51. Princeton, N.J.: Princeton University Press, 1988.

Compares the two novels, focusing on the portrayal of sexuality and sensuality in the works.

Wilt, Koos van der. "The Author's Recreation of Himself as Narrator and Protagonist in Fragmented Prose: A New Look at Some Beat Novels." *Dutch Quarterly Review of Anglo-American Letters* 12, No. 2 (1982): 113-24.

An analysis of *Naked Lunch,* Jack Kerouac's *On the Road,* Lawrence Ferlinghetti's *Her,* and Alexander Trocchi's *Cain's Book.*

Additional coverage of Burroughs's life and career is contained in the following sources published by Gale Research: *Contemporary Authors,* **Vols. 9-12, rev. ed.;** *Contemporary Authors New Revision Series,* **Vol. 20;** *Contemporary Literary Criticism,* **Vols. 1, 2, 5, 15, 22, 42;** *Dictionary of Literary Biography,* **Vols. 2, 8, 16;** *Dictionary of Literary Biography Yearbook, 1981;* **Major 20th-Century Writers; and** *World Literature Criticism.*

Elias Canetti

1905-

Bulgarian-born Swiss novelist, essayist, playwright, non-fiction writer and autobiographer.

The following entry provides an overview of Canetti's life and career. For further information on his life and works, see *CLC,* Volumes 3, 14, and 25.

INTRODUCTION

The recipient of the 1981 Nobel Prize for Literature, Canetti is best known for his novel *Die Blendung* (*Auto-da-Fé*) and his treatise on mass behavior, *Masse und Macht* (*Crowds and Power*). Both of these works probe the ways in which individuals are affected by participation in a group. While often criticized for the unscientific methods and subjective conclusions presented in his writings, Canetti is recognized for his insightful analysis of crowd psychology and vivid depictions of crowd phenomena.

Canetti was born in Rutschuk (now Ruse), Bulgaria, to parents who were descendants of the Sephardic Jews of Spain. Because of this heritage, he was exposed to numerous languages early in his life, especially Bulgarian, Hebrew, and Ladino, a fifteenth-century patois of Spanish and Hebrew spoken in his home and in the Sephardic community. His parents were ardent students of German literature and spoke to each other in German when they did not want their children to understand their conversations; remembering his fascination at the air of mystery which he perceived in these conversations, Canetti later adopted German as the language of his intellectual and literary pursuits. In 1911 the family moved to London. When Canetti's father died suddenly in 1912, his mother moved the family first to Vienna, then to other cities in the German-speaking countries of Europe. Fearing that he would become "soft" without the guidance of a father, Canetti's mother taught him German and pressured him to study chemistry, deriding his growing interest in literature and writing. During the 1920s he immersed himself in the cultural life of Berlin and Vienna, where he met such figures as satirist Karl Kraus, artist George Grosz, and novelists Robert Musil, Hermann Broch, and Thomas Mann. In 1922 he joined a demonstration in reaction to the murder of the German-Jewish industrialist Walter Rathenau, and in 1927 he was part of a crowd that burned down the Vienna Palace of Justice while protesting the acquittal of men indicted for killing workers in the Austrian province of Burgenland. These events confirmed in him the desire to make a life's work of the study of mass psychology. After receiving his doctorate in chemistry from the University of Vienna in 1929, Canetti produced his first and only novel, *Auto-da-Fé*. During the 1930s he translated the writings of Upton Sinclair into German and completed one play, *Die Hochzeit* (*The Wedding*), before he fled to

England after the annexation of Austria by Germany and the anti-Semitic violence of Krystallnacht. Canetti continued to write in German during his wartime exile in England, devoting time to works such as *Crowds and Power*. In ensuing decades, Canetti has divided his time between London and Zurich, and has published essays, collections of aphorisms, and three volumes of autobiography.

Critics of Canetti's works have focused their attention on *Auto-da-Fé* and *Crowds and Power,* praising their insight into individual and mass psychology. *Auto-da-Fé* details the ruin of Peter Kien, a world-renowned sinologist whose life revolves around his 25,000-volume library. Kien is obsessed with his books, which he regards as companions. The other major characters in the novel also exhibit obsessions that dominate their lives: Kien's housekeeper, Therese Krumbholz, is preoccupied with satisfying her appetites for money and sex; Benedikt Pfaff, the manager of Kien's apartment house, with seizing money and power; and the dwarf Fischerle with becoming a wealthy and famous chess champion. *Auto-da-Fé* satirizes the greed, cruelty, and intolerance of each of these individuals, who all readily join in the persecution of one another and at the same time are themselves victimized. In discussions of *Auto-da-Fé,* some critics have complained that Canetti's characterization is superficial. Furthermore, they argue, the world of invariably deranged personalities depicted in Canetti's novel bears little resemblance to actual life, and, with the exception of Kien, the characters do not evolve, while Kien himself only sinks into insanity before finally destroying himself. A particular point of objection to the novel is that none of its characters comes to any realization of his or her folly, and the reader is ultimately offered only a biting satire of dementia. In addition, critics describe the structure of *Auto-da-Fé* as difficult because the narrative perspective shifts without transition or explanation from the viewpoint of one character to that of another character or an omniscient narrator. Nevertheless, many commentators praise the book for its treatment of the dual nature of human beings as both individuals and members of a group. Critics observe that Canetti's portrayal of a world populated by cruel, obsessive personalities accurately reflects European society in the 1920s and 1930s, and his complex narrative technique provides a penetrating understanding of the characters' psychopathy.

Crowds and Power, which Canetti worked on for thirty years, draws on the resources of his erudition in numerous fields, including literature, anthropology, and science, in an attempt to explain the origins, behavior, and significance of crowds as forces in society. Organized as a large volume of brief, aphoristic essays explaining various aspects and examples of mass psychology, the book scrutinizes crowds and crowd phenomena found in nature, mythology, and history. As with *Auto-da-Fé,* many commentators consider *Crowds and Power* a flawed work, observing that its scholarship is unscientific and that the book advances assertions without the support of arguments or scientific proof. Moreover, critics maintain that without supporting arguments, readers have little reason to believe some of the premises on which Canetti grounds his explanation of crowds and crowd behavior. In an effort to take a fresh look at his subject, Canetti created his own terminology for discussing mass phenomena, disregarded modern scientific study of the crowd, and ignored important contemporary examples of crowd behavior and crowd manipulators, most notably Nazism and Adolf Hitler. However, because Canetti avoids scientific techniques and language, his study is highly original in its approach and accessible to the average reader.

Canetti's autobiographical writings, dramas, essays, and aphorisms are considered amplifications of the principal themes set forth in his two major works and are most often studied as documents which further critical understanding of *Auto-da-Fé* and *Crowds and Power.* In these two works, through detailed explorations of conflicts between the individual and the group, Canetti developed what one critic has termed "a poetics of crowds" which illuminates the violence and obsessiveness of human nature.

PRINCIPAL WORKS

Die Hochzeit (drama) 1932
   [*The Wedding,* 1986]
Die Blendung (novel) 1935
   [*The Tower of Babel,* 1947; also published as *Auto-da-Fé,* 1963]
*Kömodie der Eitelkeit (drama) [first publication] 1950
   [*Comedy of Vanity* published in *"Comedy of Vanity" and "Life-Terms,"* 1983]
Die Befristeten (drama) 1952
   [*Life-Terms* published in *"Comedy of Vanity" and "Life-Terms,"* 1983; also published as *The Numbered,* 1984]
Masse und Macht (nonfiction) 1960
   [*Crowds and Power,* 1962]
Die Stimmen von Marrakesch: Aufzeichnungen nach einer Reise (travel essay) 1967
   [*The Voices of Marrakesh: A Record of a Visit,* 1978]
Der andere Prozess: Kafkas Briefe an Felice (criticism) 1969
   [*Kafka's Other Trial: The Letters to Felice,* 1974]
Macht und Überleben: Drei Essays (essays) 1972
Die Provinz des Menschen: Aufzeichnungen, 1942-1972 (aphorisms) 1973
   [*The Human Province,* 1978]
Der Ohrenzeuge: Fünfzig Charaktere (sketches) 1974
   [*Earwitness: Fifty Characters,* 1979]
Das Gewissen der Worte (essays) 1975
   [*The Conscience of Words,* 1979]
Die gerettete Zunge: Geschichte einer Jugend (autobiography) 1977
   [*The Tongue Set Free: Remembrance of a European Childhood,* 1980]
Die Fackel im Ohr: Lebensgeschichte, 1921-1931 (autobiography) 1980
   [*The Torch in My Ear,* 1982]
Das Augenspiel: Lebensgeschichte, 1931-1937 (autobiography) 1985
   [*The Play of the Eyes,* 1986]
Das Geheimherz der Uhr: Aufzeichnungen, 1973-1985 (aphorisms) 1987
   [*The Secret Heart of the Clock,* 1991]

*This work was written in 1933-34.

CRITICISM

Edward A. Thomson (essay date October 1972)

[*In the following excerpt, Thomson discusses the portrayal of madness in* Die Blendung.]

The depiction and symbolic function of madness in literature has been subject to a series of changes in the last two centuries. Primarily they have arisen from an interest in new medical theories concerning the origins and interpretation of insanity and from the growing consciousness of its relevance to normal processes of thought. Its earliest appearances, in the satires, farces and tales of classical and medieval literature, ascribe to the madman the role of prophet or fool: he may be the vehicle of divine revelation or the incarnation of human folly. In either case he is an outcast, condemned by the abnormality of his behaviour to exist as a warning to man of the power of supernatural forces or as a mirror in which the extremes of human stupidity are reflected. With the rise around 1800 of the asylum devoted specifically to the care of the insane and therefore with the acceptance of insanity as a legitimate subject for medical examination, the image of the madman changes in literature also. For the Romantics he is neither the mouthpiece of the divine nor a symbol of folly: he has become a guide to unexplored states of consciousness, to problematic modes of awareness. Madness no longer points out to the supernatural or rests on the surface of behaviour, it points inwards to the processes of human consciousness, to the way in which reality is apprehended and interpreted. The realisation, therefore, that insanity is an illness in need of a cure like any other occurs at the same time as the madman appears in literature as a valid metaphor for the presentation of psychological conflicts which are not necessarily of a pathological nature. [In his *Dimensions of the Modern Novel: German Texts and European Contexts*] Theodore Ziolkowski, although following Michel Foucault in his dating of the modern attitude to madness from the end of the eighteenth century, sees in the Romantics' depiction of insanity only 'a condition of pathologically exaggerated sensibility, of subjectivism carried to an absurd extreme' with 'no typological value'. This tends to underestimate the modernity of the Romantics' interpretation of the phenomenon; their concern to present what they took to be the transcendental realities of their solipsism should not obscure the existential predicament which underlies it. In the novels of E. T. A. Hoffmann, for example, madness is a means of examining the question of human identity, the search for the true self under the conflicting demands of conscious will and unconscious emotion. Problems of cognition, of the experiences of reality, posed by the distortion of perception in madness underline a non-pathological condition rather than contradict it. This does not differ fundamentally from modern portraits of similar states; it is a matter of a less developed knowledge of the mechanics of insanity, not of a basic difference in interpretation and symbolic function. [In *Mitteilungen der E. T. A. Hoffmann Gesellschaft* (1968)] Karin Cramer points this out in relation to the works of Hoffmann: 'Nur wird hier gemäss der romantischen Tradition das Geschehen, das sich im modernen Roman fast gänzlich im Innern des Menschen vollzieht, stets von aussen durch natürliche oder übernatürliche Kräfte hervorgerufen und damit erklärt.' The madman of the Romantics was liable to meet his double as a more or less concrete being; the dynamics of psychic projection were as yet not fully explored.

It is with the advent of psychoanalysis and advances in psychiatry at the end of the nineteenth century that the madman once more emerges as a common figure in literature. In the plays and short stories of Hugo von Hof-

mannsthal the old idea of the double reappears both in totally non-pathological cases and in cases of a distinctly pathological kind. In the fragment of the novel *Andreas oder die Vereinigten* there are instances of both: the character of Maria/Mariquita is drawn from an actual case of schizophrenia, while the confusions Andreas experiences are not pathological and his *alter ego* is represented by an autonomous character. In the first case the dissolution of a firm sense of identity, the schizophrenic's 'regression' to a state parallel to that of childhood, is used as the metaphor for the existential search for identity and balance; in the second a similar situation is presented but from a non-pathological perspective, it is seen as part of normal human growth and development. In *Ein Brief* a near psychotic state is again the means of depicting a situation which is not necessarily connected with madness; the abnormal is used for a better understanding of the normal. Chandos's difficulties with language, his wavering periods of heightened perception and emotional deadness, are typical of psychosis; yet their significance is that they point to the more general question of how the individual consciousness can function when its own experience and interpretation of reality no longer coincides with that of the culture in which it finds itself. These are the directions in which the symbolic depiction of madness moves in the twentieth century.

The emergence of characters with a clinically accurate background of insanity in the literature of the 1920s and 30s has been noted by Ziolkowski: 'The psychiatric interest of a generation schooled in Freud reveals itself both in the careful motivation and in the factual description of the psychosis.' He adduces the examples of Franz Biberkopf in Döblin's *Berlin Alexanderplatz*, of the stonemason Gödicke in Broch's *Die Schlafwandler* and of Moosbrugger in Musil's *Der Mann ohne Eigenschaften*, emphasizing the symbolic quality of their madness: 'these cases of insanity symbolize an entire civilization that is shot through with insanity'. But Ziolkowski stops short of differentiating between the madness of these figures. The experiences of schizophrenia and paranoia include a multitude of physical and psychic phenomena and therefore denote an equally large set of non-pathological experience. Biberkopf's paranoia is closely related to the position in which he finds himself in a hostile society; Gödicke's schizophrenia only gains its full symbolic value in the light of Broch's concept of 'Zerfall der Werte', the fragmentation of value systems; equally, the two phases of Moosbrugger's schizophrenia, the mystical unity of the periods when he 'dances' and the confusion and paranoia of the other state, are pathological reflections of Ulrich's non-pathological experiments with the 'anderer Zustand'. A more carefully differentiated typology of madness is needed; one which not only points to the fact of madness, but which also examines more fully the symbolic functions of its psychic and physical symptoms.

In Elias Canetti's novel ***Die Blendung*** (1935) all but one of the characters are insane. It has frequently been pointed out that it is the symbol of a world gone mad: 'der Entwurf einer paranoischen Welt' [Hans Daiber, "Elias Canetti" in *Wort in der Zeit* (1957)], or: 'Naturgeschichte des Bösen, Ansicht von der Wahn- und Nachtseite der Mitmenschen' [Joachim Schickal, *Der Monat* (1964)]. Dieter Dissinger goes further [in his dissertation *Elias Canettis Roman* Die Blendung *und seine Stellung im Werke des Autors*] by specifying the kind of madness from which Peter Kien, the novel's main character, suffers; he is 'ein ausges-prochener Schizothymiker und verkörpert einen extrem leptosomen Typus'. But this kind of labelling hardly does justice to the role insanity plays as the central metaphor of the novel.

The first section, 'Ein Kopf ohne Welt', introduces the character of Peter Kien, a sinologist who lives on a private income. He seems at first well placed in the tradition of the ivory tower academic; an eccentric who prefers the company of his books to that of his fellow human beings. He lives in his private library which also serves him, secondarily, as a home. The novel begins at the point where this situation shows signs of the tensions which underlie it. An 'Angsttraum', described by Freud as a frequent precursor of a psychotic outburst, is the first real indication of the exact nature of Kien's psychic state. In this dream he finds himself the unwilling sacrificial victim of two Mexican 'Opferpriester' dressed in jaguar skins. The images of the jaguars is significant, belonging to a set of images (blood, fire, the colour red, carnivorous animals) which symbolize all that he tries to suppress in his own consciousness. They point not only to violence, aggression and sexuality but also to the whole world of normal human emotion and communication. To Kien both belong together as irrational and therefore uncontrollable. He allows only the products of a rational intellect to touch his life: 'Es war, als hätte sich jemand gegen die Erde verbarrikadiert; gegen alles bloss materielle Beziehungswesen'. But unlike Monsieur Teste, the monster of pure intellect created by Valéry, he is far from successful in eliminating this part of his personality. His reaction to the dream is symptomatic: he dissects it, discovers the origin of each episode by delving into his reading over the previous few days. Although using the mechanics of Freudian dream-analysis Kien ignores its purpose. He uses the explanation he discovers to dismiss the dream and all its warnings. Obstinately he clings to the position he has adopted:

> Unplastische, farblose, verschwommene Visionen seien den Träumen, die er bis jetzt berücksichtigt habe, fremd. Nie stelle bei ihm die Nacht etwas auf den Kopf; Laute, die er höre, hätten ihren normalen Ursprung; Gespräche, die er führe, blieben durchaus vernünftig; alles behalte seinen Sinn.

Once rational consideration has explained a phenomenon its mystery is irrevocably solved and it can safely be ignored.

Kien caricatures the values and modes of thinking of a predominantly rational age; an age which sets greatest store by logical connection and impersonal, universal laws. In the form of scholarship he exemplifies he parodies its ideals: by the power of a 'wahrhaft phänomenales Gedächtnis', by the accumulation of knowledge, he thinks he can master the world he lives in and make it completely safe. His self-deception consists of making his library into a world and in his microcosm reigning unchecked. Books and people, library and world, he soon fails to notice any

difference. His much vaunted logic turns out to be the logic of the madman, floating in a vacuum, obeying only its own laws detached from a basis of real experience in the phenomenal world.

The schizophrenic loses his hold on reality and withdraws his interest from his surroundings; he therefore lacks the ability to make meaningful connections with other human beings. Interest can sometimes be fixed on objects which act as substitutes. So it is with Kien: the only things he ever communes with are his books; 'So sehr liebte er seine Bibliothek; sie ersetzte ihm die Menschheit'. Yet even his books are not really necessary for he carries 'eine zweite Bibliothek im Kopf, ebenso reichhaltig und verlässlich wie die wirkliche'. It is to the reality of this second, imaginary, library that he in fact relates when he is cast out of his apartment through the plotting of his house-keeper, Therese, who also tricks him into marrying her.

Not only does the schizophrenic suffer a split with the outside world, his own ego is subject to conflicts also. The reasoning, conscious faculties are beset by unconscious instinctual drives. Thought is split from feeling, different levels of consciousness, of perception, fail to integrate. The rather strange and disembodied conversation which opens the novel introduces the image of the Great Wall of China; a wall built by a highly civilized culture to keep out barbarism is used to symbolize in Kien the psychic mechanism of repression. It is the wall he has built across his mind to split one form of awareness from another. The meticulous routines and the exaggerated emphasis on order, 'seine übertriebene Sorgfalt', 'eine hartnäckige Gewöhnung an peinlichste Ordnung' reveal themselves as more than the exaggerations of a pedant; they are the typical defences of a schizophrenic in such a situation. The threat the schizophrenic feels to his tenuously held sense of identity reveals itself in Kien's behaviour towards Therese; to protect himself from her he tries to turn himself into a granite statue, sitting motionless for hours. His mind too is 'erstarrt'; his actions are directed solely 'zur Erhaltung seines bedrohten Selbstgefühls'. He cannot face reality and must therefore falsify his own experiences. His mind is over-loaded with paralogical, abstract schemata which he must constantly and forcefully impose upon his actual experience of the world. Thus reality becomes a product of these rigid patterns of thought instead of their creator. The private library and its books are the means he uses to implement this vision; they are the arbiters of his world. His dream ends with the image of a giant book, 'das nach vier Seiten hin wächst und Himmel und Erde, den vollen Raum bis zum Horizont erfüllt'. His mind is a vast compendium of the knowledge he has amassed from these volumes; their wisdom has by-passed him. Reality is subject to their confirmation: on one of the rare occasions he notices something in his surroundings, namely the noise pigeons make, he acknowledges with surprise that this agrees with what he has read, ' "Stimmt!" sagte er leise und nickte, wie immer, wenn eine Wirklichkeit ihrem Urbild im Druck entsprach'. The word does not succeed reality to describe it, but precedes, determines, even excludes it. Experience is made to conform to mental concepts. Delusion and insanity are the inevitable results.

Impotence characterizes all spheres of Kien's life: intellectual, emotional and sexual. He retreats into an ever smaller and more unyielding set of beliefs which are totally inaccessible to new stimuli. His fear and hatred of life are expressed in the paranoia with which he greets the unexpected and with which he defends his microcosmic universe.

The central act of his self-deception is his relationship to his books. He uses them as a substitute for real experience; he literally invests them with the power to speak and act. Their failure to respond adequately drives him deeper into madness. He unconsciously acknowledges guilt when in the final scene he finds himself the victim of a physical assault by them. The letters rise up from the page and strike him; ironically the means he has used to protect himself from reality become the means of his initiation to it. But this is achieved only in madness. Topographically this transition is expressed by the expulsion from his library, with its windows sealed against the outside world and its skylights opening onto the light of the heavens, into the demi-monde of the 'Kneipe' (ironically called 'Zum idealen Himmel') frequented by Fischerle, his guide and persecutor during the second part of the novel ('Kopflose Welt'). His final resting place (before the brief, fatal return to the library) is the dungeon-like room of the house caretaker, Benedikt Pfaff. From the light of reason he descends into the darkness of insanity which leads to his final irrational self-immolation.

But before this he is forced to encounter the real world in the form of the hunch-backed dwarf Fischerle, his Sancho Panza. Kien's Quixotic attempt, not merely to impose the word upon reality but to substitute it for reality, produces a series of 'Wahnideen', fixed ideas. The idea that he carries a second library around in his head, which at first seemed no more than the figurative expression of his remarkable memory, he takes as a literal truth. He acts out this delusion by unpacking every night all these volumes from his head; the weight would otherwise prevent him from sleeping. He becomes obsessed with the idea of books being held prisoner in the state pawnshop, the Theresianum (characterized, like Therese, by a ruthless avarice). His fear of fire returns: one of the main reasons he married Therese was for the extra protection her presence would offer against this risk. These ideas mingle in his thoughts, his speech becomes incoherent, guided only by the associations of his fixed ideas: 'Raubkatzen in der Nacht. Tiere träumen auch. Aristoteles hat alles gewusst. Erste Bibliothek. Zoologische Sammlung. Zoroasters Leidenschaft fürs Feuer'. He continues to treat his wishes as reality by insisting that Therese has been starved to death and eaten by carnivorous dogs. When she appears before him, very much alive, he cannot admit that his hypothesis is wrong and he must therefore deny his sensory experience. Therese cannot be real, his mind tells him so—therefore he is seeing an hallucination. This is the ultimate consequence of his logic: he pronounces himself insane in order to stay sane. Only at the very end, shortly before his death, does he admit that his reason was mistaken and his senses right. This is the point he becomes hopelessly mad and sets fire to himself and his library. But before this final descent into psychic chaos the location of the novel shifts briefly: from the encapsulated worlds of Kien and his almost equally insane persecutors it moves to the mental asylum in Paris run by Kien's brother Georg.

This chapter, 'Ein Irrenhaus', depicts a very different kind of insanity to that which dominates the rest of the novel. From the very personal, associative perspective of Kien, Therese and Pfaff (conveyed almost entirely by interior monologue and 'erlebte Rede') it turns to an objectivity and restraint more typical of the classical 'Novelle': 'An einem aufregend warmen Abend des Spätmärz schritt der berühmte Psychiater Georges Kien durch die Säle seiner Pariser Anstalt'. It seems that only in the lunatic asylum is there an escape from the solipsism of insanity into a world of balance and understanding. Yet this is not a simple reversal of normal expectations: the world may be a madhouse according to the rest of the novel, but the madhouse is not the retreat of sanity. Georg is sane (the only character in the novel who is) but his patients certainly are not. Their madness is, however, quite different to that of Kien and the others.

The most important of Georg's patients is known simply as the 'Gorilla'. As this name implies he is a primitive; that is, he experiences the world and himself in a way analogous to that of primitive man. Both the psychotic and the primitive are subject to what the anthropologist Lucien Lévy-Bruhl termed a 'participation mystique': that is, a condition of affective identity with the external world produced by the projection of unconscious emotions onto it. This 'a priori' feeling of unity with their surroundings precludes the sense of individual separateness, of personal identity. The 'Gorilla' is a severe case of catatonic schizophrenia. He does not possess the ability to distinguish clearly the boundaries of his own ego from the external world, to form a stable identity with which to confront others and form relationships. Yet as a contrast to the rigid idea of his own identity held by Kien (his 'Erstarrung') this becomes a positive rather than negative experience. He is surrounded by 'ein einziger furchtbarer Zauberbann'; he invests his surroundings with emotion instead of withdrawing it from them as Kien does: 'hier waren die Beziehungen das Ursprüngliche, beide Zimmer und was sie enthielten, lösten sich in ein Kraftfeld von Affekten auf'. He stands in a direct and dynamic relationship to his environment and to the people he comes in contact with; whereas of Kien it is said: 'Statt sich in die andern zu verteilen, mass er sie, wie er sie von aussen sah, an sich, den er auch nur von aussen und vom Kopf her kannte'. Subject and object are no longer separate for the 'Gorilla', abstraction is impossible. Language is therefore concrete and direct: 'Die Gegenstände hatten, darin behielt der erste Eindruck recht, deine eigentlichen Namen. Je nach der Empfindung, in der sie trieben, hiessen sie'. Thus interpreted, schizophrenia means an escape from the isolation and sterility of Kien's kind of madness. Here fragmentation means unity, an immediate experience of reality, and meaningful human contact. It means personal motivation rather than impersonal causality, the personal experience of time and place rather than subjection to immutable universal laws (compare the equally associative and personal experience of causality, time and place in Benjy's monologue in the first part of Faulkner's *The Sound and the Fury*). The 'Gorilla' dwells permanently in a world of undifferentiated vision: his perspective is synthetic, Kien's analytic. Georg sums up the positive argument embodied in his patient:

> was für traurige und verstockte Bürger wir sind, gegen diesen genialen Paranoiker gehalten. Wir sitzen, er ist besessen; auf den Erfahrungen andrer wir, von eigenen er. . . . Wir brauchen Visionen, Offenbarungen, Stimmen—blitzartige Nähen zu Dingen und Menschen—, und wenn wir sie nicht in uns haben, holen wir sie in der Überlieferung. Aus eigener Armut werden wir Gläubige . . . Wir sitzen auf unserem dicken Verstand, wie Habgeier auf ihrem Geld. Der Verstand, wie wir ihn verstehen, ist ein Missverständnis. Wenn es ein Leben reiner Geistigkeit gibt, so führt es dieser Verrückte!

For this reason Manfred Durzak sees in this part of the novel, 'die Auf hebung, die Züge der Utopie tragende Synthese, dargestellt am Beispiel jenes sich seine eigene Welt und seine eigene Sprache erschaffenden Tier-Verkleideten' ['Versuch über Elias Canetti', *Akzente* (1970)]. He answers the objection that this is just another case of the praise of 'geist-loser Natur' by claiming, firstly, that Georg raises 'das, was als Möglichkeit in Gorilla-Verkleideten faktisch erscheint' to the level of reflection, that is, that he sees the need for a reconciliation of intellect and instinct; and secondly that 'die Reflexion zu diesem mythischen Zustand gehört: sie erscheint verwandelt in der neuerschaffenen magischen Sprache'. The first is true to a certain extent: Georg does recognize the need for such a reconciliation of conflicting forces and does try to implement it in his own life. But he must admit his failure; at one point he says to his brother:

> Beides zusammen, Gefühlsgedächtnis und Verständesgedächtnis, denn das ist das deine, ermöglichen erst den universalen Menschen . . . Wenn wir zu einem Menschen verschmelzen könnten, du und ich, so entstünde ein geistig vollkommenes Wesen aus uns.

Even Georg does not see the real synthesis coming from the irrational behaviour of his patients. For all their 'magic' participation in their surroundings they are permanently on the brink of chaos and must be kept virtual prisoners. Their undifferentiated vision points to what is missing in a civilization which limits and distorts its apprehension of reality in the way Kien does.

Schizophrenia functions as the metaphor for two opposing ideas: pure reason beset by irrational, instinctive emotions and pure affectivity, uncontrolled by reason. Both ideas are to be found in the apocalyptic final scene of the novel. Kien briefly regains, with Georg's help, the library from which he had been driven. Sanity seems about to return to him; of this even the psychiatrist Georg is sure and he departs. But the themes of Kien's obsessions have never been far below the surface even when he seemed to be talking rationally. Left alone in the library, the symbol of his faith in reason, he breaks down. His obsessions run chaotically through his mind; in the belief that he is extinguishing a fire he sets the library ablaze. He climbs the ladder he uses to fetch books. On the sixth rung, penultimate to

Nirvana, he halts and laughs louder than he has ever laughed before. Fire, a symbol of unity as well as of the irrational, engulfs him. From one kind of insanity he enters the moment before his death into another. He briefly experiences the world of the 'Gorilla' and of the mystics, but by now it is too late. Only in death does he achieve the unity which has so long eluded him.

Kien is a representative figure, a scapegoat, the sacrificial victim he sees himself as in his dream. By developing and differentiating his portrait of madness Canetti extends its value as a metaphor. It is no longer the symbol of a particular insanity or folly, nor merely a general symbol for the climate of an age. Through the depiction of a particular 'Grenzsituation' *Die Blendung* presents the conflicts of a civilization whose experience of reality is revealed as based, like that of the schizophrenic, on a process of fragmentation and repression. It also points to the possibility of change, revealed ironically in the experience of another madman. (pp. 38-46)

> *Edward A. Thomson, "Elias Canetti's 'Die Blendung' and the Changing Image of Madness," in* German Life & Letters, *Vol. XXVI, No. 1, October, 1972, pp. 38-47.*

Canetti on disorder:

When everything fits together, as it does with the philosophers, it no longer means anything. Disconnected, it wounds and it counts.

Elias Canetti, in his
The Secret Heart of the Clock, *1991.*

David Turner   (essay date 1980)

[*In the following essay, Turner surveys Canetti's works, concluding that they ultimately fail as critiques of modern political and industrial power structures.*]

In that most Austrian of stories, *Der arme Spielmann* (*The Poor Musician*), Grillparzer depicted the attempt of one man—part saint, part fool—to avoid contact with 'sordid' everyday life, including sex and commercialism, and to assert the independence and supremacy of the inner world of 'Geist'. He also depicted the failure of the attempt: the metaphorical flood, symbol of the mass against which the hero determinedly sets his face, becomes in the end a literal flood that engulfs him. The same basic theme, which was to be reworked in later generations, for example in Hofmannsthal's *Märchen der 672. Nacht* (*Tale of the 672nd Night*), now in the context of late nineteenth-century aestheticism, appears again in the twentieth century as the central focus of Elias Canetti's only novel and most widely read work, *Die Blendung* (*The Delusion*). Indeed, it is a paradigm of Canetti's entire work as a writer and thinker. For here is a man who, although acutely aware of the most disturbing manifestations of political and economic life in twentieth-century Germany and Austria—two world wars, massive inflation, the seduction of the masses, the brutal exercise of power—as well as of the pernicious effects of individual human egoism and monomania, has become suspicious of action and has chosen instead to rely on his intellectual and moral powers to counter such intractable realities. To some extent of course his background and upbringing have made him a homeless outsider. He has done much of his writing in a foreign country (England) and all of it in a language (German) which was not his mother tongue; and this had inevitably led to a strange mixture of involvement in and detachment from those realities. Yet over and above that, it is as though Canetti has wanted to demonstrate the power of mind over matter, to halt the tide of even political events by the sheer force of the intellect.

The paradox is that long before the publication of the work which, more than any other, was to express the unshakable tenacity of that will, the study *Masse und Macht* (*Crowds and Power*), his imaginative works, notably *Die Blendung* and the play *Die Befristeten* (*Their Days are Numbered*), had already called the possibility of success into question. But this should come as no surprise from a man whose whole attitude to human nature is summed up in a paradox: 'Es gibt wenig Schlechtes, was ich vom Menschen wie der Menschheit nicht zu sagen hätte. Und doch ist mein Stolz auf sie noch immer so groß, daß ich nur eines wirklich hasse: ihren Feind, den Tod' ['I've had a great deal of bad to say about both individuals and mankind in general, but I'm still sufficiently proud of them to hate one thing only: their enemy, death'].

In his novel, first published in 1935 and later revised, Canetti follows the basic pattern set by Grillparzer's story, but pushes matters to much greater extremes of both intensity and extensity, in that, on the one hand, the protagonist's attempt to preserve his inner world from contamination by the realities that surround him is pursued with an unprecedented, obsessive force and, on the other, the background against which he is set is made up almost entirely of other individuals whose admittedly very different aims are subject to the same single-minded compulsion. The result is a picture of chaos, a free-for-all between *idées fixes* which are equal in intensity and differ only in direction, a plot which contains more double-crossings than a spy-thriller, a rapid succession of ironies deriving from the thwarting of so many designs.

The philologist Peter Kien represents the world of pure intellect, where books have taken the place of people, the written word in its apparently clear and immovable content has supplanted the messy involvement of the spoken word, and where truth can shine out unhindered by such complicating factors as people and everyday objects. Women in particular pose a threat to this world and are the objects of hatred and fear, while sex, which entails the most intimate human contact, is the ultimate horror.

In a novel full of ironies it is the central irony that this intellectual recluse should be tempted out of his isolation and become entangled in the most squalid manner with the world he so despises, exposed to its most predatory representatives. He is first caught at his weakest point, when he observes the care with which his housekeeper Therese handles his books and falsely assumes an intellec-

tual curiosity. Thereafter, the sexual fiasco of his wedding night and the solid domestic furniture which she introduces into the inner sanctum of his library mark only the first of many humiliations and exploitations to which he is increasingly subjected, until his mind is overwhelmed and he finally sets fire to his precious library and is himself engulfed by the flames. There have been brave attempts to put some positive construction on his end, to see it as a modern variant of Goethe's mystical 'Stirb und werde' ('Die to be reborn') or as a return from isolation to an all-embracing unity. But what the novel convincingly depicts is the defeat, the mental disintegration of the hero, brought about not only by the exploitation of those around him, but by his own refusal to acknowledge all that within himself which links him with other human beings, by his self-imposed isolation, by the denial of any personal mutability, of what his brother calls 'the mass within the individual'. He dies moreover without the enlightenment that comes to the young aesthete of Hofmannsthal's *Märchen*, who comes to hate his premature death so much that 'he hated his life because it had brought him to this point'. Kien dies rather in delusion, resembling nothing so much as those paranoiac rulers whom Canetti will later describe in his study of crowds and power: taking his troops (i.e. books) with him into death so that none should survive his defeat or pass into the control of another.

Of the three most important figures who are variously ranged against Kien his housekeeper and subsequent wife, Therese, is dominated by lust for money, while her undoubted sexual appetite is to be regarded as the chief means to this end; Benedikt Pfaff, the former policeman, now caretaker of the house where Kien has his appartment, seeks power over others by naked terror and brute force; and Fischerle, the hunchbacked dwarf, who is no less keen than Therese to lay his hands on Kien's money, is governed by the 'higher' motive of seeking to establish himself as world chess champion.

Behind the individual *idées fixes* of these three it is not difficult to detect the common search for domination, nor to relate them to some of the manifestations of power discussed subsequently in *Masse und Macht.* What is only too easy to overlook, however, is that the representative of pure 'Geist', who has many of the attributes of the *ingénu,* careless of money and doomed to destruction at the hands of his more cunning fellows, is scarcely less preoccupied with the exercise of power. And it is not only in death that he betrays characteristics of the paranoiac ruler; they are there from the beginning in his attempt to build a protective space around himself; they are revealed in his mobilization of an army of books against the arch-enemy Therese; they are present too in that sense of uniqueness with which he justifies to himself his supposed killing of her. Altogether his relationship with Therese represents a constantly-shifting power struggle, described in terms of victory and defeat. And what emerges most forcibly from all this, what is perhaps the most compelling lesson of the whole novel, is the fundamental impotence and self-contradiction of the intellectual ivory tower. Kien's victories are either imaginary or of such a purely intellectual kind as to have no force whatsoever in the world of real power. And in effect he implicitly acknowledges the powerlessness of his mental armoury: when Therese begins to extend her domestic domain and encroach too palpably on his intellectual reserve, he has little hesitation in enlisting the muscle of Pfaff to try and get rid of her. 'Geist' cannot divorce itself from the everyday realities of life; even as it seeks to assert its power, it betrays its impotence in isolation; and in the very attempt to free itself from its mortal enemy, matter, it must needs make use of the enemy's weapons. Nor should Kien's usual carelessness in financial matters, in such stark contrast to the crass materialism of those around him, blind us to the simple fact that this is only possible because he has inherited money for which he has not had to work.

That Kien's undoubted achievements as a scholar are bought at a price accounts in part for the title Canetti eventually chose for his novel. The title denotes, first, the blinkered concentration of his existence, which requires not only a library without windows on to the world, but ultimately also the practice of closing his eyes quite literally to everything that does not belong to his academic work, thereby attempting to overcome the categories of time, space, and matter altogether. The title also relates, however, to a blindness which affects all the characters equally and is less of a self-imposed condition than a simple consequence of their monomania. They are so possessed by their egocentric purpose, so locked in their private vision, that they cannot grasp the reality of their situation and are particularly susceptible to illusions, never more so than when they imagine they can see through their opponent. The culmination of this collective blindness occurs in a scene at the police station, a setting where, ideally, truth should be brought to light. In a masterly passage of comic writing Kien confesses to the murder of his wife even as she stands, a supposed hallucination, in front of him, while she believes he is admitting to the murder of an earlier wife and so imagines she has discovered the secret of his early morning activities, and the caretaker Pfaff construes the confession as a sly means of bringing his own act of brutal murder to the attention of the police. This travesty of an investigation, in which each person is blinded by his own obsession, is under the theoretical control of an officer whose proud but empty boast is: 'Mir macht keiner was vor' (You can't fool me).

Critics have not been slow to recognize in *Die Blendung* a reflection of that theme which has so fascinated the modern Austrian (though not only Austrian) mind: the problem of language. But it is important to note crucial differences from what Hofmannsthal describes in his 'Chandos Letter' or Musil depicts as part of the confusions of his young Törless. There the problem lies in language itself, in the deceptive ease with which it masks the problematic nature of things and our uncertain understanding of them, or in its inadequacy as a rational medium to deal with the irrational, emotional, intuitive areas of life. In the case of Canetti the problem lies rather with the people who use language; in his novel, as also to a large extent in his first two plays, the characters are so blinded by their own *idée fixe* that their patterns of speech have become fossilized and they themselves have become incapable of conducting a dialogue. The conversations of *Die Blendung* are typically therefore a series of juxtaposed monologues.

The blindness of the characters also finds a concrete counterpart in the locations of the novel. The atmosphere is as claustrophobic as a Kafka novel, and that not merely because we rarely move out of doors and only once, as we follow the hero's brother, leave the confines of a city we assume to be Vienna (although in its presentation of a chaotic society full of possessed people it is also modelled on the Berlin Canetti got to know in the nineteen-twenties). The atmosphere is still more a result of the way in which the four main characters inhabit confined spaces even within the interiors available to them: Kien his windowless library; Therese her kitchen, that powerhouse of the material basis of life; Pfaff the small cabinet from which he keeps a tyrannical eye on all who seek entrance to Ehrlichstraße 24; Fischerle the space under the bed on which his wife prostitutes herself, the space from which he also offers her customers a game of chess!

Canetti clearly has considerable gifts as a comic writer. His exposure of monomaniacal absurdity, his ability to create sheer Bedlam, provoke irresistible laughter. Repeatedly, however, even as we laugh at the characters, a chill horror overtakes us. Its chief source is the grotesque distortion of humanity we are being made to witness. For just as the inanimate objects of this world can assume a life of their own in the imagination of the characters, so also the characters themselves can be debased into animals or reduced to one exaggerated attribute: Therese to her stiff blue skirt, Pfaff to his naked fist. Although we may be tempted to dismiss such phenomena as the products of distorted, subjective vision, there is no escaping the implications, horrific as well as comic, of the things the characters do, the perverse tenacity with which they pursue their aim, the disproportionate effort they devote to its fulfilment, and the mental and even physical contortions they perform along the way. Moreover, even the subjective vision of the characters cannot in practice be dismissed so easily by the reader. And this is an important consequence of Canetti's narrative method, which deliberately renounces the possibility of a unified, authoritative stance in favour of a multiplicity of perspectives, not for the sake of experiment, but as a natural expression of the fragmented world of conflicting monomanias he is depicting. No one perspective is binding; and as we enter in turn the private world of the main characters, we adjust our understanding accordingly. But for the time being we are subjected to the full force of each individual conviction, which is frequently magnified by the way in which the narrator adopts the vocabulary of the particular character and, more especially, by his habit of presenting their fantasies with all the seriousness and immediacy of real events. The novel nowhere attempts to provide a resolution of these discordant private visions; and the perspective with which it closes is insane as well as private. That *Die Blendung* thus denies us the consoling sense of some universal order or harmony that remains intact may be related to Canetti's concern to do full justice to the reality of a world that seemed to have fallen apart.

Whether in general, however, he is able to persuade us that his novel presents a valid and recognizable picture of the world, however partial, foreshortened, or caricatured, is open to question. When he records that one of the most important influences on the writing of the novel was the burning of the Viennese Palace of Justice in 1927, a mass response—in which he himself felt caught up—to the brutal murder of a group of workers in the Burgenland, some engagement with contemporary social and political reality would seem to be involved. Yet it is hard to find. Although there may be some link with Kien's act of incendiarism as a mass experience, it would be absurd to understand the destruction of this ivory-tower scholar and his esoteric library as a meaningful commentary on the actions of those workers. It is possible to see the ironic description of the Theresianum, the vast building which performs the function of state pawnshop, as a criticism of institutionalized exploitation of the poor and of a national scale of values according to which the luxuries are placed first, necessities second, and works of the intellect last of all; but the force of the criticism is reduced by our growing realization that it is being presented from the idiosyncratic point of view of the scholar Kien. The novel may provide flashes of insight into the mentality of fascism—in the descriptions of the brutal tyranny of Pfaff or the readiness of the crowd at the Theresianum to fasten on a scapegoat—but no sustained correspondence emerges; Canetti has not attempted a more coherent political allegory such as we find in Thomas Mann's *Doktor Faustus*.

Much of the difficulty in relating the fictional world to that of the reality we know may be traced, however, to the author's manner of presentation. Distortion and exaggeration are legitimate weapons of the satirical artist, but when taken beyond certain limits they can defeat their object. In *Die Blendung* it is probably less a matter of individual extravagance than of collective exaggeration. Stefan Zweig, on whom Canetti has spent only a few contemptuous words, was similarly fascinated by monomania and loved to depict it in his stories. Leaving aside his different conception of the phenomenon as a blind, demonic, instinctive force which, typically, breaks through the civilized surface of life, it is instructive to note how he used his favourite framework technique to isolate the exceptional quality of his central characters, yet at the same time provide a sympathetic bridge between them and the reader. In *Die Blendung,* by contrast, Canetti has renounced the possibility of a consistent, reliable narrator to provide a context, a standard by which to measure the monomaniacal hero; the background is populated by other monomaniacs. Although this may be seen as part of the modernity of the novel, it also entails the danger of blunting the satirical edge, since the alternatives presented are equally horrifying. In such a world of physical and mental freaks freakishness becomes the norm. There may admittedly be something of the satirical aim which Canetti was later to discuss in connection with Swift: that is, the attempt to define the limits of what is human, terrifying people into an awareness of those limits. But it is doubtful whether things work out like this in practice. For despite the sensation of horror the reader can all-too easily shrug his shoulders at a fictional world in which he fails to perceive an image, however distorted, of his own world.

The world of *Die Blendung* is not, however, entirely made up of monomaniacal freaks. With the appearance of the protagonist's brother, Georg Kien, a breath of something like normality comes into the novel. And it is not for nothing that he is presented as a literal outsider, who has to travel in from abroad. He seems altogether more sympathetic and humane than the rest, having renounced 'Macht', having abandoned a lucrative position as a successful gynaecologist in favour of psychiatric medicine, where, in the sharpest contrast to the others, who are locked in their own private world, he seeks to enter into the mentality of each of his patients. At several points his views echo those of Canetti himself, especially when he talks of the necessity for man to acknowledge the 'mass within himself'. His creator has indeed spoken of him as representing the positive side of the mass. Yet, for all the insight he brings into the novel as an internal commentator, his position remains dubious. Although he manages to extricate his brother from his immediate enemies, he fails to assess his mental state adequately and leaves him to his suicide—a considerable failure of judgement for a psychiatrist. Furthermore, the experience which seems to govern his present life, the encounter with a human 'gorilla', a man whom he regards as having renounced the stereotypes of conventional life—like Musil's 'man without qualities'—and discovered its authentic, primitive basis, can only be seen as a dangerous foundation on which to build any meaningful society in the modern world. In the end it seems appropriate that the voice of Georg Kien should take its place structurally as one of the many perspectives offered. The voice of humanity crying in the wilderness is drowned by the howl of the jackals and their demented victim.

Twentieth-century literature has often been concerned with cultural disintegration, the collapse of traditional values, former certainties, and nowhere more so than in Austria, where the end of a centuries-old dynasty and the fragmentation of a vast, multi-national empire provided its most telling visible symbol, so that for a writer like Joseph Roth the nostalgic hankering after universalism and traditional values could take the form of a desire to restore the Hapsburg monarchy. If Canetti had been able to complete his original plan to write a series of eight novels, each having as its central character a man possessed by a different monomania, we might have possessed an extensive documentation of this cultural disintegration, such as we find, for example, in Broch's trilogy *Die Schlafwandler* (*The Sleep Walkers*), most explicitly in the passages interwoven into the third novel which appear under the heading 'Zerfall der Werte' ('The Collapse of Values'). In spite of its structure and presentation the novel which alone remains of Canetti's original project is unable to achieve this: the scholar Peter Kien is certainly alienated from the rest of the world, but those around him do not embody, even negatively, a wide range of cultural values, but only an all-too similar crude egoism. What has gone is not an ancient culture, but the capacity for human love and understanding.

A similar sense of rampant egoism and a denial of any consoling ideals or compensating values also pervade the three plays which Canetti has written and still acknowledges. They are experimental plays in the sense that they conduct experiments with the human condition, by asking the question: 'What would life be like if . . . ?' The characters emerge therefore, even more markedly than those of Horváth, like clearly profiled puppets, lacking development, manipulated by the author and placed in a series of situations that perform the function of laboratory tests. Our interest is directed to their various attitudes and responses and not, for example, to any dramatic clash of personality. They elicit no sympathetic identification; instead, by virtue of their egocentric nature and the author's widespread use of such traditional devices as catch-phrases and 'sprechende Namen', they maintain a distance that encourages detached observation.

Since all three plays are to a large extent demonstration pieces, most of those who appear on the long lists of *dramatis personae* clearly serve an illustrative purpose, representing the widest possible variety of responses to the experimental question posed. And it is here that Canetti displays his greatest skill: in giving linguistic life to such a wide range of figures, especially so in the two earlier plays, where his fine ear for Viennese dialect comes into its own. The theoretical background to this gift, which owes much to the linguistic satire of Karl Kraus, is the concept of what Canetti has called the 'akustische Maske', the distinctive linguistic profile—based on pitch, speed of delivery, and a nuclear vocabulary of some five hundred words—which marks off each person from the rest. And the practical skill, which, as in *Die Blendung,* also establishes the individual's limited vision, his stereotyped responses, often even his *idée fixe,* undoubtedly owes much to the author's own conscious eavesdropping on the conversations of others in public places such as cafés.

Each play is built around a single idea, an idea basically so simple that it might have been expressed in the form of an aphorism. And it is no surprise to find that Canetti's *Aufzeichnungen* (*Notes*) abound in such aphoristically expressed hypotheses, which question the norms of human life. Any one of them might have been expanded into a play; and some of them even come close to the situations tested in the plays we already have. In *Die Hochzeit* (*The Wedding Feast*), written between 1931 and 1932 but first performed in 1965, the question posed is essentially that which is central to the tradition of the morality play, including its modern revivals in Hofmannsthal: what would happen if we were suddenly faced with death? Here, however, it is not a solitary individual but a whole society, symbolized by the varied inhabitants of a block of flats, which is put to the test. It is an effete, predatory, sexually lax society, bearing all the marks of a modern *fin de siècle,* enjoying a 'high time' (the original meaning of 'Hochzeit'), looking to its inheritance, the house, to provide solutions without attempting to contribute anything to it; and it is presented by Canetti with such satirical pungency that the scandal caused by its first performance can only be construed as a combination of obtuseness and misplaced moral fervour. [In his introduction to *Welt im Kopf,* his selection of Canetti's works] Erich Fried relates the play to the nineteen-thirties, under the threat of the Second World War, but it might equally well reflect the doomed world of pre-1914 Vienna. As long as the threat of an earthquake remains theoretical, part of an idle game, the 'immoral', frivolous surface prevails, but as soon as it becomes real—and the heart of the play is reached—the pitiful essence of the characters is laid bare: many return to the security of conventional behaviour; some foolishly refuse to take the catastrophe seriously; while others speculate commercially on the ruin that will follow. It is characteristic of Canetti that in adopting some of the conventions of the morality play he stops short of any firm advocacy of positive, lasting values. When the admonitory figure of the dying Frau Kokosch is finally permitted to speak, having been silenced for so long, she utters no words of wisdom, but only domestic banalities. And the last word is left to a parrot!

In the *Komödie der Eitelkeit* (*Comedy of Vanity*), written between 1933 and 1934 but not published in book form until 1950, we might suppose the central idea to be man's inability to live without some degree of vanity. For we are transported here to a world where photographs and mirrors, those symbols of human vanity, have been outlawed, but where men find ready substitutes and prohibition follows its customary course, increasing the fascination of what it seeks to destroy and begetting an underworld of black-marketeering and mirror-brothels. We are also shown how philanthropic acts and political involvement in even the worthiest of causes can be, and perhaps always are, an indirect means of self-flattery. But over and above these satirical points, which are scored with relative ease, over and above the incidental comments the play makes on the workings of a totalitarian state, fanaticism, and mass psychology, Canetti reveals a yet more profound insight into human nature: that we cannot live without some form of image of ourselves, whether it be an ideal, a fantasy, the flattery of others, the impression we make on them, or simply the reflection that comes from conversation with them. Without some 'mirror' our sense of identity is lost. At the end of the play therefore the selfhood celebrated by the crowd comes not through the pseudo-Nietzschean self-confidence proclaimed by Heinrich Föhn, but through the re-instatement of the mirror. It is moreover—and this is the gloomy irony of the conclusion—a dangerously egocentric self-hood, easily manipulated by the demagogic Föhn, who is himself seeking only self-glorification. Once again the seemingly positive values of the piece are ultimately called into question and founder on what Canetti seems to regard as the fundamental human weakness: egoism.

In *Die Befristeten,* at which Canetti worked during the early nineteen-fifties, the focus of interest is again death, or—more precisely—our attitude to death. He explores that strange mixture of certainty and uncertainty that follows from the fact that we do not know when our appointed hour will come, but does so negatively, by creating a futuristic world in which this no longer obtains. Here people are known not by name, but by a number which denotes the span supposedly allotted to them. Whether this clinical world of certainties leads to greater happiness is the question posed by the play. Certainly it helps to bestow a mental and social calm and forms an apparently solid basis for planning ahead. But it is unable to banish fear of the moment of death itself; and the very knowledge of the appointed hour can produce an intolerable mental burden. It instils a glowing confidence into many, but in doing so establishes an unfeeling hierarchy in which those who are to live longest enjoy a position of privilege and a sense of superiority in survival, that dangerous attitude which Canetti will later explore, notably in connection with the study of power. The calm surface of life in the play is maintained only because the individual accepts outward conformity, but is otherwise locked in his own egocentric world, shunning all compassion, the very quality which, as Canetti argues elsewhere, makes us human. Compassion, we are led to conclude, depends on the common fears and uncertainties of the 'old' order. Moreover, this very calm presupposes, indeed embodies, to an unusual degree that acceptance of death which the author universally and strenuously resists.

The smooth surface of this world is in fact ruffled in the play itself by the questioning mind of a sceptic and searcher after truth, who, acting to some degree at least as the author's spokesman, unmasks its whole basis as a piece of official deception. And from the moment when tradition has to defend itself the play begins incidentally to shed light on the workings of both an authoritarian state and zealous religious orthodoxy, as well as on mass psychology. Although the doubter seems to gain a victory, the play as a whole follows the pattern of the earlier ones in turning its back on easy, comforting solutions. Instead, just as in Kafka's *Das Schloß* or *In der Strafkolonie* (*In the Penal Colony*), the questioning of the sceptical outsider is itself questioned. Those whom he has freed from the oppression of superstition submit themselves to a new superstition, a new orthodoxy: that they will not die at all. In enjoying their new freedom they rob others of their freedom. Canetti's avowed intention was to show that truth cannot be divorced from responsibility, but what he has managed to do is to cast doubt on the course of all forms of revolution, however just their original premises.

While the two earlier plays still move largely in the orbit of *Die Blendung,* with its strong Viennese flavour, it is also true that, even from the time of the *Komödie der Eitelkeit,* Canetti was formulating with increasing insistence some of the issues that were to be central to his monumental study *Masse und Macht.* Among the most important of these are: death and man's attitude towards it; the pervasive and potentially dangerous urge to outlive others; the behaviour and psychology of crowds; the effects of authority and, specifically, of commands.

Masse und Macht occupied Canetti's attention for some thirty-five years. It grew out of experiences of crowd behaviour during the years following the first world war: mass protests against inflation, demonstrations after the assassination of Walter Rathenau, the burning of the Palace of Justice mentioned earlier, even the sounds of the crowds at football matches. But it was not until the nineteen-thirties that he came to realize that any account of crowds would be incomplete if it did not also include a study of the complementary phenomenon of power. That the book did not appear until 1960 bears witness to the foresight of Broch, who warned the author as long ago as 1933 that it would be a life's work—but who himself proceeded to work on a study of mass psychology. It is also, like the vast bibliography it includes, a testimony to the high seriousness of Canetti's purpose.

His method is to try and illuminate his twin subjects from various angles: historical, anthropological, and ethnographical; mythological and folkloristic; ethological and psychological, even psychiatric. Transitions from one to the other are often spare or even absent, so that the reader is left to fill out many gaps in the argument, while, as in the plays, ready-made solutions of whatever social, political, psychological, or religious persuasion are avoided. The result is that what may seem to some an integrated approach will appear to others merely eclectic and inconclusive.

Much of the work is taken up with classification and description: with distinctions, for example, between 'open' crowds, which constantly need to grow and fear nothing so much as their own collapse, and 'closed' crowds, which seek permanence in self-limitation; with distinctions according to the speed of formation and dispersal of the crowd; with distinctions according to the motivating force behind the mass (flight, pursuit of a victim or enemy, prohibition experienced in common, the overthrow of an old order, a shared celebration); with discussions of those features of the natural world (fire, sea, river, forest, corn, wind, sand) which, through myth and dream, have come to impress themselves on the human consciousness as symbols of particular facets of the mass; with the isolation of those mass symbols which belong in a special way to individual nations (the sea to England as a symbol of what has to be mastered, a source of change and danger; the army or its natural equivalent, the forest, to Germany as a symbol of that upright, steadfast, well-regulated mass in which the individual may lose himself); or with an examination of the ways in which power relationships are expressed by posture (sitting, standing, kneeling, and so forth).

Interesting as these descriptive sections are, Canetti is at his most fascinating when dealing with those areas which touch, explicitly or implicitly, on the realities of recent history. Here, as he examines crucial aspects of his subject, he has some memorable and stimulating observations on the psychology of both mass experience and dictatorship. Explaining the galvanizing effect of the name 'Versailles' on the German mentality, he argues that the army was the decisive factor in the sense of national unity after the Franco-Prussian war and that, although the army was a closed mass, the First World War provided the opportunity for the whole German people to become an open mass, full of an enthusiasm which embraced even the supposedly international Social Democrats. The outbreak of war in 1914 also begat National Socialism, because it was then that Hitler experienced himself for the only time as a mass. And his subsequent life was an attempt to recreate that experience from outside: Germany was to become again what it was then, to be unified in the consciousness of its military impetus. But Hitler would never have succeeded if the Treaty of Versailles, in robbing Germany of its army, had not thereby robbed it of its 'closed' mass. For it is a law of masses that if a 'closed' mass is thwarted, it forms itself into an 'open' mass, in this case the party, which could embrace all, including women and children.

Studying the characteristics of masses has also led Canetti to trace a development from the inflation of the nineteen-twenties to the later persecution of the Jews. He sees a close relation between man and his money. And what happens in a period of rapid inflation is that, just as the individual character of each unit is lost and the clear hierarchy of the coins collapses as the mass increases, so too individual people lose their identity and self-confidence, while the nation as a whole feels itself devalued. In this situation the natural desire is to discover something that is even more worthless, that can be thrown away like money or stamped on like vermin. The Jews, because of their traditional associations with money, met the requirement ideally.

Equally compelling in their relevance to some of the more gruesome aspects of recent history are those passages where Canetti deals with power as it is exercised in its clearest and most extreme form: by absolute rulers and dictators ('Machthaber'), whose inner mechanism is here laid bare and explained. The importance of knowledge is revealed in the dictator's need to preserve his own secrets but penetrate those of everyone else and in the function of questions and questioning in the practice of power. His desire to inhabit spacious rooms and keep others at a distance is shown to betray a sense of threat which, the more active it becomes, requires more and more executions, since the only safe subjects are dead ones. His subjects indeed, the mass on which his power feeds, are regarded as inferiors, pests which may be exterminated in millions. And if this sounds like paranoia, it is no accident. For Canetti draws close parallels, amounting virtually to identification, between the dictator and the paranoiac and devotes considerable space in this study of crowds and power to the hallucinations of a famous psychiatric patient.

Death, the central issue for Canetti, looms large throughout the work. It forms the background to that pleasurable sense of superiority in survival ('Überleben') which affects us all even as we mourn, but which appears in its starkest form in the behaviour of the ruler, as the ultimate token of power. As commander-in-chief on the field of battle his power lies not only in disposing over the lives of thousands of men, but finally in surviving a great mass of dead, as though he himself were personally responsible for their death. And when at other times he orders the execution of subjects he is not merely eliminating real or imaginary traitors, but enjoying the pernicious power of survival. In this respect too the ruler feeds on the mass, since the larger the number of dead, of those whom he has survived, the greater will be his sense of invulnerability and uniqueness ('Einzigkeit').

Death also plays its part in the crucial question of commands ('Befehle'). For behind every command there stands ultimately the threat of death from a superior power. In the one who receives it, Canetti argues, the command leaves behind a 'sting', which may be stored up for years unless he can rid himself of it by passing it on to an inferior. Only if a command is received collectively, in a mass where it affects all equally, does it not leave behind a sting. Yet no one needs a mass more than the individual who is full of stings, the accumulated burden of the commands received. And revolution is seen therefore as a mass formation created from those who suffer from similar stings, from which they seek to free themselves, directing their action against any who represent the commands they have received. For the ruler who issues a command it is an assertion of power, which gives him a sense of victory; yet even in his success he is left with the threat of recoil, which grows into what Canetti calls 'Befehlsangst', the fear that the inferior will one day take his revenge. And with that we again approach the realm of paranoia.

Considering the time and effort which went into the writing of *Masse und Macht* it is not surprising that many of its central ideas have coloured Canetti's other writing too. We have already noted, for example, the characteristics of the paranoiac ruler in the protagonist of *Die Blendung* and some of the manifestations of the search for power and superiority in the other characters; we have observed the exercise of institutionalized power (especially in prohibitions), various patterns of crowd behaviour, and the centrality of death in the plays, and the role of the 'Überleben' motif in the social hierarchy of *Die Befristeten.* The pervasiveness of these ideas is even more pronounced, however, in a volume entitled *Das Gewissen der Worte* (*The Conscience of Words*), which gathers together essays and talks from as far apart as 1936 and 1974. One piece, **'Macht und Überleben'** ('Power and Survival'), has direct links with the larger work; another, sparked off by the memoirs of Hitler's architect Albert Speer, is principally concerned with Hitler himself, the largely unseen presence behind the whole of *Masse und Macht* with his quest for permanence, invulnerability, and survival in the sense of outliving all others or, if he should fail, taking his entire people with him into death; with his grandiose architectural schemes, buildings designed to accommodate his masses or, more properly, allow them to expand, intended to outdo in size all his historical rivals and so assert his superiority and somehow extend his own life. Even where we might not expect it, however, the same basic ideas are an insistent presence. When Canetti records how he first came under the spell of Karl Kraus but later resisted his dominance, he speaks not only in terms of the satirist's ability to incite an intellectual witchhunt, 'eine Hetzmasse aus Intellektuellen', but also of his stifling dictatorship in matters of taste. In Confucius he sees a man who avoided the exercise of power, even feared contamination by it, and whose attitude to death was such that he refused to answer questions about the time after death, seeking thereby to diminish the desire to survive, which Canetti regards as one of the most delicate problems even today. Of his beloved Kafka, whose letters to Felice Bauer provoked Canetti to write his longest and most absorbing essay, he says that, although he was an expert in power, he himself remained powerless, seeking constantly to escape from its domain; his only weapons against it were silence and the attempts to transform himself into something small; the freedom he asserted was that of the weak man who finds salvation in failures rather than victories. And in a shorter piece, **'Dr. Hachiyas Tagebuch aus Hiroschima'**, in which Canetti praises the honesty of a man whose diary records his first bewildered reactions to the dropping of the atomic bomb, he again brings out the importance of 'Überleben', especially in the writer's sense of having outlived his friends and relatives, which is present even as he mourns their loss.

Psychological illumination is clearly Canetti's great strength—and here the influence of Freud is surely greater than he openly acknowledges. But psychological illumination is also a severely limiting factor. This is barely noticeable in the essays of **Das Gewissen der Worte,** many of which have some biographical starting-point: diaries, memoirs, letters. But in the more ambitious **Masse und Macht** the restriction is painfully obvious. Although he provides valuable new insights into the psychology of the dictator, of crowd behaviour, of power relationships within hierarchical structures, although there is much suggestive force in his juxtapositions of ancient myth and modern psychology or of the customs of primitive peoples and the workings of modern states, his conclusions must remain partial. For he has chosen to treat a subject of considerable social, political, and economic import without any of the methods and arguments of the sociologist, political scientist, or economist. His avowed aim has been to think through everything himself and so overcome the specialisms of others with a universalism or synthesis of his own. But it has proved a problematic undertaking; in deciding what secondary help to use and what to ignore he has acted with an arbitrary selectivity. **Masse und Macht** represents the 'observations of a non-political man', to use a phrase of Thomas Mann. In this Canetti could be said to be conforming to an Austrian pattern, whereby judgement of social and political issues is made according to criteria which could be aesthetic (Musil), metaphysical and cultural (Roth), or psychological (Freud, Stefan Zweig). Another way of putting it would be to say that, notwithstanding Canetti's much broader concerns, there is in the end too much of Peter Kien in his creator, too much of the intellectual's fear of involvement with the sordid facts of life, to permit the confrontation with contemporary political reality which the origins of the work seemed to promise. And the concluding proposal, that the way to attack power, which may manifest itself in contemporary political or industrial structures in both East and West, is to look the command straight in the eye and find some way of robbing it of its sting, is a feeble anticlimax, as impotent a gesture as the chalk line which Grillparzer's poor musician draws across his room to keep an unpleasant reality at bay. (pp. 79-95)

> *David Turner, "Elias Canetti: The Intellectual as King Canute," in* Modern Austrian Writing: Literature and Society After 1945, *edited by Alan Best and Hans Wolfschütz, Oswald Wolff, 1980, pp. 79-96.*

Stephen I. Gurney   (review date Summer–Fall 1983)

[*In the following review of Canetti's* The Human Province, *Gurney observes that the unrelenting brutality of Canetti's works poses a warning about human nature to the reader.*]

One does not settle back comfortably with a volume of Elias Canetti. He is the least belletristic of writers, and his style—stark, astringent, and direct—repels both the formalist and the connoisseur. We read Mr. Canetti with an excruciating sense that both we and our civilization are being judged. We may not want to hear these things about

ourselves, about human nature, about the present historical hour, but, like Coleridge's wedding guest, we are riveted and mesmerized by a speaker who compels us to recognize the terrible authenticity of his vision.

Implicit in Canetti's works is the assumption that, in the latter half of the twentieth century, the vocation of the writer no longer permits a preoccupation with "words as such." In austere and unambiguous language, Canetti bears witness to a world where "light is dethroned," "the last . . . myths destroyed," and "the atomic bomb has become the measure of all things." Canetti's difficulty is not a consequence of his style (though one critic, Phillip Toynbee, protests [in *Horizon* (1947)] that "blow after blow is directed at the reader's head with the bluntest possible of instruments") but rather a result of the disquieting nature of his message—a message which we neglect to our own impoverishment and deny at our own peril. As Canetti observes:

> The public and private can no longer be separated, they overlap in ways that would never before have seemed possible. The enemies of mankind have rapidly gained power, coming very close to an ultimate goal of destroying the earth. It is impossible to ignore them and withdraw to the contemplation of only spiritual models that still have some meaning for us. These models have become rarer; many that may have sufficed for earlier times do not contain enough in themselves, comprise too little to still serve us today. Hence, it is all the more important to speak about those who have withstood our monstrous century.

Canetti's message radiates from a nucleus of interrelated themes: the menace of mass psychology, the ambiguous nature of survival, the paranoia of power, the craven acceptance of our own and others' deaths. While these concerns pervade the entirety of his works, they find, perhaps, their most compendious expression in extracts from a private journal written between the years 1942 and 1972 and published under the title, **The Human Province.** These "meditations, epiphanies, and idle jottings" in **The Human Province** adumbrate those themes whose full significance emerges most forcibly in Canetti's principal works: the post-Kafkaesque novel, **Die Blendung** (1935); the ritual act of expiation for the crimes of this author's generation, **Crowds and Power** (1960); the drama of a society in which each person carries the year of his death inscribed on a chain around his neck, **The Deadlined** (1952); the haunting record of Canetti's visit to an impecunious Islamic village where the ubiquity of suffering and the struggle for survival wring his most eloquent pleas on behalf of stricken humanity, **The Travels of Marrakesh** (1967); the collection of essays, public addresses, and, in Canetti's words, "summing[s] up of the spiritual stations of my entire adult life," **The Conscience of Words** (1976); and the memories of the author's European childhood, **The Tongue Set Free** (1977).

Die Blendung (literally *The Blinding,* though it appears in English as **Auto-da-Fé**) initiates those themes to which Canetti returned obsessively in his subsequent career as a writer. Conceived against an historical backdrop the recollection of which is necessary to counter those critics who claim that this novel is merely a "case history . . . several case histories" [Anne Fremantle, *Commonweal* (1947)], "a portrait of mankind as a predatory and brutal race totally incapable of expressing any kind of love, warmth, or tenderness" [Peter Russell, "The Vision of Man in Elias Canetti's *Die Blendung*," *German Life and Letters* (1974-75)], *Die Blendung* is an allegorical commentary on the psychic, moral, and spiritual dissolution of Vienna on the eve of Hitler's Anschluss. The events which led to the burning of the Palace of Justice in July 1927—the periodic molestation of Jews and social democrats; the rise of anarchist groups such as the Front Fighters and Swastika Men; the indignation of the worker's party at the failure of an acquiescent government to prosecute acts of aggression by these groups; and, finally, the firing of shots by a nervous police force into a crowd of workers, students, and social democrats who retaliated by incinerating the Palace of Justice—all of these phenomena of mass psychology were witnessed by Canetti (at the time, a student of chemistry at the University of Vienna). Eighty-nine people were killed and the resultant anarchy initiated "a new epoch of slow descent" culminating in a "rising Fascism" [Charles A. Gulick, *Austria: From Habsburg to Hitler*].

In *Die Blendung* fire becomes for Canetti a principal symbol for crowd psychology and the atavistic yielding to the subterranean horrors and inner divisions of our own psyches. The novel's protagonist, Peter Kien, eventually destroys himself in a bonfire built from his own books, anticipating, as Dagmar Barnouw claims, "the 1933 burning of books, ordered by Goebbels" ["Doubting Death: On Elias Canetti's Drama *The Deadlined*," *Mosaic* (1974)]. And, indeed, fires, literally and symbolically, have plagued Canetti's career. Two excerpts from *The Human Province* testify to Canetti's sense of human outrage at the omnipresence of this destructive element. In 1943 he observes, "I cannot look at any more maps. The names of cities reek of burnt flesh"; and, in 1945, "wherever I sniff, all is heavy with the smell of extinguished fire." However one may criticize *Die Blendung* for the absence of any but "psychotic" and "pitifully deranged" [Russell] characters, we are obliged to grant it its significance as a diagnostic and prophetic indictment of a defunct civilization.

The degree to which human relationships have disintegrated in the modern age, the uprootedness, chaos, and loss of direction that have dissolved generational ties and violated the traditional rhythms of living are probed here to chilling effect. Each of these characters (who share the same address at a large and ramshackle Viennese rooming house) are isolated fragments of a single fractured ego: Kien, the obsessed sinologist, who lives surrounded by books in a room without windows; his housekeeper, Therese, a libidinous harpy, who seeks revenge against the inhuman detachment of her employer by trapping him into a perverse and destructive marriage; and, most sinister of all, the pathological sadist, Pfaff, an embodiment of pure id who has brutalized his wife and daughter and protects Kien from the importunities of life and human relationships so that he may pursue his studies unmolested. In post-Freudian Vienna, super-ego, libido, and id no lon-

ger exist in healthy interdependence: they break apart, each asserting its superiority and in doing so bring ruin and irretrievable destruction.

No author has levelled a more devastating blow at that evil which is a consequence of the steady, obsessive, and unrelieved activity of the pure intellect cut off from the saving efficacy of life, human relationships, and spiritual community. As George Steiner has observed, *Auto-da-Fé* "is a classic study of the violence subtly but steadily present in abstract thought" [*New Yorker* (1980)]. Though hailed by Raymond Williams as "the most important literary presentation of delusion within the last forty years" [*Literatur und Kritik,* (1966)], *Die Blendung* has not been without its critics. Some opine "that there is no character at all with whom we may identify" [Russell]. That may well be true, but it underscores the pertinence of Canetti's comment from *The Human Province:* "The dissolution of the character in recent literature: the figures that our time would need are so monstrous that no one is daredevil enough to invent them." No one, perhaps, except Canetti. Individualism and collectivism, isolation and absorption—these are the polar alternatives experienced by the characters in *Die Blendung.* Community, mutuality, otherness have all disappeared.

It is precisely these aforementioned polarities that inform Canetti's vision in *Crowds and Power.* This work absorbed Canetti for twenty-five years, during which time "my best friends lost faith in me . . . it took too long, I couldn't blame them." Yet on the eve of its publication, Canetti could rightfully claim, "I have succeeded in grabbing this century by its throat." The hypotheses of *Crowds and Power* are multiform and complex; one cannot imagine this work appearing in any age other than our own or under any circumstances other than those endured by Canetti. (As George Steiner remarks, our awareness of Canetti's being the "sole survivor" of the numerous "Canettis of Adrianople" is indispensable for our understanding of this work.)

For Canetti the most fundamental fear in the modern age is "the fear of being touched" [*Crowds and Power*]. Touch is no longer an index of human contact, tenderness, or warmth, but rather a signal of aggression, an encroachment on our nakedness, a reminder of our vulnerability. In consequence, each person is driven to surround himself with walls, barriers, securities, to forestall "the clutch out of the darkness." But this, of course, creates an intolerable burden and tension which is only released by immersion in crowds. "It is only in a crowd that man becomes free of this fear of being touched"—a fear which frequently has its origins in a man's own unconscious aggressions and which may now be permitted to surface safely in the anonymity, cover, and protection which a crowd provides. In a collateral remark from *The Human Province,* Canetti thus observes: "The worst crowd one could think of is a crowd consisting solely of acquaintances." Uniformity and uniforms—the stepping-stones of dictators—provide a delusory sense of impregnable power and eradicate the demands of individual conscience. Hence, the individual flees to a crowd to escape from the strain of his own exposure and through the heightened sense of strength produced by sheer numbers, willingly dies for the symbol of pure survival—dictator, demagogue, or general—whose unquestioned authority and ability to survive embody the ultimate triumph over "the clutch of darkness" (that is to say, the fear of death).

The most disturbing, profound, and controversial chapter of *Crowds and Power* deals with the question of survival. "Few readers can have finished the chapters on survival without some feeling of disgust," Canetti writes in the epilogue to this work. For Canetti survival is always survival over someone else. Despite the grief that we feel at the deaths of others, there is also, for Canetti, a suppressed sense of triumph in our having survived those persons. [The critic adds in a footnote: "Thus Canetti observes in *The Human Province:* 'Guilt feelings towards my father: I'm now nine years older than he became.' "] A sense that our own life is enhanced and our own power increased by virtue of the contrast between their lifeless bodies and our breathing flesh is an indisputable though repressed component of our grief: "The illusion that a man is or would like to be the only one among corpses is decisive for the psychology of both the paranoic and the extreme practitioner of power." The modern age has brought this feeling out of its hiding place—the paranoia of power, the desire to outlast, to achieve "onlyness," as a means of strengthening one's sense of invulnerability, are the chief motives behind the political atrocities of our times. Yet today "measured by our potentialities, Genghis Khan, Tamerlane, and Hitler seem pitiful amateurs . . . one man today has the power of surviving at a single stroke more human beings than could generations of his predecessors together."

Canetti pursues his thesis with exhaustless patience and assiduity: rummaging among tribal myths, primitive societies, mania-possessed minor officials, African kings, the memoirs of the obscure and the demented. Hitler is mentioned only once but his presence is all the more eloquent precisely because of Canetti's reticence. Two essays from *The Conscience of Words,* "Power and Survival" and "The Arch of Triumph," apply the ideas in *Crowds and Power* to the policies of the Third Reich. Here Hitler's proposed arch—a vainglorious monstrosity twice the size of Napoleon's monument—becomes the architectural embodiment and confirmation of Canetti's thesis. Hitler proposed that "everyone of our 1,800,000 casualties will be carved in granite." And, of course, at the top of the arch the most conspicuous name would be Hitler's.

The omnipresence of death finally becomes Canetti's most persistent preoccupation—a preoccupation which led to an attitude that is perhaps without parallel in Western literature: "The more intensely Canetti experienced death during the war, the more his hatred grew; he began to doubt the 'natural law' of death" [Barnouw]. Death, war, history, and finally God himself—insofar as the deity has appointed death as a natural structure of being—become the objects of Canetti's incredulity, scorn, defiance, and derision. In these pronouncements, no less than in his examination of mass psychology, Canetti speaks with the voice of an Old Testament prophet—daring God to reveal his ways, to absolve himself from the earned denuncia-

tions of his people. One is reminded of Elie Weisel's account of three Rabbis in a concentration camp who put God on trial, proclaim his guilt, and dare any but Satan to deny the justness of their accusations—a paradox further enforced by the words of the principal Rabbi at the trial's conclusion: "We must now go and pray." Canetti's Hebraism is strongly in evidence here; he demands justice not in terms of abstract metaphysics but in the only terms which are humanly conceivable and will not quit until those terms are met.

Canetti's purpose here, as one critic observes, is "to set the largest, most *edifying* standards of despair" [Susan Sontag, *Under the Sign of Saturn*]. This defiant dialogue with God may appear heterodox but its roots are biblical and fully characteristic of those Old Testament patriarchs and prophets whose passion for justice and moral intensity engage God himself in the most contumacious of arguments. Canetti's religious stance recalls the words of another radical theologian, Simone Weil: "Religion insofar as it is a sense of consolation is a hindrance to true faith; and in this sense atheism is a purification."

A Sephardic Jew of Turkish descent who grew up in Bulgaria, was exiled to England, and writes in German, Canetti—in his pilgrimage, his Jewishness, his uprootedness—refuses to regard himself as a marginal member of a persecuted minority or an isolated instance of social discrimination, but as one whose destiny and fate are fully representative of homelessness, horror, and violated humanity, the strains of which wail all through "this monstrous century." "It is only in exile," writes Canetti, "that one realizes to what an important degree the world has always been a world of exiles." His Jewishness, therefore, is non-sectarian, universal, and transnational in its significance and implications. In 1944 Canetti observed:

> The greatest intellectual temptation in my life, the only one I have to fight very hard against is: to be a total Jew. . . . But aren't the new dead everywhere, on all sides, in every nation? Should I harden myself against Russians because there are Jews, against the Chinese because they are far away, against the Germans because they are possessed by the devil? Can't I still belong to all of them, as before, and nevertheless be a Jew?

With uncommon magnanimity Canetti, during the darkest days of the Third Reich, proclaims: "The language of my intellect will remain German—because I am Jewish. . . . I want to give back to their language what I owe it. I want to contribute to their having something that others can be grateful for" [*The Conscience of Words*].

In his hatred of war ("Oh for a stethoscope, a fine stethoscope to identify the generals in their wombs"); in his detestation of death ("conclude peace with everything, but never with death"); in his defiance of historical determinism ("I hate the respect of Historians for *Anything* merely because it happened"); in his power of self-identification with the mendicant and oppressed ("[The poet] should be able to become *anybody* and *everybody,* even the smallest, the most naive, the most powerless . . . "); and finally, in his passion for the absolute ("I seek after all holinesses, and they break my heart for being past")—Canetti incarnates the indomitable vision of a people whose successive trials he seems to embody. In a word, Canetti radiates those qualities which the Catholic theologian, Jacques Maritain, discerns in the history of the Jewish people:

> If the world hates Jews, it is because the world clearly senses that they will always be outsiders in a supernatural sense, it is because the world detests their passion for the absolute and the unbearable stimulus which it inflicts. . . . [It is because] like an activating ferment injected into the mass, it gives the world no peace; it bars slumber; it teaches the world to be discontented and restless as long as the world has not God. . . . It was not because the Jews killed Christ but rather because they gave Christ to the world that Hitlerian anti-Semitism in its rage dragged the Jews along all the roads of Europe, through filth and blood, tore from their mothers children from thenceforth not even possessed of a name, undertook to dedicate an entire race to despair.

It is scarcely surprising that Canetti should be the 1981 recipient of the Nobel Prize. His diatribes against war and death clearly reflect the contemporary European spirit and sound the note of "never again" with matchless urgency. His acceptance speech, delivered on December 10, 1981, is a consummate extract of his principal themes spoken with his customary moral strenuousness: "Today since Hiroshima, everyone knows what war is, and the fact that everyone knows is our only hope." In a world, as Canetti reminds us, where motives of profit and material production have made war lucrative and where considerations of humanity are dismissed as misdirected indulgences, the ultimate standards of life, of art, of civilization have been eclipsed. "We have no standards anymore for anything," writes Canetti, "ever since human life is no longer the standard." Cynics may question the legitimacy of Canetti's claim to the Nobel Prize by citing its coincidence with the European Peace Movement; and, to be sure, much that we expect a great writer to comprehend is absent from Canetti's vision of the world: the rich and significant interplay of human relationships, the lyrical celebration of life, the laughter which reconciles us to our condition or the tragic vision which lifts us above it. But Canetti has written against a background of national uprootedness, physical deprivation, and spiritual crises. Inevitably, this has made its mark. The period of history which irretrievably silenced a novelist like E. M. Forster and drove Virginia Woolf to suicide pushed Canetti, in his own words, to "the wailing wall of humanity, and that is where I stand."

And yet we sense that this indefatigable opponent of war and death, whose corrosive aphorisms seem uttered between clenched teeth, is capable—were the times less intractable and modern history less recalcitrant—of the rich, spacious, comprehensive vision that we admire in the great novelists of the nineteenth and early twentieth centuries.

As the first volume of his reminiscences abundantly illustrates, Canetti's capacity to achieve delicate insights into human relations and to speak in the lyrical voice of a

psalmist as well as the truculent tones of a prophet is there to be developed. But the supervention of less savory truths has curtailed such an efflorescence: "The worst thing, always, is history and I must not escape it; the fact that history has actually kept getting worse forces me to be its anatomist; I slice about in its rotting body and I am ashamed of the profession I have chosen." Still, like Socrates in his later years (and the comparison is not farfetched), this indignant sage has earned the right and could develop the capacity to sing. Canetti's passion for universal longevity, for a rich and patriarchal maturity wherein to realize and articulate all those "important things" that are carried "for forty or fifty years," wins our partisanship to his crusade against death. In his unyielding campaign on behalf of humanity Canetti is a living witness to this injustice. May he continue to defy death, to rage against the dying of the light, and (in his own words) "to keep making room, on and on, and as long as I can do so, to merit my life." (pp. 355-60)

> *Stephen I. Gurney, "Speaking the Dreadful," in* Modern Age, *Vol. 27, Nos. 3-4, Summer-Fall, 1983, pp. 355-60.*

John Bayley   (essay date 1984)

[*Bayley is an English critic, poet, novelist and educator. He has remarked: "As a critic, I don't use any special approach. I brood over an author a long time and say whatever seems to me worth saying." In the following excerpt, Bayley examines how Canetti depicts power in his major works.*]

Henry James writes of a very grand lady that she had 'an air of keeping, at every moment, every advantage'. Paradoxically, the same would be true of the literary personality of Elias Canetti. Behind its approachable modesty, its avoidance of every publicity and image-making process, there is a loftiness, an assurance, a stance of absolute superiority. Indeed the modesty and the dignity make the same point: why make a fuss about your greatness?

Great writers usually do, nonetheless. 'Fame wants to find safety', as Canetti has put it. Thomas Mann was notorious for his self-importance and his suspicion of anyone whom he felt might be detecting signs of weakness in him; Thomas Hardy spent his last days writing venomously bad verses against fellow authors whom he felt had patronized him. Across the Atlantic the Hemingways and Mailers positively seethe with anxiety about their status and reputations. Such unease does not mean they are not great: it just shows the extreme vulnerability which usually goes with true creative powers.

Canetti's superiority is reverenced and proclaimed by his disciples, who feel something different from enthusiasm for an admired writer. He is sage and master of an art which only the initiated can fully perceive. The American firm which has begun to publish all his books—the novel, the essays, the play—simply print 'Canetti' in big black letters on top of the jacket, as it might be 'Socrates' or 'Confucius', and the full name and title in smaller print below. A critic writes of his memoir **The Tongue Set Free** that 'all readers'—even those not yet exposed to the writings of Elias Canetti—will appreciate 'this self-portrait.' The idea of such an 'exposure'—a magic ordeal yet to come—is typical. Nor, in this case, does it seem absurd.

The Unknown God, dwelling in splendid intellectual isolation, is always a potent cult figure. Canetti chose a language and its literature, but his genius has no setting or home. He was born in 1905 in Ruschuk, Bulgaria, into a merchant clan of Sephardic Jews originally from Spain, and retaining from it a four-hundred-year-old cultural memory. Among themselves, they spoke the Spanish dialect called Ladino, and they had until recently been Turkish citizens. The Canetti and Arditti clans were acquainted for business purposes with some fifteen or seventeen languages, and the importance they attached to this kind of fluency was shown by the story handed down from Canetti's great-grandfather of the journeys on Danube river steamers, when each merchant kept his heavy money-belt round his waist. Because he knew some Greek, the Canetti patriarch could understand the plotting of two passengers who thought it secure: they were plotting to rob him or another rich man.

Language became an art of magic and a key to power—one language in particular. Canetti's grandfather cursed his son for wanting to leave Ruschuk and set up with his brother-in-law in the cotton-exporting Sephardic community in Manchester. But the family did move, and not long afterwards Canetti père died of a heart attack at the breakfast table while reading the *Manchester Guardian.* The little Canettis had loved England, and with their father's help had joyfully learnt its language: relatives rolled about laughing when Elias recited a French story he had learnt at school with a strong British accent. The father, a gentle, civilized man, hoped that his eldest son would go to university in England and perhaps become a doctor or teacher. Had he lived, his son's destiny would have been very different.

English, then, was not to be—could it ever have been?—the magic language. Canetti's mother, who was intensely proud of her family's status—as an Arditti, she ranked above a Canetti—was devoted to Vienna where she had lived as a child: 'Vienna loves you', a later admirer was to remark. Elias became, at the age of nine, the head of the family, his mother's confidant and helpmate. He had heard with envy his parents talking the magic language, German, and now his mother set out to teach it to him, with a ruthless single-mindedness that made his days a nightmare and estranged him from his English governess and his two younger brothers. His portrait of his mother in the memoir is of the deepest interest. He adored her, but she was not, like Proust's, a worshipping and self-abnegating mother. Her eldest son, to whom she confided her fitful and spontaneous literary enthusiasms—she loved Strindberg and Baudelaire and her favourite character was Shakespeare's Coriolanus—was like a lover with several rivals. Jealousy was an early and lasting obsession. With her half-reluctant connivance he learned to dispose ruthlessly of his mother's admirers, and later came to feel that his childish and adolescent egotism had wilfully failed to realize her need for another husband or sexual relation. This was indeed an apprenticeship in power, its infliction

and reception. 'I recognise the words that Genghiz Khan's mother spoke to him', noted Canetti, when he was working on *Crowds and Power* and reading *The Secret History of the Mongols.*

Years later, his mother told him what had really happened when his father died. Relatives supposed it had been the shock of the Balkan war, announced in the headlines, but in fact for a day and a sleepless night he had refused to speak to his wife, who had just returned from a spa cure in her beloved Austria. Radiantly communicative, she had told her husband of a doctor there who had wanted her to elope with him. Her husband could not believe that nothing else had occurred. Her pride was at stake. Mother and son shared the same pride, but the son came to understand its mysterious connections—as in the case of Kafka—with powerlessness and humility.

They were in Vienna when war came, the moment which both Canetti and Akhmatova write of as the real beginning of the twentieth century. No personal problem—the Canettis are now British citizens. They leave for Zürich, but not before the boy sees, and will always remember, a trainload of Jewish refugees from Galicia (what struck him was how motionless the freight cars were, and the faces of those looking out of them). Canetti loved his Swiss school and Zürich, where he now lives, but his mother was contemptuous of his love for a complacent and self-approving provincial society. She wants him to be educated in Vienna, and after the war they return there. He studies for a doctorate in chemistry, and at the age of twenty-five begins to write a novel. His secret and steadfast intention, to study and make a general theory of power, will now manifest itself.

The novel which emerges, *Auto da Fé,* has been seriously called the most remarkable of this century. A meaningless judgement, and yet what could be said is that it is the most remarkable attempt at an intellectual imagination of the true nature of the twentieth century, an apotheosis of the immensely weighty and serious Faust tradition of German letters. It could only have been written *in* German, and yet it could hardly have been written *by* a German, a man too physically at home in the *gemütlichkeit* of his native speech. Canetti's use of the language is enormously mental, magical and dynamic. During a thirty-year residence in England after his return in 1939, he often suffered what he called 'word attacks', a compulsive urge to make lists and patterns of German words as if they were counters in a spell to conjure, or to abjure, power. He also began to keep the extended diary of thoughts and aphorisms now published as *The Human Province.* Full of fascination but verging on the portentous as such compilations in an English translation unavoidably do, it contains such comments as 'So long as there are people in the world who have *no power whatsoever,* I cannot lose all hope', and 'I have never heard of a person attacking power without wanting it.' Portraits of the powerful in history rekindle his hatred of power, 'and warn me of my own power over people'.

Everything Canetti writes is obsessed with and transformed by this abstract passion, even his academic but strangely haunting play *The Numbered,* written in England after the war. His own creative dynamism comes from the love-hate relation with power, and from 'confronting' its special nightmare in our own century. *The Human Province* is a sort of Caesar's *Commentaries* on power geography. One of Canetti's strengths is that he never discriminates between the public and the private spheres of power, just as he never admits, even tacitly, a division between his own abstraction of it and the thing itself. A profound admirer of Hobbes, he wastes no time on the anatomy of modern power systems—Communism, Fascism—which absorb the individual into an ideal of overall social cohesion. He sees the crucial area both of power and of freedom in the private life, the area which Hobbesian authority exists to encourage and protect. Yet it is here also that the worst abuses take place, as is shown by the vision of a father and daughter relation in the chapter of *Auto da Fé* called 'The Kind Father'.

For Canetti, it is self-evident that *Auto da Fé* engrosses as a novel the most central significances of our time, and in his other writings he speaks of it as Goethe spoke of *Faust*. What about such a novel as *Ulysses?* That would be by comparison a piece of random jewellery, a plaything with the popular appeal of such a craft object. The same with *A la Recherche du Temps Perdu,* even with *The Magic Mountain.* They are essentially independent of their time, floating above it: they are *literature*. In art Canetti had, as he tells us, a contempt for 'salvation and joy', for anything that was 'relaxing'. Art should have the atmosphere of revolution, the excitement, as in Goethe, of a potential, 'manifest in each of its moments'. A favourite text of Canetti is Stendhal's account of growing up in the French Revolution, *La Vie de Henri Brulard*. Dostoevsky, Büchner, Kafka also point the way to *Auto da Fé*. Writers who don't, even great ones like Tolstoy, are of minor interest; Canetti's essay on Tolstoy, one of his very few pieces lacking in compulsive interest, merely makes the point that Tolstoy at the end of his life became like the hero of *Auto da Fé*.

'Truly to confront the age'—great art does not often do that so self-consciously. Stendhal does it with lightness and élan; the painter Beckmann did it after the First World War with mythic violence and horror. Beckmann's painting is probably the closest parallel in art to Canetti's novel. Canetti does not mention him, but when writing his novel he surrounded himself with reproductions of Grünewald, who also inspired Beckmann. And apart from the intention, an art that confronts the age must not give way to it. It must be highly organized technically, to survive its own picture of disintegration.

> The thought came to me that the world should not be depicted as in earlier novels, from one writer's standpoint as it were; the world had *crumbled,* and only if one had the courage to show it in its crumbled state could one possibly offer an authentic conception of it . . . When I ask myself today where I got the rigour of my work I come to heterogeneous influences . . . Stendhal it was who made me stick to clarity. I had just finished the eighth chapter, now titled 'Death', when Kafka's 'Metamorphosis' came into my hands. Nothing more fortunate could have happened to me at this point. There, in ut-

most perfection, I found the antipose to literary noncommitment which I hated so much; there was the rigour that I yearned for. There, something was achieved that I wanted to find for myself. I bowed to this purest of all models, knowing full well that it was unattainable, but it did give me strength.

Kafka seems to be not so much an influence on *Auto da Fé* as totally absorbed by it, almost as Shakespeare's sources were absorbed by Shakespeare, and it is revealing to find out that Canetti discovered him in the actual process of writing his novel. But the greatest formative influence in Vienna at that time was Karl Kraus, the extraordinary nature of whose achievement—partly because it was histrionic, acted out in his recitals—can probably never be adequately presented to an Anglo-Saxon readership. Indeed, it would probably not be too much to say that *Auto da Fé,* which has been effectively translated, and which contains beside the potent forces of Canetti's internationalism, even his 'Englishness', his Shakespearean side, gives the best intuition that a non-Germanist can get of Kraus's peculiar genius.

It is, above all, a genius of commitment—to language and to emotion. That was the same with Kafka. How to combine, in art, a pure, fastidious rigour with the simplest feeling of rage and sorrow against the dreadfulness of life, the domination of the powerful, the torture of beetle Gregor by his family, of Woyzeck by the captain, of Jews by Nazis, Russians by Communists, Oliver Twist by Bumble, of Smike by Squeers (*Nicholas Nickleby* was one of Canetti's early and passionate enthusiasms)? For such an artist, the inner world, the world of his invention, cannot and should not be any different from the world of human and historical reality. In his study of Kafka Canetti writes that his strength was increased by the horror with which he saw the 'mass events accompanying the outbreak of war'. The rigour, the totality of his art is a direct expression of the wholeness of that sense of horror, the 'bond between the external hell of the world and his inner hell'. 'He did not have for his private and interior processes that disregard which distinguishes insignificant writers from writers of imagination. A person who thinks that he is empowered to separate his inner world from the outer one has no inner world from which something might be separable.'

Canetti has written nothing more significant than that. Most people do, in fact, feel empowered to achieve a normal equilibrium by separating their own world from the outer one. What is more, most art exists to aid, comfort and satisfy that natural urge. Our inner world is supported and confirmed by it against the outer world—which is the reason thoughtful Nazi officials could read Goethe and Schiller, and listen to Mozart, while going about their business of persecution and domination. Many artists of real honesty will admit the fact, tacitly or openly. Jane Austen, possibly not a genius in whom Canetti takes much interest, writes in a letter about a bloody battle in the Napoleonic war: 'How dreadful that so many poor fellows should be killed, and what a mercy that one cares for none of them.' There speaks the voice of a certain kind of common sense, the kind that most of us have to live by.

Not Canetti's great masters, however. Shakespeare may

not have wept over King Lear, may indeed have written the play in a passion of relish, but he *suffered:* the play is a correlative of his total capacity to suffer. That is perhaps self-evident and tautologous. In a climate of pseudo-scientific structuralism, a bloodlessly mechanistic approach to literature, Canetti's insistent emphases are decidedly salutary. In what sense, though, is Kafka for him the 'purest of all models'? That in which suffering is most absolute, most evident? But the message of great works of art is more ambiguous than that, and in a sense more comforting. As Auden wrote in Jane Austen's vein: 'You can only tell them parables, from which each according to his immediate and peculiar needs may draw his own conclusions.' And as with the client's need, so with that of the artist himself. Kafka suffers all in himself, but by writing he accepts and takes possession of that suffering. By becoming a beetle, his hero paradoxically has found how to keep, 'at every moment, every advantage'. There is nothing 'pure' in the spectacle of Kafka's pleasure in discovering the perfect way of separating himself from his hated family: for the reader, it is too touching for that, too 'human, all too human'.

That vulnerability is not to be found in Canetti's novel, a work of pure schematic power and ferocity, in which every sentence crackles with violent intelligence, violent humour.

> There was not *one* voice that he did not hear, he was possessed by every specific timbre of the war and rendered it compellingly. Whatever he satirically foreshortened was foreshortened effectively; whatever he exaggerated was exaggerated so precisely that it only first existed in this exaggeration and remained unforgettable . . . unsparingly, uncomfortingly, without embellishment, without reduction, and above all and most important, without habituation. Whatever was repeated . . . remained horrifying through every single repetition.

What Canetti wrote of Kraus's play *The Last Days of Mankind* is true of his own novel. As the First World War 'completely entered' Kraus's play, so a horrifying sense of the modern world completely enters his novel. But it is not in the slightest degree a self-consciously 'black' work, like Céline's; nor does it parade a ready-made metaphysic of gloom, like the novels of Graham Greene and Patrick White. It is not apocalyptic but dreadfully and intently domestic, like Dickens's world of Todgers.

It is divided into three parts: 'A Head without a World', 'Headless World' and 'The World in the Head'. Kien, the hero, a recluse and a distinguished Sinologist, with an enormous library, is the head; the library his inner world. His housekeeper Therese, the most memorable portrait in the book, is a world without any head. Everything in the novel can be distinctly 'heard', Therese and her speech particularly so. Having no contact with life, Kien has no speech, only an interior utterance. But he (and his creator) are painfully sensitive to what Canetti apropos of Kraus calls 'acoustic quotations': the sense that everything in the world—newspapers, people, and now radio and television—has a *voice,* its own sort of unique propaganda, which the artist must render unsparingly. He must 'let everybody speak', though most artists do not know how to listen: 'It is the hereditary vice of the intellectual that for him the world consists of intellectuals.' This no doubt is why the greatest acoustic artists, like Dickens and Shakespeare, are not in the German sense 'intellectuals'—they are naive rather than reflective. And it is perhaps the greatest achievement of Canetti to fuse in himself as artist the massive endowment and consciousness of a modern European thinker with an absolutely precise and humble sense of other people, their irreducible, untranslatable utterance of being.

Significant, then, that the speech reality of the novel is in its headless world, the world of Therese, the red-haired porter Benedikt Pfaff, the chess-playing dwarf Fischerle, his prostitute wife the Capitalist, and the other denizens of the café called The Stars of Heaven. Kien, a profound student of Confucius, becomes aware that Therese, whom he finds wearing white gloves to read a tattered book he has given her, *The Trousers of Herr von Bredow,* has a greater respect and feeling for books than he has. Amazed and humbled by this revelation, he decides to marry her. The sequence is one of the funniest in the novel and echoes the range of meaning in its German title *Die Blendung,* a noun which combines the literal with the metaphorical to signify blinding, dazzlement, delusion, deception. The married Kien is crumbled willy-nilly into the horrors of the headless world, beaten, driven out, and forced into the company of the denizens of The Stars of Heaven—particularly the dwarf Fisherle, who sets out to exploit him (there is a sort of grotesque reversal hereabouts of the adventures of Little Nell and her father).

Unhinged, Kien is convinced that he has removed his entire library into his head, whence it has to be laboriously unpacked when he lies down at night, and repacked again in the morning. 'Anything that appears in reality is seen in terms of the delusion as a whole.' This fantasy is remarkably like that set forth in a 'real' madman's book—*Denkwürdigkeiten,* by Schreber, a former president of the Senate of Dresden, whose paranoia was examined by Freud in an essay of 1911. Canetti suggests, rightly, that Freud has missed the point, and that Schreber's is really a very typically twentieth-century case of what he calls 'Power and Survival'. Schreber's delusion was that he was the one man left alive after some vast catastophe—the nuclear bomb, as it might now be. He was aware of other people around him in the asylum, but he explained their presence away by knowing that they were 'fleetingly sketched men', not real, manikins whom he can repack into his head as and when he needs, as Kien repacks the books, though for Kien books are the only reality, which is why in the headless world his survival depends on his continuing to hold them in his head. Kien, like Schreber, has entered, though by another route, what Canetti calls the extreme phase of power—the certainty of onlyness. Power is, ultimately, nothing but the refusal to believe that other people exist, and to act on that belief.

Kien is thus, by a grim paradox, reduced simultaneously to the state of ultimate survival power and of total degradation and powerlessness. As Gogol's Akaky can only apprehend the world through the reality of a new overcoat, so Kien survives by haunting the state pawnshop, 'releasing' by purchase all the books which headless people have brought to pawn, and repacking them in his own head. This is, among other things, a parable of the way in which we try to serve the world and come to terms with it, while retaining our own kinds of solipsism. The most important and terrifying statement of Kafka, says Canetti, is that fear and indifference made up his deepest feeling toward human beings. 'If one thinks about it with a little courage, our world has indeed become one in which fear and indifference predominate. Expressing his own reality without indulgence, Kafka was the first to present the image of *this* world.' The head without a world can only feel those emotions towards it, and it is the task of the artist like Kafka to bring the world into the head, to compel the two into coincidence. That is also what happens in the last section of *Auto da Fé.* Reunited with his library, Kien sets fire to it and perishes in the flames. The world has got into his head and he has voluntarily joined the crowd, the mass, the headless world, as Gregor in *The Metamorphosis* joins it by his humble death as an insect, something dry to be swept up off the carpet. Canetti records that his ending was suggested by the burning of the Justice Palace in Vienna by crowds protesting against the shooting of some workers, and against the acquittal of those responsible. He himself witnessed the scene and, like his puppet Kien, felt at last truly one with and a part of the crowd.

Schematic as it certainly is, the novel's extraordinary richness, the density of its wit and style, can only be travestied by such a brief sketch of its contents. It is not without faults, though these are more evident in the English version than in the German original. Even though it was translated by the historian Veronica Wedgwood 'under the personal supervision of the author', English linguistic forms and models cannot quite accommodate themselves to an outburst of *Kunstprosa* that was in every sense intended for the German language. There its fierce abstractness, its almost paralysing intelligence, are wholly at home: even the tedium which it by no means lacks seems, as it were, a wholly genuine and necessary tedium, as essential and even dynamic part of its massive mental specification. For the Anglo-Saxon reader accustomed to less demanding works of fiction, even the endless multiplication of the grotesque can be a little wearing, as if a computer had been programmed to turn out an infinite series of scarifying intellectual jokes, sometimes at its own expense. An example would be Kien's comment to a student who brings a set of Schiller to pawn. 'Why Schiller? You should read the original. You should read Immanuel Kant.' In classic German literature there is nothing opaquely 'original': the prismatic radiance of intellect is reflected from one work to another. Canetti's novel seems, in one sense, like the pinnacle of every brilliant and transparent work in its language: in another sense, as if it was already immanent in all of them. Exhilarating as it is, and also so physically disturbing that some of the author's friends and fellow writers hated it and couldn't bear to read it, it is at the same time a purely intellectual and philosophic exercise. This tension between a mental and physical plane is by no means unique in German literature, and it continues today in massive fantasy novels probably influenced by *Auto da Fé,* like those of Günther Grass.

It is also a tension unknown in naive art—art which slips without a purpose into a particular perfection of its kind. *The Bronze Horseman,* or *The Golden Bowl,* are just as much graphic studies of power as *Auto da Fé,* but they are also halcyon structures of consummated art, by their very natures tranquil and uninsistent. The high-pressure blast of ruthless clarity in *Auto da Fé* seems to blow away the whole world of art. This may be the reason some of its greatest admirers, though they may also admire Proust or Musil, tended in England to be intellectuals to whom it would never occur to read and enjoy the standard English poets and novelists. Like Voltaire or Nietzsche, Canetti seemed to them quite separate from the mere banal arts of literature.

Nonetheless, it may be that the predicament of *Auto da Fé*'s puppet hero, although he has none of the physical reality and emotional pathos of Gogol's Akaky or Kafka's Gregor Samsa, has for intellectuals not only a strong masochistic appeal, but conventional fiction's charge of fascination and suspense. Canetti has himself written, as any good novelist might do, that 'true writers encounter their characters only *after* they've created them': and yet his hero is obviously and by intention not a character in this sense. While the book was in progress, he was called simply B, or Bookman, and later Kant (the novel had the provisional title 'Kant catches fire'), finally becoming the combustible Kien (Pinewood) when the conflagration nears which ends the novel. Therese was based on Canetti's first impression of his Viennese landlady.

The finally completed novel was dispatched out of the blue to Thomas Mann, the author being confident that he would recognize it for the masterpiece it was. Mann replied apologetically that he found himself unable to read it. It remained in manuscript for a further four years and was published in 1935, achieving an immediate success. To Canetti's amusement, Thomas Mann wrote a warmly enthusiastic letter. But Canetti wrote no more novels: in that form there was no other subject for him. He had always been obsessed by the need to write his theoretical study of power and the mass, for which he had never ceased to read omnivorously. It was written mostly in England, and was finally published in Germany in 1960.

Crowds and Power could be said to ingest history, all stories about themselves and their behaviour which human beings have told, in the same way that *Auto da Fé* ingested the works of art that told in their different way the truths about power that Canetti was seeking. His favourite historian is Herodotus, a story-teller, with whom it hardly matters whether the story told is factually true or not, because it is always true to the psychology of the society it relates to. Conversely, he has little use for Aristotle the rationalist, who is more interested in the processes of knowledge than in those of suffering, of who does what to whom. As an analyst of the power process, Canetti is equally contemptuous of the empirical and factual historian and one of the men-of-destiny school, noting that both are on the side of power and have a vested interest in it, either because of their theories or from their very function as investigators.

Muhammad Tughlak has been defended by

Canetti with his cousin, Mathilde Camhi, in Vienna in 1930.

other man were left alive. 'This is precisely what he brings the Romans: the enhanced sense of his own life, feeding on the deaths of those he had led.' This power he is able to sell, as it were, to Vespasian and his son Titus, in the form of a prophecy that they will become Emperors of Rome. Josephus's distinction as a survivor is so great that it quite outweighs his betrayal of his fellows and desertion of his country.

Surviving the crowd implies having been once a part of it. Hitler's survivor complex was based on the amazing deliverance from his enemies of Frederick the Great. When Roosevelt dies a few weeks before the end of the war, Hitler is convinced he is saved, as Frederick had been saved by the sudden death of his arch-enemy the Empress Elizabeth of Russia. This clutch of a precedent shows an almost pathetic stupidity—and the paranoiac's ignorance of and separation from the realities of the outside world. Yet Hitler had once been truly a part of that world, and of the German and European crowd at the beginning of the First World War.

> He described how, at the outbreak of war, he fell on his knees and thanked God. It was his decisive experience, the one moment at which he himself honestly became part of a crowd. He never forgot it, and his whole subsequent career was devoted to the recreation of this moment, but *from outside.*

Hitler's response had been that of the crowd, which was given the same expression by men like Péguy and Rupert Brooke. His paranoia devotes itself to recreating that erstwhile solidarity, and his immediate instrument is the crowd: he perceives how to turn the old *closed* crowd of the German army, now forbidden under the Treaty of Versailles, into the *open* crowd of the National Socialist Party. The orders, exercises and expectations essential to German psychology had to be procured again at all costs. 'Every closed crowd which is dissolved by force transforms itself into an open crowd to which it imparts all its characteristics.'

The many categories which Canetti makes—invisible crowds, double crowds, crowds as packs—claim to quasi-scientific status. So clearly and forcefully does he set them out that we seem to be recognizing something we have always known, as Molière's hero discovers that he has been speaking prose all his life. The human condition in history is seen as Montaigne might have seen it, in pictures and conversations: the mode of discourse is itself entirely open. This very openness can lead to a sense of repetitiveness: the reader may feel that he has got the point quite early on. But it is the strength of Canetti's mode of creative exposition that he is not out to prove anything and that his terminology does not imprison enquiry. *Masse* and *Macht* are more resonant and more menacing than their English equivalents—the word 'crowd' suggests flower-shows and football matches rather than the forces inherent in a human mass—and the material of Canetti's book is mythic and historical rather than contemporary, though it can also be curiously prophetic, as is indicated by cant modernisms like 'student power' and 'gay power'.

The nemesis of such an undertaking, steadfastly through

modern Indian historians. Power has never lacked eulogists, and historians, who are professionally obsessed with it, can explain anything, either by the *times* (disguising their adulation as scholarship), or by *necessity,* which, in their hands, can assume any and every shape.

He is instructive, as I have already indicated, on the psychology and powers of the survivor, and has two chapters on the paranoia of Schreber, which are far more illuminating than any of the 'explanations' of Freud. (We might note that Canetti is implacably hostile to Freud's view of literature as both a substitute for life and a way of achieving power in it. For him, great literature is the truest expression possible of the predicament of living and of its need to understand and renounce power.)

The survivor may be detested, as in the example of Muhammad Tughlak, who killed all those returning from an unsuccessful expedition, or he may be credited with almost magical powers, as in the case of Josephus, or Hitler. Josephus, probably the only historian to have actually been in this physical sense a survivor, drew lots with his soldiers in a cave after the fall of the fortress he was commanding. They were to kill each other on this basis, but Josephus cooked the deal in such a way that he and one so long a period of intellectual growth, must be that its director becomes himself charged in its emotional field. To study the operation of power is in some sense to love it; and Canetti's scorn for historians who enjoy the spectacle of power involuntarily and aesthetically cannot dissociate him entirely from their predicament. As a character of Saul Bellow's observes, the deepest ambiguity in intellectuals is that they despise the civilization which makes their lives possible, and prefer to contemplate one, or to create one mentally, in which this would cease to be so. But Canetti never commits that particular *trahison*. His calm, which is never ironic, can be directed against himself (he repeatedly queries the possibility of self-knowledge and praises Kafka for having come as near to it as a writer can). Some of the best things in *Crowds and Power* are detached essays or meditations, like that on immortality, the last infirmity of power, and the way a walk among the silent crowd in a cemetery feeds the sensation of it ('We draw from them the strength to become, and to remain for ever, *more* than they are'). Stendhal is again a favourite here, the least pretentious aspirant to immortality: such a writer 'will still be here when everyone else who lived at the same time is no longer here'. To live for ever in this way is Canetti's own expressed ambition.

His aura of extreme exclusiveness seldom irritates; even when, in his most brilliant essay, he does not so much explain Kafka as absorb him, the process seems biologically natural and benign—Kafka was the thinnest of men and Canetti is corpulent. *The Other Trial,* first published in Germany in 1969, analyses Kafka's correspondence with Felice Bauer, to whom he was twice engaged. Canetti sees these letters as decisive in Kafka's writing life: by writing to her, he discovered both how to love her and how himself to be a writer. Two nights after his first letter he writes 'The Judgement', the first tale which liberates his characteristic genius, in a single ten-hour sitting, by night, and a day or two later, 'The Stoker'. He produces six chapters of *Amerika,* and after an interval his finest short story of all, *The Metamorphosis.* It is a *mensis mirabilis* comparable to Pushkin's Boldino autumn, the most fertile writing period in Kafka's career.

He can feel she expects something of him, and he in turn expects of her an equal precision in recording her days and her feelings. 'He succeeds in imposing upon her his own obsession', his own way of being in love, which he would later transfer to her friend Grete Bloch. Felice has given him what she could, but he cannot give her marriage in return. He confronts her family and the two girls in Berlin, at what he called the 'Tribunal', with the war already impending, and a little later he begins *The Trial,* with its culminating scene of the two executioners leaning over Josef K like the two girls, their cheeks touching.

Canetti uses the word 'obduracy' to describe the way Kafka protected 'the tremendous world he felt to be in his head'—a new world in which the human situation appears in art in a new way. Canetti rejects any idea that Kafka is exploring the nature of God or the Divine Law: it is power itself, in its ultimately and impersonally human shape, which executes Josef K and oppresses the hero of *The Castle.* The implication of Canetti's short book, which

reads like one of Kafka's own compelling stories, is that the truest and most significant modern literature can be seen as a withdrawal from power, even from literature's own magnificent pageant of mastery as it appears in the great creations of naming, recording and enjoying, in the worlds of Homer, Shakespeare, Milton or Dante. Kafka must find mastery in minuteness, in disappearance.

> Kafka's sovereign perspective on psychoanalysis ought to have helped critics to detach from its constricting domain his own person at least. His struggle with his father was essentially never anything but a struggle against superior power as such . . . Since he fears power in any form, since the real aim of his life is to withdraw from it, in whatever form it may appear, he detects it, identifies it, names it, and creates figures of it in every instance where others would accept it as being nothing out of the ordinary . . . *Macht* and *mächtig* are his unavoided, unavoidable words.

Marriage is out of the question. The place of smallness in it is usurped by children, whom Kafka envied and disapproved of because they are not actually small beings who want to dwindle and disappear, as he wants to, but 'false smallnesses' who want to grow bigger. Himself an expert on Chinese literature, where the idea of smallness—in insects or animals—is subtly explored and imagined, Canetti claims that Kafka 'belongs in its annals', and quotes for this the authority of Arthur Waley, for whom Kafka was the one Western prose author to be read with passionate attention.

Canetti's feeling for the Orient is perceptible in *The Voices of Marrakesh,* a unique travel book, and, together with *Kafka's Other Trial,* the most formally satisfying of his works. A sentence referring to Kafka's letters gives the clue to the way he enters into and conveys to us the baffling and yet familiar quality of strangers met in such a scene: 'They are so enigmatic and familiar to me that it seems they have been mental possessions of mine from the moment when I first began to accommodate human beings entirely in my mind, in order to arrive, time and again, at a fresh understanding of them.' That sort of accommodation is the key to Canetti's creative vision, with its peculiar blend of intense abstraction and equally stunning physical reality, constantly creating images of power where others would see 'nothing out of the ordinary'.

Though he is a scholar and a man of the mind, Canetti's sense of human societies and his gift—as in the Marrakesh book—for familiarizing out-of-the-way places have something in common with the art of another and earlier Nobel Prize-winner, Rudyard Kipling. But the timely comparison and contrast is with a more recent winner, the Polish poet Czeslaw Milosz. Both authors have written in a wide range of forms and both are exiles—Milosz in America—though in Canetti's case exile is itself a mode made for genius, for his country is the entire European tradition. Milosz's wonderful record of a Polish-Lithuanian childhood, *The Issa Valley,* should be enjoyed together with Canetti's *Geschichte* of his own early years in Bulgaria and England, Switzerland and Vienna. Both are subtle analysts and historians of national fixations and complexities.

There are, it is true, poems by Milosz—one of the great poets of our time—which move the reader more directly than anything by Canetti, who is by adoption a German *Dichter* but not in the naive and direct sense a poet. He enchants and enlightens but does not make the tears flow. But what a pair! The fact that two such remarkable writers should have won it in recent years almost makes one believe in the prize as an 'award' to literature. (pp. 176-91)

> John Bayley, "Canetti and Power," in his Selected Essays, *Cambridge University Press,* 1984, pp. 176-91.

Roger Kimball   (essay date September 1986)

[*In the following excerpt, Kimball maintains that Canetti's works are "deeply flawed."*]

In a room somberly decorated with a print of Grünewald's Isenheim altarpiece and looking out on the Steinhof insane asylum [Canetti] was seized with the inspiration for what would become *Auto-da-Fé.* He originally envisioned an eight-part epic to be titled the *Human Comedy of Madmen.* He spent the year 1929-30 in an ecstasy of writing. It was, he recalled, "the richest, most unbridled year of my life." He worked in a fever, sketching his various madmen, among them a religious fanatic, a technological visionary, a spendthrift, a man obsessed with truth, and a *Büchermensch,* a "Book Man" who lives only for and among his books. In the end, it was the Book Man who emerged from the crowd of characters to capture Canetti's imagination. He postponed his epic ambitions, devoting the following year, 1930-31, to writing a novel about him.

Essentially, *Auto-da-Fé* is a cautionary tale, depicting in graphic detail how reality can be capsized by obsession. It tells the story of Professor Peter Kien, "man of learning and specialist in sinology," whose ruling passion is his personal library of more than twenty-five thousand volumes. *Auto-da-Fé* is a long and involved novel, complicated by several subplots. But the main action recounts Kien's violent though celibate marriage to his uneducated housekeeper, Therese, who with her starched blue skirts and her own obsessive personality is perhaps Canetti's most successfully realized character. Kien grows increasingly out of touch with reality as the novel unfolds, until in the third and last section, "The World in the Head," he is a full-fledged paranoiac. This is the "blinding" to which the book's German title primarily refers. The tale ends with Kien's self-immolation in his beloved library. "When the flames reached him at last," the narrator concludes, "he laughed out loud, louder than he had ever laughed in all his life."

Canetti knew from the start that the novel would end with the Book Man's self-immolation; the symbolic significance of fire, soon to be developed at length in *Crowds and Power,* was already one of his main preoccupations. He had accordingly named his protagonist "Brand," that is, "conflagration," in his first sketches. As work on the novel progressed, "Brand" was rechristened "Kant" and the book was provocatively entitled *Kant Catches Fire.* It was Hermann Broch who insisted that the name "Kant" be changed. Canetti settled finally on "Kien"—"resinous

pinewood"—thus preserving a hint of the combustibility he had tokened with "Brand." [The critic adds in a footnote: "The suggestion of fire is of course also preserved by the ecclesiastical title given to the book in English—*Auto-da-Fé,* Portuguese for "act of the faith," that is, the public announcement or execution of sentences imposed by the Inquisition, especially the burning of heretics at the stake."]

In tone, outlook, and texture, *Auto-da-Fé* may be described as a cross between Kafka (Canetti mentions that he first read *The Metamorphosis* around this time) and the Borges of stories like "The Library of Babel." It possesses, at any rate, something of the nightmarish quality of Kafka's tales as well as the cosmically displaced intellectuality that Borges specialized in. In a 1973 essay on the composition of *Auto-da-Fé,* Canetti recalls that "One day, the thought came to me that the world should not be depicted as in earlier novels, from one writer's standpoint as it were; the world had *crumbled,* and only if one had the courage to show it in its crumbled state could one possibly offer an authentic conception of it." Surely, *Auto-da-Fé* succeeds in depicting the world in a "crumbled state." And in this respect it is undoubtedly an imaginative triumph of sorts; in sheer *relentlessness,* at least, it can have few rivals.

But I doubt whether even Canetti's most ardent admirers could wish that he had gone on to complete his epic. The idea that there might have been eight volumes like *Auto-da-Fé* is a prospect unpleasant to contemplate. For notwithstanding its obvious force and integrity, *Auto-da-Fé* is a brutal book. I suspect that most readers will agree with Hermann Broch when he accuses Canetti of being deliberately, even gratuitously, "terrifying" and complains of the "grotesqueness" of his characters. "You believe in alarming people to the point of panic," Canetti quotes Broch as saying. "[Y]ou end cruelly, mercilessly, with destruction. . . . Does it mean that you yourself have not found a way out or that you doubt the existence of a way out?"

Canetti answers no, but his response to completing the book suggests a more ambiguous reply. He begins *The Play of the Eyes* by claiming that he, too, had been devastated by the fire that consumed his character Professor Kien and his twenty-five thousand books. "What happens in that kind of book is not just a game, it is reality," he tells us solemnly. Like many of Canetti's more portentous comments about his own work, it is probably best not to consider this statement too closely. It seems designed mostly to underscore the existential pathos with which he would have us invest the work. At any rate, Canetti never really returned to the *Human Comedy of Madmen.* In his search for a "way out" of the chaos of modern life he embarked upon different paths: his satirical plays and, especially, his monumental study of mass behavior, *Crowds and Power.* (pp. 22-3)

Echoing throughout Canetti's memoirs is the theme that he himself identifies as his central preoccupation: the rebellion against death. In fact, it is a theme that Canetti *invokes* rather more than deals with concretely. The truth is, it would require considerable hermeneutical ingenuity to discover it as a theme of any consequence in his literary work. Yet "the rebellion against death" can do much to infuse one's statements with an air of noble gravity, and so Canetti is only too happy to adopt it as a kind of motto for his work: "I have spent the best part of my life figuring out the wiles of man as he appears in historical civilizations," Canetti observes at the beginning of *The Tongue Set Free.* "There is almost nothing bad that I couldn't say about humans and humankind. And yet my pride in them is so great that there is only one thing I really hate: their enemy, death." Canetti's response to the fact of death—"the only fact," as he sometimes puts it—is a tragic stance of rebellion against an ineluctable fate. The overriding question for every individual, he writes in *The Torch in My Ear,* is "whether he should put up with the fact that a death is imminent for him."

Canetti has never worked out his thoughts on death in any systematic fashion. His basic message would seem to be the unexceptionable admonition not to go gentle into that good night. Yet he also uses the rejection of death as the starting point for other, often more questionable, sorts of statements. At one point, for example, his insistence that the individual take a stand against death leads him to the pious declaration that "I care about the life of *every* human being and not just that of my neighbor." And in one of his essays, he goes beyond the posture of stoically resisting death to tell us that "So long as death exists, no beauty is beautiful, no goodness is good." We must of course be grateful that Canetti cares about the lives of all of us, even if the word "cares" is rendered practically empty in this context. But as for the relation between death and beauty and death and goodness—well, here I think we must question Canetti's dictum. For it seems at least equally plausible that beauty and goodness can emerge as compelling forces in our lives only against the background of mortality; in this sense, death, as Wallace Stevens put it, is the mother of beauty. Things matter to us precisely because neither we nor they last forever. Now, I do not doubt that Canetti's meditations on death betray a core of genuine pathos. But in the end I'm afraid that they amount to little more than a collection of sentimental exhortations; their chief function would seem to be to perpetuate the atmosphere of intellectual melodrama within which Canetti prefers to operate. Indeed, they would hardly be worth scrutiny, except that Canetti insists on placing them at the very center of his thought.

If the rebellion against death is Canetti's underlying "philosophical" preoccupation, the phenomenon of the crowd has proven to be the theme that has most absorbed his attention over the years. In the winter of 1924-25, he had the "illumination" about the nature of crowds that, he writes, was to determine the rest of his life. Here again, we must make allowances for Canetti's rhetoric: the version of his intellectual development disseminated in these memoirs is too neat, too novelistic, too full of determining "illuminations" and single-minded passions to be credited without reservation. But there is no doubt that in the phenomenon of the crowd Canetti believed he had found a key to perennial mysteries. As he put it in *The Torch in My Ear,* "I realized that there is such a thing as a crowd instinct which is always in conflict with the personality in-

stinct, and that the struggle between the two of them can explain the course of human history."

Canetti's first conscious experience of a crowd was in 1922, when he witnessed a mass demonstration protesting the assassination of Walter Rathenau, the German-Jewish industrialist and statesman. In the crowd, he discovered "a total alteration of consciousness" that is both "drastic and enigmatic." As he describes it, in fact, this first encounter with a crowd was little short of the kind of experience one finds recounted in certain species of mystical literature. It was

> an intoxication; you were lost, you forgot yourself, you felt tremendously remote and yet fulfilled; whatever you felt, you didn't feel it for yourself; it was the most selfless thing you knew; and since selfishness was shown, talked, and *threatened* on all sides, you needed this experience of thunderous unselfishness like the blast of the trumpet at the Last Judgment. . . . How could all this happen together? What was it?

After such an experience—which Canetti came to call "the discharge" in *Crowds and Power*—it is not surprising that the phenomenon of the crowd should become "the enigma of enigmas" for him. "In the crowd," he wrote, "the individual feels that he is transcending the limits of his own person." The problem is, however, that this intimation of transcendence "is based on an illusion": after the crowd disperses, as it must, the individual is catapulted back to himself, as alone and isolated as ever.

What crystallized Canetti's preliminary reflections on the phenomenon of the crowd was a second, and far more dramatic, experience on July 15, 1927, the day that Canetti describes as the "most critical day of my life after my father's death." In response to a headline in a government newspaper proudly announcing the acquittal of the men being held for the recent murder of several workers in Burgenland, an angry mob spontaneously formed from all over Vienna. And just as spontaneously, it marched to the Palace of Justice and set it afire. Canetti himself was swept along with the crowd. The entire experience engraved itself deeply into his imagination. A man standing on the sidelines lamenting loudly "The files are burning! The files are burning!" when the Palace of Justice was burning down and the police were firing into the crowd became a prototype for the character of the pyromaniacal Book Man, Professor Kien. And the spectacle of the crowd exploding into violence provided him with some of the central insights of *Crowds and Power*—the crowd's spontaneous formation, its lack of a recognizable leader, its culmination in destruction by fire: all these are aspects of the crowd that Canetti dwells upon at length in his book.

A text of nearly five hundred closely printed pages, *Crowds and Power* is a study *sui generis.* It is part ethnological study, part contribution to mass psychology, and part exercise in comparative religion. But above all it is an exposition of one man's personal philosophy, his vision of the world. Only as such can we understand how the struggle between the so-called "crowd instinct" and the "personality instinct" can be proposed to "explain the course of human history." The book belongs to that voluminous literature in which intellectuals have attempted to come to terms with the intractably unintellectual phenomenon of mass society. From Max Weber to Hannah Arendt, intellectuals in this century have been fascinated by the spectacle of mass society—its expression in modern democracies and its perversion in totalitarianism; Hermann Broch, to take someone from Canetti's orbit, devoted most of his energies from the mid-Thirties until his death in 1951 to a study of mass psychology. Canetti's contribution attempts to provide us not with a scholarly reflection on mass society but with what we might call a poetics of the crowd, and this, perhaps, is one reason he did not bother to supply *Crowds and Power* with an index.

Nevertheless, the book is the product of remarkable—if somewhat idiosyncratic—erudition. It is divided into twelve sections with scores of short chapters dealing with everything from "The Domestication of Crowds in World Religions" to "The Rain Dances of the Pueblo Indians," from reflections on "The Psychology of Eating" to "Human Postures and Their Relation to Power." Like many such works, it abounds in categories—there are open crowds and closed crowds, "flight" crowds and "slow" crowds, even, Canetti tells us, crowds that are invisible. One must also mention that the book is written with a masterful and beguiling clarity; nor is there any doubt that it contains many revealing, even brilliant, observations on the psychology of crowds, the nature of power, and the way they have interacted across cultures and millennia; indeed, simply as a testimony against the infatuation with power—an infatuation that our century has suffered from greatly—*Crowds and Power* must be counted among the most eloquent and compelling of documents.

Yet for all this, the book is deeply flawed. It proceeds not by argument but by assertion. Thus, it opens with the statement: "There is nothing that man fears more than the touch of the unknown." An arresting proposition. But is it true? Unfortunately, this is a question seldom broached in these pages. In *The Torch in My Ear,* Canetti remarks that he scrupulously avoided "abstract philosophy" in his reading and meditations on the phenomenon of the crowd, hoping thereby to avoid the distance from lived experience that philosophy typically demands. But by avoiding the strictures that philosophical analysis presupposes, Canetti has not made his book more compelling, only less rigorous. Because it lacks any consistent argument, *Crowds and Power* threatens to disintegrate into a collection of observations, of *aperçus,* some telling, some banal, some simply false.

On the other hand, if *Crowds and Power* is weakened by a paucity of argument, it is rendered practically surreal by Canetti's elevation of his main idea into a universal explanatory principle. He often writes as if all human behavior, and even abstract moral principles, are best interpreted as species of "crowd behavior." Of a man listening to a sermon, for example, Canetti writes that "he would have felt astonished or even indignant had it been explained to him that the large number of listeners present gave him more satisfaction than the sermon itself"—but, *pace* Canetti, who could blame him? Similarly, we learn that the

real significance of the Sermon on the Mount was that it was "directed against the confinement of the crowd which wants to feel the sensation of its own growth again," and that "All demands for justice and all theories of equality ultimately derive their energy from the actual experience of equality familiar to anyone who has been part of a crowd." Such passages give weight to Susan Sontag's observation [in "Mind as Passion," in her *Under the Sign of Saturn*] that much of the book "is really a rationalist's discourse about religion." And with the application of his ideas about crowds to areas beyond conscious human endeavor, Canetti's "rationalism" steps beyond the questionable into the realm of the fantastic. Thus he adduces the action of sperm swimming toward an egg as an example of the behavior of an "invisible crowd." "It is unnecessary to point out that a crowd of spermatozoa cannot be the same as a crowd of people," he concedes later in the book. But then goes on to insist that "there is undoubtedly an analogy between the two phenomena, and perhaps more than an analogy." Yet what more than an analogy can there be? The truth is, that in his eagerness to "explain the course of human history," Canetti is all too willing to distort the phenomena he treats in order to make them fit his pre-ordained schema.

In his essay on Hermann Broch in *The Conscience of Words,* Canetti tells us that in order to be truly representative of his time, a writer must possess three qualities: he must be original, he must sum up his time, and he must stand against his time. There can be no doubt that Canetti presents us with an original sensibility; nor need we question whether he stands against his time sufficiently: his work has always stood resolutely against the forces of commercialization and glib popularity. But can Canetti really be said to sum up his time? His work, especially the plays and *Auto-da-Fé,* are certainly *symptomatic* of their time. But in the end we must admit that they lack that scope and representativeness that make, say, *The Man Without Qualities* or even Hermann Broch's *The Sleepwalkers* artistic epitomes that seem to crystallize an age without being bound to it. Indeed, in attempting to place these volumes of Canetti's memoirs within his *oeuvre,* it is difficult not to conclude that his real masterpiece was not his life's work but his life, not the story of Professor Kien or the nature of crowds but his own story, the story of becoming Elias Canetti. It is for the account they give us of this absorbing story that they will be read long after *Auto-da-Fé* and *Crowds and Power* become historical curiosities. (pp. 25-8)

Roger Kimball, "Becoming Elias Canetti," in The New Criterion, Vol. V, No. 1, September, 1986, pp. 17-28.

Philip Purser (review date 6 December 1990)

[*In the following excerpt, Purser offers a mixed review of Canetti's* The Play of the Eyes.]

At the beginning of the third volume of his autobiography, Elias Canetti is still in his twenties. He has been cooped up for a year in a bed-sitter on the outskirts of Vienna with only a print of the Isenheim altar as company, working on the grim novel that was eventually to be called *Auto da Fé.* Early one morning he catches the first workman's train into town, dashes through empty streets and lets himself into the apartment of his loved one, later his wife, Veza—she has given him a latchkey against such an eventuality. Is it the old Adam stirring? With the manuscript finished at last is it time for a little *Beinüber*? No such luck, if that is what Veza has been hoping: Elias is bursting to tell her about the book he's just discovered and been reading all night, Büchner's *Wozzeck.* When Veza sleepily says it's been one of her favourites for ages, and rolls out of bed to find her copy, there's an almighty row. What does she mean by having known *Wozzeck* all these years and never even mentioned it? It's as if she has been unfaithful—no, worse! Because in Canetti's estimation, or anyway in the estimation which he applies so rigorously to every figure he encounters in *The Play of the Eyes,* affairs of the mind are far more important than those of either body or personality.

One by one the literary heroes of these Viennese years are summoned up, re-examined and found wanting in essential seriousness. Wittgenstein attracts only a passing mention, identified as 'a philosopher, the brother of the one-armed pianist Paul Wittgenstein'. Robert Musil occupies the summit of Canetti's esteem until he is demoted after a show of petulance at a tactless mention of his arch-rival Thomas Mann. Herman Broch was Canetti's great friend at the beginning of the period but fades out of the narrative as it continues. As for poor Karl Kraus, the mentor who had urged and inspired Canetti to write *Auto da Fé,* his is the most summary dismissal of all. His offence was to support Dollfus, the Austrian Chancellor subsequently murdered by the Nazis, rather than the ineffectual Austro-Marxists. When Kraus dies, Canetti doesn't bother to attend the funeral. 'I didn't feel that I was missing anything,' he explains in a sentence anyone might be ashamed of.

The one man who is never diminished in Canetti's eyes is the shadowy Dr Sonne. With Broch, Canetti has been conducting a ponderous game of going through the lists of everyone they know to see if they can light upon an absolutely good man. By 'good', Canetti makes it clear, he means untainted by any trace of levity, self-interest or obeisance to fashion.

Broch finally remembers Dr Sonne and suggests how the other can meet him. Canetti does so and is captivated. Henceforth he meets this hero of heroes for two hours every day in the Café Museum. They talk and talk—or rather, Dr Sonne talks and Canetti listens. Sonne is lucid, penetrating and knowledgeable about everything. He is exhaustive but concise. 'He spoke with the ice-cold clarity of one who grinds perfect lenses, who will have nothing to do with anything murky until it is clarified. He examined an object by taking it apart, yet preserved it in its wholeness. He did not dissect; he irradiated.'

Most prized of all the good doctor's qualities is his aloofness. He will not talk about himself, never makes use of the first person, rarely addresses his hearer in the second person. Canetti knows nothing of his past, his present circumstances or where he lives. He can't even be sure whether Dr Sonne really is a doctor or—in line with local

custom—chooses to call himself one. When he learns by accident that Sonne wrote Hebrew poetry in his youth, he is so ashamed of this inadvertent violation of the admired one's privacy that for a whole week he avoids the Café Museum. Then he starts to imagine the doctor sitting there behind his newspaper wondering what has happened to his disciple, and in this shaft of fellow-feeling the whole pretence of an impersonal, purely cerebral affinity tumbles like a house of cards.

Canetti and Dr Sonne have become friends, for heaven's sake: why won't either admit it? You begin to wonder exactly what empyrean topics, what proofs of the existence of God or the General Theory of Relativity, they could have discussed so memorably. Canetti doesn't say at the time, but later in the book he lets slip—and really it comes as no surprise, if rather a let-down—that the day's news from the newspaper, particularly of the Spanish Civil War, furnished the stuff of most of their conversations. You are also aware by now of the cunning with which Canetti is presenting this impersonal person Dr Sonne. As in a screenplay, he has first been glimpsed behind his paper in the Café Museum, a solitary, mysterious, but at this stage unidentified figure. When he is formally introduced, it is as a disembodied intellect. Then gradually, and against Canetti's professed intentions, the bits of information emerge which flesh him out as a human being: what Veza thinks of him (not a lot), a story about his giving away a legacy, the accident in his youth which left him with a stiff-legged gait, his mute despair at the bombing of Guernica, and finally, flashed up this once and immediately withdrawn again, as if revealing it were the ultimate presumption, the doctor's first name: Gabriel.

The notion of true wisdom confined in a truly private, inviolate life is always attractive, and doubly so when all around you—as on the radio and television in our day or in the coffee-houses of Vienna in the Thirties—is endless, self-promoting chit-chat. Canetti makes the society in which he moves sound very much like a perpetual version of Melvyn Bragg's *Start the week* on Radio 4. But he is part of it, and for all the austerity of his views, a party to it. Disdainful of gossip, scornful of show-offs, he is not averse to showing off himself, always ready to give readings from his unpublished novel or unperformed plays; and as for gossip—wow! up in the class of Richard Aldington, particularly when the target is someone he doesn't like.

Alma Mahler is that 'noisy, witless woman' who 'dominates the scene through boasting, greed and liquor'. At the funeral of her daughter Manon Gropius, she produces giant, perfectly-formed tears like pearls. Her new husband Franz Werfel sighs and fidgets through one of Canetti's readings before finally stalking out, to be damned as a philistine as well as a non-stop, vacuous talker and, worst of all, a popular novelist. James Joyce makes a brief appearance at another reading, in Zurich. Canetti declaims his Expressionist play *The Comedy of Vanity,* in which mirrors are smashed as forbidden objects, though one character raises the problem of men who shave with open razors. Joyce's sole observation in the interval is that he shaves himself with a cut-throat razor and no mirror, whereupon, like Werfel before him, he departs. Canetti broods and broods over the remark. It seemed distinctly hostile in tone. Was this because Joyce was nearly blind, and therefore touchy about the need for a mirror? Or was he only bragging of his courage in risking his jugular every morning? Later, the razor is forgotten and the theory is that, in common with most of the Swiss who were present, he was unable to understand the Viennese patois and thick Viennese accent which Canetti had obstinately retained in his performance. By the end of the book the author is half-convinced that he was being paid a mysterious compliment.

Throughout the period covered in **The Play of the Eyes,** Canetti has been pondering a study of the behaviour of crowds: how they exercise power, how they can be manipulated. He discusses the subject with Dr Sonne. It's a timely idea, and what better vantage-point from which to pursue it than a country caught between two populist dictatorships? Alas, when it appeared more than twenty years later, **Crowds and Power** turned out to be mainly a compendium of bits of this and that from the History and Anthropology and Zoology and Psychology shelves. Some three hundred and fifty sources are listed, and they are only a part of the books and papers he consulted, the author claims. There are chapters on the finger language of monkeys or self-castration among the Skoptsy, but of Nuremberg Rallies, Goebbels at the Sportpalast, or Hitler's very pointed theories in *Mein Kampf* about the theatre and theatre audiences, not a word. When Canetti does offer original observation, as in a piece on the power of an orchestral conductor, or a set of national characteristics (the Dutchman, the Spaniard etc), he presents it as bare assertion, without illustration, without evidence and, come to that, without any remarkable perception.

I was going to say that in England we've never bred writers of such relentless, uncompromising, Nobel Prize-winning seriousness—our only novelist to be tagged an intellectual was Aldous Huxley, and by the side of Canetti he was Fred Astaire. I was forgetting that not only did Canetti live in Hampstead from 1939 until quite recently (he's still in the London telephone directory) but he also spent—as related in his first volume of autobiography, **The Tongue Set Free**—a couple of childhood years in Manchester. So we must own up to being partially responsible. This is not just flippant English resistance to seriousness. I am seriously suggesting that when Canetti, who writes in German, took his Teutonic regard for *gravitas* to its logical extreme he ended up with a lost opportunity and an unreadable book. The autobiographies are saved from that by the very ingredients which he affects to despise but which make the world a more interesting place: gossip, vanity, inconsequential stories and a modicum of spite. There is even a joke somewhere in **The Play of the Eyes,** or anyway a pleasantry, a bit of British self-deprecation, though I can't find it again to quote chapter and verse. It comes when Veza reads **Auto da Fé** and like many other readers of that book, says Canetti wrily, is greatly relieved to get to the end.

> Philip Purser, *"Serious Dr Sonne,"* in London Review of Books, *Vol. 12, No. 23, December 6, 1990, p. 22.*

> **Canetti explaining in 1944 his reasons for continuing to write in German, despite his exile in England:**
>
> The language of my mind will continue to be German, because I am Jewish. Whatever remains of that country, ravaged in every sense, I will protect in myself as a Jew. It is also *their* fate that is mine; but I bear a universal human inheritance. I want to give back to their language what I owe to it. I want my contribution to add to the reason for being grateful to them for something once again.
>
> *Elias Canetti, in his*
> The Human Province, *1973.*

Michael Hofmann   (review date 4 October 1991)

[Hofmann is a German-born English poet and critic. In the following excerpt, he argues that Canetti's aphorisms are less successful than his longer works.]

As the Saturday editions of German newspapers will attest—where whole pages are set aside for them—the German language is abuzz with aphorists and would-be aphorists. People will introduce themselves with perfect seriousness with the words "ich schreibe Aphorismen", as though unaware that such an arrogation is a denial of the modesty, the self-questioning and the mockery inherent in the form. The writing of aphorisms is a kind of national recreation, by definition practised largely by non-writers: a minimal form for people only minimally interested in writing.

The exception that proves the rule is Elias Canetti, the pre-eminent living writer of German, who has been writing aphorisms or "notes" or "notations" (*Aufzeichnungen*) for half a century now. He has done so while primarily engaged on far more ambitious and taxing projects; the aphorisms were a relaxation, a return to himself, they kept his mind broad and supple. The first book, **The Province of the Human** (originally **Aufzeichnungen 1942-1972**), was largely drawn from notebooks he kept while researching and writing **Crowds and Power. The Secret Heart of the Clock,** its sequel—if a collection of aphorisms can be said to have a sequel—contains notes from the years 1973 to 1985, during which Canetti was again embarked on a long formal task, the three-volume autobiography of his youth, **The Tongue Set Free, The Torch in My Ear** and **The Play of the Eyes** (can anyone match Canetti's titles, so exquisite and distinctive?) These two books of reflections, ideas, opinions, are like the pendulum weights of a clock, keeping the machinery of his writing ticking over.

Apart from their role as counterweights to important works, their epiphytic and hygienic function, there is little to set Canetti's aphorisms apart from those of the named and nameless thousands in the papers. I wonder whether all aphorisms are not the work of a single mind anyway, with perhaps an assistant to write the funny ones. (There is not even a smile in the new book; **The Province of the Human** had managed to contain such things as: "A love letter from Sweden. Strindberg on the stamps.") Canetti occasionally voices similar doubts about the form himself: "Die großen Aphoristiker lesen sich so, als ob sie alle einander gut gekannt hätten" ("The great aphorists read as though they were all good friends of one another"). Or, in *The Secret Heart of the Clock:* "Shouldn't everyone be capable of a successful sentence? To collect the sentences of those who fail at everything else." As for his own aphorisms, there is something arbitrary, careless or brutal about them: "Er legt Sätze wie Eier, aber er vergißt, sie zu bebrüten" ("He lays sentences like eggs, and then forgets to brood on them"). They exist by fiat: "That is an aphorism, he says, and quickly shuts his mouth again."

I take the aphorism to be an anonymous sort of form, with its own strongly marked character, of which to be self-questioning is certainly a part (hence the absurdity of the introduction, "I write aphorisms"). Its space is too brief to be anything but a mask (of rage, of loathing, of cynicism) or a mirror. One can either be cruel in an aphorism, or preen. It is a single mental movement, a first thought let stand, a tiny arena for aggression, vanity or some combination of the two. Sentences which are too unbalanced or preposterous to stand in context stand alone: "Drunk with incontestability, he tosses out single sentences"; "The new lust: rejecting all publicity"; "To live in secret. Could there be anything more wonderful?"

Undoubtedly, the reason why *The Secret Heart of the Clock* exists is the habit of almost fifty years: the writing of aphorisms has become an integral part of Canetti's productive process. This book rehearses his familiar concerns: with writing and language, with enemies, names, fame and death. The writing about characters—there is a fine note on John Aubrey—takes up the publication of his *Earwitness,* while his work on his autobiography is often evident, for instance in this sad little thought: "To repeat one's life—not as an archivist—is very tempting." In years in which he won the three major German literary prizes—and the Nobel in 1981—he is much exercised with the subject of fame, mostly rather sourly and, I'm afraid, trivially: "Most terrible of all fates: to become fashionable before your death"; "The honors line up and grab their candidates". Of the outside world very little comes through: space exploration (more moonshots and satellites), animals and trees (years in which the Greens made their appearance).

It is hard to care very much for this part of Canetti's production without a very strong prior commitment to the rest of it. Canetti clearly needs the short form and cherishes his practice of it, but the reader is not bound to follow suit. The virtues of Canetti's work are the opposite of the aphoristic virtues: he is not a quick, witty, memorable writer. He has breadth, patience, scrupulousness, unsparingness of others and himself. Heroically, he takes things to the point—or beyond the point—at which they cease to be dignified, interesting or tolerable. He has the hallucinatory thoroughness of a plasterer. But to read these aphorisms is to be presented with the fossil of a creature prized for its succulence. "Before the words begin to sparkle", he writes, and he is quite right about this, "he cuts himself short." Is that any way to write an aphorism? "Put on the brakes *better*. You feel too *far*." Here he does, and

these are the results, these lugubrious, strangled paradoxes and joyless quips and squeals.

Michael Hofmann, "The Mask of Aphorism," in The Times Literary Supplement, *No. 4618, October 4, 1991, p. 34.*

Ralph Willingham   (essay date March 1992)

[*In the following essay, Willingham scrutinizes Canetti's treatment of conformity in the dramas* Comedy of Vanity *and* Life-Terms.]

The future England of Aldous Huxley's *Brave New World* controls its people by conditioning them, from the moment of conception, to accept their stations in life. Artificially conceived in a "hatchery," people are divided into classes ranging from the upper-crust Alphas to the moronic Epsilons, a servant class. Instead of entrusting social stability to laws, religious faith, and customs, this world relies on chemical treatments during gestation, sleep-hypnosis and aversion techniques in childhood, unlimited sexual freedom, and liberal doses of drugs.

Two plays by Elias Canetti explore less drastic means of achieving utopia, dramatizing the effects of the forces of law and/or faith in combination with the human willingness to conform to social pressures. But the conclusions of both dramas suggest that conformity as a tool is not only inadequate but counter-productive. Ultimately, the external pressure to conform crumbles under the force of the individual's more powerful internal drive to fulfill personal needs. Meanwhile, laws and customs designed to perpetuate stability breed social decay. In view of the enormous changes sweeping Eastern Europe, these plays, written as they were in the mid-'30s and mid-'50s respectively, seem especially topical at the present time.

Canetti, a Bulgarian Jew born in 1905, lived in Vienna and Berlin during the rise of National Socialism, which forced him to flee to England. As a result of these events, he became deeply interested in crowd psychology and eventually made it the subject of *Masse und Macht (Crowds and Power,* 1960), his principal literary work. Earlier, however, he had explored crowd behavior in two plays, *Komödie der Eitelkeit* (1933-34) and *Die Befristeten* (1956), translated by Gitta Honegger and published together in 1983 as *Comedy of Vanity & Life-Terms.* Neither drama is well known outside German-speaking territories; they remain Canetti's least-known works, despite the attention he has received since winning the 1981 Nobel Prize.

One reason for this lies in the fact that much of the humor in *Comedy of Vanity,* for example, is culturally specific and difficult to convey in English. Translator Gitta Honegger explains that the dialogue is written in a Viennese dialect whose variations indicate social status, ambitions, and other characteristics constituting a person's "acoustic mask," a concept which Canetti borrowed from the Viennese satirist Karl Kraus. [The critic adds in a footnote: "In an early interview with the Viennese weekly newspaper *Sonntag,* Canetti explained that the acoustic mask is 'the linguistic form of a person—that which remains constant in his speech, the language which grew up with him, which is his alone and which will pass away only with him.' "] Canetti himself tried to get this play produced after completing it in 1934: "I thought it an appropriate answer to the burning of the books. . . . But I had no connections in the theatrical world" [*The Play of The Eyes;* subsequently cited as *Play*]. *Comedy of Vanity* was not performed until 1965, in Braunschweig, Germany. According to Klaus Völker, however, its meaning was then distorted by the director's decisions to paper the setting with photographs of Hitler and to project unnecessary slides.

Two phenomena inspired Canetti to write *Comedy of Vanity:* the crowd hysteria generated by the National Socialists, and the way men looked at themselves in barbershop mirrors:

> They studied themselves, they scrutinized themselves, they made faces to broaden their knowledge of their features. . . .I asked myself: What would happen if men were forbidden this most precious of moments? Could any law be stringent enough to divert men from their image and likeness? And what detours would vanity take if such a barrier were placed in its path?
>
> (*Play*)

In Canetti's play, a society bans all forms of image worship, on the theory that vanity impedes human progress. Taking photographs, making motion pictures, manufacturing mirrors, and even painting portraits are declared capital crimes, and anyone owning a mirror or an image of a human being is subject to a prison sentence. At first, citizens eagerly flock to a huge public carnival to smash mirrors and burn photographs. But the demands of human nature soon create a black market. An ex-photographer, now a social pariah, charges women a fee for a glimpse of themselves in a shiny piece of metal. Professional flatterers hang around street corners and fawn on passersby, who reward their lavish compliments with cash. Teenage girls peer into one another's eyes to admire their reflections. The poor fulfill their needs by collapsing at the feet of strangers and groaning in agony until revived with praise. Eventually even public officials flock to a sanitorium opened by a former brothel owner. There they gaze into mirrors for hours.

Canetti has borrowed from the traditional comic formula which the Roman playwright Plautus popularized, and which critic Northrop Frye described in his famous essay, "The Argument of Comedy" (1948); according to this formula, an individual disrupts social stability by behaving in some aberrant, non-conformist fashion, and has to be brought back into line by the collective efforts of the community. Canetti, however, reverses the Plautine formula. His entire society goes against nature until an individual inspires a collective return to normal behavior. Meanwhile, the law which was to create an ideal world serves only to worsen the old one.

Initially, the citizens are swept up in the crowd fervor against image worship. Window glass is replaced with a non-reflecting gray material. Swimming is banned, because people might see their faces in the water. Natural behavior thus becomes intolerable. But destroying the tools of vanity cannot destroy the urge. In fact, the new law actually fans the flames of vanity. Even at the carnival, people boast of how many photos and mirrors they have brought to be burned and smashed. Later, deprived of mirrors, citizens quickly become preoccupied with what they have thrown away—that is, the opportunity to admire themselves. But the risk involved in breaking the law is too great and they must settle for praise.

Praise is no substitute for the mirror, however; and soon one of the characters, Madam Fant, becomes rich by admitting people to her mirror-filled sanitorium, which the authorities do not close because they patronize it themselves. Madam Fant capitalizes on her customers' desperate condition. She offers three types of service: First Class, Economy, and No Frills; but everybody winds up sitting in the same hall, staring at the same mirrors. The cheated customers are too mesmerized to notice the deceit. Only Henry Breeze, who is enjoying the sound of his own voice by making a speech in praise of vanity in the luxury suite, can rouse them from their trances, as his speech carries into the hall of mirrors:

RAGING VOICE

> Each of us carries a noble image in his heart. When will we be able to truly claim it as our own? . . . It can't go on like this. The world is falling apart! Must we suffer all our lives the consequences of a tiny flaw? . . . What we need now is the rebirth, the resurrection of our commitment to what is true and authentic, real and genuine, to purity and perfection. For only he who is beautiful knows what beauty is . . . and only the strong man appreciates strength!

Breeze's rhetoric sweeps the sanitorium customers into the street, where they shout "I! I! I!" Thus the play ends as it began, with the image of a crowd of self-centered individuals overcome by mass hysteria. Beneath the humorous surface, Canetti exhibits the same seriousness of purpose which characterizes the comedies of Plautus, Shakespeare, and Molière; he reaffirms the virtues of the old order by holding up alternatives to ridicule.

The Numbered (Life-Terms) is not a comedy, but it employs the same basic premise: that individual urges are stronger than the structures of social conventions. In this play, a nameless future society has abolished the fear of death by claiming to control the moment of its occurrence. At birth, all children receive lockets containing their dates of birth and dates of death. Only an official known as the Locketeer can open this locket, and it is he who christens each child according to the age he will be when his "moment" comes—Forty-five, Sixty, Eighty-one, and so on. When individuals die, the Locketeer opens their lockets and verifies that the dates are correct. Everyone knows by the person's name how old he or she will be when the "moment" arrives, but only the individual knows his or her own birth date, and thus how many years he or she has left. The reason for this secrecy is that all the lockets are empty; exposing dates of birth would discredit the illusion that society controls the moment of death. By perpetuating that illusion, society can perpetuate a myth of social advancement over past ages, when people lived in fear of death. This society can assert its elimination of accidental death and even murder, for the Locketeer can claim the victim died because the moment of death had come. Anyone else who opens a locket is branded a "murderer," a person with a low number attempting to steal years which are not due him or her.

Despite the surface consensus that defeat of death makes for a happier populace, knowing one's "moment" actually breeds social unrest. The inequality of life spans creates a social hierarchy in which people type one another according to the behavioral expectations which their names imply. Inevitably, resentments emerge. A woman in her 40s complains to an acquaintance that "Eighty-eighters" are conceited:

> How could he love anyone? How could he get attached to anyone? He doesn't know pity, he can't help anyone. His years belong to him alone. He can't give them away. But he wouldn't want to, anyway. Because he has become tough, as if nothing else existed besides him. And for this he is admired! I detest Eighty-eighters!

On the other hand, people with low numbers are low-class citizens and can be exploited by those who will outlive them. One high-numbered man marries only low-numbered women, one after another, because their low expectations of life make them submissive.

In addition to social inequality, controlling the "moment" leads to psychological unrest and irresponsibility. A boy named Seventy is disturbed that he will outlive his mother, named Thirty-two. A boy named Ten becomes a delinquent because no one sees any point in teaching him discipline. Finally, a man named Fifty begins to suspect that the "moment" is a fraud and tries to convince other citizens of this. When he upsets a mother with questions about the truth of her child's death, the Locketeer brings Fifty before the assembled people and condemns him to "the public moment." Fifty responds that he cannot be executed, for he is not yet 50; his "moment" has not yet come. Taken aback, the Locketeer offers Fifty a reprieve if he will repudiate his claim that the "moment" is a hoax. Fifty recants. But he later tells a friend that he has outfoxed the Locketeer:

> First I forced him to insist that my moment had come. He was absolutely sure and everybody heard him say so. Then I recanted for which he granted me mercy. I am still alive. Either he made a mistake and knows no more about my *moment* than I do or it is possible *to survive the moment itself.* From now on everybody has to believe in either of these two possibilities. (emphasis in original)

Fifty tricks two old women into giving him their lockets; he opens them, and his own, to discover they are empty. Fifty runs through the streets like a town crier, declaring that the lockets are empty. Thinking themselves free of death, people christen Fifty the Deliverer and tear off their lockets. But soon they become dissatisfied with the truth. First, they begin to realize that it has brought back the uncertainty of death. Second, discrediting the "moment" has

eliminated the social hierarchy. Those whose high numbers gave them status now have nothing.

Unlike **Comedy of Vanities** in its conclusion, **The Numbered** does not settle for an exuberant return to the natural order. Like the Avocatore in Ben Jonson's *Volpone*, Canetti makes his characters suffer for having deviated from that order in the first place. He leaves Fifty in a state of remorse at the social discord he has sown, realizing that no matter how evil the status quo may have been, to upset it without an alternative is to compound the evil. Thanks to Fifty's reckless fervor, society is worse off than before.

Though he discredits human willingness to conform as a key to utopia, Canetti does demonstrate that individual will is the key to freedom from totalitarian oppression. The success of the rebels Henry Breeze and Fifty makes the endings of Zamiatin's *We* and Orwell's *1984* seem less gloomy, for such individuals as D-503 and I-330, Winston Smith and Julia at least have the capacity to feel skepticism towards authority. Huxley's society is far more monstrous, for its people believe that they are already happy and thus they will never dream of rebellion. If Canetti is right, the Zamiatin and Orwell rebels are not aberrations in their societies, but symptoms of a ground swell which must ultimately engulf and eradicate their oppressors. The swiftness with which Eastern European regimes have fallen in recent years would seem to validate Canetti's vision. (pp. 69-73)

Ralph Willingham, "Dystopian Visions in the Plays of Elias Canetti," in Science-Fiction Studies, *Vol. 19, No. 1, March, 1992, pp. 69-74.*

FURTHER READING

Biography

Rosenfeld, Sidney. "1981 Nobel Laureate Elias Canetti: A Writer Apart." *World Literature Today* 56, No. 1 (Winter 1982): 5-9.
    Overview of Canetti's life and career.

Criticism

Barnouw, Dagmar. "Mind and Myth in *Masse und Macht.*" *Modern Austrian Literature* 16, Nos. 3-4 (1983): 65-79.
    Discusses Canetti's use of myth to explain crowd psychology in his nonfiction and the influence of his psychological studies upon the portrayal of characters in his fiction and plays.

Cohen, Yaier. "Elias Canetti: Exile and the German Language." *German Life and Letters* XLII, No. 1 (October 1988): 32-48.
    Examines Canetti's relationship with his "spiritual language," German.

Demet, Michel-François. "The Theme of Blood in Elias Canetti's *Die Blendung.*" *Modern Austrian Literature* 16, Nos. 3-4 (1983): 147-53.

Explores the symbolism of blood imagery in Canetti's novel.

Durzak, Manfred. "From Dialect-Play to Philosophical Parable: Elias Canetti in Exile." In *Protest—Form—Tradition: Essays on German Exile Literature,* edited by Joseph P. Strelka, Robert F. Bell, and Eugene Dobson, pp. 35-56. University: The University of Alabama Press, 1979.

> Contemplates Canetti's place in the literary tradition of World War II and postwar European exiles.

Essays in Honor of Elias Canetti. Translated by Michael Hulse. New York: Farrar, Straus, and Giroux, 1987, 322 p.

> Festschrift containing studies, reviews, and appreciations of Canetti's life and works.

Hinderberger-Burton, Tania. "The Quixotic in Canetti's *Die Blendung.*" *Modern Austrian Literature* 16, Nos. 3-4 (1983): 165-76.

> Compares Canetti's character Peter Kien with Miguel de Cervantes's Don Quixote.

Karst, Roman. "Elias Canetti's *Die Blendung:* A Study in Insanity." *Modern Austrian Literature* 16, Nos. 3-4 (1983): 133-145.

> Maintains that Canetti's novel is a pioneering work which treats madness as "a phenomenon in which the deepest truth of man is hidden."

Russell, Peter. "The Vision of Man in Elias Canetti's *Die Blendung.*" *German Life and Letters* XXVIII, No. 1 (October 1974): 24-35.

> Finds *Die Blendung* "seriously deficient" in its portrayal of human nature.

Schmidt, Hugo. "Narrative Attitudes in Canetti's *Die Blendung.*" *Modern Austrian Literature* 16, Nos. 3-4 (1983): 93-109.

> Scrutinizes Canetti's narrative devices.

Sokel, Walter H. "The Ambiguity of Madness: Elias Canetti's Novel *Die Blendung.*" In *Views and Reviews of Modern German Literature: Festschrift for Adolf D. Klarmann,* edited by Karl S. Weimar, pp. 181-87. München: Delp Verlag, 1974.

> Argues that insanity as portrayed in *Die Blendung* represents both the ultimate individuality and the eradication of the individual.

Steiner, George. "A Tale of Three Cities." *The New Yorker* LVIII, No. 40 (22 November 1982): 186, 188, 191-95.

> Positive review of *The Torch in My Ear* in which Steiner provides an overview of Canetti's life.

Zorach, Cecile C. "The Outsider Abroad: Canetti in Marrakesh." *Modern Austrian Literature* 16, Nos. 3-4 (1983): 47-64.

> Analyzes Canetti's departures from the conventions of travel writing in his *The Voices of Marrakesh: A Record of a Visit.*

Additional coverage of Canetti's life and career is contained in the following sources published by Gale Research: *Contemporary Authors,* Vols. 21-24, rev. ed.; *Contemporary Authors New Revision Series,* Vol. 23; *Contemporary Literary Criticism,* Vols. 3, 14, 25; *Dictionary of Literary Biography,* Vol. 85; and *Major 20th-Century Authors.*

Fernand Crommelynck

1885-1970

Belgian playwright.

The following entry provides an overview of Crommelynck's career.

INTRODUCTION

Best known for *Le cocu magnifique* (*The Magnificent Cuckold*), Crommelynck wrote plays in which he depicted humanity's propensity for illusions and the destructive nature of such personality traits as avarice and jealousy. Described as a mixture of cynicism, comedy, and tragedy, Crommelynck's work exhibits many typical elements of the farce, including crowd scenes, extravagant plots, physical violence, and pantomime. While some critics have attacked Crommelynck for the coarseness of his language and plots, most have praised him as a major force in the development of modern French drama.

Crommelynck was born in Paris. Expressing an early fascination with the theater and a hatred for the constraints of formal education, he spent much of his early youth roaming the backstreets of Montmartre and frequenting the theaters and cabarets in which his father, an actor, performed. At the age of fourteen Crommelynck began his own career in the theater with his acting debut at the Bouffes Parisiens. Soon afterward his family moved to Brussels, where in 1906 he published two works in a Belgian magazine: a one-act version of *Le sculpteur de masques* (*The Sculptor of Masks*) and "Clématyde," a short story with macabre and erotic overtones. That year also marked the first production of *Nous n'irons plus au bois*, a pastoral comedy that demonstrated his talent for arresting dialogue. While living in Ostend, Crommelynck met James Ensor, a Belgian artist whose grotesque paintings of masks influenced Crommelynck's work. In his succeeding plays, such as *Le marchand de regrets* and *Les amants puérils*, Crommelynck used masks to portray fantastic, nonhuman characters. In 1916 Crommelynck established the Flying-Theater, an acting company that performed plays in Brussels until insufficient finances forced the troupe to disband two years later.

With the 1920 Paris production of *The Magnificent Cuckold*, Crommelynck achieved his greatest popular success. In the five plays that Crommelynck wrote between 1920 and 1934 he attacked the values and constraints of society and continued to refine his style, a bizarre mix of slapstick comedy, satire, and tragedy. After 1934 Crommelynck produced relatively few works. During World War II he lived in Paris and then Brussels, where he served as director of the Théâtre des Galeries. In 1954 Crommelynck wrote *Le chevalier à la lune ou Sir John Falstaff de William Shakespeare*, an adaptation of Shakespeare's *Henry*

IV, which focuses on the character of Sir John Falstaff, whom Crommelynck considered the quintessential comic figure. Crommelynck died in 1970.

Three subjects dominate Crommelynck's dramas: destructive personality traits, sexuality, and the nature of society. In such plays as *The Magnificent Cuckold* and *Tripes d'or*, Crommelynck chronicled the death or descent into insanity of an individual who embodies a particular character flaw. In *Tripes d'or* the miser Pierre-Auguste Hormidas is so consumed by avarice that he eats his gold and dies from constipation. In *The Magnificent Cuckold* the character Bruno is also the victim of an overwhelming obsession. Doubting the fidelity of his wife Stella, he forces her to sleep with various men in order to determine with whom she has been unfaithful. Although Bruno's plan fails to substantiate his original concerns about her fidelity, Stella is unable to endure her husband's mistrust and leaves him for one of the other men. Critics have noted that Crommelynck's emphasis on a single personality trait, rather than the overall psychology of an individual, illustrates the influence of German Expressionist drama, which often exaggerated particular psychological qualities in a character.

Crommelynck addressed some aspect of sexuality in all of

his plays. He portrayed the consequences of sexual repression in *The Sculptor of Masks* and depicted voyeurism and other sexual perversions in *The Magnificent Cuckold.* Critics have also noted a fundamental conflict between Crommelynck's male and female characters, who fail to communicate with each other. In several plays Crommelynck satirized various aspects of society, particularly those related to religion. In *Chaud et froid ou l'idée de Monsieur Dom,* a religious movement develops around the memory of Monsieur Dom, a drab, prosaic person who, according to a story fabricated by his mistress, had an "idea" on his deathbed. Critics contend that *Chaud et froid* reveals Crommelynck's belief that society needs myths to provide structure and security but that these myths are essentially false.

Despite their humor, Crommelynck's plays are often characterized as pessimistic, with critics arguing that he tends to debase his characters without redeeming them. As Bettina Knapp has observed: "There are no heroes in Crommelynck's plays; his characters represent a carnival of human folly in which man's vanity, egotism, and cruelty are brought forth in all of their disquieting grandeur."

PRINCIPAL WORKS

Nous n'irons plus au bois (drama) 1906
Chacun pour soi (drama) [first publication] 1907
Le sculpteur de masques (drama) 1911
   [*The Sculptor of Masks,* 1982]
Le marchand de regrets (drama) 1913
Le cocu magnifique (drama) 1920
   [*The Magnificent Cuckold,* 1966]
Les amants puérils (drama) 1921
Tripes d'or (drama) 1925
Carine ou la jeune fille folle de son âme (drama) 1929
Chaud et froid ou l'idée de Monsieur Dom (drama)
   1934
Une femme qu'a le coeur trop petit (drama) 1934
*Le chevalier à la lune ou Sir John Falstaff de William
   Shakespeare* (drama) [first publication] 1954
Théâtre. 3 vols. (dramas) 1967-68

CRITICISM

Ashley Dukes (essay date 1923)

[*Dukes was an important English dramatist and drama critic during the first half of the twentieth century. He is most noted for his writings on modern European theater, particularly poetic drama. He had a broad knowledge of continental drama and, both as a translator and as the manager of his own theater, introduced English audiences to the work of several important French and* German *dramatists, including Ernst Toller, Georg Kaiser, and Lion Feuchtwanger. In the following excerpt, he praises Crommelynck for enlarging the scope of the traditional French sex drama.*]

It is the fashion to say of plays like *Le Cocu Magnifique* that they are vastly entertaining, but their subject will not bear analysis in the cold light of the English language. We must leave them, it is urged, to our Gallic cousins, who have so graceful a gift for the handling of impropriety. It would be a crime to translate such scandalous persiflage into terms of reason; and so forth and so forth. Now this is the greatest nonsense that ever served to fill ten lines of a newspaper column. If a work of art has any meaning, that meaning can be decently expressed and universally understood. The English language is as good as the French language, and cuckold is as good a word as its equivalent, and *The Magnanimous Cuckold* is as good a title as any comedy can hope to bear. Let us, therefore, look at M. Crommelynck's play with the unprejudiced eyes proper to a nation that possesses not only the finest but the coarsest dramatic literature in the world. It may reasonably be conjectured that however scandalous the plot and however shocking the dialogue, they will not compare with those of the old English plays revived by the Phœnix Society. But first let us look into the question of the drama of sex in general.

It is a question concerning which the French are obstinately conservative. With them savagery and the social equality of the sexes go hand in hand. With them pornography and high comedy hob-nob together, and the grossest cynicism is matched by the most dishevelled sentiment. The wittiest scenes of contemporary French comedy have not a word in them that might not have been written by Henry Becque in 1880, or for that matter by Molière in 1650, while the sentimental scenes appear to have been lifted bodily from the stage of the younger Dumas. Where men and women are concerned this drama changes as little as do the young ladies of *La Vie Parisienne* with their roseate insipidity and flagrant disarray.

The tradition is in part excellent and in part despicable; but it must be exceedingly hard for a French author to write a comedy of marriage when he reflects that all the dramatists of his native theatre have said the same thing about the subject. If there be any advantage of originality, it lies with the older and not with the younger school. Some of the youngest writers, like MM. Duhamel and Vildrac, refuse to mount the treadmill of convention. They seek for subjects in which, if the sexual interest be not entirely eliminated, it plays at least a secondary part. This is an evasion that carries with it a certain conscious weakness. On the other hand, M. Crommelynck accepts the old tradition and proceeds boldly to enlarge its scope. *Le Cocu Magnifique* and *Les Amants Puérils*—these are the chosen titles of an author who takes the comedy of sex at its face value and yet laughs heartily at the imposture. He is no realist. By placing the scene of his action "des nos jours en Flandre" he achieves a singular detachment. We can believe anything of these Flemings, whose babes are surely as rosy as Rubens cherubs and whose skies luminous as the backgrounds of "Velvet" Brueghel. The inexhaustible generative force of Nature is in this people. They inhale exuberance from their flax-fields and cruelty from their cattle. When Bruno, the cuckold, points out the beauties of his wife's form, he falls naturally into a lyrical and Rabelaisian profusion:—

> Et c'est une ligne, celle-ci, une seule ligne! Et il y en a mille comme elle, cent mille, que dis-je? mille milliards de lignes selon que je tourne autour de ce modèle unique, chacune aussi parfaite, et qui toutes, en faisceaux réunies, festonnées, volutées, onduleuses, droites ou contournées, grasses ou déliées, jaillissantes ou retombantes, vibrantes ou reposées, longues ou ramassées, roulées, ondées, frisées, nouées, distendues, dévidées, fouettantes ou pleuvantes, cinglantes ou pleureuses, ou caressantes, ou tremblées, ou vaguelées, en spire, en hélice, en torsade, l'une après l'autre ou ensemble, ces lignes-la n'ont qu' une trajectoire, une seule, qui porte l'amour dans mon cœur!

This is no ordinary language; but Bruno is no ordinary man. He is a dweller in a windmill. He is composer-in-chief of love-letters to an illiterate peasantry, who pay him twenty *sous* apiece for his effusions. He is adviser-in-chief to the mayor in delicate questions of public policy. He is the chief character of the countryside; his doings are the talk of every fair. He is a well of jocundity, a fountain of high spirits, a volcano of human nature in active eruption. When such a man doubts the honour of his wife the affair is portentous. The rankling uncertainty in which other husbands live is intolerable to him. He must have knowledge at whatever cost:

> BRUNO. J'ai le remède a ce doute, le remède absolu, immediat, la panacée universelle: pour ne plus douter de ta fidélité, que je sois certain de ton infidélité! . . . Tu me tromperas donc aujourd' hui, sous mon toit. . . . Un mari doit être cocu, inévitablement, et je veux l'être. Il n'y a pas de remission. Le ridicule et la souffrance naissent de l'ignorance et du doute. Je serai instruit de mon infortune et je le serai le premier. Pas de compromis, je serai cocu ce jour-même ou je serai mort. Les cornes ou la corde!

He throws his wife into the arms of his friend Pétrus, and is instantly consumed with jealousy. He loads a gun to shoot the pair of them; his frenzied shouts bring the mayor to the house at the head of a throng of villagers. He declares himself cuckolded and receives the tactful condolences of the civic power. But when his wife and friend reappear, the instincts of the immemorial husband are too much for him. His cry is "Ah! ah! la bonne farce! Ils veulent m'en faire accroire!" They are trying to frighten him, he declares; he'll not believe a word of it. The unhappy Stella is reduced to convincing him not only with Pétrus, but with Tom, Dick and Harry. She is pursued by joyous hordes of swains, she is execrated by all good wives and maids. Still Bruno will not believe; still he looks for one unknown lover among the men who surround her. He disguises himself and comes to her as a serenader, and she, who no longer loves him, is about to yield when the house is raided by indignant matrons seeking their missing menfolk. Stella is ducked in the river, and she returns clad in the cloak of the herdsman who is the most vigorous of her

suitors. The herdsman has sworn to share her with nobody, not even with her husband. She boxes his ears, and Bruno, who is listening, observes "C'est lui, c'est donc lui!" The blows are proof for him that this is the unknown lover. But when Stella begs the herdsman to assure her that she will be able to be faithful to him, Bruno cries, "Ah, non, non, pas si sot! C'est encore un de ses tours! Tu ne m'y prendras plus!" His magnanimity is sustained to the end.

Imagine these personages transferred to the drawing-room, and you have one of the hundred polite and weary comedies of sex—such a comedy as Capus or Donnay or François de Curel might have written. M. Crommelynck, who abandons the plane of realism and seeks for the ludicrous essentials of his situation, escapes at the same time from the urbanity and the lassitude of these contemporaries. His *reductio ad absurdum* of the sexual motive imparts a new vigour to the theme. His comedy is cruel and grandiloquent, but it is elemental. The sap of nature runs in this tree that leans against the wind of Flanders and casts a fantastic shadow on the plain. (pp. 85-90)

Ashley Dukes, "Comedians," in his The Youngest Drama: Studies of Fifty Dramatists, *Ernest Benn, Limited, 1923, pp. 85-106.*

Charles Morgan   (review date September 1932)

[*An English novelist, essayist, and dramatist, Morgan was the chief drama critic for the London* Times *from 1926 to 1939. In his fiction, he emphasized the transcendence of violence and the triumph of the good and the beautiful. Morgan believed that art should be a spiritual experience that reaffirms human values as it penetrates appearances to reveal ideal beauty, which he considered an aspect of God. In the following review, he gives* Le cocu magnifique *a mixed assessment.*]

Le Cocu Magnifique is a play of fluid violence that will beget in its audiences, if it proceeds beyond the Stage Society's performance, excessive praise and excessive antagonism. There is no good reason in Monsieur Crommelynck's work itself for rushing to either extreme, for, though it is a bold and interesting experiment in theatrical method, it has not behind its bludgeoning assault the strength to wound deeply nor, in its many ingenuities of symbolism, the wisdom to create an enduring delight. Perceiving this, we do well to be moderate in judgment of it—or as moderate as our temperament permits. The play's power of provocation is greater than its substance. Those who found much to their taste in its cruel humours or were able to discover pleasure in its perpetual leaping between tragedy and farce may yet beware how they proclaim a masterpiece; and those of us who were less fortunate may, if we are urged to attack, recognize that it is, perhaps, our own temperament as much as the play's demerit that urges us. To say that the thing is Maeterlinck without beauty and Strindberg without genius may be to express too personal a repulsion.

Charles Morgan, in a review of "Le Cocu Magnifique," in Theatre Arts Monthly, *Vol. XVI, No. 9, September, 1932, p. 714.*

David I. Grossvogel   (essay date 1958)

[*An American educator, Grossvogel has written extensively on French drama. In the following excerpt from a chapter that first appeared in his* The Self-Conscious Stage in Modern French Drama *(1958), Grossvogel analyzes the themes, characters, and language of Crommelynck's plays.*]

By the time [Fernand Crommelynck] was twenty he had already written three successful plays. In chronological order of publication, these were *Nous n'irons plus au bois* (1906), *Chacun pour soi* (1907), and the first version of *Le Sculpteur de masques* (1908). André Berger (*A la rencontre de Fernand Crommelynck,* 1947), in an endeavor to dispel some of "the bitter northern mists" with which André Bellessort has associated Crommelynck (*Le Plaisir du théâtre,* 1938), omits mention of *Le Sculpteur de masques* in order to point out that the author's very first play is a lighthearted *bluette* utterly devoid of gloom or philosophy. True, *Nous n'irons plus au bois* is a *bluette* and, admittedly, Crommelynck's next play is a farce with no underlying design, whose types and situations appear to imitate Molière while its language and tone sometimes recall Marivaux. However, it seems that if one is to speak of the author's initial endeavors, one cannot omit *Le Sculpteur de masques* (called by the author *symbole tragique*) which, notwithstanding its date of publication, was written in 1905. Even if some light piece should antedate this drama, it might well be remembered that at twenty the author was already preoccupied by the horror upon which laughing masks brood.

That by 1905 Crommelynck had definitely conceived laughter to be as huge, as grotesque, and as superficial as the mask, is confirmed by the fact that three years later, he expanded his one-act tragic symbol into a full-length play, and that his succeeding work, *Le Marchand de regrets* (1913), overshadows laughter with mysticism and human suffering, though at first glance the plot appears to be that of a farce. The *marchand* is an antiquary more in love with his antiques than with his young wife. The young woman ultimately elopes with the village miller. But there is a crime: the antiquary kills his pandering neighbor and *Le Marchand de regrets* acquires the fuller meaning of its tragic title.

Such had been the texture of Crommelynck's plots and people when his next play burst upon the stages of Europe. *Le Cocu magnifique* (1920), "Farce in three acts," was to link Crommelynck's name with that genre—though it is noteworthy of changing times that Hébertot's first postwar *reprise* (December 31, 1945) made it a *pièce triste.* Bruno, village scribe and poet, is in love with, and loved by, his wife, the simple, pristine Stella. One day, the malignant virus of jealousy grips him. In order to relieve suspicions that soon dwell in him stronger than any other feeling, he forces Stella into the arms of every male villager in the hope of discovering *the* figment that obsesses him. He ends by losing Stella completely though still believing, as she is carried out the door, that this is merely another trick to hide from him the "real one." Such a plot, superficially related or superficially treated, would be little more than an ordinary farce. The caricature which the ageless

Bruno has become by the end of the play is gross portrayal also. (When a hero's hair turns grey, it is usually an invisible function of tragedy; should he lose his hair completely, in sight of the audience, a farcical note has been injected, though both changes may be due to identical emotions.) Still, no one placed within the play can forget that every line distorting Bruno's face is incised by pain.

Lest anyone be misled by Stella's poetry and the sincerity of her love, Romanie, her old *nourrice,* early in the first act clouts the *bouvier,* Stella's first suitor and her ultimate one, to remind the spectator that blow-dealing leaves no marks upon the tough surface of the Farce. This is the first bastinado, a common activity on Crommelynck's stage. There are others later in the play, when wrathful village women belabor one of Stella's numerous lovers, but by this time something of the play's harshness has gone into their blows and Farce has verged on drama.

This element of bitterness communicates itself to, and redeems, many of the comic props. Those who escape and remain simple creatures of laughter are the unregenerate, the occasional characters on whom tragedy has no grip because they have been drawn as mechanical agents of mirth with no further purpose. Such is the *bourgmestre* who reappears often in Crommelynck casts, generally endowed with the braggadocio, cowardice, venality, and stupidity which are the traditional Farce attributes of officialdom.

Types such as these pursue their course with no regard to, with no comprehension of, the latent tragedy building up about them. Their surface is scrupulously realistic but houses no soul. They are, however, rare. Estrugo, Bruno's secretary, is awkward and funny when he must resort to pantomime, pressed for words which, in him, are always too slow in coming. At such times he is a clown. However, when his silence becomes fuel for the suspicions of Bruno, he unwittingly grows to demoniacal stature. The pains which the author has taken to paint him as "Bruno's double" suggest Iago living within the body of Othello. The comic symbol need not represent only those whose meaninglessness makes them amusing. Through his character, or through the situation in which he has been placed, a stage personage builds up an expectation of superficial emotions, actions, or words, which he then abruptly shatters according to the laws of some inner consonance. This sudden departure from what had been anticipated—and usually the departure is from the falsely sublime to the very prosaic—brings about a twist which is humorous and which, because it is so disrespectful of the elevated tone it interrupts, can act but as a comic trigger, very similar to Herbert Spencer's "descending incongruity."

The character, however, has not been necessarily robbed of a more essential fiber which the audience had singled out in him and which will lead him, or the over-all action, to a grimly significant and wholly acceptable conclusion. When Bruno, obsessed by his monomania, is warned by the *bourgmestre* that the whole village is after his wife, Bruno's persistence in his dementia might lend deep tragedy to his reply. Crommelynck, nevertheless, turns it into a farce speech by the tone and words used: "Ah . . . Oh! wild imagination. What will they invent next? *Bourgmestre,* your mind is as flat and as twitching as a monkey's ass. Begging your pardon, begging your pardon!" And thereafter, the author abets his comic figure of tragedy with the aid of the genuine Farce type, the official, who rises deeply stung to mimic and speak the following retort: "To a magistrate! (*He looks around him in fear. No one. He feels better.*) Mum's the word!"

Likewise, the tone of the Farce, that is to say the use of vernacular for humorous effect, frequently dominates the poetic language, spoken in this play chiefly by Stella and Bruno. The mob scenes, the choruses of men and women that enter towards the end of the play, are frankly crude and reminiscent of the similar scenes which Peter Breughel once painted. The difference between Crommelynck's and Breughel's colorful, lusty mobs is that they are agents of sorrow in the scenes of the Belgian playwright, a suggestion not always apparent in his compatriot's canvases.

Some of, or all, these superficial disguises of tragedy come back in Crommelynck's succeeding plays, though their paucity in *Les Amants puérils,* which he staged during the following year (1921), suggests that this play might have been conceived earlier. Yet even here, in this somber drama concerned wholly with the incommunicability of souls, Crommelynck uses comic characters. Such are the servants, notably Zulma with her heavy, naïve laughter, and old Quasiment, whose deafness occasions amusing pantomime. There is also a coarse, carnal tone, much more pertinent to Farce than to tragedy, and again it is granted to those traditional comic heirs—the servants.

Tripes d'or (1925) has often been linked to Molière's *L'Avare.* The link is slender: both plays deal with avarice, one of the oldest Farce themes, and through the intensity of the drama they convey, both have soared beyond the realm of mere laughter. The dramatic impact of Crommelynck's play does not prevent, once more, the comic elements from dominating. The very ludicrousness of the situation stamps the work as Farce. Pierre-Auguste Hormidas (the names of the main characters are frequently meaningful) inherits a fortune which soon becomes the cause of his nightmares and his insanity. Barbulesque, the cosmically wise horse-doctor who attends him, advises him to eat his gold as a cure. After a month's constipation, Pierre-Auguste can no longer keep the gold in his system and he dies—the masque of comedy has become death mask.

Clearly, such a plot is symbolistic, but the author has given the symbols humble life by placing their acts under the aegis of Folly, and one must fall back on the conventional *bourgmestre* for harmless fun. Beneath their superficial insanity, these people exhibit fiendish implacability and coldness in their acts, "logical as only madmen can be," in the words of Maurice Coindreau (*La Farce est jouée,* 1942). When Pierre-Auguste's manservant Muscar, whose name and cruelty are reminiscent of Ben Jonson's Mosca, brandishes a whip, he sends a chill through cast and audience, for there are tales of murder about him, rampant even before the play is fully under way. Froumence, Muscar's wife, the clairvoyant chorus whose insights are penetrating to the point of discomfort, becomes the nearly monstrous conscience of Pierre-Auguste.

In line with the rest, Barbulesque, the veterinary in attendance on the hero, is revealed early in the play to be as broadly omniscient as the Knock of Jules Romains. After narrowly skirting satire throughout the first two acts, he assumes cosmic significance at the last when he rises before the dying Pierre-Auguste, and "burlesquing a terrible menace," exposes in a horrendous version of Creation the futility of men's acts.

In spite of the otherworldly implications of these characters and their inevitable didacticism, Crommelynck has been very careful to remain *terre à terre* in most of his scenes (even relieving Barbulesque's rather terrifying apocalyptical speech with the image of "millions of little Adams fornicating throughout the world"). Where he might have had Pierre-Auguste eating his gold pieces as such, thereby placing the scene in a symbolic light, he makes the hero grind each piece into fine powder which he eats with a hash—the dog's, incidentally. Such painstaking realism preserves in the most meaningful moments a caricatural surface: insignificant details are magnified while the substance of the theme is understated.

Furthermore, faithful to his method, Crommelynck inserts fun into moments of greatest pathos. At the height of his agony, Pierre-Auguste makes puns. Talking of the gold he has kept in him for a whole month, he blurts out, sobbing, "And now I can hold out no longer. The microbes are waging, with modern weapons, an intestine war."

But the true quality of these people's laughter becomes apparent when contrasted with that of the unalloyed Farce character, the customary *bourgmestre,* in scenes such as that during which, trimming by trimming, he is bribed into performing a marriage by proxy for the price of a handsome uniform. However, his is indeed a feeble voice in the mad chorus assembled here by Crommelynck.

Carine, ou La Jeune Fille folle de son âme (1929) is not a comedy. The play is about a young girl who says, "I do not believe that there is a single natural thing in the world into which candor might not enter," and who dies when the brutal coarseness of the world finally breaks through to her. This brooding drama affords a glimpse of the self-conscious author unable to curb the superficial strain of his mockery even though the heavy gloom of the drama makes it an awkward echo. Flippant language burlesques the speech of many of the characters, if not that of the two protagonists, though the characters be normally as disquieting as the ominous and sexually perverted uncle whose veiled and symbolic speeches contain discordantly humorous fillips. Such language would not be called for usually in a play as intensely tragic as this one. However, it echoes distantly the farcical types that do circulate even here, such as the servants or some of the sillier young girls.

Even the sentence that Carine speaks about her young husband Frédéric, "Frédéric is not a man," though it is innocent in her mouth, soon becomes fraught with more lurid meaning when bruited about by a girl friend, and acquires singular resonance in that the misunderstanding which it brings about starts the fatal unwinding of the tragedy. The *quid pro quo* in tragedy, the tablets in *Hippol-*

ytus, like the handkerchief in *Othello,* even if unseen, have the credible substance of tangible objects. It is more typical of the Farce that a similar mechanism be, if not unbelievably real, at least close to the shallow pun if it is not to jar the Farce tone.

By contrast with the semi-caricatures around them, the realistic Carine and Frédéric occasionally sound awkward and ultimately unreal. Divested of all humorous attributes, they have become overstatements of purity and this exaggerated realism makes them morbid counterparts of the missing *bourgmestre.* Crommelynck experiences here some of the difficulties that were to beset Giraudoux and Anouilh a few years later.

Thus, the lack of tonal unity by which Crommelynck had hoped to single out his heroes creates an unpleasant dissonance and frustrates the communion intended. A Farce character can be accepted as real no matter what his exterior if his fundamental conflicts are accepted, but a soul too heavily swelled with its own pathos remains a vulnerable target for the pin pricks of his Farce associates. Stylized figures of unrelieved tragedy must dwell on their own stage if the spectator is not to be encouraged to throw them off the precarious pedestals which they would assume on a stage that also allowed comedy.

With *Une Femme qu'a le cœur trop petit* (1934), Crommelynck turns the subject of *Carine* inside out and gives the Farce aspects freer rein. If these are less assertive than in either *Le Cocu magnifique* or *Tripes d'or,* it is because there is no tragic vein in this comedy, and the whole tone being subdued, the Farce, which needs the full ferocity of tragedy to maintain its exacerbated pitch, will be perforce paler also.

The situation is, however, farcical, for attempts to unbend a prudish woman are bound to be humorous if successful. Crommelynck has turned even the prudery of Balbine into farce, since it is on this account that the servants are driven to concupiscence, her solidly constituted husband to hypochondria, and her stepdaughter to marry her timid lover. Balbine dresses her evidently indecently exposed servant Minna, thereby repeating in her own household the trouble that followed upon the original sin. Her steadfastly puritanical demureness makes her husband conscious of his age and starts him taking his temperature. She confuses Patricia's romantic lucubrations with threats of seduction and drives her into the arms of the agronomist who would have been too shy to act of his own accord.

The comic situation is granted echoes of Molière in the two servants, Minna and Xantus, and, as usual, the Farce actuates what little drama will be vouchsafed this play:

> BALBINE. Stand straight! There, you see: your knees are frowning at me.
>
> MINNA. Frowning, my knees?—Oh, no, Madam, I beg of you.
>
> BALBINE. And you have nothing under that dress.
>
> MINNA. I have nothing under that dress, I?

> BALBINE. Nothing at all, my poor child.
>
> MINNA. (*proudly*) Nothing at all? Oh, yes, Madam, I have what it takes!
>
> BALBINE. What did you say?
>
> MINNA. I beg Madam's pardon—I have what it takes, under my dress.
>
> BALBINE. (*surprised*) What "what it takes"?
>
> MINNA. (*overflowing with pride*) Yes, Madam— but I have my innocence!

And at this point, Balbine who finally understands, faints, revealing her physical (and symbolic) weakness: a heart too small to countenance the fuller implications of life. However, in spite of these Farce devices, and others, such as the pantomime scenes enacted by the servants, and that performed by Balbine herself, the archhousekeeper who goes about her chores even while sleepwalking, this same Balbine, never wholly farcical, never wholly tragic, sets the tone of this mild comedy. The Farce crackles throughout, but never sufficiently to kindle significant action.

With *Chaud et Froid, ou L'Idée de Monsieur Dom* (1934), Fernand Crommelynck seemed to reach his apogee. Here are blended elements of Farce, satire, and drama in the story of an adulterous wife who is compelled after her husband's death to become a vestal to his memory. When Mr. Dom dies, and he does so early enough never to be seen, his wife Léona discovers that he had had a mistress. She is crushed when she further finds that this man, who was nearly an abstraction to her, loved another woman enough to find in himself unsuspected lyricism, images such as "Félie, your eyes are longer than the days in June, longer than even happy memories," or, "Your eyes, when nearly closed, just like a soft horizon, eternize the gentle sadness of a subtle twilight," which first stagger Léona and then start torturing her.

Meanwhile, Alix, the abnormal servant-girl of Léona, spreads the rumor that Mr. Dom died mumbling, "I have an idea." This "spiritual legacy" is pounced on by the *bourgmestre* and other leaders of the community, with the result that the colorless Mr. Dom starts living a truly epic life the minute he is dead. Humiliated, frustrated, Léona finds herself trapped between the intense public life that has suddenly been conferred upon her husband in the form of political factions vying for the support of his "idea," and his just as suddenly revealed private life personified by her husband's mistress, Félie. This dual development has been blamed by many critics, namely Bellessort (*Le Plaisir du théâtre*) as plot-padding. But Léona must be driven ultimately to the pathetic expedient of convincing others, if not herself, that her husband's lovewords to Félie were really addressed to her. In order to achieve this denouement, Léona's jealousy and her frustration must first be exacerbated. This can happen only if Mr. Dom becomes formidably real after his death, a man of sufficient stature and sufficiently alive to flog Léona with humiliation she cannot return. The Farce lining of this drama confers that grandeur upon Mr. Dom and its non-farcical significance forces his wife into the submission which this ironic drama demands.

Notwithstanding the secondary motor-plot, the play escapes Farce appellation. The mental form of the humor and of its implications make this high comedy. But harmonious integration of the forms sprinkles Farce situations and types throughout the action. Relying solely on the stupidity of the official, Crommelynck has created here his most comic *bourgmestre*—a slow-witted individual whose laboriously contrived sentences are usually open to amusing innuendos. He is the inadequate character who is unwittingly drawn into the growth of the "idea" whose birth is reminiscent of a similar one in Jules Romains's *Donogoo:*

> ALIX. He is repeating softly: "I have an idea. . . I have an idea . . ." (*Amazement. Alix leaves. The men look at each other, astonished.*)
>
> EVERYONE. (*on every sort of note*) An idea? An idea? An idea?
>
> BELLEMASSE. (*laughs mockingly*) Mister Dom's idea? Ha! ha! ha! can you imagine that?
>
> THE BOURGMESTRE. Who can tell?
>
> BELLEMASSE. It would be properly his first one and his last.
>
> THE BOURGMESTRE. We must unfortunately admit that he belonged to no clan, to no group . . .
>
> BELLEMASSE. . . . to no party.
>
> THIERRY. (*brutal, all of a sudden*) Not to yours, assuredly!
>
> BELLEMASSE. (*pale with rage*) Not to yours, assuredly!
>
> THIERRY. (wild) My party!!
>
> BELLEMASSE. My party!!! You old cocoon!
>
> THIERRY. You dung-beetle's crap!
>
> BELLEMASSE. You fart's skin!
>
> THIERRY. You rabbit's leavings! You jaundiced excrement!
>
> BELLEMASSE. You moth dust! You microbe's rump!!!
>
> THE BOURGMESTRE. (*moves between them, arms upraised, indignant*) Gentlemen!!! (*The pitch has so risen that the Bourgmestre intervenes. He takes from his pocket a small, golden bell, whose ring is shrill and tiny, and shakes it frantically. This minor melodic shower seems so unusual that it calms the antagonists, as if by miracle.*)

And after this reminder of Métaphraste's bell in Molière's *Dépit amoureux,* the second-act curtain will come down on this note of mock exaltation:

> THE BOURGMESTRE. (*calls*) Amédée-Jacques-Louis Dom!
>
> ALL THE OTHERS. (*together*) Here!

> THE BOURGMESTRE. (*exalted*) Amédée-Jacques-Louis Dom!
>
> ALL THE OTHERS. Here!!!

These are instances of Farce seeking the fun of its caricature in a stylization that affords it, nevertheless, crude realism. However, that same fun has more somber extensions. When in the concluding moments of the play, Léona, who has alienated Félie's affection for Dom by forcing her own lover upon Félie, quotes to Alix a sentence purloined from Félie's love affair: "Do you know, one afternoon, we were running together on the meadow, and as I was gaining on him, he shouted to me 'Léona, you are cheating, your feet do not touch ground!' " Alix's answer is grossly amusing: "You were walking on your hands, of course." But it is this same abnormal servant in whom are detected undertones of sexual irregularity and a devotion to her mistress which is more like possessiveness—this same Alix brings the curtain down upon an obviously pathetic Léona who has stolen only an illusion and who stands bereft of all but this empty token, with the words, "Yes, yes, you are his entirely."

What might be said about this play can apply in general to the theater of Crommelynck. Here, the very deep frustration of a central figure has been drawn from the broader element of the comedy, just as elsewhere a deep suffering ultimately is differentiated from the Farce setting. The plays of Crommelynck recall the fine, feminine hands Rodin has carved and polished out of the coarse stone which he left rough-hewn for contrast.

A carnal obsession lies at the core of Crommelynck's drama—in the words of Léon Ruth ("Fernand Crommelynck," 1922): "Everything in him is translated through the senses or mysticism." Although written in reference to **Les Amants puérils,** something of that appraisal is valid for the other plays as well. In **Carine,** one of the masks says: "What are you doing there, without a mask or coat? Come with me into the only world that is real—the world of faceless beings. No more brain, no more superfluous names! Good-bye, cares, torments of the mind, waiting and useless seeking. Put on your mask. Come to the park, come join the essential play of mankind!" This atmosphere fashions not only Carine's world but that of nearly every drama of Crommelynck from the earliest.

In **Le Sculpteur de masques,** written at twenty, the author had already sketched the hermetic nature of the protagonists in the larger carnal scene. Pascal has loved Magdeleine and now his own wife, Louison—Magdeleine's sister—is dying. Haunted by a sensuality which frustrates both art and sensitivity, Pascal dreams of a world that might integrate beauty and his own passionate drives. Presently, the symbol of temporal lusts, a drunken lot of bacchanals, breaks upon the scene. They are followed by a leper whose terrible isolation sets off the heavily voluptuous atmosphere. It is to this leper that Magdeleine's own seclusion and remorse finally draw her. But even that contact is not to be effected for their worlds are already sealed. Meanwhile Pascal, whose longing makes him a supreme outcast amidst the others, falls prey to his horrible masks that become the mad Erinyes of his despair.

Giacomo Antonini (*Il Teatro contemporaneo in Francia*, 1930) has seen in **Carine** the inability of human love to succeed, doomed as it is by the libido of man: the Italian critic could have found substantially the same thesis in Pascal's torment. He could have found it also in **Les Amants puérils** that anticipated **Carine** by nearly a decade. This was the undoing of Elisabeth de Groulingen grown old under her make-up and the veil of twilight in which she hides. A "stranger" loves the ideal mask of her, the flesh which he imagines:

> I have seen you dressed in wind, behind the silk of banners, between the clouds whose slow shadows stroke the ridge of the sea, and beneath the leaves of young poplars that trembled as you tremble against me, Elisabeth! It was you, I swear it, who danced upon the beach, in the transparent dress of the tumultuous sands. I have seen you a thousand times, reclining, warm, and altogether naked in the shadeless dunes.

But Elisabeth is old. The baron Cazou who is senile and broken was her lover in the days beyond time and its punishing. All the while, two children, Marie-Henriette and Walter, act out in counterpoint a similarly hopeless love story suggesting that the basic incommunicability of souls may be due to causes deeper than the barriers of the flesh.

The statement of this incommunicability is presumably more important than that of the flesh which is a mere vehicle. The flesh, although a latent presence in every play, will simply be used to describe different aspects of the failure of love, a frail agency, weaker than jealousy (**Le Cocu magnifique**), weaker than avarice (**Tripes d'or**), conceivably even weaker than fraud (**Chaud et Froid**). However, the vehicle has frequently obscured the statement. André Rouveyre ("*Carine,*" 1930), who could not find very much to salvage in Crommelynck ("Let him be exported as quickly as possible; that will be best,") saw the Belgian playwright's drama as "Solely an object of venereal functions [. . .] that gives its characters the shabby aspect of maniacal patrons in a bawdy house."

André Rouveyre was not allowing, in such condemnation, for one of the primary attributes of Farce that dates back to days when coarseness was accounted for by the greater intimacy then existing between art and life. This part of the theater is properly its own and escapes mental confines: it is the primal spectacle whose communion harks back to the days of a more essential drama. Referring to Bruno's exhibition of Stella to Pétrus, Léon Ruth ("Fernand Crommelynck," 1922), has said with scarcely disguised enjoyment: "Not only Pétrus, but the entire audience as well partakes at great length of this spectacle."

However, this element of immoderation before the problems of the flesh is also part of a greater excessiveness—and of it, the same Rouveyre has said (*"Le Cocu Magnifique,"* 1928): "The Crommelynck hero is, in a word, cracked, and cracked people are not funny on stage." This assertion calls for amplification and, especially, qualification.

Implicit in the remark is an admission that these characters are something more than mere vehicles for comedy since automata could not be disturbing. Those automata that do circulate on these boards are neither new, nor more debased than is the average subject of laughter. They are the servants, the *bourgmestres,* and occasional characters whose life-span is measured in terms of a few humorous cues. They are the recognizable descendants of the medieval Farce. They have no life of their own, they are stock characters, and for that reason could not be offensive even if they were actually "cracked."

Another category of Crommelynck personae comprises the tragic characters such as Pascal, Carine, or Elisabeth de Groulingen. These people never depart from the dignity which is a fundamental attribute of their flesh and blood reality. They never attempt therefore to create laughter, and can obviously not be the ones drawing Rouveyre's criticism. As noted, Farce context—if it exists for them— tends to rob them of their credibility: French authors such as Apollinaire and even Giraudoux had already experienced this.

In the third group are those mysterious hybrids, such as the *chasseur,* Carine's malevolent uncle, or the previously encountered Estrugo. They are obviously "real" people though their quiddity appears to be part of a vaster supernatural scheme. If they are crazy, they dominate their insanity and channel it with uncanny malignity. In them madness is not an oppression but a weapon.

The last, and most important body of characters in Crommelynck's dramatic roster, is made up of those true-to-life creations that go mad as the play progresses. These are the ones whom insanity subjugates—though to call them "cracked" is to indulge a hasty apriority that neither situates nor renders the true quality of their dementia. These, and the creatures in the third group, are presumably the ones that disturbed Rouveyre. They are Crommelynck's distinctive contribution to the theater, the types that recur most frequently in his later drama and consequently the ones that come to mind when one thinks of "the Crommelynck hero."

The hybrids, of whom it would be rash to say that they are actually mad, though they are clearly not "normal," have a symbolic value which accounts for the disproportionate shape they acquire at times and which might have been confused with madness by critics writing in 1928. Since that time they have become recognizable in contemporary drama thanks to certain of the mythological transpositions of Cocteau, Sartre, Giraudoux, etc. Notable in Crommelynck's work are Froumence, Barbulesque, the *chasseur,* and Estrugo.

Froumence, in **Tripes d'or,** starts out merely as Pierre-Auguste's very down-to-earth housekeeper. As Pierre-Auguste gradually grows more insane and more incoherent in his words, Froumence appears by contrast to be more and more tight-lipped and progressively more formidable, eventually towering over the insane hero as the silent but thundering voice of his conscience. She ultimately dominates the entire stage, making even the terrible Muscar, Pierre-Auguste's demoniacal shadow, cringe before his own whip which she now wields.

Froumence actually exists only in relation to Pierre-

A 1959 production of Le cocu magnifique.

Auguste, and later, as a result of his death. She is more important as a presence than as a creature exhibiting autonomous life. The impassioned ending of the first act calls for her to remain immobile while the hero tries to disculpate himself from accusations never leveled at him: such and other instances throughout the play indicate a physical projection of what might have been a simple verbal or intellectual statement in a genre relying more on mental synthesis.

In the same play, the already-mentioned Barbulesque is a similar character with no intrinsic life. His function is that of an omniscient and satirical chorus, in the same sense as the beggar in Giraudoux's *Electre*. This fantastic horse-doctor knows the inner thoughts of all and, by exposing them divested of their social wraps, he enriches the play with incisive comment. It is he, at the end, who presides over the sumptuously grotesque death of Pierre-Auguste to whom he has ministered all along, following his degeneracy with the cool detachment of a doctor or an otherworldly judge, both of which he embodies.

The disquieting uncle of Carine, the hunter (*le chasseur*), is somewhat more disconcerting because the tangible part of his being, that part which is not symbolic, is fixed within the incidents of the drama instead of belonging to the more broadly sketched Farce world where his physical acts might have been discounted. He too knows the lives of everyone beyond the mask. When Nency speaks of Car-

ine as "the young girl in love with her soul," the uncle asks her, "Is that what Carine was called in the convent?—And you, who have no soul, you have come to find out how roughly hers is being handled?" He thus shows an insight into Carine's soul (and into Nency as well) which even Carine's own fiancé will not attain until it is too late—Frédéric being able to achieve such comprehension only through her death. Yet the uncle appears as a wholly perverted figure when he ends the words of his insight with the following, "Ah! I love you, dear child." (*He takes her head in both his hands, draws her close and kisses her on the mouth.*) He is an anti-Carine, a wholly sensual organism. But if this is the drama of Carine, his suprahuman wisdom imperils her own symbolism.

Nevertheless, the hunter is granted the habitual function of such symbols—that of becoming epilogue—for he too comes back to stand over the deaths of the two principals. But this man, whom Crommelynck has created laughing harshly and saying while the calls of hunting-horns are heard outside, "Fury, disgust, terror, everything lashes my desire!" is by no means an abstraction in his final impersonation, since he has contributed to the pollution of the air from which Carine dies.

Solely for the comic aspects which it seeks, the Farce demands realism in detail; the discrepancy thus created by an unreal situation arouses unessential laughter. The drama can allow those same details to be unreal, but only if they, in so becoming, acquire symbolic value, because the genre demands a reality in depth—the note which must echo in the soul and marrow of the spectator. Therefore, in this drama, the hunter is a disturbing element since, truly, a hybrid, he is pure only symbolically while remaining corrupted by his physical action throughout the play.

Estrugo, Bruno's second self, is a clown until his slow-wittedness is given the amplitude and the significance of Froumence's damning silence. He is, essentially, the rejected part of Bruno's soliloquies. Like all Crommelynck's hybrids, he is only semi-real. These people are born on the stage as symbols, even though they may occasionally have one or both feet on the ground of the general Farce life. Inversely, the main protagonists—the all-important fourth group—appear as real people when the curtain rises, or at any rate people as real as is the surface of the Farce. They end up tortured, wracked, demented; figures of whom, when their realistic body has withered away, the truer significance is clear.

They are hypersensitive. This abnormality, enlarged to the scope of a psychosis, is the source of all their other infirmities. They are relatively weak until the moment when their full energy is compacted into the one obsession of their madness and the fury of their monomania powerfully exalts them. Until then, their hypersensitivity irritates their every nerve ending exposed to a world within which they cannot integrate themselves. But contrary to Anouilh's heroes, they achieve at least artistic integration in that a harmless prelude to their ultimate and significant madness knits them and the Farce cast from the first.

When they are passive, these inadaptable people, like Carine or Balbine, are ultimately stifled. When they are active, and this is more frequently the case, they are soon unable to keep their exasperation in check; their passions are intensified to such an extent that at the final curtain they escape from the physical framework of the drama.

It is by this uprooting, by cutting the individual adrift from all reserve, all modesty, all worldly conventions that might conceal a fragment of the true self, that Crommelynck analyses the ravages of an emotion upon the individual possessed. He is a laboratory technician isolating a mainspring of the human being in order to watch it as it runs down, unhampered, in the vacuum of an observation chamber. If this blunt removal clashes with the physical aspects of a more familiar world, the momentary laughter of such an awareness is Farce, but it does not affect the central concern.

Henri Clouard (*Histoire de la littérature française du symbolisme à nos jours,* 1949) has called this technique "the ripping out of what is real from the depths of the infinite." And Léon Ruth, ("Fernand Crommelynck,") a compatriot and a keen analyst of Crommelynck, details the method thus:

> Take a man whose character is genuine and generous, cut him along an incisive line that frees him from the very first of contingencies, and then continue that line according to its own logic, work the dough according to its own con-

sistency, and cut deeper, knead further, systematically, beyond existence, into the sheer and enormous truth, right in the midst of life pure and simple.

It is meaningless to say that these people are pathological. They might be pathological in a transitional stage, as when their disease first manifests itself, but such moments are those of dawn or twilight: very soon the character will become an abstraction—the essence of the vice from which he is suffering. Only a part of the individual, of the former physical individual, remains.

That part moves about in a world rife with the madness it has engendered at least to some extent and is surrounded by deceptive liaisons—the nonsymbolic part of the hybrid in attendance upon the nonsymbolic part of the hero, false contacts with a bygone world. That is the dolorous part of the individual, the memory of a lost being suffering from the distorting passion that feeds upon it—the sacrificed part that must nevertheless still bear the rigor of a meaningless present. Such is the anatomy of Farce: a garish masque bleeding to death.

In this world, the destructiveness of time continues, as does the corrosiveness of love, of lonesomeness—for like those of Anouilh, these protagonists always remain alone, though in this drama, both they and those around them attempt repeatedly to bridge the insuperable breach. It is this live outline of anguished flesh that gives the abstractions of Crommelynck their pathetic, their sometimes mystical appearance.

The typification of such a personage is Bruno. He is the embodiment of jealousy—"Jealousy [. . .] bursting suddenly, like a horrible, implicit flower, from a love that has simply become too strong, too expansive; the struggle of the hero with his suspicions" (J. Rivière, *"Les Amants puérils,"* 1921). Bruno—ever seeking "the one who will not come, Him, the only One," losing his wife unconcernedly to all his neighbors while he lies in waiting for the ghost of his madness, *that* Bruno ends up logically and climactically insane. But the remnant of the old Bruno that loved, and that still loves his wife in moments when his lunacy assumes through some grotesque coincidence a posture reminiscent of his former self, that remnant nails the symbol to a suffering body.

Stella who prostitutes herself for the love of her husband, Stella, the ideal of love, does not for a moment understand her husband. She is able only to drive him deeper into his madness. Between the devoted Estrugo and the loving Stella, Bruno is helplessly alone. The hands they reach out to him and toward which he vainly strives can never extend into his hermetic world. It is Stella who becomes the true pathological type, for she is never to achieve martyrdom, that is to say abstraction.

Pierre-Auguste, the pathetic Tripes d'or, similarly lives in an atmosphere replete with demented people. He is in love with the never seen, and consequently ideal, Azelle. Once his gold possesses him, it forces him to give her up. When she has been driven away, there remains Muscar, disinterested and faithful, to whom he might turn for help. Unfortunately Muscar, the grotesque and terrifying jester, "whose untamed heart has never forgiven"—Muscar is mad. He is the one chosen to read the will, for who better than he can render the demented voice of old man Hormidas, its author? . . .

> Item, I give, yield and cede to the *bourgmestre* of the municipality, my body with all that it contains, lean and fat, coarse and delicate, inert and subtle, in a word, my earthly remains with all of their dependences, incumbent upon him to have engraved atop my tombstone the following epitaph:
>
> Here lies a sinner without remorse
> Who lived that he might diddle life.
> Now since in hanging, 'tis said, a corse
> Relieves the urge with which he's rife,
> He hanged himself and gave up breath
> That dying he might diddle death.

This Muscar is the man who remains the bond between the Pierre-Auguste that once was and the world he has lost, and who, through this semi-isolation within the pales of insanity, preserves just enough of the hero's body for his delirium to prey upon.

Carine enacts the tragedy of unmitigated sensitivity. Not only is the coarseness of the world too brutal for her, the pure ones about her are too brutal also, for she is seeking in them responses to the most tenuous feelings of her deepest soul. Marcel Arland (*"Carine,"* 1930) has called this "The intimate struggle of a primordial and unsullied chastity upon which are forced, nearly inevitably, circumstances, traditions, the character's aging, and perhaps some jealous demon hitherto dormant within the very depths of his being." In analyzing Carine, that demon might well be invoked, for is not her world first created in rebellion against that which she has rejected? And is not the area rejected again one of insanity—specifically that caused by the flesh this time? Carine's hypersensitivity is more exacerbated by the incomplete comprehension of her very pure husband than by more objectionable aspects of the outer world. But might one not assume that through Frédéric, she is attempting to reach her mother, a pathetic madwoman fighting, like so many of Crommelynck's characters, the depredations of time and carnal love?

And here, of course, lurks the uncle, the one who *does* see through to Carine, but who is part of the over-all mania:

> LE CHASSEUR. How goes your soul?
>
> CARINE. (*far away*) Badly . . .
>
> LE CHASSEUR. So much the better, my girl. Listen to this. In the Paradise lost, there was a proliferation of beasts and plants. Were they then mortal? For if they weren't, one of each kind would have sufficed. But let that be. Inevitably, then, these will be found in the Paradise regained. Thus, beasts have a soul. The lecherous dog, the lascivious ape have a soul—or you do not. Choose.

Perhaps these words are meant to save Carine. But there is of course no contact to be established with those who are sacrificed to a fixation.

The ambivalence of the attempted comprehension which is due to the dual nature of those closest to the central figure, and the failure of that attempt which further isolates the victim, are operative even upon as strong a character as Léona in *Chaud et Froid.* This is the already observed Léona, significantly named, who says to an outraged rival, "You have come to beat me. Strike! I am in a hurry." That rival, Ida, is one of the pathological creatures that surround every principal. She has momentarily lost her husband to Léona and comes to exact physical pain from her. (Later, when she has found that this has little effect, she will try mental pain. Such an instance shows how close are some of the Farce elements to the neurotic expressions of these people. Ida slapping Léona all through a fairly long scene is a bastinado whose bitterness has robbed it of its mirth. Similarly, uncontrolled women beat their husbands in *Le Cocu magnifique* and the tragic Pierre-Auguste beats his gold.)

The first evidence of a lesion in the tough Léona is a teardrop: a certain Félie has come to the bedside of the deceased Mr. Dom and "She is crying! She is crying with irresistably contagious strength," acknowledges Léona, who has never cried until then. It is the harsh Alix who presently tells her that Félie was the mistress of Dom. Léona fights the preposterous idea with all the fire of her past self-confidence: "Quiet! It is not true! Or I did not know Mr. Dom!" But evidence soon compels her to recognize the facts. Her reaction is a savagely violent outburst—for an instant, the atavistic woman is seen in the full grip of her madness. At this point, however, she wrestles the beast in her and subdues it. Though still quivering, she reassumes an appearance of normality but she is already alone. Odilon, ready to do anything Léona might command him (he had previously volunteered to kill Dom while the latter was still alive) and the supremely devoted Alix can reach only an exterior part of Léona, who, as a result, is locked within her incipient insanity.

The obsession of Mr. Dom's deceit is now building up in her to tremendous proportions:

> ODILON. You were deceiving him too!
>
> LEONA. (*carried away*) You lie by every hair on your body!
>
> ODILON. With me!
>
> LEONA. You lie! Is that deceiving? I at least lived without a mask!

Perhaps because she is stronger than most of Crommelynck's heroes, she continues to fight. Her torment is measured by the fury with which she strikes her blows. She first attempts to destroy Félie's Dom with the Dom she knew. To the panic that grips her when she finds herself unable to break Félie's unruffled hold on her past is added Félie's unalterable serenity, reflection of the love which is a constant flagellation to Léona. A culminating blow is the reading of the will in which Dom has bequeathed to Félie a place next to his in the family vault. Mystically confident, Félie is about to kill herself. Should she die, she too will escape Léona just as Dom has. Léona is now a Cornelian heroine because of the choice forced upon her, and she will effect that choice in Cornelian fashion, for ultimately she must win her tremendous and pointless battle. She destroys Félie's faithfulness to Dom by forcing his mistress to accept her own lover Odilon. She slights the dead man just as he, from the grave, had slighted her. She exacts the right to be the sole keeper of a symbol that never existed for her. Exalted, like a triumphant Medea, she ultimately stands alone, drawn to the full height of her pathetic victory, having triumphed over an illusion.

In order that she might suffer, like Bruno, the full measure of her tragedy, Léona wins out over a figment. More mercifully created personages usually succumb, but it is always to a similar illusion, for there is little material interference and little essential action in these dramas for which the Farce is a separate shell indeed. But there can scarcely be anything humorous in the struggle which these people wage with the shadows of their own minds.

The part of the hero that laughs is the mortal part, that crucible not yet destroyed by the fire it contains. When it does laugh, it is in response to a Flemish atmosphere, which French critics like Clouard, Coindreau, Bellessort, Brisson, etc., have termed that of the *kermesse*. The word implies a world of boisterous, cheerful, rough, and rather primitive people—people already sufficiently detached from the polish of a more affected society to give the radically abstracted hero an initial modicum of credibility.

Discounting native biases, the atmosphere of the *kermesse* with its farcical implications might nevertheless be questioned as a dramatic medium. The quest for "the sheer and enormous truth" undertaken by Crommelynck provides one of the reasons for the choice. That truth can be found only in an archetype whose divorce from standardizing patterns is complete enough to make it an absolute. Such a figure lies beyond everyday normality, of course, and, in the case of Crommelynck's creation, even beyond everyday abnormality, so sharply has he been cut off from all avenues whereby he might have approached assuaging norms. Placed in a realistic drama, this character would have been bound to the limitations and the leveling of realism and those necessary compromises would have altered his make-up radically.

Moreover, any hero who corresponds to an excessive vision might easily grow beyond the spectator's reach, as have, for example, Carine and Frédéric. Dramatic logic calls for this kind of character to perform in a world of similar exaggeration wherein he can more easily assume his symbolic value, enabling the spectator to establish new links within an intellectual sphere.

Lastly, the very excessiveness of such heroes might be open to question. However, should they achieve beyond the stage the sought-for integration of their symbolism, their superficial stage life becomes part of the life of the theater—the often-stressed spectacle, its color, and its fun. In this realm, ambient insanity is justified in that it affords artistic homogeneity, blending the act resulting from comedy with that brought about by folly. But although such laughter integrates the world of the hero and that of his surroundings, it is never directed at that which is essentially tragic in the hero.

All through the drama of Crommelynck that hero will suf-

fer, but usually within physical surroundings as mad as are those who people it and as funny as will always be the incongruous object to which no moral stigma can be affixed. Ferocious in his damnation of gold, the author has it kill Pierre-Auguste in the midst of bodily pain that adds to the latter's obvious mental pain. But the hero's Gethsemane is the most grotesque of seats—his *chaise percée*. In the broadly sketched world of the Farce, logic extends beyond its normal limits. Death is exacted by tragedy. The Farce indicates the place of death.

Mr. Dom who comes back from the grave to thwart the lovers Léona and Odilon, and who exacts from his wife the life-long faithfulness she never granted him during his own lifetime, is very reminiscent of the commander's statue in *Don Juan*. And yet he is an unreal presence, the creation of the abnormal Alix. And his ectoplasm is given reality by the frantic, and not altogether sane, leaders of the community. Everything around Mr. Dom is tragedy except his very real, though posthumous, self, which is unmitigated Farce.

Bruno allows a body obviously separate from his mind to become the principal Farce figure in a play wherein his substance is the titular hero. Like the clowns of Rouault, this one is transfigured in spite of his stage paint. Yet his most desperate cry in the play belongs to the over-all Farce. It rings out when, masked, having brought Stella to the verge of giving in to him, he comes tumbling down the stairs, screaming, "With me! With me! Estrugo! With myself, if I had wished it! Estrugo! I am cuckolded as much as one can be!" He is a forceful reminder that, originally, the Candaules myth was not a farce.

The mysticism of the Flemish, that curious admixture of the flesh and the supernatural grotesque, establishes a world that is close to the medieval atmosphere of the original Farce. It is fixed on the canvases of Jerome Bosch. It is apparent in the work of Charles van Lerberghe and of Michel de Ghelderode. Just as naturally, it seeps through the tamer writings of Maeterlinck. The French—including the French mystics, such as Claudel, or even Péguy or Jammes—are usually more urbane, and even when primitive seldom tend towards caricature.

Although Crommelynck has, on occasion, disclaimed his Flemish heritage, it is in Belgium that he learned the theatrical trade, and, in interviews that Belgian newspapers have published, he showed himself less anxious to reject the country in which he was brought up. The meticulous attention which the Farce pays to details stamps Crommelynck, for in his work these are Belgian. No draughty castle halls here, as in Maeterlinck, subject to otherworldly rustling and temporal ridicule. Rather, these are opulent Flemish interiors, never very different whether farmhouse, living room, or mansion hall, with a door ever open onto the real world—the bedroom.

Water, symbol of Flanders, canals, and the endless passing of time, is seldom far away. It is specifically indicated or implicit because of the action. The Belgian Northland is sketched in the solidity and the cleanliness of the sets, such as that of *Tripes d'or*—"Heavy oak furniture that is well polished, painted earthenware, copper, and pewter utensils." Similarly, Léona's interior is one of "luxury, order, stability." If the notation of order and cleanliness is absent, there is someone dusting or decorating as the curtain goes up—diligent hands of *huisvrouwen* are ever present.

Inevitably, this setting of regularity and bourgeois solidity is disrupted by the entrance of more significant symbols, but these grotesque intruders remain as Belgian as the surroundings they invade. True to another Flemish vein that fuses what is coarse with what is sublime, the most incensed of these performers will see a light in moments of desperate aspiration away from the direction of his madness. Such is the symbol Azelle, towards whose soothing sanity the body of Pierre-Auguste still strains. Such are the drives toward their past in Elisabeth, Bruno, or Carine. Ever does the aspiration remain within the individual; outer forces are never called on or brought into play. Evil is in the blood, salvation in the past—and the hopeless pattern within which these people are mured is ceaselessly repeated.

In this hallucinatory world, love is not one of the primordial forces as in Maeterlinck. The great forces are the primal passions that have endured since a much earlier drama and that are not subject to social or superficial psychological contingencies. The only ambient atmosphere strong enough to contain them is that of the flesh, the essential world that antedates morality. But if a moral might be derived from dramatic foundations, it might well be that taught Balbine: the senses whence flow all spiritual values are necessary rather than evil and are an essential constituent of the healthy, sane, and full individual. They have given birth to the Farce and its tragedy: they are now the spectator's to assume.

If the tone of these plays leaves an impression of earthiness, their language remains poetic in the main. The combination of these qualities has been called by André Bellessort "a coarse and precious style." "Coarse," this style is indeed, as are unpolished the people who speak it. If "precious" refers to the constant images through which their words express their immediate concerns, then this preciosity is indeed an attribute of lyric style. Expressions of the tragic and of broad farce are intermixed as naturally as are the genres. "Lyricism elbows bestiality. And even within the figure of the public scribe Bruno, poetry does not disdain to appear, though it may be suddenly interrupted by a burst of laughter that mocks it" (Jean-Richard Bloch, *Destin du théâtre,* 1930).

The achievement of Fernand Crommelynck has been to maintain poetry even through the coarsest passages of his work, so that the melodic flow seldom appears to be broken. It was this aspect of his drama, coming at a time when the taste of theater-goers was still accustomed to the language of the naturalistic play, that occasioned some of the *littérature* accusations that were leveled at him as they were at Giraudoux. Crommelynck replied to these in the same manner as did Giraudoux. In 1934, just before the Belgian première of *Une femme qu'a le cœur trop petit,* he declared to a journalist: "The drama that will be performed must first be a written drama. There is in language a plastic beauty that will have spoken value only if it has written value."

Maintaining these dramatic ideals, Crommelynck was, by obtaining recognition, one of the very first able to free the French stage of naturalism by creating a language—as well as a world—of the theater. J. R. Bloch (*Destin du théâtre*) placed Crommelynck's **Le Cocu magnifique** alongside Giraudoux's *Siegfried* in listing plays which, he believed, were leading the French drama into new and more spacious realms. He saw in these plays a confirmation: "The public is desirous of and expects a dramatic *style* whose architecture will be at once ideological and imaged, with diamondlike poetry and terse prosody, fit to remain in the spectator's mind and able also to create its own aura."

Crommelynck's men are usually artists or are sufficiently cultured to warrant an imaged expression. Barring such innate distinction, the supernatural significance of the protagonist soon confers that right upon him. The women are, of course, essentially lyrical. The deep sadness of Carine's last speeches to Frédéric is spangled with poetic visions of the past, and her language makes her a sister of the prototypal Stella. It also echoes the speech of those naturally poetic people, the young, the lovers, the dreamers that are found in nearly every one of Crommelynck's plays.

Even the more sinister people in this drama couch the unpleasantness of their symbol in agreeable terms, and it is noteworthy of the author's gift for words that even his buffoons use a rich imagery in their harshest moments. Their adjectives are meaty, concrete, and smack of the fertile loam. Their speech comes effortlessly in a flow whose amplitude echoes Rabelais more convincingly than does that of Jarry for at such moments there is no intellectual notation intended—whether humorous or ideational.

Like Baudelaire, like Valéry, Crommelynck might be called the painter of the feminine body, so thoroughly are all of his people steeped in the essential flesh. But the extreme sensuality of the language hardly ever detracts from its beauty, though, on occasion, Crommelynck's poetic verve needlessly extends certain scenes. This fault parallels, and stems in part from, the garrulity and the argumentativeness of the Flemish. In spite of Crommelynck's farcical virulence, a forensic interest in the problems which they embody occasionally keeps his personages weighted down, intellectual symbols, but also didactic ones that become awkward within the huge, unalloyed life of the Farce.

Some of the author's dramatic mannerisms may be due also to the fact that like Ghelderode's, his style was still being shaped at a time when the German expressionists held sway. Although Crommelynck's work appears less influenced by this school than is that of his compatriot, Clouard deems it significant that the brutal, satirical form from beyond the Rhine was an important current during the author's formative years, while noting too the coeval vogue of Synge's *Playboy of the Western World.*

As early as 1924, Ashley Dukes, whose vision enabled him to see the dramatic world that would succeed the naturalists' and who assayed the contemporary plays in that light, had hailed Crommelynck as a new force in the theater and one for whom he demanded wider audiences, correctly epitomizing in *The Youngest Drama* the Belgian's art:

> Mr. Crommelynck who abandons the plane of realism and seeks for the ludicrous essentials of his situation, escapes at the same time from the urbanity and the lassitude of these contemporaries. His *reductio ad absurdum* of the sexual motive imparts a new vigor to the theme. His comedy is cruel and grandiloquent but it is elemental. The sap of nature runs in this tree that leans against the wind of Flanders and casts a fantastic shadow on the plain.

Within the broader perspective offered by an additional quarter of a century, it is possible to discern that shadow falling across a whole era in drama and in literature. (pp. 220-53)

> *David I. Grossvogel, "Crommelynck," in his* 20th Century French Drama, *Gordian Press, 1967, pp. 220-53.*

The dialogue [of *Le cocu magnifique*], it can be said without hesitation, revivified the language of the Belgian theatre. Nobody until then had so thoroughly explored verbal resources. Crommelynck not only scored points for poetry, but loosened the ties language has with the rational and explored the power of suggestion it contains.

—*Suzanne Lilar, in her* The Belgian Theater Since 1890, *1950.*

Bettina Knapp   (essay date Winter 1976-1977)

[*An American educator, Knapp has written extensively on French literature and employs the psychoanalytic theories of C. G. Jung in her approach to criticism. In the following excerpt, she underscores Crommelynck's relation to German Expressionist drama and describes his use of farce and mythic elements in his plays.*]

Crommelynck's brand of expressionism as dramatized in *The Magnificent Cuckold* (1920), *Golden Tripe* (1925), and *Hot and Cold* (1934) is innovative. He enhanced expressionism, defined traditionally as a subjective presentation of a bitter vision of humanity, by introducing farce into the stage happenings, thereby enabling him to point up and then cut down social convention, organized religion, and political organizations. To the lyrical language, so important a factor in expressionist plays, Crommelynck added other means of articulating feeling: onomastically, semiotically, and onomotopeically. The farce, then, dismembered the stifling, narrow, and rigid society under scrutiny, while language exteriorized the hostility implicit in the play's themes. To this combination of elements Crommelynck included a mythmaking device. By inter-

weaving a structured view of humanity onto the plot, he rebuilt and solidified what the farce had destroyed during the course of the play. But this fresh view of the collective as depicted in the myth (no better than the earlier situation) became in Crommelynck's hands an added weapon to deride and caricaturize a society for which he felt contempt.

Crommelynck's theatre is neither a civic festival nor a morality lesson, nor is it designed for relaxation. It is a theatre of action, of psychological probing, of violence and of fascinating and bizarre machinations. It is a composite of opposites: serious drama and farce. On stage, therefore, there are beatings and whippings; a series of visual dialectics that divest the happenings of all sensitivity; and cacophonies that include raucous speech, screeching, jeering and snickering. The hilarity of Crommelynck's monstrous emanations as viewed in *The Magnificent Cuckold, Golden Tripe, Hot and Cold,* or *The Puerile Lovers* is only apparent. The fun lies on the surface; it is a mask which hides a bent for the macabre and somber, a need for the grotesque, a derisive tendency to debase what is beautiful in life and to destroy the tenuous spiritual climes. Treachery, eroticism, and satiric ferocity are *de rigueur* in Crommelynck's theater. We are made privy to a dramatist who cuts his characters open and who inflates their traits and ridicules their propensities with carnal delight in the unforgettable manner of a Kokoschka, a Wedekind, and a Strindberg. Understanding and tenderness have been banished from Crommelynck's world. We are at the antipodes of Giraudoux's golden realm or of Anouilh's illusory domain. Rather, we are closer to the nightmarish and fiendish ghouls of an Arrabal, Vauthier, or Ghelderode—each wearing the gargoyle's smirk. Crommelynck's theatre flagellates in spectacular ways.

Crommelynck's plays such as *The Magnificent Cuckold, Golden Tripe,* and *The Sculptor of Masks* are written in the expressionist tradition of Wedekind, Kokoschka, and Strindberg. Like Wedekind whose plays depict bizarre and absurd situations, and who has been labeled "the father of expressionism and the prophet of sexuality in modern drama," so Crommelynck's theatre also focuses on the pathological, distorted, offensive, and bewildering facets of human nature. Just as Wedekind in *The Awakening of Spring* (1891) indicated bourgeois society for its failure to give sex education to children—his two protagonists die at the end, one from an abortion and the other from suicide—so Crommelynck shocked audiences by introducing *voyeurism*, phallus worship and all types of sexual perversions in *The Magnificent Cuckold.* The blame for these anomalies was directed at the spectators and their culture. In Wedekind's two Lulu plays, *Earth Spirit* (1895) and *Pandora's Box* (1903), the dramatist satirized society's attempts to mask man's enslavement to sexuality, thus increasing its power over the individual and the collective. In *The Sculptor of Masks* Crommelynck expressed the negative side of instinctual repression with excoriating results. To reinforce his anger, Wedekind had his actors proclaim their lines in an unrealistic, impersonal manner, exaggerating every word, phrase, and clause, thus reflecting through rhythmic and tonic structures the hardness and frigidity of some of his characters. Although Crommelynck's language is poetic—even lyrical at times as was Wedekind's, particularly during love-duets—its beauty is hard, cold, and puppetlike, underscoring the inability of man to communicate with his fellow beings even on the most superficial of levels. An abraded world is concretized for the viewer.

Kokoschka who is said to have written the first expressionist drama, *Murder, Hope of Women* (1907), expressed his rancor for humanity through a conflict between the sexes. Here too Crommelynck follows his predecessor's lead. In nearly all of his plays, whether it be in *The Sculptor of Masks, The Puerile Lovers* or *Hot and Cold,* a fundamental *mésentente* exists between man and woman. Rather than love each other they attempt to destroy their mates, overtly or covertly, consciously or unconsciously, in a traumatic power struggle. In Kokoschka's dramas, *Murder, Hope of Women* or *The Burning Bush* (1910), the protagonists are prey to the worst of agonies and passions and are, as in Greek drama, finally cleansed of their suffering and resurrected into new beings—a fresh life. Such rebirth is nonexistent in Crommelynck's theatre.

Crommelynck's theatre is neither a civic festival nor a morality lesson, nor is it designed for relaxation. It is a theatre of action, of psychological probing, of violence and of fascinating and bizarre machinations. It is a composite of opposites: serious drama and farce.

—Bettina Knapp

Unlike realism and naturalism, Crommelynck's plays follow in expressionist tradition. They go beyond the usual verisimilitude and explore personality traits and social inadequacies on an impersonal level. Ibsen, Zola, and Brieux, for example, fought specific social evils, whereas Crommelynck was enraged by general wrongs. The same may be said for Strindberg's expressionism. In *A Dream Play* he depicts society through the dream of Indra's daughter. She enters the earthly sphere to better comprehend the ways of man. In order to experience the dramatist's ego-centric universe spectators must enter into the protagonist's nervous system—experience her unconscious and her perception of reality as a dynamic force. In Crommelynck's *Hot and Cold* or *The Sculptor of Masks* activity also revolves around a central figure. The play's action and the rest of the cast serve to exteriorize the main personality. The secondary characters are devoid of individual traits with no lives of their own. They are seen through the protagonist's eyes and colored by her or his temperament, remaining appendages, subsidiary beings—abstractions.

Crommelynck added the farce technique to expressionism. It enabled him to point up more incisively, he felt, society's foibles as well as to discredit the protagonists and

their entourage. Crommelynck's farce, based on the visual delights of frenetic physical activity on stage, is a combination of Franco-Belgian techniques. The bizarre machinations of his buffoon-like creatures, their instinctuality and crudeness, bring to mind the seventeenth-century *farceurs:* the antics and verbal routines of Tabarin who would abash his viewers with his exaggerated visual and auditive compositions. Crommelynck's creatures are also reminiscent of Turlupin and Gros-Guillaume who used to perform their acrobatic and clowning feats, their jokes, and their seemingly unlimited repertoire before a delighted Molière. Crommelynck's imagination also ripples along and is accompanied by truculent dialogue. But while he captures the rudimentary temperament of the farceurs, a Flemish tonality is likewise present in his characterizations. The comic tradition of *sotternyen* ("tomfooleries"), the *boerden* ("comic farces"), and the *klutchten* ("farces"), performed during the Middle Ages, emphasized man's absurd side and excited humor by ridiculing, derogating, profaning, and deforming what was considered sacred: church and state. They elicited laughter by pointing to man's vices—his cupidity, hypocrisy, and gluttony—sparing no classes from cleric to nun to king and courtier. Comedy as delineated in *klutchten* has much in common with Crommelynck's acerbic and macabre humor as manifested in *Golden Tripe* and *The Magnificent Cuckold.* Both destroyed the logical order of things by using humor of all genres: interruptions, mispronunciations, profanations, coincidences, catch phrases, quid pro quos, exaggerated pantomime, or beatings in the best of Franco-Belgian traditions.

Hot and Cold is one of Crommelynck's typical expressionist farces. It is not a happy work. Nor are his other plays. In this respect it is in keeping with expressionist theatre as defined by one of its most significant theorists, Paul Kornfeld, who labeled this genre "a drama of the soul" where man reveals himself, smudged, ego-centric, but never "crystal-clear." Clothed under the garb of fun and frolic, *Hot and Cold* emerges as a sharp commentary on human nature. In keeping with expressionist drama, the female lead, Léona, is the play's pivotal force. All situations, climaxes, and the dénouement radiate and coalesce as a result of her needs, deficiencies, and qualities. For Crommelynck she represents the living incarnation of faulty values in the marriage structure and in society in general: its need for illusion, for the lie, for a credo or banner that will take people out of themselves—a placebo. Léona and the world from which she emerges are viewed as empty, destructive entities. Those who function within this framework do so with a kind of macabre hilarity—black humor which, as defined by André Breton, banishes all sentimentality and tenderness.

Hot and Cold tells the story of M. Dom's wife, Léona, who finds her husband dull and prosaic. She therefore has taken a series of lovers: Thierry, Bellemasse, and Odilon. Each time she tires of one, which happens frequently, she elicits the aid of her clever servant Alix to free her from the unwanted suitor. Odilon, the latest in line, is so passionately in love with Léona that he wants to poison M. Dom. The situation reaches a crisis point when M. Dom is brought home one afternoon in a semicomatose condition. Shortly before his demise a young attractive girl, Félie, enters M. Dom's home in great distress. Unbeknown to Léona she had been M. Dom's mistress for ten years. Her pride hurt, Léona grows jealous of Félie's past happiness and is angered by her husband's hypocritical attitude toward her. Alix, aware of Léona's suffering, tries to distract her and spreads the rumor that just before he died M. Dom said: "I have an idea." This statement spreads throughout the town like wildfire. It is magnified to such an extent that M. Dom is transformed into a hero. Léona, meanwhile tries to get rid of Félie. She forces Odilon to seduce her. The ruse works. Félie is no longer interested in M. Dom's memory nor in his "spiritual legacy," which has turned into a credo. The new "belief" gives Léona's life purpose and teaches her the meaning of love. She can now admire M. Dom and proudly say that she has come out the victor: "He is mine, completely mine." Her relationship with her husband was cold during his lifetime but is now hot after his death. An altar will be set up in her home that will be a sanctuary where homage may be paid to the founder of the Domist cult.

Crommelynck's protagonists in *Hot and Cold,* in keeping with the farce technique, are "worse than average." He scorns them. They become the butt of his ridicule and the target of his satire. Léona represents blind amorality. We are far from Plautus' universe as dramatized in *The Haunted House* and *The Rope,* in which lively love affairs and confusion abound; nor may *Hot and Cold* be compared to Terence's sprightly works *Eunuchus* and *Phormio,* in which the characters in all of their subtle vagaries arouse bouts of laughter in the viewer. A certain healthiness and spirited verve are evinced in these ancient comedies; a judicious outcome reinforces the ludicrous and impossible pattern of events.

Crommelynck's expressionist-farce is nihilistic and despairing. Léona never experiences any kind of conflict; nor does she struggle to suppress certain tendencies within her or to resolve what gnaws at her vitals. Her inhibitions are perpetually bubbling on the surface. No reason or critical judgment, no power of evaluation or perception ever emerge. The world, then, peopled with this type of superficial and sordid individual, thrives on excitement generated by every new incident; it pursues its peripheral course and lives for and by webb-spinning. Life as experienced by Léona is bare, devoid of meaning, and although comic, is in effect humiliating tragedy. Unlike the existentialist Camus, whose characters in *The Misunderstanding* and *Caligula* attempt to face themselves, Léona skirts surfaces and finds extravagant ways of relieving the routine axis of her life. Her lovers, she hopes, will bring her some semblance of merriment and joy. The rate at which she changes them, however, attests to her own failure; such activity does not give birth to a long term solution. Her lies, deceits, and slanders usher in what expressionist dramatists view as a paradigm of the ugliness of man's soul, the paucity of his vision, and the inferior nature of his being. Although one may argue that the protagonists in Camus' theatre or in Sartre's *No Exit* and *The Devil and the Good Lord* are similarly gruesome, they demonstrate nevertheless courage and willingness to muster their energies in an attempt to confront their inner beings—thus cre-

ating a more lucid but not necessarily happier vision of life. Even in Lenormand's play *Time is a Dream* or in *The Simoon,* in which man's pathetic and nihilistic nature is examined and exteriorized and is found to be bereft of beauty, one is made privy to a redemptive quality, a metaphysical grandeur resulting from the experience and the pain implicit in it. In *Man and his Ghosts* and *The Eater of Dreams,* Lenormand depicts a world in which neuroses, incest, murder, and sexual anomalies of all types are the corpus of the drama, but so is man's desire to transcend his negative destiny.

No positive ideas emerge in Crommelynck's theatre. In *Hot and Cold,* for example, the characters are carried along by their own vices. The slow erosion of a personality is viewed as a humorous state of affairs. Thus the grotesque and farcelike beings peopling Crommelynck's stage are forever circumventing the truth and accepting illusion. Life in *Hot and Cold* is built on egotism, deceit, and the acceptance of subterfuge by an individual and a community. Yet, the entire sequence of comic-tragic events is billed as a side-splitting joke. Léona becomes a kind of master of ceremonies, a *psychopomp,* a leader of the game called life—in which man puts something over on himself. Léona, the butt of Crommelynck's ire, is a *femme fatale.* Women such as her are all things to all men. To Thierry she took on the stature of a goddess; to Bellemasse, a divine object; to Odilon, a flesh-and-blood sensualist. She ordered them about as she saw fit and they yielded to her will; spellbound they became votaries of this powerful force.

In keeping with expressionism, Crommelynck used language as a theatrical device to discredit the protagonists involved. But he went further than Wedekind or Kokoschka, even Strindberg, in this regard. He used all types of figures of speech to express a variety of emotions from passion to hatred: antitheses and repetitions ("hatred, hatred, hatred"), slang phrases ("the trollop," in French *la garce*), neologisms (Domism), clichés ("I have plunged into love as a swimmer into water"), puns ("Ephé-mère"), onomatopoeias used semiotically: "More slippery than an eel!", injecting character traits into the visual image. Signified and signifier blend into one when Léona's hatred is described in terms of ice: "Nothing but pure, naked hatred, salubrious as the air of glaciers" will help her face her ordeal. Language gave birth to M. Dom's *idea* and its "spiritual legacy" to mankind which is the generating principle around this absurd yet paradoxically plausible play.

Crommelynck's theatre, linguistically speaking, is one of violence insofar as man's needs and personality are concerned. His characters' speech, their situations, and their personalities are objects: wooden, hard, unbending. Yet, lyricism frequently prevails when experiencing love crises. Odilon reveals his passion to Léona: "I knew that our bodies would join each other immediately, even despite ourselves." Félie expresses her love as "Adorable day: the flowers brighten as at dusk, the shadow takes on a spangled hue under the trees, and I saw groups of flying ants displaying their golden halo in the valleys!" Seconds later, their words become choppy, frigid, and brittle, like hammer strokes. Harsh effects are now dealt out visually and accoustically as rhythms accelerate and groups of staccato-like enumerations follow, each mounting in intensity. As in the plays of Kokoschka and Wedekind, so here too language explodes and becomes a quasiautonomous factor in the stage happenings. "I want her punished," screams Léona. "And you heard me . . . Félie will not enter the cemetery; never . . . ".

Onomastics are also used by Crommelynck to underscore the chicanery, knavery, and lust of his protagonists. Léona, *leo, leonis,* from Latin "lion," resembles the animal. She has lionlike force, a kind of solar energy and courage that enables her to destroy what she thinks to be inimicable to her needs. The lion (which figures on the French, German, and English coat of arms) not only represents power, but an irascible appetite, instinctual force, avidity, and vigor as well. In many myths and fairy tales the lion has been equated with the dragon who protects great treasures (the "Lion Knight" in the Arthurian cycle, for example) and in this instance uses all means, whether brutal or not, to gain his ends. Implicit in Léona are these cruel, tension-filled and ruinous features. She is an aggressive, energizing, excitable element, and her flamboyant ways are a replica of her inner being. Throughout the play she acts in a chaotic, demonstrative, and episodic manner. Her disorderly nature causes the play's jagged structure. The scenes frequently give the impression of improvisation, the characters forever barge in and out in a quite uncausal nature; the dialogue is interrupted by the sudden appearance and disappearance of characters, and bursts of anger from Léona's rejected suitors also impose themselves spasmodically on the stage happenings. The derision provoked by Léona's emotional upheavals or Alix's eruptions into the picture trigger off protests from other characters, not only adding to the suspense factor, but also creating a series of rhythmic and imagistic reverberations. Although only Léona's voice dominates the situations enacted, a plurality of voices is heard as cacophonous background music, all of which is integrated into the Crommelynckian construct.

We are first introduced to Léona through Ida, Thierry's jilted wife. She erupts onto the stage ready to tear Léona apart with her bare hands: "It won't be the first time," she screams, that "the beautiful Léona" will be beaten. "She will pay for having taken him and leaving him." Alix is also rambunctious. As a kind of alter ego for Léona, she too is a catalyst. Her namesake, Alix de Champagne, Queen of France and wife of Louis VII (1160), mother of the illustrious Philip Augustus, is transformed by Crommelynck into a servant, thus discrediting what had been highly valued: queenship. It is Alix's obligation to play hide-and-seek with Bellemasse, one of Léona's rejected lovers. As planned by the two ladies but still unbeknown to the audience, Léona finds Alix and Bellemasse ensconsed in an armchair, kissing madly. Léona wears a mask of anger and hurt, thus deceiving her suitor and audience who believe her pain to be real. The entire amorous escapade is handled with brio and permits Léona on grounds of *flagrante delicto* to rid herself of Bellemasse. As a final flourish she allows her fiery temperament to explode, thus compelling him to depart. Léona now flits about the stage in a joyful interlude as she awaits her next lover, Odilon.

Alix remarks, thus including the audience in their complicity: "It is so pleasurable to change men. One effaces the other."

To Odilon Léona makes known her needs and the course her love will take: "You will work for me, for both of us?" And the cumbersome, awkward bumpkin believes her passion to be real and lasting. As in *The Marriage of Figaro,* the entire scene with Odilon rests on a series of skirmishes and contretemps—the fool and the clever hetaera—the one acting in all sincerity though a bit dull-witted in his ways, the other basking in her delightful machinations, in her quest and conquest. The motility of the sequences featuring Odilon and Léona depends upon the points of controversy at stake and their resolution.

As Odilon's passion grows, so does his jealousy of M. Dom. He decides to poison him and confesses the plan to Léona. Wearying of Odilon's ardor, she assures him there are no grounds for jealousy. Then she turns around and deprecates him by asking him to go on an errand for her; to further irritate him, she adds insidiously: "And what will I do to forget you while you're away? I'll deceive you." Odilon reacts as she expected; he threatens to kill her. But his fury heightens his sexual joy, which now grows to unparalleled heights.

M. Dom's demise does not subdue Odilon's temper. He is so outraged by Léona's obsession with her late husband's memory that he is ready to strike her. To relieve the tension and inject humor into the sequence, Alix pokes her head through a window and screeches: "Yes, strike, strike, strike her!" The comic interruption of course has the opposite effect. Odilon stops short and falls into the armchair in shock and disbelief, humiliated at the thought that another has witnessed his emotional display.

M. Dom's death arouses Léona's anger, however. Her wounded pride, her gullibility at her husband's deceit, and her jealousy over the unhappiness he had experienced with Félie alter her opinion of him. Indeed, she is caught up in Félie's lyricism, in her passionate love and devotion to his memory, and responds dramatically to the image created by the rival. M. Dom begins to attain epic grandeur in Léona's imagination. And as her admiration increases, the once flighty, superficial, and amoral hetaera is transformed into a statuesque, elegant kind of vestal virgin. Her house becomes a Domist sanctuary and fills with guests in the last scene, all come to pay homage to the great M. Dom. Thierry, once her lover, but now the apostle of a new religion, suggests that "The Altar to the Idea" be built in the home: "These three steps seem to have been placed here for this express purpose." The room will be elevated, isolated, and thus a "special solemnity" will be conferred on it. The Burgomaster speaks of the rituals involved in Domist worship and the heights of spirituality these may attain. Thirty delegations are to arrive and declare themselves Domists. As the crowd enters, Léona, caught up in the Domist myth, confesses to Alix that she has finally found love; her soul now experiences its true calling. In a burst of lyrical frenzy she glorifies M. Dom's new image and the lasting love to which it has led.

Crommelynck's satire of organized religion and of the

femme fatale is incisive. His brand of expressionism draws upon the inner and outer ugliness of individuals, their bestiality and cruelty, their distorted views of life. These are then painted onto the stage happenings in the manner of a Kokoschka, Wedekind, or Strindberg—along with the farce, thereby depicting a world bereft of tenderness and sensitivity.

But equally as significant as the farce element in Crommelynck's dramaturgy is the mythmaking factor. The myth, according to Mircea Eliade [in his *Aspects du mythe*], is defined as a primordial and numinous experience. "Refined, modified, and systematized" during the course of centuries, these "sacred" and "true" narratives have become the bases of religious belief. They also express "a cultural reality." As a living and dynamic force, myths answer a need of the society over which they prevail. Whether dealing with creation, transformation or any of the countless types of myths which have become part of man's heritage, each in its own way gives structure and security to individuals and collectives. Crommelynck, aware of man's dependence upon the myth to pursue a relatively optimistic course in life, used this genre as a theatrical vehicle to deflate and then inflate his puppetlike creatures. The myth of the artist with all of his needs and wants is fleshed out in **The Sculptor of Masks;** the myth of the eternal return is cut open and crushed in **The Puerile Lovers;** in **Hot and Cold** we learn of man's dependence on cult and cult objects.

Crommelynck's mythmaking process is strictly a ruse, a hoax, a joke humanity plays upon itself in order to be able to walk about the earth blind and deaf to its realities. It is a satiric-comic view of life; in contrast is Genet's use of the mythmaking technique. In *The Screens,* the myth takes on the dimension of a religious ritual; it enables the votaries within its framework to acquire stature, to step away from their mortal activities and penetrate an immortal realm—thus from the individual they move into the transcendental sphere. Genet's view is, nevertheless, ambivalent. Although he takes man's mystical quests and the rituals inherent in these seriously, he nevertheless is able to objectivize and satirize man's inability to come to grips with certain realities, such as the notion of death and the need for illusion. While Genet is spiritually oriented, Crommelynck is earthbound. His life is firmly rooted in *tellus mater* and not in some nebulous, spacial, celestial, or infernal region.

In **Hot and Cold,** M. Dom is unwittingly the catalyst for the mythmaking process. Onomastically Dom comes from the Latin *dominus,* "master." It was a title given in the Middle Ages, Renaissance, and Classical era to certain men of religion; it was also an honorary title attributed to nobles in Portugal. In fact, when Molière wrote his *Dom Juan,* he spelled it *Dom* and not, as later interpreters insisted, *Don.* In addition, D.O.M. is an abbreviation for the Latin *Deo optimo, maximo,* "To God the best, the greatest," a formula used to dedicate religious edifices. By using the name Dom, which lends historicity, continuity, and religious overtones to the play, Crommelynck was carefully setting the stage for the birth of some "fabulous" situation. In this manner, he set the terrain for the mythmaking

process. The fact that M. Dom never appears onstage, that he dies in some mysterious manner, and that the details surrounding his life are never subsumed, injects an aura around his being. He takes on the attributes and dimensions of a remote divinity, a kind of powerful father figure who will dominate all the events in the play.

Strangely enough, a countermovement also comes into being. Léona, who had considered her husband pedantic and had been a seducer of men, is now transformed—through religion—into a dignified priestess of sorts, a female votary to the new Domist cult. Whereas Félie, who had loved M. Dom for ten years in secret and knew felicity during his lifetime (as her name indicates), takes on another aspect after his death. Onomastically, Félie is feline, catlike. She insinuates her way into Léona's house, into its activities. Félie is also a felon; she betrays her dead lover. Seduced by Odilon thanks to Léona's machinations, Félie becomes an apostate. She rejects Domism and its cult for the dead in favor of the alive, attractive, and virile Odilon.

The mythmaking mechanism is expertly interwoven into the fabric of the play. The nuances of Léona's anger, jealousy, and feelings of rejection are countered by M. Dom's growing reputation, the rumors that declare him an unrecognized genius, the creator of an idea the townspeople interpret as a boon to humanity. As is the case of most cult objects or patriarchal images, M. Dom becomes a kind of placebo, a hierophany—capable of solving all of life's problems. The collective psychosis so brilliantly evoked by Jules Romains in *Dr. Knock* (where the doctor through the power of suggestion controls the personalities of a group of mountain people) and in *Crommedeyre-le-Vieil* (when some kidnapped girls are assimilated into the substance of some remote village) is dramatized step by step by Crommelynck—leading to collective intoxication.

The energy generated by M. Dom's *idea* (which is never elucidated upon), concocted by Alix in order to dispel Léona's wounded ego, takes on the power of an avalanche. M. Dom's genius arouses the admiration of the Burgomaster, the teacher, and the political leaders of the community. His doctrine—ultra vague and in keeping with the mythical device—influences neighboring towns until a mob psychology comes into being. Like a plague, news travels quickly; instant communication is experienced as the gullible adopt the new religion. The masses and the irrational element predominate as the promise of a *fontaine de jouvence* is offered to everyone who converts to Domism.

"M. Dom's ideas have conquered the entire province," Léona states as she is herself overwhelmed by the greatness of her late husband. A veritable epiphany occurs, a miracle that gives authenticity and stature to the newly created religion. On the third day after M. Dom's death rumors have it that he appeared in various towns and districts: "M. Dom passed through Villou and Beauvisu and Pranet—he is at this very moment at Terres-Meubles." To reinforce the mythico-religious flavor of the miraculous event, Alix intones: "The morning of the third day." Thus Crommelynck satirizes Christ's resurrection on the third day while also derogating organized religion and the power it holds over humanity.

As the events near their climactic finale, each county seat articulates its own interpretation of Domist doctrine, setting up dialectical situations: "The doctrine enunciated by the Jury committee is diametrically opposed to ours, without its being any the less Domist." The "spiritual legacy" is of such value to the various people involved and the communities they represent, they are filled with emotion as they talk of the new cult. Léona, the guiding spiritual force now, the mystical Queen of Domism, accepts her new role as religious leader of the community. Statuesque in her black gown, her visage now wears the countenance of saintliness and is marked by deep gravity.

Crommelynck's theatre, expressionistic in focus, makes audiences privy to a world viewed subjectively from the standpoint of a single protagonist. His intention is to exteriorize the essence of man, to impel audiences to experience the underlying truth concerning the human condition in schematized, direct, and violent means. Crommelynck, along with Wedekind, Kokoschka, and Strindberg, expressed dissatisfaction with society by having characters speak in hysterical and choppy tones which some German critics labeled "telegraph style." To these auditive devices Crommelynck added onomastics and semiotics which further depotentiated what he disliked most in man and society. His masterful use of the farce and the mythmaking techniques enabled the skirmishes and reversals of fortune that oscillated throughout each of his plays to underscore the crudeness and uncouth nature of his beings: their chicanery, knavery, lust, and desire for evil. There are no heroes in Crommelynck's plays; his characters represent a carnival of human folly in which man's vanity, egotism, and cruelty are brought forth in all of their disquieting grandeur. (pp. 314-27)

> *Bettina Knapp, "Crommelynck's Farcical and Mythmaking Expressionism," in* Comparative Drama, *Vol. 10, No. 4, Winter, 1976-77, pp. 314-27.*

Bettina Knapp   (essay date 1978)

[*In the following excerpt from her study* Fernand Crommelynck, *Knapp considers Crommelynck's relation to Flemish and French theater and categorizes his plays according to theme and style.*]

Crommelynck's theater is a composite of Flemish and French traditions combined with his own personal style.

When speaking of Flemish theater—as one does of Flemish painting—one usually refers to an area extending from Bruges to the coast region from Calais to the Scheldt. In the Middle Ages this area was divided into two parts: the west of Flanders—which included the towns of Bruges, Ostend, Courtrai, Ypres—and the east of Flanders—which included Antwerp, Ghent, and the rich area watered by the Scheldt.

Generally speaking, Flemish characteristics may be described as an attitude of extreme realism toward existence and, paradoxically, a penchant for mysticism. These characteristics were said to have been introduced by the Spaniards during their occupation of this area, but according to J. A. Goris were present long before that time. The Flemish felt a deep-seated need to transcend their workaday world. They yearned for some spiritual realm that would bring them serenity and create unity where there was diversity—in the phenomenological world. They needed the surreal realm of their imaginations to create their masterpieces. Compelled to contend with the rigors of their climate and the multitude of economic difficulties facing a nation surrounded by enemies seeking to divest it of its sovereignty, the Flemish had to deal with reality on solid footing. But Flemish reality must not be confused with French nineteenth-century Naturalism and its attempt to duplicate what the Naturalists saw scientifically in their arts and letters. Flemish reality includes the phenomenological realm as well as the surreal world: fantasy and phantasmagoria, where the logical and intangible cohabit.

> Their reality surpasses reason. The Fleming is essentially a man for whom the supernatural exists. Jan van Eyck paints with utmost precision the sumptuous raiment of the Arnolfini, the little dog of the Arnolfini, the precious shoes ready for wear, and the rosary of crystal beads—all these personal objects arranged around the young man and his bride as tokens of security in a quiet, well-ordered home. But he will not forget the convex mirror that opens the room to the outside world, and even to the world of magic. Such is Flemish realism. It opens onto the unknown, on the unusual. [Suzanne Lilar, *The Belgian Theater Since 1890*]

The distinctly Flemish brand of mysticism and realism, of pathos and merrymaking, are expressed most spectacularly in Pieter Brueghel's *The Battle Between Carnival and Lent.* In this canvas, people are crowded together; they are at play. Suddenly, their revelry turns to madness as the long wild night of the Mardi Gras is slowly transformed into the depressing dawn of Ash Wednesday and the beginning of Lent. Two opposing spirits are present in Brueghel's work: the penitent and the carouser; the roisterer and the reveler. In *Peasant Wedding,* another Brueghel canvas, the rustic tables and benches upon which the peasants are seated as they indulge in an abundance of food and drink are crudely depicted and may be compared with the restrained elegance of the city folk—and perhaps their hypocritical ways. Coarseness of feelings (considered another Flemish characteristic), is frequently injected in the tavern scenes depicted by Adriaen Brouwer. Hieronymus Bosch's repulsive and monstrous forms, demons who attack, gape at, and assault the holy man in *The Temptation of St. Anthony,* also inhabit the Flemish soul. The violent and instinctive visions of Maurice de Vlaminck, with their strident reds, blues, greens, their fast and furious rhythms, the harshness of their brushstrokes and explosive qualities of the trees, rivers, and skies, are likewise part of Flemish nature.

These characteristics are also implicit in the Flemish comic tradition of the *sotternyen* ("tomfooleries"), the *boerden* ("comic farces"), and the *klutchten* ("farces") performed during the Middle Ages. These plays brought into focus man's more absurd side and elicited laughter by ridiculing, derogating, profaning, and deforming what was considered sacred: church and state.

The comic tradition in both France and Belgium aroused humor by pointing to man's vices—his cupidity, hypocrisy, and gluttony—sparing no classes from cleric and nun to king and courtier. Comedy as delineated frequently in the farce destroyed logical order of things through slapstick humor of all types: interruptions, mispronunciations, profanations, coincidences, catch phrases, quid pro quos, exaggerated pantomime, or beatings. In all of their deformities, clowns and buffoons represented man's physical imperfections. But these clowns who aroused laughter in others spoke their words pointedly in bitter, satirical tones, revealing the deficiencies in those around them— less obvious, perhaps, but far more insidious.

In more recent centuries Verhaeren, Maeterlinck, van Lerberghe, and Rodenbach continued in the medieval tradition but introduced new elements. In *Princess Maleine, The Intruder,* and *The Interior,* Maeterlinck created a symbolic theater with sparse language, short scenes, and a mystical frame of reference. Writing about *Princess Maleine* in *La Jeune Belgique,* Iwan Gilking declared it to be "an important work which should be considered a landmark in the history of contemporary theater." Charles van Lerberghe's *The Detectors,* which Lugné-Poë directed at the Odéon, could be labeled a mystery play as well as a symbolic drama because it featured a girl forced to face death—a prominent theme in Flemish and German literature throughout the Middle Ages. Georges Rodenbach's *The Veil* and *The Miracle* is weighted down with symbolism, frequently quite obvious: antique bells, candles, crystals, and a panoply of other objects that encourage a macabre and supernatural atmosphere. Cyriel Buysse wrote in Flemish but with the naturalism of a Becque and Zola. His *De Plaatsvervangende Vrederechter* was a satire on the judiciary system. Its humor was biting and sardonic; its characters pointed out the ugliness of human nature.

Crommelynck was imbued with the spirit of these writers, past and present; to their innovations he added his own. His theater may be divided into two loosely knit categories: "The Theater of the Unexpressed and the Tragic Farce" and "Toward the Boulevard."

Like the Symbolist theater, the Theater of the Unexpressed (which includes Crommelynck's *The Merchant of Regrets, The Sculptor of Masks,* and *The Puerile Lovers*) sought to delineate an inner vision through suggestive imagery, nuanced sensations, and tenuous ideas. Unlike symbolist theater, however, the Theater of the Unexpressed did not have recourse to fairy tales or to myths; insofar as Crommelynck was concerned, its recourse was to the complexities and chaotic nature of human beings in everyday surroundings and situations. Psychology was an important factor in Crommelynck's Theater of the Unexpressed, but not the intellectual assessment and pathological situations that mark H. R. Lenormand's *Time is a Dream* or *The Eater of Dreams.* Rather, Crommelynck's method was to portray an underlying morbidity that leads to outbreaks of jealousy and even deaths, as in *The Sculptor of Masks.* In *The Puerile Lovers,* the inability to face the ravages of age leads to a pronounced schizophrenic condi-

tion that is never expressed as such but is subsumed, felt, or sensed by the characters. Crommelynck never includes dream sequences nor any curative agent. He dramatizes; he cuts open; he offers no remedies.

In the Theater of the Unexpressed the action usually takes place in some prosaic area, for example, a store in *The Sculptor of Masks,* a large living room in *The Puerile Lovers.* The plot is simple and devoid of complicated intrigues. All unnecessary chatter is banished. Words no longer reveal "soul states" as they did in the plays of Henry Bataille, Henri Bernstein, and Paul Hervieu. Such inner architecture had to be communicated through sighs, silences, or lyrical poetic passages.

The Theater of the Unexpressed is rooted in French classical tradition. Marivaux, a master in delving into the secrets of the heart, left much unsaid in *Game of Love and Chance,* in *The Second Love Surprise,* and in *Conquered Prejudice.* Although his plays are comic, neither laughter nor satire is essential. His characters are for the most part finely etched, in elegant, nuanced, and sometimes imperceptible lines. The love between the protagonists is hidden or repressed at the outset of the play and is allowed to blossom forth during the course of the acts. Marivaux wrote: "I observed all the different niches within the human heart where love could hide, where it is afraid to show itself; each of my comedies has as its goal to allow this love to emerge from its niche." A century earlier Molière also used "zones of silences" to exteriorize his characters' feelings. The unexpressed in certain cases was far more powerful, he felt, than what was said. We know how annoyed Molière was by the pompous and dogmatic acting styles of the Comédie-Française tradition. Molière opted for a more attenuated method. (pp. 22-6)

Chekhov was a master of the Theater of the Unexpressed. His characters in *The Cherry Orchard, The Three Sisters,* and *Uncle Vania* are resigned and remote in their thoughts and sentiments. They inhabit a strange world, an atmosphere imbued with melancholy based on a past that will never be revived. Their world, with its mysteries, includes moments of intense suspense and anguishing climaxes where conversation simply ceases.

In Crommelynck's *The Merchant of Regrets, The Sculptor of Masks,* and *The Puerile Lovers,* a whole inner world is focused upon but never really brought to light in the dialogue. Its impact on the viewer is marked through the imagery of sensuous poetry and the expert use of the mask, facial expressions, and versatile acting techniques. In *The Puerile Lovers* a dream quality is interjected into the stage happenings; vagueness of plot and character delineations propel viewers into a world where the fine demarcation lines between illusion and reality no longer exist—a world tinged with anguish and despair.

Elements of the Theater of the Unexpressed co-mingle with the spirit of the Tragic Farce in *The Magnificent Cuckold* and *Golden Tripe.* A violent and cruel yet humorous world is set before the viewer. In these plays Strindberg's influence—his pessimism as delineated in *The Father, Miss Julie,* and *The Dance of Death*—is strongly felt: man doomed to suffer forever—since Adam's fall for the crimes committed in some past existence. Although Crommelynck was an agnostic and did not believe in Strindberg's mystic lucubrations, Strindberg's nihilistic approach, his sharp repartees, and his excoriating types prevailing onstage did make their mark on Crommelynck.

Crommelynck's farces are not happy; indeed, they are touched with tragedy. In this respect they are in keeping with Ionesco's definition of the Tragic Farce: stage happenings of a violent, cruel, and absurd nature. For Ionesco, logic must be disrupted by the onslaught of improbable situations, eliciting nonsensical activity, unbelievable coincidences, and terminating in a crescendo of virulence. In *Victims of Duty,* Ionesco attempted to "drown the comic in the tragic; in *The Chairs,* the tragic in the comic . . . to oppose the comic with the tragic and to blend them into a new theatrical synthesis." Crommelynck reveals a crumbling and disintegrating society whose values hamper man's evolution rather than encourage it. His world is peopled with grotesque characters making their plight known through horrendous outbursts. Absurd and unreal qualities enter into the frenetic antics of the protagonists; but, as in the delirious fantasy of Armand Salacrou's *Breaker of Plates,* humor clothes an underlying spirit of anguish and revulsion. Crommelynck's protagonists are jealous, frequently without reason; they live in a fantasy realm that makes reality painful to face. With the introduction of the absurd and the unreal into the stage happenings, anything can take place in the illogical world of the obsessed. Humor is experienced as an agent of destruction in **The Magnificent Cuckold** and is death-dealing in **Golden Tripe.**

Crommelynck's tragic-farce technique is phallus-oriented, originating in the ancient farces given in Megara in the fifth century B.C. It rests on the scabrous as well as on the intensity of the activities pursued on stage and the developments that arise from them. Comedy is more intellectual than farce. It is an outgrowth of character study, as demonstrated in *Tartuffe, The Miser,* and *The Misanthrope.* Farces, pointing up the humorous side of life, frequently use masks and stock characters from the *commedia dell'arte* repertoire. The characters speak with a particular accent, use stereotype expressions, and indulge in a variety of set behavior patterns. (pp. 26-8)

Crommelynck uses the slapstick routines of the farce in **Golden Tripe** and **The Magnificent Cuckold,** and his technique is precise, perhaps even mechanical at times. But the truculent dialogue and the buffoonlike natures of his characters provoke tragedy amid laughter. Henri Bergson was right, stating in his essay on "Laughter" that certain types of comedy are marked with "insensitivity," "automatism," and an "absence of feeling on the part of the observer."

The ugliness of Crommelynck's characters is striking. They are like concretized monsters, scoundrels for the most part. The situations of marriage, inheritance, and law and order are unpleasant. Unlike Molière's usually light and bantering satire, Crommelynck's is heavy and negative. He seeks to destroy, not to rectify; to vilify and humiliate, not to reform and strengthen. Crommelynck's plots are mostly anarchic; he uses them to give free reign

to his creatures. The madness of the situations he engenders and the amorality of the protagonists, who act on impulse, give rise to a nightmarish atmosphere—comparable to the surrealistic dramas of Vitrac (*The Mysteries of Love* and *Victor*). Obscure motivations reveal the complex and incomprehensible nature of man's psyche, and satire is used to provoke a dissociation between thought and expression.

Crommelynck's adaptation of Shakespeare's *Falstaff* (1954) was undertaken in this vein. A great admirer of the Elizabethan dramatist, Crommelynck decided to restore the original unity of *Falstaff,* which Shakespeare had divided into Parts I and II in *Henri IV.* To Crommelynck, Falstaff was the ultimate of comic figures, a kind of *miles gloriosus:* parasite and fool. Crommelynck was attracted to this "tun of flesh" who fed on deceptions, lies, and roguishness; who was as "gross as earth," ridiculous, a coward, and a blind lover. (p. 28)

Carine, Hot and Cold, and **A Woman Whose Heart Is too Small** are lighter comedy and more in the boulevard tradition. This kind of comedy aims to please: its characterizations are more superficial, and its verse and power less virile. In his boulevard plays, Crommelynck avails himself of a central idea, or themes, and expands upon it. Sacha Guitry using a similar method successfully, expressed his belief: "What I call point of departure is frequently a minute idea . . . Once I constructed an entire scenario after having heard just a simple remark one person made to another." Guitry's play *Jealousy* was based on the old proverb, "It's a jealous husband that makes for an unfaithful wife." His plays were so popular that when speaking of him and his father, an actor, Lugné-Poë, said they were "a national treasure."

Jules Romains' influence is clearly discernible in **Hot and Cold,** in which the concept of unanimism is dramatized with felicity. The play deals with the collective's need for the myth and the individual's longing for a religious credo. Romains gave dramatic form to his unanimistic doctrine in *Donogoo Tonka:* a "famous" professor, a candidate for the French Institute, mentions a nonexistent town in South America, which then has to be founded so that he will not lose face. Romains used the same form in *Doctor Knock,* in which sickness becomes a collective phobia. His brand of humor is special, that of the *canulard*—dry, biting, and sardonic; so is Crommelynck's in **Hot and Cold** and in **A Woman Whose Heart Is too Small.** These plays reveal a blend of roguery with a dash of Voltarian piquancy. But Crommelynck's characters are anthropophagous in addition to their wit. They symbolically eat each other up during the course of the events.

Crommelynck's theater ridicules, destroys, inflates, and deflates amid a series of frequently incongruous situations. His plays are "as disorderly as his life," said Roger Blin; his protagonists as "irascible" as he—bitter, jealous, and tormented. Crommelynck clothes his beings in garbs of fun and frolic, but in reality they emerge as vehicles expressing his own sharp commentary on human nature. (pp. 29-30)

Bettina L. Knapp, in her Fernand Crommelynck, *Twayne Publishers, 1978, 160 p.*

FURTHER READING

Goris, Jan-Albert. Introduction to *Two Great Belgian Plays, about Love,* by Fernand Crommelynck and Suzanne Lilar, translated by Marnix Gijsen, pp. vii-xiv. New York: James H. Heineman, 1966.
> Brief introduction to *The Magnificent Cuckold.*

Grossvogel, David I. "The Plight of the Comic Author and Some New Departures in Contemporary Comedy." *The Romanic Review* XLV, No. 4 (December 1954): 259-70.
> Traces the development of comic theater in France and Belgium from the late nineteenth through the twentieth century and points to Crommelynck as a principal figure in the development of Flemish farce.

Knapp, Bettina L. "Fernand Crommelynck's *Golden Tripe: The Miser Type and the Farce.*" *The USF Language Quarterly* XV, Nos. 3-4 (Spring-Summer 1977): 25-30.
> Discussion of Crommelynck's use of farce in his plays and his depiction of the miser type in *Tripes d'or.*

——. *Fernand Crommelynck.* Boston: Twayne Publishers, 1978, 160 p.
> Analyzes the themes, characters, and techniques of Crommelynck's major plays.

——. "Introduction to Fernand Crommelynck (1885-1970)." In *An Anthology of Modern Belgian Theatre: Maurice Maeterlinck, Fernand Crommelynck, and Michel de Ghelderode,* translated by Alba Amoia, Bettina L. Knapp, and Nadine Dormoy-Savage, pp. 147-53. Troy, N.Y.: The Whitson Publishing Co., 1982.
> Introduction to *The Sculptor of Masks.*

Knowles, Dorothy. "Studio Theatre: Cocteau and Company, Intelligence Unlimited." In her *French Drama of the Inter-War Years, 1918-39,* pp. 48-89. London: George G. Harrap and Co., 1967.
> Comments on Crommelynck's major plays.

Law, Alma H. "Meyerhold's *The Magnanimous Cuckold.*" *The Drama Review* 26, No. 1 (Spring 1982): 61-86.
> In-depth review of the Soviet director Vsevolod Meyerhold's 1922 production of Crommelynck's *The Magnificent Cuckold.*

Lilar, Suzanne. "Contemporary Theater . . . Crommelynck and the Others." In her *The Belgian Theater Since 1890,* pp. 27-43. New York: Belgian Government Information Center, 1950.
> Praises Crommelynck as a playwright who "loosened the ties language has with the rational and explored the power of suggestion it contains."

Mallinson, Vernon. "The Theatre of French Expression." In his *Modern Belgian Literature, 1830-1960,* pp. 173-97. New York: Barnes and Noble, 1966.
> Argues that Crommelynck transcended the influence of German Expressionism of the Flemish theater and points out ways in which Crommelynck was influenced by Maurice Maeterlinck.

Additional coverage of Crommelynck's life and career is contained in the following source published by Gale Research: *Contemporary Authors,* Vols. 89-92.

Robertson Davies

1913-

(Full name William Robertson Davies; has also written under the pseudonym Samuel Marchbanks) Canadian novelist, playwright, essayist, journalist, short story writer, editor, and critic.

The following entry provides criticism on Davies's *The Papers of Samuel Marchbanks, The Cornish Trilogy,* and *Murther & Walking Spirits.* For further information on his life and works, see *CLC,* Volumes 2, 7, 13, 25, and 42.

INTRODUCTION

Davies established himself as a leading figure in Canadian literature with the novels *Fifth Business, The Manticore,* and *World of Wonders,* collectively published as *The Deptford Trilogy.* Typical of his fiction, these densely plotted works incorporate religious symbolism and the supernatural, underscore the mystery and wonder of life, and are infused with a Jungian sensibility that informs the individual's quest for identity. Related to this concept of self-awareness is Davies's self-prescribed role as a Canadian man of letters. Believing that Canada must distinguish itself from England and the United States, Davies consequently sets many of his novels in Canada and often satirizes Canadian provincialism, which he perceives as a hindrance to his homeland's cultural development.

Born in Thamesville, Ontario, Davies later moved to Renfrew, a small town in the Ottawa Valley, and then to Kingston, Ontario, regions which provide the backdrop for much of his fiction. He attended Queen's University in Kingston from 1932 to 1935 and then enrolled in Balliol College, Oxford, England, where he became active in student theater productions and contributed to university magazines. After graduating from Balliol in 1938 with a degree in literature, Davies remained in England and joined the Old Vic theater troupe. He returned to Canada in 1940 and contributed to the liberal journal *Saturday Night* before assuming editorship of the *Peterborough Examiner* newspaper in 1942. Davies was named vice-president and publisher of the *Examiner* in 1946 and served with the newspaper until 1962. During this time, he also helped found the Canadian Stratford Shakespearean Festival and was elected governor of its board of directors in 1953. In 1960 he began teaching English literature at Trinity College in Toronto and the following year was appointed first master of Massey College, a graduate school at the University of Toronto, where he taught until his retirement in 1981.

During his years with the *Peterborough Examiner,* Davies wrote and directed such plays as *Overlaid* and *Fortune, My Foe.* Examining the relationship between art and life and the consequences of repressed hopes, these works reflect

Davies's interest in psychology and signal themes that are central to his fiction. It was also during this period that Davies wrote many journalistic essays under the pen name Samuel Marchbanks. A curmudgeon who has been likened to Samuel Johnson and Canadian satirist Stephen Leacock, Marchbanks is humorously excessive in his bitter attacks of provincial life, Canadian politics, and contemporary culture. These essays have been collected in *The Diary of Samuel Marchbanks, The Table Talk of Samuel Marchbanks, Samuel Marchbanks' Almanack,* and *The Papers of Samuel Marchbanks.* Although *The Papers of Samuel Marchbanks,* which brings together essays from the three previous volumes, has been described as dated and one of Davies's lesser works, it is often considered a successfully veiled parody of the contemporary academic publishing world, with Davies frequently editing, footnoting, and annotating Marchbanks's diatribes.

In the 1950s Davies began writing novels, the genre for which he has received his greatest recognition. His first three works—*Tempest-Tost, Leaven of Malice,* and *A Mixture of Frailties*—comprise *The Salterton Trilogy,* which examines life in the small university town of Salterton, Ontario. *Tempest-Tost* recounts the local theater group's attempts to stage Shakespeare's *Tempest*. The company's ineptitude and churlish behavior are the source of much of the novel's humor and represent characteristics which, according to Davies, limit Canada's cultural growth. The plot of *Leaven of Malice* revolves around the placement of a false engagement announcement in Salterton's newspaper, linking a young man and woman from rival families. The pretentiousness of the two families is satirically exposed as they go to great extremes to humiliate each other. Love triumphs, however, and the couple eventually marry. A young Salterton woman who travels to Europe to train as a singer is the subject of *A Mixture of Frailties*. Her development from a rustic small town girl to a sophisticated woman reflects Davies's belief that education and experience are necessary for a complete life.

The Salterton Trilogy was followed by Davies's critically acclaimed *The Deptford Trilogy*, which Claude Bissell described as "the major piece of prose fiction in Canadian literature." Focusing on the individual's need to accept the irrational, unconscious side of the self in order to achieve a state of mental and emotional well-being, this series centers on the seemingly inconsequential incident of a snowball fight that ultimately alters the lives of three men. In *Fifth Business*—the first novel in the trilogy—Dunstan Ramsay suffers remorse and guilt because a snowball intended for him strikes a pregnant woman. He attempts to rationalize his feelings by studying religious biographies, magic, and psychology. *The Manticore* opens with the mysterious suicide of Boy Staunton, who, as a child, initiated the infamous snowball incident, and recounts the psychoanalysis of Boy's son, David. In this novel Davies employs Jungian archetypes and ancient myths to unravel the mysteries of David's unconscious and depict David's growing self-awareness and acceptance of his father's actions. *World of Wonders* is the story of Paul Dempster, whose mother was hit by the snowball—an event which caused his premature birth and her mental breakdown. As in Davies's other works, magic and illusion figure prominently; Dempster is kidnapped by a carnival magician and eventually becomes the world-famous prestidigitator, Magnus Eisengrim. The dominant themes displayed in these novels reflect Davies's interest in the individual's search for identity and the moral necessity to examine all facets of life.

Like *The Salterton Trilogy*, *The Cornish Trilogy* centers on individuals living in a Canadian college town. *The Rebel Angels* concerns a group of professors who serve as executors of the estate of Francis Cornish, a collector and patron of the arts. Among the eclectic subjects Davies discusses in this novel are the works of French satirist François Rabelais and Swiss alchemist Philippus Paracelsus, gypsy customs, and "filth therapy." Short-listed for England's Booker Prize for Fiction, *What's Bred in the Bone*, ostensibly a biography of Francis Cornish as narrated by two angels, explores the influence of external forces upon one man's life. Containing a frame story involving characters from *The Rebel Angels*, *What's Bred in the Bone* dramatizes the protagonist's pursuit of self-knowledge and is infused with supernatural, psychological, and religious elements. In *The Lyre of Orpheus*, which focuses on the complexities of artistic representation, Cornish's biogra-

pher, Simon Darcourt, discovers that a painting that had been attributed to a sixteenth-century artist in *What's Bred in the Bone* is actually the work of Cornish. Concurrent with this plot are events that revolve around characters who, on behalf of the Cornish Foundation, are attempting to reconstruct E. T. A. Hoffmann's unfinished opera about the fictional kingdom of Camelot. While the production is accepted as an obvious attempt to complete Hoffmann's work and imitate his style, Cornish's painting, originally construed as the genuine work of a medieval artist, is nevertheless regarded as a fake with no artistic merit. Additionally, *The Lyre of Orpheus* is a parody of the academic world that relies heavily on myth and delineates the effect that the past has on the present; Davies's characters in this work are viewed as Jungian archetypes of King Arthur, his knights, and Queen Guenevere and are doomed to repeat the mistakes of their mythic counterparts. Several critics consider *The Lyre of Orpheus* a culmination of Davies's artistic philosophy, which is rooted in nineteenth-century Romanticism rather than in the aesthetics of contemporary fiction; David Lodge noted that *The Lyre of Orpheus* "has all Davies' wit, learning, and inventiveness in abundance, and brings to a satisfying conclusion a trilogy that stands as a major fictional achievement independent of literary fashion."

Davies's other works, which have earned him various awards and honors, include numerous plays, essay collections, and a volume of short stories entitled *High Spirits*. Nevertheless, Davies remains best known for *The Deptford Trilogy* and his work as a novelist. In summarizing Davies's career and literary stature, Anthony Burgess declared that "Robertson Davies' claim to world renown as expressed in the Nobel laureateship, I think, is undoubted. There we have Canada's greatest living writer, greatest living novelist, who must be universally acclaimed."

PRINCIPAL WORKS

Shakespeare's Boy Actors (nonfiction) 1939

Shakespeare for Young Players: A Junior Course (nonfiction) 1942

The Diary of Samuel Marchbanks (journalism) 1947

Overlaid (drama) 1947

At the Gates of the Righteous (drama) 1948

Eros at Breakfast (drama) 1948

Fortune, My Foe (drama) 1948

Hope Deferred (drama) 1948

Eros at Breakfast, and Other Plays [first publication] (drama) 1949

The Table Talk of Samuel Marchbanks (journalism) 1949

At My Heart's Core (drama) 1950

King Phoenix (drama) 1950

*Tempest-Tost (novel) 1951

A Masque of Aesop (drama) 1952

Renown at Stratford: A Record of the Shakespeare Festival in Canada, 1953 [with Tyrone Guthrie and Grant Macdonald] (nonfiction) 1953

A Jig for the Gypsy   (drama)   1954
*Leaven of Malice   (novel)   1954
Twice Have the Trumpets Sounded: A Record of the Strat-
      ford Shakespearean Festival in Canada, 1954   [with
      Tyrone Guthrie and Grant Macdonald]   (nonfic-
      tion)   1954
Hunting Stuart   (drama)   1955
Thrice the Brinded Cat Hath Mew'd: A Record of the Strat-
      ford Shakespearean Festival in Canada, 1955   [with
      Tyrone Guthrie, Boyd Neal, and Tanya Moisei-
      witsch]   (nonfiction)   1955
*A Mixture of Frailties   (novel)   1958
†Love and Libel   (drama)   1960
A Voice from the Attic   (addresses, essays, and lectures)
      1960; also published as *The Personal Art: Reading to*
      Good Purposes,   1961
A Masque of Mr. Punch   (drama)   1962
Samuel Marchbanks' Almanack   (journalism)   1967
‡Fifth Business   (novel)   1970
Stephen Leacock   (nonfiction)   1970
Hunting Stuart, and Other Plays   [first publication]
      (drama)   1972
‡The Manticore   (novel)   1972
Question Time   (drama)   1975
‡World of Wonders   (novel)   1975
One Half of Robertson Davies: Provocative Pronounce-
      ments on a Wide Range of Topics   (addresses, lec-
      tures, and short stories)   1977; also published as *One*
      Half of Robertson Davies,   1978
The Enthusiasms of Robertson Davies   (journalism and
      essays)   1979
§The Rebel Angels   (novel)   1981
The Well-Tempered Critic: One Man's View of Theatre
      and Letters in Canada   (addresses, essays, and lec-
      tures)   1981
High Spirits   (short stories)   1982
The Mirror of Nature   (lectures)   1983
The Papers of Samuel Marchbanks   (journalism and es-
      says)   1985
§What's Bred in the Bone   (novel)   1985
§The Lyre of Orpheus   (novel)   1988
Murther & Walking Spirits   (novel)   1991

*These works were published as *The Salterton Trilogy* in 1986.

†This work is an adaptation of Davies's novel *Leaven of Malice.*

‡These works were published as *The Deptford Trilogy* in 1983.

§These works are collectively referred to as *The Cornish Trilogy.*

CRITICISM

Robertson Davies   (essay date 1968)

[*In the following excerpt from an essay that was first de-*
livered as a lecture at Glendon College in York Universi-
ty, Davies defines and describes the conscience of the se-
rious writer.]

My subject is 'The Conscience of the Writer', and I have
accepted your invitation to speak not because I think I
have anything new to say about it, but because I think that
the familiar and basic things demand constant repetition,
in an age when familiar and basic things are so often cast
aside, as if we had outlived them. The writer's calling has
been greatly romanticized—more so, I believe, than that
of any other artistic creator. Painters, sculptors, and com-
posers are regarded with a degree of awe by the public in
general, but writers possess a special sort of magic, and I
believe that in part it is the magic of what seems to be a
familiar and attainable, yet somehow unrealized, element
in the lives of many people who are not artists of any kind.
Anybody can see that he is not going to paint like Picasso,
or write music like Benjamin Britten; he is not so sure that
he is not going to write like somebody whose writing he
admires. He has learned the humblest techniques of the
writer at school; he can put down words on a page; he has
some idea of grammar, or he may have decided that grammar is an unworthy shackle on his inspiration; he is constantly meeting with experiences, or observing people,
that seem to him to be the stuff of writing. But somehow
he never writes.

He could do so, of course. Every writer is familiar with the
person who buttonholes him and tells him about the book
he would write—if he had the time. Or else they have fathers or uncles who are screamingly funny characters
whose lives ought to be written at once. These people
sometimes offer to collaborate with the author, providing
the raw material if he will do the actual work of writing.

Such people are usually middle-aged. Younger people
with the urge to write do not want to collaborate; they are,
on the contrary, often suspicious that older writers will
snatch their splendid inspirations and capitalize on them.
These young people are often daring experimenters in
technique, because their ideas can only be given adequate
form in some wholly new way of writing—leaving out all
the verbs, or perhaps writing nothing but verbs, but most
often in the present day by describing, with gloating particularity, various sexual acts which they have just discovered, and of which they wish to make the innocent old
world aware. But after a few months during which they
burn with a hard, gem-like flame, these people cease to
write.

The world is full of people who think they could write, or
who have, at some time, written. But they do not stay with
it. Why?

Is it because the real writer, the serious writer, who is a
writer all his life, is a special kind of person? Yes, it is. And
what kind of person is he? I do not pretend to be able to
answer that question fully, for there are many kinds of
writers, some of whom I do not understand at all, and
some whom I understand but do not admire, although I
am well aware of their talents. But they all have a characteristic—indeed a distinguishing trait in their psychological make-up—which makes them recognizable, and it is
this that I have called the writer's conscience, although
that is not a very satisfactory name for it. I use that phrase
to describe the continuing struggle that goes on in the psyche of every writer of any importance. And by that expres-

sion 'of any importance' I exclude the journalistic word-spinners, the ghost-writers, the concocters of literary confectionery, although some of these are remarkable technicians. I am talking about the writers who try—perhaps not all the time but certainly during the greater part of their careers—to write the best they can about the themes that concern them most.

This is not a moral judgement, and has nothing to do with the themes that writers choose. Perhaps I can make myself clear by instancing two books—Dostoevsky's *Crime and Punishment* and Max Beerbohm's *Zuleika Dobson.* One is an agonized exploration of the psychology of a criminal intellectual; the other is a charming joke about youth and love. One is clumsily written, with long passages of overheated and perversely sensitive emotion; the other is elegantly and exquisitely written, in a fashion so subtle that it yields up its secrets only after several careful readings. Both are great books, and I think it is foolish to say that one is greater than the other, as if one were marking an examination, and giving Dostoevsky higher marks because he tries harder. He didn't try harder. He just wrote the best book he could in the circumstances in which he found himself. So did Max Beerbohm. Both books appeal strongly to large numbers of readers, who encounter them at particularly fortunate moments in their lives. And I believe that it is because both writers wrote under the domination of conscience, and it is the subsequent revelation that gives the books their particular weight and value.

There are no absolutes in literature that can be applied without reference to personal taste and judgement. The great book for you is the book that has most to say to you at the moment when you are reading. I do not mean the book that is most instructive, but the book that feeds your spirit. And that depends on your age, your experience, your psychological and spiritual need. These days I find myself reading poetry rather a lot. But when I was ten what I liked to read best were bound volumes of a boys' paper called *Chums.* It had just what I needed, and it extended my world remarkably; however, when I looked at some of that stuff recently I could not endure it. But I am sure I should not be reading what I read now if I had not read *Chums* then, and I am grateful. We do not read to make ourselves cultured, but to nourish our souls. Real culture is the evidence, not the reality, of the fully realized spirit.

This is one of my great quarrels with university courses in English; they require students to read lists of fine books, and to profess a knowledge of them that is usually superficial, though even this sort of knowledge is better than none at all. But for every masterpiece that is on the reading-list, there are five that are not, and many students fall into the trap of thinking that anything that is not on the list is not Blue Brand Literature, and may be disregarded. This is not the intention of English courses, but it is what happens. The great difficulty is that the emphasis in universities is likely to be on criticism of literature, rather than on delighted discovery and surrender to it. Every student—BA,MA, or PH D—knows what is wrong with Charles Dickens, though they have probably read nothing but *Great Expectations,* and read it once, when they were too young to understand it. The reason for this is perfectly clear: criticism is comparatively easy in its showy but superficial aspect. Anybody can pick up its techniques and use them with a display of skill, just as anybody can make a spectacular cut with a surgeon's scalpel, simply because it is so sharp. But the vastly more difficult business of discovering literature, and giving oneself wholly into its embrace, and making some of it part of oneself, cannot be done in large classes, and not everybody can do it even in small classes. A surprising number of people can get PH D's in criticism; to be a worthy reader of what writers of conscience have written is a very different matter.

Which brings us back to our theme—the writer and his conscience. Moral judgements based on the themes a writer chooses, I have said, are irrelevant. Evelyn Waugh was a writer of extraordinary conscience, and his novels, even when most serious, have a comic guise, and are spare and elegant in form. Tolstoy was similarly a writer of extraordinary conscience, but *Anna Karenina* and *War and Peace* are solemn and almost portentous in tone, and their greatest admirers will admit that they might have been the better for the cutting of large passages. It is of little use to say that *War and Peace* is a masterpiece because it tells us all there is to say about war; it tells us wonderful things, but Waugh's little novel *Scoop* tells us something that Tolstoy did not. This is not to say that the two books are equally 'great' or 'good' but only that every good book is good in its own way, and that comparisons are of extremely limited value. Unless, of course, you are a superficial critic, in which case you had better banish all humility in the face of genius and get on with your self-appointed task of awarding marks and establishing hierarchies. But if you want to know and feel what genius knows and feels, you must be a reader first, and a critic a very long way afterward.

Now—what is this conscience I have been talking about? It is the writer's inner struggle toward self-knowledge and self-recognition, which he makes manifest through his art. Writers, and artists generally, are notoriously resistant to psycho-analysis, and to put hundreds of thousands of words by both Freud and Jung into a nutshell it is because they are continuously psycho-analysing themselves in their own way, which is through their work, and it is the only way to peace of mind, to integration, open to them. It is a life process, and in the work of a writer of great abilities who has been so fortunate as to live long it presents an awesome achievement. Consider the case of Thomas Mann; from *Little Herr Friedemann,* which he published when he was twenty-three, and *Buddenbrooks,* which appeared when he was twenty-five, the succession of his books reveals to us, beneath the themes, the fables, and the philosophical explorations, the development of an extraordinary spirit: *The Magic Mountain* (1924), the great *Joseph* tetralogy, which was sixteen years in the writing, *Lotte in Weimar* (1939), *Doctor Faustus* (1948), and that extraordinary book which appeared when the writer was eighty, *The Confessions of Felix Krull*—these are a few mountain peaks in a career of an artist's self-exploration. And what is revealed? A deep preoccupation with themes of death and disease, of sin and remorse and redemption, of myth and the irrationalities of life, of the wellsprings of the creative spirit, and at the last, in *Felix Krull,* a triumphant return and exploration of one of Mann's lifelong preoccupations, which was the link between the artistic and the criminal instinct, embodied in what I regard as quite the subtlest and most hair-raisingly erotic novel I have ever read. A concern, as you see, with some of the deep and continuing problems of human life.

Here we have what the great literary artist does; he explores his own spirit to the uttermost, and bodies forth what he finds in a form of art that is plain to anyone who can read it—though not necessarily to anyone who picks up his books.

The struggle is not easy and its results are sometimes disastrous, for reasons that we shall explore a little later. Psycho-analysis is notoriously demanding and disagreeable, when undertaken by a sympathetic and skilled physician: consider what it means when it is a solitary venture, undertaken as a life sentence and carried out under the circumstances in which most authors live. Is it any wonder that the domestic lives of some of them are rumpled and unseemly? Or that many of them take to drink? Or that others escape into that attractive world of action where they can get so much easy acclaim by protesting or sitting-in or freaking-out or setting themselves up as great friends and patrons of youth, or whooping it up for the Pill or LSD—doing anything, in fact, except getting on with the laborious task to which their gift and their temperament calls them?

Henrik Ibsen knew all about it, and he was one of the heroes who remained chained to his task until finally it broke him; for the last years of his life he toiled painstakingly every day over a copybook, trying to force his hand to learn, for the second time, the skill of making readable writing. Did you know that Ibsen was a poet? Here is a translation of one of his verses, full of meaning and of warning for writers:

> To live—is a battle with troll-folk
> In the crypts of heart and head;
> To write—is a man's self-judgement
> As Doom shall judge the dead.

'A man's self-judgement'—that is the conscience of the writer. Whatever he writes, and whatever the summing-up of that mysterious inner court may be, if it is carried through truthfully and manfully, we shall sense in it that quality that makes literature one of the greatest of the arts, and well worth the sacrifice and the frequent misery of a writer's life.

Sometimes I laugh when aspiring writers assure me that if they could get enough money—usually in the form of a grant from some handout agency subsidized by the government—they would go to Mexico, or the Mediterranean, or to Capri, and there they would be able to write—so readily, so fluently, so happily. Fools! 'A man's self-judgement' will go with him anywhere, if he is really a writer, and he will not be able to command either inspiration or happiness or serenity. Of course if he is a mere scribbling tourist, or a work-shy flop, or both, it does not really matter much where he goes. But if he is a writer he will be wise to write wherever he finds himself. The history of literature is full of writers who have thought that the judgement of the inner court would be easier in some country outside his own.

This is not to say, of course, that a writer should not travel or gain experience. But if he is really a writer his task may be, not to seek experience, but to survive the experience that crowds upon him from every quarter. As Aldous Huxley has written, 'experience is not a matter of having actually swum the Hellespont, or danced with the dervishes, or slept in a doss-house. It is a matter of sensibility and intuition, of seeing and hearing the significant things, of paying attention at the right moments, of understanding and co-ordinating. Experience is not what happens to a man: it is what a man does with what happens to him.' Many years ago I read a book by the travelling journalist Richard Halliburton; he had climbed a very high mountain somewhere—I forget where because the book was not of the sort that sticks in the mind—and he recorded the reflection of his companion at the top. It was 'Now I can spit a mile!' We are familiar with the reflections of Wordsworth, who climbed a few quite unremarkable hills in the Lake District. There is the contrast in what experience meant to a man of trivial mind, and to a poet. (pp. 119-25)

How does the real writer—the man with the writer's conscience, or temperament, or whatever label you choose—set about his work? There are as many ways as there are writers, but there are a few well-worn paths, and of these I can only speak with certainty about the path I have chosen for myself. It would be more correct to say, the path my temperament has chosen for me. I combine writing with other sorts of work. For twenty-eight years I have been a journalist—not just a writer, but an editor, an employer, a man who had to make sure that his newspaper did not lose money, who had to worry about new machinery, new buildings, new contracts with unions, and continually to be concerned with an obligation to a community. When I had spent the day doing this I went home and wrote, altogether, works that fill eighteen volumes; I am at work on the nineteenth, and the twentieth exists in the form of extended notes. I am not counting four full-length plays that were produced but are not yet in print. I am not saying this to dazzle you with my industry, but to tell you how I do my work. I have always been grateful for my journalistic experience, which amounts to millions of words of writing, because it kept my technique in good muscular shape. I can write now without that humming and hawing and staring at the ceiling which plagues so many writers who have trouble getting started.

I have of late become a university professor and head of a college, and these tasks can hardly be regarded as a rest-cure. My most difficult work in this realm is the correcting of student essays and marking examinations. Reading inexpert writing is deeply exhausting. It is like listening to bad music.

I have also had the ordinary family experiences. I am married and have three children, now all grown up, and I have spent countless happy hours in domestic pursuits—gardening, family music-making, getting together some modest but pleasant collections of things, amateur theatricals as well as some professional theatre-work, and a kind of family life that seems perhaps to be more characteristic of the nineteenth century than of our streamlined era. I have sat on committees, and boards; I have made a great many speeches, and I have listened to what seem, in recollection, to be millions of speeches.

All of this I consider necessary to my life as a writer. It has kept me from too great a degree of that fruitless self-preoccupation which is one of the worst diseases of the literary life. It has provided me with the raw material for what I write. The raw material, you observe; before it becomes the finished product it must undergo a process of distillation and elimination. An author is a very different thing from a reporter, or an autobiographer. This way of living has confirmed a theory I formed many years ago, when I was at the age you have reached now, that myth and fairy-tales are nothing less than the distilled truth about what we call 'real life', and that we move through a throng of Sleeping Princesses, Belles Dames sans Merci, Cinderellas, Wicked Witches, Powerful Wizards, Frog Princes, Lucky Third Sons, Ogres, Dwarves, Sagacious Animal Helpers and Servers, yes and Heroes and Heroines, in a world that is nothing less than an enchanted landscape, and that life only seems dull and spiritless to those who live under a spell—too often a spell they have brought upon their own heads.

Do not misunderstand me. I am not being whimsical, and my world is not the cosy nursery retreat of Winnie-the-Pooh. It is a tough world, and it only seems irrational or unreal to those who have not grasped some hints of its remorseless, irreversible, and often cruel logic. It is a world in which God is not mocked, and in which a man reaps—only too obviously—what he has sown. I do not think I understand it all, but I think I am acquainted with a few corners of it. And I may as well tell you that I regard the writing I have done as little more than a preparation for the work I mean to do.

Although I have been telling you about what I have done that is not the primary work of a writer, I would not have you believe that I have merely fitted my writing into odd corners of my life. Writing has always been central to my life, and my real work. But I said that I was glad to have the ordinary occupations of a busy man to protect me against that self-preoccupation that is one of the worst diseases of the literary life. Let me explain: I do not write in my spare time, I write all the time; whatever I may be doing, the literary aspect of my mind is fully at work: it is not only the hours at the desk or the typewriter, but the hours spent in other kinds of work and in many kinds of diversion when I am busily observing, shaping, rejecting, and undergoing a wide variety of feelings that are the essential material of writing. Notice that I said feelings—not thoughts, but feelings. One of the burdensome parts of the writer's temperament, as I understand it, is that one feels quite strongly about all sorts of things that other people seem to be able to gloss over, and this can be wearisome and depleting. This is the famous 'artistic sensitivity' that one sometimes hears people boasting about—very often people who show no other awareness of it. It is not a form of weakness. A writer is very rarely a wincing, delicate kind of man; in my experience he is often rather a tough

creature, though given to hypochondria and sudden collapses of the spirit. I rely on a routine of daily work, and the necessities of a busy life, to keep me from succumbing too completely to the demands of a particular kind of temperament. My kind of writer—I can speak for no other—needs other work and a routine to keep him sane.

Let me return once again to the emphasis I laid on feeling, rather than thinking, in the writer's temperament. All sorts of people expect writers to be intellectuals. Sometimes they are, but it is not necessary to their work. Aldous Huxley was an intellectual, but he was not so good a novelist as E. M. Forster, who is not and does not like to be considered one. The writer is necessarily a man of feeling and intuition; he need not be a powerful original thinker. Shakespeare, Dickens, Dostoevsky—we do not think of them as intellectuals; Tolstoy's thinking was vastly inferior to his fiction; Keats was a finer poet than Arnold, though no one would deny Arnold the title of intellectual. I do not say that writers are child-like creatures of untutored genius; often they are very intelligent men: but the best part of their intelligence is of the feeling and intuitive order. Sometimes they are impatient and even rude with people who insist on treating them as intellectuals. It is not pleasant to be treated like a clock by some clever but essentially unsympathetic person who wants to take you apart to see what makes you tick. But the modern passion for this sort of thing has led to the establishment on many campuses of a man called the Writer in Residence, who is there, in part at any rate, for intellectuals to pester, take apart, and reassemble, under the impression that they are learning something about writing.

As I draw to a conclusion, I want to return to something I said at the beginning of this address, which is that the life of a writer may be likened to a long self-analysis. I suggested that the process was painful, and indeed it frequently is so. But it is something else—something that Freud never mentioned, because of his preoccupation with neurosis, but which Jung suggests: it is sometimes joyous, victorious, and beautiful. It is not fashionable nowadays to say that one's life has moments of piercing beauty, or that it brings hours which are not merely recompense, but ample and bounteous reward for all the anxieties and dark moments. But I am not a fashionable person, and I am saying that now.

The degree of self-examination that is involved in being a writer, and the stringency of the writer's conscience, which holds you to a path that is often distasteful, necessarily takes you on some strange journeys, not only into the realm of the personal Unconscious, but into the level below that. It is assumed, by many people who have read Freud and Jung, that these descents must always be alarming experiences, because Freud and Jung were so much occupied with people who were very seriously disordered. But the writer is not necessarily disordered, and great rewards await him in this realm, if he approaches it with decent reverence. He will have serious struggles, but sometimes his struggles are like those of Jacob when he wrestled with the angel at Peniel, and cried in his extremity, 'I will not let thee go, unless thou bless me.' And he received the blessing, and bore it all his life. That realm of the Unconscious, which is the dwelling-place of so many demons and monsters, is also the home of the Muses, the abode of the angels. The writer, in his traffic with that realm in which dream, and myth, and fairy-tale become mingled with the most ordinary circumstances of life, does not lack for rewards and very great rewards. Self-examination is stern and often painful, as Ibsen tells us in the verse I quoted to you, but it is not all bitterness.

I have spoken to you seriously, because I presume that you are serious people. Certainly I am one, though such reputation as I have as a writer rests—rests perhaps a little too heavily—on my qualities as a humorist. Never be deceived by a humorist, for if he is any good he is a deeply serious man, moved by a quirk of temperament to speak a certain kind of truth in the form of jokes. Everybody can laugh at the jokes; the real trick is to understand them.

I have spoken of the conscience of the writer, trying to give you some insight into what it is that distinguishes the writer by temperament, the writer who cannot help being a writer, from someone who may write very well, but who writes for a different purpose—to instruct, to explain, to criticize—and for whom therefore writing is a necessary technique rather than an all-absorbing art. If I have discouraged anyone, I am sorry, but honesty comes before even courtesy in such matters as this. And if I have made anybody look searchingly into himself, to determine whether or not he has the kind of artistic conscience I have described, I shall think myself greatly rewarded. (pp. 130-34)

> *Robertson Davies, in his* One Half of Robertson Davies, *The Viking Press, 1977, 286 p.*

Robertson Davies with Donald Cameron　(interview date 1971)

[*In the following excerpt from an interview which took place in 1971 at Massey College in Toronto, Canada, Davies discusses such subjects as psychology, religion, the contrast between his public image and personal identity as a writer, and the role of the reader in fiction.*]

[*Cameron*]: *I sense a good deal of Freudianism in your thinking. Is Freud someone you've read seriously and thought about a lot?*

[*Davies*]: Yes, I have, as a matter of fact. I am, I guess, one of the very few people I know who has read Freud's collected works from end to end. Freud was an enormous enthusiasm of mine before I was forty; after forty I came to examine the works of his great colleague Carl Gustav Jung, and I have been, over many years, reading and re-reading and reading again the collected works of C. G. Jung.

What gave you that serious an interest in psychoanalytic thought in the first place?

Well, I had been interested in the notion that this line of thought existed even when I was a schoolboy; when I went to Queen's University there was a remarkable professor of psychology there, Dr. George Humphrey, a notable man who later on became Professor of Psychology at Oxford

and wrote a great book on the theory of learning. Humphrey talked a great deal about Freud, about whom he knew a lot, and so I was led to read some Freud. One of the things that enchanted me was that Freud was saying explicitly things which I had vaguely apprehended as possibilities. This whetted my appetite enormously, so on I went. Later on I discovered the same thing in Jung: he had had the intellect and the ability to go into very deeply, and to talk about superbly, things which I had dimly apprehended, and so I was eager to follow.

Was there something that you became unsatisfied with in Freud?

Yes, there was. It was Freud's reductive train of thought, which is very welcome to the young mind but becomes, I find, less welcome to the older mind. Freud didn't indulge in this kind of thing, but a great many of his disciples do: you're afraid of thunder because when you were little you heard your father fart and then he spanked you, or something of that sort. Well, this seems to me unworthy of the human race. It's not the kind of cheap wares in which Freud dealt, but it's a thing that people have rather developed from his line of thinking, and much of his thought *is* violently reductive—the tendency to feel that the sexual etiology of neurosis explains everything, and that sort of thing. As Jung pointed out, a surprising number of people seemed to turn up in Jung's consulting room with manifest neuroses which were not primarily related to any sort of sexual hangup. As Jung also pointed out, Freud was an extraordinarily brilliant and very, very successful young man—the darling of his doting mother—who had always lived a city life. Jung had led much more the kind of childhood I myself had had—going to country schools, living with country children, knowing country things, being quite accustomed to animals and the sort of rough and rather sexually oriented—but in an ordinary, daily way—life of the country person.

Robert Kroetsch, who lives in the States, feels that Freudianism had great success there because it really appeals to something in American experience, in American ideology: the stress between the good guy and the bad guy, the id and the ego, a kind of Manichean view of the psyche.

That's extremely interesting.

And he felt that Canada was a much more Jungian society.

Ooooh, this is music to my soul! I think we're a much softer-focussed country. In the intellectual life of the United States, there seems to be such a very, very strong Jewish strain—I would not for an instant suggest that that was a bad thing, but it is an intensely *conditioning* thing. This intellectual ferocity and sort of black/white quality is very strong there. We're fuzzier, but I think we're more humane, and that's what I think about Jung, too. (pp. 35-6)

Has religion something to do with your interest in Freud and Jung?

Yes. One reason I was drawn to the study of Freud and of Jung was my religious interest, because I very quickly found that for my taste, investigation of religion by orthodox theological means was unrewarding. You never got down to brass tacks, or at least nothing that I ever read did so. You started off by assuming that certain things were true, and then you developed all kinds of splendid things on top of that. I wanted to see about the basic things, so I thought that I would have a look at people who had had a wrestle with these very, very basic things, and Freud was one of them. Freud decided that religion is essentially an illusion: well, I read that, I studied it and chewed on it and mulled it over for quite a long time, but it never fully satisfied me, because it seemed to me that brilliant as Sigmund Freud was, there have been men of comparable brilliance or even greater brilliance who had been enormously attached to this concept which seemed to him to be nothing better than an illusion. One of the figures which bulked very large in my ideas was St. Augustine. I was very interested as a very young boy to discover that I was born on the day of St. Augustine, the 28th of August, and also on the birthday of Tolstoy and Goethe; and I thought, Oh, that's great stuff, splendid! This is an omen. But St. Augustine was a man of the most towering intellectual powers, and if he was willing to devote his life to the exposition of this thing which Freud called an illusion, I felt that the betting couldn't all be on Saint Sigmund; some of it conceivably ought to be on St. Augustine. And there were other figures whom I thought intensely significant. I thought a great deal about it, and then I gradually began to look into the works of Jung and found a much more—to me—satisfying attitude towards religion, but it was not an orthodox Christian one. Orthodox Christianity has always had for me the difficulty that it really won't come, in what is for me a satisfactory way, to grips with the problem of evil. It knows an enormous amount about evil, it discusses evil in fascinating terms, but evil is always the other thing: it is something which is apart from perfection, and man's duty is to strive for perfection. I could not reconcile that with such experience of life as I had, and the Jungian feeling that things tend to run into one another, that what looks good can be pushed to the point where it becomes evil, and that evil very frequently bears what can only be regarded as good fruit—this was the first time I'd ever seen that sort of thing given reasonable consideration, and it made enormous sense to me. I feel now that I am a person of strongly religious temperament, but when I say "religious" I mean immensely conscious of powers of which I can have only the dimmest apprehension, which operate by means that I cannot fathom, in directions which I would be a fool to call either good or bad. Now that seems hideously funny, but it isn't really; it is, I think, a recognition of one's position in an inexplicable universe, in which it is not wholly impossible for you to ally yourself with, let us say, positive rather than negative forces, but in which anything that you do in that direction must be done with a strong recognition that you may be very, very gravely mistaken. This is something which would never satisfy the humblest parish priest, but I live in a world in which forces are going on which I am unable to tab and identify so that the tickets will stick. I just have to get on as well as I can. Various kind people in writing about my books have called me an existentialist, and they won't believe me when I tell them I don't know what an existentialist is. I've had it explained to me many times, but the explanation never really makes enough sense to me to cling. But I have tried to state for

you what my position is, and I fear that I've done so clumsily and muddily—but if it comes in clumsy and muddy, it's just got to be that way. Better that than slick and crooked.

Perhaps people find it difficult to believe that you don't know what an existentialist is because of your public persona, your image, to use the ad-man's word, which—

—my image, if I've got an image—I suppose I have—has been made for me by other people. Nobody wants to listen to what I want to say. They want to tell me what I think.

Well, the image presents you as a man of formidable learning, formidable intellect, and fearsome wit, a man who would know about things like existentialism.

I am not of formidable learning; I am a very scrappily educated person, and I am not of formidable intellect; I really am not a very good thinker. In Jungian terms I am a feeling person with strong intuition. I *can* think, I've *had* to think, and I *do* think, but thinking isn't the first way I approach any problem. It's always, What does this say to me? And I get it through my fingertips, not through my brain. *Then* I have to think about it, but the thinking is a kind of consciously undertaken thing rather than a primary means of apprehension. Also intuition is very strong in me; I sort of smell things. As for this wit business, it's primarily defence, you know. Witty people are concealing something.

What are you concealing?

I suppose I'm concealing—hmmm. Well, you see, if it were easy for me to tell you, I wouldn't be concealing. I think I am concealing a painful sensitivity, because I am very easily hurt and very easily rebuffed and very easily set down; and very early in life I found out that to be pretty ready with your tongue was a way of coping with that. You know that is a thing which is attributed to Dunstan Ramsay in *Fifth Business.* He was always "getting off a good one". If you can get off a good one once or twice a day, people don't rasp you as much as they otherwise might. They'll do it enough, however defensive you are. (pp. 40-2)

There's a very interesting interplay in your work between theatre and fiction. I suspect that for you theatre is a metaphor of some dimensions.

It's the element of illusion in life, the difference between appearance and reality. In the theatre you can be in the know about what makes the difference, and it is fascinating that you can know what creates the illusion, know everything about it, be part of it, and yet not despise the people who want the illusion, who cannot live without it. That's important, you know. So frequently it is assumed that if you know how something's done you despise the people who don't. You don't do that in the theatre. You respect them; you know that they know a good thing when they see it. (pp. 43-4)

You are very strongly Canadian, aren't you, in that you have a very clear sense of who you are and which national community is yours.

Yes, indeed, and this became very very clear to me within

ROBERTSON DAVIES THE PAPERS OF SAMUEL MARCHBANKS

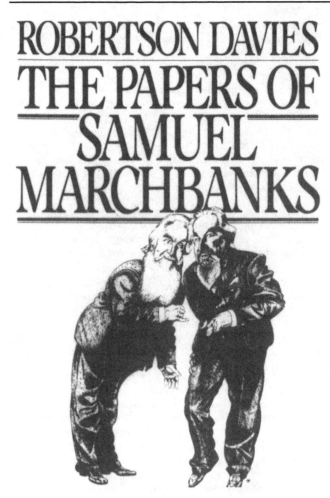

Cover of the first American edition of The Papers of Samuel Marchbanks.

the last two or three years. I've always felt strongly Canadian, which doesn't mean complacently or gleefully Canadian, but Canadian; and my father, who was a Welshman, had always, during the latter part of his life, spent all his summers in his native country, in Wales. My mother was Canadian and her family had been here for a very long time—since 1785 as a matter of fact—but my father always had this extraordinary pull back to his home country. Living in this college, I live in a house which is attached to the college, which is not mine, and when I retire I will not, of course, continue to live there. So my wife and I thought the time had come when we ought to have some place where we'll be able to go when we retire. Distant though that time may be, now is the time to get on with doing it, because when you're retired you don't want to plunge right into the business of finding a dwelling or building one. So we thought, what'll we do? Will we acquire some place in England and retire there? Now this would have been comprehensible because there was this very strong pull of my father's towards the old land, and my wife's family, who were Australians, were always drawn back to England as the great, good place in which all important things happened. We talked it over and decided that my wife had been a Canadian far longer than

she'd been an Australian, and that I was really a Canadian, and that to leave this country would be like cutting off my feet. So we built a house in the country in Canada. That was a decision which went far beyond a matter of bricks and mortar. It would be impossible now to leave with the feeling that you'd left for good. We like to travel, we like to get around to see what's doing, we're both terribly interested in the theatre, which means we like to get over to England where the theatre is most lively, and to the continent. But to live, to have your being, to feel that this is where you're going to get old and die, that's another thing—and that's *here*.

That doesn't surprise me now, but it might have before I met you.

Well, as we've said, the popular notion of what I am and why I do things is very wide of the mark. The mainstream of what I do is this sense which I can only call a religious sense, but which is not religious in a sectarian, or aggressive, or evangelistic sense. And also, you know, I really think I've now got to the age where I have to consider what I am and how I function, and I can only call myself an artist. Now people hesitate very much in Canada to call themselves artists. An extraordinary number of authors shrink from that word, because it suggests to them a kind of fancy attitude, which might bring laughter or might seem overstrained—but if you really put your best energies into acts of creation, I don't know what else you can call yourself. You'd better face it and get used to it, and take on the things that are implied by it.

What sorts of things are implied?

A duty to be true to your abilities in so far as you can and as deeply as you can. I think this is where Leacock didn't trust himself, didn't trust his talent. He never thought of himself as an artist, which he started out, I'm sure, to be; his early work has a lot of that quality about it. He decided he was going to be a moneymaker instead, so he didn't become the writer he might have been, and I think that's what you've got to do if you have a chance. I couldn't have said this until fairly recently—you know, you step out in front of the public and say, I am an artist, and they shout, Yeah? Look who's talking, and throw eggs. If you step out in front of them and say, I am a humorist, they say, All right, make us laugh. You can do that fairly easily, but if you say, I can make you feel; I can maybe even make you cry, that's claiming a lot.

And do they want you to do it?

They really do, but they want to be sure that they're in safe hands before they let you do it, because you might be kidding them: you might make them cry and then say, Yah, yah, look who's crying; I did that as a trick—and that's what would hurt them. They're sensitive too. It's an awareness of approaching and retreating sensibilities that is not very easy to acquire.

W. O. Mitchell refers to the reader as a "creative partner".

Yes! Exactly! And you've got to find the way to make it possible for him to create without being ashamed of himself afterwards. Only an artist can do that. (pp. 44-6)

Robertson Davies and Donald Cameron, in an interview in Conversations with Canadian Novelists, *Macmillan of Canada, 1973, pp. 30-48.*

Robert Jones   (review date 20 December 1985)

[*In the following excerpt, Jones faults Davies as a writer who is "concerned with pretentions to greatness and the compulsion to be Significant, not with art itself."*]

[In] allegedly "serious" fiction, it is virtually a unique occurrence to find a writer who was born to write one novel and yet who continues to produce at an astonishing rate. Canadian novelist Robertson Davies has written more than twenty-four books. His *Deptford Trilogy,* consisting of *Fifth Business, The Manticore,* and *World of Wonders,* is his most widely known work in the United States, but it is *Fifth Business* alone by which he stakes any claim to respectability. His new novel, *What's Bred in the Bone,* is a peculiar rehash of everything he has done previously, but it is a caricature of his other books, like a hammy performance by a fading actor reduced to repeating his glory in small towns and sideshows.

Davies is the perfect example of what we have come to know as the "middle-brow" writer. He has prevailed because in the context of most glib, popular fiction, the issues he raises appear to be substantial. He has taken as his theme the idea of the supernatural, usually represented through the figure of the magician, and the tricks and turns of perception which reveal a world beyond that of appearances. In *Fifth Business,* the narrator says of his childhood, "But what I knew then was that nobody—not even my mother—was to be trusted in a strange world that showed very little of itself on the surface." The foundation of Davies's work has been the desire to lead his readers into this world of wonders, but he never penetrates beyond its surface.

His characters speak volumes (literally) about art, religion, and the meaning of life, but even in *Fifth Business,* he fails to follow the primary lesson of all fiction workshops: don't tell me, *show me.* All the references to Faust and damnation, to God and the afterlife, never amount to anything but glitter. To refer to oneself as "damned," as Dunstan Ramsay does in *Fifth Business,* is a different matter entirely from giving any indication through characterization or action of the state of damnation. Whenever the reader is treated to a lengthy conversation about God or the supernatural, he or she becomes lost in the voices. Unless each character is identified after each statement, it becomes difficult to determine who is speaking. They exist as mouths who lip-synch the author's views.

The writer Davies would most like to imitate is Iris Murdoch, but he lacks the sophistication of her best novels or the ease by which philosophical ideas become the backdrop to her characters' motivations. We don't feel the threat of Julian in *A Fairly Honorable Defeat* because Murdoch tells us he is evil, but by the way he so cheerfully and successfully victimizes each character. It is from Julian's ability to manipulate and conquer that we see the

horror of a mechanistic universe, not from any chatter about the fate that determines our lives.

To read several of Davies's novels in succession is to suspect that he is no match for his intentions. He has clearly been struck by the presence of angels and demons, but he has never gone beyond the original perception. He pastes spirits onto the scenery and by that act attempts to persuade the reader that they exist. But they have no substance and become little more than another disappearing act in his bag of tricks. It is like sitting in a theater and seeing the props and settings and realizing after several hours that there will be no play.

As a writer, Davies may be the victim of his own conservatism. The unnerving message underlying the real, if precious, charm of *The Deptford Trilogy,* and which is increasingly manifested in his most recent novels, is that the fundamentalist view is essentially correct. The invisible universe is populated by angels and devils at battle for human souls. There is nothing to suggest that these spirits are meant as metaphors of benevolence or malevolence unloosed by human power and desire. Or that they represent a terrifying capacity to compromise with evil as we see in a book like Thomas Mann's *Dr. Faustus.*

In Davies's work, and especially in *What's Bred in the Bone,* these spirits have personality. He believes in pitchfork-carrying devils and in angels who tell jokes. If his narratives seem structurally flimsy and pallid intellectually, and if his mechanistic view of the cosmos irritates rather than disturbs, it is because he has accepted as his vision the most retrograde view of human existence possible. He cannot create motivation in his characters or sustain dramatic tension because his understanding of the universe is antithetical to human action and responsibility. Since Davies sees people as cardboard cutouts pulled along by cosmic strings, his characters cannot be anything but flat, ventriloquist dummies. All the talk of Freud and Jung and the unconscious is a smokescreen for a determinist view that should be the delight of creationists the world over.

This is not to suggest that literature is the property of liberals. But the conservatism of writers like Waugh and Eliot evolved as a response to their particular experiences of the bleakness of modern life. Ideology ruins aspects of each of their work, but when they break through and render their vision meaningful, it is always in those moments when private opinion finds itself translated into something larger than the self and its tedious autobiography. It is impossible to understand much about the creation of art, or to determine how or why that odd confluence between writer and audience happens, but we know when it does.

We also know when it does not. Writers like Robertson Davies are concerned with pretentions to greatness and the compulsion to be Significant, not with art itself. If his work has never evolved from the one book by which he is best known, it is because of his basic misperception of ideology as in any way credible as a vision. His grandiloquent, quasi-nineteenth-century prose is an artificial attempt to find a style to match his moralizing about a past he fails to grasp historically, yet wields as an image by which he damns the present. His work gives no indication of the natural or instinctual play by which an author's voice speaks through the form. The structure of his novels has become increasingly creaky and full of gimmicks as he repeats the same ideas over and over within an identical framework.

Both *Fifth Business* and *What's Bred in the Bone* begin with a mystery about a central character and both seek to reveal their secrets by the retelling of that character's life. Both even share the device of a newspaper article in the opening scenes which is meant to demonstrate that the facts known about the character illuminate little about him. And they each include the birth of a hideous, misshapen child who haunts the action of the novel and who, perhaps unwittingly, betrays much about the mind of Robertson Davies.

In *Fifth Business* a pregnant woman is hit by a snowball as she walks with her husband and immediately gives birth to a premature, deformed child. The birth of the tiny monster unhinges this woman completely. She disappears from her sick bed, only to be found copulating with a tramp in the woods. When her bewildered husband asks the reasons for her betrayal, she replies, "He was very civil, 'Masa. And he wanted it so badly."

Davis clearly thinks he is making a coy joke by abbreviating the husband's name, Amasa Dempster, so that it sounds like a slave addressing a master when spoken. But this idea of women as mindless dolts eager to succumb to any bum with a zipper never leaves us and clouds Dunstan Ramsay's quest for the great magician, Magnus Eisengrim. And once Ramsay finds himself under the spell of the magician and is finally able to seek answers to his questions about the supernatural, he experiences a crisis of belief. Not because he has glimpsed anything revelatory about another world, but because he stumbles upon Eisengrim's two women, Liesl and Faustina (get it?), embracing. The sight of the two women with legs and arms intertwined is enough to undermine Ramsay's entire quest for truth. As he says, "I have never known such a collapse of spirit even in the worst of war. And this time there was no Little Madonna to offer me courage or ease me into oblivion."

The devil is a woman. In case the reader fails to grasp Davies's point, he states it explicitly in a later conversation between Ramsay and Eisengrim. One begins to suspect that all the talk of damnation, of the mysteries of the universe, and the journey of the soul have nothing to do with theology or the life of the spirit, but with a dread of sexuality and an alarmist view of women as the "other." Suddenly all the references to harlots and virgins, to private parts and masturbation, become evident not as aspects of a vision, but as part of a private pathology.

What is Robertson Davies trying to tell us? The life of Francis Cornish as portrayed in *What's Bred in the Bone* culminates in a castle owned by Saraceni, a shady Teutonic art collector. Francis, like Dunstan Ramsay in *Fifth Business,* has become an apprentice, but this time our hero yearns to discover everything there is to know about art. Enough scoundrels, prostitutes, Nazis, and plot contrivances abound to rival the convolutions of a grand opera

(Goering even buys the fake triptych Francis paints in the style of the Old Masters), but as always with Davies, the real story comes down to the talk. Saraceni and Francis indulge their love of conversation with much bombast about the modern world versus the past, the role of art in society, and the misuses of tyranny and power. And while there is no suggestion that Davies admires the teachings of the German Reich, there is a confusion and ambiguity in Cornish's conversations with Saraceni that remain unsettling.

Be it the sorcerer's apprentice, the magician's apprentice, or the Nazi's apprentice, Davies is fascinated by servitude and the violence of the oppressor towards the oppressed. His view amounts to a kind of reactionary Darwinism with religion thrown in for good measure. In the hierarchy of domination, celestial bodies reign over the earth, the strongest men rule the weaker, and of course, even the feeblest wimp is the *sine qua non* master of women.

Or this is how life should be in Davies's zen heaven. Francis's spiritual guides, a recording angel and a daimon, frequently interject interpretations of events as they occur in the novel. These spirits are intended to represent opposing voices of reason in Francis's life and, by extension, the world itself. What, then, are we to make of the daimon's comment following one of Francis's and Saraceni's dialogues about art, "Those who find a master should yield to the master until they've outgrown him"?

Master and slave, oppressor and victim: these are the categories by which Robertson Davies imagines the world. History has taught us much about the truth of this dynamism, but seldom has the matter-of-fact benefit of slavishness to authority been embraced with such apparent reasonableness. The evolution of life is a ceaseless process of outwitting the opponent and struggling for position. The apprentice looks to the master to glean the tricks of appearances by which he gives the illusion of strength. But it is all a fantasy. This is why Davies is fascinated by magic. For him there is no netherworld to encounter, but only masks of deception, one giving way to another. The master is the one who learns to manipulate them and dazzle the observer with his sleight of hand.

We are left with a curiously despairing idea of experience, but one that includes neither tragedy nor even pathos. Its source is not hopelessness, but the rage of the insignificant man who has peeked into the void and glimpsed his essential powerlessness. So he dreams of greatness as a way back and worships those he believes have conquered the emptiness he has felt at the core of life. Davies's concept of apprenticeship is the act of initiation into this world of artifice and duplicity through which one learns the tricks of domination that others misbelieve as power.

This fragile control is proclaimed as the natural order of things because only such an extreme response to nothingness returns the world to a necessary, if illusory, harmony. And this is the source of Davies's misogyny. For all of his novels portray the figure of the crumbling, desperate man. What could be a more telling episode of this figure than Francis's reaction to his abandonment by his wife? He goes out onto the street to find a prostitute he can pay to beat up. One woman is the same as another. Each possesses a lethal magic to beguile away his power and unnerve the ground beneath him by restoring him to doubt.

To enter Davies's universe is like walking into a fun house and losing one's way among the mirrors. One feels the initial exhilaration of what might be a new way of seeing. But it is quickly replaced by the exhaustion of having spent too long among clever distortions, and one rushes to escape to the world of truer size. Davies's problem begins with his very understanding of art. As Francis Cornish engages in a bit of summing up at the end of his life, he reflects upon his painting and decides that, "the division between art and deviousness and—yes, it had to be admitted—crime, was sometimes as thin as a cigarette paper." In the circus, maybe. But to see art as a partner to crime is to give up entirely on whatever we might imagine as the possibility of truth. And it is to see the artist as that cliché of the explorer who flicks his lighter just before he is to be eaten by cannibals and finds himself hailed as a god. (pp. 705-08)

> Robert Jones, "A Company of Daimons," in Commonweal, Vol. CXII, No. 22, December 20, 1985, pp. 705-08.

Davies on the editorial process:

I go through several drafts, and work over a manuscript very very carefully. But I feel that any work of art—and I try to make my novels works of art—are inevitably going to have some imperfections; but if you level off and grind down and polish and shine too much, you may get a very glossy novel but it may have lost its life on the way. And sometimes I wonder if that isn't what happens in the work of a writer whom I used to admire very much—not so much now—and that was Aldous Huxley. I always thought his novels were too finely honed. Much better to be Evelyn Waugh, whose novels present some obvious imperfections and infelicities and abound with life.

Robertson Davies, in an interview with Michael Hulse, in The Journal of Commonwealth Literature, *1987.*

D. O. Spettigue   (review date Spring 1986)

[*In the following excerpt, Spettigue examines how Davies's work emphasizes the individual's search for identity.*]

The Papers of Samuel Marchbanks is an attractively bound, 540-page compilation of the three Marchbanks volumes [**The Diary of Samuel Marchbanks, The Table Talk of Samuel Marchbanks,** and **Samuel Marchbanks' Almanack**]. I think my preference might have been for a judicious abridgement that would have given us the best of Marchbanks in paperback, to be sampled on the train or at bedtime. Nobody but a reviewer or an academic would want to read **The Papers** right through. This is not a criticism of Marchbanks; I wouldn't read three volumes of [Stephen] Leacock non-stop either, unless they were narrative. Rather, it is an acknowledgement that these

were light pieces from newspaper columns written over many years, and it may be a mistake to put too much light fare in a heavy book. Having made this ill-tempered, Marchbanksian pronouncement, I have to add that I am fond of Marchbanks and welcome **The Papers.** But I like them in two different ways. I like to sample them, to give them the humour test, as well as to study them. The humour test is simply to ask whether, on successive readings, dipping here and there, the reader discovers new nuances each time, finds himself chuckling where earlier he had missed a point, discovers in short that the material grows in the reading. Marchbanks, who would scorn the test, passes it easily.

The second interest is more academic: what is Marchbanks' place in the Davies canon? If this sounds critically old hat—surely you're not still looking for unity?—my defence is the obvious one: Marchbanks is stubbornly old hat, and the Davies canon represents the life-long search for unity in the form of the integrated self.

Marchbanks' age is now about x + forty. That is, it's about forty years since his name began to appear in print, so **The Papers** makes a handsome anniversary gift. From book to book, the **Diary,** the **Table Talk** and the **Almanack** spread over twenty years, from 1947 to 1967, and so are a kind of counterpoint to the early plays and the Salterton novels. The first volume was a newspaper diary, and may well have been, as Davies claims, originally intended as a spoof on Eleanor Roosevelt's "My Day," the Marchbanks diary recording the trivia of one eccentric citizen's daily life in a provincial town, as Mrs Roosevelt recorded the sociopolitical excitements of Washington. In this, Marchbanks of course had one advantage: he could afford to be eccentric as the international figure could not. At any rate, the **Diary,** as a short column in the Peterborough *Examiner* and the Kingston *Whig-Standard,* made much of Marchbanks' epic conflict with his furnace, his trials with the neighbourhood dogs ransacking his garbage, his comments on items he has read about or observed in the street, his altercations with fellow citizens, his occasional observations of Toronto, and a rare vacation. The tone of most of these is acerbic: Marchbanks does not suffer fools gladly, he has no patience with politicians, proselytizers, do-gooders, and other professional hypocrites. Moreover, he is a radical conservative in his social views: he has no illusions about the honest working man or the deserving poor. Besides, writing in the 1940s, he can make anti-social remarks—about women, about foreigners, about minorities—that our more repressed times cannot allow. Part of the attraction of Marchbanks is his outspokenness, even though the reader is aware that much of it is calculated; Davies is creating a character for Marchbanks to live up to.

The **Table Talk** is in the same voice, but does not have to follow the demands of chronology. Where the **Diary** names days of the week (but not dates), and occasional parodic saints' days, the **Table Talk** organizes itself around courses. In the foreword, called **"On the Nature and Use of this Book,"** we are told that Marchbanks likes a proper dinner (though he considers it modest) which includes Soup, Fish, Entrée, The Remove, Sweet, Savoury and

Dessert, as well as appropriate wines. The book is divided into seven sections corresponding to the seven courses. This is not pursued as far as it might be—again we're viewing retrospectively what was light fare written under pressure for the editor's page of the daily paper. So there is no significant relation between the day and the column in the *Diary* (apart from the obvious ones, such as Christmas and New Year's), and in the *Table Talk* we do not find a sweeter voice in the Sweet section or a more substantial offering in The Remove. There are bits of dramatic monologue at intervals; on occasion the woman on Marchbanks' right will be offended or will make some unstated rejoinder to cause him to turn away to the partner on his left. These supply the equivalent to the more evidently narrative element in the *Diary* provoked by letters arriving, the furnace going out, encounters with neighbours and so forth.

The equivalent slight organizing structure in the "Garland" section was, originally, the astrological material appropriate to an almanack, combined with fictional correspondence "from my Archive," and random bits "from my Notebooks." The introductory almanack material—drawings of the signs of the Zodiac, for instance—is missing from the new Marchbanks anthology, and I am puzzled by the absence of any explanation in the foreword. Was there ever a Marchbanks "Garland", and if so, when was it published? *Samuel Marchbanks' Almanack* was published in 1967, by McClelland and Stewart, and this is it, with a few deletions intended to make it look less like an almanack and more like the miscellany it is. Its longer title was "Marchbanks' Almanack: an Astrological and Inspirational VADE MECUM Containing Character Analyses, Secrets of Charm, Health Hints, How to be a Success at Parties, Fortune-telling by the Disposition of Moles on the Body and divers other arcane knowledge here revealed for the First Time; As Well As Generous Extracts from the Correspondence, *Pensées,* Musings, *Obiter Dicta* and Ruminations of Wizard Marchbanks." Of course this delightful parody of an almanack title had to be replaced in *The Papers* by something more suited to a garland: "A Nosegay plucked from the Musings, *Pensées, Obiter Dicta,* and Apophthegms as well as the Letters of Samuel Marchbanks and Some of his Friends (to say nothing of his Enemies) provided with Notes and Explanatory Matter by Robertson Davies." It may be that the editor, seeing *The Papers* as a whole, decided that the wizard role was not really in keeping with the Marchbanks persona.

In fact there is a contradiction in the Marchbanks role that *The Papers* do not resolve. In various places—in the forewords, in **"The Double Life of Robertson Davies"** and in Marchbanks' comments on himself—it is made apparent that Davies is dull and conventional, Marchbanks is exuberant and Dionysian. Yet Marchbanks also appears on occasion as reclusive, retiring, readily defeated by the complexities of the modern world. What we observe is Marchbanks taking on a "real" character and creating his own persona, as well as being, psychologically, Davies' "shadow," as the foreword now acknowledges. It would evidently have been too much of a muddle to have made him a wizard as well.

While the comments in the "Notebook" are reminiscent of the *Diary* and the *Table Talk,* most of the "Garland" section is made up of letters to and from Marchbanks' acquaintances. Some of these are *alter egos,* if we can have *alter egos* of an *alter ego;* Amyas Pilgarlic, notably, was an early (pre-Marchbanks) pseudonym that never developed. Minerva Hawser "was a maiden lady of Scottish antecedents," a former teacher of Marchbanks'. Like Marchbanks' neighbour, Dick Dandiprat, she presumes on slight acquaintance to bully Marchbanks into doing favours for her. Dandiprat borroweth and returneth not, Minerva wants Marchbanks to take her sewing machine to Edinburgh as she understands he will be visiting there. Marchbanks is equal to them, however, refusing their requests with pungent sarcasm. Dandiprat, however, though outwardly genial, manages to defeat Marchbanks in a lawsuit, but here the satire is clearly directed at the legal profession rather than, or as well as, the neighbour.

This suggests more narrative than in fact *The Papers* has. Some elements of recurrent plot are visible, and do contribute to the unity of the whole, but in general the entries are isolated and occasional. It is not story that we read Marchbanks for, but personality.

The personality is a complex one, and there is a corresponding range of tone, from the casual and the light-hearted through the witty, the sarcastic, the satiric, the stern. Marchbanks presents himself as a gourmet, despising dull cuisine; as a connoisseur of good wines, deploring the Ontario liquor laws; as a *bon vivant,* defying Canadian insipidity; as a conversationalist and etymologist appalled at our ignorance and our slack speech; as a sophisticated and fastidious reader contemptuous of our reading habits, or lack of them; as a champion of the arts aghast at public and political philistinism; as a sceptic about women, and children, and dull, hollow men. His trademark is his refusal to accept the thoughtless, popular view of anything. There are no "motherhood" topics for Marchbanks; he even has some harsh comments on motherhood.

As a "shadow" Marchbanks has the function of expressing the repressed attitudes and hence the suppressed energy of his author. In his role as Dionysian reveller and exuberant iconoclast, Marchbanks' public function is to expose and counteract the Canadian and modern fear of free and individual expression. Like Davies, Marchbanks is noticeably a nationalist, not in a narrow sense—he is very much a cosmopolitan—but in that he openly scolds Canadians for their shortcomings. He wants us to be a more interesting, a more aware, a more informed, a more culturally sophisticated and hence a better people. From Davies' earliest book to his latest there has always been a didactic nationalist strain. So, in the most recent novel, Frank Cornish's astrologer tells him:

> Of course you're a Canadian. Do you know what that is? A psychological mess. For a lot of good reasons, including some strong planetary influences, Canada is an introverted country straining like hell to behave like an extrovert. Wake up. Be yourself, not a bad copy of something else.

As the occasional editorial notes indicate, many of Marchbanks' early targets have since been destroyed or have faded away; some of the freedom he argued for has been achieved, at least in the sense of more open public discussion. But Davies has no illusions: permissiveness without self-knowledge is not progress. Marchbanks is a conservative radical; the barriers we must break down are barriers to understanding, to knowledge of our past, to knowledge of our cultural inheritance, and knowledge of ourselves.

In the Marchbanks material, in *One Half of Robertson Davies,* and in *A Voice from the Attic,* which together constitute the journalistic or critical or public statements, Davies reveals a self-consistent and yet always developing, always growing, body of thought. As Patricia Monk demonstrated, it was a progression from Freud to the works and thought of C. G. Jung. In Marchbanks, Davies found his first vehicle, though at first he was not aware that the intellectual superstructure was primarily psychological. But early in his reviewing, when in the 1940s he was literary editor for *Saturday Night,* he reveals an enthusiasm for the writings of Sigmund Freud. At first he did not think much of C. G. Jung. Freud showed the primitive roots of much that was troubling society; Jung was the more literary thinker, and more complex, demonstrating the close link between the arts and psychology, and hence in the long run would prove more congenial to writers and critics. Contemporary criticism has moved away from archetypal psychology; Davies has assimilated and expanded beyond it, as the novels reveal.

What's Bred in the Bone is the second volume in what promises to be Davies' third trilogy of novels. Davies functions in threes, no doubt for some occult reason that has not yet emerged. There were the three Stratford books (in collaboration), the three Marchbanks books, three volumes of essays/critical writings, the three Salterton novels, the three Deptford novels, and now two-thirds of a new trilogy which, like the others, beds itself solidly on Canadian rock but reaches around the world. The Salterton novels, beginning with *Tempest-tost* in 1951, may have been 'prentice work; Davies has said that he made the deliberate choice to become a novelist. They are clever comedies, but they reveal their cleverness and their rather straightforward application of the Jungian notion of individuation, in the context of a satirical portrait of the small city that was so obviously Kingston, Ontario. Only with the third of them, *A Mixture of Frailties,* did the thesis and the character, and the characteristically Davies humour and insight, fully blend. In *The Salterton Trilogy,* the concern with the nature of identity, the necessity to confront and to recognize the archetypal human patterns in our own lives, emerged as Davies' trademark.

The Deptford Trilogy, inaugurated with *Fifth Business* in 1970, withdrew from the small provincial city—the Kingston where Davies had been an undergraduate—back to the small town, the Thamesville where he had been a child. Deptford is harshly treated: the small town is characterized by ignorance, prejudice, religious and economic bigotry, and a narrow puritanism that may have its positive side but is more likely to be destructive. The targets here are the same ones Marchbanks railed at, but in the novels the response of most of the protagonists is to try to

escape. In *Tempest-tost* and *Leaven of Malice* the escape is only begun, and is internal. But Monica Gall must escape physically from Salterton in order to become both an artist and her own person. Dunny Ramsay joins the army to escape from Deptford and his mother; physical removal is both symbolic and a practical necessity for him as it was for Monica. For both, too, a narrow and joyless religion is one of the nets to be avoided. Paul Dempster escapes via a shabby circus—actually he is kidnapped, buggered and enslaved—but the childhood of horror that he endures is also his initiation into the art of illusion, of which he will become a master. He also flees from his mother in fleeing Deptford. He has suffered from the taint of "hoor" that attaches to her, whereas for Dunny Mrs Dempster is a saint who initiates him into love, into mystery, into the world of wonder that is his lifelong pursuit. Paul's story, his series of apprenticeships that lift him beyond Deptford to wealth and international fame, is told in *World of Wonders,* the last volume in *The Deptford Trilogy.* The middle volume, *The Manticore,* records the psychoanalysis of David Staunton, heir of the wealthy Boy Staunton whose stone-in-the-snowball, thrown at Dunny Ramsay, precipitated the whole Deptford story.

The new series may become the Toronto trilogy, as Davies almost abandons the provincial scene for the sophistications of the big city. Nevertheless the small town remains as a background and an undeniable influence, part of the personal and national self that has to be put behind us, assimilated, controlled, escaped from, but never entirely rejected. For Frank Cornish, of *What's Bred in the Bone,* the ugly Ottawa Valley childhood is the wellspring of his art.

This latest trilogy began with *The Rebel Angels,* a novel whose setting is a fictionalized Massey College, Toronto, called in the book The College of St John and the Holy Ghost, and nicknamed "Spook." (The nickname will remind Davies readers of the little volume *High Spirits,* a collection of the ghost stories Davies wrote for an annual presentation at Massey. The aim was to give the college a past and a mythology to counteract its newness; the stories are all therefore "in" stories in their jokes and allusions, but learned in reference and never very far from the larger Davies subject of "wonder" and its manifestations in the individuated life.) The cast are therefore academics, and not surprisingly they are a bizarre and eccentric lot. What may be surprising is that Davies does not satirize them, or not very much. Whatever the real Massey College may be like, these academics are remarkably learned, dedicated researchers, living earnestly narrow, spartan, almost monkish lives within the College. Two of them, Darcourt and Hollier, have similar literary, humane and classical interests. So, in part, does McVarish, though he has an unsavoury reputation—well earned, and in the end it costs him his life. A quite different and younger man, Ozy Froats, is a scientist who has drawn some fire upon the College because he is doing research in excrement, a notion that might have been culled from Swift, though of course it is fully assimilated to the Davies theme. Connected with these four is the beautiful and brilliant graduate student Maria Theodoky, every academic's dream, and also the villainous ex-monk Parlabane. As the academic talk of Maria and her professors centres on Rabelais, Paracelsus and Faust, we are not surprised to find Parlabane both a jolly friar and a devil, and quite explicitly the Mephistopheles of the piece.

In *The Rebel Angels* the Cornish fortune and art collection intrude into college life as Hollier, Darcourt and McVarish are asked to sort out, identify and appraise the Cornish collection of paintings and *objets d'art.* Their involvement also involves Maria and the demonic Parlabane, and that involvement ends in a murder, a suicide, a visit to the sorceress to pronounce a curse, and then the marriage of Maria and the wealthy Arthur Cornish, as money-brains wins out over academic-brains. The elaborately involved murder within the cloister, accompanied by the scholarly medieval trappings, may remind readers of Umberto Eco, but Davies is still pursuing his own chimera.

The ever-expanding—rather, the ever-refining—Davies subject has been the nature of the internal being, how it becomes what it is, and how it is that a select few people—artists, saints, inspired eccentrics—are able to transcend the stultifying littleness of daily human life. For Davies, there is more than one royal road to transcendence: religion, analytic psychology, art, and the occult are all possibilities. Even a "mystery," in the old sense of a handicraft fully entered into, can lift one above the mundane. This does not, of course, eliminate the physical. Again like a medievalist, Davies grounds the transcendent fully in the mundane, even, like Yeats, in the mire. This is the point of the gypsy woman's wrapping violins in dung, and Froats' research in excrement.

What's Bred in the Bone gives us Arthur and Maria, now married and squabbling, urging Darcourt to continue with the biography he has been commissioned to write of the life of Francis Cornish, Arthur's uncle, the eccentric multimillionaire artist and art collector whose chaotic collection was the focus of interest in the previous novel. Darcourt is discouraged because he cannot get a handle on his subject. He knows that the secret is "what's bred in the bone," because whatever that viaticum is must eventually reveal itself. But what's bred in the bone is a compound of heredity and early environment, together with a mysterious something that in this book is represented by Maimas, the Daimon. Maimas makes it clear that he is responsible for what in Davies' middle works would have been called "synchronicity," the coincidences or unexpected encounters that change our lives and that are not quite coincidences but occur only because our psyche is ready for them at that point. Maimas appears here as a bit of a manipulator, though of course he can do only what Cornish's particular combination of genes and family/environmental influences has made possible for him. It is still psychology we are getting, but perhaps an older form of it, as Davies moves always away from orthodoxy to his own doxy of the *anima mundi* in the mundane.

The Rebel Angels marks a slight shift from the Deptford novels in that it did not so specifically ask Jung to provide the structure of the book. The confrontations with the archetypes are still there, the balancing of personalities is still there, and the tripping-up of characters by those ele-

ments of personality they had repressed is reminiscent of *Tempest-tost.* But the handling of the gypsy woman is less Jungian than Spenglerian, or perhaps neither. She represents an acceptance of the world of wonder as accessible to the twice-born artist, though she is less an artist in fact than a sybil, the wise old woman whose art is magic. It is interesting to see here how far Davies has travelled—talk of the romantic journey—from the faintly Rabelaisian Marchbanks to a shoplifting, smuggling, cheating gypsy, and in Francis Cornish to an artist who is also a spy.

The academics in *The Rebel Angels* remind us of Dunny Ramsay, in that their governing myth seems to be history. But their actions are the familiar revelations of the shadows behind or below the public personae. Balancing the sybil is the demonic Parlabane, much more a devil-figure than Liesl was in *Fifth Business.* Presumably he is to be seen, more positively, as the modern Paracelsus, but his function is demonic—allowing for the devil to have his "good fellow" side, perhaps, or at least to be potentially useful to those self-possessed souls who can confront him without fear. But this devil has, rather gratuitously, a gift for parody. Rather, he is writing a bad novel whose thesis he outlines in terms that repeat the four levels of meaning expounded most recently by Northrop Frye. Who is the target then? Frye? Renaissance critical theory? A generation of academics and graduate students? Or Davies himself, whose own fictions are almost too neatly structured in psycho-critical terms?

Like *Fifth Business, Bred in the Bone* begins with a written account—in this case an obituary—of the protagonist, which is palpably inadequate and must be corrected. But whereas Dunny Ramsay was privileged to tell his own story, in this latest novel an angel and a daimon—the Lesser Zadkiel and Maimas—listen to, and between sections comment on, the celestial record of Francis Cornish's life. Daimons are defined by the Rev Simon Darcourt, after Hesiod, as spirits of the Golden Age, who act as guardians to mortals, but their own comments suggest that "guardian," as applied to a daimon, needs qualification. One's daimon is really what's bred in the bone, what allows us to become what we might be, as opposed to the angel, here, who only records and comments. It is the remarkable Maria, now domesticated as wife of the wealthy banker, Arthur Cornish, who tells us:

> The name of the Recording Angel was Radueriel, and he wasn't just a book-keeper; he was the Angel of Poetry, and Master of the Muses. He also had a staff . . . a civil service staff. One of its important members was the Angel of Biography, and his name was the Lesser Zadkiel. . . . He is an angel of mercy, though a lot of biographers aren't. The Lesser Zadkiel could give you the low-down on Francis Cornish.

What follows in the novel is the low-down on Frank Cornish, everything that Darcourt as official biographer for the Cornish Trust cannot know. The low-down—technologized for mortal comprehension as the play-back of some sort of record or tape—takes the form of a *Bildungsroman,* a portrait of the artist as genius, eccentric, snoop, miser, crook, and normal man. It is quite conventionally presented, after this opening frame, the Lesser

Zadkiel proving to be a rather conservative recorder in some ways, but the material is not conventional except within the Davies conventions. Numerous Davies characteristics are evident in the story: his fondness for eccentric characters, which dates back to Marchbanks and the plays, his preference for the artist as protagonist, his recognition that if one is going to be eccentric it is helpful to be rich, and his conviction that the world of wonder, of the transcendent, is at least as real as the mundane. The use of the daimons as a mild sort of classical chorus maintains our awareness of the transcendent throughout, however forcefully the mundane in the action may impinge.

The "key" information Darcourt needs is the story of Frank Cornish's childhood. To this extent Davies is still a Freudian. What he will eventually show us is the reappearance in Cornish's art of the figures who had haunted his childhood, and in his lonely, reclusive later life a pattern that childhood began.

In a rather Tristram-Shandyish way we are required to understand first the significance of Frank's begetting, but even before that we have to have a sketch of the grandfather's success in early Ontario lumbering, his political connections and senatorship that allow him to have his daughter presented at court, and therefore to have too much champagne, and therefore to enjoy a brief fling with a hotel employee, and hence the begetting of Frank—well, actually Francis Cornish the first. As a visitation upon her sin, perhaps, her father has virtually to buy a wedding with the opportunistic Major (later, Sir) Francis Chegwidden Cornish, and the inopportune child is born a monster—shapeless, unintelligent, and kept out of sight in the attic, cared for by a discreet nurse, all in the best Victorian tradition. The secret is so well kept, indeed, that the parents apparently think the monster—known to the younger Frank as The Looner—has died. There is even a funeral for it, and a grave, but the Looner remains in his upstairs apartment, cared for by the maid and entertained by a sympathetic embalmer named Zadok. The Looner supposedly having gone to heaven, a second son is born and given the same name, Francis Cornish, who thus has a natural *alter ego,* his "Dark Brother." The younger Frank grows up as a privileged but alienated child in the stultifying little town, which has even less to offer than Deptford. And like the Stauntons, Frank's parents cut a wider and wider social swath outside the town, so that the boy is virtually raised by the servants and older members of the household. As they are mostly ardent Catholics, he gets a mixed but intensive religious training. He knows little about his parents: his mother is beautiful, his father distant. His grandfather is closer, and gives the boy his first technical artistic training in the sense of urging upon him the importance of light in photography—we are to see this as the beginning of his eventual career in painting, reinforced by the religious pictures his aunts collect. The notion, connected with the concept of the universe as energy, that nothing is ever wholly lost, is back of this "justifying" of the later painter and art collector.

Apart from his miserable experience at school—he is like both Dunny Ramsay and Paul Dempster in this—Frank's future is most directly influenced by his awareness of the mysterious presence of the Looner upstairs, and by the friendship of Zadok, who functions not only as a servant for the family and as the community undertaker but also, thanks to the complexities of thesis and plot, as the Looner's father. Zadok allows Frank to visit the morgue with him, where the boy eagerly sketches the corpses being prepared for burial. Much later in his life the critics of his anonymous paintings will puzzle over the recurrent image of a small, misshapen figure in them—the obsessive memory of the Looner—and the figure of a dwarf, whom no one will ever identify, whose corpse Frank sketched after the dwarf had been driven to suicide by persecution in the small town.

A relatively minor character, appearing late in the novel, is Aylwin Ross, a physically attractive, smooth, rising civil servant, evidently evil, who remains a bit of a puzzle. He seems destined to become Frank's lover, but suicides instead, when he fails to get Frank's support in procuring a supposed Renaissance German painting for the National Gallery. Of course Frank himself painted it—it was literally his "masterpiece," signalling the end of his apprenticeship to Saraceni, the brilliant restorer of old paintings. Ross caps the "bad luck" that prevented Frank from becoming a painter. Once Frank's restorations were accepted as genuine, he could not go on to paint in that style. The style was his own development from the masters; he finds he cannot work in the modern mode, and hence his creative genius is blocked—he becomes a collector, not an artist.

Perhaps Ross will figure in some way in the third novel, but the painting that causes his suicide remains the focus of *What's Bred in the Bone.* The subject of the painting is the Marriage at Cana, where Christ turned water into wine. Its motto is "Thou has kept the good wine until now." Alchemically, it is said to represent "The Chymical Wedding. The alchemical uniting of the elements of the soul." In terms of the novel, it is virtually a *peinture à clef,* incorporating the figures who have influenced Frank's life. As such, it represents the whole point of the novel, and may have significance for the author as well.

In his own career, C. G. Jung reached a critical point where he found he had to pause to learn alchemy because so much of the world of archetypes depended on that ancient science. I have always assumed that when Northrop Frye made the same decision he was not only making it for the same reason but was consciously following in the footsteps of the master. Now we see Robertson Davies making, at a much later stage in his career, a similar discovery: you can't go very far in literary symbolism without encountering the occult. Of course Davies would say that he was interested in the fully lived life, not in literary symbolism, but the pattern he is following is the same. This also explains the shift in literary models in the recent books to Rabelais, Paracelsus and Ben Jonson.

What will the next shift be? Davies seems to be the green pine that keeps on growing, and while for some readers the burden of learning may seem heavy, knowledge has traditionally been one of the rewards offered by fiction. Davies stubbornly refuses to withdraw into the smaller infinity, as so many of his contemporaries have done both in prose and verse, giving their readers only the private images of-fered by their subconscious. He insists on the public func-tions of art, while acknowledging, and representing, its or-igins in the individual psyche. Art is bred in the bone, and the artist must descend into the unconscious, into "The Mothers," to use Davies' new term, in order to find it.

Perhaps the Toronto series will prove to be a trilogy *à clef.* At any rate, **What's Bred in the Bone** has its appropriate-ness for its vigorous but aging author. Presumably it is not only Frank Cornish whose life has kept its best wine until now; Davies may interpret his own life that way. Certainly he has much to say about art in this book, and all in de-fence of a method that makes no concessions to modern-ism. Early in his career, Frank is told by his master, "I don't get on very well with the modern manner, either. But I must warn you: don't try to fake the modern manner if it isn't right for you. Find your legend. Find your per-sonal myth."

The Davies protagonists have sought and found their per-sonal myth. That was the quest, the heroic life. Davies has not scorned modern subjects, but through psychology, ha-giography, religion, astrology, alchemy, a lifelong study of the principles of metaphor in art and cultures generally, he has found his own manner and his own myth, and if to adhere to these seems to some to be old hat, so be it— the hat will wear that much better in the long run. Davies lets Saraceni, the master, make the traditionalists' case against the modernists:

> The best of them are doing what honest painters have always done, which is to paint the inner vi-sion. . . . But in an earlier day the inner vision presented itself in a coherent language of mytho-logical or religious terms, and now both mythol-ogy and religion are powerless to move the mod-ern mind. So the search for the inner vision must be direct. The artist solicits and implores some-thing from the realm of what the psychoana-lysts, who are the great magicians of our day, call the Unconscious, though it is actually the Most Conscious. And what they fish up . . . may be very fine, but they express it in a lan-guage more or less private. . . . And the great danger is that such private language is perilously easy to fake. Much easier to fake than the well-understood language of the past.

Is this Davies' last trilogy? Is there another series down there? He neither talks nor writes as though from an empty well, but we notice the fondness for theory over ac-tion in this last book. **What's Bred in the Bone** is not so engaging a novel as **Fifth Business** was, or **The Rebel An-gels.** Perhaps the very best wine is being kept to the last. (pp. 123-34)

> *D. O. Spettigue, "Keeping the Good Wine until Now," in* Queen's Quarterly, *Vol. 93, No. 1, Spring, 1986, pp. 123-34.*

Humphrey Carpenter   (review date 20 July 1986)

[*An English critic and author of children's books, Car-penter is best known for his biographies of J. R. R. Tolkien and W. H. Auden. In the following re-view, Carpenter offers a negative appraisal of* The Pa-pers of Samuel Marchbanks *through a comparison to the satirical diaries of Auberon Waugh.*]

Until a few weeks ago, readers of the British satirical mag-azine *Private Eye* were regularly regaled by the diary of Auberon Waugh, son of Evelyn. This diary was conducted on the premise that Mr. Waugh was a bastion of the En-glish squirearchy, a Tory in the 18th-century meaning of the word, surrounded by feudal vassals and possessed of political assumptions that made Mrs. Thatcher seem like a card-carrying Marxist-Leninist. From his supposedly castellated country seat, where (one was led to assume) unwanted visitors would be greeted by a cascade of boiling oil, Waugh penned observations upon the contemporary scene that were healthily unbridled by any regard for the niceties of fact or the law of libel. I wish I could quote a few lines to illustrate, but Waugh has not seen fit to pre-serve his ephemera in volume form, and the diary has, alas, now terminated with his removal to the editorship of a literary journal.

The real Waugh was, one gathered, rather a different char-acter from the diarist: mild of visage, living in modest cir-cumstances without a feudal vassal to his name, offering kindly hospitality to travelers rather than boiling oil. Such political feelings as he displayed in private were said to be tinged with at least a mild shade of pink. He was in other words a master-hand at the Spoof Diary: a genre in which a diarist only superficially resembling the real writer makes observations of a calculated outrageousness. In-deed, until I received my copy of **The Papers of Samuel Marchbanks,** I was under the impression that Waugh was the inventor and sole exponent of this genre. But, as I opened the **Papers** and dipped at random, it seemed to me that here was, at the very least, an affinity:

> Somebody told me a few days ago that they got the impression that I disliked children. Not at all: I love the little dears. But I have no patience with ill-mannered, noisy, destructive, rude, ram-paging little yahoos and it is my misfortune, from time to time, to come in contact with herds of these, roaming wild in the streets; can anyone blame me if I drive them away with curses and blows?

This is Marchbanks writing, but it might well be Waugh. And when I read in the introduction to the **Papers** that Marchbanks describes himself as "one of the last of a breed of Canadians whose racial strains and mental habits derive from those Loyalists who came north after the American Revolution of 1776," I was perfectly sure I had stumbled on a vital literary discovery: that Auberon Waugh's Diary was modeled on the "Samuel March-banks" column, which appeared from 1943 to 1953 in the *Examiner* newspaper of Peterborough, Ontario. Small matter that Waugh, in those days an English schoolboy, was not likely to be a regular reader of a newspaper pub-lished in Peterborough, Ontario. It is upon such hunches, however improbable, that great literary scholarship is built.

Unfortunately I have to record that random dipping (the tried and tested method of the reviewer) was in this case a strikingly inaccurate gauge of the real facts in the case. A reading of **The Papers of Samuel Marchbanks** from cover to cover reveals the following: (1) That "Samuel Marchbanks" (unlike Auberon Waugh) is a pseudonym. The real author of the diary is Robertson Davies, the distinguished Canadian man of letters. (2) That during the years in which the Marchbanks diary appeared in the *Examiner*, Davies was that paper's editor and owner. (3) That Davies subsequently published three volumes extracted from the Marchbanks column. (4) That **The Papers of Samuel Marchbanks** is an omnibus edition of these three volumes, consisting of 540 pages. (3) That Elisabeth Sifton, a distinguished New York editor and publisher, has issued this omnibus edition because she believes that Americans will be driven to uncontrollable spasms of mirth by Samuel Marchbanks. (6) That I am not of the same opinion as Ms. Sifton.

Marchbanks is certainly not without his charm, but it is the charm of a Pooter rather than a Waugh. Marchbanks' domestic trials—such as his endless battle with his central-heating furnace—occupy a substantial proportion of the chronicle, and inevitably recall the hero of *The Diary of a Nobody* trying to survive the rigors of domesticity rather than the asperities of a Waugh. Asperities, indeed, are not really in Marchbanks' line. They tend to peter out:

> To the bank this afternoon, and was once again amazed by the nonchalance with which the young women behind the bars treat my balance. To me it is matter of the most profound significance; to them it is a mere sum in addition and subtraction. Without being in the least aware of it, they can drive their cruel pens deep into my heart. That is, they are not aware of it unless I sink upon the floor with a despairing cry and attempt to disembowel myself with my pen-knife; then they call the assistant manager to throw me out. Banks hate suicides on the premises—looks bad.

I fancy that Waugh, writing on the same topic, would have implied that he had several millions in his bank account (all in gold sovereigns) and that he had arrived at the bank by hansom cab, or maybe in a sedan chair carried by four crippled retainers. And without that element, something essential has gone. Marchbanks should lord it over his oppressors; instead, he cringes.

It is a pity, for he is far from devoid of humor. In one of the footnotes added to the omnibus volume, he (or his alter ego Davies) observes that the present-day computerized address machine "scorns anyone whose name contains more than twelve letters," and so has reduced him to "Samuel Marchb," who "sounds like the kind of Middle European poet who gets the Nobel Prize because the Russians (probably quite rightly) can't stand him." Indeed, I shall probably be deluged with abusive letters from the inhabitants of Peterborough, Ontario, assuring me that they have not stopped laughing since Marchbanks first set pen to diary in '43. But I do wish that the Marchbanks features wore a little less of the Pooter humility and had a touch more of the Waugh *hauteur*. (pp. 5, 9)

Humphrey Carpenter, "Robertson Davies Conjures Up a Columnist," in Book World— The Washington Post, *July 20, 1986, pp. 5, 9.*

Davies on the themes of his novels:

The theme which lies at the root of all my novels is the isolation of the human spirit. . . . I have not attempted to deal with it in a gloomy fashion but rather to demonstrate that what my characters do that might be called really significant is done on their own volition and usually contrary to what is expected of them. This theme is worked out in terms of characters who are trying to escape from early influences and find their own place in the world but who are reluctant to do so in a way that will bring pain and disappointment to others.

Robertson Davies, in an interview with Contemporary Authors, New Revision Series, *Vol. 17, Gale Research, 1986.*

John Kenneth Galbraith   (review date 3 August 1986)

[*Considered among the most influential economists of the twentieth century, Galbraith is the Canadian-born author of such classic economics texts as* The Affluent Society *(1958),* The New Industrial State *(1967), and* Economics and the Public Purpose *(1973). He has served as advisor to several U.S. presidents and as the U.S. ambassador to India. In the following review, Galbraith praises* The Papers of Samuel Marchbanks *as a perceptive, humorous, and satirical commentary on Canadian life, culture, and society.*]

Some 40 years back the city of Peterborough in eastern Ontario had a distinction in the Canadian urban pantheon about on a level with that among American cities of Springfield, Mass. It was principally renowned for the giant lift lock on the canal that passed by the town; this engineering marvel lifted not only the boat but the lock and the water in which the vessel floated. It was considered something of a flaw, in a commercial way, that the canal didn't go much of anywhere. *The Peterborough Examiner*, the newspaper of the town, had a standing about like that of *The Springfield Republican*.

It will surprise no one nowadays that this anonymity of place and paper, much appreciated by residents and readers, was being gravely jeopardized at the time by the editor (later the publisher) of *The Examiner*. Following World War II, the person so employed was Robertson Davies, an unfailing contributor to the pages of the newspaper and on the way to becoming one of the best and best-known writers of our time. Not many journalists would wish to risk having their daily efflux dug out and published after a lapse of 40 years—not Walter Lippmann; not Arthur Krock; not Westbrook Pegler; not even, conceivably, Mr. William F. Buckley Jr. This writing of four decades ago [collected in **The Papers of Samuel Marshbanks**] is consistently incisive, insulting, funny, relevant and altogether interesting.

It succeeds partly because Mr. Davies separates himself

from himself and speaks with the voice of one Samuel Marchbanks. Marchbanks is not the editor or publisher of the paper; he is but one of the reputable citizens of the town, exceptional only in his pride in his own foibles and eccentricities. As a result, Marchbanks has a degree of freedom not available, alas, to anyone of journalistic position and importance. Of this he makes truly impressive use.

In a journal, alleged table talk and imagined correspondence, he touches but rarely on current politics and events and then only as they illustrate some point—including the public character of Canadians, of which he is a relentless critic. Marchbanks dwells on his day-to-day preoccupations, observations and resulting reflections, all of which escape the rapid and greatly deserved obsolescence to which solemn political comment is subject. His coal furnace in the wintertime is a constant source of inspiration. So also his income tax and, during (as he sees it) the momentary Canadian summer, his lawn and garden. In all these matters he combines physical reluctance with unquestioned incompetence, and these regularly lead him on to larger reflection:

> Cut my grass today. I neglected it over the weekend, thinking that the atomic bomb might settle all such problems forever. As I plodded back and forth I reflected miserably upon my own political rootlessness, in a world where politics is so important. When I am with Tories I am a violent advocate of reform; when I am with reformers I hold forth on the value of tradition and stability. . . . The presence of a person who has strong political convictions always sends me flying off in a contrary direction. Inevitably, in the world of today, this will bring me before a firing squad sooner or later. . . . Tiger, my kitten, has wandered away.

Without ever quite telling what he does, he also contemplates his working life at the office:

> I spent a busy day today, but got little done. This is because I am at last becoming perfect in the art of seeming busy, even when very little is going on in my head or under my hands. This is an art which every man learns, if he does not intend to work himself to death. By shifting papers about my desk, writing my initials on things, talking to my colleagues about things which they already know, fumbling in books of reference, making notes about things which are already decided, and staring out the window while tapping my teeth with a pencil, I can successfully counterfeit a man doing a heavy day's work. Nobody who watched me would ever be able to guess what I was doing, and the secret of this is that I am not doing anything, or creating anything, and my brain is having a nice rest. I am, in short, an executive.

Two hundred words, more often less than more, is all he allows himself for his daily observation, sometimes as republished in *The Papers of Samuel Marchbanks* with a note to explain some now obscure allusion. There is frequent comment on films, for he goes once or twice a week to the movies, and no motion picture actor or actress

pleases him except Gypsy Rose Lee. It is a problem as to why he continues to go. Marchbanks's health is also consistently bad, and he greatly enjoys being bedridden. This, however, does not entirely relieve him of misanthropy. Ending one such confinement, he even gives away a little information on his occupation:

> During my stay in bed I have done my best to keep up with my work as a book-reviewer, and have waded through a mountain of muck. Every day in every way I agree more and more with the anonymous reviewer who wrote:
>
> And much though each new book keeps lit my light,
> Defrauding me of sleep by dubious sleight,
> I often wonder what the authors read
> One half so rotten as the stuff they write.

Marchbanks comments also on children and politicians he encounters, and toward politicians he is uniformly adverse—"The proper democratic attitude seems to be that a national leader should be the intellectual peer of a barbershop loafer, and as illiterate and undistinguished as possible." He goes occasionally to Toronto, a city which, in its righteousness in that earlier age, he greatly deplores. In Toronto, he notes, good females are ladies without "discernible sex" and:

> There is nothing a Lady hates so much as a Woman, and women are occasionally sleek, ravishing and sexy. The idea that women have invaded Toronto would of course be repugnant to the City Council, which distinguishes itself every year or so by banning *The Decameron* or insisting that male and female authors be kept apart on the shelves of the public libraries, lest an unlicensed pamphlet make its appearance.

Occasionally in these pages Marchbanks becomes a trifle repetitious in the pleasure he derives from his personal inconsequence, his inability to cope with the common problems of everyday life. The misanthropy becomes a bit predictable. But overall there should be no doubt: as the enduring claim of *The Baltimore Sun* to fame is H. L. Mencken, that of *The Peterborough Examiner* is the comparably distinguished gift of Marchbanks, a k a Robertson Davies.

> *John Kenneth Galbraith, "Proud of His Foibles, Busy as a Lazy Bee," in* The New York Times Book Review, *August 3, 1986, p. 9.*

Roger Clarke (review date 9 May 1987)

[*In the following review, Clarke provides a mixed assessment of* The Papers of Samuel Marchbanks, *finding it an anachronistic record of Canadian life.*]

Reading Robertson Davies' *The Papers of Samuel Marchbanks* is not unlike browsing through an edition of 1950s *New Yorker* cartoons. Davies invented this alter-ego to write a regular postwar column in the Canadian *Peterborough Examiner.* As with the *New Yorker,* there is (or was) that slightly alien American patrician sense of humour, gently massaging everyday life rather than challenging it, or rendering it vivid or satirical. It was already old-fashioned then. Now it creaks, with more bearing on anthropology than wit.

Add to the dated feel the obscure interests of another culture spawned from our own, which Marchbanks constantly upbraids for its philistinism, and you have a book like a stuffed parrot in a belljar. This is not to demean it. Davies is a writer of considerable stature, and this is a collection of writing I doubt he ever believed for a minute would be republished outside its contemporaneous context. Its journalistic quality heightens the cultural divide. Many of the references require footnotes—an unfortunate necessity (in my book a joke explained is a failed joke) which Davies, to his credit, manages to turn into a source of further rueful witticisms. In these and in the introduction he deliberately sets himself up in conflict with his creation, who personifies the author's tetchy and conservative side, with a bantering irascibility bred of a poor digestion.

Many of Marchbanks' observations on Canadian life which may have been amusing once now seem quaint and dusty; for example, his constant daily battle to light a recalcitrant boiler. Others are surprisingly fresh, and often his diction is not unlike Auberon Waugh's, but with additional carbuncles. If you thought the 'young fogey' to be a product of our era, look again, for here is a 1940s attack on them. In Canada? What were they doing there?

Whether the stereotypes of Canada as mauled by Marchbanks still hold true 40 years on we are not told. There is a very real frustration with the national attitude to arts at the time, though perhaps, and ironically, this has been cured by the international success of Davies himself, or just re-exported back to the colonial masters.

The book is a bulky one. Davies' editorial tinkering has divided up the Marchbanks effusions into various categories: there is a straightforward diary sequence, then a meal allegory, then a final section of tabletalk. Most of the writing is interchangeable between the three, and the categories are pretty but little else. Superfluity is another 'no-no' in humour.

As a slimmer and more judiciously edited book it might have made that select band of bestsellers left in the lavatory, or at the bedside table of the spare room. But if anyone reads this in bed they are liable to do themselves an injury. Its self-conscious image as a monument to a famous writer conflicts with its purpose to entertain, and perhaps not much thought was given to who is going to buy it and why.

Perversely, its very anachronistic qualities might prove the source of its appeal, its anti-modishness and raillery against popular culture nearer to the modern ethic than at any other time since it was written. For it is the humour of bent pipe-cleaners and drying tweeds, with that edge of misanthropy the crotchety bachelor conceals with a beady interest in the goings-on about him. Marchbanks has plenty of opinions on everything, from ancient films to the modern child and even the modern dog. He has fine-tuned his natural dyspepsia and intolerance into a source of acidic interest; he professes an admiration of Waugh and Bernard Shaw, taking after them both.

It is not a book to wade through, and the effect of doing so can be stultifying. It is a book to be dipped into before you give it to a cantankerous and aged relative, who at least may appreciate the obscurer reaches of its humorous vocabulary. What is essential is that it be kept away from first-time readers of Davies, and that they are instead pressed to read *The Deptford Trilogy.* He is much more than a scribbler of now yellowed newspaper articles.

> Roger Clarke, "Bad Temper Once More in Fashion," in The Spectator, Vol. 258, No. 8257, May 9, 1987, p. 40.

James Mulvihill   (essay date June 1987)

[*In the following essay, Mulvihill discusses* The Rebel Angels *as a novel of ideas.*]

In the Jamesian house of fiction, according to Mary McCarthy, ideas are "expelled by a majestic butler at the front door." What puzzles McCarthy is that this attitude still prevails, that "ideas are still today felt to be unsightly in the novel," whereas so many other aspects of human life, such as sex, are freely admitted there. [In *Ideas and the Novel*] McCarthy wittily puts this down to "modernism in its prim anti-Victorian phase," but the fact is that the novel of ideas *per se* is an anomaly in English fiction. This is not to deny the existence of a minor tradition of sorts, including Aldous Huxley and Thomas Love Peacock, as well as much lesser figures like W. H. Mallock and Norman Douglas. However, it is not a well-defined tradition, for the simple reason that the genre itself is not well-defined, and the term is often applied to works that are not really novels of ideas.

In **The Rebel Angels,** the first novel of Robertson Davies's [*Cornish Trilogy*], we have in fact a genuine novel of ideas that has not been recognized as such. In a review [appearing in *Canadian Forum* (1981-82)] of several works by and about Davies, including this novel, Sam Solecki traces the development of Davies's fiction, from the first Salterton novels, "comedies of manners relatively free of any burden of ideas," to the works after 1958, which he finds "explicitly ideological." Although Solecki concedes that **Fifth Business** is Davies's masterpiece, he finds it somehow predictable in its thematic preoccupations and its manner of presentation. Moreover, "The tedium increases between **The Manticore** and **The Rebel Angels** because the novels become increasingly static, cluttered with the flotsam of Davies's store of learning and, surprising in a drama scholar and critic, less dramatic. After **Fifth Business** the scholar-didact has prevailed over the novelist in Davies's fiction." A practical critic, Solecki insists that there are fundamental questions to be asked of any literary work—" 'Can it walk? Even more can it dance?' " **The Rebel Angels,** he decides, stumbles.

If in the end Solecki is simply bored by Davies's later novels, there is not much to be said. But while it would be rather silly, and presumptuous, to argue with him about his personal likes and dislikes, it is surely valid to question his critical expectations. Even more fundamental than "Can it dance?" is "Is it supposed to dance"—at least according to Solecki's lights? Solecki betrays his critical bias early on in his essay:

Davies is a teacher, an intellectual and a writer who uses fiction as a medium for ideas—to the point that we recognize Davies as one of our few explicitly didactic and ideological novelists. Reading any of his novels of the past two decades we sense the author's guiding hand on our shoulder—just as we sense something similar happening when reading *Voices in Time* and *The New Athens* but not *Coming Through Slaughter* and *The Invention of the World.*

Is there something of the prim anti-Victorian modernist in this? Davies's fiction is "witty, elegant and informed," and yet despite this—or perhaps because of it—Davies fails to give "adequate fictional expression" to his themes. Whereas ideally we should "experience" directly the "reality" of a novel, in Davies "we all too often sense that we have been *told* about it." John Mills voices a similar objection: "The point is that Davies trots this stuff out— theology, psychology, epistemology, etc.—as though it meant nothing real to him, as though it existed somewhere in his prefrontal lobes and not in his feelings." In this rather Lawrentian view, nothing experienced in the pre-frontal lobes is "real," apparently.

Measured against such conventional standards, perhaps Davies does stumble somewhat. Another possibility, however, is that Davies's fiction has been inclining (not declining) towards something other than the tactile realism we have come to regard as synonymous with the novel. "[T]he subject-matter of Rabelais . . . filtered through the fictional method of Thomas Love Peacock" is how W. J. Keith aptly describes *The Rebel Angels* in a review of two quite different works by Davies. *The Rebel Angels* and a collection of essays entitled *The Well-Tempered Critic,* both published the same year. This accident of publication leads Keith to contemplate an approach to Davies "that ignores the formal generic distinctions of novel and criticism, fiction and non-fiction, and considers the unifying interests and attitudes that characterize Davies's writings as a whole." Perhaps, though, it is not necessary to drop generic distinctions entirely, so much as to find one that accommodates at once the fictional and (supposedly) non-fictional elements of a work like *The Rebel Angels.* Keith's references to Peacock and Rabelais provide some clue. More conclusively, Keith suggests that beneath the "paradoxical richness" of this work "lies the organizing form of a symposium." From here it is only a short step to the novel of ideas.

The classic definition of this rather specialized literary form is provided by Aldous Huxley in the notebook jottings of Philip Quarles, the novelist within the novel in *Point Counter Point:*

> Novel of Ideas. The character of each personage must be implied, as far as possible, in the ideas of which he is the mouthpiece. In so far as theories are rationalizations of sentiments, instincts, dispositions of soul, this is feasible. The chief defect of the novel of ideas is that you must write about people who have ideas to express—which excludes all but about .01 per cent of the human race.

How this latter difficulty is dealt with varies—as Quarles

notes, "the real, the congenital novelists don't write such books"—but the common solution is to isolate the novel's characters in some way. Peacock puts his in country houses, though a sanatorium or a cancer ward will do just as well, or even a prison. Or the isolation can be moral, as with the over-cultivated and world-weary cliques in Huxley's early novels. The other, most important element is talk, copious amounts of talk on every conceivable subject, for the hallmark of the novel of ideas is an inexhaustible, exuberant eclecticism. The novels of Thomas Love Peacock and Aldous Huxley are in this sense novels of talk, their characters seeming to exist solely for the sake of what they have to say. (Solecki, significantly, complains that Davies's characters "treat living and talking as synonymous terms.") And in the end it is the ideas that these characters utter that determine who they are, what they do, even what happens to them. Their tensions and conflicts arise when these ideas clash, as they often do. A novel of ideas is a novel in which ideas not only take precedence over character and plot but largely determine them.

The first two novels of Davies's **Salterton Trilogy, Tempest-Tost** and **Leaven of Malice,** are both conceived in the provincial comedy of manners tradition, but certain of their characters—the voluble Humphrey Cobbler, for instance—and even particular episodes would not be out of place in a novel of ideas. One of these episodes, in **Tempest-Tost** (chapter 5), is uncannily like something by Peacock or the young Huxley. Depicting a small informal party held in the rooms of Solly Bridgetower, it features a significantly "ill-assorted group" of revellers: Solly himself, an ineffectual Prufrockian type (common in Huxley's early novels); Roger Tasset, a worldly-wise extrovert; Hector Mackilwraith, a high-school mathematics teacher with a drably practical view of life; and, presiding over the festivities, the Rabelaisian Humphrey Cobbler. Add to this inordinate amounts of drink (and drinking songs, courtesy of Cobbler), even a dash of slapstick when Solly and Roger briefly come to blows, and all the ingredients are present for the contest of faiths that characterizes the novel of ideas. The following exchange between Cobbler and Macilwraith dramatizes the opposition of two radically differing world-views. Cobbler leads off:

> "Oho, now I know what you are. You are an advocate of Useful Knowledge."
> "Certainly."
> "You say that a man's first job is to earn a living, and that the first task of education is to equip him for that job?"
> "Of course."
> "Well, allow me to introduce myself to you as an advocate of Ornamental Knowledge. You like the mind to be a neat machine, equipped to work efficiently, if narrowly, and with no extra bits or useless parts. I like the mind to be a dustbin of scraps of brilliant fabric, odd gems, worthless but fascinating curiosities, tinsel, quaint bits of carving, and a reasonable amount of healthy dirt. Shake the machine and it goes out of order; shake the dustbin and it adjusts itself beautifully to its new position."
> "As a mathematician I can hardly agree with you that disorder is preferable to order."
> "Mathematician my foot! Do you know any-

thing about linear algebra? How are you on dio-
phantine equations? Could you tell me, in a few
words, what Bertrand Russell has added to
modern mathematical concepts? You are a
mathematician in the way that a teacher of be-
ginners on the piano is a musician!"
"I know what I know," said Hector, "and it is
sufficient for my needs."

Useful Knowledge versus Ornamental Knowledge, Order
versus Disorder, Efficiency versus Brilliance: throughout
the passage, Mackilwraith and Cobbler become mouth-
pieces for these antithetical ideas, their dispute representing not so much a clash of personalities as of intellectual
attitudes (although temperament and opinion are closely
related in the novel of ideas). Granted, there is not much
give and take in this particular exchange; such discussions
in Peacock or Huxley can often be little more than punctuated monologues, particularly those involving Huxley's
social seers. As well, throughout most of *Tempest-Tost* it
is Mackilwraith as a character, rather than as an embodied
attitude, who mainly interests us. Cobbler, on the other
hand, stubbornly resists such conventional casting. He remains, throughout the novel, very much a "humours" figure, a personification of the eccentric, disordered ideal of
intellect that he champions in the passage above (and that
continues to have its spokesmen in subsequent novels, particularly in *The Rebel Angels*). His erudition and his penchant for song and drink alike are two traits that would
gain him instant entry to Peacock's convivial country-
house fêtes. And for the duration of this exchange at least,
he and Mackilwraith are part of the lively play of ideas
that animates such occasions in Peacock.

Ideas begin to come to the fore in Davies's fiction with the
last Salterton novel, *A Mixture of Frailties.* The small-
town comedy of manners is left behind as this novel's
heroine. Monica Gall, leaves Salterton to pursue a musical
education in England. Thereafter, the anarchic intellectualism which is the sole province of Humphrey Cobbler in
the earlier two novels is allowed freer play. " 'I'm living
in a novel by Peacock,' " exclaims John Scott Ripon, a
character who, viewing life exclusively in terms of literary
associations, seems himself a likely Peacockian crot-
cheteer. (Indeed, Monica and Ripon spend a Christmas as
guests at a country house in Wales, although Davies slips
up when he cites Peacock's *Gryll Grange* rather than
Headlong Hall, which *is* set in Wales.) Most of the novel's
action takes place in London, however, where Monica
mixes with a diverse set of artists and artists *manqué,* including a group known as the "menagerie," and here the
imprint of Huxley—the Huxley of *Point Counter Point*
and *Antic Hay*—is evident. The "menagerie," for example,
is ruled by Giles Revelstoke, a "Satanic genius" who has
clear affinities with Huxley's diabolists (cf. Spandrell in
Point Counter Point). As we might expect, the clash of attitudes noted in the passage excerpted from *Tempest-Tost*
is more prominent in this novel. Monica's mentor, Sir
Benedict Domdaniel, divides mankind into two opposing
parties, Eros and its genteel antithesis Thanatos, and the
novel as a whole concerns Monica's struggle to find her
place in this scheme.

Beneath the antithesis, however, is an element of synthesis. According to Huxley's Philip Quarles, the key to the
novel of ideas is "multiplicity": "The biologist, the chem-
ist, the physicist, the historian. Each sees, professionally,
a different aspect . . . a different layer of reality." A similar premise underlies a scene in *A Mixture of Frailties*
when Monica and Ripon admire the Welsh countryside:
" 'Look at that view! Now I'm appreciating it in literary
terms, and you're interpreting it in some kind of inner
music which is incomprehensible to me. So I ask you
again: what does it mean to the people who live here? By
what means do they interpret it to themselves?' "

Separate yet parallel modes of perception similarly inform
the novels of *The Deptford Trilogy.* Jungian psychology,
hagiography, jurisprudence, magic, theatre craft, anthropology, cinematography: these are the different intellectual systems that Davies's characters variously employ as
they attempt to reconcile apparently conflicting aspects of
themselves and of the world. Throughout the trilogy Davies increasingly presents a drama of individualized ideas
and attitudes, from Dunstan Ramsay's vinous debates
with Father Blazon in *Fifth Business* and the Jungian dialogues of *The Manticore* to the work that most closely approaches in form a novel of ideas, *World of Wonders.*

Although Magnus Eisengrim's account of his life occupies
much of it, *World of Wonders* as a whole is structured on
the framing device of a symposium. During the shooting
of a film about the French illusionist Robert-Houdin,
Eisengrim, who plays the title role, tells his life story off-
camera to a group of listeners all associated in some way
with the film. Well supplied with food and drink, these sessions take place, significantly, in an improbably eccentric
Swiss castle owned by Liesl Naegeli. Throughout the narrative, Eisengrim's listeners freely contribute their own
highly characteristic impressions and opinions. The Swedish director, Jurgen Lind, sees the story in terms of his film
obsession with evil, while his cinematographer, Kinghovn,
sees it solely in terms of camera angles and lighting. Dunstan Ramsay is preoccupied with Eisengrim's story as documented history, while the literary Roland Ingestree—in
his youth a devotee of Huxley—is wittily facetious
throughout. In the end, we are left not so much with any
single view of Eisengrim and his life, as with a multiplicity
of views, each separate and self-contained, each coloured
by a particular attitude of mind. With this final novel of
the Deptford trilogy, the way is clear for the genuine comedy of ideas enacted in *The Rebel Angels.*

While elements of the novel of ideas may be found
throughout Davies's fiction. Davies fully incorporates
these elements only in *The Rebel Angels.* Indeed, Davies
seems to have returned to the *bildungsroman* form of *A
Mixture of Frailties* in his newest novel. *What's Bred in
the Bone.* There are, it is true, still strong traces of the
novel of ideas in the latter work. Good talk is a staple in
this novel, as the master-pupil dialogues between the
young Francis Cornish and his mentor Tancred Saraceni
testify. Startling erudition, a sheer pleasure in ideas for
their own sake, as well as for their thematic relevance, is
also in ample evidence. Nevertheless, "the organizing
form of a symposium," which Keith finds in *The Rebel
Angels,* has receded in *What's Bred in the Bone,* to be re-

placed by a more conventional narrative line set against a much broader historical and geographical backdrop.

As much as anything else, the setting of *The Rebel Angels* makes the novel of ideas an apt vehicle for Davies's concerns in this work. Peacock gave his fictional banquets at country houses hosted by generous patrons of the arts and sciences. In post-Massey Canada, however, a more appropriate setting is the university, its syllabus providing the diversity of views necessary to a novel of ideas. " '[E]very kind of creature here.' " exclaims a character in *The Rebel Angels,* " 'and all exhibiting what they are so much more freely than if they were in business, or the law, or whatever.' " In Peacock it is always the host who brings together a varied, sometimes ill-matched, party of guests, essentially acting as a catalyst to the ensuing clash of opinions. The closest thing to a host in *The Rebel Angels,* the collector Francis Cornish, is deceased when the novel opens, yet as a host *in absentia* he indeed acts as a catalyst for what follows.

Cornish has died leaving an estate of immense value, including books, paintings, and manuscripts, which it is the task of Cornish's three executors—Professors Simon Darcourt, Clement Hollier, and Urquhart McVarnish—to sort out and catalogue. Trouble begins when Hollier suspects McVarnish of having unscrupulously kept for himself an undiscovered Rabelais manuscript from the collection. Narrated in turns by Darcourt and a beautiful graduate student named Maria Theotoky (who is suffering a painful infatuation for Hollier, her thesis supervisor), the novel concerns Hollier's obsession with obtaining this manuscript, a quest in which he is abetted by a diabolical character named John Parlabane. At the end of the novel, Urquhart has died grotesquely at Parlabane's hands, and Hollier will get his manuscript, while Maria, sadder but wiser, marries the sensible Arthur Cornish, a nephew of the collector.

The Rebel Angels has been described [by Solecki] as "A combination of a murder-mystery novel and comic love story," which is accurate as far as it goes. In the first instance, however, there is no drawn-out mystery surrounding the murder of Urquhart McVarnish, sensational though it is, and, in the second, romantic love in itself is a relatively minor concern in this novel. In each case, the real interest lies in the complex of ideas, complementary and conflicting, that informs the event, whether murder or marriage. Although McVarnish's perverse end reveals some very odd aspects of his life and character—which the reader has had good reason for suspecting anyway—the significance of his murder lies more in the conflict going on within Clement Hollier between modern rationality and the dark, primal forces that have moved him finally to will the death of his rival. In the same way, underlying Maria Theotoky's various attachments is a deep split in Maria's allegiances between the ordered, modern life of the intellect lived at the university and her superstitious Gypsy background. In both instances, plot and character are subordinate to this complex of ideas, which manifests itself on many levels in the novel and in many different forms, not unlike a musical theme and variations (a favou-

rite metaphor for Huxley and Peacock and incidentally one found in this novel as well).

Neither a murder mystery nor a love story, indeed not appearing to fit into any category of fiction, popular or highbrow, *The Rebel Angels* seems like nothing so much as a muddle—but a rich muddle. Like the "extraordinary, precious mess" that Francis Cornish has left for his executors to sort out, its offerings are plenteous and mixed. The "excess of intellectual baggage" that Solecki complains of is in fact a distinguishing formal element, for this novel is broadly conceived in the tradition of Menippean satire (as Eugene Benson has pointed out), of which the novel of ideas is a specialized sub-genre. "The Menippean satirist," in Northrop Frye's definitive account [in *Anatomy of a Criticism: Four Essays.*], "dealing with intellectual themes and attitudes, shows his exuberance in intellectual ways, by piling up an enormous mass of erudition about his theme or in overwhelming his pedantic targets with an avalanche of their own jargon." Clearly aware of his novel's Menippean ancestry, Davies pays tribute, directly and indirectly, to such predecessors as Rabelais, Erasmus, Robert Burton, Peacock, and Huxley (all cited by Frye). Moreover, two of the novel's characters, Simon Darcourt and John Parlabane, are engaged in writing works which, their artistic merits notwithstanding, are Menippean in nature. In the case of Darcourt it is his *New Aubrey,* a "ragbag of information" about the university and its personalities; and Parlabane's *"roman philosophique,"* that "rat's-nest of fiction," is clearly in the Menippean tradition, if not in the best Menippean tradition. These broad hints should be enough to forestall hasty critical judgements such as those of Mills, who feels that the novel's encyclopaedic frame of reference burdens an "already disordered plot." As Frye points out, the appearance of disorder in Menippean satire is deceptive and "reflects only the carelessness of the reader or his tendency to judge by a novel-centered conception of fiction."

Disorder plays an important role in *The Rebel Angels* nevertheless. A big brain, as one character points out, does not necessarily mean a " 'well-managed intellect,' " and Davies's principal theme in the novel concerns just this, the management of the intellect. The tidy, efficient ideal advocated and embodied by Hector Mackilwraith in *Tempest-Tost* is out of the question in the world of *The Rebel Angels,* for the latter is characterized on all levels by profuseness, " 'a rich diffusion, and profusion, and—,' " and even " 'Confusion.' " *The Cornish Collection,* indeed, is less a collection than an accumulation, a vast, chaotic accumulation of culture to be systematized and made sense of by Cornish's academic executors. In one of Huxley's later novels, *After Many a Summer Dies the Swan,* an English scholar named Jeremy Pordage is hired for a similar purpose by a wealthy American collector, whose California mansion is "positively stuffed with the best that has been thought and said." Huxley uses the huge, indiscriminately amassed collection as a metaphor for cultural and intellectual disorder. It is, Pordage finds, like living "inside a cultural idiot. . . . Inside a patchwork of mutually irrelevant words and bits of information."

The Cornish Collection and indeed the university itself

carry much the same significance in *The Rebel Angels.* " 'Universities,' " as one character observes, " 'are great repositories of trivia,' " and the disciplines pursued within them reflect at once this disorder and the attempt to resolve it. Professor Clem Hollier's field, for example, is an interdisciplinary farrago of medieval studies, psychology, and anthropology:

> It's really digging into what people thought, in times when their thinking was a muddle of religion and folk-belief and rags of misunderstood classical learning, instead of being what it is today, which I suppose you'd have to call a muddle of materialism, and folk-belief, and rags of misunderstood scientific learning.

If Hollier's field cuts across many other fields, however, such breadth of inquiry remains largely an ideal in *The Rebel Angels.* A common disclaimer in universities, and in this novel, is " 'it's not my field.' " Hence the incomprehension and even distrust that exist among the muddle of mutually exclusive specialities comprising what is called knowledge and that rare spirits like Clem Hollier attempt to break down.

Intellectual obsession, of course, are, along with talk, a staple of the novel of ideas. Not even Hollier, indeed per-

THE·REBEL·ANGELS

A novel by the author of FIFTH BUSINESS
ROBERTSON DAVIES

Dust jacket of the first American edition of The Rebel Angels.

haps he least of all, is free from a limiting obsession. Although his scholarly preoccupation with bridging the gap between the modern and the primitive mind is worthy, it is nevertheless an *idée fixe,* an intellectual crotchet of the kind that types and traps characters in the novel of ideas. Thus throughout *The Rebel Angels* he and the other characters talk at each other from their particular intellectual viewpoints, seemingly failing both to understand and to be understood.

University life is a perfect arena for the clash of creeds and opinions that characterizes the novel of ideas. Significantly, Davies's centre-piece is a Peacockian banquet hosted by Simon Darcourt's college. The guests are mainly academics, drawn from a diversity of fields:

> There was Gyllenborg, who was notable in the Faculty of Medicine, Durdle and Deloney, who were in different branches of English, Elsa Czermak the economist, Hitzig and Boys, from Physiology and Physics, Stromwell, the medievalist, Ludlow from Law, Penelope Raven from Comparative Literature, Aronson the computer man, Roberta Burns the zoologist, Erzenberger and Lamotte from German and French, and Mukadassi, who was a visitor to the Department of East Asian Studies. With McVarish from History, Hollier from his ill-defined but much-discussed area of medievalism, Arthur Cornish from the world of money, the Warden who was a philosopher . . . and myself as a classicist, we cast a pretty wide net of interests, and I hoped the conversation would be lively.

Such specialization would seem to preclude any genuine understanding among these guests—there are even two specialists from separate branches of English! As in Peacock's fictional banquets, each topic of conversation is discussed from a multiplicity of differing viewpoints: murder, for example, from the perspective not only of a jurist, but of a physicist as well; sex from the perspective of a historian, a French literary scholar, and a zoologist. The concept of original sin is discussed from the points of view of theology, physiology, and psychology. Yet Darcourt observes that "We were a coherent group, in spite of the divergence of our academic interests." There is in fact an underlying harmony beneath this miscellany of subjects and views, for as Roberta Burns, the zoologist, observes (undoubtedly from the viewpoint of evolutionary theory), " 'Everything matters. The Universe is approximately fifteen billion years old, and I swear that in all that time, nothing has ever happened that has not mattered, has not contributed in some way to the totality.' "

Like Parlabane's *roman philosophique,* which serves as something of a reference point for Davies's method, *The Rebel Angels* presents " 'A multiplicity of themes, interwoven and illuminating each other.' " The key to the "muddle," indeed, lies in the implicit connections that exist among seemingly disparate elements in the novel. Hollier's rooms, for example, "were, by ordinary standards, a mess, but they had a coherence, and even a comfort, of their own. Once you stopped being offended by the muddle, neglect, and I suppose one must say dirt, they were oddly beautiful, like Hollier himself." Similarly,

Maria at one point reflects that her life is all "confusion, but at least an intensely interesting confusion." It is in the very midst of this "interesting confusion," the discord and the muddle, that Davies's characters attempt to sort out themselves and their world. The resolution, moreover, only tentatively glimpsed, does not stand apart from the muddle like a Platonic idea, but lies deep within it.

"Totality" is the sought for ideal in a novel of ideas. "The problem for me," according to Huxley's Philip Quarles, "is to transform a detached intellectual scepticism into a way of harmonious all-round living." In like wise Theodore Gumbril of *Antic Hay* wishes to become the Complete Man (and his conception of this creature is distinctly Rabelaisian, incidentally). A similar theme runs through *The Rebel Angels.* Simon Darcourt, amidst a "muddle of committees and professional university groups," is attempting to "make manifest the wholeness of Simon Darcourt." During the unsettling period of his infatuation for Maria, his "diurnal" man struggles with his "nocturnal" man as he strives to realize this ideal in the object of his love: "For me Maria was wholeness, the glory and gift of God and also the dark earth as well, so foreign to the conventional Christian mind." Maria herself, as mentioned earlier, suffers a similar "duality of mind," divided as she is between her ancient Gypsy ancestry and her life as a modern rational-minded academic—in Parlabane's terms, her "root" and her "crown": " 'No splendid crown without the strong root that works in the dark, drawing its nourishment among the rocks, the soil, hidden waters, and all the little, burrowing things'."

While Maria and Darcourt struggle to reconcile these conflicting elements in themselves, two other characters in the novel, Clem Hollier and Ozy Froats, are striving to reconcile them in humanity as a whole, if by quite disparate means. Due to his exclusively intellectual nature Hollier leads a "lopsided life," and yet the object of his investigations is "wholeness," for in uncovering the obsolete, forgotten lore of ancient superstitions he hopes to restore balance to the sceptical, overly-rational modern mind. Thus he is attempting " 'to understand the world: the whole world, not just the world of little Here and little Now.' " His current interest in this connection is the "Filth Therapy" of the Middle Ages, the use of urine or excrement for healing purposes. " 'It's astonishingly similar to alchemy in basic principle.' " marvels Hollier, " '—the recognition of what is of worth in that which is scorned by the unseeing.' " Moreover, while Hollier pursues this line of research from a humanistic perspective, his colleague Ozy Froats is proceeding on a similar premise, but from the perspective of the scientist.

Pursuing their separate but parallel lines of investigation, Hollier and Froats exemplify the "multiplicity" central to the novel of ideas—the "biologist" and the "historian" of Huxley's earlier cited example, each seeing "a different aspect . . . a different layer of reality." But it is the same reality, seen from different perspectives, which, taken together, form a "totality." Underlying this phenomenon, as Maria remarks in a different connection, is "synchronicity," the notion that "some things happened that ran on separate but parallel tracks, and occasionally flashed by

one another with blazes of confusing light, like trains passing one another in the light." Realizing this Hollier wonders: " 'is Froats the scientist looking for the same thing, but by means which are not ours, and without any idea of what we are doing, while being on much the same track?' "

Indeed, though the means are different, the end is identical, "dissimilars solving the same problem," according to Huxley. In the following exchange, Maria and Froats contrast two very different thinkers, the medieval physician Paracelsus, who worked by intuition, and the nineteenth-century scientist W. H. Sheldon, needless to say an empiricist. Maria speaks for the intuitive approach; Froats, for the empirical:

> "He [Paracelsus] may have said it, but he couldn't prove it."
> "He knew it by insight."
> "Now, now, Miss Theotoky, that'll never do. You have to prove things like that experimentally."
> "Did Sheldon prove what Paracelsus said experimentally?"
> "He certainly did!"
> "That just proves Paracelsus was the greater man; he didn't have to fag away in a lab to get the right answer."
> "We don't know if Sheldon got the completely right answer; we don't have any answers yet— just careful findings. Now—"

Yet, firmly committed as he is to scientific method, Froats does eventually come around to appreciating the common ground between a Sheldon and a Paracelsus. " 'Some extraordinary insights,' " he admits of the latter, " 'but of course without any way of verifying them. Still, it's amazing how far he got by guesswork.' "

Indeed, this rather cautious admission by Froats is as far as Davies himself is prepared to go. A fine line separates the novel of ideas from the tract (as the didactic novels of the later Huxley testify), and the synthesis of ideas in the *The Rebel Angels* is necessarily tentative, an implicit answer underlying the factious surface dialectic. It is significant that Hollier and Froats never compare notes face to face; rather, Maria—Darcourt's symbol of wholeness— serves as intermediary, tentatively uniting past and present, intuition and rationality, root and crown. In the end it is the fate of the characters in a novel of ideas to live, like Parlabane's sceptic, " 'in a constant atmosphere of carefully balanced dubiety about everything.' "

"Satura," according to Dryden's derivation of satire, "signifies a dish plentifully stored with all variety of fruit and grains." It is surely in this broad, copious spirit that Davies has conceived *The Rebel Angels* with its generous store of ideas and talk. " 'Conversations and jokes together, mutual rendering of good services, the reading together of sweetly phrased books, the sharing of nonsense and mutual attentions' " is the motto of Simon Darcourt's university classes, and indeed it might serve as the motto of *The Rebel Angels* as a whole (Maria in fact adopts it for her marriage to Arthur Cornish at the novel's end). Davies's characters seem always to be talking, and more often than not over a meal. Maria and Parlabane (whose name indi-

cates his garrulous habit) dine and argue in a restaurant with the very Menippean name of "The Rude Plenty": the spirit of Peacock is surely present alongside that of Rabelais on the last occasion, which dissolves in a spate of drinking songs. The college dinner described by Simon Darcourt is more obviously Peacockian in provenance, the Christmas dinner at Maria's home being essentially a variation on this theme, with its animated conversation and hospitable table. Thus even at Parlabane's interment a conventional funeral oration is dispensed with as Darcourt proposes talk among the deceased's friends instead; the service ends in laughter and is followed by a festive lunch.

" 'Conversations and jokes together' "; the latter element is as important in a novel of ideas as the former. Parlabane's *roman philosophique,* with its "long philosophical pow-wows," is finally a "dull muddle," for its author is a lively talker who lacks the broad comic perception of the true novelist of ideas. " 'You can't make a novelist out of a philosopher,' " observes one of Davies's characters, but as *The Rebel Angels* amply demonstrates you can make a novel out of philosophers—many different philosophers, gathered together, sharing " 'conversations and jokes.' " (pp. 182-94)

> *James Mulvihill, " 'The Rebel Angels': Robertson Davies and the Novel of Ideas," in En-glish Studies in Canada, Vol. XIII, No. 2, June, 1987, pp. 182-94.*

Anthony Burgess on Robertson Davies:

Robertson Davies is one of the most important of living novelists, I may say this, now, I think, to Canadian ears. I've just come back from Stockholm where I've been trying to persuade the Nobel Committee to at least *read* the work of Robertson Davies and consider him as, I think it must be, Canada's first Nobel Prize man. The trouble with the Nobel committee is this: they're not omniscient, they don't read everything. They ought to be told what to read, and it's the function of writers like myself who tend to be—I think I am a fairly omnivorous reader—to tell them what they ought to be doing. . . . I think Robertson Davies' claim to world renown as expressed in the Nobel laureateship, I think, is undoubted. There we have Canada's greatest living writer, greatest living novelist, who must be universally acclaimed.

Anthony Burgess, quoted by Peter Gzowski in a CBC radio interview with Davies, October 20, 1985. Reprinted in Conversations with Robertson Davies, *edited by J. Madison Davis, 1989.*

Jack Matthews   (review date 10 November 1988)

[*In the following review, Matthews examines Davies's treatment of artistic representation, truth, Jungian psychology, and mythology in* The Lyre of Orpheus.]

No novelist can bring off a committee meeting with quite the flourish and high style of Robertson Davies. So it is good to report that his latest novel, *The Lyre of Orpheus,*

opens (the theatrical metaphor is appropriate) upon a meeting in a Canadian city, presumably Toronto, of the board of the Cornish Foundation. They are gathered to decide whether they should subsidise a project which Arthur Cornish characterises as 'crack-brained' and 'absurd,' adding that it 'could prove incalculably expensive, and violates every dictate of financial prudence,' after which he recommends that, in view of all these disadvantages, they should, of course, vote to go ahead with it. And with this breezy paradox, Davies's latest novel—last in *The Cornish Trilogy,* which includes *The Rebel Angels* and *What's bred in the bone*—is off and running.

The project under discussion is an opera to be called *Arthur of Britain, or The Magnanimous Cuckold*—a work said to have been left unfinished by E. T. A. Hoffmann at his death; the score now to be completed by a singularly unattractive and difficult young genius named Hulda Schnakenburg ('Twaddlesville'?), who will thereby earn her PhD in Music. To help things along, the famous and redoubtable musicologist, Dr Gunilla Dahl Soot, is brought in as an adviser—surely bringing coals to Newcastle, for all of Davies's characters are spilling over with advice, and hardly have time to listen to one another.

The term of the opera's creation, from the committee phase of its conception to its public performance over four hundred pages later, provides the basic temporal frame of the novel: but this is only one of many thematic bonds intricately woven into the text not simply of *The Lyre of Orpheus* but of the entire trilogy. Simon Darcourt's biography of Francis Cornish, for example, was begun early in *The Rebel Angels* and is completed at approximately the same time as the opera. Cornish was Arthur's uncle and eponym of the Foundation—a man who had gathered great wealth and great art during a life that began and ended in Canada, although much of it was lived in England and Europe, where he was occupied with intelligence work during World War Two.

During those of his investigations into Cornish's life which are recounted in *The Lyre of Orpheus,* Darcourt discovers that his subject's greatness lay not only in his collecting money and art, but also in his secretly painting an astonishingly 'authentic' 16th-century masterpiece, *The Marriage at Cana,* hitherto assigned to some anonymous 'Alchemical Master': this discovery is one of the major satisfactions for the reader who has read the works of the trilogy in the order of their publication.

This is not the same, however, as the chronological order of the events they describe. *The Rebel Angels,* the first novel of the trilogy, begins shortly after the death of Francis Cornish, with the setting-up of the Cornish Foundation, and with Simon Darcourt's initial brooding over the artistic problems of fitting such a man into a book. *What's bred in the bone* carries the reader back in time, focusing upon the life of Francis Cornish himself—the *fons et origo* of so much that has to be lived out by his heirs and successors, who seem destined to explicate in terms of their own preoccupations and realities what he has so cunningly complicated. In writing this novel, Davies is doing Darcourt's job, as it were—but from a greater distance, so that his view includes Darcourt. He is painting a portrait of

Francis Cornish, showing the back of Simon Darcourt in the foreground as he paints *his* portrait of Cornish within this lesser frame. Now, with *The Lyre of Orpheus,* we pick up temporally where *Rebel Angels* left off.

As for Francis Cornish's biographer, Simon Darcourt: he is a priest, a bachelor, and a professor of Greek in the College of St John and the Holy Ghost (familiarly known as 'Spook'); he is also a man of acute observation and humane understanding. In addition, since much of the action of all the novels derives from Francis Cornish's life and accomplishments, Darcourt provides a sort of artistic mediation, and if any character other than Cornish himself may be said to possess the action of the trilogy, it is Darcourt. He is in many ways worthy of the role, although he suffers, I think, from an affliction which is shared by some of Davies's other characters: he often does not quite measure up to his talk.

Davies possesses rare insight into human dividedness, and can argue a contrary case with admirable conviction. In his essay, **'Truth in Melodrama'** (in *Voice from the Attic*), he wrote: 'Melodrama stirs us, and stirred our forefathers, because we sense its basic truth.' The argument is not unfamiliar, but in Davies's essay **'From the Attic'** (i.e., from Canada to the US), the argument finds a unique relevance to an age that seems to be working with all its might to destroy history.

The pervasive belief in hidden truths is closely connected with melodrama, for what melodrama can exist without a secret? Certainly, there are secrets and hidden truths in *The Lyre of Orpheus,* for, like all of Davies's fiction, it is to some extent about art itself—which is concerned with the truth of appearances—and gives pleasure to the extent that we are momentarily, willingly deceived, and then edified, only to be deceived again—and so forth, in a sort of dialectical progression in which hiddenness and revelation play thesis and antithesis, turn and counter-turn, until their final various syntheses and revelations.

The title of this new novel derives from E. T. A. Hoffmann's observation that 'the lyre of Orpheus opens the door of the underworld of feeling.' The utterance is germane to all of Davies's fiction, for his subject never drifts far from magic, and that special institutionalised form of magic we call art. Davies has been labelled a Jungian, and the elemental divisions Jung found in human experience provide rich material for his special gifts and interests. Most of these divisions are variations on the classical separations of truth from appearance which, with the advent of modern epistemology, have begun to seem simplistic, even disreputable: for today we are evidently condemned to experience a world of graded appearances, providing endless opportunities for a novelist who understands and delights in fictional games employing levels of deceit.

I have claimed that Davies creates committee meetings in his fiction that are wonderfully interesting and unlike those of any other writer. No doubt his experience in the theatre (he is a playwright and studied acting at the Old Vic, where he was Tyrone Guthrie's literary assistant) has been useful in his mastering the craft of fiction: but while his dialogue may have been learned in the theatre, it is still

his own. Fictional dialogue is an art in itself, and, by everyone's admission, a very difficult one. And for all his gifts, Davies does not always create 'pure' dialogue— which is to say, his characters do not always speak as they alone could speak. In fact, when they are inspired by topics of a scholarly nature, they almost inevitably begin to sound exactly like Davies himself in his literary essays. Since I value these essays as models of grace and insight, however, I am content to let his people step out of character long enough for the voice of the magician who has created them to be clearly heard.

Over a large dinner one-third of the way though *The Lyre of Orpheus,* while all the guests are 'chirping over their cups', Geraint Powell announces that their opera needs a story. This idea seems to catch everyone by surprise, and they are immediately launched into several pages of delicious haggling. Probably the drink has something to do with the scene's reminding one of Alice's mad tea party: but drink, together with Powell's remark, is only the catalyst, for all of these characters are madly articulate, madly informed, madly outspoken, and madly partial in their views. The mention of such a scene, however, should not be taken to suggest that *Lyre,* or the trilogy it completes, lacks either a complex and interesting architectonics or good storytelling. The narrative lines are interwoven, contrapuntal, and bound together by various themes that are sounded over and over in different ways, and with a gratifying sense of authenticity. The quest motif is everywhere apparent, and it functions in different ways just as it means different things to different people. If the Arthurian analogue in *Lyre* is focused upon, the quest becomes twofold: the opera itself, as a completed work of art, as well as a properly more mystical possession. But possession of what? Of knowledge, of course—beyond that, of understanding; and beyond that, of wisdom. Nothing in the world of sensation proves to be exactly what it seems, and yet what is perceived always carries within itself a seed of mystic revelation.

Like Jung before him, Davies is infatuated with the constant discovery of human wisdom in ancient knowledge. All his work, and *The Cornish Trilogy* especially, teems with old and half-forgotten lore—Tarot, astrology, the chemistry of pigments in Renaissance painting, alchemy, Gypsy lore, Arthurian legend, the old and discarded subtleties of the Schoolmen. *The Rebel Angels* also includes a treatise on somatotypes and features a biologist named Ozy Froats (how John Cowper Powys would have liked that name!) who is earnestly engaged in what might be termed 'scatomancy'—the biological analysis of human feces and what they might reveal of what we are, and are not.

One of the motifs in *The Lyre of Orpheus* is supplied by the ghost of E. T. A. Hoffmann, who is heard periodically (in italics, naturally) commenting upon the action. He speaks from that limbo which is reserved for artists who have not done their best or have left work unfinished, and his function here is somewhat that of a Greek chorus. His sections are analogous to the phased commentaries of 'the Lesser Zadkiel, Angel of Biography, and the Daimon Maimas' in *What's bred in the bone.* With considerable panache, these two explain one of the most astonishingly melodramatic coincidences in all literature, underscoring Davies's defiant insistence upon the event happening, and to hell with plausibility. Hoffmann's comments upon the completion of his own imagined work are dim and uncertain—which is perhaps only natural for an artist in limbo. 'Operas devour incident,' a character remarks in *Lyre:* and, indeed, this opera acts as a mirror and metaphor for the novel itself, as *it* devours incident. When works of art are given prominence in a novel, they inevitably tell us something about the novel. How could they not? Like Darcourt's biography of Cornish, all that talk about how to conceive an opera, and produce it adequately, reflects upon and energises the action of the novel in which the talk takes place.

Davies's many years of theatrical experience enliven these scenes, and one can feel that special shared excitement that comes when artistic collaboration moves to a public performance. But there is another sort of personal experience Davies has evidently drawn upon to enrich his fiction: his tenure as Dean of Massey College at the University of Toronto. One is not invited to identify Spook with any specific aspect of the university life Davies has known personally and from within; nevertheless, there are sorts of madness that are equisitely peculiar to academic life. Most of these have to do with the curse/blessing of over-specialisation, so that—unbalanced by profession—scholars occupying neighbouring territories can suddenly turn vicious over matters the world must view as trivial. Spook is a microcosm, as well as the setting for most of the trilogy's shenanigans: in its great rooms the committees meet and the banquets are held. Alma Mater continues to nourish all within—the faculty and administration especially—and even favours deans and sub-committees with xeroxed agendas. Davies's playfulness with the academic mind contributes to wonderfully comic scenes, scenes so exuberant and so good-natured in the Horatian mode that the satire is more joyful than bitter. Notable exceptions are the only three 'Americans'—those living beneath the attic—so grubby and silly a trio of specimens that it would have been better had they been distributed over the trilogy, one to a novel.

As the theme of the opera suggests, cuckoldry is a dominant motif—but it is not limited to *Lyre,* for there are two other cases—if one can call Francis's aristocratic father a cuckold (he married knowing that his wife was pregnant with a child begotten by champagne, by accident and by a stranger). Arthur Cornish himself is the magnanimous cuckold in *Lyre,* and it is unfortunate that he is not especially convincing as a character. Possibly he is not meant to be, for his existence as a rather pale symbol possessed of the kingly power of money might seem justification enough. His wife Maria (née Theotoky—she is half-Gypsy, and her mother, Mamusia, has a lively part in the earlier action) is another matter altogether. She is the learned and subtle protégé of Clement Hollier, a 'paleo-psychologist' who seduced her at the very beginning of **The Rebel Angels.** Her scholarly interest is Rabelais, and, like most of Davies's characters, she is interestingly at odds with herself, divided between her half-Gypsy heri-

tage (embodied in her terrible, fascinating Mamusia) and the Western world of higher learning.

Now, having been married to Arthur, Maria is again 'seduced'—this time by the flamboyant Geraint Powell, who comes to her at night wearing Arthur's robe. To a sleepy and amorous woman, whose husband has just become sterile from mumps, her acquiescence might seem no more than a willing suspension of disbelief. Geraint Powell is a guilt-tormented con man with a handsome profile and a flair for the theatrical. His dividedness, too, is spectacular, manifest in his ambivalence towards his father, an evangelical pastor in Wales whom poor Geraint can neither forgive nor forget.

The novel is about cuckoldry, art and salvation. But, like virtually everything in the mirror-muddled world these novels present, none of them is exactly what it seems. For example, cuckoldry is not simply the deceiving of basically good men by women, two of whom would hardly be accounted wicked even from a Victorian point of view (the third, however, is one of the great bitches in all literature—she appears in **What's bred in the bone**). It is also a metaphor which suggests that all of our truths are merely appearances, that there is a compassion, or *caritas,* that accepts what fate has dumped into our nests, and that such magnanimity and acceptance can help us to find our humanity. This wisdom parallels artistic creation, which does not really operate independently and personally, but rather participates always in the perpetuation of old skills and old knowledge.

I found the ending of *Lyre* crowded, hurried, with important issues tossed dismissively aside (Darcourt's completion of Cornish's biography is given little more than footnote status). And yet, perhaps, this is in one sense as it should be: perhaps every trilogy should be thought of as consisting of four books, the last unwritten. (pp. 19-20)

Jack Matthews, "Magnanimous Cuckolds," in London Review of Books, *Vol. 10, No. 20, November 10, 1988, pp. 19-20.*

David Lodge   (review date 13 April 1989)

[*An English novelist, critic, short story writer, and dramatist, Lodge is best known for his novels* Changing Places *(1975) and* How Far Can You Go? *(1980), in which he lampoons the world of academia, and for such theoretical works as* The Language of Fiction *(1966),* The Modes of Modern Writing *(1971), and* Working with Structuralism *(1981). In the following review of* The Lyre of Orpheus, *Lodge places Davies outside the realm of contemporary writers, arguing his fiction is more typical of nineteenth-century authors.*]

Robertson Davies started writing novels fairly late in life, and has come into his prime as a novelist at an age when most men are glad if they can summon up enough energy and concentration to read a book, let alone write one. Born in Thamesville, Ontario, in 1913, he was an actor (with the London Old Vic company), then a playwright, theater director, essayist, and newspaper editor for many years before (and after) he published his first novel, **Tempest-Tost** (1951). This and its sequels, **Leaven of Malice**

(1954) and *A Mixture of Frailties* (1958), which make up the so-called *Salterton Trilogy,* aroused little interest outside Canada. *Fifth Business,* which appeared more than a decade later (1970), and *The Deptford Trilogy,* which it inaugurated, continued in *The Manticore* (1972) and completed by *World of Wonders* (1975), enjoyed some success in America, but made little impact in England. I have to confess that the first time Robertson Davies impinged on my own consciousness was when I was asked (by an American journal) to review *The Rebel Angels* in 1982.

What's Bred in the Bone, a related, though free-standing novel, was widely praised, and was short-listed for the Booker Prize in 1984. It put Robertson Davies in that small group of novelists whom anyone professing a serious interest in contemporary fiction has to read. His impressively bearded countenance, staring challengingly from the review pages of newspapers and magazines like a reincarnation of Tolstoy (whose birthday he shares, to his obvious pleasure, along with Goethe and Saint Augustine), has become a familiar literary icon. The publication of *The Lyre of Orpheus,* which completes another, as yet unnamed, trilogy, is an important literary event.

There are several possible reasons why Robertson Davies's novelistic reputation has ripened so slowly. One is that he is Canadian, and the Anglo-American world has only recently begun to take seriously the idea of a Canadian literature. He was once told by the secretary of a famous London theatrical management to whom he had submitted one of his plays, "Mr. Davies, you must realize that nobody—literally nobody—is interested in Canada." Such an attitude is not unknown in the United States— some years ago an American magazine competition to invent the most boring book title imaginable was won by *Canada—Our Neighbor to the North.*

This dismissive attitude toward Canadian culture becomes increasingly difficult to sustain in the presence, literal or metaphorical, of writers like Margaret Atwood, Alice Munro, and Robertson Davies himself, but it is not without some historical foundation, as Davies would readily acknowledge. When he returned to his native country in 1940, after completing his education and theatrical apprenticeship in England, Canada seemed to him "like a dull, ill-rehearsed show that someone should put on the road," and his novels are peppered with satirical observations on the Canadian ethos that have not endeared him to his fellow countrymen.

The narrator of *The Lyre of Orpheus* says of his characters, "They were not wholly of the grey majority of their people. . . . They did not murmur the national prayer: 'Oh God, grant me mediocrity and comfort; protect me from the radiance of Thy light.'" This is something of an understatement: any foreigner who took Robertson Davies's novels as his only guide to Canadian society would acquire a somewhat distorted image of it. Davies deals for the most part with rich, eccentric, artistic, and scholarly personages, who enjoy good food and good wine, old books and old masters, and engage each other in witty and learned conversation—characters who seem to have strayed out of the pages of Thomas Love Peacock or George Meredith rather than the kind you might meet at, say, a neighborly barbecue in a Toronto suburb.

The affinity with bookish nineteenth-century writers suggests another reason why Davies's novels have taken a long time to find a large appreciative audience. When he hit his stride as a novelist, in the 1970s, new fiction claimed attention by being formally "experimental" in the postmodernist style (lots of discontinuity, fragmentation, contradiction, randomness, and "metafictional" openness of form) and/or by a boldly explicit exploration of sexuality and sexual politics. Though Robertson Davies's novels are not without their erotic, sometimes kinkily erotic, passages, he has made clear, both in these texts and outside them, that he regards the contemporary Western obsession with the physical mechanics of sexual intercourse, and especially with what an uncouth character in *The Lyre of Orpheus* calls "the organism," as encouraging a fatally limited view of human relationships. As for literary experimentalism, he has characteristically observed:

> We all know what the avant-garde was. It was the group that was sent forward to encounter the worst of the fire, and to fall bravely in the service of their country, and then the real army came up and took over and won the battle. And I think that's what happens in literature. Those who want to be in it, are just inviting their destruction, because the avant-garde has changed its clothes and its uniform and its underwear three or four times in my lifetime. Who wants to get into that?

Certainly there is at present a lull, indicating either exhaustion or disillusionment, in the polemical and creative struggles of postmodernism, and a literary climate, therefore, receptive to the old-fashioned pleasures of texts like *What's Bred in the Bone* and *The Lyre of Orpheus.* Robertson Davies has observed that "great literature always has plots," and although he likes to group his novels in sequences of three, each has a beginning, a middle, and an end in true Aristotelian fashion. He has called them "romances," perhaps acknowledging that he takes some liberties with probability in the interest of narrative complication or symbolic design, and uses supernatural machinery (for example the interventions of the Recording Angels in *What's Bred in the Bone,* and of the limbo-confined composer Hoffmann in *The Lyre of Orpheus*), but it is all done in a style hallowed by traditional literary convention, and does not in any way subvert or challenge ways of reading derived from the classic realist text. The word that constantly comes to mind in reading Davies is "gusto": he seems to have taken huge pleasure in the creation of his imagined world, and this pleasure conveys itself infectiously to the reader. His prose is brisk, supple, and well-balanced. The enigmas of the narrative, and the amusing, cultivated chatter of the characters, draw us effortlessly through the text, intrigued and stimulated, if seldom deeply moved. His novels are (I do not regard this as faint praise) the thinking man's good read.

The sequence completed by *The Lyre of Orpheus* may become known as *The Cornish Trilogy,* since its stories revolve around the enigmatic figure of Francis Cornish, a well-to-do Canadian art connoisseur who has left his mysteriously acquired fortune to found a charitable trust for patronage of the arts, administered by his businessman nephew, Arthur Cornish, and a number of other trustees drawn from the University of Toronto—in particular from the College of St. John and the Holy Ghost, which seems to bear some humorous resemblance to Massey College, of which Robertson Davies was master from 1962 to 1981. *The Rebel Angels* concerns the intrigues and struggles between several of these academics for possession of a rare collection of holograph letters from Rabelais to the Renaissance magus Paracelsus.

What's Bred in the Bone backtracks in time to relate the life of Francis Cornish and explain some of the mysteries of his life. This is a more serious and ambitious novel than its predecessor, moving confidently in time and space, vividly evoking the hero's childhood in provincial Ontario, his aesthetic and sentimental education in England, and his experiences during World War II, when he served on an Allied commission for tracing and identifying old paintings. One of the works he discovered was a depiction of *The Marriage Feast of Cana* by an unidentified genius of the sixteenth century known as the Alchemical Master, following an explication of the painting's esoteric symbolism by an art critic associated with Cornish.

One of the main plot strands of *The Lyre of Orpheus* concerns the discovery by Simon Darcourt, a theology professor and Anglican clergyman who is writing a biography of Francis Cornish, that this interpretation of the painting is quite mistaken. The other strand concerns the production of an opera subsidized by the Cornish Foundation—not so much a production, in fact, as the reconstruction and completion of a complicated original work by the German Romantic composer E. T. A. Hoffmann. The subject of the opera is the story of King Arthur, and Hoffmann's working title was *Arthur of Britain, or the Magnanimous Cuckold.* Its theme was to be "King Arthur's recognition of the love of Lancelot for Guinevere, and the great pain with which he accepts that love." The project foundered because Hoffmann was unable to reach agreement with his London-based libretist, Planché. All that survives (in Francis Cornish's valuable manuscript collection) are Hoffmann's notes and rough drafts of the score, and the correspondence with Planché.

On the basis of these documents, Hulda Schnakenburg, a brilliant if unprepossessing graduate student of music at Toronto, undertakes to reconstruct the opera as a Ph.D. project, supervised by the Swedish composer and musicologist Dr. Gunilla Dahl-Soot (Davies's gusto is very evident in his invention of names). Darcourt supplies the libretto (deftly plagiarized from Sir Walter Scott) and the performance is directed by the ambitious and eloquent Welsh director Geraint Powell. The ghost of the composer himself watches over the whole enterprise with some excitement, from his vantage point in the limbo of forgotten artists from which the production promises to release him.

Robertson Davies makes full use of his theatrical experience in relating the story of this production, and the account of its first night is genuinely thrilling even to a reader (like myself) who has little enthusiasm for opera. One acquires from this book a great deal of fascinating information about the history of operatic form, early-nineteenth-century stage design, and the mechanics of libretto writing ("Do you know a two-syllable word meaning 'regret' that isn't 'regret'? Because 'regret' isn't a word that sings well if it has to be matched up with a quarter-note followed by an eighth-note"), not to mention Arthurian legend, the Tarot pack, art history, pony breeding, old Ontario figures of speech, and Romany proverbs. The apparently effortless deployment of specialized and arcane knowledge about many different subjects is one of Davies's great strengths as a novelist.

The production of the opera is enmeshed in various amorous intrigues. The lesbian Dr. Gunilla Dahl-Soot seduces Hulda Schnakenburg, who falls in love with Geraint Powell, who, by a device reminiscent of the bed tricks in Shakespeare's problem plays, impregnates Arthur Cornish's barren wife, Maria (née Theotoky, a former graduate student of the College of St. John and the Holy Ghost, and a major character in *The Rebel Angels*). By magnanimously accepting the child, Arthur Cornish reenacts the theme of Hoffmann's opera—Maria corresponding to Guinevere and Powell to Lancelot.

"Let us, I entreat you, explore the miraculous that dwells in the depths of the mind," Hoffmann writes to Planché. "Let the lyre of Orpheus open the door of the underworld of feeling." The lyre of Orpheus stands metonymically for music and mythopoeia, which break through the crust of rationality and materialism concealing our real desires and fears from ourselves. Davies, a self-confessed Jungian, invokes archetypes in his novels for the same purpose. The fact that the characters are all well aware of these archetypes makes the mythic level of the novel seem somewhat artificial and contrived, but Davies tries to mitigate this effect by a kind of mythic overdetermination. Thus it is not only the Grail legend but also the Tarot pack that offers clues—confusing clues—to the fortunes of the characters. Darcourt, for instance, who supposes himself to be the Hermit in the pack, turns out to be the Fool.

But a wise fool, whose disinterested pursuit of the truth about Cornish, to the point of endangering his own reputation (it entails his stealing some drawings from the National Gallery in Ottawa), enables him to unravel the mystery of *The Marriage Feast of Cana.* It proves to be the work of Francis Cornish himself, executed in a flawless imitation of sixteenth-century painting, every figure of which is a portrait of some member or associate of the artist's family.

Darcourt feels that his discovery "establishes Francis as a very great painter. Working in the mode of a bygone day, but a great painter nonetheless." Arthur Cornish is not so sure: "He may be a great painter, but that makes him unmistakably a faker." This exchange seems to bear obliquely on the art of Robertson Davies himself, which some critics have seen as skillful pastiche of an obsolete fictional style rather than an authentic contribution to modern literature.

The Lyre of Orpheus ends with a discussion of Keats's remark "A Man's life of any worth is a continual allegory"; and in the invented life of Francis Cornish Davies seems to be writing an allegory of his own artistic career. Like Cornish, Davies has "dared to be of a time not his own"; like Cornish he has been fascinated by the figural tradition in late medieval and early Renaissance art and literature, "all that allegorical-metaphysical stuff, all that symbolic communication" that, according to Darcourt, post-Renaissance Europe rejected. Through the theme of the fake or imitation painting which is indistinguishable from its revered models, Robertson Davies seeks to undermine the arrogant historicism of modern aesthetics that would condemn his highly crafted and highly enjoyable novels as "irrelevant."

The Lyre of Orpheus is not perhaps as powerful and *surprising* a novel as *What's Bred in the Bone,* but it has all Davies's wit, learning, and inventiveness in abundance, and brings to a satisfying conclusion a trilogy that stands as a major fictional achievement independent of literary fashion. Davies's own spiritual home, however, is not so much the sixteenth century as the early nineteenth. He is essentially a latter-day Romantic who believes in man's unconquerable mind, and the expressive function of art. *The Marriage Feast of Cana,* when decoded by Darcourt, turns out to be a work not of alchemical symbolism but of Romantic biography and autobiography, rather like Benjamin Haydon's huge canvas *Christ Entering into Jerusalem,* in which Haydon himself and most of his acquaintances, including Keats, were portrayed. Does this imply that underneath the highly contrived plotting and archetypal patterning of the Cornish trilogy there is a kind of confessional, autobiographical novel waiting to be discovered? Davies has hinted as much, and in the process given another explanation for the late maturing of his formidable talent. In a very recent interview he told Herbert Denton of *The Washington Post* that "he was able to write more frankly as he grew older because 'people died.'" We must be grateful for his own vigorous longevity. (pp. 35-6)

> David Lodge, "Hermits and Fools," in The
> New York Review of Books, *Vol. XXXVI, No.*
> *6, April 13, 1989, pp. 35-6.*

Sally Eckhoff (review date 25 April 1989)

[*In the following excerpt, Eckhoff characterizes* The Lyre of Orpheus *as an exposition of the pedantic world of academia.*]

The Lyre of Orpheus, the last installment in Robertson Davies's [third] trilogy, charts the magic zone where knowledge and education intersect. The book is situated smack dab in the middle of uptight Scottish Presbyterianism, at a provincial Ontario college nicknamed Spook. From its small, serious population, Davies assembles a cast of contentious scholarly characters infiltrated by one smart businessman and a suitably slovenly artist. These citizens of academia are irritating and challenging messengers of Davies's notions of true intelligence.

When Spook is presented with a lavish and unexpected gift, its inhabitants' wits are tested in a way that surprises them. An eccentric local patriarch dies, leaving behind his art collection and heaps of money. A foundation of Spookians and other qualified parties gathers to decide what to do with Frank Cornish's wealth. The dead man's nephew Arthur, his wife, and a bunch of crusty professors focus on a strange project: they want to fund the production of an unfinished opera. They pick filthy bohemian music whiz Hulda Schnakenburg, otherwise known as Schnak, to complete E. T. A. Hoffmann's *Arthur of Britain, or The Magnanimous Cuckold* for her doctoral thesis.

As the plans get hashed out at the foundation's round table, life begins to imitate Arthurian legend. Arthur Cornish is going to be cuckolded by some modern-day Lancelot whether he likes it or not. Maria, his stunning wife, must betray him. And the reader, who saw all this coming as soon as the shape of the table was announced, wonders if the story is already over.

The big question is whether *Orpheus*'s academic hotshots will choose to think their way out of this mythic mess, or succumb to the power of the muse. Since they are True Aesthetes, the art must have its way: Maria, her husband, and the professors are swept away, taking Schnak with them. This is their passion, and Davies's. But all those years of quoting New Testament Greek and Rabelais haven't given them or their author a clue as to what kind of person makes art or why. They would like to put their young artist on a leash—they can't seem to say enough about what a directionless slob Schnak is. If they were less squeamish, they might learn something crucial about the forces that drive her, and the pleasures these forces can unleash.

But pleasure, especially the physical variety, is a shrunken, gnarled presence in any Davies novel. His descriptions of sex have a fishy offhandedness, as if he rather enjoys the fact that people still Do It, but considers it an unseemly pastime for anybody with a brain. He also renounces any seductiveness in the sound of his prose. From the galumphing names of the characters (Dr. Gunilla Dahl-Soot is one of the chunkier ones) to the choppy dialogue, Davies's writing can fall mighty heavy on the ear.

There's only one person in *The Lyre of Orpheus* who doesn't go around talking like a concordance with legs. She's Maria Cornish's mother, Mamusia, and a gypsy to the soles of her unwashed feet. She oils her hair more than she shampoos it, lades her wrists with clanking bangles ("You can tell the ring of real gold," she says), reads the tarot, fixes violins, and fears neither her past nor her future. Davies suggests that it's she who holds the cards in her world: her perspicacity gives her power. Her speech is wry and funny. She has a fire within her. Yet she spends the entire book literally in the basement, forced to move into the underground floors of the building that houses her daughter's penthouse when her old tenement burns down.

Davies introduced Mamusia two books ago in *The Rebel Angels* as someone whose intelligence had reached full flower without benefit of a conventional education. She then said, "The kind of sensitivity that made it possible for a man to hear an army marching several miles away without any kind of artificial aid has almost disappeared from the earth. The recognition of oneself as a part of nature, and reliance on natural things, are disappearing for hundreds of millions of people who do not know that anything is being lost." Maria and her teachers in *The Lyre of Orpheus* have striven to repress their intuitive powers, and discredit the areas of knowledge that Davies describes as feminine. Mamusia has become not only a minor character, but an insensitive one. Now she thinks that artists "thrive on hunger and destruction" and that they are best left constantly deprived. Is this the voice of the wild Magyar fiddler who broke hearts all over Europe when she was young? No, it's her creator talking. Davies hints that blood will out and Maria will get her comeuppance for thwarting her past, but readers wait in vain.

There are joys in *The Lyre of Orpheus,* the greatest of them being that the author makes the reader feel smart. Davies's polymathic knowledge of etymology, stagecraft, Hungarian food, Welsh slang, Latin, Old French, and Hoffmann contes is fascinating. But I would trade an earful of his encyclopedic knowledge for lunch with Mamusia. In Davies's world, the academic mind is so sure of its own worth that it feels no need for the intuitive or the sensual. This says a great deal about why Davies's artist is more like a poorly domesticated animal than a woman, and why Schnak's scholarly advisers are ultimately destructive to themselves and to her. I hope that in his next work, Davies will get Mamusia out of the basement in time to save Maria and her toffee-nosed friends from themselves. (pp. 49-50)

> *Sally Eckhoff, "Mind Set," in* The Village Voice, *Vol. XXXIV, No. 17, April 25, 1989, pp. 49-50.*

Aram Bakshian, Jr.   (review date May 1989)

[*An American editor and critic, Bakshian has written extensively about American politics. In the following review, he praises* The Lyre of Orpheus *as an examination of humanity's preoccupation with myth, religious figures, and transcendental truth.*]

If you are among the growing number of readers who resort to fiction as a mental muscle relaxant, Robertson Davies is not your kind of novelist. The doyen of Canadian authors refuses to succumb to the trite or trendy. With Davies, the easy read is eschewed for the intelligent read; timelessness triumphs over timeliness, and a measure of literacy, wit, and mature thought is required of the reader as well as the author.

An accomplished critic, essayist, and novelist, Davies has also served time as an actor and academician, experiences that enrich most of the pages of his latest novel. *The Lyre of Orpheus,* as strummed by Davies, evokes myth, magic, music, theatre, ivory-tower oddities, poetry, and generous insights into the Old Adam and his Maker. All this combines to tell a story that, excellent in itself, also neatly concludes the latest Davies trilogy. Those unfamiliar with the preceding volumes, *The Rebel Angels* and *What's Bred in the Bone* (both still in print as paperbacks), will derive maximum enjoyment by reading them in sequence. But each stands as a distinctive work, much in the manner of Trollope's ecclesiastical and parliamentary novels, though covering murky areas of the human psyche and behavior which that Victorian worthy may never have dreamt of.

Not that the Victorians didn't know a thing or two about sin, which gives their best work more depth than most contemporary fiction. As Davies himself has observed, "Sin is the great unacknowledged element in modern life. The great Freudian revolution diffused old sins. No one believes in spite anymore. People call it objectivity and then act mean as hell on very high-minded grounds." To the extent that psychology has something to tell us, says Davies, the key lies more in Jung than Freud, in seeking to understand the meanings of dream and myth not to explain individual quirks, but to know why human beings have an inbred desire "to believe in certain things. . . . Why do people wish to believe in saints? Why do they develop legends that are manifestly untrue but they wish to be true?" And, ultimately, does a greater truth about man and the universe lie rooted beneath this mythic topsoil?

The Lyre of Orpheus explores these questions in a triple-tiered allegory: an early form of the Arthurian legend of chivalry, cuckoldry, and redemption that inspires a present-day attempt to complete an operatic fragment based on the legend by the nineteenth-century German romantic author-composer E. T. A. ("Tales of ") Hoffmann. This, in turn, triggers another cycle of idealism, betrayal, and cleansing on the part of the modern roundtable of philanthropists, scholars, and artists who work on the opera and its premiere in contemporary Canada. The theme, taken from a real line of Hoffmann's, is that "The Lyre of Orpheus opens the door of the underworld." And in the course of 472 entertaining pages, it does.

If all this sounds a bit labored, it should not. Davies is a master of plot, character, dialogue, and irony. Minor comic figures and comic moments abound, and he has a poetic gift for language. Nor, despite his erudition and academic background, does Davies ever succumb to pedantry, a scholarly affliction which his years as master of Massey College in Toronto have taught him to despise. Some of his best needling is reserved for learned philistines such as the lady scholar who

> had a critical system, unfailing in its power to reduce poetry to technicalities and to slide easily over its content. It was a system which, properly applied, could put Homer in his place and turn the Sonnets of Shakespeare into critic-fodder. Without intending to be so, it was a system which, once mastered, set the possessor free forever, should that be his wish, from anything a poet, however noble in spirit, might have felt and imparted to the world.

There is also the occasional graceful swipe at academic bluffers, as when two faculty members, discussing the opera project but totally ignorant of the identity of the nineteenth-century theatrical hack, James Robertson Planche (who was originally intended as its librettist), engage in a professional battle of witlessness: "Neither the dean nor Darcourt knew who Planche was, but they sparred in the accustomed academic manner to find out what the other knew, and worked up a cloud of unknowing which, again in the academic manner, seemed to give them comfort."

It is not surprising that Davies's disdain for learned flummery, and his strong sense of civilized tradition and the darker reaches beneath, should annoy and perhaps genuinely puzzle some of the more literal-minded *literati* of today. Even an essentially friendly critic, Professor Phyllis Rose, complained in the *New York Times* that Davies's approach is "ahistorical, conservative" and that, despite "wild invention and bizarre plot turns, he does not believe that human nature changes." Professor Rose, who apparently believes that the human race redefines itself and grows a new soul every few years, found this a bleak perspective for a novelist because:

> If circumstances do not affect the soul, if each person lives out a quest to achieve personal integration and only the terms of the quest change, then truly there is nothing new under the sun. . . . Create characters who have no vital connection to their times and they will have no depth.

Professor Rose got it backwards. By proving that his characters have depths and dimensions that go back far beyond 1980s North America, Davies gives their feelings and conflicts a larger meaning and recognizes human nature as a spiritual creation of infinite complexity rather than a fickle mutation subject to change without notice, rather like each season's hemlines.

For all his barbs, Davies takes a basically humane view of his characters and the world, best articulated by Simon Darcourt, the bemused Anglican priest through whose eyes most of the novel's action—and underlying passions—is sensed. The priestly role of both author and character is flawed and limited by human nature, as Darcourt confesses to Arthur Cornish, the millionaire benefactor who, like his namesake of the opera and legend, has tried to create a Camelot and ends up a noble cuckold:

> I know we are supposed to love mankind indiscriminately, but I don't. That's why I gave up practical priesthood and became a professor. My faith charges me to love my neighbor but I can't and I won't fake it, in the greasy way professional lovers-of-mankind do—the professionally charitable, the newspaper sob sisters, the politicians. I'm not Christ, Arthur, and I can't love like Him, so I settle for courtesy, consideration, decent manners, and whatever I can do for the people I really do love . . .

Perhaps Darcourt's—and Davies's—personal creed is best summed up in a passage describing the baptism of the baby conceived as a result of Arthur's cuckolding, a product of adultery that reunites an estranged couple with a bond of love:

> Its solely Christian implications apart . . . [baptism] was the acceptance of a new life into a society that thereby declared that it had a place for new life; it was an assertion of an attitude toward life that was expressed in the Creed which was a part of the service in a form archaic and compressed but full of noble implication. The parents and godparents might think they did not believe that Creed, as they recited it, but it was plain to Darcourt that they were living in a society which had its roots in that Creed. . . . The Creed was one of the great signposts in the journey of mankind from a primitive society toward whatever was to come, and though the signpost might be falling behind in the march of civilization, it had marked a great advance from which there could be no permanent retreat.

Even at his most fantastic, Robertson Davies clings to this basic truth, recognizing along the way that "one of the most difficult tasks for the educated and sophisticated mind is to recognize that some clichés are also important truths," a lesson lost on most of today's novelists, and the reason why they will be forgotten long before this brilliant mixture of Merlin, Falstaff, and moralist, Robertson Davies—quite possibly the worthiest novelist writing in the English language today. Tired London and trendy New York have been trumped by a white-bearded old eccentric in, of all places, Toronto.

> *Aram Bakshian, Jr., in a review of "The Lyre of Orpheus," in* The American Spectator, *Vol. 22, No. 5, May, 1989, p. 46.*

David Rollow on Davies's use of the archetype:

Robertson Davies sees everything in the world as substitutable for something else. Nothing exists in isolation, but it is not just that things are related or interconnected. What happens in life echoes something that has happened before, and Davies is after the whole long chain of resemblances. Like an astrologer, a gypsy fortune-teller, or a certain kind of priest . . . Davies believes that ordinary life is less real than the archetypes it suggests. The whole culture is raised on the ruins of half-forgotten mythologies. The remarkable thing is that Davies takes all this gaseous material and makes it work.

> *David Rollow, in his "Lying beneath the Surface, in* The Spectator, *8 October 1988.*

Michael Peterman (essay date Fall 1989)

[*A Canadian critic, educator, editor, and scriptwriter, Peterman has written extensively about Canadian writers associated with Peterborough, Ontario, and is the author of the biography* Robertson Davies *(1986). In the following essay, Peterman discusses the structure and style of* What's Bred in the Bone, *which he considers an artistic and thematic extension of Davies's other works.*]

The typical Robertson Davies novel blends two narrative patterns. The first is the struggle of a young man—often of wealthy or socially prominent parentage—to find his own self-sustaining direction in life. Despite the crippling social restrictions of a provincial Canadian upbringing and the powerful personalities of parental figures, the Davies hero, be he Solly Bridgetower, Dunstan Ramsay, or David Staunton, enacts not only a psychological success story but also an apology for wealth and power in twentieth-century Canada. In the smallest nutshell, Jungian individuation triumphs over social and Freudian constraints, and the hero makes his determined pursuit of what matters most to him, alert to the advantages inherent in "the freemasonry of the rich."

The second narrative pattern, which has become increasingly more complex with each of Davies's recent novels, concerns the education of the conscious artist. It involves a close study not only of the factors that go into the making of the artist, but also of the ramifications of the artist's "double consciousness." Davies is particularly interested in the way in which a serious artist is compelled to pursue his spiritual goals, often at the cost of appearing duplicitous, ungrateful, cruel, even traitorous. Sharply rejecting the clichés that would have artistic worth flourishing in Bohemian circles or in the school of poverty, Davies depicts with relish a pattern of developing egoism that involves not only recognition of and loyalty to one's best teachers, but also the pure pursuit of "The Mothers," the deepest voices of the artist's soul.

What's Bred in the Bone clearly fits this two-pronged pattern. As such it offers an intriguing extension of the artistic and personal concerns first dramatized in depth in *A Mixture of Frailties* (1958), then in *World of Wonders* (1975) and *The Rebel Angels* (1981). It presents the "inside story" of the life of Francis Cornish, a wealthy and eccentric artist-connoisseur-patron-collector whose sudden death in Toronto made for the academic antics and paper chase that comprise *The Rebel Angels.* In Davies's playful hands that inside story is provided not by an observer or biographer, but by a pair of "guardian" angels named the Lesser Zadkiel and the Daimon Maimas. In lieu of available evidence about Francis Cornish's inner life, they provide a *"record, or film, or tape, or whatever fashionable word Francis's contemporaries would apply to it,"* of that life, along with italicized commentary upon those events and their consequences.

As is often the case with Davies's fiction, the novel opens with a frame. The Reverend Simon Darcourt, one of *The Rebel Angels*'s two narrators, has been at work as official biographer of Cornish but has been frustrated in his attempts to unearth crucial knowledge about his friend. Teased by hints of forgery and homosexuality, he strives on a deeper level to know "what lies behind" the known events of Cornish's life, what constitutes the "extra energy" of "the artistic conscience" Cornish developed and lived by. In a device recalling the beginning of *Fifth Business, What's Bred in the Bone* employs a formal London *Times* obituary to place before the reader, as a challenge to interpretation, the public record of Cornish's life. Then, by means of a little literary/celestial lamp rubbing, Davies enlists the participation of the two off-duty angels who seem glad to recall the life they have previously overseen. Freed from the constraints of the realistic frame, the reader is cautioned to "think medievally," that is, in terms of personifications and symbols, of Heaven and Hell.

Though the narrating angels claim that "Nobody ever knows the whole of anything," their collective authority is unquestioned and masterful. The Lesser Zadkiel functions as a rather literal-minded and sentimental *"Angel of Biography."* He plays straight man and recorder of events to the more opinionated, toughminded guardian of Cor-

nish's soul and artistic spirit, the Daimon Maimas, who was assigned by fate to encourage the possibilities dictated by Cornish's special *"destiny."* A grotesque and androgynous figure who unites Hermes and Aphrodite, the Daimon is *"A simulacrum of a complete human figure."* He embodies (if that is the right word) the spirit of Mercury or Hermes ("patron of crooks, the joker, the highest of whatever is trumps, the mischiefmaker, who upsets all calculations" even as he is "the reconciler of opposites—something out of the scope of conventional morality") at work in the artistic temperament of Cornish. Without the timely enterprise of the Daimon, it is made clear that Francis Cornish could never have become great, escaped stupidity, and risen above the moral muddle that entraps most people. Hence, special destiny and celestial determinism are irrevocably linked.

As readable and chatty as *What's Bred in the Bone* is (and it is the longest of Davies's eight novels to date), it creates for itself certain problems. Most striking of these is the angelic commentary in which the author invests so much narrative authority. Writing in *The New Republic,* Jack Beatty wondered why "a device that's perfectly acceptable in Frank Capra movies [should] seem so ludicrous in a novel?" There is a Laurel and Hardy kind of *badinage,* heightened by Davies's relish for one-upmanship and browbeating, that characterizes and inadvertently trivializes these narrators. Hence, while at first promising so much by way of special insights beyond the limits of mere biography, the gambit never quite measures up to its intention. In seeking yet another way to probe and articulate the unseen elements of destiny at work in human life, Davies gambles grandly but misfires with his angels. It is difficult to take them as seriously as is required.

Equally problematic are the novel's structure and pacing. Arguing that it is essential to get into a character's make-up *"right from the instant of his conception,"* *What's Bred in the Bone* outdoes *Tristram Shandy* by spending an unusually long time describing the circumstances surrounding the conception not of the hero but of his older brother. It takes some 60 pages in fact to bring the protagonist into the novel. Much later, with Cornish still a relatively young man, the angels tell us that *"Time in his outward life will run much faster for him now."* As such, the presentation of Cornish's last three decades is as hurried as that of his formative years is leisurely. The novel thus underplays "the new beginning in the middle of life" that the Daimon prophesizes for Cornish. For a writer so devoted to celebrating what intelligent, unusual, and successful men make of their lives, given the way they begin, such an approach may seem surprising. Whatever Davies's intention, the reader senses a slackness and sprawl once Cornish is launched upon his peculiar artistic career.

One of the richest elements of *What's Bred in the Bone* also carries with it elements of difficulty. Setting the novel of Blairlogie, a fictionalized version of Renfrew, one of the towns in which he grew up (roughly 60 miles northwest of Ottawa with a population, at the time, of about 5 thousand), Davies was able to draw upon his memories of the most painful and disturbing years of his youth. Outsider, polymath, and teacher's pet, he was made the victim of his rougher schoolmates, even as he was appalled by certain glimpses he had of Renfrew social behaviour. As Francis's English-born father understatedly puts it, "a little of Blairlogie was enough." What Francis, who has to endure far more of Blairlogie than his father, suffers, among other things, is a formative bath in Christian excesses and contradictions. The son of a "lukewarm" Anglican, raised by an aunt fervently committed to "hot, sweet Catholicism," watched over by a housekeeper who practised "a stern and unyielding Calvinism" and a maid of Salvation Army persuasion, Francis is presented as one whom *"Christianity cost . . . dear."* Hence, even as Davies leads his readers deep into the cruel, contradictory, and unforgiving religious tensions of a turn-of-the-century rural and provincial community like Renfrew, he practises a kind of dramatic overkill. Francis Cornish must not only be the artist, impulsively led to follow the direction of his own spirit, but he is also presented as the experiential sop, the target and victim of an extraordinary range of religious tyrannies and fanaticisms. To his European "father in art," Tancred Saraceni, Francis obligingly defines himself as "A Catholic soul in Protestant chains." While such a background helps to account for Francis's allegorical propensities as a painter and his strong moral outlook, it makes him seem to bear the weight of too much provincial Canada, to be, as it were, the victim of everything.

But to question excess, the layering on of wounds, out-of-the-way detail, allegorical possibility, and the grotesque, is perhaps to overlook the kind of writer Robertson Davies, since *A Mixture of Frailties,* has sought to become. Characteristically a tart critic of "modern" values and satirist of Canadian manners, he has evolved, according to Robert Fulford, into Canada's "leading fantasist." Realism and fantasy, the ordinary and the grotesque, are so deftly mixed in the novels, beginning with *Fifth Business,* that one is led willingly, happily, to enter unusual fictional worlds that seem to promise much by way of insight and illumination. *What's Bred in the Bone* integrates Davies's personal experience of Renfrew; his interest in the lives of prominent Canadians such as Alan Jarvis (the novel's Aylwin Ross) and Douglas Duncan (Cornish); aspects of the life of, and his relationship with, his father; and, most importantly, his own personal quest to be a successful artist on his own terms. If some narrative elements work better than others (compare the effectiveness of Francis's experiences with Zadok Hoyle to his amorous relation to his cousin, Ismay Glasson), if there is a sense of Davies forcing certain events and characters to be interesting and significant, what holds the novel together is its commitment to the study of Cornish as an artist.

A sensitive boy whom experience made a misanthrope and, eventually, something of a hoarder, if not a miser, Francis Cornish is an unusually sweet-tempered and gentle protagonist within the Davies canon. His fate is a curious one. Blessed with talent and aptitude along the lines of the Great Masters, he creates his greatest work in the form of two "religious" allegories meant to deceive the German experts who collected art during World War II for the inner circle of Hitler's Reich. When later critics discover these paintings and come to hail the unknown artist as the "Alchemical Master," Cornish's fate is sealed;

he is doomed to be unrecognized in his own time for his extraordinary achievement. Unable at this point to adapt to modern style and technique, Cornish takes refuge in Picasso's famous and "bitter confession" about his subservience to contemporary fads and tastes. To be a modern artist is to be "only a public entertainer," Picasso lamented; it is to be held to "the imbecility, the vanity, the cupidity of his contemporaries."

While Cornish's dilemma fascinates Davies, and allows him to explore the extent to which a serious and pure artist may (must) engage in deception and must detach himself from the priorities of Christian, conventional, and contemporary morality, Davies, as an artist himself, is doubtless offering something of a self-reflective subtext. Paul Roberts sees him as "clearly working on his own myth." To be sure, Davies would be hard-pressed to pin a more pleasing label upon himself than that of Alchemical Master. A writer who has always been conspicuously anti-modern (see his *A Voice from the Attic* [1960]) in his values and outlook, who endlessly quotes Ben Jonson, who borrows a great deal from other writers, and often, as in the case of Alan Jarvis, uses real lives with little fictional variation, who seems to side with the narrow perimeters of deterministic destiny and poetic license, Davies uses the Cornish situation as a screen for his own particular aesthetic and moral concerns. Hence, for all its flourish and excess, and despite certain problems that mar its presentation, *What's Bred in the Bone* must and will be seen as one of Davies's most significant novels. In it, he takes us close to what's bred in his own bone and, by means of Francis Cornish, shows us not only the respect he has for, and the pride he takes in, his deceptive aesthetic vocation, but also his own self-conscious sense of his precarious relation to the time and world in which he writes. (pp. 29-34)

> *Michael Peterman, "Manifestations of the Artistic Conscience," in* Essays on Canadian Writing, *No. 39, Fall, 1989, pp. 29-34.*

Wilfred Cude   (essay date Winter 1990)

[*In the following essay, Cude discusses* The Cornish Trilogy *as a melodramatic examination of artistic and academic fraud.*]

Fiction lives on as a means of telling truths that nobody wants to hear. The reasons for not wanting to hear are legion, varying in urgency and subtlety from community to community, nation to nation, people to people. Perhaps the truth is deemed to threaten a powerful vested interest, political or economic. Perhaps the truth is deemed to threaten a cherished concept, philosophic or theological. Perhaps the truth is deemed to threaten a central cultural institution, social or academic. Such a truth cannot be boldly stated, and linked to harsh fact, for fear of unleashing punitive disruption. But state the truth as fiction, disguise it and distance it by placing it in the realm of not-there, not-now and not-exactly-us, and a few venturesome souls will consider what was said. Despite the uproar attendant upon releasing the stark realism of *One Day in the Life of Ivan Denisovich* or the complex fantasy of *The Satanic Verses,* a few will consider what was said. Thus fiction anticipates a more frank and accurate history, Thalia acting as handmaid to Clio—here in our carefree Western world, every bit as much as behind the Iron Curtain or in the heartland of Islamic fundamentalism. Witness the phenomenal international success of the latest trilogy by Robertson Davies, a melodramatic rendering of intellectual posturings and strivings, all focusing on the very real but hitherto shunned topic of fraud in art and scholarship.

"Faking is the syphilis of art," Davies writes in the concluding pages of *The Lyre of Orpheus,* "and the horrid truth is that syphilis has sometimes lain at the root of very fine art." This sort of pronouncement is not what scholars want to hear, for the Master is speaking in his own voice with this passage, and the fakery he has in mind ultimately embraces the whole apparatus of art criticism. Like *The Rebel Angels* and *What's Bred in the Bone* before it, *The Lyre of Orpheus* is set squarely in the intellectual community of our time, depicting with unmistakable clarity the always-convoluted and often-squalid intrigue surrounding the authentication of great art. We have in these volumes the Oxbridge realm of the Old World and the New, from Oxford to a transparently-veiled variant of the University of Toronto, all in a turmoil over a misappropriated manuscript, an incomplete opera and—right at the centre, dominating everything else—"a fine, poxy piece of painting" (*Lyre*). Much of the turmoil is recorded by Professor the Reverend Simon Darcourt, Anglican priest and professor of ecclesiastical languages at Spook, more reverently (if less frequently) known as the College of St. John and the Holy Ghost. And Simon's record contains many a detail that, offered in a historical context, would profoundly disturb academic complacency.

Simon's record, however, is not always (and even Davies couldn't resist the pun) Simon Pure. And that, of course, proves to be the redeeming touch for most academic readers. [In *Rebel Angels*] Simon hears a colleague confess his seduction of a beautiful graduate student, and dismisses the event with an appropriately erudite summation: "Abelard and Heloise lived again for approximately ninety seconds." Well, that's one way of putting it. Our portly Prof the Rev, as his students known him, can garnish with scholarly sauce any number of distasteful doings on campus: and it all becomes, if not exactly palatable, then at least excitingly spicy. Seduction, intimidation, theft, even murder: Simon gives us every detail, almost frightening in his zest for verisimilitude, yet no supporter of our universities has taken offense. After all, these novels are classic melodrama, a comic mode of presentation that nobody would seriously apply to the intellectual life. It's all a joke, right? Well, that's one way of seeing it.

The careful reader should be very alert, nevertheless, to the full context of Simon's activities. In *The Rebel Angels,* he is one of the two narrators, an observer and commentator rather than participant. In *What's Bred in the Bone,* he is reduced to a cameo appearance as the frustrated biographer of Francis Cornish, an art forger, critic and minor spy whose later life as eccentric patron serves as cover for earlier breaches of propriety. But in *The Lyre of Orpheus,* he at last plays an active role, piecing together the full story of Francis and his unconventional past—

achieving, in the process, a startlingly realistic exposure of extraordinary scholarly misbehavior. For a serious involvement in an active role, he learns, means coming to terms with some rather nasty little games. He discovers that an early drawing by Francis Cornish is featured in the elegant advertisements of a cosmetics firm headed by the Princess Amalie, a West German aristocrat. The Princess wants her public to regard the drawing as coming from the hand of a renaissance master, and Simon—as biographer of the real artist—could tell the world something quite different. Yet he chooses not to, since the Princess can give him information about a blank space in his subject's life: and if the suppression of some of the truth is part of the price for success in his biographical venture, then Simon will suppress the truth. A true scholar, he is [described in *The Lyre of Orpheus* as] consumed by "the feverish lust of a biographer."

Much to Simon's dismay, though, that is only a small installment on the Princess's price. A shrewd businesswoman whose family motto declaims, "Thou shalt perish ere I perish," the Princess wants to acquire all the drawings by Francis Cornish on the subject of her advertisements—who just happens to be herself. Her motive [as described in *The Lyre of Orpheus*] is largely, but not exclusively, commercial: the revelation of the artist's real identity would leave her, "in the idiom of the advertising world," with "egg all over her beautiful face." The drawings she hopes to obtain are in the National Gallery of Canada, and she wants Simon to steal them for her. Which he does in the neatest possible fashion, first by taking five uncatalogued Cornish sketches from his own University Library, then by switching those with the ones that Amalie wants in the National Gallery. Simon's dismay, we might note, has nothing to do with his scruples as priest and scholar: rather, it has everything to do with the practical question of "how could he steal without being found out." He manages, naturally, by trading upon the righteousness of his priestcraft and scholarship. He is trusted, and he successfully abuses that trust—once with a colleague who is also an old friend. "Nothing like a good reputation when you are about to commit a crime." When he finally delivers the swag to the Princess, Simon has come to think of himself as the Clerical Cracksman. And there is far more of praise than condemnation in the name.

Because he is a clergyman, Simon might have been expected to reflect sombrely upon the new character he has assumed. But because he is also a tenured academic, he is toughened to turns of scholarship that rarely suffer exposure, let alone the indignity of hard names. Just as he calmly accepts the seduction of one student in *The Rebel Angels,* so he accepts the seduction of another in *The Lyre of Orpheus,* this time in a lesbian encounter. He listens tolerantly as the magisterial Dr. Gunilla Dahl-Soot, herself no Abelard, explains that the relationship wasn't "love"— only "a teacher-and-pupil thing." The pupil in question, a doctoral candidate named Hulda Schnakenburg, would undoubtedly have acquiesced in her mentor's account: after all, there was far worse awaiting her. In one of the most scathing renditions of the modern doctoral examination process available in Western literature, Davies shows how a single pompous and unprincipled professor can em-peril a gifted student's entire career. Andreas Pfeiffer, distinguished musicologist and external examiner at Hulda's final oral defense, is "let loose upon her." Pfeiffer is "a matador of immense skill, and for thirty-five minutes he nagged and harassed the wretched Schnak, who had no verbal ease": disappointingly, though, "the bull had no style, no pride of the ring, seemed really unworthy of a matador of his repute." So unfitted for this ordeal was Schnak that she actually attempts suicide during an intermission in the examination. Out of a grudging spirit of compensation, she is awarded the degree as an ambulance rolls away with her: "and Schnak, dead or alive, was therefore a Doctor of Music." When students are to their teachers as flies to wanton boys, how can even a clerical prof avoid turning cracksman—or worse?

Thus equipped for his biographical sport, Simon is off in pursuit of his subject, a man described by a former colleague as having "a whiff of brimstone" about him. For the Byronic figure of Francis Cornish dominates the trilogy, with his major work of art at last enshrined in a special gallery at the National Gallery of Canada, under an excerpt from the letters of John Keats rendered in handsome calligraphy: "A Man's life of any worth is a continual allegory—and very few eyes can see the Mystery of his life—a life like the scriptures, figurative." Prior to the appearance of Simon's book, which "received attention not only in Canada but throughout the English-speaking world, and indeed everywhere that books about extraordinary painters are read," Francis had been known to very few—including his fellow experts in the strange business of art authentication. Those that knew him best would recall his brilliance in exposing a spurious Hubertus van Eyck, an audacious bit of forgery created by Jean-Paul Letztpfennig, sometime art expert and luckless dealer in old canvases. The exposure was quite a "sensation" and demonstrates that Davies had taken some pains to familiarize himself with certain of the more ingenious techniques of art criticism.

"Truth, the daughter of Time, reveals indications of another age, another temper and taste, in a picture which is painted long after the period to which it has been attributed." Thus Francis ruminates [in *What's Bred in the Bone*], as he scrutinizes every inch of the supposed Hubertus Van Eyck, a composition entitled *The Harrowing of Hell.* He is looking for a definitive detail, one revealing the work as indisputably of an era later than that of the brothers Van Eyck. His intuition is in harmony with that of his master, the Italian art restorer Tancred Sarceni, whose own craft often borders on fraud—and occasionally crosses right over. What Sarceni suspects, Francis must prove: and he does so by isolating that definitive detail, one compelling assent from all the other assembled experts, each a specialist of far greater experience and formal training in the discipline. He draws their attention to a monkey hanging by its tail from the bars of Hell, a symbol of fallen humanity: since it had a tail, it was a New World monkey, and Huburtus Van Eyck had died in 1426. Davies, revelling in his own presentation of criticism as monkey business, cannot deny himself the appropriate dramatic flourish. "In the melodrama of the nineteenth century there may frequently be found such stage directions as *Sensation! Astonish-*

ment! Tableau!" he writes [in *What's Bred in the Bone*] "this was the gratifying effect produced by Francis's judgement."

With such a forceful gesture, Francis ranks himself as first among his intellectual equals, the haughty arbiters of artistic value. Through peace and war and back again to peace, these would reign over "that world of scholarship, of connoisseurship, of hair-splitting, haggling, wrangling and quarrelling which was their very own, and in which they moved like wizard kings." And Davies, drawing selectively from the historical record, easily persuades his readers of the dark undercurrents in this world. Art fraud establishes authentication as an economic necessity, a process initially subverting scholarship by reducing the appraisal of truth and beauty to a technique for certifying valuable commodities. Nonetheless, the same process can also move the appraisal of truth and beauty beyond commerce and into politics, thus investing scholarship with an occasionally terrible majesty. Courtesy of his commission from Saraceni, Francis learns as much immediately. Saraceni is conducting a fine little scam of his own, doctoring relatively worthless old German paintings to resemble something better, and swapping them for genuine non-German masterpieces with Reichsmarschall Hermann Goering—Hitler's "Director-General of the Delights of

First American edition of What's Bred in the Bone.

My Eye." It was this pleasing and noble commerce of artistic liberation that the hapless Letztpfennig's forgery indirectly threatened: and for that, Saraceni dispatched Francis to destroy him. Literally, as well as intellectually. Word of Letztpfennig's suicide follows Francis back to Saraceni's studio, and the Meister allows his stricken journeyman to "take the day off." Criticism can involve high enough stakes, ethical and otherwise, by anybody's measure.

Driven by these intense pressures, Francis renders his own life's vision in a perfectly characteristic way, painting on a centuries-old triptych with traditional colors and the late renaissance style he had come to command so easily. "I am not talking of course of faking, for that is contemptible," Saraceni explains, setting him to this last and greatest of artistic tests: "but the ability to work truly in the technique and also in the spirit of the past." Deciding that "he would paint the myth of Francis Cornish," taking as his subject *The Marriage at Cana,* Francis produces a memorable rarity. The work is indeed, even to the expert eye, a renaissance masterpiece: an important but not commonplace Christian event, captured with an assurance that attests the most subtle genius. "The vigour and brilliance of the colour, and the calligraphic line, the distortion of some of the figures and the *grotesquerie* (that word again!) supported such an attribution." Yet it was nothing less than the principal people in Francis's life, all waiting attendance upon himself and his wife-to-be, at the moment when an enigmatic and almost idiotic angel proclaims, *"Tu autem servasti bonum vinum usque adhuc."* There is a literal truth in the triptych that at last raises the work to prophecy, as far as the artist's personal life is concerned. And Saraceni is more than satisfied, first privately, and then publicly. "You have found a reality that is not part of the chronological present," he tells Francis during an emotional meeting just prior to the outbreak of World War Two, as both of them inspect the work alone: "you seem not to be trapped, as most of us are, in the psychological world of today."

At the outset, Francis has no intention of committing fraud: his masterpiece is a personal exercise, nothing more, and he must leave it behind in Germany when he returns to England for wartime duty. After the war, his MI5 service and critic's reputation win him a post with the Allied Commission on Art, an international forum of experts convened to classify and return major works of art misappropriated during the fighting. Saraceni is one of his associates, and both are more than startled when *The Marriage at Cana* is placed before the forum to be appraised. Francis quickly suppresses the urge to acknowledge what he has done: while his colleagues plunge "into an orgy of happy haggling, of high-powered knowing-best," he realizes that any admission from him would expose Saraceni's pre-war patriotic hoax on the Reichsmarschall. Out of the same realization, Saraceni glibly fabricates a plausible provenance for the picture, describing it in terms at once false and true. And so Davies demonstrates how adept scholars can be, under some circumstances, at distorting the truth. Their approach is no surprise, really: they merely apply the same intellectual tools devised to reveal the truth, but in a contrary manner.

Since the process involves equal ingenuity, whatever the purpose of the scholar, controversy in an intuitive and subjective field like aesthetics can rage for decades without resolution. Hence, Saraceni's smooth attribution to "The Alchemical Master, whose name, alas, we cannot determine," soon becomes fixed in the discipline.

Once initiated, and by that action sent moving in a specific direction, the process of authentication almost takes on a life of its own. Present at the committee meeting so cunningly manipulated by Saraceni is a young Canadian critic named Aylward Ross, whose aesthetic intuition is sharp enough to sense something of the truth: the painter who created an enigmatic little panel entitled *Drollig Hansel* was also the one who produced *The Marriage at Cana.* Intoxicated by his own cleverness, Ross later builds upon Saraceni's fabrications, spinning a very convincing background for the triptych and further strengthening its bogus provenance. Francis, as one of Ross's closest friends, now has another reason to keep silent: if he spoke out, he would not only create difficulties for the Saraceni ring and all the national institutions that had benefitted from their activities, but for Ross as well. Still, like Letztpfennig before him, he hungers for some recognition of the quality of his work: and money definitely won't do, since he has a comfortable surfeit of that. His solution to this dilemma with "a bewildering array of horns" is to include irrefutable evidence of his creation of the triptych in the immense array of material he is leaving to the National Gallery of Canada: truth, that unerring daughter of time, will do the rest—long after Francis and his professional associates have ceased to care.

This is the intellectual inheritance that Simon must unravel, after sorting at length through the Cornish family documents: and he makes rapid progress, once he happens to glimpse *The Marriage at Cana,* delivering his stolen goods to the penthouse of Princess Amalie. The triptych had been returned to the Princess's mother, the Grafin von Ingelheim, who never allowed any scholar other than Aylward Ross to examine it. On the Grafin's death, the work became the Princess's property, and that lovely aristocrat has very firm convictions about its value—financial, as well as aesthetic. Yet again, Simon's scholarly insight brings him hard into conflict with the vested economic and social interests of some very powerful people. The Princess doesn't want to lose the monetary value of the supposed renaissance rarity, and the Cornish family doesn't want to have Uncle Francis identified as the creator of a splendid fraud. Simon's solution is wonderfully igenious, evading every one of the bewildering array of horns studding the dilemma that had so baffled Francis. In his book [as recounted in *The Lyre of Orpheus*], Simon depicts his artistic old friend as a genius who had "many times laughed at the notion of contemporaneity . . . , mocking it as a foolish chain on a painter's inspiration and intention." Throughout the text, he argues for accepting the *Marriage* as a modern masterpiece; and then, quietly over the next two years, he arranges for the Cornish family to buy it from the Princess at a fabulous price, in order to donate it to the National Gallery. Simon has his book, complete with a gratifying blaze of academic notoriety; the Princess has her money, and her integrity acknowledged; and the Cornish family ensures that Uncle Frank's memory is properly honored. And nobody, miracle of miracles, thinks to take offense.

In melodrama, as Simon's own masterstroke would indicate, extremely difficult problems can vanish with the whisk of an authorial wand. There is nothing enduring, or even seriously dismaying, about all the scholarly misadventures chronicled within these novels. The abuse of helpless academic apprentices, the misuse of priceless artifacts, the mishandling of library resources, the truckling to persons of power and privilege, everything is finally resolved within the parameters of decorum and reason. Sometimes, to be sure, the resolution is attained through very rough treatment: and there, the fate of professor Baudoin [presented in **What's Bred in the Bone**] is doubly instructive. Baudoin is as malign a caricature as any to be found in the trilogy. Foul of breath and foul of disposition, his every exhaltation "suggested that he was dying from within, and had completed about two-thirds of the job." Opinionated, argumentative, technically informed though spiritually unimaginative, he stands for academic obstructionism at its arbitrary and authoritarian worst. He is first silenced by Francis, on the occasion of destroying the wretched Letztpfennig, through an adroit deployment of the definitive detail. And he is next silenced far more expeditiously by Saraceni, on the occasion of certifying *The Marriage of Cana*. Saraceni has a reputation for the Evil Eye, and glances savagely at Baudoin through "ill-coordinated blazing eyes." The foul-breathed nuisance "retreated to his chair as if a fierce gust of hot air had passed him," and later tumbles down a flight of marble stairs, breaking his hip. Where logic fails, magic can triumph: thus is establishment obstructionism rendered impotent in melodrama's groves of academe. (pp. 67-75)

For most readers today, Robertson Davies is the master of comic charm, creating through his novel adaptations of the melodramatic mode a relief from the pressures of reality. In this, they overlook the possibility that his enduring reputation may well rest upon the sophisticated technique by which he accomplishes that task while nonetheless introducing the most vital intellectual concerns, developing his melodrama—to use the definition he sketches out in

---

Davies on the creative process:

You can't sit down and say, "Now, I think I'll think up a funny Jesuit," and do it because you'll get a mass of eccentricities; you won't get a live person. But if one arises in your mind, and he's got all his oddities and you see him hopping around and doing things, then you just write down about it. This is what imagination is. It's not invention, you're more passive than that. You listen to your ideas; you don't tell them what to do.

Robertson Davies, in an interview with Renée Heatherington and Gabriel Kampf, in Acta Victoriana, *April, 1973. Reprinted in* Conversations with Robertson Davies, *edited by J. Madison Davis, 1989.*

Feast of Stephen—"as a way of looking at life, and of giving it some of the compelling immediacy of a dream." The dream of life, to Davies, should not be a nightmare: and who would have it otherwise? (p. 78)

Wilfred Cude, "Robertson Davies and the Not-So-Comic Realities of Art Fraud," in The Antigonish Review, *No. 80, Winter, 1990, pp. 67-78.*

Muriel Whitaker   (review date Winter 1990)

[*In the following review, Whitaker compares the characters and themes of* The Lyre of Orpheus *to their mythic counterparts in Arthurian legend.*]

The Lyre of Orpheus, the third volume of Robertson Davies' [*Cornish Trilogy*], completes the story of characters who appeared in *The Rebel Angels* (1981) and *What's Bred in the Bone* (1988). The title derives from a comment by the early nineteenth-century Romantic author, composer, and critic, E. T. A. Hoffman: "The lyre of Orpheus opens the door of the underworld." Davies' lyre is an imaginary opera which the composer supposedly roughed out as he was dying of syphilis and drink. The process of completing *Arthur of Britain or the Magnificent Cuckold* as a doctoral "dissertation" and staging it at the Stratford (Ontario) Festival reveals that lust, greed, anger, envy, in fact, the full complement of Deadly Sins run rampant among the participants. At the same time, music effects the eventual sublimation of base passion.

While the title suggests an archetypal pattern derived from classical mythology, the major influence on Davies' mythopoeic imagination is the legendary material about King Arthur and his Knights of the Round Table. Malory's *Morte Darthur* (1485) is the obvious source, though one suspects that Davies has also browsed in *The Arthurian Encyclopedia* (1986). He is not the first to update medieval Arthurian romance by presenting it as contemporary fiction. G. A. Lawrence's *Guy Livingstone* (1857) depicted an aristocratic cast drawn from Victorian gentry of the horse and hounds type, army officers, and public school graduates. The Canadian version of an élite features academics at the University of Toronto and a well-heeled businessman who presides over their deliberations and funds their "noble actes" with the resources of the Cornish Foundation. As in medieval romances, "le génie feminin" dominates the cultural scene. Female professors and graduate students prove to be as powerfully aggressive and amorous as were the courtly ladies and fées.

Each major character has an Arthurian prototype who represents a "buried myth." "Fish up a myth from the depths and it takes you over," observes Professor the Reverend Simon Darcourt whose predilection for giving advice, skill in machination, and bardic contributions make him a Merlin figure. The beautiful graduate student, Maria Theotoky, now married to Arthur Cornish, is both Guenevere (proud to be the wife of a noble spirit but a little bored) and Elaine of Corbenic (the mother of Galahad). In a manner suggesting both King Uther's begetting of Arthur and Lancelot's begetting of the Grail hero, she is seduced and impregnated by a man "disguised" as her husband. Geraint Powell, a "self-seeking bastard," is the pseudo-Lancelot. Arthur Cornish, rendered infertile by an attack of mumps, must endure the role of cuckold. Yet he sustains the attribute of magnificence (the virtue which Prince Arthur represents in Spenser's *The Faerie Queene*) not only by presiding over the Round Table and footing the bills but also by practising patience, forgiveness, and love (Tennyson's Arthur is not an appropriate co-relative!). The composer, Hulda Schnakenburg, a grubby graduate student cleaned up and seduced by the lesbian musicologist Dr. Gunilla Dahl-Soot, unconvincingly enacts an Elaine of Astolat role when her hopeless love for Geraint-Lancelot leads to her attempted suicide. The illegitimate Wally Crottel, an ignominious Mordred recast as a schoolyard drug-pusher, is easily thwarted when he threatens the mythic society.

The Tarot pack provides a second layer of mythic correspondences. In order to foresee the opera's fate, Maria's gypsy mother lays out for Darcourt the nine-card deal, "a very womanly hand" that includes the Empress, ruler of worldly fortune (Arthur); Force, a lady subduing a lion by opening its jaws (Gunilla); the Lover (Geraint); Judgement (Maria); and the Fool with the little dog nipping at his bare arse "to make him go in a path that the mind would not think of." Simon's appropriation of the Fool figura enables him to rationalize the thefts he commits in order to complete his biography of Francis Cornish.

On the literal level, the functions involved in producing the opera are distributed among the major characters. "Schnak" and her advisor turn Hoffman's sketches into an operatic score. Darcourt fits a libretto to the music, lifting his best parts, he confesses, from Sir Walter Scott whose metrical romances—"Marmion," "The Lady of the Lake," and "The Bridal of Triermain" (in which Arthur fathers an illegitimate daughter)—are similar in diction and metre. Geraint Powell, who is responsible for the staging, attributes his schema to Malory and Hoffman. In fact, both the projected drama which Powell describes at Maria's Arthurian feast and Stratford performance which forms the novel's climax Davies has appropriated from the Victorian dramatist J. Comyns Carr (1849-1916). His *King Arthur* was produced at London's Lyceum Theatre on January 12, 1895, with Henry Irving as King Arthur, Forbes Robertson as Launcelot and Ellen Terry as Guenevere. Edward Burne-Jones designed sets and costumes and Arthur Sullivan provided music. As in *The Lyre of Orpheus,* the drama begins with a Magic Mere prologue: Arthur receives his sword from the lake spirit and sees in a vision his "fate," Guenevere. In Act I (the great hall at Camelot) Arthur and the knights depart on the Grail Quest, leaving Launcelot to rule and Morgan with her son Mordred to plot. Act II in both productions is "The Queen's Maying," followed by "The Black Barge," where the dying Elaine of Astolat reveals the love between Lancelot and Guenevere. Both conclude with the final conflict, Mordred's death and Arthur's departure across the Enchanted Mere to Avalon.

Davies does not assume his readers' familiarity with the conventions of Romantic opera or with the literary sources. One authorial voice belongs to Hoffman (ETAH)

who from limbo provides autobiographical details, information about early nineteenth-century theatres, disquisitions on Romantic art, and sardonic assessments of the Torontonians. A psychologically appropriate technique of exposition is that of allowing know-it-all academics to instruct the less informed. We get discourses on everything from the Questing Beast's anatomy to the Madness of Lancelot. The frequent interpolations not only slow plot development but also, by reminding us of their noble predecessors, emphasize the moral inferiority of the modern characters. Foul-tongued Hulda, self-centered Geraint, and casuistic, toadying Simon re-enact a story that has "its shape and its pattern somewhere outside our daily world." The result borders on farce.

Davies is at his best when satirizing academia. His sharp ear accurately catches and pen records the hectoring tones of the upwardly mobile female professor, the American graduate student's woolly-minded jargon, the dissertation committee's bitchiness and sly maneuvuring, the professional propensity for dragging apt quotations into every conversation. At times Davies' eclecticism strains our patience. There are too many characters introduced for no better reason than to get a cheap laugh or provide a link with previous novels. And the dash of lesbianism, dash of gnosticism, and snide characterizations of "the Canadian identity" have a formulaic modishness that seems forced.

Despite the irony inherent in juxtaposing the idealized Arthurian society of medieval romance and the realistic Kater Murrish Ontario world, Davies chooses a fairy tale ending to conclude [*The Lyre of Orpheus*] and his trilogy. Arthur and Maria are accepted as genuine patrons of the arts when they establish the Francis Cornish Memorial Gallery. Simon Darcourt, whose explication of Francis Corning's great painting, *The Marriage at Cana,* (and a couple of thefts) has enabled him to complete the biography, receives the critics' accolades. Schnak is "on her way" to becoming an established composer; Powell has produced a terrific "Orfeo" in Milan. And Robertson Davies has effected a synthesis of Arthurian romance and Canadian setting that is a witty, plausible expression of his thesis: " 'A Man's life of any worth is a continual allegory.' " (pp. 166-68)

Muriel Whitaker, "Satire & Romance," in Canadian Literature, *No. 127, Winter, 1990, pp. 166-68.*

George Woodcock   (essay date Autumn 1990)

[*Woodcock is a Canadian educator, editor, critic, poet, essayist, historian, and travel writer. The founder of Canada's most important literary journal,* Canadian Literature, *he has written extensively about the literature of Canada. In the following essay, Woodcock examines* The Lyre of Orpheus *as a return to themes of Davies's earlier trilogies and a statement of his aesthetic philosophies.*]

With the publication in the autumn of 1988 of *The Lyre of Orpheus,* Robertson Davies has completed the third of his fictional trilogies, each centred on a different Ontario town, and each dominated by a central group of characters through whose varying perceptions and memories the current of events that characterizes the trilogy is perceived.

The completion of the triple triad is, as Davies has undoubtedly recognized, an event that stirs a multitude of numerological, folkloric, and mythological echoes. Nine was one of the three mystical numbers of the Pythagoreans, and though three was a perfect number which Pythagoras made the sign of the deity, nine had its specific significance as a trinity of trinities, the perfect plural. For Pythagoras, and later for the great classical astronomer Ptolemy, the universe moved in nine spheres. In various contexts we find the number particularly associated with inspiration and imagination. There were nine Muses, nine Gallicenae or virgin priestesses of the Druid oracles, and nine Sibylline books transmitted from Cumae to Rome. Echoed constantly in Davies' novels is the ancient concept of a nine day's wonder: as the old proverb has it, "A wonder lasts nine days, and then the puppy's eyes are open." But most relevant of all in considering *The Lyre of Orpheus* as the last Davies novel to date—and perhaps the last of the kind to which we have become accustomed since *Fifth Business* appeared in 1970—is the role which nine plays in music, for nine was the Pythagorean *diapason,* man being the full chord, or eight notes, and nine representing the deity, ultimate harmony.

The Lyre of Orpheus is not merely a novel about music; it is a novel about the nature of art in general and its relation to reality and time and the human spirit. But the main plot carrying this theme concerns a musical event, and in doing so it takes us back with striking deliberation to the first group of Davies novels, the Salterton series. For, like the last of that series, *A Mixture of Frailties* (1958), *The Lyre of Orpheus* is built around a family trust which offers a phenomenally generous grant to a young woman musician from a Philistine background, and finds itself sponsoring a controversial opera, so that a contribution is made to the art of music in a general way at the same time as the young musician, aided by wise teachers, undergoes an inner transformation that opens to her what in Davies terminology one might call "a world of wonders"; in Jungian terms she is taken out of the anonymity and personal incompleteness of common life and achieves individuation.

There are indeed important ways in which *The Lyre of Orpheus,* written thirty years later, goes beyond *A Mixture of Frailties.* While Monica Gall in the earlier novel is a singer whose talents are trained by inspired teachers, and the opera in which she becomes involved is the original work of another—a wayward modern genius—in *The Lyre of Orpheus* we edge nearer to the creative role, for the musician, Hulda Schnackenburg (generally called Schnak), is a composer engaged not in an original composition but in a task of inspired reconstruction. She is making an opera, *Arthur of Britain,* out of scattered fragments left by E. T. A. Hoffman (better known as a Gothicist taleteller than as a musician) of an opera he was unable to complete before his early death from the nineteenth-century endemic, syphilis. At the same time the priestly scholar Simon Darcourt (one of the narrators of an earlier

Davies novel, *The Rebel Angels*) constructs the libretto around which the score that Schnak develops from Hoffman's fragments is built up. Schnak and Darcourt, with their various collaborators, manage to recreate an authentic sounding early nineteenth-century opera which pleases the spirit of E. T. A. Hoffman who makes a ghostly appearance in the comments from the underworld that appear as interludes between the narrative chapters.

Related to this major plot is a strikingly similar sub-plot devoted to the visual as distinct from the audial arts. As well as acting as pasticheur-librettist, Simon Darcourt is engaged on a biography of Francis Cornish, the celebrated connoisseur and art collector whose bequest has funded the preparation and production of *Arthur of Britain.* Darcourt stumbles on the clues which reveal to him what readers of *What's Bred in the Bone* already know, that Cornish was actually the painter of a famous triptych, *The Marriage of Cana,* done so authentically in the fifteenth-century German manner that it has been plausibly attributed to an unknown painter working five centuries ago who was given the name of the Alchemical Master.

Simon Darcourt manages to convince everyone involved, including the owners of the painting and the reluctant mandarins of the National Gallery to which it is eventually given, that a work done sincerely and without intent of fraud in the style of a past age is not a fake and can be as authentic as the best work in a contemporary manner. The argument put forward by Darcourt's colleague Clement Hollier, an expert on myths, is not only interesting in itself but important for what it tells us about Davies' own attitudes towards the arts and about his own literary achievement. Here is Darcourt's paraphrase of Hollier's statement:

> If a man wants to paint a picture that is intended primarily as an exercise in a special area of expertise, he will do so in a style with which he is most familiar. If he wants to paint a picture which has a particular relevance to his own life-experience, which explores the myth of his life as he understands it, and which, in the old phrase, "makes up his soul", he is compelled to do it in a mode that permits such allegorical revelation. Painters after the Renaissance, and certainly after the Protestant Reformation, have not painted such pictures with the frankness that was natural to pre-Renaissance artists. The vocabulary of faith, and of myth, has been taken from them by the passing of time. But Francis Cornish, when he wanted to make up his soul, turned to the style of painting and the concept of visual art which came most naturally to him. Indeed, he had many times laughed at the notion of contemporaneity in conversation . . . , mocking it as a foolish chain on a painter's inspiration and intention.
> It must be remembered . . . that Francis has been brought up a Catholic—or almost a Catholic—and he had taken his catholicity seriously enough to make it a foundation of his art. If God is one and eternal, and if Christ is not dead, but living, are not fashions in art mere follies for those who are the slaves of Time?

In musical terms the chapter in which these matters are

resolved can be regarded as a coda, a concluding passage after the main pattern of the work has been developed and completed; it states the theme of the novel more definitely and succinctly than in early renderings. *Arthur of Britain* has been completed and successfully launched as a new work in the operatic repertoire, Schnak had found herself and her career, and now, three years later in a chapter free of the ghostly voice of E. T. A. Hoffman (a ghost now actually laid), we can consider what is the meaning of it all, assisted by our reflections on Francis Cornish's strange master work. And so, just as *The Lyre of Orpheus* as a whole, with its deliberate reordering and retelling of the plot of *A Mixture of Frailties,* completes the circle of Davies' mature fiction, so this final chapter of the latest of his novels acts, I suggest, as a veiled *apologia pro vita sua,* a justification for the uncontemporary aesthetic underlying Davies' life work.

George Orwell once remarked on the striking fact that the best writers of his time—and among them he included the great apostles of literary modernism—have in fact been conservative and even reactionary in their social and political attitudes. This is certainly true of most of the great moderns in the Anglo-American tradition; Eliot, Pound, and Wyndham Lewis were all to be found politically somewhat to the right of old-style Toryism, and James Joyce failed to join them only because of a massive indifference to anything outside his own linguistic experiments.

Robertson Davies has not spoken of his political views in any detail or with much directness. I have no idea how he votes, though it is clear that he has the kind of Tory mind which judges politics ethically; his treatment of Boy Staunton's political career in *Fifth Business* suggests that he probably has little patience with what passes for a Conservative cause in late twentieth-century Canada.

What distinguishes Davies from the reactionary modernists is that his Toryism runs into his art as well as his political ethics. He is an unrepentent cultural élitist. "There is no democracy in the world of intellect, and no democracy of taste," he said in *A Voice from the Attic* (1960) and he has not since shown a change of attitude. He has never posed as an avant garde writer of any kind. In spite of occasionally expressed admiration for *Ulysses* as a great comic work, he has never followed Joyce's experiments in language, and despite a loosely stated interest in Proust, he has never tried to emulate Proust's experiments in the literary manipulation of time and memory. Indeed, in this respect he has been far less experimental than other writers we do not regard as particularly avant gardist, like Margaret Laurence and Marian Engel. Though in his two later trilogies he may view the same sequences of events in different novels through different eyes, he still tends within each novel to follow a strictly chronological pattern, with effect following cause, whether the causes are the inner ones to be dragged out by Jungian analysis or the outer ones which we see a character's social ambiance and physical environment imposing on him.

Not that, even taking into account the clear, serviceable and declarative prose that Davies writes, we should regard him as a plain realist. If he is a realist, it is not in the docu-

mentary sense, but in the theatrical sense of wishing to give plausibility to the implausible, in his early novels to farce and in his later ones to melodrama. There is always in his writing a heightening of the use of language that goes beyond the demands of ordinary realism, and, given his special interests, Davies might justly be called a magic realist rather than a surrealist. It is true that he shares with the surrealists a preoccupation with depth psychology and its resources of imagery, but while most of the surrealists tended to put their faith in Freud, Davies has found Jung a richer source.

Just as his magicians are technicians of illusion rather than true thaumaturges, so Davies himself takes a pride in artifice, yet he is too conservative a writer to fit in with the postmodernists, metafictionists and destructionists of our own day. Far from being destructionist, indeed, his novels are as Edwardianly well-made as Galsworth's Forsyte novels or Arnold Bennett's fictional chronicles of the Five Towns, while among his contemporaries the one novelist he has regarded as undeniably great, and whom he has admitted to be an influence, is Joyce Cary, whose virtues lay not in his experimental daring, but rather in a zest for the language, "a reaffirmation of the splendour and sacredness of life," and the same kind of restless and active erudition as Davies displays in his own fiction.

While recognizing that a novel is a work of artifice in which verisimilitude is part of the illusion, and often using contrived fictional devices, Davies manifests little of that preoccupation with the relationship between writers, readers, and the work which has led metafictionists ever since Cervantes and Sterne in their smoke-and-mirror games with reality. He is too didactic, too much concerned with developing lessons about life, and with displaying knowledge and expertise, to subordinate the central narrative, the line of purpose in his works, to any speculative process that might seem to weaken its validity. He is, essentially, a novelist in the central English tradition of Fielding and Dickens and Cary, intent on using artifice to entertain and to instruct. He is brilliantly inventive and has an extraordinary power of assimilating information and presenting it acceptably. But he has little formal originality, little of the power of imaginative transfiguration, so that his novels are still influenced by the conventions of the theatre where he began his writing career, and large sections of them are dominated by the kind of didactic dialogue we used to associate with Bernard Shaw and his disciples. Art comes, when it does, at the end of the process, in the accidental way which also accords with the main English fictional tradition. The kind of deliberate artistry that distinguished the main French tradition from Flaubert onwards, and the tradition of deep social criticism that distinguished the central lineage of Russian fiction from Turgenev onwards, find no place in Davies' books.

Nor, for that matter, does one find much in common between Davies' novels and those of the writers, like Hugh MacLennan and Sinclair Ross and Margaret Laurence, whom we regard as most faithful in their projection of the climate and character of Canadian life and its relation to the land. Davies' novels are restricted geographically to a tiny fragment of Canada—Toronto and the small towns of western Ontario—and to a restricted social milieu of Old and New Money, of the false and true intellectual and artistic aspirations of the middle class, and working-class people are introduced only for comic relief, as in the case of the Morphews in *Leaven of Malice* or the elder Galls in *A Mixture of Frailties,* or on condition that they become transformed and find their way into the cultured bourgeoisie, as Monica Gall does in *A Mixture of Frailties* and Hulda Schnackenburg seems about to do at the end of *The Lyre of Orpheus.*

Davies did indeed define his attitude to Canada in an interview in *Maclean's* in 1972, two years after *Fifth Business* was published, when he replied to the complaints he had heard that "my novels aren't about Canada."

> I think they are, because I see Canada as a country torn between a very northern, rather extraordinary mystical spirit which it fears and its desire to present itself to the world as a Scotch banker.

Davies and his critics tend to use the term "mystical" in a rather loose and general way which has nothing to do with the genuine experiences of mystics like St. John of the Cross or Jakob Boehme, but if we interpret this statement to mean that Canadians hover between an intuitive acceptance of their environment which leads them to see their history in mythic terms, and a grey and materialist attitude in everyday life, I think we have perhaps a good point at which to begin a reconsideration of the triple fictional triads of which *The Lyre of Orpheus* represents the conclusion.

Looking back at *Tempest Tost* (1951), the first of the early novels of manners which Davies set in the small town of Salterton (Kingston transmogrified), we notice how limited is the range of situations in Davies' novels, for here already we have the theatrical producer, Valentine Rich, coming into a Canadian town to direct the amateur actors of the Little Theatre in a production of *The Tempest,* just as in *The Lyre of Orpheus* the formidable Dr. Gunilla Dahl-Soot will descend on Toronto to preside over the Canadian metamorphosis of Hoffman's *Arthur of Britain.* And in the very choice of the play that is produced in the earlier novel—*The Tempest*—we have the favourite Davies theme of the interchangeability of life's pretences of reality and art's frank and open illusionism.

The main satirical device of *Tempest Tost* is a relatively simple one: the effort to find among the inadequate citizens of Salterton the types who will adequately project Shakespeare's characters. The results of the casting are ludicrous: Prospero is played by an arrogant and insensitive pedant, Professor Vambrace, Ferdinand by a young army officer whose aim in life is to seduce as many girls as he can, and Gonzago by an owlish middle-aged schoolteacher, Hector Mackilwraith, who falls lugubriously in love with the rich man's daughter Griselda Webster, who is half his age and plays Ariel.

As this is a novel of manners, people are rarely illuminated from within, but are seen usually as they react to each other in social situations. At this stage Davies was still obviously much affected by the theatrical world in which he

had recently been so closely involved, and the dialogue reads like a cross between that of early twentieth-century English farce and—when ideas are uppermost—that of Thomas Love Peacock's conversational novels. All the Davies novels give off a perceptible whiff of Peacock, though I have been unable to find any reference that might show Davies took a direct interest in him; the way of transmission may have been through Aldous Huxley, whom Davies certainly read with attention, since in *The Rebel Angels*—with oblique acknowledgement—he made extensive use of W. H. Sheldon's theories linking temperament with physical types which Huxley had already introduced extensively into his later books.

The disadvantage of this kind of dialogue, as Hugo McPherson pointed out in an early issue of *Canadian Literature,* is that it reveals very little of the private as distinct from the social personalities of the characters, and this creates an extraordinary formal awkwardness, since Davies then saw no other way to reveal his people in depth than to explain them in long narrative passages; in one instance, twenty pages of narrative are spent giving the history of Hector Mackilwraith so that we know how this amorous clown—the would-be lover of Griselda—came to be what he is. The shallowness of this approach to characterization ends in simplistic contrasts; Valentine Rich strikes us as being much too good and Professor Vambrace much too bad to be true.

Yet *Tempest Tost* prefigures in its own way much of the later Davies: the preoccupation with mystery as illusion, with art as artifice and—personified in those who variously court Griselda—the absurd complexities of the emotional life—with love and sex as rich sources of comedy.

Like *Tempest Tost, Leaven of Malice* anticipates the later novels with the kind of display of practical knowledge that often makes one think, while reading a Davies novel, of Zola and the naturalists. Davies is not so brutally obvious as Zola in presenting his characters as the products of material circumstance; even in his later novels when he shows his characters strongly conditioned by childhood experience and social ambiance, he allows them ways of liberation for which the iron determinism of the naturalists left no space.

But he does share with the naturalists the urge to present very circumstantially the activities and interests in which his characters become involved; it is part of the verisimilitude on which convincing illusions depend, as his magicians constantly insist. He began—and this perhaps shows the caution of a writer who is craftsman by intent and artist by good fortune—with areas where he already had knowledge through experience. His involvement in the theatre—both professional and amateur—gave him the background for *Tempest Tost,* and his occupation of editing a newspaper, the *Peterborough Examiner,* gave him that for *Leaven of Malice,* which combines a satirical picture of small-town feuds with the tension of a rather mild detective mystery, for the plot centres on a false and maliciously placed newspaper announcement of the coming marriage of Sollie Bridgetower and Pearl Vambrace. Like the Montagues and the Capulets, the academic families of Bridgetower and Vambrace are ancient enemies, and the notice results in splendid histrionics as Professor Vambrace threatens legal action in all directions. However, in the end all is well, since, by the kind of glib twist that was common enough in London West End comedies at the time, Solly and Pearl fall in love during the feuding process, and after the perpetrator of the hoax is discovered the malicious announcement is in fact fulfilled when they marry.

Leaven of Malice, though a more tightly constructed book, is flawed in the same ways as *Tempest Tost.* The satire moves at the surface level of manners, so that the characters are two-dimensional, and the didacticism of the book is largely unassimilated; Davies will break up the action for several pages at a time to give—say—a disquisition on who reads newspapers and why. Thus the novel moves haltingly as a series of dialogues and slapstick encounters interrupted by essays. At best it and *Tempest Tost* are reasonably good entertainment, but like most mere entertainment they seem very dated a third of a century after writing.

A Mixture of Frailties is an altogether more satisfying book—and much more of a real novel—than its predecessors, as Davies himself seems to suggest by repeating its essential situation in *The Lyre of Orpheus.* There are several reasons for this. First, though satire is not absent, it is given depth by the comparison of two worlds of manners and taste, those of Salterton and those of Britain. Then, through the concentration on the training of Monica Gall and the emotional adventures that accompany it, we are shown for the first time not merely a character getting wise to his own inadequacy, as with Hector in *Tempest Tost,* but the awakening and development of a whole personality as her various masters introduce Monica to the splendours and miseries of life and art. In the process a deeper and less facile element of romance enters into *A Mixture of Frailties,* and the tension between satire and romance, between comedy and the tragedy that eventually breaks in, gives the narrative an element of dramatic *chiaroscuro* and a depth of perspective that the earlier novels lacked. *A Mixture of Frailties* broadens because of its multiplicity of locale, and deepens psychologically because we are no longer seeing people merely in terms of their behaviour, but as individuals who feel deeply and speak their feelings. They also speak their knowledge, and sentention in a sub-Wilde way as Sir Benedict Domdaniel may be when he talks of life and artifice and art, his aphorisms are an improvement on the interpolated essays of the earlier works.

With *A Mixture of Frailties* in 1958 Robertson Davies seemed like a novelist who after some clever failures was really beginning to find his way, and yet he waited twelve years before publishing his next novel, *Fifth Business,* in 1970. During the intervening period he moved from the newspaper world into that of academe, becoming Master of Massey College at the University of Toronto in 1961 and shortly afterwards he began to teach dramatic literature as a graduate study. During this interlude his writing was very scanty and almost entirely journalistic. Whatever the reason for the silence, it was a productive one. The world changed, and Davies changed his mind with it. He

paid attention to the deep theological and political debates of the 1960s, and though he became no easy convert to any novel doctrine, he quietly modified his attitudes to life and kept his mind open to anything he might be able to use when he returned to fiction again. It was a time of rapidly growing permissiveness both in behaviour and in the ways in which people expressed themselves, and though Davies was too conservative at heart to make any great changes in his use of language, he was ready, by the time he came to write *Fifth Business,* to write openly of things he had not even hinted in his earlier novels, so that while both *Tempest Tost* and *Leaven of Malice* were devoid of any active sexual irregularities, and *A Mixture of Frailties* contented itself with a little heterosexual living in sin, such hitherto unmentioned pursuits as sodomy began to find their place in later Davies books, and invariably as negative manifestations of the quasi-Gnostic dualism that had turned the novels from 1970 onwards into the skirmishing grounds of good and evil.

Good and evil, truth and falsehood, reality and illusion— the oppositions continue through the rest of Davies' novels, and there has never been a resolution of the struggle. There is much calling up of "the vasty deep," much conscious and unconscious seeking for God, but, as Dunstan Ramsay admits in *Fifth Business,*

> I had sought God in my lifelong . . . preoccupation with saints. But all I had found in that life-long study was a complexity that brought God no nearer.

In practice, Davies' characters are much nearer to Hotspur than to his own fellow Welsh sage, Owen Glendower; they too seek to "shame the devil, and tell the truth." In fact the whole of the so-called *Deptford Trilogy* (which extended so far beyond Deptford), beginning with *Fifth Business,* is an attempt by three different people, Ramsay himself, David Staunton (the son of his friend Boy Staunton), and Paul Dempster, to discover the truth about themselves and about the strange series of events in which they are involved. All their enquiries proceed on a human level. The wonders that occur among them, at the hand of Paul Dempster metamorphosed into the magician Magnus Eisengrim, are man-made illusions, not supernatural marvels. Mary Dempster, the "fool saint" through whom Ramsay seems to get a whiff of the divine, is in fact a woman turned half-witted by misfortune, and the miracles he attributes to her are not such as the church would accept. In the end the wise and eccentric old Jesuit, Father Blazon, calls upon him to abandon his quest for saintliness if not for saints.

> Forgive yourself for being a human creature, Ramezay. That is the beginning of wisdom; that is part of what is meant by the fear of God; but for you it is the only way to save your sanity. Begin now, or you will end up with your saint in the madhouse.

Similarly, when the devil appears to Ramsay, it is in the form of a human being, the rich Swiss woman Liesl who is Eisengrim's impresario and eventually becomes Ramsay's friend.

In all this, Davies is not suggesting that the good represented by the saints or the evil represented by the devil do not exist. What he tells us is that—unless we belong to the privileged and scanty ranks of the mystics who have been vouchsafed the ecstatic vision of deity—we see both the divine and the diabolical in fleeting manifestations in our human existence, hinted rather than stated in dreams, in myths, in puzzling personal encounters. That is why Ramsay, like Clement Hollier in the third trilogy that begins with *The Rebel Angels,* will operate as a scholar in the interface between history and myth; why Jungian analysis with its underworld of archetypical beings mysteriously residing in the collective unconscious which we all share, will play such an important role in the novels; why the illusions that Marcus Eisengrim creates by mechanical means will shadow forth a different "world of wonders" as mysterious and inaccessible as the world of Plato's Forms. In the end, one is left after reading Davies' later novels with a sense of the enormous ambivalence of one of the key phrases of the religious quest: "Seek, and ye shall find." Davies' characters, or at least the significant ones, seek and indeed they find, but what they find is not the Grail of which they have gone in search. If they are fortunate they find self-realization, and often it is in some way self-realization through creation. The individual may not find God in the whole and all-consuming way of the great mystics, but he will realize the fragment of God, the creative spark, that is within himself.

All this represents an enormous thematic advance on the early Davies novels, and it is clear that the twelve years of literary silence were spent in much study and thought. Still, in the last resort the success or otherwise of the novels lies not in what they tell us, which an intelligent tract could probably do as well, but in how they tell it. And here also *Fifth Business* is a great advance on even *A Mixture of Frailties.* Indeed, there are some who say it represents the peak of Davies' achievement, the best of all the nine novels, and, as we shall see, there is some justification for such an opinion.

In *Fifth Business* Davies departs from the old-fashioned form of third-person narrative with somewhat theatrical dialogue which he used in the Salterton trilogy. Now he uses a direct and rather aggressive first-person approach as Ramsay, a retiring master at Colborne College, protests to the Headmaster about the patronizing farewell notice accorded him in the *College Chronicle*. His letter of protest extends into a whole book, but once we accept this basic implausibility we find ourselves involved in the account of a strange life told with a becoming idiosyncrasy and with a vigour of language and imagery, and a grasp of the grubby glory of life, that is quite beyond anything in the Salterton stories. What makes the book so successful is a remarkable unity of tone which extends into an appropriateness of speech to character and character to action that rarely lapses.

With the ingenuity of a dedicated mythographer, Ramsay traces how a misaimed snowball, intended for him and wickedly loaded with a stone, set the three main characters of the novel, and of the rest of the trilogy, on their often parted but always interweaving paths in life.

The stone-laden snowball, intended by Boy Staunton for

Ramsay, knocks down Mary Dempster and brings on the premature birth of her son Paul. It also results in her permanently losing her reason and becoming what the local Catholic priest calls a "fool saint," eccentric in her behaviour and indiscriminating in her generosity, up to the point when she scandalizes the town by giving herself to a wandering tramp, whom the trauma of their discovery by a search party in the local hobo jungle turns into a missionary in the city slums.

Ramsay, whose evasion of the snowball resulted in Mary Dempster's misfortune, not only feels a lifelong guilt towards her, but, in observing actions he can only interpret as saintly, is started on his career as a high-class hagiographer, tracing the various kinds and conditions of sainthood, and treating the phenomenon of hagiolatry as one of the points where myth and history most illumine each other and where illusion may lead to the recognition of truth.

Ramsay's other boyhood passion is the deceptive magic of conjuring; himself too ham-handed to succeed, he passes his knowledge on to young Paul Dempster who has the necessary manual facility. And when Paul has endured enough of his Baptist minister father's fundamentalist disciplines, and of the mockery to which his mother's actions subject him at the hands of Boy Staunton and the other Deptford children, he lets himself be seduced into a freak show by the homosexual conjuror Willard, one of Davies' most chilling personifications of evil. After years of virtual slavery during which he learns his art, Paul falls in with the formidably ugly and intelligent and also very rich Liesl Naegeli, who establishes him as the internationally famed magician Magnus Eisengrim. Meanwhile, Boy Staunton, the author with his hard-centred snowball of all these strange metamorphoses in the lives of others, goes on blindly with his self-obsessed career as financier and politician, impervious to the sufferings of others until, in a fatal encounter where he and Paul and Ramsay for the first time come together as a trio, he gains a kind of enlightenment into the emptiness of his life, goes off with the stone which Ramsay has religiously preserved, and dies mysteriously, drowned in his car with the stone in his mouth.

It is the single, consistent, idiosyncratic, eloquent voice of Ramsay that gives *Fifth Business* its impressive and convincing power and unity, which neither of the later volumes in the trilogy projects to the same degree. Bizarre as much of it may seem to him, the reader is aware of the essential, devil-shaming truth of *Fifth Business,* its authenticity as the account of a failed search for the divine. Ramsay's letter, of course, is a piece of artifice, a literary contrivance, but it is a contrivance that we accept as easily as we might accept a magnifying glass as an aid to reading a difficult text. The character evoked by it seems to live with his own inner vigour, and so all that happens to him seems fictionally authentic.

In his trilogy Davies sets out to show the consequences of the snowballing from the standpoints of the three Deptford boys who were most affected, but in *The Manticore* he actually circumvents the problem of how to perceive and present the insensitive and monstrously self-conceited Boy Staunton by showing Boy's life through the eyes and feelings of his son, the brilliant and alcoholic lawyer David Staunton, "who had a dark reputation because the criminal world thought so highly of him, and who played up to the role, and who secretly fancied himself as a magician of the courtroom."

Realizing that the shock of his father's dramatic death has pushed him to the edge of a mental breakdown, David decides to subject himself to psychoanalysis, and it is this analysis, conducted in Zurich by the Jungian Dr. Joanna von Heller, that forms the frame of the book. It consists of conversations with Dr. von Heller, interspersed by sections of a narrative of the past which the analyst requires David to write. In the process we are given not only a picture of the kind of upbringing that by middle age had carried Boy Staunton's son to the verge of madness, but also a portrait of that startlingly soulless man, his father, who was evil by default of goodness.

But the framework is too rigid for events to move easily and too awkward to be evocative of character. Neither of the Stauntons stands in the mind's eye as a living person with the same kind of depth and complexity as Ramsay in *Fifth Business.* One of the reasons is that in *The Manticore* Davies is even more eager than in previous novels to perform as the Canadian latter-day Zola, exhibiting too painfully and at times all too dully his Jungian scholarship and his carefully acquired knowledge of the working of the Canadian legal system.

The third novel of the series, *World of Wonders,* tells of the transformation of Paul Dempster, the wretched Deptford boy, into the famous and accomplished stage magician, Magnus Eisengrim. Again there is a rather contrived frame, for the story is told when Eisengrim is playing the role of an earlier magical illusionist, Jean-Eugène Robert-Houdin, in a film directed by the famous Swede, Jurgen Lind. Evening after evening, at the urging of Ramsay who wishes to prepare an authentic biography of Dempster as well as the lying life of Eisengrim he had earlier written to give his friend publicity, the magician tells of the terrifying experiences in the lower levels of the entertainment world by which, like an ancient shaman being ceremonially reborn, he was transformed from a parson's tyrannized son into a wonder-worker. The framework gives the narrative a formality that does not always accord with the spirit of what is told, and acts as a kind of hobble to the narrative. Yet the content is so dark and compelling in its evocation of evil and so fascinating in its use of the illusory wonders of the magician's art to suggest by analogy the true wonders of existence, that the knowledge so broadly displayed of early twentieth-century English theatre and of the life and crafts of American show people becomes far more thoroughly assimilated into the narrative than happened with Jungian analysis in *The Manticore.* In form, as in content, *World of Wonders* impresses one as a work of consummate artifice, in which the protagonist, Paul Dempster, is barely perceived as a human being through the multitude of bright mirror images and the endless argumentative evasions he displays in offering his conversational autobiography. One feels that this is Proteus, and that his creator has never really got him by the heels. At the end of the novel it is not Paul Dempster but once again

canny old Ramsay who emerges as the one thoroughly convincing, because thoroughly revealed, character. Such are the perils to a novelist of entering too deeply and deliberately into the world of illusion.

A different kind of writer's peril emerges in the third group of Davies novels, the Toronto campus trilogy as one might call it. For these books—*The Rebel Angels, What's Bred in the Bone,* and *The Lyre of Orpheus*—are partly at least *romans à clef,* based on Davies' experiences of educational and cultural institutions, so that readers in the know have had no difficulty recognizing some of the people whom Davies has embellished into often bizarre characters: John Pearson transmogrified into John Parlabane in *The Rebel Angels,* for instance, and Alan Jarvis made over into Aylwin Ross in *What's Bred in the Bone.* Such mergings of fact into fiction always arouse doubts in one's mind about the writer's motives and ultimately about the nature of his achievement. Is he playing metafictional games with the reader? Or is he lazily offering us memory half raw? As distinct from the youthful autobiographical novel, which is a *rite de passage* many readers undergo in the development of their fictional imagination, the *roman à clef,* in the hands of an experienced novelist, is always an equivocal achievement in which the power of imagination remains in doubt.

Still, the three novels are more than *romans à clef;* if the Deptford series is concerned with the relationship between illusion and reality as mediated by artifice, this later group tends to be dominated by the relationship between true art and artifice, played out, as in the earlier novels, against the shifting scenes of a stage where history and myth are seen as merging.

In a literal way the central figure is Francis Cornish, whose life is told in the middle novel, *What's Bred in the Bone.* Cornish is known to the world as a discriminating connoisseur and a voracious collector of art. In the first volume, *The Rebel Angels,* he has just died and left to three professors the task of sorting the great accumulation of objects he has acquired and of distributing them in accordance with his will. The narrative is a curiously divided one, part of it being written by one of the three professors, Simon Darcourt, as a gossiping journal of academic life he called "The New Aubrey," and alternating chapters forming a kind of interior diary of Maria Theotoky, a half-Polish, half-Gypsy graduate student; she thinks herself in love with Clement Hollier, the second of the professors, a great mythographer who has seduced her in a fit of absent-mindedness. The third professor, the leading villain, is an unprincipled academic poseur, Urquhart McVarish, who steals from the Cornish collection a remarkable unknown Rabelais manuscript after which Hollier lusts academically.

These high eccentrics, consumed by scholarly passions and academic greeds, and reinforced by such colleagues as the sinister ex-monk John Parlabane, present academe as the terrain of such strange conflicts that one feels often Davies is trying to compensate for his frustration with the dullness of real Canadian academic life. The action mounts to a suicide (Parlabane's) and a bizarre murder (of McVarish by Parlabane) among sexual orgies as strange in their own way as anything in Petronius. The novel slides—as so many of Davies' do—into the serene harbour of a happy ending, out of tone with the rest of the book, in which Maria, having recovered from her infatuation with her professor, marries Arthur Cornish, the rich nephew of Francis and the real administrator of the Cornish estate.

Once again we are treated to displays of knowledge. There is a fascinating oddity about the arcane lore of gypsies rejuvenating and faking old violins which provides some of the most entertaining pages of the book. There is also an unfortunate bit of stale derivativeness when the Sheldonian theory of the effect of physique on temperament is warmed up in a weakly humorous scene when Ozias Froats expounds his theories on the qualities and virtues of human excrement. It is a more disunited novel than any of Davies' previous works; the central intrigue over the Rabelais papers is too weak to carry the burden of so many extraneous interests, and no character—not even wicked Parlabane or the brooding offscene presence of Francis Cornish is sufficiently realized to sustain one's interest.

Francis Cornish comes fully onstage in **What's Bred in the Bone,** which is really a classic *bildungsroman,* in form, language, and in the handling of the trilogy's central theme, the relationship between artifice and art. A whimsical structure, in which the chapters are interspersed with angelic conversations, does not disguise the fact that the novel is told in a very conservative third-person narrative. Cornish's life begins in Blairlogie on the Ottawa River, which is clearly a fictional presentation of Renfrew, where Davies spent much of his childhood, and the money that will eventually finance Francis as a collector comes originally from the destruction of the northern Ontario forests. Like Ramsay's, his childhood is dominated by an obsession, in this case with "the Looner," his idiot brother, the first Francis, whose survival has been concealed and who becomes one of the earliest subjects of the second Francis's pencil when he begins his lonely apprenticeship as an artist.

Following a picaresque line, the novel takes Francis to Oxford, where he falls in with the famous restorer of classical paintings, Tancred Saraceni; he eventually joins Saraceni at a castle in Bavaria where their task is to restore—and improve in the restoring—a cache of German late medieval paintings which are passed on to the credulous Nazis in exchange for authentic Italian masterpieces from German collections. Here—and the opportunity is not lost for a display of the knowledge Davies has acquired of the methods of the old masters and how their effects can be reproduced in materials now available—Francis perfects his grasp of the technique of painting. When he has reached this point Saraceni proposes to test his aesthetic imagination by leaving him to paint—on an old ruined altarpiece—the work that will show he is a true artist as well as a fine artisan. The result is *The Marriage of Cana* which, when it surfaces before a commission established to send European paintings back to their proper homes, Saraceni proclaims to be an original by an unknown early painter, whom he calls The Alchemical Master; later Aylwin Ross publishes an analytical essay that seems to

set the picture firmly in the political and social context of the times. What we—as readers—know to be the work of a modern man has been accepted by the artistic establishment as the work of a man five centuries before, and we enjoy the ironies that our knowledge allows us.

But Davies is after more than irony. There is serious business on foot here, as *The Lyre of Orpheus* reveals. I have already shown, in opening this essay, how in plot *The Lyre of Orpheus* circles back to the early Davies novels, as if to signify that a cycle is being closed, and how, thematically, it brings to a conclusion questions regarding the nature of literary art that are implicit in Davies' fiction from the beginning.

Here, in [*The Lyre of Orpheus*] the artistic conservatism of Robertson Davies is clearly displayed, in argument and in practice. Once again the narrative is a traditional third-person one, given a touch of metafictional contrivance by the introduction of the beyond-the-grave commentaries of Hoffman, which in fact deepen the conservatism of the narrative by presenting the views on art of a nineteenth-century musician, which the twentieth-century musicians in the novel are seeking to bring to fruition. The enthusiastic account of Schnak's dedicated toil in completing another musician's work abandoned so long ago is a clear denial of the cult of originality that has dominated western art and literature since the days of the romantics. Allied to the cult of originality is that of contemporaneity, the idea that the true artist must speak of his time in its own verbal or visual language; Darcourt's triumphal assertion of Francis Cornish's genius, which finds in *The Marriage of Cana* an expression that is neither original nor contemporary but is true to his talents and his life, is a negation of that doctrine too.

Thematically, *The Lyre of Orpheus* projects a viewpoint that is reactionary rather than classicist in formal terms, for, though Davies has adhered increasingly in his most recent English novels to the traditional methods of mainstream English fiction, his interests have placed him on the verge of Gothic romanticism in selecting his content, while his approach to characterization has brought him close to a comic tradition in fiction that, as we have seen, runs from Fielding through Peacock and Dickens to Joyce Cary. In denying the importance of originality and contemporaneity he is in fact guarding his own territory, for he is neither a strikingly original novelist, nor, in the sense of representing any avant garde, a notably contemporary writer.

Here lie the main reasons for the popularity of Robertson Davies, which some critics have found offensive to their ideas of what Canadians should be expecting of their writers. It resembles the current popularity of realist painters like Alex Colville, Christopher Pratt, Ivan Eyre, and Jack Chambers. Most people, in Canada and elsewhere, are artistically conservative; only the avant gardes of the past are—though not invariably—acceptable to them. It is true that the permissiveness of the 1960s made the broader public open to certain kinds of content that were once unacceptable. But, as the totalitarians have always known, it is in the formal aspects of a work that the deepest rebellion declares itself, and it is at this point that general readers, feeling the boundaries of normal speech and perception slipping away, become disturbed; the nihilism of much of modern art and literature bewilders and repels them. They need reassurance, and the novels of Robertson Davies, which present no real formal challenges, and whose essential optimism is shown in upbeat endings, with quests completed, wishes fulfilled, evil routed, and villains destroyed, are admirably suited for the calming and comforting of uneasy Canadians. They exist on the edge of popular fiction, where Pangloss reigns in the best of possible worlds. (pp. 33-48)

> George Woodcock, "A Cycle Completed: The Nine Novels of Robertson Davies," in Canadian Literature, No. 126, Autumn, 1990, pp. 33-48.

My books are not novels in the sense of being artistic constructs formed on something which reaches back to a French origin, or Henry James, or something. They're romances. I just write romances, and when you write romances you have to be Scheherezade and bear in mind that if you do not hold the Caliph's attention he will cut your head off in the morning.

—Robertson Davies, in an interview with Michael Hulse, in The Journal of Commonwealth Literature, *1987*.

Jo Allen Bradham   (essay date Fall 1990)

[*In the following essay, Bradham analyzes how Davies's use of biography, allegory, art criticism, and satire in* What's Bred in the Bone *reflects the philosophical and artistic heritage of Western culture.*]

Robertson Davies's ***What's Bred in the Bone*** takes its title from an English proverb traceable to a 1290 Latin version: *Osse radicatum raro de carne recedit.* The antiquity of the title discloses much about the book; as Davies concentrates on the power the past exerts on the present, the implications of the title reach far beyond the maxim that what is bred in the bone of the artist-protagonist Francis Cornish will come out in his flesh. Davies also affirms a literary inheritance of theme and form bred in the bone of the author. This inheritance focuses on four genres: biography, allegory with its emphasis on ambiguity and on symbolic transformation, art and art criticism, and satire. The 1985 novel is summary and synthesis of matters bred in the bone of the Western thinker and artist. What's bred in the bone of a writer will be apparent in the flesh of his novel.

One of the forms bred in the bone is biography, an old genre but one popular and extensively analyzed since the eighteenth century. The framework narrative of the novel focuses on Simon Darcourt, who is in the process of pre-

paring a biography of his deceased friend, Francis Cornish. In the handling of biography, Davies joins the tradition of Virginia Woolf's *Orlando* and Steven Millhauser's *Edwin Mullhouse: The Life and Death of an American Writer, 1943-1954, by Jeffrey Cartwright.* Fiction, masked as biography, provides literary criticism on the conventions of biography and on the routine and frequently misleading methods of its practitioners. Like Woolf and Millhauser, Davies both laughs at and laments the poses, strategems, and personal inadequacies of those who define biography and make lives out of stacks of papers in shoeboxes. *Orlando, Edwin Mullhouse,* and ***What's Bred in the Bone*** form a nucleus in biographical satire. All integrate the genres of satire, biography, novel, and criticism to analyze biography and to create a central figure who suffers just because he or she is the focus of biographical consideration.

Davies recalls familiar problems in the history and development of biography in his handling of Darcourt, official biographer of the deceased expert in art. Cornish will live on in the image Darcourt creates, but the subject is a man of gift and vision; the biographer, conventional and hesitant. The episode with the monkeys, in which Cornish identifies a fake painting by pointing out that the New World monkeys on the canvas could not have been known to Hubertus van Eyck, the artist to whom the painting was attributed, shows a Francis who misses nothing and concludes well. His biographer, however, is not someone who has a similar reach and scope, but the timorous and bibulous Simon Darcourt, clergyman and critic. In Davies's earlier volume ***The Rebel Angels,*** Darcourt is sensitive, interesting, and fully capable of interpreting subtleties, but the frame which fixes him in ***What's Bred in the Bone*** recalls little of the scholar, lover, dreamer, and teacher of the preceding book. Darcourt's weaknesses, not his strengths, are now in evidence. Darcourt and Francis had been friends; they shared similar interests and attended concerts together. As biographer, Darcourt satisfies Samuel Johnson's argument that the best biography will come from the person who has eaten with and known personally the subject. Darcourt can supply the little telling details and, thereby, meet the Johnsonian standard that small things reveal major things in a man's character. At first glance, Darcourt recalls Boswell; he met his man fairly late in the subject's life but talked with him often and attended events of mutual interest with him. The two moved in the same circle and shared many friends and associates. The similarity to Boswell cannot go much beyond these basics because Darcourt, in the few passages in which he appears, comes across as a decidedly limited man who wants to find sources so that he can put them together in routine scholarly fashion. We see him at his note cards, diligent and meticulous, an eternal writer of term papers, but a man in whom the imagination seems conspicuously lacking. Darcourt himself describes the way he prefers to work: "I'm a disciplined worker, I don't mess about, waiting for inspiration, and all that nonsense. I sit down at my desk and wire in and make prose out of my copious notes." Francis Cornish may deserve a Boswell; he gets the equivalent of Joseph Spence.

Professor the Reverend Simon Darcourt's first words in

What's Bred in the Bone are "I haven't any idea. It would take experts to decide, and they could be years doing it. All I have is suspicions. I'm sorry I ever mentioned them." This speech is neither a dramatic entry nor a convincing recommendation for a biographer. The diction establishes him as a man of negatives, evasion, escape, and indecision. He is a man limited in seeing; yet, ironically, it is his task to capture and explain a man who could see into the heart of art and allegory. The job is for the best of biographers, not for the "Reverend Simon Darcourt, pink, plump, and a little drunk, [who] looked precisely what he was: a priest-academic pushed into a tight corner."

Darcourt conveys indecision and timidity. To Arthur and Maria, his fellow trustees of the Cornish Foundation, Darcourt confides, "You know, of course, that Francis and Ross were thought to be homosexual lovers." The phrasing is indirect, the parenthetical phrase "of course" breaks the line to suggest gossip; the "were thought to be" continues the indirection and damns by insinuation. The redundancy of "homosexual lovers"—since the two men could hardly be lovers in any other way—hints of Darcourt's shortcomings as he faces the biographical task. The teller ruins the subject but keeps his own skirts clean. It is not talk appropriate to a biographer, who, ideally, contributes vision and clarifies meaning but refrains from intensifying confusion.

Later Darcourt confesses, "I simply don't know who he was." About all that Darcourt can document is that Francis Cornish did not bathe with sufficient frequency and was a miser. Although both notations may be true, they hardly capture the Alchemical Master—the identity that Cornish's work earns for him. Equally damning to Darcourt's biographical credentials is his letter to the *Times*. The style is turgid, and evasion is dominant. The concluding line—"When his collections have been examined it may emerge that he was a more significant figure in the art world of his time than is at present understood"—defines Darcourt as one unequipped to interpret the mercurial artist. The two passive verbs and the conditional verb in Darcourt's sentence diminish him as a writer—at least on this particular subject—and whimper that Francis Cornish will not be known.

Darcourt, of course, wants to do a good job, but he is not equal to his task. Inevitably, he will blur the image of Francis Cornish and suggest meanings that are invalid. The Lesser Zadkiel, the Angel of Biography, and Maimas, Cornish's Daimon who serves as definer and protector, conclude that "poor Darcourt [will] never know the whole truth about Francis Cornish." In choosing, arranging, and writing up the events of Francis's life, Darcourt, like any literary biographer, will convey meaning as he sees and reads it in the life he studies. The meaning will be based on the events, but the mind of the biographer will be the shaper and interpreter. The Cornish Darcourt may present seems likely to bear little resemblance to the real Cornish.

Conscientious biographer that he is, Darcourt has made the required trip to Blairlogie, Cornish's birthplace sixty miles from Ottawa, so that he could see and feel the community and interview those who knew Cornish or his relatives. Not only does he make the proper investigatory trip, recommended by all schools of biography; but Darcourt also explains to Maria that he has only contempt for the popular fictionalized biography that lacks sound scholarship. Through this conversation, Davies, like his predecessors who use fiction to criticize accepted methods of biographical procedure, weighs the different schools and approaches of biography and comes out not too far from the much quoted position of Desmond MacCarthy: "A biographer is an artist who is under oath." Darcourt is "an artist chained to biography." The idea of bondage, of the chained biographer, finds discussion in all who have wrestled with a theory of the genre; but Virginia Woolf, whose experiments with biography are now bred in the bone of any writer who turns to the form, makes the case clear. In "The Art of Biography," Woolf stesses the bounds: "the art of biography is the most restricted of all the arts" and the biographer, unlike the novelist, "is tied." Behind Davies and Darcourt remains Woolf's summary that "the biographer complained that he was tied by friends, letters, and documents. . . . "

While Davies touches on the current controversy of biographical theory and practice, he neither minimizes the problems that face even the best trained and most conscientious of biographers nor ignores the possibility for transformation. The Lesser Zadkiel, the Angel of Biography, and Francis Cornish's Daimon, Maimas, both of whom are immortal and have seen all, do not possess all answers. They argue frequently (but in more good-humored fashion than most biographers do) about the significance and effect of events; and even with their perspective and power, they face the problems of interpretation that beset the mortal biographer. And a growth in awareness is always possible for that mortal. Darcourt knows very little in the beginning; but there is the suggestion in the subsequent action that because of the prophecy of fame for Cornish, Darcourt may grow into his task as an artistic and critical inheritance descends to him.

Bred in the bone of *What's Bred in the Bone* is a tradition of biography that has produced many conspicuous practitioners, considerable critical controversy, some parody, and much fragmentation into types and schools ("pure," popular, "new," scholarly, scholarly-historical, literary, socio-, psycho-, mediated, fictionalized, novelistic, silhouette, life-and-times, warts-and-all, objective, artistic-scholarly, narrative, hagiographic, interpretative, compilation). This inheritance of biography underlies Darcourt and Davies, who plays on and with it. Biography informs the book just as the long tradition of painting with its practitioners and schools is the giant on the shoulders of which Francis stands and by which his *oeuvre* must be studied.

Davies's treatment of biography is inseparable from his adaptation of allegory, a second form bred in the bone of a Western writer. Allegory, with frames and multiple levels, provides the structure of the book. Davies adapts the conventions of the old dream vision allegory; but rather than have a real man fall asleep and dream the inner and complex narrative, Davies uses the framework narrative of Simon Darcourt, the official biographer. Only the first and last sections, approximately 20 pages, focus directly on Darcourt, the biography, and the discussion within the Cornish Foundation about the advisability of the biography. Darcourt and Maria Cornish, as trustees of the Foundation, mention Zadkiel and Maimas, who then control the internal—but truly significant—narrative. The Daimon Maimas reviews with Zadkiel the events of Francis's life. In the heart of the telling, but included at the will of Maimas and Zadkiel, Francis Cornish paints the story of his life in a work entitled *The Marriage at Cana.* The painting is as much narrative and biography as the other levels are. It is biography within biography within biography. The painting and the Maimas-Zadkiel narrative correspond to the vision of truth within the earth-bound action of the old dream vision allegory.

Recalling the old form that Davies appropriates is simple. The writer (Robertson Davies) sets up a fictional biographer (Simon Darcourt) to tell a tale, but then interrupts what would be an incomplete rendering for a vision of truth offered by two supernatural agents and by the true subject (Francis Cornish). All strive to interpret the story of Cornish on his quest. What is simple to see is not, however, easy to evaluate because Darcourt has picked up a rumor that Francis Cornish may be a faker. Certain sketches in the National Gallery have begun to arouse suspicion. Francis, in his turn, tells his story, as he sees it, in the guise of *The Marriage at Cana;* and Francis's *Meister* (Master), Tancred Saraceni, publicly interprets the painting, not as *The Marriage at Cana* or overtly as Francis's own story, but as the alchemical marriage. With so many levels of meaning and so many variations on truth, knowing the truth is problematic. Time and his daughter Truth appear frequently in the text, but Davies's attention to allegory and ambiguity discourages any claim that truth is easy to determine.

The Maimas-Zadkiel narrative brings truth and recalls that the moral level of allegory offers direction for living and understanding life. It focuses on the trials that the human spirit undergoes in its diurnal progress. The spirit confronts obstacles; it grows; it learns; it suffers defeat. But there is purpose to the trials, for the journey of life is part of the pilgrim's way. That the Daimon and the Angel of Biography tell this level affirms that Francis's journey has purpose and that each encounter embodies meaning. The two tellers repeatedly emphasize that they deal with the timeless, with perspectives that those who exist in time will never find.

Francis's level of telling, in the painting *The Marriage at Cana,* is the anagogic core. As artist and as human being, Francis deliberately sets out to paint the myth of Francis Cornish; and he holds the focus steady on his soul and its search for ascent and the mystical marriage through which it would achieve *unitas.*

Allegory, of which the dream vision frame was a popular manifestation, was the glory of the late Middle Ages and the early Renaissance. Dante's *Divine Comedy,* Chaucer's *House of Fame,* Langland's *Piers Plowman,* and Spenser's *Faerie Queene* are probably the most familiar examples of a form intended to explain man's journey and to show "as above, so below." Allegory teaches and allegory allows for the search of the soul for unity with truth. For a novel about an artist who worked in the style of the late medieval-early Renaissance period, Davies adapts a favorite narrative structure of those years. Like his protagonist, Davies restores an old form and spreads it out rich and bright in its own colors. He is not a faker. He does not sign the name of Dante or William Langland or Geoffrey Chaucer. He does essentially what Francis does; he creates in a form outside of his own time.

Many of the names Davies crafts are those of allegory. The pivotal action—the painting of *Drollig Hansel* and *The Marriage at Cana*—takes place at Schloss Düsterstein. *Düster* means *melancholy* or *gloomy* and *stein* means *rock.* The place is Castle Gloomyrock for many reasons. Here, for the Profession (British military intelligence), Francis counts the cars of the railroad train that passes nightly with human cargo bound for extermination. Here, the young artist experiences initiation into fraud on the level of high art and international politics. Finally Castle Gloomyrock becomes the estate of Prince Max, the resilient survivor of the Hohenzollern, and his beautiful wife, Amalie, direct inheritor of Düsterstein, who "never gave a damn about the pictures" but for money, will widen the circle of fraud. Aptly named, Castle Gloomyrock is the successor to the countless castles of allegory—the Castle of Perseverance, the Castle of Pleasure, or the House of Fame.

Personal names also work in the way of allegory. The artist who paints *The Harrowing of Hell* is Jean-Paul Letztpfenning, which means *last farthing* or *pennyless,* as indeed he is. Zadok recalls the high priest in the days of David; as the strongest man during Francis's boyhood, Zadok Hoyle guides, guards, and initiates the youth much as a priest might. Amalie calls Francis *Le Beau Tenebreux,* which means the *lovely gloomy or mysterious one.* The allegoric tradition of symbolic names—Mankind, Good Deeds Mr. Worldly Wiseman, Herr Letztpfenning—runs unbroken from the earliest medieval effort through the characters in **What's Bred in the Bone.**

Allegory typically dramatizes the change humanity experiences in its journey, and alchemy remains the dominant symbol for change. Davies relies on the fund of ideas and associations that alchemy holds to deepen his characterization of Cornish as a man who experiences spiritual transformation. Cornish is the Alchemical Master; but whether his final state is one of pure gold or base lead depends on interpretation. He is locked out from love throughout life. Because of the reputation of *Drollig Hansel* and *The Marriage at Cana,* he cannot paint in the style he feels fulfills him; and once he reads the comments of Picasso about the failure of contemporary art and its capitulation to "the imbecility, the vanity, the cupidity of . . . contemporaries," he is stopped in the attempt to develop another style. What was gold to him—painting— is forbidden. Called to art the way many of his relatives are called to the Church, Cornish honors his novitiate, but then is not allowed to serve the host or administer the sacraments of art. By this progress in denial, he appears base lead. But in the corrupt application of alchemy, as a chemical rather than a spiritual process, Francis is eminently successful. He is unbelievably rich at the end. If the coin of the realm is gold, he has turned all into gold.

Tancred Saraceni calls Francis the Alchemical Master during the session when the art experts come upon and attempt to deal with Cornish's painting of *The Marriage at Cana.* Admiration for the painting is high; but as soon as one expert insinuates that he suspects that it is not genuine, Saraceni rises to the occasion and offers the long and intricate interpretation of the painting as an allegory of the alchemical marriage. Because no painter can be determined, Saraceni concludes that the work and the similar *Drollig Hansel* must be attributed to a painter known only as the Alchemical Master. Immediately after the public attribution, when Saraceni and Francis are alone, Saraceni calls Francis, Meister, defining him as the Alchemical Master. In the world of art, Francis is the master of alchemy; he transforms. The canvas is his alembic.

In a manner appropriate to the ambiguities of alchemy and the intricacies of allegory, Francis Cornish stands as both painter and canvas, the canvas on which Tancred Saraceni paints his most nearly original work. The style in which Francis excels is the one to which Saraceni directs him; the circle in which Francis moves while he is in Europe is that which Saraceni dominates; the identity of Alchemical Master is the one Saraceni gives him; and the great fortune that Francis inherits is that Saraceni leaves him. Francis becomes what Saraceni crafts. In this case, Francis is the transformed, not the transformer; the product, not the master of alchemical alteration. Much that Saraceni effects is good within the Kingdom of Art, but Saraceni is also Judas.

Into one panel of the triptych of *The Marriage at Cana,* Cornish incorporates Saraceni, changing only the color of his hair, as the figure who controls the purse and calls "the attention of his brethren to figures in the central panel." Saraceni recognizes himself in the figure of Judas and acknowledges that identification to Cornish. The portrayal is correct: Saraceni controls the purse (by refusing to pay Cornish); he calls attention to other figures (by forcing the young Cornish to examine in a new way all the events and people in his life); and Saraceni betrays Cornish (Christian iconography identifies Judas primarily as a betrayer).

Saraceni's betrayal resembles Judas's kiss of death. Once the renowned restorer, said to have the Evil Eye, acknowledges Francis as one set apart, as the Alchemical Master, Francis is marked. The event reenacts the occurrences that followed Saraceni's other markings. One art critic goes blind; old Baudoin, Saraceni's enemy in art criticism, breaks his hip. Francis Cornish suffers no physical crisis, but he loses the means to paint just as surely as if he had lost an arm. Tancred Saraceni leaves Francis Cornish a fortune but only after he has betrayed him by the curse of the Evil Eye. Saraceni's praise, acknowledgment, and celebration precede the crucifixion of Francis's talent.

Saraceni, after completing his public analysis of *The Marriage at Cana,* the Judas kiss in the Gethsemane of art, reassures Francis that he has not spoken an untruth. By a narrow scale of logic, that statement is true. Furthermore, if one reads the book the way Saraceni reads a canvas, the statement is entirely true and in a far more convincing way. Francis may be the Alchemical Master, not in the sense of the alchemist who effects transformations or the artist who paints the apogee of transformation, but in the sense of *master* as a basic form from which copies may be made. Francis is an alchemical master in that he shows the synthesis of time and experience; he has known the ugliness of Carlyle Rural, his rough provincial grade school, and the beauty of the peony. His totality combines the evil of Ismay, his zealous and unprincipled wife of a few months, and the charity of Ruth, the woman of generous spirit and sincere love with whom he is allowed to share an equally brief alliance. The destruction of Blairlogie and the creativity of Rome, the terror of loneliness and the splendor of aloneness come together in Francis. Cornish combines what is bred in the bone and what is impregnated by means of art. Within him are Victoria Cameron, the family cook who befriends and loves the young Francis while inculcating a grim Presbyterian conscience, and Aunt Mary-Ben, his aunt who attempts to imbue him with the sweet piety of a sentimental Catholicism. These two women from Blairlogie are the old painters, who colored the canvas with their opposing strokes and their disparate concepts of love and duty. Saraceni, whose name recalls the ancient, hated Saracens against whom the Christian crusaders claimed to fight for the soul of man, attempts to rub clean the canvas of the colors of the two women. Unable to do so, he performs in his usual way. He overpaints and enhances. Saraceni applies quite specific methods to the portraits on canvas he finds at Düsterstein:

> But Saraceni would place one of these competent, uninteresting daubs on his easel, and study it with care for hours before removing certain portions with a solvent so that the painting beneath was blurred, or else the undercoating of the panel was revealed. Then he would repaint the face, so that it was the same as before but with a greater distinction—a keenness of aristocratic eye, a new look of *bürgerlich* astuteness, a fuller beard; women, if they had hands, were given rings, modest, but costly, and better complexions. Sometimes, he placed in the upper left-hand corner of the panel, some little heraldic device, which might indicate the status of the sitter, and on one picture, rather larger than the rest, he introduced an ornamental chain, the collar and emblem of the Saint-Esprit.

To transform Francis, Tancred Saraceni uses the same process in the alchemical or metaphorical sense and the results are similar. Francis "had absorbed [the philosophy], and ingested it, and had made it part of his own wholeness. . . . He had consumed the wheat and discarded the chaff, and the wheat was now bone of his bone. It was his belief, not his lesson."

Tancred Saraceni is part of Francis Cornish, "bone of his bone," just as Victoria Cameron and Mary-Ben McRory are. Francis is the mystical union of forces disparate in the extreme. He may be an original (a master) from which copies may be made, a kind of prototype of alchemy, the evidence, not the generator, of transformation. Even Darcourt, at the prompting of Maria, confesses that "if ever there was a true son of Hermes ['the reconciler of opposites,' according to Maria], it was Francis Cornish."

Davies adapts the old structure of medieval and Renaissance allegory; he revives alchemy from its medieval grave and handles it convincingly. Both traditions are bred in the bone of the artist. Art and art criticism are also part of his inheritance. It is hardly surprising that a biography of an artist gives attention to the techniques of art, but the degree to which plastic art becomes literary art may be unprecedented. Allegory has always claimed a strong pictorial quality, in obvious fashion in illustrations of fables or in the emblem books and in complex Renaissance works. Davies explores the literary variant of the interlocking of art and allegory. On the simplest level, he emphasizes the patterned and pictorial quality. He describes scene and character as if he were offering a commentary on a picture. The characters become figures posed in spatial relationships to other figures; to each is attributed some visual detail that can strongly suggest, if not actually symbolize, an identity or function. Their actions evoke the effect of a painting:

> Arthur Cornish, who was pacing up and down the room, was unquestionably a business man; a Chairman of the Board to his business associates, but a man with interests that might have surprised them if he had not kept his life in tidy compartments. The Reverend Simon Darcourt, pink, plump, and a little drunk, looked precisely what he was: a priest-academic pushed into a tight corner. But the figure least like a trustee of anything was Arthur's wife Maria, barefoot in gypsy style, and dressed in a housecoat that would have been gaudy if it had not been made by the best couturier of the best materials.

The three people form a composition of line, color, size, gestures. The manner of that presentation matches that of Davies writing as art critic in the description of three figures within the composition of *The Marriage at Cana:*

> . . . on their left stood a stout old man of a merry, bourgeois appearance, who seemed to be making a sketch of the scene on an ivory tablet, and somewhat behind him, but clearly to be seen, was a woman, smiling like the Virgin, who was holding an astronomical, or perhaps an astrological, chart. Completing this group was a man who might have been a superior groom or huissier, with a smiling, sonsy face, richly liveried; he held a coachman's whip in one hand, but in the other what might have been a scalpel, or small knife; almost concealed behind his back hung a leather bottle; obviously this guest was feeling no thirst.

Davies not only picks up the orientation of any painter but also emulates many of the distinguishing traits of mannerism, the school of painting that captures the imagination and then controls the hand of Francis Cornish. This vocabulary of mannerism dominates the book; and its technique is that of the writer. *What's Bred in the Bone* is a narrative embodiment of the mannerist manner. The very structure suggests some of the features. Mannerism, according to Jacques Bousquet, relies on elongation, a device Davies applies to figures just as the mannerist painters did.

Francis Cornish repeatedly looks at his long face in mirrors; and when he visits relatives in Cornwall, he is aware that all the family faces have the same elongation, or what he calls on one occasion a horse face. The bride, groom, and parents in *The Marriage at Cana* all have the elongated face: "Their faces seemed to be male and female versions of the same features: a long head, prominent nose, and light eyes." Faces in this style are essentially obligatory in mannerism; thus, what Davies does with architectonics is probably more noteworthy. The book delineates in painterly detail the early life of Francis Cornish but runs summarily through the second half. Davies uses the foreshortening effected by the mannerists on the postwar career of Francis, thus elongating his early life in time, detail, length, and number and fullness of supporting characters. The elongation exposes meaning; among other things, it illuminates what's bred in the bone. Because what's bred in the bone won't fade from the flesh, the foreshortened presentation of the last 30 or 35 years is appropriate. Nothing is lost.

Mannerism also shows a tendency toward cubism, an extreme clarity of design and a tendency to include architectural elements that constitute a frame within a frame. Davies is very much the mannerist in this respect. Davies's frame surrounds Darcourt's frame, which surrounds the Maimas-Zadkiel frame of the major narrative that surrounds Cornish's painting, which itself is a triptych with the two side panels framing the couple on whom the light falls in the central panel. Creating the effect of another frame around the painting is the horoscope Ruth records. That portrait is a narrative of biography within the other narratives of biography. A diagram of *What's Bred in the Bone,* showing its structure from above, would expose a series of boxes within boxes all leading to a painting that some would call a fake and some would call the final truth. The elaborate and ambiguous triptych at the center is a puzzle. Similarly, Franzsepp Wurtenberger writes of mannerist painting as a puzzle, "complicated and many layered."

What's Bred in the Bone opens with a question and ends with the metaphor of chance: "Blow your whistle, Arthur, and let the sport begin." Chance is central in the novel. Francis's mother and grandmother are obsessed with card games and play to win. At Oxford Francis becomes involved with the self-styled revolutionary Buys-Bozzaris, through his ability at bridge. Card games expand into metaphor because Zadok Hoyle functions as father figure, and Francis learns to play the game of life "according to Hoyle." Financial speculation adds another dimension of chance. And coincidences offer the most conspicuous and important manifestations of chance: in Zadok, the father of the Looner, coming to love and care for him; and in Francis Cornish bringing Tancred Saraceni exactly the capacities the older man needs to complete his most nearly original work. The book combines questions and chance to generate riddles, encourage multiple meanings, and crown ambiguity. The many-leveled narrative is a texture of questions; it provides no easy answers. At the heart of the book is ambiguity: the nexus of truth—the explanation of Francis Cornish—appears to be fake, a painting with provenance in the early sixteenth century.

Cover of Davies's The Lyre of Orpheus.

Like *The Marriage at Cana,* **What's Bred in the Bone** can "give the wiseacres a great deal to chatter about, anatomize, and discuss in articles and even books." That possibilities for different interpretations spread out in a tantalizing array gives Davies a chance to satirize the academic, critics, and criticism. The tradition of satire that lambastes false learning is bred in the bone of Western writers, an inheritance from Swift and Pope. *The Memoirs of Martinus Scriblerus* is another biographical satire that creates a fictional character in order to show how not to write a biography and, specifically, to indict superficial learning and misguided criticisms.

Sketched lightly in the background of **What's Bred in the Bone** always seems to be Robertson Davies himself, who, like a Bronzino figure of Time, Truth, or Irony, hovers and laughs. The satire on scholars, critics, and academics with their egocentric territoriality is never far from the surface of the novel and breaks out in full force in any scene where the art experts gather. The indictment is particularly cutting in the scene in which Ross explains to Francis that the critic, not the creator, understands and finally makes the work of art what it is. The satiric dimension of the narrative indicts scholars and critics as the fakers who create what was not and then perpetuate

trumped-up readings. Saraceni's explications of *The Marriage at Cana* and Ross's historical interpretation of it are fake; and Ross's argument that only critics, not artists, know what the artist meant and what art means, shows the so-called scholar as false creator. Davies's book constitutes another entry into the canon of satiric allegory; and although **What's Bred in the Bone** does not conform in all ways to the definition of satiric allegory, as Ellen Douglass Leyburn formulated it in her book *Satiric Allegory: Mirror of Man,* the term is apt and helpful. *Allegory,* in the noun position, recalls works multilevel in structure, allusive in technique, symbolic in names, and timeless in scope. *Satiric* refers to attitude, Professor Leyburn points out—a stance that in **What's Bred in the Bone** exposes incompetent biographers, self-inflated critics, stick-figure Communist organizers, petty politicians, and religious zealots of any stripe. Like its predecessors in satiric allegory, **What's Bred in the Bone** depends on allusiveness and inclusiveness; like its predecessors, it insinuates many meanings while focusing on vivid, pictorial details.

Throughout the novel Davies both illustrates what is bred in the bone of the fictional protagonist and implements what is bred in the bone of his own historical inheritance as an artist. The work itself fuses on a single literary canvas many old forms and methods: theories of biography, methods of satire, structures of allegory and its accompanying ambiguity, the transformation of alchemy, and the practices and theories of art. Cornish and Davies, protagonist and writer, have the Old Masters of Western culture bred into their bones. What's bred in the bone comes out. (pp. 27-38)

> *Jo Allen Bradham, "Affirming the Artistic Past: The Witness of 'What's Bred in the Bone',"* in *Critique: Studies in Contemporary Fiction, Vol. XXXII, No. 1, Fall, 1990, pp. 27-38.*

George Woodcock   (review date August 1991)

[*In the following review, Woodcock offers a negative appraisal of the fantastical* Murther & Walking Spirits.]

Robertson Davies's theatrical past hangs heavy over his novels, which tend to combine saucily implausible plots with a good deal of creaking stage machinery, a romantic realist manner, and a shameless display of knowledge in some mildly esoteric field. It is a precarious kind of mixture, but sometimes it has worked well, as in **The Rebel Angels,** where the faults of structure are negated by the effrontery and the rhetorical and histrionic skills of the writer. For there always, whatever the characters he manipulates, is Davies himself strutting the stage, Owen Glendower *in parvo* with his melodious Cymric voice as he declaims the elaborate narrative. The ingredients of the plot may vary; the basic recipe does not. And so Davies leaves one always with a curiously contradictory final impression. On one level he resembles those Edwardian novelists—Arnold Bennett or H. G. Wells in his comic moments for example—who woo their mass readerships with social realism laced with fantasy, and on the other he is the kind of frank melodramatist who dominated the Victorian stage in both Britain and North America.

Davies has always traded on Coleridge's good old phrase about the "willing suspension of disbelief" by framing plots so unlikely that once we accept them we accept the rest. But this time, with *Murther & Walking Spirits,* the machinery is so absurd that I am no longer willing to suspend my disbelief, and so my attitude to the rest of the book immediately becomes less trustful. A newspaper man, Gilmartin, finding his wife and one of his colleagues (the newly appointed film critic) *in flagrante delicto,* is coshed and killed by the lover. He finds himself a spirit, following his murderer day after day to the sensational film festival that has just begun. What he finds, seated beside his killer, is that the film shown him is different from the film seen by the living audience. Day after day he is watching a vast family chronicle, a kind of Anglo-Celtic *Buddenbrooks* enacted in Wales and Canada, with a beginning scene in the newly rebellious America of the 1770s.

This is in fact *his* family, one side Dutch-English Loyalists escaping from New York and the other side unsuccessful merchants from an Anglicized Welsh border town—my own childhood country, so I can vouch for the reasonable authenticity of the detail. This is a tale mainly of those 19th-century nightmares, bankruptcy and failure, in which the proud insolvent grandfathers are more interesting than the milder sons in a modern world that supplies fewer opportunities of spectacular downfall—though we do have, after all, our Campeaus! As always with Davies, the urge to romanticize contends with the urge to document, and here the two seem less successfully reconciled than in the earlier novels, for the narrative is more liable to clog into doughiness and the stagy devices (like that film just for Gilmartin) are more unacceptably absurd. Not, by a long shot, the best of Davies!

> *George Woodcock, "Atwood's Dark Parables, Davies's Ballad of Bankruptcy," in* Quill and Quire, *Vol. 57, No. 8, August, 1991, p. 14.*

John Bemrose   (review date 23 September 1991)

[*In the following review, Bemrose examines Davies's treatment in* Murther & Walking Spirits *of the relationship between past and present, a theme that Bemrose asserts is common to all of Davies's works.*]

Robertson Davies has always been fascinated by ancestors, that vast company of the not-quite-dead who live on in photographs and old letters—and in the dreams and personalities of the living. In most of his novels, from *Fifth Business* and *The Manticore* to *What's Bred in the Bone,* he has explored the ways in which the past haunts the present. That theme is partly what makes him such a deeply conservative writer—conservative in the best sense. He knows that the changes that obsess the modern world are often illusory, and that the sense of freedom that comes with speed is a hoax. In his skilful but flawed new novel, *Murther & Walking Spirits,* he makes clear that many of the voices that clamor at the edge of consciousness, many of the problems that dog the living, are the legacy of the ghostly line of men and women long gone into the earth.

Murther & Walking Spirits pushes Davies's emphasis on the past to a comic extreme, beginning with the novel's marvellous first sentence: "I was never so amazed in my life as when the Sniffer drew his concealed weapon from its case and struck me to the ground, stone dead." The speaker is Connor (Gil) Gilmartin, entertainment editor of a Toronto daily. "The Sniffer" is Randal Allard Going, a film and drama critic for the same paper. When Gil surprises his own wife and the Sniffer in bed together, the Sniffer jumps up and kills him. Now a ghost, Gil follows his murderer into a film festival that Going is covering. But he does not see the same images that Going does. Instead, he witnesses a hallucinatory series of films portraying the lives of his own ancestors.

Meanwhile, Gil carries on a very funny posthumous battle with Going. Unused to his new ghostly powers, Gil wonders how he can haunt his killer. He does not want to be the traditional "crude spectre . . . discovered squatting by the fireside when people enter rooms." Besides, he reflects, Going has no fireplace, and "I shall certainly not make a fool of myself squatting by his thermostat."

Such impish humor is largely confined to the Going plot line. The actual film epic of Gil's forbears—which takes up most of the book—is more sombre, but eminently readable. Indeed, Davies is a born storyteller who could probably spin a good yarn out of tying his own shoe. And his language, while never particularly original, pours out of him like eloquence from a Welsh preacher: it is easy to be carried comfortably forward on its endless tide.

Such fluency is necessary since *Murther & Walking Spirits* covers a good 200 years. Oddly, the book says almost nothing about Gil's mother and *her* ancestors: a rather major omission in what purports to explain a man's past. The ancestors who count in the narrative are Gil's father, Brochwel, and the two family lines, Welsh and United Empire Loyalist, from which he is descended. The Loyalist saga begins with Anna Gage, the widow of a British officer in the American Revolution. Escaping by canoe to Canada, she becomes the matriarch of a long line of farmers. The other side of the family, the Welsh Gilmartins, are staunch Methodists and cloth-trade men. After a family bankruptcy, Gil's grandfather, Rhodri, emigrates to Canada, where he eventually becomes a newspaper magnate.

With so much ground to cover—so many failures, romances, brave deeds and family secrets—it is hardly surprising that *Murther & Walking Spirits* seems more like a collection of story fragments than a fully realized novel. Yet many of the stories stick in the mind. One of the best concerns Thomas Gilmartin, a Methodist preacher in the remotest hills of Wales. Trapped by a band of foulmouthed brigands, he convinces them that *real* cursing is not a matter of using dirty words, but of condemning the godless to damnation. Davies commonly illuminates such tales with his wide knowledge of social history. He can build an entire anecdote on long-forgotten customs—such as people's habit, in pre-central-heating days, of making love with their clothes on.

Yet, despite its learning, epigrammatic wit and narrative

drive, something essential is missing from Davies's novel. Gil's experience of his ancestors gives him, he claims, "a sense of life more poignant and more powerful than anything I ever knew when I was a living man." Reading *Murther & Walking Spirits,* however, does not reproduce that feeling. Gil—and Davies—seem to float above the novel's events with an overly cool detachment. What they observe is always interesting, but only rarely moving. A strange, invisible barrier separates *Murther & Walking Spirits* from the quick of life. So much of it is energetically and gracefully told, yet its characters are ghostly, half-realized caricatures: the heat of those past generations has evaporated.

> John Bemrose, "The Living Dead: A Master's Ghost Story Spans Generations," in Maclean's Magazine, *Vol. 104, No. 38, September 23, 1991, p. 68.*

Adam Mars-Jones   (review date 27 September 1991)

[*In the review below, Mars-Jones offers a mixed assessment of* Murther & Walking Spirits.]

Robertson Davies has a high regard for ghost stories, going so far as to say in one essay that few authors of any consequence die without leaving at least one behind them. He himself is no mean provoker of gooseflesh, and the title of his new novel [*Murther & Walking Spirits*] promises a fuller working of that vein. The epigraph, from Samuel Butler (*Hudibras* Butler, not *Erewhon* Butler), strongly endorses the promise: "Printers find by experience that one Murther is worth two Monsters, and at least three Walking Spirits . . . But where Murthers and Walking Spirits meet, there is no other narrative can come near it." The first sentence of the book then clinches the matter: "I was never so amazed in my life as when the Sniffer drew his concealed weapon from its case and struck me to the ground, stone dead." What an author promises three times is guaranteed. It is a ghost story.

Not quite. Davies's prose has always possessed a certain sprightly swing, and the opening of *Murther & Walking Spirits* is suitably rollicking (Davies must be one of the few contemporary novelists who would welcome the adjective). But Connor Gilmartin, the dead narrator, turns out to be a Spirit less Walking than Sitting, and the book takes on a correspondingly sedentary quality. Gilmartin finds himself accompanying his murderer, a critic on the *Colonial Advocate,* to a film festival.

At first, this seems to be the metaphysical consequence of his last living thoughts being devoted to Randal Allard Going, alias the Sniffer. The *Bhagavad Gita* warns—and an erudite friend of Gilmartin's has passed the suggestion on to him—that the dead attain the state they were thinking of at the moment of their transition. The film festival, though, turns out to have different programmes for the living critic and for the dead man who, in life, was his editor. The Sniffer sees, for instance, Paradjanov's *Shadows of Our Forgotten Ancestors,* but Gilmartin sees his ancestors in person. He sees films that, he gradually realizes, tell the story of his lineage, or one side of it, variously Scottish, Welsh and Dutch, from the eighteenth century on.

Death, as the narrator remarks, is full of surprises. There is an undoubted beauty in the idea of death as not only a dispossession—Gilmartin is aware of the doings of his unfaithful wife and of his murderer, but cannot communicate with them—but also the coming into an inheritance. The film festival of the spirit, however, takes up four-fifths of the book, and it begins to look as if this novel, its genre so unambiguously announced, is actually a family saga dressed in a white sheet rather than a ghost story proper.

The problem is not that the pageant is insubstantial; rather the reverse. Davies materializes the past with all its furniture, literal and metaphorical—its politics, its slang. Within each section, each "film", his ambition is to make the past immediate, using the narrator's intervention to point out, for instance, that eighteenth-century characters fleeing by canoe past landscapes of rugged beauty have a pre-Romantic response to mountains, or that doughnuts at a particular period were still called "fried cakes".

The book's overall structure, though, requires the narrator to be overwhelmed emotionally by his genetic past, and this is likely to have a lower order of reality for the reader. Davies divides his talents between making a past world stand four-square before us—solid households, their keyholes cleaned once a week with an oiled feather—and filtering that world through a dead mind, open to emotion as it never was in life. His great success in the first task entails mild failure in the second.

At least one of the sections, "The Land Of Lost Content", contains a strong autobiographical element. Davies's father, like his narrator's grandfather, bought on his retirement a large house in Wales, Belem Manor in the novel, Leighton Hall in fact. The fictional character strikes a bargain with the two countries, Canada and Britain, in an attempt to stave off a double dose of death duties, but dies before the stipulated period of residence is up. The fictional house boasts a number of the real house's treasures—Victorian garden statuary, an unusual tower clock—and in the account of the auction that disperses them, there can be detected a certain stoic pain. By the same token, there is no sense, such as the book's overarching structure calls for, of disavowed feeling flooding an unsuspecting narrator.

Murther & Walking Spirits is finely written and always entertaining. Even a minor character, like the ineffectual medium Mrs Salenius, gets the benefit of some first-rate phrase-making: she speaks English "in a quiet, regretful voice, the voice, as it were, of Garbo, speaking through a mouthful of chocolate".

The sections are variably successful, the best perhaps being an account ("Of Water and the Holy Spirit") of a Wesleyan taking on a gang of hostile Welsh brigands with storytelling, a cursing competition and only then, having exhausted them, with preaching. "Scenes From A Marriage", a portrait of an unhappy household done in four contrasting interior monologues, is the least dynamic part of the book, for all the accuracy of its evocation. But what prevents *Murther & Walking Spirits* from being top-flight Robertson Davies is less the variability of its episodes than the relative weakness of the thread that ties them together, which lacks something of the infinite holding properties of ectoplasm.

> *Adam Mars-Jones, "Death at the Festival of the Spirit," in* The Times Literary Supplement, *No. 4617, September 27, 1991, p. 24.*

FURTHER READING

Biography

Peterman, Michael. *Robertson Davies.* Boston: Twayne Publishers, 1986, 78 p.
> Biographical and critical study that attempts to present Davies as a "many-sided writer . . . as man of letters."

Criticism

Burgess, Anthony. "Alter-Ego's Joke Book." *Observer,* No. 10208 (31 May 1987): 23.
> Mixed review of *The Papers of Samuel Marchbanks* which Burgess characterizes as a "frivolous bedside book" of farce and "British facetiousness."

Clute, John. "Forging a Life." *The Times Literary Supplement,* No. 4460 (23 September 1988): 1040.
> Praises *The Lyre of Orpheus* as "the most Canadian book Davies has written in decades," but finds it is the weakest book in *The Cornish Trilogy.*

Danziger, Jeff. "Ruminations of an Arch Curmudgeon." *The Christian Science Monitor* 78, No. 159 (14 July 1986): 21-2.
> Positive assessment of *The Papers of Samuel Marchbanks.*

Davis, J. Madison, ed. *Conversations with Robertson Davies.* Jackson: University Press of Mississippi, 1989, 285 p.
> Collects interviews conducted with Davies between 1963 and 1988. Topics include Davies's career, his interest in Freudian and Jungian psychology, and Canada's search for a national identity.

Deveson, Richard. "Early *espièglerie.*" *The Times Literary Supplement,* No. 4411 (16 October 1987): 1137.
> Argues that the satirical essays collected in *The Papers of Samuel Marchbanks* are most valuable when read as a precursor to Davies's later and better-known works.

French, Sean. "Third Time Unlucky." *New Statesman & Society* 1, No. 19 (14 October 1988): 35.
> Mixed review which faults *The Lyre of Orpheus* for its "garrulousness," sentimentality, and blatant mythic parallels.

Fuller, Edmund. "The Canadian Curmudgeon." *The Wall Street Journal* CCVIII, No. 10 (15 July 1986): 26.
> Positive assessment of *The Papers of Samuel Marchbanks.*

Godard, Barbara. "Robertson Davies's Dialogic Imagination." *Essays on Canadian Writing,* No. 34 (Spring 1987): 64-80.
> Applies Mikhail Bakhtin's theory of the novel, which emphasizes the dynamics of dialogic and monologic discourse, to Davies's fiction.

Guttridge, Peter. "Kindred Spirits." *The Sunday Times,* No. 8719 (29 September 1991): 12.
> Interview in which Davies briefly discusses *Murther & Walking Spirits,* his life, career, and affinity for metaphysics and psychology.

Hamilton, Janet. "Davies Completes His Cornish Trilogy." *Quill & Quire* 54, No. 8 (August 1988): 24.
> Positive assessment of *The Lyre of Orpheus* which views the novel's predominant theme as "the relationship between what one produces and who and what one is . . . and how the past gives meaning to the present."

Harvey, Elizabeth D. "Property, Digestion, and Intertext in Robertson Davies's *The Rebel Angels.*" *English Studies in Canada* XVI, No. 1 (March 1990): 91-106.
> Analyzes how the self-reflexive processes and metaphors of digestion, assimilation, ownership, and transformation are depicted in *The Rebel Angels* and reflect Davies's preoccupation with individual, national, and artistic identity.

James, Geoffrey. "Moonshine and Masterful Storytelling." *Maclean's* 101, No. 38 (12 September 1988): 116.
> Positive assessment of *The Lyre of Orpheus,* which, James says, defines *The Cornish Trilogy* as an "extended meditation on the nature of artistic creation."

Kakutani, Michiko. "Arthurian Legend Wrapped in a Tale of Hoffmann." *The New York Times* CXXXVIII, No. 47733 (28 December 1988): C24.
> Delineates Davies's use of mythic archetypes and Arthurian legend in *The Lyre of Orpheus.*

Klinkenborg, Verlyn. "Mr. Myth." *The New Republic* 200, No. 17 (24 April 1989): 38-40.
> Compares *The Lyre of Orpheus* to Davies's other fiction and characterizes it as the typical Davies novel: a romance compromised by Davies's dependence on myth.

McWilliam, Candia. "Cornish Pastiche." *Observer,* No. 10278 (2 October 1988): 42.
> Asserts that the predominant themes and metaphors in *The Lyre of Orpheus* derive not from Arthurian legend but from opera.

Mills, John. "Robertson Davies (1913-)." In *Canadian Writers and Their Works, Fiction Series, Vol. 6,* edited by Robert Lecker, Jack David, and Ellen Quigley, pp. 19-78. Toronto: ECW Press, 1985.
> Biographical and critical survey of Davies's career through *The Deptford Trilogy.*

Monk, Patricia. "Somatotyping, Scatomancy, and Sophia: The Relation of Body and Soul in the Novels of Robertson Davies." *English Studies in Canada* XII, No. 1 (March 1986): 79-100.
> Argues that the relationship between the physical and the spiritual is present in all of Davies's fiction but most fully realized in *The Rebel Angels.*

——. "Robertson Davies Recently." *Dalhousie Review* 66, No. 3 (Fall 1986): 363-67.
> Relates the theme of *What's Bred in the Bone* and *The Papers of Samuel Marchbanks* to what Samuel March-

banks has termed the "savage and often melancholy" nature of wisdom.

Rollow, David. "Lying beneath the Surface." *The Spectator* 261, No. 8361 (8 October 1988): 35-6.

>Mixed review of *The Lyre of Orpheus* which praises Davies's use of myth but faults Davies for being more interested in "stagey effects" than in ideas.

Rose, Phyllis. "King Arthur in Toronto." *The New York Times Book Review* (8 January 1989): 7.

>Extols *The Lyre of Orpheus* for its focus on "the risks of art versus the self-satisfaction of Philistia . . . [and] the eternal forms of human nature versus the changing garb of history," but laments that Davies's preoccupation with myth results in superficial characters.

Twigg, Alan. "World of Wonders: Robertson Davies." In his *For Openers: Conversations with 24 Canadian Writers,* pp. 31-44. Madiera Park, British Columbia: Harbour Publishing, 1981.

>Interview in which Davies discusses his childhood and education, his role and identity as a Canadian writer, and the relationship between religion and psychology.

Tyler, Anne. "Robertson Davies' Pictures from an Institution." *The Washington Post Book World* XVIII, No. 51 (18 December 1988): 3.

>Asserts that the development of plot and character in *The Lyre of Orpheus* is hampered by Davies's fascination with the academic world and its preoccupation with theoretical discourse.

Additional coverage of Davies's life and career is contained in the following sources published by Gale Research: *Contemporary Authors,* **Vols. 33-36, rev. ed.;** *Contemporary Authors New Revision Series,* **Vol. 17;** *Contemporary Literary Criticism,* **Vols. 2, 7, 13, 25, 42;** *Dictionary of Literary Biography,* **Vol. 68;** *Major 20th-Century Writers***; and** *World Literature Criticism.***

Shelby Foote

1916-

American nonfiction writer, novelist, and short story writer.

The following entry provides an overview of Foote's life and career.

INTRODUCTION

Foote is highly regarded both for his expansive historical work *The Civil War: A Narrative* and for his novels and short stories concerning the heritage of the American South. He expressed his view on the relationship between literature and history in his foreword to the first volume of *The Civil War:* "The novelist and the historian are seeking the same thing: the truth—not a different truth: the same truth—only they reach it, or try to reach it, by different routes." Although frequently considered a regionalist writer whose works evoke the traditions and the consciousness of the American South, Foote is praised for the universality of his vivid settings and characterizations.

Foote was born into a distinguished Southern family in Greenville, Mississippi, a city recognized as the cultural and literary center of the Delta region. As a young boy, he moved frequently throughout the region with his parents. When his father died suddenly in 1924, Shelby and his mother returned to Greenville, where he later met the writer William Alexander Percy and became close friends with his nephew Walker Percy. Foote attended the University of North Carolina in 1935. There he wrote his first stories for the school's literary journal *Carolina Magazine* but spent most of his time independently reading modern and classical literature. He dropped out of college in 1937 to write his first novel, a work derivative of James Joyce which was rejected by publishers. In 1939 Foote entered the Mississippi National Guard and was sent to Northern Ireland. After leaving the military base without permission to meet his girlfriend in Belfast, Foote was court-martialed and discharged from the army in 1944. He returned to the United States and worked briefly as a reporter in New York City before enlisting in the United States Marine Corps in 1945. Following his release that year, he returned to Mississippi, where he worked various jobs and continued to pursue his writing interests.

Foote drew upon the draft of his unpublished novel for his first short story, "Flood Burial," which was published in the *Saturday Evening Post* in 1946. Portions of the book were also reworked for his first published novel, *Tournament.* Devoted to maintaining a strict writing schedule, Foote entered a highly prolific period between 1946 and 1954, publishing four novels and a short fiction collection. Following the success of his historical novel *Shiloh,* he was contacted to write a brief history of the Civil War in 1954.

Twenty years and over 1.5 million words later, he completed the three volumes that comprise *The Civil War.* After finishing this immense task, he returned to fiction and published the novel *September September* in 1978. Interest in Foote was renewed when he appeared as a commentator in Ken Burns's adaptation of *The Civil War,* which aired on PBS in 1991 to wide critical and popular acclaim.

Much of Foote's fiction, including the novels *Tournament, Follow Me Down,* and *Love in a Dry Season,* and his short fiction collection *Jordan County; A Landscape in Narrative,* are set in the fictional locale of Jordan County, Mississippi, and delineate themes associated with Southern history. While not as frequently studied by American critics as his historical work, Foote's fiction is nevertheless praised as an impressive analysis of the American South, and French critics have written numerous studies of his fiction, comparing the interlocking settings and characters in his fictional world of Jordan County to those of William Faulkner's Yoknapatawpha County. In his first novel, *Tournament,* Foote chronicles the transformation of Hugh Bart from successful landowner to destitute gambler following the sale of his plantation. This same plantation appears in subsequent novels, and the lives of its various residents mirror social changes of the South throughout the nineteenth and twentieth centuries. Foote's thriller *September September* also explores themes based on the importance of history. The novel concerns three white Southerners who kidnap the grandson of a wealthy black man. Utilizing such incidents as the racial integration crisis in Little Rock, Arkansas, and the launching of Sputnik in 1957 as a backdrop for his story, Foote relates factual events of the period to his characters' racial attitudes, creating a microcosm of American society during the 1950s.

In his historical novel *Shiloh,* Foote dramatically recounts the circumstances surrounding the crucial Civil War battle of Shiloh by interweaving a series of monologues spoken by Confederate and Union narrators who convey various perspectives on the battle. *Shiloh* has frequently been compared to Stephen Crane's *The Red Badge of Courage* for its graphic fictional treatment of modern warfare, and several critics consider Foote's work a more complex depiction of the multitudinous aspects of war. Commentators have recognized Foote's ability to create memorable characterizations of both fictional and historical figures of the battle, frequently citing Nathan Bedford Forrest as the novel's hero. Recounting the moving description of Forrest's final efforts to defeat his Northern enemy, Thomas H. Landess wrote: "In this episode Foote transcends the view of modern war as a mass movement of faceless bodies and pushes the action of the novel toward the level of pure epic, the creation of a mythic hero who embodies the ultimate virtues valued by society."

The Civil War is noted for its balanced treatment of all fronts of the American Civil War: northern, southern, eastern, and western. Foote patterned his work on Homer's *Iliad* and Marcel Proust's *A la recherche du temps perdu* (*Remembrance of Things Past*), hoping to evince their grand-scale significance. Foote's mastery of such features as character, plot, setting, and narrative voice—traits of fiction not traditionally integrated into historical writing—distinguish *The Civil War* as narrative history. Characterization is considered a key element of *The Civil War,* and Foote has been lauded for his insightful depictions of such principal figures as Jefferson Davis and Abraham Lincoln. Through precise and telling visual descriptions as well as a series of revealing anecdotes, he presents balanced and sympathetic portraits of these key figures as well as ordinary soldiers and lesser known military and political characters. The work's structure has also garnered praise. In Foote's nonpartisan narrative, he creates a sequence of events in which two occurrences take place simultaneously while a synchronous reference is also made to a past episode, thus evoking a panoramic view of the entire conflict.

While many critics have lauded *The Civil War* as the most impressive study of that conflict yet written, some detractors have questioned the intellectual merit of the work, maintaining that because Foote concentrated on military aspects of the war, he ignored important political, social, and economic factors. Other critics have focused on the comprehensiveness of Foote's work, which, while predominantly focused on the battles and the men who fought them, is so far-reaching in scope that all components of the war are incorporated into the narrative. Foote did not intend to advance a thesis in writing *The Civil War,* but rather, in the tradition of such great narrative historians as Thucydides and Gibbon, sought to create a work of literature that accurately recreates the complete story of a decisive historical period. Unlike studies written by academic historians, *The Civil War* is not documented by footnotes. However, most critics—including professional historians—do not question the validity of the factual information contained in the text. Foote achieved accuracy and realism in his work by gleaning data from an abundance of established historical sources as well as by studying photographs. He also attended to such nuances as the weather and conditions of a battlefield, visiting each field he wrote about at the same time of month that the battle had been fought. James M. Cox voiced the opinion of numerous critics when he stated that "the authenticity of [Foote's] narrative, coming from its comprehensiveness, its discipline, its clarity, its graphic conception and vision, and its capacity both to see and hear the action of the moving forces, produces a living and informed faith in the reader: living, because the reader will never have felt the war so vividly and intimately; informed, because he will never have known or seen it so illuminatingly."

PRINCIPAL WORKS

Tournament (novel) 1949
*Follow Me Down (novel) 1950
*Love in a Dry Season (novel) 1951
Shiloh (novel) 1952
*Jordan County: A Landscape in Narrative (short stories and novellas) 1954
The Civil War: A Narrative. 3 vols. (history) 1958-74
September September (novel) 1978

*These works were published as *Three Novels* in 1964.

CRITICISM

Michael Ravenna (review date 25 September 1949)

[*In the following review of* Tournament, *Ravenna praises Foote's delineation of the past and evocation of the Mississippi Delta region.*]

It is manifestly impossible to write a serious book about Mississippi and ignore the past. And tell the truth, that is. Yesterday and today are too much tangled together. John and William Faulkner, Edward Kimbrough, Eudora Welty, W. A. Percy, Hodding Carter, David Cohn and a passel of others have proved that. Now Shelby Foote of Greenville, Miss., has written a first novel that proves it again. It's a good novel, too.

In *Tournament* the main character, Hugh Bart, thinks back over his life and reflects that "to tell it properly would require as much time as had been required to live it." Mr. Foote doesn't take quite that long—indeed, his novel moves swiftly and holds the interest—but to explain Hugh Bart and his period, he does find it necessary to go back in time to years before Bart was born and to explore many facets of Delta life.

Bart, a boy of 18, came to the rich farming land of the Delta around Reconstruction times to make his fortune. He was likable, courageous and willing to work, and he made the fortune. He farmed a little, served a term as sheriff. Eventually he acquired the finest plantation in the county and married a daughter of one of the most prominent families. Yet Bart, for reasons which he did not understand himself, remained a lonely man. His loneliness was increased by his disappointment in his children—none of whom was capable of carrying on what Bart had created.

Although Bart, for the most part, seems strangely untouched by the hardships, rewards, disappointments and achievement of his life, it is not for any lack of attention to them on the part of Mr. Foote. He gives us the facts and searches behind the obvious incidents for the less obvious relationships that will explain them. This includes Bart's background in the Black Prairie of east Mississippi, the coming of the first settlers into the Delta wilderness long before Bart's time, his adventures as sheriff, fairly exact details on how a plantation is run and financed, Bart's brief courtship and his relations with his wife and children and his part in the social and business life of town and county.

It is a moving, many-sided narrative, in which the Delta, perhaps, comes more alive than Hugh Bart. Mr. Foote controls his material well. In a novel of this sort, chronology and incident might well have gotten out of hand; but the writing is clear, the narrative well pruned. This is generally true in spite of occasional lapses into such things as "incult" (to describe a beard), "impervious stasis," "catabasis" and at least one sentence thirty-two lines long. (But, after all, Mr. Foote is Mr. Faulkner's neighbor).

While it cannot be said that Mr. Foote has made use of any new or striking material, he has demonstrated that it is still possible to write of his region freshly and effectively.

> *Michael Ravenna, "Mississippi Delta," in* The New York Times Book Review, *September 25, 1949, p. 30.*

Charles J. Rolo (review date May 1952)

[*In the following review of* Shiloh *excerpted below, Rolo commends Foote's realistic and engaging portrayal of the Battle of Shiloh.*]

Shiloh, a Civil War novel, is focused on the bloody battle fought on April 6 and 7 of 1862. The author, Shelby Foote, is a young writer with three novels behind him, the best of which was *Follow Me Down. Shiloh* is a better one: a fine accomplishment.

"Historical characters in this book," Mr. Foote notes, "speak the words they spoke and do the things they did at Shiloh. Many of the minor incidents also occurred, even when here they are assigned to fictional persons." But though the action sticks closely to historical facts, *Shiloh* bears the stamp of a genuinely creative talent. The combat episodes have the realism which only art can impart to reality.

Mr. Foote unfolds the various phases of the battle through the eyes of a succession of officers and men on both sides, each speaking in the first person singular. He weaves in life sketches of the leading generals and brings them sharply before the reader's eye in the course of the action. The novel does not take sides, and strictly speaking it has no hero—though the swashbuckling cavalryman, Forrest, with his magnificent charges, was possibly the hero of Shiloh. The author's achievement is that he has fused the landscape, the weather, the generalship, the fighting, the atrocious suffering of the wounded, the thoughts and feelings of the living, the shattered bodies of the dead, into a single dramatic entity which takes possession of the reader. (pp. 81-2)

> *Charles J. Rolo, in an originally unsigned essay titled "Men Fighting," in* The Atlantic Monthly, *Vol. 189, No. 5, May, 1952, pp. 81-2.*

Robert L. Gale (essay date January 1955)

[*Gale is an American educator and critic who has written numerous studies of American literature. In the following essay, he negatively reviews the short stories of* Jordan County, *arguing that their interlocking plots, characters, themes, and use of description and dialogue are derivative of Foote's novels.*]

Shelby Foote's *Jordan County* is a collection of seven crisp, often summary stories of various lengths leading back in time from the present to the late eighteenth century and revealing a parade of tragic people against the almost changeless backdrop of the Delta. The narratives in order are **"Rain Down Home,"** *Ride Out,* **"A Marriage Portion,"** *Child by Fever,* **"The Freedom Kick,"** **"Pillar of Fire,"** and **"The Sacred Mound."**

The book should have been entitled *Jordan County Continued* (or *Revisited*), since all of the novels of Shelby Foote to date, except *Shiloh* (1952), have interlocking episodes involving persons in mythical Jordan County (really Washington County), and even in *Shiloh* Jordan County is mentioned and there is a Colonel Jordan. *Tournament* (1949), Mr. Foote's splendid first novel, seems to have grown out of two short stories. One is **"Flood Burial"** (1946), in which Asa Bart tries to help a dying man, Major Henry Dubose, who is endangered by a flood. And the other is **"The Merchant of Bristol"** (1947), which concerns the victimizing of a businessman in Bristol (really Greenville), the main city in Jordan County: the merchant shoots himself when he cannot promptly repay a loan to Lawrence Tilden, agent for the innocent Asa Bart. Asa is renamed Hugh Bart and becomes the hero of *Tournament,* in one chapter of which, called "Solitaire" after Bart's plantation home, the merchant's story is retold with little change; then in a later chapter eccentric Major Dubose's pathetic story is repeated almost verbatim from **"Flood Burial."** In *Follow Me Down* (1950), Mr. Foote's second novel and surely his best thus far, the murderer is caught because his name and address, "Luther Eustis, Solitaire Plantation," were seen on the flyleaf of his Bible. Then in his next novel, *Love in a Dry Season* (1951), Mr. Foote introduces Amy Carruthers, who has inherited Briartree, a plantation similar to Solitaire and also near Lake Jordan, from an aunt whose lover a generation earlier was quite rightly killed by our friend Hugh Bart. The episode, touched on in *Love in a Dry Season* was elaborately told in *Tournament* and then summarized in *Follow Me Down.* Furthermore, in *Love in a Dry Season* we also meet Mrs. Carruthers' lover, Harley Drew, who works in Bristol's leading bank, now run by Lawrence Tilden, Jr.

Such plot links connecting Foote's novels are too numerous to list, nor do they stop before we get to *Jordan County.* For example, imbedded in *Tournament* is an incomplete summary of the career of Isaac Jameson, who was the first white explorer and settler in the Lake Jordan area and who built palatial Solitaire, gutted during the Civil War. In *Jordan County* the story **"Pillar of Fire"** is an amplified retelling of Jameson's life, which ends when Union Army reprisal troops under Colonel Frisbie burn the mansion and watch the stricken owner die on his lawn. Also, when Luther Eustis, the murderer in *Follow Me Down,* is assigned a cell in the Bristol jail, a local reporter who comes to interview him recalls that a Negro cornet player nine years before left the same cell to walk to his electrocution. *Ride Out,* which originally appeared in 1947 in the *Saturday Evening Post* as **"Tell Them Goodby"** and is the second chapter of *Jordan County,* relates the story of Duff Conway, the brilliant Negro jazz artist. Late in the narrative Duff returns from the North to his mother Nora, planning to die of the tuberculosis which has almost silenced his cornet, but instead shoots a gambler in a dispute over a worthless, sensual Negress, and is tried and executed. Incidentally, Duff's mother Nora works for Amanda Barcroft, the odd, frustrated spinster in *Love in a Dry Season* whom Harley Drew originally remains in Bristol to wed for her probable inheritance; and Jeff Carruthers, the blind husband of erotic Amy in the same novel, finds much-needed solace in Duff's recorded music. Finally, several minor characters link most of Foote's work. One is Dr. Clinton, precise and confident as he prescribes for Hugh Bart in *Tournament* but worried and faltering as he attends Ella, pregnant wife of Hector Sturgis III, the grotesque hero of *Child by Fever* which is the fourth and by far the longest sequence in *Jordan County.* Similarly, the Reverend Mr. Clinkscales marries both Bart of *Tournament* and Sturgis of *Child by Fever.* And Colonel Frisbie, who orders Solitaire burned in **"Pillar of Fire,"** had an eye shot out at Shiloh and huddled among the stragglers, seemingly saying, "If you wont tell on me, I wont on you"; precisely the same line appears in Foote's 1952 fictional *Shiloh.* But the busiest as well as undoubtedly the most gruesome minor character shuttling from novel to novel is Mr. Barnes, Bristol's pushing undertaker, whose nickname "Light-Hearse Harry" is repeatedly explained to us. It is "Light-Hearse Harry" who in *Follow Me Down* arrives almost with the police after the murder

victim is found. He also is quickly on hand in *Love in a Dry Season* when Amanda's long-dead father is discovered. And he efficiently takes charge in *Child by Fever* when Ella's body is discovered and later when Hector's suicide in the attic is tardily detected. (Foote appears to have a decomposition obsession.)

Not only does *Jordan County* repeat plot and character elements from much of its author's previous fiction, it repeats description, dialogue, and imagery as well. For instance, in **"Rain Down Home,"** which opens *Jordan County,* as the confused World War Two veteran is eyeing the Bristol signboard erected in memory of his comrades who died, we are informed that ugly talk prevented the naming of whites and Negroes together. But in *Follow Me Down* the memorial was far more graphically described. In **"The Freedom Kick,"** the short and bitter satire appearing in fifth place in *Jordan County,* the Negro narrator speaks ominously of the Kluxers immediately after the Civil War: "They burnt crosses every night all round us, and a man who'll burn what he prays to, he'll burn anything." But the same point was sufficiently made in **"The Merchant of Bristol."** In *Child by Fever* the night-clerk gossips about Ella: "Let me tell you, Pete, if thats blueblood I'm glad I didn't have any to pass on to my kids." But in *Tournament* a barber has already said of Hugh Bart's daughter-in-law Kate: "If thats blueblood I'm glad I didn't have none to pass on to my daughters." And both Ella and Kate are identically pictured as flirtatiously walking past barber shop and pool hall windows "wobbly on high heels," etc. (*Jordan County; Tournament*). Perhaps a more serious instance of Mr. Foote's borrowing from himself is contained in his description of Katy, Jameson's wife in **"Pillar of Fire,"** as her wildness ends following the death of her first-born (Foote has too many babies born dying or malformed):

> Five months after the death of the infant, this second and furious period ceased. It did not play out: it just stopped, gave way to her original placative manner. The frenzy was finished, gone. She became calm again, almost bovine. Isaac recognized the symptoms, the quiet, careful movements, the attitude of inward listening. . . .

But in *Tournament* we may read this description of the change in Bart's wife Florence, who oddly is the granddaughter of Jameson:

> Not four months after the death of the child, this second and furious period ended. It did not play out: it just stopped, gave way to her former passive manner. The frenzy was finished, gone. She became meek again, almost bovine. Bart recognized the symptoms, her careful movements, her attitude of inward listening. . . .

And in *Ride Out* it is written that Duff Conway's horn leads the reform school orchestra, "the other instruments falling in behind . . . like leaves sucked into the rearward vacuum of a speeding truck"; but *Love in a Dry Season* similarly images a rich widow and her Continental lover: "She had him in tow; he was being sucked along in her rearward vacuum, like a leaf behind a speeding truck." Finally, we are I think too monotonously told by Mr. Foote of hair glinting like brass, of eyes slapped by sunlight, of Jordan Countians who yell "Yair!" . . .

Jordan County, then, is the latest of Shelby Foote's fictionalized pictures of the Delta he knows from his Greenville days. Its originality lies neither in characterization nor in description, both of which are superior in his earlier works. The freshness is instead in the unique trip through the same place back, back in time. But the end of the journey is most disquieting, for **"The Sacred Mound,"** the closing story, contains a hypnotic scene of horrible violence, too typical of Foote, so nauseous that the final tiny note of hope and tolerance is almost unheard.

Mr. Foote is now at a crucial step in his career. He insists that he will not stop, but that he plans to write a novel a year; we may therefore assume that he will either continue to exploit the now evidently overworked vein of Bristol or begin digging elsewhere. His interviewers speak of a new novel from him, to be entitled *Two Gates to the City,* about Bristol folk in 1948; and it is reported that he is going to center some fiction at Memphis, his present home. Let us hope that the work to come will be more original than much of *Jordan County.* (pp. 56-60)

> *Robert L. Gale, "Shelby Foote Repeats Himself: A Review Article," in* The Journal of Mississippi History, *Vol. XVII, No. 1, January, 1955, pp. 56-60.*

[The short story is] a form that's unsatisfactory to me unless it's tied in with other things. Then I can get some interest. But to create a perfect little thing doesn't interest me at all.

—Shelby Foote, in an interview with Evans Harrington,The Mississippi Quarterly, *1971.*

Richard N. Current   (review date 23 November 1958)

[*Current is an American historian and editor. In the following review of the first volume of* The Civil War, *he applauds Foote's efforts to assume the dual role of novelist and historian.*]

Of all the Civil War writings in the centennial harvest now coming, Shelby Foote's projected three-volume work [*The Civil War: A Narrative*] is one of the most ambitious in scope. The first volume, now published, opens with Jefferson Davis' resignation from the Senate and Abraham Lincoln's departure from Springfield, Illinois. It closes—nearly two years and more than 400,000 words later—with Lincoln's "We cannot escape history" message to Congress in December 1862.

In between, the reader is treated to a grand, sweeping narrative made up of many narratives. It includes the course of battle along the entire front, from Chesapeake Bay and the Carolina coast to the Mississippi Valley and the desert of New Mexico. It includes also the political events that bear most pertinently upon the fighting. All the themes are carried forward together, clearly and without confusion, by means of marvelously skillful transitions.

Throughout, the characters and careers of Davis and Lincoln provide a kind of unity in duality. Foote writes:

> In Richmond and in Washington, one hundred miles apart—the same distance as lay between Fairview and Hodgenville, their birthplaces in Kentucky—Davis and Lincoln toiled their long hours, kept their vigils, and sought solutions to problems that were mostly the same but seemed quite different because they saw them in reverse, from opposite directions.

Both of the Presidents are viewed with sympathy and understanding. Davis being pictured as a man of courage and consistency, one who was loyal to those who were loyal to him, one who "sustained them through adversity and unpopularity." Viewed with sympathy also are the officers and men on both sides. The author, a Mississippian, by birth and upbringing, is no biased partisan of the Lost Cause.

Politicians, generals, soldiers—all appear in these pages as unique, living individuals, their appearance and personality convincingly suggested with an economy of descriptive detail. Here, for example, is the boastful General John Pope, as he addressed the Committee on the Conduct of the War before taking his Virginia command:

> He had shaved his cheeks and his upper lip, retaining a spade-shaped chin beard that bobbed and wagged decisively as he spoke, lending weight and point to his utterances and increasing the over-all impression of forcefulness and vigor.

The reader puts down the book with the feeling that he actually has met and known the actors in it. He feels, too, that he has experienced the events they took part in. He has been in battle with them, seen the fire and smoke, felt the shock, heard the shouts and the moans, smelled the dust and afterwards the stench, sensed the exultation, the terror, and the weariness.

This sounds like history written by a novelist, and in fact it is. "Accepting the historian's standards without his paraphernalia"—such as footnotes—"I have employed the novelist's method without his license," Foote explains. "Instead of inventing characters and incidents, I searched them out, and having found them, I took them as they were. Nothing is included here . . . without the authority of documentary evidence which I consider sound." After all, he says, the novelist and the historian are seeking the same truth.

And Foote is as good as his word, or almost as good. Certainly he makes up no conversations, presents no stream-of-consciousness stuff, indulges in no empty "poetic" prose. He writes with transparent honesty.

Yet one may question whether the novelist and the historian, even when both are writing history, are always after quite the same kind of truth. The novelist is interested in the lifelike detail, which often is derived from a single, unsupported source. The historian insists upon the verifiable fact, which usually lacks sharp outlines and specific color, because it has to be somewhat generalized; it has to be reduced to the lowest common denominator of several more or less conflicting sources. The novelist, confronted with various bits of evidence, chooses the one that gives a realistic touch. Then he goes boldly ahead and makes the most of it. For him to hem and haw, as the historian often must, would destroy for the reader the precious sense of verisimilitude.

Choosing his sources by a storyteller's instinct as well as the historian's standard, Foote relates as accepted truth a number of things that historians question or dispute. At Lincoln's inauguration, he says, Stephen A. Douglas took and held the President's tall hat. Once in office, Lincoln knew he must unite the North, "and he knew, too, that the most effective way to do this was to await an act of aggression by the South, exerting in the interim just enough pressure to provoke such an action." During the Sumter crisis he agreed to give up the fort if Virginia would adjourn its secession convention. And after the war Robert E. Lee, when asked who was the ablest Federal general he had opposed, replied: "McClellan, by all odds."

Now, all those propositions are dubious at best, and so are a number of others like them in Foote's narrative. Downright misstatements of fact, however, are few. One of these concerns the Second Confiscation Act, of 1862, regarding which Foote says: "No slave was to be freed by it until the master had been convicted of treason in a Federal court." In fact, as Lincoln himself remarked in objecting to the measure, it would forfeit property, including slave property, "without a conviction of the supposed criminal or a hearing given him in any proceedings."

On the main points Foote probably is as accurate as most historians writing a book of comparable coverage. Certainly he is more interesting. Any one who wants to relive the Civil War, as thousands of Americans apparently do, will go through this volume with pleasure and then await the next one with impatience. And, years from now, when the centennial ephemera have been forgotten, Foote's monumental narrative most likely will continue to be read and remembered as a classic of its kind.

> *Richard N. Current, "A Novelist as Historian Shows Blue and Gray in a Mighty Panorama," in* New York Herald Tribune Book Review, *November 23, 1958, p. 5.*

John Cournos (review date 9 January 1959)

[*Cournos was a Russian-born American novelist, poet, translator, and critic who achieved his greatest notoriety as a novelist during the 1920s. In a review of the first volume of* The Civil War *below, he objects to Foote's deviations from traditional methods of historical writing.*]

The shoemaker should stick to his last, the novelist to his fiction. This reflection is engendered by Mr. Foote's "narrative," or rather by the first third of it (a little matter of

over eight hundred pages), for two more hefty volumes are promised. In an autobiographical note Mr. Foote frankly boasts: "I am a novelist, and what is more I agree with D. H. Lawrence's estimate of the novel as 'the one bright book of life.'" This is a strange confession to make for a youngish Mississippian, already with five novels to his credit, basing his argument on the hypothesis "that the novelist and the historian are seeking the same thing: the truth—not a different truth: the same truth—only they reach it, or try to reach it, by different routes."

This is a fallacious idea, and if scholars permitted themselves to put it into practice we'd be a long way from the truth indeed. What a confusion of thought there is in Mr. Foote's statement: "Accepting the historian's standards without his paraphernalia, I have employed the novelist's methods without his license!" He confesses to having left out the footnotes on the ground that they would "detract from the book's narrative quality. . . ." But footnotes are the very thing the careful reader may want. He may want to know on what authority the author has made this or that statement and has drawn certain conclusions therefrom. For example, quite early in the book we have the insinuation that Lincoln wanted the attack on Fort Sumter, that he had in fact "more or less maneuvered him [Jefferson Davis] into firing the first shot," so that the South, it is averred, would be branded as aggressor "in the eyes of history and Europe." There is nothing in the previous pages, however, to show this to be a fact. Is the Machiavellian idea in the author's own mind, a bit of novelist's license he has promised to shun?

"The novelist's touch"—a phrase which D. H. Lawrence, of all people, used derisively—is ever present. Thus:

> On the one hand there was Davis, "ambitious as Lucifer," with his baleful eyes and bloodless mouth, cerebral and lizard-cold, plotting malevolence into the small hours of the night. On the other there was Lincoln, "the original gorilla," with his shambling walk and sooty face, an ignorant railsplitter catapulted by long-shot politics into an office for which he had neither experience nor the dignity required.

In his portrayal of persons Mr. Foote most reveals his predilection as a novelist. Thus in describing Beauregard: "The Creole's big sad bloodhound eyes were rimmed with angry red and his hands were fluttering as he spoke." And on the same page he refers to Polk's "deep pulpit voice." At times he fascinates with backstage reports of conversations held in both Northern and Southern camps; they would be valuable if he didn't scorn the scholars, and supplied the necessary footnotes of sources to establish their authenticity. (pp. 393-94)

> *John Cournos, "Bright Book of the Civil War," in* The Commonweal, *Vol. LXIX, No. 15, January 9, 1959, pp. 393-94.*

T. Harry Williams (review date 25 December 1963)

[*An American historian who was highly regarded as an authority on the American Civil War, Williams published such works as* Lincoln and the Radicals *(1941),*

Lincoln and His Generals *(1952), and* P. G. T. Beauregard, Napoleon in Gray *(1955), which have been praised for their dramatic retellings of historical events as well as thought-provoking theses. Williams is best remembered, however, for* Huey Long: A Biography *(1969). A comprehensive narrative biography of the flamboyant Depression-era Louisiana politician,* Huey Long *is distinguished as the first biographical study which incorporates oral transcripts as research sources. In the following review of the second volume of* The Civil War, *Williams compares Foote's methods of writing as a novelist with those of academic historians.*]

To open his projected three-volume history of the Civil War, Shelby Foote focused on the tall, thin Mississippian who arose in the Senate on Jan. 21, 1861, to announce that his state had seceded from the Union and he was going with it. The words of Jefferson Davis on that occasion were eloquent and sad, for, though he was a firm secessionist, he could not but regret the dissolution of the old Union.

To open this, the second volume of his massive work, Mr. Foote again focuses on Davis—this time as President of the Confederate States of America, addressing the Mississippi Legislature on Dec. 26, 1862. His tone that day was not sad but solemn. He had been traveling far and talking often and usually well, and when he returned to Richmond on Jan. 5, a very weary man, he felt that his exertions had been worth while. His remarks seemed to have struck fire with the people, and, better than speeches, victories in the field seemed to promise a lift in the country's will to fight on.

There had been several minor successes on both sides of the Mississippi: Lee had again bloodily repulsed a Federal army, this time at Fredericksburg; and, at Murfreesboro in Tennessee, General Bragg reported a triumph that was, however, even then beginning to look dubious. Davis recited these achievements in yet another speech on the night of his arrival home. Mr. Foote skillfully combines the events of Davis' tour, "The Longest Journey," and the battles the President described in his opening chapter. Despite Davis' apparent bright auguries of victory, the reader immediately senses, although the author does not say it, that the doom is on the Confederate cause.

Mr. Foote does not make any predictions because to do so would violate his concept of how history should be written. His favorite practitioners of the art are Tacitus and Thucydides, and his aim is to write narrative history. That is, he wants to set the reader before the scene and the scene before the reader without intruding himself on either. He quotes as his ideal Hobbes' compliment to Thucydides as one who never digressed "to read a Lecture, Moral or Political, upon his own Text, nor enter into men's hearts, further than the Actions themselves evidently guide him." Undoubtedly, it is because Foote was a novelist before he was a historian that he believes in this method of presentation. It invests his work with some unique features.

The academic historian is likely to object to some of these features. For one thing, Mr. Foote never pauses, as the professional would, to argue the evidence, which on some points is highly controversial, and confusing, but rushes on to reconstruct his story. Nor does he, in the manner of the professional, stand off to contemplate events and utter his judgment as to their meaning.

In thus deviating from the pattern, he is, in this reviewer's opinion, quite right. For his purpose, it is enough that he places before the reader the story of the war in all its varied splendor and sweep. For this is a full record of those four years, as comprehensive a treatment as we are likely to get. Although the emphasis is on military episodes, there are good sections on such matters as politics and economics, conscription and army life, the social scenes in the capitals of Washington and Richmond, and the relation of Europe to the American conflict.

The coverage of the campaigns is encompassing and astonishing. The big set battles receive the major attention—Fredericksburg, Murfreesboro, Chancellorsville, Gettysburg, Vicksburg, Chickamauga and Chattanooga. But adequate space is devoted to the minor engagements, to Prairie Grove, Port Hudson, Charleston and to smaller meetings that are only names to even the specialists. Moreover, the battles are described so clearly and accurately that it is apparent the author has thoroughly mastered his sources.

It is on the question of sources that the academic historian may wish to quarrel again with Mr. Foote. Although the work contains neither footnotes nor a formal bibliography—the latter is to come in the final volume—it is evidence that Foote has drawn his material from published documents and secondary accounts. But again it is necessary to discount a possible criticism. The published records on the Civil War are so staggeringly immense that it is a considerable feat in itself to digest them—and another feat to reproduce them in narrative form. In fact, Mr. Foote has so many notes at hand that he sometimes repeats quotations within a short space.

This, then, is narrative history, a kind of history that goes back to an older literary tradition. It may have, from the modern viewpoint, certain shortcomings. But for what it is conceived to be, it must be set down as outstanding.

The writing is superb. Occasionally the author gets involved in some long sentences—there is one whopper of at least 118 words—that force rereading. But every page contains a delight—a sparkling description, a vivid characterization, a moving record of a man or an event. Even in retelling such familiar accounts as Gettysburg and Vicksburg, Mr. Foote is able to maintain an element of suspense. This skill also appears in the sketches of personalities. The portraits of Lincoln and Davis, of Lee and Grant, and of other figures are among the best in Civil War literature.

The writing is so good that one is tempted to quote. On Davis:

> The gray eyes, one lustrous, the other sightless, its stone gray pupil covered by a film, were deeply sunken above the jut of the high cheekbones, and the thin upper lip, indicative of an iron will and rigid self-control, was held so tightly against the teeth, even in repose, that you saw their shape behind it.

Or the devastating disposal of Joe Johnston:

> On the evidence, Old Joe's talent seemed primarily for retreat: so much so, indeed, that if left to his own devices he might be expected to wind up gingerly defending Key West and complaining that he lacked transportation to Cuba in the event that something threatened one of his flanks.

The last passage indicates something about the work that deserves emphasis. Despite his protestation that he is just setting the scene before us, Mr. Foote frequently does introduce his own opinions and interpretations. For these we may be thankful, since nearly always they are extremely shrewd and illuminate broad aspects of the war. Sometimes he intervenes with a revealing ancedote: the paradox of the Southern mind as shown by the Richmond F.F.V.'s who suspected Mrs. Davis of disloyalty because she employed a white nurse for her baby; or the chivalry still clinging to a cruel war, as epitomized in the Confederate officer on the Rappahannock line who recognized a tall top-hatted figure on the other side and respectfully bowed to Abraham Lincoln.

More often, Mr. Foote simply tells us what is in his mind. Thus he comments sharply that the trouble with Braxton Bragg was that he wanted to win battles only according to his preconceived plan; and when he found, at Murfreesboro and Chickamauga, that he could win by using a different method, he did not want to switch plans.

And like all of us who write about this war, Mr. Foote cannot resist second-guessing the strategy of its commanders. His summation of the Confederate failure at Gettysburg is excellent—"the army had slipped back to the disorganization of the Seven Days." The gray army had fought as bravely as ever, but its quality "could not make up for the crippling lack of direction from above and the equally disadvantageous lack of initiative just below the top."

Equally good is his evaluation of the enervating effect on Confederate efficiency of the activities of the states' rights men who insisted that the conflict be prosecuted by the precepts of legal dogma.

When completed, the three volumes will stand as one of the historical and literary achievements of our time, and one of the best things to come out of the centennial.

Now and later, the work will inevitably be compared with another and somewhat similar project, Bruce Catton's centennial history of the war. Mr. Catton's history was also planned as a three-volume affair, but as the second volume comes down only to the end of 1862 it seems unlikely that the author will be able to stay within his prescribed limits.

The two collections are alike and yet different. Both are narrative rather than analytical, both are beautifully written, and both emphasize the military aspect. Catton utilizes a wider variety of sources, including manuscripts, but Foote's treatment is broader. The largest diversity is an unconscious reflection of the authors' sectional and cultural origins. Catton is at his best in describing things Northern, Foote in depicting things Southern. Their books are not competitive but complementary. (pp. 5, 10)

> *T. Harry Williams, "Drawing the Lines Then Battling It Out," in* Book Week—New York Herald Tribune, *December 25, 1963, pp. 5, 10.*

Foote on historians:

Novelists know instinctively not to do things that historians do all the time. It's what makes historians such poor reading, and I'm not talking about being entertaining, I'm talking about what makes you dissatisfied with an historian, a dry, unskilled historian's history. There are great historians, I'm not talking about them. There has never been a greater novelist or writer of any kind than Tacitus, for instance, who was a great historian by any standards; Gibbon, Thucydides. It's just that a lot of modern historians are scared to death to suggest that life has a plot. They've got to take it apart and have a chapter on slavery, a chapter on "The Armies Meet," chapters on this, that, and the other. There's something almost low-life about trying to write about events from a human point of view. So they say. The result is they have no real understanding of the Civil War because they don't understand what Lincoln's problems were. They don't see them as problems impinging on a man; they see them as theoretical problems. I'm not saying what they do has no validity; I am saying it has no art. Of course, without their work I could have done nothing. They get along without me very well, but I couldn't get along without them.

Shelby Foote, in an interview with John Griffin Jones, Mississippi Writers Talking, I, *University Press of Mississippi, 1982.*

Thomas H. Landess   (essay date Fall 1971)

[*In the following excerpt, Landess surveys important themes in Foote's fiction and the first two volumes of* The Civil War.]

The work of Shelby Foote is of particular interest to students of Southern literature because it reveals within the framework of a single sensibility the evolution of the South's historical consciousness from a time of minimal self-awareness to an ultimate moment when the region began to call the very nature of its being into question, a moment which, according to Donald Davidson, produced that literary phenomenon known as the Southern Renaissance ("Why the Modern South Has a Great Literature," *Still Rebels, Still Yankees*). Thus an examination of Foote's career suggests a number of significant truths about the nature of the Southern experience while at the same time shedding light on the special quality of one writer's considerable achievement.

Central in much of Foote's work is a preoccupation with the theme of masculinity, which involves not only the idea of a classic heroism in the struggle for survival, whether in economic competition or in war, but also the proper relationship between man and woman, where the male either assumes a strong stance or is emasculated and rendered ineffectual in the pursuit of his proper vocation. Most of the author's earlier volumes deal with this theme in an historical context, that of the changing South. Thus one can see his growing awareness of the meaning of Southern history in each of his succeeding novels, an awareness that culminates in his latest work-in-progress, an ambitious account of the Civil War.

Ride Out, Foote's first sustained narrative, published as a short novel, is a story almost devoid of those historical and sociological superimpositions so familiar to readers of recent Southern fiction. In its austerity it is curiously akin to a folk ballad, and this kinship is all the more remarkable because the action is concerned with the trial and execution of a Mississippi Negro who, though guilty of murder, is basically goodhearted and deserving of a better fate. Yet one does not feel that the piece is devised to describe the ills of Southern society any more than one feels that Sir Patrick Spens was composed as an indictment of the Scottish monarchy. In both works there is an implied political structure which undergirds the incidents; but it is the central action, its moving and tragic thrust, which is the true subject matter of the artist. Indeed, Foote, with admirable economy, flirts with the stereotypes only to reject them for characters which emerge as vigorous and complex. His hero, a Negro jazz musician named Duff Conway, is misunderstood and unappreciated in his native state. His executioner is a callous redneck. And his last visitor is a sympathetic and tolerant Easterner. These characters by their very nature, then, hover on the brink of popular abstractions, yet Foote renders them so precisely and compassionately that they are always believable as human beings, and the conflict evolves from their humanity rather than from any social values they might exemplify.

For this reason the story is a tragedy in the traditional mold, spare and sharp in its subtle irony, which, once again, is the higher irony of the folk ballad rather than the irony of political satire or the so-called "ballads of social protest" that have as little in common with real ballads as the novels of, say, Shirley Ann Grau, have with the poetry of Homer. In this regard Foote's avoidance of the stereotype and the consequent credibility of his work are doubly remarkable when one remembers that *Ride Out* appeared in the forties, when the Southern protest novel was in its ascendancy. One has to go back twenty years or more to find a time when other Southerners were writing as unselfconsciously about their region and its particular institutions.

The true theme of the narrative is similar to that of Eudora Welty's short story "Powerhouse," which employs the jazz musician as an embodiment of the artist. Duff Conway's commitment to his art is absolute, an obsession with vocation that leaves little room in his life for anything else. But the artist is subject to the same mortality as other men and to the same human weaknesses. Duff's tuberculosis, which he inherits with his cornet from a dead inmate in a reformatory, illustrates that mortality; and the crime for which he is executed, the murder of a man who steals his woman, is evidence that despite his singleminded devotion to music, he is still a man whose other needs must be satisfied. Foote has written other works in which an artist is

the central character, but *Ride Out* is the only one which deals explicitly with the nature of art itself, and its relationship to the world at large.

There is no hint that this work is the first significant piece of an elaborate historical jigsaw puzzle in which the mythical Jordan County and its chief "jewel," the plantation house Solitaire, emerge as dominant images of a Southern society in the process of evolution from its lusty and primitive beginnings to its defeat in the Civil War.

Duff's mother, it develops, has worked for the Barcroft family, rendered fully in Foote's later novel, *Love in a Dry Season.* Thus, viewed in the context of his fiction as a whole, this excellent narrative has greater historical implications than can be understood from a strictly formal analysis. Like Faulkner's, Foote's career must be considered in its totality before the full meaning of every individual part is realized.

In *Tournament,* published in 1949, the author for the first time reveals his intense preoccupation with the broader scope of Southern history. Here he focuses on the plantation Solitaire: and though he is primarily concerned with Hugh Bart, whose proprietorship begins after the Civil War and extends well into the twentieth century, Foote devotes a significant amount of space to the origins of the plantation itself and to the character of Isaac Jameson, who first carved a cotton empire out of the wilderness and lived to see that empire and the house which was its primary symbol destroyed by the Northern invaders. The span of history covered in the career of Jameson is from the period when the early settlers first arrived to the time when the region was drawn into a devastating war which completely wrecked it.

Thus the action in *Tournament,* which is primarily concerned with the rise and fall of the heroic Hugh Bart, grows out of the historical circumstances surrounding the war and its aftermath. For in many ways the lives of Jameson and Bart are parallel. Both are men of immoderate character and virtue who succeed and then fail because their ambition and talents, sufficient to overcome the external obstacles which stand in their way, are not tempered by a necessary insight into the true nature of their enterprise. Bart's stewardship of the land can be viewed as the historical equivalent of the Southerner's efforts to "come again" after the ravages of the War and Reconstruction, but these efforts are in part made difficult by the same natural and economic problems to be found in the Old Order and are further complicated by a brand of capitalism new to the region, a force which is both hostile and tempting to Hugh Bart and to the generation he represents. Bart, who begins his rise to power as a tough and fair-minded sheriff, has something of the same dynastic dream as does Thomas Sutpen in *Absalom, Absalom!;* and his early activity is characterized by a capacity for fierce competition conducted within the bounds of propriety defined by his age. As suggested by the title, life for him is a "tournament" in which the game itself, played by the rules, is as important as the prize. And here he differs significantly from Sutpen, who is something of an affront to his more respectable neighbors and who knows precisely the goals he wishes to achieve. Both characters share in common the failure of their sons to assume the responsibility of their heritage; but in Foote's narrative there is an implicit commentary on the younger generation, a falling off from greatness, while in *Absalom, Absalom!* Henry Sutpen is in many ways the victim of his father's early excesses. In **Tournament,** Bart's downfall does not grow directly out of his efforts to rebuild Solitaire but out of a deep-seated restlessness which makes him finally dissatisfied with the realization of his ambitions. For a while he is content to amuse himself with such games as poker and trap shooting, an obvious sublimation of the heady competition of agricultural enterprise; but, disappointed in his son's lack of character and strangely restless, he sells the plantation, puts his money in the bank to draw interest, and moves to town. This act is disastrous, for it not only separates him from the land and the world he knows best, but it also places his fortune in the hands of the money manipulators; and when the bank fails he is a ruined man, who finally betrays himself and everything his life has represented by becoming a "professional" poker player, pitting himself against those friends whose respect and admiration he has earned by his earlier triumphs. His ensuing death, then, is a confirmation of the deeper tragedy he has suffered.

Tournament is not essentially a novel about history but is concerned with the struggle for survival and supremacy, an archetypal role of the male in society. As such the book cannot be called an historical novel in the narrowest sense. Yet history is the matrix in which the central action takes place, and Foote carefully constructs his enveloping action in order to emphasize the historical dimensions of his major characters. In so doing he has defined for his readers a significant transitional period in Southern life, the shift from agriculture to an economy grounded in business and finance, and the narrative marks the true beginnings of a saga of the region which he continues in succeeding works.

Follow Me Down (1950) is perhaps Foote's most powerful work of fiction, and once again the thematic focus is not primarily historical. As Walter Sullivan has written, the novel is concerned with "man's moral responsibility in the face of an inscrutable and pitiless fate" (*South: Modern Southern Literature in Its Cultural Setting*). Foote's story, then, does not take place in a cultural vacuum, and, in fact, he deliberately recaps some of the background of Solitaire and Jordan County in order to make certain that the reader understands the extent to which his characters are exemplary of their own time and place.

The major figures in the action are Luther Eustis, a middle-aged tenant farmer, the latest resident of Solitaire, and a teen-aged girl named Beulah, whose loose morals are the result of her mother's perversive influence and the vicissitudes of fortune. The two meet, are irresistibly attracted to each other, and flee to an island where they live for a while in what appears to be perfect sexual bliss. Luther, however, obsessed by guilt, begins to hear voices commanding him to kill Beulah, and the girl, failing to understand the conflict broiling within him, allows herself to be drowned, thinking in her ignorance that love, as she would define it, will triumph over his moral inhibitions.

In *Follow Me Down* the historical implications of the story are more profound than those in the earlier works and consequently more difficult to discern. Foote is specifically interested in a subtler ingredient of Southern society than the agrarian economic consideration important to **Tournament.** The key to an understanding of that ingredient, as Mr. Sullivan has suggested, is to be found in Foote's use of the Bible as a frame of reference. Luther Eustis (his first name is obviously significant) is basically a religious man whose adult life, up until the time he meets Beulah, is dominated by a desire to follow the letter of the Holy Word. As such he represents the intrinsically protestant morality which has informed nineteenth-century Southern society and provided the real basis for the conservatism of the region, a conservatism which has always differed radically from that of the financial interests in the Northeast. Beulah, on the other hand, represents a force in the modern world which is something more than merely pagan, though it is certainly that in its origins. Pathetically ignorant, she is a believer in sexuality as the ultimate truth of existence. Nor does she recognize the necessity for any moral or social inhibitions which restrict man's sexual conduct; and consequently she is symptomatic of a widespread modern malaise contrary to the nature of a traditional society. Indeed in earlier times it was the woman's responsibility to confine sexual relationships within the bounds of propriety, that is to say, within the institution of marriage; and adulterous though it may have been, even courtly love had its rules and prohibitions.

Of course there have always been women of easy virtue, and men of a religious temperament (St. Augustine, for example) have often been tempted by them, but the uniquely modern ramifications of this love story are emphasized both by the rendering of several significant minor characters and by the presence of a well-defined enveloping action.

Among those characters are two which pinpoint the moment of time in which Luther Eustis is trapped. One is an old-fashioned preacher who picks up a young sinner and dashes him against a tree with a physical strength suggestive of his stern and powerful traditional faith, and the other is a disillusioned lawyer who convinces both Luther and the jury that any irrestible sense of guilt is fanaticism, a form of insanity, and therefore undeserving of capital punishment. It is between these two views of human error, the old and the new, that Luther finds himself, confused and therefore susceptible to spiritual disaster.

Then, too, Luther is now the inhabitant of Solitaire, which Foote through his emphasis on history has already defined (and defines again) as the symbol of Southern society. For this reason, therefore, he must be understood in contrast with the earlier proprietors and the age which they represent. It is true that Ike Jameson and Hugh Bart are never rendered in explicitly religious terms, but the orthodox nature of the world in which they lived was a given, so much a part of the times that its definition is unnecessary.

Perhaps Foote's concern with the defeat of fundamentalism at the hands of modern sexuality represents a new development in the author's understanding of his region. Whatever, his consistent emphasis on the origins of Luther Eustis—his family history and its associations with the plantation Solitaire—point both to a past of moral certitude and to a future of increasing decadence.

In his next novel, *Love in a Dry Season* (1951), this decadence is rampant, and has almost completely undermined the foundations of the society represented by such men as Jameson and Bart. Here one sees the consequences of the defeat of Southern society in a cast of characters almost totally devoid of the virtues of their nineteenth-century forefathers, and even their vices are petty and demeaning by comparison. The only one who is faintly reminiscent of the old order is Major Malcolm Barcroft, and he is no more than a pale copy of the old-style heroes he attempts to emulate. He does not become master of an economic empire by conquest. Instead he marries, his father-in-law dies, and as a result he assumes a fortune in securities. (By contrast, Bart, who marries Jameson's daughter, does so only after he has acquired Solitaire and restored it to its former splendor.) Then, too, Major Barcroft is never given the opportunity to prove himself as a military man, the career he envisions for himself. Born during Reconstruction and nurtured on the lore of Confederate heroism, he is unable to continue his military education because of financial reversals, and must take a job as a cotton broker in his uncle's office. Later, during the Spanish-American War he is given a commission, but he never sees combat. With the retired rank of major, however, he plays the role of military hero to the hilt, comports himself with martial bearing, tries to teach his reluctant son to shoot and hunt, and then is utterly confounded when the boy's head is blown off in a hunting accident, leaving him with two unmarriageable daughters. Hardly the beginnings of a dynasty.

He is by turns sadistic, ridiculous, and cold-hearted. Yet, he is by no means the worst of his time, and indeed is very nearly the best. For there is a new breed of man abroad in the cotton community—it is now no more than a "business" controlled by a powerful Eastern trust. This type is represented in Jordan County by Harley Drew, a weak and unscrupulous adventurer who sees in Amanda, the Major's daughter, his opportunity for the main chance. She is hopelessly unattractive and is saddled with the burden of a malingering sister; yet she is rich and the major old; so Drew settles in the town, takes a job at the bank, and when Major Barcroft refuses him permission to marry Amanda, courts her surreptitiously and bides his time.

Though, as the title suggests, the novel is about love, or rather its absence, there is an obvious relationship between Drew the courtier and Drew the businessman, and in this relationship Foote is making an explicit commentary on the role of the male in the twentieth century. A man who will see a woman as no more than a means to achieve his economic goals is no man in the full sense of the word. In the classical heroic tradition, the woman, after all, is a prize to be won through fair and vigorous competition in the tournament, and in this novel these values are hopelessly confused.

That confusion is given added dimension by the introduction of two characters who are, in their own way, as empty and immoral as Harley Drew. These people, Amy and Jeff Carruthers, come to town after a life of dissipation which

reaches its climax when they join the international set and tour the fashionable playgrounds of Europe. During the course of their adventures, highlighted by adulteries and excessive drinking, Jeff is blinded in an automobile accident and becomes almost totally at his wife's mercy, a clear example of male impotence in the new society. The couple comes to Jordan County at the insistence of Amy, who wants to restore Briartree, a counterpart of Solitaire, partly for something to do and partly because she finds the notion quaint and romantic.

Inevitably Amy and Drew discover each other, enter into an affair, and talk about murdering her husband. Blind though he is, Jeff is able to understand something of what is going on between the two and shoots Drew in the very act of adultery, thus in a small sense redeeming a fragment of his manhood. But the episode is more comic than tragic. Drew is only wounded and, seeing his opportunities at an end, decides to try his luck in Memphis, leaving things as they were when he came: Amy and Jeff still trapped in an impossible marriage and Amanda resigned to spinsterhood and a life of charitable works. Later Drew marries an older woman with money and is soon a frequent face on the society pages of the Memphis papers.

The temper of this novel is similar to that of Fitzgerald's best work, and is an excellent example of Foote's virtuosity as a novelist. The ironic tone, the complexity of plot, the theme of pervasive decadence are something new to his fiction, and yet the archetypal patterns, what Faulkner calls "the old verities," still lie at the heart of the story and the enveloping action is the historical South, captured once more at a crucial time of change.

Love in a Dry Season ends on an interesting note, which not only directs the reader's attention to the obvious similarities between Major Barcroft and Harley Drew, but also points the way to Foote's growing concern with the importance of the Civil War as the single most significant factor in the perceptible degeneration of Southern society. During World War II Amanda sees in the newspaper a picture of her former lover leading the grand march at the cotillion: he is dressed in the uniform of a colonel in the Tennessee Home Guard. In addition to the more evident ironies, these details, contained in the final sentence of the novel, lead the reader inevitably back to the origins of Major Barcroft's dreams, and to the military glories of the Lost Cause. It is there that one finds the extravagant masculine virtues so absent in latter-day society, the courage and courtliness which go hand in hand and in another age were considered the mark of proper manhood.

It is no surprise then, that *Shiloh,* published in 1952, should concern itself with the Civil War; and the choice of this particular battle, with which the narrative is exclusively concerned, is singularly appropriate, since it was one of the crucial encounters of the war. For one thing, the Union successes in the West made an ultimate Southern victory highly unlikely because they split the Confederacy down the middle and made any concentrated defense of the region all but impossible. And Shiloh was, in many ways, the turning point, not only because of the loss of Albert Sidney Johnston, the most able professional soldier serving the Confederacy in that part of the country;

but also because it gave Grant an advantage which he pressed with relentless determination until he had conquered a major portion of the West, thereby preparing the way for his fateful confrontation with Lee's Army of Northern Virginia.

But there are also dramatic values to be found in the battle which exist quite apart from its strategic importance. It was, in a sense, a perfect miniature of the entire war—an encounter in which both sides fought fiercely and incurred staggering losses. The engagement, characterized by a blind ferocity peculiar to modern warfare, provided a new test of manhood for all involved, a sense of the futility of individual action in the face of an overwhelming and anonymous force. And it was a first encounter with the enemy for a majority of the troops, both Northern and Southern.

Foote's narrative method is interesting and innovative. The battle is viewed through the eyes of five soldiers, Union and Confederate, and a squad of Indiana men. Most of these characters cross each other's paths during the course of the battle: some are wounded, some are killed, all are irreparably altered by their terrifying experiences. As the action unfolds, the reader feels a sense of the tremendous power of battle, an irresistible ebb and flow similar to that which Stephen Crane depicts in *The Red Badge of Courage*. There is something of the same confused exaltation during a successful charge and a good deal of the wild panic that seizes men when they are overrun by the enemy.

However, Foote is not simply rewriting *The Red Badge of Courage*. There are other thematic complexities which inform the novel. For example, in the character of Lieutenant Palmer Metcalfe, aide-de-camp to Albert Sidney Johnston, one finds the key to an important meaning of the narrative. Metcalfe, deliberately placed by the author at the center of strategic planning, participates in a minor way in the formation of the Southern army's Napoleonic battle plan, which is so perfect on paper and turns out so badly in practice. Later, after the disaster of the engagement is apparent, he is able to tell himself that the fault lay in the plan itself, created by men who in their enthusiasm and pride failed to see that they were, in fact, not devising a strategy for victory but a blueprint for their own defeat. Here Foote goes far beyond the dimensions of war as defined by Crane, whose picture was essentially one of uncontrollable chaos. In *Shiloh* the fortunes of war ultimately have their origins in the character of men; and the theme of Metcalfe's account is classical in its implications—nemesis earned by an identifiable hybris.

The broader historical meanings of the battle are to be found in Metcalfe's recollection of an early warning he had left unheeded: "I remembered what my father had said about the South bearing within itself the seeds of defeat, the Confederacy being conceived already moribund. We were sick from an old malady, he said; incurable romanticism and misplaced chivalry, too much Walter Scott and Dumas read too seriously. We were in love with the past, he said, in love with death."

However Foote does not end his narrative on this note.

Metcalfe himself recalls that his own father, who posed as "a realist and straight thinker" was in truth "a highly romantic figure of a man himself and he knew it . . . " And the final scenes of the novel, again as viewed through the eyes of Metcalfe, are devoted to the stirring figure of Nathan Bedford Forrest who, as the army is retreating, turns on his pursuers and leads a violent and dramatic attack. Riding fifty yards ahead of his cavalry, he enters the enemy lines and is momentarily trapped. Though sustaining a severe wound from a musket ball, he hacks his way toward freedom, grabs up one of the enemy soldiers, and dashes him against a jagged stump as he rejoins his men.

In this episode Foote transcends the view of modern war as a mass movement of faceless bodies and pushes the action of the novel toward the level of pure epic, the creation of a mythic hero who embodies the ultimate virtues valued by society. In the person of Forrest one sees the ideal against which to measure not only the lesser figures in *Shiloh* but also such thoroughly emasculated characters as Jeff Carruthers and Harley Drew. Here, Foote is saying by implication, is the paradigm of manhood. One need only look at the contemporary world to measure the decline of Southern society since its earlier era of greatness. And because of these final scenes of unmitigated heroism *Shiloh* is unique as a twentieth-century chronicle of war.

Jordan County (1954) is a collection of Foote's stories and short novels (including *Ride Out*) which treat the span of Mississippi history from the early days of Spanish occupation to the present; and though it cannot be considered as a significant step in Foote's development as a novelist and historian, since it contains material published over the years, most of the selections illustrate his lifelong concern with the problems of Southern society. (pp. 321-33)

Child by Fever, a short novel of 150 pages is, with the possible exception of *Ride Out,* the most ambitious piece in the volume. It is concerned with the life of Hector Sturgis, a weak and ineffectual socialite whose failure as a man drives his wife Ella to numerous adulteries and finally leads to his own suicide. For, after Ella dies accidentally from gas fumes while in the arms of another man, he is haunted by her memory. Indeed her ghost speaks to him out of the darkness of their room, which is the darkness of his own soul, taunting him for his cowardice and sexual inadequacy. His love of this ghost, which indicates his inherent love of death itself, finally drives him to the one act of violence he is fully capable of, his own self-destruction.

Here as elsewhere Foote clearly equates manhood with the capacity to act violently when the occasion demands such action, and there are two isolated incidents in Hector's life which show his deep-rooted and healthy desire to strike out at the world as well as his final inability to do so with any manly grace. One occurs in his childhood when he is badgered by the other children and begins to pummel them, to the cheers of the Negro servants. Foote's precise description of this scene is important since it again involves history as a frame of reference:"Then, drawing on some atavistic reserve—received perhaps from the man [his great-grandfather] who fell near the apex of the V at Buena Vista—he stood on the seat, facing backwards over the tonneau, and swung the oilcloth book satchel at their heads." But his revulsion at his own action, which later causes him to vomit, is so great that the lesson he might have learned is lost.

The second time in his life he resorts to violence occurs when, overcome by anger at his wife, he slaps her in the face with his open hand. Instead of tears or anger, she is suddenly transformed into a tender, receptive woman, and invites him in soft tones to "Hit me. Hit me again." He knows what he must do to regain her respect, but in this instance, too, he is incapable of transforming his temporary rage into a permanent and mature manhood; and instead of vomiting, he throws himself down and weeps uncontrollably, forever the weak and contemptible woman-child.

Hector's problem, specifically defined in an historical context which includes references to the Civil War as well as to the Mexican expedition, is perhaps Foote's most overt statement of his views on the nature of masculinity; and as such it can be used as a touchstone in determining the values inherent in such earlier works as *Tournament* and *Shiloh* and in the later volumes of history. But apart from this significance, it is a superb piece of fiction and one of the author's most successful narratives. (pp. 333-35)

One is tempted to say that Shelby Foote's massive work-in-progress, *The Civil War: A Narrative,* is his greatest achievement; but to do so would be to slight the novels, which must be ranked among the best in twentieth-century American literature. And for many reasons excellent fiction is harder to come by at the present time than excellent history, though both, to be sure, are extremely rare. Foote makes any absolute choice unnecessary, however, by making it clear that he does not regard the two as discrete genres. Both the historian and the novelist, he writes, "are seeking the same thing: the truth—not a different truth: the same truth—only they reach it, or try to reach it, by different routes" (*Mississippi Quarterly,* Fall, 1964). He continues by suggesting that historians have much to learn from novelists about style, plot, and characters and must transcend the pedantic urge to tie themselves too closely to facts, which provide the basis for good history but are not its sole resources. Thus *The Civil War,* as its subtitle indicates, is "a narrative"; and predictably it contains all of the virtues of the author's best works of fiction.

Before discussing these virtues, however, it might be well to consider the new problems which he must encounter in writing pure history and to indicate in what ways those problems have possibly led him astray. In the first place, any full-blown account of the Civil War must of necessity involve political considerations. The most important failure of Douglas Southall Freeman in dealing with Lee is his unwillingness or inability to come to terms with the larger political ramifications of the battles he is describing, the enveloping action of his chronicle. And yet politics, in addition to being a pragmatic game played by human beings, is also philosophy, as Aristotle knew. Thus Foote, as well as other Civil War historians, must deal to some extent in abstractions; and abstractions are abhorrent to the instincts of the true novelist.

As a consequence, he seems to have adopted too simple a view of the political implications of the War and to have allowed that view to color his renditions of such a "character" as Abraham Lincoln, who, one suspects, was far more complex than he seems to be in Foote's account and (though it is surely a matter of opinion) far more devious. Foote seems to have derived his version of Lincoln from Carl Sandburg and from such "revisionist" historians as James B. Randall and T. Harry Williams. This Lincoln is "the man of sorrows," a highly practical loner whose upbringing on the Midwestern plains, removed from abolitionist New England, made him less of an ideologue than the radicals, more of a compromiser, a chief of state dedicated to reconciliation and peace.

To be sure Foote does not idealize Lincoln out of all proportion, as Sandburg does. He mentions his ambitions, hints at their self-seeking nature, and dutifully chronicles the unconstitutional actions the newly elected president initiated prior to the convening of Congress: the raids on Northern telegraph offices to confiscate copies of telegrams; the imprisonment of innocent men on the mere rumor of Southern sympathy; the holding of prisoners incommunicado and the denial of *habeas corpus;* the transference of federal funds to private accounts for the purchase of arms. Of course Foote excuses Lincoln by adding that "there were guilty men among the innocent, and a dungeon was as good a place as any for a patriot to serve his country through a time of stress." Yet this wry humor and the questionable rationalization that underlies it are forgiveable. The times were extraordinary and Lincoln felt he was acting to preserve the very life of the nation.

What is wrong with Foote's composite picture of Lincoln's career is his failure to understand the political motives that lay behind it, the president's concept of his own destiny which is suggested in the works of such contemporary political philosophers as Henry Jaffa and David Potter, the former an inordinate admirer of Lincoln. Indeed in many respects the Great Emancipator was as thoroughgoing an abstractionist as the abolitionists (who were not themselves in total agreement about the final solution of the slavery question), and he shared many of their assumptions about the nature of American society. His own inviolable absolute, however, perhaps more radical in its own way than that of the abolitionists, was the idea of Union. This preoccupation seems innocent and practical enough; indeed, it is an ideal with which most Southerners would sympathize in retrospect, unless they examined it further; and then it would begin to assume monstrous proportions. For Lincoln, almost from boyhood, as Jaffa and Potter show, saw himself as the "second founder," a man destined to purify the first founding which was imperfectly conceived by Washington and his contemporaries. Thus when he speaks of "Union," Lincoln does not mean the Old Republic which existed prior to the outbreak of hostilities. He is speaking of a Union which exists only in the future and hence a Union more abstract than Foote and the revisionists have recognized. Such a Union would be devastatingly homogeneous, would abolish the comity of sections, and more to the point, would not allow the South to return (despite the Emancipation Proclamation) except as an indistinguishable component of the total state, a participant in the New Birth of the nation. This "second nation," as Lincoln envisioned it, would have as its single absolute doctrine the idea of equality; and it is clear, if one considers the matter, that equality and freedom are inevitably antithetical propositions. If one carries this argument to its logical conclusion, it is plausible to view Lincoln not as the defender of the old Union, but as the first Caesar of the new.

A second misunderstanding of the political implications of the war (or so one could argue) is to be found in Foote's basic assumption, despite his own evidence to the contrary, that slavery lay at the heart of the South's struggle for independence and that what Frank Owsley calls "the plain people" were conscious of exploitation at the hands of the slavocracy and hence by nature lukewarm in their support of secession and the ensuing hostilities. The incredibly small number of significant slaveholders is one argument against such a view, since, however powerful its economic resources, the slavocracy could hardly have mustered from its own ranks and from those it controlled sufficient popular support to initiate such a drastic political move as secession. But a more persuasive argument is to be found in the nature of Southern society. What, after all, would have happened had millions of slaves been freed by the legislative action of a Northern majority? The plain people would have sustained an economic and social shock almost as great as that felt by the large planters. And from where did the racist populists of the post-Reconstruction era derive their primary support? In truth, as distasteful as it may seem to contemporary egalitarian sensibilities, the average nineteenth-century Southerner probably viewed slavery as a means of social control and therefore had a vested interest in its perpetuation, until such time as a better solution than instant abolition could be advanced. What Foote ignores and Lincoln never understood, any more than an orthodox Marxist would, is that class distinction in the South was a private matter among men and did not severely undermine the sense of Southern community. Hence the failure of John Hay's expedition to Florida for the purpose of setting up a Republican state among people who had no economic investment in slavery, people who might be called in today's vernacular "peckerwoods." But the slaveless peckerwoods mustered an impressive militia and drove out the invaders in a battle which Foote describes with great skill and obvious relish. This action, with its attendant political implications, suggests the true reason for the unity of Southerners on most of the important issues of the day: their survival as a corporate people was at stake and hence their manhood. They could not bear the thought of political defeat at the hands of their enemies any more than they could bear the thought of military defeat. Indeed the prewar abolitionists, by the nature and intensity of their vituperation, had created a true nation of people where none had existed before, and though "the South" at first was no more than an abstraction in the abusive rhetoric of New Englanders, it became a flesh-and-blood reality long before the firing on Fort Sumter.

If these points seem labored and overly argumentative it is because they are highly relevant to a complete understanding of Foote's treatment of the military actions. In his accounts of the battles themselves, probably the best ever written on the subject, he gives ample evidence to undercut his questionable political assumptions (his handling of the other political questions, such as the internal workings of the Confederate government, is admirable and beyond reproach). Like Winston Churchill, he seems to see the war itself, the actual combat, as the last great display of Anglo-Saxon manhood, a spectacle which, however gallant it may have been on both sides, insured by its extravagant expense the ultimate destruction of that manhood. And in their discipline, the loyalty they displayed toward their commanders, and the heroic way in which they fought, the plain people, as Foote presents them, lend authority to those who argue that there was a basic unity in Southern society, one which derived from something more than slavery and other economic considerations.

To put it in fictional terms, Foote's enveloping action is not always consistent with the central action itself, which is predictably the military prosecution of the war. Here the masculine role in society is once again an important part of the thematic substance of his narrative; and in dealing with the two armies, their leaders and the rank and file, he constantly raises the question of whether or not they are adequate to the violence which is expected, indeed required of them. As for Foote's Southerners, they *fight* as if they were unified in their ultimate goals, and the way they regard the invasion of the North to establish Mr. Lincoln's Union is certainly implicit in the manner in which they conduct themselves on the field of battle.

Unlike the author's treatment of the political scene, in his battle accounts there are few villains, though he regards "book soldiers" and ideologues with more contempt than he does incompetency or bemusement, which he treats with admirable compassion—a virtue he praises in his *Mississippi Quarterly* article and which he says is absent from most histories, too often the product of simplistic and doctrinaire political theses that refine the principle of humanity out of the action. Thus Custer, Bragg, and Beauregard emerge as more complex figures than, for example, Freeman would have been willing to admit; and by the same token, Grant and Lee are likewise complex.

In Foote's treatment of the war in the West, which is the most thorough and competent ever written, Grant is not presented as the invincible commander who always knew precisely what he was doing. The narrative of the attack on Fort Donelson is a case in point, and he clearly shows that the great Union general was feeling his way into the action, unsure of himself and at times highly fallible in his judgements. One feels after reading this and other accounts, that the author must surely be right in his assessment of a man who has been too facilely idealized by historians like Kenneth P. Williams and Bruce Catton.

In the same vein, his Lee is not the Lee of Freeman, a figure who totally embodies the virtues of ideal Southern manhood. Lee has often been an enigma to those who have dealt with him. Stephen Vincent Benét in *John Brown's Body* expresses some doubt as to the validity of the public myth which surrounds this benevolent patriarch, though Benét was not man enough to come to grips with the truth; and even a vastly superior artist such as Robert Penn Warren has said on occasion that Lee would provide poor subject matter for fiction since the surface of his character is as smooth and perfect as an egg. The problem, of course, is how to reconcile Freeman's gentle perfect knight with the successful field commander who enthusiastically destroyed so many of his enemies. But Foote is not troubled by this problem, since he regards the capacity for violent action as an essential ingredient of manhood; and he reveals his character as made of sterner stuff than the old mythology would allow. His Lee is the man who, as his career reveals, rejoiced in the goriest successes of his army, pressed for attack with no quarter given, shot his stragglers, brooded excessively in later life, and died in a delirium telling Hill he must come up; in fact, where Lee's genteel courtesy interfered with his conduct of war, as at the battle of Gettysburg, Foote seems to reprove him for weakness.

And his most striking hero is, of course, Nathan Bedford Forrest, whose life and character in many ways are clearly a contrast to Lee's. A "diamond in the rough" whose vocation as slave trader (not merely slave owner) made him suspect in polite company, he abhorred excessive ceremony and dealt with his peers and subordinates in tough and peremptory fashion when the circumstances required it. One feels from Foote's depiction of him that he would never have allowed Stuart or Longstreet to get off so lightly at Gettysburg, nor would they have dared to deviate from his orders had he been their commander.

Then, too, Forrest, unlike Lee, was a native military genius without the formal advantages and disadvantages of a West Point education, and as a consequence understood more clearly than most the new type of warfare that Grant and Sherman were waging, a warfare which was far removed from the Napoleonic battles which served as the models for most professional soldiers. Forrest was best in guerrilla actions; and his chief tools as a general were tactical innovations, movement, and surprise, combined with an almost animal ferocity that made him all but invincible. Lee possessed these qualities, otherwise he would not have been one of the great generals of all time, but they were muted in him by an elaborate civility; Forrest is a man very much like the early Hugh Bart, and Foote finds him particularly attractive and exemplary of those masculine virtues he deems indispensable to the survival of a society.

Besides the complexities of the human condition inherent in Foote's rendition of history, there is also a careful devotion to minute detail which is present in the brilliant texture of the author's fiction. In addition to a characteristic concern with the personal history of his major figures, in which he renders significant scenes and dialogues from their private lives, he is always aware that in order for a character to "exist" in a narrative he must be created for the reader in terms of concrete sensory impressions. Thus one sees, hears, smells, and therefore fully experiences the world in which the action takes place. Undoubtedly Foote garnered many of his specific details from *Battles and Leaders of the Civil War* and from numerous memoirs, accounts of a personal nature which often focused on bits of trivia absent from the chronicles of formal historians. But while these small and apparently irrelevant facts lie dor-

mant in his sources, he revitalizes them and gives them a relevance to the overall action as only a seasoned writer of fiction, steeped in the narratives of Faulkner and Proust, could do. Consequently almost every page abounds with images of life itself. At Jefferson Davis's inauguration, for example, he describes the Episcopal bishop as he raises his arms to pronounce the invocation: "his lawn sleeves hung limp and his heavy vestments were splotched with wet." When Farragut attacks the *Arkansas* at Vicksburg, his difficulties are emphasized by the blurred image of the enemy: "For one thing, in the ruddy murk between sunset and dusk, the rust-red boat was almost invisible under the red clay bank." And the full meaning of that histrionic gesture known as Pickett's Charge is brought into focus by the physical description of its controversial leader: "Jaunty on a sleek black horse, he wore a small blue cap, buff gauntlets, and matching blue cuffs on the sleeves of his well-tailored uniform. Mounted or afoot, he carried an elegant riding crop. His boots were brightly polished and his gold spurs glinted sunlight, rivaling the sparkle of the double row of fire-gilt buttons on his breast."

Within the framework of Foote's overriding purpose—which is to depict the human dimensions of the war—he does not neglect the minor engagements, where, for example, bravery is just as important an ingredient as it is in the major battles such as Shiloh, Chancellorsville, and Gettysburg. Two of his best accounts, one in the first volume, and another in the second, will serve as illustrations. The first is Henry Sibley's abortive campaign into New Mexico to clear the area of federal troops and open the way to a western seaport, and the second is Hay's landing at Hilton Head and subsequent march into Florida (the political purpose of which Foote, alas, refuses to take seriously). In a sense both ventures can be described as fool's errands, since the objectives and obstacles involved were too great for the meager forces dispatched. And the author suggests their quixotic nature from the outset; yet he renders them fully, sparing none of the talents and resources he brings to the rest of his narrative. Thus the reader senses his deep concern for men as men and not merely as two-dimensional figures in an abstract drama. His attention to these out-of-the-way encounters also suggests his desire to recapture in a Proustian sense the totality of Southern (and Northern) experience as contained within this crucial era.

These accounts, small masterpieces in themselves, also reveal something about the work as a whole. Foote, despite his obvious admiration for the heroism of the forces involved, treats much of their activity with ironic humor. Most often his irony is gentle, comic in the highest sense of the word. On rare occasions it reflects his scorn for pretense and blind ideology. But the presence of humor serves as a foil for the heroic moments of the action and thereby underscores them for posterity to admire.

Thus it is obvious that what the author is creating is not history in the narrow contemporary mold but an epic not unlike Homer's, modern in that it lacks a uniform tone of high seriousness, but an epic nonetheless. For the nature of the epic mode is to elevate and sustain an existing society by preserving within its consciousness the memory of its own glorious past, and the central image by which this purpose is achieved is that of the hero. Such poems as *The Iliad* and *Beowulf*, then, though oral in nature, are akin to the Renaissance books of conduct, which created paradigms for an age which was in the process of forgetting how to behave. In his later fiction—and particularly in such novels and stories as *Follow Me Down, Love in a Dry Season,* and *Child by Fever*— Foote indicates that contemporary society has already forgotten; and for this reason the task he has set out for himself is more difficult. It is further complicated by the fact that fiction is no longer regarded as a "relevant form of communication" by a new generation of secular puritans. Hence the necessary transition from a book like *Shiloh* to the more "acceptable" type of discourse exemplified by *The Civil War: A Narrative,* a transition which could be viewed as a considerable personal sacrifice, since, at the time he undertook this monumental task, the author's reputation as a novelist was just beginning to burgeon.

Taken as a whole the work of Shelby Foote is an achievement of importance, and one which has been shamefully neglected by the literary establishment; for, as suggested earlier, there is a sense in which his evolving career may be viewed as symptomatic of a profound self-consciousness that has been characteristic of many Southern writers over the past three decades. This phenomenon is not merely a mutation of the modern hyperrationality which has been the subject of so much poetry and fiction; it is peculiar to the twentieth-century Southerner, who has found himself the central figure in a mythology so rigid and persuasive that he can reach the point where he actually begins to doubt the reality of his own unique existence and that of the phenomenal world which surrounds him, a world peopled by relatives, friends, and flesh-and-blood acquaintances. Such a writer, when he comes to this moment of self-doubt, will either cross over into the unreal world of abstraction and write about characters as essentially stylized as any found in *The Faerie Queen,* or else he will rebel as Foote has done, and in constructing his own "antimyth" create a tension in his poetry or fiction which is an ingredient of the best literature in the language.

Obviously some sort of confrontation with self is inevitable for the Southerner, just as it is inevitable for the Negro or the Jew. The myth—really no more than a puritanical reading of United States history—is too powerful to ignore, too deeply entrenched in the minds of Americans, who, while carefully purging themselves of less-fashionable stereotypes, still cherish a notion of the South which is so simple and pure it would seem almost a surrender of innocence to abandon it. But Foote's view of Southern history represents a credible antimyth to combat this stereotype, which has been religiously merchandised to the nation as a whole; and while he is not blind to the imperfections of his own section, he is aware of its virtues as well, the better traditions of an essentially heroic past. That he is pessimistic about the future is understandable. There are few Hugh Barts and Bedford Forrests left in the world, and the Harley Drews are legion. But for what it

is worth, at least one writer has called them by their proper name. (pp. 337-47)

Thomas H. Landess, "Southern History and Manhood: Major Themes in the Works of Shelby Foote," in The Mississippi Quarterly, *Vol. XXIV, No. 4, Fall, 1971, pp. 321-47.*

Louis D. Rubin, Jr.   (review date 30 November 1974)

[*Rubin is an American critic and educator who has written and edited numerous studies on Southern literature. In the following review of the third volume of* The Civil War, *he extols what he considers to be Foote's original and vivid retelling of the Civil War.*]

When novelist Shelby Foote first began work on his narrative history of the American Civil War, there were still six years to go before the centennial observance of the war was scheduled to begin. In publishing circles the boom market was on for Civil War books. Bruce Catton was in command of the field with his vividly written trilogy on the Army of the Potomac, and all over the land, historians both professional and amateur were preparing to contribute to the great bonanza. Wartime diaries, journals, memoirs were being assiduously edited and annotated. Entrepreneurs such as Ralph Newman were stocking up wares for the bookfest. Meanwhile the associated travel promoters of the states in which the battles had been fought were laying plans to collect the financial harvest from battlefield reenactments, pageants and other tourist-luring observances. It was going to be a great show.

But the centennial never developed in quite the way that was expected. For one thing, the book market crested too far in advance. By the year 1961, when the actual centennial began, readers were already wearying of encountering the same stories about the same battles and the same commanders, told over and over again in only slightly different accents. Too much shoddy work, too many contrived "non-books" operated to drive out the good books.

Then the centennial itself was abruptly upstaged by the civil rights movement. In order to take proper satisfaction in the reenactment of a war that had been fought years earlier, one had to be able to feel that it was truly past history, and that the antipathies and injustices that had caused the fighting were gone, and only the recollection of heroism and valor was now important. But when one realized only too well that the passions that had been inflamed into civil war were still alive, if no longer on quite the same sectional basis, it was difficult to contemplate the blood-letting of a century ago with anything like the requisite antiquarian detachment. How celebrate a war in which some 600,000 persons died, when before one's very eyes, in the daily newspapers, there was so much testimony that the underlying causes of the strife were not yet laid to rest? Thus the centennial, all told, so far as its reenactment went, was mostly a bust.

It is Shelby Foote's good fortune, I think, that his narrative of the fighting of the American Civil War was not finished and published during or immediately following the years of the centennial, but comes to completion only now, when it can be read for the majestic work of history that it is. For essentially it is different from most of the other Civil War books—and perhaps the circumstance that the first two volumes were published in 1958 and 1963, respectively, may account for the fact that, however they were well received and widely praised, the originality was not properly recognized. Now that Volume III, *Red River to Appomatox,* is ready and the long-time project is complete, it may be that some will go back and reread Volumes I and II as well, and thus be able to discern something of Foote's full achievement.

His is not the vicarious refighting of battles in print, though these are well chronicled and vividly described. Neither is his work a ranking and rating of the various commanders, though their individual capabilities come through clearly and unarguably. Nor, finally, is it an attempt to fasten upon the strategic mistakes and advertise the missed tactical opportunities, *i.e., if* only the Confederates had followed up First Manassas, *if* McClellan had stayed in place and pressed on toward Richmond after the Seven Days, *if* Beauregard had continued the assault after the initial rout at Shiloh, *if* Meade had struck Lee's beaten army before it could recross the Potomac and so on. The material for such second-guessing is there, and lost opportunities are identified, but they are not what Foote has been after.

What he has written instead is a disenthralled narrative of just how the war was fought out, from beginning to conclusion. He has sought to show what happened, to describe the way that the commanders on both sides planned their campaigns and fought their battles. This is old-style history; Foote's models have been Tacitus and Gibbon. Written with flowing style and unfolding narrative art, drawing upon massive research but with all material thoroughly incorporated and placed in the service of his narrative, he has told the story of the war.

This volume begins with the appointment of U. S. Grant as chief of all the Union armies in the late winter of 1864, and follows the war through Grant's onslaught against Lee that spring and summer, Sherman's move southward against Joe Johnston, the replacement of Johnston with Hood and the subsequent destruction of the Confederate army in the west, the besieging of Petersburg, the march of Sherman's troops through Georgia and the Carolinas, the final dislodgement of Lee's army from the Petersburg defenses, and the subsequent surrenders.

As always Foote gives devoted attention to the characters and personalities of the principal figures—the two opposing chief executives, Lincoln and Davis; Lee and Grant; Sherman and Johnston; Forrest, Hood, Sheridan, Thomas, Farragut. As in his first two volumes, what is striking is Foote's almost complete emancipation from the partisan evaluations of these figures that have been handed down, unconsciously for the most part, from generation to generation by subsequent historians. Because the South lost the war despite the battlefield achievements of its soldiers, the civil government, and in particular Jefferson Davis, was in effect made into scapegoat and explanation. Had Davis been wiser and less inflexible, the war would have turned out otherwise. But Foote's Jefferson Davis is

an able and resourceful man, who did well for a cause doomed to defeat by overwhelming military and industrial force. Foote is not out to find scapegoats, but to tell what happened.

I know of no other military historian of the Civil War who has written with so much objectivity and freedom from inherited partisanship. The late Douglas Southall Freeman, for example, for all his matchless skill at research and his ability to piece together what actually took place on confused battlefields, inherited some of the loyalties and biases of the postwar generation. His handling of Gen. James Longstreet was thoroughly colored by the detestation of that general felt by most white Southerners because of Longstreet's having turned Republican after the surrender. Foote by contrast views Longstreet's performance in terms of what the wartime records show, and we get a completely different and far more reasonable depiction. But not a verdict—Mr. Foote is not in that business. He is not identifying heroes and villains, but describing a bloody war.

The best section of *Red River to Appomatox,* surpassing even the account of the Fort Donelson campaign in Volume I, is Foote's depiction of the Wilderness campaign. I have never read a better, more vivid, more understandable account of the savage battling between Grant's and Lee's armies that began on the Rapidan in May of 1864 and ended 40 days later at Cold Harbor. It is a model of what military history can be.

But for that matter, so is the entire book [*The Civil War: A Narrative*]—all three volumes, the finest writing to have come out of the centennial. Foote stays with the human strife and suffering, and unlike most Southern commentators, he does not take sides. In objectivity, in range, in mastery of detail, in beauty of language and feeling for the people involved, this work surpasses anything else on the subject. Written in the tradition of the great historian-artists—Gibbon, Prescott, Napier, Freeman—it stands alongside the work of the best of them. (pp. 44-5)

> *Louis D. Rubin, Jr., "Old-Style History," in*
> The New Republic, *Vol. 171, No. 22, November 30, 1974, pp. 44-5.*

George Garrett (essay date Winter 1974-75)

[*Garrett is an American novelist, poet, and critic whose satiric and darkly humorous works often concern the processes of history and the significance of family tradition in the American South. In the following essay, he studies how Foote applies novelistic techniques, particularly methods of characterization, to the writing of* The Civil War.]

One of the pleasures coming with the appearance of each of the three volumes of Shelby Foote's *The Civil War: A Narrative*—"Fort Sumter to Perryville" (1958), "Fredericksburg to Meridian" (1964), and now "Red River to Appomattox" (1974)—has been the "Bibliographical Note" published at the end of each book. These can be read independently, of course; for they dutifully acknowledge each time the essentially unchanging primary sources, where, as Foote says, "you hear the live men speak." But they can also be examined in sequence, representing the changing and cumulative library of secondary sources, including what might be termed the "competition," the work of Bruce Catton and Allan Nevins, all the sources which have expanded in wild growth, in startling quantity, over the years. (Perhaps not so startling; for both scholars and publishers aimed to make the most of the centennial years.) In any case, Foote's bibliographical notes offer a careful accounting of the historical research which has been going on during the twenty years or so that went into the making of *The Civil War.* Equally important, and perhaps more interesting, has been the stance of the author, his attitude and his tone of voice, as he explained his aims, his ways and means, and his models of excellence, in the process of creating this work. The note to the first volume is thorough, solid, inclusive, and appropriately humble without false modesty. The anticipated problem is that of the novelist who invades the territory of the specialist. He does not retreat from his badge and chevrons as novelist, nor does he shy away from his commitment to that art: "Well, I am a novelist, and what is more I agree with D. H. Lawrence's estimate of the novel as 'the one bright book of life.' " But he is at pains to make clear the integrity of his method, if not to defend it:

> Accepting the historian's standards without his paraphernalia, I have employed the novelist's methods without his license. Instead of inventing characters and incidents, I searched them out—and having found them, I took them as they were. Nothing is included here, either within or outside quotation marks, without the authority of documentary evidence which I consider sound . . . In all respects, the book is as accurate as care and hard work could make it.

By the time Foote had finished the second volume he had passed through, unscathed, his baptism of fire from the historians. His work had been praised and appreciated by honorable and demanding critics. And he was now past the halfway mark in his own enormous task. The "Bibliographical Note" to the second volume is a virtuoso piece, threaded with some brilliant sentences of silver and gold. There is the veteran's earned swagger and no longer any necessity for self-defense. In fact, the mood expressed is expansive in its confidence. Concluding his particular list of debts to scholars, he writes:

> Other, less specific obligations were as heavy. The photographs of Mathew Brady, affording as they do a gritty sense of participation—of being in the presence of the uniformed and frock-coated men who fought the battles and did the thinking, such as it was—gave me as much to go on, for example, as anything mentioned above. Further afield, but not less applicable, Richmond Lattimore's translation of the *Iliad* put a Greekless author in close touch with his model. Indeed, to be complete, the list of my debts would have to be practically endless. Proust I believe has taught me more about the organization of material than even Gibbon has done, and Gibbon taught me much. Mark Twain and Faulkner would also have to be included, for they left their sign on all they touched, and in the course of this

exploration of the American scene I often found that they had been there before me.

For historical method he very gracefully invites comparison of his work with that of Tacitus and Thucydides. In context, then and now, none of this seems self-serving or outrageously illusionary. His pride is just.

The tone of the "Bibliographical Note" to the newly published and final volume is more relaxed, more casual, and more confident in a different way—the confidence of a survivor. The final paragraph says and shows it all:

> So, anyhow, "Farwel my book and my devocion," my rock and my companion through two decades. At the outset of this Gibbon span, plunk in what I hope will be the middle of my writing life, I was two years younger than Grant at Belmont, while at the end I was four months older than Lincoln at his assassination. By way of possible extenuation, in response to complaints that it took me five times longer to write the war than the participants took to fight it, I would point out that there were a good many more of them than there was of me. However that may be, the conflict is behind me now, as it is for you and it was a hundred-odd years ago for them.

That is how it ends, not the story, but the task, the largest and most ambitious single piece of work attempted and completed by any American novelist in this century. In total, something over a million and a half words, it is longer than all of Proust and, give or take, just about the size of Gibbon's masterpiece. Begun in 1954 and worked at steadily, fulltime, since then, it is a remarkable achievement, one which would be remarkable at any time, but is all the more so in our own time when our artists, like everyone else, have shunned the high risks of real adventure, hoping and settling for the hoarded privileges of easy recognition and, sometimes, a fast buck. Foote's choice and his commitment to it are simply unique. He could easily have taken the more popular, easier way. For by 1954 he had established himself as a serious, very productive, and, in the best sense, successful young novelist. If art were a horserace (as so many seem to think it is), Shelby Foote had already gained a good lead, a couple of lengths at least, on the rest of the pack, including some of the novelists who have since come to be regarded as our contemporary masters. He had already moved beyond the merely promising. Which is to say a number of things. The conception and execution of *The Civil War* was not a case of a writer "finding himself " or finding his proper form, not, then, a turning away from one form to another; rather it is the rarer example of a mature artist adapting and assimilating all his skills and applying these to a different sort of problem. It is not a question of loss, but of gain and change. The chances for loss, the risks involved, were staggering. For example, even assuming the good fortune of living to complete his marathon enterprise and doing it tolerably well, the odds were strong, if not overwhelming, that in a time of instant attention and instant oblivion, he would find himself and his work cheerfully forgotten. And to a degree that has happened, though there have been a few critics through the years who have preserved the

memory of his reputation and accomplishments. (A notable example was the *Mississippi Quarterly*'s Fall 1971
"Special Issue on Shelby Foote.") But indicative of the
risks and temporary losses is the fact that the announcement of the publication of the final volume of *The Civil
War* was not "newsworthy" enough to place the book
among the lists of promising and "significant" titles due
to appear in the fall of 1974. (At this writing there are
good signs that the newspaper and magazine reviews may
make up for that oversight.) Most important, Foote was
freely willing to take all those risks in order to give himself
to his great subject. The word for that is dedication.

It is probable that he will return to the novel now, according to the most recent interviews; but even if he does not,
it is more than likely that his earlier novels will have a kind
of second life, if only to be re-examined in the light of what
he has done since then. With the advantage of time between, we can see some general things more clearly. For
one thing, Foote's novels hold up very well. They have not
"dated" much; they are, therefore, not to be taken as exemplary of any particular school or movement or, for that
matter, any single *period*. They are highly individual, independent works. It used to be said by some that he was
deeply under the influence of William Faulkner. Well, it
is impossible for any Southern writer aware of his place
and people and aware of his own literary tradition *not* to
be influenced by the towering energy and example of
Faulkner. Those who pretend otherwise (and there are a
number) are either trying to fool themselves or us or both
at once. It might be expected that Foote would be singularly susceptible as a Mississippi writer who knew William
Faulkner as well and as closely as any other writer could.
Yet, with the passage of time, it is clear that Foote was not
influenced in any of the obvious and negative ways. His
style and language were, from the beginning, and remain,
distinctly different. Rhetorical tropes and certain trade-
marks of the Faulkner manner, including specific forms of
verbal texture, now widely used (and often misused) by
American writers of all kinds, are chiefly absent from
Foote's prose. Which is characterized by a kind of classic
clarity and condensation, often transparent, though the
materials he deals with may be complex and dark. Foote's
approach to the presentation of character is different in intent and may be described, with obvious oversimplification, as a method of continuing *development* rather than
characterization by discovery. There is one major characteristic in common. In Foote's five novels, as in all of
Faulkner's, the basic pattern, a combination of structure
and point of view, is different for each story. But Foote is
a conservative innovator, which is to say that he neither
invents new forms for storytelling, nor in any of his work
is the means or strategy anything more (or less) than a precision tool for his overall purpose. None of which makes
him "better" or "worse" than William Faulkner, but all
of which makes his work different in its qualities. And
these qualities stand out now even more distinctly from
the more recent habits of deliberate overt and self-
conscious innovation which have been fashionable in serious American fiction for the past decade or so. Finally,
and in this he perhaps inevitably comes close to much of
Faulkner, all of Foote's stories have been, to one degree

or another, rooted in history. No present action is presented without a real or an implied historical shadowing.

> **I'm working with a very large canvas, but at the same time I'm trying to do each paragraph the way you'd write a sonnet. I'm trying for precision on a large scale.**
>
> —*Shelby Foote*

Together with a rigorous fidelity to fact and a mastery of
the materials, all the qualities already evident in his fiction
were perfectly transferable to the writing of narrative history. The clarity and the compression of style and language are great strengths in the history. He put it very accurately in an interview for the Memphis *Commercial Appeal* (July 15, 1973): "I'm working with a very large canvas, but at the same time I'm trying to do each paragraph
the way you'd write a sonnet. I'm trying for precision on
a large scale." Characterization presents another sort of
challenge. Conventional history, even the best written,
most often, for the sake of convenience and efficiency if
nothing else, introduces each character in the prose equivalent to the unveiling of a statue. The figure is revealed,
all at once, solidly and in three dimensions, and, in exposure, is judged. Then we are shown actions and events involving the character, and such suspense as there is, lies
in the analytical game of determining to what extent the
character conformed to or deviated from the initial judgment. Foote used the novelist's means, his own, allowing
the individual characters to develop and change in and
with action and events. We have first impressions, not
judgments, and these impressions change continually as
we go along. The consistency, the core of the character,
is there by inference and implication. Which is to say characterization is dramatic and dynamic and becomes a
source of narrative suspense, thus of forward motion in
the whole narrative. There are a thousand ways to do this,
and a cast of thousands to handle; but one way is in finding
the exact and appropriate moment in the action, and usually only once in the entire narrative, to present certain
relevant details. A superb example of this typical care
comes in the opening pages of the final volume when Foote
describes General Grant and his son checking into Willard's Hotel prior to receiving his promotion to lieutenant
general and assuming his final command. We see him as
others—the desk clerk and observers in the lobby—in fact
saw him, unimpressive, another major general in a town
full of stars. When he signs the register and is known,
there is a classic "double-take" and we are given, the only
time in the book, the objective physical facts of Grant's appearance ironically just at the moment that, by virtue of
his name and fame, he is magically transformed in the eyes
of his beholders.

> Here before them, in the person of this undistin-
> guished-looking officer—forty-one years of age,
> five feet eight inches tall, and weighing just

under a hundred and forty pounds in his scuffed boots and shabby clothes—was the man who, in the course of the past twenty-five months of a war in which the news had been mostly unwelcome from the Federal point of view, had captured two rebel armies, entire, and chased a third clean out of sight beyond the roll of the southern horizon.

It is a question of dealing out bits and pieces, shards, of information. The effect is that these figures are seemingly in constant motion. Combined with a similar arrangement of psychological details, this novelistic method results in a suspension of the habit of snap judgment until such time as judgment becomes both dramatic and requisite. To put it another way, in conventional historical prose judgments are regularly rendered (and, indeed, are required) by the author. In Foote's narrative history there is a narrator who must, from time to time, enter in, "intrude" directly; but when this happens in Foote's story it is direct and dramatized, usually in terms of one character's judgment or misapprehension of another's actions or motives and is justified by coming with a slight shift in point of view. An excellent, and typical, example of the careful entrance of the narrator into action comes in Volume II. Forrest has just given his commander, Braxton Bragg, an outrageously insubordinate, personal denunciation, called him a coward and threatened his life. The scene ends with Forrest riding away with a companion whom he reassures that no real trouble will come from his outburst, that Bragg will not mention it or do anything about it. Since Forrest has long since been established as one of the narrative's genuine heroes, and since Bragg has revealed himself in many ways as a serious scoundrel, we are delighted. *Then,* and only then, we are given the benefit of intrusive judgment which, among other things, gives us a single fact about Bragg that subtly changes our view of him and Forrest as well.

> Forrest was right in his prediction; Bragg neither took official notice of the incident nor disapproved the cavalryman's request for transfer, which was submitted within the week. He was wrong, though, in his interpretation of his superior's motives. Braxton Bragg was no coward; he was afraid of no man alive, not even Bedford Forrest.

Foote then moves to explore the real, and on the whole laudatory, motives behind Bragg's willingness to shrug off Forrest's misconduct. We learn two things from the brief episode, some sense of the limits of Forrest's imagination, intelligence, and judgment, and some awareness of strengths in Bragg's flawed character. Both become more complex figures as a result. The same rigor is observed throughout the entire narrative. Which means that direct acts of judgment are few and far between, and when they occur they are functional. That in turn creates what critics used to call a "tension"; for, to a greater or lesser extent all readers of this story know much of the story in advance and come to it with preconceived notions and with a baggage of prejudicial judgments. The methods of characterization work actively to unsettle us from certainties; and, thus, by narrative devices and construction, old events are renewed and engage us with the demands of raw experi-

ence itself. Which means, further, that *Foote's* judgments of characters, of Lincoln and Davis, of Lee and Grant, and of all the others, can be apprehended only in terms of the whole story, the accumulated revelations of details in the presented sequence of the entire work. (This is exactly the opposite of the mingling of fact and fiction which has been named "The New Journalism.") With that roundness and complexity of characterization and with strict adherence to the angles of point of view, within the omniscient scheme, goes the capacity to treat some of the less than worthy characters more fairly, thus more accurately. And so Foote is able to do justice to high-placed scoundrels like Bragg and Henry Halleck and Edwin Stanton, men who have been scorned because they were scoundrels. In answer to a question about this, Foote has replied, succinctly enough: "Pricks too have their point of view, and sometimes it's an interesting one to investigate, especially if what you're after is a sense of 'how it was.' "

His interests in innovation and his structural skills as novelist have been applied to enable him to achieve what very few historians of any stripe have managed, a sense of the simultaneity of diverse actions. And it is this feeling of simultaneous actions which gives us, in my opinion, for the first time in accounts of the Civil War, a real and continuing awareness of the war in the West and, as well, of the war at sea. All this adds up to a larger awareness of the whole war, its size and scope; and, so, for example, in this context, the war in the West assumes its proper weight of importance. Foote, in his final "Bibliographical Note," states that he has no "thesis" about this to maintain, but he is willing to claim "that Vicksburg, for example, was as 'decisive' as Gettysburg, if not more so, and that Donelson, with its introduction of Grant and Forrest onto the national scene, may have had more to do with the outcome than either of the others had, for all their greater panoply, numbers, and documentation."

Because *The Civil War* is primarily, though not entirely, a combat history of the war, the other elements, political and social and economic, are realized dramatically and in that context. They, too, are shown and implied, or are to be inferred, in action and in character. It would be a serious misreading to conclude that any of these elements are missing, but it would be a critical mistake to look for their exploitation in conventionally analytic and expository terms. The richness of mid-nineteenth-century America in a multiplicity of forces and details, large and small, is there in the narrative; but these appear, occur to us, *happen* to us much as they happened to those who were too much involved in the experience of the war to be self-conscious or especially analytical about either the larger ghostly patterns within and behind events or the small, taken-for-granted things on the surface of daily life. Reading *The Civil War* is, then, an experience, one which is analogous to the experience of a novel with a richly sensuous affective surface rather than a recapitulation of events. It is superb history by any standards, but it is unique history as well.

It is far too early (and it would be purely presumptuous) to report anything more than these most general reactions. My judgment is that the work is, without question or qualification, a masterpiece, one of the very few genuinely great literary works of our time. Time will tell. And one can't say that much about many books in a lifetime. We shall be a long time coming to know *The Civil War* deeply and in detail. Perhaps our children and grandchildren will know it better; for it seems most probable to be the version of our most tragic time which will be passed on to them. It may well have been a knowledge of what he had achieved and of its likely continuity and posterity which led Foote to take his story on beyond the war's end, the series of surrenders, parade's end, and the Reconstruction, to the death of Jefferson Davis in 1889 for its curtain. For this allowed him to suggest—again, as in the unbroken line of the narrative, by inference and by dramatic perception—some of the things that all of it means, most especially in what it meant to those who fought the war and survived it. In terms of casualties we have never experienced anything like it.

> Approximately one out of ten able-bodied Northerners was dead or incapacitated," Foote writes, "while for the South it was one out of four, including her non-combatant Negroes. Some notion of the drain this represented, as well as the poverty the surrendered men came home to, was shown by the fact that during the first year of peace the state of Mississippi allotted a solid fifth of its revenues for the purchase of artificial arms and legs for its returning veterans.

But the last word of the veterans and survivors is chosen by Foote to be represented by twice-wounded, former Captain Oliver Wendell Holmes, who came close to matching the eloquence of Lincoln's Gettysburg Address with a speech in Keene, New Hampshire, in 1884, in the midst of what Mark Twain called the Gilded Age, a time in which these soldiers, old from their youth, were out of place. What Holmes said for them becomes, in essence, the summing up of the whole experience of *The Civil War*:

> The generation that carried on the war has been set aside by its experience. Through our great good fortune, in our youth our hearts were touched with fire. It was given to us to learn at the outset that life is a profound and passionate thing. While we are permitted to scorn nothing but indifference, and do not pretend to undervalue the worldly rewards of ambition, we have seen with our own eyes, beyond and above the gold fields, the snowy heights of honor, and it is for us to bear the report to those who come after us.

(pp. 83-92)

George Garrett, "Foote's 'The Civil War': The Version for Posterity?" in The Mississippi Quarterly, *Vol. XXVIII, No. 1, Winter, 1974-75, pp. 83-92.*

M. E. Bradford   (review date 14 February 1975)

[*Bradford is an American educator and critic who specializes in American literature of the South. In the following review of* The Civil War, *he favorably assesses Foote's emphasis on military history.*]

Almost transfixed by what they saw, Generals James Longstreet and Robert E. Lee paused at the crest of a ridge overlooking a considerable portion of the field at Fredericksburg. It was December 13, 1862. And beneath their fascinated gaze unfolded in panorama the bruit of that momentous day. Out of a line of woods, driving before them with the bayonet the flower of Hooker's infantry, came a portion of the ragged host commanded by these professionals in grey. The air was filled with the distinctive war cry (half Celtic, half Indian) which had already become the signature of the Confederacy under arms. Then Lee, lifted in spirit to meet the spectacle, turned to his dour lieutenant and said, "It is well that war is so terrible—we should grow too fond of it!"

In the spirit of these words, novelist Shelby Foote has given twenty years to a penetration of the pattern which they suggest, to an inclusive, almost hieratic retelling of what may properly be denominated *the* American story. His most considerable achievement [of *The Civil War*] lies in rendering what was epitomized for Lee and Longstreet as they stood, silent, watching—in employing his skills to "make . . . live again" as one high, heroic narrative, America's second (and most serious) "revolution." There is, of course, a majesty inherent in the subject. Some sense of that ineluctable fact, however reluctant its expression, is evident in every honest consideration of our history. But the credit for recovering such majesty to the attention of our skeptical and unheroic age will hereafter belong peculiarly to Mr. Foote.

The War itself, gathered to a point in the epiphany at Fredericksburg, is indeed Foote's subject: the *war,* the *fighting*—and not its economic, intellectual, or political causes. And therefore the persons who made, died in, or survived that conflict. Good novelists have a proper horror of abstractions. Foote's subtitle is thus not casually intended. Nor is it an exaggeration to speak of the total effect produced by this emphasis as epic. Or perhaps the appropriate analogy is to Shakespeare's history plays. For men and the spirit with which they perform, not momentous events, are what distinguish *Beowulf* and *Henry V* from quantitative reports of the clash of hordes and the fall of kingdoms. Epics may, however, have a composite hero, a whole nation, as in Shakespeare's two tetralogies. The America that ended in 1865 is the central character in this *Heldenleben*.

Foote does not neglect his facts and is lavish of detail in drawing a scene. Little people and great captains are marshaled in their proper places. Also failures, fools, and knaves. And the complete accounts of discrete campaigns are intertwined with skill. Yet Foote's strong suit is in matching purpose and design. He has a tale to tell, one that few Americans understand as a complete action. And, like the epic poets of old, he assumes that the character of a society is revealed for once and all in struggle. For he writes of the Americans measured in these days that " . . . It was their good fortune, or else their misery, to belong to a generation in which every individual would be given a chance to discover and expose his worth, down to the final ounce of strength and nerve." Sir Winston Churchill once observed that Anglo-Saxon manhood achieved an apotheosis at Gettysburg not elsewhere equaled, except perhaps on that other ridge at Hastings. He would have understood Shelby Foote's unfashionable decision to put his military history first. For like the accounts of love and faith, it too has power to exalt the spirit of man.

But, if this history is martial and "shown," not intellectual and explained, it is to be expected that it will attempt to embody its significance in a total action, a dialectic of men and circumstances: that it will find in the order and emphasis of the telling the form that is its meaning. This is, as every social scientist will admit, the hard way around. One and one-half million words on these archaic assumptions are enough to demonstrate that Foote was serious about his enterprise, almost as heroic as the subject itself. In telling, he has neglected nothing.

For one thing, he gives us a balanced emphasis on the war in the West, something usually omitted in the orthodox accounts. On these campaigns, and on other lesser actions, he is at his best. And also in implicit portraiture—Jackson, once the enemy is in flight, crying "now let's holler"; Grant, almost in shock after his first encounter in the Wilderness; Lee, drawn by his men from the midst of battle at Spotsylvania. Lincoln and Davis had to be included in these images—both as politicians and as something more. Lincoln is visible throughout. But with Davis Foote begins. And with Davis he ends—impertinent, honored, and alone. Here inevitably what looks like a touch of ideology enters in. For what made the war and for what came after, a glance at political history had to be included in so thorough a report. Foote is less satisfactory in these matters, more likely to be misled by respect for futurist authorities and a desire to keep his subject from contamination by comparison with contemporary sectional disputes. His emphasis and his pieties fortunately protect him even here. And especially in the recently published final volume of the three, covering from "Red River to Appomattox."

Events occurring in the twenty years since the author began his work have perhaps recovered to him the wisdom of his fathers—wisdom concerning what Union based on force would come to be, what Father Abraham's "little engine" of ambition left us all once his second founding was complete. But Foote had it there, in fragments, all the time. I choose two instances for a demonstration. First a quotation from an 1861 editorial in the *New York Times:* "We must remain master of the occasion and the dominant power on this continent." Then the words of an ordinary Virginia private who, when asked upon capture why he had been drawn to the rebel colors, answered simply, "Because you're down here." Set off against each other, these two statements give us all the political framework we need, to live again in spirit where the issue remains in doubt, the battle is yet to be joined, and a man may yet lift his hand in some worthy deed to live at the top of his bent. With so much at stake, who could stand aside? (pp. 173-74)

M. E. Bradford, "Else We Should Love It too Well," in National Review, *New York, Vol. XXVII, February 14, 1975, pp. 173-74.*

C. Vann Woodward   (review date 6 March 1975)

[*Woodward is a preeminent historian of the American South whose studies, including* Origins of the New South, 1877-1913 *(1951; rev. ed., 1971) and* The Strange Career of Jim Crow *(1955), are praised as insightful interpretations of Southern history and identity. A frequent contributor to such journals as* Commonweal, Harper's *and the* New York Review of Books, *Woodward has gained popularity for his intelligent and accessible commentary. In the following review of the third volume of* The Civil War, *he evaluates the intellectual merit of Foote's narrative military history.*]

Professionals do well to apply the term "amateur" with caution to the historian outside their ranks. The word does have deprecatory and patronizing connotations that occasionally backfire. This is especially true of narrative history, which nonprofessionals have all but taken over. The gradual withering of the narrative impulse in favor of the analytical urge among professional academic historians has resulted in a virtual abdication of the oldest and most honored role of the historian, that of storyteller. Having abdicated—save in the diminishing proportion of biographies in which analysis does not swamp narrative—the professional is in a poor position to patronize amateurs who fulfill the needed function he has abandoned.

In no field is the abdication of the professionals more evident than in military history, the strictly martial, guns-and-battle aspect of war, the most essential aspect. The burden of this kind of history has to be borne by narrative. The academic professionals are prolific with books on the political, diplomatic, economic, ideological, and psychological history of wars, but not on the purely military history. The leading chroniclers of the most important American military experience, that of the Civil War, have been Douglas Southall Freeman, Bruce Catton, Kenneth P. Williams, and Shelby Foote—none of them trained academicians. Allan Nevins did become a professor, but he was jealous of his amateur standing as a military historian.

Shelby Foote is the author of five novels, yet most of his writing has gone into his huge history of the Civil War, which he unabashedly describes as "A Narrative." ["Red River to Appomattox"] is the third, the largest, and the final volume of a work that has been twenty years in the writing. Like his predecessors named above (with the exception of Nevins) his subject has been military history in the strictest sense. Within these limits, however, he has attempted a more comprehensive treatment than the others. Freeman viewed the war from the standpoint of the Confederate Army of Northern Virginia and was concerned primarily with the eastern theater. Catton treated the western theater as well as the eastern, but from the standpoint of the Union Army. Williams also covered both theaters, but from the outlook of the Union command. When one of these writers calls a chapter "A Season of Reverses," you know whose reverses he is talking about. Save for river gunboat actions, they do their fighting ashore.

Foote undertakes to cover it all, all the military history—Union and Confederate, east and west, afloat and ashore. As narrator he is omnipresent, shifting from Grant's headquarters to Lee's, from Sherman's to Johnston's, from the eastern theater to the western and back again, and from dry land to blue water. Disavowing any "thesis to argue or maintain," he does profess a desire "to restore a balance," lacking in previous accounts, between the eastern and western theaters, and to correct the impression of the war in the West as "a sort of running skirmish [that] wobbled back and forth, presumably as a way for its participants, faceless men with unfamiliar names, to pass the time while waiting for the issues to be settled in the East." In spite of his Mississippi origins, Foote also attempts to keep an even hand in giving North and South their due measure of praise and blame. Yet somehow a bit more adrenalin goes into his accounts of campaigns west of the mountains; there is more dash in a cavalry charge of Forrest's than in one of Sheridan's, and the heroes in gray were a bit more heroic than those in blue. And maybe that was the way it was.

It is the last year of the war—from the Red River Campaign in Louisiana in April, 1864, to Appomattox in April, 1865—that is covered in this volume. The conventional view is that by this time the Rebels had lost their will to win and that the action was essentially reduced to mopping-up operations. It did not seem that way to General Sherman, who was in a position to know. At the beginning of that last year he wrote his wife that "no amount of poverty or adversity seems to shake their faith, . . . niggers gone, wealth and luxury gone, money worthless, starvation in view, . . . yet I see no sign of let up—some few deserters, plenty tired of war, but the masses determined to fight it out." They needed more persuasion, and he was prepared to give them all that was required, and more. "All that has gone before is mere skirmishing," he told his wife as he set forth on the task—his knock-out blow to Georgia and his rape of South Carolina.

General Grant opened his Virginia campaign of that horrible last year with the same relentless savagery. Within one month after it crossed the Rapidan River the Army of the Potomac under Grant had lost no less than half as many men as it had lost in the previous three years of bloody fighting in Virginia. "For thirty days it has been one funeral procession past me," protested one of Grant's generals, "and it has been too much." Yet it was only the beginning. By the time he had crossed the James and besieged Petersburg, Grant's losses came to nearly 75,000 men—more than Lee and Beauregard had had in both their armies at the start of the campaign a month and a half before. In one charge before Petersburg a Maine regiment of 850 lost 632 men, more than 74 percent, in less than half an hour. Casualties among the graybacks were nearly always much smaller in numbers but larger in proportion to their available manpower and therefore more costly in military terms. With that fateful knowledge, Grant ruthlessly swapped casualties on unequal terms and never abandoned his meat-grinder tactics, pouring black meat after the white into the grinder.

While he is willing to admit that there is "a good deal more to war than killing and maiming," Foote has little space for the other aspects. We are admitted to a few of Lincoln's cabinet meetings and some of the president's public speeches and private conversations. We are taken backstage occasionally in the Richmond theater of politics. We are permitted a passing glance at an election, a diplomatic exchange, and (particularly in the South) an economic crisis that had immediate military consequences. The politics of command in both armies—personal rivalries, political animosities, and power plays among the brass—are adequately kept before the reader. But always the main matter before us is the "killing and maiming."

To the predominantly analytical historians of the schools, this flood of action provides little of what they call "insight." That means clues to mass motivation, keys to puzzles of grand strategy and policy, and answers to large questions of "why"—why the North won and the South lost, for example. I suppose the narrative historian's answer might be that there is something to be said for knowing how a cataclysm was experienced as well as explaining why it happened. Problems of motive and explanation acquire a new dimension in the presence of surviving veterans of the battle of Spotsylvania. They

> went through the motions of combat after the manner of blank-faced automatons, as if what they were involved in had driven them beyond madness into imbecility; they fought by the numbers, unrecognizant of comrades in the ultimate loneliness of a horror as profoundly isolating in its effect as bone pain, nausea, or prolonged orgasm, their vacant eyes unlighted by anger or even dulled by fear.

The intimacy of combat in that age of warfare lends itself to Shelby Foote's impressive narrative gifts and to his dramatic purposes. In World War II, battleships opened fire at a range of thirteen miles or more—beyond sight of their targets. In the Battle of Mobile Bay the opposing flagships rammed each other head-on, and the *Tennessee's* guns were so close to the *Hartford* that the powder blackened her side. In the latter ship, Admiral Farragut had himself lashed to her rigging the better to command, and his opponent and friend Admiral Buchanan attacked Farragut's fleet of seventeen vessels with his one surviving ship outgunned twenty to one. Rebel taste for histrionics supplies embarrassing riches of color. The duel between the *Alabama* and the *Kearsarge* in the English Channel is right out of Scott, with Admiral Semmes flinging his glittering sword into the sea as his ship sinks. Jeb Stuart whirls through cavalry actions in red-lined cape, bright yellow sash, black ostrich plume, and golden spurs—no less dangerous for it all.

Where possible, however, Foote tends to let his beloved Army of Tennessee upstage the easterners. The western spirit of desperate improvisation best typified the expiring rebelion. General Joe Johnston, the Virginian, whom Sherman described as "a sensible man who only did sensible things," yielded command to General Hood, the Texan, an unsensible man who did desperate and unsensible things. One leg missing, one arm paralyzed, strapped to his saddle, he led his army of barefoot scarecrows to their doom. Three regiments that started the war with an average of 1,250 effective troops fought on with sixty-five, fifty, and sixty-four present for duty. In five weeks Hood lost 20,000 veterans in casualties, including sixteen generals. He was loyally supported by that genius of improvisation, General Forrest, whose engineers constructed bridges out of grapevines—literally.

For all this "the butcher's bill" was a North-South total of 623,026 dead from all causes and 471,427 wounded, or a total of 1,094,453 for both sides, in and out of more than 10,000 military actions. Another historian, Eric McKitrick, has calculated that a casualty rate in World War II comparable to Union deaths in the Civil War would have required nearly 2.5 million deaths as against actual losses of 384,000. Southern losses in dead or incapacitated were fewer in number but greater in proportion to the number available for service-one out of four (including noncombatant Negroes) as against one out of ten in the North. Of generals the Unions lost one out of twelve killed in action, the Confederates one out of five.

But what has all this to teach our "psychohistorians," our "cliometricians," and our crypto-analysts busy with their neat models, parameters, and hypotheses? It is hard to say for sure. It is possible, however, that the 1,100 pages of this raw narrative, bereft as it is of "insight," might serve to expose them to the terrifying chaos and mystery of their intractable subject and disabuse them of some of their illusions of mastery.

> *C. Vann Woodward, "The Great American Butchery," in* The New York Review of Books, *Vol. XXII, No. 3, March 6, 1975, p. 12.*

James I. Robertson, Jr. (review date June 1975)

[*Robertson, an American educator and historian who specializes in the American Civil War, has stated: "I am a social historian in a military period, for my interests are not primarily in battles and leaders. Rather, I am more concerned with the feelings of the soldiers and the common folk." In the following review, he offers a balanced judgement of* The Civil War, *focusing on the merit of Foote's work according to the criteria of professional historians.*]

Our historical profession of late has come under widespread attack because of a simple, growing and potentially fatal weakness. Historians, it is charged, have abandoned popular history. Turned around, the criticism is more biting. Professional scholars seemingly devote too much time to studies with limited readability. Too often historical works are ponderous if not pontifical; too often rebuttal and revision prevail at the expense of revelation; too often "scholarly studies" are designed for fellow historians and graduate students rather than for interested laymen and the buying public. In other words, a feeling persists that the study of history is slipping into a closed shop exclusively for the professionals. Such an occurrence would be disastrous for all concerned.

The possibility of that transpiring in the Civil War field is unlikely, thanks in great part to a corps of writers who have so popularized the conflict between North and South as to make it far and above the nation's favorite historical period. For example, Carl Sandburg, Clifford Dowdey, V. C. Jones and—especially—Bruce Catton have shown through numerous studies that history can be human, ap-

pealing at all levels, and enjoyable if the narrator can use a broad base and a gifted pen. These attributes have rarely been wielded in more brilliant fashion than by Shelby Foote; and now, with the completion of . . .[*The Civil War: A Narrative*] encompassing decades of labor, Foote hereby surges forth as one of the half-dozen major figures in Civil War writing. His trilogy is at once important and imposing. It offers a direct and competent challenge to Catton's *Centennial History of the Civil War.*

Foote is a native of Mississippi who long ago adopted Memphis as his home. His literary fame first developed with five novels. Two of them—***Follow Me Down*** and ***Shiloh***—had Civil War themes. Then, in 1954, he was persuaded to embark on a full-scale narrative history of the war. Neither Foote nor the publisher realized at the time the dimensions that the project would ultimately take: twenty years of work on three widely spaced volumes containing a total of 1,500,000 words.

Volume I, first published in 1958, begins the story with secession and preparations for war, skillfully carries the reader through the early crises, and concludes with the autumn, 1862, campaigns at Perryville and Antietam. Volume II, released in 1963, opens with preludes for battle at Prairie Grove, Stone's River and Fredericksburg. It provides an in-depth study of the major and awesome 1863 contests: Vicksburg and Chattanooga in the West, Chancellorsville and Gettysburg in the East. Some 900 pages later, it is March, 1864, and U. S. Grant arrives in Washington to take supreme command of the Union armies.

Now the long-awaited and concluding third volume is at hand. It fulfills every expectation. Certainly it is the most dramatically written of the three installments, in part because it treats of the war's most dramatic months. Sherman slashes his way across the Deep South, and Sheridan blackens the Shenandoah, while Grant methodically pounds Lee into the immobility of the Richmond-Petersburg defenses. A short series of blows in the spring of 1865 and, for the South, a dream ends but a heritage begins.

Comparing Foote with Catton is inevitable, and not merely because each is the author of a three-volume narrative history. The two men possess such writing talent as to put them in a special category to themselves. Both rely on printed sources—although Catton came to depend on research assistant E. B. Long for a wealth of manuscript material. Catton uses documentation; Foote disdains footnotes. Catton is a Northerner and Eastern-oriented. He concentrates on military matters and gives excellent discussions of a selected number of Civil War subjects. He writes in a moving, poignant prose style unequalled by any other current historian. Foote is a Southerner and Western-oriented. He is also interested primarily in army actions, and he is given to a far broader but somewhat more shallow coverage of the struggle. His prose is powerful, tending more toward the overwhelming than toward the incisive.

Punctilious scholars will charge that historian Foote is assailable on at least four separate counts. First is his total reliance on printed sources. That is not as serious as it might seem. Indeed, it is difficult to criticize Foote's research because the literature of the Civil War is so immense that it is actually a compliment to any writer who can wade through thousands of volumes and glean informational nuggets to the successful degree demonstrated by Foote. He has carefully digested a mass of printed material and then rewritten the story to suit the tenets of his own presentation. This can hardly be branded as slipshod work. In fact, Foote regularly presents little human-interest stories that give personality to history. A Johnny Reb once shouted across no-man's land to a Billy Yank: "Why don't you come over to our side? We're fighting for honor and you're fighting for money." The Union soldier hollered back: "Well, I reckon each of us is fighting for what we need the most."

The absence of documentation is a more serious flaw in this study. No one will challenge the authenticity of statements made by Foote, but it would have been extremely helpful to serious readers and working historians to know the sources for some of his facts. One case in point will suffice. At Gettysburg, Foote states, all Confederate corps and division commanders were West Point graduates save one—and he had attended Virginia Military Institute. Foote then points out that only 14 of 26 corps and division leaders in the Army of the Potomac had attended the Military Academy. The majority of Meade's generals were non-professionals who suddenly found themselves immersed in the most professional war then known to man. Such contrasting situations would be worth pondering further, if one only knew where to start the search for additional information. With no leads provided, frustration results.

Foote's stated aversion to making interpretations would seem to violate one of the historian's most basic obligations. He refuses to pause to render judgments or to argue conclusions. He makes no judicious observations, predictions or the like, he asserts, because in his mind this would be a gross encroachment on what he is primarily interested in producing: a narrative history in which he puts the action before the reader and the reader before the action and then allows no intrusion on his presentation. Foote takes pride in keeping the story free from opinion.

The irony of it all is that, in spite of Foote's efforts, interpretations abound throughout the text. Braxton Bragg is repeatedly portrayed as a general too narrow-minded for the intricacies of battle. William T. Sherman is "a violent-talking man whose bite at times measured up to his bark, and whose commitment was to total war." Following Gettysburg, Lee's army "had slipped back to the disorganization of the Seven Days" because it "could not make up for the crippling lack of direction from above and the equally disadvantageous lack of initiative just below the top." Foote's evaluation of Joseph E. Johnston is especially barbed. "On the evidence, Old Joe's talent seemed primarily for retreat; so much so, indeed, that if left to his own devices he might be expected to wind up gingerly defending Key West and complaining that he lacked transportation to Cuba in the event that something threatened one of his flanks."

Whether Foote admits it or not, these are interpretations—not facts.

Finally, some purists will allege that Foote says little not already well-known and readily accessible in other works. This is only half-true. Foote does present the usual stereotypes of the war's leading figures, and he sometimes displays an equalitarian tendency to lower or raise men to the same level. However, what sustains these three volumes—what Foote utilizes that others missed—is a prose ranging from powerful to adroit.

It alternately brims with natural movement, constructed excitement, allegory, color and force. On a few occasions, it overflows badly when Foote's sentences become hopelessly long and sometimes end with a damaging, dangling participle. Yet practically every page in this set contains at least one quotable passage. It might be a battle description such as Foote's statement after "Stonewall" Jackson's men delivered a point-blank volley into an assaulting Federal column at Fredericksburg: "The blue line stopped, flailed ragged along its forward edge, and then reversed its flow."

Or it might be a succinct assessment of one man, such as this comment on the Northern president: "Nothing pleased Lincoln more than to have an opponent think he was an idiot. It was like swiping somebody with a razor and then telling them to shake their head." Or the prose could be a simple rendition of one human story. Foote has obvious (and commendable) admiration for Jefferson Davis. Volume I begins with Davis' farewell speech in the Senate on the eve of war. Volume II opens with his 1862 inaugural address in Richmond. Foote fittingly ends Volume III—and the study—with a statement Davis made just before he died: "Tell the world I only loved America."

Whether from a publisher's stinginess with review copies or from editors' apathy with widely spaced installments of an undocumented history, America's major historical journals largely ignored the first two volumes of Foote's study. The set is now complete. Foote no longer can be, or will be, ignored. He has provided a superb view of the forest rather than the usual and tiring look at a few trees; and he has done so in a writing style both fluid and appealing. The inclusion in this set of no less than 140 maps, each placed just where it is needed, is but a dividend to a sweeping history impressive to read and impossible to forget. (pp. 172-75)

> *James I. Robertson, Jr., in a review of "The Civil War: A Narrative," in* Civil War History, *Vol. XXII, No. II, June, 1975, pp. 172-75.*

Simone Vauthier   (essay date Fall 1975)

[*In the following essay, Vauthier examines narrative perspective and the relationship between fiction and reality in Foote's short story "Rain Down Home."*]

Although, on the surface, the work of Shelby Foote is representational—fostering the illusion that the world it creates is continuous with the real world—it also obliquely insists, through a number of devices, on its fictionality. The literary allusions in *Love in a Dry Season,* the manipulation of two narrative stances in **"Pillar of Fire"** serve this function. In **"Rain Down Home"** it is essentially the end which rearranges the story along different lines and obliges us to reconsider the relation of fiction to reality.

"Rain Down Home" is the story of a World War II veteran who spent several years in institutions and who, on returning home to Bristol at last, finds the town changed from everything he remembers; he wanders about trying to establish some kind of communication with the people he meets; after several such unsuccessful attempts—and one too successful conversation with a nihilistic old man—he shoots up a café and its proprietor. While Bristol and Jordan County are imaginary places, they are explicitly located in a real state, Mississippi; and though fictive, the central character is supposed to live in chronological, historical time. As for the *donneé* of the story, it is one of those incidents that make the front page of the local newspapers only to disappear the next day and, at a first (and casual) reading, the story might be dismissed as tenuous. Indeed it has been called by one critic "a very silly anecdote about a love-starved lunatic who bumps up against this hostile world of ours" [Marvin Mudrick, *Shenandoah,* Winter, 1954].

But it seems to me that even the inattentive reader should be perturbed by the end of the story. The dramatic action is completed with the coming of the police on the scene: "He was sitting there eating the pie, quite happy, with the empty pistol and the four empty clips on the table in front of him, when the police arrived. He even smiled when they shook him up, roughed him up. 'Do your duty, men,' he said, 'just like I did mine.' " The veteran's exit line might be a perfect ending. Yet the narration goes on for another paragraph:

> Next day it was in all the papers, how he shot up the place for no reason at all. The Greek proprietor, whose injury had been more bloody than serious—all he lost was the lobe from one of his ears—used that day to date things from, the way old people once spoke of falling stars. The waitress was quoted too: "I knew it was something wrong with that one from the minute I laid eyes on him." [sic] DERANGED VETERAN the headlines called him, and the stories gave a list of the various institutions he had been in and out of since the war. Everyone agreed that that was what he was, all right, deranged.

Considered as information, these lines are to a great extent redundant, or unnecessary. We have already been told that Pauly Green was a veteran; we have guessed that he was mentally disturbed and had been in hospitals. The only unforeseen detail is the news that the Greek did not die. That the papers should take the matter up or the waitress boast of her insight was only to be expected. But this very redundancy works in the narration as a sort of "inner duplication" which has far-reaching effects. By including a report on the newspapers' accounts of the event, the narration itself stresses at once the anecdotal character of the basic situation and designates its own literarity, thus in fact denying that it presented us with an anecdote. Although in terms of the action, the end may seem superfluous, tagged on to the ending, it sounds a note that rever-

berates back through the story and reactivates the whole of **"Rain Down Home."** Furthermore, it deeply alters our relation to the story. Paradoxically it contests our reading of the fictional event by confirming it. The narration offers us a summary of the case that appears objective since it is the general consensus: "DERANGED VETERAN the newspapers called him. . . . Everyone agreed that that was what he was, all right, deranged." Now, as readers, confronted with a character we know nothing about, we have been warily picking up clues that would enable us to place him, to define who and what he is and the goal towards which the story has him headed. We have noticed his aggressive awareness that others find him different: "You think I'm drunk or something"; we have been sensitive to the connotations of his pronouns which lack referents: "*They* changed *it,*" he said to the man. "*They* changed *it* on me while my back was turned" (emphasis added); we have seen our growing doubts as to his balance supported by his allusions to the strait jacket or his horrified reaction at the blase old man's advice on how to stay out of the asylum. So his final act of violence comes to some degree as a satisfying confirmation of our diagnosis—and cleverness. Like the waitress, we brashly think that it is what was to be expected.

What is unexpected, however, is that the waitress' self-satisfaction cannot but strike us as dreadfully complacent and our diagnosis, once phrased in the collective discourse, as insensitive and somehow inadequate. Its finality—which we would like to reject—is impressed on us by the repetition of the word "deranged" and its strategic position at the beginning of the sentence before last and at the very end of the story. Far from concurring in this glib judgment—which accuses us—we realize that in spite of everything, we have been made to think of the protagonist as one Pauly Green and not as a "deranged veteran"; we realize that the picture which we have been given of his predicament is far too complex to be thus cursorily assessed. The end creates a double effect of distance and is an invitation to read the story as fiction, and the fiction as more than just a case-history.

When it purposely reminds us that the events narrated are in the nature of a news item, the conclusion calls our attention to one of the choices made by the novelist. Indeed one common way of fictionalizing the *donneé* veteran-shoots-up-restaurant would have been to build up the psychological evolution that may lead to such an outburst, to supply the actor with a past, an unloving mother or a too-loving one, a traumatic war experience, in brief, with motivations. But free as we are to venture our own suppositions, none is propounded by the narration. Shelby Foote has chosen to deprive himself of some of the advantages of the novelist over the serious reporter—the use of flashbacks, the dramatization of the character's inner life. An alternative fictional course, however, which he also refused, would have been to draw away from the mimetic and to embrace the hyperbolic or surrealistic modes of illusion. But Pauly is no grotesque, however ill-adjusted he may have become. Neither is the Bristol world nightmarish, though it is alienating.

The evacuation of both Pauly's past and his actual

thoughts is made possibly by a third-person narration in which most of the time the focus is external to the protagonist: a camera eye now fixes images of Pauly, "rumpled and unshaven," with his "aggressive chin," his eyes "threaded with red," and the "coppery glint" in his stubble of beard, now turns to the objects he sees, "the traffic lights suspended between poles, the lidless glare of red and green," the Mississippi, "tawny, wide, dimpled and swirled by eddies," "the graveled paths [of the park] glittering in sunlight." Only occasionally is the focus internalized, as in "Singing woke him. At first he did not know where he was, nor then how long he had been there." Such shifts, being unfrequent and smoothly made, do not disrupt the even tenor of the narration. One, perhaps, may be felt as obtrusive: when Pauly drops the letter he has found into the mailbox, we are told: "As always, when he turned it loose there was the sense of having done something irretrievable," but here to the shift in focus there is added the intrusion of the effaced narrator, in *as always*. Through most of the narration we can only guess at Pauly's feelings from his facial expressions (e.g., his frown, smile or stiff lips) or from his gestures, and of course, from his quoted words, all the more revealing since he often talks to himself. Besides, the instance of internal focalization all occur in the first part of the story. They signally disappear from the climactic scene. There in a series of close-ups and reverse shots, the camera eye cross-cuts from Pauly to his targets in a manner that *formally* contributes to the "Western" style of the episode, thus tying it in with ritualized versions of violence in another narrative medium.

Such a technique is of course strongly reminiscent of that of Hemingway, especially in the Nick Adams stories. However, **"Rain Down Home"** modulates in a way quite characteristic of the author the two complementary aspects of the narrative instance, which is both voice and vision. Whereas in Hemingway's fiction, the voice as well as the eye strives for a sort of stylised transparency, in *Jordan County,* the voice comes through at times very clearly, neutral yet somehow slightly Southern, conversational yet compact and crisp. **"Rain Down Home"** prismatically decomposes the narrative instance: it begins with a dominant eye which registers, from some spatial distance, the dawning day and the speeding train; it ends with a pervasive voice, reporting, at some temporal remove, a collective discourse. In between, voice and vision merge, or disjoin as in the explanation of the Negro mourners' troubles.

Moreover, the management of point of view enables Shelby Foote to "thicken the texture by bringing in the background" [Foote, in an interview with Evans Harrington, *Mississippi Quarterly,* Fall, 1971]. The Delta scenery and the Bristol sights are sketched in brief but vivid vignettes, and the weather in the streets is as present to us as Pauly Green. Rain turns to "mizzle" or "drizzle," or to a hard pattering; the sun shines, "brilliant" or "pale yellow," "the glitter [leaves] the rain-washed streets but then [comes] back as bright as ever." The basic anecdote is expanded into a longer narrative through the structuring of a verbal space which is largely devoted to the creation of a fictional place—Jordan County. In that sense, the short story is a fitting introduction to a collection that purports to be "a landscape in narrative."

The brief recourse, at the end, to a passage of temporally unlocated summary and commentary also highlights the fact that the *donneé* is developed almost entirely through *showing*. The predominance of this method emphasizes the fictionality of the treatment. **"Rain Down Home"** is one scene broken down into micro-scenes. The links between these seem at first to be purely chronological and topographical. The hero wanders about Bristol as in a dream, covering the same ground several times. But, as a matter-of-fact, there is an underlying similarity between all the micro-scenes insofar as they all show Pauly's encounters with an indifferent, loveless world. Besides, through the frequent juxtapositions of descriptions of the weather and descriptions of his movements, narrational connections are set up between the natural world and the character, which, taken together, form a pattern.

Indeed the extensive network of recurrences that reticulates the story sharply distinguishes it from the merely anecdotal. And the weather pattern, for instance, clearly functions as an objective correlative of the protagonist's unstable mood; on occasion the relation is even accentuated: "When he reached the crest the rain stopped as if by signal." But the spells of rain and sunshine also contrast, in their unpredictability, with the regular blinking of the traffic lights "relaying the orders of some central brain peremptory, electric, and unthinking," representative of the artificial, inhuman organization of city life. In addition they connote the larger cycles of alternation in the natural world, that is to say in an equally unthinking but nevertheless reassuring cosmic order. Meshing with, but distinct from, the sunshine-rain cluster are the references to all sorts of lights and light effects; the railroad man's brass buttons "as bright as the sun itself," "the lidless glare of red and green, the momentary blink of amber," the parking meters "twinkl[ing] in steady metallic progression," the sparkling river, the "glittering gravel paths," the "peculiar glint" in Pauly's eyes. Together with the numerous allusions to the sun, they form another paradigm which unites the abrupt "bloodred" sunrise in the first paragraph and the final bloody outburst, through the recurrence not only of iconic images but of verbal ones as well, since the story links the "fiery" dawn to the "fireworks" of Pauly's display.

Because of such features of the narration, we have all along been reading **"Rain Down Home"** as imaginative literature. Although we may have been more consciously preoccupied with deciphering the enigma of Pauly Green, we have also been encoding all the other elements of the short story into a total impression of the world in which he moves and which must needs appear to us as cold and dehumanized.

The end in no way detracts from this impression. It rather reinforces it. When we are told how Bristol dealt with its native son, we understand more clearly what Pauly was fighting against. To the newspapers, he is above all a case, whose name, in the report we have, is not even mentioned, whose connections with the town are unimportant. "DE-RANGED VETERAN, the newspapers *called* him" (emphasis added). Not that our assessment of the affair is completely reversed. It would be an oversimplification of a deceptively complex story to interpret it as meaning only that the loveless outside world is mad and Pauly Green sane because he rebels against its inhumanity. But the intrusion of the narrative voice at the end operates a dislocation of our viewpoint by shifting the story's point of view, and leads us to question the created world's, the story's, and our own values, to ask with new humility: what is madness—what is manhood?

Perhaps more than anything else in particular it is the phrase "deranged veteran" that turns the trick. On the one hand it works in consonance with other elements of the narration, thereby making the theme of anonymity and obliteration, which sounds mutely through the story, ring loudly at the end. Absorbed in Pauly's statements on the lack of love and on suffering, we may have tended to see his plight mostly in terms of a search for love, an interpretation which is implicit in the epithet Marvin Mudrick applies to the hero and in his summary of the action. But Pauly would in fact settle for much less than love. Back in his hometown, what he asks for is *recognition*. However, first Mr. Nowell is too preoccupied to recognize "little Pauly Green that used to deliver [his] paper," too hurried even to hear that the young man addresses him by name. Later Pauly complains: "I came back from the war and all, back here where I was born and raised, and people don't even know me on the street." While *he* asks the little girl who must not talk to strangers for her dolls' *names*, there will be no one to inquire after his, let alone greet him by it. He has already disappeared from the collective memory of Bristol. But significantly, so have those who died in World War II, only a few years back. For racial reasons, the names of the war dead have not been recorded on the War memorial. Nor can the void thus created be filled by the inscriptions which have been put there, the absence of names merely stressing the emptiness of the words: IN MEMORY OF THOSE WHO SERVED IN WORLD WAR II . . . MAY THE SPIRIT OF OUR BOYS WHO FELL IN BATTLE LIVE FOREVER. Against this devastating (but unobtrusive) irony, another inscription serves as a ludicrous and pathetic reminder of World War II and as a debased testimony to man's innate desire to leave some trace of his passage, be it obscene and/or facetious, be it even anonymous. The sentence "Kilroy was here," scrawled in several places on the walls of the men's room, does not simply add a picturesque detail to the story but glances at its major theme. Pauly is too fastidious, too much concerned, too, with human misery, to express his need through *graffiti*. But his outburst of violence is to be understood as his way of saying to an unresponsive society "Pauly Green was here," of making his mark in the world, appropriately enough through his marksmanship. Hence, this is the terrible irony of the headlines which refer to him by generic name instead of by patronym. At the level of the action, the Bristol discourse cancels the signification of Pauly's gesture. But at the narrative level the phrase "deranged veteran," on the contrary, reverberates and intensifies a major polarity of the short story, the extraordinary power of obliteration of the contemporary world versus man's profound desire to be named and to assert himself. At yet another level, of course, what **"Rain Down Home"** says is "Shelby Foote was here."

Moreover the expression "deranged veteran" also endistances us from the communal judgment for a different reason. The operative word, in this light, is the epithet "deranged." While it is less charged than "crazy" or "lunatic," less technical than "paranoid" or "schizophrenic," and may well be the most appropriate word experientially, it affects us as somewhat inaccurate fictionally because we have been made to apprehend some sort of *arrangement* in Pauly's action. Certainly, the lack of apparent cause for the shooting, the link which the narration establishes between Pauly's displeasure at the lewd joke of the men in the adjoining booth and his consecutive decision, the sexual ambiguity of some of his remarks—"I know what they need. And I'm the one can give it to them too," or "This is doing me a lot of good"—all this may suggest the senselessness of his act. But paradoxically, some of these remarks, together with other details, are evidence that Pauly's outburst is not uncontrolled. Not only does it make sense to him, but he inserts it in a societal context. Realizing what people "need," seeing himself as the one who can give it to them, he truly assumes the role of *hero* and accomplishes a sacrificial rite. "Let's do this right." He pins to his coat the badge which the Army conferred upon him, and that, like the Sheriff's silver star, gives him authority and guarantees his fitness for the role. He is doing his "duty" in full awareness that it clashes with some requirements of society and will therefore be punished: after the shooting, when the police rough him up, he smiles: "Do your duty men . . . just like I did mine." Deranged he may be, but he has not lost all sense of reality.

Moreover, the ritual enacted by Pauly also proceeds from a desire which readers of fiction all share in—the desire to transform the meaningless successiveness of contingent instants into a purposeful time—redeeming moment, or, in Frank Kermode's terms, *chronos* into *kairos* [*The Sense of an Ending*]. Time seems to expand. Although "the whole affair took less than three minutes by the clock," it "seemed considerably longer to those who crouched beneath the tables." Pauly himself "[takes] his time" to make the most of his adventure. He knows how to space out his gestures, telling himself to "wait" first until he has drunk his coffee, then until he has pinned on his marksmanship badge. He knows when the proper moment has arrived: " 'Now,' he said. He was talking to himself by then. . . ." The change in the nature of time is reflected in the slowing of the narrative tempo: twelve pages are devoted to the hours going from dawn to two o'clock, two pages to the five minutes of the crisis. Under the circumstances, the metamorphosis of *chronos* into *kairos* must be achieved by violence, but this violence makes a concord of the anti-social present and the past which Pauly Green was trained for, and became expert in, institutionalized patriotic shooting. Thus the *now* is full and free and satisfying, invested with goodness: "This is doing me a lot of good," says the hero. Pauly has triumphed over the indifference of the socio-spatial world and over the emptiness of mere successiveness.

Here again, the importance of the last paragraph cannot be underestimated. It throws a new light on the transfiguration of time achieved by the protagonist, whatever his own feelings. On the one hand, the newspapers, to which the shooting is just an item in the local chronicle, turn it into *chronos* again and significantly reduce Pauly's life to dead time, to a "list of the various institutions he had been in and out of since the war." And part of our frustration when he read the newspaper account proceeds from this diminishing of an event which *we* had felt as *kairos*. For what satisfaction the shooting gave us was not simply a feeling of smugness at having been proved right; it sprang from much deeper sources as well, from an identification with Pauly's release, perhaps, and certainly, too, from the pleasures of seeing a pattern emerge and time redeemed from the contingency.

Nor is this impression purely subjective. To one other character in the story the event is at least outside of ordinary time. The Greek proprietor "used that day to date things from, the way old people once spoke of falling stars." The comparison between the "fireworks" at the café and the fall of shooting stars over the Lower South in eighteen thirty-three, a prodigy that deeply affected the public mind with its connotations of prophecy and apocalypse, again strengthens the portentousness of the incident and at the same time undercuts it ironically, adding a new twist to its ambiguity.

Till the end, therefore, the narration produces and superimposes new visions of Pauly and of the changed town, of the young man's relation to Bristol and to experience. Similarly, to the very end, we have to keep focusing our sight, shifting our vision.

The result, however, is not so much a brighter illumination of the (fictive) reality as an exploration of fiction—of different sorts of fiction.

Obviously, the collective newspaper report, factual as it may claim to be, is a fiction. It articulates for the community the version of the case that is most socially acceptable. There is "no reason at all" for the shooting that the communal vision can perceive and record, but there is the very convenient explanation of the man's former history of mental illness. So a violation of the rules intended to make some impact on the outside world is easily reduced to private, psychological *dis*order. And everything else can be left out. To this extent the newspaper accounts illustrate the discrepancy between socialized verbal fiction and (fictive) reality.

But their order-denying fiction counterpoints two other fictions that operate at different levels. In the first place, it counterpoints Pauly's attempt to give meaning to his life. This attempt obviously owes something to the historical context of World War II and perhaps to the role which was assigned to Pauly and/or fantasied by him. But it is also shaped by a cultural context of Westerns and thrillers, obscurely derived from the Ur-myth of Natty Bumppo, Lawrence's "Saint with a gun," and it is shadowed as well by the Southern legend of a pregnant and glorious past. In any case, this is a (fictive) *experiential* fiction, which Pauly acts out, pleasurably making up for past frustra-

tions and the sense of loss: "He appeared to *enjoy the whole display* from start to finish." (emphasis added). In the second place, as a story within a story, the journalistic fiction counterpoints the overall fiction of **"Rain Down Home."** To expand a remark made at the beginning of this essay, it highlights the literarity of the text, its inherent duplicity. Dealing with the vacuity of modern organization and the randomness of life, the narration presents us with an action undertaken to impose an order of sorts, to overcome insignificance, death-in-life. It could be argued that the story exists in the tension between two concepts or reality—two fictions as it were. But our concern is with the narration. Although it seems almost plotless, although— or because—it avoids developing character or building up tension and suspense, two major devices of narrative structuring, it heavily relies upon the repetitions of actions (he smiled, he frowned), upon a network of images, and upon verbal arrangements. Capitalizing on some of the requisites of narrative, **"Rain Down Home"** enriches the impoverished, meaningless reality which is its subject. Even the images that suggest random sequence, like the numerous allusions to the fickle weather, contribute to give a particular rhythm to the story and to create certain expectancies. Thereby the incarnational order of literary fiction is both opposed to the abstracting order of pseudo-journalistic and to that of pseudo-existential fictions. But this order is itself fictitious. Not only insofar as it actualizes aspects of a basic narrative paradigm which presupposes order—so much so that the novel can only mime disorder, but also in the sense that this has no existence beyond the words on the page and is merely the functioning, from the beginning forwards *and from the end backwards,* of these words. In this respect the third-person narration is again an important element. The implicit narrator obtrudes upon us a way of viewing reality—or a virtual reality—and would efface the marks of his presence so that we may mistake his vision for reality itself. Concurrently, and cunningly, he gives us signs—and above all those presented at the end—warning us that this, or any fictional vision is in fact a verbal construction.

"Rain Down Home" illuminates what it seems to deny— the discontinuity between literary fictions and "life." It also raises the problem of the reader's activity and of his need for novelistic form. That we read the story partly through the inner journalistic fiction is an emblem of the way in which we read all literature—through expectations, that may be either frustrated or fulfilled, created in us and for us by other patterns of order, other fictions. But again, what is the relation of these aesthetic fictions to reality? To take but one example from **"Rain Down Home,"** it is largely because of the lack of casual linkages *in the narration* between the outward events and Pauly's reactions that we believe him to be unbalanced. Yet to what extent is our need for such linkages conditioned by the traditional novel which makes great use of casual concatenation? To what extent is it related to some deep psychic demand for rhythm and order, shadowed by the paradigm of the *fort/da* game, which, as Freud has shown [in his *Beyond the Pleasure Principle*], is manchild's earliest game with reality—probably, therefore, our most primoridal fiction? And what is, in the final analysis, this interpretation of the story if not another critical fiction which proves that my existential fictions must be different from Marvin Mudrick's, but which also evinces the critic's unavowed desire to substitute his fiction for that of the author, i.e., to displace the father?

Classically smooth, like a sea-worn pebble, **"Rain Down Home"** is on closer sight glittering with the tiny reflective mirrors of mica particles. It confronts us, as we enter the fictive universe of Jordan County, with the fundamental issue of the nature of fiction (s). Perhaps this explains why in the "landscape in narrative" which is *Jordan County* the movement should be time-bound, from the present of **"Rain Down Home"** back to the past of *Child by Fever,* further back to **"Pillar of Fire,"** until we come to **"The Sacred Mound,"** in an ever-renewed, because ever failing—and ever satisfying—search for the origins. (pp. 35-49)

> *Simone Vauthier, "Fiction and Fictions in Shelby Foote's 'Rain Down Home',"* in Notes *on Mississippi Writers, Vol. VIII, No. 2, Fall, 1975, pp. 35-50.*

Foote on the influence of Marcel Proust:

Along with *The Iliad,* the model for *The Civil War* is Proust's *Remembrance of Things Past.* It's the handling of multiple themes. It's tying them all into one thing, and Proust taught me that. Proust taught me so very much in so many ways, and for the same reason the writer who taught me more than anyone else is probably Shakespeare. The better he is, the more he teaches you. I'd be hard put to say where Proust's chief talents lie, whether it's the telling of a little incident or the drawing of character or looking at life as to what it's all about, or what's the nature of memory. God knows where his chief talent is. It's a broad, marvelous talent. And anybody can learn from him. I certainly did—especially . . . in the handling of a large-scale thing. *Remembrance of Things Past* is a miracle.

[What] interests me perhaps more than anything else—on the repeated reading of it—is how [Proust] moves that story, the *whole* time. No matter how many digressions there seem to be, that story is moving forward. It may be a little incident that's nothing, whether it's looking through a window at Montjouvain or whatever little incident it is; later on you'll find out why it was there. And it's that way all through Proust. He's nudging the story forward *all the time.* And *that* was the thing I had very much in mind while writing *The Civil War:* keep the story moving. Proust does that and he does it superbly. And the paradox is, he's thought to depart from the story so frequently. He *never* departs from the story.

> *Shelby Foote, in an interview with William C. Carter,* The Georgia Review, *1987.*

Helen White and Redding S. Sugg, Jr.   (essay date Spring 1979)

[*White and Sugg are American critics whose works include* Shelby Foote *(1982). In the following excerpt, they study the themes, characters, and stylistic elements* in The Civil War *which underscore what they consider its modern epic quality.*]

In posting the bald phrase "A Narrative" as the subtitle of his history, *The Civil War,* Shelby Foote, previously known as a novelist, advanced a claim for literary sensibility and art in a field where the palms were going to analysis and schemes of quantification. His challenge to the preferences of academic historians is the greater in that he wrote what is often deprecated as "mere" military history. The academics, C. Vann Woodward observed in a review of Foote's book, not only honor "the analytical urge" while tending to dismiss "the narrative impulse"; they ignore "the strictly martial, guns-and-battle aspect of war, the most essential aspect." During Foote's Gibbonian labor of 20 years, however, a number of theorists of historiography, notably Leo Braudy, W. B. Gallie, and Morton White, argued the intellectual validity of historical narrative. John Keegan, moreover, must see in Foote's work a vindication of his demands for liquidation of the 19th-century tradition of the sentimental "battle piece" and correction of the institutional military historian's urge "to generalize and dissect." Keegan would require him rather "to qualify and particularize and above all to combine analysis with narrative—the most difficult of all the historian's arts." Woodward, at any rate, has suggested that the brilliance of Foote's work ought to moderate the prejudice of academic historians who think narratives of battle yield no "insight" or "clues to mass motivation, keys to puzzles of grand strategy and policy, and answers to large questions of 'why' " [Woodward, "The Great American Butchery," *The New York Review of Books,* 1975].

Foote, confident of his capacities as "a serious writer," has commented that most academic historians never become serious about writing but skip "the sweatshop apprenticeship" through which alone they might obtain "command of language" and "a way of looking at the world: Proust called it 'a quality of vision.' " This implies the necessity for mature sensibility in the writer of history no less than in the writer of fiction or verse, for the reader must sense behind the work a credible author and find in his pages an artistically constructed point of view. Credibility depends in part on the reader's confidence in the author's scholarship; but, that taken for granted, as one may with Foote on the basis of the bibliographical notes appended to each of the three volumes of *The Civil War,* one accords belief as a result of what Foote calls "narrative quality." The hallmark of this, in his opinion, is the reader's feeling that he "is not so much reading a book as sharing an experience." What Braudy has said of Gibbon may be applied to Foote: taking written history "as preeminently a construction, a literary work with aesthetic rather than systematic order and coherence," Foote, too, has controlled "the rush of time's multiplicity" by relying upon "the firmness of his own point of view and an almost Virgilian sense of the existence of a geographic site through time."

The reader does not doubt Foote's assertion, "Nothing is included here, either within or without quotation marks, without the authority of documentary evidence which I consider sound"; and the "evidenced" narrative (to borrow a term from Gallie) is never diverted in the service of bias. Foote's decision to omit footnotes in order to enhance narrative quality is aesthetically right and intellectually acceptable because he earns, by the particularity, amplitude, and balance of his presentation, the reader's confidence that authenticity was no less a consideration than vividness in the telling. Foote says that nowhere does he argue a thesis, for he "never saw one yet that couldn't be 'proved' . . . to the satisfaction of the writer who advanced it." He acknowledges, however, that he wished "to restore the balance" of emphasis on campaigns in the East and West which he found lacking in most sources. The effect of his "western-mindedness" is only to project the whole war and make us appreciate, among many examples of the rightness of his emphasis, the emergence of U.S. Grant in the West as the general-in-chief Lincoln had sought so long who could "face the arithmetic" of the war and arrive at the grim sum of victory in the East.

Foote took as his task what he asserts is the task of any novelist, any historian, the presentation of *"how it was."* He hoped to have said of him what Hobbes said of Thucydides, that he was "one who, though he never digress to read a Lecture, moral or political, upon his own Text, nor enter into men's hearts, further than the Actions themselves evidently guide him . . . filleth his narrations with that choice of matter, and orderth them with that Judgment, and with such perspicuity and efficacy expresseth himself that (as Plutarch saith) he maketh his Auditor a Spectator." So well has Foote served his noble ambition that he has made his readers not merely spectators but participants in the epic, folk-shaping events of the Civil War.

The vision that shapes the narrative can be described as "Modern"—the informed, disabused vision of the writer who approaches his work as a craft to which, far from pretending to impossible detachment, he brings the accidents of his own breeding as part of his materials. We find in Foote's book the formalism—attention to structure and design, balance, symmetry, proportion—which distinguishes the great moderns and is a first tenet of modern criticism. The narrator is balanced, generous, seeing many sides from many angles, and from a late position within a long tradition—one almost says Christian-humanist—with a Southern quality, involving piety real but rueful and pervasive irony. Foote's complex irony bears family resemblance to that of major writers of "the Southern Renaissance" and beyond them to that of other artists and critics usually associated with literary modernism.

The distinguishing marks of the Southern in Foote's history certainly do not include vulgar chauvinism. *The Civil War* exemplifies, preeminently, the "sense of place" in its economical, functional use of concrete details, the sensory effects that anchor the narrative, the human story, to "the world's body." Years ago, in attesting the authenticity of various details in his fictional narrative of *Shiloh* (1952), Foote said he hoped that in that novel "the weather is accurate too." In *The Civil War,* he has again and again rendered the particulars of place, season, and weather so as to discriminate in the reader's apprehension one engagement from another in the long sequence. We are given the theatrical lifting of the fog at Fredericksburg, the surrealistic atmosphere of the Wilderness, the band music on the

eve of Stones River "carrying sweet and clear on the windless winter air." In the account of the U.S. Navy's river campaign in the Yazoo-Mississippi Delta, Foote's native region, he rises to sustained comedy in rendering the Yankees' stunned encounter with that intractable climate and all it had bred in the way of impossible geography and intransigent men, black and white.

A Southern relish for the humorous or absurd aspects of the situations narrated, especially the quiddities of persons and places, has dictated the choice of much of the matter and colored much more. Although epic in magnitude, seriousness, and scope and tragic in impact, the book conveys much of the human quality of events through humor. Foote appreciates and features Confederate humor, shares it, and develops it by the special touches of the literary man. Whether there was actually less Yankee humor, we cannot say; where it was to be had, as in Lincoln, Foote shows impartial relish in rendering it. In spite of destruction, carnage, and pain—unforgettably rendered, as in the account of Sharpsburg, where the wounded crept into hayricks for shelter only to be burned when fire swept the field—Foote blends humor into whole sections. That devoted to the Red River campaign in central Louisiana, with its scenes of U. S. ships caught in shallows above the rapids at Alexandria and being taught by a clever engineering officer to lurch back downstream like disoriented salmon, is as richly amusing as the tales of the Yazoo. The section on "the fiasco of The Crater"—in which Union forces under the slightly comic Ambrose E. Burnside, tagged with his Homeric epithet as "the ruff-whiskered general," mined and blew up a Confederate fort with an unheard of quantity of explosives—is laced with the humor of "mismanagement at or near the top" and Rube Goldberg ingenuity. The humor only enriches and gives hysterical edge to the presentation of an incident which Foote uses as a forward allusion to the better managed explosion at Hiroshima and as a symbol of the lasting effects of the war: the Crater, he says, "in time would green over and lose its jagged look, but would never really heal."

Humor glints in the development of many personages, for example, the sloppy fanatical Stonewall Jackson and his tatterdemalion men when they were doing their famous worst against Union troops overpaid, overfed, possibly oversexed, and in any case "down here." He cites the reaction of a Northern reporter wounded near Harpers Ferry and captured who, on learning that the redoubtable Jackson was passing, asked to be raised from his stretcher, took one look, and cried, "O my God! lay me down." Foote repeatedly thereafter invites in the reader what he calls the "O-my-God-lay-me-down" reaction to extreme types and situations. Humor pervades the handling of the feisty, as for example Earl Van Dorn, or the political, such as Benjamin F. Butler, or the grandiose such as Pierre G. T. Beauregard and John Charles Frémont.

Foote's vision is Southern, too, in its alertness to the historical and literary traditions he has sought to reflect in his book. Both in bibliographical notes and by allusion, quotation, and parallel in the text he acknowledges admiration for Thucydides, Tacitus, and Gibbon among other historians. The reader is frequently put in mind also of

Homer, Tolstoy, and Proust. Foote has referred to his book as "my iliad," and the epic is undoubtedly the ground note against which he plays the obbligato of modern irony. Even in formal outline, *The Civil War* alludes to the epic. It celebrates the heroic individual exploit, though it may also point up its anachronistic quality; it mourns the deaths of heroes. It deploys the stylistic features of epithet and simile and relieves battle scenes with those of council and the domestic hearth.

Eschewing the novelist's license to render psychological time and the play of memory upon his personages' present experience, Foote has used his own position in after time to provide perspectives on Civil War events which lend them consequence and meaning. He has repeatedly shifted from the past tense to an anterior perspective as well, writing of a vividly rendered "now" in a present-participial, future-conditional mode which invests often-rehearsed events with a developmental, contingent aspect. He has further retrieved the problematical sense of historical events in the making by approaching them from a variety of contemporary points of view, thus reviving the forces which played for or against the determinations we take retrospectively for granted as "the facts."

Foote has avoided the looseness of mere chronicle by shuttling back and forth between component narratives of campaigns East and West, political effects North and South, actions on land and sea, and background developments in government and diplomacy. He takes one forward to a high point of suspense, a deferred or suspended resolution, in a given campaign, only to turn and develop more or less simultaneous actions to *their* heights and the mutual influences on eventual conclusions. There may be a lapse of weeks or months as between the several perspectives on the given action, so that the reader, though he knows the outcome, is alive to the anxieties felt by participants and observers. A temporal dialectic results which gives progression. Foote manages the transitions with constant regard for the cumulative effect of the whole, and a "plot" emerges in which momentum mounts from climax to climax and finally to the scene at Appomattox and a gathering of all the scattered parts.

Imbued with the sense of place, the sense of history, the sense of literary tradition, *The Civil War* is most profoundly Southern in projecting the sense of tragedy. This has, of course, been attested to by the major critics of Southern literature as a defining characteristic imposed by Southern history. C. Vann Woodward has declared, "The experience of evil and the experience of tragedy are parts of the Southern heritage that are as difficult to reconcile with the American legend of innocence and social felicity as the experience of poverty and defeat are to reconcile with the legends of abundance and success." Without intending paradox, we suggest that insofar as Foote's vision of the Civil War is Southern by virtue of the ironic and the tragic, it transcends the parochial and may prove to be the version for all Americans.

Its chief competitor in the professionally approved analytical and ostensibly objective kind, Allan Nevins's *War for the Union,* advertises in its title the victors' bias and evasion of the difficulty of reconciling the losers' experience with the later American legends and complacency. Although Nevins observed in his preface that any writer on the war itself must give "equal emphasis to the Southern and the Northern story," he explained that, because his work covered a period longer than the war years, its emphasis "falls on what is permanent in the life of the nation. From this standpoint much of the Confederate effort appears too transitory to require detailed treatment." He was prepared to leave "tactical military operations" and "the Confederate story" to others in order to deal with "political, administrative, economic, and social history"—as this was influenced and, after the war, dominated by the victor. But it was a *civil* war, so intimately and protractedly fought that honor—one of Shelby Foote's concerns—attached as much to the loser as to the victor; and the heirs of either side delude themselves if they imagine that the effect of what was lost—nothing less than "the Second American Revolution"—has been less permanent in the life of the nation than what was gained. Foote skimps neither side in narrating the tactical military operations, for these were the fires in which the modern American nation was forged.

Through the encompassing narrator's voice, with its intricate shifts, varying of pace, and adjustments of tone, the voice of Shelby Foote tactfully breaks from time to time. We take it as expressive of him at his best, consciously representing the best of contemporary Southern culture and sensibility. It is a humane, variously bitter, humorous, ironic, or poetic voice which the reader is pleased to hear for its own sake as well as for what it conveys or chooses to emphasize, without ever suggesting that another writer might not deploy other and equally acceptable emphases. The most frequent sort of authorial intervention is the brief aside, usually between dashes, serving to tie the action being narrated to others, to comment, to draw a literary or historical parallel, to provide perspective. More extended authorial interventions come in the form, for example, of judgments or acknowledgments that judgment must remain moot on individuals and events. Repeatedly, the author's voice sounds at the end of a battle narrative, however excitedly it may have been told, to tot up "the butcher's bill" and compare the appalling totals increasing from battle to battle as the Civil War turned into "the Thing," that is, industrialized total war. Thus in a chapter headed "The Thing Gets Under Way," we are given Shiloh as "the first great modern battle" and the shock of it even to the professionals. Beforehand, the author gives us Albert Sidney Johnston, who had husbanded his meager forces and bluffed as long as he could: "He was faced now with the actual bloody thing"; afterward he gives us Grant, soberly realizing that nothing short of absolute conquest was going to settle matters.

Stemming no doubt from Shelby Foote's predilections as a serious writer, love of language is everywhere evident both as a quality of the authorial voice and as a selective factor determining which facts the narrative voice relates or stresses. It would be possible to write a respectable history of the Civil War without featuring the articulateness, so surprising in contrast to the banal expression of 20th-century Americans, of the participants. Foote savors even the overblown rhetoric of some of the 19th-century figures though he is also quick to deflate it by juxtaposing, for example, General John Pope's grandiloquent dispatches dated from his "Headquarters in the Saddle" to the private soldiers' "jibe that he had his headquarters where his hindquarters ought to be."

It was love of language that dictated the development of a minor figure, the Union General Samuel R. Curtis, in a memorable passage in which he is proved a commander of language as well as of men and valuable on both counts in Foote's view. Curtis, a homely, unromantic, but uxorious man who loved the natural world and the singing of birds, is presented after the battle of Elkhorn Tavern through and partly for the sake of a letter to his wife. He "moved his headquarters off a ways" under Pea Ridge, Foote tells us, because of the taint of decay rising from the dead on the field of which he was victor. Foote writes:

> "Silent and sad" were the words he used to describe the present scene of recent conflict. "The vulture and the wolf have now communion, and the dead, friends and foes, sleep in the same lonely grave." So he wrote, this highly practical and methodical engineer. Looking up at the tree-fledged ridge with its gray outcroppings of granite, he added that it would serve hereafter as a monument to perpetuate the memory of those who had fallen at its base.

This passage illustrates the many controlled "poetic" compositions which enrich *The Civil War,* sometimes using the words of participants, sometimes Foote's own, and often, as above, skillfully blending them. (pp. 234-42)

For all its amplitude and concreteness, the narrative is firmly organized into three volumes and each of these into three books, the whole comprising in effect an epic prologue and 24 chapters. The first chapter of Volume III serves as an epilogue. The work comes to well over 1,500,000 words.

Foote has erected in symbolic proportions the figures of Jefferson Davis and Abraham Lincoln, stationing them at the beginning and end and reverting to them frequently throughout. "All men were to be weighed in this time," he tells us early on, "and especially these two." Beginning with Davis's farewell speech to the U. S. Senate on Jan. 21, 1861, the prologue moves to Lincoln's furtive entrance into Washington after election to the presidency. Volume I closes with the preparations of Davis, now President of the Confederate States, for his trip to "the troubled western theater" to rally his people as they began to apprehend the seriousness of the war. Foote follows this with an evocation of "the Lincoln music" in an account of the message to Congress in December 1862, in which the Union heard itself eulogized, jug-jug to Confederate ears, as "the last best hope of earth." We hardly need add that Foote, with his love of language, does all justice to the Lincoln music.

Volume II opens with Davis's trip west, which gives Foote an occasion to develop his Western-mindedness, not as a contribution to the sometimes tendentious debate as to the relative importance of Virginia and the rest of the South, but as a presentation of the whole Confederacy and its sense of a distinct manifest destiny in the Southwest and Latin America. He had memorably struck this note in the first volume with a bravura narrative of Henry H. Sibley's horrendous march on Albuquerque and Santa Fe, which Jefferson Davis, chief mover of the Gadsden Purchase, cheered against the odds. The second volume closes on a Confederacy, not only cut off from fantasies of expansion to the Pacific, but severed at the Mississippi River, and on William T. Sherman's articulation of the doctrine of total war, which he had already tested in the devastation of central Mississippi after the fall of Vicksburg—"to the petulant and persistent secessionists, why, death is mercy. . . ." The whole immense work is brought to a climax in the Cincinnati conference between Sherman and Grant, the latter finally recognized by Lincoln as the general who faced the arithmetic, as they concert the Western and Eastern strategies to bring the war to an end by waging it totally. Foote sets the two figures earnestly talking in a Cincinnati hotel room against the chiaroscuro of the Confederates' liquidating their pretensions to wage a Second American Revolution. They have had to enact conscription some time back, feeling that they thus sacrificed the classic rights to the necessities of "the Thing." Now they must extend it to all white males from 17 to 50, and Jefferson Davis mourns the necessity "to grind the seed corn of the nation."

The final volume, after moving inexorably with sustained narrative skill to the laying down of arms on all fronts, comes to a quiet and thoughtful epilogue, a look into the future. The ghost of the murdered Lincoln is summoned, and Foote employs Lincoln's words to suggest his own motivation in writing Civil War history:

> What has occurred in this case must ever recur in similar cases. Human nature does not change. In any future great national trial, compared with the men of this, we shall have as weak and as strong, as silly and as wise, as bad and as good. Let us therefore study the incidents of this, as philosophy to learn wisdom from, and none of them as wrongs to be revenged.

Foote, we suspect, would approve the amendment of this by the addition of a phrase—" . . . or as complacencies to be defended." He goes on to quote Davis, the worn and hounded survivor, though acknowledging that he "could never match that [Lincoln] music, or perhaps even catch its tone," as he asserts at the end his love of America. The reader supplies, "All passion spent."

Within the grand epic design, Foote has been unflaggingly ingenious in weaving, stitching, and binding the parts by recurrent themes and characters, meant to function, he has said, like the armature within a sculpture. The most pervasive theme, already alluded to, is the one Foote has said comes as near as he gets to a thesis, the redressing of the balance between the East and West theaters. He develops Western actions as fully as Eastern ones and makes mutual influences clear. Thus he narrates the events at "Bull Run and Wilson's Creek, near opposite ends of the thousand-mile-long fighting line" and takes his opportunities to show the reader how a twitch at either end was felt the length of the line. He gives added coherence to the book by maintaining in the reader's eye, with the aid of numerous maps and images, the whole of the Confederacy as this becomes one enormous battleground and then is contracted under the pressure of Winfield Scott's Anaconda strategy, in time split down the Mississippi, and dismembered as the Sherman-Grant strategy and tactics take over.

A related theme is the changing character of the war, begun, especially by the Confederates, under romantic illusions about individual honor only to develop into the prototype of modern mass technological warfare. At First Manassas and repeatedly thereafter, there were exploits by mounted heroes with plumes in their bonnets. Foote does justice to these, often ironically but also with affection, admiration, and tears as he follows, for example, the superbly mounted and plumed Jeb Stuart to his Homeric death scene. He brings us on grimly to Cold Harbor and there gives us a glimpse of Colonel Lawrence Keitt of South Carolina thinking to take his chance for glory by leading a green but dashingly uniformed brigade into the fray. "Long on rank but short on combat experience," Foote comments, "he went into his first attack in the gallant style of 1861, leading the way on a spirited gray charger; only to be killed by the first rattling clatter of semiautomatic fire. . . ."

Foote makes themes illuminate one another often, again, with ironic effect. It is obvious that in narrating the changes in the character of the war he would have repeated occasion to illuminate another major theme, that of the searches by the presidents for generals competent to understand modern war and prosecute it effectually. It is less obvious that, in giving thematic prominence to the contrast between Northern plenty and Southern poverty, he should have clarified certain tactical issues faced by the presidents and their generals. There is powerful human interest in repeated scenes of hungry, tattered Confederates falling ravenously upon abandoned Yankee supply dumps or stripping Yankee dead, not in Homeric lust for trophies but to obtain food to eat, shoes for bleeding feet, and guns to fire. Cumulatively, such scenes help the reader to understand in concrete fashion that in certain circumstances what Foote terms their "philosophy of abundance" was a tactical drawback for the Yankees while the Confederates necessarily traveling light arrived at stunning victories under officers such as Jackson and Nathan Bedford Forrest.

Lincoln's long frustration in getting one general after another to move south of the Potomac was caused in part by the generals' preoccupation with the development and defense of immense commissaries which they believed had to follow the armies. Foote prepares the reader to recognize an important development when U. S. Grant finds in December 1862, after Earl Van Dorn has destroyed his quartermaster stores at Holly Springs, that he could subsist his troops on the countryside deep in enemy territory. Foote quotes Grant's remark, "This taught me a lesson"—and the reader grasps, before Lincoln can, that in his ability to learn this lesson Grant was proving himself to be the long-sought general-in-chief.

Foote's human sympathies are so inclusive and skill in characterization so great that he brings historical personages hauntingly alive. Their presence is felt even when off-stage, with the result that they function as ligaments binding and articulating the narrative. As figures appear and reappear, Foote develops them in terms of their responses to successive crises and engagements. He never presumes to judge absolutely but is only fascinated to observe men of whom he declares, "It was their good fortune, or else their misery, to belong to a generation in which every individual would be given a chance to discover and expose his worth, down to the final ounce of strength and nerve." His discretion is constant; if he admires a Forrest or a McClellan or dislikes a Joseph E. Johnston or a Phil Sheridan, the reader must infer the fact from characterizations fairly developed until the weight of evidence tells.

In characterizing historical figures, Foote generally uses their own words, supplementing them with those of contemporaries and his own, varying tone and language to suit his man. He may provide a brief background or a glimpse of a postwar career to suggest, at least, the rounding for which he cannot halt his narrative. He uses parallel and contrast, for example in developing the "immovables," McClellan on the Union side and Joseph E. Johnston on the Confederate, or in pitting the rash, mercurial Van Dorn against the stolid Curtis at Elkhorn Tavern. He enlivens history by exhibiting the interplay of personalities, as in narrating the rise of Grant against the prejudice of Henry Halleck or the frustration of Beauregard's Napoleonic strategies by the realism of Jefferson Davis colored by the incompatibility of WASP and Creole. The play of personality is nowhere more effectively used than in the narration of the battle of Nashville. Foote shows us Halleck and Grant prodding the commander in the field, "Slow Trot" Thomas, and follows Thomas, who like Kutuzov sometimes fell asleep in councils, on his deliberate way to his apotheosis in victory over John Bell Hood. Foote multiplies varieties of "single combat," sometimes between champions on the same side, as in the encounter between Huger and Longstreet at Seven Pines, or between prewar friends or enemies now on opposing sides, as when Hood faces his old West Point roommate John M. Schofield in the final battles for Middle Tennessee.

Foote touches to life not only figures with pervasive roles but many whom he brings forward on account of some one signal action or speech. Often he accords the cameo treatment to men responsible for technological advances, thus crosslighting the theme of modernizing warfare. An example is the treatment of Charles Ellet, Jr., who developed with U. S. Navy backing and proved the effectiveness of rams as naval weapons on the Mississippi, his numerous sons commanding them. Another, more exquisite instance is Foote's introducing handsome Major Roberdeau Wheat of Louisiana into the account of First Manassas where, wounded and told by a doctor his wound was mortal, the young man said, "I don't feel like dying yet." The doctor insisted, "There is no instance on record of recovery from such a wound." "Well then," replied Wheat, "I will put my case on record." He did so, and Foote notices him again the next spring at New Market and then records his death two months later at Turkey Hill. Again a participant's language has commanded space in the narrative, and the narrative profited. The reader remembers with a pang Roberdeau Wheat putting his case at last on record and that pang helps discriminate and memorialize these battles as human experience.

The handling of John Bell Hood is an admirable instance of Foote's use of a major figure, not to bootleg suggestions of historical causation, but to unify and humanize his long narrative without retarding the pace with biographical digression. Brought on casually at the age of 30 in 1862, Hood is impressed upon the reader as an exciting aggressive type, six feet two, blond-bearded—"a Wagnerian hero" in the eyes of Mrs. Chesnut. In an incremental presentation, Foote shows Hood through his men's enthusiastic responses, his interaction with military superiors and peers, and the reactions of society women in Columbia and Richmond; shows him also in the height of the action at repeated engagements, receiving wounds—the maiming of an arm, the loss of a leg—but returning fierily to the field. By the time Hood is given command of the Army of Tennessee following the loss of Atlanta and dismissal of Joseph E. Johnston, Foote has provided so many views of him that the reader understands, without being instructed, why Hood was the choice for the high command and equally why it was a desperate choice.

Hood was ambivalent himself, and Foote affectingly renders his agony of self-knowledge so that we are the more impressed—and alarmed—by Hood's ability to reassert his aggressiveness, reinvigorate his demoralized army, and attempt to return to the enemy's frontiers in the Lee-Jackson style of 1862. When he has led the army to fearful destruction successively at Spring Hill, Franklin, and Nashville, Foote is unsparing in assessing responsibility yet still *presents* Hood in all the ambiguity of his human character and in the light of all the long narrative of the war. He failed, but the threat he mounted was real, as Foote makes us realize through the alarmed communications between Washington and Slow Trot Thomas, who might have been the Rock of Chickamauga but was by no means certain yet of his third sobriquet, the Sledge of Nashville.

Shelby Foote exhibits in this book undeviating interest in human character and enjoyment of human experience. He knows that there is always a mixture of qualities in men, that heroism is not exclusive. There *are* heroes here, however, North and South, no matter how ironic Foote's view may be and no matter how unfashionable the idea of the hero may be in our day of psychoanalytical reductionism and impertinent revisionism. There is magnanimity for the men who break or fail, such as Hood or the Union General William S. Rosecrans, who abandoned the field at Chickamauga; for the tests they had to meet are rendered in all their formidableness. So the reader is prepared to credit the virtual apotheosis of Robert E. Lee when, after Chancellorsville, Foote presents "the jubilant Confederates, recognizing the gray-bearded author of their victory" and tending him "the wildest demonstration of their lives." The reader is prepared to credit yet more when Foote, discreetly avoiding authorial assertion, quotes one of Lee's staff: "I thought that it must have been from such a scene that men in ancient times rose to the dignity of gods."

We think it probable that the passion which powers *The Civil War,* informs the narration with novelistic life, and

makes it history rather than analysis or essay is Foote's fascination with men as they are proved in such scenes. He is something more and other than the expert sportscaster, excitedly guiding the reader and enhancing his appreciation of a complex sequence of actions, to whom Gallie compares the historian in one of his functions. He is an aficionado, not necessarily of war, but of the testing of men under extreme pressure; for he has faith that some, at least, will rise to the occasion and set a standard while others, if they fail, earn understanding or pity. Although on reflection he may be appalled, Foote pays steady attention to the organized carnage, feels in it ritualistic value, and conveys the supra-sexual male transport of battle as ritual played out to actual death. This is the fuel of the narrative vigor of his hour-by-hour rendering, for example, of the terrible suicidal scenes at Gettysburg or Cold Harbor. And it is vigor generated in such scenes which, throttled by considerations of art, guarantees the steady pace of the dominant narrative voice, through which the author's personal tones, humane, ironic, sometimes freely excited, break with effect also artistic. (pp. 243-50)

Helen White and Redding S. Sugg, Jr., "Shelby Foote's 'Iliad'," in The Virginia Quarterly Review, *Vol. 55, No. 2, Spring, 1979, pp. 234-50.*

Jan Nordby Gretlund (review date Fall 1979)

[*In the following review of* September September, *Gretlund faults Foote's emphasis on historical events over theme and character development.*]

When I met Shelby Foote briefly in May, he made a point of his *having been* a historian. He is still very much the historian in his return to literature. **September September** is a contribution to Southern history and to Southern mythology. But history alone does not make a novel, and Foote will have to re-qualify for the title of "fiction writer" by doing better than this novel.

With a Proustian accumulation of detail, he here sends a gambler, a thief, and the promiscuous daughter of a preacher from Arkansas into Memphis to kidnap an eight-year-old black boy, who is to be ransomed at $60,000. This elaborate build-up of suspense, which takes up the better part of the novel, is more successful than the final climax of the book.

Time and place are so important in **September September** that plot and characters are dwarfed by comparison. The novel is set during the reign of Gov. Orval Faubus, a time of abortive space rockets and gas at 30 cents a gallon. The Edsel, "with a radiator that looks like a toilet seat," is used as a humorous *leitmotif.* In the Memphis of 1957 people rode in segregated cabs, so the three kidnappers ride Yellows, whereas the black characters ride Little Johns. Memphis is very much here in these pages, the Memphis of W. C. Handy, its Negro sections and its Peabody Hotel.

The history of blacks in the South is revealed through the history of one black family: that of Theo. G. Wiggins. Their history is an American success story, from Booker T. Washington ideals to success in business. The best part of the novel is its savage comment on the racial situation in the South in the '50s. The kidnappers can count on the blind prejudices of both the Memphis police and the black community to help them carry out their plan. With the racial situation in Arkansas being what it was, the police would not be overly concerned with the disappearance of one black boy, though he is the grandson of the richest black man in Memphis.

We also get an insight into the ambitions and fears of the Wiggins family. They tend to see their African background as something negative, and their criterion of beauty is white. They hold a non-military view of the racial situation. The grandfather's experience is summed up in his view of the law: "You got to remember, the law is first of all the white man's law. He wrote it, he enforces it, and he sits in judgment of it." In presenting this family, Foote parodies several black classics, in particular Ralph Ellison's *Invisible Man*. (There is also a wonderfully comic page on William Faulkner, which, however, is totally superfluous in the novel.) It is to Foote's credit that he can show us why a black family would think and act in a certain way in Memphis in the '50s and that he can suggest the disastrous and long-lasting consequences of the Civil War for the Southern blacks. Yet, as the novel progresses, the reader may begin to suspect that the characters exist only to illustrate a historical period. The history of the month of September 1957 *is* the structure of the novel; but it seems to be the theme, as well.

Take, for example, the case of Reeny Perdew, originally trained to be a Southern lady, who now works with two ex-cons on a kidnapping. The girl has guts and sense, but finally her pocket-philosophy does not do her much good. While the facts make her a well-rounded character, Foote does not permit her fate the emphasis that could have made it *more* than just information. Time is allowed to carry the whole burden of our interest. Besides, Reeny's thoughts about her role as a woman seem to belong more to the time of Women's Lib than to the '50s. Furthermore, while her two male companions, Podjo and Rufus, are both from Jordan County, *September September* has only echoes of the creative madness which produced the early Foote book by that title. In Foote's new novel there are too many details which are comic or interesting enough, but which contribute nothing towards a theme, or to the reader's understanding of the novel.

The attempted Faulknerizing of language and style does not help the novel either. Stylistically, Shelby Foote could do worse than study [Madison Jones's] *Passage Through Gehenna*. From that novel Foote might learn how to make a convincing shift from one so-called "voice" to another. One possible stylistic influence may have been Virginia Woolf's *The Waves*. But Foote's transitions are not up to Woolf's standard.

Shelby Foote has written five earlier novels and his Herculean three-volume Civil War History. We can only hope that with *September September* Foote has rid himself of his excess of facts and that he plans to deal in *ideas* in his future fiction. (pp. 361-62)

Jan Nordby Gretlund, in a review of "September September," in The Southern Humanities Review, *Vol. 13, No. 4, Fall, 1979, pp. 361-62.*

James M. Cox (essay date Spring 1985)

[*Cox is an American educator and critic. In the following excerpt, he analyzes* The Civil War *as a work of modern literature, highlighting what he regards as Foote's mastery of narrative structure, sequence, and character.*]

Shelby Foote's *The Civil War: A Narrative* is a great work of literature, surely one of the great works written in this or any other country—a work to rank with that of Thucydides, Clarendon, Gibbon, or Henry Adams. Like those writers, Foote chose a great subject, and, like them too, he proved himself equal to it. But what chance is there that this splendid achievement will be recognized and supported? It will be classified as history and, in this age of departmentalization, will remain largely outside the ken of teachers of literature and literary critics. Yet historians will not really welcome it either. Faced with the onslaught of cliometricians, they have become more and more suspicious of narrative. Even Vann Woodward, who reviewed it for the *New York Review of Books,* tended to lament the increasing absence of narrative in historical studies rather than to devote his attention to Foote's remarkable narrative achievement. Part of Woodward's defensiveness came from his own troubled sense that Foote's concentration on battle action opened him to a charge of having neglected the political and social history of the Civil War. Then too there is the dominant antiwar culture in which we live. (p. 329)

Considering its forbidding length, considering the specialization separating history from literature, and considering too the general cultural recoil from war and military history, we can see that access to these volumes is all but reduced to that group of readers depressingly called Civil War Buffs. But Foote's subject is the Civil War that forever looms like a beacon upon our sense of ourselves. Southerners are prone to fight the war over again in their minds; northerners, adamantly attached to the ideals of freedom that the war guaranteed, are ready to send federal troops to Little Rock or Oxford on one more invasion of a recalcitrant and lawbreaking region.

This state of affairs serves to remind us of how central the Civil War remains as a presence defining both the American nation and the American identity. If the white southern mind too much remembers the actual military conflict in order to distract itself from the paramount issues of slavery, race, and secession, the white northern mind too much represses the actual war in its precise fixation on the moral certitudes about slavery, race, and constitutional law that were established and secured by the bloodiest and most violent war in American experience. (pp. 329-30)

The very title—*The Civil War: A Narrative,* as true a title as we shall meet in our lifetime—is telling in the full sense of the word. It is indeed a narrative, and the Civil War, in all the meaning of those words, is its subject. No one who reads these three volumes will find the account incomplete, if by completeness we mean the full comprehension of the entire field of action of that war. Considered in such terms, I have not the slightest doubt that this narrative is the single most complete narrative of the war that has yet been written or yet will be written. His three volumes panoramically encompass the war, which is to say that they fully comprehend it from its beginning to its conclusion. To achieve this comprehension, Foote has to *see* the war, as if from above, which meant that he had to imagine its tremendous space from the air. It is no accident that he defines distance, whether from Washington to Richmond or Memphis to Vicksburg, in terms of airline miles even as he fully recognizes the agonizing discrepancy between such an abstract measurement and the overland distances across which the armies had to toil. Indeed, the economy of his perception, combining a modern overview of the war with an incisive recognition of the true, which is to say relative, resistance of both actual and historical terrain, is one of the chief sources of his authority as a narrator. It is truly a double view, at once characterizing his overall, swift, and mobile vision and his close-up, penetrating, and intense pursuit of individual engagement.

Then there is his impartiality. In a small note appended to the first volume, he contends that, aside from having a typically American sympathy for the underdog, he believes that, for all his being a Mississippian, he has written an impartial account of the war. His narrative is, if anything, even better than his word. Some reviewers, evidently trapped by the modest confidence of Foote's frankness in his endnotes to each volume, have observed that the pulse of his prose beats faster as he follows southern armies toward victorious exploits. Admitting that my own southern pulse might beat faster as it follows Foote's narrative before Second Manassas, Fredericksburg, and Chancellorsville, I still can see nothing but an awesome impartiality in Foote's narrative—an impartiality utterly related to its comprehensiveness of scope. One could well say that because the narrative is complete, it is never partial.

The most visible basis of the impartiality lies in Foote's balanced structure—balanced not only between North and South but between East and West. This balance is evident from the opposing portraits of Jefferson Davis and Abraham Lincoln, which constitute Foote's prologue to the conflict. Born in Kentucky log cabins within a hundred miles of each other, Davis and Lincoln moved in divergent directions—the one southwest to Mississippi, the other northwest to Springfield. For all that, and for all their differences in temperament—Davis serious, formal, and intensely principled; Lincoln humorous, relaxed, and shrewdly skeptical—they were yet western in their vision. Thus both knew how utterly crucial the Mississippi River was to their opposing causes. Foote's vision of the two men therefore equips him both narratively and thematically for his task of achieving a balance between the eastern and western theaters of war. Thus he balances those two arenas of action from the outset, showing just how the battle of Wilson's Creek in Missouri followed hard upon First Manassas, and how Lee's failures in Western Virginia were juxtaposed to Grant's success at Donelson. The very subtitles of his three volumes—*Fort Sumter to Perryville, Fredericksburg to Meridian,* and *Red River to Appomat-*

tox—are an index to both the balance and the coverage of his narrative.

Foote's balance between North and South measures the historical conflict at the heart of the war, giving the narrative remarkably economic access to the social and political issues at stake. To be sure, he does not treat those issues as extensively as Allan Nevins does in *The War for the Union.* But Nevins' commitment to the political aspect of the struggle makes him see the war itself as a result of the political forces, whereas Foote sees the war as the essence of his narrative and is determined to make that dramatic action revolve around the men who fought it. That is why he begins with the portraits of the two men, Davis and Lincoln, who represented the warring sections. Yet anyone who concluded that Foote's paramount interest in the actual battles resulted in a military history of the manner of K. P. Williams' *Lincoln Finds a General* would be profoundly mistaken. Having portrayed Davis and Lincoln at the outset, Foote is always poised to show the reciprocal relationship between battlefield action and political skirmishing at the seats of government. He sees and tells, with remarkable acuity, how both northern armies and politicians were at war with each other as well as with the South. At pains throughout the war to reconcile the deep division within his political constituency, Lincoln was perpetually threatened by political rear guard action almost as much as he was by Lee's tattered army. Even as late as 1864, when Sherman boldly decided to move seaward from Atlanta instead of pursuing Hood's retreating army northward and westward into Tennessee, both Lincoln and Grant knew that failure of such a strategy might cost the Republicans the election.

Not only did Lincoln, in order to consolidate and maintain power, have to reconcile the opposing political factions within the North; he had to reconcile politics and principle. Thus, however, much he was against slavery in principle, he had to manage affairs in such a way that principle *politically* prevailed. That prevalence was the unity he sought in order to save the Union in which he believed. However much he was against slavery, he was for Union more.

With Davis things were different. Since the Confederate constitution provided for a six-year presidential term, Davis neither faced nor had the opportunity of an election. Spared the deep division of a two-party system, he could fall back confidently on the unity of principle and could call on his nation for sacrifices necessary in war. The severity of Davis' adherence to principle kept him on the brink of self-righteousness and made him brittle in brooking differences from colleagues; at the same time, if he experienced loyalty from his subordinates he returned it with fervor. While Lincoln was moving cagily and at times almost humbly before the ambitious and popular McClellan even as he was listening sensitively to the growing cabinet criticism of this Young Napoleon, Davis was discovering in Robert E. Lee the man who could at once lead armies yet constantly defer to his President's political authority. But if Davis had a particular unity of principle that held him above the scuffle of politics, and if he had unquestioned authority of command, he was presiding over a nation increasingly isolated and increasingly driven in on itself. Seeing its hopes of European recognition dwindle, its economy at the point of disintegrating, its armies more and more overborne, he, along with his nation, looked at principle being converted into starvation and ruin. If its head was held high, there was less and less body to hold it.

Of course, readers versed in history can say that they knew about these matters. Yet emerging as they do in the course of Foote's recurrent returns from battles to the opposing capitols, these interpretations become actualities that are at once economically and unforgettably etched in the reader's mind.

They are unforgettable because of the particular perspective of Foote's whole narrative. By putting the war not only in the foreground but *as* the foreground, it no longer seems the result of political force. *It* is the violent action to which politics and history have surrendered; by being narratively true to its dominance, Foote implicitly reveals a superior political vision of those four years. The war was, in all its intensity and bloodiness, the superior reality of that long moment to those who fought it and to Lincoln who ultimately presided over it. He was not indulging in mere self-serving rhetoric when he said at Gettysburg that the world would little note nor long remember what he said but could never forget what the soldiers did. Because his own death sealed the conclusion of all the battles and because he himself had the language equal to his large vision of the nation, there are many who feel that his language is more permanent than the battle, but that is only because the battle has not yet found itself in language. If we had to wait a hundred years for Lincoln's vision to begin to be fulfilled in the action of history, we have also waited—not passively but actively through attempt after attempt—for that battle and all the battles of the war, to find the writer equal to their reality. For me, Shelby Foote is that writer.

Knowing both historically and imaginatively the full reality of the war, he does not have to be for or against it; instead, he believes in the war, believes in it enough to believe that the men who fought it were as real as its reality. His great task as a writer is to render their reality. That rendering draws on all his skill as a novelist and at the same time requires all of his energy as a reader of all the Civil War histories and narratives that have preceded him. His novelistic skill is deployed in two ways. First he has literally to mobilize his immense panoramic action in a linear narrative. Thus he has the difficulty not only of moving from battle to battle in cumulative sequence but also of determining a sequence for actions that took place almost simultaneously in time but in far different space. The deep structure of such a subject all but requires the "meanwhile back at the ranch" transition, which is as old as Homer. Yet such a transition implies subordination of one action to another; it also subverts the true nature of historical process, implying as it does a fictive closure of events. Equally important, it denies the very nature of the war as Foote envisions it. He sees the whole cumulative force of the war as pushing forward; thus the retroactive moves he perforce has to make in order to bring his war

forward in all theaters of action are necessarily at variance with his deepest recognition of the war's forward thrust. Though there might be retreats on any given field, both sides went relentlessly forward not so much toward each other—though there were furious encounters of opposing forces—as in the powerful direction the war took, a direction beyond the management or even victory of either side. There could be no real "meanwhile back at the ranch," since such a transition implies that things in one place are not affected by actions in another. But Foote knows that this was a war where telegraphic communication all but instantly relayed results of one action to the opposing nerve centers of Washington and Richmond and from thence out to the extremities. Yet he also knows that the war cannot be reduced to this acceleration, since there were men still laboring with muzzle loaders to the extent that breach loading carbines couldn't make headway against them; and the presence of Federal balloon observers didn't keep Jackson from becoming obscurely lost until he burst in fury upon Hooker's flank. All the troop transport by train didn't annihilate the old inertial resistance of land and weather any more than all the machines of war could quite obliterate the recalcitrant individual soldier. The old order of making war and the old resistance of nature to technology were as much in conflict with the new technology as the South was in conflict with the North. How else could the war have been so very big and very long?

Yet all these conflicts, ideologically and historically large though they are, remain for Foote the subordinate and implicit aspects of the struggle. The battles themselves are, and must be, the explicit conflict. They are the violent resolution of the irresolvable political and historical conflicts. The measure of Foote's achievement is that he fully recognizes the violence and at the same time never forgets that it is human violence—more human than politics and history because it is so mortal.

Foote's forward movement in his narrative sequence is directly into that mortality. Though the necessities of his scope and comprehensiveness require him to make temporal retrograde movements in his narrative, these are offset by the breadth and intensity of his cumulative and panoramic action. Beyond that, Foote possesses sufficient narrative resources to make the most telling references to his past narrative. He tolls anniversaries of past battles or deaths of commanders; in the midst of narrating one action, he interpolates reminders that it is taking place simultaneously with another action that he has already dealt with; he emphasizes the haunting repetition of action—the returns to Manassas, to Fredericksburg, to the Wilderness; he amasses cumulative references to past battle behavior in building the characters of his commanders. These rhetorical tactics not only keep the whole mass of his accumulating narrative in mind; they sustain his narrative strategy of treating past battles and past narrative as the reserve force of lived experience. Thus the reader's experience tallies with the dominant strategy of Grant and Lee and Sherman, whose remarkable reading of each battle became the experience on which they relief as they moved on and on into the terrible responsibility of command.

If Foote's problem in relation to his own narrative past is to mobilize it by means of the lifelines he keeps throwing back to it, thus attaching an immense reserve force to his own forward movement, he has a vastly different relation to his future. For the broad and deep outlines of his great subject are known. Almost every reader knows that the South will begin with victory at First Manassas, that Jackson will be brilliant in the Shenandoah Valley, that Pickett's charge will fail at Gettysburg, that Grant will win Vicksburg on the same day, that he will ultimately come east and push relentlessly forward to Appomattox, and that Lincoln will die in the aftermath. And the vast majority of the relatively limited audience sufficiently interested and arduous enough to contemplate these three massive volumes will know much more. Such knowledge and such inevitability suspend for both writer and reader possibilities of novelistic suspense. A writer who knows this inevitability too well will allow his knowledge to overdetermine both his judgment of participants and his selection of narrative incident and direction. Such overdetermination results in a cheapened authority—cheapened because the authorial advantage of hindsight is deployed to foreknow the future. Knowing the conclusion too easily, the writer forgets that the participants didn't know it.

Yet the writer of historical narrative who tries to suppress the inevitability of the "future" is more and more seduced into faking suspense and excitement by tuning up descriptions, dramatizing action by making it "colorful"—in other words, by making it read "like a novel." Though Foote had written novels before entering on this monumental project, and though he uses many novelistic resources in his narrative, he never resorts to such techniques to gain excitement for the simple reason that he never doubts the reality of his subject. Instead, his whole effort is to get into that subject by using all the resources of the historian. The result is that he pushes deeper and deeper into the conflict even as he pushes forward through it. Knowing how much inevitability he confronts yet possessing so much more knowledge of the entire conflict than those who know the primary inevitabilities, he displaces mere narrative excitement in order to gain suspense, or prejudgment of character and behavior in order to reach foregone conclusions, with the plenitude of both action and evidence. Thus, the reader who knows all about Grant and Lee, or about Stuart and Sheridan, finds that he does not know about Henry Sibley's campaign through Texas into New Mexico, or about Richard Taylor's brilliant Red River campaign, or about Isaac Newton Brown's remarkable achievements in the naval war on the Mississippi, or about William Cushing's incredible efforts to torpedo the Confederate ironclad *Albemarle,* or about the battle of Mobile Bay, or about the intricate Florida campaigns, or about Pea Ridge, or about Buck Van Dorn's death, or about a hundred other engagements and ironies that were vital parts of the war.

Foote does not try to make these "minor" events major so much as he allows his narrative to discover their importance, and discover it not merely by covering it but by integrating and weaving it into the comprehensive web of inclusion. Thus the reader, or this one at least, is perpetually astonished at how little he knows and at the same time profoundly gratified by his mounting grasp of the largeness, fullness, and pervasiveness of the Civil War. And throughout this massive narrative comprehension, Foote maintains clarity of progression without visible resort to showing off or belittling others for neglecting these episodes and incidents that flanked the central theaters of action. Instead, he gives to every action he comprehends the great vitality of his imaginative embrace. If he knows that they are subordinate in any conventional view of the war, he also knows that they are actions—participations—in the general conflict, just as he knows that subordinates, all the way down to privates, participated in the individual battles. And if he remembers that some of these actions are diversions from the main lines of the struggle, he does not forget the diversionary delight that is incipient in them.

To appreciate Foote's comprehensive coverage is to be brought back to my point about his impartiality and to be brought forward from the balance, continuity, and comprehensiveness of his structure to his treatment of character. For if structure and sequence are at the heart of narrative, so also is character. And character, as his initial portraits of Davis and Lincoln fully signal, is utterly central for Foote. If the war was a clash of forces, institutions, and ideas, it was fought by men. Although the war with its battles was larger than the men and though in a deep sense it made or broke or killed them, they nonetheless fought it. Because battles are violent efforts toward decision, and because the Civil War was decisive in the extreme, and because we helplessly know the outcome, the same inevitability that both we and the writer encounter in relation to action and incident is operative in relation to character. Once we know a battle is going to be lost, the evaluative mechanism that runs like a constant dynamo in our minds begins to take precedence in relation to the persons fighting it. We helplessly conceive the completed action, to which we know the conclusion, in terms of prejudgment masquerading as detached judgment.

There is no way for the historical narrator to evade this problem completely; it goes with the territory. Even Bruce Catton, an able, lucid writer committed to genuine narration rather than thesis, confronts the decisive Confederate victory at Ball's Bluff with the following paragraph:

> [McClellan] did not have to wait much longer [for a larger object than his having won the good will of the army], for the Army of the Potomac was about to suffer one more public disgrace, and the shock of it would force a change—and, in the end, would arm and perpetuate a bitterness that would be felt to the last day of the war and beyond. One October 21 [1861], a small Federal detachment was routed in an engagement at Ball's Bluff, on the Virginia side of the Potomac thirty-five miles upstream from Washington. The engagement had little military significance, but it was one more dreary licking. The Confederates inflicted heavy losses and they killed, in hot battle action, a prominent Union commander—Colonel Edward D. Baker, an unskilled soldier but an orator and politician of much renown, a member of the United States

Senate, and for years an intimate friend of Abraham Lincoln.

Here is extremely serviceable prose, but it reverses the order of narrative in order to put the meaning of the battle before the battle. We are not told just what the significance is—other than that it will perpetuate a bitterness much more significant than the battle itself, which is *militarily* insignificant. Catton then proceeds to give an extremely condensed version of the battle, and concludes by showing that the "disgrace" of the defeat led Zechariah Chandler, Lyman Trumbull, and Ben Wade to see the President and demand some decisive action from the senile Winfield Scott and the overcautious McClellan. Their pressure led to the retirement of Scott—which thoroughly suited McClellan, since he was promoted to general-in-chief.

By putting the battle in a secondary position, Catton is able to put the unspecified significance in the primary position, thus making it the withheld narrative action. That significance is the promotion of McClellan, which had been the larger object for which the Young Napoleon was waiting at the outset of Catton's paragraph. But that decision has great cost for Catton, since he has to return to the battle of Ball's Bluff a hundred pages later, showing how those three abolitionist senators went on to lead the Joint Congressional Committee on the Conduct of the War, the first action of which was summarily to investigate the possibly treasonous behavior of Brigadier General Charles P. Stone, who was in command at Ball's Bluff. And here again Catton concludes that the charges leading to Stone's imprisonment and the wreckage of his career were unfounded.

Foote's narrative is far different. He begins with the battle itself in the larger context of McClellan's confrontation with Joseph E. Johnston, his Confederate counterpart. Both of them were cautious and at the same time immensely popular, and Johnston had just tricked McClellan by retreating under cover of Quaker guns (logs painted to look like cannon) which held McClellan sufficiently at bay while Johnston conducted his retrograde movement. Smarting under the public criticism of his exposure, McClellan, upon hearing that Johnston was apparently preparing to evacuate Leesburg, determined to find out whether the Confederates were really retreating in that sector. He therefore sent one division, under McCall, up the Virginia side of the Potomac to make a reconnaissance and ordered Stone's division, stationed on the Maryland side, to assist. McCall "halted at Dranesville, ten miles short of Leesburg, content to do his observing from there," but Stone, "who read his instructions as permission to push things—believed that the best way to discover the enemy's strength was to provoke him into showing it." He thus sent two regiments across the river at Edwards Ferry and his others across at Harrison's Island, three miles upstream in order to envelop whatever opposition might exist:

> Here the operation was necessarily slow, being made in three small boats with a combined capacity of 25 men. By dawn one regiment was on the island looking out across the other half of the river at the wooded Virginia bank. It reared up tall there, over a hundred feet steep and mean

looking; Ball's Bluff it was called, and from beyond its rim they heard a nervous popping of musketry, each shot as flat and distinct as a handclap, only more so. They were Massachusetts boys, and they looked at one another, wondering. No one had told them on the drill field or bivouac that the war might be like this. They continued the crossing, still in groups of 25, herded by their officers, and took a meandering cowpath up the bluff toward the hollowsounding spatter of rifle fire.

Foote goes on to show that the rifle fire is coming from an exchange between another Massachusetts regiment that, having crossed the river earlier and engaged the Confederates in the bush, has retreated to the edge of the bluff. Both are reinforced by a Pennsylvania regiment under Colonel Edward D. Baker. Foote carefully outlines Baker's character, showing his long-time friendship with Lincoln, whom he had known in Illinois before going to the Mexican War, participating in the California Gold Rush, and finally becoming a senator from Oregon. Baker could have had a major general's commission but remained a colonel in order to stay in the Senate, where he was Lincoln's chief far-western spokesman. He had ridden in the presidential carriage on inauguration day and introduced Lincoln for the inaugural address. A fine speaker who loved to quote poetry to the troops, he was eager for the battle that was taking shape and greeted the Massachusetts colonel who had brought his troops up the bluff with a quotation from "The Lady of the Lake." Minutes later he, who on the Senate floor "had called for a sudden, bold forward, determined war received it in the form of a bullet through the brain, which left him not even time for a dying quotation."

Foote does not stop with Baker's death, but narratively pursues the battle action as Shanks Evans' Mississippi and Virginia regiments drive the retreating Federals back down the bluff and into the water pouring fire "into the huddled, leaping rout of blue-clad men as fast as they could manipulate ramrods and triggers." The horror of the developing scene caused some Confederates to pause momentarily, but only momentarily, before they rushed to the rim of the bluff, where they poured a furious fire that lashed the water "until the surface boiled 'as white as in a great hail storm,' one participant declared." The panicked soldiers leaped into the small boats and swamped them, and one flat boat "was scrambled into until it was almost awash . . . but presently, live men ducking and dodging and shot men falling heavily on the gunwales, it capsized, and thirty or forty were drowned."

This, then, was, as Foote narrates it, the battle that Catton sees as a bungled fumble of no military significance. It is not merely the concentration of novelistic ability, producing a graphic account of the battle that distinguishes Foote's account. Rather, his deployment of the battle as the primary cause of a narrative sequence distinguishes his conception of the war. The war itself, in this early stage of his narrative, is revealed in the very act of becoming the reality that generates political response. Thus Baker, who has declaimed on war, is drawn into the conflict he has weakly imagined—and slaughtered. Equally important, there are men out there *on both sides* who, though nameless, are as real as Baker. They are at once more deadly yet as frail as Baker proves to be. That is what those bullets, charges, and retreats are all about. Foote's great strength is to conceive the action of that reality as both the gripping and generative force of his narrative sequence.

He is then in position to pursue his sequence. The news of Baker's death galvanizes the Senate into indignation at the same time that it reduces Lincoln to helpless tears at his sense of personal loss. Out of the indignation comes the Joint Committee on the Conduct of the War, whose first act is to scapegoat the hapless Stone. And from that initial step, the Committee, with all the virulence of the generating battle, can implicate and threaten anyone suspected of sympathy for the enemy. At the same time, Lincoln, still struck to the heart with his personal loss, yet faced, only eleven days after Ball's Bluff, with the task of telling McClellan of his promotion to the place of the aging and increasingly discredited Scott, shows fatherly concern for the Young Napoleon even as he knows that this youthful and ambitious general has coveted the rank of general-in-chief. He knows how McClellan has snubbed Scott not only because he has seen it but also because McClellan has patronizingly lectured him on the nature of military science. For all his knowledge, Lincoln yet shrewdly feels both the burden and responsibility that his commission places upon McClellan's youthful and ambitious shoulders:

> "Well," Lincoln said, "draw upon me for all the sense I have, and all the information." Still wondering, however, if McClellan was aware of the weight that had been added as he was of the weight that had been taken away, he returned to the point. "In addition to your present duties, command of the army will entail a vast labor on you."
>
> "I can do it all," McClellan told him.

Such is the conclusion of this particular sequence. It leaves Foote ready to proceed with McClellan's farewell to General Scott, to give a masterful appraisal of Scott's Anaconda Plan (which Foote believes was the abstraction of the strategy Lincoln and Grant would materialize more than three years later), and to go on to all that McClellan could not do. It also leaves him in position, a hundred and fifty pages later, to show how the Joint Committee on the Conduct of the War had spawned a progeny of committees to implicate anyone suspected of treason. When the Lincolns lost their son Willie, and Mrs. Lincoln's ensuing hysteria made her, with her southern parentage, subject to rumors of disloyalty, Lincoln himself, aware of the mounting slander and accusations, came unexpectedly to a secret session of a congressional investigating committee to announce in a sad voice:

> "I, Abraham Lincoln, President of the United States, appear of my own volition before this committee of the Senate to say that I, of my own knowledge, know that it is untrue that any of my family hold treasonable communication with the enemy."

These are the far-reaching consequences of Ball's Bluff, and Foote's sequence shows how the battle, far from being a fumble, was itself of vast military significance in that it brought the war home to both the President and Senate, thus intensifying and widening the conflict by spawning a militant indignation in the political sector that accelerated a change in command and led ultimately to the grief-stricken heart of the President who had lost a real son. My selection of this sequence is likely to conceal what is perhaps the finest quality of Foote's writing: his essential restraint. The words may seem all wrong in light of Foote's dramatic intensity and vividness of description, but this sequence is but a thread in his comprehensive narrative web, and its tensile strength lies in Foote's refusal to call overt attention to his own connective operations and designs. The battle itself is where he finds the impetus, and he lets the battle do its work. (pp. 331-42)

Seeing Foote's balanced structure and comprehensiveness of scope, seeing his conceptual vision of battle as the inescapable action and reality of the Civil War, and seeing too his capacity to describe that action in such a way that it discovers the character of the participants—the generals, the politicians, the men—seeing all this still leaves the texture of the narrative to be accounted for. And here again it is not sufficient to begin praising Foote's "art," as if he had merely applied his novelistic skill to his great subject. Just as his concern with battle action involves him in a truly conceptual vision of the war, his profound research into and knowledge of historical detail is completely wedded to his narrative skill. Thus the texture of his narrative is a translation of all his enormous reading of prior texts into a living and not merely a lively account of the action. He unfailingly sees both the ground and the actors in his battles in such a way that his capacity to make things appear—to create the images of his scenes and actors—is the very current of his narrative.

There are no illustrations in his volumes—indeed, illustrations would be an affront to the narrative he accomplishes—because he must have looked so long and searchingly at photographs as to have resolved them into verbal vision. Here is his description of Lee:

> On horseback, deep-chested and long-waisted, with his big leonine head set thick-necked on massive shoulders, he looked gigantic. Partly that was the aura. It must have been; for when he dismounted, as he often did, to rest his horse—he had a tender concern for the welfare of all animals, even combat infantrymen, aside from those times when he flung them into the crackling uproar of battle like chaff into a furnace—you saw the slight legs, the narrow hips, and realized, with something of a shock, that he was no larger than many of the men around him, and not as large as some. The same contrast, above and below, was apparent in his extremities; the hands were oversized and muscular, the feet tiny as a woman's. He was in fact just under six feet tall and weighed less than 170 pounds. Quickly, though, you got over the shock (which after all was only the result of comparing flesh and perfection. However he was was how you preferred him) and when you saw him thus in the field your inclination was to remove your hat—not to wave it; just to hold it—and stand there looking at him: Mars Robert.

This is unabashedly an idealized portrait, as the prose frankly acknowledges. As a matter of fact, Foote immediately follows it by referring to less flattering accounts of Lee by Robert Toombs and the editor of the Charleston *Mercury.* But there are so many insights in it, not least of which is the parenthetical recognition that Lee's gentleness does not obscure the fact that he was able, ready, and willing to sacrifice his men to the furnace of battle. The fierceness and gentleness are borne out by the large trunk of the rider, whose horse obscures the delicacy of the lower body. And finally the descent into the solid facts of weight and height which lead to the mysterious generosity of the figure who leaves preference to his beholder, but a preference which gives back authority to the figure who is not Marse Robert, as we have always seen it spelled, but Mars Robert, whose name at once pronounces the gentle patriarch yet designates the mailed essence of the warrior.

If the idealism of this particular portrait is rare for Foote—and it is—the vividness is not. There are literally hundreds of unforgettable images of the officers who led men to battle. There is of course Grant, walking always with his body pitched forward; and Sherman, "red bearded, tall and thin, with sunken temples and a fidgity manner"; and Judah P. Benjamin, Confederate Secretary of War and later of State, whose rotund, smiling face stood always between the administrative dispatch with which he kept his desk cleared and the military men who approached him and upon whom he exercised his talent in dialectics with a "precision of logic that could lead men where they would not go, making them seem clumsy in the process"; and the redoubtable Edwin M. Stanton, who had once snubbed Lincoln before the war, and whose moral savagery in dealing with men who were culpable was offset by "the joy he took in fixing a frightened general or petitioner with the baleful glare of his black little near-sighted eyes behind small, thick-lensed, oval spectacles"; and Jackson, dust covered on horseback in the Seven Days, "the dingy cadet cap pulled so far down over his face that the bill almost touched the lemon he was sucking"; and Philip Kearney, who had lost an arm in the Mexican War, riding in the darkness into A. P. Hill's men at Chantilly, and, upon being called on to surrender, whirling his mount and "leaning forward on its withers with his arm around its neck" as he tried to escape, but shot down in the dark where the Confederates found him "lying one-armed in the mud, the back of his coat and the seat of his trousers torn by bullets"; and Charles S. Winder, sick with fever but leaving his ambulance at Cedar Mountain, where "tall and wavy-haired, he kept his post . . . calm and cool-looking in his shirt sleeves," until "a shell came screaming at him, crashing through his left arm and tearing off most of the ribs on that side of his chest."

Unforgettable as these images are, it is the voices of the war in Foote's narrative that are to me the most haunting. When Winder lies quivering on the ground, for example, a staff lieutenant rushes to him to ask, "General, do you know me?"

> "Oh yes," Winder said vaguely; and his mind began to wander. The guns were banging all around him, but he was back at home again in Maryland. In shock, he spoke disconnectedly of his wife and children until a chaplain came and knelt beside him, seeking to turn his thoughts from worldly things.
>
> "General, lift up your head to God."
>
> "I do," Winder said calmly, "lift it up to him."
>
> Carried to the rear, he died just at sundown, asking for the welfare of his men, and those who were with him were hard put for a comforting answer.

And when Kearney's body is brought into the Confederate lines, A. P. Hill, looking on the man he had known in the old army, remarks, "Poor Kearney. He deserved a better death than that." Foote's sensitivity to this and similar moments reminds us, even in the midst of violence, that there was yet civility in Civil War.

It is not generals alone who speak in this narrative. Foote finds between the *Carondelet* and the Confederate ironclad *Arkansas,* the badly damaged *Carondelet* fires back:

> The return shots glanced off the *Arkansas'* prow, doing no considerable damage except to one seaman who, more curious than prudent, stuck his head out of a gunport for a better view and had it taken off by a bolt from an 8-inch rifle. The headless body fell back on the deck, and a lieutenant, fearing the sight would demoralize the rest of the guncrew, called upon the nearest man to heave it overboard. "Oh, I can't do it sir! It's my brother," he replied.

These examples in no way suggest the range of the voices in these volumes. There are, for example, the speeches of Lincoln and Davis, which are reminiscent of the crafted speeches in Thucydides' history of the Peloponnesian War. Davis' speeches have the oratorical formality of state speeches, yet in Foote's carefully orchestrated context, they disclose a genuine stateliness. And Foote hears the music in Lincoln's speeches, and places them so ably in his narrative that no reader will miss it. Beyond the political speeches, there are the rallying cries to battle, ranging from the bluntness of Bedford Forrest demanding surrender unless his opponents wish him to give them no quarter, to the martial flourish of Sherman addressing his troops during the course of their destructive march across Mississippi. Then there are the taunting cries of the men of the armies, whether in the midst of battle or during the lull between. Finally there is the irrepressible humor of the soldiers, which Foote catches superbly. There is, for example, the southern soldier, suffering from the "Tennessee quick-step" from having eaten green corn, who boasted that "he could hit a dime at seven yards." And when John Pope announced that his headquarters were in the saddle, there was the wry observation that his headquarters were where his hindquarters should be. Then there is Lincoln's humor, forever present, indicating how rich his musical range really was. He had a penchant for unerringly discovering appropriate barnyard imagery and activity with which to illuminate or explicate the behavior of politicians and generals. But I think my favorite Lincoln joke has to do with Stanton, whose prancing and bouncing put Lincoln in mind of a Methodist preacher out west who got so wrought up in his prayers and exhortations that his congregation was obliged to put bricks in his pockets to hold him down. "We may have to serve Stanton the same way," Lincoln drawled. "But I guess we'll let him jump a while first."

There are two reasons for the great effectiveness of these voices in the narrative. First, they are embedded in the narrative in such a way that they wonderfully serve it, giving it the tenor of dramatic authenticity without once reducing it to scenes of dramatic dialogue. Second, these speeches are never footnoted, a fact that has drawn complaints from some reviewers. I must confess that there were times when I wished for footnotes that might have conveniently located the sources of certain speeches or anecdotes. Yet I think that Foote was boldly right in dispensing with them. As he says in his bibliographical note to the first volume, "Accepting the historian's standards without his paraphernalia, I have employed the novelist's methods without his license." By freeing himself from footnotes, the speeches and anecdotes are freed from their prior textuality to become voices in this text. Any reader familiar with the *Official Records* or histories and memoirs of the Civil War will recognize some or even many of these voices, though no such reader, I venture to say, will read these volumes without *hearing* the war far better than ever before. And no reader, whether reading about that war for the first time or the hundredth time, will doubt Foote's assertion that "nothing is included here, either in or outside quotation marks, without the authority of documentary evidence that is sound." I am glad that Foote made the assertion, but he would not have had to. The authenticity of his narrative, coming from its comprehensiveness, its discipline, its clarity, its graphic conception and vision, and its capacity both to see and hear the action of the moving forces, produces a living and informed faith in the reader: living, because the reader will never have felt the war so vividly and intimately; informed, because he will never have known or seen it so illuminatingly.

But these volumes illuminate more than those four years. They were written during the twenty-years (1954-1974) when the Civil War centennial approached, came, and passed; when a southerner, who succeeded to the Presidency by virtue of an assassination, sought, and largely achieved, a political realization of Lincoln's unforgettable vision of Gettysburg, which was in turn a monumental rededication, on a field almost still bloody, of Jefferson's original vision in the Declaration. And yet, almost simultaneously, this same southerner carried out a moral and ideological imperialism, also inherited from the Civil War, leading us into the Vietnam War and finally resulting in a radical disunion in the body politic as well as a radical aversion to war. That aversion, flourishing under the umbrella of nuclear threat, makes war "unthinkable," as we are told by those who imply that the old "conventional" wars were easy to fight. Those who, easily willing to think the unthinkable, emerge with visions of technological deterrents multiplying with ever-increasing "refinements," which inevitably assume the identity of star wars. The one side reduces history to simplicity, voiding the old wars of their terror and courage; the other futuristically invents

machines which make the warrior obsolete. Both are fantasy.

These same twenty years witnessed the exhaustion of the great movement in art and literature denominated as the *modern,* which came to full fruition in World War I, when a whole civilization experienced the expression of a profound nihilism in the very trench warfare—really initiated, as readers of Foote will discover, by Longstreet before Chancellorsville—presently referred to, with unbelievable complacency, as conventional war. The modern has died into the postmodern, the very term disclosing the devastation wrought by one period on another. What was profoundly dislocating and revolutionary in the fracturing of representation and reference has run its course into acutely self-reflexive forms on the one hand and into an instantaneous technological communication and information system on the other, both of which combine to displace narrative and deconstruct the self. In the flood of images, facts, and language pouring from the information system, the novelistic imagination has pursued paranoid strategic retreats into structures of discontinuity as a means of escaping narrative plot.

It is surely of great critical importance that, during these twenty years, Shelby Foote, coming from the world of the novel, should have narratively discovered a larger, wider, and more complete Civil War than anyone before him. He discovered it precisely because narrative was never device or technique but vision itself, a means of seeing, through language, a historical reality that he never doubted. The ground of the battlefields was still solid beneath his feet; the weather of Mississippi, Tennessee, Georgia, and Virginia—and, yes, of Texas, Louisiana, Arkansas, Missouri, Kentucky, Alabama, Florida, Maryland, and Pennsylvania—was present to his senses; and the war itself must always have been living for him, so that he never had to bring it to life but had to reach the sure life it had in his mind and blood and bone. To reach it he went relentlessly outward to the fields, the woods, the weather—how well he realizes that Napoleon's fifth element of war was mud—and to the records, letters, memoirs, and histories, there to quarry out the lives, actions, character, and, above all, the battle of a nation for its life.

And so he sees at the end of his narrative the two figures, Lincoln and Davis, with whom he began—the one victorious at the moment of his death, yet his death the very measure of the loss in victory; the other captured, imprisoned, abused, yet unreconstructed and, some might say, unvanquished. But Foote knows better than easily to use that word which was to become a shibboleth for southerners, most of whom had not faced the fury of Lincoln and Grant's arithmetic of war. Having recorded both the valor and defeat of the nation that fought and died, and having recorded too the death of Davis' own children, he comprehends how profoundly Davis represented his nation. Yet if Davis was defeated, he remained unyielding, ready to challenge in court the constitutionality of secession. And no court, supreme or otherwise, was ready to face the challenge. Yet beyond Davis' refusal to renounce his cause, he lived long enough to say to a reporter who asked him for the underlying motivation that might account for four years of war, "Tell the world that I only loved America."

To read this great narrative is to love the nation too—to love it through the living knowledge of its mortal division. Whitman, who had seen, in the amputated limbs heaped beneath a tree at Fredericksburg, the true dismemberment of the body politic and who intimately knew and loved the bravery and frailty of the soldiers, observed that the real Civil War would never be written and perhaps *should* not be. For me, Shelby Foote has written it. Unlike Thucydides, he was not a participant in the war he narrates; but like him, he is boldly sure that his subject is as great as any in the past and that, as a writer, he is equal to it. He never says so much, but the writing—which he wonderfully calls his "devocioun"—emboldens me to say that this work was done to last forever. (pp. 344-50)

> *James M. Cox, "Shelby Foote's Civil War," in* The Southern Review, *Louisiana State University, Vol. 21, No. 2, Spring, 1985, pp. 329-50.*

FURTHER READING

Bibliography

Kibler, James E., Jr. "Shelby Foote: A Bibliography." *Mississippi Quarterly, Special Issue: Shelby Foote* XXIV, No. 4 (Fall 1971): 437-65.

> Thorough listing of primary works and annotated listing of secondary sources, including interviews, essays, and reviews.

Criticism

Adams, Phoebe. Review of *The Civil War,* Volume II, by Shelby Foote. *The Atlantic Monthly* 212 (December 1963): 156, 160, 162.

> Commends Foote's detailed retelling of the Civil War, noting that "[Foote] has an acute sense of the relative importance of events and a novelist's skill in directing the reader's attention to the men and episodes that will influence the course of the whole war, without omitting items which are of momentary interest."

Burger, Nash K. "The Blue and the Gray Ran Crimson." *The New York Times Book Review* (15 December 1974): 2-3.

> Summary review of *The Civil War,* praising Foote's exhaustive and balanced treatment of the war.

Carmignani, Paul. "Jordan County: Going Back to the Roots." *Journal of the Short Story in English (Les cahiers de la nouvelle),* No. 11 (Autumn 1988): 93-8.

> Discusses the significance of the past, landscape, and traditions of the South in Foote's short story collection *Jordan County.*

Carter, William C., ed. *Conversations with Shelby Foote.* Jackson: University Press of Mississippi, 1989, 276 p.

> Collects eighteen representative interviews from 1950

through 1987 in which Foote discusses his development as a writer of fiction and history.

Daniels, Jonathan. "Immortal Story Begun at Sumter." *The Saturday Review* XLI, No. 50 (13 December 1958): 18.

> Review of the first volume of *The Civil War* in which the critic praises Foote's engaging account of the war, yet notes with disappointment the author's emphasis on military actions over social, political, and economic factors.

Donald, David. "The Turning of the Tide." *The New York Times Book Review* (1 December 1963): 36.

> Reviews the second volume of *The Civil War,* ranking Foote's work "as one of the three major comprehensive histories to be produced during the current centennial celebration" with Allan Nevin's *War for the Union* and Bruce Catton's *Centennial History of the Civil War.*

Freedman, Richard. "Trouble in Memphis and Boston." *The New York Times Book Review* (5 March 1978): 15, 37.

> Review of *September September* in which the critic provides a plot synopsis of the novel.

Fuller, Edmund. "Deep South Vignettes." *The New York Times Book Review* (25 April 1954): 29.

> Summary review of the short stories and novellas collected in *Jordan County,* denoting the work uneven in quality.

Gaither, Frances. "Dry-Rot in Dixie." *The New York Times Book Review* (23 September 1951): 26.

> Review of *Love in a Dry Season* in which the critic discusses Foote's characterizations, maintaining that the novel "is a book about fear, greed, lust, frustration, cruelty—never love. None of the several main characters ever did or ever can experience anything of the sort."

Geismar, Maxwell. "New Novels: But Not Very." *The Nation* 178, No. 17 (24 April 1954): 367-68.

> Survey of several works by contemporary writers in which the critic acknowledges the technical merit of *Jordan County,* yet contends that Foote's short stories lack originality.

Green, Michelle, and Hutchings, David. "The Civil War Finds a Homer in Writer Shelby Foote." *People Weekly* 34 (15 October 1990): 61-2.

> Biographical profile occasioned by the popularity of Foote's commentary in the PBS program *The Civil War.*

Hartje, Robert. Review of *The Civil War,* Volume III, by Shelby Foote. *The American Historical Review* 81, No. 4 (October 1976): 975-76.

> Favorable assessment of *The Civil War* in which the historian praises Foote's narrative treatment of the individuals and events of the war, asserting that "though history written as literature may cease to be history as we should define it, it may still retain validity as an art form and as another source."

Krim, Seymour. "Faulkner Country." *The New York Times Book Review* (9 July 1950): 20.

> Briefly reviews *Follow Me Down,* praising Foote's technical abilities, yet dismissing his handling of subject matter as sensationalized and cheap.

The Mississippi Quarterly, Special Issue: Shelby Foote XXIV, No. 4 (Fall 1971): 321-65.

> Contains essays on *The Civil War* and Foote's fiction, in-

terviews with the author, and a bibliography of primary and secondary sources.

Phillips, Robert L., Jr. *Shelby Foote: Novelist and Historian.* Jackson: University Press of Mississippi, 1992, 261 p.

Traces the development of Foote's literary career, focusing on his artistic achievements as a novelist and writer of history. Phillips also includes a primary and secondary bibliography.

Robertson, James I., Jr. Review of *The Civil War,* Volume II, by Shelby Foote. *The American Historical Review* LXIX, No. 3 (April 1964): 790-91.

Compares Foote's study with Bruce Catton's *Centennial History of the Civil War,* discussing methods of research and narrative focus.

Rubin, Louis D., Jr. "Shelby Foote's Civil War." In his *A Gallery of Southerners,* pp. 174-96. Baton Rouge: Louisiana State University Press, 1982.

Characterizes various military histories of the American Civil War that emerged prior to and during the years of the Civil War Centennial, denoting Foote's *The Civil War* "the best military account of the four years of conflict that has thus far been written."

Shepherd, Allen. "Technique and Theme in Shelby Foote's *Shiloh.*" *Notes on Mississippi Writers* V, No. 1 (Spring 1972): 3-10.

Studies the themes and such narrative techniques as point of view in *Shiloh* to demonstrate that the novel "exhibits a careful craftsman, completely in control of his material, shaping it into an effective memorable narrative."

Skei, Hans H. "History as a Novel: Shelby Foote's *The Civil War: A Narrative.*" *Notes on Mississippi Writers* XIII, No. 2 (1981): 45-63.

Analyzes the relationship between history and fiction, focusing on narrative forms and strategies used to convey facts in *The Civil War.*

Smith, Frederick Rutledge, Jr. Review of *Tournament,* by Shelby Foote. *The Saturday Review* XXXII, No. 47 (19 November 1949): 44.

Commends Foote's depictions of southern characters and place in *Tournament.*

Stone, Jerome. Review of *Jordan County,* by Shelby Foote. *The Saturday Review* XXXVII, No. 23 (5 June 1954): 34.

Considers Foote's prose descriptive and vital but faults his character development as shallow.

"Novel Thrillers." *The Times Literary Supplement,* No. 2583 (3 August 1951): 481.

Reviews several works by contemporary authors, commenting on Foote's style, narrative perspective, and characterization in *Follow Me Down.*

Vauthier, Simone. " 'Pillar of Fire': The Civil War of Narratives." *Delta, Special Issue: Shelby Foote,* No. 4 (May 1977): 159-76.

Textual analysis of Foote's short story "Pillar of Fire," highlighting its frame narrative structure.

Ward, Geoffrey C. "Telling How It Was." *American Heritage* 38, No. 8 (December 1987): 14, 18.

Extols Foote's engaging narrative and balanced treatment of events in *The Civil War.*

White, Helen, and Sugg, Redding S., Jr. *Shelby Foote.* Boston: Twayne Publishers, 1982, 150 p.

Critical study of Foote's career, including a primary and annotated secondary bibliography.

Additional coverage of Foote's life and career is contained in the following sources published by Gale Research: *Contemporary Authors,* Vols. 5-8, rev. ed.; *Contemporary Authors New Revision Series,* Vol. 3; and *Dictionary of Literary Biography,* Vols. 2, 17.

Jacques Lacan

1901-1981

(Full name Jacques Marie Emile Lacan) French psychoanalyst, lecturer, and essayist.

The following entry provides an overview of Lacan's career.

INTRODUCTION

One of the most influential and controversial thinkers of the twentieth century, Lacan disseminated a radical interpretation of psychoanalytic theory through popular public lectures and notoriously difficult writings, thereby attracting a school of adherents and influencing scholars in numerous fields of study. Although his work originated within the tradition of psychoanalysis established by Sigmund Freud, who postulated a psychological theory emphasizing unconscious mental processes, Lacan's teachings incorporate a variety of philosophies and social sciences. Most notably, Lacan employed structuralism and linguistics to create a model of the unconscious, which he argued constitutes a linguistically structured system of cultural symbols and social patterns.

Lacan was born in Paris to middle-class parents and educated in Jesuit schools. He graduated from medical school, completed his training as a psychiatrist, and presented his first professional paper by the age of twenty-six. In 1932 he became clinical director of the Paris Medical School after delivering his doctoral thesis, "Paranoiac Psychosis and Its Relation to the Personality"; considered an able if unremarkable exegesis of Freud's work on paranoia, his thesis is remembered primarily as an early example of his tortuous, allusive, digressive writing style. Loosely associated with the artistic and literary movement known as Surrealism, Lacan contributed essays on psychopathological crime and the writings of schizophrenics to the surrealist journal *Le minotaure* in 1933. He worked in relative obscurity until the International Psychoanalytic Congress in 1936 when he presented his most famous paper, "Le stade du miroir" ("The Looking-Glass Phase"), which contains the essence of his thought. That year Lacan started a private practice while also serving on the staffs of various mental hospitals in Paris. He became a full member of the Paris Psychoanalytic Society in 1939, officially joining the ranks of orthodox Freudianism in France, and by the late 1940s was recognized as France's leading theorist of Freudian psychoanalysis.

In 1951 Lacan began a long-running series of public seminars that examined Freud's principal texts and attracted increasingly large numbers of students, over a thousand per session in his last years; many influential thinkers attended these lectures, including the Marxist philosopher Louis Althusser and the philosopher-historian Michel

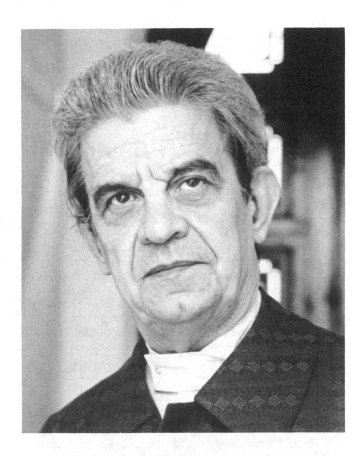

Foucault. In 1952 the Paris Psychoanalytic Society objected to Lacan's assertion that the psychoanalytic session requires a dialectical interaction between the patient and the analyst, whom Lacan viewed as a participant rather than a neutral observer. Due to this dispute, Lacan and colleague Daniel Lagache left the Paris Psychoanalytic Society to form the French Society for Psychoanalysis. At the Society's inaugural meeting in Rome in 1953, Lacan presented a paper entitled "Fonction et champ de la parole et du langage en psychanalyse" ("The Function and Field of Speech and Language in Psychoanalysis")—commonly known as the Rome Discourse—which has been described as Lacan's manifesto and the nearest thing that he ever wrote to a summation of his theories. In 1954 Lacan's disagreements with professional bodies continued when the International Psychoanalytic Association (IPA), led by Sigmund Freud's daughter Anna, rejected the French Society for Psychoanalysis as an affiliated member; observers contend that in rejecting the group on the grounds that it lacked adequate training facilities, the IPA's leaders were really objecting to Lacan's dictatorial personality and unorthodox methods—such as his disregard for a standardized session length, which they saw as the flouting of established practices. Despite the controversy, the French

Society prospered in the 1950s. In 1962 the IPA granted the group affiliation on condition that Lacan be prevented from teaching and training students. Effectively robbed of authority, Lacan resigned and founded the Freudian School, which continued his challenge to psychoanalytic orthodoxy by waiving formal requirements for admission and graduation. Lacan remained with the Freudian School until 1979 when some of the younger staff members tried to depose him. Lacan closed the school, stating that it had strayed far from the basic tenets of Freudianism, and retired, preferring not to participate in the resulting sectarian disputes among his followers. Lacan died in Paris in 1981.

Lacan's interpretation of Freud draws on the principles of many disciplines. Commentators note that his ideas are strongly influenced by Ferdinand de Saussure's structural linguistics, which suggests that meaning does not inhere in words or symbols but is a result of their relational positions within a linguistic or semiotic system. In addition Claude Lévi-Strauss's work, which applied structuralism and linguistics to the study of human interaction and culture in order to identify universal laws regulating societies, influenced Lacan's notion that the unconscious is structured like a language and constitutes a system of culturally derived images and patterns. His most famous theoretical construct is the "mirror stage." During this stage of psychological development, which, according to Lacan, occurs between the ages of six and eighteen months, an infant—whose experience has been one of undifferentiated sensory stimulation—comes to perceive itself as a distinct and unified entity. The cause of this identification is either the infant's reflection in a mirror or the mother's gaze, both of which convey to the infant an idealized mental image of itself and a sense of independence from its mother and the environment. For Lacan, the infant's recognition of itself during the mirror stage is really a misrecognition, for the infant is not the idealized image of itself; this misrecognition forms the basis for the ego or the sense of self, which Lacan viewed as fictional. The significance of the mirror stage for Lacan is that it brings about an awareness of the distinctions between the self and the world and initiates the process by which the infant will acquire language. According to Lacan, the awareness of distinctions allows language acquisition and alienates the infant from its previous experience. Lacan stated that language is an illusory assuagement of the condition of alienation because it continuously reinforces the fiction of the substantive, unified ego through the use of pronouns ("I" and "you") and the assumed roles of speakers and listeners.

Lacan rarely agreed with the interpretations of his work whether put forth by supporters or critics. Contemptuous of commentators who charge him with obscurantism, he responded to the "idea of speaking so as to be understood by idiots" by stating: "I am speaking to those who are savvy, to the nonidiots, to the supposed analysts." Lacan intended his discourse to pose interpretive difficulties. Critics note that because of the emphasis he placed on the role of language in human development, particularly its importance to ego formation and a sense of self, the opacity of Lacan's writing represents an attempt to encourage interpretation and critical self-examination; sharing the dialectical quality of his psychoanalytic method, Lacan's writing makes the reader work and participate in the construction of meaning just as his patients did. Commentators have noted that the inherent difficulty of his work is further compounded by the actions of the academic community Lacan so influenced. As Catherine Clément has said, "Lacan's thought, now fashionable, has been reduced to jargon, turned into a parody of itself" by academics who have kept his work "jealously protected in the most traditional way, by shrouding it in esoteric language." Nevertheless, Lacan's work has had tremendous impact, extending into such wide-ranging fields as literary and film studies, and has provided a new vocabulary and framework for the theoretical work of social critics and philosophers.

PRINCIPAL WORKS

Ecrits   (treatises)   1966
  [*Ecrits: A Selection*   (selected translation), 1977]
"The Seminar on 'The Purloined Letter'"   (essay)
  1972; published in journal *Yale French Studies*
Le séminaire de Jacques Lacan. Livre XI. Les quatre concepts fondamentaux de la psychanalyse   (lectures)
  1973
  [*The Four Fundamental Concepts of Psychoanalysis*, 1978]
La télévision   (lecture)   1974
  [*Television: A Challenge to the Psychoanalytic Establishment*, 1990]
Le séminaire. Livre I. Les écrits techniques de Freud   (lectures)   1975
  [*The Seminar of Jacques Lacan. Book I: Freud's Papers on Technique, 1953-1954*, 1988]
"Desire and the Interpretation of Desire in *Hamlet*"   (essay)   1977; published in journal *Yale French Studies*
Le séminaire. Livre II. Le moi dans la théorie de Freud et dans la technique de la psychanalyse, 1954-1955   (lectures)   1978
  [*The Seminar of Jacques Lacan. Book II: The Ego in Freud's Theory and in the Technique of Psychoanalysis, 1954-1955*, 1988]

CRITICISM

Louis Althusser   (essay date January 1964)

[*Althusser was one of the world's foremost Marxist philosophers. An outspoken critic of Soviet communism, he gained an international following in the late 1960s with the publication of* Lire "Le Capital" (*1965;* Reading "Capital," *selections, 1970) and* Pour Marx (*1965;* For Marx, *1969), which reinterpret Marx's theories in rela-*

tion to modern structuralism. In the following excerpt from an essay originally published in French in 1964, Althusser defends Lacan's assertion that the unconscious evinces a linguistic structure which gives meaning to experience and enables psychological development.]

What is the *object* of psycho-analysis? It is *what* analytical technique deals with in the analytical practice of the cure, i.e. not the cure itself, not that supposedly dual system which is tailor-made for any phenomenology or morality—but the *'effects'*, prolonged into the surviving adult, of the extraordinary adventure which from birth to the liquidation of the Oedipal phase transforms a small animal conceived by a man and a woman into a small human child.

One of the 'effects' of the humanization of the small biological creature that results from human parturition: there in its place is the object of psycho-analysis, an object which has a simple name: *'the unconscious'*.

That this small biological being survives, and not as a 'wolf-child', that has become a little wolf or bear (as displayed in the princely courts of the eighteenth century), but as a *human child* (having escaped all childhood deaths, many of which are human deaths, deaths punishing the failure of humanization), that is the test all adult men have passed: they are the *never forgetful* witnesses, and very often the victims, of this victory, bearing in their most hidden, i.e. in their most clamorous parts, the wounds, weaknesses and stiffnesses that result from this struggle for human life or death. Some, the majority, have emerged more or less unscathed—or at least, give this out to be the case; many of these veratans bear the marks throughout their lives; some will die from their fight, though at some remove, the old wounds suddenly opening again in psychotic explosion, in madness, the ultimate compulsion of a 'negative therapeutic reaction'; others, more numerous, as 'normally' as you like, in the guise of an 'organic' decay. Humanity only inscribes its official deaths on its war memorials: those who were able to die on time, i.e. late, as men, in human wars in which only *human* wolves and gods tear and sacrifice one another. In its sole survivors, psycho-analysis is concerned with another struggle, with the only war without memoirs or memorials, the war humanity pretends it has never declared, the war it always thinks it has won in advance, simply because humanity is nothing but surviving this war, living and bearing children as culture in human culture: a war which is continually declared in each of its sons, who, projected, deformed and rejected, are required, each by himself in solitude and against death, to take the long forced march which makes mammiferous larvae into human children, *masculine or feminine subjects.*

This object is no business of the biologist's: this story is certainly not biological!—since from the beginning it is completely dominated by the constraint of the sexed human order that each mother engraves on the small human animal in maternal 'love' or hatred, starting from its alimentary rhythm and training. History, 'sociology' or anthropology have no business here, and this is no surprise for they deal with society and therefore with culture, i.e. with what is no longer this small animal—which only be-

comes human-sexual by crossing the infinite divide that separates life from humanity, the biological from the historical, 'nature' from 'culture'. Psychology is lost here, and this is hardly strange for it thinks that in its 'object' it is dealing with some *human* 'nature' or 'non-nature', with the genesis of this existent, identified and certified by culture itself (by the human)—when the object of psycho-analysis is the question with absolute priority, whether to be born or not to be (*naître ou n'être pas*), the aleatory abyss of the human-sexual itself in every human scion. Here 'philosophy' loses its bearings and its cover (*'repères'* and *'repaires'*), naturally!—for these unique origins rob it of the only origins it renders homage to for its existence: God, reason, consciousness, history and culture. It is clear that the object of psycho-analysis may be specific and that the modality of its material as well as the specificity of its 'mechanisms' (to use one of Freud's terms) are of quite another kind than the material and 'mechanisms' which are known to the biologist, the neurologist, the anthropologist, the sociologist, the psychologist and the philosopher. We need only recognize this specificity and hence the distinctness of the object that it derives from, in order to recognize the radical right of psycho-analysis to a specificity of its concepts in line with the specificity of its object: the unconcious and its effects.

Lacan would be the first to admit that his attempted theorization would have been impossible were it not for the emergence of a new science: *linguistics.* It is in the nature of the history of the sciences that one science may often not become a science except by recourse to a detour through other sciences, not only sciences that existed at its baptism but also some new late-comer among sciences that needed time before it could be born. The temporary opacity of the shadow cast on Freudian theory by the model of Helmholtz and Maxwell's thermodynamic physics has been dispersed today by the light that structural linguistics throws on it, making possible an intelligible approach to that object. Freud himself said that everything depended on language. Lacan makes this more precise: 'the discourse of the unconscious is structured like a language'. In his first great work *The Interpretation of Dreams* (which is not anecdotal and superficial as is frequently suggested, but fundamental), Freud studied the 'mechanisms' and 'laws' of dreams, reducing their variants to two: *displacement* and *condensation*. Lacan recognized these as two essential figures of speech, called in linguistics metonymy and metaphor. Hence slips, failures, jokes and symptoms, like the elements of dreams themselves, became *signifiers,* inscribed in the chain of an unconscious discourse, doubling silently, i.e. deafeningly, in the misrecognition of 'repression', the chain of the human subject's verbal discourse. Hence we were introduced to the paradox, formally familiar to linguistics, of a double yet single discourse, unconscious yet verbal, having for its double field only a single field, with no beyond except in itself: the field of the 'Signifying Chain'. Hence the most important acquisitions of de Saussure and of the linguistics that descends from him began to play a justified part in the understanding of the process of the unconscious as well as that of the verbal discourse of the subject and of their inter-relationship, i.e. of their identical relation and non-relation in other words, of their reduplication and dislocation (*décalage*). Thereby philosophico-idealist interpretations of the unconscious as a second consciousness, of the unconscious as bad faith (Sartre), of the unconscious as the cankerous survival of a non-current structure or non-sense (Merleau-Ponty), all the interpretations of the unconscious as a biologico-archetypical 'id' (Jung) became what they were: not the beginnings of a theory but null 'theories', ideological misunderstandings.

It remained to define (I am forced into the crudest schematism, but how could I avoid it in such a short [essay]?) the meaning of this *primacy* of the formal structure of language and its 'mechanisms' as they are encountered in the practice of analytical interpretation, as a function of the very foundations of this practice: its object, i.e. the 'effects' still present in the survivors of the forced 'humanization' of the small human animal into a *man* or a *woman*. This question cannot be answered merely by invoking the factual primacy of language as the sole object and means of analytical practice. Everything that happens in the cure does take place in and through language (including silence, its rhythms and scansions). But it is necessary to show *why* and *how* in principle the factual role of language in the cure as both raw material of analytic practice and means of production of its effects (the passage, as Lacan puts it, from an 'empty speech' to a 'full speech'), is only founded in fact in analytical practice because it is founded in *principle* in its object, the object that, in the last analysis, founds this practice and its technique: hence, since it is a science, in the *theory* of its object.

Herein no doubt lies the most original aspect of Lacan's work, his discovery. Lacan has shown that this transition from (ultimately purely) biological existence to human existence (the human child) is achieved within the Law of Order, the law I shall call the Law of Culture, and that this Law of Order is confounded in its *formal* essence with the order of language. What are we to understand by this formula, at first sight so enigmatic? Firstly, that the *whole of this transition* can only be grasped in terms of a recurrent language, as designated by the language of the adult or child in a *cure situation,* designated, assigned and localized within the law of language in which is established and presented all human order, i.e. every human role. Secondly, that in this assignment by the language of the cure appears the current, constant presence of the absolute effectiveness of order in the transition itself, of the Law of Culture in humanization.

To give some idea of this in a very few words, I shall indicate the two great moments of this *transition*. I.The moment of the dual pre-Oedipal intercourse, in which the child, concerned with nothing but one alter-ego, the mother, who punctuates its life by her presence (*da!*) and absence (*fort!*), lives this dual intercourse in the mode of the imaginary fascination of the ego, being itself *that* other, *any* other, *every* other, all *the others* of primary narcissistic identification, never able to take up the objectifying distance of the third *vis-à-vis* either the other or itself; 2. the Oedipal moment, in which a ternary structure emerges against the background of the dual structure, when the third (the father) intrudes on the imaginary satisfaction of dual fascination, overthrows its economy, destroys its fas-

cinations, and introduces the child to what Lacan calls the Symbolic Order, the order of objectifying language that will finally allow him to say: I, you, he, she or it, that will therefore allow the small child to situate itself as a *human child* in a world of adult thirds.

Hence two great moments: I. that of the imaginary (pre-Oedipal); 2. that of the symbolic (Oedipal resolution), or, to use a different language, that of objectivity recognized in its (symbolic) use, but not yet known (the knowledge of objectivity arising at a quite different 'age' and also from a quite different practice).

And the crucial point that Lacan has illuminated is this: these two moments are dominated, governed and marked by a single Law, the *Law of the Symbolic.* Even the moment of the imaginary, which, for clarity's sake, I have just presented as *preceding* the symbolic, as distinct from it—hence as the first moment in which the child *lives* its immediate intercourse with a human being (its mother) without recognizing it practically as the symbolic intercourse it is (i.e. as the intercourse of a small human child with a human mother)—*is marked and structured in its dialectic by the dialectic of the Symbolic Order itself,* i.e. by the dialectic of human Order, of the human norm (the norms of the temporal rhythms of feeding, hygiene, behaviour, of the concrete attitudes of recognition—the child's acceptance, rejection, yes and no being merely the small change, the *empirical* modalities of this constitutive Order, the Order of Law and of the Right of attributory or exclusory assignment), in the form of the Order of the signifier itself, i.e., in the form of an Order *formally* identical with the order of language.

Where a superficial or prejudiced reading of Freud has only seen happy, lawless childhood, the paradise of 'polymorphous perversity', a kind of state of nature only punctuated by stages of a biological type linked with the functional primacy of some part of the human body, the site of a 'vital' need (oral, anal, genital), Lacan demonstrates the effectiveness of the Order, the Law, that has been lying in wait for each infant born since before his birth, and seizes him before his first cry, assigning to him his place and role, and hence his fixed destination. Each stage traversed by the sexed infant is traversed in the realm of Law, of the codes of human assignment, communication and non-communication; his 'satisfactions' bear the indelible and constitutive mark of the Law, of the claims of human Law, that, like all law, cannot be 'ignored' by anyone, least of all by those ignorant of it, but may be evaded or violated by everyone, above all by its most faithful adherents. That is why any reduction of childhood traumas to a balance of 'biological frustrations' alone, is in principle erroneous, since the Law that covers them, as a Law, abstracts from all contents, exists and acts as a Law only in and by this abstraction, and the infant submits to this rule and receives it from his first breath. This is the beginning, and has always been the beginning, even where there is no living father, of the official presence of the Father (who is Law), hence of the Order of the human signifier, i.e. of the Law of Culture: this discourse, the absolute precondition of any discourse, this discourse present at the top, i.e. absent in the depths, in all verbal discourse, the discourse of this Order, this discourse of the Other, of the great Third, which is this Order itself: *the discourse of the unconscious.* This gives us a hold, a *conceptual* hold on the unconscious, which is in each human being the absolute place where his particular discourse seeks its own place, seeks, misses, and in missing, finds its own place, its own anchor to its place, in the imposition, imposture, complicity and denegation of its own imaginary fascinations.

That in the Oedipal phase the sexed child becomes a sexual human child (man or woman) by testing its imaginary fantasms against the Symbolic, and if all 'goes well' finally becomes and accepts itself as what it is: a little boy or little girl among adults, with the rights of a child in this adult world, and, like all children, with the full *right* to become one day 'like daddy', i.e. a masculine human being with a wife (and no longer only a mother), or 'like mummy', i.e. a feminine human being with a husband (and not just a father)—these things are only the destination of the long forced march towards human childhood.

That all the material of this ultimate drama is provided by a previously formed language, which, in the Oedipal phase, is centred and arranged wholly around the signifier *phallus:* the emblem of the Father, the emblem of right, of the Law, the fantasy image of all Right—this may seem astonishing or arbitrary, but all psycho-analysts attest to it as a fact of experience.

The last Oedipal stage, 'castration', shows us why. When the small boy lives and resolves the tragic and beneficial situation of castration, he accepts the fact that he *has not* the same Right (phallus) as his father, in particular, that he has not the same Right as his father over his mother, who is thereby revealed as endowed with the intolerable status of double use, mother for the small boy, wife for the father; but by accepting that he has not the same right as his father, he gains the assurance that one day, *later on,* when he grows up, he will get the right which is now refused him through his lack of 'means'. He has only a little right, which will grow big if he will grow big himself by taking care to 'mind his p's and q's' (*'manger sa soupe'*). For her part, when the little girl lives and assumes the tragic and beneficial situation of castration, she accepts that she has not the same right as her mother, and hence she doubly accepts that she has not the same right (phallus) as her father, since her mother has not this right (no phallus), although she is a woman, because she is a woman, and she simultaneously accepts that she has not the same right as her mother, i.e. that she is not yet a woman as her mother is. But she thereby gains in return her own small right: the right of a little girl, and the promise of a large right, the full right of a woman when she grows up, if she will grow up accepting the Law of Human Order, i.e. submitting to it if need be to deflect it—by not minding her p's and q's 'properly'.

In either case, whether it be the moment of dual fascination of the Imaginary (I) or the (Oedipal) moment of the lived recognition of the insertion into the Symbolic Order (2), the whole dialectic of the transition in all its essential details is stamped by the seal of Human Order, of the Symbolic, for which linguistics provides us with the *formal* laws, i.e. the *formal* concept.

Psycho-analytic theory can thus give us what makes each science no pure speculation but a science: the definition of the *formal* essence of its object, the precondition for any practical, technical application of it to its *concrete* objects. Thereby psycho-analytic theory escapes the classical idealist antinomies formulated by Politzer for example, when, while demanding of psycho-analysis (whose revolutionary theoretical scope he was the first in France to realize) that it be a science of the true 'concrete', a 'concrete psychology', he attacked it for its *abstractions:* the unconscious, the Oedipus complex, the castration complex, etc. How, said Politzer, can psycho-analysis claim to be the science of the *concrete* it aims to be and could be, if it persists in *abstractions* which are merely the 'concrete' alienated in an abstract and metaphysical psychology? How can one reach the 'concrete' from such abstractions, from the abstract? In fact, no science can do without abstraction, even when, in its 'practice' (which is not, NB, the theoretical practice of that science but the practice of its concrete *application*), it deals only with those peculiar and unique variants that constitute each individual 'drama'. As Lacan thinks them in Freud—and Lacan thinks nothing but Freud's concepts, giving them the form of our scientificity, the only scientificity there can be—the 'abstractions' of psycho-analysis are really the authentic scientific concepts of their object, insofar as, as concepts of their object, they contain within them the index, measure and basis for the necessity of their abstraction, i.e., the measure of their relation to the 'concrete', and hence of their specific relation to the concrete of their application, commonly called analytic practice (the cure).

So the Oedipal phase is not a hidden *'meaning'* which merely lacks consciousness or speech—it is not a structure buried in the past that can always be restructured or surpassed by 'reactivating its meaning'; the Oedipus complex is the dramatic structure, the 'theatrical machine' imposed by the Law of Culture on every involuntary, conscripted candidate to humanity, a structure containing in itself not only the possibility of, but the necessity for the concrete variants in which it *exists,* for every individual who reaches its threshold, lives through it and survives it. In its application, in what is called its practice (the cure), psychoanalysis works on the concrete 'effects' of these variants, i.e. on the modality of the specific and absolutely unique nexus in which the Oedipal transition was and is begun, completed, missed or eluded by some particular individual. These *variants* can be thought and known in their essence itself on the basis of the structure of the Oedipal *invariant,* precisely because this whole transition is marked from its beginnings in fascination, in its most 'aberrant' as well as in its most 'normal' forms, by the Law of this structure, the ultimate form of access to the Symbolic within the Law of the Symbolic itself.

I know that these brief suggestions will not only appear to be, but are, summary and schematic; that a number of notions put forward here require extended development if they are to be justified and established. Even if their well-foundedness and the relations they bear to the set of notions that underly them were clarified, even if they were compared with the letter of Freud's analyses, they would pose their own problems in their turn: not only problems of conceptual formation, definition and clarification, but real, new problems, necessarily produced by the development of the work of theorization we have just discussed. For example, how can we rigorously formulate the relation between the *formal* structure of language, the absolute precondition for the existence and intelligibility of the unconscious, on the one hand, the concrete kinship structures on the other, and finally the concrete ideological formations in which the specific functions implied by the kinship structures (paternity, maternity, childhood) are lived? Is it conceivable that the historical variation of these latter structures (kinship, ideology) might materially affect some or other aspect of the instances isolated by Freud? Or again, to what extent may the simple definition of the object and location of Freud's discovery, rationally conceived, react on the disciplines from which it distinguished itself (such as psychology, social psychology, sociology), and raise for them questions as to the (often problematic) status of their objects? And selecting one more from among so many possible questions: what relations are there between analytic theory and I. the historical preconditions of its appearance, and 2. the social preconditions of its application? (pp. 189-200)

Louis Althusser, *"Freud and Lacan," in his* Lenin and Philosophy and Other Essays,

translated by Ben Brewster, NLB, 1971, pp. 177-202.

Fredric Jameson   (essay date 1977)

[*Jameson is considered America's most eminent Marxist critic. While his literary studies have focused on the works of Jean-Paul Sartre, Jameson has written prolifically on the ideological aspects of mass culture, drawing on and analyzing the work of such noted critics and philosophers as Theodor Adorno, Ernst Bloch, Herbert Marcuse, and Walter Benjamin. In the following excerpt, Jameson examines the definitive role of language in Lacan's concepts of the Imaginary, the Symbolic, and the Real, expanding on the notion that the unconscious has a linguistic structure which both enables and limits the understanding of human experience.*]

The difficulties involved in an exposition of [Lacan's concepts of the Imaginary, the Symbolic, and the Real] spring at least in part from their inseparability. According to Lacanian epistemology, indeed, acts of consciousness, experiences of the mature subject, necessarily imply a structural coordination between the Imaginary, the Symbolic, and the Real. [In "A la recherche des principes d'une psychothérapie des psychoses," in his *La Solution psychiatrique* (1958), Serge Leclaire states:] "The experience of the Real presupposes the simultaneous exercise of two

Lacan when he was a medical student.

correlative functions, the imaginary function and the symbolic function." If the notion of the Real is the most problematical of the three—since it can never be experienced immediately, but only by way of the mediation of the other two—it is also the easiest to bracket for purposes of this presentation. We will return to the function of this concept—neither an order nor a register, exactly—in our conclusion; suffice it to underscore here the profound heterogeneity of the Real with respect to the other two functions, between which we would then expect to discover a similar disproportion.

Yet to speak of the Imaginary independently of the Symbolic is to perpetuate the illusion that we could have a relatively pure experience of either. If, for instance, we overhastily identify the Symbolic with the dimension of language and the function of speech in general, then it becomes obvious that we can hardly convey any experience of the Imaginary without presupposing the former. Meanwhile, insofar as the Imaginary is understood as the place of the insertion of my unique individuality as *Dasein* and as *corps propre,* it will become increasingly difficult to form a notion of the Symbolic Order as some pure syntactic web, which entertains no relationship to individual subjects at all.

In reality, however, the methodological danger is the obverse of this one, namely, the temptation to transform the notion of the two orders or functions into a binary opposition, and to define each relationally in terms of the other—something it is even easier to find oneself doing when one has begun by suspending the Real itself and leaving it out of consideration. We will however come to learn that this process of definition by binary opposition is itself profoundly characteristic of the Imaginary, so that to allow our exposition to be influenced by it is already to slant our presentation in terms of one of its two objects of study.

Fortunately, the genetic preoccupations of psychoanalysis provide a solution to this dilemma: for Freud founded his diagnosis of psychic disorders, not only on the latter's own aetiology, but on a larger view of the process of formation of the psyche itself as a whole, and on a conception of the stages of infantile development. And we shall see shortly that Lacan follows him in this, rewriting the Freudian history of the psyche in a new and unexpected way. But this means that, even if they are inextricable in mature psychic life, we ought to be able to distinguish Imaginary from Symbolic at the moment of emergence of each; in addition, we ought to be able to form a more reliable assessment of the role of each in the economy of the psyche by examining those moments in which their mature relationship to each other has broken down, moments which present a serious imbalance in favor of one or the other registers. Most frequently, this imbalance would seem to take the form of a degradation of the Symbolic to an Imaginary level [a process elucidated by Anika Lemaire in her *Jacques Lacan,* 1970]: "The problem of the neurotic consists in a loss of the symbolic reference of the signifiers which make up the central points of the structure of his complex. Thus the neurotic may repress the signified of his symptom. This loss of the reference value of the symbol causes it to regress to the level of the imaginary, in the absence of any

mediation between self and idea." On the other hand, when it is appreciated to what degree, for Lacan, the apprenticeship of language is an alienation for the psyche, it will become clear that there can also be a hypertrophy of the Symbolic at the Imaginary's expense which is no less pathological; the recent emphasis on the critique of science and of its alienated "sujet supposé savoir" is indeed predicated on this overdevelopment of the Symbolic function: "The symbol is an imaginary figure in which man's truth is alienated. The intellectual elaboration of the symbol cannot disalienate it. Only the analysis of its imaginary elements, taken individually, reveals the meaning and the desire that the subject had hidden within it" [A. Vergote, quoted by Rifflet-Lemaire].

Even before undertaking a genetic exposition of the two registers, however, we must observe that the very terms themselves present a preliminary difficulty which is none other than their respective previous histories: thus Imaginary surely derives from the experience of the image—and of the imago—and we are meant to retain its spatial and visual connotations. Yet as Lacan uses the word, it has a relatively narrow and technical sense, and should not be extended in any immediate way to the traditional conception of the imagination in philosophical aesthetics (nor to the Sartrean doctrine of the "imaginaire," although the latter's material of study is doubtless Imaginary in Lacan's sense of the term).

The word Symbolic is even more troublesome, since much of what Lacan will designate as Imaginary is traditionally designated by expressions like symbol and symbolism. We will want to wrench the Lacanian term loose from its rich history as the opposite number to allegory, particularly in Romantic thought; nor can it maintain any of its wider suggestion of the figural as opposed to the literal meaning (symbolism versus discursive thought, Mauss' symbolic exchange as opposed to the market system, etc.). Indeed, we would be tempted to suggest that the Lacanian Symbolic Order be considered as having nothing to do with symbols or with symbolism whatsoever in the conventional sense, were it not for the obvious problem of what then to do with the whole classical Freudian apparatus of dream symbolism proper.

The originality of Lacan's rewriting of Freud may be judged by his radical reorganization of this material which had hitherto—houses, towers, cigars and all—been taken to constitute some storehouse of universal symbols. Most of the latter will now be understood rather as "part-objects" in Melanie Klein's sense of organs and parts of the body which are libidinally valorized; these part-objects then, as we shall see shortly, belong to the realm of the Imaginary rather than to that of the Symbolic. The one exception—the notorious "phallic" symbol dear to vulgar Freudian literary criticism—is the very instrument for the Lacanian reinterpretation of Freud in linguistic terms, for the phallus—not, in contradistinction to the penis, an organ of the body—now comes to be considered neither image nor symbol, but rather a signifier, indeed the fundamental signifier of mature psychic life, and thus one of the basic organizational categories of the Symbolic Order itself.

In any case, whatever the nature of the Lacanian Symbolic, it is clear that the Imaginary—a kind of pre-verbal register whose logic is essentially visual—precedes it as a stage in the development of the psyche. Its moment of formation—and that existential situation in which its specificity is most strikingly dramatized—has been named the "mirror stage" by Lacan, who thereby designates that moment between six and eighteen months in which the child first demonstrably "recognizes" his or her own image in the mirror, thus tangibly making the connection between inner motricity and the specular movements stirring before him. It is important not to deduce too hastily from this very early experience some ultimate ontological possibility of an ego or an identity in the psychological sense, or even in the sense of some Hegelian self-conscious reflexivity. Whatever else the mirror stage is, indeed, for Lacan it marks a fundamental gap between the subject and its own self or *imago* which can never be bridged: "The important point is that this form [of the subject in the mirror stage] fixed the instance of the ego, well before any social determination, in a line of fiction which is forever irreducible for the individual himself—or rather which will rejoin the subject's evolution in asymptotic fashion only, whatever the favorable outcome of those dialectical syntheses by which as an ego he must resolve his discordance with his own reality." In our present context, we will want to retain the words "dans une ligne de fiction," which underscore the psychic function of narrative and fantasy in the attempts of the subject to reintegrate his or her alienated image.

The mirror stage, which is the precondition for primary narcissism, is also, owing to the equally irreducible gap it opens between the infant and its fellows, the very source of human aggressivity; and indeed, one of the original features of Lacan's early teaching is its insistence on the inextricable association of these two drives. How could it indeed be otherwise, at a moment when, the child's investment in images of the body having been achieved, there does not yet exist that ego formation which would permit him to distinguish his own form from that of others? The result is a world of bodies and organs which in some fashion lacks a phenomenological center and a privileged point of view:

> Throughout this period the emotional reactions and verbal indications of normal transitivism [Charlotte Bühler's term for the indifferentiation of subject and object] will be observed. The child who hits says he has been hit, the child who sees another child fall begins to cry. Similarly, it is by way of an identification with the other that the infant lives the entire spectrum of reactions from ostentation to generosity, whose structural ambiguity his conduct so undisguisedly reveals, slave identified with despot, actor with spectator, victim with seducer.
>
> ["**Aggressivity in psychoanalysis,**"
> in *Écrits: A Selection*]

This "structural crossroads" (Lacan) corresponds to that pre-individualistic, pre-mimetic, pre-point-of-view stage in aesthetic organization which is generally designated as "play," [as labeled by Hans-Georg Gadamer in "Der Begriff des Spiels" in his *Wahrheit und Methode,* 1965,]

whose essence lies in the frequent shifts of the subject from one fixed position to another, in a kind of optional multiplicity of insertions of the subject into a relatively fixed Symbolic Order. In the realm of linguistics and psychopathology, the fundamental document on the effects of "transitivism" remains Freud's "A Child is Being Beaten," which has had considerable emblematic significance for recent theory.

A description of the Imaginary will therefore on the one hand require us to come to terms with a uniquely determinate configuration of space—one not yet organized around the individuation of my own personal body, or differentiated hierarchically according to the perspectives of my own central point of view—yet which nonetheless swarms with bodies and forms intuited in a different way, whose fundamental property is, it would seem, to be visible without their visibility being the result of the act of any particular observer, to be, as it were, already-seen, to carry their specularity upon themselves like a color they wear or the texture of their surface. In this—the indifferentiation of their *esse* from a *percipi* which does not know a *percipiens*—these bodies of the Imaginary exemplify the very logic of mirror images; yet the existence of the normal object world of adult everyday life presupposes this prior, imaginary, experience of space: It is normally by the possibilities of a game of imaginary transposition that the progressive valorization of objects is achieved, on what is customarily known as the affective level, by a proliferation, a fan-like disposition of all the imagination equations which allow the human being, alone in the animal realm, to have an almost infinite number of objects at his disposition, objects isolated in their form.

The affective valorization of these objects ultimately derives from the primacy of the human *imago* in the mirror stage; and it is clear that the very investment of an object world will depend in one way or another on the possibility of symbolic association or identification of an inanimate thing with the libidinal priority of the human body. Here, then, we come upon what Melanie Klein termed "part-objects"—organs, like the breast, or objects associated with the body, like feces, whose psychic investment is then transferred to a host of other, more indifferent contents of the external world (which are then, as we shall see below, valorized as good or as evil). [Lemaire states:] "A trait common to such objects, Lacan insists, is that they have no specular image, which is to say that they know no alterity. 'They are the very lining, the stuff or imaginary filling of the subject itself, which identifies itself with these objects.' " It is from Melanie Klein's pioneering psychoanalysis of children that the basic features of the Lacanian Imaginary are drawn: there is, as we might expect for an experience of spatiality phenomenologically so different from our own, a logic specific to Imaginary space, whose dominant category proves to be the opposition of container and contained, the fundamental relationship of inside to outside, which clearly enough originates in the infant's fantasies about the maternal body as the receptacle of part-objects (confusion between childbirth and evacuation, etc.).

This spatial syntax of the Imaginary order may then be

said to be intersected by a different type of axis, whose conjunction completes it as an experience: this is the type of relationship which Lacan designates as aggressivity, and which we have seen to result from that indistinct rivalry between self and other in a period that precedes the very elaboration of a self or the construction of an ego. As with the axis of Imaginary space, we must again try to imagine something deeply sedimented in our own experience, but buried under the adult rationality of everyday life (and under the exercise of the Symbolic): a kind of situational experience of otherness as pure relationship, as struggle, violence, and antagonism, in which the child can occupy either term indifferently, or indeed, as in transitivism, both at one. A remarkable sentence of St. Augustine is inscribed as a motto to the primordiality of this rivalry with the imagoes of other infants: "I have myself seen jealousy in a baby and know what it means. He was not old enough to speak, but, whenever his foster-brother was at the breast, would glare at him pale with envy [et intuebatur pallidus amaro aspectu conlactaneum suum]."

Provided it is understood that this moment is quite distinct from that later intervention of the Other (Lacan's capital A, the parents) which ratifies the assumption of the subject into the realm of language or the Symbolic Order, it will be appropriate to designate this primordial rivalry of the mirror stage as a relationship of otherness: nowhere better can we observe the violent situational content of those judgements of good and evil which will later on cool off and sediment into the various systems of ethics. Both

Nietzsche and Sartre have exhaustively explored the genealogy of ethics as the latter emerges from just such an archaic valorization of space, where what is "good" is what is associated with "my" position, and the "bad" simply characterizes the affairs of my mirror rival. We may further document the archaic or atavistic tendencies of ethical or moralizing thought by observing that it has no place in the Symbolic Order, or in the structure of language itself, whose shifters are positional and structurally incapable of supporting this kind of situational complicity with the subject momentarily occupying them.

The Imaginary may thus be described as a peculiar spatial configuration, whose bodies primarily entertain relationships of inside/outside with one another, which is then traversed and reorganized by that primordial rivalry and transitivistic substitution of imagoes, that indistinction of primary narcissism and aggressivity, from which our later conceptions of good and evil derive. This stage is already an alienation—the subject having been captivated by his or her specular image—but in Hegelian fashion it is the kind of alienation from which a more positive evolution is indistinguishable and without which the latter is inconceivable. The same must be said for the next stage of psychic development, in which the Imaginary itself is assumed into the Symbolic Order by way of its alienation into language itself. The Hegelian model of dialectical history—as Jean Hyppolite's interventions in Lacan's first Seminar make clear—remains the fundamental one here:

In 1963. From the left: Lacan, Serge Leclaire, and François Perrier.

This development [of the human anatomy and in particular the cortex] is lived as a temporal dialectic which decisively projects the formation of the individual as history: the *mirror stage* is a drama whose internal dynamic shifts from insufficiency to anticipation—a drama which, for its subject, caught in the mirage of spatial identification, vehiculates a whole series of fantasies which range from a fragmented image of the body to what we will term an orthopedic form of its unity, and to that ultimate assumption of the armature of an alienating identity, whose rigid structure will mark the subject's entire mental development. Thus the rupture of the circle in which *Innenwelt* and *Umwelt* are united generates that inexhaustible attempt to square it in which we reap the ego.

["**Le stade du miroir**"]

The approach to the Symbolic is the moment to suggest the originality of Lacan's conception of the function of language in psychoanalysis. For neo-Freudianism, it would seem that the role of language in the analytical situation or the "talking cure" is understood in terms of what we may call an aesthetic of expression and expressiveness: the patient unburdens himself or herself, his "relief" comes from his having verbalized (or even, according to a more recent ideology, from having "communicated"). For Lacan, on the contrary, this later exercise of speech in the analytical situation draws its therapeutic force from being as it were a completion and fulfillment of the first, imperfectly realized, accession to language and to the Symbolic in early childhood.

For the emphasis of Lacan on the linguistic development of the child—an area in which his work necessarily draws much from Piaget—has mistakenly been criticized as a "revision" of Freud in terms of more traditional psychology, a substitution of the psychological data of the mirror stage and of language acquisition for the more properly psychoanalytic phenomena of infantile sexuality and the Oedipus complex. Obviously Lacan's work must be read as presupposing the entire content of classical Freudianism, otherwise it would be simply another philosophy or intellectual system. The linguistic materials are not intended, it seems to me, to be substituted for the sexual ones; rather we must understand the Lacanian notion of the Symbolic Order as an attempt to create mediations between libidinal analysis and the linguistic categories, to provide, in other words, a transcoding scheme which allows us to speak of both within a common conceptual framework. Thus, the very cornerstone of Freud's conception of the psyche, the Oedipus complex, is transliterated by Lacan into a linguistic phenomenon which he designates as the discovery by the subject of the Name-of-the-Father, and which consists, in other words, in the transformation of an Imaginary relationship to that particular imago which is the physical parent into the new and menacing abstraction of the paternal role as the possessor of the mother and the place of the Law. (pp. 349-59)

The Symbolic Order is thus, as we have already suggested, a further alienation of the subject; and this repeated emphasis further serves to distinguish Lacan's position (what we have called his Hegelianism) from many of the more facile celebrations of the primacy of language by structuralist ideologues. Perhaps the link with Lévi-Strauss' primitivism may be made across Rousseau, for whom the social order in all its repressiveness is intimately linked with the emergence of language itself. In Lacan, however, an analogous sense of the alienating function of language is arrested in Utopian mid-course by the palpable impossibility of returning to an archaic, pre-verbal stage of the psyche itself (although the Deleuze-Guattari celebration of schizophrenia would appear to attempt precisely that). Far more adequately than the schizophrenic or natural man, the tragic symbol of the unavoidable alienation by language would seem to have been provided by Truffault's film, *L'Enfant sauvage,* in which language learning comes before us as a racking torture, a palpably physical kind of suffering upon which the feral child is only imperfectly willing to enter.

The clinical equivalent of this agonizing transition from the Imaginary to the Symbolic is then furnished by an analysis, by Melanie Klein, of an autistic child, which makes it clear that the "cure," the accession of the child to speech and to the Symbolic, is accompanied by an increase, rather than a lessening, of anxiety. This case history (published in 1930 under the title "The Importance of Symbol-Formation in the Development of the Ego") may also serve to correct the imbalance of our own presentation, and of the very notion of a "transition" from Imaginary to Symbolic, by demonstrating that the acquisition of the Symbolic is rather the precondition for a full mastery of the Imaginary as well. In this case, the autistic child is not only unable to speak but unable to play as well—unable, that is, to act out fantasies and to create "symbols," a term which in this context means object substitutes. The few meager objects handled by Dick all represent in a kind of undifferentiated state [what Melanie Klein described as] "the phantasied contents [of the mother's body]. The sadistic phantasies directed against the inside of her body constitute the first and basic relation to the outside world and to reality." Psychic investment in the external world—or in other words, the development of the Imaginary itself—has been arrested at its most rudimentary form, with those little trains that function as representations of Dick and of his father and the dark space or station that represents the mother. The fear of anxiety prevents the child from developing further symbolic substitutes and expanding the narrow limits of his object world.

Melanie Klein's therapy then consists in the introduction into this impoverished realm of the Symbolic Order and of language; and that, as Lacan observes, without any particular subtlety or precautions ("Elle lui fout le symbolisme avec la dernière brutalité, Melanie Klein, au petit Dick! Elle commence tout de suite par lui flanquer les interprétations majeures. Elle le flanque dans une verbalisation brutale du mythe oedipien, presque aussi révoltante pour nous que pour n'importe quel lecteur"). Verbalization itself superposes a Symbolic relationship upon the Imaginary fantasy [suggested by Klein] of the train rolling up to the station: "The station is mummy; Dick is going into mummy."

It is enough: from this point on, miraculously, the child begins to develop relationships to others, jealousies, games, and much richer forms of substitution and of the exercise of language. The Symbolic now releases Imaginary investments of ever new kinds of objects, which had hitherto been blocked, and permits the development of what Melanie Klein in her paper calls "symbol formation." Such symbol or substitute-formation is a fundamental precondition of psychic evolution, since it can alone lead the subject to love objects which are equivalents for the original, now forbidden or taboo, maternal presence: Lacan will then assimilate this process to the operation of the trope of metonymy in the linguistic realm, and the profound effects of this new and complex "rhetorical" mechanism—unavailable in the pre-verbal realm of the Imaginary, where, as we have seen, only the rudimentary oppositions of inside/outside and good/bad are operative—may serve to underscore and to dramatize the extent of the transformation language brings to what without it could not yet have been called desire.

We may now attempt to give a more complete picture of Lacan's conception of language, or at least of those features of articulate speech which are the most essential in the structuration of the psyche and may thus be said to constitute the Symbolic Order. It will be convenient to consider these features in three groups, even though they are obviously all very closely interrelated.

The first of these groups—we have already seen it at work in the Oedipal phenomenon of the Name-of-the-Father—may be generalized as that naming function of language which is not without its profound consequences for the subject himself. For the acquisition of a name results in a thorough-going transformation of the position of the subject in his object world: "That a name, no matter how confused, designates a particular person—this is precisely what the passage to the human state consists in. If we must define that moment in which man [sic] becomes human, we would say that it is at that instant when, as minimally as you like, he enters into a symbolic relationship." It would seem fair to observe that Lacan's attention to the components of language has centered on those kinds of words, primarily names and pronouns, on those slots which, like the shifters generally, anchor a free-floating syntax to a particular subject, those verbal joints, therefore, at which the insertion of the subject into the Symbolic is particularly detectable.

Even here, however, we must distinguish among the various possible effects of these types of words: nouns, in particular the Name-of-the-Father itself, awaken the subject to the sense of a function which is somehow objective and independent of the existence of the biological father. Such names thus provide a liberation from the here-and-now of the Imaginary; for the separation, through language, of the paternal function from the biological father is precisely what permits the child to take the father's place in his turn. The Law, as Lacan calls it, the order of abstraction, is thus also what releases the subject from the constraints of his immediate family situation and from the "bad immediacy" of the pre-Symbolic period.

Pronouns, meanwhile, are the locus for a related, yet distinct, development which is none other than the emergence of the Unconscious itself. Such is indeed for Lacan the significance of the bar which divides signifier from signified in the semiotic fraction: the pronoun, the first person, the signifier, results in a division of the subject or *Spaltung* which drives the "real subject" as it were underground, and leaves a "representative"—the ego—in its place:

> The subject is figured in symbolism by a stand-in or substitute [un tenant-lieu], whether we have to do with the personal pronoun "I", with the name that is given him, or with the denomination "son of". This stand-in is of the order of the symbol or the signifier, an order which is only perpetuated laterally, through the relationships entertained by that signifier with other signifiers. The subject mediated by language is irremediably divided because it has been excluded from the symbolic chain [the lateral relations of signifiers among themselves] at the very moment at which it became "represented" in it.
>
> [Lemaire, *Jacques Lacan*]

Thus, the discontinuity insisted on by linguists between the *énoncé* and the subject of the enunciation (or, by Humboldt's even broader distinction between language as *ergon* or produced object, and language as *energeia* or force of linguistic production) corresponds to the coming into being of the Unconscious itself, as that reality of the subject which has been alienated and repressed through the very process by which, in receiving a name, it is transformed into a representation of itself.

This production of the Unconscious by way of a primary repression which is none other than the acquisition of language is then reinterpreted in terms of the communicational situation as a whole; and Lacan's redefinition of the signifier, "the signifier is what represents the subject for another signifier," now illuminates what it may be artificial to call a different form of linguistic alienation than either of the above features, but what is certainly a distinct dimension of that alienation, namely, the coming into view of the inescapable mediation of other people, and more particularly of the Other with a capital O or A, or in other words the parents: yet here the Law represented by the parents, and in particular by the father, passes over into the very nature of language itself, which the child receives from the outside and which speaks him just as surely as he learns to speak it. At this third moment of the subject's alienation by language we therefore confront a more complex version of that strategy which we have elsewhere described as the fundamental enabling device of structuralism in general, namely, the possibility—provided by the ambiguous nature of language itself—of imperceptibly shifting back and forth between a conception of speech as a linguistic structure, whose components can then be tabulated, and that which, now on the contrary understanding speech in terms of communication, permits a virtual dramatization of the linguistic process (sender/receiver, destinaire/destinateur, etc.). Lacan's "capital A" is the locus of this superposition, constituting at one and the same time the dramatis personae of the Oedipal situation (but most particularly the father or his substitutes) and the very structure of articulate language itself.

So it is that this third aspect of Symbolic alienation, the alienation by the Other, passes over into the more familiar terms of the accounts of the "chaîne du signifiant" given in Lacan's mature doctrine, which, embattled in a struggle against ego psychology, and emerging from a long polemic with the neo-Freudian emphasis on the analysis of resistances and the strengthening of the subject's ego, has found its fundamental principle and organizing theme in "a conception of the function of the signifier able to demonstrate the place at which the subject is subordinated to it to the point of being virtually subverted [suborné]." The result is a determination of the subject by language—not to say a linguistic determinism—which results in a rewriting of the classical Freudian Unconscious in terms of language: "the Unconscious," to quote what must be Lacan's best-known sentence, "is the discourse of the Other." For those of us still accustomed to the classical image of the Freudian Unconscious as a seething cauldron of archaic instincts (and inclined, also, to associate language with thinking and consciousness rather than the opposite of those things), the Lacanian redefinition must inevitably scandalize. As far as language is concerned, the references to Hegel have a strategic role to play in confronting this scandal with the philosophically more respectable idea of alienation in general, and alienation to other people in particular (the Master/Slave chapter is of course the basic text here): thus, if we can bring ourselves to think of language itself as an alienating structure, particularly in those features enumerated above, we are halfway towards an appreciation of this concept.

The other half of the way, however, presents the more serious obstacle of our preconceptions, not about language, but rather about the Unconscious itself. To be sure, the relationship between the Unconscious and the instincts will seem less problematical when we recall the enigma posed by Freud's notion of the *Vorstellungsrepräsentanz* (or "ideational representative"), one of those rare moments in which, as with his hypothesis of the death wish, Freud himself seems terminologically and theoretically inarticulate. Yet the function of the concept seems clear: Freud wants to avoid giving the impression that instincts or drives (*Triebe*) are conceivable in a pure state, even for the purposes of building a model of the psyche, and his tautological term is meant to underscore the indissociable link, no matter how far back we go in the history of the psyche, between the instincts to be found there and the fantasies or objects to which they are bound and through which alone they must express themselves. What is this to say but that the instincts, indeed, the libido itself, no matter how energetically boiling, cannot be conceived independently of their representations, in short, that, in Lacanian terms, no matter how archaic they may be, the instincts are already of the order of the signifier? So it is that the place A of the Lacanian topology indifferently designates the Other (the parents), language, or the Unconscious, now termed the "treasurehouse of the signifier," or in other words, the lumberroom in which the subject's most ancient fantasies or fragments of fantasy are still stored. Two well-known, if less well understood, graphs illustrate this topology, in dynamic as well as in static forms. The static version is, of course, the so-called L-schema, in which the subject's conscious desire, which he under-

stands as a relationship between the desired object (a) and his ego or self (*â*), is mediated by the more fundamental relationship between the real subject (S) and the capital A of the Other, language or the Unconscious. In the dynamic version of this topology (the so-called "graphe du désir"), this structure of the subject is as it were put in motion by the movement of desire, considered as a *parole* or act of enunciation: the inexhaustible fascination of this graph comes from the difficulty of thinking its intersections, in which the speech act of the subject, on its way from sender to receiver, is traversed by the retroactive effect of the "chain of the signifier" travelling, *nachträglich*, in the opposite direction, in such a way that the capital A constitutes the source and the fulfillment of both trajectories.

Still, it will be observed that even if language can be invested to this degree with the content of the subject's alienations, it remains to square the Lacanian linguistic bias with the predominantly sexual emphasis of psychoanalysis' inaugural period. Even if, in other words, one were willing to grant the phallus provisional status as a signifier, the relationship between language and sexuality remains to be defined, the suspicion lingering that a system which permits you to talk about language instead of sexuality must betray a revisionist, if not a downright idealistic, impulse. The connection is made by way of the distinction between need ("pure" biological phenomenon) and demand (a purely interpersonal one, conceivable only after the emergence of language): sexual desire is then that qualitatively new and more complex realm opened up by the lateness of human maturation in comparison with the other animal species, in which a previously biological instinct must undergo an alienation to a fundamentally communicational or linguistic relationship—that of the demand for recognition by the Other—in order to find satisfaction. Yet this alienation also explains why, for Lacan, sexual desire is structurally incapable of ultimate satisfaction: "plaisir"—as the momentary reduction of a purely physical tension—not being the same as "jouissance," which involves that demand for recognition by the Other which in the very nature of things (in the very nature of language?) can never be fulfilled. This structural distance between the subject and his own desire will then serve as the enabling mechanism for the Lacanian typology of the neuroses and the perversions; and nowhere is Lacan more eloquent than in his defense of the ontological dignity of these primordial malfunctionings of the human psyche:

> Hieroglyphics of hysteria, blazons of phobia, labyrinths of the *Zwangsneurose*—charms of impotence, enigmas of inhibition, oracles of anxiety—armorial bearings of character, seals of self-punishment, disguises of perversion—these are the hermetic elements that our exegesis resolves, the equivocations that our invocation dissolves, the artifices that our dialectic absolves, in a deliverance of the imprisoned sense, which moves from the revelation of the palimpsest to the pass-word of the mystery and the pardon of speech.
>
> **["The Function and Field of Speech and Language in Psychoanalysis,"** in *Ecrits: A Selection*]

Meanwhile, this conception of desire as a proto-linguistic demand, and of the Unconscious as a language or "chain of signifiers," then permits something like a rhetorical analysis of psychic processes to come into being. As is well known, not only is desire for Lacan a function of metonymy, the symptom is a product of metaphor, and the entire machinery of the psychic life of the mature subject—which consists, as we have seen above, in the infinite production of substitutes, or, in other words, in Melanie Klein's "symbol-formation"—may be said to be figural in its very essence, figuration being that property of language which allows the same word to be used in several senses. The correlative of the chain of signifiers is thus the conception of a "glissement du signifié" or slippage of signifieds which allows the psychic signifier to be displaced from one object to another. Here once again, the material of the Imaginary serves as a useful contrast by which to define the Symbolic: for not only does the latter, with its slippage of signifieds, know a structural malfunction in the language of the schizophrenic (whose syntagmatic experience of the signifying chain has broken down, on account of a radical *forclusion* or expulsion of the Other), it may be said to have something like a zero degree in the so-called animal languages which constitute the very prototype of the code proper to the Imaginary, involving no demands on the Other, but simply a fixed one-to-one relationship between signifier and signified, between signal and place, from which the more properly human phenomenon of figuration is absent. (pp. 359-68)

[What] is at stake, in Lacan as well as in psychoanalysis in general is truth. . . . For that very reason, it seems arbitrary to class as logocentric and phonocentric a thought which—insofar as it is structural—proposes a decentering of the subject, and—insofar as it is "existential"—is guided by a concept of truth, not as adequation with reality (as Derrida suggests), but rather as a relationship, at best an asymptotic approach, to the Real.

This is not the place to deal with Lacan's epistemology, but it is certainly the moment to return to this term, the third of the canonical Lacanian triad, of which it must be admitted that it is at the very least astonishing that we have been able to avoid mentioning it for so long. Just as the Symbolic Order (or language itself) restructures the Imaginary by introducing a third term into the hitherto infinite regression of the duality of the latter's mirror images, so we may hope and expect that the tardy introduction of this new third term of the Real may put an end to the Imaginary opposition into which our previous discussion of Lacan's two orders has risked falling again and again. We must not, however, expect much help from Lacan himself in giving an account of a realm of which he in one place observes that it—"the Real, or what is perceived as such,—is what resists symbolization absolutely" (it would however be useful to have a compilation of all of these lapidary comments on the Real which are to be stumbled on throughout his work).

Nonetheless, it is not terribly difficult to say what is meant by the Real in Lacan. It is simply History itself: and if for psychoanalysis the history in question here is obviously enough the history of the subject, the resonance of the word suggests that a confrontation between this particular materialism and the historical materialism of Marx can no longer be postponed. (pp. 383-84)

[These] two systems—each one essentially a hermeneutic—have [much to offer] each other in the way of method. Marxism and psychoanalysis indeed present a number of striking analogies of structure with each other, as a checklist of their major themes can testify: the relation of theory and practice; the resistance of false consciousness and the problem as to its opposite (is it truth or knowledge? science or individual certainty?); the role and risks of the concept of a "midwife" of truth, whether analyst or vanguard party; the reappropriation of an alienated history and the function of narrative; the question of desire and value and of the nature of "false desire"; the paradox of the end of the revolutionary process, which, like analysis, must surely be considered "interminable" rather than "terminable"; and so forth. It is therefore not surprising that these two nineteenth-century "philosophies" should be the objects, at the present time and in the present intellectual atmosphere, of similar attacks, which focus on their "naive semanticism."

It is at least clear that the nineteenth century is to be blamed for the absence, in both Marxism and psychoanalysis, until very recently, of a concept of language which would permit the proper answer to this objection. Lacan is therefore in this perspective an exemplary figure, provided we understand his life's work, not as the transformation of Freud into linguistics, but as the disengagement of a linguistic theory which was implicit in Freud's practice but for which he did not yet have the appropriate conceptual instruments; and clearly enough, it is Lacan's third term, his addition of the Real to a relatively harmless conceptual opposition between Imaginary and Symbolic, which sticks in the craw and causes all the trouble. For what is scandalous for contemporary philosophy in both of these "materialisms"—to emphasize the fundamental distance between each of these "unities-of-theory-and-practice" and conventional philosophies as such—is the stubborn retention by both of something the sophisticated philosopher was long since supposed to have put between parentheses, namely a conception of the referent. For model-building and language-oriented philosophies, indeed (and in our time they span an immense range of tendencies and styles from Nietzsche to common language philosophy and from pragmatism to existentialism and structuralism)—for an intellectual climate dominated, in other words, by the conviction that the realities which we confront or experience come before us pre-formed and pre-ordered, not so much by the human "mind" (that is the older form of classical idealism), as rather by the various modes in which human language can work—it is clear that there must be something unacceptable about this affirmation of the persistence, behind our representations, of that indestructible nucleus of what Lacan calls the Real, of which we have already said above that it was simply History itself. If we can have an idea of it, it is objected, then it has already become part of our representations; if not, it is just another Kantian *Ding-an-sich,* and we can probably all agree that that particular solution will no longer do. Yet the objection presupposes an epistemology for which knowledge is in one way or another an identity with the thing: it is a presupposition peculiarly without force over the Lacanian conception of the decentered subject, which can know union neither with language nor with the Real, which is structurally at distance from both in its very being. The Lacanian notion of an "asymptotic" approach to the Real, moreover, maps a situation in which the action of this "absent cause" can be understood as a term limit, as that which can be both indistinguishable from the Symbolic (or the Imaginary) and also independent of it.

The other version of this objection—that history is a text, and that in that case, as one text is worth another, it can no longer be appealed to as the "ground" of truth—raises the issue of narrative fundamental both for psychoanalysis and for historical materialism, and requires us to lay at least the groundwork for a materialist philosophy of language. For both psychoanalysis and Marxism depend very fundamentally on history in its other sense, as story and storytelling: if the Marxian narrative of the irreversible dynamism of human society as it develops into capitalism be disallowed, little or nothing remains of Marxism as a system and the meaning of the acts of all those who have associated their praxis with it bleeds away. Meanwhile, it is clear that the analytic situation is nothing if not a systematic reconstruction or rewriting of the subject's past, as indeed the very status of the Freudian corpus as an immense body of narrative analyses testifies. We cannot here fully argue the distinction between this narrative orientation of both Marxism and Freudianism and the non-referential philosophies alluded to above. Suffice it to observe this: that history is not so much a text, as rather a text-to-be-(re-)constructed. Better still, it is an obligation to do so, whose means and techniques are themselves historically irreversible, so that we are not at liberty to construct any historical narrative at all (we are not free, for instance, to return to theodicies or providential narratives, nor even the older nationalistic ones) and the refusal of the Marxist paradigm can generally be demonstrated to be at one with the refusal of historical narration itself, or at least, with its systematic pre-preparation and strategic delimitation.

In terms of language, we must distinguish between our own narrative of history—whether psychoanalytic or political—and the Real itself, which our narratives can only approximate in asymptotic fashion and which "resists symbolization absolutely." Nor can the historical paradigm furnished us by psychoanalysis or by Marxism—that of the Oedipus complex or of the class struggle—be considered as anything more Real than a master text, an abstract one, hardly even a proto-narrative, in terms of which we construct the text of our own lives with our own concrete praxis. This is the point at which the intervention of Lacan's fundamental distinction between truth and knowledge (or science) must be decisive: the abstract schemata of psychoanalysis or of the Marxian philosophy of history constitute a body of knowledge, indeed, of what many of us would be willing to call scientific knowledge; but they do not embody the "truth" of the subject, nor are the texts in which they are elaborated to be thought of as a "parole pleine." A materialistic philosophy of language reserves a status for scientific language of this kind, which designates the Real without claiming to coincide with it,

which offers the very theory of its own incapacity to signify fully as its credentials for transcending both Imaginary and Symbolic alike. "Il y a des formules qu'on n'imagine pas," Lacan observes of Newton's laws: "Au moins pour un temps, elles font assemblée avec le réel."

The chief defect of all hitherto existing materialism is that it has been conceived as a series of propositions about matter—and in particular the relationship of matter to consciousness, which is to say of the natural sciences to the so-called human sciences—rather than as a set of propositions about language. A materialistic philosophy of language is not a semanticism, naive or otherwise, because its fundamental tenet is a rigorous distinction between the signified—the realm of semantics proper, of interpretation, of the study of the text's ostensible meaning—and the referent. The study of the referent, however, is the study, not of the meaning of the text, but of the limits of its meanings and of their historical preconditions, and of what is and must remain incommensurable with individual expression. In our present terms, this means that a relationship to objective knowledge (in other words, to what is of such a different order of magnitude and organization from the individual subject that it can never be adequately "represented" within the latter's lived experience save as a term limit) is conceivable only for a thought able to do justice to radical discontinuities, not only between the Lacanian "orders," but within language itself, between its various types of propositions as they entertain wholly different structural relations with the subject. (pp. 386-90)

Fredric Jameson, "Imaginary and Symbolic in Lacan: Marxism, Psychoanalytic Criticism, and the Problem of the Subject," in Yale French Studies, *Nos. 55-6, 1977, pp. 338-95.*

Alan Sheridan (essay date 1977)

[*In the following excerpt from the "Translator's Note" in* Ecrits: A Selection, *Sheridan comments on some key terms in Lacan's thought.*]

The short glossary below is not intended to provide adequate definitions of concepts. To do so would be quite alien to the nature of Lacan's work, which is peculiarly resistant to interpretation of a static, defining kind. (p. vii).

The first italicized word in brackets in each entry is Lacan's French word, the second, where necessary, Freud's German. It is assumed that the reader is familiar with the terminology of 'classical' Freudian psychoanalysis.

AGENCY (*instance, Instanz*). Lacan's use of the term '*instance*' goes well beyond Freud's '*Instanz*'. It represents, one might say, an exploitation of the linguistic possibilities of the French equivalent of Freud's German term. In the absence of any exact equivalent of Lacan's French term, one is thrown back to the term used by Freud's English translators, 'agency'. In Freud, the reference is most often to the three 'agencies' of the id, ego and superego. In Lacan, one must bear in mind the idea of an 'acting upon', even 'insistence', as in the title of the essay, **'L'instance de la lettre'**.

COUNTERPART (*le semblable*). This notion of the 'specular ego' was first developed in the essay, **'The Mirror Stage'**.

DEMAND (*demande*). See DESIRE.

DESIRE (*désir; Wunsch, Begierde, Lust*). The *Standard Edition* [of Freud's writings] translates Freud's '*Wunsch*' as 'wish', which corresponds closely to the German word. Freud's French translators, however, have always used '*désir*', rather than '*voeu*', which corresponds to '*Wunsch*' and 'wish', but which is less widely used in current French. The crucial distinction between '*Wunsch*' and 'wish', on the one hand, and '*désir*', on the other, is that the German and English words are limited to individual, isolated acts of wishing, while the French has the much stronger implication of a continuous force. It is this implication that Lacan has elaborated and placed at the centre of his psychoanalytic theory, which is why I have rendered '*désir*' by 'desire'. Furthermore, Lacan has linked the concept of 'desire' with 'need' (*besoin*) and 'demand' (*demande*) in the following way.

The human individual sets out with a particular organism, with certain biological needs, which are satisfied by certain objects. What effect does the acquisition of language have on these needs? All speech is demand; it presupposes the Other to whom it is addressed, whose very signifiers it takes over in its formulation. By the same token, that which comes from the Other is treated not so much as a particular satisfaction of a need, but rather as a response to an appeal, a gift, a token of love. There is no adequation between the need and the demand that conveys it; indeed, it is the gap between them that constitutes desire, at once particular like the first and absolute like the second. Desire (fundamentally in the singular) is a perpetual effect of symbolic articulation. It is not an appetite: it is essentially excentric and insatiable. That is why Lacan co-ordinates it not with the object that would seem to satisfy it, but with the object that causes it (one is reminded of fetishism).

DRIVE (*pulsion, Trieb*). Lacan reinstates a distinction, already clear in Freud, between the wholly psychical *pulsion* (*Trieb*) and *instinct* (*Instink*), with its 'biological' connotations. As Lacan has pointed out, Freud's English translators blur this distinction by translating both terms as 'instinct'.

ENUNCIATION (*énonciation*). The distinction between '*énoncé*' and '*énonciation*' is a common one in contemporary French thinking. '*Énoncé*', which I translate as 'statement', refers to the actual words uttered, '*énonciation*' to the act of uttering them.

IMAGINARY, SYMBOLIC, REAL (*imaginaire, symbolique, réel*). Of these three terms, the 'imaginary' was the first to appear, well before the Rome Report of 1953. At the time, Lacan regarded the 'imago' as the proper study of psychology and identification as the fundamental psychical process. The imaginary was then the world, the register, the dimension of images, conscious or unconscious, perceived or imagined. In this respect, 'imaginary' is not simply the opposite of 'real': the image certainly belongs to reality and Lacan sought in animal ethology facts that brought out formative effects comparable to that described in 'the mirror stage'.

The notion of the 'symbolic' came to the forefront in the Rome Report. The symbols referred to here are not icons, stylized figurations, but signifiers, in the sense developed by Saussure and Jakobson, extended into a generalized definition: differential elements, in themselves without meaning, which acquire value only in their mutual relations, and forming a closed order—the question is whether this order is or is not complete. Henceforth it is the symbolic, not the imaginary, that is seen to be the determining order of the subject, and its effects are radical: the subject, in Lacan's sense, is himself an effect of the symbolic. Lévi-Strauss's formalization of the elementary structures of kinship and its use of Jakobson's binarism provided the basis for Lacan's conception of the symbolic—a conception, however, that goes well beyond its origins. According to Lacan, a distinction must be drawn between what belongs in experience to the order of the symbolic and what belongs to the imaginary. In particular, the relation between the subject, on the one hand, and the signifiers, speech, language, on the other, is frequently contrasted with the imaginary relation, that between the ego and its images. In each case, many problems derive from the relations between these two dimensions.

The 'real' emerges as a third term, linked to the symbolic and the imaginary: it stands for what is neither symbolic nor imaginary, and remains foreclosed from the analytic experience, which is an experience of speech. What is prior to the assumption of the symbolic, the real in its 'raw' state (in the case of the subject, for instance, the organism and its biological needs), may only be supposed, it is an algebraic x. This Lacanian concept of the 'real' is not to be confused with reality, which is perfectly knowable: the subject of desire knows no more than that, since for it reality is entirely phantasmatic.

The term 'real', which was at first of only minor importance, acting as a kind of safety rail, has gradually been developed, and its signification has been considerably altered. It began, naturally enough, by presenting, in relation to symbolic substitutions and imaginary variations, a function of constancy: 'the real is that which always returns to the same place'. It then became that before which the imaginary faltered, that over which the symbolic stumbles, that which is refractory, resistant. Hence the formula: 'the real is the impossible'. It is in this sense that the term begins to appear regularly, as an adjective, to describe that which is lacking in the symbolic order, the ineliminable residue of all articulation, the foreclosed element, which may be approached, but never grasped: the umbilical cord of the symbolic.

As distinguished by Lacan, these three dimensions are, as we say, profoundly heterogeneous. Yet the fact that the three terms have been linked together in a series raises the question as to what they have in common, a question to which Lacan has addressed himself in his most recent thinking on the subject of the Borromean knot (*Séminaire 1974-75*, entitled '**R.S.I.**').

JOUISSANCE (*jouissance*). There is no adequate translation in English of this word. 'Enjoyment' conveys the sense, contained in *jouissance*, of enjoyment of rights, of property, etc. Unfortunately, in modern English, the word has lost the sexual connotations it still retains in French. (*Jouir* is slang for 'to come'.) 'Pleasure', on the other hand, is pre-empted by '*plaisir*'—and Lacan uses the two terms quite differently. 'Pleasure' obeys the law of homeostasis that Freud evokes in 'Beyond the Pleasure Principle', whereby, through discharge, the psyche seeks the lowest possible level of tension. '*Jouissance*' transgresses this law and, in that respect, it is *beyond* the pleasure principle.

KNOWLEDGE (*savoir, connaissance*). Where 'knowledge' renders '*connaissance*', I have added the French word in brackets. Most European languages make a distinction (e.g. Hegel's *Wissen* and *Kenntris*) that is lost in English. In modern French thinking, different writers use the distinction in different ways. In Lacan, *connaissance* (with its inevitable concomitant, '*méconnaissance*') belongs to the imaginary register, while *savoir* belongs to the symbolic register.

LACK (*manque*). '*Manque*' is translated here as 'lack', except in the expression, created by Lacan, '*manque-à-être*', for which Lacan himself has proposed the English neologism 'want-to-be'.

LURE (*leurre*). The French word translates variously 'lure' (for hawks, fish), 'decoy' (for birds), bait (for fish) and the notion of 'allurement' and 'enticement'. In Lacan, the notion is related to '*méconnaissance*'.

MECONNAISSANCE. I have decided to retain the French word. The sense is of a 'failure to recognize', or 'misconstruction'. The concept is central to Lacan's thinking, since, for him, knowledge (*connaissance*) is inextricably bound up with *méconnaissance*.

NAME-OF-THE-FATHER (*nom-du-père*). This concept derives, in a sense, from the mythical, symbolic father of Freud's *Totem and Taboo*. In terms of Lacan's three orders, it refers not to the real father, nor to the imaginary father (the paternal imago), but to the symbolic father. Freud, says Lacan, was led irresistibly 'to link the appearance of the signifier of the Father, as the author of the Law, to death, even to the murder of the Father, thus showing that although this murder is the fruitful moment of the debt through which the subject binds himself for life to the Law, the symbolic Father, in so far as he signifies this Law, is certainly the dead Father' (*Écrits*, **'Of a question preliminary to any possible treatment of psychosis'**).

NEED (*besoin*). See DESIRE.

OBJET PETIT a. The '*a*' in question stands for '*autre*' (other), the concept having been developed out of the Freudian 'object' and Lacan's own exploitation of 'otherness'. The '*petit a*' (small 'a') differentiates the object from (while relating it to) the '*Autre*' or '*grand Autre*' (the capitalized 'Other'). . . . [However,] Lacan insists that '*objet petit* a' should remain untranslated, thus acquiring, as it were, the status of an algebraic sign.

OTHER (*Autre, grand Autre*). See OBJET PETIT a.

PLEASURE (*plaisir*). See JOUISSANCE.

REAL (*réel*). See IMAGINARY.

STATEMENT (*énoncé*). See ENUNCIATION.

SYMBOLIC (*symbolique*). See IMAGINARY.

WANT-TO-BE (*manque-à-être*). See LACK. (pp. vii-xii)

Alan Sheridan, in a translator's note to Ecrits *by Jacques Lacan, W. W. Norton & Company, 1977, pp. vii-xii.*

William Shullenberger   (essay date 1978)

[*In the following essay, Shullenberger argues that Lacan's notion of desire is embodied in the relationship between poetry and the literary audience.*]

This essay is a partial meditation on a key term in the vocabulary of Jacques Lacan, "desire," and how this term plays itself out in the activity of poetry. Lacan's own ruminative style, dense, prolix, allusive, asymmetrical, confronts its reader like a riddle or parable. His language sorts out a fit audience, though few: those who are willing to attend to the rumination in order to arrive at a full understanding of those axioms with which Lacan's work is studded. Now Lacan, in one of those axioms, calls "desire" a metonymy, thus linking it to a particular rhetorical gesture, one of the two primary figures which govern literary discourse [in a footnote, the critic identifies metaphor as the other figure]. If "desire" can be recovered from the obscurity by which Lacan separates out his readers, it may provide a way by which we can understand how the world inscribes itself in us, and how we try to write outselves into the world.

The first step toward understanding Lacan's "desire" is to strip ourselves of the commonplace notion of desire as sexual instinct or appetite. "Desire," as Lacan designates it, is not a bodily phenomenon, but a kind of thinking. Our bodies satisfy themselves in one way or another, whatever we will or say or think; but desire, for Lacan, is a psychic remainder, that which is left over when an original demand for fullness is reduced to the satisfaction of bodily needs. "Desire is neither the appetite for satisfaction, nor the demand for love, but the difference which results from the subtraction of the first from the second, the very phenomenon of their split." Troilus mourns this difference when he tells Cressida, "This is the monstruosity in love, lady, that the will is infinite and the execution confined; that the desire is boundless and the act a slave to limit" [William Shakespeare, *Troilus and Cressida*, III, iii, 82-5]. Desire is what is always in excess of bodily need, and it is always boundless, according to Lacan, because it is generated by a primal loss, the loss established by a child's constitution of himself as a "subject" in the symbol-system of language.

How are we to understand this original rupture? It is not simply a child's separation from the oral paradise of the breast into the oral diaspora of language. It is more truly the child's falling away from a timelessness of pure presence, in which there is neither self nor other, into a condition of self-exile, in which the "self" is constituted *as* other. Lacan locates the child's origination of a sense of "self" in what he calls the "mirror phase." Between the ages of six and eighteen months, the child recognizes in the significant others around him/her the potential for an organismic integrity and power of which he/she is not yet capable. In the mirror of others as coherent beings, the child creates the fiction of him/herself as a bodily and psychic totality, not only like the others, but according to the desire of the others. "Desire," according to Lacan, is always "desire of the other." Once the original awareness of difference takes hold, the child has no way but to conceive him/herself according to the signifying system which is always other, and which always appears to be mastered by others. The original structure of desire must be what the child conceives that the powerful Other desires for him/her. Desire, then, is not bodily instinct but an expression of loss; even more; desire is the linguistic institutionalization of loss, for desire itself, organized around the "desire of the Other," is structured as the very alienation which it forever seeks to overcome. "The very structure at the basis of desire always lends a note of impossibility to the object of human desire." Whatever object desire summons is inevitably a diminished substitute, offered by the symbol-system by which desire has been composed, for a wholeness whose absence is sealed by desire.

The key to Lacan's untangling of the knot in which language joins desire and loss is located in his reference to a moment in Freud's *Beyond the Pleasure Principle,* which takes on the authority of a psychoanalytic parable. Freud describes the child playing with a toy, repeatedly throwing it away and drawing it back, all the time practicing the vowel sounds which Freud interpreted as the words "Fort!" ("gone!") and "Da!" ("here"). What was at stake in the game, according to Freud, was nothing less than the child's struggle to master, through the substitute mastery of language, the disappearances and appearances of his mother. Lacan accords this moment the status of a myth of origins:

> There is consequently no further need to have recourse to the outworn notion of primordial masochism in order to understand the reason for the repetitive utterances in which subjectivity brings together mastery over its abandonment and the birth of the symbol.

> These are the acts of occultation which Freud, in a flash of genius, revealed to us so that we might recognize in them that the moment in which desire becomes human is also that in which the child is born into Language.

The humanization of desire is also the inauguration of the tragedy of desire, for in this moment, the child learns the limits of his/her mastery over presence and absence, which is always to be substitute mastery, a mastery over the fantasy of an object which is always already missing. Desire becomes bound in "the chains of the signifier," and its structure will always be metonymic. Lacan understands metonymy not only in the classical sense, the representation of a thing by an attribute or association, but in a sense informed by what he considers Freud's rhetoric of the unconscious: whereas "metaphor" corresponds to Freud's description of the process of "condensation," "metonymy" corresponds to the Freudian "displacement." Desire seeks continually to replace that which was suffered in the original displacement; but each substitute object, each "signifier" available from the symbol-system,

reconfirms its difference from what was originally lost, and so sustains desire in its metonymic inertia.

This is the point where Lacan's insight may be brought to bear upon poetry. A primal totality is not conducive to poetry because it is not conducive to language; there is no need to signify if there is no absence. Language emerges as the condition and the structure of our exile, and poetry—"strong" poetry, Harold Bloom would say—is a repetition-compulsion of this primal catastrophe, language returning to its genesis in loss, and playing out the scene "yet once more" [a phrase quoted from John Milton's poem "Lycidas"]. Yet repetition-compulsion involves a refusal to remember, a getting stuck at the threshold of trauma; this is particularly true of the occasion of poetry, because it cannot make present a time when language was not. There is no regression out of symbolization once one has been caught in "the chains of the signifier," and if desire dreams of a passage into pure presence, the language which keeps desire alive also reminds it of its own impossibility of fulfillment.

Every poem harbors the awareness of the conditions of desire, though perhaps no poem is more riddled by that awareness than Keat's "Ode to a Nightingale." This poem is an undisguised wish for pure presence, from which the condition of writing constitutes itself as exile. As the poem approaches the pure voice of the nightingale, and seeks to erase its difference from that pure voice, it discovers that the erasure of difference, the recovery of presence, would be death, the loss of the language by which the poet's merely human consciousness tries to write itself into existence. Before its final dissolution, the poem offers a serial perspective in which the reader locates him/herself among the "hungry generations," (l. 62), in line with emperor and clown, with the writer and with the figure of Ruth, whom the poem foregrounds, to represent the exile in which we all stand as scriptural beings, beings "sick for home," (l. 62), who have been claimed and constituted by language.

"Was it a vision, or a waking dream? / Fled is that music—do I wake or sleep?" (ll. 79-80). The final movement of Keat's Ode is a dissolution of voice brought on by the writer's having tested the limits, and exhausted the possibilities, of desire. The radical questioning of the last two lines may have less to do with the verifiability of the experience inscribed in the poem than with the nature of the scriptor: does the "I" of the final question survive the tracings of the poem's quest for presence, or does it exist in those tracings, as a literary phantasm? If desire composes a person, and a person discovers, as the writer of the Ode does, the impossibility of desire, what choice does a person have but to dwell in the phantasmagoria of substitute images or to fade far away into the voicelessness which is death? Keats goes beyond this impasse, though always very tentatively, in his conception that poetry composes those who read, write, and are written into a community of loss, in which the memory and the desire of each "I"—an entity which cannot survive beyond its own utterances—are kept alive through the sympathy by which we know ourselves to be bound to each other, implicated in each other, by the language we share. Keats knew that we exist not in isolation, but in dialogue, or as Lacan says, "intersubjectively." When, in reading the "Ode to a Nightingale," I speak the "I" which Keats wrote, I am participating in the repetition-compulsion by which poetry courts yet staves off death; I am not only resurrecting "yet once more" the poet whom death has barred from me, but I am committing myself to the community of discourse which his original desire composed in the composition of the poem.

If Ruth is stationed as a solitary representative of this scriptural community, which exists neither spatially nor temporally, but intersubjectively, that is to say imaginatively, Keats offers a more inclusive emblem of the community in the "little town" emptied of its residents in the "Ode on a Grecian Urn." The poem has arrived at this town through a series of metonymic displacements of more superficial figures for the desire which generates it: first, the hectic sexual pursuit of the initial stanza, with figures scrawled like graffiti across the surface of the inviolable urn; then, the indefinitely drawn-out adolescent foreplay of the second and third stanzas, "forever warm and still to be enjoyed" (l. 26); finally the stable and solemnized forestalling of a ritual sacrifice. The play of desire in this poem cannot satisfy itself in any of these images, because Keats demystifies the illusion, suggested by each image, that the process of art interrupts the fulfillment of desire. This is the paradox where most interpretations of the poem come to rest: there can be no ravishing, no sexual consummation, no atonement with the gods, in the Cold Pastoral of the urn by which these moments of desire are immortalized, or in the poem which desires to represent and interpret the urn. Yet I would argue that Keats goes beyond this subtle commonplace to an understanding that is more likely to tease us out of thought: that art is the expression wherein desire can find itself more truly than in any other activity, that the poem represents the final circumference of desire. This circumference is rounded by the gnomic chiasmus, "Beauty is Truth, Truth Beauty," (l. 49), which sets a limit to the desire which is interpretation by presenting a riddle so abstract and so redundant that it will be forever still unravished by the critical mind. The image of the "little town," however, is of a different order than those which precede it in the poem, for it provides an opening in the frieze, a home for the imaginative sympathy which Keats believes to be the highest possibility of human desire. Note that this town which the poem asks us to ponder and to mourn has never existed anywhere, on earth or on urn, before Keats imagined its desolation in the Ode. Although the poem dreams of the town's inviolable silence, it only denies a return to those who would break that silence by trying to explain. The image desires a silent completion by the reader. The town does not even "exist" until the reader, called on by the writer, can share in the imagination of its existence. And in so imagining, the reader shares in its repopulation. Who will dwell there but the community of loss, whom poetry, which is desire made conscious of its own terms, has called out of the exile which is being human? (pp. 33-8)

William Shullenberger, "Lacan and the Play of Desire in Poetry," in Massachusetts Studies in English, *Vol. VII, No. 1, 1978, pp. 33-40.*

Richard Wollheim   (essay date 25 January 1979)

[*Wollheim is an English philosopher, critic, and novelist who has written extensively on the philosophical and psychological ramifications of art. In the following essay, he examines the fundamental tenets of Lacan's thought, finding that a significant debt to structural linguistics and an emphasis on symbolism lead his theory to implausibilities and logical inconsistencies and allow Lacan to indulge in obscurantism.*]

It is commonly said, by way of depreciating Freud, that he left us not a new science of man but a new picture of man. He opened our eyes.

This is to give Freud less than his due, but also more. For there is no complete picture of man that emerges autographically from Freud's own hand. There are several reasons for this. The chief one is that Freud never got the two sets of concerns, theoretical and clinical, between which he divided his working life, fully to cohere. And there are several ways in which this shows, one of which is the absence of any account of cognitive development—of how functions like reasoning, perception, and memory mature in the individual. Another (and related) way is the absence of any account of symbolism, of how the individual acquires and uses the system of internal representations with which he encodes reality. What Freud has left us is a sketch toward a picture of man, but he never worked this up into the finished thing.

Awareness of the need to say something about cognitive development and about symbolism is now common in the two principal schools that can make a good claim to be within the Freudian tradition: the New York school of ego psychology, and the so-called "English school" which derives from Karl Abraham and Melanie Klein. There is also an awareness that, since the two topics are connected, something needs to be said about how they connect. Does cognitive development presuppose symbolism (as philosophers tend to think), or does symbolism emerge in response to the needs of cognition (as psychologists tend to think)? And on all these topics both schools have made contributions of insight and interest.

But the thinker who would appear to have taken the challenge of making good these deficiencies most seriously is the legendary Jacques Lacan. For many years now Lacan's name has been widely known as that of someone who not only is a practicing analyst whose technique has been the topic of much controversy, but who has, largely through a series of seminars, magisterially conducted and faithfully recorded, brought about an extensive revival of interest in Freud's thought among French intellectuals and *littérateurs*. In the Anglo-Saxon world, he has been professionally taken up by some non-psychoanalysts, and he has been professionally ignored by nearly all analysts; but his name remains the best-known thing about him. Now, with the long-awaited translation first of a selection of his *Ecrits* [*Ecrits: A Selection,* 1977], which includes his most important lectures and addresses, and then of the transcript of a seminar conducted through the first half of 1964 and put together under the title *The Four Fundamental Concepts of Psycho-Analysis,* something of an opportunity has been given to the English-speaking reader to assess the phenomenon.

"Something of an opportunity." Two things make the qualification necessary. One is that the translated work is still only a small fraction of the total output. The other is that the translator, set no easy task, can claim only partial success: he has got Lacan's prose out of French but barely into English, with the result that the reader who can manage it would be best advised to have both text and translation in front of him and to use each to decipher the other. He may also want to consult Anika Lemaire's study [entitled *Jacques Lacan*], which is agreeably modest, straightforward, and workmanlike.

If we start by thinking of Lacan's work as an attempt to elaborate the sketch Freud left us, there are three observations to be made about the way he goes about it.

In the first place, Lacan assigns clear priority to symbolism over cognitive development. Advances in cognition depend upon the entry into symbolism. Secondly, symbolism is entered into in two stages. In the earlier stage the infant makes do with a form of pre-symbolic representation, which Lacan calls "the Imaginary," and only in the later stage does it acquire symbolism proper, or language. Before these two stages, for which there is direct evidence, we have to guess at an inaugural phase. The newly born infant, victim of the prematurity of birth peculiar to man, is at the mercy of unbounded and unmediated instinct: it is (Lacan tells us) a broken egg, *"une hommelette."* Thirdly, Lacan treats the whole process as best understood through its outcome, so that to ask at any point what stage of development the infant has reached is to ask how close it is to, or how far from, being a language-user. The crucial question now is what is language, and Lacan's answer is that he follows Saussure, who has been the major influence upon that whole body of European thought loosely called "structuralist."

Ferdinand de Saussure, professor of philology at Geneva from 1891 to 1913, was preoccupied all his working life with the question of the fundamental subject of linguistics: how it should be defined. The book toward which all his intellectual efforts were directed was never written and the posthumous *Cours de linguistique générale* on which we have to rely for his ideas is a compilation of students' notes taken from his lectures. We remain ignorant how far the difficulties in the book stem from Saussure himself or whether they are not partially due to misrepresentation.

The central idea in the *Cours,* which must be authentically Saussurean, is that theoretical linguistics, as opposed, say, to various historical inquiries, fundamentally treats of the *sign,* and the sign is best represented in the formula [S:*s*] where "S" stands for "signifier" or *signifiant,* and "*s*" for "signified" or *signifié.*

Saussure understood his formula to convey two essential facts about the sign. The first, which it does convey, is that the sign is a complex: it is made up of two constituents which may be distinguished though they may not be separated. The second fact, which it doesn't seem to convey, is that the sign is inherently arbitrary. But by arbitrariness Saussure had in mind two different things which he took

to be linked. He had in mind that—with the rare exception of onomatopoeia—there is no natural accord between the signifier and the signified that make up a given sign. Generally it is a convention how any language pairs off Ss and *s*s. Saussure also had in mind that any given signifier and any given signified have the value that they have solely because of the system to which they belong and the relative position that they occupy within it. Each signifier, each signified, is what it is because of the other signifiers used in, or the other signifieds articulated by, the same natural language. The value of the signifier and signified is differential or "diacritical."

Saussure illustrates his formula with the example ["TREE": *image a tree*]. Lacan, perceiving that this example conveys the complexity of the sign and its conventional character, but barely its diacritical nature, substitutes his own example ["LADIES": *image of a lavatory door* just as "GENTLEMEN": *image of a lavatory door*] which he thinks makes the latter point more perspicuously. We may wonder if it does, just as we may wonder why Lacan thinks it an advantage of Saussure's example that *"arbre"* (= "tree") and *"barre"* (= "line in the formula") are anagrams. But he does.

Set out so skeletally, Saussure's conception of the sign presents certain fundamental problems of interpretation which further reading in the *Cours* doesn't conclusively resolve, and which any account that makes use of it is therefore bound to inherit.

The most fundamental question is the most persistent, and it is just how labor is divided between signifier and signified. Over the centuries most of those who have reflected hardest upon language have had forced on them, in some form or another, a distinction which ordinary consideration of the "meaning" of a word easily overlooks. Roughly, the distinction is between that about a word which allows it to pick out things in the world and those very things (if there are any) which it thereby picks out. The distinction has been variously pinned down by the contrast between intension and extension, connotation and denotation, sense and reference. Not all these contrasts are equivalent: some theorists of language have ultimately dispensed with the distinction altogether. But the trouble with Saussure is that he gives one no clear indication how his formula stands to this tradition. Does connotation (to use one dichotomy) go on the side of signifier or signified? Or (to use another) is signified equivalent to sense, or is it just reference? In Saussure's diagram does the drawing of the tree represent a tree or does it represent some internal representation we have of a tree?

And there are other problems. If every signifier and every signified is to be understood entirely (the crucial word) in terms of all the other signifiers, all the other signifieds, how does meaning ever get started? Will Saussure's formula do for all signs—or has it been worked out with only one part of speech particularly in mind, i.e., that part which can occupy a subject-place in a judgment? Finally, is it Saussure's hope that the whole of syntax can be covered by the way signifiers may be permissibly combined— and then the whole of semantics by the way signifieds get linked up by the permissible combinations of signifiers—

or do we need from the start something that provides more structure, like the sentence or the fact?

It will be surprising, I have suggested, if Lacan's account of the infant's entry into symbolism avoids all these problems. Let us look at this account.

Lacan's account opens, like Freud's account of the origins of human culture in *Totem and Taboo,* on a single catastrophic event. In each case, if it seems mythical to assign such weight to a single event, some sense of reality may be restored by thinking of it as summing up a series of interrelated happenings. In Freud's account, it is the slaying of the primal father. In Lacan's account, it is the infant's first sight of its own reflection, which cuts short the inaugural phase of its life and precipitates it toward language. This hypothesis of the *stade du miroir* was formulated as long ago as 1936 and first presented to the International Psychoanalytical Congress at Marienbad. The original paper was heavily reworked for the 1949 congress, and it is this version that appears in *Ecrits* [entitled **"The Mirror Stage as Formative of the Function of the I as Revealed in Psychoanalytic Experience"**].

Characteristically Lacan adduces no evidence for the significance of the *stade du miroir,* and it seems that the idea was first suggested to him by studies of animal behavior. Nor is the precise significance of the event all that clear. The crucial thing is that the infant is presented with an image, for it is typical of the ensuing stage, which, as we have seen, Lacan calls "the Imaginary," that the infant lives with images or its mind is inhabited by them. Lacan gives several different descriptions of how these images function, some positive, or saying what the image does for the infant, some negative, or saying what the image doesn't do for it. In keeping with what I have said about the nature of Lacan's account I take the negative descriptions, which in effect say how images fall short of language, as the more fundamental or informative.

Briefly, according to Lacan, the image lacks generality. The infant's confrontation with it is a confrontation with brute fact. What the infant cannot do is to put it to use. It can take various attitudes toward it or experience various emotions in front of it. Struggling to overcome the gulf between itself and the image, it tries to assume it or get inside it: Lacan calls this "primary identification." Primary identification with the mirror image is going to be of major importance in the infant's development, and it is crucial for Lacan that the pre-history of the individual—for that is where we are still at—originates in an "alienating" experience.

What the image denies the infant is just what language, once acquired, grants it. The infant gains a way of articulating reality, outer and inner, and it can now have thoughts, form desires, and enter into relations with others. And this is so because language isn't brute; it possesses generality, it bears meaning.

A favored and ultimately highly significant way in which Lacan distinguishes between the two stages of symbol-acquisition is to say that, whereas in the Imaginary stage the infant is involved in a dyadic or two-term relation, in the Symbolic stage it is involved in a triadic or three-term relation. The two terms to the Imaginary relation are, of course, infant and image, but what is crucial is how Lacan characterizes the third term of the Symbolic relation. The three terms are infant, sign—and the Other. The Other—properly spelled, though not always by Lacan, with a capital O translating *l'Autre* with a capital *A*—is a highly powerful Lacanian concept and is notable for the voracity with which it swallows up ever new connotations.

For the moment, however, it is adequate to think of the Other as something like this: it is what mediates between the mind and the world, or it is meaning. Or, if there is a further connotation that already needs to be taken note of, it is that meaning is essentially something public. The Other is that preexistent "world of rules" into which we are born. Though the most evident influence here is Lévi-Strauss, Lacan is also in the mainstream of mid-twentieth-century philosophy which, irrespective of tradition, is intent on denying the possibility of an inherently private language. "The notion of egocentric discourse," Lacan writes against Piaget, "is a misunderstanding."

If, however, it is through language that the infant becomes constituted as an individual, this transformation is, according to Lacan, achieved at a price. Language makes distinctions and thus causes divisions. It splits the inner world from the outer. Within the inner world it divides the "I," the spoken pronoun, from the self which it vainly claims to denote. Then, rustling about in the mind among materials left over from the Imaginary stage, language translates the self's new double into the illusory *ego*—which, Lacan charges, American ego-psychology solemnly proceeds to study. This alienating effect is only intensified by the way in which, as the child realizes himself in language, he is thereby bound into an external and collective entity—the community—whose values and, above all, whose prohibitions he absorbs from its speech. He becomes the mouthpiece (literally) of an external agency. And, finally, if language-learning makes knowledge possible, it makes the failure to recognize or a tendency to misconstrue inevitable. *Connaissance* brings in its train *méconnaissance.*

So long as we continue to think of Lacan's work as primarily an attempt to supplement Freud, to work up the sketch into a picture, it cannot be thought of as very original either in the materials it uses or in the ends to which it puts them.

Apart from his general indebtedness to Saussure, Lacan produces an account of the good consequences of language, or of language in its constitutive role, from which only the crassest empiricist would dissent. His account of the bad consequences of language, or its alienating effect, is borrowed, exaggerations and all, from standard Hegelianism. If there is something to the idea that language distorts even while it describes, and that, more particularly, introspective language falsifies internal reality, Lacan does not seem the man to make it clear. The need to distinguish within symbolism, taken broadly, between a primitive or more concrete and a developed or more discursive kind of representation has been felt by psychoanalysts at least since Ernest Jones; and, in the work of both Jones and Melanie Klein, the distinction has been developed not only with greater elegance but also with a regard for the clinical material that makes it necessary.

Again the two places within Freudian theory where Lacan stresses the importance of symbolism would be worth emphasizing only if one thought that they had been overlooked.

In the first place, Lacan points out that nearly all the mental phenomena that psychoanalysis deals with—desires, beliefs, anxieties, thoughts—are invariably *of* something. They are directed on to an object, or are what philosophers call (technically) intentional, and Lacan argues that it is hard to see how they could get their objects without the aid of symbolism. The point is sound, but has not been neglected by psychoanalysts. Indeed the dispute that has long raged within psychoanalysis between those who ascribe a very early psychosexual development to the infant and maintain that at the age of four or five months it entertains Oedipal phantasies and those who hold to a much later psychosexual development has in large part been a dispute about the age the infant can have the kind of symbolism that these phantasies require for their representation. (Incidentally Lacan identifies the "intentionalist" thesis with the denial that the mind has any biological basis. So he thinks it an obvious philosophical error to believe that "drive," which is mental, is grounded in "instinct," which is physical. In his glossary of terms the translator concurs, but neither of them gives an argument.)

Secondly, Lacan stresses that speech is the medium of the psychoanalytic process and that, in a session, at least as important as what is said is how or when it is said. The point is correct, but if there are readers likely to be ignorant of this, surely the best thing would have been for him to include some case histories, which Lacan never gives us. It is also true that Lacan exaggerates the point. For him speech is everything, and his neglect of the nonverbal aspects of the analytic process may be partly responsible for some of his more extreme innovations in technique: for instance, the ten-minute session.

But to criticize Lacan on the assumption that his aim is to supplement Freud's work is beside the point. We can look at it in this way, but to do so is to leave out what is most distinctive, most original about it. Lacan's aim is not to add on to psychoanalytic theory, it is to provide a base or ground, and this he claims to find in the theory of symbolism. His recipe is this: Take the best available theory of symbolism. (This for Lacan is the Saussurean theory.) Construct around it the most plausible account of how such symbolism is acquired. (This we have seen Lacan doing.) And from this psychoanalytic theory follows. "Everything," he writes in *The Four Fundamental Concepts of Psycho-Analysis*, "emerges from the structure of the signifier."

To this bold claim Lacan adds a coda: Freud thought so too. For years now Lacan has been saying that he is different from other psychoanalysts. But the difference, according to Lacan, lies not in his greater intelligence, or in his more powerful imagination, or in his familiarity with philosophy and mathematics and classical learning: it is not

[Lacan's] recipe is this: Take the best available theory of symbolism. . . . Construct around it the most plausible account of how such symbolism is acquired. . . . And from this psychoanalytic theory follows.

—Richard Wollheim

his high culture or his high spirits or the high priestliness of his personality that sets him apart—all claims for which we might be prepared. What sets him apart is his Freudian fundamentalism. It is total. Eroticizing, like other French intellectuals, *le texte,* Lacan exhibits himself as the Slave of the Freudian text. If Freud too thought that psychoanalysis came out of psycholinguistics, it is Lacan's pride that it was left to him to discover this and the pride of discovery notably inflates one of the best-known *écrits,* the **"Discours de Rome."**

In the *New Introductory Lectures* Freud contrasts the different ways we would react to someone who speculates (against all good evidence) that the interior of the earth is filled with water saturated with carbonic acid and to someone who tells us that it is filled with marmalade. Lacan's hypothesis that Freud anticipated Lacan seems to me to fall into the second category. Evidence passes it by, and our curiosity soon shifts from the hypothesis to the kind of person who put it forward. So rather than get involved in the labyrinthine reinterpretations of the text that Lacan encourages—excellent examples are to be found in **"On a Question Preliminary to Any Possible Treatment of Psychosis,"** which is Lacan's reading of the Schreber case—I suggest that we let the question of fidelity to Freud take second place and ask whether Lacan's interpretation of psychoanalytic theory is of intrinsic interest. One feature of his presentation we must be prepared for. And that is that the constant appeal to case histories, the making sense of everyday actions, the richness of psychological detail, all of which make the reading of Freud such a remarkable and vivid experience, give way, in Lacan's prose, to a far more abstract mode of exposition. All is either argument or rhetoric.

To assess Lacan's project it is necessary to get the resultant theory into some kind of shape, and it is a good idea to think of it as layered like a cake. At the bottom of the pan Lacan places his account of the infant's entry into symbolism. Then he builds it up layer by layer, each more specific than that below, and the secret of the dish is that any gap or split referred to in the base gets itself reflected all the way up. When the theory is complete, the test is, does it have, in richness, in subtlety, the quality of that confected in Vienna?

The first layer that Lacan lays down concerns the affective side of the subject's life or what could be called the "instincts" if it weren't that for Lacan this implied an undesirable biologism. Anyhow, he is referring to aggression and sexuality, and he calls them "drives."

In *The Four Fundamental Concepts* Lacan produces a general argument to show that "drives" are impossible without some progress toward symbolism. The argument runs: No drives without subjective experience, no subjective experience without some approximation to meaning. As he says elsewhere, drive "implies in itself the advent of a signifier." But more interesting are the specific histories ascribed to aggression and to sexuality.

The origins of aggression, which are treated in the *écrit* "Aggressivity in Psychoanalysis," are placed in the Imaginary stage. Aggression is the infant's reaction to early mirror-derived images of its body. The simpler account is that the infant reacts aggressively to certain particular images it entertains which have a brutal and mutilated character. Surely such images are themselves expressions or projections of the infant's aggression. So a more sophisticated account is that aggression is the infant's reaction to its general relationship to images. Aggression breaks out for, having internalized its image, the infant now finds within its inner world a rival to itself—the rival in the mirror. Aggression is the infant's response to the tensions, threats, and, above all, confusions attendant upon primary identification.

Lacan's account of the origins of sexuality—for which a good source is "The Transference and the Drive" in *The Four Fundamental Concepts*—is more complex both in the materials it surveys and in the time span it allows them to work themselves out. For not only does this account spread itself forward into the Symbolic stage, it reaches back into the inaugural phase. Indeed the early start that Lacan allows sexuality ought to make it difficult for him to insist on the full dependence of sexuality on symbolism and to deny its biological base. Sometimes Lacan bows to this difficulty and settles for only a partial dependence of sexuality on symbolism. But at other times Lacan circumvents the difficulty. How does he manage this?

[It] is typical of Lacan to think that the nature of something very material like sexuality comes out clearest when thought of most abstractly.

—Richard Wollheim

Lacan, as we have seen, thinks of the inaugural phase as originating in the anatomical incompleteness of the newly born infant. This incompleteness is experienced as what Lacan calls *"déhiscence"* and what his translator (on mature reflection presumably) translates as "dehiscence": that is, the opening-up of a gap to be filled. This sense of a gap precipitates the infant into symbolism—Lacan's idea being, I think, that language through its capacity to represent absence offers to make good this gap. Now Lacan finds a very significant parallel between the trajectory de-

scribed by the process of symbol-acquisition and the trajectory described by the sexual drive. The parallel is on a highly abstract level, but it is typical of Lacan to think that the nature of something very material like sexuality comes out clearest when thought of most abstractly. Both articulate a loop. The sexual drive sets out from some part of the subject's body, moves outward, encircles some thing or object in the environment, controls it, and then returns with it to find satisfaction in that very part of the subject's own body from which it set out. This is the erotogenic zone.

But what of the erotogenic zone itself? The sexual drive may be given some kind of symbol-linked function, but surely the erotogenic zone is not to be explained as a psycholinguistic phenomenon?

Freud, as we know, identified four such zones—the mouth, the anus, the phallus, the genitals. His treatment of them as functionally equivalent throughout the body's maturation, in that the libido organizes itself around each in turn, together with his account of how one libidinal organization gives way to another underlie his spectacular extension of the concept of sexuality. Now Lacan accepts the zones that Freud identified. But he denies any biological account of how they get singled out and how they succeed one another. For him the central feature of an erotogenic zone and that which he thinks gives it its significance is—that it is a zone. The significance of the mouth, the anus, the phallus, the genitals, for the developing infant, is, in each case, that it is an area of the body marked off from those other areas which it is not. Answering an interlocutor after one of his seminars Lacan is recorded as saying:

> It is precisely to the extent that adjoining, connected zones are excluded that others take on their erogenous function and become specific sources for the drive. You follow me?
> [*Four Fundamental Concepts*]

This assimilation of the erotogenic zone to the "diacritical" sign as Saussure conceived of it is for Lacan confirmed by the way that each zone is demarcated by a rim and that sexual pleasure is always experienced at the rim. Pleasure *at* the rim, Lacan implies, is pleasure *in* the rim.

But doesn't the reference to pleasure invalidate this whole "semiotic" account of the erotogenic zone? Surely it is the fact that pleasure can be got out of them that explains why we esteem certain parts of our body—and why we esteem different parts at different stages of development? Lacan finds it in him to deny this too, and suggests that it reverses the order of explanation. The primary item in a libidinal organization is an organ, and that we use it, for instance to gain pleasure, comes second. (In *The Four Fundamental Concepts* he traces the way in which the use of the eye is an antidote to the dominance of the eye in our thinking.)

The second layer that we might expect from Lacan concerns the conative side of the infant's life; that is, the striving, effortful side of life through which the drives get realized. In the inaugural phase the infant is confined to the single conative state of Need. Need is an "intransitive" state, in that, when the newborn child has needs, there is nothing of which it can be said that this is just what it needs. This is because the infant at this stage cannot represent to itself an object. So, when the infant acquires a system of representation, we should expect it to move into a "transitive" state, or a conative state with an object, which is what Desire is. To express the dependence of Desire on symbolism, Lacan reuses his notion of the Other and says, "Desire is the desire of the Other."

But if symbol acquisition is a prerequisite to Desire, it also puts obstacles in its way. From Need the infant may graduate to Desire, but it may be shunted into what is mysteriously called Demand. So, to be faithful to Lacan, let us consider the smooth transition from Need to Desire as a preliminary idealization, look at the obstacles across its path, and then return.

The third layer of Lacan's theory concerns the formation of the unconscious or repression. In the *écrit* **"The Agency of the Letter in the Unconscious"** Lacan denies any original or instinctual unconscious. Everything that is in the unconscious has to find its way there. And there is only one way to get there: it must first get symbolized, and only then is it ripe for repression. In the preface provided for Lemaire's book Lacan defines his theoretical position by contrasting it with one he assigns to the French analyst Jean Laplanche. For Laplanche the unconscious is the precondition of language; for Lacan "language is the condition of the unconscious."

But for Lacan language is not just the precondition, it is also the content, of the unconscious. Lacan constantly says that the unconscious is like, or is structured like, a language. What he appears to think is that the unconscious *is* a language. It is a language having three distinctive features. In the first place, it is made up not of signs but just of signifiers. Secondly, the signifiers that make it up are those which have undergone repression and also those signifiers related to them by principles of association.

Freud too thought that unrepressed material gets dragged into the unconscious through association with the repressed. Freud specified what he thought the principles of association were. He called them "condensation" and "displacement." Following Roman Jakobson Lacan calls his principles "metonymy" and "metaphor" and, of course, claims they are identical with Freud's. "Metonymy" and "metaphor" seem to me to have all the disadvantages and none of the advantages of technical terms, and here I only want to point to one significant difference between Freud's principles of association and Lacan's. It is we, speakers of the language, who condense and who displace: we forge associations within the system of language. But for Lacan metonymy and metaphor are intrinsic features of language itself. So in holding that the unconscious is formed in accordance with such principles, he edges himself a little further toward where he wants to be: that is to say, to a view of human psychology as constituted by the impersonal reality of language.

Thirdly, the chains of signifiers that form the unconscious are inaccessible to the subject. Access to them is gained through the dialectic of the analysis which restores to the patient "true" or "full" speech. If psychoanalysis is psycholinguistics in its theory, in its technique it is speech therapy.

A slogan which expresses the Lacanian view of the unconscious and also exemplifies the Lacanian form of the slogan is "The unconscious is the discourse of the Other." Whereupon "the Other" acquires two further connotations. It means first "the unconscious," and then he who restores the discourse of the unconscious to its owner or "the analyst."

Lacan sets out his notion of the unconscious in the **"Discours de Rome," "The Agency of the Letter in the Unconscious," "The Direction of the Treatment,"** and the untranslated ***Position de l'Inconscient***: and it might be thought feasible to work back from this to his notion of repression and to reconstruct how the unconscious presupposes symbol acquisition.

One account immediately suggests itself: In repression what happens essentially is that the link between signifier and signified gets broken, and the signified slips out of the picture. The signifier now rides free, and the associative links with other signifiers, effected through metonymy and metaphor, become all-important. One signifier gets freely exchanged for another signifier in accordance with these links so that the subject loses all grip upon what his signifiers mean. He fails to understand them either when he asserts them (in speech) or when they assert themselves (in symptoms). Understanding returns only with the reconstitution of the sign in the analytic process.

Such an account has a certain amount to recommend it, including its comparative clarity, but whether we are right to attribute it to Lacan depends on how we think he interprets the Saussurean distinction between signifier and signified when he says that the unconscious is populated entirely with signifiers. Does he mean, as I take him to mean, signs which have lost their sense? Or does he interpret Saussure differently? Or is it possible, as some commentators suggest, that Lacan is much more casual with Saussurean terminology than his professions of discipleship prepare us for?

Both repression and the unconscious have a dual aspect in Lacan's theory. Once a thought is repressed, the person who has the thought does not recognize it. Additionally, he cannot recognize it as his thought. He misunderstands what his speech says, and where it comes from.

This symbiosis of alienation and repression becomes significant when we turn to the fourth layer that Lacan lays down, which concerns what he calls Need, Demand, and Desire. This is the realistic version of that simple progression from Need, which life does not offer. The crucial difference between Demand and Desire seems to be that Demand has its roots in the Imaginary, whereas Desire is structured within the symbolic order. Each has the defects of its origins, and each brings with it its own attendant dissatisfactions.

Being represented within the Imaginary order, the object of Demand is always brute. The infant demands it for its immediate allure, not because of any meaning it has for him. Accordingly, when one demand is met, a new demand is presented. Being represented within the symbolic order, the object of Desire is never brute, it is always sought after as if for its meaning. But the "as if" here is crucial. Rooted in symbolism, and therefore prone to repression, desire is essentially a substitutive phenomenon, so that one desired object always does duty for another, with a third lying in wait to take over. "Man's desire is a metonymy," is how Lacan puts it, adding, "however funny people may find the idea." And this process of substitution goes back historically to the very beginnings of desire in the individual's life, or to the earliest attempt to formulate that lack or gap, which is the original psychic representation of need. Accordingly, desire too is insatiable, but not because when one desire is satisfied a new desire arises, as with demand, but because, more radically, desires do not thus split themselves up: there is one desire, which is continuous.

There is for Lacan another dimension to the difference between Demand and Desire. So far we have contrasted them as they relate to their objects: but they also relate differently to the individual. In breaking out of the miasmic condition of Need, the infant claims recognition and love, and every demand and every desire is also a vehicle of this general claim. They express a kind of primitive assertiveness.

But they carry the claim in different ways. Demand invariably makes the claim from the outside, peremptorily, and therefore, when it gets what it asks for, this invariably seems extorted and therefore unacceptable. By contrast Desire makes the same claim from the inside, insinuatingly, in that it tries to take over the desire of the person upon whom the claim is made. (A young girl, the daughter of a paranoiac impotent father and a frightened authoritarian mother who is terrified of change, goes mad. She is retarded, her speech is incoherent, she has phobic attacks. Her madness is the assumption of her mother's desire that nothing should be different, that mother and daughter should never be separated [in a footnote, the critic adds that this "example comes from the work of an analyst working within a Lacanian framework, Maud Mannoni, *The Child, his 'Illness,' and the Other*"]). The fact that desire is from the beginning an encroachment upon another extends the meaning of "Man's desire is the desire of the Other." For, since the earliest encroachment is upon the mother's desire, the Other is, in appropriate contexts, the mother.

Buried in this rather confusing material—and I regard it as no accident that I have failed to find a coherent account of the distinction between Demand and Desire in any of Lacan's commentators—are several reasons why Desire has ultimately more to offer the individual than Demand.

In the first place, Desire, being registered in language, can be understood. And understanding may be the best we can achieve. Secondly, the registration of Desire in language, being a social phenomenon, automatically gives the individual part of what he claims: it gives him recognition—if not love. Thirdly, however fugitive or elusive the object of desire may be, at the causal end Desire is firmly fixed. It is rooted in the original lack or *manque-à-être,* or (better

perhaps) in that primitive phantasy in which the filling of this lack was hallucinated. This original moment of bliss, which Lacan calls "*l'objet petit a*" ("*a*" for "*l'autre,*" "the other" as opposed to "*A*" for "*l'Autre,*" "the Other"), and which a less abstract psychology might think of as the mother's breast, lies at the back of all the intersubstituted objects of desire, and at one point Lacan suggests that this, the cause of the desire, may also be its (true) object. If we can only recognize this in ourselves, or that what we desire stands in for a lost object, at least we may get beyond the stop-go of "demand."

But with four layers laid down, how far on are we toward psychoanalytic theory? Not very far, it might be said. Out of rather unpromising elements Lacan has elucidated the chief categories of the mind and the general principles of its functioning. But this is about the same point that Hegel reached by the end of *The Phenomenology of Mind,* starting from roughly similar material. Lacan, it is true, has updated Hegel by adding certain twentieth-century ideas about symbolism, but the enterprise he set himself was, after all, that of backdating Freud, or showing that he can be derived from the general principles of symbol acquisition. Where Freud differs from Hegel is that he described not only the structure of the mind but its content. He talked not just about the general possibilities of human development but about how these are actualized: he talked about the Oedipus complex, and castration anxiety, and penis envy, about the origins of homosexuality and about paranoia. Does Lacan think that these too can be derived from psycholinguistic material?

The answer is that he does, and accordingly the fifth layer he lays down concerns man's psychosexual development. One peculiarity about this layer is that, though everything gets explained through language, some phenomena get deep explanations and others shallow. So the incest prohibitions, which are intrinsic to the Oedipal situation, are connected with language in the most superficial way. They are said by Lacan to be messages explicitly written into the natural languages which we all learn: with presumably the utopian consequence, convenient for Lacan, that they could just as easily be written out of these languages, should society agree. By contrast, the two phenomena crucial and also peculiar to the Lacanian account of psychosexuality—the phallus and what he calls the Name-of-the-Father—get deep explanations. They are located within the profoundest moments of symbol acquisition. Just how is at best obscure, but also ambiguous.

What are the phallus and the Name-of-the-Father? The best way of looking at them, which Lacan encourages, is as phantasies that the infant entertains. The phallus is the earlier phantasy, originating in the Imaginary stage but persisting. The Name-of-the-Father dates from the Symbolic stage.

If we now ask what the content of these phantasies is, Lacan's implicit answer is that they are about what their names indicate. The phallus is a phantasy about the erectile sexual organ. The Name-of-the-Father is a phantasy about the male parent: or more specifically the male parent in so far as he issues commands—and, more specifically yet, in so far as he commands in absence, or from beyond the grave.

However, each of these phantasies, bound up as it is with the most elementary movements toward expression, acquires further significance. The phallus dominates the infant's moments of blissful merging with the mother: it is the phantasized point of union between them. And so it comes to stand for totality, or a state in which all is union and nothing is differentiated, and ultimately, when the symbolic stage is entered into, for the completeness of the system of signs. The Name-of-the-Father gets similarly extended. It comes to stand for rule-governed activity, and then for the supreme example of such activity, speech.

So Lacan's implicit answer shows the importance of symbol acquisition for psychosexuality, but not its priority. Hence Lacan's explicit answer about the content of the phallus and the Name-of-the-Father. This reverses the whole story, and makes the phallus primarily a phantasy about the totality of a symbol system and the Name-of-the-Father primarily a phantasy about the rules of language.

Plausibility apart, this explicit answer just won't do because it renders incomprehensible many of the quasi-Freudian things Lacan says about the infant's life.

For instance, Lacan regards phallic phantasies as, for a variety of reasons, peculiarly precarious. As they crystallize around the symbolic system, they get more precarious. But how does this precariousness evince itself? Phantasy converts itself to anxiety, and the anxiety is experienced as fear of castration. But doesn't this require that phallic phantasies are indeed about what their name indicates?

Again, the phallus, or phallic fantasy, is at its most precarious when it collides in the infantile mind with the Name-of-the-Father. Why is this? Because the Name-of-the-Father claims the mother from the infant. Because the Name-of-the-Father seeks to subject the mother to its will. And because the Name-of-the-Father instills into the infant's mind, alongside the warm, primitive hallucination of being the phallus, the more evolved, the more discursive, the more reality-testable thought of having the phallus. But, if we are to make sense of this collision and its baneful aspects, does this not require that we think of the Name-of-the-Father too as being about what its name indicates?

And a final consideration in favor of the implicit over the explicit answer is this: Freud, as we know, thought the appearance of the father in the infant's awareness sets up a three-cornered conflict in its mind in which the actors are father, mother, and infant, and the stake is the infant's sexual organ. This is the Oedipus conflict. Lacan also talks of a psychic drama in the infant's mind. He gives it the same structure as Freud does, he gives it the same *dramatis personae* as Freud, and he borrows the Freudian title. The Lacanian drama is set into being by the Name-of-the-Father and it is fought over the phallus. Is this a coincidence, or does it show that whatever may be in doubt about the Lacanian scenario, the Name-of-the-Father and the phallus must be given a literal significance primarily, if an extended one derivatively? With this, the attempt to ground psychosexuality in the phenomenon of language collapses.

In expounding Lacan's theory of the mind I have shown where Lacan takes Freud's name in vain, which may not be serious, and I have indicated certain confusions and mistakes, which may be eliminable. The big question to which everything leads is whether, charitably read, adequately repaired, Lacan's theory can be put beside Freud's—which, after all, has its defects too.

My answer would be a qualified No.

The reason for the No is that Lacan's theory lacks the explanatory force of Freud's. Freud's theory has the following form: It shows man to be endowed with a very complex internal structure. This internal structure changes. It matures, and also it is modified by experience which can be both of outer and of inner reality. But if experience modifies structure, structure mediates experience. It determines how man reacts to experience, and this reaction, like the experience it reacts to, can be either external or internal. Structure, experience, reaction—Freudian theory shows these to be interdependent, and yet capable of being independently studied.

Precious little of this survives in Lacan's theory. In the first place, Lacan assigns no place to maturation. Indeed, he looks upon any attempt to treat the mental as resting upon the state of the body as an abdication of psychology.

Secondly, Lacan is extremely hazy about the internal structure that he presumes. He talks of the mechanisms of repression and rejection, and treats them as impairments of the symbolic function. But he says next to nothing about other mechanisms like introjection, projection, projective identification, which later psychoanalysts have carefully and fruitfully distinguished. And we are never told why any of the mechanisms should get employed. As long ago as 1909 Freud thought that internal conflict could not be explained simply by reference to consciousness and the unconscious, but that separate agencies in the mind had to be invoked. Lacan antedates this.

> **Lacan totally depreciates the contribution of experience to psychoanalytic explanation, and it becomes clear that the absence from his writing of case histories and clinical illustration is not just an eccentricity of presentation. It reflects his theory.**
>
> **—Richard Wollheim**

Thirdly, Lacan totally depreciates the contribution of experience to psychoanalytic explanation, and it becomes clear that the absence from his writing of case histories and clinical illustration is not just an eccentricity of presentation. It reflects his theory. For his favored form of explanation is not by reference to the internal structure of the individual plus his experience. He appeals only to how the individual is internally structured.

An artificial example might help. In her account of early development, Melanie Klein laid great emphasis upon the moment when the infant is able to conceive of whole persons, at once good and bad, and not just part-persons, some altogether good, some altogether bad. It can now recognize that it has hated the person whom it also loves, it can feel remorse, and it can desire to set the harm right. This is the "depressive" position, and Klein goes on to make use of it in order to explain how an infant who achieved this position will then respond to subsequent experiences. But if Lacan were a Kleinian, we can imagine him simply appealing to the depressive position to explain an infant's reactions, and there would be no reference to experience. The Lacanian individual typically reacts to himself or to his own being rather than to what happens to or within him.

But the No I would give to Lacanian theory is a qualified No. For judgment must be qualified if it respects the difficulties inherent in any text which disdains examples, which concedes no second thoughts and denies all change of opinion, which modulates from rhetoric to buffoonery to self-pity, which is laden with formulas that respect no formation rules and diagrams that require conflicting principles of interpretation, which uses technical terms like "topology," "metalanguage," *"Gestalt"* decoratively, which is elusive and obscure, and consciously and deliberately so.

And for the reader who is still uncertain what I have in mind in talking about Lacan's obscurity, the following examples must suffice.

1) On the connection between psychoanalysis and science:

> If we can couple psychoanalysis to the train of modern science, despite the essential effect of the analyst's desire, we have a right to ask the question of the desire that lies behind modern science. There is certainly a disconnection between scientific discourse and the conditions of the discourse of the unconscious. We see this in set theory. At a time when the combinatory is coupled to the capture of sexuality, set theory cannot emerge. How is this disconnection possible? It is at the level of desire that we will be able to find the answer.
>
> [*Four Fundamental Concepts*]

2) On the mirror image:

> The fact is that the total form of the body by which the subject anticipates in a mirage the maturation of his power is given to him only as *Gestalt,* that is to say, in an exteriority in which this form is certainly more constituent than constituted, but in which it appears to him above all in a contrasting size that fixes it and in a symmetry that inverts it, in contrast with the turbulent movements that the subject feels are animating him.
>
> [*Ecrits*]

3) And:

> What one ought to say is: I am not wherever I am the plaything of my thought; I think of what I am where I do not think to think.
>
> [*Ecrits*]

Obscurity is not the worst failing, and it is philistinism to pretend that it is. In a series of brilliant essays written over the last fifteen years Stanley Cavell has consistently argued that more important than the question whether obscurity could have been avoided is whether it affects our confidence in the author.

Confidence raises the issue of intention, and I would have thought that the primary commitment of a psychoanalytic writer was to pass on, and (if he can) to refine while passing on, a particular way of exploring the mind. Indeed this is how Lacan himself proposes that his work should be judged. "The aim of my teaching," he writes, "has been and still is the training of analysts."

For decades now Lacan has been insisting that the nature of this commitment has been systematically obscured, particularly in North America. Training has become "routinized," and analysis itself has become distorted into a process of crude social adaptation. There is much here to agree with. Yet two questions must be raised. Has Lacan devised a more effective method of training analysts? And, would one expect this from his writings?

Neither question gets a favorable answer. All reports of his training methods, over which he has now brought three distinct secessions within the French psychoanalytic movement, are horrifying. It is now, I am told, possible to become a Lacanian analyst after a very few months of Lacanian analysis. And what pedagogic contribution could we expect from a form of prose that has two salient characteristics: it exhibits the application of theory to particular cases as quite arbitrary, and it forces the adherents it gains into pastiche. Lacan's ideas and Lacan's style, yoked in an indissoluble union, represent an invasive tyranny. And it is by a hideous irony that this tyranny should find its recruits among groups that have nothing in common except the sense that they lack a theory worthy of their cause or calling: feminists, *cinéastes,* professors of literature.

Lacan himself offers several justifications for his obscurity, about which he has no false modesty. At times he says that he is the voice, the messenger, the *porte-parole,* of the unconscious itself. Lacan's claim stirs in my mind the retort Freud made to a similar assault upon his credulity and by someone who had learned from Lacan. "It is not the unconscious mind I look out for in your paintings," Freud said to Salvador Dali, "it is the conscious." (pp. 36-45)

> *Richard Wollheim, "The Cabinet of Dr. Lacan," in* The New York Review of Books, *Vol. XXV, Nos. 21-2, January 25, 1979, pp. 36-45.*

Ellie Ragland-Sullivan   (essay date Summer 1981)

[*Ragland-Sullivan is the author of* Jacques Lacan and the Philosophy of Psychology *(1986). In the following essay, she discusses Lacan's central place in the history*

mushroomed beyond comprehension in the 1970s, making Lacanian analysis to this era what existentialism was to the 1950s. The opportunity of being analyzed by a Lacanian is seen as an apprenticeship in a philosophical discipline, as well as a socially prestigious honor. The standard Anglo-American view, that a person being treated by an analyst is someone with a lack or deficiency, has been reversed in Lacanian circles where only the very bright and able are admitted, either as analysts or analysands. Such an attitude corresponds with the Lacanian view of neurosis as that level of "knottedness" which endures in each person's life story. Lacan, thus, removes from the concept of neurosis the stigma of failure and pathology, and focuses, rather, on the idea that the ego is itself a neurotic and conflicted "organ."

Turkle shows how Lacan's thought has reshaped the thinking of a culture in a decade, making Lacan the most influential French thinker since Sartre. His antipsychiatry contains an essentially human and experientially meaningful conceptualization of the psyche. It criticizes the notion that medical training *per se* might lead psychoanalysts to some knowledge which could effect a cure of psychic pain. In Lacan's picture of Being, madness is not a thing apart, a genetic deficiency or environmental blight, but rather a human potential which reveals the structural limits of human freedom. Looking away from biology, Lacan has problematized the standard view of the ego as a whole entity, as well as the role played by language in structuring both perception and identity. The Lacanian ego is a linguistic, symbolic, divided structure whose autonomy is largely illusory. The unconscious ego (the *moi*) is a representational "intelligence," structured from earliest infancy by symbolic effects whose sources are visual images, auditory effects, and mimesis. The conscious ego (the *je*) evolves concurrently with the capacity to use language in which it becomes progressively fixed and alienated. Language itself (sounds, codes, conventions, myths, etc.) and mimetic identification are the *modus vivendi* of imposing both meaning and unity on an inherently meaningless and chaotic biological nature. Thus Lacan depicts the ego as a faithful mirror of his idea that Man is determined by the linguistic and social structures which are *outside* him, and which transcend him, culture giving meaning and shape to biology.

Lacan's thought is in contradiction to the neo-Cartesian, empirical basis of most contemporary Western thought which views both perception and identity as innate, instinctual, and—if not theologically—then genetically determined, and language as a thing apart. Lacan's *moi* is the subject of dreams, intentionality, identity, and Desire, and is formed, not by instincts or genes, but by a composite of visual and verbal introjections. The *moi,* although essentially a non-verbal subject, is not, however, relegated to the static realm of sleep and unconscious repression. For, although they are actually two different structures, the *moi* and *je* function most of the time as an intertwined unit. The *moi* is reflected in relationship dynamics (mirroring of the self in the eyes of the other) and is "translated" by the *je* through the medium of language. Throughout life the *moi* seeks in a dynamic fashion to affirm its own alien and tenuous being, implicitly asking the identity

questions: Who am "I"?, What am "I" here in my parents' discourse? Lacan's *moi,* then, is a more powerful subject than the *je* which it controls, for the *moi* is that motivating, personal force which Lacan has put in place of Freud's impersonal, instinctually-controlled "drives." However, if one were to equate his *moi* with Freud's Id, thereby assuming that psychoanalytic cure lies in the direction of replacing *moi* with *je* ("Wo Es war, soll Ich werden"), Lacan's basic point would be missed. Ever-present both temporally and spatially, the *moi* flouts human myths of ego unity and rational truth by surfacing in mysterious repetitions and unexpected responses. By taking such aspects of human behavior seriously, Lacan throws new light on issues of autonomy, control, clarity, and intrinsic logic. Twentieth-century Western culture is a world in decomposition, says Lacan, a world which is only too faithful a reflection of the essential de-centered, alienated, anxious, ex-centric nature of the ego.

One begins to see how antithetical Lacan's thought would be to Anglo-American ego psychologists who consider a healthy ego to be conflict-free, integrated and whole, a view of the ego which is interchangeable with the idea of personality as a fixed singularity. Lacan has called the promise of integration, happiness, and cure held out by ego psychologists—whose path American psychoanalysts have tended to follow—merely a "capitalist discourse," based on the notion that health lies in adaptation to prescribed cultural norms. Lacan insists that he, on the contrary, has remained faithful to Freud's idea of cure as passing from unbearable psychic pain to normal unhappiness. While Lacan holds out the possibility that his analysands will discover the personal truths of their own unconscious identities, which may or may not lead to "symptom relief," he stresses that there is no cure for the human condition. Psychic pain and conflict are eternal and universal and derive from the inherently fragmented, narcissistic, aggressive structure of the ego itself.

Lacan's epistemology has polarized his students, followers, patients and intimates, making of the 79-year-old harbinger of a new psychoanalysis a legend in his own time. But the road to his position of eminence has been filled with obstacles and clashes. His first major disagreement with the orthodox psychoanalytic establishment dates from 1936 when he presented his theory of the mirror stage to the 14th International Psychoanalytic Association. At that time most analysts were following Anna Freud with her emphasis on the ego's powers to marshal mechanisms of defense and adaptation, while Lacan was maintaining that the ego did not exist at all as a unified entity. By 1953, the year of Lacan's now celebrated **"Discours de Rome"** (*The Function and Field of Speech and Language in Psychoanalysis*), Lacan and Daniel Lagache broke with the Paris Psychoanalytic Society. In that same year the International Psychoanalytic Association excluded Lacan's new group, The French Psychoanalytic Society, allegedly because of their "insufficient training facilities" for future analysts. Since 1953 there have been at least five major splits within Lacan's group, not unlike the quarrels and divisions which characterized Freud's circle of intimates.

In the February 1, 1980 issue of the *Times Literary Supplement* Galen Strawson's review of Turkle's book concludes that it "makes an important contribution to the debate, and should be a valuable agent of *rapprochement.* For once one gets the facts straight about Lacan's life and works, what need can there be to hurl abuse? Lacan has doubtless caused a great deal of suffering as Turkle records; suffering which doubtless outweighs what good he has done in any plausible felicific calculus, and *tout comprendre n'est pas tout pardonner.* . . . " "Doubtless," Strawson's conclusions will please the ever-growing body of Lacan's critics. But the so-called "empirical" evidence of the rage which Lacan elicits among his naysayers and *abandonnés* might just as well be proof that he is no sham, on the principle that "where there's no smoke, there's no fire." However, a more intellectually interesting fact is the passion with which Lacan's critics insist on reducing the man's thought to the reputedly negative aspects of his behavior. In viewing the emotional turbulence surrounding Lacan, I cannot but think of the human preponderance for creating masters and heroes, only to dismantle them and replace them with new ones. And Lacan unabashedly throws this fact in the face of young idealistic students by statements such as: "Comme révolutionnaires, vous aspirez à un maître. Vous l'aurez" (Lacan, *Télévision*). He thus outrages his would-be followers even further. His style of speech and writing is hermetic, impenetrable, circular, opaque, like his thought. Yet, Lacan has the courage or audacity, depending on one's point of view, to maintain that if one spends seven to ten years reading him, one will understand him. Lacan refuses to compromise with the human desire for easy, even clear, answers. He claims to demonstrate by his own discourse not only the complexities of Being, but the aggrandizing propensities of the ego as well. More outrageous still, he has the arrogance to proclaim himself a genius while telling his disciples that each one of them cannot be a genius; cannot find the path which synthesizes already existing knowledge into new and astounding configurations.

He claims to demonstrate by his own discourse not only the complexities of Being, but the aggrandizing propensities of the ego as well. More outrageous still, he has the arrogance to proclaim himself a genius while telling his disciples that each one of them cannot be a genius.

—Ellie Ragland-Sullivan

Strawson is incorrect, however, in supposing that Turkle's book will "go a long way towards setting an ill-tempered and ill-informed debate on a more even keel." Precisely because Turkle's aim is to sketch a "sociology of superficial knowledge" in regard to Lacan, she does not provide, nor does she intend to, the necessary "translation" of Lacan's concepts from their French context to an Anglo-

American one that would permit the degree of understanding needed in order to even *enter* the debate. For the French Freudian revolution, when understood, will automatically join psychoanalysis to literary criticism in a way that American psychoanalysis never has. With its biological orientation, American psychoanalysis leans toward medical theories and has thus remained isolated from both main-stream and academic cultures. Although Jungian psychoanalysis and ego psychology have influenced literary criticism, Lacan's postulate that language shapes Man and then inhabits him is so subversive a doctrine that it takes a considerable amount of familiarity with his reasoning to begin to contemplate its vast implications for literary criticism and theory. The idea that, at the very least, one can control what one thinks and says in most circumstances, is shattered in Lacan's epistemology wherein sense is seen to follow sound in many instances, rather than the reverse, and wherein structural and associational relations in the unconscious call into question developmental concepts based on logical, genetic, and maturational theories. Although ideology and belief are still seen to center around theological and economic issues, Lacan finds no absolute truth in either, only situation, condition, tradition, and myths. Language, in such a context, is far-removed from the classical, transparent, reliable vehicle one unquestioningly assumes it to be. Language is, rather, that which creates History and then serves as its museum.

Lacan's impact on literary theory would imply an explosion of the assumed boundaries between text and reader. The explanation of our reliable way of reasoning by oppositions (as modern linguistics and philosophy have revealed to us) is called into question in Lacanian thought. Distinctions between inside/outside, fantasy/reality, objective/subjective, deep and surface structures, are blurred, if not obliterated. For language permeates the universe and the human psyche, setting up associations in an infant's perceptive capacities, long before meaning is attached to them. Language, moreover, acts as a *material* tool which aids an infant in the painful task of separating from the Other (usually Mother) of early continuity and care, by providing a means to manage distancing through substitution and displacement. Naming and labeling give both form and meaning to the chaotic, fragmented inner world of the infant. Yet, underlying the imposition of language on biological nature is Lacan's explanation for why Man later attaches oppositional, binary values to perceptions and renders them thus in language.

Humans are born without an innate ego or identity. They can perceive, mimic, and demand food, but in this are no different from other animals. To complicate life even further, human infants have less motor control and coherence than most other animals do. At around six months of age an infant begins to perceive totalities, faces and bodies of those in the environment, as well as his/her own body image if reflected in a mirror. But the capacity to perceive totalities in no way reduces the inner feeling of fragmentation and incoherence which characterizes life for the infant. Gradually, however, both totalized images (the Mother's body, etc.) as well as part-object images (the breast, etc.) impress themselves on the infant's perception as the first fragments which will gradually compose a "bric-à-brac" identity (the *moi*). In this imprinting process, the images provide a sense of unity which the infant lacks. At the same time the infant is recognized, looked at, responded to. This metaphorical "mirroring" actually creates the human ego as a structure, intimately linked to the dialectic of self and other throughout life. When the recognition is forthcoming and positive, the narcissistic slope of the ego is further built up, and in later life is gratified by these dynamics. When the sought-after recognition is withheld, the aggressive slope of the ego is reinforced or, in later life, activated. This tendency of the ego to feel good through positive identifications and recognitions, as well as the reverse, insures that the most basic of human predispositions is towards totalizing experience in a good/bad, right/wrong kind of framework. Lacan has named this underlying order of human experience and reaction the Imaginary order.

In interaction with Lacan's Symbolic order (the realm of language, culture, History), the Imaginary ceaselessly imposes meanings and values on experiences and perceptions which tally with the absolute needs of the unconscious—albeit ever active—Imaginary domain. The unique subject of the Imaginary is the *moi* whose particular dictates issue from the images and words and sounds which have come together over time to build it into a forceful intentionality (with its own opinions, beliefs, and out-of-sight dictates). Lacan speaks then of the unconscious ego as an amalgam built into a structural gap in being, caused by a prematuration at birth. Thus, such familiar things as the pluralities of belief, the permutations of ideology, the human need to affirm and reaffirm self through "communication," become interrelated phenomena, all connected to the structure of the ego, and to the fact of its extending and realizing itself in and through language. Substance *per se,* that is, refers to the multiple and varied means which the fragmented ego has of filling itself up, of giving itself unity and cohesion through meanings. Although the unconscious ego never ceases to "write its story," its structural limits are fixed by given Symbolic codes and by the particular effects of early Oedipal experiences. Still, the boundaries of the ego of intentionality and Desire are always open to challenge and change, although the core is set. Faith in human images and introjected words are Man's earliest religion, the only means by which an identity is created which will be strong enough to survive the pain of separation and of an impersonal cosmos. Language will forever after be the medium which not only conveys information, but reifies identity as well.

If Lacan is correct, then Man is a representational, symbolic creature, his ego created by the effects of the symbolic world around him. The *human* capacity for reflection and consciousness is, ultimately, inseparable from language. Bound *a priori* in an intricate web of verbal and symbolic meanings from which there is neither distance nor escape, both reader and text are made from the same cloth, so to speak. Nor can textual boundaries or stylistic conventions create an entirely different language—a metalanguage—to provide a shelter of objectivity. Within a Lacanian worldview, there can be no rational, classical, objective reader who approaches a text which is a discrete, contained, and separate entity, for each was structured by the language surrounding it and each will operate its own linguistic possibilities on the other in an intersubjective dialectic. The ambiguities in literary texts and the malleability of interpretation bear witness, in a Lacanian epistemology, to the inherent properties of the unconscious which make language an open-ended system and render impossible the task of pinning down *The Meaning* or *The True Interpretation.*

As Ferdinand de Saussure demonstrated early in this century, language is an ever-shifting, elusive, endlessly flowing, referential, differential, and thus arbitrary, system. While Saussure's genius was to disconnect the "word" from the "thing" in any natural one-to-one relationship, he made the understandable error of believing that concept comes first and is followed by sound which describes or represents it. Saussure's linguistic world, then, is a closed, Formalist, neo-Platonic one where form plays second-fiddle to idea. Lacan contradicts Saussure on several major points. First, he sees sense as often created by sound, rather than the opposite. This idea has yielded brilliant Lacanian reinterpretations of many of Freud's case histories. Yet, in this Lacan maintains that he is only following the examples set forth by Freud in *The Interpretation of Dreams* (1900). Whereas Saussure gave primacy to the Signified (concept or idea) which is conveyed by the signifier (sound or form), Lacan reverses this order. He redefines Signifier as a combination of sound and concept—articulated language in other words—which has not only the function of naming and representing, but also the function of structuring the unconscious. In his redefinition of signified, Lacan dispenses with the intellectual idea of concept and equates the signified with unconscious discourse and Desire (Freud's *Wunsch* plus identity). In one of the many paradoxes which Lacan presents, and does not resolve, the signifiers (language and its effects) which actually create signifieds, in turn furnish the means for signifieds (unconscious realities) to surface, gluing themselves to language in discourse units which are no longer linguistic. In this sense identity and unconscious Desire have become paramount, and language their subjectivized servant. Yet, signifiers and signifieds possess different kinds of power which they alternate. For signifiers continually reshape signifieds. In historical retrospect one can see this phenomenon at work. New verbal messages change old myths whether one refers to modern issues such as sexual and racial stereotypes being rethought and restated, or to Erasmus's introduction of exegesis which ultimately marked the end of neo-Scholastic reasoning.

Thus Lacan has opened up Saussure's closed world of language by adding an unconscious ego which has identity, "intelligence," verbal reality, and a need to try to find (or deny) itself through the very dialectical form of language. Lacan's unconscious system parallels Saussure's linguistic system, however, for it too is an ever-flowing discourse, although its logic of association and intention are not altogether arbitrary or random. Still, Lacan postulates that the unconscious meaning system functions *like* language in terms of its *basic* laws, condensation being to metaphor as displacement is to metonymy. What Lacan has done, then, is to eliminate the Saussurian possibility for a one-to-one correspondence between signifier (sound) and signified (concept). For Saussure the ultimate reality is language itself, divorced from any relationship to real factors *per se*. Such a theory has led to Structuralism in literary studies, as well as to the post-Structuralist theories of Jacques Derrida who finds the only reality to be sheer textuality (*l'écriture*). For Lacan verbal realities are the "material" means by which one describes and represents the Real—that which *is*—but can only ever be indirectly apprehended in language. Thus, words stamp on Man's perceiving capacities certain concepts which persons and eras take to be "true," and even natural, i.e. unquestioned postulates, until the unconscious must rethink its perceptions of natural and "true" when it is once again challenged by the linguistic/social order.

Lacan's idea that signifieds attach themselves to signifiers at "points like a button attached to a mattress" (*points de capiton*) destroys the belief that language-use is a willed, unified, autonomous, rational process. Condensations and substitutions are continually at work in the unconscious, interacting with the perceptions of the *moi*—the subject of identifications—to make conscious verbal interchange and daily discourse as overdetermined as any dream symbol or pathological symptom. Thus, in Lacan's hands language becomes a *Pantagruelion*-like material, inhabited by unconscious Desire whose truths are those of verbal effects, narcissistic fixations and identifications, mysterious intentionalities, as well as those of cultural myths and fictions. This essentially nonverbal Imaginary realm lives like a parasite on a host in and through language. While *parole* was originally Saussure's term for the personal aspect of language-use, Lacan uses the same term to mean unconscious "messages" attached to language, both in content and form. Lacan also reshapes Saussure's *langue*, the system of language, to refer only to the information-providing aspect of language-use.

In Lacan's epistemology people speak in order to seek recognition and validation of their own sense of self, as well as to provide unity and continuity to an inherently divided ego. Furthermore, people write and read literary texts for the same reasons. It is the manna-like power of symbols which underlies the human capacity to speak, read, and write, and thus attempt communication. For Lacan even words themselves are symbols in the sense that they function to represent direct experience, although they can never replace lived events. In this sense, symbols underlie all language-use, conscious and unconscious, each symbol pointing to a thousand possible meanings, or a thousand possible meanings towards one symbol. In Lacan's view, then, the real human mysteries lie on the surface of behavior and in identity, in the movement of speech, and in the spatio-temporal presence of language. The idea of an inner reality to be found, or a deep structure to be uncovered—whether one refers to philosophical truth or psychological experience—are merely examples of comforting myths of wholeness and ontological resolution. If, as Lacan maintains, the controlling ego (*moi*) of human motivation is unconscious, yet directs choices and dictates intentions, then substantive realities of the conscious realm are seen in a new light. Humanistic philosophies and psychologies which elevate Man as an actor who can will his own actions and find his *raison d'être* in abstract ideologies or theologies, seem vain and shallow hopes. In Lacan's view the conscious ego (*je*) is not the ally we automatically assume it to be, but should actually be greeted by psychoanalysts, and other searchers of truth, with daggers drawn, because it is an inherently fictional structure and thus both deceived and deceiving.

Lacan's "baroque" style is of a piece with his thought wherein the comforts of hierarchy and security of labels disintegrate along with the idea of an objective, finally knowable reality. Familiar dualities such as emotion/intellect, subjective/objective, fantasy/reality, dream/discourse, and so forth, seem simplistic and non-serviceable. Rather, one is brought into a universe where science and poetry are wed, where the abstract has been concretized, and the concrete made porous and opaque. While the act of looking (*le regard*) is made tangible in Lacan's thought, actually possessing the power to create and destroy, language is granted the same power. But the seeming transparency and well-made system aspects of language have disappeared and it is shown to be, rather, a gaping, slippery and confusing, albeit dynamic, force. "Knots" are the topographical image which Lacan uses to describe intersections of the Orders of identity-fixations, words, sounds, social conventions and Real events. "Knots" link the seeable and unseeable, the conscious and unconscious.

[Lacan is] a spokesman of the times in that his use of anthropology, philosophy, linguistics, and mathematics, in place of biology, mechanistic physics, and the positivistic metaphors which characterized Freud's psychoanalysis, have a Renaissance ring, in keeping with the interdisciplinary movements of our day.

—*Ellie Ragland-Sullivan*

Lacan builds a bridge between language and psyche. The unconscious, he says, is structured by the effects of language and subsequently functions analogously to the laws of language. Ultimately, it reveals its own intersubjective dialectic in verbal interchanges. Lacan has raised the very issue of using language—whether in spoken or literary discourse—to an interpretative act. Distinctions between intellect and affect, literature and daily speech, fiction and fact, are among the many which become blurred. And those differences which clearly do exist no longer appear innate or natural, but attributable to specific structuring codes and languages. Lacan's verbal ego and linguistic/structural unconscious are fitting outgrowths of the current academic interest in language and structures. He is also a spokesman of the times in that his use of anthropology, philosophy, linguistics, and mathematics, in place of biology, mechanistic physics, and the positivistic metaphors which characterized Freud's psychoanalysis, have a Renaissance ring, in keeping with the interdisciplinary movements of our day. His view of the ego as disunified and divided, and his portrayal of "the world in decomposition" not only resemble the fragmented literature to which we have become accustomed, but offer an explanation for its underlying causes as well. Techniques of the "new novel" which abolish character, and linear, well-constructed plots, as well as experiments with various narrative forms find their theoretician in Lacan's conception of a decentered subject, and in his portrayal of the multi-leveled aspects of discourse. The meaninglessness of ontology and ideology as depicted in the Theater of the Absurd finds an echo in Lacan's epistemology, where substance becomes in reality "a style," and the unconscious a deontologized, Desiring system of networks. In the current era of post-Formalism and "beyond structuralism," Lacan's relocation of intentionality in an unconscious subject strikes the final blow at the hoped-for linguistic formulae which were bent on making literary studies just one more scientific, empirically verifiable operation. In Lacan's thought, the fondest of all dreams of unity and stability is that of an objective, empirically quantifiable "I," which is for him but the most illusory of fictions. The very criterion for an empirical science—the unity of the perceiving subject—is false, says Lacan. Science can only exist in theory, he counterposes, not in praxis or technique.

Lacan's future value for literary theory and criticism remains an imponderable. Turkle herself points out one reason, beyond the apparent incomprehensibility of his thought and style, why many intellectuals reject Lacan. His reputed megalomania supposedly makes of him the intolerant *Maître* whom he has so aptly described in his own discourse. Turkle makes much of the significance of this contradiction in the current, passionate climate of French academic and analytic communities. But though Lacan's supporters and detractors doubtlessly do see the *Maître*/disciple relationship as central to much of the controversy which surrounds the man, I wish to take issue with Turkle on her use and understanding of the Lacanian concept of the *Maître*. His use of this term is as unique and enigmatic as are all his other unexpected reformulations of standard terms (such as symbolic, imaginary, signifier, signified, metonymy, Desire, phallus, castration, and so forth). In his *Séminaire XX* (*Encore,* 1972-73) in the lecture-cum-essay entitled **"A Jakobson,"** Lacan develops the idea of four different discourse-structures which signal various relationships or links between language-use and the unconscious of a given speaker or writer: those of the *Maître,* the hysteric, the analyst, and the academic. Lacan shows each discourse to be delineated by different psychic structural patterns which link the social aspect of language-use to the direction of psychic intention.

The *Maître* is depicted as one who speaks a discourse of opinion, animated frequently by what Lacan calls the passion of ignorance. The criterion of authority for the *Maître's* discourse is an identification with "phallic" supremacy, then, although one need not actually be male to represent such authority. Lacan's Phallus is not a reference to the penis, but instead a metaphor which symbolizes power and dominance. The fact that social power and public status have been predominantly associated throughout history with maleness, suggests to Lacan that the key to the enigma lies not in natural biological or genetic dictates, but in early structuring processes and in the representation of gender in language. If all infants are born without an inner self, or core identity, then the earliest and most constant source of nurture and mirroring will provide the missing center. Separation from that source—the rupture of a symbiosis—will be felt as a loss of self or ego. The force (third term) which symbolizes the growing distinction of infant from the nurturing Other (usually Mother) is usually male, whether it be the father, mother's brother, or the social group itself. The effect of this painful separation on the infant's developing unconscious ego is what Lacan terms "castration." Anglo-American psychologies refer to adult neuroses and psychoses as involving difficulties with "individuation." In Lacanian terms this means that the father's power never penetrates an individual's unconscious sense of self. However, since the father has no intrinsic magic or no biological supremacy *per se,* it is the symbolic effect of his dividing presence to which Lacan points. The father's very presence is an implicit "no" to total possession of the Mother, and coincides with an infant's dawning realization of its own separateness, its limits and boundaries, both physical and psychological. Lacan refers, then, not to the biological father, but to the "law of the *name* of the father." Moreover, at the same time that an infant begins to sense its separateness from its Mother (18 months of age), it is also beginning to use language with some degree of coherence. Thus law ("no"), separation, and language become indissolubly linked in unconscious associations and in the structure of the *moi.* Language, even then, acts as a paradoxical, yet potent force, both enforcing the ever-growing sense of a lawful and ordered universe (culture), and also enabling the infant to manage and tolerate separation ("individuation") by the substitutive act of naming objects. Language, thus seen, is the condition of culture imposing itself on nature.

Now a person who identifies with powerful social forces and positions uses language in order to represent his/her ego as on the side of the *Maître*. Two of the other discourse patterns described by Lacan in **"À Jakobson"** are those of the hysteric and the analyst, not dissimilar in pattern. The hysteric is, in Lacan's view, one who poses the question of non-being (*non-être*) by finding the truth of his/her identity in a *Maître,* whom the hysteric views as one who pronounces on and defines Being by incarnating it. Lacan plays on the pronunciation of the French word *Maître* here, calling it *m'être.* The *Maître* does not see that he or she merely signifies or represents authority and power, but actually considers him or herself to *be* it. The value of such a stance is that ego division is masked. The analyst, on the other hand, studies the ways in which individuals manage to deal with ego incompletion and alienation (fill up the inherent lack in Being) by looking at the underside of conscious discourse, that part of Being which gives silent witness to the inadequacy of the *Maître's* sense of self totality. The analyst waits for irruptions, "knots," surprises, verbal repetitions, and *non sequiturs,* which reveal how an individual's discourse is an elaboration of his/her unconscious truth or identity. While many of Lacan's pupils and followers wish to spend their time in a series of disputes and finely-honed quibbles, Lacan insists that as the bringer of a new knowledge, he does not wish continually to justify his insights by the argumentation that is the province of the *Maître* and of university discourse. Lacan's own discourse, he maintains, is unlike that of the *Maître* in that it alternates between those of analyst and hysteric whose language-use is linked to the psyche by means of unconscious truth: that of the self in the case of the hysteric, and that of the other in the case of the analyst.

The essential elements in all these discourses are represented by Lacan's controversial mathemes, formulae which are made up of little letters lacking signification of their own. The four letters which Lacan uses to describe the varying patterns in the discourse-structures are: S1 = the "phallic" signifier which reflects the link between language and power; S2 = knowledge as the conscious elaboration of unconscious perception and its reflection in relationships where one implicitly poses one's identity question to others (objects); $ = the conscious subject (*je*) as reflection of its own unconscious ego (*moi*); a = the link between knowledge, love, repetitious patterns and symptoms as indications of how individuals complete their own inherent lack of unity (*Séminaire XX*). But the *Maître* grounds his discourse in "phallic" authority *per se*. Having tried to exclude disruptive elements, the *Maître* takes the surface transparency of his/her own perceptions to be the sum of knowledge and truth. This discourse is, of course, in the imperative mode. The mirror reflection (object relation) which reinforces its power base is the hysteric's discourse, since the hysteric actually takes the opinions and beliefs of the *Maître* to be final statements of truth merely because he/she represents "phallic" power. As law-giver, the *Maître* is seen to be the one who knows/no's. The university discourse bases its authority—more securely—on academic knowledge which Lacan somewhat iconoclastically terms *doxa*. Such knowledge, he says, consists of the multiple efforts made by academics to pin down final answers, but, in fact, consists largely in elaborations of linguistic effects, social codes and myths, as well as personal fictions. This is not to say that facts are not discoverable; some truths have indeed been pinned down throughout history. But much less often than professorial dictate would have it.

Lacan's effort to divorce his conception of truth from the mainstays of tradition, both in terms of "phallic" authority (*Maître* discourse) and academic bodies of knowledge (university discourse), makes his thought a natural ally of literary criticism. The truth of Lacan's own discourse is that of poetry, dream, fantasy, and creation. He views language as always significant, and interpretation as inherent in the use of language. His view that language creates realities depicts Man as a representational, symbolic being who believes that he autonomously originates ideas which, in fact, he only acts out. We are born into a vast symbolic network of words, codes, and meanings which inhabit, direct, and control us, but which we megalomaniacally take to be thoughts and truths which originated with and in ourselves. Rather, the unconscious dwells in language, waiting to "write itself," inviting hearers to decode messages whose meaning is opaque and intentionality unfathomed. In this sense, literature is the expression *par excellence* of the opaque, ambiguous surface of language, an

open invitation to dialectical interchange. Lacanian literary interpretation would be like a Lacanian cure, an interminable process, characterized by the analysis of an infinite regress of words, sounds, images, and identifications. The literary critic, however, would not be a psychoanalyst, looking for final meaning or truth in the biographical details of an author's life. Rather, the Symbolic codes of historical context must be analyzed along with the diachronic and synchronic variables of the author's life and the reader's life, and historical context. In such a literary criticism text and reader would merge indissolubly in a synthesis much like that of creation itself. Lacan could furnish the means to offset the labeling, categorizing limitations of historical Positivism and contribute a means for talking about aesthetics (perception) in a more global and dynamic way. "Meaning" would not have to be sought through meta-languages or Formalist codes if, as Lacan proposes, language always means something more than it says. (pp. 562-77)

> *Ellie Ragland-Sullivan, "Lacan, Language, and Literary Criticism," in* The Literary Review, *Fairleigh Dickinson University, Vol. 24, No. 4, Summer, 1981, pp. 562-77.*

Robert Con Davis   (essay date December 1983)

[*Davis is an American scholar, critic, and educator who has written extensively on the literary implications of Lacan's theories. In the following essay, he outlines ways in which Lacan's theories apply to the study of narration and addresses the difficulty of understanding Lacan's work.*]

Jacques Lacan as narrative theorist? A Lacanian narratology? The answer to both questions . . . is a qualified yes. Jacques Lacan's concern with the Freudian subject suggests a position in regard to narration—an approach, even (with some elaboration) a narratology. It is an approach derivable from his view—his central insight into psychoanalysis—that *l'inconscient est structuré comme un langage*. It says simply that narration, too, operates like a language, is a language, and manifests linguistic operations in various ways. Narration exists, finally, within the context of an unconscious "discourse," within the bounds of what Lacan calls the "discourse of the Other." Since the early 1970s, though earlier in France, literary theorists have busily sought to understand this central insight of Jacques Lacan's rethinking of psychoanalysis—in a sense to reverse it, not to disprove it necessarily, but to grasp how language in literary texts is constituted, buoyed up, permeated, and decentered by the unconscious. The aim has been to understand (reversing Lacan's statement) how *"literature,"* in Shoshana Felman's words [in "To Open the Question," *Yale French Studies,* Nos. 55/56 (1977)], *" . . . is the unconscious of psychoanalysis."* (p. 848)

[The] theoretical melding of *l'inconscient* and *le langage*—psychoanalysis and linguistics—[takes] place *before* Lacan, as Lacan himself insists, in Freud, particularly in *The Interpretation of Dreams* (1900), *The Psychopathology of Everyday Life* (1901), *Jokes and Their Relation to the Unconscious* (1905), and many of the metapsychology

In 1955. From the left: Martin Heidegger, Kostas Axelos, Lacan, Jean Beaufret, Mrs. Heidegger, and Lacan's wife Sylvia.

pieces. Freud, unlike Lacan, did not have access to Ferdinand de Saussure's formulation of semiotics on which modern linguistics is based (the *Cours de linguistique générale* was not published until 1916, sixteen years after *The Interpretation of Dreams*). But, as Lacan shows, Freud was simultaneously "discovering" the sign and semiotics for psychology just as Saussure was doing so for linguistics. In that Freud's major work on dreams "appeared long before the formalizations of linguistics," Lacan argues even that psychoanalysis "paved the way [for linguistics] by the sheer weight of its truth."

This "discovery" of semiotics can be seen in a passage in *The Interpretation of Dreams,* a central Freudian "scene of writing" that Lacan discusses, where Freud describes two different modes of narrative interpretation. In this passage Freud gives a sample dream about a "house with a boat on its roof, a single letter of the alphabet, [and] the figure of a running man whose head has been conjured away." Now as he might interpret it, or as Lacan might, this brief narration is actually *about* semiotics. We see this in the placement of a house with too much of a top (a head) in relation to its contrary, to the image of a running man "whose head has been conjured away." The images form a binary opposition. There is an excess of presence in the boat-head, and there is a stark and inappropriate absence in the man's missing head. In this contrast, further, is a theatrically distinct opposition between presence and absence, the condition of difference in a binary system that

makes a sign (and semiotics) possible. That is, what stands apart from and yet represents a semiotic difference is the possibility of representation itself, the signifying possibility (as represented in the dream) of "a single letter of the alphabet." This signifying capability, further, exacts a human cost in that the subject of language is signified within and, simultaneously, is alienated from language—hence the man's symbolic castration in being headless. The dream's figures or elements—Lacan calls them "sliding signifiers"—thus move over certain "positions" in the dream in a kind of articulation structured *in* language and, through interpretation, actually *about* language. That is, they inhabit the "binarity" of language and semiotics. Freud speaks, as does Lacan, in several registers simultaneously—in both his commentary and choice of an example so that his discourse foregrounds the structurality of language and semiotics.

Thus, Freud's main interest in this "scene of writing" is interpretation itself, the principles by which we read the dream as essentially a picture, at one extreme, or as a narrative, at another. His first approach to the dream focuses on the "*manifest* content" of the narrative details as if they are in a "pictographic script" where all of the pieces are present simultaneously for inspection as in a "picture-puzzle, a rebus." In this pictographic approach the disjunctive quality of the picture—"house with a boat on the roof," etc.—creates a problem for interpretation. The dream elements, dislocated from a familiar context and yet fixed in place, have no significance except possibly as icons with preexistent and fixed meanings. If they are icons, the dream narrative may be read as an intelligible picture-story, a deciphered rebus with its meaning available on its surface. For the second mode, instead of being a picture, the dream functions like a language governed by, as Freud says, "syntactic laws." In this approach, by contrast, the dream elements are not seen, at least not exclusively, as if in a picture or as inherently meaningful. Rather, now they are arbitrary "signifiers" occupying "positions" in discourse with no intrinsic or assigned meaning. In this "linguistic" approach, Freud explains, we "replace each separate element by a syllable or word that can be represented by that element in some way or another." This kind of interpretation, in other words, takes place through the substitution of one element for another according to certain narrative codes. Crucial here is the interchangeability, the substitutability, of dream elements—signifiers—which can hold particular places in the dream. The dream is an interpretable text only according to the possible substitutions of elements. While in Freud's pictographic approach particular dream elements are meaningful (or lacking in meaning) as they are locked in a particular pattern, in the linguistic approach dream elements lack inherent meaning but can stand in for (be replaced by) other elements within a certain structure or set of possibilities.

In view of the choices—the interpretive dilemma—that Freud sets up in this discussion, we must say that Lacan chooses to go the second way of interpretation, that of language and linguistics—of, as Lacan says, "writing rather than of mime." The apparent simplicity of such a choice, however, is misleading in the extreme. Freud's pictographic approach, on closer examination, actually contains important aspects of the linguistic approach and so cannot be completely discarded. If the dream elements are not icons, Freud's picture-dream is reduced to being a structure of juxtaposed elements. Since the particular elements themselves are without meaning, what is left are the combinatory possibilities of dislocated and yet co-present elements—contiguous and/or simultaneously adjacent to each other. In the second or linguistic approach, Freud emphatically does not attribute inherent meaning to the dream elements; he does say that their relative positions, their existence in a system of differences, affect another process, that of elements being selected to go in the dream initially and to replace other elements as interpretation takes place, especially to replace the "original" (or manifest) elements that would otherwise form a pictograph. In short, the pictographic approach, as Freud describes it, emphasizes combinatory possibilities; the linguistic approach, as we are using the term here, indicates a selective process of one element substituting for another. In both approaches, elements in a series are placed in different relationships, but in being so placed they are also being selected and then substituted so as to represent any number of combinatory possibilities.

This is the distinction of post-Saussurean linguistics in which "combination" emphasizes purely relational concepts such as syntax, concepts inconceivable, however, apart from the selective (or paradigmatic) possibilities of

words and word parts, such as morphemes, available in language as a whole. Roman Jakobson insists that—to point up the interdependence of combination/selection as a single system of discourse—necessarily in any one "utterance (message) is a COMBINATION [syntagmatic dimension] of constituent parts (sentences, words, phonemes, etc.) SELECTED [paradigmatically] from the repository of all possible constituent parts (the code)" ["The Twofold Character of Language," in Roman Jakobson and Morris Halle, *Fundamentals of Language,* 1971]. Thus, while Freud for his own purposes separates these analyses into two approaches to narrative, insofar as they represent syntagmatic and paradigmatic analyses they are interdependent and imply each other. Pictography and linguistics, Freud's commentary aside, are not finally different modes of analysis.

And yet, and perhaps this is Freud's real point, such extremes of analysis—especially for narration—do exist usefully as ideals. We surely can imagine a narrative criticism that, merely tending toward the ideal (the "lure," as Lacan says) of naturally meaningful pictographic inscription, would emphasize spatial form in narration. This approach, of course, actually exists in the narrative tradition associated with modernist fiction and spatial form (for example, in much criticism of Virginia Woolf's fiction). Joseph Frank imagines "modern" narrative structure as somehow escaping temporality, yielding its intended content when narrative elements are arranged as adjacent and copresent in the semblance of a picture, an organization Frank calls a nontemporal unity. Here narrative form resides inherently in the pattern of individual elements which are presented metonymically as if in a still life. At another extreme, we can imagine narration as tending toward being an operation of substitution; that is, narration is created as elements, signifiers, stand in for other elements in a sequence, the selective process that Roman Jakobson identifies as metaphoric. This possibility, too, is a reality; there is the tradition of modern narrative interpretation inspired by Ferdinand de Saussure, Vladimir Propp, and Marcelo Mauss, developed by Claude Lévi-Strauss, A. J. Greimas, and the structualists, and which continues on to Lacan and the post-structuralists—a tradition of narration as language process, not a pictograph, but a linguistic system of substitutions and alterations in time. Freud's discussion of the dream is, in fact, a rough but reliable map of two main areas of narrative theory—pictographic and linguistic—that have existed and dominated literary criticism since 1900. It is Lacan's contribution to all of this to show that the operation of the unconscious, encompassing the extremes of what Freud calls pictographic and linguistic analyses, is itself a linguistic process and to bring this insight intensely to bear in the psychoanalytic critique of the subject as inscribed in language.

Lacan's interpretive choice, then, is not linguistics over pictography, or selection over combination—choices not available theoretically. It is, rather, a move to show the explicitly linguistic structure of the subject within an unconscious discourse. By "subject" Lacan means both the agency of knowing *and* the site at which this agency functions, has form, and is meaningful. Lacan's view here has implications for the narrative terms we have been using: what Freud calls the manifest content of a dream (or narration)—the pictograph—does not stand alone as a privileged structure. It is already a repetition, the result of a previous interpretation, of an interpretive process—Freud's "dream work"—that already having taken place (and fated always to be a repetition) has produced the pictographic representation of a dream thought. Lacanian analysis takes this manifest content, this monument to a previous interpretation, and—treating it as one phase of interpretation—places it (in importance) on narration's margin, decentered, as a part and just one effect of the unconscious process involving metonymy and metaphor. As manifest content, this "literal" story or plot is "real," just as it is "real" when it displays the traces—"gaps" in meaning or "lapses" of logic—that represent the unconscious system that produced it.

In this way, the so-called manifest content (really an "old" interpretation) is resubjected in interpretation to the same process of combination *and* selection, metonymy and metaphor, that produced the manifest content in the dream work initially. Narrative interpretation actually mimics and repeats the dream work analytically, as if to give the message back to its sender "in an inverted form" in narration. The actual dream work began with unconscious desires and dream thoughts and moved the thoughts through displacement (metonymy) and condensation (metaphor). Lacan's analysis of narration, as Lacan's readings of *Hamlet* and "The Purloined Letter" show, begins with language, the product of a previous interpretation, and proceeds to rediscover—by giving attention to certain "gaps" or "lapses," the indications of the unconscious process—the Other discourse that previously produced the so-called manifest text. In this way, narrative interpretation from a Lacanian viewpoint in fact does reverse Lacan's statement (as Lacan himself reverses it) about the unconscious and language and finds the unconscious structure of language, which, in turn, is structured like a language, which, in turn—and so on. Freud's dream narrative, then, as Lacan might say, is *structured like a subject* in that it has the unconscious structure of language.

What is narration à la Lacan? It is certainly the work of the signifier as it can be known in its metaphoric and metonymic operations, the fortunes of the signifier, its history, in relation to its own repressed origin in unconscious discourse. Narration—irremediably diachronic *and* synchronic—repeats and represents unconscious discourse in the only way the unconscious can be known: as a sequence of opportunities for linguistic substitution and (re)combination. The potential for continuity and unity in such sequences makes possible the "gaps" or "lapses" that indicate the "Other" scene of signification, the repressed scene of writing not a part of manifest narration but which (like a buoy, or series of buoys) holds it up and enables it to exist at all. In this formulation we are already assuming three fundamental propositions that characterize—though will not limit—a Lacanian concern with narration: 1.) Narration is structured like a (subject in) language. This places Lacan in a tradition of narrative theory with a linguistic orientation. 2.) Narration's manifest content

is a product of the unconscious discourse that is both the precondition of narration and the site of its appearance. This says essentially that the subject of narration, what gives it form and meaning, will always be other than what is signified *in* narration, or what is signifiable *as* narration. 3.) Last, the unconscious discourse of language and its processes are revealed in the "gaps" or "lapses" (inconsistencies, failures of speech and signification, etc.) that appear in a narrative's manifest text. This final proposition situates narrative interpretation, too, as a movement, a trajectory, a contingent effect, within the larger (unconscious) discourse of the Other.

In practice, a Lacanian narratology based on these propositions is likely to be a triple reading: of the manifest text, of the unconscious discourse that buoys up the manifest text, and then of the reconstituted (repositioned) manifest text—a new interpretation. The *text* read here obviously is neither the New Critical, positivistic text—ambiguous and ironic but absolutely knowable—nor is it a rebus in which one reads and finds whatever one wants. To the question, "is there a text in this classroom?" we can answer yes; the Lacanian text is definitely *there,* but it is exclusively text-as-textual-production. This narrative text differs from Jakobson's structuralist one in that Jakobson's communication model of sender/receiver (addresser/addressee) is absorbed by Lacan's formulation of a split subject and a set of "positions" existing *within* narration—not necessarily between sender and receiver. This shift—marking an important shift from structuralist to poststructuralist modes of thought—occurs largely because "the conception of language as communication," as Rosalind Coward and John Ellis explain, "tends to obscure the way in which language sets up the positions of 'I' and 'you' that are necessary for communication to take place at all" [*Language and Materialism: Developments in Semiology and the Theory of the Subject,* 1977]. The key phrasing here is "sets up the positions of 'I' and 'you' "— that is, "sets up" positions through structuration within the subject and within narration itself, in time. And, finally, the Lacanian text differs from the deconstructionist (problematic) text, to which it bears a resemblance, in that the "positions" of narration ("I" and "you," for example) are anchored, held down, by Freudian desire, which enforces a curb on the infinite textual regress opened by *différance.* The "signifier"—subject to desire, as Lacan states—"stops the otherwise endless movement (*glissement*) of the signification." Hence the Lacanian text—to Derrida's outraged dismay—may speak its own "truth"— the Other's "truth," what Jacqueline Rose calls "the truth of the unconscious [that] is only ever that moment of fundamental division through which the subject entered into language and sexuality, and the constant failing of position within both" ["Introduction—II," in *Jacques Lacan and the "école freudienne," Feminine Sexuality,* edited by Juliet Mitchell and Jacqueline Rose, translated by Jacqueline Rose, 1982]. Thus, there is no knowable subject in Lacan's text or in Derrida's (no Other of the Other); Lacanalysis and deconstruction do not differ here. But the desire of the Other—not part of the Derridean program— positions and limits the free play of signification through the continual resubjection of the signifier (the subject) to the Other's desire, through the continual "passage into the semiotic triangle of Oedipus."

One can scarcely contemplate [the study of] of narration à la Lacan without being mindful of the famous "difficulty" of reading Lacan's own narration, his *écrits*—a "difficulty" vaguely embarrassing (for [Lacan disciples] at least) and more often spoken than written about. He is at times maddeningly elliptical, playful, and (at his worst and best) polyphonic in his pronouncements. As George Steiner says [in "On Difficulty," in *On Difficulty and Other Essays,* 1978] about similarly "difficult" writers, it can seem as though "at certain levels, we are not meant to understand *at all,* and our interpretation, indeed our reading itself is an intrusion." "For whom"—and here Steiner could be interrogating Lacan's texts—"was the Master composing his cryptograms?" Why *should* reading Lacan be this difficult? Where and what is the difficulty?

Steiner sheds light on four different types of difficulty (*contingent, modal, tactical,* and *ontological*) that are relevant—especially *ontological* difficulty—to the task of reading Lacan's discourse. *Contingent* difficulties, in brief, are those problems we might have with the obscurity of Lacan's text, possibly psychoanalytical, linguistic, and philosophical terms that we, as Steiner says, "need to look up." Either we look up "primary process," "foreclosure," and "aphanisis" and understand them, or we do not. And since Lacan is highly allusive and steeped in the debates of psychoanalysis and twentieth-century thought in general, the difficulty here is a formidable one. Next, *modal* difficulty, rather than being an obscurity in the text, is a problem of receptivity for the reader in regard to a text's mode of presentation. Lacan's major publications, mostly transcripts of lectures, are addressed to us as students who are supposedly in diligent pursuit of this Master's teachings (imagine the audacity of entitling one's own book simply *Écrits!*). This magisterial mode can pose problems of tone and can generate resistance enough to become a great obstacle in reading. Then, *tactical* difficulty, strangely enough, is created by Lacan's strategies for communicating efficiently and powerfully. In his discourse Lacan may explain a point about the "gaze" quite fully and then refuse to expound on a related concept, or suddenly break off all explanation. This practice, like his erratically short therapy sessions, is intended to prompt his listeners to a deep and direct engagement with psychoanalysis, to bring them face-to-face with "real" (impossibly continuous) discourse. The potential for such strategies to succeed is a great difficulty when they fail or only partially succeed.

[As] a post-Saussurean psychoanalyst, [Lacan] offers a paradigm of possibilities which seemingly scandalize common sense, especially as seen in the tradition of American Freudian thought.

—*Robert Con Davis*

These difficulties—enough to be fatal to a single reading—are certainly common enough and are ultimately (though at times it may seem otherwise) surmountable. The greatest difficulty in reading Lacan, and the far more interesting one to contemplate, is *ontological,* the "difficulty," as Steiner writes, that breaks "the contract of ultimate or preponderant intelligibility between poet and reader, between text and meaning." "Difficulties of this category," he continues, "cannot be looked up" because " . . . they confront us with blank questions about the nature of human speech [and] about the status of significance." In other words, an *ontological* difficulty arises—that is, the contract may break between writer and reader, text and meaning—when a text posits (in Thomas Kuhn's terminology) a whole new paradigm of understanding entailing a new grasp of phenomena, their relations, and the horizon of possibility that moves up behind them. This "difficulty," though not inherently insurmountable, can be an absolute obstacle to understanding.

The ontological difficulty here is that Lacan as a post-Saussurean psychoanalyst offers a paradigm of possibilities which seemingly scandalize common sense, especially as seen in the tradition of American Freudian thought. Lacan's project, for example, is worlds away from the psychoanalytic criticism that Frederick C. Crews rejected in *Out of My System* (1975), Freudian criticism developed between 1900 and the 1960s as a distinctly formalizing and allegorizing tendency. The prior movement, strongly akin to New Criticism, existentialism, and archetypal interpretation, flourished during what may be called the Age of the Critic, an age of expert critical strategies formulated under the authority of T. S. Eliot, the southern Fugitives, I. A. Richards, and Northrop Frye. Lacan's Freud, by contrast, is read in quite different company, intertextually (in Julia Kristeva's sense and in the popular meaning of "influence") with Ferdinand de Saussure, Martin Heidegger, Claude Lévi-Strauss, and Maurice Merleau-Ponty during our own Age of the Reader. It has connections with deconstruction, reader-response criticism, and feminism—to a critical era under the strong sway of Jacques Derrida, Geoffrey Hartman, J. Hillis Miller, Stanley Fish, Julia Kristeva, and Lacan himself.

Most scandalizing about Lacan's paradigm, and this goes to the heart of ontological difficulty, is a figure that can be described rather simply, that of a division, a *split.* For Lacan the pervasive figure of the split indicates a fundamental division in psychic life, in selfhood, and even within the things we know. In literary studies, it is a permanent division within the text and narration. Lacan's model of narrative, accordingly, is not that of a unified thing but of a split process, a two-fold process that swings metronome-like from side to side between product and production (manifest text and unconscious discourse), back and forth, and never reaches a point of stability or wholeness. This narrative model poses a serious threat to the empirically-based tradition of interpretation as a transparent and focusable lens, an open subjectivity, through which a detached investigator peers into a stable (possibly pictographic) narrative structure. Positioned in a different paradigm, Lacan's concept of narration *and* of narrative interpretation rests squarely on an ontological fault line, the radical split of a subject irretrievably unwhole—the subject of what Lacan calls *aphanisis.* Lacanian analysis, in this regard, is difficult because it is revolutionary (literally so) in its promotion of this paradigm.

Lacan's greatest "difficulty," then, in Steiner's sense—and for which we need feel no embarrassment—is precisely here: since the subject (narration), for Lacan, is marked by this irrevocable split, what we are accustomed to calling unity and wholeness in form and seeing as concepts centrally important to narration and interpretation are unceremoniously ousted. But these concepts do not just vanish; we still have some reason to speak of wholeness and unity. Such concepts are relegated, however, to the status of being (in Jacques-Alain Miller's term) a mere "suturing" over of the fundamental split with the various commitments (threads) of ideology, the inevitable ideological bias that we bring to any one approach to the subject in a narration in hopes of promoting a view of meaningful significance and wholeness. In shifts such as these (dislocating and potentially painful)—in which sense and nonsense, the central and the marginal, are seen to switch places—we stand witness as the lines of understanding (as if seeking a new haunting) palpably move from one paradigm to the other, from a world in which they (already) made sense to a world in which they are (just now) making sense. This revolution of the subject's status, and the resultant shift in the way we understand narration, poses an ontological difficulty of the highest order. (pp. 848-58)

> *Robert Con Davis, "Introduction: Lacan and Narration," in* MLN, *Vol. 98, No. 5, December, 1983, pp. 848-59.*

William Kerrigan   (essay date Fall 1989)

[*Kerrigan is an American scholar and educator who has written extensively on Renaissance literature and the influence of psychiatry on the humanities. In the following excerpt, he criticizes Lacan's psychoanalytic theory as a rigid, abstract philosophy that is unable to account for the variable, irrational reality of existence.*]

[The Lacan tradition in psychoanalysis] looks more and more like a pretentious, personless, metaphysically inspired variation on psychoanalysis, caught up in absolutist styles of thought and insufferably nationalistic polemics. We already have, moreover, a perfectly decent alternative to do for us those limited things that psychoanalysis can alone perform—the tradition of Freud.

It is not *just* that Lacan's version of psychoanalysis in unrelievedly biased toward one gender, though it is, more so than Freud's, despite the enthusiasm of some feminists for **Encore,** a text that must be either a muddle or above my head, and despite the disturbed women who seem to have influenced his early work. If Lacan had illuminated male psychology, that would not be everything, but it would be something.

It is not *just* that Lacan's work has little in the way of empirical confirmation or clinical utility. We may indeed wonder whether the universal route to egohood is to respond with jubilation to being held up before a mirror, an event that seems more provocative in the context of mirror-ridden Western literature and philosophy than in the presumed experience of infants. We may indeed raise an eyebrow at the technique of the "punctuated" session, which might or might not help the patient, but will certainly expand the case load and therefore the bank account of the analyst. However, this kind of objection fails to address shortcomings specific to Lacan. The awesome weight given to the word "clinical" in some quarters is mostly the residue of Freud's idea, amply qualified in his own texts, that psychoanalysis is a positive science, and must be understood in terms of the charges leveled against contemporary psychoanalysis by rival therapies whose alleged efficiency is more popular with medical insurance companies. When invoked in the context of literary theory, "clinical" reserves an authority for practicing analysts in a discussion they do not comprehend very well: there is no reason why they should. As for samplings and statistics, no genuinely controversial, unobvious, countercommonsensical Freudian idea has ever passed the test of hard-core empirical confirmation. Psychoanalysis does not belong to the genre of things we have to believe—to the uncontroversial. In this respect, then, Lacan succumbs to the usual fate. The sense of the descriptive power of psychoanalysis does not derive from checkable empirical items put together one by one into a cumulative system. It stems holistically from the wisdom we gain by assimilating an entire body of thought, the feeling that we have come into the possession of a vocabulary that makes a difference, and must now be cross-referenced with a good deal of what we know, do, and value. Still, Lacan looks worse from a positivist perspective because his characteristic proposals for psychoanalysis are almost entirely metapsychological. Where Freud was equivocal, moving from fiction to fiction as he tried to hammer out causes and reasons, Lacan seems committed to indispensable laws, or to the posture of laying down such laws, however obscure they may actually be in his oblique but always self-important expositions.

Nor is it *just* that Lacan as an author exploited the gross recuperative strategy of denouncing the bonds of narcissism while flagrantly surrendering to his own, though he did, and passed on the lure of this recuperation to some purveyors of truth who now work in his name, so basic is it to his seductiveness. But anyone doing psychoanalysis—at least I assume that this is a point in common, and therefore uncontroversial—knows how little we enjoy giving up our earliest satisfactions. So let an ego without sin cast this stone. Colossal vanity in the intellectual life is not by itself enough to disqualify somebody's thought; Petrarch, after all, was our modern prototype. I do think that the mannered narcissistic indulgence of Lacan's intellectual style was more massive and primitive than most. He once referred, brilliantly, to the analyst managing a transference as the dummy in a bridge hand. Yet in his published texts he played no other role but the all-knowing master, telling us how very good his hand is while we wait around, page after page, for some glimpse of his cards. Few readers of Lacan doubt that whatever else may be said of the imperial expositor enthroned in his texts he is for sure, to put the language of the street on it, a sonuvabitch. It is astonishing that this defect should recently have emerged in his defense. "After years of study," Jane Gallop writes [in her *Reading Lacan,* 1985], "I have come to believe Lacan's text impossible to understand fully, impossible to master—and thus a particularly good illustration of everyone's inevitable 'castration' in language." This seems a plausible lesson to have learned from years of studying Lacan. But it is desperate apologetics to go on to argue, as Gallop does to some extent and Shoshana Felman does to the hilt [in "Psychoanalysts and Education: Teaching Terminable and Interminable," *Yale French Studies,* 63 (1982)], that Lacan was a world-class innovator among scribbling teachers because he deployed his pompous expositor therapeutically, to psychoanalyze his readers by inviting them to project onto his texts a "subject supposed to know" who would then never come clean, never impart to them the knowledge on which his mastery rested, leaving the wisest of them to recognize his supposed mastery as their desire, and their prolonged tantalization as his scourging of that desire. We probably have encountered world-class students here, who want to take responsibility for even the vanity of their master. It is defensible to say that "frustrated understanding, unable to correspond with the knowledge supposed by the expositor, is the effect of reading Lacan." The argument becomes an excuse and an occasion for praise when it is assumed, in the old-fashioned way, that this effect was the author's intention. Like all questions of intention, it's a judgment call. Emerson said that "true genius seeks to defend us from itself." Lacan does not belong among that crew. I cannot believe for a moment that he had achieved such control over his narcissism. The spell of the literary transference that Gallop took years of study to dissolve was cast by a lordly and preemptive analyst, a vain practitioner wholly devoted to our enthrallment.

I want out of the traffic in Lacan because I don't like what he did to Freud, I don't want him to replace Freud; I don't want there to be people thought to be making psychoanalytic sense who have read Lacan in depth and Freud scarcely at all. Lacan, it is true, showed us how psychoanalysis might fit together with certain ideas of his generation of French intellectuals. His so-called "return to Freud" made a number of passages in Freud appear newly interesting or decisive. But the overall effect is that of a premature burial, as Freud's wonderful lucidity—modest lucidity—gets covered over and lost in murky, sometimes outrageous metaphysics. That, in my view, was Lacan's wrong turn. He welcomed into psychoanalysis far too much of the metaphysical claptrap that Freud wisely suspected.

Few readers of Lacan doubt that whatever else may be said of the imperial expositor enthroned in his texts he is for sure, to put the language of the street on it, a sonuvabitch.

—*William Kerrigan*

A considerable proportion of Lacan's work, including the part derived from structural linguistics, can be described as a fusion of Freud and various fragments of the metaphysical tradition. Sometimes he hid these debts behind contemptuous polemics. As M. Guy Thompson has astutely observed [in his *The Death of Desire: A Study in Pathology,* 1985], Lacan posed as the scornful mocker of "phenomenological theories which approximate Lacan's own in ways he is loathe to admit." Lacanian topics like the gaze that changes subject into object and the unrepresentability of the *objet petit a* have blue-ribbon pedigrees in the history of philosophy, and also appear in the work of two contemporaries rooted in phenomenology, Sartre and Merleau-Ponty.

Sometimes the debts are conceded. Thus, in place of Freud's several fictions about ego genesis, Lacan gave us the emanations of the ego as set down in Hegel's parable about self-consciousness, mastery, and slavery. I call it a parable, or a way we might talk, for example, about stoicism and empire. . . . But for Lacan, the metaphysician of psychoanalysis, this venerable dialectic cuts the psyche at the joints and marks off the psychological spaces of a System—the famous triad of the Imaginary, the Symbolic, and the Real. It is not difficult to see what Lacan has done in this instance, if we come to him with the history of metaphysics in mind. He has simply made Kant speak Freud, producing yet another variation on the phenomenon (the Imaginary), the noumenon (the Symbolic), and the thing-in-itself (the unrepresentable Real). By plotting out psychic development as our appropriate or inappropriate "entrance" into these quasi-epistemological sectors, Lacan commits an error similar to the one found in countless theories of language acquisition. The familiar and wrong assumption is that language must be learned in logical stages (words before sentences, say, and sentences before quotations) corresponding to the constructs of one or another epistemology. As Donald Davidson has maintained [in his *Inquiries into Truth and Interpretation,* 1985], we do not learn language part by logical part, passing lockstep through a sequence of logical priorities: we just, again and again, *partly learn* it. Lacan thought we grew up quasi-epistemologically, that psychic stages rounded off the logical parts (images before words, mother before father). Like other constructivist system-makers, Lacan built as an idealist, keeping the parts as clean and precise as possible. Hence his refusal to consider that language comes from the mother, for that would put the Symbolic in the Imaginary and question the distinctness and sequential necessity of the parts of his System.

In place of Freud's gratefully unprofessional maxims about the psychoanalytic cure, the metaphysical Lacan gave us Heidegger on full and empty speech. What a bizarre role for Heidegger! His Dasein in *Being and Time,* a moody placeholder for the ancient theme of human essence, is never once said to be hungry or horny—the two key "wants" in psychoanalysis. Lacan himself dropped some words full of pompous piety over having translated Heidegger and given this philosopher to his students sans paraphrase. Most students of psychoanalysis believe that Heidegger, in spinning out one of his Grecian fantasies, happened to stumble onto the best available distinctions for describing psychic health? We should be keeping the credible lean and feisty, not gorging it with reification. We do not need this kind of tortured prescription to measure our health. *Thinking we need it* is one of the illnesses specific to theory building. We only need, as Freud admirably saw, to do our work, care for those we love, and enjoy our cigars. The cigars are parabolic.

Lacan's most discussed innovation was to yoke Freud's unconscious to the *langue* of Saussure, Jakobson, and Lévi-Strauss. In the 1970s, when many of us in the English-speaking part of the world began to feel the influence of Lacan, this element in his work seemed to be unphilosophical. Lacan was on solid ground, exactly as he claimed to be, in appealing to the painstaking science of structural linguistics. We might have known better had we achieved a better grasp on Derrida, who drew some of his first and most telling examples of unrealized metaphysical servitude from this movement. Today, it almost goes without saying among people following literary theory that the structuralists have put out the latest edition of Western rationalism. Structuralism is rationalism retreating one step and counterattacking: if we cannot fulfill the rationalist desire to see reality naked because language keeps getting in the way, then perhaps we can develop a special science for seeing language itself naked. This ambitious movement, modeling itself on science as the paradigm of worthwhile thought, achieved some success with topics like literary genre. It reformed ethnography by treating culture as a differential system of binary classifications and working out homologies in the form of "as A to B, so X to Z." But most of us have come to realize that structuralism is entranced above all by its own taxonomic elegance. It is weak on specific historical process, on the individual and the idiosyncratic, and in its lofty vision of ubiquitous system invites a nominalist reaction: everything is individual and idiosyncratic. Its cherished polarity of metonymy and metaphor, precisely like its medieval and Renaissance ancestor, the distinction between time and eternity, trails with it a whole array of metaphysical binaries (visible and invisible, sensible and intelligible, presence and absence), and proves to be by its very ubiquity a trivial truth. The abstract taxonomies of structuralism resemble some aspects of Freudian psychoanalysis—diagnostics, for example, and certainly metapsychology.

As Lacan brings these aspects of Freud to the center of his thought, he reveals the underlying kinship between structuralism and metaphysics. Neither has the patience for psychology. People, idiosyncratic people, drop out in the work of Lacan. In Freud, metapsychology provides something like a set of thematic expectations for the real work of constructing idiosyncratic and contingent narratives of human lives. In Lacan, there are no people, just theory. He fills the vacuum with airy metaphysical statements about the character of the sign, the question of reference, the meaning of meaning, and other philosophical puzzles that have little to do with human behavior. Since Lacan purports to be doing psychology, he has to claim otherwise. This leads him to make ripe melodramas out of structuralist trivialities, such as the undoubted fact that a child does not invent language, or even name herself. We have problems more serious than that. It hardly scratches

the surface of, is not even a start on, human disillusionment.

Freud gave us more than a fresh way to narrate our lives. Psychoanalysis is also, and perhaps most importantly, a postphilosophical and postreligious morality. It teaches us tolerance for the idiosyncracies of others and, in a rigorous way, forgiveness for our own. It is in certain respects a stoic vision, keyed to the ineradicable hardships of life, but a stoicism leavened with humor. It shrinks grandiosity. Lacan offers us little if anything of unprogrammatic moral wisdom. His humor is caustic and superior. Even his playfulness seems to demonstrate that he is grander than we are, that he alone gets the point of the most precious jokes. If, reading Freud, we tone down the scientific treble and bring up the base of his skepticism, his works sound almost brand-new. The teachings of Lacan, by contrast, appear old-fashioned today, like the remote island of science fiction whereon the dinosaurs still flourish. He got rooted in our literary practice before we saw through structuralism all the way. He repeats the most questionable gestures of the major structuralists, especially the staged resignation before some vast systematic determinism, which turns out to be, since we are supposed to know the "laws" of this system, another way of worshipping reason. It is increasingly evident today that we do not best appreciate the power of language by isolating global features of the system, but by attending to the local matter of how it is used, what the language-games are, how language functions in specific activities. About this down-to-earth, pragmatic sense of discourse Lacan has not an inkling. He goes for the quasi-metaphysical response to language "as such," the sort of cognition that wants to grasp it all in a single thought, and to record, better than ever before, the Really Appropriate Human Mood in the face of the Really True. Freud told us that analysts listen and listen, propose interpretations, and check for confirmation, trying to forge a good fit, a working alliance. But psychoanalysis in Lacan is not something between people that will slowly move toward a particular human coherence. It is a high-tech philosophical system, waiting at the flick of a switch to chew up data in its classificational machine. People would just get in the way of all this portentous theorizing about language and meaning.

> **[For Lacan psychoanalysis] is a high-tech philosophical system, waiting at the flick of a switch to chew up data in its classificational machine. People would just get in the way of all this portentous theorizing about language and meaning.**
>
> —*William Kerrigan*

People from the point of view of grandiose theory are paltry and unworthy units, merely individual, merely idiosyncratic. There are few interesting universal truths about them. In literary criticism the influence of Lacan usually produces, whatever may be said up front about postmodern sympathies, a patently essentializing disposition toward literature. At the beginning of his Lacanian anthology, *The Fictional Father,* Robert Con Davis maintains with a metaphysical confidence that might have shocked even the Schlegel brothers that "a primordial want-to-be is pre-ontological and, as such, is a theoretical precondition of all structure" and "an originary feature of every narrative." Pre-ontological? That must be a name for a substrate that is really and truly ontological, here, there, and everywhere. After backtracking in the epilogue, having seemingly become aware in the course of assembling his book that there is more than one genre of heart in the universe, that women, Marxists, and others make and consume narratives, he still wants to peddle us the numbing bromide that love "comes ultimately from the father." Davis has a bright idea. He might have told us that some narratives search for paternity, or for something often associated with the paternal imago in psychoanalysis, and do not find it because it is already assumed by signification itself, and that by studying these narratives under this description we can observe a novel and interesting alignment of their features. Instead, encouraged by the example of Lacan, he is driven to make a particular bent, a partiality, one among many kinds of psychological quest, into an indefensible universal of universals ("primordial," "pre-ontological," "all structure," "originary feature," "every narrative," "comes ultimately": the language fairly pants with metaphysical ambition). This is the Lacanian style. Never acknowledge your quirks, seize the high ground of absolutes and universals, and leave it to others, if they dare, to laugh in your face. It is about time we started doing so.

Here is another example of the Lacanian manner, from the psychologist John Muller. He is discussing the "structure" of language, by which he seems to mean that language makes the absent symbolically present. Some of us, conceding that this of course is what language does, would wonder why we need a metaphysically loaded term like "structure" to point out this uncontroversial truth about language, and Muller's answer is not far to seek. Structure gives us law with a capital letter:

> This structure radically determines our lives as human subjects, as subject to its Law: it subjects us to primordial loss, the loss of fantasized totalization in symbolic castration, the loss incurred in separation from the immediacy of maternal symbiosis, the loss of that part of ourselves and our desire that henceforth finds expression only in the bits and pieces of metaphoric substitution and an unending metonymic displacement. To be finitely human means to live as decentered subjects, split and barred from unconscious desire, forced to channel our wants through the narrow defiles of the signifier, which offers a limited satisfaction by affording us symbolic presences. The alternative is either death or psychosis, where there is neither presence nor absence and no speaking subject.
>
> ["Language, Psychosis, and the Subject in Lacan," in *Interpreting Lacan,* edited by Joseph Smith and William Kerrigan, 1983]

In other words, if you do not get through the Oedipus complex having accepted your castration, you are likely to become psychotic, and when psychotics speak, the unconscious interferes grossly. I suggest that everything else about this paragraph, everything Lacanian—the radically determining structure, the play on the word "subject," the evocation of even healthy language as somehow a fracturing into "bits and pieces" that render castration manifest, the attempt to give voice to the indignation of the poor immediate desires that have to put up with "the narrow defiles of the signifier," the posing of a stark binary choice between death or psychosis, the coercive threat that readers had better choose death, and think of language as Muller thinks of language, since the alternative is the existential failure of psychosis—all of this serves to retrieve, in the rhetorical pomposity of laying down the Law, the "fantasized totalization" that the passage seems to recommend losing. The metaphysical ambition of the Lacanian style is, in effect, a defense mechanism against assimilating its own account of psychic well-being.

I conclude with a parable. Lacan did one thing well. It needed doing at his historical moment, and he was so close to accomplishing this task that we probably need not do it again. He psychoanalyzed several hundred years of French intellectual history. The ego on his couch was Descartes, and he developed an interpretive language sure to get his patient's attention. He rewrote Freud's "where id was, ego shall be" as the antithesis of *cogito ergo sum.* His patient was the father of *clarté,* and he had somehow to break into his encasement in clear and distinct ideas. Lacan came up with the notion—fair enough in this analysis, though monstrous when passed along as general theory—that the ego is solely a narcissistic construct, is purely and simply pathological. He dreamed up the state of the mirror, and informed Monsieur Descartes that his *res cogitans* were formed unknowingly from the lineaments of his *res extensa.* He stressed in his interpretations the materiality of the signifier, which he would not have done had his patient been, say, a poet, since among poets the materiality of the signifier is an old chestnut. But Lacan remembered that Descartes had never doubted the language extended before his eyes and ears. In mounting other interpretations, Lacan took advantage of the fact that his patient possessed a spectatorial ego and also happened to believe that the rest of nature was written in mathematics. So Lacan introduced visual aids in graphs and diagrams and formulae, developed a pseudo-algebraic notation for symptomatology, and showed this ego images of itself drawn from advanced products of the tradition of analytic geometry such as Borrorean knots and mobius strips. Since the patient had fallen ill from rationalist narcissism, the therapeutic frustration in this case—and the abstinence of the analyst—lay in making all these signs of Cartesian clarity *absolutely impenetrable.* Surreal sense is what a healthy ego makes when it plays with rationalist sense; the empty solitude in Cartesian thought follows in some measure from its effort to subtract or deny the unconscious, which can result only in a bleak and unplayful reality. So Lacan went about spoiling the clear and distinct ideas of his influential patient.

> **This is the Lacanian style. Never acknowledge your quirks, seize the high ground of absolutes and universals, and leave it to others, if they dare, to laugh in your face. It is about time we started doing so.**
>
> —*William Kerrigan*

But, as I have tried to show, Lacan gave in to a powerful countertransference. He kept losing sight of the surrealism of his own interpretations. He entertained the seductive thought that his patient was Everyman, and claimed that the human ego was through and through narcissistic. He embarked on the countertransferential venture of making psychoanalysis into a system in the metaphysical sense, and welcomed into his system the work of philosophers apparently opposed to Descartes, such as Hegel and Heidegger, using them in such a way as to bring out their latent solidarity with the Cartesian tradition. Denouncing the living Cartesianism of phenomenology, he took from it everything he could use. He invested deeply, fatally, in the retrenched rationalism of the linguistic structuralists. He misread Freud as someone who, if structuralism had been available to him, would have embraced its abstract taxonomies as the answer to his dreams, when Freud would no doubt have preferred a good Greek myth, an anthropological speculation about prehistory, or a play by Shakespeare. As a result of these instances of mismanagement, Lacan himself now stands in the way of terminating his own case. To cure Cartesian rationalism, we must terminate its analyst.

To me the word "postmodernism" gathers up a related set of beliefs about how things stand just now in the most consequential debates among intellectuals: rationalism having failed to pan out, we must all get along without Enlightenment desirables such as a decisive philosophical argument, or, better yet, truths so good that they do not require argument, self-evident truths, or versions of the same thing in moral and political thought, such as natural justice or inalienable rights; we must rethink in this light everything from the intellectual history of our nation to the need for a new paradigm in the humanities and sciences; as we proceed with caution in this task, we must be especially careful of reaffirming in a self-deceived way the tradition we want to discard, since rationalism has a demonstrated penchant for resurrection. As a postmodernist in this sense, I have been attacking the popular assumption that someone with postmodern sympathies who also wants to do psychoanalytic literary criticism should as a matter of course, on the grounds of common sense, work in the name of Lacan or the movement he inspired. Most of that work is on another road altogether. It leads straight back to the bogs and mires of philosophy. It is a logophallocentric, nostalgic countertransference to rationalism, a marked regression from Freud's prescient distaste for philosophy. It encourages us to preserve unearned postures

of mastery that have hurt us enough already. For the time being, we ought really to return to Freud, and leave Lacan behind, remembering him as the exorcist who identified with the demon. (pp. 997-1007)

William Kerrigan, "Terminating Lacan," in South Atlantic Quarterly, *Vol. 88, No. 4, Fall, 1989, pp. 993-1008.*

John Sturrock   (essay date 26 March 1992)

[*In the following excerpt, Sturrock assesses the stylistic differences between the "malicious complications" of Lacan's prose and the more lucid articulations of his transcribed seminars.*]

Sessions with Dr Jacques Lacan were famously short, but none I dare say as short as mine. We met professionally not as doctor and patient, but as author and editor, and over the telephone, voice to voice. Newly taken on at the *TLS,* I was the one appointed to give Lacan the bad news, that an article he had been commissioned to write could not be used. He had sent in an absurdly knotted French text which had been turned by a translator into a blankly unmeaning English one, and it was not thought sensible for the paper to publish something that none of its editors could understand. Lacan was incensed at knowing that he had been spiked, on what to him seemed insultingly practical grounds. He thought it was enough that his name should be on the piece for it to have to be published, I that unintelligibility was a ground for rejection, irrespective of whose unintelligibility it was. Since the disputed article was not echt-Lacan but only Lacan in translation, the argument from authorship was strong but not irresistibly so: the article did not appear.

This two-minute dialogue of the deaf was nothing much as Lacan stories go, for no one was ever more generative of good gossip than that dazzlingly rude and fissile man; but it serves to raise the question which is slow to die in the case of Lacan, of how far we should feel obliged to go in order to understand him. At the time when he was asked to write in the *TLS,* he was known outside France— and outside the psychoanalytical profession to which he had long stood in the relation of charismatic Other—only through the *Ecrits,* the large volume of his theoretical papers that had been published in 1966. With the *Ecrits,* the claim was that Freud had finally been brought to France, and that France would have now, as Lacan himself might have franglicised it, to *faire bye-bye* to a smug and superannuated Cartesianism for which the idea of an unconscious mind was a contradiction in terms. But whether they were pure Freudianism or no, the *Ecrits* nowhere read with the benign clarity of Freud, but rather as the work of an inordinately subtle concettist whose warped syntax and cultural presumption seemed designed to separate those who read him into the two mutually impermeable classes of worshippers and dropouts. Only later did those of us who dropped out discover that the *Ecrits* were Lacan at his most obstructively difficult, and that we should have paused over the title he gave to that book: writings were what it contained, not speakings, and when he wrote Lacan believed that he should complicate his prose to the point where it stands in illustration of the riddling discourse the psychoanalyst hears when he is at work.

In the consulting-room the Lacanian analyst is hired to elicit 'the discourse of the hysteric', which is the old Free Association by another name and the more liberating in its effects the wilder it can be brought to be, the function of the analyst being to 'hystericise' a patient's discourse artificially. In the *Ecrits* Lacan seems to have combined the two roles and 'hystericised' his own discourse, crossing the method of the analyst with the madness of the patient, and giving free rein to the verbal promptings of his unconscious—so proving on the page his most celebrated dictum, that 'the unconscious is structured like a language.' But there is a counterfeiter at work here. Lacan was nothing if not magisterial and quite implausible when arguing as he did that we fantasise if we imagine ourselves to be masters of our own discourse because as users of language we come willy-nilly under the impersonal empire of the Signifier, which makes greater or lesser hysterics of us all. According to Lacan, once conscripted into the Symbolic Order of language we no longer function as gratifying wholes but as subjects divided, the unconscious mind being bound to have its say in collaboration with the conscious whenever we write or speak. But if the Speaking Subject can but go blindly ahead, signifying freely, the Writing Subject is in a different case, because he or she—or better, it—can go back over what has been written, to give greater order to it. To go back over it like Lacan in an opposite intention, to make it harder for others to understand, merely suggests that his discourse had proved over-lucid and insufficiently hysterical first time around. As the ventriloquist of the unconscious, Lacan is a consummate performer; but so arrogant in the demands he makes on the intelligence of his readers as to lead one to reject the rationale of what he is up to; readers of the *Ecrits* have habitually felt more taunted by them than taught.

It was and remains a relief to turn from the malicious complications of the written Lacan and meet with him in the spoken version, as he is contained in the volumes of his *Séminaires.* In these are to be found the transcripts of the annual courses of lectures which he gave in Paris from 1953 almost up until his death, in 1981. As a lecturer, Lacan drew the crowds because he entertained them, his caustic digressions, his polemics, his erudite ad-libbing, along with the assurance and wonderful energy of his psychological theorising, having made him into a star metropolitan turn. Allusive and acrobatic of mind though he still was on these oral occasions, he used them to exercise his pedagogical cure with a certain responsibility, coming back again and again to the repertoire of key axioms or concepts around which his grand theoretical design should be seen to turn, and explicating and expanding on them to the point where they make consistent and impressive sense. It is usually possible to follow Lacan and surprisingly often to enjoy him in the *Séminaires,* the public performer being more congenial and instructive than the oracular author of the *Ecrits.* (p. 22)

John Sturrock, "Above the Consulting-Room,"

in London Review of Books, *Vol. 14, No. 6, March 26, 1992, pp. 22-3.*

FURTHER READING

Bibliography

Clark, Michael. *Jacques Lacan: An Annotated Bibliography.* 2 vols. New York: Garland Publishing, 1988.
> Extensive bibliography which "lists and describes works by and about Jacques Lacan published in French, English, and seven other languages including Japanese and Russian."

Biography

Clément, Catherine. *The Lives and Legends of Jacques Lacan.* Translated by Arthur Goldhammer. New York: Columbia University Press, 1983, 225 p.
> An attempt, according to Clément, "to go beyond the life and death of [Lacan] and treat him as I always experienced him, as a shaman, a sorcerer possessed by a poetic inspiration—which he was at least as much as he was the unbending founder of a new psychoanalytic theory."

Criticism

Bär, Eugen S. "The Language of the Unconscious according to Jacques Lacan." *Semiotica* III, No. 3 (1971): 241-68.
> Sympathetically discusses Lacan's "linguistic model of unconscious processes" but adversely criticizes his prose style, arguing that "the reader, like a student of Socrates, is left feeling that Lacan is right, without knowing precisely what it is he is right about."

——. "Understanding Lacan." In *Psychoanalysis and Contemporary Science: An Annual of Integrative and Interdisciplinary Studies, Volume III,* pp 473-544, edited by Leo Goldberger and Victor H. Rosen. New York: International Universities Press, 1974.
> Discusses Lacan's use of structural linguistics and explains the necessary failure of attempts to draw "a strict correspondence between linguistic data or processes and those of psychology, sociology, and anthropology."

Bird, John. "Jacques Lacan—The French Freud?" *Radical Philosophy,* No. 30 (Spring 1982): 7-14.
> Presents the main themes of Lacan's work, concluding that Lacan had "much *less* to say than might appear to be the case" and that "Freud had already said all that is important in Lacan in a far more accessible form."

Bruss, Neal H. "Re-Stirring the Waters, or The Voice That Sees the World as Patients." *The Massachusetts Review* XX, No. 2 (Summer 1979): 337-54.
> Reviews *Ecrits: A Selection* and *The Four Fundamental Concepts of Psychoanalysis,* offering an overview of Lacan's thought. Bruss states that "virtually all of Lacan's papers are militant efforts to epitomize the meaning of Freud."

——. "Lacan and Literature: Imaginary Objects and Social Order." *The Massachusetts Review* XXII, No. 1 (Spring 1981): 62-92.

Summarizes Lacan's major ideas and interprets passages from Homer's *The Iliad,* Marcel Proust's *Remembrance of Things Past,* Shakespeare's *Hamlet,* Frank Herbert's *Dune,* and a fifteenth-century book of Muslim poetry, *The Kabir Book,* according to Lacan's notions of the Imaginary, the Symbolic, and the Real.

Carroll, Noël. "Lacan and the Construction of the Subject." In his *Mystifying Movies: Fads and Fallacies in Contemporary Film Theory,* pp. 62-73. New York: Columbia University Press, 1988.

Finds deficiencies in the logic Lacan used to formulate his notions of the Imaginary, the Symbolic, and subject construction.

Evans, Martha Noel. "Introduction to Jacques Lacan's Lecture: 'The Neurotic's Individual Myth'." *The Psychoanalytic Quarterly* XLVIII, No. 3 (1979): 386-404.

Analyzes Lacan's 1953 lecture "The Neurotic's Individual Myth," which addresses the mirror phase and the Oedipus complex and "serves as an especially valuable preliminary to Lacan's special reading of Freud."

Felman, Shoshana. "Turning the Screw of Interpretation." *Yale French Studies,* Nos. 55-56 (1977): 94-207.

Employs Lacan's theories in an analysis of Henry James's *The Turn of the Screw,* demonstrating the implications for literary study of Lacan's theories.

———. "Lacan's Psychoanalysis, or The Figure in the Screen." *October,* No. 45 (Summer 1988): 97-108.

Discusses the broadcast and published forms of Lacan's *Television,* examining how he "invites us not to take 'the little screen' for granted, but to rethink through it, provocatively, his complex structure of address."

Fisher, David James. "Lacan's Ambiguous Impact on Contemporary French Psychoanalysis." *Contemporary French Civilization* VI, Nos. 1-2 (Fall-Winter 1981-82): 89-114.

Examines the nature of Lacan's contribution to Freudian theory and the extent of his influence on French psychoanalysis.

Kurzweil, Edith. "Jacques Lacan: French Freud." *Theory and Society* 10, No. 3 (May 1981): 419-38.

Discusses the evolution of Lacan's thought and the specific responses it has engendered in other psychoanalysts.

Lavers, Annette. "Some Aspects of Language in the Work of Jacques Lacan." *Semiotica* III, No. 3 (1971): 269-79.

Discusses the importance of structuralism and linguistics in Lacan's work, focusing on Lacan's interpretations of key passages from Freud's work.

Leavy, Stanley A. "The Significance of Jacques Lacan." *The Psychoanalytic Quarterly* XLVI, No. 2 (1977): 201-19.

Presents an overview of Lacan's ideas from the perspective of a practicing psychoanalyst.

Lemaire, Anika. *Jacques Lacan.* Boston: Routledge & Kegan Paul, 1977, 266 p.

Examination of Lacan's thought which includes a preface by Lacan.

Lyotard, Jean-François. "The Dream-Work Does Not Think." *The Oxford Literary Review* 6, No. 1 (1983): 3-34.

Discusses Lacan's notion of metaphor in relation to Freud's theories on dreams.

Macey, David. "Fragments of an Analysis: Lacan in Context." *Radical Philosophy,* No. 35 (Autumn 1983): 1-9.

Closely examines several essays from the original French edition of *Ecrits* and discusses Lacan's doctoral thesis.

McCauley, Karen A. "Lacan and Questions of Desire in Psychosis and Feminine Sexuality." *Literature and Psychology* XXXVII, No. 4 (1991): 47-62.

Discusses concepts presented in Lacan's 1955-56 seminar on psychosis with the aim of demonstrating "how Lacan's relatively early work on psychosis contains the embryonic outlines of his later analytic, and certainly more polemical, thoughts on feminine sexuality."

McKenna, Ross. "Jacques Lacan: An Introduction." *The Journal of the British Society for Phenomenology* 7, No. 3 (October 1976): 189-97.

Examines the main points in Lacan's theories, addressing the mirror stage, the Imaginary, the Symbolic, and the Real, as well as Lacan's debts to Ferdinand de Saussure.

Miel, Jan. "Jacques Lacan and the Structure of the Unconscious." *Yale French Studies,* Nos. 36-37 (1966): 104-11.

Discusses Lacan's disputes with the psychoanalytic establishment and the importance of language in his conception of the unconscious.

MLN, Special Series. 98, No. 5 (December 1983).

Includes a collection of essays by various scholars that examine Lacan's theories in relation to literary narration.

Montag, Warren. "Marxism and Psychoanalysis: The Impossible Encounter." *The Minnesota Review* 23 (Fall 1984): 70-85.

Relies heavily on the ideas of Lacan in an attempt to determine how—according to Marxist thought and psychoanalytic theory—ideology and the unconscious interact in the individual.

Muller, John P. "Ego and Subject in Lacan." *The Psychoanalytic Review* 69, No. 2 (Summer 1982): 234-40.

Examines Lacan's concept of the ego and the extent to which he was influenced by G. W. F. Hegel's phenomenology.

Mykyta, Larysa. "Lacan, Literature, and the Look: Woman in the Eye of Psychoanalysis." *SubStance,* No. 39 (1983): 49-57.

Examines Lacanian theory from a feminist perspective "in order to illuminate women's enigmatic position and function in psychoanalytic theory." Mykyta focuses on the dynamics of speaking and seeing, finding both acts masculine in nature.

Ragland-Sullivan, Ellie. "Explicating Jacques Lacan: An Overview." *University of Hartford Studies in Literature* 11, No. 2 (1979): 140-56.

Introduction to Lacan's major ideas which includes discussions of Lacan's published works and the implications of his theories for literary study.

Richardson, William J. "Lacan's View of Language and

Being." *The Psychoanalytic Review* 69, No. 2 (Summer 1982): 229-33.

> Discusses the importance of language and "the role of the social milieu" in the formation of the personality.

Roudinesco, Elisabeth. *Jacques Lacan and Company: A History of Psychoanalysis in France, 1925-1985.* Translated by Jeffrey Mehlman. Chicago: University of Chicago Press, 1990, 766 p.

> Chronicles the development of psychoanalysis in France with particular attention to the role of Lacan.

Roussel, Jean. "Introduction to Jacques Lacan." *New Left Review,* No. 51 (September-October 1968): 63-70.

> Discusses Lacan's three basic orders of consciousness: the Real, the Imaginary, and the Symbolic.

Schneiderman, Stuart. "Afloat with Jacques Lacan." *Diacritics* I, No. 2 (Winter 1971): 27-34.

> Former member of Lacan's Ecole Freudienne provides an overview of Lacan's theories, comparing them with those of Sigmund Freud, Jacques Derrida, Martin Heidegger, and others.

——. "The Most Controversial Freudian since Freud." *Psychology Today* 11, No. 11 (April 1978): 50-9.

> Introduction to Lacan's theories and career.

——. *Jacques Lacan: The Death of an Intellectual Hero.* Cambridge: Harvard University Press, 1983, 182 p.

> Recounts the experience of studying under and being psychoanalyzed by Lacan and provides an introduction to Lacan's thought.

Scott, Charles E. "The Pathology of the Father's Rule: Lacan and the Symbolic Order." *Thought* 61, No. 240 (March 1986): 118-30.

> Criticizes Lacan's conceptions of language, the Symbolic, and the name-of-the-father from a perspective influenced by Jacques Derrida and Martin Heidegger.

Silverman, Kaja. "The Subject: The Lacanian Model." In her *The Subject of Semiotics,* pp. 149-93. New York: Oxford University Press, 1983.

> Account of Lacan's theory of subject construction focusing on his three registers of consciousness: the Imaginary, the Symbolic, and the Real.

Staten, Henry. "The Difference between Lacan and Derrida." *Western Humanities Review* XLV, No. 2 (Summer 1991): 98-109.

> Compares and contrasts Lacan's idea of the phallus with Derrida's notion of *différance,* concluding in part that, despite similarities, the use of these concepts indicates that "Lacan is *trying* to talk about the real world, whereas Derrida thinks there is no real world."

Wright, Elizabeth. "Another Look at Lacan and Literary Criticism." *New Literary History* 19, No. 3 (Spring 1988): 617-27.

> Discusses the influence of Lacanian psychoanalysis on literary criticism and suggests that the work of philosophers Gilles Deleuze and Félix Guattari points the way toward a post-Lacanian critical method.

Additional coverage of Lacan's life and career is contained in the following source published by Gale Research: *Contemporary Authors,* Vols. 104 [obituary], 121.

John Patrick Shanley

1950-

American playwright, scriptwriter, and film and stage director.

The following entry provides an overview of Shanley's career through 1992.

INTRODUCTION

Shanley is best known as the author of *Moonstruck,* for which he won an Academy Award and Writers Guild of America Award for best screenplay in 1988. His movies and plays are usually set in New York City and frequently feature eccentric working- or middle-class characters from various ethnic backgrounds. Shanley's works are especially praised for their insightful depictions of sexual intimacy and abuse, alienation, infidelity, and unrequited love.

The youngest child of devout Irish Catholics, Shanley was born and raised in the Bronx, New York. He was an avid reader and began writing poetry at age eleven. After being expelled from several different parochial schools, he was sent to a private academy in New Hampshire. Shanley briefly attended college before enlisting in the United States Marines. Following two years of service, he resumed his studies and graduated from New York University as class valedictorian. After beginning work on a master's degree in drama, Shanley left school, worked a series of odd jobs, and eventually pursued a literary career. His earliest plays, *Rockaway* and *Welcome to the Moon,* both produced in 1982, achieved little success, and Shanley did not attract critical acclaim until the 1984 premiere of *Danny and the Deep Blue Sea: An Apache Dance.*

Danny and the Deep Blue Sea focuses on individuals attempting to overcome their feelings of loneliness. Set in a New York City bar, the play delineates the romantic relationship that develops between a boxer and a young woman who was sexually abused by her father. His best-known drama is *Italian American Reconciliation,* which is set in New York's Little Italy and which, with its effective use of dialect, provides a realistic portrait of a highly individualized ethnic group. In this play Shanley documents one man's endeavors to reunite with his embittered ex-wife and the efforts of his girlfriend and best friend to prevent such a reconciliation.

Moonstruck, Shanley's first screenplay, caricatures New York's Italian community. A whimsical tale of romance and adultery, the script centers on the recently engaged Loretta Castorini and her growing love for her fiancé's brother, a one-handed baker. The movie's plot revolves around the conflicts that arise among family members as Loretta tries to confront her guilt, desires, and obligations as a woman in a patriarchal society; her moral crisis is heightened when she is forced to recognize her parents' own faults and infidelities. Pauline Kael praised *Moonstruck* as "an opera buffa in which the arias are the lines the characters deliver, in their harshly musical Brooklyn rhythms. . . . And when you see that the whole cast of family members are involved in libidinal confusions the operatic structure can make you feel close to deliriously happy."

In subsequent screenplays Shanley explores several new themes. Set in the Bronx during the turbulent 1960s, *Five Corners* examines social and political activism, rape, murder, and child and drug abuse. Critics have praised the film as an insightful commentary on the nature of violence in America. Also set in New York, *The January Man* follows a nonconformist cop's search for a serial killer. Ostensibly a mystery, *The January Man* has been faulted for overambitiously trying to comment on the problems of sibling rivalry, betrayal, sexual revenge, and political corruption. *Joe Versus the Volcano,* which Shanley also directed, is a lighthearted fantasy that depicts one man's growth from an insecure hypochondriac to an individual who learns to take personal and emotional risks.

PRINCIPAL WORKS

Rockaway (drama) 1982
Welcome to the Moon (drama) 1982
Danny and the Deep Blue Sea: An Apache Dance (drama) 1984
Savage in Limbo (drama) 1985
The Dreamer Examines His Pillow: A Heterosexual Homily (drama) 1985
Women of Manhattan (drama) 1986
Italian American Reconciliation (drama) 1987
Moonstruck (screenplay) 1987
Five Corners (screenplay) 1988
The January Man (screenplay) 1989
The Big Funk: A Casual Play or Talk around the Polis (drama) 1990
*Joe Versus the Volcano (screenplay) 1990
Alive (Screen play) 1993

*This movie was also directed by Shanley.

CRITICISM

Mel Gussow (review date 14 October 1982)

[*An American drama critic, Gussow has written a biography of film producer Darryl F. Zanuck and has won numerous awards for his drama and art criticism. In the following excerpt, he offers a negative assessment of* Rockaway.]

The time is 1957 and the scene is a rundown bar in Rockaway. The whisky is cheap—and so is the sentiment. John Patrick Shanley's **Rockaway** is a commonplace situation comedy about the triumph of good will.

Blackie the bartender sums up the play's pennyworth philosophy by saying, "People are grand and the world's a joke." That line and the character could have been borrowed from William Saroyan's *The Time of Your Life,* except for the fact that in this neophyte effort, Mr. Shanley is far from a Saroyan.

The story has to do with a doctor who has told a patient she has six months to live. The patient sells her family bar to her barkeep and embarks on a high-spending world tour. When the diagnosis proves incorrect, she is miserable and she declares war on the malpracticing physician. By the end of the evening, the two dedicated enemies are suddenly planning a course of connubial bliss.

Such unmotivated switches are characteristic of **Rockaway.** A young woman who has told a cold-blooded local Lothario, "I'm not goin' anywhere wi' choo, ya goofball," eats her unappetizing words the instant he says, "I love you." And the bartender, who has been battling for the entire evening to keep his establishment, casually gives it back to its original owner simply because someone points out that as a socialist he is miscast in the role of owner. . . . As a bar play, **Rockaway** is bonded in blather.

Mel Gussow, " 'Rockaway' by John Patrick Shanley," in The New York Times, *October 14, 1982, p. C15.*

Frank Rich (review date 24 November 1982)

[*Rich is an American editor and performing arts critic. In the following excerpt, he offers a negative assessment of* Welcome to the Moon.]

"It's a relief to say things, even if they are sophomoric," says one of the many young lovers in John Patrick Shanley's **Welcome to the Moon.** No doubt that's true for the person who's doing the talking, but what about those who have to listen? In this collection of eleven playlets . . . , Mr. Shanley says many sophomoric things, and, however relieved he may feel by evening's end, the audience is bored silly.

The brief sketches of **Welcome to the Moon** are each written in ostensibly different idioms, but, . . . they all seem identical. Over and over, a few lost young strangers stroll on a bare stage, and, a few whimsical lines later, reach out to each other (or to someone just offstage) for love.

Among the settings are the Wild West, World War II-era New York, Tennessee Williams country, a contemporary singles bar, the Bronx, Central Park Lake at 2 A.M. and a Runyonesque gangsterland. What makes the characters blur together is that they all tend to use the same buzz words ("lonely," "dreams," "moon," "suicide attempt") and arrive at the same epiphany about the saving powers of romance. Though only the opening sketch involves a high-school couple, everyone seems permanently frozen at the emotional age of 16.

Mr. Shanley dresses up his material with many pretentions—ersatz poetry, wan stabs at literary pastiche, fairytale conceits—but his parade of old-fashioned, sentimental endings makes one wonder if he is trying to write compressed parodies of the entire oeuvre of William Inge. The endings are never earned, in any case, and there is little energy or pungency to the dialogue. The author seems to feel that the conciseness of his chosen format is a style in itself: though he uses words sparely, he doesn't bother to choose or shape them precisely.

Frank Rich, in a review of "Welcome to the Moon," in The New York Times, *November 24, 1982, p. C14.*

John Beaufort (review date 18 June 1984)

[*An American film, theater, and arts critic, Beaufort is a member of the New York Drama Critics Circle, the New York Drama Forum Association, and the Critics Circle of London. In the following excerpt, he provides a mixed review of* Danny and the Deep Blue Sea.]

Notwithstanding its rough language and recurrent violence, *Danny and the Deep Blue Sea* could be described as soft-core realism. John Patrick Shanley's new play . . . is subtitled: "An Apache Dance." The program helpfully defines this as "a violent dance for two people, originated by Parisian Apaches," who are "gangsters or ruffians."

Since the long-titled, short work (three scenes without intermission) takes place in the Bronx, the alienated Shanley characters can be taken as Bronx Apaches. Their aggressions bristling, Roberta and Danny perform their first verbal pas de deux in a gloomy bar. Danny is a belligerent bruiser who fears he may have killed a man in his latest brawl. Roberta is guilt-haunted by an incestuous incident involving her father. As the night wanes, the lonely pair discover a romantic tenderness that transforms their lives and induces at least a degree [of] maturity.

Or so Mr. Shanley would have the spectator believe. The dialogue unfolds in an authentic flow that reflects the author's familiarity with the street jargon of his native Bronx.

The action possesses the spontaneity of an impromptu. In some respects it resembles a workshop improvisation that developed into a play rather than a script that received its professional première at the Actors Theatre of Louisville. For all of its groping eloquence, psychological probings, and wry comic touches, *Danny and the Deep Blue Sea* winds up being less than five fathoms deep.

> *John Beaufort, in a review of "Danny and the Deep Blue Sea," in* The Christian Science Monitor, *June 18, 1984, p. 22.*

Edith Oliver   (review date 7 October 1985)

[*In the following excerpt, Oliver offers a mixed assessment of* Savage in Limbo *and finds loneliness the play's predominant theme.*]

[John Patrick Shanley's *Savage in Limbo*] was first done as a staged reading at the O'Neill Playwrights Conference, at Waterford, Connecticut, and I acted as a kind of adviser during rehearsals. Now it is billed as a "concert play," and in a program note Mr. Shanley writes, "In a concert play the audience . . . is included in the world which the characters inhabit. And the play itself is more a series of related emotional and intellectual events than a conventional story." The "Savage" of the title is one Denise Savage, a woman of thirty-two, who announces in a bar in the Bronx that she is a virgin—to the astonishment of the patrons and the bartender. "What's it like?" asks one of them. "I feel you know something I don't know." All those present, we soon find out, are the same age and went to the same parochial school. There is Murk, the bartender; April White, his crazy girlfriend, who sleeps on the bar and dreams of Christmas and Santa Claus; Linda Rotunda, whose boyfriend has suddenly lost interest in her; and Tony Aronica, the boyfriend himself. The underlying theme is loneliness, which has devastated April, looms over and terrifies Savage, and now suddenly threatens Linda and, perhaps, Tony. All of them are desperate, although Savage's desperation is the most acute, and all of them spend a good deal of time trying to express the inexpressible, often at the top of their lungs.

These characters, as I say, talk a lot, in a rough language that seems appropriate, but time and again I felt I heard the playwright speaking. Unlike Ring Lardner, say, or John O'Hara, Mr. Shanley cannot quite conceal his own hand in the lines, or, for that matter, in the events; and one is also aware that the events are "made up." Nevertheless, many of the lines are funny and shrewd, and the characters are certainly actable.. . . . (pp. 110-11)

> *Edith Oliver, "Noise in the Bronx," in* The New Yorker, *Vol. LXI, No. 33, October 7, 1985, pp. 110-11.*

Dan Sullivan   (review date 5 February 1986)

[*Sullivan is an American journalist, music reporter, and drama critic. In the following excerpt, he provides a positive review of* Danny and the Deep Blue Sea.]

He's 29 and brutal. She's 31 and needy. They meet, clash, go to bed, share their secrets (he's afraid he killed a guy last night; she can't get over a sexual experience with her father) and start to heal one another.

That's the ground plan in *Danny and the Deep Blue Sea* . . . , a 90-minute mood play that playwright John Patrick Shanley might easily have placed on Philco Theater or Studio One back in the golden days of live TV.

The sex and the rough language would have been a problem, but Danny and Roberta are very much the kind of lovers that Marty and his girlfriend were—groping for the words to express the big feelings they are having.

They also might remind you of Rocky and Adrian. "I lock horns with *anybody*!" roars Danny, known to the guys at work as The Beast. "You got a nice nose," chirps Roberta, the battered gamin. "It looks at you and says hello."

Being street people, they go from one emotion to the other as quick as lightning. Even from one mental level to another. Sometimes Danny seems retarded, and Roberta pretty smart. Sometimes Roberta seems the out-of-it one, Danny the on-the-ball one.

We are pleased when Danny starts to soften and Roberta learns to trust. Two little people finding each other in the dark—only a cynic would knock it. But underneath we're aware that, in the real world, which *Danny* is supposed to be a transcript of, people don't start spilling their inmost secrets within 10 minutes of meeting one another—especially not wary people like Danny and Roberta.

In the end it's a wouldn't-it-be-nice play. Wouldn't it be nice if we could heal our scars this easily? Wouldn't it be nice if one night with the right stranger could turn our lives around? Yes, it would, and taken as a modern fairy tale, *Danny* has charm. . . .

Danny's an adorable pug, not a stolid brute. Roberta's a smudged waif, not a desperate neurotic. There's no danger that these characters will make any claims on us. We're dealing with lovable stereotypes who know their place. . . .

It's all so familiar that some will confuse it with life.

Dan Sullivan, "Boy Meets Girl in 'Deep Blue Sea'," in Los Angeles Times, *February 5, 1986, p. 4.*

John Simon   (review date 20 October 1986)

[*An American essayist and critic, Simon has served as a drama critic for* New York *magazine as well as a film critic for* Esquire *and the* New Leader. *In the following excerpt, he examines Shanley's use of language in* The Dreamer Examines His Pillow.]

You would expect the worst, wouldn't you, from a play called *the dreamer examines his pillow,* which caps its decapitalized title with the subtitle "A Heterosexual Homily"? But you'd be wrong. John Patrick Shanley's three-character play . . . is all talk, but much of it of high quality: pungent, thought-provoking, original, poetic in both the good and bad senses, and leading by stylized, fantasticated ways to genuinely startling illuminations.

Tommy, a ne'er-do-well on whom Donna, his girl, has walked out, sits in his terminally shabby apartment and apostrophizes his antiquated refrigerator containing nothing but beer. Refrigerator, young man, and dilapidated recliner in which he sits seem to be slowly decomposing. Enter Donna, furious, ostensibly to stop Tommy from screwing around with her sixteen-year-old sister, but groaning under a huge hidden agenda, hidden even from herself. They remonstrate, argue, fight, and analyze themselves and each other into a stupor.

In the second scene, Donna seeks out her dad, whom she hates, loves, and besieges with questions. A painter who became very successful, Dad stopped painting at the death of his wife, whom he bullied, betrayed, and destroyed out of—yes—love. Now he just sits, drinks, and sneers. Donna wants answers about who she was and is, and also wants Dad to force Tommy to marry her: "I want you to beat him up till his head is ringing like a bell. Will you do this for me, Dad?" The scene is an orgy of reciprocal revelation. In the third scene . . . but enough of that.

The language gushes forth in great gobs of sense and absurdity, but absurdity with its own slanted, devious sense. Though this language is an uneasy mixture of the plebeian and the elevated, it does—when it doesn't take pratfalls—work. The characters have a way of sounding discomfitingly alike, but that, it turns out, is one of the points. There are impressive lines galore: "God is bigger and more rotten than you know"; "People don't usually part with their weird shit, because they know it's too easy to punch holes in it"; (concerning reproduction) "It was the first time sex went dead for me—when I found out what it was for"; and "I saw all women bald. I was deceived by hair. So I shaved them clean as a hardball." And many, many more, interwoven into a glinting tissue of tenderness and obscenity, pain and promise of redemption. Shanley is least persuasive in his arias about the raptures of sex; most when he lets his characters have at one another and themselves in torrents of rage and despair, sarcasm and sudden epipha-

ny. Funny or moving, the play is a consistent challenge. (p. 106)

John Simon, "By the Beautiful Sea," in New York *Magazine, Vol. 19, No. 41, October 20, 1986, pp. 104, 106.*

Edith Oliver   (review date 20 October 1986)

[*In the following excerpt, Oliver briefly summarizes the plot of* The Dreamer Examines His Pillow *and praises Shanley's use of humor.*]

John Patrick Shanley's *the dreamer examines his pillow* (the lowercase title doesn't mean much of anything), . . . was first produced last year, as a staged reading at the O'Neill Playwrights Conference, where I work as a kind of adviser. If Mr. Shanley has made any changes in his script, I failed to detect them. The play is composed of three conversations in three scenes. The first conversation is between two lovers, [Donna and Tommy], who broke up some time ago but are obviously still deeply attracted to each other. She enters his basement room in a rage, because she has heard that he is sleeping with her teen-aged sister, and tries to make him promise to quit, which he refuses to do. The second is between Donna and her father, whom she visits to demand that he beat Tommy up. The father, a painter who has done nothing but sit and drink since the death of his wife, is a complex, combative, and very funny character; he is in no mood to be drafted as an indignant parent, but changes his mind after an emotional and affecting scene with Donna. The third is between the father and Tommy, and it is full of surprises. Mr. Shanley is a born playwright, if not a born self-disciplinarian. Too many patches of guff get in the way of his strong, often witty lines; his seriousness may be suspect, but there is no question about his sharp, original humor.

Edith Oliver, in a review of "The Dreamer Examines His Pillow," in The New Yorker, *Vol. LXII, No. 35, October 20, 1986, p. 105.*

David Ansen   (review date 21 December 1987)

[*In the following excerpt, Ansen offers a positive assessment of* Moonstruck.]

Opening with Dean Martin's "That's Amore," *Moonstruck* lets you know it knows it's going to revel in—and tease—every Italian-American stereotype in the book. A family-style roundelay of inappropriate passions, transpiring under the magical influence of a full moon, the tale focuses on Brooklyn bookkeeper Loretta, a no-nonsense widow with lowered romantic expectations who agrees to marry the steady, uninspiring [Johnny]. But while he's off in Sicily tending to his dying mother, she meets—and beds—her fiancé's tormented younger brother, a hot-blooded baker with a wooden hand and a passion for opera. Appalled by her inappropriate lust, Loretta agrees to one final date—to see *La Bohème* at the Met—where she discovers her father with *his* secret tootsie. Meanwhile, her worldly-wise mother is being courted by a skirt-chasing NYU professor, her aunt and uncle are rediscovering their own passion and her Old World grandfather is trying to make sense of the bewildering *opera buffa* transpiring under his roof.

Inventively written, wittily scored and seductively photographed, *Moonstruck* is enchanting, mock-operatic fluff, marred only by its occasional need to push its "heartwarmingness" (beware the moon motif). . . . Underneath *Moonstruck*'s gossamer artifice, you hear the beating of real hearts.

> *David Ansen, "When the Moon Hits Your Eye," in* Newsweek, *Vol. CX, No. 25, December 21, 1987, p. 69.*

Pauline Kael   (review date 25 January 1988)

[*A highly respected American film critic, Kael is the author of* I Lost It at the Movies *(1965);* The Citizen Kane Book *(1971);* Deeper into Movies *(1973), for which she won a National Book Award; and* Reeling *(1976). In describing her philosophy of film criticism, Kael said: "I try to use my initial responses (which I think are probably my deepest and most honest ones) to explore not only what a movie means to me, but what it may mean to others: to get at the many ways in which movies, by affecting us on sensual and primitive levels, are a supremely pleasurable—and dangerous—art form." In the following excerpt, Kael provides a positive assessment of* Moonstruck.]

[*Moonstruck* focuses on] Loretta, a widowed bookkeeper in her late thirties, who lives with her Italian-American family in a big old brownstone in Brooklyn. Doing the levelheaded thing, she accepts the marriage proposal of a timid dullard, a bachelor in his forties, and, when he has to fly to Palermo, she does what he asks: she invites his estranged younger brother, a baker, to come to the wedding. Up to that point, you may not be sure how to take the flat-out, slightly zonked dialogue.

Moonstruck is an opera buffa in which the arias are the lines the characters deliver, in their harshly musical Brooklyn rhythms. Looking as if he's in a sick trance, the baker tells Loretta he's in love with her; she has just been to bed with him, but when she hears this she slaps him two quick whacks and says, "Snap out of it!" In her dry way, she's more irrational than he is. And when you see that the whole cast of family members are involved in libidinal confusions the operatic structure can make you feel close to deliriously happy.

Working from a script by John Patrick Shanley, the director, Norman Jewison, doesn't go for charm; he goes for dizzy charm. And that's what wins you over. . . . [They have] blended a slapstick temperament with the pleasures that the synthetic elements in American movies used to give us. And so you get such counterpoint as the baker, whose thought processes are primeval, telling Loretta about the accident that turned him against his brother, and Loretta calmly explaining what happened, in a parody of Freudian explanations that's pure bughouse. . . . [The] picture has a warm, fluky dazzle. Its originality is that the mockery doesn't destroy the overblown romanticism—it intensifies it.

This is ethnic comedy, but it's not noisy or monotonous. . . . And Shanley's theatrical artifice works, partly because he accepts the characters as comic stereotypes—he doesn't try to give them depth—and partly because the actors love their lines, and, as characters, they can flaunt the excessiveness of their emotions. These characters make comedy turns out of everything they do.

Moonstruck is slender, and at times it's a little too proud of its quaintness. When the characters raise their champagne glasses in a toast "To family!" you may dimly recognize that this picture could become a holiday perennial. But you're probably grinning anyway, because the toast has a flipped-out quality. *Moonstruck* isn't heartfelt; it's an honest contrivance—the mockery is a giddy homage to our desire for grand passion. With its own special lushness, it's a rose-tinted black comedy. (pp. 99-100)

> *Pauline Kael, "Loony Fugue," in* The New Yorker, *Vol. LXIII, No. 49, January 25, 1988, pp. 99-100.*

David Ansen   (review date 25 January 1988)

[*In the following excerpt, Ansen praises* Five Corners *for its portrayal of American violence and descriptions of life in the Bronx during the 1960s.*]

Good screenwriting, it's always said, never calls attention to itself. Dialogue, it follows, should never sound written. This may be useful advice, but it's also hogwash—a rule that was made for talented writers to break. Playwright-turned-screenwriter John Patrick Shanley clearly does not subscribe to the invisible-author theory. His distinctive voice can be clearly heard in two recent scripts—first in the mock-operatic romanticism of *Moonstruck* and now in the unexpected comic quirks of *Five Corners*. This modestly scaled movie, which covers 36 hours in the year 1964 in a lower-middle-class Bronx neighborhood, is far from perfect, but it contains a dozen characters capable at any moment of taking you by surprise. Shanley isn't afraid to take chances—mixing artifice and realism, switching tones and styles in midstream, bouncing from whimsy to melodrama. He'd rather give you too much than too little, and when his gambles pay off you find yourself delighted in original ways.

This is not a generic view of the '60s. Shanley's idiosyncratic Bronx is a place where a high-school algebra teacher is shot dead with a bow and arrow, penguins get pummeled and thrill seekers ride on top of elevator cars to the accompaniment of "Lakmé." *Five Corners* is a seriocomic meditation on American violence seen through the prism of a half-dozen blue-collar kids in the dawning era of the civil-rights movement. The key figure is Harry, the son of a murdered cop, who has been inspired by Martin Luther King Jr. to take up nonviolent activism. He's hoping, when the summer ends, to join the Freedom Riders in Mississippi. His opposite number is Heinz, a hulking psychopath just released from prison for the attempted rape of a neighborhood girl, Linda. When the looming Heinz reappears, Linda turns to the beefy Harry for protection, driving her skinny boyfriend Jimmy wild with jealousy. Harry saved her before, back in his brawling "caveman" days, but now that he's a born-again idealist he'd rather tell Heinz he loves him than fight.

Woven into this damsel-in-distress story are several other strands: two glue-sniffing girls out on the town in pursuit of thrills and two singular cops on the trail of the dead algebra teacher's killer. . . . *Five Corners* bops along in its unexpected, oddball way, always on the edge of farce and danger. Unfortunately, Shanley feels compelled to bring events to a rip-roaring melodramatic conclusion, and the climax gets out of hand. You can see he's making a point about the inevitable collision between Harry's nonviolent ideals and Heinz's irrational savagery, but he's forcing his theme into a form more appropriate to *King Kong*. Still, check this one out: even when *Five Corners* misfires, it does so boldly, with a craziness it can call its own.

> David Ansen, "Fort Apache, the Bronx," in Newsweek, *Vol. CXI, No. 4, January 25, 1988, p. 69.*

[Shanley's] characters confront alienation, betrayal, guilt and love. The keenly observed street-tough dialogue has a vivid realism, but a strong poetic streak and humor are also scattered throughout scenes of heartbreaking poignance.

—Polly Roberts, "Stages of Life: Bard of the Bronx," in Harper's Bazaar, February 1988.

Charles Champlin   (review date 5 March 1988)

[*The host of the Public Broadcasting System's "Film Odyssey," Champlin is an American film critic, journalist, and educator. In the following excerpt, he praises Shanley's ability to evoke time, place, and a personal narrative voice in* Five Corners.]

John Patrick Shanley, the author of **Moonstruck,** which seems as nearly as perfect a script ever gets (in terms of defining and realizing its romantic, comedic intention), is these days also represented on the screen by another of his works, **Five Corners. . . .**

Five Corners is linked with **Moonstruck** by its New York setting and by Shanley's genius for conveying the way the people of that peculiar place live and think, feel, act and talk (or *tawk* or *tork,* as the case may be).

It is a more personal, daring, ambitious and tentative work. At a guess, it was written earlier. It has much more the impressionist feeling of a film envisioned as a film, less the feeling, which **Moonstruck** has, of being a succession of set-piece scenes, theatrically shaped.

The film is a mixture of the remembered realities of growing up in the Five Corners section of the Bronx in 1964, enriched by what might well be remembered daydreams

presented as reality (a hated algebra teacher is felled by an arrow, a villain is thwarted by a later arrow, as in a dream of narrow escapes and happy endings).

The reminiscences hang from a hard narrative line of melodrama. One of the old neighborhood crowd, a wacko loner comes home from prison to pursue his obsessive courting of . . . the girl in the pet store. (p. 1)

Beyond the melodrama, **Five Corners** is fundamentally about coming of age in a time of change—change that affected the whole country but nowhere more dramatically than the Bronx.

There the older ethnic patterns of working-class and lower-middle-class Jews, Irish and Italians co-existing in seldom perfect harmony were to be sundered and reconstituted by the expansion of Harlem and Spanish Harlem.

Shanley is recollecting the old neighborhood as it was before wedding bells and everything else conspired to break up that old gang of his and made Five Corners some other place.

In the film, Martin Luther King Jr. is all over the television, and one of Shanley's characters—perhaps his alter ego . . . —is an idealistic and courageous young man who wants to go off and join the civil rights movement.

It involves a kind of hazing by humiliation to test his sincerity, but there's no doubt he is riding the wave of the future. There is also no doubt, although it is understated, that social change, positive in the longer run, will bring its own tensions and dislocations to the neighborhood.

Much of the neighborhood, in fact, simply no longer exists. [The director] shot in Astoria Park, Queens, which still looks as Five Corners did a quarter-century ago.

By its nature, diffused and documentary, ranged between serious comedy and farcical tragedy (Momma gets thrown from a window), **Five Corners** is unlikely to command the mass audiences of **Moonstruck.** Yet it is original, unpredictable and capturing.

The linking strength of both films is the power of the personal voice, Shanley's, saying this is how things are, or were, and probably will be. (pp. 1, 7)

The familiar moral, as of all film stories, is that it all begins on the scripted page. (p. 7)

> Charles Champlin, " 'Five Corners' Knows Its Place and Has Its Say about It," in Los Angeles Times, *March 5, 1988, pp. 1, 7.*

John Simon   (review date 14 November 1988)

[*In the following excerpt, Simon provides a mixed review of* Italian American Reconciliation, *applauding the vitality of the drama while faulting the second act as contrived and awkward.*]

Italian American Reconciliation is a small play, though that in itself is no drawback. Most of John Patrick Shanley's works have smallness built into them, so that the clash of two to four characters can reverberate to its heart's content or discontent. The play concerns Huey

Maximilian Bonfigliano, who, still depressed three years after his divorce from Janice, wants to come to terms with it by talking and sleeping with her at least once more. No easy project, for Janice tried to shoot him, and definitely shot his dog. Then there is his likewise Italian-American buddy Aldo Scalicki (which sounds more like Polish), a man obsessed with his mother and devoted to Huey; this suggests homosexual overtones, but Shanley won't pursue such leads.

Aldo agrees to woo and soften up Janice for Huey until the melancholy ex arrives to claim his *jus ultimae noctis.* But Huey has a waitress girlfriend, Teresa, whom the neighborhood considers (rightly) more loving and lovely than Janice; still, Huey is prepared to sacrifice her for one more shot (not of the dog-killing kind) at Janice. Aldo drops by the souphouse where Teresa works. She has just been telling her Aunt May that she is tired of Huey and about to send him packing, when Aldo informs her of Huey's imminent coming to give her her liberty, whereupon she becomes so enraged and enamored as to resolve to keep her lover. Aldo promises to seduce Janice himself, and so save Huey for Teresa. Thus far the first, better, act.

This act is heartwarmingly zany. From the very start, when Aldo chats up the audience with sweet and wry talk while also announcing that tonight is special because his mother is attending, things proceed bouncily and giddily along a gibbously cobblestoned road. Huey is comically weird, Aldo weirdly comic; together, they spell wacky mayhem. "Why should your life mean anything? *My* life doesn't mean anything." "In many ways, Teresa is better than Janice. I mean, if you put them both on television, she'd get better ratings." "Takes a woman with big feelings to kill a man's dog." There's no loss of jollity when the scene shifts to the souphouse. "Do you really love him?" Aunt May asks Teresa. "Yeah—to the best of my knowledge." And: "I've got feelings, you know. I've got pride and a s—load of other things, too." When Aldo joins the two women, the existential small talk plumbs comic depths.

Alas, in Act Two, which begins with a neo-Cyranesque balcony scene for Aldo and Janice, things bog down under a load of other things. One applauds the author's self-proclaimed attempt to digest his divorce from his first wife, but one would prefer to applaud his writing. Here Shanley rather grandly rediscovers psychoanalysis, but whereas old-fashioned crazies have a comic glow, it is hard to get a sentimental comedy out of grinding neurosis: Janice is too realistically hysterical, and Aldo's attempts to seduce her are too steeped in self-pity. "That guy is another example of why I should become a nun," Janice moans. . . . "I have a very full and real fantasy life," Aldo declares in an oxymoron that, at least as delivered, is almost too sad to be funny. Yet Shanley's way with excess still intermittently scores: "There was a time when women stuck to men till the ship went down and there were no more bubbles." By the time Huey appears, Aldo has indeed, however circuitously, softened up—or worn down—Janice.

The last scene, set at the souphouse, really lands in the soup. Teresa is gone to Canada; May (who, a trifle myste-riously, takes over as waitress) and the men cannot generate enough heat. There are still funny moments ("Oedipus didn't mean to marry his mother, but he did." "That's true. But Oedipus really did have exceptionally bad luck"), but Shanley doesn't know how to conclude and stumbles over ending after ending without finding a graceful way to let go. (p. 103)

But there is a raciness, a joy in hyperbole, a savoring of the juices of living, that makes *Italian American Reconciliation* a tasty enough pizza, though a bit bottom-heavy on the crust. (p. 104)

> *John Simon, "Puccini without Music," in* New York *Magazine, Vol. 21, No. 45, November 14, 1988, pp. 103-04.*

Mimi Kramer   (review date 14 November 1988)

[*In the following excerpt, Kramer likens* Italian American Reconciliation *to* Moonstruck *and characterizes it as "a pretty story," but faults its depictions of women as superficial.*]

[*Italian American Reconciliation*] is John Patrick Shanley's latest offbeat comedy about the difficulty of finding love and married bliss in an imperfect world. Set in Little Italy, and directed by the author himself, it completes Mr. Shanley's semi-autobiographical tetralogy about love and loneliness and the war between men and women. . . . (p. 121)

Today Shanley is best known as the author of *Moonstruck,* but before he was a hot young screenwriter he was a hip young playwright: our premier poet of singles anxiety. His plays mixed raw, searing emotions with sitcom tendencies. Rough-hewn, they tended to put college-bred ideas into the mouths of blue-collar street toughs and to be full of lost, solitary young people. They juxtaposed psychological acuity with incredibly young-seeming moments of self-conscious whimsicality. They had a pretentious streak a mile wide, but they were very, very funny. Shanley has the gift of gab. He writes wonderful Runyonesque dialogue—a sort of gritty, downtown version of sparkling drawing-room comedy—and highly rhetorical speeches that are fun to hear, because actors love to perform them.

The current play, which takes the form of a flashback—a story, Aldo tells us, with which he means to "teach" us something—concerns Aldo's best friend, Huey, and the time Aldo tried to prevent him from going back to his ferocious ex-wife, Janice. Aldo feels, on the whole, that Teresa, the perfectly nice waitress Huey has been seeing, is better for him than Janice, who shot Huey's dog. He nevertheless agrees to act as an emissary and pave the way for a midnight reconciliation between Huey and Janice—planning, all the while, to save Huey by going after Janice himself.

Dogs, midnight reckonings, stolen women—at times *Italian American Reconciliation* seems to be patched together from whatever of *Moonstruck* wound up on the cutting-room floor. Nearly every element in the movie has a counterpart in the play—from the plot (the idea of a diplomatic mission gone awry) to the bits of Puccini and schlock music with which Shanley tries to achieve an ironic distance from what is essentially a hip version of a gothic romance. Not that the play isn't funny and entertaining: like all Shanley's urban fairy tales, it has charm and a certain theatrical elegance. In the past, though, his whimsical premises have been vehicles for the dramatic exploration of an idea. *Italian American Reconciliation* doesn't really tell us anything. Like *Moonstruck,* it's just a pretty story. . . .

Shanley might at least have set up a great confrontation. But nothing of any import is revealed in the climactic scene between Aldo and Janice. It isn't enough for us to discover that Janice's abuse of Huey was an attempt to make him really "look at" her, that a desire for someone to "take charge" of her "like a man" lurks behind her fierceness, that her hatred of men stems from an unsatisfying relationship with her late father. These are Hollywood clichés. (p. 122)

[Before Shanley] was a hot young screenwriter he was a hip young playwright: our premier poet of singles anxiety. His plays mixed raw, searing emotions with sitcom tendencies. Rough-hewn, they tended to put college-bred ideas into the mouths of blue-collar street toughs and to be full of lost, solitary young people.

—*Mimi Kramer*

[In *Italian American Reconciliation* Shanley] had three things to unify: the idealized relationships between Aldo and Janice, between Janice and Huey, and between Aldo and the audience. But there's no connection between the pat moral that concludes the evening—"The greatest, the only, success is to be able to love"—and the story that purports to illustrate it; no consistency between Huey's avowal to Janice—"If I have to go back to the beginning, right or wrong, and win you again . . . I am willing"—and his announcement the next day that, with Janice's ghost laid to rest, he's now ready to go off in pursuit of Teresa, whom he really loves. The moral would appear to be that women are interchangeable. Perhaps Janice was right to be fierce.

If Shanley's play is disappointing, that's partly because it's so vague on the subject of women. Not that plays have to be "about" women, but women have always been Shanley's strong suit. He is genuinely interested in them, in the same way that he's captivated by Little Italy, and possibly for the same reason: he seems to find us shabby but charming. Ordinarily, that combination makes for good theatre, and at a time when almost no one was writing interesting parts for women Shanley was. It may be that he has run out of ideas about us. If so, I hope this is only a temporary condition and the result of married bliss. (p. 123)

Mimi Kramer, "Divorce Italian Style," in The

New Yorker, *Vol. LXIV, No. 39, November 14, 1988, pp. 121-23.*

Brian D. Johnson   (review date 23 January 1989)

[*In the following excerpt, Johnson argues that Shanley's desire to include a variety of themes, subplots, and numerous literary and cinematic devices in* The January Man *undermines the film's effectiveness.*]

The combination sounds irresistible. *The January Man* is based on an original script by New York City's John Patrick Shanley, who won an Oscar last year for *Moonstruck.* . . . [But] *The January Man* falls short of its promise.

Shanley's script plays a teasing game of hide-and-seek with cinematic convention. Flirting with comedy, mystery and romance, it avoids making a commitment to any of them. The story starts with the murder of a young woman as she returns to her Manhattan apartment on New Year's Eve—the latest target of a serial killer who has strangled a new victim in each of the past 11 months. Although New York City's homicide rate produces a murder about every five hours, the strangler's steady output seems to have struck a sensitive chord with the city's jaded populace. As public hysteria mounts, the mayor is literally screaming for an arrest. Apparently, the only person capable of cracking the case is a brilliant but eccentric ex-cop named Nick, the estranged brother of the police commissioner, Frank, who is married to Nick's former love, Christine.

Under pressure from the mayor, Frank reluctantly reinstates his brother into the force. Nick, now happily working as a fireman, accepts the assignment—hoping to rekindle his romance with Christine. As Nick sets up camp at police headquarters, his unorthodox methods put the precinct captain in a rage: he moves in with a stereo system, a talking parrot and an artist who treats the office as his studio. Nick's investigation leads him to the mayor's daughter, Bernadette, who was with the strangler's last victim on the night she was murdered. They waste no time falling in love. "I don't want to ask you a lot of pushy questions," Nick tells her, "because I want you to like me." Meanwhile, guided by quirks of mathematics and astrology, he closes in on a killer who is just slightly crazier than he is.

Like Nick's investigation, Shanley's story unfolds with a sense of serendipity. An iconoclast who seems bent on having it both ways, the screenwriter sabotages cinematic conventions even as he uses them. On the night before Nick's attempt to ambush the strangler, Bernadette reassuringly tells him, "We'll go to bed and then we'll sleep, and tomorrow after a good breakfast you'll catch the killer and save the girl." Shanley cannot resist the impulse to deflate dramatic tension: irony and sincerity keep cancelling each other out. That can result in flashes of fine comedy—including a memorable fight scene. . . . But behind all the narrative sleight of hand and off-kilter dialogue, the story never finds its footing.

Like an overly ambitious juggler, Shanley has thrown up too many balls without enough concern for where they might land. A number of plot tangents spin off into nowhere, including an intrigue about a cancelled cheque that has something to do with police corruption. And the romantic subplot involving [Christine] is especially ill-fated. . . .

Above all, *The January Man* is an artifact of New York—although it was mostly filmed in Toronto. Like Shanley's two previous movies, *Moonstruck* and *5 Corners,* it deals with the strangely provincial quality of life in America's largest city, from the romance of meeting in Central Park to the idiosyncrasies of a serial killer. Shanley, a native New Yorker, displays the sort of bemused affection for Manhattan that Woody Allen features in his work. And the movie's gargoyle-like city officials, looking for scapegoats and villains to feed a frenzied media corps, recall Tom Wolfe's satiric novel of New York City, *The Bonfire of the Vanities.*

However, *The January Man* tries to be too clever. . . . Too often, the characters seem like marionettes designed to show off the writer's dexterity. Shanley has quickly acquired a reputation for invincibility. Insisting that no one rewrite his work, he has defied industry traditions and created a unique place for himself in the Hollywood sun. But *The January Man's* script cries out for a little judicious tampering. After the triumph of *Moonstruck,* the screen's hottest new writer seems to be suffering from a touch of sunstroke.

> Brian D. Johnson, "Manhattan Mayhem," in Maclean's Magazine, *Vol. 102, No. 4, January 23, 1989, p. 45.*

John Morrone (review date 23 January 1989)

[*In the following excerpt, Morrone argues that Shanley's focus in* The January Man *is not on the development of a murder mystery but the examination of middle-class individuals who have become corrupted by political ambition.*]

In the prologue to *The January Man,* two fashionable young women, dressed to the nines for New Year's Eve, step sleekly into their cars and are driven away. [Bernadette] purrs contentedly to the chauffeur, "Gracie Mansion, please." The other heads home, to a posh but more modest address, and is promptly murdered upon arrival. The identity of the victim goes largely undiscussed throughout the film, other than that she is the best friend of the survivor, who turns out to be the daughter of an Irish-American mayor of New York named Eamon Flynn. . . .

Mayor Flynn and his up-from-the-ranks commissioner of police, Frank Starkey, are facing political heat because the murder of Bernadette's friend has hit too close and is too much before the public. "Miss December," as I'll call her, was the 11th in a series of unsolved "blue-ribbon" strangling murders begun almost a year before. To avoid the possibility of a 12th corpse in January, the Mayor, Frank and a retrothinking, pasta-gutted precinct captain, Alcoa, are forced to bite a very hard biscotto: to hire back to the force the Commissioner's gifted brother Nick, a "Beatnik"

ex-cop marking time in the Fire Department who just might crack the case. Nick isn't exactly thrilled. Flynn once made him the scapegoat in a bribery scandal concocted to protect Frank. Now the brothers are barely on speaking terms, and their working together is further made unpalatable because of a woman they have shared. Christine, a gal with patrician ambitions, ditched Nick for his power-mongering brother and still has the paperwork that could prove Frank actually took the bribe. . . .

Shanley, a playwright, became last year's most visible new screenwriting talent for his disarming treatments of Italian and Irish neighborhood neuroses in *Moonstruck* and *Five Corners.* But trapping a serial killer sits most uneasily upon the volatile social fabric he has created here. His intention, apparently, was to enrich the stale police-procedural plot while setting the characters' personal conflicts in motion, but the result is a dissipation rather than a heightening of suspense. Since Shanley shows little interest in the killer (who at the end is apprehended and dismissed with amazing dispatch), we don't either.

What, however, is he trying to say about this bunch of working-class blokes who have sold out by climbing the political ladder, or have flaked out by becoming the vivacious socialite or the underappreciated genius? As Shanley has it, if you haven't entered public service for personal advancement, you concentrate on private pursuits. (When not grubby from fire fighting, Nick practices a particularly indigestible style of cuisine and talks art and economic injustice with his neighbor, . . . the crankiest of nonconformists.)

You may be tempted to dismiss the film as "All in the Family" dressed up like *Serpico.* Rarely have I seen the duplicity of civil servants so linked with their middle-class ethnicity. . . .

Though on the outskirts of the story, the most revealing character is Christine. Dressed WASPily in a severe black sheath dress, a plain string of pearls and far too much hairspray . . . she looks simply terrible knowing she's wed the wrong man, the wrong class, the wrong way of life. The film telegraphs what a dumb move this was (Nick baldly asks her, "How can you sleep with him after you've been with me?"—and, frankly, we're inclined to agree). How Christine will resolve the frustration induced by her greed, and what she will do with the bribery evidence, are practically the only sparks of suspense in *The January Man.* Of course, both questions are tangential to the plot, but if this is a thriller, so is *Abie's Irish Rose.*

> John Morrone, "Patrician Ambitions," in The New Leader, *Vol. LXXII, No. 2, January 23, 1989, p. 23.*

Charles Champlin (review date 9 February 1989)

[*In the following excerpt, Champlin praises Shanley's use of dialogue and creation of bizarre characters in* The January Man, *finding the film's strengths characteristic of Shanley's work.*]

One of the East Coast film observers has announced that the makers of *The January Man* can now relax. Theirs is no longer the worst movie of 1989, he said. *Her Alibi . . .* has taken its place at the bottom of the barrel. (p. 1)

What is true, as has been attested by the East Coast critic and many others, is that *The January Man* contains plot holes of immense size, has astonishing inconsistencies of tone and attack and leaves a curious general impression that the next time they'll get it right.

But what is also true is that even in its artifices and its incoherences, *The January Man* does offer those laughs and some quite beguiling performances, even if you do leave the theater whistling, "What was *that* all about?"

The most interesting thing about *January Man* is that it is the third film written by John Patrick Shanley. *Five Corners,* loosely inspired by his boyhood in the Bronx in the 1950s, was quirky, original and not very successful. *Moonstruck* was quirky, original and, of course, hugely successful with (most) critics and audiences. (Shanley won an Oscar for original screenplay.)

January Man is nothing if not quirky and original. It is not a rousing success, to say the least of it, but it offers a chance to triangulate on Shanley.

The three scripts are clearly the work of the same idiosyncratic imagination. They have a consistency that, like it or not, is uncommon in film work—or has been since Preston Sturges departed.

Shanley appears to have a unique line on magical Eastern urban realism, a variant of the magical realism found mostly in contemporary Latin-American writers. It is an often paradoxical blending of the observed and the imagined, verisimilitude and wild fancy.

In *Five Corners,* Shanley gave us the unlovely reality of Bronx streets plus a kidnaped penguin, a true psychopath and victims killed by bows and arrows by other persons whose presence was never quite satisfactorily explained. (pp. 1-2)

Weird, all of it, although you could see that a certain amount of less-than-wonderful social truth was being diluted, so to speak, by the improbable, mildly fantastical imaginings.

So it was in *Moonstruck,* which was called *Moonstruck* for good reason. That old mythic moon was left over from Eugene O'Neill and several centuries' worth of predecessors. The realities of the city streets, double-entry bookkeeping and a sweatshop bakery were ameliorated by characters with one foot in farce and the other on the rim of tragedy.

What *Moonstruck* proved beyond argument was that Shanley has a rare gift for dialogue. I'm not sure that an *ear* for dialogue is the way to say it. Real speech rarely has the economy, the timing, the polish that Shanley gives his talk. Like the dialogue in John O'Hara's best short stories, it is a simulation, but the disguise is perfect.

Shanley also has a dramatist's feeling for scenes—scenes with beginnings, middles and exits. They're his building blocks, and . . . they gave *Moonstruck* an odd sense of orderliness, no matter how zany the goings-on got to be.

With *The January Man,* you do get the feeling that there is a great cutting-room in the sky someplace where all the missing exposition can be found. The back story never got out of the back room and there are moments when watching *January Man* is like trying to follow the third episode of a miniseries mystery after you've missed the first two. It doesn't matter a great deal, you tell yourself, but what *was* that business about the check?

Shanley has evidently watched or read a bunch of mysteries himself and taken umbrage at the dazzling intuitions by which the sleuth perceives the pattern that produces the villain. [The protagonist's] tracking of a serial killer is the reduction to absurdity of all such intuitions, deriving the pattern from the moon, a constellation, a song title and mathematics—and discovering a killer who doesn't look as if he could find his way to a subway station.

The Shanley gifts for wonderful dialogue and for inventing characters who are poised somewhere between the abnormal and the bizarre remain intact in *January Man.* (pp. 2-3)

Like the two earlier films, *January Man* is full of what the Elizabethan poets called *conceits,* small, glittering and unexpected inventions: wonderful if they work, rather dismal when, as happens here, they don't. For example, [the hero] likes to cook meals of repellent unattractiveness for the women he loves, I guess as a test of their faith. But it is a notion that falls flatter than a diseased scrod. . . .

[With *January Man* you] are left with some genuine laughter, with a renewed awareness that Shanley is a special and considerable talent, and with an equally renewed feeling that nobody wins 'em all. (p. 3)

> *Charles Champlin, "Getting Acquainted with 'January Man',"* in Los Angeles Times, *February 9, 1989, pp. 1-3.*

John Patrick Shanley with *American Film* (interview date September 1989)

[*In the following excerpt, Shanley discusses his decision to write professionally, the creative process, and his work as a playwright, screenwriter, and director.*]

[*American Film*]: *What brought you to writing?*

[Shanley]: Well, I was always a writer. I wrote poetry from the time I was 11 years old. I was looking for an art form that was satisfying and, when I stumbled onto playwriting at NYU, that was pretty exciting. I realized that I had found a social life and that I wasn't going to have to stay in my room for the rest of my life, which frightened the daylights out of me. Also, just being a poet and going to parties and meeting other people who were poets made me decide that I didn't want to be a poet anymore. [Laughter] Poets are a rather dour lot. But when you're a playwright, which is very similar to being a screenwriter, it's a collaborative effort that begins with you. Screenwriting provides that—and also provides a lot of cash at the same time.

You've said in the past that you decided to write your first screenplay for the money—that you had finally started making a living as a playwright. . . .

Just barely. I'd made enough money from a play called *Danny and the Deep Blue Sea* to survive in New York City for a year. And I realized then—I'd made a living painting people's apartments—I was going to be back painting apartments. It's very hard to do that and write, because it's enervating work. So I decided to write a screenplay.

When you were making this decision, were you looking at films, were you looking at screenplays?

Oh yeah, I looked at films, and I got hold of some screenplays. I wanted fresh screenplays; I didn't want a screenplay from 20 years ago, because I found that the things that were done 20 years ago don't help me. They may be totally great, but they don't help me to understand how I, as somebody existing now, would do something. So I read 10 screenplays, just completely willy-nilly. One of the 10 screenplays was called *Scarface*, by Oliver Stone. And as I read this, I started laughing because I thought it was very silly—the prose was so purple. Stone had all this stuff about this guy standing at the head of the boat, his black hair blowing in the wind, his heroic face twisted by his anger against the injustice that happens to every man. And I'm, like, How can the guy write this? [Laughter] How can he do it? And then I thought about it, and I said, You know, you're looking at this like it was something you picked up in the store to read, like a novel. Think of this as an image. Would you buy it? I said, Yes, I'd buy it immediately if you didn't ask me to say it out loud.

And I realized that in order to write an effective screenplay, you have to have no distance from your material. You have to be in the scene with the characters. You cannot be cynical, you cannot be removed, you cannot be in a place where you think you know more than they know. Emotionally, you have to respect your characters and you have to be there with them. And also, after all is said and done, there *are* heroes in the world. If you point the camera at somebody real, or somebody's spirit you recognize as real, and say, this person is a hero—that's a heroic thing for you to do.

The idea of looking at things from a critic's point of view when you're writing is disastrous. You have to go in and be a fool, a true believer. You have to find a solid place in yourself to stand on—a single vantage, a value system from which you can view the world. If the ground underneath you is shifting, the movie will have no point of view.

Whatever you do in terms of telling a story, the most important thing that you can define is who you are. The stories are all out there; it's finding a place where *you* are in relationship to the story that will tell the story.

After you decided to write a screenplay to make money, how did you come to write **Five Corners,** *a script without a central character?*

Well, that's the tragedy of being an individual. I discovered a long time ago that I can't write anything that I can't write. I could write a screenplay, but I couldn't write what popular wisdom said was a commercial screenplay. And when I finished it, I said, My God, it doesn't have a main character, I'm in big trouble, nobody's going to want to do this. The first person I showed it to said, "You've just blown it." And the second person I showed it to said, "I want to make this film." Which goes to show you.

The only thing you can do is be true to yourself, because then, even if nobody wants to make this film, you can sleep at night. It's like marrying somebody. You are, like, wonderful to this person, you know? You take her out on these great dates, and you have these wonderful dinners. But you know you are bullshitting this person: You are not showing her your true face and that, in fact, some of the things this person does are enraging you, but you haven't told her that. And, in fact, you're not as you have presented yourself to be. And this person, at least to the best of your understanding—loves you, but the person that she loves is a lie. So, even though you've gotten this person to love you, it doesn't mean anything to you because it's not *you* that she loves.

If you write a movie and everybody loves it but you know it's a big lie, who cares whether you get a lot of accolades or you get a lot of money? You have got to protect your ability to work and to live by being true to yourself.

I did a panel discussion a couple of years ago, with, I guess, six of us onstage. This one guy, who was, like, the head of a movie company, made this statement about how the first thing that he asked anybody when they brought him a project was, Why would anybody besides you want to see this movie? And I said that if I went into this guy's office and he said that to me, I would tell him to go fuck himself. [Laughter] That is a really hostile statement designed to put me on the defensive and has absolutely nothing to do with the merit of [a screenplay] on any level, commercial, artistic or anything else. It ain't necessarily my job to explain how to market this thing, how to build it, whether or not he should do it. That's his decision to make, but to put the onus on you to tell him what this thing is. . . . I don't think you necessarily have to buy into it. If it's good, somebody's going to want to do it, and it'll be much more likely to be good if you were true to yourself when you did it.

How do you approach writing a screenplay?

I write a lot. I've written a lot of plays and a few movies now, and the more you write, the more it helps you to write more clearly. Also, the pain of having to redo it starts to teach you where those big mistakes are. The biggest mistake that you can make is to wander in the first 10 pages and then start to get going. The first five pages of the script are the world—you establish all of the physical laws of the world that you are going to inhabit for the rest of the film. So it's really nice to spend a lot of time cultivating in yourself the reality of that specific world. What are the colors, what are the smells, what does it look like? Who are the people, and where would be, to you, a cinematic place to begin? And then take your time and outline just three scenes ahead. And know, if you can, the end of the movie, because you will have that in the back of your head, and it will show up in the structure that all along you aimed toward that. Now, if you structure it too much, if you outline all the way through, then it gets mechanistic, and you lose your ability to be off-the-cuff, where a lot of your best stuff comes from.

What happens in the collaborative process? How much do you change the finished screenplay based on ideas from others?

The best people in a collaboration are the people who look over at somebody else and say, "You be the hero." The job of everybody in a collaboration is to have the best idea in the room, unattached to an ego. If it's not your idea, recognize it and say, "That's the best idea." When I sat down with Norman [Jewison] to go through the [*Moonstruck*] script, we read it aloud. We acted out the entire movie together. He wanted to hear me read it, and he wanted to understand the humor of it. We share a similar sense of humor, basically, about death. If you go back and really look at *Moonstruck,* all they talk about is death, through the whole film. And both Norman and I think this is very funny for some reason, so we had a lot of good laughs over that and we hooked up on that level. (pp. 20, 23)

With **Joe Versus the Volcano,** *the film you're currently working on, you've joined the ranks of playwrights who have crossed over to filmmaking as writer-directors. How would you say your education in the theater has prepared you for filmmaking?*

Well, one of the things about having a lot of time in theater is, you spend a lot of nights hearing audience reaction, night after night. And you get a sense of what plays and what doesn't, and a sense of pace. When I was in theater, I discovered something that there was no way I could have known, and that is, when I revealed the innermost depths of my worst pain, the audience was on the floor. They just thought that was hilarious. I had no idea that I was going to get this reaction. So I think screenplays are very good to read with an audience. You may think you have a tragedy and the audience will be on the floor, and you should know that as soon as possible.

When did you decide that you wanted to direct?

I did a 20-minute, 16mm film about a year ago, called *I Am Angry,* which was an interesting experience and one that I enjoyed very much. And I came out of it saying, I like directing films. It's very relaxing, which really puzzled the shit out of lots of people who knew more about it than I did.

The film [*Joe Versus the Volcano*] that I happen to be making my directorial debut with—and I would not have chosen it this way—is a huge picture. I mean, it's not *Moonstruck.* It takes place over half the world, and it has typhoons and volcanoes and mythical cultures and extended aquatic sequences and animals. It's unbelievable.

The way that I got this job was not by clawing my way to the top. I was minding my own business, and I got a phone call. It says, "Steven Spielberg is calling. Hold on for Steven Spielberg, hold on." "Hello, John, this is Steven Spielberg." I said, "Hello, it's nice to talk to you." He says, "I just read this movie you wrote, *Joe Versus the Volcano,* and I think it's terrific." I said, "Well, thank you." He says, "I want to make it." I said, "Great!" He

said, "I understand that you want to direct it." And I said, I swear, I said, no different than this: "Uhh, yeah." He said, "Great! I think it's a great idea." That's how I got the job. [Laughter] So now, I've been living in a hotel room because of this conversation.

Why did you write this story?

This particular thing is about a guy who's a terrible hypochondriac. He's diagnosed as having a terminal illness, and this puts him in a very good mood [laughter] and sets his life in motion for the first time in several years because he's finally been released from the thing that had him in its thrall—the fear. And I wrote the film because I was having unbelievable hypochondriacal feelings. I was at the edge of the grave. I was in the tomb looking up, and I had to . . . I write about whatever my problems are. So I sat down and I said, I can't go on like this. I have to find a way to solve this phobic attack that will probably lead to my having to ask the question, Why am I having this experience? Why do I have these feelings?

You have to find a way to solve the problems of your own life. That's why you're here. And if you want to do something, if you see a guy starving on the street, or if you see a man you would like to kiss, or if you see that things are getting very aesthetically ugly around you, that people are building ugly houses all around you, whatever it is, you might sit down and spend some time thinking. What should I do about this? Maybe there's a movie in this, and maybe it'll be a good movie. If you really do it passionately, it'll probably be funny. And it may also be moving. If you try to write a movie while reading the mind of somebody else, you're not going to have any passion in it, and it's just going to be a hollow effort.

> **Whatever you do in terms of telling a story, the most important thing that you can define is who you are. The stories are all out there; it's finding a place where *you* are in relationship to the story that will tell the story.**
>
> —*John Patrick Shanley*

Is your work important to you?

Yes, very. My work has saved my life. It has revealed to me that everything that I knew when I was a child is true. And that we are in the grip of enormous powers and beauty beyond our comprehension. I think that our whole culture has been generated in a vain attempt to stop the incredible influx of beauty that was overwhelming us and making us so humble.

It seems like everything you've been writing, you've been writing on celluloid. Does that, in the back of your mind, affect what you choose to write next—because it'll probably get made?

I have made the attempt to write each thing [as if] it would never get made. When I wrote *Five Corners,* I didn't say, I hope this never gets made. But I said, I don't care, I'm going to write this, and I'm going to see the movie when I write it so at least I'll have seen the movie that I want to see. And then with *Moonstruck,* it was pretty much the same way. *The January Man,* I don't particularly remember. I just wanted to try it. I wanted to try this form. I read a bunch of murder mysteries and stuff, and I wanted to say something, so I decided to get into it.

Then I wrote *Joe Versus the Volcano,* and I remember very clearly reading that aloud to a group of playwrights, and they really enjoyed it and said, "Oh, that'll make a great movie." And I said—and I meant it—"I don't think anybody's ever going to make this movie." Because it was so big, it just required such production value. They're usually looking for something that's not that expensive to do, not that hard to do.

I was talking to the marketing guy for Warner Bros., and he had been at some vendor thing in Las Vegas. He's telling me, "I went down there, and they said, 'So, Joel, what're you doing?' And I said, 'Well, we're doing a movie called *Batman.*' 'I love that movie; we want that movie.' I said, 'We're also doing a movie called *Joe Versus the Volcano.*' They said, 'Joel, what kinda *farchachdah* title is that? What kind of *farchachdah* movie is that? Who's in it?' 'Tom Hanks.' 'I love that movie.' [Laughter] And I have written another film that I haven't shown anybody, which I feel confident nobody will make. But my dreams have been dashed before. [Laughter] Yes, sir. (p. 24)

> *John Patrick Shanley and* American Film, *in an interview in* American Film, *Vol. XIV, No. 10, September, 1989, pp. 20, 23-4.*

Brian D. Johnson   (review date 19 March 1990)

[*In the following excerpt, Johnson praises the campy and fantastical aspects of* Joe Versus the Volcano.]

It begins with "once upon a time" and ends with "happily ever after." *Joe Versus the Volcano* is a lavish fairy tale for grown-ups that snaps together two far-flung territories of American moviemaking—the quirky imagination of New York City's John Patrick Shanley and the Hollywood might of Steven Spielberg. Shanley is the screenwriter who won an Oscar for *Moonstruck,* 1987's offbeat romantic comedy about star-crossed lovers in Brooklyn. Spielberg is the Midas behind such on-beat mega-hits as *E. T. The Extra-Terrestrial* and the *Indiana Jones* trilogy. The first three movies that Shanley scripted—*Five Corners, Moonstruck* and *January Man*—never strayed from the writer's home turf, his idiosyncratic version of New York. But with *Joe Versus the Volcano,* which marks his feature directing debut, Shanley does not just leave town. Using executive producer Spielberg as his travel agent, he escapes to a preposterous world of Kon-Tiki kitsch on a Hollywood sound stage.

Funny, frivolous and charming, *Joe Versus the Volcano* is as enjoyable—and forgettable—as a ride down the water slide in the West Edmonton Mall. As usual, Shanley's

writing is riddled with unlikely twists and turns. But, as a novice director plugging into Spielberg's dream factory, he concocts a visual universe to match the wildness of his verbal wit. It is like watching an acoustic guitarist going electric for the first time, with the volume cranked up to maximum. (p. 54)

The opening scene of *Joe Versus the Volcano* shows zombie-like hordes of dark-suited workers filing into a factory that looks like a nightmare of industrial modernism. The company is American Panascope—"home of the rectal probe" and of "50 years of petroleum jelly," according to the signs outside. Joe works as a drudge for the advertising department in the greenish pallor of buzzing, flickering fluorescent lights. Joe hates his job, his boss and himself. He feels and looks perpetually sick.

But one day, Joe's doctor informs him that he has a strange terminal disease. "You have a brain cloud," says the doctor, "a black fog of tissue running right down the centre of your brain." Told that he has just six months to live, Joe suddenly perks up. He wants to make every moment count. And a wealthy industrialist named Graynamore gives him an opportunity to do just that. Promising a bottomless expense account, Graynamore agrees to send Joe on a luxurious voyage to a fictional South Seas island named Waponi Woo. The catch: Joe must leap into the island's live volcano, as a human sacrifice to the islanders' volcano god. In return, the islanders have agreed to let Graynamore exploit a rare mineral required for the manufacture of superconductors.

That absurd premise sets the stage for an outlandish odyssey that takes Joe from New York to Los Angeles to a luxury schooner heading into a mythic world of typhoons and volcanoes. Joe encounters three women . . . —DeDe, his mousy officemate at Panascope; Angelica, a fatuous redhead who escorts him around Los Angeles in a sports car; and Patricia, a fabulous blonde who serves as his hostess on the boat. Joe's voyage is male fantasy run wild—relentless upward mobility. It starts with a shopping spree and a make-over in uptown Manhattan, all charged to the American Express Gold Card provided by his benefactor. And before it is over, he is afloat in the Pacific, staring deliriously at a full moon that almost swamps the screen.

That image is an immodest tribute to Shanley's own *Moonstruck.* But then, Joe's trip to the moon has obvious parallels to the filmmaker's own excursion from good, grey New York to the mock-tropical heart of Hollywood. After his meteoric success as a screenwriter, Shanley, now 39, says that he "no longer had to worry about making a living and paying the rent." He finally had time to ask, "What am I doing on this planet and what do I do with my limited time here?" And that question, he adds, inspired the screenplay. After writing it, he sent it to Spielberg, the Gold Card benefactor who helped make his fantasy island a reality.

The result is a campy parody of old-fashioned Hollywood art direction. The sets are built in a deliberately unreal style. The windows of the Manhattan skyline behind the Panascope factory twinkle with the colors of the rainbow. Waponi Woo's erupting volcano looks like it is made of papier-mâché. And its natives look as if they have been costumed from a fire sale at a 1950s studio warehouse. (According to Shanley's script, Waponi Woo's culture is "a mixture of Polynesian, Celtic, Hebrew and Latin influences"—the island was colonized 1,800 years ago by a Roman galley manned by Jews and Druids that got swept off course.)

Shanley created his polymorphous Polynesia—and his make-believe Manhattan—on two gigantic Hollywood sound stages, including the former site of the yellow-brick road in *The Wizard of Oz* (1939). Unlike *Oz*, *Joe Versus the Volcano* offers little in the way of magic. Instead, it features abundant wit and a stagy victory of sentiment over cynicism. . . . On the fairy-tale scaffold where Shanley's brain meets Spielberg's brawn, that is a considerable feat. (pp. 54, 57)

> *Brian D. Johnson, "Love and Lava," in* Maclean's Magazine, *Vol. 103, No. 12, March 19, 1990, pp. 54, 57.*

Terrence Rafferty   (review date 26 March 1990)

[In the following excerpt, Rafferty offers a negative review of Joe Versus the Volcano.*]*

There's a gigantic special-effects moon in John Patrick Shanley's *Joe Versus the Volcano.* It looks about ten times the size of the luminous sphere that hovered in the sky of *Moonstruck,* which was written by Shanley. . . . In the two years since that film, Shanley's sense of proportion seems to have deserted him. By the end of *Moonstruck,* all the script's excesses—the florid characterizations, the cartoon-Italian ambience, the over-the-top romanticism—made charming sense, partly because the director's dexterity helped tone down the cuteness, and partly because the movie's operatic motif created a world of sublime unreality. Everything in *Joe Versus the Volcano,* which Shanley directed from his own script, just seems too big—everything, that is, except the characters; they have quirks in place of personalities.

Joe is a depressed-looking average guy who works in the advertising department of American Panascope, a medical-supply business specializing in rectal probes and petroleum jelly. The office looks as if it hadn't been decorated—or even cleaned—since the late fifties; Joe's boss is an idiot and a bully; the coffee is undrinkable; and Joe, a world-class hypochondriac, has felt listless and unwell for the four and a half years he's worked there. A doctor tells him that he's suffering from a condition known as a "brain cloud," and has only a few months to live. Soon after he quits his job, he's approached by a wealthy businessman, who offers him a paid trip to a South Seas island so that he can end his life gloriously by leaping into an active volcano. (The businessman will derive some financial advantage from this; the details are whimsical and boring.) After stops in Manhattan and Los Angeles, Joe sets sail for the island on a yacht piloted by the businessman's daughter Patricia . . . ; a shipwreck, tropical high jinks, and a romantic happy ending ensue. The message—one of Hollywood's current favorites—is "Seize the day."

Shanley's wild, ambitious screenplay, with its abrupt changes of setting and mood, would be a challenge for a veteran director; it's much too tricky for a beginner—even one who knows exactly what the writer had in mind. As a director, Shanley doesn't serve himself very well. He overemphasizes his most fragile bits of comic invention—the drifts of dandruff on [Joe's boss's] jacket, the island natives' fondness for canned orange soda. He kills his throwaway ideas with repetition. The movie loses its tempo every time the setting shifts, and has to work up a rhythm again, so it has a lurching, manic-depressive pace. And too many important scenes, like the one with that big moon, require a kind of visual lyricism that Shanley hasn't mastered; they end up either puzzling or merely flat. Worst of all, the tone of some of the more elaborate sequences is disastrously off: Joe's office is depicted so grotesquely that the movie seems to be laughing at people who work at low-paying, dead-end jobs; the scenes in which Joe goes on a shopping spree in Manhattan look uncomfortably like advertising for expensive Madison Avenue stores. (pp. 81-2)

The actors are on their own, trying to work the oddball traits they've been given in the characters.

Shanley has a talent for weird, off-kilter dialogue, and the movie has a few bright moments. But his inspirations are much too fragile for the hard sell he gives them in *Joe Versus the Volcano.* This sort of crackpot comic fantasy works only if it's done with a light touch—in a style like Bill Forsyth's or Jonathan Demme's. It's dangerous to make too big a deal out of eccentricity. (p. 82)

> *Terrence Rafferty, in a review of "Joe Versus the Volcano," in* The New Yorker, *Vol. LXVI, No. 6, March 26, 1990, pp. 81-2.*

Mimi Kramer   (review date 24 December 1990)

[In the following excerpt, Kramer faults The Big Funk *for being a series of plotless sketches.]*

[*The Big Funk*] is the sort of play that leaves you marvelling at what some people think they can get away with. Written and directed by John Patrick Shanley, . . . the play, which has classical allusions galore and purports to tell you the meaning of life, is so incoherent. There's a setting, all right ("Place: Here. Time: Now"), and characters (they're called Jill, Fifi, Omar, Austin, and Gregory). What's missing is a plot.

The Big Funk, doubly subtitled "a casual play or talk around the Polis" (as though Shanley were afraid that someone, recognizing *The Big Funk* for what it is, might call it a poor excuse for theatre), begins with four of the five characters stepping out and introducing themselves. One, dressed like a Greek goddess, declares herself the villain of the piece. Another, dressed like a tightrope walker, tells us about her past. A third, who claims to be a knife-thrower and to be married to the woman dressed like a tightrope walker, tells us his problems. A fourth claims to be the hero of the story, and an argument about this ensues. All of which would be fine if one had never seen a play by Christopher Durang or heard of Pirandello. Actually, all of it would probably be fine, in spite of Pirandello *of psychoanalysis in France and examines some of the main points of his thought, asserting that the fragmented literature and turbulent, factious nature of recent world history are both reflected and explained in Lacan's work.*]

[In *Psychoanalytic Politics: Freud's French Revolution*, 1978, a work which describes] the explosion of psychoanalysis into French psychoanalytic, academic and popular cultures, Sherry Turkle takes as her point of departure the student revolt of May 1968. The long-standing view of France as unified, rational, and stable was no longer feasible or workable after 1968, she maintains, and one of the symptoms of the new era is the country's unexpected capitulation to psychoanalysis. Given France's sixty-year rejection of Freudian psychoanalysis, its current infatuation seems to vindicate Freud's prediction that the USA would adopt psychoanalytic concepts quickly, apply them broadly, and thus misunderstand their revolutionary nature; whereas the final battle for understanding the subversive power of psychoanalysis would be waged in France, precisely because of the strength of Gallic resistance. France owes its "conversion" to psychoanalyst Jacques Lacan.

Although Turkle's book has already aroused interest among Europe-watching audiences of socio-historians, sociologists, and some literary theorists, its major importance for literary studies in the USA is its suggestion that Anglo-American critics should seriously consider studying Lacan's thought. If Lacan's theories are even partially correct, then language itself will have to be seen as a far more dynamic, powerful and mysterious force than heretofore suspected. Rather than a static medium which one consciously manipulates, Lacan proposes that language shapes perception and identity by symbolic effects; that the structural laws of linguistics (metaphor and metonymy) work like the structural laws of the unconscious (condensation and displacement); that unconscious messages, intentionality, and identity themes adhere in conscious language use, ultimately making any purely rational, logical or objective use of language an impossibility. Thus—unlike linguists who study language in components smaller than a sentence—Lacan looks at large units of language discourse in their dialectical form of question/response, in their direction of movement and intention, and in terms of those patterns and repetitions which move at the surface of apparent linguistic clarity. Mixed into conscious verbal expression, unconscious associations and intentions destroy the illusion of linguistic transparency, rendering language itself inherently porous, opaque and plurivalent in meaning.

Turkle provides excellent and lucid summaries of the highlights of Lacan's interpretations of the contradictions in Freud's texts, but does not go into any detailed explanations of the complexities of Lacan's thought. Thus, despite the brilliant resumé of the history of psychoanalysis in France which she provides, one will remain just as mystified by Lacan's elusive theories after reading Turkle as before. Lacan's ideas run so utterly counter to entrenched American ways of thinking about language, the unconscious, and empirical science that his thought will have to be exposed again and again before it can even begin to create an atmosphere of receptivity. Lacan's interlocutors,

like his analysands, will suffer a "time-lag in assimilation" (*le temps pour comprendre*).

In 1964 Lacan founded *l'École freudienne de Paris* as a place for contact with representatives of disciplines other than psychoanalysis. Unlike American psychoanalysts who find the university setting to be incompatible with psychoanalysis, Lacan is committed to the idea that psychoanalysis is a science and for that reason must have a place within the university structure. By science, however, he does not refer to the empirical conceptions which our century has come to equate with science. For him a science is not defined by its praxis or technique, but by its theory. In this way Lacan is able to separate psychoanalytic clinical practice which is characterized by talking (*l'acte de la parole*) from analytic theory which he is currently intent on formalizing mathematically. Lacan's mathemes (small letters in formulae) express his attempt to pin down that knowledge in psychoanalysis which *can* be expressed without equivocation. It is not surprising then that Lacan is now discussing the future of psychoanalytic theory with philosophers and mathematicians. Nonetheless, this swing toward theory and away from practice has been interpreted by many of his followers as an abandonment of interest in clinical experience or even in validating his theories about the connections between language and the unconscious. Even since the 1978 appearance of Turkle's book, Lacan has dissolved (*la dis-solution*) his 1,200 member Freudian School as of January, 1980. Proclaiming anew that he is Freud's true successor, he insists that the real meaning of psychoanalysis is continually distorted when theory veers toward meaning, and practice quickly follows suit. The only hope for a solid core of psychoanalytic knowledge, says Lacan, lies in setting out a theory as formal and carefully weighed as Einstein's formulations, a theory closer to mathematics than to metaphysics.

The standard Anglo-American view, that a person being treated by an analyst is someone with a lack or deficiency, has been reversed in Lacanian circles where only the very bright and able are admitted, either as analysts or analysands.

—*Ellie Ragland-Sullivan*

The French psychoanalytic revolution of the 1970s is not dissimilar in nature to the American 1960s swing toward group therapies and psychologies of multiple varieties. The major difference is to be found in the "mass," even anti-intellectual nature of the American phenomenon, and the intrinsically intellectual nature of the French revolution. Freud and Lacan have begun to infiltrate French lower schools as well as the universities, and are frequently included in regular school curricula. French intellectuals, whatever their academic or political persuasions, pride themselves on some knowledge of basic psychoanalytic concepts. The number of French psychoanalysts has and Durang, if there were only a story. Shanley has proved his gifts as a raconteur before now, but he's usually hung his self-consciously zany brand of dialogue and imagery on a definite structure—a play that has a moral (*Italian American Reconciliation*); a movie in which events in five different groups of lives converge in one place (*Five Corners*); a movie in which all the women are played by one actress (*Joe Versus the Volcano*). Some unifying element, in other words, has made one willing to put up with the forced whimsy of Shanley's style.

Italian American Reconciliation, Shanley's last play, promised to teach the audience an important lesson about life, but when the lesson came it turned out to be pretty banal: that love is what it's all about. *The Big Funk* offers a lesson—that nudity is what it's all about—without a story. Instead, we get a series of sketches, most of which Shanley has written before: the one about two guys in a bar talking about Life; the one about the quaint young man seducing the difficult woman; the one about the wacky meal. There's a scene in which [one individual]— playing the fifth character, who never turns up again— smears Vaseline all over [another character's] face and hair. And then, as I say, there's the nudity that ends each act and is probably gratuitous—in the absence of a context, it's hard to tell. Still, the premise is clear: the characters are lunatics of various kinds, and they all have problems, just like us, and Shanley is going to explain it all for us—this indefinable malaise that besets everyone.

By now, though, we're tired of Shanley's lunatics and the wacky things they say and do, and now we have, in addition to Pirandello and Durang, "Twin Peaks" and "Cop Rock," in which characters do the kinds of surprising things that used to happen only in stage plays. Shanley's problem is that television has caught up with him, revealing how little he has to say. In *The Big Funk,* there's a certain amount of talk about the possibility of God, happiness, and life after death, as characters pontificate and face off with each other. Individual lines or deliveries are occasionally funny, but nothing adds up. When a character refers to "the verities," there's something almost self-congratulatory about it. It's as though Shanley had gone from being our premier poet of singles anxiety to being a sort of thinking man's Andrew Lloyd Webber—providing the excuse for a lot of spectacle that will make members of the audience feel hip or sophisticated, the way certain musicals make audiences feel opulent.

Mimi Kramer, in a review of "The Big Tease," in The New Yorker, *Vol. LXVI, No. 45, December 24, 1990, p. 75.*

John Simon (review date 7 January 1991)

[*In the following excerpt, Simon provides a negative review of* The Big Funk.]

Although I was more often than not well disposed toward John Patrick Shanley's earlier work, I am sorry to say that *The Big Funk,* which he wrote, directed, and wallows in, resoundingly unites his formerly scattered blemishes. Excesses of malignity, overfantasticated sappiness, brain-storming garrulity are all there and looking especially vulnerable when free-wheeling in a vacuum.

To begin with, the characters introduce themselves in monologues to the audience. Omar is a professional knife-thrower who wears weirdly operatic headgear; his wife, Fifi, a tightrope walker who will give birth to twins tomorrow, shows no sign of pregnancy; Austin, a somewhat amorphous young man, claims to be the hero of the story, which is promptly disputed; Jill, a toothsome young woman in a vaguely mythological costume, purports to be the villain, though she is soon revealed as a masochistic victim. They all have cute problems or chores. Omar: "My life is falling apart; I'll never hit the dot again." Fifi: "I work with the Battered Women's Bowling League." Jill (I think): "Being really bad made you feel skinny." Jill (definitely): "Somebody recently got honest with me and I didn't like it." Funky stuff, *The Big Funk.*

Not much happens in the first act until a fifth character, Gregory, who oozes evil and speaks with a British accent, produces an oversize jar of Vaseline into which he sticks his arm to the elbow, and proceeds to smear the jelly all over Jill's submissive hair, face, and shoulders. (It turns out later that Jill's father was given to buttering his daughter's nose, which now elicits an impeccably logical proposition from Fifi: "I got to tell you something, Jill. Grease is not love.") Gregory leaves, and Austin, a stranger, comes on and charmingly coaxes Jill into his bathroom, where, with platonic propriety, he administers a degreasing and liberating bubble bath. Cleansed and heartened, she emerges in glorious nudity before donning a pristine bathrobe; Austin, the psychic spot remover, has hit the spot.

The second act features a sort of sub-Lewis Carroll mad dinner party at which outsize portions of steak and salad are either gobbled up or barely nibbled at, and Jill, recidivous, douses herself with salad oil. The talk turns heavily philosophical (to live up to the lengthy passage from Jung reprinted in the program), e.g., "You think there is life after death?" "Yes. Maybe not my life, but there's life." Again, "We've come up against the verities." "What are the verities?" "Well, the first is. I don't know." Unfortunately, as far as Shanley is concerned, that seems to be the last one, too.

It is all subsumed by a message from the author that, printed on a placard, greets the incoming audience. It reads in part: "I want to talk about something that's at my throat and your throat." That something is the Big Funk that apparently envelops us. "I want to know if you disagree with me. Or if we should do something. Or what." As you can see from the lack of actual questions, Mr. Shanley is not really interested in our answer.

There is a happy resolution: Austin and Jill are in love. He now comes on mother-naked and carrying a mirror in which he sometimes contemplates his genitals. This nudity he offers us as our road to salvation. The emperor clearly knows that he has no clothes; does he know also that he has no ideas? . . . There may have been plays of equally self-indulgent emptiness, but surely never such emptiness without a play. (pp. 66-7)

John Simon, "Wire Swingers and Word-slingers," in New York *Magazine, Vol. 24, No. 1, January 7, 1991, pp. 66-7.*

FURTHER READING

Ansen, David. "The Galloping Sleuth-Gourmet." *Newsweek* CXIII, No. 5 (30 January 1989): 70.
 Negative review of *The January Man.*

Johnson, Brian D. "Writing His Own Ticket." *Maclean's* 101, No. 15 (4 April 1988): 40.
 Interview in which Shanley discusses his upbringing and his success as a screenwriter.

Kauffmann, Stanley. "Candor and Contraption." *The New Republic* 200, No. 6, Issue 3864 (6 February 1989): 24-5.
 Negative review of *The January Man.*

Kehr, Dave. "*Joe Versus the Volcano* Revels in the Fake Look." *Chicago Tribune*, No. 68 (9 March 1990): 7C-D.
 Praises Shanley's use of artifice and superficiality in *Joe Versus the Volcano.*

Novak, Ralph. A review of *Joe Versus the Volcano. People Weekly* 33, No. 12 (26 March 1990): 10.
 Positive assessment of *Joe Versus the Volcano* in which Novak describes it as a comedy that is "unrealistic in almost poetic ways."

Roberts, Polly. "Stages of Life: Bard of the Bronx." *Harper's Bazaar* 121, No. 3315 (February 1988): 110, 112, 206.
 Recounts Shanley's childhood and his family's influence on his writing.

Travers, Peter. A review of *Joe Versus the Volcano. Rolling Stone* 576 (19 April 1990): 38.
 Mixed assessment of *Joe Versus the Volcano*. Travers praises the script as "a gentle fable about the fear of love, responsibility, and commitment," but criticizes Shanley's abilities as a director.

Additional coverage of Shanley's life and career is contained in the following sources published by Gale Research: *Contemporary Authors,* **Vols. 128, 133.**

John Steinbeck
Of Mice and Men

(Full name John Ernst Steinbeck) Born in 1902, Steinbeck was an American novelist, short story writer, playwright, nonfiction writer, journalist, and screenwriter. He died in 1968.

The following entry focuses on Steinbeck's novel and play *Of Mice and Men* (1937). For further discussion of Steinbeck's life and works, see *CLC,* Volumes 1, 5, 9, 13, 21, 34, 45, and 59.

INTRODUCTION

Of Mice and Men, which revolves around the relationship of two migrant farm workers in Depression-era California, garnered immediate popular acclaim as a novel and a play, establishing Steinbeck as a leading American writer. Unlike his earlier novels, this work was written as a play in novel form and therefore exhibits many qualities common to drama: brevity, simplicity of plot, and emphasis on speech and action. Commentators have identified the major themes of *Of Mice and Men* as friendship and isolation, hope and futility. Critical reaction has been extremely diverse, with some reviewers faulting the novel as sentimental or predictable and others praising it as realistic and moving.

Steinbeck began writing *Of Mice and Men* in January 1936. Like his previous novel *In Dubious Battle,* the characters and setting for *Of Mice and Men* are derived from his experiences as a farm laborer in California in 1922. Originally entitled "Something That Happened," *Of Mice and Men* was completed during the summer and published in February 1937. Although Steinbeck did not expect the novel to do well, *Of Mice and Men* appeared on best-seller lists from April into the fall, allowing him to finance his first trip to Europe. Upon returning to the United States in August, he worked with George Kaufman on the theater adaptation of the novel, which required few changes. With Kaufman as director, the play opened in New York at the Music Box Theatre in November 1937 and won the Drama Critics Circle Award over plays that included Thornton Wilder's *Our Town.*

Of Mice and Men relates the experiences of itinerant field hands Lennie Small and George Milton over a three-day period. Simpleminded and gentle, Lennie possesses great physical strength and becomes unwittingly destructive when startled. He relies upon George for guidance as the pair move from one ranch to another. Rather than squander their earnings in town saloons and whorehouses, the two workers try to save money in the hope of eventually buying property of their own. They find work on a ranch and meet a coworker who offers his savings to help finance the purchase of a farm. Before the acquisition can be

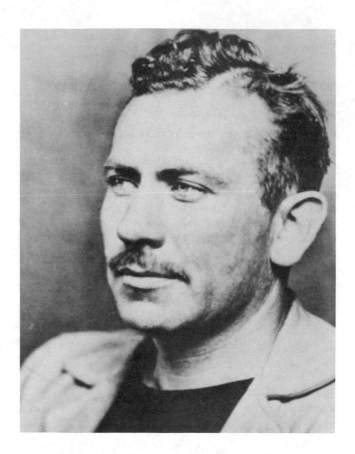

made, however, Lennie unintentionally kills the coquettish wife of the boss's son when her frightened reaction to his innocent overtures scares him. George finds Lennie in hiding and shoots him—knowing that the lynch mob would have murdered Lennie in a more cruel and frightening fashion. The novel concludes as George walks to town to spend his money, abandoning his dream of buying a farm. For the stage version, Steinbeck expanded the role of the flirtatious wife and altered the conclusion so that the play ends just before Lennie's death.

Of Mice and Men has engendered surprisingly diverse interpretations, considering its length and ostensible simplicity. Much of the criticism perceives the story to be either an allegory or a tragedy. Critics who consider the story allegorical point to the contrasts between George and Lennie as the key to interpreting the novel. For example, some consider George representative of the rationality of the mind and Lennie representative of the appetites of the body; accordingly they interpret Lennie's dependence on George and the necessity for George to kill Lennie as the mind's responsibility for the actions of the body. Other critics who consider the novel allegorical argue that Steinbeck based *Of Mice and Men* on the biblical tale of Cain and Abel, in which Cain is banished from his family to wander alone, and interpret George's loss of Lennie as Steinbeck's confirmation of the individual's destiny to live in isolation. Commentators who view *Of Mice and Men* as a tragedy emphasize the seemingly fated end of the sole friendship in the novel and George's abandonment of a noble dream despite the standing offer of assistance from a coworker. A few observers, however, have responded that George and Lennie lack tragic character flaws and that Steinbeck's use of foreshadowing de-emphasizes the characters' ability to make choices, therefore mitigating any sense of tragedy in the classic tradition.

Other areas of critical concern include discussion of the novel as social criticism, realism, and as a reflection of Steinbeck's philosophical views. Although most critics agree that Steinbeck did not intend *Of Mice and Men* to be social criticism on the same level as *In Dubious Battle* or *The Grapes of Wrath*, the novel nonetheless describes the aimless existence of migrant laborers who work hard yet perpetually lack the money to purchase farms of their own. Many observers have noted the realism of the work as well, particularly Steinbeck's rendering of the farm workers' speech and prosaic lives. However, a few ardent detractors have insisted that *Of Mice and Men* is an overtly theatrical, sentimental melodrama which does little more than arouse a reader's sympathy. *Of Mice and Men* has also been perceived as the embodiment of a nonteleological philosophy, according to which events are beyond humankind's comprehension and control: despite the efforts of George and Lennie, their plans fail and two people senselessly die. Noting that the original title of the novel was simply "Something That Happened," Peter Lisca has argued that "the ending of the story is . . . neither tragic nor brutal but simply a part of the pattern of events."

PRINCIPAL WORKS

Cup of Gold: A Life of Henry Morgan, Buccaneer, with Occasional References to History   (novel)   1929
The Pastures of Heaven   (novel)   1932
To a God Unknown   (novel)   1933
Tortilla Flat   (novel)   1935
In Dubious Battle   (novel)   1936
Nothing So Monstrous   (short stories)   1936
Saint Katy the Virgin   (short stories)   1936
Of Mice and Men   (novel)   1937
Of Mice and Men: A Play in Three Acts [with George S. Kaufman]   (drama)   1937
The Red Pony   (novella)   1937; revised edition, 1945
The Long Valley   (short stories)   1938
The Grapes of Wrath   (novel)   1939
The Forgotten Village   (novel)   1941
The Moon Is Down   (novel)   1942
How Edith McGillicuddy Met R. L. S.   (short stories) 1943
Cannery Row   (novel)   1945
The Pearl   (novella)   1947
The Wayward Bus   (novel)   1947

Burning Bright: A Play in Story Form   (novel)   1950
East of Eden   (novel)   1952
Viva Zapata!   (screenplay)   1952
Sweet Thursday   (novel)   1954
The Crapshooter   (short stories)   1957
The Short Reign of Pippin IV: A Fabrication   (novel) 1957
The Winter of Our Discontent   (novel)   1961
Travels with Charley: In Search of America   (nonfiction) 1962

CRITICISM

Mark Van Doren   (review date 6 March 1937)

[*One of the most prolific American men of letters in the twentieth-century, Van Doren wrote poetry, novels, short stories, plays, literary and film criticism, social commentary, and several accomplished studies of prominent literary figures. In the following review, he judges* Of Mice and Men *mechanical.*]

All but one of the persons in Mr. Steinbeck's extremely brief novel [*Of Mice and Men*] are subhuman if the range of the word human is understood to coincide with the range thus far established by fiction. Two of them are evil, one of them is dangerous without meaning to be, and all of them are ignorant—all of them, that is, except the one who shall be named hereafter. Far from knowing the grammar of conduct, they do not even know its orthography. No two of their thoughts are consecutive, nor for that matter do they think; it is rather that each of them follows some instinct as a bull follows the chain which runs through a hole in his nose, or as a crab moves toward its prey. The scene is a ranch in California, and the bunkhouse talk is terrific—God damn, Jesus Christ, what the hell, you crazy bastard, I gotta gut ache, and things like that. The dialect never varies, just as the story never runs uphill.

George and Lennie, the itinerant workers who come to the ranch one day with a dream of the little farm they will own as soon as they get the jack together, seem to think their new job will last at least that long; but the reader knows from the beginning that it will not last, for Lennie is a half-witted giant with a passion for petting mice—or rabbits, or pups, or girls—and for killing them when they don't like it. He is doomed in this book to kill Curley's wife; that is obvious; and then—. Lennie, you see, cannot help shaking small helpless creatures until their necks are broken, just as George cannot relinquish his dream, and just as Curley cannot ever stop being a beast of jealousy. They are wound up to act that way, and the best they can do is run down; which is what happens when Mr. Steinbeck comes to his last mechanical page.

What, however, of the one exception? Ah, he is Slim the jerkline skinner, the tall man with the "God-like eyes" that get fastened on you so that you can't think of anything else for a while. "There was a gravity in his manner and a quiet so profound that all talk stopped when he spoke. . . . His hatchet face was ageless. He might have been thirty-five or fifty. His ear heard more than was said to him, and his slow speech had overtones not of thought, but of understanding beyond thought. His hands, large and lean, were as delicate in their action as those of a temple dancer." He looks through people and beyond them—a feat never accomplished save in mechanical novels. And he understands—why, he understands everything that Mr. Steinbeck understands. It is the merest accident of education that he talks like the rest; "Jesus, he's jes' like a kid, ain't he," he says. If he had his creator's refinement of tongue he could write such sentences as this one which introduces Lennie: "His arms did not swing at his sides, but hung loosely and only moved because the heavy hands were pendula." It wouldn't have done to write pendulums. That would have given the real sound and look of Lennie, and besides it is a real word.

Mr. Steinbeck, I take it, has not been interested in reality of any kind. His jerkline skinner (mule driver) is as hopelessly above the human range as Lennie or Candy or Curley's painted wife is below it. All is extreme here; everybody is a doll; and if there is a kick in the story it is given us from some source which we cannot see, as when a goose walks over our grave, or as when in the middle of the night the telephone rings sharply and it is the wrong number. We shall remember it about that long.

> *Mark Van Doren, "Wrong Number," in* The Nation, *New York, Vol. 144, No. 10, March 6, 1937, p. 275.*

Burton Rascoe (essay date March 1938)

[*An American literary critic noted for his perceptiveness in recognizing new or obscure talent, Rascoe wrote for several influential periodicals during the early and mid-twentieth century. In the following excerpt from an essay originally published in* English Journal *in 1938, he identifies* Of Mice and Men *as an overt tragedy whose success arises from Steinbeck's storytelling ability and character delineation.*]

On the evening of November 23, 1937, an aesthetic miracle was performed on the stage of the Music Box Theatre in New York City. It was the occasion of the first presentation of John Steinbeck's play *Of Mice and Men.* The more literate portion of the reading public had become familiar with the story or theme of the play because *Of Mice and Men* had first appeared in book form as a novel and had met with great critical acclaim, and, fortunately, this critical acclaim had been followed by purchases of the book in large quantities. (p. 57)

I am very glad Mr. Steinbeck did not attend the opening performance of *Of Mice and Men* in New York and that he has not, as yet, seen a performance of the play. For, although the play was an instantaneous hit and although it drew from the drama critics the most gravely and warmly worded notices of praise that have been accorded any native drama since *Tobacco Road* (and hence is likely to enjoy a run as extended as the Erskine Caldwell drama),

a distressingly large part of the audience on the opening night took the tragic, heart-breaking lines of George and Lennie to be comedy. They laughed outrageously when tears should have been streaming down their faces. They appeared to think that the lumbering, dimwitted, pathetic Lennie was supposed to be funny. Village idiots laughing at the village idiot all over again. I am told that this laughter at the wrong places occurs during at least part of the first act at every performance.

But the consummate art of Steinbeck conquers every time even the more insensitive elements of a New York theater audience before the first act is over. Compassion for the misfits of life, for those who are handicapped by the imponderables of heredity and environment and for those who are warped physically and emotionally, is so deeply and so understandingly felt and expressed by Steinbeck that, before the curtain comes down on the first act, the light, superficially cynical mood of the less sensitive members of the audience has changed, and pity and wonder has taken possession of them.

This is the miracle I referred to in the opening sentence of this discourse.

It seemed to me after my first reading, subsequent re-readings, and careful analysis of the novel, *Of Mice and Men,* that Steinbeck as a literary artist had deliberately posed for himself the most difficult problem conceivable to a writer of fiction and that he had resolved it in a Sophoclean manner, that is, without poetic or rhetorical fault. He had even done a braver thing than Sophocles had done (though, please, let no one be so silly and so supercilious as to imagine that, in my saying this, I am comparing Sophocles and Steinbeck to the disadvantage of Sophocles or even that I am ranking Steinbeck as remotely in the class of Sophocles: he may be, before he is finished, a greater poetic dramatist than Sophocles, for he strives to learn the most delicate nuances and the most meaningful emphases of—in the Aristotelian sense—the arts of poetry and rhetoric; but he is thirty-eight years old, and Sophocles was only twenty-eight when he triumphed over the long preeminent tragic poet, Aeschylus, by writing *Antigone;* so, in order to be classed with Sophocles, Steinbeck has much ground, in little time, to cover). I am talking about a writing problem. Sophocles chose to treat in poetic and dramatic form the legends already familiar to the Athenian audiences who had witnessed tragic dramas since the days before Aeschylus. Steinbeck, on the other hand, chose as the most important character of his novel, and of his play, *Of Mice and Men,* a believable contemporary figure—a man who would be described on any police docket or in a detective's dossier as a sexual pervert or degenerate and in almost any psychiatrist's case history as, probably, a man afflicted with gigantism, with an abnormally low I.Q., unusual thyroid deficiency, excessive pituitary secretion with resulting imbalance, a tactile fetish, psychic and/or physical impotence, and with improperly functioning adrenals which caused him in moments of fear to act destructively without intention—and Steinbeck chose to, and *did,* make this monstrosity a sympathetic figure, one whom you, if you had heart in you, would regard with all the despair but also with all the affection with which the giant Lennie is regarded by his bindle-stiff guardian and companion, the more astute and intelligent George.

In the novel and in the play the relationship between George and Lennie is a paradigm of all the nonphysical, nonsexual (let us use the so tritely inadequate and now almost meaningless word "spiritual" to help out in indicating the meaning) emotions, concerns, and aspirations in the world. George has toward Lennie the tenderness and the protective instinct which some of even the most hard-bitten and most hard-boiled have toward the helpless, the maimed, the dependent. A lonely, itinerant bindle-stiff, a migratory ranch hand, barley bucker, mule skinner, fruit picker, and general handy man, without a home or family, George has encountered and embraced a responsibility, a social responsibility, a humanitarian responsibility. It is to take care of, protect, save from hurt, the dim-witted, loyal, and devoted Lennie.

George nags and rags Lennie at times like a distracted, exasperated harridan wife; scolds him like a long-suffering mother whose child is a constant worry and trial. He gives way at times to eloquent fancies as to how much more enjoyable, unconstrained, and livable life would be if he were only free—if he didn't have Lennie as a burden, a yoke, a ball and chain to hamper him. But as George speaks and as his character becomes plain, you know that life would be wholly meaningless and empty for him without Lennie to take care of. And he has his emotional recompense in Lennie's pathetic and doglike devotion to him, a loyalty so great and so intense that Lennie's weak brain scarcely comes alive except where George is concerned—when George is angry with him, when George is planning a future for them wherein they will have a little farm of their own and won't be subject to the whims of bosses or to the seasonal variations in employment, or when harm seems to threaten George.

The never-quite-realized, too often tragically shattered dreams of men toward an ideal future of security, tranquillity, ease, and contentment runs like a Greek choral chant throughout the novel and the play, infecting, enlivening, and ennobling not only George and Lennie but the crippled, broken-down ranch hand, Candy, and the twisted-back Negro stable buck, Crooks, who begs to come in on the plan George has to buy a little farm. Lennie is so enthralled by the prospect that he begs George to tell the story over and over again:

> LENNIE. (*pleading*) Come on, George. . . . . Tell me! Please! Like you done before.
>
> . . . . .
>
> GEORGE. Guys like us that work on ranches is the loneliest guys in the world. They ain't got no family. They don't belong no place. They come to a ranch and then they go into town and blow their stake. And then the first thing you know they're poundin' their tail on some other ranch. They ain't got nothin' to look ahead to.
>
> LENNIE. (*delightedly*) That's it, that's it! Now tell how it is with us.
>
> GEORGE. (*still almost chanting*) With us it ain't

like that. We got a future. We got somebody to talk to that gives a damn about us. We don't have to sit in no barroom blowin' our jack, just because we got no place else to go. If them other guys gets in jail, they can rot for all anybody gives a damn.

> LENNIE. (*who cannot restrain himself any longer; bursts into speech*) But not us! And why? Because. . . . because I got you to look after me. . . . and you got me to look after you. . . . . And that's why! (*He laughs.*) Go on, George!
>
> GEORGE. You got it by heart. You can do it yourself.
>
> LENNIE. No, no. I forget some of the stuff. Tell about how it's gonna be.
>
> GEORGE. Some other time.
>
> LENNIE. No, tell how it's gonna be!
>
> GEORGE. Okay. Some day we're gonna get the jack together and we're gonna have a little house and a couple of acres and a cow and some pigs and. . . . .
>
> LENNIE. (*shouting*) And live off the fat of the land! And have rabbits. Go on, George! Tell about what we're gonna have in the garden. And about the rabbits in the cages. Tell about the rain in the winter. . . . and about the stove and how thick the cream is on the milk, you can hardly cut it. Tell about that, George!
>
> GEORGE. Why don't you do it yourself—you know all of it!
>
> LENNIE. It ain't the same if I tell it. Go on now. How I get to tend the rabbits.
> (GEORGE *continues to elaborate the story of the dream place.*)

And now you must observe that Steinbeck has compassion without maudlinity, sentiment without sentimentality, a stern, realistic, very observant and deductive sense about the realities and about the consequences in a chain of causes. Anyone with any deductive sense at all needs to read only five pages of the novel *Of Mice and Men* to discover the "plot," to know what is going to happen. The intelligent reader knows that poor Lennie is going to "do a bad thing again" as he did before when he wanted to stroke a girl's dress (and that was all he wanted to do), and the girl got frightened and screamed because she thought she was being attacked, and Lennie and George had to run away and hide in a swamp in water up to their necks to escape the mob that was going to lynch Lennie.

You know that *this* time Lennie, who likes to stroke soft things and who has killed a pet mouse because his hands are so strong and he is so dumb, is going to kill a girl, unintentionally, because of all the things wrong in his disordered brain. The impatient, plot-minded reader doesn't have to turn to the back of the book to see how it comes out. Steinbeck tells you, in effect, in the first five pages just about how it is "going to come out."

And that is his terrific moral. Also it is his gambit to the reader to prove his power as a convincing and enthralling narrator. The reader who, having read that far, fails to go on, is a reader whose mentality is equal only to, and has been conditioned by, very bad, tricky, detective stories, which have no true relation to literature any more than have crossword puzzles, or, indeed, any more than crossword puzzles have (as they are alleged to have) to the increase of the vocabulary you would ordinarily, or potentially, use.

You see, Steinbeck not only indicates to the sentient reader in those first five pages that Lennie is going "to do a bad thing" unintentionally: he also indicates to the sentient reader that Lennie will have to die for it this time and, also, that it is highly necessary and just that Lennie should die. For Lennie's condition is an inimical and destructive force. It is a condition he is not responsible for. It is something he cannot help. One can have all the feeling for him in the world—but Candy in the second act of the play has an old, rheumatic, blind, crippled dog, smelly with age and disease, of whom Candy is very fond because this old dog is the only thing left to Candy on which, or on whom, to lavish human affection, warmth, and care; and Candy has to carry the old dog around in his arms until the dog's disintegrating smell so permeates the bunkhouse that the other ranch hands can no longer stand it, and they have to persuade Candy, with the utmost kindness and consideration, to let them put the old dog out of his misery.

Therein, truly, is a displayed sense of the *lacrimae rerum* of which John Steinbeck is a master. For, when the posse is seeking poor Lennie to string him up and "blow his guts out," as the egoistically inflamed and sadistic leader of the posse demands, George humors Lennie by telling him again about the place they are going to have. He tells it all over, word for word, with promptings by Lennie, who knows it all but wants to hear it from George. He tells it to keep Lennie in ecstasy until the shouts and other noises disclose that the posse is near upon them. Then:

> GEORGE. And you get to tend the rabbits!
>
> LENNIE. (*giggling with happiness*) And live on the fat o' the land!
>
> GEORGE. Yes. (LENNIE *turns his head. Quickly*) Look over there, Lennie. Like you can really see it.
>
> (GEORGE *pulls* CARLSON'S *Luger from his side pocket and fires at the base of* LENNIE'S *brain, to put him out of his misery, just as* CARLSON *had told* CANDY *he could put* CANDY'S *old dog out of his misery and the dog wouldn't know or feel it, because the bullet would go right into the base of the brain.*)

After that, it seems to me that many of the "hard-boiled" writers who imitate Hemingway's hard-boilism (and including Hemingway who now imitates himself) are like just so many Lennies parroting what George has said, except that their George was about as unimaginative in the brainpan as Lennie and even much more undeveloped, however facile and neat were the hard-boiled word patterns their George was able to patter out. The George of Steinbeck's novel and play was hard-bitten and hard-boiled; but he had imagination, a sense of reality, true compassion, and the dream of life.

Steinbeck abhors and abjures the tag "mystic" which some critics have used in describing him. He is deeply concerned with the problem of Good and Evil, not in any conventional, moral, or philosophical sense but as phenomena in life and as animating principles in life. I have heard him use no word indicating the nature of his beliefs and intimations; but I should vaguely describe them as comprising a curious, very modern Manicheanism, derived perhaps in part from the Indians of the West Coast he has known since boyhood, from acute observation of cause and effect operating among primitive or untutored men, and from a frank facing of the evidence of his own hidden resources of mind and will. Although I have not heard him mention the late Mary Austin or give any evidence of having read her studies of the mind and will, it occurred to me that his psychic beliefs and convictions are probably akin to those of Mrs. Austin. Mrs. Austin believed that will, thought, and emotion are forces that are immediate, dynamic, and kinetic and that they can bring about definite ends, for good or evil, without the employment of any physical means whatever.

It would appear from a long conversation at my house which followed upon Steinbeck's bland, resolute affirmation that what is commonly called witchcraft and the "hexing" of one person by another person is not a superstition but a fairly common and attestable fact. It is, he says, merely the operation of the kinetic and highly destructive emotion of hate. This is, he says, a disturbing and terrible fact. He says that he knew of a man who had reason to hate another man greatly and did so hate him with such concentrated emotion that he was able to say to that man, "You are going to die next Tuesday. At 2:15 next Tuesday you are going to step in front of a truck." And the man did step in front of a truck at 2:15 the following Tuesday and was killed. Steinbeck denied that this was hypnotism, although he believes that all of us daily perform hypnotism and are subjects of hypnotism almost daily in degrees depending upon the force unconsciously exercised upon us, our resistance to it, and upon the strength of our own will and purpose.

He said that he was mortally afraid of hate and that he never wanted to hate anyone or have anyone hate him—very much. The only defense against concentrated hate, he said, was immediate surrender, capitulation; and this must take the form of humility, benevolence, friendliness. The only way to combat hate is to remove from within yourself the reasons for this hate; only thus can you disarm the one who hates you; only thus can you render the terrible force of his hate impotent. "If I knew a man hated me a great deal," he said, "I would try to make friends with him; if I had done him harm I would try to undo that harm quickly. I wouldn't try to hate him back, no, no, because then the only reason I would have for hating him was because he hated me, and that isn't reason enough to generate any strong, counteracting emotion. This would only intensify his hate and he might take it into his head to will disaster or death upon me."

Presently I perceived that Steinbeck's metaphysics was

having to do, in a language and ratiocination of his own, with what in the Greek consciousness was the high sin of *hubris* or arrogance or insolence and its consequences. In Greek tragedy there are degrees and kinds of *hubris* each with degrees and kinds of punishment extending up to dire suffering and disaster, the reasons for which the victim in his *hubris* or unwarranted and exaggerated self-conceit cannot figure out; he does not know why he has offended the gods; but the audience knows; he thought too well of himself and so aroused hatred by insolence without even knowing he was insolent and so brought punishment upon himself.

In *Of Mice and Men* Steinbeck's thematic intention, not wholly obvious, was, in a way, to expound the complete nonmorality of Nature in her physical aspects and of the morality of expediency that must necessarily arise from Nature's blundering. The giant imbecile was certainly not responsible for being what he was, and nothing could right the bungling of Nature, and yet this giant imbecile, fully meriting our pity, sympathy, and tenderness, must be killed; for society cannot permit, out of pity, the dumb, destructive force of bungling, nonmoral Nature to operate. (pp. 59-66)

Burton Rascoe, "John Steinbeck," in Steinbeck and His Critics: A Record of Twenty-Five Years, *edited by E. W. Tedlock, Jr. and C. V. Wicker, University of New Mexico Press, 1957, pp. 57-67.*

Critical opinion on John Steinbeck's *Of Mice and Men* is surprisingly varied, miscellaneous, and contradictory.

—William Goldhurst, in his "Of Mice and Men: *John Steinbeck's Parable of the Curse of Cain,"* Western American Literature, *1971.*

Stark Young   (essay date 4 May 1938)

[*An eminent American drama critic in the 1920s, Young was also a dramatist, director, and author. His most successful publications are* So Red the Rose *(1934) and a translation of Chekhov's* The Seagull *(1939). In the following excerpt, Young states that* Of Mice and Men *evinces a very deliberate structure which contributes to the realism of the work.*]

Not everyone among us might be sure of knowing it, but *Of Mice and Men* is marked by delicate and sensitive perceptions that are quite equal to anything in [Thornton Wilder's *Our Town*]. As a matter of fact, I should say it is more sensitive. Its characters and incidents suggest the clarity and outline of legend; but within them there is a kind of quivering suspense and an almost fatalistic giving of yourself to life.

More elusively, perhaps, but just as certainly, *Of Mice and*

Men is as much arranged, built on artifice, left as a work of art, with its own kind of reality and wholeness, as *Our Town* is. Sharp bits of the naturalistic, or whatever we may call it, streaks of brutality, frank outbursts of expression, or a locale of violent light and shade, might seem at times to disprove this, but the whole play remains dominated by its mood; the element of design in it is unusually marked.

And instead of losing, as some followers of realism might have said it would, by this evident manipulation for the effect, the play gains in its total impact and imaginative compulsion.

In the characters, too, we get a sense of arrangement or design, so definitely carried through that we have almost a sense of types, an almost classic designation and completeness to each. But again there is no loss on that account. The figures strike sharply on our minds, simply and inexhaustibly; and they have variety even in their degrees of distinctness. The two leading characters, farm laborers, one of them a defective, the other leading and guarding him, are remarkably well carried through by the dramatist, with boldly repeated motifs, tender, half-muted revelations, and a profound sense of the theatre.

Stark Young, "Drama Critics Circle Awards," in The New Republic, *Vol. LXXXXIV, No. 1222, May 4, 1938, p. 396.*

Desmond MacCarthy   (review date 22 April 1939)

[*MacCarthy was one of the foremost English literary and dramatic critics of the twentieth century. As a member of the Bloomsbury group, which included Leonard and Virginia Woolf, John Maynard Keynes, E. M. Forster, and Lytton Strachey, MacCarthy was guided by its primary tenet that "one's prime objects in life were love, the creation and enjoyment of aesthetic experience, and the pursuit of knowledge." In the following review occasioned by a performance of the play in England, he describes* Of Mice and Men *as a sentimental tragedy.*]

Of Mice and Men by John Steinbeck is admirably acted at the Gate Theatre. The play, founded on a successful novel in which, I am told, the Simple Simon has more time to endear himself to readers, is American; so is the cast. This is fortunate since the scene is laid in central California, and the types are indigenous. Neither the atmosphere nor the characters would have been convincing had they not been interpreted by actors entirely at home with them. The play itself is a sentimental tragedy. By that I mean that it touches us rather than moves us deeply, and that the climax (too easy to foresee) does not awake that strange, still exhilaration which springs from looking fate in the face. It is not the passion of man that brings about the catastrophe, but the accident that the central figure is a congenital half-wit. Lennie, with his gigantic muscular strength, was—to use the words of the sister of a lovable village simpleton I knew myself—"not exactly quite all right." And when George, who loves him, is forced to shoot him, because Lennie has absent-mindedly strangled a girl—the chase is up and he would be lynched unmercifully—we, the audience, feel: "Well, it is sad. But in a rough world where no man has time to be his brother's keeper, Lennies are a danger and better dead." *Of Mice and Men* is a play hard on the surface and tender underneath; it is about "tough guys" with warm hearts. The confidence of its appeal to the conviction that at bottom plain human nature is sound and splendid is characteristic of America. This is the deepest difference between America and Europe. In Europe such a feeling is apt to be merely sentimental—a pretence which people leading sheltered lives nourish in themselves because it looks kind and is comforting. But in America it is instinctively believed and common property. It is the main prop of their traditional passion for equality and of their generosity. To-day, it is speaking through the mouth of President Roosevelt. It is the most heartening element in the make-up of a suspicion-ridden modern world. The grudging response it meets here (often to the dismay of practical Englishmen who are eager to make use of it) is due to the reproach generosity of faith conveys. A by-effect of this faith in human nature is that it leaves the American playgoer free to revel in a surface cynicism of comment and laughter such as horrifies English audiences; for he cannot be frightened—*Man* is all right. This is not the theme, but it enters into the spirit of this play.

The lives of the men who compose the wandering mass of casual labour in America are very lonely. They have no roots; few are married. They compete against each other for temporary jobs, well-paid enough to dangle before them perpetually a seldom realised hope of some day settling down on a piece of land of their own and of being at last their own masters. They seldom hunt in couples, for each must take his chance as it comes; a pal may be as great a drawback as a wife in finding one. The curtain goes up on two such men, a big one and a small one, who are exceptions. Evidently they are bound together; they are on their way to a farm where they hope to get a job together. We soon learn from their talk that the smaller of the two, George, has found the great hulking fellow Lennie a confounded nuisance. Lennie has got into trouble by unintentionally frightening a girl, and George has had not only to fly with him but to supply the wits which enabled them both to escape. He is afraid that Lennie will do something, or say something, which will lose the next job too, and then they will have to wander about together, hungry. And no wonder he is afraid of that. It is soon obvious from their talk that the giant is a child—a kindly, helpless simpleton. Like a child, Lennie loves to make George repeat over and over again the story of how happy they will some day be together in a shack of their own, "living on the fat of the land" and keeping (this is indispensable to Lennie's dream) rabbits. Like a child, he is never tired of hearing George repeat how they will always stick together. He corrects him when he does not use the same words he has used before. Lennie is very fond of small, soft, furry animals—rabbits, mice, puppies, but if the pet he is caressing shows signs of fear, a spasm of instinctive sympathetic terror seizes him and he is apt unintentionally to kill the little creature he loves with a child's concentration.

Well, thanks to George's speaking up for him, they both get the jobs they are seeking. Lennie as a worker gives full satisfaction, doing the work of four. But unfortunately the son of the "boss" employing them has married a poor little floosey of a girl, whose only notion of getting into friendly contact with the men about her is to give them the glad eye. Her husband, Curley, is a bully who can use his fists and is fiercely jealous. George and the other hands on the farm are terrified of getting involved with Curley's wife, and George warns Lennie against speaking to her. You can guess what happens. She can't stand her life on the farm and plans to run away. That very day she finds Lennie alone in the barn and persuades him to stroke her hair. He can't stop; she, like the little puppy he was so fond of and killed, gets frightened, struggles—the nervous sympathetic spasm seizes him. Lennie flies to the place where George had told him to go *if* he ever got into trouble. And there George finds and shoots him, while telling him to look where the little house stands which had so nearly become their own. Yes, nearly. For on the farm was an old man who had saved money and had been ready to come in with them. This old man's sheep-dog had been to him what Lennie was to George, and it had had to be shot. The great merit of *Mice and Men* is the way in which it conveys that these "tough guys' " need above everything some outlet for affection.

The other men on the farm, with the exception of Curley, understand what Candy's dog meant to him and what Lennie, who was a gigantic child, meant to George; and yet that both had to be shot. (pp. 605-06)

> *Desmond MacCarthy, "The American View of Human Nature," in* The New Statesman & Nation, *Vol. XVII, No. 426, April 22, 1939, pp. 605-06.*

Joseph Wood Krutch   (essay date 1939)

[*Krutch is widely regarded as one of America's most respected literary and drama critics. A conservative and idealistic thinker, he was a consistent proponent of human dignity and the preeminence of literary art. In the following excerpt from his noteworthy study* The American Drama Since 1918, *Krutch praises Steinbeck as a skilled writer but nonetheless concludes that* Of Mice and Men *lacks the imagination, realism, and tenderness for which others have praised it.*]

[In *Of Mice and Men,* Steinbeck] deals with the lives of the lowly and he owes an obvious debt to the style of Hemingway, but for all the effectiveness of his writing and the equal effectiveness of the dramatization it is difficult, on sober consideration, to find in either novel or play the high imagination, stunning reality, and almost ineffable tenderness which many profess to find there.

The story—difficult to tell without seeming to do it an intentional injustice—is concerned with a strange friendship between two migratory harvest workers, one of whom is a witless but amiable giant given to fondling all soft and helpless things with a hand so unintentionally heavy that, sooner or later, he infallibly breaks their necks. The theme is tenderness taking strange forms in a brutal environment, and the dramatic tension arises out of our foreknowledge of the fact that at some time and for some reason the heavy hand will be laid with fatal results upon the camp's only member of the female sex—a pathetic little nymphomaniac married to the boss's cruel son. All the grotesqueness inherent in the tale is emphasized rather than concealed (we first meet the strange pair when the giant is being unwillingly deprived of a dead mouse he has been keeping too long in his pocket), but the skill of the writing is such that the whole is carried off far better than one could well imagine and that success is absolute in so far as it consists merely in forcing the spectator to take the whole with perfect seriousness. The only question is whether he is right so to take it, whether what we are presented with is really a tale of eerie power and tenderness, or whether, as it seems to me, everything from beginning to end is completely "literary" in the bad sense and as shamelessly cooked up as, let us say, the death of Little Nell.

After all, Dickens, as well as thousands of his readers, sincerely believed that Little Nell was the real thing. A fascinating but largely unexplored field lies ready for any psychologist-critic who wishes to examine the reasons behind the demand of every age that sentiment be served up according to some formula, the peculiar charm of which no previous age would have recognized and which every succeeding age finds patently ridiculous. Your Victorian was ready to weep over the fate of any sentimental monster if that monster could be described in sufficiently convincing terms as "innocent." Today nothing arouses the suspicions of any audience more infallibly than either that word or that thing, but a tough Little Nell, thoroughly familiar with four-letter words, would be a sensation on any stage, and the moronic giant of Mr. Steinbeck seems real because all the accidents of his character and surroundings are violent and brutal. Mr. Steinbeck, as I have already suggested, writes with great technical adroitness. But neither that adroitness nor all the equal expertness of staging and acting exhibited in the performance of his play would avail if the whole were not concocted according to a formula which happens to be at the moment infallible. Sentiment flavored with a *soupçon* of social criticism and labeled "Ruthless Realism" is well nigh certain to be applauded by thousands quite unaware that they are responding to an appeal as old—not as the theater itself—but as the rise of the middle-class public. Mr. Steinbeck's most recent novel, *The Grapes of Wrath,* is written in quite a different style and may possibly indicate that he himself realizes the extent to which *Of Mice and Men* was meretricious. (pp. 128-30)

> *Joseph Wood Krutch, "Tragedy: Eugene O'Neill," in his* The American Drama Since 1918: An Informal History, *Random House, 1939, pp. 73-133.*

Harry Thornton Moore   (essay date 1939)

[*An American educator, critic, and author, Moore is best remembered for his studies of the life and works of D. H. Lawrence; he also wrote and edited works on several other noted literary figures. In the following excerpt, he faults* Of Mice and Men *for possessing violence without tragedy.*]

Of Mice and Men was written as an experiment. Steinbeck told his publisher not to disturb himself about the book if he didn't like it, and to send it back if it didn't interest him. But Pascal Covici was immediately enthusiastic about it and published it early in 1937. It was taken as a Book-of-the-Month Club selection and it entered the best-seller lists. Then as a play, adapted by Steinbeck with very little change, it ran for a crowded season on Broadway. The Drama Circle of the New York critics awarded it a prize for being the best play of the year.

Of Mice and Men tells the story of two drifting ranch hands, George and Lennie, who dream, as rootless men do, of a piece of land of their own, where they will "belong." They have never been able to work up a stake because big, blundering, simple-witted Lennie keeps getting them into trouble. He can never remember things. He tenderly loves puppies and mice, but always forgets about not squeezing them too hard, and kills them. Fabulously strong but very timid, he is docile under the control of George, the pilot-fish of the pair. George, little and clever, feels that Lennie has been given into his keeping. He holds him in check by telling him about the rabbit-farm they will have one day, where Lennie may look after the rabbits when he is good—George too is webbed in the dream. They come to work in the Salinas Valley, and it is there, amid the people they meet at the ranch, that their story is worked out, with doom hanging in the warm dry air.

Structurally, the novel was from the first a play: it is divided into six parts, each part a scene—the reader may observe that the action never moves away from a central point in each of these units. Steinbeck's manner of writing was coming over quite firmly to the dramatic. The process had begun in the latter part of *In Dubious Battle* (which the novelist John O'Hara once tried unsuccessfully to dramatize), where some of the most exciting happenings in the story take place offstage. After *Of Mice and Men* was published and the suggestion was made that it be prepared for the stage, Steinbeck said it could be produced directly from the book, as the earliest moving pictures had been produced. It was staged in almost exactly this way in the spring of 1937 by a labor-theater group in San Francisco, and although the venture was not a failure it plainly demonstrated to Steinbeck that the story needed to be adapted to dramatic form. The San Francisco *Chronicle's* report of the performance admitted that the staged novel had power, though it "seems slightly ill at ease in the theater . . . Its climaxes need sharpening," for "some of the scenes end lamely, tapering off without the pointed tag-lines that might crystallize or intensify the action. And there are certain passages of dialogue that caused embarrassed titters in the audience; it would do the play no harm to leave these out altogether." But when Steinbeck transferred the story into final dramatic form for the New York stage he took 85% of his lines bodily from the novel. A few incidents needed juggling, one or two minor new ones were introduced, and some (such as Lennie's imaginary speech with his Aunt Clara at the end of the novel) were omitted. A Hollywood studio bought the film rights to *Of Mice and Men,* but the picture has not been made yet.

Although there are few descriptive passages in the novel

Of Mice and Men, Steinbeck's presentation of ranch life has once again the gleam of the living. The people, human beings reduced to bareness of speech and thought and action, are on the sidetracks of the main line of western culture. They exist in a hard reality, but most of them are susceptible to dreams. Some of them are lost in a compensatory dream-image of themselves, others are set afire by the wish-dream of George and Lennie. But in one way or another all the dreams and some of the people (the good along with the bad) are smashed. The spirit of doom prevails as strongly as in the pages of Hardy or of Steinbeck's fellow-Californian, Robinson Jeffers.

A writer deep in the lore of his own people feels (in many cases unconsciously) a folkways compulsive: the actual and mythical experience of his people helps to generate his material. But the final shaping of it depends upon the artist's own vision. Lennie in *Of Mice and Men* is cast up from the midst of us and we all know him. Baffled, unknowingly powerful, utterly will-less, he cannot move without a leader. And we also know many Georges, good-heartedly trying to help the Lennies of life muddle through; but all the while, despite their courage and good intentions, none too certain of themselves. John Steinbeck sees them as unable to prevent their charges (and often themselves) from steering into catastrophe. In book after book his protagonists, tragic or comic, are shattered, and it goes hardest with those who had the brightest dreams. It is disturbing to find so many of these likeable heroes going down so consistently in spiritual defeat or meeting with a brutal death.

Violence without tragedy: that is the weakness of this book. Socially considered, most of the people are what could legitimately be called "tragic," but there is no tragedy as we understand the word in reference to literature. On the social side, we have George's ritual of dreaming aloud with Lennie, which begins with this incantation:

> Guys like us, that work on ranches, are the loneliest guys in the world. They got no family. They don't belong no place. They come to a ranch an' work up a stake and then they go into town and blow their stake, and the first thing you know they're poundin' their tail on some other ranch. They ain't got nothing to look ahead to . . .

and continues:

> With us it ain't like that. We got a future. We got somebody to talk to that gives a damn about us. We don't have to sit in no bar room blowin' in our jack jus' because we got no place else to go . . . Someday—we're gonna get the jack together and we're gonna have a little house and a couple of acres an' a cow and some pigs . . .

This has roots of social tragedy, despite the sentimental manner of its statement. (Steinbeck once said he writes this way because he is a sentimental guy.) George and Lennie and Candy and Crooks and some of the others are caught in this situation, they are lonely and homeless and yearning. But the social tragedy never really gets beyond that static proposition: its potentials are never exercised. It affords a background but it doesn't motivate the catastrophe.

On the literary side there is no authentic tragedy, which comes out of character. There is no basis for it. Even if we slur over the criticism that Lennie is a poor choice for a central figure in the story because from the start the odds against him are too great—even if we get beyond this and admit George as the true protagonist, we still don't find tragedy. George is no more than pathetic. He attracts sympathy because he has to lose his friend Lennie, to whom he has been so loyal, and whom he has to kill at the last in order to save him from the others. But because this isn't genuine tragedy it gives the reader a brutal shock when George kills Lennie, and it cannot be anything else no matter how many little tricks have been used throughout the story to prepare us for Lennie's death. One of the most noticeable of these is the obvious comparison of Lennie with a worthless old dog that must be shot, as Lennie must be at the last.

It is true that Elizabethan tragedy ended with corpses and horror, and one doesn't protest against them when they are necessary ingredients to tragedy: it is the misuse of corpses and horror that is objectionable. It can become a trick. All that side of the *Of Mice and Men* story is crude and shoddy. The writing comes to reflect this, and although there are occasionally excellent terse descriptive passages, projections of atmosphere as well as superb descriptions of physical actions, the prose finally comes to seem as if it were stretched too tight—it gives an effect of bright artificiality. The projection is really too bare for narrative; since the main story is so slight it should have been filled in more at the sides. Its very narrowness emphasizes the awkward attempt to resolve pathos by brutality. (pp. 48-52)

Harry Thornton Moore, in his The Novels of John Steinbeck: A First Critical Study, *Normandie House, 1939, 102 p.*

Peter Lisca   (essay date Winter 1956-57)

[*An Italian-born American educator and critic, Lisca has written several major works on Steinbeck, including the highly praised studies* The Wide World of John Steinbeck *(1958) and* John Steinbeck: Nature and Myth *(1978). In the following essay, he analyzes the significance of motifs in* Of Mice and Men.]

Shortly after sending off the manuscript for *Of Mice and Men,* Steinbeck wrote to his agents, "I'm sorry that you do not find the new book as large in subject as it should be. I probably did not make my subjects and symbols clear. The microcosm is difficult to handle and apparently I did not get it over." Despite the agents' initial disappointment, *Of Mice and Men* became a great success as novel, play, and motion picture. That Steinbeck's audience found his "subjects and symbols clear" is doubtful; that the critics did not is certain. For the most part, those critics who saw nothing beyond the obvious plot disliked the work immensely. Those who suspected more important levels of meaning were unable to offer specific and thorough explication. Today, almost twenty years later, it is generally accepted that the success of *Of Mice and Men* was an accident of history: Steinbeck merely cashed in on his audience's readiness to shed a tear, even a critical tear, over the plight of lonely migrant laborers. As one critic put it ten years later, "This is a negligible novel, seemingly written with a determined eye on the cash register" [George D. Snell, in his *The Shapers of American Fiction,* 1947].

This essay is a much belated attempt to discover just what Steinbeck's "subjects and symbols" are and how they are utilized in *Of Mice and Men,* which he once referred to as "a study of the dreams and pleasures of everyone in the world."

To present his larger subject in terms of a microcosm Steinbeck makes use of three incremental motifs: symbol, action, and language. All three of these motifs are presented in the opening scene, are contrapuntally developed through the story, and come together again at the end. The first symbol in the novel, and the primary one, is the little spot by the river where the story begins and ends. The book opens with a description of this place by the river, and we first see George and Lennie as they enter this place from the highway to an outside world. It is significant that they prefer spending the night here rather than going on to the bunkhouse at the ranch.

Steinbeck's novels and stories often contain groves, willow thickets by a river, and caves which figure prominently in the action. There are, for example, the grove in *To a God Unknown,* the place by the river in the Junius Maltby story, the two caves and a willow thicket in *The Grapes of Wrath,* the cave under the bridge in *In Dubious Battle,* the caves in *The Wayward Bus,* and the thicket and cave in *The Pearl.* For George and Lennie, as for other Steinbeck heroes, coming to a cave or thicket by the river symbolizes a retreat from the world to a primeval innocence. Sometimes, as in *The Grapes of Wrath,* this retreat has explicit overtones of a return to the womb and rebirth. In the opening scene of *Of Mice and Men* Lennie twice mentions the possibility of hiding out in a cave, and George impresses on him that he must return to this thicket by the river when there is trouble.

While the cave or the river thicket is a "safe place," it is physically impossible to remain there, and this symbol of primeval innocence becomes translated into terms possible in the real world. For George and Lennie it becomes "a little house an' a couple of acres." Out of this translation grows a second symbol, the rabbits, and this symbol serves several purposes. By the figure of synecdoche it comes to stand for the "safe place" itself, making a much more easily manipulated symbol than the "house an' a couple of acres." Also, through Lennie's love for the rabbits Steinbeck is able not only to dramatize Lennie's desire for the "safe place," but to define the basis of that desire on a very low level of consciousness—the attraction to soft, warm fur, which is for Lennie the most important aspect of their plans.

This transference of symbolic value from the farm to the rabbits is important also because it makes possible another motif, the motif of action. This is introduced in the first scene by the dead mouse which Lennie is carrying in his pocket (much as Tom carries the turtle in *The Grapes of Wrath*). As George talks about Lennie's attraction to mice, it becomes evident that the symbolic rabbits will come to the same end—crushed by Lennie's simple blundering strength. Thus Lennie's killing of mice and later his killing of the puppy set up a motif of action, a pattern, which the reader expects to be carried out again. George's story about Lennie and the little girl with the red dress, which he tells twice, contributes to this expectancy of pattern, as does the shooting of Candy's dog, the crushing of Curley's hand, and the frequent appearances of Curley's wife. All these actions are patterns of the mice motif and predict the fate of the rabbits and thus the fate of the dream of a "safe place."

The third motif, that of language, is also present in the opening scene. Lennie asks George, "Tell me—like you done before," and George's words are obviously in the nature of a ritual. "George's voice became deeper. He repeated his words rhythmically, as though he had said them many times before." The element of ritual is stressed by the fact that even Lennie has heard it often enough to remember its precise language: " 'An' live off the fatta the lan'. . . . An' have *rabbits.* Go on George! Tell about what we're gonna have in the garden and about the rabbits in the cages and about. . . . ' " This ritual is performed often in the story, whenever Lennie feels insecure. And of course it is while Lennie is caught up in this dream vision that George shoots him, so that on one level the vision is accomplished—the dream never interrupted, the rabbits never crushed.

The highly patterned effect achieved by these incremental motifs of symbol, action, and language is the knife edge on which criticism of *Of Mice and Men* divides. Mark Van Doren, for example, sees this patterning of events as evidence of a mechanical structure: "Lennie, you see, cannot help shaking small helpless creatures until their necks are broken, just as Curley cannot help being a beast of jealousy. They are wound up to act that way, and the best they can do is to run down; which is what happens when Steinbeck comes to his last mechanical page" ["Wrong Number," *The Nation* CXLIV (6 March 1937)]. This view is shared by Joseph Wood Krutch, who insists [in his *The American Drama since 1918,* 1939] that "everything from beginning to end" is "as shamelessly cooked up as, let us say, the death of Little Nell." On the other hand, Mr. Stark Young sees this patterning as a virtue: "And instead of losing . . . by this evident manipulation for effect, the play gains in its total impact and imaginative compulsion. In the characters, too, we get a sense of arrangement or design, so definitely carried through that we have almost a sense of types, an almost classic designation and completeness to each" ["Drama Critics Circle Award," *The New Republic* XCIV (4 May 1938)]. Frank H. O'Hara comes to a similar conclusion [in his *Today in American Drama,* 1939], though admitting that "the constituents of melodrama are all here."

Thus while Steinbeck's success in creating a pattern has been acknowledged, criticism has been divided as to the effect of this achievement. On one side it is claimed that this strong patterning creates a sense of contrivance and mechanical action; and on the other that the patterning actually gives a meaningful design to the story, a tone of classic fate. What is obviously needed here is some objective critical tool for determining under what conditions a sense of inevitability (to use a neutral word) should be experienced as catharsis effected by a sense of fate, and when it should be experienced as mechanical contrivance. Such a tool cannot be forged within the limits of this study; but it is possible to examine the particular circumstances of *Of Mice and Men* more closely than has been done in this connection.

Although the three motifs of symbol, action, and language build up a strong pattern of inevitability, the movement is not unbroken. About midway in the novel (chapters 3 & 4) there is set up a counter movement which seems to threaten the pattern. Up to this point the dream of "a house an' a couple of acres" has seemed impossible of realization; the motifs have been too insistent. But now it develops that George has an actual farm in mind (ten acres), knows the owners and why they want to sell it: " 'The ol' people that owns it is flat bust an' the ol' lady needs an operation.' " He even knows the price—" 'six hundred dollars.' " Also, the maimed workman, Candy, is willing to buy a share in the dream with the three hundred dollars he has saved. It appears that at the end of the month George and Lennie will have another hundred dollars and that quite possibly they " 'could swing her for that.' " In the following chapter this dream and its possibilities are further explored through Lennie's visit with Crooks, the power of the dream manifesting itself in Crooks' conversion from cynicism to optimism. But at the very height of his conversion the mice symbol reappears in the form of Curley's wife, who threatens the dream by bringing with her the harsh realities of the outside world and by arousing Lennie's interest.

The function of Candy's and Crooks' interest and the sudden bringing of the dream within reasonable possibility is to interrupt, momentarily, the pattern of inevitability. But, and this is very important, Steinbeck handles this interruption so that it does not actually constitute a reversal of the situation. Rather, it insinuates a possibility. Thus, though working against the pattern set up by the motifs, this counter movement makes that pattern more aesthetically credible by creating the necessary ingredient of free will. The story achieves power through a delicate balance of the protagonists' free will and the force of circumstance.

In addition to imposing a sense of inevitability, this strong patterning of events performs the important function of extending the story's range of meanings. This can best be understood by reference to Hemingway's "fourth dimension," which has been defined by Joseph Warren Beach as an "aesthetic factor" achieved by the protagonists' repeated participation in some traditional "ritual or strategy," and by Malcolm Cowley as "the almost continual performance of rites and ceremonies" suggesting recurrent patterns of human experience. The incremental motifs of symbol, action, and language which inform *Of Mice and Men* have precisely these effects. The simple story of two migrant workers' dream of a safe retreat, a "clean well-lighted place," becomes itself a pattern or archetype.

Thus while John Mason Brown [in his *Two on the Aisle*,

1938] calls the play "one of the finest, most pungent, and most poignant realistic productions," Frank H. O'Hara says that ". . . we are likely to come away with more . . . feelings for the implications of the story than the story itself . . . sketching behind the individual characters the vast numbers of other homeless drifters who work for a toe hold in a society which really has no place for them." [In "Steinbeck of California," *Delphian Quarterly* XXIII (April 1940)] Carlos Baker sees the book as an allegory of Mind and Body. Edmund Wilson calls the book "a parable which criticizes humanity from a non-political point of view" [*The Boys in the Back Room,* 1941]. The French critic, Mme. Claude-Edmonde Magny sees George and Lennie as "l'homme et le monstre," or "la conscience et l'humanité" [*L'Age du roman américain,* 1948].

As these remarks make clear, three levels have been observed in *Of Mice and Men.* There is the obvious story level on a realistic plane, with its shocking climax. There is also the level of social protest, Steinbeck the reformer crying out against the exploitation of migrant workers. The third level, is an allegorical one, its interpretation limited only by the ingenuity of the audience. It could be, as Carlos Baker suggests, an allegory of Mind and Body. Using the same kind of dichotomy, the story could also be about the dumb, clumsy, but strong mass of humanity and its shrewd manipulators. This would make the book a more abstract treatment of the two forces in *In Dubious Battle*—the mob and its leaders. The dichotomy could also be that of the unconscious and the conscious, the *id* and the *ego,* or any other forces or qualities which have the same structural relationship to each other as do Lennie and George. It is interesting in this connection that the name *Leonard* means "strong and brave as a lion," and that the name *George,* of course, means "husbandman."

The title itself, however, relates *Of Mice and Men* to still another level which is implicit in the context of [Robert] Burns' poem:

> But, Mousie, thou art no thy lane,
> In proving foresight may be vain:
> The best laid schemes o' mice and men
>
> Gang aft a-gley
>
> An' leave us nought but grief an' pain
>
> For promis'd joy.

In the poem Burns extends the mouse's experience to include mankind; in *Of Mice and Men* Steinbeck extends the experience of two migrant workers to the human condition. "This is the way things are," both writers are saying. On this level, perhaps its most important, Steinbeck is dramatizing the non-teleological philosophy which had such a great part in shaping *In Dubious Battle* and which was to be explicated in *Sea of Cortez.* This level of meaning is also indicated by the book's tentative title while it was in progress—"Something That Happened." In this light, the ending of the story is, like the ploughman's disrupting of the mouse's nest, neither tragic nor brutal but simply a part of the pattern of events. It is amusing in this regard that a Hollywood director suggested to Steinbeck that someone else kill the girl so that sympathy could be kept with Lennie.

In addition to these meanings which grow out of the book's "pattern," there is what might be termed a subplot which defines George's concern with Lennie. It is easily perceived that George, the "husbandman," is necessary to Lennie; but it has not been pointed out that Lennie is just as necessary to George. Without an explanation of this latter relationship any allegory posited on the pattern created in *Of Mice and Men* must remain incomplete.

Repeatedly, George tells Lennie, "God, you're a lot of trouble. I could get along so easy and so nice if I didn't have you on my tail." But this getting along so easy never means getting a farm of his own. With one important exception, George never mentions the dream except for Lennie's benefit. That his own "dream" is quite different from Lennie's is established early in the novel and often repeated: " 'God a'mighty, if I was alone I could live so easy. I could go get a job an' work, an' no trouble. No mess at all, and when the end of the month come I could take my fifty bucks and go into town and get whatever I want. Why, I could stay in a cat house all night. I could eat any place I want, hotel or any place, and order any damn thing I could think of. An' I could do all that every damn month. Get a gallon of whiskey, or set in a pool room and play cards or shoot pool.' " Lennie has heard this from George so often that in the last scene, when he realizes he has " 'done another bad thing,' " he asks, "Ain't you gonna give me hell? . . . Like, 'If I didn't have you I'd take my fifty bucks—' "

Almost every character in the story asks George why he goes around with Lennie: the foreman Curley, Slim, and Candy. Crooks, the lonely Negro, doesn't ask but he does speculate about it, and shrewdly—" 'a guy talkin' to another guy and it don't make no difference if he don't hear or understand. The thing is, they're talkin'. . . . ' " George's explanations vary from outright lies to a simple statement of " 'We travel together.' " It is only to Slim, the superior workman with the "God-like eyes," that he tells a great part of the truth. Among other reasons, such as his feeling of responsibility for Lennie in return for the latter's unfailing loyalty, and their having grown up together, there is revealed another: " 'He's dumb as hell, but he ain't crazy. An' I ain't so bright neither, or I wouldn't be buckin' barley for my fifty and found. If I was even a little bit smart, I'd have my own place, an' I'd be bringin' in my own crops, 'sted of doin' all the work and not getting what comes up outa the ground.' "

This statement, together with George's repeatedly expressed desire to take his fifty bucks to a cat house and his continual playing of solitaire, reveals that to some extent George needs Lennie as a rationalization for his failure. This is one of the reasons why, after the murder of Curley's wife, George refuses Candy's offer of a partnership which would have made the dream of a "safe place" a reality. The dream of the farm originates with Lennie; and it is only through Lennie, who also makes it impossible, that the dream has any meaning for George. An understanding of this dual relationship will do much to mitigate the frequent charge that Steinbeck's depiction of George's attachment is concocted of pure sentimentality. At the end of the novel, George's going off with Slim to "do the town" is more than an escape from grief. It is an ironic and symbolic twist to his dream.

The "real" meaning of the book is neither in the realistic action nor in the levels of allegory. Nor is it in some middle course. Rather, it is in the pattern which informs the story both on the realistic and allegorical levels, a pattern which Steinbeck took pains to prevent from becoming either trite or mechanical. (pp. 228-34)

> *Peter Lisca, "Motif and Pattern in 'Of Mice and Men'," in* Modern Fiction Studies, *Vol. II, No. 4, Winter, 1956-57, pp. 228-34.*

Steinbeck on *Of Mice and Men*:

Of Mice and Men was an attempt to write a novel in three acts to be played from the lines. I had nearly finished it when my setter pup ate it one night, literally made confetti of it! I don't know how close the first and second versions would prove to be. This book had some success, but as usual it found its enemies. With rewriting, however, it did become a play and had some success.

John Steinbeck, in his "My Short Novels," Wings, 1953.

Winifred L. Dusenbury   (essay date 1960)

[Dusenbury is an American educator and critic. In the following excerpt, she comments on the theme of loneliness in Of Mice and Men.*]*

[John Steinbeck's *Of Mice and Men* and Clifford Odet's *Night Music* both treat the loneliness that is engendered by homelessness.] In both plays the intense hunger for a home burns in the main characters, as well as in many minor ones; but otherwise—in character, in setting, in structure, in dialogue, in mood, and in form—the two plays vary. Set in the Western ranch country of the Salinas Valley, California, mainly on a river bank, in a bunk house and in a hay barn, *Of Mice and Men* is a realistic depiction of the life of transient ranch hands. The characters are particularized in that they cannot be said to represent man lost in America, as Suitcase Steve [in *Night Music*] might, nor is there any semblance of a guiding spirit to aid them. They are one kind of man lost. The plays are similar, however, in that although both Odets and Steinbeck have shown intense interest in the sociological and economic causes of the unfortunate situations of various kinds of Americans, here they have turned from sociological to personal drama, and Burns Mantle's description [in *The Best Plays of 1937-38*] of *Of Mice and Men* might apply to both. He praises the play for "its appealing exposure of the tragedy that is found in human loneliness."

The dominant cause of George and Lennie's lonesomeness and of that of all the ranch hands is lack of a home. George and Lennie's dream is: "Someday we're gonna get the jack together and we're gonna have a little house, and a couple of acres and a cow and some pigs and. . . . " The stable buck, Crooks, cynical and doubting, expresses the theme of the play:

> I seen hundreds of men come by on the road. . . . Every damn one of 'em is got a little piece of land in his head. And never a God damn one of 'em gets it. Jus' like heaven. Nobody never gets to heaven, and nobody gets no land. . . . I seen guys nearly crazy with loneliness for land.
>
> (II, ii)

Steinbeck has made bitterly real the impulsive hunger of the ranch hand for a home of his own. Nothing of the sentiment of the "little grey home in the West" or "land where the tall corn grows" regulates his dreams. He understands the hard work of a farm; he recognizes that farm animals involve a daily responsibility; but his happiness would be in belonging to the land and to the house and to the animals upon the land. Crooks' opinion proves to be correct, however, that for a ranch worker a farm of his own is as unlikely as heaven. Something in his character makes him forever a hired hand, and never a land owner.

In this hopeless longing for a home on the land George and Lennie are like the other ranch hands. In their friendship for each other they are not. Steinbeck makes use of their close relationship to point up the loneliness of the typical ranch hand. Their affection—almost a mother-child relationship—is convincingly illustrated by their great pleasure in conversational byplay. To George's "What I could do if I didn't have the burden of you," Lennie usually replies, "I'll go and hide in a cave." George contritely answers, "No, I didn't mean it. Stay with me." Then Lennie leads into the subject dearest to them both. "I will if you'll tell me about the farm." George now has an audience ecstatically rapt in every well-worn phrase. Emerson, for all his words on friendship, has not expressed the feeling so vividly as has Steinbeck in a few short conversations.

That such a relationship is unusual is evidenced in the doubt of the boss that George's interest in Lennie can be unselfish. He suspects that George is taking Lennie's pay. One of the hands, Slim, also is skeptical: "I hardly never seen two guys travel together. . . . Most hands work a month and then they quit and go on alone." George himself says, "Guys like us that work on ranches is the loneliest guys in the world." "But not us!" continues Lennie, "because . . . I got you to look after me . . . and you got me to look after you." Steinbeck points up the unusual friendship to enhance the tragedy of George's having to shoot Lennie to save him from being lynched, but also to emphasize the aloneness of the typical ranch hand.

So unusual is the obviously genuine feeling between George and Lennie that their dream of a home seems possible of fulfillment to the old bunkhouse keeper, Candy, and finally even to the cynical Crooks, both of whom beg to be allowed to help in buying a small farm. Crooks goes so far as to offer to work for them for nothing if they will take him along. The friendship blows like a breath of love through the lonely world of the ranch hands, who are moved by it to think all things possible, but it inspires the hate of the cowardly boss's son, and proves in the end an

ill-fated relationship among workers destined for loneliness. A kind of meanness, which even the dim-witted Lennie senses, pervades the air of the ranch where the two men start work. George's reiterated warnings to Lennie to stay away from Curley and Curley's wife are well founded, but the inevitability of Lennie's becoming entangled with them makes the warnings fruitless. The sustaining dream of a home, which is so vivid as to inspire other lonesome ranch hands with belief, is blasted at the end by the death-dealing shot from the German Luger.

In structure Steinbeck's drama resembles the "well-made play" in its careful plotting and its pointing up of properties and incidents which will play an important part in later scenes. Were it not for the fact that the theme of lonesomeness is made so poignantly real, the play would seem melodramatic. It contains several violent climactic scenes, which, if they had not been motivated by the suffering of the characters, would be only sensational. This is not to say that it deteriorates into mediocrity, however, for, instead of imposing the action upon the characters, the violence resulting from their loneliness is a logical outcome of it, and the technique of the plot does not weaken the encompassing theme.

The obvious framework which contains the play is the use of the riverbank scene at the opening curtain and at the closing, with George's admonishing words in the first scene, "Lennie, if you just happen to get in trouble, I want you to come right here and hide in the brush," fulfilled by his shooting of Lennie in the last. In between there are references to the possibility of trouble and to the place by the river, where the two men first camp for the night. After the boss's son speaks to Lennie with a chip on his shoulder, George reminds Lennie, "Look, if you get in any kind of trouble, you remember what I told you to do." The big, stupid man finally remembers, "Hide in the brush until you come for me." Later Lennie, in response to George's warning to stay away from Curley's wife, senses trouble. "Let's go, George. Let's get out of here. It's mean here." Later when attacked by the sullen Curley, he complains to George, "I didn't want no trouble." Finally when he has killed Curley's wife and realizes that trouble has hit him broadside, he rushes to the riverbank, where in darkening twilight like that of the opening scene, George shoots him while describing the "little place," which had been their dream.

Added to the carefully prepared build-up of the likelihood of Lennie's getting into trouble is dramaturgical preparation of the kind of trouble to which Lennie is prone. In the beginning George takes a dead mouse away from Lennie, while Lennie protests that he needs something soft to pet and that he has always tried to be gentle with the mice which his Aunt Clara used to give him, but "I'd pet 'em . . . and then I pinched their heads a little bit and then they was dead." Lennie wishes they could get the "little place" of their own soon, because the soft, furry rabbits would not get killed so easily. To arrive at a ranch where one of the hands is trying to give away a litter of new pups is perhaps what Aristotle would call a possible improbability. It is not long after he has been given a puppy that, as could have been prophesied, Lennie has "petted" it to death. By exposition in the opening scene, George makes clear that Lennie has barely escaped lynching in Weed because of this predilection for fondling soft things.

> You just wanta feel that girl's dress. Just wanta pet it like it was a mouse. . . . You didn't mean for her to yell bloody hell. . . .
>
> (I, i)

And shortly after the men first reach the bunkhouse, Curley's wife, whom George rightly calls "jail bait," appears sluttishly perfumed and evokes the comment from the staring Lennie, "Gosh, she's purty."

As if the forecast by incident and exposition of the kind of trouble coming were not enough, Steinbeck has strengthened the play's structure by the pointed use of Carlson's German Luger. Carlson first produces the gun from the bag under his bunk to shoot Candy's old dog. He cleans it obviously before replacing it. Later when George, having found the dead woman, is seen to rush into the empty bunkhouse, the audience is prepared for Carlson's announcement that his gun is missing and recognizes that it is not Lennie, as the men assume, but George, who has taken it. And while George makes Lennie sit and look across the river in the final scene, it is no surprise to see him slowly draw it from his side pocket.

Thus, it is with Ibsen-like precision that Steinbeck lays the stage, but also with Ibsen-like purpose he portrays the tragic loneliness of life on a Western ranch. The isolation which George and Lennie feel pervades every other character. Candy, the old bunkhouse keeper, who has lost his right hand, clings to his blind, stinking dog, until with despairing resignation, he lets the men shoot the miserable animal because of his recognition that they do it with understanding pity for his grief and not with brutality. Curley's wife hangs around the bunkhouse relentlessly, although she is not encouraged by any of the men. To the charge that she is a tart, she pleads innocent and claims that she is only lonesome.

> I got nobody to talk to. I got nobody to be with. . . . I want to see somebody. Just see 'em an' talk to 'em.
>
> (II, i)

Crooks, the black stable buck, complains to Lennie:

> You got George. S'pose you din't have nobody. . . . A guy goes nuts if he aint got nobody. . . . I tell you a guy gets too lonely, he gets sick.
>
> (II, ii)

Even the boss, after stern questioning of George and Lennie, "relaxes, as though he wanted to talk but felt always the burden of his position." After some jocular remarks, which are turned aside by George, who feels that "He's the boss first an' a nice guy afterwards," the boss "realizes there is no contact to establish; grows rigid with his position again."

So besides the loneliness of the ranch hands because of their homelessness, there is in the play the lonesomeness of debilitated old age, of the Negro because of his color, of the lone woman on the ranch, and of the man in author-

ity. There is a sense of homelessness and temporariness among all these characters and some elemental discussion of the needs of mankind for privacy as well as for companionship. Whereas the hands who live in the bunkhouse long for a room of their own, the black stable buck laments that he must live by himself. George's dream of a farm includes "a room to ourselves," and Candy says to Crooks, as he enters the stable room for the first time, "Must be nice to have a room to yourself this way." But Crooks replies satirically, "All to myself. It's swell. . . . Guys don't come in a colored man's room." There is lonesomeness in being one bunk-inhabitant among many as there is lonesomeness in being segregated. There is lonesomeness in old age and in authority, as there is lonesomeness in being homeless.

Although the suitcase is not the much-used property it is in *Night Music,* Steinbeck, like Odets, has accented the idea of homelessness by its use. Carrying their possessions in blanket rolls, or "bindles," George and Lennie make their first entrance, and in a later scene arrive with them at the ranch bunkhouse, where they stow their few belongings by their bunks. A reminder that all the men are temporarily working at the ranch is Carlson's pulling his bag from under his bunk to take out his gun and the placement of all the hands' possessions from their bags onto the little shelves by their bunks. At the end it is with a "small, cheap suitcase" that Curley's wife arrives in the barn to prepare for her running away from Curley. The suitcases or bindles are used as visual reminders of the homelessness which haunts the characters. They contribute to the theme as well as to the plot.

It is because Steinbeck has made his theme more important than his plot that the play becomes a meaningful aesthetic expression of a phase of American life. The technique of creating suspense by exposition and incident is obvious upon analysis, but its use is justifiable, for the final effect of the tragedy of human loneliness is what remains with the audience. Of far more importance than the plot is the portrayal of the friendship which is blasted; of the isolation of each character; of the mood of meanness which is engendered in the atmosphere of lonesomeness on the ranch; and of the homelessness of the ranch hands. Here loneliness is not only pitiful; it is tragic.

Steinbeck does not share Odets' hopeful attitude that Americans (at least these particular Americans) can have homes by fighting for them. His play may perhaps more properly be called one of homelessness than can *Night Music,* in which a home is seen to be possible within oneself even in unpromising circumstances. In *Of Mice and Men* a home remains forever a dream which only temporarily assuages the lonesomeness of the dreamers. (pp. 45-50)

Winifred L. Dusenbury, "Homelessness," in her The Theme of Loneliness In Modern American Drama, *University of Florida Press, 1960, pp. 38-56.*

Warren French   (essay date 1961)

[French is an American educator and critic. In the following excerpt, he remarks on the style, themes, and characterization in Of Mice and Men.*]*

Although other critics have not noted to what extent *Of Mice and Men* is an Arthurian story, the fundamental parallels—the knightly loyalty, the pursuit of the vision, the creation of a bond (shared briefly by Candy and Brooks), and its destruction by an at least potentially adulterous relationship—are there. They are, however, so concealed by the surface realism of the work that one unfamiliar with Steinbeck's previous Arthurian experiments would be hardly likely to notice them. The one obvious Arthurian hangover is George, who is not only remarkably loyal to his charge—the feeble-minded Lennie—but also remarkably pure.

George not only warns Lennie against the blandishments of Curley's wife, but is himself obviously impervious to her charms. While the other ranch hands are excited by her presence, George says only, "Jesus, what a tramp!" When invited to join the boys in a Saturday night trip to a neighboring town's "nice" whorehouse, George says that he "might go in an' set and have a shot," but "ain't puttin' out no two and a half." He excuses himself on the ground that he is saving money to buy a farm, but not even Galahad might have found it politic to profess chastity in a bunkhouse. George seems to have stepped, in fact, not out of Malory's Arthurian stories but Tennyson's. When he is told that Curley boasts of having his glove full of Vaseline in order to keep his hand soft for his wife, George says, "That's a dirty thing to tell around."

George is noticeably more critical of Curley's wife than Steinbeck is. *Of Mice and Men* is not so completely objective as *In Dubious Battle;* Steinbeck editorializes occasionally, for example, after the girl has been killed:

> . . . the meanness and the plannings and the discontent and the ache for attention were all gone from her face. She was very pretty and simple, and her face was sweet and young.

George shows no such sympathy, and it is important to notice that the author is more flexible than his character, because it is a sign that he is not being carried away by his vision as are the characters sometimes assumed to represent his viewpoint. The Arthurian flavor here is faint, but unmistakable. Like Jim Nolan [in *In Dubious Battle*], George is a last Galahad, dismounted, armed only with a fading dream, a long way from Camelot. Steinbeck is his historian, not his alter ego.

One does not need to justify a search for an allegory in *Of Mice and Men* since the author has spoken of the book as symbolic and microcosmic. Just what the universal drama enacted against a Salinas Valley backdrop may be is not, however, so obvious as first appears. Unquestionably it concerns a knight of low estate and a protégé who share a dream, a dream that cannot come true because the protégé lacks the mental capacity to be conscious enough to know his own strength or to protect himself from temptation.

At first glance, it appears that nature is the culprit and that this is an ironic, deterministic fable like Stephen Crane's "The Open Boat." It is an indifferent nature that makes men physically strong but mentally deficient; dreaming is man's only defense against a world he never made. "The best-laid schemes o' mice an' men aft agley," Burns said, providing Steinbeck with a title, because man is at the mercy of forces he cannot control which ruthlessly but indifferently destroy the illusions he has manufactured. The book may be read in this naturalistic manner, and those who speak of it as sentimental must think of it as an expression of Steinbeck's outraged compassion for the victims of chaotic forces.

Such a reading, however, does not do the story justice. If George stood helplessly by and saw Lennie destroyed, the novel might be called deterministic; but he doesn't. George has a will, and he exercises it to make two critical decisions at the end of the novel—to kill Lennie and to lie about it.

George could, of course, have killed Lennie simply to protect the giant brute from the mob; but, since Lennie doesn't know what is going on anyway, it is easy to oversentimentalize George's motives. Actually he has reasons of his own for pulling the trigger. Steinbeck makes it clear that George had tremendous difficulty bringing himself to destroy Lennie, although Lennie will not even know what has happened. What George is actually trying to kill is not Lennie, who is only a shell and a doomed one at that, but something in himself.

[In "Motif and Pattern in 'Of Mice and Men'," *Modern Studies Fiction* II, No. 4 (Winter 1956-57)] Peter Lisca points out that Lennie's need for George is obvious, but that George's need for Lennie, though less obvious, is as great. In his most candid appraisal of himself, George says, "I ain't so bright neither, or I wouldn't be buckin' barley for my fifty and found. If I was even a little bit smart, I'd have my own little place. . . ." He needs him, however, as more than just a rationalization for his own failure; for George not only protects but *directs* Lennie. Lennie doesn't speak unless George permits him to; and, in the fight in which Curley's hand is broken, Lennie refuses even to defend himself until George tells him to. George, of course, directs Lennie partly to protect him from committing acts he could not mentally be responsible for, but George is not a wholly altruistic shepherd. Another aspect of the relationship becomes apparent when George tells Slim that Lennie, "Can't think of nothing to do himself, but he sure can take orders." Since George gives the orders, Lennie gives him a sense of power.

One aspect of the dream that George repeatedly describes to Lennie also needs scrutiny. The ritual ("George's voice became deeper. He repeated his words rhythmically.") begins "Guys like us, that work on ranches, are the loneliest guys in the world. . . . They ain't got nothing to look ahead to" and continues "with us it ain't like that . . . because [here Lennie takes over from George] I got you to look after me, and you got me to look after you, and that's why." The dream not only gives a direction to their lives, but also makes them feel different from other people. Since this sense of difference can mean little to Lennie, it is part of the consolation George receives from the dream. George wants to be superior. With Lennie gone, his claim to distinction will be gone. Thus when George shoots Lennie, he is not destroying only the shared dream. He is also destroying the thing that makes him different and reducing himself to the status of an ordinary guy. He is obliged to acknowledge what Willy Loman in Arthur Miller's *Death of a Salesman,* for example, could never acknowledge but what Henry Morgan accepted when he turned respectable in *Cup of Gold*—his own mediocrity. George is much like Willy Loman; for he is forced to recognize the same self-deflating realization Biff Loman vainly tries to impress upon his father: he is a "dime a dozen." Because of their relationship, George has actually been able to remain as much a "kid" as Lennie; shooting him matures George in more than one way.

It is equally important that George lies to the posse after the shooting. If the experience had not matured him, he had here his opportunity for a grand gesture. He could either destroy himself along with Lennie and the dream or, by an impassioned confession, force his enemies to destroy him. George, who by Romantic standards has little left to live for, chooses to go on living and to say that he had to shoot Lennie in self-defense. Actually the maturing effect of the experience upon George has been apparent from the moment when, in reply to Candy's offer to help him carry out the dream, he says: "—I think I knowed from the very first. I think I know'd we'd never do her. He usta like to hear about it so much I got to thinking maybe we would." With Lennie gone, George will not try to keep the dream alive. When Slim leads George up toward the highway at the end of the novel, the wonder is not that George is badly shaken by his experience, but that he is alive at all.

[*Of Mice and Men*] is a story not of man's defeat at the hands of an implacable nature, but of man's painful conquest of this nature and of his difficult, conscious rejection of his dreams of greatness and acceptance of his own mediocrity.

—*Warren French*

Despite the grim events it chronicles *Of Mice and Men* is not a tragedy, but a comedy—which, if it were Shakespearean, we would call a "dark comedy"—about the triumph of the indomitable will to survive. This is a story not of man's defeat at the hands of an implacable nature, but of man's painful conquest of this nature and of his difficult, conscious rejection of his dreams of greatness and acceptance of his own mediocrity. Unfortunately, the allegory is less clear in the play version than in the novel, since Steinbeck, probably to provide a more effective curtain, eliminates George's last conversation with Slim and ends with the shooting of Lennie. The original ending would also probably have been too involved for playgoers to follow after experiencing the emotions engendered by the climactic episodes.

Lennie has been viewed sometimes as an example of Stein-

beck's preoccupation with subhuman types; actually Lennie is not a character in the story at all, but rather a device like a golden coin in *Moby Dick* to which the other characters may react in a way that allows the reader to perceive their attitudes. So intensely focused upon the relationship between George and Lennie is the novel that the other characters are likely to be overlooked; yet each makes an important contribution to the narrative and provides a clue to Steinbeck's conception of the human condition.

The protest against racial discrimination and the treatment of the aged through the characters of Brooks and Candy needs no elaboration. The symbolism of Curley and his ill-fated bride is perhaps summed up in her statement that they married after she "met him out to Riverside Dance Palace that same night." There is a sordid echo of Fitzgerald and the "lost generation" here; for, like the Buchanans in *The Great Gatsby,* these are "careless people" who smash up things and "let other people clean up the mess." It is true that the girl is smashed up herself, but, unlike Curley, she did have dreams and disappointments. He simply, like the Buchanans, retreats into his "vast carelessness." The wife, not George, is the one in the novel who is destroyed when, instead of controlling her dreams, she allows them to control her; and Curley, not Lennie, is actually the willfully animalistic type.

The most interesting characters—except for George and Lennie—are Carlson and Slim, two other ranch hands, who have the last words in the novel. They are complements, symbolizing, on one hand, the insensitive and brutal; on the other, the kindly and perceptive. "Now what the hell ya suppose is eatin' them two guys?" are Carlson's words—the last in the book—as Slim and George sadly walk off for a drink. Undoubtedly this sums up Steinbeck's concept of an unperceptive world's reaction to the drama just enacted. The uncomprehending responses to his books had given Steinbeck sufficient grounds for being aware of this "practical" attitude and through Carlson he strikes back at the men to whom Doctor Burton in *In Dubious Battle* attributes the world's "wild-eyed confusion." But Steinbeck also suggests that such men have the last word.

This bitterly ironic view is expressed through the major incident involving Carlson: the shooting of Candy's old dog. All Carlson can see about the dog is that "he don't have no fun . . . and he stinks to beat hell." He has no feelings about the animal, and, because his reactions are entirely physical, no concept that anyone else might have feelings about it. He is the same kind of man as the agitators Steinbeck condemned in *In Dubious Battle*—insensitive, violent, fanatical. This "practical" man's only contributions to the group are destructive.

To balance this destructive force, Steinbeck introduces and awards the next-to-last word to the jerkline skinner, Slim, the man who alone understands and tries to comfort George at the end of the novel. Steinbeck breaks his editorial silence, as he does in speaking of Curley's wife, to make it absolutely clear to the reader how Slim is to be regarded. "His ear heard more than was said to him," the author writes, "and his slow speech had overtones not of thought, but of understanding beyond thought." "His authority," the reader is told, "was so great that his word was taken on any subject, be it politics or love." What matters most, however, is the professional standing of this paragon:

> He moved with a majesty only achieved by royalty and master craftsmen. He was a jerkline skinner, capable of driving ten, sixteen, even twenty mules with a single line to the leaders. He was capable of killing a fly on the wheeler's butt with a bull whip without touching the mule.

The important thing about this passage is the emphasis placed upon skill and craftsmanship; here is the really "practical" man—not the callous boor, but the man who is able to do his job exceedingly well. We are to meet him again in *Cannery Row* and *The Wayward Bus.* It is notable that he is not a dreamer, but a doer. In another editorial aside that sets the tone for the whole book, Steinbeck points out that among other things with which the shelves where the ranch hands kept their personal belongings were loaded were "those Western magazines ranch men love to read and scoff at and secretly believe." Underneath the surface most men are not only dreamers, but unsuccessful dreamers; the real heroes are not these dreamers, but the doers. The heroic "doers," however, are not those who act only for personal aggrandizement, but those who try to do their best out of an affection for their craft and who feel compassionate rather than scornful toward the dreamers. With *Of Mice and Men,* Steinbeck himself unmistakably joins this class of craftsmen, for he not only shows compassion for the plight of the dreamer, but he accomplishes in the manner of a master craftsman his intention to sort out and evaluate the categories of men. Having mastered his craft, he was ready to execute his masterpiece [*The Grapes of Wrath*]. (pp. 73-9)

> *Warren French, in his* John Steinbeck, *Twayne Publishers, Inc., 1961, 190 p.*

Joseph Fontenrose   (essay date 1963)

[*Fontenrose is an American educator and critic. In the following excerpt, he asserts that in* Of Mice and Men *Steinbeck suggested that the desire for immediate gratification prohibits the actualization of dreams.*]

Man's longing for the land, a favorite Steinbeck theme, appearing in some form in nearly every novel, is [in *Of Mice and Men*] expressed in the farmhand's and bindlestiff's desire for a few acres of his own, so that he can be his own boss. George said, "I'd have my own little place, an' I'd be bringin' in my own crops, 'stead of doin' all the work and not getting what comes up outa the ground." And Candy said,

> "Everybody wants a little bit of land, not much. Jus' som'thin' that was his. Som'thin' he could live on and there couldn't nobody throw him off of it. I never had none. I planted crops for damn near ever'body in this state, but they wasn't my crops, and when I harvested 'em, it wasn't none of my harvest."

Only in such speeches as these does *Of Mice and Men* seem to relate this land hunger to contemporary social issues. But this is hardly the author's intention: he is simply reporting a mode in which the yearning is really expressed by men whose chances of acquiring land are well-nigh hopeless—altogether hopeless, as Crooks, the Negro stable buck, saw it:

> "I seen hunderds of men come by on the road an' on the ranches, with their bindles on their back an' that same damn thing in their heads. Hunderds of them. They come, an' they quit an' go on; an' every damn one of 'em's got a little piece of land in his head. An' never a God damn one of 'em ever gets it. Just like heaven. . . . Nobody never gets to heaven, and nobody gets no land. It's just in their head."

Yet Crooks too had the dream. When he saw that Candy and Lennie had a real proposition, backed by real money, he offered to work for them for nothing, just to share their independence—until Curley's wife made him realize the futility of his wish. And Crooks was right after all, as the story is told: these were but three more men with that "thing in their heads." The land hunger of impoverished farm workers, a dream of independence, usually remains a dream; and when it becomes a real plan, the plan is defeated.

Of Mice and Men was meant to be a non-teleological tale, and the first title that Steinbeck gave it was "Something That Happened." Something that happens may be accidental, coincidental, atypical, and surely the concluding events and deeds in this novel are neither typical nor commonplace. For George and Lennie, being who they are and where they are, the outcome may be inevitable, and we may see a personal tragedy in the tale. Steinbeck, however, meant the story to be a parable of the human condition, as his final title indicates. It is a good title, because the story itself tells us just what Burns meant when he said, "the best-laid schemes o' mice an' men gang aft agley": one unlucky fieldmouse lost its nest when the field was plowed. But not all fieldmice suffer that fate; Burns did not mean that no man's scheme is ever realized. Steinbeck reads, "All schemes o' mice an' men gang ever agley." Crooks said, "Nobody never gets to heaven, and nobody gets no land," and George said to Candy, "—I think I knowed from the very first. I think I knowed we'd never do her," thus reading destiny—the inevitable failure of his plans—in Lennie's terrible deed. It is the message of *Cup of Gold,* the vanity of human wishes. In a letter to his agents, written soon after completing the manuscript of *Of Mice and Men,* Steinbeck said that Lennie represents "the inarticulate and powerful yearning of all men," and referred to its scene as a microcosm, making it plain that this novel was meant to express the inevitable defeat and futility of all men's plans. But the tragic story of George and Lennie cannot carry the load of cosmic pessimism placed upon it. It tells us only that it is hard for bindlestiffs to buy land, and that even when they get the money they cannot be sure of making the purchase. Nevertheless, migratory workers have acquired land, even in California, and George could have done so. Not Lennie who died, but Candy who lived, had $350, and Candy still wanted to carry out the plan. Objectively considered, the prospects for success were better without Lennie, who would surely have killed every rabbit on the place. But without Lennie the plan had no meaning for George. The sweeping pessimistic thesis is thus imposed upon the story and obscures its true meaning: that our pleasures often oppose and thwart our schemes. Steinbeck came nearer to an adequate statement of thesis when he said in another letter that *Of Mice and Men* was "a study of the dreams and pleasures of everyone in the world."

After shooting Lennie, an act that the others assumed he had done in self-defense, George went off with Slim to get a drink. This means that George had turned to his counter-dream of independence: freedom from Lennie. This dream, as well as the other, George recited in both the opening and closing scenes among the willows by the river:

> "God a'mighty, if I was alone I could live so easy. I could go get a job an' work, an' no trouble. No mess at all, and when the end of the month come I could take my fifty bucks and go into town and get whatever I want. Why, I could stay in a cat house all night. I could eat any place I want, hotel or any place, and order any damn thing I could think of. An' I could do all that every damn month. Get a gallon of whisky, or set in a pool room and play cards or shoot pool. . . . An' whatta I got, . . . I got you! You can't keep a job and you lose me ever' job I get."

It is a recital that Lennie often heard. At the end the contrite Lennie expected to hear it again and urged George to say it. George started half-heartedly, but soon turned to the other recital about the land and the rabbits. And what George longed for in his dream of individual freedom was exactly what he deprecated in his dream of living with Lennie on a small ranch. He recited this dream too at the beginning and end of the story, and once in the middle; but only the first time is it given in its complete ritualistic form:

> "Guys like us, that work on ranches, are the loneliest guys in the world. They got no fambly. They don't belong no place. They come to a ranch an' work up a stake and then they go into town and blow their stake, and the first thing you know they're poundin' their tail on some other ranch. They ain't got nothing to look ahead to. . . . With us it ain't like that. We got a future. We got somebody to talk to that gives a damn about us. We don't have to sit in no bar room blowin' in our jack jus' because we got no place else to go."

Then he went on to describe the little place that they would buy when they "[got] the jack together," where they would *"live off the fatta the lan'."*

So the "dreams and pleasures" of Steinbeck's statement are both synonymous and contrasting terms. The lonely bindlestiff dreams of owning land (and although George said that others did not have "a future," Crooks said that all ranch workers had that dream); yet he enjoys cards, whisky, women. His pleasures take his little money and he never begins to realize the dream. For George, who was tied to Lennie, freedom to enjoy these pleasures was as much a dream as having a ranch; in fact, any indulgence in them was severely limited, since Lennie prevented his earning more than a few dollars at a time. Thus George was split between genuine affection for Lennie, who was company, someone to control and look after, and a desire to be free of an inconvenient burden. When he shot Lennie he was not only saving Lennie from Curley's cruelty, but was also making a choice between dreams: events had forced him to a decision. "I'll work my month an' I'll take my fifty bucks an' I'll stay all night in some lousy cat house. Or I'll set in some poolroom . . . ,"—thus George answered Candy's question "Then—it's all off?" and realized without joy that one dream was dead and another, the dream of lonely independence, had come true.

Of Mice and Men has no recognizable mythical pattern. The central image is the earthly paradise, visible in nearly every Steinbeck novel. This has meant for Americans an agrarian economy of small farms, worked by their owners for their own benefit. It is part of the American dream, finding expression in such nineteenth-century visions as "the garden of the west" and "the garden of the world." It is a vision of Eden, a land of peace, harmony, prosperity; it includes both individual independence and fellowship. And in Steinbeck's world you aren't likely to get there; as Crooks said, "Nobody never gets to heaven."

We should also notice that this novel ignores the group organism, unless we say that Lennie, representing "the inarticulate and powerful yearning of all men," symbolizes it. Like the group Lennie has an elementary mentality, lacks initiative and originality, and can follow but not lead. The association of George and Lennie, leader and follower, is held together by a religion, complete with myth, ritual, and litany. When George makes his formulaic recitation, as quoted above, Lennie responds at the right place with *"But not us! An' why? Because . . . because I got you to look after me, and you got me to look after you, and that's why."* From loneliness, from blowing our money in barrooms and cat houses, from jails, good Lord deliver us— and grant us the blessings of fellowship on the land. It is a religion of cooperation, but, as in other religions, deprecated evils are powerful to keep men from paradise. The individual's desire for carefree enjoyment of pleasures is the serpent in the garden. (pp. 56-9)

> *Joseph Fontenrose, in his* John Steinbeck: An Introduction and Interpretation, *Barnes & Noble, Inc., 1963, 150 p.*

Bryant N. Wyatt   (essay date Spring 1969)

[*In the following excerpt, Wyatt applauds* Of Mice and Men *as technically well-written but adds that the work lacks substance.*]

[In his *Cavalcade of the American Novel* (1952) Edward Wagenknecht] maintains that "*Of Mice and Men* is unsatisfactory because it tries to squeeze tragedy out of characters who lack tragic stature." But such an indictment does injustice to the author as well as to the novel, for it is doubtful that Steinbeck should or does *wish* to present tragic characters in the classic sense (which seems essentially to be the sense Mr. Wagenknecht has in mind); rather, he wishes to examine *unfortunate* characters, persons upon whom suffering and misfortune are imposed. His concern is with the more representative, the *human,* tragedy. Additionally, Steinbeck attempts here to subordinate his interest in specific characters as individuals to that of analyzing abstract and universal human values and conditions—those which must be recognized and properly responded to, in his view, if man is to have stable and meaningful existence. Upon deliberate examination of the novel in the light of Steinbeck's motives, and keeping in mind his effort to obtain greater novelistic control, we appreciate more fully the competence with which its materials are treated.

It is evident that a primary construct of the work is the loneliness-togetherness motif, and Steinbeck expediently places the bulk of the novel's action in the environs of an isolated ranch, a setting where both poles may exist in conjunction. The inhabitants form a family group, constantly together; yet virtually every one of them yearns for a sense of belonging, a feeling of community, an escape from solitude.

The novel abounds with conflict of various types—between characters as well as within individual personages. The contrast between the two central figures is made graphic upon the initial entrance of George and Lennie. Though they are dressed similarly (emblematic of their common bond), Lennie appears to be almost the antithesis of George. Whereas George is small, perceptive, and swift of action, Lennie is huge, slow, and dull-witted. His subordinate status is accentuated by the fact that he is relegated to walking behind his companion. This literal devaluation on Lennie's part is sustained throughout, and intentionally so, for such apparent debasement accords with Steinbeck's overall thematic concerns. Lennie is repeatedly depicted in animalistic terms: he drags his feet "the way a bear drags his paws," obeys George "like a terrier," and threatens to leave George and find a *cave* to live in. Furthermore, he associates himself with animals (wishing to pet mice and sleep with puppies) and his most cherished goal is to be able to feed rabbits for the rest of his life.

The basis of the seeming conflict between the two is revealed in the very first chapter when George tells Lennie what an encumbrance the latter represents. If he were not burdened with responsibility for Lennie, George would be free to lead his life as he desires. Yet it is here that the essential aspect of their inseparability is revealed. George tells Lennie, "I want you to stay with me," and Lennie, in one of his least inarticulate moments, announces the unifying motives of their relationship when he proclaims, *"I got you to look after me, and you got me to look after you"* (ch. 1). Both wish to procure a little farm where they can live simply and happily. They are united in a dream.

A nearly identical relationship is that involving the old ranchhand, Candy, and his dog. The implications surrounding the necessary killing of the dog are paralleled by those relating to the "mercy killing" of Lennie at the end of the story. Candy has owned the dog a long time and has much affection for it. But it is agreed that the animal is of no use to anyone, even to itself; so it is put to death. George has been associated with Lennie in a similar manner and takes care of him just as Candy does the helpless dog. But Lennie ostensibly is of no use either, and he too is mercifully killed—shot in the back of the head just as the dog was. But Steinbeck believes that Lennie *is* of value, and the entire novel is grounded primarily in the unrecognized worth of Lennie and what he symbolizes. It is ironic, therefore, that although Lennie is debased throughout the literal account, so many of the positive values with which the book is concerned should take their origin with him, as will be examined presently in greater detail.

The multiple conflict of the novel is further illustrated in the case of other prominent characters. Both inner and external conflict arises from the relationship between Curley and his wife. He mistreats her in order to bolster his own ego, to compensate for his deficiencies. She is hostile toward him because he neglects her and because, by ensconcing her on the secluded ranch, he has thwarted her ambition to make a more conspicuous place for herself in the world. She too is lonely. The Negro stable buck, Crooks, aside from the racial slurs he must endure, has a twisted spine. He is not allowed to play cards with the other men (one of the few pastimes available at the ranch) and lives alone in a bleak harness room at one corner of the barn. Nobody pays him much attention. He is lonely.

The one character who seems untroubled is the jerkline skinner, Slim. He is the most humane and convincing figure of all. At the same time, he is the most nearly perfect. Slim is described as "the prince of the ranch" (ch. 2). Infallible, he is the mediator of all disputes, the solver of all problems, the authority whose word is law, whose judgment is never questioned, who is respected almost to the state of reverence by all. Only with his consent may Candy's dog be killed. Except the boss, whose duties occasionally require it, Slim is the only character who will customarily visit Crooks. Like Doc Burton [from *In Dubious Battle*], he refuses to divide people up. The cold authority of [*In Dubious Battle*] personified in Jim has been tempered and is handled here in more acceptable terms, for in Steinbeck's microcosmic ranch setting Slim takes on the attributes, in an inconspicuous way, of a Christ figure. Mention is made of his "God-like eyes" (ch. 3) and he is ever beyond fallibility. He operates at both the literal and the symbolic levels of the novel: he is another "insignificant" ranch hand and at the same time a kind of god. His position and Lennie's (similar, as we shall see) are the twin axes upon which the story revolves.

These alliances, this intensified conflict, and the atmosphere which they create are essential to the themes and significance of the novel. A major theme (and one typical of Steinbeck) is that of the need for unity in pursuit of a common worthwhile goal. This is what Mac was so interested in achieving in *Battle.* Such a bond between human beings must be secured by the solidifying qualities of kindness, loyalty and, especially, love—and by the ridding of the disintegrative ones of fear and mistrust. Lennie is an ideal character for the function which he serves in this aspect of the novel. He is character and symbol. He is Man (in God's own image) but among the most abject of men.

Lennie's proximity to the animal world has been already established. There is no denying that he also represents a segment of mankind. Aside from the fact that he *is* human, he is, in the eyes of the other workers, "a nice fella," is termed such by all the other important characters—George, even Crooks, and most importantly, Slim. When Slim is first introduced the concrete feature which sets him above the other men is his perfection as a worker: he is capable of driving "ten, sixteen, even twenty mules with a single line to the leaders" and of "killing a fly on the wheeler's butt with a bull whip without touching the mule" (ch. 2). Lennie is the only other character whose superlative ability as a worker is mentioned. His strength enables him to exhibit the one feature which only he is shown to possess in common with Slim. Slim himself pays Lennie the supreme tribute: "I never seen such a worker. . . . There ain't nobody can keep up with him. God awmighty I never seen such a strong guy" (ch. 3).

Lennie, then, in certain respects is equated with an animal, a man, and a god. His function is a catalytic one. Because he is "burdened" with Lennie, George has aspirations of purchasing a farm where the two of them can live. Without Lennie, George would be free, but free to do what?—to, by his own admission, take his money to town every payday and spend it in a "cat house." Their common aim and mutual responsibility bind them in a unity suffused with love.

Candy, left alone after the loss of his dog, becomes a third party to the plan. He now shares the dream of settling down with them, and a purposeful dimension is added to his life thereby. Crooks too comes to share the dream for a few brief moments, but he is promptly and brutally reminded of "his place" by Curley's frustrated and also lonely wife. He is jolted back to reality, is made aware of his position in a world rife with fear, mistrust, and hate. He sees his dream deferred.

At the climax of the novel Lennie's accidental killing of the woman shatters the dream shared by George, Candy and (for a time) Crooks, and founded upon Lennie himself. The plan is smashed and the dictum which provided the book's title is confirmed:

> The best laid schemes o' mice an' men
>
> Gang aft a-gley,
>
> An' lea'e us noght but grief an' pain
>
> For promised joy.
> [Robert Burns, "To a Mouse"]

Rather than see Lennie tragically abused, rather than let someone else kill him (as Candy let another kill his dog and afterward regretted having done so), George must perform the deed himself. He alone has the right, for he and Lennie have become one, made so by love and a shared dream. They are *responsible* for each other. The implication here is that man, without hope and love, without a dream, is perhaps better off dead; and at the story's end both God and man symbolically condone the murder when Slim says, "You hadda, George. I swear you hadda.' "

The book is a vastly underrated artistic achievement. One critic remarks of it, for example, that "one could forgive the ham in that novel-play, or digest it, just as one realized

that the paisanos of *Tortilla Flat* were not quite authentic" [Maxwell Geismar, *American Moderns: From Rebellion to Conformity*, 1958]. But the sentimentalism for which Steinbeck has been justly censured is remarkably muted in this work, and here he produces a highly symbolic novel without permitting the symbolism to dislocate the narrative, as he fails to do in *Battle*. By devising a microcosmic setting so appropriate, he is able to limit his gallery of characters and at the same time treat universal issues, for this restricting of setting does not force Steinbeck to forego the handling of his chief concerns. They all appear: the importance of family ties (compare the unwarranted pains which he takes to detail the disintegration of Jim's family in *Battle*) and the resultant aimlessness when such ties are broken; the need for solidarity; the disruptive effects of suspicion, fear, and group prejudice; and the functioning of Group-man in general. These concerns place his works squarely within the American proletarian tradition. But one of the features which distinguish his work from that of Dos Passos or Edward Dahlberg is the intense sympathy which he projects for the characters he treats. It is primarily this strong attachment that is responsible for the sentimentality which mars even the best of his writings.

Despite its artistic merits, however (or perhaps because it *is* so successful artistically), *Of Mice and Men* is not quite satisfactory as social criticism. Its failure offers support to the hypothesis that a literary work's success as polemic is inversely proportional to its esthetic stature. Because Steinbeck *did* modulate the extensive symbolism in the novel to make it compatible with the realistic situation and dramatic mode, the symbolism and the philosophic assumptions which it renders are all but submerged, and their impact mitigated. Thus the story is likely to strike one as being just that—an entertaining little tale. In this transitional piece (it has been called "probably the only one of Steinbeck's books which is satisfying as a whole" [R. W. B. Lewis, "John Steinbeck: The Fitful Daemon," in *Modern American Fiction: Essays in Criticism*]) the author evinces the artistic control he sought, but finds it still inadequate to his purposes. (pp. 147-51)

> *Bryant N. Wyatt, "Experimentation as Technique: The Protest Novels of John Steinbeck,"* in Discourse: A Review of the Liberal Arts, *Vol. XII, No. 2, Spring, 1969, pp. 143-53.*

Lester Jay Marks   (essay date 1969)

[*In the following excerpt, Marks examines* Of Mice and Men *in terms of thematic and structural similarities shared with Steinbeck's* In Dubious Battle.]

[Although in *In Dubious Battle* Steinbeck addressed the subject of the social group] because it was "more than the sum of its parts", he also knew that the individuals who composed the group must also be studied—if only because each is more than the sum of his cells, because each is a vital human being. So the question arises, because a group *is* men: What is it in the nature of men, considered as individuals, that motivates them to struggle towards ideals which are invariably lost in a shuffle of circumstances? The striking group of *In Dubious Battle* gets its energy after all from the hundreds of migrant workers—wanderers upon the earth—who have been dispossessed by natural and economic forces. What yearnings, what illusions must they share, must perhaps all men share, to make them turn their energy towards ends which are, at best, dubious?

Steinbeck's handling of these questions in *Of Mice and Men,* and his shift in focus from groups to individuals, will be better understood if I first examine certain thematic similarities between that novel and *In Dubious Battle.*

In Dubious Battle did not entirely bypass the individual's illusion. Implied by the action of men coming together to search for a world in which they would no longer be "migrants", is a great religious dream of utopian peace and prosperity. The strikers . . . move on faith, resenting "high-falutin ideas" that might weaken their resolution. Even when Doc Burton gives a name to Jim's passionate faith in the illusion, Jim is resentful:

> "You've got something in your eyes, Jim, something religious. I've seen it in you boys before."
>
> Jim flared, "Well, it isn't religious. I've got no use for religion."
>
> "No, I guess you haven't. Don't let me bother you, Jim. Don't let me confuse you with terms. You're living the good life, whatever you want to call it."
>
> "I'm happy", said Jim. "And happy for the first time. I'm full-up."
>
> "I know. Don't let it die. It's the vision of heaven."

The sense of fulfillment Jim feels when he is working with other men for a cause is later described by Doc as "pure religious ecstasy".

In *Of Mice and Men* this theme is carried over and developed. Steinbeck focuses, instead of on the group, on two individuals, migrant workers who might well have been among the strikers of *In Dubious Battle* but who are now removed from the body of the group and examined as its microcosms. The strikers clung together to protect themselves from doubting the success of their utopian vision. Similarly, George and Lennie need one another to keep alive their dream of finding "a little piece of land" where they might cease their wandering and live in simple, domestic peace.

Steinbeck's technique in *Of Mice and Men* is still disciplined by his non-teleological methods of observing "phenomena". He is concerned not with the *why* but with the *what* and *how* of the individual's illusions. The title that Steinbeck originally intended for the novel, "Something That Happened", is a typically unsentimental comment upon the tragic reversal of fortunes experienced by George and Lennie. And the lines from Burns' poem ["To a Mouse, on Turning Her up in Her Nest with the Plow, November, 1785"], which provided the title finally used, even more explicitly illustrate the illusory condition of man's highest hopes:

> But, Mousie, thou art no thy lane,

> In proving foresight may be vain:
> The best laid schemes o' mice an' men
>   Gang aft agley
> An' lea'e us nought but grief an' pain
>   For promis'd joy.

George and Lennie, like the strikers and like the mouse, are frustrated in their plans by the nature of things, by "something that happened". Since we can never track down the *cause* of life's ironies, both Steinbeck and Burns are saying, we had best accept them for what they *are*—conditions of human existence.

The theme of this novel, however, is not only its non-teleological observation that man is the victim of amoral Nature. This is something we know, if not from the title, then certainly after a very few pages of reading when we see how the well-intentioned Lennie cannot avoid destroying with his great idiot clumsiness all the simple things he loves most. Mindless Lennie is not responsible for what he does, but society nevertheless cannot tolerate him. Hence, when the old ranch hand, Candy, delivers his decrepit and foul-smelling dog into the hands of his bunk-mates, to let them kill the dog mercifully, we know that Lennie will have to die for his socially obnoxious act of violence. Lennie's unintentional destructiveness will therefore block his dream of tending the rabbits on the farm where he and George would "live on the fat o' the land". The failure of the dream, in fact, is implied by Lennie's tendency to crush the small animals he loves to feel and which he intends only to stroke.

But *Of Mice and Men* may also be read as a social protest and as an allegory. [In his *The Wide World of John Steinbeck* (1958),] Peter Lisca efficiently summarizes the first as "Steinbeck the reformer crying out against the exploitation of migrant workers", and the second as an

> interpretation limited only by the ingenuity of the audience. It could be, as Carlos Baker suggests [in "Steinbeck of California," *Delphian Quarterly* XXIII (April 1940)], "an allegory of Mind and Body." Using the same kind of dichotomy, the story could also be about the dumb, clumsy, but strong mass of humanity and its shrewd manipulators. . . . (or) that of the unconscious and the conscious, the id and the ego, or any other forces or qualities that have the same structural relationship to each other that do Lennie and George.

These symbolic interpretations may suggest to the reader that the relationship between George and Lennie closely resembles that which existed between Mac and the strikers in *In Dubious Battle.* The ranch hands often ask the intelligent George why he bothers to burden himself with Lennie. What they do not see is that George "uses" Lennie to sustain his own dream of the farm, that if he did not believe that Lennie needed him for protection his illusion would dissipate under the pressures of the workaday world. Without the "earth longings" of the primitive, asocial Lennie, George would fall prey to the literally hopeless life pattern of his peers. His faithfulness to Lennie belies his words: " 'God a'mighty, If I was alone I could live so easy. . . . I could take my fifty bucks and go into town and get whatever I want. Why, I could stay in a cat house all night. I could eat anyplace I want . . . , get a gallon of whiskey, or set in a pool room . . . !' " But when Lennie pathetically offers to leave him alone, George responds quickly: " 'No—look! I was jus' foolin', Lennie. 'Cause I want you to stay with me.' " George (seen as mind) is just as certainly welded to Lennie (seen as body) as Mac (the "brain" of the group animal) is to the body of strikers. Both George and Mac want to believe that they control the great primordial forces with which their own fates are bound; for only if they do control can they make progress towards their dream worlds. Mac attempts to use the strikers in ways that will aid the cause of communism; George puts Lennie to work to earn money needed to buy a farm. As we have seen, the carefully laid plans of Mac and George get nowhere because the forces they would manipulate are as unpredictable and uncontrollable as Nature itself.

There is another way in which *Of Mice and Men* may be likened to *In Dubious Battle,* and that is in its inclusion of Slim, a character whose qualities we recognize as similar to those of Doc Burton. There is one major difference: in the evolution of his hero type, Steinbeck has made Slim less of a talker than Doc and more of a doer, more of a man of the people; less of an abstract "voice" and more of an individual in his own right. Still, like Doc, he is gentle, understanding, and quietly wise in his acceptance of the way things are. We see him in this passage as he first appears to the reader:

> Like the others he wore blue jeans and a short denim jacket. When he had finished combing his hair he moved into the room, and he moved with a majesty only achieved by royalty and master craftsmen. He was a jerkline skinner, the prince of the ranch, capable of driving ten, sixteen, even twenty mules with a single line to the leaders. . . . There was a gravity in his manner and a quiet so profound that all talk stopped when he spoke. His authority was so great that his word was taken on any subject, be it politics or love. . . . His hatchet face was ageless. He might have been thirty-five or fifty. His ear heard more than was said to him, and his slow speech had overtones not of thought, but of understanding beyond thought.

Slim does not participate in George's dream, perhaps because he has no need for it in his position of honor on the ranch. But this is only to say that Slim's "understanding beyond thought" includes an acceptance of what *is,* which removes him from the futile struggle to remake the world as it *should be.* Thus detached, Slim is the only one who is capable of seeing George's tragic loss when George is forced to kill Lennie to save him from the mob. George kills a part of himself, the part that was his dream. Slim comforts George with a gentle reminder that it is better to kill the dream yourself (" 'a guy got to sometimes' ") than to deliver it into the hands of society, who would tear it apart in order to preserve itself.

I have been trying to illustrate that *Of Mice and Men* bears a strong thematic and structural relationship to *In Dubious Battle.* Both stories involve the hopeless pursuit of an illusion—the same illusion. As social protest, both

decry the maltreatment of migrant laborers. The allegorical structure of each is based upon Steinbeck's group-man theory and its conjunctive aspect of leadership (the several possible interpretations of the allegory stemming from the conflict that arises when an intellective force attempts to impose its will upon its mindless physical counterpart.) Finally, both novels are fictive enactments of Steinbeck's non-teleological philosophy; no blame or cause is ascribed to the patterns of action, and a dispassionate narrator in each case describes the action simply as "something that happened". To give credence to this philosophy, Steinbeck includes in each novel a character whose non-teleological view of life illustrates dramatically what is otherwise an abstraction.

What, however, differentiates *Of Mice and Men* from *In Dubious Battle?* What makes it a work of greater emotional impact even though its thematic and philosophic concerns are almost identical with those of its predecessor? The answers seem to lie, as I implied [at the beginning of this essay], in the earlier novel's reliance on protagonists of an organically *impersonal* nature. Steinbeck depended, for allegorical effectiveness, upon characters and groups of characters that were nearly flat representations of ideological forces. For example, much more important than "roundness" in the character of Doc Burton is his personification of intellectual independence. It is the tensions that arise between these ideational forces when they are placed in a setting of violent social flux, rather than "human" elements of conflict, that invite the reader's excitement. In contrast, *Of Mice and Men* focuses upon two individuals who, while they serve allegorical purposes, retain their individuality. George and Lennie are unusual characters, but they are believable. And because they are believable their tragedy also seems real and gains the reader's sympathy. Burton Rascoe, discussing Steinbeck's handling of character, writes [in "John Steinbeck," *The English Journal* XXVII (March 1938)]:

> [Lennie is] a believable contemporary figure—a man who would be described on any police docket . . . as a sexual pervert or degenerate and in almost any psychiatrist's case history as, probably, a man afflicted with gigantism, with an abnormally low I.Q., unusual thyroid deficiency, excessive pituitary secretion with resulting imbalance, a tactile fetish, psychic and/or physical impotence, and with improperly functioning adrenals which caused him in moments of fear to act destructively without intention— and Steinbeck chose to, and did, make this mostrosity a sympathetic figure, one whom you, if you had heart in you, would regard with all the despair but also with all the affection with which the giant Lennie is regarded by . . . the more astute and intelligent George.

And about George, Rascoe continues:

> George has toward Lennie the tenderness and the protective instinct which some of even the most hard-bitten and most hardboiled have toward the helpless, the maimed, the dependent. A lonely, itinerant bindle-stiff, a migratory ranch hand, barley bucker, mule skinner, fruit picker, and general handy man, without a home

or family, George has encountered and embraced a . . . humanitarian responsibility. It is to take care of, protect, save from hurt, the dimwitted, loyal, and devoted Lennie.

Lennie, however, is not merely a moron of fantastic strength, and George is not merely his bindlestiff protector. Their search for a safe place away from a world they never made is, after all, a ritual act as old as man himself. The dialogue between George and Lennie, recurring in almost identical language whenever either of them feels despondent, is like the chant of a priest and the response of his congregation. It is the ritual of earth-bound man listening to and being reassured by his hopeful inner voice:

> George's voice became deeper. He repeated his words rhythmically as though he had said them many times before. "Guys like us, that work on ranches, are the loneliest guys in the world. They got no family. They don't belong no place. . . . They ain't got nothing to look ahead to."
>
> Lennie was delighted. "That's it—that's it. Now tell how it is with us."
>
> George went on. "With us it ain't like that. We got a future. We got somebody to talk to that gives a damn about us. . . . If them other guys gets in jail they can rot for all anybody gives a damn. But not us."
>
> Lennie broke in. *"But not us! An' why? Because . . . because I got you to look after me, and you got me to look after you, and that's why."* He laughed delightedly. "Go on now, George!"
>
> "You got it by heart. You can do it yourself."
>
> "No, you. I forget some 'a the things. Tell about how it's gonna be."
>
> "O.K. Someday—we're gonna get the jack together and we're gonna have a little house and a couple of acres an' a cow and some pigs and . . ." *"An' live off the fatta the lan."*

It is a curious thing that audiences to the play, which Steinbeck adapted from the novel with only minor changes, invariably laughed at the antics of dimwitted Lennie—but that the laughter was short-lived; before the end of the first act, compassion had replaced their "light, superficially cynical mood" [as described by Rascoe]. The audience changed as, despite themselves, "pity and wonder [took] possession of them". The experience is, it seems to me, no different for the reader of the novel; he begins with the reader's typical attitude of detachment from the fictional events before him, but before long he is in sympathy with the tragically shattered illusions of George and Lennie, perhaps because he sees in them something of his own illusions and his own tragedy. (pp. 58-65)

> *Lester Jay Marks, in his* Thematic Design in the Novels of John Steinbeck, *Mouton, 1969, 144 p.*

Howard Levant   (essay date 1974)

[*Levant is an American educator, poet, and critic. In the following excerpt, he critiques* Of Mice and Men *as an example of Steinbeck's play-novelette form, which Levant considers inherently flawed.*]

John Steinbeck's only published excursion into literary theory is an effort to justify the form of the play-novelette—a term he invented. Also, in the span of thirteen of the middle years of his career, Steinbeck published three play-novelettes. These facts suggest that for Steinbeck the play-novelette is an important novelistic form. It is therefore appropriate to consider the theory and the practice of the form as well as its implications in the larger frame of Steinbeck's development of a simplified novelistic structure in longer fiction after about 1940.

The tale of George and Lennie . . . is more than social criticism; it is also the story of human hopes and human obligations. Steinbeck's antipathy towards the middle class is even more powerfully created here than in *In Dubious Battle* because of the tenderness with which Lennie and George are drawn.

—*James Woodress, in his "John Steinbeck: Hostage to Fortune,"* The South Atlantic Quarterly, *1964.*

Steinbeck presented the theory in an oddly titled article, " . . . the novel might benefit by the discipline, the terseness . . . ," in the January 1938 issue of *Stage*. Steinbeck's view is that a play-novelette is a pure dramatic structure—in the theatrical, not in the Jamesian, sense. He argues that if a novelist can simplify narrative and characterization by ordering a novel as if it were a play, the result must be an immediately powerful communication of theme and an enormous intensification of all the other novelistic values. He adds that *Of Mice and Men,* one of his efforts in the genre, is a failure as a play-novelette.

One can praise Steinbeck's intention to vitalize the novel through a new form, but without doubt his theory is absurd. (It should be added that Steinbeck's practice does little to redeem the theory.) Foremost, a novel is not a play, and terms do not make it so. Consider a key passage in Steinbeck's argument:

> For some years the novel has increasingly taken on the attributes of the drama. . . . To read an objective novel is to see a little play in your mind. All right, why not make it so you can see it on a stage? This experiment, then, is really only a conclusion toward which the novel has been unconsciously heading for some time.

The argument is serious, as the tone suggests. But the logic is unconvincing because the analogy is false. To know that Henry James and his literary heirs succeed in making the novel a direct rendering of experience does not mean that a novelist can remove every vestige of form and, in that sense, "make it so you can see it on a stage." Steinbeck takes the issue beyond the limits of analogy in an effort to sharpen a point; he confuses what a novel and a play are and can do; in short, he loads the argument in his favor.

The logical trick is not worth consideration, as Steinbeck seems to know, since he uses a second argument that is based on a quite different theory: The best way to reach an audience is by a direct effect. He asserts that the trouble with the novel as a form is that it is made for the individual "alone under a reading lamp," whereas a play depends on a group response:

> Now if it is true, and I believe it is, that the pre-occupation of the modern novelist lies in these themes which are most poignantly understood by a group, that novelist limits the possibility of being understood by making it impossible for groups to be exposed to this work.

Again the logic is unconvincing because the analogy is false. The argument rests only on Steinbeck's feeling that the group responds to a literary effect with more emotional validity than any individual can generate. Even if a measure of emotion could be devised, and if the private reading of drama were outlawed, the fact remains that a play is not a novel. Finally, the analogy is qualified by the direction of much modern writing, including the novel, into private or subjective content and form.

The *Stage* article is an aberration of logic and of literary history, but it is more illuminating to consider how deeply the aberration is rooted in Steinbeck's practice.

Much of the longer fiction is organized around some abstraction, a technical device or an intellectual point of view that operates as a "universal," giving a spurious dramatic structure to panoramic materials. Steinbeck can overcome this tendency by accident (as in *Tortilla Flat*) or by exorcising a part of his skill that is dangerous to cultivate (as in *The Grapes of Wrath*—but only in part). The excellent work and the aberrant work are both characteristic. Dates of publication alone prevent critical simplicity: *Of Mice and Men* and the *Stage* article were published between *In Dubious Battle* and *The Grapes of Wrath*. It is quite probable, as Moore [in his *The Novels of John Steinbeck* (1939)] and Lisca [in his *The Wide World of John Steinbeck* (1958)] suggest, that the beginnings of the play-novelette form can be seen in the more objectively rendered chapters of *In Dubious Battle*. The factual and probable evidence indicates that the play-novelette form, aberration as it may be, nevertheless is rooted deeply in some of the best of Steinbeck's previous work. Further, the evidence suggests why Steinbeck engages in so patently absurd a confusion of form over a period of thirteen years. He tries to achieve a harmony between structure and materials in every novel, but the effort is a constant struggle, open in part to accident. Now, the play-novelette form is eminently a way to *formulate* a harmony—to remove accident and struggle by a formula. To a novelist like Steinbeck, afflicted with artistic ambitions but limited in structural insight, the attraction of the play-novelette form is obvious. Its theory may rest on false analogy, may be only a gimmick, may indicate Steinbeck's lack of judgment with a terrifying clarity. But we must keep in mind that the theory and the practice of the play-novelette, in Steinbeck's hands, is a continuation of his constant effort to achieve a harmony between structure and materials. To do less is to limit criticism to a club. (pp. 130-33)

Despite Steinbeck's disclaimer in *Stage, Of Mice and Men* is certainly a play-novelette according to Steinbeck's own theory. Biographical information supports this view. Steinbeck reported to his agents, at the beginning of his work in February 1935, "I'm doing a play now," and Harry Thornton Moore records several illuminating contemporary facts:

> After *Of Mice and Men* was published and the suggestion was made that it be prepared for the stage, Steinbeck said it could be produced directly from the book, as the earliest moving pictures had been produced. It was staged in almost exactly this way in the spring of 1937 by a labor-theater group in San Francisco, and although the venture was not a failure it plainly demonstrated to Steinbeck that the story needed to be adapted to dramatic form. . . . But when Steinbeck transferred the story into final dramatic form for the New York stage he took 85% of his lines bodily from the novel. A few incidents needed juggling, one or two minor new ones were introduced, and some (such as Lennie's imaginary speech with his Aunt Clara at the end of the novel) were omitted.

It would seem that the novel was intended to function as a play, and Steinbeck did not alter the novel in any essential during the tinkering in preparation for the New York stage production. Aesthetic considerations support the biographical information, as in Moore's observation:

> Structurally, the novel was from the first a play: it is divided into six parts, each part a scene—the reader may observe that the action never moves away from a central point in each of these units.

And clearly the novel does "play": Characters make entrances and exits; plainly indicated parallels and oppositions that are characteristic of the drama exist in quantity and function as they should; suspense is maintained; characters are kept uncomplicated and "active" in the manner of stage characterization; since there is little internal or implicit development, events depend on what is said or done in full view; the locale is restricted mainly to one place; the span of time is brief; the central theme is stated and restated—the good life is impossible because humanity is flawed—and in itself is deeply poignant, as Steinbeck had defined a play-novelette theme. In short, I do not see how *Of Mice and Men* could meet more completely the specifications of a play-novelette as Steinbeck listed them. If critics have been displeased with *Of Mice and Men,* as Steinbeck was, the trouble cannot lie in the application of the theory but in the assumption that inspired the theory. I shall explore this point in detail.

As a dramatic structure, *Of Mice and Men* is focused on Lennie and occurs within the context of the bunkhouse and the ranch. Within these confines, Steinbeck develops theme and countertheme by exploring the chances for the good life against the flawed human material that Lennie symbolizes most completely and the code of rough justice that most people accept. Even this initial, limited statement points to the central difficulty in the novel. The "well-made" dramatic form that Steinbeck defined in *Stage* and did construct in **Of Mice and Men** is conducive to abstraction because it is limited to visible action. Lennie is limited in much the same way. As a huge, powerful, semi-idiot who kills when he is frightened or simply when he is thoughtless, Lennie is a reduction of humanity to the lowest common denominator. It may be possible to construct a parable out of so limited a structure and materials, but it is impossible to handle complex human motives and relationships within those limits. **Of Mice and Men** is successful to the extent that it remains a parable, but the enveloping action is more complex than the parable form can encompass.

Lennie is the most fully realized character, yet he is presented necessarily as a personification, an exaggerated, allegorized instance of the division between mind and body; the sketch that is Lennie is incapable of conveying personality. The other characters are personified types rather than realized persons. Though less pathetic than Lennie, they do not have his moral impact. In short, every structural device except personification is sacrificed to highlight Lennie's moral helplessness. The sacrifice is much too great. It thins out the parable. The stripped language furthers this effect of extreme thinness. For example, Lennie's one friend, George, is not a realized man but a quality that complements Lennie's childlike innocence. George fills out Lennie's pattern to complete a whole man. He is a good man, motivated to protect Lennie because he realizes that Lennie is the reverse image of his own human nature. George is a representation of humanity that (unlike Lennie) is aware of evil. An extended abstract passage, makes this clear.

Everything in the development of the novel is designed to contribute to a simplification of character and event.

The opening scene of the green pool in the Salinas River promises serenity, but in the final scene the pool is the background for Lennie's violent death. George's initial hope that Lennie can hide his flawed humanity by seeming to be conventional is shattered in the end. Lennie's flaw grows into a potential for evil, and every evil is ascribed to him after his unwitting murder of Curley's wife. The objective image of the good life in the future," a little house and a couple of acres an' a cow and some pigs," is opposed sharply to the present sordid reality of the bunkhouse and the ranch. Minor characters remain little more than opposed types, identifiable by allegorical tags. Curley is the unsure husband, opposed to and fearful of his sluttish, unnamed wife. Slim is a minor god in his perfect mastery of his work. His serenity is contrasted sharply with Curley's hysterical inability to please or to control his wife, and it contrasts as easily with the wife's constant, obvious discontent. Candy and Crooks are similar types, men without love. Both are abused by Curley, his wife, and the working crew. (Lennie might fall into this category of defenselessness, if he were aware enough to realize the situation; but he is not.) These sharp oppositions and typed personae restrict the development of the novel. The merely subordinate characters, such as Carlson and Whit, who only begin or fill out a few scenes, are strictly nonhuman, since they remain abstract instruments within a design.

The climax of that design is simplified in its turn, since it serves only to manipulate Lennie into a moral situation beyond his understanding. The climax is doubled, a pairing of opposites. In its first half, when Curley's wife attempts to seduce Lennie as a way to demonstrate her hatred of Curley, Lennie is content (in his nice innocence) to stroke her soft hair; but he is too violent, and he snaps her neck in a panic miscalculation as he tries to force her to be quiet. In the second half, George shoots Lennie to prevent a worse death at the hands of others. The melodramatic quality of these events will be considered at a later point. Here, it is more important to observe, in the design, that the climax pairs an exploration of the ambiguity of love in the rigid contrast between the different motives that activate Curley's wife and George. Curley's wife wants to use Lennie to show her hatred for Curley; George shoots Lennie out of a real affection for him. The attempted seduction balances the knowing murder; both are disastrous expressions of love. Lennie is the unknowing center of the design in both halves of this climax. Steinbeck's control is all too evident. There is not much sense of dramatic illumination because the quality of the paired climax is that of a mechanical problem of joining two parallels. Lennie's necessary passivity enforces the quality of a mechanical design. He is only the man to whom things happen. Being so limited, he is incapable of providing that sudden widening insight which alone justifies an artist's extreme dependence on a rigid design. Therefore, in general, **Of Mice and Men** remains a simple anecdote.

It would be a mistake to conclude that the limited scope of the materials is the only or the effective cause of the simplification. Writers frequently begin their work with anecdotal materials. Most often, however, they expand the reference of such materials through a knowing exercise of their medium. It is Steinbeck's inability to exercise his medium or, perhaps more fundamentally, to select a proper medium, which ensures the limited reference, the lack of a widening insight.

In his discussion of the play-novelette form in *Stage*, Steinbeck dismisses the objection that allegory is an overly limited form, but the objection is serious. **Of Mice and Men** is not merely a brief novel. It is limited in what its structure can make of its materials. Moreover, Steinbeck hoped to achieve precisely that limitation—the *Stage* essay leaves no doubt of this—although, it is true, he felt the form would ensure a concentration, a focus, of the materials. Instead, there is a deliberate thinning of materials that are thin (or theatrical) to begin with.

In fact, Steinbeck uses every possible device to thin out the effect of the materials. Foreshadowing is overworked. Lennie's murder of Curley's wife is the catastrophe that George has been dreading from the start. It is precisely the fate that a fluffy animal like Curley's wife should meet at the hands of Lennie, who has already killed mice and a puppy with his overpowering tenderness. When Curley's wife makes clear her intention to seduce the first available man and the course of events abandons Lennie to her, the result is inevitable. But that inevitability does not have tragic qualities. The result is merely arranged, the characters merely inarticulate, and the action develops without illumination. Lennie can hardly distinguish between a dead pup and the dead woman:

> Lennie went back and looked at the dead girl. The puppy lay close to her. Lennie picked it up. "I'll throw him away," he said. "It's bad enough like it is."

The relative meaninglessness of his victims substitutes pathos for tragedy. Curley's rather shadowy wife underlines the substitution: She is characterless, nameless, and constantly discontent, so her death inspires none of the sympathy one might feel for a kind or a serene woman. Others respond to her death wholly in light of Lennie's predicament—from George's loving concern to Curley's blustering need for revenge—not his character. Everything that is excellent in the novel tends to relate, intensely if narrowly, to that emphasis. Within these limits, much that Steinbeck does is done excellently. The essential question is whether the treatment of the materials is intense enough to justify their evident manipulation, their narrowed pathos.

The novel communicates most intensely a theme of unconventional morality. Lennie does commit murder, but he remains guiltless because he is not responsible for what he does. Yet the morality is only a statement of the pathos of Lennie's situation, not an exploration of guilt and innocence. A development through parallels and juxtaposi-

View of the Salinas River, southeast of Soledad, possible locale of Of Mice and Men.

tions does little to expand the stated theme. Carlson parallels Lennie's violence on a conventional level when he insists on killing Candy's ancient, smelly dog. Carlson's reasoning is that the group has a right to wrong the individual. Lennie is incapable of any logic, even of this twisted sort, and he is never cruel by choice; that potential moral complexity is neglected in the design to permit the brutal simplicity of the group's response to Carlson's argument and to Lennie's crime. Carlson's crime is approved by the group: He abuses power to invade another man's desire for affection, reduced to a worthless dog. Lennie's crime is an accident in an attempt to express affection; murder is too serious for the group to ignore, so Lennie is hunted down. We are intended to notice the irony that Carlson's crime inverts Lennie's. That simple, paralleled irony substitutes for a possible, intense, necessarily complex, and ambiguous development of the materials. The rendered development, not the materials themselves, produces this simply mechanical irony.

Certainly the theme of unconventional morality offers tragic possibilities in a dimension beyond the anecdotal or the sketch of a character or event. From that viewpoint, the oppositions can expand into tragic awareness, at least potentially. They can even be listed, as follows. Lennie is good in his intentions, but evil in fact. The group is good in wanting to punish a murderer, but evil in misunderstanding that Lennie is guiltless. Counterwise, George, Candy, and Slim are endowed with understanding by their roles as the friend, the man without hope, and the god, but they are powerless against the group. Curley's wife is knowingly evil in exploiting Lennie's powerful body and weak mind. Curley is evil in exploiting all opportunities to prove his manhood. These two are pathetic in their human limitations, not tragic. George enacts an unconventional morality less by accident than any of the others. He feels strongly that, in being compelled to look after Lennie, he has given up the good times he might have had, but he knows the sacrifice is better, that he and Lennie represent an idealized variety of group-man. Slim's early, sympathetic insight makes this explicit:

> "You guys travel around together?" [Slim's] tone was friendly. It invited confidence without demanding it. "Sure," said George. "We kinda look after each other." He indicated Lennie with his thumb. "He ain't bright. Hell of a good worker, though. Hell of a nice fella, but he ain't bright. I've knew him for a long time." Slim looked through George and beyond him. "Ain't many guys travel around together," he mused. "I don't know why. Maybe ever'body in the whole damn world is scared of each other." "It's a lot nicer to go around with a guy you know," said George.

This important passage centers the theme of unconventional morality. It celebrates a relationship "the whole damn world" is incapable of imagining, given the ugly context of ranch life and sordid good times, and it locates the good life in friendship, not in the material image of the little farm. This passage is the heart of the novel.

But a novel cannot be structured solely on the basis of a theme, even a fundamental theme. Too much else must be simplified. Worse, the unconventional morality located in friendship produces Lennie's death, not only because Steinbeck can see no other way to conclude. Lennie dies necessarily because friendship can go no further than it does go, and nothing can be made of the dreamlike ideal of the little farm. The extreme simplification is that Steinbeck can do nothing with Lennie after he has been exhibited. These limitations derive from the simplification required by the play-novelette form. Steinbeck appears to be aware that formal limitations need some widening, since he imbeds Lennie's happiest and most intense consciousness of the good life of friends in an ironic context:

> George said, "Guys like us got no fambly. They make a little stake an' then they blow it in. They ain't got nobody in the worl' that gives a hoot in hell about 'em—" *"But not us,"* Lennie cried happily. "Tell about us now." George was quiet for a moment. "But not us," he said. "Because—" "Because I got you an'—" "An' I got you. We got each other, that's what, that gives a hoot in hell about us," Lennie cried in triumph.

The passage extends friendship beyond its boundary; it celebrates a species of marriage, minus the sexual element, between Lennie and George. But the content of the passage is qualified heavily by its position; George shoots Lennie after retelling the story about the little farm that always quiets Lennie. As further irony, precisely the responsibilities of a perfect friendship require George to shoot Lennie. The mob that would hang Lennie for murder is in the background throughout the scene. The situation is moving, but the effect is local. The ironies relate only to Lennie's pathetic situation; they do not aid an understanding of Lennie or account (beyond plot) for his death. Too, the scene is melodramatic; it puts aside the large problems of justifying the event in order to jerk our tears over the event itself.

To say that Steinbeck avoids the problems of structure by milking individual scenes is not to say that *Of Mice and Men* is a total failure. As mature work, it is not a depot for the basic flaws in Steinbeck's earliest work. Many of the scenes are excellently constructed and convincing in themselves. Considerable attention is given to establishing minor details. For example, George shoots Lennie with the Luger that Carlson used to kill Candy's old dog. The defenseless man is linked by the weapon with the defenseless dog in the group's web of created power. George does his killing as a kind of ritual. If the police or the mob had taken Lennie, the death would have been a meaningless expression of group force, the exaction of an eye for an eye rather than an expression of love. The background of language is the workingman dialect that Steinbeck perfected in *In Dubious Battle,* realized here to express a brutally realistic world that negates idealism and exaggerates the sadistic and the ugly. Its perfection is enhanced by a factual context—the dependence of the men on their shifting jobs, the explicit misery of their homelessness, and the exposure of their social and economic weaknesses. The more sensitive men dream of escape into some kind of gentleness. The thread of possible realization of that dream tends to hold the novel in a focus. The opposite pole of

man's imperfect moral nature motivates Curley's wife and Carlson. Steinbeck's fine web of circumstance reaches from the ideal possibility to the brutal fact.

Of Mice and Men is strongest in precisely this plot sense, in a sequence and linkage of events controlled by ironic contrast and juxtaposition. The result is limited to the rendering of a surface, yet the necessarily external devices of plot are used with artistic care and skillful tact.

Just after George, Lennie, and Candy agree to realize the dream of the little farm by pooling their savings and earnings, Curley appears, searching for his wife. Frustrated, Curley punches Lennie without mercy until (on George's order) Lennie grabs and crushes Curley's hand. This violent event suggests that Curley's sadistic vision of the world will not be shut out by the idealized vision of cooperative friends. More closely, the ugly inversion of "the good, clean fight" serves to contrast Lennie's innocence with his surprise and helplessness before evil. The other men in the bunkhouse are unconcerned; violence is an ordinary element in their lives. The incident enacts and announces the implicitly universal moral imperfection of humanity—an insight that broadens and becomes more overt in the following scenes. When Curley has to go to town to have a doctor care for his crushed hand, the men take the chance to go into town for a spree. Crooks, Candy, and Lennie—the Negro, the old man, and the idiot—are left on the ranch with Curley's wife. The circumstances provide her with an opportunity to seduce Lennie; she hates Curley, and the Hollywood ideal of the seductive movie queen is her only standard of love. Crooks cannot protect Lennie because his black skin leaves him open to sexual blackmail; Candy's feeble efforts are useless; and Lennie does not understand what is happening. The ultimate irony in this tangle of violence is that none of the characters is evil or intends to do evil. The irony is more explicit and more powerful than the crux of the Munroe family in *The Pastures of Heaven,* in that all of them are trying to express some need of love. In her need as in her amoral unawareness of good and evil, Curley's wife is not unlike Lennie, just as the various moral defects of other people conspire by chance to leave Lennie alone and defenseless with Curley's wife. Yet "love" has different meanings for Lennie and for Curley's wife; the clash of meanings ensures their deaths.

The death of Curley's wife switches the narrative focus to George and to the device of the split hero. Steinbeck is fond of this device of a divided (not a duplicated) hero, usually two men of opposite nature, one distinctly secondary to the other, but both sharing the center of the novel. For a few suggestive, not inclusive, examples: Henry Morgan, Jim Nolan, and Aaron Trask are coldly thoughtful, knowing men, either selfish or idealistic in what they do; Coeur de Gris, Mac, and Caleb Trask are relatively warmer men, possibly as knowing as their opposites, but usually more subject to their emotions. Jim Casy and Tom Joad extend and complicate the pattern as they become suggestive types of Christ and Saint Paul, the human god and the coldly realistic organizer, but they do not break the pattern. There are obvious narrative virtues of clarity in a device that is recognizable as well as flexible. The secondary hero is subordinate in Steinbeck's fiction—except in *Of Mice and Men.* There, Lennie's murder propels George into a sudden prominence that has no structural basis. Is the novel concerned with Lennie's innocence or George's guilt? The formal requirements of a play-novelette mandate a structural refocus. Steinbeck needs a high point to ring down the curtain. With Lennie dead, Steinbeck must use and emphasize George's guilt. The close is formulated—the result of a hasty switch—not structured from preceding events, so it produces an inconclusive ending in view of what has happened previously. And the ideal of the farm vanishes with Lennie's death, when George tells Candy the plan is off.

Here the difficulty is with a structure that requires a climax which cannot be achieved once Lennie, the center of the novel, is removed; but Lennie must be killed off when his existence raises problems of characterization more complex than the play-novelette form can express. Materials and structure pull against each other and finally collapse into an oversimplified conclusion that removes rather than faces the central theme.

The abrupt "solution" rests on melodrama, on sudden, purely plot devices of focus and refocus. Such overt manipulation indicates that in its practice the play-novelette is not a new form. Steinbeck's experience, his mature technical skill do not finally disguise his wish to return to his earliest fictional efforts to realize complex human behavior by way of an extreme simplification of structure and materials. His deliberate avoidance of an organic structure and his consequent dependence on a formula, on the exercise of technique within an artistic vacuum, exhausts the significance of the play-novelette theory. His practice, as in *Of Mice and Men,* does not lead to serious efforts and to a real achievement in the art of the novel. Rather, it leads to manipulations designed to effect a simplification of structure and materials. So much skill, directed toward so little, is disturbing. But the skill is absolutely there. (pp. 133-34)

> *Howard Levant, in his* The Novels of John Steinbeck: A Critical Study, *University of Missouri Press, 1974, 304 p.*

Sandra Beatty   (essay date 28 December 1977)

[*In the following excerpt from an essay originally presented at the 1977 MLA Steinbeck Society meeting, Beatty comments on the role of Curley's wife in* Of Mice and Men.]

Steinbeck's female characters in his plays warrant critical attention first because they are significant in their own right and also because they perform a number of important functions in relation to the drama as a whole. For example, influential in determining the fate of the major characters, George and Lennie, Curley's wife in *Of Mice and Men* is the deciding factor in the outcome of the play. In addition, she serves to reinforce the theme of loneliness, isolation, and the idea of a personal dream which is central to the play. She commands both our sympathy and respect because of her naive yet genuine pursuit of a life-long dream. (p. 7)

Of Mice and Men has received wide critical acclaim both as a stage drama and as a film, primarily because of its simple yet poignant treatment of one of Steinbeck's recurring themes: the inherent loneliness of the itinerant farm laborer and his desperate desire for land of his own. Loneliness and the land dream are both personified in the characters of George and Lennie in *Of Mice and Men* and so critics' attention has traditionally focused on them. However, there is another character in the play who is portrayed as equally lonely and commands an equal measure of our understanding and sympathy because she, too, had a dream that was never realized.

Curley's wife may, at first, appear to play a relatively minor role in relation to the male characters in *Of Mice and Men* and also to the development of Steinbeck's overall theme. However, closer study of her character reveals that she is not only a major influence in the play but a well-developed character in her own right. Curley's wife has not been given a name, consequently, she is seen merely as an extension of her husband. This is not to say that Steinbeck considered her an unimportant character; rather, he is deliberately delineating her role insofar as it is seen by the male characters in the play.

We are introduced to Curley's wife by the farm hands, men who have been on the place for a while and who "know" her. We are tempted to pre-judge her in light of the comments made by these men. Candy remarks to George that "she got the eye" and "I think Curley's married himself a tart. . . . You look her over, mister. You see if she ain't a tart."

Steinbeck's initial description of Curley's wife seems to reinforce the opinion of the farm hands. She has "full, heavily rouged lips. Widespaced, made-up eyes. Her fingernails are bright red, her hair hangs in little rolled clusters like sausages. She wears a cotton house dress and red mules, on the insteps of which are little bouquets of red ostrich feathers." Unfortunately, many characterizations of Curley's wife, particularly stage productions, begin and end with this superficial impression of her as a "cheap hustler". Curley's wife may come on to the men as playful and seductive, but she is acutely aware of the hostile reception she is receiving from them. She realizes that they will tolerate her presence around the bunkhouse only if she uses her usual excuse, "I'm lookin' for Curley." Her more honest explanation and appeal, "I'm jus' lookin' for somebody to talk to. Don't you never jus' want to talk to somebody?" meets with coldness and resentment from the men. As we get our first glimpse of the loneliness of this woman, we begin to sympathize with her repeated attempts to befriend the men.

It is interesting to compare the initial reactions of George and Lennie to Curley's wife. George's evaluation of her reinforces the opinion already voiced by the other farm hands—"Jesus, what a tramp!" Lennie provides a characteristically simple and honest response, "Gosh, she's purty!" Lennie's straightforward statement triggers an alarmed reaction from George. For the first time, he sees Curley's wife as a potential threat to their job security, their plans to "get a stake" and, ultimately, to their land dream. George threatens Lennie harshly. "Don't you even look at that bitch. I don't care what she says or what she does. I seen 'em poison before, but I ain't never seen no piece of jail bait worse than her."

We begin to appreciate the intense loneliness and the desperate need for companionship in Curley's wife from a comment made by Whit later in the play. He says, "She's just workin' on everybody all the time. Seems like she's even workin' on the stable buck. I don't know what the hell she wants." It is difficult to understand why a group of men who, by their own admission, are lonely most of the time and who crave companionship, cannot recognize the same need in a woman. The fact that Curley's wife would attempt to befriend the Negro stable buck, indicates the degree of her loneliness.

For the men, at least, there is an emotional outlet. The male need for warmth and female companionship is satisfied, in part, by the whore. Susy in *Of Mice and Men* is typical of the whores found in Steinbeck's fiction. The matronly owner of the whorehouse knows and understands the men she serves. "I know what you boys want. . . . My girls is clean . . . and there ain't no water in my whisky." The men enjoy Susy's company. "Old Susy is a laugh. Always cracking jokes. . . . She never talks dirty neither." A good whorehouse is like a home to these men. "Susy's got nice chairs to set in. If a guy don't want to flop, why he can just set in them chairs and have a couple or three shots and just pass the time of day. . . . A guy can set in there like he lived there."

Unfortunately, there is no such outlet for the loneliness which Curley's wife feels. She tries to make the men understand her situation: "Sure I got a man. He ain't never home. I got nobody to talk to. I got nobody to be with. Think I can just sit home and do nothin' but cook for Curley? I want to see somebody. Just see 'em an' talk to 'em. There ain't no women. I can't walk to town. And Curley don't take me to no dances now. I tell you I jus' want to talk to somebody." Curley's wife is totally isolated on the farm. She admits that her husband provides little company, and because she has no female companionship, she turns to the men. They misinterpret her friendly advances and her attempts to be nice and try to get rid of her. George demands, "If you're just friendly, what you givin' out the eye for an' floppin' your can around?" She counters his abuse with, "I try to be nice an' polite to you lousy bindle bums—but you're too good."

It is sadly ironic that Curley's wife's understanding of Lennie's passion for touching soft things and her final gesture of allowing him the pleasure of stroking her hair, leads to the simultaneous destruction of both their dreams.

—Sandra Beatty

As a result of the hostility of the other men towards her,

a kind of affinity develops between Curley's wife and Lennie. In the conversation in the barn, Steinbeck creates one of the most moving scenes in the play. For the first time, we are allowed to get close to two characters who have always been overshadowed by others and who have been afraid to speak openly because of the threat of the consequences. Even though the two are not speaking directly to one another, we sense that they are growing closer together as the scene progresses because they are sharing their feelings and their own personal dreams. Curley's wife confides in Lennie about her true feelings for her husband and about her plans to leave him. "I ain't tol' this to nobody before. . . . I don't like Curley, he ain't a nice fella. . . . I don't have to stay here. . . . I'll go in the night an' thumb a ride to Hollywood." Our sympathy is aroused for this woman who married a man she met at the Riverside Dance Palace in order to get away from her home and a mother who she felt did not understand her. We are also sympathetic towards her naivety in being taken in by the smooth talk of the big city boys who deceived her into believing that she could become a part of the glamorous life. But Curley's wife's dream of becoming a famous movie star in Hollywood is as real to her as Lennie's dream of being allowed to tend the rabbits on their own farm is to him: "Gonna get in the movies an' have nice clothes. . . . An' I'll set in them big hotels and they'll take pichers of me. . . . All them nice clothes like they wear . . . because this guy says I'm a natural." We instinctively sense that Curley's wife's dream will never be realized, but we must credit her for her determination and courage in pursuing that dream, just as we credit the men for their single-minded perseverance in working to buy their own farm.

It is sadly ironic that Curley's wife's understanding of Lennie's passion for touching soft things and her final gesture of allowing him the pleasure of stroking her hair, leads to the simultaneous destruction of both their dreams. Curley's wife becomes a pivotal force in the play at this point because her unselfish gesture triggers all the succeeding action and the ultimate outcome for the major characters. We are brought to this grim realization near the end of the play when Candy bitterly addresses Curley's wife's dead body: "You goddamn tramp. You done it, didn't you? Everybody knowed you'd mess things up. You just wasn't no good." Candy's harsh words serve to generate additional sympathy for Curley's wife—a woman whose intense loneliness and dream for the future was as real and human as the men's. (pp. 7-10)

Sandra Beatty, "Steinbeck's Play-Women: A Study of the Female Presence in 'Of Mice and Men', 'Burning Bright', 'The Moon Is Down', and 'Viva Zapata!' " in Steinbeck's Women: Essays in Criticism, *edited by Tetsumaro Hayashi, The Steinbeck Society of America, 1979, pp. 7-16.*

Michael W. Shurgot   (essay date Winter–Spring 1982)

[*In the following excerpt, Shurgot explores the symbolic importance of George's card games.*]

Midway through section two of *Of Mice and Men,* after

George and Lennie have met Candy, the boss, and his son Curley, Steinbeck describes George walking to the table in the bunkhouse and shuffling some of the playing cards lying there. Often during the rest of section two and throughout section three, Steinbeck pictures George playing solitaire with these cards. Although George's card-playing may seem just a means of passing time during his and Lennie's first night on the ranch, the frequency of George's card games and Steinbeck's careful juxtaposition of them with the prophetic events of sections two and three indicate that the game of cards is the central symbol of the entire novel.

George's card games are generally symbolic in three ways. Lester Jay Marks writes [in *Thematic Design in the Novels of John Steinbeck,* 1971] that Steinbeck's novel is "disciplined by his non-teleological methods of observing 'phenomena.' He is concerned not with the *why* but with the *what* and *how* of the individual's illusions." Steinbeck's original title, "Something That Happened," is, according to Marks, an unsentimental comment upon the "tragic reversal of fortunes" that George and Lennie experience. A non-teleological world is one of chance, of reversals of fortune beyond man's comprehension or his power to control. And a game of cards is an exact symbol of this kind of world. In card games there is no pattern to the cards' random appearance; their sequence is solely a matter of chance. Analogically, although George tries to control Lennie's activities and movements on the ranch, he cannot prevent Lennie's tragic meeting with Curley's wife in the barn.

Further, George's card game is solitaire. From the opening dialogue between George and Lennie, to the novel's final, terrifying moments, Steinbeck's characters talk about the isolation, rootlessness, and alienation of their lives. Steinbeck introduces the theme of isolation shortly after George and Lennie arrive at the clearing in part one. George laments,

> "Guys like us, that work on ranches, are the loneliest guys in the world. They got no family. They don't belong no place. They come to a ranch an' work up a stake and then they go inta town and blow their stake, and the first thing you know they're poundin' their tail on some other ranch. They ain't got nothing to look ahead to."

George's sense of the loneliness and rootlessness of ranchhands is echoed several times in the novel. In section two, Slim observes, "Ain't many guys travel around together. . . . I don't know why. Maybe ever'body in the whole damn world is scared of each other." Early in section three, Slim elaborates on the uniqueness of George's relationship with Lennie:

> "Funny how you an' him string along together. . . . I hardly never seen two guys travel together. You know how the hands are, they just come in and get their bunk and work a month, and then they quit and go out alone. Never seem to give a damn about nobody. It jus' seems kinda funny a cuckoo like him and a smart little guy like you travelin' together."

George tells Slim he "ain't got no people," and insists that, although Lennie is a "God damn nuisance most of the time," nonetheless traveling with him is preferable to the loneliness and misery of most ranchhands' lives:

> "I seen the guys that go around on the ranches alone. That ain't no good. They don't have no fun. After a long time they get mean. They get wantin' to fight all the time."

Later, after George has told Candy about his and Lennie's dream of owning their own place, Candy, obviously enthralled at being included in their plans, says that he would leave his share of the place to them " . . . 'cause I ain't got no relatives nor nothing."

On the ranch itself, the most hopelessly alienated characters besides Candy are Crooks and Curley's wife. Crooks, the crippled black stable buck, although serving an important function, is nonetheless isolated in a world of physically powerful white men. Because he is disfigured, and thus less mobile than the ranchhands, he is ironically more permanent than they, but he is barred from their quarters and sleeps in a "long box filled with straw," a symbolic coffin. Echoing George's remarks about the psychological effects of constant loneliness, Crooks complains bitterly to Lennie, "A guy goes nuts if he ain't got nobody. Don't make no difference who the guy is, long's he's with you. . . . I tell ya a guy gets too lonely an' he gets sick." Curley's wife is equally lonely, frustrated, and alienated. She hates staying in the "two-by-four house" with Curley, who "spends all his time sayin' what he's gonna do to guys he don't like, and he don't like nobody." She insists that at one time she "could of went with shows," and that "a guy tol' me he could put me in pictures." But instead, she now spends Saturday nights "talkin' to a bunch of bindle stiffs—a nigger an' a dumdum and a lousy ol' sheep—an' likin' it because they ain't nobody else." Although the circumstances of their lives on the ranch are quite different, Crooks and Curley's wife are similarly isolated within and segregated from the white, predominantly masculine world of the novel. Fortune has been kind to neither Crooks nor Curley's wife, and their lives emphasize the pervasive isolation (and occasionally despair) that haunts Steinbeck's characters.

Besides symbolizing the lonely, disjointed lives of the ranchhands and the alienation of Crooks and Curley's wife, George's games of solitaire are symbolic in a third way. George tries, quite naturally, to "win" his games of solitaire, and when considered along with several of his remarks to Lennie, such efforts at victory become quite ironic. Early in section one, after pleading with Lennie not to "do no bad things like you done in Weed," George describes, as he does frequently in the novel, what he could do if he were alone:

> "God, you're a lot of trouble," said George. "I could get along so easy and so nice if I didn't have you on my tail. I could live so easy and maybe have a girl."

Twice more in part one, George repeats this sentiment. The first time, Lennie's innocent wish for some ketchup precipitates one of George's most violent explosions against him in the novel. George angrily recounts their narrow escape from Weed—"You crazy son-of-a-bitch. You keep me in hot water all the time"—and brutally claims, "I wish I could put you in a cage with about a million mice an' let you have fun." Moments later, after Lennie pathetically insists that had they any ketchup George could have all of it, George says, "When I think of the swell time I could have without you, I go nuts. I never get no peace." Just after returning to the clearing in part six, Lennie says, "George gonna wish he was alone an' not have me botherin' him." Shortly after Lennie's remark, George is alone, and as lonely as the other ranchhands he describes earlier in part one. Although he certainly wants and needs Lennie to fulfill their dream together, George's frequent wish to be alone, to be free of the burden of minding Lennie, is ironically forecast in his frequent resorts to solitaire in the first half of the novel.

Steinbeck enhances the general symbolism of George's games of solitaire by carefully interweaving them into the narrative of sections two and three. George first plays with the cards during his conversation with Candy about Curley and his wife. Candy explains that Curley is a fighter and has become "cockier'n ever since he got married." George remarks that Curley had better "watch out for Lennie," walks to the table and picks up the cards, and fumbles with them continually as Candy describes Curley's "glove . . . fulla vaseline" and his wife:

> "Wait'll you see Curley's wife."
>
> George cut the cards again and put out a solitaire lay, slowly and deliberately. "Purty?" he asked casually.

Steinbeck's careful positioning of Candy's description of Curley's wife and George's first hand of solitaire juxtaposes the immediate cause of the failure of George and Lennie's dream and the ultimate consequence of that failure for George: his solitude. A similar juxtaposition occurs moments later. Candy says to George, "Well, you look her over, mister. You see if she ain't a tart." Steinbeck writes:

> George laid down his cards thoughtfully, turned his piles of three. He built four clubs on his ace pile. . . . George stared at his solitaire lay, and then he flounced the cards together and turned around to Lennie.

George warns Lennie about Curley, whom he correctly perceives as a threat to their plans, and repeats his instructions to him about returning to the pool in the river should trouble occur. Curley's wife enters immediately, and Lennie's twice-repeated "She's purty" elicits George's fierce warning to him about her being "jail bait" and his insistence that he and Lennie must stay at the ranch until they make their stake:

> "We gotta keep it till we get a stake. We can't help it, Lennie. We'll get out jus' as soon as we can. I don't like it no better than you do." He went back to the table and set out a new solitaire hand.

George's card games precede and follow the appearance of Curley's wife and Lennie's reactions to her, thus symbolically framing their first meeting in a realm of chance. Further, when Slim enters he sits down at the table across from George. While Slim plays with the cards, he talks to Carlson about his dog's pups and Candy's old dog. This conversation foreshadows Lennie's death; and the sense of his and the dog's similar fates is suggested by the hand of cards that George and Slim, with ironic nonchalance, manipulate during this scene. Section two closes with George's return to the cards amid his promise to Lennie to ask Slim about a pup, thus initiating the chain of events that leads to Lennie's presence in the barn when Curley's wife tempts him the following Sunday.

Section three opens with George's confiding in Slim about Lennie's troubles in Weed. Twice during their dialogue Steinbeck describes George playing solitaire:

> " 'Course he ain't mean. But he gets in trouble alla time because he's so God damn dumb. Like what happened in Weed—." He stopped, stopped in the middle of turning over a card.

And

> Slim's eyes were level and unwinking. He nodded very slowly. "So what happens?"
>
> George carefully built his line of solitaire cards.

Steinbeck's careful interweaving of George's hand of solitaire with his narrative of Lennie's seizure of the girl in Weed is his most effective apposition in the novel. Lennie's actions in Weed clearly presage his killing Curley's wife, and George will be alone after he shoots Lennie.

Steinbeck employs this card symbolism variously in the rest of section three. Just before Carlson shoots Candy's dog, George and Whit start a game of euchre, but when Whit mentions Curley's wife, he drops his cards and George immediately lays out another hand of solitaire. After Carlson and Lennie return to the bunkhouse and Curley inquires about his wife and Slim, Lennie joins George at the table:

> He got up from his bunk and sat down at the table, across from George. Almost automatically George shuffled the cards and laid out his solitaire hand. He used a deliberate, thoughtful, [sic] slowness.

George's "automatically" laying out his solitaire hand as he sits across from Lennie is acutely ironic and prophetic, for George will be as solitary as the rest of the ranchhands after Lennie's death. A moment later, as George "look[s] carefully at the solitaire hand," he mentions that Andy Cushman is "in San Quentin right now on account of a tart." As an anonymous tart was responsible for Andy Cushman's fate, so Curley's wife, whom Candy describes as a "tart" in section two, will be responsible for Lennie's. Even as he and Lennie talk, George's conversation obliquely foreshadows the novel's climactic scene and ironically reinforces the symbolism of his game of solitaire.

Lennie's repetitive questioning about their "little place" abruptly changes the mood in the bunkhouse. "George's hands stopped working with the cards. His voice was growing warmer." Significantly, George abandons the cards while describing their dream, as if its fulfillment were within their own control, beyond chance. Indeed, Candy's unexpected offer of his $300 suddenly convinces George that his and Lennie's long quest may finally be successful. "They all sat still, all bemused by the beauty of the thing, each mind was popped into the future when this lovely thing should come about." But their illusion is quickly shattered. It is sheer chance, like the unexpected appearance of a card, and brutal irony that Lennie is still smiling "with delight at the memory of the ranch" when the enraged Curley, after being repulsed by Slim, enters the bunkhouse spoiling for a fight and misinterprets Lennie's smile. In the ensuing battle between Lennie and Curley, Steinbeck vividly and prophetically describes the terrible strength that will destroy the dream and insulate George: "The next minute Curley was flopping like a fish on a line, and his closed fist was lost in Lennie's big hand." Steinbeck uses the same image to describe the death of Curley's wife: " 'Don't you go yellin',' he said, and he shook her; and her body flopped like a fish."

In the final moments of section three, Steinbeck's disciplined non-teleological vision is clearly evident; chance rules in the bunkhouse as later it will in the barn. The genius of Steinbeck's narrative in **Of Mice and Men** lies in the consistency of this vision, and in George's card games Steinbeck provides an exact symbol of the unpredictable, often merciless world in which his characters vainly strive to maintain their dignity and fulfill their dreams. (pp. 38-43)

> *Michael W. Shurgot, "A Game of Cards in Steinbeck's 'Of Mice and Men'," in* Steinbeck Quarterly, *Vol. XV, Nos. 1-2, Winter-Spring, 1982, pp. 38-43.*

FURTHER READING

Bibliography

French, Warren. "John Steinbeck." In *Fifteen Modern American Authors: A Survey of Research and Criticism,* edited by Jackson R. Bryer, pp. 369-87. Durham, N.C.: Duke University Press, 1969.

> Appraises bibliographies, books, and articles on Steinbeck.

———. "John Steinbeck." In *Sixteen Modern American Authors, Volume 2: A Survey of Research and Criticism since 1972,* edited by Jackson R. Bryer, pp. 582-622. Durham, N.C.: Duke University Press, 1990.

> Appraises bibliographies, books, and articles on Steinbeck.

Hayashi, Tetsumaro. *A New Steinbeck Bibliography: 1971-1981.* Metuchen, N.J.: The Scarecrow Press, 1983, 147 p.

> References to criticism on Steinbeck written from 1971 through 1981.

Biography

Benson, Jackson J. "Poverty and Success." In his *The True Adventures of John Steinbeck, Writer,* pp. 163-468. New York: Viking Press, 1984.

> Chronicles Steinbeck's life and career during the 1930s.

Criticism

Bellman, Samuel I. "Control and Freedom in Steinbeck's *Of Mice and Men.*" *The CEA Critic* XXXVIII, No. 1 (November 1975): 25-7.

> Argues that George comes to depend on Slim for guidance in the same way that Lennie depended on George.

Burgum, Edwin Berry. "The Sensibility of John Steinbeck." *Science and Society* X, No. 2 (Spring 1946): 132-47.

> Argues that Steinbeck's depiction of working people in his novels fluctuates between admiration and sentimentality. Discussing *Of Mice and Men* specifically, Burgum adds that social issues and capitalism condition the relationships between the characters.

Cardullo, Robert. "On the Road to Tragedy: The Function of Candy in *Of Mice and Men.*" In *All the World: Drama Past and Present, Vol. II,* edited by Karelisa V. Hartigan, pp. 1-8. Washington, D.C.: University Press of America, 1982.

> Asserts that the depiction of Candy in *Of Mice and Men* contributes to an understanding of the work as a tragedy centered on George.

Davison, Richard Allan. "*Of Mice and Men* and *McTeague:* Steinbeck, Fitzgerald, and Frank Norris." *Studies in American Fiction* 17, No. 2 (Autumn 1989): 219-26.

> Examines F. Scott Fitzgerald's claim that Steinbeck incorporated scenes from Frank Norris's *McTeague* in *Of Mice and Men.* Davison concludes that Steinbeck appropriated some of Norris's dramatic effects but did not plagiarize.

Demott, Robert. " 'Voltaire Didn't Like Anything': A 1939 Interview with John Steinbeck." *Steinbeck Quarterly* XIX, Nos. 1-2 (Winter-Spring 1986): 5-11.

> Questionnaire in which Steinbeck comments briefly on *Of Mice and Men.*

Everson, William K. "Thoughts on a Great Adaptation." In *The Modern American Novel and the Movies,* edited by Gerald Peary and Roger Shatzkin, pp. 63-9. New York: Frederick Ungar Publishing Co., 1978.

> Considers *Of Mice and Men* nearly unique to the history of film adaptations because the novel and the film "stand side by side as producing the *same* emotions at the *same* junctures, even if not quite in the same way."

Ganapathy, R. "Steinbeck's *Of Mice and Men:* A Study in Lyricism Through Primitivism." *The Literary Criterion* V, No. 3 (Winter 1962): 101-04.

> Maintains that *Of Mice and Men* is lyrical in theme, characterization, and narrative.

Goldhurst, William. "*Of Mice and Men:* John Steinbeck's Parable of the Curse of Cain." *Western American Literature* VI, No. 2 (Summer 1971): 123-35.

> Explores religious and allegorical elements in *Of Mice and Men,* particularly parallels with the biblical account of Cain and Abel.

Gurko, Leo. "*Of Mice and Men:* Steinbeck as Manichean." *The University of Windsor Review* VIII, No. 2 (Spring 1973): 11-23.

Contends that *Of Mice and Men* is a parable based on principles of dualism and opposition.

Hill, Rodney. "Small Things Considered: *Raising Arizona* and *Of Mice and Men.*" *Post Script* 8, No. 3 (Summer 1989): 18-27.

Maintains that the movie *Raising Arizona,* by Joel and Ethan Coen, is a retelling of Steinbeck's *Of Mice and Men.*

Kauffmann, Stanley. *"Of Mice and Men."* In his *Persons of the Drama: Theater Criticism and Comment,* pp. 156-59. New York: Harper and Row, 1976.

Reprint of a 1975 review in which Kauffmann criticizes *Of Mice and Men* for the inevitability of its conclusion.

Lisca, Peter. *"In Dubious Battle* and *Of Mice and Men:* The Macrocosm and the Microcosm." In his *John Steinbeck: Nature and Myth,* pp. 63-86. New York: Thomas Y. Crowell Co., 1978.

Discusses Steinbeck's use of foreshadowing, hand imagery, and allusions to the story of Cain and Abel which, Lisca claims, enhance the theme of loneliness in *Of Mice and Men.*

Loftis, Anne. "A Historical Introduction to *Of Mice and Men.*" In *The Short Novels of John Steinbeck: Critical Essays with a Checklist to Steinbeck Criticism,* edited by Jackson J. Benson, pp. 39-47. Durham, N.C.: Duke University Press, 1990.

Examines the historical and biographical context in which Steinbeck wrote *Of Mice and Men* and summarizes the critical history of both the novel and drama.

McCarthy, Paul. "Conflicts and Searches in the 1930s." In his *John Steinbeck,* pp. 46-64. New York: Frederick Ungar Publishing Co., 1980.

Considers *Of Mice and Men* a novel about elusive dreams and friendship, stating that "George and Lennie

symbolize something of the enduring and hopeful as well as the meaningless."

Millichap, Joseph. "Realistic Style in Steinbeck's and Milestone's *Of Mice and Men.*" *Literature-Film Quarterly* VI, No. 3 (Summer 1978): 241-52.

Compares Steinbeck's novel and Lewis Milestone's 1939 film adaptation, both of which, Millichap claims, exemplify realism.

O'Hara, Frank Hurburt. "Melodrama with a Meaning." In his *Today in American Drama,* pp. 142-89. Chicago: The University of Chicago Press, 1939.

Characterizes *Of Mice and Men* as a distinctly contemporary melodrama.

Spilka, Mark. "Of George and Lennie and Curley's Wife: Sweet Violence in Steinbeck's Eden." *Modern Fiction Studies* 20, No. 2 (Summer 1974): 169-79.

Psychological analysis of *Of Mice and Men,* centering on Steinbeck's concern with men's sexual impulses and women as exploiters of those impulses.

Wilson, Edmund. "The Boys in the Back Room." In his *Classics and Commercials: A Literary Chronicle of the Forties,* pp. 19-56. New York: Farrar, Straus and Co., 1950.

Describes *Of Mice and Men* as both "a compact little drama, contrived with almost too much cleverness, and a parable which criticized humanity from a non-political point of view."

Woodress, James. "John Steinbeck: Hostage to Fortune." *The South Atlantic Quarterly* LXIII, No. 3 (Summer 1964): 385-97.

Survey of Steinbeck's career. Woodress claims that Steinbeck wrote *Of Mice and Men* before an artistic decline that began as a result of the popular and critical success of *The Grapes of Wrath.*

Additional coverage of Steinbeck's life and career is contained in the following sources published by Gale Research: *Concise Dictionary of American Literary Biography, 1929-1941; Contemporary Authors,* Vols. 1-4, 25-28 (rev. eds.); *Contemporary Authors New Revision Series,* Vols. 1, 35; *Contemporary Literary Criticism,* Vols. 1, 5, 9, 13, 21, 34, 45, 59; *Dictionary of Literary Biography,* Vols. 7, 9; *Dictionary of Literary Biography Documentary Series,* Vol. 2; *Major 20th-Century Writers; Something about the Author,* Vol. 9; and *World Literature Criticism.*

Andrei Tarkovsky

1932-1986

(Full name Andrei Arsenyich Tarkovsky; also transliterated as Tarkovskii) Russian film and stage director, scriptwriter, and memoirist.

The following entry presents an overview of Tarkovsky's life and career.

INTRODUCTION

Tarkovsky is recognized as one of the Soviet Union's preeminent film directors. A visionary filmmaker whose contemplative, dreamlike works reflect both the despair and hope of modern life, Tarkovsky garnered international acclaim for producing a body of work in which landscapes, even colors, assume thematic significance. His characters grapple with spiritual considerations while struggling against the mediocrity and seeming hopelessness of earthly existence. The acclaimed Swedish film director Ingmar Bergman called Tarkovsky "the greatest, the one who invented a new language, true to the nature of film, as it captures life as a reflection, life as a dream."

Born in the village of Zavrozhne, near Moscow, Tarkovsky was raised by his mother after his father, the Russian poet Arseny Tarkovsky, abandoned the family following his service in World War II. Tarkovsky's early education included seven years of music studies and three years of art classes. In 1951 he enrolled in the School of Oriental Languages to study Arabic but dropped out during his second year for medical reasons. In 1954 he entered the Moscow State Film School, where he studied for six years under the tutelage of the noted Soviet film director Mikhail Romm. Tarkovsky's final project under Romm, *Katok i skripka* (*The Steamroller and the Violin*), a short film concerning the friendship between a young musician and a construction worker, was awarded first place at a student film competition in New York. After graduating in 1960, Tarkovsky pursued a career as a film director. During the next two decades he made such films as *Ivanovo Detstvo* (*My Name Is Ivan*), *Andrei Rublev, Solaris,* and *Stalker.* While his films were generally well received abroad, Soviet cultural officials frequently censored or restricted their distribution because of the films' spiritual and often enigmatic content, which conflicted with government doctrines of socialist realism in the arts. In 1982 Tarkovsky obtained permission to leave the Soviet Union to work in Italy on *Nostalghia.* Two years later, despite longing for his homeland, Tarkovsky refused to return to the Soviet Union, citing immense artistic differences with Soviet officials. He settled in Italy, then traveled to West Germany and, eventually, to Sweden, where he made his final film, *Offret* (*The Sacrifice*). Before completing *The Sacrifice,* Tarkovsky was diagnosed with cancer; he died in a Paris hospital in 1986.

Tarkovsky first earned critical acclaim for his films dealing with the Russian past. *My Name Is Ivan,* a black-and-white film set during World War II, presents the war from the perspective of a twelve-year-old boy who volunteers for dangerous reconnaissance missions behind enemy lines and who is ultimately captured and executed by German forces. Like many Soviet war films, *My Name Is Ivan* has been faulted for clichéd subject matter but has garnered praise for its dreamlike visual imagery and innovative narrative structure. *My Name Is Ivan,* which is also known as *Ivan's Childhood* and *The Youngest Spy,* was awarded a Golden Lion of St. Mark at the 1962 Venice Film Festival.

Tarkovsky earned several major awards for his next film, *Andrei Rublev,* a quasi-biographical film focusing on the life of the title character, a fourteenth-century Russian monk revered for his icon paintings. The film depicts several important episodes in the life of Rublev, contrasting the brutality and suffering of the era with the artistic inspiration and spirituality of his works. At the conclusion, the film switches from black-and-white to color to present a series of close-up shots of Rublev's paintings. *Andrei Rublev* was completed in 1966, but Soviet cultural officials, objecting to the film's violence, nudity, religiosity, and celebration of the artist as an individual, withheld it from circulation. A censored version was shown in the United States in 1968 and at various international film festivals the following year, where it earned numerous major awards and prompted demands for release of the uncensored version. *Andrei Rublev* has been widely applauded for its powerful evocation of the Middle Ages and skillful dramatization of Rublev's spiritual development. Mark Le Fanu observed that "*Andrei Rublev* as far as I know is the first and maybe (for the time being) the last Russian film to look at the historical culture of Christianity not in terms of a so-called 'reactionary' content, but in terms of its own profound inner rightness and grandeur."

Tarkovsky is also widely known for his science-fiction films, including *Solaris* and *Stalker*. *Solaris,* an adaptation of Polish writer Stanislaw Lem's novel, focuses on Kris Kelvin, a psychologist assigned to investigate reports of mysterious phenomena at a distant space station orbiting the planet Solaris. The film opens at the home of Kelvin's father, where Kelvin plans his mission and meets with Burton, a scientist who returned from Solaris in a state of extreme anxiety, contending that the sea-like landscape of the planet is actually a vast consciousness. After arriving at the space station, Kelvin discovers that Burton's contentions were accurate: the entire planet is a living organism capable of materializing the thoughts of others. Kelvin, who had been obsessed throughout his trip by the suicide of his wife, soon finds that the planet has transformed his thoughts into a simulacrum of his wife. Initially horrified, Kelvin sends her away in a rocket, but after she reappears he gradually adjusts to her presence. When she commits suicide again, Kelvin decides to return to Earth. At the end of the film, Kelvin is shown returning to his father's home, which has materialized on the surface of Solaris. Often called the "Soviet reply" to Stanley Kubrick's *2001: A Space Odyssey, Solaris* is considered a masterpiece of Russian science-fiction filmmaking, less concerned with futuristic technology than with understanding the psychological and spiritual concerns of humanity. Le Fanu commented: "Kelvin muses that if there is one reason for going up into space, it is so that we can look back again on Earth with renewed understanding and tenderness. The whole 'adventure' of space is regarded sceptically. The film seems to say that our destiny is on this planet or nowhere."

Stalker is Tarkovsky's adaptation of Arkadii and Boris Strugatsky's novel *Piknik na obochine* (*Roadside Picnic.*) The film depicts a journey by two men, Writer and Scientist, and their guide, Stalker, through a mysterious, polluted region called the Zone and into a magic room where wishes are supposedly granted. After leaving their barren industrial environment, the party crosses through lush fields and arrives at the building containing the room, which appears to be a flooded basement displaying various magical phenomena. Once at the room's threshold, Writer and Scientist succumb to introspection and doubt. It becomes apparent that faith is needed for wishes to be granted. After the three men return from the Zone, Stalker finds that his crippled daughter, somehow affected by her father's journey, has begun to display telekinetic ability. Some Western critics have faulted *Stalker* for its slow pace

and obscurity; others, however, have interpreted the film as an allegorical exploration of the nature of faith in a world of futility and spiritual desolation. Soviet officials expressed dissatisfaction with the themes of *Stalker* and restricted its distribution.

In *The Sacrifice,* Tarkovsky's final film, a former actor named Alexander becomes convinced that a nuclear holocaust is imminent. He consequently makes a pact with God to free himself from material possessions in order to save the world. Later, perhaps in a dream, Alexander encounters his eccentric mailman, who informs him that a tryst with a local witch will save the world. After acting accordingly, Alexander awakens to find his life in a familiar state of absurdity and despair. Believing that he has saved the world, he torches his family's home to fulfill his earlier vow. At film's end, Alexander is straitjacketed and presumably taken to an asylum while his son tends a fragile tree that the two had planted earlier. *The Sacrifice* was awarded four prizes at the 1986 Cannes Film Festival, including a special grand prize. Praising the technical and thematic aspects of the film, many reviewers regarded *The Sacrifice* as Tarkovsky's masterpiece as well as a profound exploration of the Christian faith.

While his work was frequently restricted by Soviet cultural officials, Tarkovsky nevertheless has been acknowledged as an important influence on his contemporaries. In 1990 the Russian film critic Peter Shchepotinnik observed: "We are still living with the gradually fading light following Tarkovsky's death. Until recently his unique presence set the standard of spirituality (a purely Russian notion!) toward which all our directors tended, for they had before their eyes an example of supreme craftsmanship, philosophic profundity, and artistic obsession. We now see only rare reflections of his style."

PRINCIPAL WORKS

Katok i skripka [with Andrey Mikhalkov-Konchalovsky] (screenplay)   1960; also released in England as *The Steamroller and the Violin,* 1981

Ivanovo Detstvo [with Mikhail Papava, adaptors; from the novella *Ivan* by Vladimir Bogomolov]   (screenplay) 1962; also released as *My Name Is Ivan,* 1963; also known as *Ivan's Childhood* and *The Youngest Spy*

Andrei Rublev [with Andrey Mikhalkov-Konchalovsky] (screenplay)   1966; censored version released in the United States, 1968; abridged version, 1971; restored version, 1983

Solaris [with Friedrich Gorenstein, adaptors; from the novel *Solaris* by Stanislaw Lem]   (screenplay) 1972

Zerkalo [with Aleksandr Misharin]   (screenplay) 1974; also released in the United States as *The Mirror,* 1983

*Beregis! Zmej (screenplay)   1979

Stalker [adaptor; from the novel *Piknik na obochine* (*Roadside Picnic*) by Arkadii and Boris Strugatsky] (screenplay)   1979

Nostalghia [with Tonino Guerra] (screenplay) 1983; released in the United States, 1984
Offret (screenplay) 1986; released in the United States as *The Sacrifice*, 1986
Sapetchatlionnoye Vremya (criticism) 1987 [*Sculpting in Time: Reflections on the Cinema*, 1987]

*Tarkovsky wrote but did not direct this film.

CRITICISM

Isabel Quigly (review date 24 January 1964)

[*In the following review of* Ivan's Childhood, *Quigly praises Tarkovsky's focus on Ivan and the horror of warfare but finds the film clichéd and formulaic.*]

The Russians are good at films about children and so long as *Ivan's Childhood* (director: Andrei Tarkovsky) sticks to Ivan, a touching, ferocious boy of twelve with beautiful hands, wrists and movements, things are fine. The title is ironic: pitchforked into the war when his family is wiped out, Ivan is used as a scout because he can get through the German lines where grown men can't. He is bitter but loving, a passionate and pathetic figure, girlishly pretty in his large fur hats and becoming chunky sweaters. Among the officers who plan his missions he has friends who plan to adopt him when the war is over and the relationships are shown as mercifully unlike those of the 'army mascot' sort of film, for Ivan is an equal, doing a man's job better than a man could do it, and finally getting a man's fate—hanging.

So far, so good; there are moments of feeling, tenseness, and strength. But it has to go wandering, and it wanders disastrously: into the 'idyllic' country of so many Russian war films, into Ivan's dreams and nightmares, all corny symbolism with apples, wells full of stars, wet sand and lapping water; into woods, interminable lyrical woods where the cupolas of trees whirl tenderly round in circles as they did in *The Loneliness of the Long-Distance Runner* and every other pretentious piece ever made involving woods, boys and sorrow; into a sketchy love affair between a friend of Ivan's and a woman doctor at the front, who, of course, goes for walks in the woods and peeps round the trunks of birch trees like a Russian Mary Pickford, forty years on; in short, into anything and everything that was ever used as a symbol of suffering, nostalgia, loneliness and regret. What's right is the film's feeling for Ivan, torn between childhood and a horror where childhood isn't admitted and a child can be hanged like anyone else; what's right, too, is its sense, even at this distance, of the unthinkable horror of the war in Russia. What's wrong is the method, soggy and second-hand, which gives way to the cinema's everlasting temptation to say nothing prettily, to use visual cliché just because it's there and to the director (presumably) seems compelling. (p. 107)

Isabel Quigly, "Lost in the Woods," in The Spectator, *Vol. 212, No. 7074, January 24, 1964, pp. 107-08.*

Lee Atwell (review date Fall 1964)

[*In the following review, Atwell favorably appraises* Ivan's Childhood.]

The Soviet war films exported to the West (*The Cranes Are Flying, Ballad of a Soldier, The Letter That Was Not Sent, Clear Skies*) increasingly appear as poetic exercises in which the directors use their material as an excuse for indulging in brilliant compositions and stylistic experiments, although on the script side they remain essentially propaganda pieces reminding us that war is a monstrous thing and that Russians are much antiwar. *Ivan's Childhood* is one of the latest to reach us, and in spite of certain similarities with earlier films, it is a significant advance in the use of the camera as an interpretive tool, and a deviation from the straightforward narrative of routine Soviet cinema.

Ivan is a small, twelve-year-old boy forced into premature manhood as a result of the war and the loss of his parents, who has become a most effective Russian spy. The story-content of the film involves his return to the Russian front and his camaraderie with two officers who have volunteered out of necessity to adopt the boy, and with whom he finds a much needed warmth and companionship between assignments. But the primary preoccupation of the film and the film-makers is with Ivan's dream-memories and fantasies which are introduced, often by direct cut, throughout the film. It is his escape mechanism, his return to the time of innocence and abandon, to happiness as he knew it—juxtaposed with his adult awareness of war which has destroyed him psychologically and emotionally. This ironic contrast of the two "Ivans" is seen in the pretitle sequence: in the bright, clear morning Ivan, a remarkably beautiful, glowing child is seen "flying" over the treetops near his village, and as he descends he meets his mother on the road; seconds later, from the depths of night we see a dark, dirty, small figure advance through a marsh as Ivan returns from the German camp.

Ivan's Childhood is an ambitious directorial debut which can stand well beside the first film of practically any director.

—*Lee Atwell*

Andrei Tarkovsky with his first film clearly demonstrates that he is a director who is taken with the refinements of "artistic" style and beautiful compositions (not unlike, say, Welles or Losey). His visual concepts are consistently stunning and often startlingly right, utilizing some of the camera and cutting devices characteristic of Truffaut and the French directors. However, in the final analysis, it is in part his technical excesses and concern with pictorial values that throw the film off balance and rob it of its full potential.

The casting is near perfect—especially the astonishing performance of Kolya Burlayaev as Ivan. He succeeds beautifully in convincing us that he is both a clever and lovable child, and circumstantially an adult and a soldier. He is a representative product of war and at the same time an unusually fascinating individual. One assumes that Tarkovsky, since he shows us practically nothing of the war itself, is concerned with the boy's mental view of the war and his lost childhood. However, we do not see these elements as Ivan sees them, but as *Tarkovsky* and his camera see them. His meticulous, lyric style can be justified, as in the dream sequences which are metamorphosed into a super-reality, but the most objective realism in the film is equally as beautiful to behold. One seldom feels the overpowering anguish and terror of war as in the work of Wajda. Ivan's last mission at the end is the only time this comes through with any impact. If the style intrudes upon the film's objective images, it succeeds brilliantly in a sequence where the real and fantasy worlds converge in Ivan's mind as he acts out a war-game in the dark, stalking the enemy to the kill: a moment of true terror.

What the film does succeed in communicating with vivid imaginativeness and power is Ivan's tormented psyche and his remembrance of a beautiful childhood which is his only source of goodness and hope. Whether it is simply meeting his mother on the road to draw a bucket of water from the well, or riding to the beach in the rain on an applecart, Tarkovsky and his cameraman Vadim Yusov invest the images with a surreal haunting beauty not easily forgotten. And after the silent, yet eloquent epilogue, in which we learn of the child's tragic end, we return to Ivan's dream vision—a final liberation, a return to paradise lost. *Ivan's Childhood* is an ambitious directorial debut which can stand well beside the first film of practically any director. (pp. 50-1)

> Lee Atwell, "Ivan's Childhood," in Film Quarterly, Vol. XVIII, No. 1, Fall, 1964, pp. 50-1.

Ivor Montagu (essay date Spring 1973)

[*Montagu was an English film director, critic, editor, journalist, and screenwriter. During the 1930s he became associated with Alfred Hitchcock and produced or coproduced several of his films, including* The Man Who Knew Too Much *(1939) and* The Thirty-Nine Steps. *(1935). In the following essay, Montagu provides an overview and assessment of* Ivan's Childhood, Andrei Rublev, *and* Solaris.]

Tarkovsky's work is not so well-known in this country, perhaps, as in several others. *Ivan's Childhood* is available in a remarkably well and sensitively dubbed version made in France with American voices. *Solaris,* with English titles for the dialogue, was shown at last year's London Film Festival. *Andrei Rublev* has not arrived yet owing to commercial complications. World rights were sold to a French firm soon after the film was made, an English language

version was made for the U.S. Who has it here and what, if anything, they intend eventually to do with it has not yet transpired. Our loss.

I suppose the most notable thing most people know about Tarkovsky is the holdup that kept *Rublev* on the shelf in U.S.S.R. for several years. The cause of the kerfuffle is not at all clear. Some say it was religion, some 'lack of historicity', some horror. The real Andrei Rublev, of course, is *the* greatest—so great as to be almost legendary—Russian icon-painter of all time. Hence the guess about 'religion'. This is, however, difficult to credit, for the religious-philosophical issues remain the intact centrepiece of the picture as released. 'Unhistorical' was certainly an accusation bandied about in the public controversy that flared up in U.S.S.R. when it was eventually shown, and I have myself heard it spoken to damp my enthusiasm by a Soviet fellow-guest at a dinner party. Considering that absolutely nothing is known about the life of Rublev, beyond the fact that he must have been a monk and lived about the turn of the 14th/15th century, this seems rather a nonsense criticism to make of any purported film biography, and Tarkovsky himself has reminded the captious that such a charge would dismiss not only *Hamlet* but *Julius Caesar* as well.

Accounts of its wonders were rife from both Soviet film colleagues and visitors who had the chance to see *Rublev* just after it was made; the 'inside' tale I heard at the time from 'those who should know' was that the censors were shocked at its brutality and that the director was being difficult about cuts. That this, not politics, may well have been the real reason is perhaps fortified by the fact that it was freely sold for abroad—not usual with any Soviet film thought bordering on the heterodox politically—several years before it was thought safe for less shock-proof Soviet stomachs, that the cuts I perceive were certainly of that character, and that there is quite enough of this sort left to shatter even audiences used to *Clockwork Orange.*

Before we go in to bat, cold-war-wise, for the woes suffered by young geniuses from the set-up in Soviet cinema revealed by the misadventures of *Rublev,* we had better reflect (*a*) how long most of our young film aspirants have to wait (or work) before they get a feature to direct; (*b*) how long *Kes* had to wait to be shown; (*c*) how many talented young directors here would be delighted to get any chance to work on at all, let alone be put at once on a colour, wide screen, three and a bit hour super-production without waiting to see how his last film—still being quarrelled about—was really going to turn out; and (*d*) what are the prospects of *Rublev* here when its remains, already mangled abroad twenty minutes more than in U.S.S.R., do at last reach the British Board of Film Censors.

Enough of the career, let us look at the work. To me Tarkovsky is one of the best things to happen in world cinema for a long time. Not everyone can be a Brigadier Gerard, but I tip him certainly as a horse to follow. Incidentally, Tarkovsky must, like Picasso, have a 'thing' about horses. In every one of his films, at a peak moment, he introduces a horse with tremendous impact.

Tarkovsky is a realist, but not in the sense in which, in

every form of society, Philistines use this word to restrict their favours to a narrow naturalism. *Realism* in the full sense implies the portrayal and exploration of reality.

It can embrace many styles, including surrealism where this relates itself to reality in content. The designation *non-realism* applies properly to: patterns and designs without any representational character, which may be appraised for their skill and liked or disliked on a basis of subjective pleasure, but are no more and no less reprehensible than any other diversion; and the rubbish misrepresenting the human character and situation that makes up the regular stock-in-trade of commercial cinema, and distortion and exaggeration—however zealous or even worthy—with propaganda object: these are falsehood however naturalistic.

Tarkovsky is a *realist poet in images:* that is, he digs deep beneath the surface structure of his narrative to load his treatment with overtones and undertones, hints, symbols suggestive of and reflecting on the theme. Stylistically he intermixes in his presentation the straight story—events in sequence—with events that happened in the past or may happen in the future, or can never happen, all represented on the same plane of actuality, without any of the fades or trick 'effects' that older techniques used to help guide the spectator to a distinction.

In *Ivan's Childhood* we turn to and from Ivan's dead parents and dead childhood and conclude with scenes that never were or will be. In *Rublev* the central character matter-of-factly continues an argument with a senior artist after the latter is dead, and in a place where he could not possibly be even were he yet alive. In *Solaris,* the hero's mother intervenes, where she cannot be, and plays scenes as a young girl, and there is a remarkable scene, Chinese box within Chinese box, in which characters watch themselves watching a film of some of them watching another film in which they are depicted. All these intricacies are treated quite straight. This cinematic equation of treatment of objective experience and subjective thoughts or imagination on the part of the character is not, of course, peculiar to or a discovery of Tarkovsky; it might almost be called a 'modern' style, used quite widely already by others. What seems to me peculiar to Tarkovsky is that whereas in others this freedom often confuses, leaving the spectator uncertain what elements are reality or imagined, and in others (among them real masters like Buñuel) deliberately presents a real content to be deciphered from an entirely imagined shape, with Tarkovsky we are never in doubt as to the objective narrative presented to us. The boundaries of natural events are broken only to deepen, clarify and enrich the essence of the real.

All truly poetic work is susceptible of varied interpretation according to the intellectual baggage (period, national, class, traditional, etc. background) of its audience, spectator, reader. Everybody knows that Shakespeare in every generation and clime can be and is interpreted in many ways, each as 'true' and illuminating as its rival. To take a less exalted example, I. A. Richards in the 1920s set his Cambridge class to paraphrasing a plain poem by D. H. Lawrence into prose and found that every student read it differently. So if I try briefly to describe the three features

of Tarkovsky I cannot pretend that I have got it 'right' or to enjoy any special authority in elucidation. This is simply how it seems to me.

All three have an extraordinary 'Ancient Mariner' power. They buttonhole you and will not let you go. They are not pleasant to watch, they are obsessive and they convince like a hammer. Part of the magic that rivets is the beauty, harmony and relevance of the graphic composition. It is perhaps significant that all three are filmed by the same cameraman, the fellow-student Vadim Yusov, that of the three features the only one not an adaptation (*Rublev*) was co-scripted with another fellow-student (Andrei Mikhalkov-Konchalovsky, since a director in his own right), that all three graduated from G.I.K. together on the same diploma short, and that other names recur in credits for art direction and for music: there is hint here of a lively creative generation. But other Soviet film directors before Tarkovsky have worked magic with graphic composition. What is especial here is that sometimes (even in *Solaris*) he has the power to evoke through his actors an anguish of empathy that is hardly to be borne.

The stories are superficially hackneyed. It is how they are presented that becomes a commentary on man, his experience and the universe.

Ivan's Childhood is a last-war film that introduces us to a boy returning to the Russian lines after a scouting expedition. We see his twelve-year-old waif's face peering through the mists and barbed wire studying the swift-flowing river that forms the No Man's Land between the armies and which he must traverse. Follows a scene in which the boy imposes his will on the under-officers in a situation reminiscent of the First Act of Shaw's *Saint Joan* and, welcomed at headquarters, refuses for the umpteenth time to be fobbed off with relegation to a military school safe behind the lines. His parents are dead, his village destroyed, he himself escaped from a concentration camp—his living can only be revenge. Eventually Ivan accompanies two officers crossing to the German side to recover the corpses of two soldiers, caught and executed while trying to help the boy back on his last expedition and now displayed on the bank 'to discourage the others'. In their task the two officers succeed, but from his intelligence mission Ivan never returns. Years later, his comrades find in Berlin after the victory a folder recording his capture and fate.

This same 'scenario' has been told a hundred times, in fiction or in fact, the young 'Red Devils' as much heroes as their elders, running the gauntlet to improbable triumph (as in *The Feather Letter*) or dying for rashness, like Petya Rostov in *War and Peace.* But this is something quite different. The film is not about a boy's death at all. Not that such tragedies do not occur, or that they cannot be told, as they have been by Tolstoy and so many others, to epitomise—indeed melodramatise—war's arbitrary injustice. The very facility and repetition of this symbol weakens its impact nowadays. The tragedy here, however, is much worse because more inescapable. Ivan's fate is sealed before ever the film begins. He is wonderfully played by Kolya Burlyayev. From the moment we see the wide-eyed creature in the mist, the contrast between the skinny, hungry, sometimes blubbering boy and the expert spy, professional, authoritative, competent, indispensable, the two bound in a single being—a soldier who has known torture and triumph alike, a child on whom grown men depend—we know he cannot survive.

The film has subtly changed its hub from that in the novel (called *Ivan*) to that designated by the new title *Ivan's Childhood;* and that, in the true sense, has already died. The film is not disfigured by the unnaturally cheery or the conventionally hysterical. With one blow it annuls a whole cinémathèque of the war films of all lands. Soldiers and officers, all are reasonably decent—samples at hazard of mean sensual man—all alike are under tension that frays and saps the nerve but against which they stubbornly endure in ways varying according to their character. We know, peace come, they will return to living. But what is there for Ivan? His parents gone, his playmates dead, the burden of responsibility even unto life and death shouldered in immaturity, he is not a real boy, he can never be a natural man. Peace would finish him as surely as a bullet.

This is No. 1 of the Tarkovsky features. Follows No. 2. The first is of a child where he should not be, in the trap of duty-death constituted by patriotic war. The second centres on the dilemma of the artist trapped helpless in a world of horror. Where the first film depended for its achievement on the performance of the boy, and the atmosphere of the unendurable tension, the second depends above all on the persuasiveness and conviction of the atmosphere of barbaric and arbitrary indifference to man.

I do not think that anyone can 'enjoy' Tarkovsky's films. They are too tense, too agonising, at their best too spellbinding with sympathies. . . . Born 1932? Remember, he comes of a generation that, in the years he was the age of the boy in his first feature, was losing in its homeland 20 million dead. But when one has seen any one of his films once, one wants to see it again and yet again. . . .

—*Ivor Montagu*

I have already noted that no one knows anything about Rublev save his approximate date, that he must have been a monk and that he painted. His icons stand out among those of his contemporaries not merely for their graphic virtues but for their expression of pity, charity, humanity. Too often contemporary masters reflected, of deliberate belief, only what they saw in the surface of the world around them, man in a losing contest with devils. Tarkovsky says that he considered the conventional imaginary Russian portrait of Rublev must be entirely wrong—the blue-eyed, fair-haired, suffering saint. To go against the then prevailing tradition of icon-painting, to go against the violence of his feudal surroundings, lord over serf, lord against lord, and Tartar destroying both, Rublev must

have been a dark, intense, stubborn and passionate man. To dramatise the significance of his 'premature' faith in man, the events around him must all tend negative to it. It is thus not derogatory to Anatoli Solonitsyn in the name part to say that his is not a bravura but a subdued, intense performance. He has no 'big' moment. The formidable power of the film derives, as is intended in its shape, from the appalling incidents and sufferings provoked or endured by those around him. The minor characters in this film all act marvellously.

Andrei Rublev is in two parts, eight episodes dated from 1400 to 1423 with the four central ones falling within one year, 1408. It opens with a bell and it ends with a bell. To start with, craftsmen are trying to raise a bell on a church in the marshes by means of hot-air balloons. A raid of skiffs puts them to flight. Rublev and his companions take refuge in a hostelry from fearsome, quagmire-producing rain. A pair of mounted retainers enter the inn and seize a vagrant serf. From the moment, taking the man each by one arm, they drag him out and suddenly, unexpectedly, crash his forehead against a gatepost, then throw his unconscious body across a packhorse, we are *in* Tarkovsky's Middle Ages.

There follows a scene of argument theological, philosophical, compounded with personal rivalries and jealousies, between Rublev, his associates and a venerable icon-painter, Theophanes the Greek. As Jeanne Vronskaya quotes Tarkovsky: 'Unlike Theophanes the Greek, who propounded the idea of Judgment Day, who found in Man only an embodiment of sin and vice, and in God a vengeful, primitive being, Rublev placed Man first. In Man he sought God, he regarded him as the house in which God lived.'

Incidents, visions of the procession of the cross and the Passion prolong the argument. A terrifying episode of peasant festival in which Rublev is bound, freed by a nude woman he rejects and who is later seized by guards and escapes flapping in the river like a great white dolphin, is succeeded by the painting of new murals in the cathedral by Rublev's group. The envious brother of the reigning prince meets a party of craftsmen in the forest on their way to join Rublev, blinds them, and then encounters a foraging party of Tartars and leads them by secret ways into the town to burn and rape and massacre. The attackers in an episode called 'Judgment Day—Summer 1408' batter in the doors of the cathedral and slaughter nearly every soul who there took refuge. Rublev, stung by the scene to kill a man who was carrying off a woman who had joined his group, sees all his effort in vain. The murals wrecked; the woman, driven mad, in spite of his care and facing the Tartars to protect her, prefers to ride off with them as a laughing-stock.

Tarkovsky, in commenting on the film, says: 'I do not understand historical films which have no relevance for the present. For me the most important thing is to use historical material to express Man's ideas and to create contemporary characters.'

What are the ideas here? Tarkovsky tells us that he and his group studied the graphics and architecture of the period for a long time—many artists contributed to the sets, many real surviving structures were used in the exteriors. Never have I seen in a historical film before so extraordinary and 'seamless' a conjunction of 'period' and nature: buildings, people, clothing, fields and weather. So far the graphics have carried us along through cruelty and catastrophe; we have identified with Rublev. He has abandoned creation and speech. He no longer works, he no longer interferes. He wanders passive. But now, in an 'appendix', the situation resolves itself, the wall crumbles. The prince's guards descend on a burnt-out village, seeking a craftsman capable of building to their master's glory a mighty bell, bigger than any before.

The village is waste, its inhabitants dead or fled. One boy remains, the son of the craftsman, who calls to the departing retainers of the prince to take him on their saddles, his father before dying imparted to him his secrets; he will build the bell. There follows the process of casting the monster bell, as the boy demands ever more and more men and metal and hurries men twice his age to do his bidding. At last all is ready, the populace is assembled, the prince and his guests ride out for the great hour. The clay cools, gingerly the craftsmen remove it. The boy—played again, brilliantly, by a now five years older Burlyayev—can stand it no longer. He runs and falls to earth, sobbing into Rublev's arms that there was no secret, he had no idea how to make a bell, but he had watched, he could not but try. There is no crack in the bell. It is hoisted successfully. It rings.

There follows, in a paean of blazing colour replacing the black and white of the film's action, image after image drawn from Rublev's icons. The point is clear. If the boy cannot forbear, but must create, how can Rublev, for very shame, accept frustration? Is this not a topical question, unanswerably answered? No words could be more explicit. Tortured, and torturing, this is yet a masterpiece.

Solaris I do not find so successful. Mainly because, I think, the director lost his way and the action does not bear out what he says he set out to do. *Solaris* is sci-fic, founded on a novel by [Stanislaw] Lem, a Polish author. Critics have pounced on the obvious contrast between the 'spectacular gadgetry' of Kubrick's *2001* (which Tarkovsky had seen) and what Tarkovsky also calls the 21st century, emphasising the 'human interest'. Contrasting it with the original novel, [Philip Strick] observes that the director 'has declined nearly all invitations to special effects and emphasises instead the novel's domestic, personal aspects.'

But Tarkovsky himself, in his own apologia, noting that, where Lem began with the entry of the scientists into the space capsule, he himself has begun with the home life of his astronaut, says that this is because what interested him, and what he intended to make the essence of his picture, was the question of the moral and ethical aspect of science. If so, this does not come off.

The surface action, stripped bare, is—as with his first film—simple and hackneyed. A scientist lives with his mother and father and son in a country *datcha* not far from Moscow. He is due for a responsible mission to the planet Solaris. Strange happenings have been reported there—he is to investigate and recommend whether the station maintained there needs to be vacated. Before he goes, there is discussion of the phenomena—of some long standing but in which at first no one had believed—a suggestion that figures personal to each observer are materialising from its pulsating surface. Life appears to exist on Solaris but in an unfamiliar form, a single continuous cover to the planet, an ocean of living matter with which no one can communicate directly but which can read the minds of the humans and materialise to them figures from their own past experience or inward fantasy. Is this entity malignant? Arrived on the Solaris station, the scientist hero, Chris Kelvin, finds his friend and predecessor dead, unable to survive the personal confrontations with which he was assailed, and himself face to face with the simulacrum of his dead wife, Hari, whom years ago he had failed, leading to her suicide. He is also isolated from his two surviving colleagues.

One of these is Sartorius (played, in utterly different character, by the actor of Rublev), a cold-blooded fish, who looks on his own materialised 'guests', in Tarkovsky's words, as a 'purely scientific phenomenon. [They] as it were do not touch him. He refuses to load his psyche with spiritual torments. In this attitude things are lighter for him than for Chris, who recognises in Hari a human being and not only an object for analysis.' The other man, Snaut (played by Kozintsev's Lear), has simply been broken by his materialisations, and become a drunkard.

Kelvin is obviously Tarkovsky's hero. 'I find myself nearer to him,' he writes, and adds: 'A man not too supple, not wanting to adapt to circumstances, he trusts himself, he does not want to change his principles and goes on to the end, even if this seems to others not too sensible. Maybe such people are a bit rigid, but they are strong and human. In a word, I wanted to show by his portrait that the problem of moral firmness, moral purity, penetrates our whole existence, appearing even in those spheres which at first glance are not linked to the moral, for example the penetration of the universe, the study of the objective world, etc.'

It is this that does not come off. On earth, Tarkovsky shows Kelvin as an apostle of the position: 'Moral and not moral, Man practises science. Remember Hiroshima!' And reproved by a colleague who says: 'I am not a partisan of knowledge at any price. Knowledge is only true when it is based on morality. Don't practise non-moral science . . . ' But when on Solaris, Kelvin is face to face with his conscience, his past deeds, he is too good a man to practise what he preaches. At first he tries in vain to destroy Hari. In vain! She is warm flesh enough for identity, feeling, sex, even love, but she cannot attain mortality. She can bleed, but she cannot be destroyed, certainly not by him in whose mind she lives. Is he to return to earth, deserting her once again, or abandon mission, parents, child and remain forever with her on this planet? It is this last he swears to her to do, but she knows he cannot.

This is how Tarkovsky sums it up. 'The point is the value of each piece of our behaviour, the significance of each of our acts, even the least noticed. Nothing once completed can be changed. If a man might 'replay' his actions, they would not be worth a groat, this would entail moral devaluation. The irreversibility of human experience is what gives our life, our deeds, their meaning and individuality . . . It appears that Chris is given a 'second chance', he as it were receives the possibility of experiencing once more the tragedy of separation from her. To repair what has been done once is impossible, but it does not mean that the meeting with the new 'Hari' has not changed our hero. He has once again undergone the experience, but now quite obviously more deeply, he has become cleaner, more humane, discovered a new moral potential.'

We see here, deliberately, the concept of the irreversibility of experience, its role as a constituent of personality, determining action, that stands out pre-eminently in Tarkovsky's work.

Here it unbalances Tarkovsky's declared primary purpose. The issue: should science be moral or amoral cannot be resolved on this plane of individual human experience. Partly it fails because of a weakness in the director himself—I do not think he understands scientists enough to grasp what makes them tick and so give relevance to his treatment of the problem. As in other fiction films of the scientific life—Soviet or other—the scientists behave not as scientists (they are only wearing hats so labelled), but as such are intellectualised concepts and otherwise might just as well be persons the director knows better, actors for instance or even newspaper reporters. But even more because of his strength—his unsurpassed power of rousing in the spectator an agonised tension and sympathy for the suffering human being (the name-part in the first film, the whole world around in the second film). Here all the arts of his transcendence of naturalism are devoted to an only partially successful effort to explore the background of the failure of Chris and Hari. But from the 'new' Hari herself (Natalie Bondarchuk, daughter of the famous actor) he has drawn so extraordinary a performance of the inhuman-human; feeling, longing, like a human, so near to being but knowing she can never be, becoming, growing closer, but forever debarred—in a word, so fey—that it quite overturns the subject of the picture and makes Chris a clot by comparison.

Indeed all the scientific chi-chi suddenly appears pseudo, the space trappings no more than the conventional 'once upon a time' that begins every fairy-tale. The planet Solaris and all the intellectualisation recede like the cheap Egyptology of *She* or *L'Atlantide*. With Hari feeling and poetry carry us back to the age-old legends of djinn-princess brides returning to the never-never lands of birds and serpents, Orkney fishermen whose seal-wives bear them children and go back to the ocean, the peasant left dumb because he cannot find his way back into the green mound. Perhaps this is not what the director meant. It is what we get from a creator who has mistaken his own strength.

I do not think that anyone can 'enjoy' Tarkovsky's films. They are too tense, too agonising, at their best too spellbinding with sympathies. Forty-one years old? Born 1932? Remember, he comes of a generation that, in the years he

was the age of the boy in his first feature, was losing in its homeland 20 million dead. But when one has seen any one of his films once, one wants to see it again and yet again; thoughts chase after one another like hares in March.

And in composition they are like Breughels. Not only are they pictures as a whole; take a lens to the parts, the details, they will strike as forcefully. Three images I cannot forget: in *Ivan's Childhood,* an incident that leads nowhere, the embarrassed girl medical attendant, newly come to the front, and the officer attracted to her; in *Rublev,* the exquisite beauty of the landscape as the prince's guards lead off their captive runaway, unconscious across a horse, along the edge of the lake; and, again from *Rublev,* the scene of the rescued woman, crazed and now unconscious, lying amid the heaps of corpses on the floor of the gutted cathedral—a riderless horse enters the building. As it halts its hoof clops on the stone floor. At the sound the woman's head jerks an inch, though she does not open her eyes. She is still a sentient being. (pp. 89-94)

Ivor Montagu, "Man and Experience: Tarkovsky's World," in Sight and Sound, *Vol. 42, No. 2, Spring, 1973, pp. 89-94.*

Lee Atwell (essay date 1974)

[*In the following essay, Atwell discusses the scientific, psychological, and spiritual aspects of* Solaris.]

The electric confluence of revolution and poetry sustained in the films of Eisenstein, Pudovkin, Dovzhenko, and Vertov, during those brief, optimistic, and unforgettable few years of the Soviet cinema's glory will undoubtedly never be revived. Yet, traces of their art emerge in occasional flickers of genius that manage to cut through the ponderous prestige of an official cinema: an unending stream of "classic" adaptations of plays, operas, and ballets. Certainly, Kozintsev's Shakespearean films are worthy, often brilliant efforts, yet the sympathetic observer must admit that film as a contemporary art form in the USSR is presently impoverished, just as it has been for the last 25 years, by narrow formal and thematic conception.

In a cultural milieu where the artist is still closely scrutinized for signs of ideological unorthodoxy and strident individualism, it is remarkable that a filmmaker such as Andrei Tarkovski has managed not only to survive but to create two of the most imposing Soviet films of the last decade. Following his bravura debut with *Ivan's Childhood,* he produced *Andrei Roublev,* a massive, but finely wrought, historical fresco depicting the personal struggles of the great icon painter, set against the painful turmoil of war and its attendant suffering that swept across feudal Russia.

Rather than create simply a biographic tribute, Tarkovski—in the tradition of Eisenstein—treats historic material as the vehicle for expressing his own beliefs and ideas, to develop the eternal and consequently always vital theme of the interrelation of an artist with his time, of the correlation between art and life. Tarkovski devoted three years to this epic work, which bears favorable comparison with the best of Eisenstein and Dovzhenko. Tarkovski himself defines the central subject as the individual suffering and sacrifice for the sake of an ideal: "The Russian people have always had a moral ideal, and Roublev endeavors to express it in his art. He succeeded in expressing this moral ideal of his epoch, the ideal of love, harmony, unity, and brotherhood."

Lofty sentiments were not sufficient, however, to endear the Russian critical front to this astonishing work as it mercilessly exposes the barbaric atmosphere of 15th century Russia with unprecedented realism, untempered by nobilized sentiments or events, though its concluding color images of the resplendent icons, suggest spiritual transcendence and rebirth. **Roublev** received limited showing in the Soviet Union, but was not distributed elsewhere for almost five years, though it registered a *succes d'estime* at Cannes in 1969 and appeared in selected European engagements the following year. (It ran for nearly a year at the Vieux-Colombier in Paris and was ecstatically received by the Paris press.)

Tarkovski's ranking in the vanguard of Soviet filmmakers and as an important creative force in modern cinema is confirmed by his most recent work, **Solaris,** a meditative parable based on the novel of the same title by the Polish science-fiction writer, Stanislaw Lem, about the nature of scientific investigation and its limitations in coping with the irrational, and incomprehensible developments of cosmic exploration. Significantly, from a political as well as artistic perspective, he has moved from the historic past to a contemporary, if somewhat theoretic subject and has again provoked considerable controversy, not only through the demanding stylistic nuance of the film, but in its direct interrogation of the morality of science and man's position in the universe.

If the ambience is technically advanced and modern, **Solaris**—astutely referred to as a "Russian answer to *2001,*" is much less concerned with the aesthetics of technology than the emotional resonances of a scientific, technocratic society, which could be anywhere on earth, as the ambiguous character names and cultural setting indicate. At the same time, its thematic grandeur is classic, characteristic of the Russian novelistic imagination, preoccupied with central human existential dilemmas, the great themes of life, love, and death.

The opening prelude suggests a biological linkage between man and nature, a metaphor which gradually establishes itself as a connection between earth and the planet Solaris. A pond, with plantlife gently swaying, opens onto a quiet, poetic, lush country (Russian) landscape, where Chris Calvin, a middle-aged psychologist, contemplates the scene of his childhood prior to his impending journey to investigate a space station near the surface of Solaris. In his father's country cottage, he confers with fellow cosmonauts, including Burton, who has returned from Solaris some years previously. They view a filmed report of Burton's interrogation by a scientific team, who in turn view films he has taken of the "visions" he experienced on the outpost. On earth scientists have hypothesized that the viscous surface of Solaris may actually be a living organism, but the science of Solaristics has run into a dead end

for lack of definite, verifiable data, though Burton still insists that what he saw there was real.

Whereas Kubrick's *2001* follows with great fascination the journey of man and his streamlined apparatus on an interstellar mission, **Solaris** presents a metaphoric passage that surprisingly eliminates almost completely scenes of space travel. A futuristic automotive transport is seen moving along an intersecting stretch of freeways and tunnels; the subjective, moving camera renders a flowing, musical sensation of movement through space, while the images, bathed in aqua tint, become increasingly darker, culminating in a full color shimmering superimposition of nocturnal traffic (astute observers have pointed out the locations as Tokyo). The interlude presents a marked contrast with the bucolic country scenes and its poetic analogue is made clear when Tarkovski cuts directly to a brief shot of distant stars as Chris approaches his destination and his space capsule descends to the orbital space station, hovering near the surface of Solaris. Here, for the first time, there is some of the awesome splendor of Kubrick's film, but only momentarily.

While the intricate, spacious decor of the space station is virtually expressionistic in design—each room and corridor suggesting a different psychological or emotional character—gadgets and machinery never overwhelm the human element nor are they endowed with anthropomorphisms. The atmosphere is at once ominous as Chris investigates the deserted, maze-like chambers and finally encounters only two remaining members of the original team of cosmic explorers: Dr. Snoutt, a scurrilous, short-tempered man, suffering from an unexplained source of psychic stress, who remains sealed off in his laboratory for long periods; and Sartorius, an older scientist whose resignation to loneliness and placid contemplation is unexpectedly interrupted by the visitor from earth who provokes in him a nervous apprehension. Learning his comrade Gibaryan has recently committed suicide after a period of severe depression, Chris wanders dazed through his disordered living quarters to discover a filmed message—a communique from the dead—that does little to clarify the mystery surrounding the suicide and Sartorius is deliberately evasive in response to Chris' questioning. Thus Tarkovski, like many other modern directors evokes numerous narrative lines for which there are no given solutions.

Amid this labyrinthian observatory, a Cocteauesque "Zone" between life and death, in which unexplained phantoms flit through corridors and compartments, Chris soon learns that the sea of Solaris—the film's central metaphor—is a source of intelligence, as suspected, and like the inexplicable monolith of *2001,* effects all within its immediate proximity. Images and visions, referred to as "visitors"—actually materializations derived from the human brain—appear periodically to haunt the men. Chris remains somewhat skeptical until he begins to experience the reincarnation of Hari, his beautiful young wife who ended her own life on earth, many years previously.

The revival of Chris' love for Hari, an emotion relegated to the museum of memory, is central to Tarkovski's thematic structure. The apparition of Hari, beautifully captured in dream images, moving from aqua tints as Chris prepares for sleep, to golden, transcendent light, evokes profound feelings in Chris. As Hari becomes more and more human, prompted by Chris' attempt to stir memories of her earthly existence, he becomes increasingly distressed by his failure and the knowledge—evidenced by Snoutt—that she is in fact, biologically, "inhuman." Chris plummets her into space in a rocket, but she reappears and twice recovers from fatal accidents; and when he ultimately surrenders to her growing love, she realizes the mental anguish it is causing and departs never to return.

The suffering brought on by this experience forces Chris to understand a universal truth: that the most vital things in life, whatever form it may assume, cannot always be verified; the cosmos is a vast reflection of the mystery of love, a phenomenon man can experience but never perfectly understand, and before which science is helpless. Experience equally directs Chris to the sea of Solaris, the enigmatic source of this mental suffering. Sartorius, the film's spokesman for scientific conservatism and tradition, proposes that risk must be minimized if their work is to continue, by beaming lethal rays at the ocean, and sees no validity in Chris' emotional attachment to his "visitor." Chris, however, asserts that science must always be guided by moral principles and that to destroy any living matter simply because man cannot understand it is unethical. In a meditative soliloquy before the sentient surface of the planet, he professes that the ocean is seeking to penetrate the ideas of man and that they must respond by providing it with precise data about mankind in an orderly way, rather than through fragments of dreams.

An encephalographic record of Chris' private thoughts is projected onto the sea of Solaris, calming its turbulence, and suddenly islands begin to surface. With awesome effect, the film's final sequence, a formal variation on the opening prelude, returns to the pond and country landscape; but as Chris observes them, natural processes are reduced to stasis, with only the movement of the man and a dog against the frozen background. But as the camera pulls back to encompass the house where Chris warmly greets his father, then moves further and further back into space, we gradually see this is a materialization on an island in the sea of Solaris. . . .

The spiritual complexity of the vision Tarkovski has derived from Lem's novel organically unites man with the mysteries of the cosmos, and finds expression in a style that is essentially metaphysical and poetic. The visual continuity is synthetic and organic, emphasizing sustained *mise-en-scène* rather than an analytical shot breakdown, and the use of Panavision ratio is perfectly suited to the stylistic mode. Inevitably, Tarkovski will be criticized for the solemn, slow pacing of the film, though it is quite intentional. Just as Kubrick indicates our experience of time will be radically affected by space travel, Tarkovski retards the movement of the individual shot, the camera and actors, to render a temporal duration that is an aesthetic equivalent totally removed from our present hectic psycho-perceptual experience. Occasionally there is a sense of *temps-morts* in Chris' prolonged preparation for sleep, fleeting memories of earth, and the haunting moments

dwelling on the viscous surface of Solaris. The film's mesmeric, poetic rhythm requires an unaccustomed patience and attention, considering its exceptional length of two and three-quarter hours, but it is arguably an integral and essential part of the director's expression. Music is sparingly but effectively used with the plaintive organ tones of Bach's F Minor Choral Prelude underscoring scenes suggesting ties between earth and outer space, supplemented by amplified percussion, an appropriate "music of the spheres."

Tarkovski's intimate acting ensemble, all experienced in theatre as well as cinema, are superbly attuned to the sustained level of dramatic understatement and introspection. Without possessing any of the physical appeal of a major film star, Donatas Banionis, a Georgian actor, is authoritative and persuasive in the central role of Chris Calvin, while his more impressive interlocutor Sartorius, is memorably etched by the cragged nobility of Yuri Jarvet, who gave life to Kozintzev's King Lear. In the brief but pungent role of Dr. Snoutt is Anatoly Solonitsyn, the lead in Tarkovski's **Andrei Roublev;** Natalie Bondarchuk, daughter of the actor/director Sergei Bondarchuk not only is strikingly beautiful but projects a tender, ethereal presence as Hari, and her enactment of revivification after a suicide attempt by drinking liquid oxygen, is extraordinarily vivid. With an art that tends to conceal its virtuosity, Tarkovski, with his co-scenarist F. Gorenchstein, and cameraman Vadim Youssov, has invested every detail of the film with the care of a Tolstoi or Cervantes. **Solaris** is at once personal and universal, timeless, and yet the most imaginative subject in modern Soviet cinema. Whether it will be seen by audiences in the West other than those at festivals such as Cannes (where it was awarded the Jury Prize) and San Francisco, seems uncertain. In any event, it remains a major work in the as yet slender and provocative body of Tarkovski's *oeuvre,* and is a testament to his creative daring that refuses to be silenced. (pp. 22-5)

> Lee Atwell, "Solaris: A Soviet Science-Fiction
> Masterpiece," in The Film Journal, (Hollins
> College), Vol. 2, No. 3, 1974, pp. 22-5.

Timothy Hyman (essay date Spring 1976)

[*In the following essay, which was originally entitled "The Return of the Prodigal," Hyman interprets* Solaris *as a prophetic vision for contemporary society and compares the structure and thematic concerns of* Solaris *with those of* Andrei Rublev.]

Solaris was the first of Tarkovsky's films to be seen at all widely in the West and, perhaps inevitably, it was misunderstood. Audiences and almost all critics brought to it the most conventional expectations—of a genre film, a sci-fi epic, "Russia's answer to 2001." And although it clearly owes part of its continuing availability to this science-fiction label, **Solaris** has never, I suspect, found the wider audience it deserves.

I want to present **Solaris** here not as science-fiction but as prophetic vision. It was of course based on a science-fiction source, but a reading of Stanislaw Lem's novel reveals Tarkovsky's entirely different intentions. Crucial is the film's new ending, with Kris's return and submission to his father. The space journey of Lem's novel is now enclosed, as a kind of dream-core, within the sequences of earth; and the planet Solaris becomes, as I hope to show, essentially a metaphysical dimension, the location of an oceanic love. Space fantasy has become moral allegory; Tarkovsky is clearly speaking in *Solaris* about our life, today; all that happens in space is intended only to return us to earth.

The film's most memorable sequences—the garden, the drive through the city, the bonfire film, the Hunters in the Snow, the ending—bear no relation to anything in the novel; they are entirely personal to Tarkovsky's vision, and it is these visionary sequences that will determine my approach to the film. What follows is not so much criticism as "interpretation"; in Wilson Knight's phrase, a "reconstruction of vision," rather than a judgment. But *Solaris* demands exegesis partly because it is full of ambiguities. Stylistically, it can easily be grouped with the cinema of Resnais and his circle, with *Je t'aime Je t'aime,* or with Chris Marker's *Le Jetée.* Tarkovsky has spoken of the film-maker having as his basic material a block of time, into which he carves, as the sculptor into stone; and this potentiality of film to shape time is particularly relevant to the theme of *Solaris*: a man has to relive the past in order to return to the present. In *Solaris,* as so often in Resnais also, we are plunged into the middle of a complex story, and the information necessary to understand it on a rational level is only slowly divulged. There is a many-layered structure, of films-within-the-film. We do not immediately recognize Burton as he watches his much younger self on television; nor the younger variants of Kris's parents, or of Kris himself, in the Bonfire Film, with its bewildering telescoping of Kris's life from childhood to marriage. Gabaryan we meet only after death, in the suicide cassette he records for Kris. Each of these is a key sequence in terms of information or "background," but in each, cinema's ability to present the past as the present is felt as undermining temporal reality. A further disorientating factor—especially during the sequence of Kris's fever—is Tarkovsky's interpolation of black and white and color. But within this world, Hari's presence is both more meaningful and more acceptable. We first see her in a photograph, and when she appears on *Solaris,* she clearly is the photographic image (imperfectly) "copied." Unlike Burton or Kris's parents, however, she is quite unchanged by, because outside, time.

All this takes a lot of unravelling, but in both Tarkovsky and Resnais, there is a serious intent; the essence of this kind of film is that the spectator should be forced to undergo a confrontation with mystery, to acknowledge the uncharted. But where I think Tarkovsky is so different from Resnais is in his going beyond the mystery to a moralistic end. *Solaris* is not another *Marienbad,* about the mysteries of love in Time: nor is it, as some have thought, about the illusiveness of love, (so that Kris never returns to earth at all, but is marooned in the mirror world of Solaris's ocean). In the final image of *The Return of the Prodigal Son,* the film's political and ideological overtones become clear. While the film is not precisely anti-Soviet (Tarkovsky gives some of the principal characters English

names, and he has Burton drive through Tokyo's freeways) yet it is clearly anti-materialistic. In Kris's return to his father's garden are implied many of the radical perspectives familiar to us in the west, though I cannot think of any significant earlier film that has embodied such protests, set as they are here within a deeply felt metaphysic. What Tarkovsky is surely saying at the end of *Solaris,* is that love carries with it the imperative to change society, to build a very different society than our own.

The film begins on Kris Kelvin's last day on earth, before setting off for Solaris. A terrible sadness is felt from these first sequences, in the film's numbed pace, its wavering, disturbing slowness. At first I think most audiences must assume this sadness reflects Kris's regret at leaving earth. Later however we will piece together Kris's earlier history: the mother to whom he was too much attached, the marriage she resented, his abandoning it, the young wife's suicide. All this has happened years before, but it has left Kris vanquished and without hope.

Yet Kris's predicament is soon seen to be representative of society as a whole. *Solaris* is centrally a prophecy; it is about a society which has lost humanity and which has, or soon will, come to the end of its tether. The landscape of these first sequences spells out a polarity, between garden and city, organic and inorganic, humanistic and anti-humanistic, which is obviously central to Tarkovsky's thought. Kris's father inhabits an anachronistic world, of protest and nostalgia for the past ("I dislike innovation") with a horse in the garage, the car beside it half-covered with hay, and a gas balloon moored to the roof. Yet directly beside the garden runs the highway, which will lead eventually to the terrible city of Burton's drive, a world with no human organic thing visible.

It is with this mechanical world of hardware and radiation that Kris, although a psychologist, is at first identified; as his father rebukes him, "Earth has adapted itself to men like you, but at a heavy price." Yet in the film's mysterious opening sequence, as Kris stares down at plants slowly waving underwater, is already a foretaste of that "contact with the ocean" by which Kris will be redeemed, and which will entail involvement with all that is most soft, fluid, and in a cultural sense, primitive.

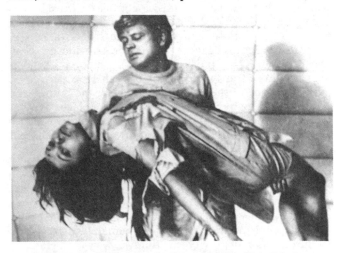

Kris Kelvin holding the simulacrum of his wife in Solaris.

If the first part of the film is essentially about society, in the second we focus almost exclusively on the individual experience of Kris. Indeed the whole story of *Solaris* has unmistakably the air of an inner adventure, a dream-sequence or a psychoanalytic exploration. The planet Solaris offers a kind of purgation; it becomes an inner dimension in which Kris, through Hari, is made to relive the experience which had brutalized him on Earth, to become once more compassionate, ready to return. The planet and its ocean can well be seen as one of many archetypal islands, familiar to us from myth and literature. On Solaris, as on the island of *The Tempest,* men "of great guilt" are forced to confront the specters of their past, and so, each one, to discover himself, "When no man was his own." For Kris, as for Prospero, the ocean is the agent of catharsis, of cleansing, and so of his release. And when the process is at an end, Kris must return to take up his role on earth, as Prospero his dukedom.

"Though the seas threaten, they are merciful." Something of Kris's sea-change the spectator is made to share also. For us, as for Kris, it is the transformation of our initial fear of the ocean, first into a sense of absurdity, of the impotence of man in the face of such a power, and then eventually into love, that constitutes the true narrative of the film. The ocean presents itself throughout as some overwhelming existential problem, which we have to come to terms with, to interpret. In the earlier sequences, where the camera will frequently pass out through windows into the blankness beyond, the ocean is experienced as a void, a threat the greater for being unspecific. Then, when Kris's dead wife appears, she is the materialization of his guilt; as Gabaryan had warned, the ocean "has something to do with one's conscience." And so long as she is no more to Kris than a threat to be destroyed, Hari retains her own sense of incompleteness, her obsessive fear of abandonment.

With Hari's reappearance, however, the whole character of the film changes. The ocean now begins to be seen as the source, not of ghosts, but of love. At this point Kris begins his return back towards society. What his growing love for Hari will reveal to him is the validity of his father's humanistic—and socially divergent—viewpoint, for which Tarkovsky has provided a complex cultural reference. We had noticed a copy of Don Quixote open in Kris's father's study; and now, in the space-station's library, Cervantes is again read from, (with Snouth as Sancho Panza to Kris's gallant madman). On one wall, moreover are large transparencies of Brueghel's *Seasons,* and in front of one of these, "The Hunters in the Snow," *Solaris*'s most remarkable sequence will take place. Kris has left Hari alone in the library, to escort the drunken Snouth to his room; now he anxiously returns, only to find her staring absorbed in front of the picture. Magically, she is *in* the landscape, and for some moments we explore it with her; the skaters and the homesteads below, the birds and trees silhouetted against the sky, the men and their dogs as they move across the brow of the hill. When she turns to Kris, we realize that through Brueghel she has been able to apprehend what it is to be a human being on earth. In the cessation of gravity that follows, we watch Hari and Kris as they float together in mid-air, in front of the Brue-

ghel, while around them slowly circles the Cervantes, with Don Quixote riding forth. This sequence must be seen as Tarkovsky's cultural testament. Cervantes and Brueghel are both felt as representative of a humanistic culture that is earthy and realistic, yet transcends naturalism, even as love transcends the weight of matter, and for Kris, redeems the past.

Kris's love for Hari restores him to humanity; but the continuing failure of their relationship opens up for him terrifying vistas of a love that goes beyond any individual. We sense his growing realization that Hari is not the victim of the ocean, "that custard," but a part of it. These sequences culminate in a kind of breakdown, at the onset of which, speaking half-intelligibly to Snouth, Kris outlines the core of the film's speculation. "Maybe we're here," he suggests, "to sense man as an object for love." He speaks of Tolstoy's shame at his inability to love all mankind. " . . . Shame, that is what will save mankind."

In the fever-sequence that follows, Hari and his mother merge and proliferate; and when Kris wakes, it is to learn that Hari and the other "guests" have disappeared. Kris's role is now clear. "Contact" with the ocean has been established. "It is time," says Snouth, standing at Kris's bedside, "to return to earth."

Clearly the central part of the film has been, on one level, about a man's discovery of what love is. But love is here viewed as a dimension both cosmic and metaphysical; and so Tarkovsky clothes his dialectical progression in a space allegory. The ocean is the "void" of undifferentiated experience, the matrix from which all experience comes. Kris's love for Hari issues from and returns to this void, and only by confronting and accepting it will its threat be transformed to beneficence. At the end of the film, the ocean is found to be the ground of being, and in the final shot the living presence of a metaphysical reality is affirmed.

The last scenes on earth begin with Kris once again lingering by the lake, staring into the vegetable life in the watery depths—images that now take on a much more explicit meaning. We watch Kris with foreboding as he comforts the dog, walks over to the house, presses his face against the window—a face of appalling compassion, as he watches his father, apparently crazed with grief, standing helplessly as water drips onto him from above.

But his father's sudden joy as he recognizes him, and Kris's wonderful gesture at the threshhold, define this ending as one of hope. When Kris returns to earth, it is to kneel before his father in an image of submission exactly echoing the great Rembrandt in Leningrad, *"The Return of the Prodigal Son."* Kris has "returned to his father's house," and so, implicitly, to the antimaterialist and divergent view his father embodies. He shares with him not only the grief of a terrible human loss—for each has lost his wife since they last met—but also a common anchorage in a transcendent love. When we left Solaris, our last image was of the plant Kris had brought from earth, flourishing on the window sill. "Once earth was beyond the reach of love" . . . And now, as the camera rises from the kneeling figure and above the house, we see that the earthly garden is indeed fully located in the ocean; and from this contact, a new society will be born.

Despite their scale, both *Solaris* and *Andrei Rublev* are very personal films. Each seems to take a panoramic view, to include the whole world, but each is in fact about the effect of that world on one character only. As Tarkovsky explained just before starting work on *Solaris*: "In all that I have done, in all that I intend to do . . . my theme is this: a man gripped by an ideal searches passionately for the answer to a question, goes to the limit in his attempt to understand reality. And he obtains this understanding, thanks to his strivings, to his experience."

The films have similar formal structures. Tarkovsky has made clear that he rejects for himself the dynamic juxtapositions of Eisenstein, in favor of building one sequence upon another, until in one last conclusive image the overall meaning of the film is made clear. In both *Rublev* and *Solaris* this final sequence is all-important in providing the affirmation Tarkovsky seeks, of "that optimism to which I hold so firmly, and about which I am constantly speaking." Yet in *Rublev* this ending may be felt to have a certain hollowness about it. Throughout the film appallingly violent episodes have been presented to us in a strangely distanced perspective; it is only in the final minutes that the film suddenly becomes emotionally full-blooded, and is allowed to move at last into color, into the warmth, tenderness and refinement of Rublev's ikons. However much we may agree with the film's argument—that spiritual values and artistic achievement come out of and redeem the brutality of experience—yet I am not sure this ending makes out a convincing case. I think a comparison with the Brueghel sequence in *Solaris* is revealing. Both sequences are an attempt to use a great work of art as a means of transcendence. But whereas, in *Rublev,* this transcendence is juxtaposed to the rest of the film, in *Solaris* it is situated at the heart of it, and Brueghel's affirmation of the natural world is embodied within the dramatic context, of Hari becoming human. It makes a very different sense to pan and zoom into Brueghel's illusionistic landscape than into the flaking color areas of a Rublev ikon; and I think it is the difference between the humanistic and the merely aestheticizing.

There are aspects of both these films that are difficult, but these difficulties are common to most significant European cinema of the last decade. As film-makers have emerged as great artists, they have inherited the same problems as the painters of the previous generation; and they have paid the same price. Even the once-loyal "serious" audiences have turned away, and above all, to the Hollywood of the thirties and forties; and I think the common factor in their choice of naivete or mediocrity in preference to obvious artistic mastery is the disturbing subjectivity of this recent cinema, its apparently dissociated, futile inwardness.

Yet a positive view of the recent work of (for example) Bergman, Resnais, Antonioni, Fellini, Pasolini, and Bresson would be to see them as attempting to forge a metaphysical cinema, whose inclusion of the mystical and the miraculous often recalls the "World-Theater" of the past. Before the advent of cinema, the stage had to be the vehicle for the cosmic flights of such works as *Everyman* or *The Tempest, The Magic Flute* or *Faust* or *Peer Gynt.* But in cinema, the "rough magic" of masque and opera can become infinitely more resourceful. And these recent films do seem to me to have greatly expanded cinema's potentiality—through its magical inclusiveness they have conveyed the scope and spectacle of life, while at the same time, chiefly through temporal ambiguities, they have given this spectacle a subjective edge, so that we sense the director's personal and mysterious experience. In its approximation to dream and to our mental processes, in its capacity to manipulate space and time without losing verisimilitude, film surely can uniquely embody this kind of vision.

In many respects Tarkovsky does belong within this new personal cinema of dream and reverie, fantasy and metaphysic. He shares with these others an interest in psychoanalysis, a use of almost self-conscious "archetypes" (the images of horses, rushing streams, and figures standing under rain or pouring water repeated in both films). And he is, even more than they, a master of the "Bead-Game" of cultural reference. Yet there is a real difference. Like Kris's father in *Solaris,* Tarkovsky "dislikes innovation." What gave him "more pleasure than anything else" in *Rublev*'s French reviews were the words "without breaking with tradition." His purpose, he says, is not to experiment, but to make "important" films.

We should not confuse such utterances with official Soviet attitudes to Western decadence. I think Tarkovsky means only that he remains committed to an art that puts content before form. And his films do in some respects stand as a corrective. Unlike that of his Western contemporaries, Tarkovsky's is a vision informed by an urgent moral content—a vision we can all share. "Dream," wrote Jane Harrison, "is the myth of the individual; myth, the dream of the collective." It is Tarkovsky's ability to project, through cinema's unique potentialities, a very inward vision, in such a way that it becomes a collective statement—a myth for our whole society—that makes *Solaris* likely to prove the "important" film its director hoped for. (pp. 54-8)

> Timothy Hyman, "Solaris," in Film Quarterly, Vol. XXIX, No. 3, Spring, 1976, pp. 54-8.

J. M. Purcell   (essay date May 1978)

[*In the following essay, Purcell discusses the visual style, narrative structure, and sources of* Solaris *from a Freudian psychoanalytic perspective.*]

It should be said first that the [version of *Solaris*] under review is discussed from a print either rented or projected with a half-hour missing from the 165-min. 1972 Soviet original. Such scissoring obviously qualifies some of the remarks I make below. I try to make it clear why the film's approach and moody style make it unlikely any very elaborate plotting disappeared. The two-plus hours remaining on screen are certainly an important contribution to live-action filmed sf; and the film is sufficiently unknown and difficult to see . . . to justify my account even of this "edited" form.

The 1972 A-budget Russian film adaptation of Stanislaw Lem's novel, *Solaris* (1961), was directed and co-scripted by Andrei Tarkovsky and has since become an important part of Tarkovsky's reputation with film historians. *Solaris* received good reviews in 1972—partly for the cynical reason, I believe, that it seems shot to draw "prestige" notices. Of cast and credits, the only participant besides Tarkovsky likely to be familiar to even the most cineastic reader, is its ingenue lead, Sergie Bondarchuk's wife, Natalia: "Natasha" in the Soviet *War and Peace.* So, for the film's full credits I refer the interested reader to such a reference source as Walt Lee's *Reference Guide to Fantastic Films.*

Solaris is, first of all, an interesting movie, with the virtue, like Eric Rohmer's films, of taking for granted an adult audience. But as an expensive, thematically pretentious adaptation of a contemporary "standard" sf author, the reader is likely to base his advance expectations on Kubrick's *2001;* and what Tarkovsky in the event has shot is a kind of "anti-*2001* " sf movie.

Tarkovsky's approach to space technology is, for example, intimate, authoritative, realistic, but anti-numinous. *Solaris* must be the first space epic to domesticate the working satellite, to make it as anti-romantic as a kitchen or factory. This unusual everyday atmosphere is partly related to the theme Tarkovsky is developing (which is a variation on that of the original novel); but the film goes to the extreme of omitting what in 1930's fantasy serials or 1950's sf-disaster / monster drive-in epics, would have been treated as the most obviously "cinematic" sections of Lem's original. The spectacular, disastrous exploratory flights over "Solaris"—a unicellular ocean-planet—have been minimized in favor of extended confrontation scenes within the satellite which seem to owe more to Chekhov's country houses than to Ray Herryhausen or George Pal.

This filmed *Solaris,* let it be said, has a consistent visual style—with the emphasis of a Kurosawa on texture: sweats, scars, bleeding, scorched burn stains. There is a general feel and mood of things wearing out, specifically including the Russian space program. One can make this point by describing what Tarkovsky has most conspicuously added to Lem's original plot.

Unlike Lem, instead of immediately isolating the hero, Kris Kelvin, with the other astronauts and with their mutual guilts and dreams from the very beginning of the story, Tarkovsky has fronted and backed Lem's plot with a prologue-epilogue frame. This is mainly set on the hero's—hero's parents' exurbanite farmhouse. This opening farmhouse section—by a fluent use of TV cassettes which package sections of the plot-background both for the hero and for the audience—is used to establish scientific points about "Solaris" that Lem spends much of the novel exploring. That is, Tarkovsky immediately announces he intends to minimize, once Kelvin gets into space, the "scientific" in favor of the "personal" story: a dichotomy acceptable enough, I suppose, for the art-film audience, but not for Lem.

Cinematographically, the order of shots for this farm-home/prologue is carefully and ingeniously mimicked and repeated during the earliest parts of the main story sequence aboard the satellite with Kelvin. Probably the reader will be relieved to hear I can't make a detailed explanation of this technical point from my one seeing of a cut print. Such an explanation would require not only a private print and cassette or movieola, but some considerable percentage of the 300-odd pages that Dumont-Monod took in their *Le Foetus-Astral* (Paris: 1970) to make a comparable structuralist examination of *2001.* (Let me tease the future sf-course grad student who accomplishes this chore for *Solaris* by reminding him that Tarkovsky is not only obviously familiar with *2001* and Lem's other work, but very likely knows something about Domont-Monod's critique!)

Tarkovsky's Kelvin—more simplistically than Lem's—is trying to displace his own guilts and past, not confronting them. And the thematic analogue for his film is not *2001,* but some reductive theatrical study of heroism like the Auden-Isherwood *Ascent of F6.* For the sf-film, *Solaris* therefore, good or bad, has the automatic historic importance of the genre's equivalent for whatever was the first postwar U.S. western in which the hero felt Freudian guilt feelings about using his—pistol.

Solaris' Freudianism is explicit and not simply read into it by academic reviewers like me. Kelvin's guilt feelings toward his wife's suicide derive heavily from his relationship toward his parents (toward the "heroic" World War Two *cum* space-exploration older Russian generation?). The film ends with a longshot Prodigal-Son-Returns sequence of Kris's reconciliation with a bearded Tolstoyan patriarch. Outside Freud, the allusions and frame-of-reference demands made on the audience by the dialogue of the three male astronauts are determinedly literary; they seem meant to suggest that space exploration—in this film, *Soviet* space exploration—is somehow at odds with the "humanistic" tradition of 19th-century Russian literature. (The three astronauts are all what we would mean by "intellectuals" as opposed to "technocrats.")

But what about the main love plot of the book and film?—which may seem to some middlebrow readers to be dissipated by all this thematic analysis. In a movie theatre, the fact is that the "dark" love story of loss, suicide, and emotional failure contrasts so strongly with the enormous social malaise that Kelvin finds when he boards the satellite, that this "dark" private love story becomes in the film its "light" emotional contrast. Kelvin finds one astronaut already a suicide, his corpse refrigerated for later home delivery. The two "survivors" are haunted by physical artifacts of inexplicable past guilts in their lives: a child or a dwarf semi-concealed in their locker-apartments. For Kelvin, the artifact (and the beginning of the main plot) will be the reappearance in 3-D form of his beautiful, young, dead wife.

For . . . readers unfamiliar with or forgetful of the original novel, the source of all this uproar is the unicellular planet's reaction to the beginning of radioactive exploration of "it" by the astronauts. (The association of the revival of guilt with the use of radioactivity seems to me much more emphasized in Tarkovsky than in Lem.) The planet thus explores the explorers in the same "scientific" spirit as they are exploring "it."

But as I suggested, despite the Freudian ambience which soaks the satellite, the film audience can only brighten up when it gets the chance to admire the young barefoot Mrs. Bondarchuk. She becomes a "3-D haunt" who appears in his bedroom, lives and sleeps with him, and forces him to relive with "her" what he first lived with Mrs. Kelvin. Indeed, the first real action-sequence in *Solaris* occurs when, from sufficient clues, Kelvin realizes he's dealing with a simulacrum. He maneuvers "her" into a ship's rocket and fires her into space. But everytime he exposes his psyche in passive dreamy sleep, the planet sends "her" back, recreated in his bedroom.

The movie simplifies the number of times Kelvin murders "her"—or that, presumably re-acting the role of dead wife, she attempts "suicide." (Her internal makeup is only the planet's substitute for human blood and doesn't do the same things when "she" cuts her "wrists.") This murder-suicide sequence ends when Kelvin "accepts" her; i.e., his emotionally disruptive past. But he fails to reach the moral heights the script obviously intends when he sternly informs his bachelorized colleagues that he's going to keep his "wife" (his past) around. The audience (and the colleagues) see not psychic resolution of a Freudian conflict, but a middle-aged monasticized scientist who would have rocks in his head if he failed to permit a dream like Natalie Bondarchuk some locker space.

The wittiest of the original novel's jokes about male sexual behavior or observation—and one which might have suggested to Tarkovsky a Lubitschian treatment of Kelvin's whole bedroom situation—is the kind of clue by which Kelvin discovers the "first" simulacrum. It so happens that "Solaris" is unable to invent a technically possible arrangement of "her" dress down the back because Kelvin never noticed clearly how Mrs. Kelvin arranged her outfits, or how they buttoned together. As I first saw this film with an audience that was reasonably sophisticated, it is not my subjective impression that Tarkovsky misses a laugh that Lubitsch would have infallibly gotten. I am aware, incidentally, that Lubitsch is almost totally out of fashion with U.S. film academics. There is even some general critical suggestion that in his interest in comic impact he lost sight of structure, but in fact his films have emotional tensions and impact that can derive only from being sensitive to emotional development. If Tarkovsky deliberately threw away a joke-situation, for example, in the dress-back scene—because he knew Kelvin would be rocketing "her" into space a minute or two later in screen-time—then Tarkovsky was sacrificing a witty, revelatory, long-range strategic point about Kelvin's marriage for short-range considerations of mood.

Just as Kelvin's keeping Natalie Bondarchuk does not, filmed, seem to equate with any long-range sexual maturing, the disappearance of the final simulacrum—her acting out of the original wife's "disappearance" from Kelvin's mind—dissipates its emotional impact by seeming the same "disappearance" of James Bond's windup dolls between the end of one Bond film and the start of the next. Paradoxically, I would argue that Tarkovsky's simplism

in making the novel's intellectual predicament "only" Freudian prevents the film's being emotionally convincing for the audience in precisely this Freudian way.

We are perhaps, in 1978 (1972, actually) past considering even a heavily financed Soviet film project as a "policy statement" except in the same obvious way that a Western audio-visual project is recognizably a "policy statement" in terms of not contradicting too badly the beliefs of Lew Wasserman, Norman Lear, or whoever else is supervising. My guess is that the Russians not so much share Tarkovsky's implicit belief that the "journey to the stars" contradicts the social activism of a Pushkin (?) or a Tolstoy (?)—but that there is a feeling of frustration that postwar Soviet films have yet to regain their unquestioned pre-World War Two prestige and eminence. If *Solaris'* attitudes, filmed, bring home Golden Bears and such from Berlin-Venice-Cannes-Chicago—or even make some of *2001*'s profit—my assumption is that the film's morals will be quite tolerable back home.

A few suggestions about the film's sources: there exists, both in Russian postwar films and books—and gravitating quite naturally toward generic sf—a large body of work comparable to Tarkovsky's treatment of *Solaris.* The huge, often attractive-seeming body of Russian films that existed in the old Brandon foreign-film catalogues—which had great difficulty even getting film-society playoffs—often intermixed love or love-triangle plots like *Solaris'* with intimately accurate treatments of the Russian educated technocratic elite. One would like, in fact, to see the Russian film industry attempt some of C. P. Snow's novels.

Solaris must be the first space epic to domesticate the working satellite, to make it as anti-romantic as a kitchen or factory.

—J. M. Purcell

Probably the best-known Soviet sf specialists, the Strugatski brothers, have published a series of (now translated) novels which deal with the moral and social challenges of technological work in a way quite as sophisticated as Tarkovsky's. It is a further complication that our experts on Soviet sf, Suvin and Rottensteiner, agree that "modern" Soviet sf from 1958 onward derives heavily from Lem.

By a publishing accident of an earlier (1970) translation, and not by merit alone, *Solaris* tends to appear in U.S. academic accounts of the "history of science fiction" as some sort of isolated achievement of Lem's. (I testify as a reviewer of non-fiction sf.) This notion gets some support from Lem's own testimony, in print, that he invented Chapter One without knowing where he or the rest of the novel was going.

If in the true New-Critical spirit we ignore what Lem says,

we can fit *Solaris* satisfactorily into an "evolutionary trilogy": *Eden* (1959); *Solaris* (1961); and the climactic *Invincible* (1964). These three novels, with their imagined genetic and technological developments, contrast yet parallel the fictions, published within the same half decade, with more playful, more satiric treatments of scientific theory: *Investigation* (1959); *Memoirs Found in a Bathtub* (1961); and *Cyberiad* (1965). Perhaps conclusively, Lem fused the sober-sided imaginatively exhaustive evolutionary novels with the "pure-theory" fictions by publishing in 1969 *Glos Pana,* "His Master's Voice" (a 1976 French edition is available).

Glos Pana and *Invincible*—like the planet "Solaris" but perhaps more deeply than the novel where the planet appears—deal with how we define all our discoveries, investigations, and explorations by our limits, our neural configurations. The point is not so much a Freudian guilt removable by appropriate media-liberal or psychiatric social actions, but our necessarily partial relationship to the "other," which Lem is able to put more scientifically, more imaginatively, and more exhaustively than does Tarkovsky.

At the same time, it will be noted that this review simply takes for granted Tarkovsky's considerable accomplishment in putting the filmed space epic into the realm of intelligible educated-adult discourse. (By contrast, *2001* copped out, "mystically.") To get Lem's thesis about the problems of human exploration on screen, we need not a replacement for Tarkovsky's attempt at *Solaris,* but treatments, preferably independent, of the rest of the trilogy: a filmed *Eden* and *Invincible.* (One might hope at least one of them would be animated, like the best hard-sf film, *La Planete Sauvage,* also adapted from a "standard" sf novel.) The simple necessity for their scripts' requiring new "angles" of theme and technical approach, would in turn necessitate the directors' going further "beyond Freud" than Tarkovsky does—perhaps in Lem's direction? (pp. 126-30)

> *J. M. Purcell, "Tarkovsky's Film 'Solaris' [1972]: A Freudian Slip?" in* Extrapolation, *Vol. 19, No. 2, May, 1978, pp. 126-31.*

Michael Dempsey   (essay date Fall 1981)

[*In the following essay, Dempsey discusses the enigmatic narrative and thematic aspects of Tarkovsky's films, focusing on* The Mirror *and* The Stalker.]

The vagaries of distribution, and probably politics, brought Soviet director Andrei Tarkovsky's two most recent films, *The Mirror* (1974) and *The Stalker* (1980), to Filmex this year simultaneously, despite the gap between their original release dates.

It is hard to think of a widely admired filmmaker who seems more enigmatic than Tarkovsky. Partly, this stems from the rarity of Russian movies on American screens, though maybe the recent art-house successes of *Moscow Does Not Believe in Tears* (surprise winner of 1981's Oscar for Best Foreign Film) and of *Oblomov* will loosen up the situation a bit. Tarkovsky's first feature, *My Name Is Ivan*

(*Ivan's Childhood*) played some American dates during the early sixties, when "art movies" were an exotic genre unto themselves here, but it has seldom been revived since then. A cut version of *Andrei Roublev* (1966) has been appearing from time to time in occasional museum or one-night theater showings lately; and *Solaris* (1972), likewise cut, has become a fixture in the cult circuit and among sci-fi lovers. Few Americans, then, can have seen his films often enough to evaluate them confidently; fewer still seem to have knowledge of enough contemporary Russian movies to place them in any adequate context. Added to which, we have the vague stories that float out of Russia from time to time about Tarkovsky's "difficulties" with the Soviet establishment, which is said to object to his style of moviemaking, supposedly because his style and concerns are too rarefied for the "masses" who, the cliché has it, must be appealed to with the clear-cut, propagandizing "boy-meets-tractor" epics of Socialist Realism. The long years between Tarkovsky's productions, the rationale for letting him work at all despite all these objections by the government, the arrangements between him and the authorities—we remain in the dark about all these, even after accounts by Westerners with good Russian contacts, like Herbert Marshall and Ivor Montagu (*Sight and Sound,* Spring 1976 & Spring 1973).

But even if all these mysteries cleared up tomorrow, Tarkovsky would still have an aura of the enigmatic, the intractable, the ineffable about him. Like his closest Western counterpart, Stanley Kubrick, he tends to make what Gene Youngblood once called "trance" films, characterized by slow, dreamlike pacing created with large, static tableaux, stately camera movements, and an extensive use of classical music. Instead of the Marxist certainties promulgated by the rulers of his country, Tarkovsky pursues a degree of uncertainty, which can be called mystical or merely vague, depending on your outlook. Implicitly, his style and his concern with large abstractions like Love and Nature deny that materialism and rationality can explain everything. His taste for cosmic mystery has a religious tinge which makes him comparable to Alekandr Solzhenitsyn, except that he replaces the writer's overbearing nineteenth-century Russian Orthodoxy with a mistier, virtually oceanic pantheism and humanism.

All by themselves, words like these might seem to be describing an impossibly dewy-eyed naif. But Tarkovsky is almost always able to ground his preoccupations in poetic, tactile images. The early shots of the anomic astronaut in *Solaris,* staring at grasses as they ripple hypnotically beneath the surface of a pond, could be his signature shots; the mesmerizing, balletic sway of the grasses bears witness to a powerfully infectious belief in the natural world as the embodiment of a primal peace which we can regain. This vision of lost harmony is what haunts every aspect of Tarkovsky's work, from his choice of colors to his liking for entranced tracking shots through forests to his recurring interest in the commingled joys and sorrows of memory. His expansive crane shots of the steppe where a teenage boy attempts to cast a mighty bell, in *Andrei Roublev,* or that film's final shift from black-and-white for the brutality and loneliness of medieval Russia to color for the vivid icons of the almost unknown title character express a heroic optimism about the force of artistic expression arrayed against all the forms of dark powers in the world. Similarly, although the memory-releasing ability of the planet Solaris unbalances the scientists who work there by conjuring up phantasms from their tormented pasts, it also enables the strongest of them to purge himself of numbing alienation from life. When the astronaut's late wife, who had killed herself over intractable problems with the marriage, reappears as a floating ghost, her very movement through the air, eerily soft and lovely, and the delicate beauty of actress Natalie Bondarchuk are Tarkovsky's means of imbuing us as well as his deadened hero with revivified pleasure in existence. At his best, Tarkovsky is enraptured, as much by movies as by his favorite abstractions, which is why he is able to prevent them from drying out into mere abstractions. He is a kind of Walt Whitman, with a sense of moonstruck awe instead of a barbaric yawp.

But something has changed in *The Mirror* and *The Stalker;* the Tarkovsky spirit of struggling but finally soaring hope has clouded. In these films, he works with much the same material as before. With its collage of memories from a boy's rural life with his abandoned mother, plus concurrent newsreels of World War II, the Stalin era, and more recent times, *The Mirror* reworks and expands the earthbound aspects of *Solaris,* which are marked by marital and father-son agonies in a pristine natural setting. *The Stalker,* contrasting a silted-over, trashed-out urban society with the allure of a mysterious, cordoned-off natural wonderland known as The Zone, is viewable as a contemporary companion piece to *Andrei Roublev,* which presents equally sharp contrasts between dazzling landscapes and the barbaric wounds inflicted on their inhabitants in the name of what passes for civilization. But in *The Mirror,* the broken home, the lost loves remain irretrievable, both in fact and through any form of contemplative consolation, including the artistry which brings them back to life for us. And in *The Stalker* the promise of The Zone—that a Room somewhere in its midst can make one's profoundest wishes come true—is not merely betrayed, it is pathetically betrayed, leaving the horrors of polluting modernity dominant and the battered title character clinging to the remnants of his quest for transcendence.

Herbert Marshall's account of how Soviet authorities and several of Tarkovsky's fellow directors reacted when they first saw *The Mirror* has them all complaining about its obscurity, its refusal (or its inability) to make itself easily understood by a mass audience. For different reasons, naturally, they all sound amazingly like baby moguls in Hollywood scratching their heads over this artsy whacko who, if you can believe it, doesn't like money. However, wrong reasons or not, they are right in their basic observation; *The Mirror* is an extremely puzzling film. The looking glass that it offers us is not merely cracked but shattered, and we are seeing the jagged, jumbled reflections of its scattered shards. Tarkovsky begins this 90-minute montage of memories, stock footage, and fantasy with black-and-white shots of a stuttering boy whom an off-screen therapist is trying to cure with hypnosis. As the boy fights his recalcitrant tongue and finally breaks through to coherent speech ("I can speak!"), we suppose that he will

turn out to be the focal figure of the movie. But he never reappears; his predicament and his victory over it are evidently meant to be metaphorical. The problem is, to extend the metaphor in a way that Tarkovsky probably did not intend, that the film's eruptions of semi-disconnected, non-narrative scenes feel like the boy's stutter yet do not break through to his final burst of clarity. *The Mirror* finally speaks only dimly because nobody, nothing quite manages to take this boy's place as either an organizing principle or a center of consciousness.

Tarkovsky tries to place another boy, Ignat, in this role. Evidently a surrogate for himself, Ignat lives with his mother during the World War II years in a small cabin-like home near a meadow, surrounded by luxuriant trees and other greenery which become seedbeds of his memories. These, in turn, reach us partially via narrated comments by a male voice which appears to represent the grown-up Ignat/Tarkovsky. Breaking into them further are occasional quotations from the poems of Tarkovsky's father, who (as fictionalized in the film) has left Ignat's mother, disgusted with his failure at the age of forty to escape what he considers his innate mediocrity as a writer. In addition, shots of the Spanish Civil War, the sufferings of bedraggled Soviet troops struggling against the Nazi invaders, and hero-worshipping Chinese crowds acclaiming Mao jump in and out of the film's imagistic flow. Sometimes immediate connections between this archival material and the other shots are instantly obvious, as when Tarkovsky shows us children in Spain forcibly placed aboard trains for removal from war-torn areas or dead soldiers dangling from tree-caught parachutes. And even when a specific reason for this or that piece of editing does not leap promptly to mind, we can view the newsreel footage in a general way—as, for instance, History, in contrast to the rest of the movie, which may be taken to represent what the capital H always fails to encompass of human existence. But this "generality" (this blurriness, in fact)—which extends to Tarkovsky's use of two actresses, one young, the other (his actual mother) old to portray Ignat's mother—eventually overcomes the film, leaving it a tantalizing but unknit collection of "haunting" shots.

But, leaving aside judgments like this one, which is based on only one look at the film, *The Mirror* is approachable as a thesaurus of Tarkovsky's past interests and the darker light that he is throwing on them here and in *The Stalker.* Again, he focuses on the breakup of family life, expressed here as an impacted mass of reveries (a neighboring house bursting into flames repeatedly, slow-motion shots of rain pouring into Ignat's home and his mother wallowing ecstatically beneath the debris that the water brings crashing down), like mental loops. Although Tarkovsky is aware of family life's psychic strains and repressions, he continually returns to it as a source of both loving intimacy and poetic imagination—which, of course, may make him as suspect in certain American circles as he may be with the Russian film establishment. Ignat's mother he makes as luminous an icon of mercurial beauty and persistent devotion as the resurrected wife of *Solaris.* The first image of her, as a young woman sitting on a fence and gazing out over a glorious meadow, is characteristic, almost a John Ford shot of the Woman Who Waits. Later, a co-worker at the printing plant where she works (ever fearful, like everyone else, of a printing mistake which might land everybody in political trouble) accuses her of being too independent, and others chime in that they are surprised her husband stayed with her as long as he did. But Tarkovsky saves a big close-up for her dismissal of these comments. Obviously, he is fascinated by the dignity that he perceives in the figure of the abandoned wife. Yet he cannot (or so one viewing makes it seem) clarify the repeated failures of his men to deal straightforwardly with these examples of female grace. *The Mirror* suggests that Ignat as an adult is replaying his father's infidelity, yet it is hard to grasp why (without dragging in one's own speculation), given the almost incandescent idealization of the wife/mother here which does not carry with it any of the ambiguous charge that so often accompanies the equivalent character in American movies and literature.

The salient emotion at the heart of *The Mirror* appears to be a deep longing for a state of Eden-before-the-Fall innocence and bliss, which Tarkovsky typically locates in exquisite images of natural flux and flow refracted through the prism of childhood, when every detail of daily life, however, commonplace, had an aura of enigma about it. Accordingly, the most resonant moments of this movie are those that capture these jewelled fragments of Ignat's "past recaptured:" a reverie of his mother levitating above her sickbed, a winter bird nesting momentarily in his cap, a sudden squall rising without warning to shake a field and then vanishing just as suddenly, to name just a few. At its best, *The Mirror* does catch the sensation which Tarkovsky's father headily evokes when he writes of "Life's swift needle (which) draws me on like a thread." But because neither Ignat nor his mother nor any other consciousness generates enough force or clarity, this vortex of images finally registers on our own memories like distant, faded recollections from past life (or movies) which, when re-examined, prove to be either distorted or even nonexistent. The result is a pervasive sense of chaos, breakdown, the beauties of the past not crystallized in art but whirling away, unrecaptured and finally extinguished. *The Mirror,* with its pantheistic-lyrical whirlpool of regret and old desire, ends up a beautiful bewilderment.

With *The Stalker,* Tarkovsky has returned to straight-line, though not conventional, story-telling. The hero, a single-minded visionary, sneaks two outlanders (American, like himself, in the film's loose source, a novel called *Picnic by the Roadside,* but evidently Russian in the movie, though metaphorically All People) into The Zone. They are a Writer and a Scientist, both as anomic as the spaceman of *Solaris* and both, like their guide, nameless. Whatever may have created the Zone and its reputed magic (hints center on a meteor, like one which is said to have crashed into Siberia some years ago), the two wayfarers, each a variation on your basic disillusioned intellectual, are making their foray, past barbed wire and border guards, in the hope that their shaman can lead them to a renewal of sapped faith and vigor. As they proceed over land which proves to have some science-fiction traits, like odorless flowers, for instance, the thought arises that Tarkovsky is presenting us with an elongated (165 minute) episode of "The Twilight Zone." At times, when the Writ-

er and the Scientist fall to discoursing about the roles and the weaknesses of art and science, the parallel with the late Rod Serling's show-ending aphorisms seems even stronger. But the climax of their sortie silences them and these thoughts, when the Room not only proves impotent to live up to its reputation but also turns out to be a near-twin of the Stalker's wretched house, where he ekes out bare subsistence with his wife and their crippled little girl. *The Stalker,* then, is a negative image of both *Solaris* and *Andrei Roublev.* Their journeys through hell end in serenity; here the result is a deepened disillusionment.

The Stalker begins in tinted black-and-white, almost as if there were mildew in the emulsion. Yet the effect is stingingly clear as the camera slowly (*slowly*) moves over the hero and his family as they sleep in their hovel on the fringes of a pollution-spewing modern city (actually located in Estonia). Just as an aura of latent, lyrical possibility emanated from the dacha, the woods, and the meadows in *Solaris* and from the wind-ruffled foliage and vistas of *The Mirror,* the opening sequences of *The Stalker* exude bleakness, rattiness, stagnation like noxious fumes. It is as though the whole world has taken on the character of a weedy, diseased railroad siding. Tarkovsky uses his slow pacing and camerawork to heighten our desire to break out and brave the Zone with his three explorers. This method links him to what Kubrick did with similar pacing in *2001,* which also centers on the lure of exploring the unknown for people mired in mundane life at its most stultifying. All through *2001,* watching apes stumble toward their great discovery of the bone as tool-weapon and astronauts float endlessly through their Jupiter Mission, we long to speed things up, only to be held back by the inexorable measured drift of the film, which will reach its goals in its own good time, not ours. This effect translates directly into cinematic terms the frustrations of exploring in any form (for knowledge or enlightenment as well as new realms)—the dogged labor, the blind alleys, the slowness of discovery, the difficulty of making leaps to new ideas or approaches. This is a primary component of the "trance" style, and Tarkovsky uses it in *The Stalker,* both before and after we and his characters make it into the Zone.

But our arrival there is not like our arrival in Kubrick's Louis XIV room after a slit-scan trip into intergalactic space or, to bring up another comparison that is not as far-fetched as it may seem at first, our arrival in Oz. Both of these are enchanted realms, alive with mystery and promise, hot with blazing colors and weird sounds. But the Zone, even compared to the hellhole from which the Stalker and his companions emerge, is quite unprepossessing, neither beautiful nor especially otherworldly, like the natural wonderlands of *Solaris, Andrei Roublev,* and *The Mirror.* Instead, it looks initially like an ordinary, dowdy wilderness. Accordingly, Tarkovsky brings up the intensity of his color just slightly from the monochrome look of the opening scenes and never makes it ravishing, as he has done in the past. For the Zone, too, proves to be a large illusion. Even though the Stalker, for instance, tries to lay down the law about how his charges must proceed if they are to reach the Room, they violate them several times without coming to any harm. Much of the land proves to be as littered with civilization's garbage as the outer world does; again reversing key images of *Solaris,* Tarkovsky shows us waterways in the Zone choked with junk; even with armed patrols and a fence to protect it, the region cannot remain clean. The trio's long struggle through some kind of subterranean culvert suggests an abandoned subway or sewer system. There is no Yellow Brick Road in the Zone.

What holds this threnody of gloom together and makes it moving is not just Tarkovsky's poeticizing style, though it functions with eerie brilliance throughout the film. It is the image created by Alexander Kaidanovsky in the title role. Looking as though he had just crawled out of a Gulag or an inner city ghetto or some post-cataclysm bomb shelter, this half-demented seer-freak, with a bald head and a contorted face that looks torn from a boulder, is the most vivid human element in Tarkovsky's work since Natalie Bondarchuk's wife. One weakness of Tarkovsky's allegorizing methods has been the tendency of most of his characters, both their natures and their very faces, to fade in recollection, like most of *The Mirror* and the Stalker's two companions. But Kaidanovsky's face is an icon of pain to place alongside Umberto D. When the Room proves to be sterile, we realize that he has lost absolutely the final glimmer of hope for something resembling a truly human life. His chastened return to the outer world produces one staggering shot of a monstrous factory beside a river, along which he and his family walk in the foreground, while the factory spews masses of putrefaction as if to poison the very universe. Yet Tarkovsky does not pitch him headlong into the utter despondency which seems to await him, for he implies a saving resilience in his crazy, dogged hero, who persists in believing that the Room has redeeming forces yet to reveal. We leave him a certifiable fool, yet perhaps a genuine seer as well.

This is also where Tarkovsky leaves us, poised between the edge of despair's abyss and the compensating incandescence of his images. Their heavy, intoxicating ether works on us even when it is at his most obscure or sententious, like some ancient mariner's spell. It is not a brew for everyone, commissar or capitalist; there is no use in pretending that his brand of work can expect any easier sledding in our commercial film world than in his own totalitarian one. Until we are able to see them more often, these strange pictures—exasperating and fascinating by turns—will remain as enigmatic to us as their maker. (pp. 12-17)

Michael Dempsey, "Lost Harmony," in Film Quarterly, *Vol. XXXV, No. 1, Fall, 1981, pp. 12-17.*

Mark Le Fanu (essay date November 1985)

[*In the following essay, Le Fanu provides an overview of Tarkovsky's films from* Ivan's Childhood *(1962) through* Nostalgia *(1983).*]

Is cinema, in the West, any longer very important? It is; but one is forced to defend that conviction in the face of a culture which increasingly sees this art-form as a standard dinosaur. Cinemas, as we know, are closing; we live in "the television age." But the exigencies of the cathode tube are less than friendly to the pictorial richness which was always part of the cinema's greatness: the enormous screen, the darkened auditorium, the invitation to dream which is our past and our fortune. We were lucky as children to be open to the cinema's romance and we may hope, in turn, that enough of it survives for future generations to learn its pleasures.

In the Soviet Union and the countries of the East, and in the Third World, the issue has not yet reached crisis point. There, city-dwellers still adore "the movies", giving them a place in their lives, as the West did in the 1920s and '30s. Yet such a contrast is already contentious as far as the Soviet Union is concerned. Soviet cinema is, of course, as old as cinema itself. Its heroic age in the 1920s was responsible for many of the medium's most enduring masterpieces, and Andrei Tarkovsky—perhaps Russia's greatest contemporary film-maker—is first and foremost a descendant of Eisenstein. Like Eisenstein he has a passion for history, which he explores with intense painterly boldness. His talents are visionary and theatrical, and as far above tendentious ideological moralising as it is possible for an artist's to be.

In a career which began in 1960 Tarkovsky has made six feature-length films, all generally considered to be masterpieces: *Ivan's Childhood* (1962), *Andrei Roublev* (1966), *Solaris* (1972), *The Mirror* (1974), *The Stalker* (1979), and *Nostalgia* (1983). His "sociological position" is complex and subtly interesting. Cinema is a popular art-form, but Tarkovsky's films are—more, perhaps, than those of any other contemporary film-maker—hermetic, experimental, intellectual to the point of obscurity. One wonders how he managed to survive in the Soviet Union for as long as he did. After the filming of *Nostalgia*—a co-production between Mosfilm and the major Italian television channel RAI—he applied to the Soviet authorities for permission to extend his stay abroad for another two years in order to carry out a couple of projects (in Sweden and Britain) arising out of assignments for the staging of operas. He received no reply. He is now in Sweden, working on his latest film, *The Sacrifice;* it is not yet clear whether he regards himself as being in permanent exile.

Tarkovsky's first film, *Ivan's Childhood*—shot in a black-and-white of striking tonal contrasts—is one of his most lovely and complex works. Set in the Second World War, it opens with a sequence of a child remembering his mother; he yearns for her with passionate longing—he seems to fly through the air to greet her. (The Tarkovskian camera possesses, always, extraordinary powers of mobility.) Later in the film, a Russian officer's care for the child is like the tender regard of a father.

In themselves, stories of the War are of little importance to Tarkovsky. Their value lies in the residue of human attachment—the bonds of loyalty, courage, memory—which at any given moment such stories can muster. They define, I believe, his thoughtful and melancholy patriotism, which is as far as it is possible to be from a strident imperial chauvinism. Tarkovsky's patriotism stems, like the boy's protectiveness towards his mother, from sentiments of pity and love.

In the ebb and flow of the Russian advance through the

Ukraine during the Second World War, the boy finds himself pitched into a position of command. His knowledge of the river crossings proves indispensable to the advancing battalions, conferring on him in the confusing delays of battle the status of minor guerrilla chieftain. An officer takes an interest in him, recognising his extraordinary qualities. A long time later, when the Russians finally enter Berlin, the same officer, sorting through the rifled files of the Chancery, comes upon a death certificate: the boy, captured by the Germans, has been executed along with hundreds of others. . . .

These Chancery scenes provide a useful route into what is distinctive about Tarkovsky's cinema. The capture of the ruined city of Berlin is dramatised on screen like no other military conquest I have seen. As the soldiers and tanks advance through the streets, the air becomes filled with a wash of the Chancery's documents, whirling and falling in multitudes. This "snowstorm" image has the power of an epiphany, not less so for the realisation, when it comes, that what we are witnessing is cleverly-cut documentary footage. For Tarkovsky's talent is as much as anything a talent for *finding* things. It is as if his gaze possessed some power, some integrity, that had only to alight on the photographed image to call into it a special beauty and meaning. All his films are imbued with this intensity of dreaming, yet his dreams (as such "documentary" incidents indicate) have their origin in the tragic determinants of history.

The film which followed in 1966, ***Andrei Roublev,*** is perhaps his best known in the West, and also the most explicitly indebted to Eisenstein. In *Alexander Nevsky* (1938) and *Ivan the Terrible* (1945-46) Eisenstein was engaged in intricate ideological manoeuvres. On the one hand, these films expose the darkness of the Middle Ages: their cruelty, superstition, unenlightenment. In the process, however, the logic of the intention collapses. The film-maker's astonishing reconstruction makes us see the very institutions of oppression as possessed of indescribable beauty. *Nevsky* and *Ivan* become a nostalgic lament on the variety of estates which in all their heterogeneous clamour and their teeming inequality have been stamped out by contemporary society. I don't think anyone can watch the sequence of Ivan's coronation in Moscow Cathedral, and not believe that to Eisenstein the lack of such pageant and music and magnificence constitutes an irretrievable loss.

Eisenstein's attraction to the Church's pageantry came from his ebullience and irrepressible aesthetic generosity. But his admiration was distanced, pagan, materialist. Tarkovsky's admiration, on the other hand, emanates from within. I would imagine that he is a Christian; but whether this is so or not, it is striking that his subject-matter deals not with the power of military victory, but with the pathos of defeat, and with the achievements of artists and thinkers. Roublev is a peripatetic painter of icons, and in his characterisation Tarkovsky says clearly what in Eisenstein may only be hinted at: that the salvation of mankind is more likely to be found, not in the glories of conquest and government, but in the activities of the individual hand and eye, in their concentrated appropriation of beauty.

The icon painter is accompanied by his apprentices. In the scenes of their instruction are drawn together with exemplary seriousness some of the great forgotten themes of humanist teaching. A trade was originally a mystery, and the artist passed on his craft to a pupil who had chosen him as master, freely and humbly. Surely one of the most unusual aspects of contemporary thinking about art is the curious refusal to acknowledge that there need be such a master. Tarkovsky's stern and ascetic stories return again and again to this classical relationship (he has spoken nobly about his own teacher, Mikhail Romm).

Apprenticeship, then, has its value. But beyond it lies a knowledge about art that comes from religious conviction. At the climax of ***Andrei Roublev*** we are present at the casting of an enormous bell on the wild hillsides outside Vladimir. The old craftsman-bellfounder having died, the work is in the charge of his son (played by the same actor, wiry and waithlike, who played the boy Ivan). The bell is to be cast in a trench dug in the side of a hill covered with fantastic scaffolding. The men believe the boy knows the formula for the alloy; we know that his confidence is bluff. In front of our eyes the casting of the bell becomes a metaphor for the indestructibility of the artistic impulse under the most exigent spiritual circumstances.

With its imaginative depiction of plunder, battle and savagery, ***Andrei Roublev*** is a most vital evocation of the Middle Ages. In England in recent decades there has sprung up a vogue among dramatists—Edward Bond and Howard Brenton are the best known—for setting their plays in a remote and barbaric period of history. But *Lear* (Edward Bond, Royal Court, 1971) and *The Romans in Britain* (Howard Brenton, National Theatre, 1981) reveal themselves as foolish and windy works, conceived in malice; they share none of the Russian film-maker's imagination and attention to physical detail. Who ever doubted that the Middle Ages were cruel? What the British playwrights seem to lack is some directed countervailing concern for the richness or mystery of life as experienced in the epoch before science. It is this that shines out in ***Andrei Roublev,*** in the shots of mists and flares and waters, massed bonfires glimpsed fleetingly in the forest, churches in their pride and ruin. And Tarkovsky floats over these reveries, as if in Leonardo da Vinci's flying boat, dreaming his events into existence.

[Tarkovsky's] talents are visionary and theatrical, and as far above tendentious ideological moralising as it is possible for an artist's to be.

—*Mark Le Fanu*

Tarkovsky turned to the future in ***Solaris*** (1972)—an adaptation from a science-fiction novel by the Polish author Stanislaw Lem—and his speculation about such matters raises itself above the normal level of childish guesswork and special effects by anchoring itself to the present. For great stretches of the film Tarkovsky seems quite reluctant to leave the earth. There are extraordinary scenes in the countryside *dacha* of the leading scientist, Burton, as the expedition to the planet Solaris is planned—scenes that have little to do, perhaps, with science-fiction proper, and everything to do with the smell of hay on summer afternoons, the gleam of polish on old floorboards, the need to live and work close to earth and water. These are ancestral moments snatched from a culture that in its official capacity frowns on the notion of ancestry, meditations on the past in a film about the future. Evidently Tarkovsky would have men live in the houses of their grandfathers. And where this is not possible, he would urge us (like the romantic injunctions of Thoreau or Stevenson) to choose a remote spot in the countryside and build a house of our own.

Eventually the rocket takes off, and the film, it turns out, does indeed have a science-fiction content. The expedition has been organised to investigate a strange cloud of gas known as "the Sea of Solaris." The peculiarity of this phenomenon is that it seems to be activated as much by the observation of the scientists as by its own chemical or physical properties. In particular, the mental turmoil of one of the astronauts (co-leader of the expedition and the hero of the film) buffets the "Sea" into mysterious awakenings. The meaning? Perhaps, by some logic of displacement, we are looking not into a "soup" of interstellar dust, but into the workings of the brain. Solaris is, interchangeably (depending on whether we use a telescope or a microscope), a galaxy in the starry heavens or that other, internal, galaxy of atoms out of which is constituted the human mind.

In some forcefully tangential way the film invites us to ask whether we think the universe into existence. The philosopher Charles Sanders Peirce wrote, at the end of the last century, a book called *Chance, Love and Logic* which purported to be a statistical proof of the existence of an Intelligent Being; and something of the spirit of these mathematical cogitations seems to animate Tarkovsky's fable. The hero's turmoil is his remembered love of his wife—or his mother; for someone, at any event, whom he has betrayed, and who comes back now from the mirror-land of Solaris in the shape of a "neutrino girl." Her coming-to-life, like the resurrection of the heroine of Carl Dreyer's great Christian epic *Ordet,* is the culminating event of a profound idiosyncratic meditation on time, memory, and survival.

After *Solaris* comes *The Mirror* (1974). *Zerkalo,* to give it its Russian name—to my mind the richest and most moving of Tarkovsky's films—is a personal and historical meditation on a child growing up under Stalinism. The film is a mosaic, weaving among scenes of childhood the reveries of more recent decades, which take the form of puzzling highly-charged documentary footage. The filmmaker seems to ponder not only his own identity but also his native land's.

The powerful maternal presence of Margarita Terekhova as the boy's mother makes one think of a deftly-woven patchwork, cherished and beautiful. Memory, more cap-

tious than narrative, gets away with audacious lacunae, and some commentators have likened the film's collage to the practices of Cubist painting, citing the "prismatic effect" of a broken mirror. But to search for a governing metaphor is to risk stranding this film at the level of formalism. Mirrors—even Cubist mirrors—don't merely "break up"; and the opacity of the film, when we allow ourselves to relax into it, is belied by its representational boldness.

In this sense the cinema has taken over the domain of the painter, as if film-makers in the end had found something rebarbative and foolish about the anti-representationism of so much modern art. Tarkovsky's "eye" is radically innocent, and films like *The Mirror* constitute an effort to demonstrate that the period of purest seeing—and thus the origin of painting—lies in the candour of childhood. Modern painting, it seems to me, has lost access to this childish and mythological groundspring. In *The Mirror* the gust of wind across a field of wheat, the bonfire glimpsed blazing through the arch of a doorway, the scurrying of animals in the winter loft, all serve to recreate from the plundered imagery of childhood a genuine and utopian subject-matter in which the noble mastery of the painter's canvas can once more come into its own.

The vision of the child is one matter; the vision of the adult another. *The Mirror* displays a dual perspective. In one vista there are unspoken epiphanies, at their most piercing in the time before language. In the other there is language, carrying along with it history and meaning and identity. In one of the key scenes of the film the boy in his grandmother's house comes across a volume of Pushkin's poems. He contemplates and reads aloud with passion the work of a writer influenced by Shakespeare and Goethe and Byron. Was Tarkovsky suggesting that Russia "belongs to the West"? If so, it was an extraordinary and daring affirmation. A related impetus governs a scene in which the boy picks up a book about Leonardo's paintings, pausing at the portrait of Ginevra de' Benci. And the audience pauses too—draws breath—since the book itself is so beautiful. Isn't this the kind of book the Revolution dispensed with? Are there books like this surviving still in private hands, handed down to each generation?

The whole meditation on country in *The Mirror* is dramatically complex. If Russia belongs to Europe in terms of its 19th-century culture, obviously it belongs, too, to "Asia." Russia's exoticism is present in the way Leonardo's mirror-writing is matched, in Western eyes, by the strangeness of the Cyrillic script that captions the book's illustrations. Later too there are extraordinary newsreel sequences of troops moving across the flat plans of Central Asia under an interminable sky. At the Chinese border, crowds of Red Guards wave Maoist booklets in the faces of their solid opponents. Who is who, and what is happening to national identities? We see only the guards in their fur-lined parkas, all so "asiatic" and "foreign", their broad Kalmuch features edging imperceptibly into the flat yellow faces of the "enemy."

Tarkovsky's sensibility is similar, I suggest, to the sensibility of a Chekhov or a Turgenev: a cultivated and European mind at home in the spiritual and cultural places of the

West. Yet, if *The Mirror* reminds one of Chekhov, *The Stalker* (1979) clearly has something of Dostoevsky, especially in its Christian pessimism. In terms of its *mise-en-scène* this film is as brilliant as the others, but for the first time in Tarkovsky's cinema the brilliance seems neurotic. Take a line of dialogue (apparently adapted from a poem by the film-maker's father): "What is soft and weak is good; hardness is closest to death." Is this simply a suggestion that we must be open to experience? But the hero's magnificent readiness becomes indistinguishable, at times, from passivity—indistinguishable almost (here Dostoevsky) from a Christian connoisseurship of suffering.

And the stalking character whom the film is about? Is his anguish motivated, or mad? Our difficulty in deciding may be due to the allegorical and abstract nature of the quest, which at the end of the journey denies the existence of a definable goal—a prey that could be adequately "netted." Still, *The Stalker* with its imagery of dank corridors, crumbling walls, subterranean rivers, moss-bedded banks of fern, is a masterpiece. The landscape appropriates the characters and the characters appropriate the landscape; even in this Slavic wilderness Tarkovsky pays a certain homage to the West. For the films that *The Stalker* most resembles are surely the early 1960s black and white masterpieces of Ingmar Bergman and Antonioni (*Persona, L'Eclisse, La Notte*); except that, with a characteristic belief in miracles, Tarkovsky manages at the last moment to extract hope, where these films had merely despair. Tarkovsky persuades his audience that even if the Stalker's child never walks again, other miracles will happen in the miraculous real-life montage of living. At his most searching and most pessimistic, it is the single conviction which illuminates his work.

The case of Tarkovsky illustrates what one might otherwise be in danger of forgetting: that the Russian land has an old and sophisticated culture. Within its borders there are still many, not all of them dissidents, who think matters out for themselves and follow their chosen paths with integrity.

Nostalgia (1983) speaks of the pain of exile from these roots of artistic being. A Soviet writer undertaking important research in Italy finds himself morose, unhappy, and longing to return to his family. The guide and translator who has been delegated to help him is a beautiful young Italian woman who ought to provide a temptation to dally. The protagonist won't have it, and dourly turns instead to a relationship with a grizzled old madman of the neighbourhood (the Tuscan spa village of Bagno Vignoni). The madman's lucubrations, so close to despair—he later commits suicide—armour the Russian at this low stage in his fortunes, so that he can face his growing personal crisis with fortitude.

In the character of Evgenia, the Italian translator, we see again Tarkovsky's distance from contemporary attitudes. The protagonist seems to be critical of her beauty and, by extension, of all proud young independent women in our modern Western society. Her designer clothes belong to the aggressive, bisexual orthodoxies of modern *couture,* but her utter self-confidence disguises insecurity. Her costume is a physical embarrassment, tripping her up in the hotel, preventing her (in Piero della Francesca's chapel) from sinking to her knees. She is attempting, of course, to short-circuit the unwelcome advances of the traditional masculine predator; but the poignant consequence is to make one wonder who it is that her beauty is for. The film is about temptation, and resistance to temptation. The Russian scholar's love for his wife is made to win out over Evgenia's obvious allurements; but the very pressure of his refusal provides the film with a sombre subliminal eroticism.

The foreignness of the girl is the foreignness, too, of her country. As in *The Mirror,* Tarkovsky tests out various possible attitudes towards the West; but with a complex and ambivalent verdict. From his base inside Russia, the West could be subtly commended; but in the West itself—as newcomer, visitor, or exile—distinctions need to be made. If a larger explanation may be conjectured for the dissatisfaction of the brooding protagonist, it lies in Tarkovsky's conviction that the West in some curious way has cut itself off from experience; above all, ironically, in Italy, where History (in its works of art, palaces and monuments) is so palpably present.

The presence of History is no guarantee of understanding. Indeed the contrary: the more it *is* present, the more wilfully it may be ignored or gainsaid (think of the *Brigati Rossi*). The West, Tarkovsky concludes—he is not the only visitor to have done so—has been spoilt in its freedoms; it has forgotten, as it were, the cost of their gradual acquisition. Descendants of the Communist convulsion who have had (supposedly on their behalf) so much of their history taken away from them, know better.

The film is both meditation and warning. One admires about it, as usual, Tarkovsky's incredible seriousness; as also the perfectionism of his camerawork, infusing each frame with his conviction, personality, and strength.

We know little of Tarkovsky's early life and efforts. Son of the poet Arseni Tarkovsky, he was brought up in comparative security in a family that had been settled in Moscow for many generations. After the War he went prospecting for gold in Siberia (into the landscapes no doubt of Kurosawa's *Dursu Uzala*). In Moscow he studied history and painting, and later (1954) enrolled in the Soviet State Film School under Mikhail Romm—the apprenticeship took him six years. His first full-length feature film, *Ivan's Childhood,* won the "Golden Lion" at the 1962 Venice Festival, and started him on his career.

Naturally, it has not always been easy. *Andrei Roublev* was "held back from distribution" for some five years. Yet the setbacks, grave as they were (and are), should not perhaps be too blackly underlined. For Tarkovsky's achievement has been to keep alive the great literary traditions of the Russian 19th century. The candle still burns in its brightness, and one of the world's foremost living artists guards its flame. (pp. 70-3)

Mark Le Fanu, "Andrei Tarkovsky," in Encounter, *Vol. LXV, No. 4, November, 1985, pp. 70-3.*

An excerpt from *Sculpting in Time*

What is the essence of the director's work? We could define it as sculpting in time. Just as a sculptor takes a lump of marble, and, inwardly conscious of the features of his finished piece, removes everything that is not part of it—so the film-maker, from a 'lump of time' made up of an enormous, solid cluster of living facts, cuts off and discards whatever he does not need, leaving only what is to be an element of the finished film, what will prove to be integral to the cinematic image.

Cinema is said to be a composite art, based on the involvement of a number of neighbour art forms: drama, prose, acting, painting, music. . . . In fact the 'involvement' of these art forms can, as it turns out, impinge so heavily on cinema as to reduce it to a kind of mishmash, or—at best—to a mere semblance of harmony in which the heart of cinema is not to be found, because it is precisely in those conditions that it ceases to exist. It has to be made clear once and for all that if cinema is an art it cannot simply be an amalgam of the principles of other, contiguous art forms: only having done that can we turn to the question of the allegedly composite nature of film. A meld of literary thought and painterly form will not be a cinematic image: it can only produce a more or less empty or pretentious hybrid.

Nor must the laws of movement and the organisation of time in a film be replaced by the time laws of theatre.

Time in the form of fact: again I come back to it. I see chronicle as the ultimate cinema; for me it is not a way of filming but a way of reconstructing, of recreating life.

Andrei Tarkovsky, in his Sculpting in Time, *translated by Kitty Hunter-Blair, Bodley Head, 1986.*

Geoff Dyer   (review date 16 May 1986)

[*In the following review, Dyer praises Tarkovsky's work as a director but finds the reflections on cinema in* Sculpting in Time *disappointing.*]

There is a reasonably precise relation between power and the nature of the dissent that power breeds against itself. In our century all art has had, implicitly, to be responsive to this fact, either allying itself with power or, increasingly, affirming that which is suppressed and becoming a crystalline form of opposition.

So, in the Soviet Union, the narrow materialism of a leaden bureaucracy has produced, in its greatest artists, an acute faith in the spirit, a sense of mystery that has nothing in common with our own commercially motivated cult of the irrational. One thinks of dancers and musicians, of Solzhenitsyn at his best and of film director Andrey Tarkovsky, creator of ***Andrey Rublyov, Solaris, Mirror, Stalker*** and ***Nostalgia.***

Tarkovsky's career has met with opposition from the Soviet authorities and he has, finally, been forced to leave. Yet art of this kind of greatness could only have been produced within the specific history of his native country. (To be pragmatic for a moment: could he ever have raised the money to make ***Andrey Rublyov*** here in the West?) ***Stalker*** is not a film about the Gulag but it is a film which could only have been made as a result of a nation's historical experience of the Gulag.

More broadly, there is a clear line of descent from the ethical imperatives of the great 19th-century novels of Tolstoy and Dostoievsky to Tarkovsky. More broadly still, his films yearn for the stillness and spatial calm of the Russian icons. But Tarkovsky owes his sense of the expressive potential of the cinema (a sense which, he rightly suggests, we are in danger of losing) to the revolutionary film makers of the 1920s. Although there is none of their frantic clamour about Tarkovsky's films (then the stress was on the artist as engineer; Tarkovsky is an artist/philosopher), a 1923 declaration from Vertov—'My way leads towards the creation of a fresh perception of the world'—could easily be Tarkovsky's.

It is these twin motivations, of reverence and revolution (or, more accurately, the consequences of revolution) that explain one of the most important aspects of Tarkovsky's art: the sense of beauty as a *force:* the casting of the bell in ***Andrey Rublyov,*** the breeze from nowhere suddenly sweeping across the meadow in ***Mirror,*** the crippled daughter telepathically moving glass beakers at the end of ***Stalker*** (the most beautiful and simple image of affirmation in cinema).

It is precisely because of his ability to conjure images like these that ***Sculpting in Time*** is such a massive disappointment. Put together with the assistance of Olga Surkova from diaries, conversations and lectures, it is a rambling and repetitive assortment of 'reflections on the cinema'—as it is sub-titled with appropriate vagueness. The problem has substantially to do with the style (whether author's or translator's I don't know) of flaccid, archaic chattiness. 'Tender and noble as an actor and as a man,' notes Tarkovsky of a colleague; 'I love him dearly. A serene soul, subtle and with great depths.' 'How true!', 'Indeed!', 'How wonderfully apposite!' are frequent interjections and even when drawn towards weightier matters—'Why does art exist? Who needs it? Indeed does anybody need it?'—his ideas are developed in an elevated version of the same style:

> Search as a process . . . has the same bearing on
> the complete work as wandering through the
> forest with a basket in search of mushrooms has
> to the basketful of mushrooms when you have
> found them. Only the latter—the full basket—is
> a work of art . . .

Elsewhere it's all 'infinite', 'absolute' and 'eternal'; it's also all 'man', 'men', 'he' and 'his'—not a quibble with the copy editor but an indication of something endemic to certain ways of thinking.

Tarkovsky's opinions, too, can lack coherence. 'I believe that sensitivity to art is given a person at birth and depends subsequently on his spiritual growth.' But two pages later: 'Not that the cinema-goer is to be blamed for his poor taste—life doesn't give us all the same opportunities for developing our aesthetic perceptions.' Which is it to be?

There may be little in *Sculpting in Time* to inform or impress, but then print is not Tarkovsky's medium and he is not the first artist to have little illuminating to say about his/her own work. His achievement lies in having created cinema's richest iconography, its deepest exploration of fundamental questions. The level of responsiveness to the world managed in his films is impossible to sustain in real life; any kind of practical activity distracts us from such receptivity but, equally, nothing can deflect us from an elemental recognition of what he shows. This is why his films are both religious and yet can exert such a hold on secular audiences.

Hope so tainted by regret as to be at times almost indistinguishable from it is one of the most authentic expressions of our secular age. The disaster at Chernobyl must have made many who have seen it think of *Stalker* and its two landscapes: the Zone and the sepia-tinted industrial wasteland which, together, worked on us like the memory of a possible future. The oft-remarked historical novelty of our epoch is that our next step into the future may be our last. It is quite possible that we will be the generation to whom it is revealed, as a character in James Thackara's *America's Children* puts it, that there has never been such a thing as progress.

A character in *Solaris* remarks that we never know when we are going to die and because of that we are, at any one moment, immortal. Rain drips in the puddles around Chernobyl; wind ripples across the Ukraine; fragments of *Challenger* lie in weeds on the ocean floor . . . In showing us how much we have lost and how much will always remain beyond our control Tarkovsky reminds us how much we still have to lose: That is why he is a politically necessary artist.

> *Geoff Dyer, "Landscapes of Resistance," in New Statesman, Vol. 111, No. 2877, May 16, 1986, p. 25.*

Karen Rosenberg   (review date Summer 1986)

[*In the following review of* Sculpting in Time, *Rosenberg discusses the influence of Soviet intellectual and cultural debates on Tarkovsky's work.*]

The discussions on art and faith in Tarkovsky's films *Stalker* and *Nostalgia* have been called weak or banal by some English speaking critics who find his visual images redolent and haunting. Words, one might conclude, are not the director's strongest suit. But [*Sculpting in Time*] presents his ideas to such advantage that one begins to suspect that the philosophical dialogues in his films suffer by their brevity. True, in *Sculpting in Time* Tarkovsky repeats old, even ancient, theories about the spiritual and regenerative power of art. Yet, if I read him correctly, his desire is not to spin new formulae but to remind venal producers in the West, cautious Eastern-bloc film bureaucrats, and consumers of celluloid entertainment in both camps of what they have blocked or perhaps never learned about the poetic potentialities of the cinema. His stance makes one wonder whether critics who demand originality above all else aren't unwittingly hurting the artistic cinema they admire. Like a good preacher or teacher,

Tarkovsky knows that other principles and values must be repeated, often and well.

In fact, the repetitiveness of *Sculpting in Time* creates its intensity. By his obsessive insistence on cinema's right to ambiguity and density, Tarkovsky demonstrates the strength of his belief and also suggests his constant irritation with his minority status. His opponents' points seem to ring in his ears although, like many a polemicist, he rarely adduces them. So this book reads like one half of a debate, and those unfamiliar with Soviet cultural history may not recognise the terms of the argument.

Tarkovsky's concern with ethics—to choose one example—is not a bland platitude but a principled response to the abortive nature of the post-Stalin liberalisation. Many younger members of the Soviet intelligentsia (Tarkovsky was born in 1932) were bitterly frustrated when the self-examination that began with the 1956 thaw was cut short. When historians, philosophers and memoirists could not use state presses to ask if an end like communism could be created by coercive means like the purges, a few figures in the arts tried to fill the breach. By claiming the right to artistic ambiguity, they staked out needed manoeuvering space. 'Honesty', 'sincerity', 'conscience' and 'responsibility' became the watchwords of Tarkovsky and others who were sick of lies and cover-ups. (When the director writes 'truth is always beautiful' he is not just paraphrasing Keats.)

A number of intellectuals took protection in—and courage from—the role of nineteenth century Russian writers: to address 'cursed' questions and direct their countrymen to the good. Some embraced Dostoevsky, who had been viewed as reactionary, pessimistic and politically undesirable during the Stalin era and whose novel *The Brothers Karamazov* had been published rarely and in small editions. So when Tarkovsky cites Dmitri Karamazov's line 'Realism is a terrible thing,' he is implicitly attacking the still-enforceable Stalinist command that artists conform to the optimism and crude symbolism of socialist realism; when the film-maker writes, 'Dostoevsky had warned people of the "grand inquisitors" who presume to take upon themselves the responsibility for other people's happiness,' he is applauding the section of the novel most controversial in the USSR, even today.

Even in translation Tarkovsky must be translated. 'I am fascinated by the capacity of a human being to make a stand against the forces which drive his fellows into the rat race . . . ' suggests, at least on one level: what made some of our parents into Stalinists and others into Mandelstam? This context would be evident to a literate Russian or, say, Slovak, but most of us in the West don't regard cataclysms in the Soviet bloc as major dates on our calendar. That history is seen as 'theirs', as very foreign indeed. It's partly our fault that this collection of essays needs a good preface. Partly, but not entirely, for Tarkovsky, even in emigration, still employs the shorthand of the tight-knit Russian intellectual milieu. Does he know yet how much *Mirror,* too, takes for granted?

An unfortunate example of Tarkovsky's failure to communicate is his interview in the March 1984 issue of the

West Berlin magazine *Tip*. Xeroxed copies of a typewritten English translation by Zsuzsunna Pal have been scandalising film circles in the States because Tarkovsky makes such statements as, 'It seems to me that . . . woman's meaning, the meaning of female love, is self-sacrifice . . . ' or, 'Women don't thirst for knowledge as much as men. Fortunately.' According to Tarkovsky, men have become independent, cold and egotistical and have all but lost their spirituality; women who want equal rights are following suit. *Sculpting in Time* makes it clear, at least, that the director would like all of us—men and women, and artists in particular—to sacrifice selflessly in the name of love and to accept responsibility for others as a moral duty. He associates these values with the feminine probably because (as his essays show) he is steeped in Goethe, Pushkin, Dostoevsky and Tolstoy. This is his patrimony and it provides the only alternative to the present which he can envision. And that's largely because so many -isms of the last half-century never made it past Soviet censors and therefore have had little or no impact in the USSR. If this book had an index (which it sorely lacks), one could easily note the absence of recent leading thinkers in psychology, sociology, history, literary and film criticism—and feminism.

As an émigré from another time, as well as another place, Tarkovsky is fascinating and often refreshing. He provides a needed link between cinema and the literary past—without making theatrical films. (In filming *Mirror* he moved so far away from theatrical conventions that he hid the plot from the actress who played his mother because he wanted her to live through—and express—each moment as his mother did, without knowing how everything would turn out.) *Sculpting in Time* confirms that Proust taught him much about the workings of memory, time and nostalgia and provided him with a lofty standard. In his attempt to prove that cinema has its own artistic possibilities equal to those of the best prose, this director has pushed himself hard. His comments on his own films are often critical. Perhaps familiarity with the nineteenth century literary masters provides an antidote to the egotism that Tarkovsky considers endemic to modern males. (pp. 213-14)

> *Karen Rosenberg, "A Russian Patrimony," in* Sight and Sound, *Vol. 55, No. 3, Summer, 1986, pp. 213-14.*

Peter Green   (essay date Spring 1987)

[*Green is the author of* Andrei Tarkovsky—The Winding Quest *(1993). In the following essay, he interprets the themes, symbolism, and meaning of* The Sacrifice.]

Within a few weeks of each other in the spring of 1986, Günter Grass' *Die Rättin* was published in Germany and Andrei Tarkovsky's *The Sacrifice* was given its first showing at Cannes. In his novel Grass describes the time after an atomic holocaust, after the end of human time, the earth ravaged by fire storms and ashes, its landscapes pitted and filled with water and debris, encrusted with mud, cleft and torn asunder. The catastrophe at the centre of Tarkovsky's film is the outbreak of a Third World War,

a final cataclysm in which 'there will be neither victors nor vanquished, neither cities nor villages, neither grass nor trees, neither water in the springs nor birds in the sky.' In the spring of 1986 the disaster of Chernobyl burst upon us, casting its warning shadow over the world. In the final days of the year Tarkovsky died.

The convulsion that sets the machinery of sacrifice in motion in Tarkovsky's film is in fact a symbolic crisis. As we shall see, it took a different form in the original project. In a general sense it can be seen as a product of man's spiritual plight, of the triumph of materialism. 'I wanted to show that man can restore his links with life by renewing his covenant with the source of his soul,' Tarkovsky said in an interview last March. The cause of the catastrophe that lies at the heart of the film is to be found in the state of disharmony in which man lives with himself and with nature. The disaster that threatens the world is more a symptom of its malaise than the root of the problem. 'Sin,' Alexander philosophises, 'is that which is superfluous; and that being the case, our whole civilisation consists from beginning to end of sin.'

Alexander's sacrifice is the liberating act of a man seeking a way out of this situation, a man who sees an opportunity of becoming an instrument of human redemption. Although he himself has retired from the stage to contemplate, to write and teach, he has grown weary of words. Like Hamlet, he sees the world ruled by procrastination and idle talk. The time has come for deeds.

Alexander has gone to live with his wife and daughter in a house they had found by the sea. About him he has a small but intimate circle of friends and servants. It is there that his son, 'Little Man', was born, a latecomer and the apple of his father's eye. Although his wife's life is evidently marred by regrets and frustrated love, to Alexander the idyll still seems intact, above all through the presence of his little son, his hope for the future.

This entire world is suddenly threatened with obliteration by a nuclear convulsion, the outbreak of a Third World War, from which there can be no escape. In a bid to avert inevitable destruction, Alexander makes a gesture of faith on behalf of mankind. Alone in the darkness, he makes a fearful vow, 'Lord, deliver us in this terrible hour. Do not let my children die, my friends, my wife . . . I will give you all I possess. I will leave the family I love. I shall destroy my home, give up my son. I shall be silent, will never speak with anyone again. I shall give up everything that binds me to life, if You will only let everything be as it was before, as it was this morning, as it was yesterday: so that I may be spared this deadly, suffocating, bestial state of fear.'

In the same night, Otto, the postman, comes secretly to Alexander in his room and suggests a possible way out. Alexander must go to the serving girl Maria, who is a witch with benign powers, and lie with her. Alexander complies with these instructions, and when he awakes the following morning, the threat of war has vanished.

He thereupon prepares to carry out his act of sacrifice. Sending everyone away on a fool's errand, he proceeds to burn the house down, and is finally taken away in an ambulance to silence and confinement by two white-jacketed men.

The Sacrifice reveals Tarkovsky's continued exploration of certain basic themes and at the same time represents the summation of his life's work. Loss or sacrifice by fire is a motif to be found in particular in *The Mirror* (the burning house and the burning bush) and in *Nostalgia.* Domenico's self-immolation on the scaffolding around the equestrian statue of Marcus Aurelius in Rome, Andrei's sacrifice to St Catherine in the emptied sulphur pool of an Italian spa, can be seen more clearly in the light of *The Sacrifice.* In *Nostalgia,* Domenico had called for a change in universal values, a return to the point in history where man had taken the wrong path. He had poured a can of petrol over himself, perched high above the onlookers, and had taken his life by fire in the cause of a better world. At the same time, at Domenico's request, Andrei had lit a candle and borne the flame across the drained pool, ultimately expiring himself, the victim of his exertions and his own weak heart.

Played by the same actor (Erland Josephson), Domenico is very much a forerunner of Alexander. In *The Sacrifice* it is almost as if Domenico had been resurrected from the dead, returned to life to continue his work and to repeat his sacrifice. Domenico had locked his family away for seven years, held them captive in a deserted Italian hill town, until the police had freed them. (On being liberated, his son had exclaimed, 'Is this the end of the world?') The sepia scenes of this liberation in *Nostalgia,* with people fleeing along the steps of a church in the abandoned town, anticipate the two black and white inserts of a devastated street in *The Sacrifice.* In the latter case the street is littered with paper, rags and the refuse of our modern consumer society. Alexander's family is also held in a congenial confinement, in the remoteness of the northern exile he has chosen as his home; where his wife in the moment of crisis levels the accusation that she has sacrificed her own career on the stage to come and live with him here.

Through his son, Alexander hopes for a new beginning, that he too may return to that point in history where man had taken the wrong turning. But whereas Domenico had given an urgent warning to turn back while there was still time, in *The Sacrifice* it is already too late. The end is not merely nigh; the final countdown has begun.

There is a new sense of urgency, something fundamental, Old Testament-like about the single-mindedness with which Alexander executes his plan. It is an act of release in itself. In his traumatic state after the outbreak of hostilities, he whispers under his breath that he has been waiting for this moment all his life—as if deriving a perverse pleasure from the occasion that now presents itself.

The destruction of his home by fire is not the only sacrifice Alexander brings, however. His renunciation of speech is a further token of this and a recurring motif in Tarkovsky's works. Roublev's vow of silence and his abandonment of painting in protest against the senseless cruelty of the world provides a close parallel; and one recalls the speech impediment of the youth at the beginning of *The Mirror,* his liberation from which generates a sense

of spiritual release that is the springing point of the film. One can interpret this as a process of growing articulacy, whereas Alexander's renunciation is in part a protest against the inflation of words, from which only his son, recovering from a throat operation and unable to speak himself at the outset, will ultimately deliver him.

．．．．．

The film opens with a coloured still of a detail from Leonardo's magical, unfinished painting 'The Adoration of the Magi' (1481-2), now in the Uffizi, Florence. It forms the background to the opening credits and in a sense to the whole film. One sees the head of one of the kings, who is proffering a cup, and the hand of the Infant Jesus reaching out to touch it. After the credits the camera slowly moves up the painting, revealing Christ and the Virgin and the foot of a tree held by the hands of angels. It continues to rise vertically up the trunk of this tree (as it does up the withered stem at the end of the film), past the wild, rearing forms of horses in the distance.

The picture provides a key to the film. At its simplest level, it is a depiction of a present-giving in celebration of a birthday; and it is for this reason, of course, that Alexander's guests are gathered about him on this day, Otto remarking that a gift must represent something of a sacrifice. In the figure of Christ surrounded by the Magi the picture conveys an image of naked innocence in the midst of worldly wealth. Furthermore, it is through the sacrifice of Christ that the world is redeemed, which is precisely Alexander's ambition in the film.

It would be taking the parallel too far and underestimating Tarkovsky's own breadth of vision and genius as a filmmaker to see a direct translation of the contents of the Adoration painting into another medium. Tarkovsky paid homage to Renaissance painting in general and to Leonardo in particular (as indeed he did to icon painting) in other films. But *The Sacrifice* is of a kindred spirit to the painting, and Leonardo's work contains not merely a similar central statement to that of the film, but also motifs that could be seen as specifically Tarkovskian. The sketched form of the white horse to the left of the tree is one of the director's most common fingerprints; and the portrayal of ruined architecture (which in Renaissance religious painting was often used to convey the idea of the decay of the old order, the old temple; Christ, in contrast, representing the rise of the new Jerusalem) finds its counterpart in the waste landscapes and crumbling buildings of many of Tarkovsky's films. In *The Sacrifice* the motif of decay can be seen as a token both of the decline of civilisation and the destruction the war is about to bring.

Otto finds this picture terrifying. He has a great fear of Leonardo, he says. The picture indeed has its fearful aspects, in the awe-filled countenances of the shepherds in the foreground, and in the animated scenes in the background and the wild, primeval character of the horses.

The picture reappears on a number of occasions in the film. A print of it hangs in the house, the protecting glass reflecting Alexander in an overlaid double image, as if he were entering the picture or emerging from it, according to the play of light and the position of the camera.

The tree in the painting also finds its counterpart in the film. In the opening scene after the credits we see Alexander planting a tall, dried up tree stem. He tells his son the legend of the old Orthodox monk Pamve, who had planted a dead tree on a mountain and had instructed a novice, Ioann Kolow, to water it every day till it wakened to life. Every morning Ioann would fill a bucket, ascend the mountain and water the tree, returning in the evening after dark. Three years he did this, until one day he climbed the mountain and found the tree covered with blossom.

In this parable one can recognise allusions to the same act of faith performed by father and son in *The Sacrifice;* to the tree of life, beneath which the Virgin and Child are seated in the Leonardo painting; and to the Cross of Christ and its ultimate burgeoning with new life as an expression of resurrection. At the close of the film we see Little Man heaving two buckets along the track to water the withered stem his father has planted. Having completed his task, he lies down beneath the tree to wait. At this moment he recovers his voice and speaks for the first time in the film, repeating the words he had heard from his father at the outset: 'In the beginning was the word.' And he adds, 'Why, papa?' Again the camera rises to the crown of the tree, where there is still neither blossom nor leaf. But as if in answer to this question, the dedication to Tarkovsky's own son is faded on.

. . . . .

In *The Sacrifice,* as in other films by Tarkovsky, there are thus certain autobiographical references to be found. It is an aspect of his work for which he frequently incurred criticism, and most severely in his native country. The autobiographical element in his films ranges from the direct personal quotations of *The Mirror* to relatively allusive parallels in other films. *Nostalgia* is dedicated to Tarkovsky's mother and contains echoes from his childhood and youth. *The Sacrifice,* as we have seen, is dedicated to his son, and the thematic material—the faith Alexander places in Little Man—is a reflection of the hopes Tarkovsky himself placed in the future.

In other realms of art the inclusion of personal motifs or experience is regarded as a valid process, through which a further plane of meaning and dialogue may be established. Tarkovsky's use of autobiographical reference could be compared in painting (to which one can trace numerous parallels in his work) with the incorporation by artists of their own portraits, often discreetly hidden among the secondary figures or in background scenes. In the 'Adoration of the Magi', for example, critics have long conjectured that the armoured figure in the bottom right-hand corner is a self-portrayal of Leonardo himself as a young man.

Tarkovsky's descriptions of the development of the screenplay for *The Sacrifice* throw an interesting light on the autobiographical elements in his films, and how they are either allowed to impinge directly on the content or are transmuted and assimilated to form a virtually indistinguishable part of the overall fabric.

The initial screenplay concept, written before the shooting of *Nostalgia* and bearing the title 'The Witch', revolved about the cure of a man suffering from cancer. In his desperation, confronted with the knowledge of an incurable disease, he encounters a strange figure (the forerunner of Otto, the postman), who tells Alexander that his only hope of recovery is to go to a woman, allegedly a witch possessed of magical powers, and to sleep with her. This he does and experiences a remarkable cure, much to the amazement of his doctor. But the witch turns up one day and stands outside his house in the rain to claim him. Alexander's sacrifice at this stage in the development of the screenplay consisted of relinquishing family and possessions and going off with this woman in the attire of a poor man.

During the shooting of *Nostalgia,* Tarkovsky was struck by a number of parallels between his preoccupations in film at that time and his own life. Andrei Gorchakov, the film's leading character, had come to Italy with the intention of remaining only a short time and had been consumed with yearning for his home; but he had been unable to return, and ultimately died in Italy. Tarkovsky himself had originally intended to return to Russia after completing the film, but had also been overtaken by illness in Italy and forced to stay. He was deeply affected further by the death of Anatoli Solonizyn, the leading actor in most of his earlier films, who was to have played the role of Gorchakov in *Nostalgia,* and who was long foreseen for the part of Alexander in 'The Witch'. Solonizyn died of the same disease that had brought the turning point in Alexander's life in the first version of the story, and 'today, years later, I too am suffering from it.'

Tarkovsky subsequently revised his treatment of this story, removing it from a realm that had become alarmingly personal, to give it a more universal validity. The autobiographical strand remains, however, inextricably woven into the texture, and the lines spoken by Alexander to his little son beneath the trees have a poignant significance: 'There is no such thing as death, only the fear of death.'

. . . . .

One has come to recognise certain recurring stylistic features of Tarkovsky's direction, personal fingerprints and structural devices. Over the years he came to refine and extend these to a point where they have acquired a semiotic content of their own.

The relationship between the iconography of his films and that of classical painting, the use of identifying attributes, the citation of the four elements has been observed elsewhere [in Green's "The Nostalgia of the Stalker," *Sight and Sound,* Winter 1984-85]. The generation of sounds, the quality of the camerawork, lighting and choreography, and the dramaturgical use of certain characters all serve to illuminate areas that are not otherwise expressed in the pictures or dialogue.

Tarkovsky developed the use of a differentiating colour code to a fine degree from its first appearance in *Andrei Roublev.* There the entire film was shot in black and white. Only the closing sequences, after Roublev has revoked his vow of silence and returned to painting, are in colour, celebrating his icons and murals. This key was used in subsequent films with increasing subtlety to distinguish between various realms, states of mind, or times. The use of such a code in this film will be considered in greater detail later in conjunction with the analysis of the ultimate significance of Alexander's sacrifice. At this point it is sufficient to remark that Tarkovsky here employs three levels of colour to distinguish between present reality, other time, dream and vision. This complexity is heightened by the fact that the range of colour used is limited in extent. The film is shot in the pale light of Sweden, where even the daylight scenes are of low contrast; furthermore, the indoor waking scenes are relatively subdued in colour, with the result that the transitions between the different realms are often slight, almost imperceptible, creating deliberate ambiguities that reflect the multi-layered quality of this film and its possible interpretations.

Manifestations of the four elements recur in Tarkovsky's works. In *The Sacrifice* water and fire predominate. He himself referred to water as a mysterious element that is extremely cinegenic, that conveys a sense of movement, depth and change; but that accounts for only one aspect of its presence in his films. In *The Sacrifice* he uses it not merely as an atmospheric background or context (the sea or the waterlogged earth), but as a specific iconographic element within the film, conveying images of life and growth and purification. Fire is of a similar visual quality, but it is also associated with ideas of light and purgation, and in this case comes to represent the central vehicle for Alexander's sacrifice.

Other personal Tarkovskian motifs are also to be found. The occurrence of mirrors, and of doors that swing open on their own; the trembling glasses, the image of spilt milk, the condensation of breath on the window pane, the pictures of the little boy asleep, the bloody nose, the phenomenon of levitation are all familiar from previous works, and in particular from *The Mirror.* Personal allusion and intrinsic content become one.

The extraordinary visual quality of this film is in large part due to the camerawork of Sven Nykvist. If *Nostalgia* was distinguished by slow zooms in and out, the striking feature of *The Sacrifice* is the use of parallel tracking and the pan. Here too camera movements are almost imperceptibly slow, and many of the uncut scenes remarkably long. (In this context, it will suffice to mention the opening two sequences and the fire scene at the end.) The lateral movement of the camera, together with the choreography of the figures, creates an exceptional sense of space. An example of this is the garden scene after the nightmare has passed. Victor and Adelaide are seated at a table in front of the house. The camera moves slowly to the right, the focus imperceptibly shifting from the foreground to explore successive planes of depth and activity, finally allowing a view through the doorway, through the entire house to the garden beyond; and as if by chance, one observes Alexander slipping unseen out of the house at the back. The viewer is in two worlds at the same time; listening to the conversation at the table and also party to Alexander's secret design.

The sense of space is enhanced both by the spare furnishing of the interiors and the careful control of lighting. Changes of light within a single scene (as in Little Man's bedroom), or classical chiaroscuro effects, in which one sees merely the expressionistically half-lit face of Maria, for example, are among the most striking aspects of the use of lighting. The tone is nevertheless subdued throughout, the night scenes often barely lit. The camera scarcely seems to move; and this still austerity creates a tension, a sense of space and movement that is one of the most remarkable achievements of the film and one of Tarkovsky's outstanding contributions to the grammar of cinema.

The collage of visual references is echoed on the plane of aural composition; and despite the spare use of music, this expression is not out of place. As in *Nostalgia,* Tarkovsky orchestrates the visual element with a host of suggestive sounds. Only at the beginning (to the Leonardo picture and the credits) and at the very end does he use music as a background, extraneous to the film. In both cases one hears a passage from Bach's St Matthew Passion. The other brief incidences of music in the film are integral to the action; i.e. both the Japanese flute music, which Alexander plays on his stereo set, and the organ prelude that he plays in Maria's house are 'live', in the sense that they are motivated by and occur within the action of the film. They are not effects added on from outside.

The soundtrack accompanying the dialogue and images is of quite another nature. Here Tarkovsky refined the technique of *Nostalgia* even further. The composition of sounds near and far, present, past or even future, in reality or dream, counterpoints the visual stream, forming a further layer of meaning that claims almost as much attention as the pictures. The sounds of the sea and gulls and the foghorn in the night establish the basic context against which the action is set; they are to be heard for much of the film. The rumble of thunder and the sounds of trembling glasses herald the approaching cataclysm and the blast of the planes roaring past overhead, shaking the whole earth. One hears the window shutters outside Little Man's bedroom swinging in the wind, opening and closing, and modulating the light in the room as they do so; and in the night, when Alexander cycles to Maria, one hears the familiar bark of a dog. Throughout the scene in Maria's house the passage of time is documented by the loud ticking of a clock; and at the close of the film the great fire is accompanied not merely by the crackle of the flames, but by the splintering and crashing of beams, the shattering of falling glass, explosions within the house, the telephone grotesquely ringing amid the conflagration, and the strings of the piano finally snapping with awful resonance.

Perhaps the most significant sound in this score is, however, the voice of the shepherd, as one might describe it. The strange voice the writer hears from the house in *Stalker,* warning him not to proceed, or the voice of God that Andrei hears in *Nostalgia,* here reappears in the form of a shepherd-like call, half cry, half song, recurring at turning points in the drama. It first occurs near the beginning, when Alexander and his son are sitting beneath the trees, Alexander philosophising about the world. Little Man slips off out of sight and Alexander notices the boy's disappearance in alarm. The call recurs, and when his son steals up on him, Alexander's reaction is one of shock or fright. He lunges out, accidentally striking the boy in the face, causing his nose to bleed. The scene is followed by Alexander's black-out, in which the vision of the devastated street appears for the first time. The cry recurs later in the house, after Otto has told his strange tale and is inexplicably struck down. We hear the voice of the 'shepherd' once more, after Alexander's terrible vow alone in the darkness of his room; and again when Otto visits him in the night to advise him to go to Maria. On this occasion they are aware of the cry, but do not know what it is. It is a cry of warning or exhortation, perhaps the voice of God or the silent call of Little Man, so faint and fleeting that one can never be entirely sure it is any more than a shepherd calling to his flock in the night; and yet, when Alexander turns back on his way to Maria, having fallen from his bicycle and hurt his knee, it sounds again, as if in admonition. Whether or not Alexander hears it consciously on this occasion, he turns once more and continues along the path to Maria's house.

Finally, mention should be made of the way Tarkovsky uses certain figures as pivots for the drama. Two characters in particular have a catalytic function in this film: Otto, the postman, a foil to Alexander; and Maria, who has a relatively small role but who appears at vital turns in the action.

Otto can be seen as providing the comic element in the film. He is a Puck-like, mercurial, ambivalent figure, constantly springing surprises with his unexpected aphorisms and naïve wisdom, much like the clown in a play by Shakespeare. It is he who philosophises with Alexander in the opening scene on fundamental existential questions, referring, much to Alexander's surprise, to the dwarf who had overcome Zarathustra—only to become the victim of Little Man's practical joke in the same scene and to be laid low a few scenes later by his own 'evil angel'.

It is Otto who brings the grandest of the birthday presents, an enormous framed map of Europe. Alexander assumes that it is a reproduction of an old print. An original would be far too valuable for the postman to give him. But as if it were the most natural thing in the world, Otto confirms that it is indeed a 17th century original and adds that any present has to be something of a sacrifice, otherwise what sort of present would it be? It is he who perceives the frightening aspect of Leonardo's picture. Asked by Victor about his background, Otto replies that he has given up his work as a history teacher to come here and concentrate on other things, and that he only works as a postman 'in his spare time'. It is Otto who collects strange phenomena and describes the remarkable parapsychological case of a mother and son who had been photographed together; shortly afterwards the boy was killed in the war, but inexplicably reappeared in a photograph the mother had taken of herself many years later. Otto is the key to the supernatural world of this film. It is he who comes to Alexander in his night of despair and tells him that Maria, the househelp, is a witch from Iceland, possessing benign powers; that Alexander's only hope of rescue is to go to her and lie with her.

It is through Maria that Alexander finds deliverance. She is a figure of many parts—mother, eternal womanhood and Virgin Mary all rolled into one. The parallels to the Madonna in the Leonardo painting are reinforced by the attributes with which Tarkovsky endows her. On Alexander's arrival at her house, one hears the bleating of sheep and sees a flock of lambs running backwards and forwards along the front of the building in the darkness. Inside the house one sees a group of objects forming a still life picture in black and white: a cross, a mirror, old photographs. Finally, Alexander, who has fallen into a puddle on his way there, washes his hands. Maria pours water from a jug into a bowl and over his hands, giving him a white towel with which to dry them. The ewer, the water and the towel denote purity and, like the lamb and the Cross, are common Marian attributes used in Renaissance painting. Similarly, the mirror, the ticking clock and the photographs are familiar vanitas symbols of transience. The memento mori is here juxtaposed with tokens of eternal life.

Alexander proceeds to tell the story of his mother's overgrown garden, which he had attempted to put in order, but the spirit of which he had in fact destroyed. This whole scene is filled with maternal references. When finally he asks, 'Could you love me, Maria? Save me! Save us all!' she tells him to leave. But Alexander places the pistol he has removed from Victor's bag to his temple, threatening to take his own life. The glasses rattle again, and the jets thunder past overhead. The shepherd-like call is heard. In their union, in the moment of deliverance, one sees Maria and Alexander swathed in sheets, turning, hovering above the bed in an act of levitation, bride and groom of the winds, mother and child, recalling perhaps the levitation scene and the pregnant mother in *The Mirror,* and the Child in the arms of the Madonna.

The visionary black and white scene of the devastated street returns, now filled with people fleeing in fear. The camera retires over their heads, to the glass balustrade, in which one sees the reflections of tall buildings above. On this occasion, however, the camera retreats even further, revealing the sleeping child. The shepherd's song-like call recurs and a series of brief images follows. Alexander lies asleep in the grass, at his side sits Adelaide, her back to the camera; but when she turns one sees that it is really Maria wearing the same dress and hairstyle as Adelaide— the characters of wife and lover, witch and Madonna now merged. The 'Adoration of the Magi' picture reappears; the last flickerings of the dream.

The dream is over and Maria disappears from the scene until the very end, when Alexander suddenly becomes aware of her presence, standing there watching the burning house. He falls to his knees at her feet, kissing her hands, before being taken away. But as the ambulance describes a broad curve past the house and turns on to the track, Maria grabs the bicycle lying in the grass and cycles off, taking a short cut towards the withered tree stem. There one sees her for the last time, united momentarily in a single picture with Little Man and Alexander, before their ways finally part.

. . . . .

The dream is over. One sees Alexander sleeping on the couch, the electric light burning next to him. He wakes; almost imperceptibly the picture fills with soft colour and light. The nightmare is banished, as he slowly comes to ascertain. The electricity and telephone are working again, and a call to his publisher confirms his hopes. It is as though nothing had happened. What then is the sense of Alexander's sacrifice? In the aftermath of the dream certain parallels with the events of the night manifest themselves. As if it were a reminder, Alexander stumbles into the piano, hurting his knee, just as he had when falling from the bicycle on his way to Maria.

In our modern world Alexander's readiness to sacrifice seems something of an anachronism. The age of sacrifice came to an end long ago; and yet, faced with destruction, he is prepared to abandon everything to accomplish the mission of his heart and save his little son and mankind.

In the first edition of his book *Sapetchatlionnoye Vremya,* which was compiled when the film was still in the project stage, Tarkovsky described his leading figure as a weak person, not a hero in the conventional sense of that word, but an upright, thinking man who brings a personal sacrifice for his high ideals. His actions are not merely performed with determination, but reveal a destructive despair, despite the fact that he risks incurring the misunderstanding of those nearest and dearest to him and although he is aware that he may be regarded as a madman. Alexander is not the master but the servant of his fate.

This distinction is significant, yet it is sometimes difficult to differentiate between the two in reality. Alexander's fate is at the same time his mission; his opportunity to take the stage again in the service of mankind. History has shown, however, that this kind of fatalism and a determination to fulfil it can prove disastrous in its own way. Alexander's calling does indeed verge on what society regards as madness; and although he may claim to have saved the world, his sacrifice is not confined to himself alone. Although he takes steps to exclude Victor from material loss and to keep everyone out of harm's way, he inevitably drags those closest to him into personal tragedy. Alexander's deed is not merely a self-sacrifice. It has something of a sacrificial offering about it.

A small price to pay, one might say, for saving the world; but at first sight Alexander's sacrifice seems superfluous and too programmatic. He has woken from a nightmare and the world is in order again. Only a lunatic would burn his house down now, surely. In fact, this turn of events provides an illustration of Tarkovsky's genius. In previous films one has seen how he goes to the borders separating the natural from the supernatural, always finding an explanation for strange circumstances that allows them to remain within the bounds of physical law. Having entered the Zone in *Stalker,* one of the men takes a direct route towards a house, despite the stalker's urging that they should follow a more circuitous course. Suddenly the man, the writer, hears a voice forbidding him to come closer. He turns in his tracks and rejoins his companions. The stalker finds a natural explanation for what at first seems to be a supernatural manifestation; he suggests that the man had been afraid in his own heart to go any further

and had created the audible warning himself to save his face. This and similar devices, to be found in particular in *Stalker* and *Nostalgia,* became a personal fingerprint of Tarkovsky's work. Ultimately they are formulations of the idea of belief, which is a major element of all his films. Just as the journey into the Zone may be seen as a quest for belief, so the casting of the bell in *Andrei Roublev* by a young boy who has never done the work before and the miraculous delivery from certain destruction in *The Sacrifice* are fundamental statements of belief.

Confronted with a global war, Alexander is forced to his knees in an act of humility and repentance. He grasps for God, promising to sacrifice everything and to take a vow of silence, if God will avert the catastrophe. But how can a process of universal destruction, once set in motion, be reversed by the prayers of a recluse? How can Alexander's strength of belief be demonstrated in a plausible manner that still observes the natural laws of the world in which the film takes place? Alexander's plea is granted. The inevitable holocaust is averted by the seemingly simple device of turning the catastrophe into a dream, from which Alexander now awakes. This is not a banal, sentimental trick, but a stroke of genius; and when Alexander, at first scarcely trusting his fortune, slowly reassures himself of the fact, he does not back out on his vow, but acknowledges this wonderful dissolution of his horror into a dream from which he may awake as an act of God, as God's active but unseen answer to his prayers. It is no mere happy coincidence and release. More than ever he must honour his vow, even if this means incurring the misunderstanding and despair of others. To keep faith and to preserve his own peace of mind, he is prepared to risk appearing insane in the eyes of the world.

In view of the 'last chance' Otto presents him with, one might of course ask whether Alexander's sacrifice was really necessary. Having sworn to forsake all worldly possessions and relationships, he is suddenly confronted with the promise of redemption through Maria. Is this an immediate answer to his prayers, the response to his vow, or is it an alternative to sacrifice? One might equally ask, in view of Alexander's readiness to honour his pledge, whether God might not have intervened at the last moment to prevent him carrying out his terrible deed, just as He had stopped Abraham taking the life of Isaac. Both questions are, however, irrelevant. There can be no room for doubt in Alexander's mind; a failure to act would be a return to the prevarication he abhors; and a direct intervention by God would invalidate the very rule the film has established.

The supposition that this whole central episode is but a dream is supported by a number of circumstances: by the many references to sleep; by the irrational, dreamlike actions that occur; and, more conclusively, by Tarkovsky's use of a differentiating colour code. The entire central nocturnal section of the film, from the time Alexander goes out into the garden to seek Little Man and finds Maria and the model of the house, to the time he wakes on the couch in the morning, is cast in the form of a dream and is photographed in darkly lit sequences virtually devoid of colour. The everyday waking reality of beginning and end is painted in the pale, natural colours of a northern summer, framing the interior world of the dream. There is also a third level of photography: the black and white or sepia sequences of the visions, or of scenes from other times, past or future, inset into the coloured reality or into the dark-hued central section.

Maria therefore stands at the beginning and end of this dark dream, the entrance to which is via the model of the house set on the blasted earth and built as a birthday present by Little Man himself and Otto. In embarking upon this apocalyptic midsummer night's dream, Alexander enters a labyrinthine realm, akin perhaps to the Zone in *Stalker.* The fact that he may awake and find the world as it was before, does nothing to lessen the horror of the vision. If anything, it demonstrates the truly nightmarish perspective of Shakespeare's own play.

Alexander's sacrifice is a parable, perhaps a vision in itself; a sacrifice we may all be called upon to make one day, the relinquishing of a materialist, expansionist world order, upheld by exploitation and nuclear power, a world of international rivalries that verge on armed conflict; a sacrifice in favour of love and a belief in a different future. Is it possible, however, for man to turn back short of the holocaust Grass describes in his book and Tarkovsky in his film? The mere threat of one would seem to be insufficient.

That this glimpse into the abyss 'no more yielded but a dream' seems certain. But one must ask whose dream it was—Alexander's or Little Man's? As in *Ivan's Childhood* and *The Mirror,* much of the film is as if seen through the eyes of a child. Furthermore, the sleeping child motif recurs throughout the film. Little Man sleeps through the entire night-war section; indeed, he dare not be woken. The dream has to be dreamt. In the second of the devastated street scenes in black and white one catches a glimpse of the little boy asleep again; and finally, at the end of the film, he lies down beneath the tree, his work done, perhaps to sleep and dream, and bring the story full circle, back to its starting point. Is the film Alexander's dream of his son, or Little Man's dream of his father; vision of the past or of the future? Past and future are fused together or are ambivalent; it is a feature one may observe in other films by Tarkovsky. The sacrifice is that which one generation brings to another, Alexander for Little Man, Christ for God.

In true Tarkovskian manner identities merge. Like the fair-haired boys in earlier films, Little Man, whose recovery of speech represents the end of Alexander's vow of silence, is his father's continuation or his alter ego. Otto's collection of strange phenomena echoes in the mind. The unity of time and place comes full circle. But this is only one of the cycles in which the film abounds, and to which Otto refers in his debate with Alexander by the sea at the beginning.

Perhaps Alexander's apocalyptic vision is but the unhappy dream of a child. Tarkovsky allows us to view the world from both ends of the telescope; and in both cases what remains is the future. Perhaps 'the tree of life, which is in the midst of . . . paradise' will bloom and Alexan-

der's sacrifice, whether it took place in reality or in the imaginings of his little son, will not have been in vain. (pp. 111-18)

Peter Green, "Apocalypse & Sacrifice," in Sight and Sound, *Vol. 56, No. 2, Spring, 1987, pp. 111-18.*

Andrei Tarkovsky with Charles-Henri de Brantes (interview date August-September 1987)

[*In the following excerpt from an interview reprinted after his death, Tarkovsky discusses the spiritual elements of his films.*]

[*De Brantes*]: *Some have spoken of overlapping in your films, especially in* **The Sacrifice,** *where you seem to hover between Christian inspiration, as in the Our Father recited by Alexander, and a more archaic, rather pagan inspiration, as in the character of Maria, the 'good witch'. This results in a certain perplexity. Are you, or are you not, a Christian film writer?*

[Tarkovsky]: I don't think it is really important to know whether I share or do not share certain ideas, certain prejudices, be they pagan, Catholic, Orthodox, or simply Christian. The important thing is the film itself. In my view, it should be judged in a general sort of way, and not used as a forum for contradictions which some would attribute to me. A work of art does not always mirror the artist's interior world, and certainly not in its finer details, though there is a certain logic in the relation of one to the other . . . but the work can also portray a point of view that is not that of the artist. Another thing, when I was shooting the film, I was very conscious that it would be seen by very different types of audiences.

When I was very young, I asked my father one day: 'Does God exist or not?' His answer was an inspiration: 'For the one who does not believe, no! For the believer, yes!' This is a very important problem. What I am trying to illustrate by that is that the film can be interpreted in different ways. For instance, for those who are interested in the supernatural aspect of human phenomena, the main point of the film will be in the relationship between the postman and the witch, and as a consequence, the chief action will spring from these two characters. Believers on the other hand, will be more sensitive to the prayer Alexander addresses to God, and for them, the entire film will evolve around this. Finally, a third category of viewers who have no particular creed, will say that Alexander is ill and psychologically disturbed because of the war or because of fear. Thus several categories of viewers can interpret the film as they please.

My point of view is that the viewer must be given the possibility of interpreting what he sees on the screen according to his own interior world, and not through an interpretation I might choose to impose on him. For my objective is to show life, to present an image, a dramatic and a tragic image, of modern man.

To conclude what we are saying, could you imagine a film like that being made by a non-believer? I couldn't!

Some people also question the reality of the faith of certain of your characters. What is its content? For instance, what quality was lacking in Alexander's faith for him to escape madness?

Personally, I do not believe that Alexander was mad, though there are probably viewers who believe that he has lost his reason. I think that he is just in a certain psychic condition, and generally speaking, in a difficult one. I think he stands for a certain type of man. His inner world is that of one who has not seen the inside of a church for a long time; of one who perhaps, was educated in a Christian family, but whose belief is no longer what one might term 'conventional' . . . or perhaps again, he is an unbeliever? I could imagine him for instance waxing enthusiastic over Rudolf Steiner and about questions of an anthroposophical nature. I can also imagine him as a man who is aware that the world of matter is not the whole world, and that there is a transcendent world too, to be discovered. And when tragedy strikes, when some terrible catastrophe is imminent, he turns to God with the logic of his own personality, as to the only hope that is left. It is a moment of despair.

Your characters always seem to remain on the threshold of an authentic spiritual life, in a sort of perpetual state of innocence . . .

For me, in spite of the torment he is suffering, Alexander is a happy man, for in the course of his torments, he found faith. With all that he is going through, it seems difficult to say that he remains on the threshold of something! The most important and the most difficult aspect of the religious problem, is believing.

But this faith, in a certain sense, borders on the absurd?

But this is normal! I think that a person who is ready to sacrifice himself, may be called a believer. Of course it's strange! Alexander sacrifices himself, and at the same time, obliges others to do likewise. It's rather crazy! But what can be done? As far as the others can see, he is probably lost, but what is absolutely clear is that he is saved.

Some people who saw **The Sacrifice** *were conscious of a Bergman atmosphere. Would you say that the Swedish film-maker influenced you in any way? or could it be due to the place where the film was made?*

I don't agree with that at all. When Bergman speaks about God, it is to say that he does not speak to his creature, that he does not exist . . . thus there is no comparison between us. Such critics are superficial ones, and if they say that because the principal actor also had roles in Bergman's films, or because one finds Swedish countryside in my film, it is proof that they did not understand Bergman at all, nor did they understand existentialism. Bergman is nearer to Kierkegaard than he is to the religious question.

Of all your films, **The Sacrifice** *seems to be the most 'theatrical'. Could you envisage some scenes being played on the stage?*

I suppose one could attempt it, though I imagine it would be easier to dramatise **Solaris** or **The Stalker.** Although I don't think such a play would be a good one . . . it

would be rather pretentious. I'm happier with the film, because it does not have to reckon with time nor with the viewers' rhythm, for it has its own rhythm. And if one were to transpose it onto the stage, it would do away with the time problem which I introduce into the film and which is very important. The thing just wouldn't work any more.

The principal actor, Erland Josephson, in his own personal life, would seem to be particularly concerned by the questions you raise. Can you say something about your relationship with him?

The principal roles of the film were in fact, specially written for Erland Josephson and Allan Edwall. The others came after.

At the end of **The Sacrifice,** *a tree burns together with the house. Were you surprised at that?*

Nothing in my films happens by chance. Why did the tree burn together with the house? If only the house had burned, it would have been just one more 'cinema fire' . . . not real . . . not unique.

Don't you think it was rather cruel?

The tree was dead, it had been replanted, it was just an element of the décor.

In your film **Nostalgia,** *you put on the lips of your hero the words 'man must now build pyramids'. Without too much analysis, what kind of pyramids were you thinking of?*

Man must aspire to spiritual greatness. He must leave after him mysteries which others will have to unravel for millions of years afterwards . . . not ruins, which will be remembered as catastrophes . . . I don't know . . . in any case not a Chernobyl, the opposite rather. . . .

You have stated that you admire Robert Bresson. But are not your films the exact opposite of his? Bresson cuts a scene, and does not resolve certain essential questions, but merely sketches them or suggests them . . .

For me, Robert Bresson is the best film-maker in the world. I have for him the greatest respect. Having said that, I can't see a lot of resemblance between us. Yes, he will cut a scene which I could never do . . . it would be like killing a living being . . .

Somebody recently talked to me about a friend of his, who had suicidal tendencies. He went to see **The Sacrifice,** *and having seen it, spent about two hours in contemplation. His desire to live has returned.*

That argument carries more weight for me than all the criticisms and opinions . . . I had the very same experience after *The Childhood of Ivan*: a criminal serving his time in a Gulag wrote to me that he had seen my film; he was so transformed by it interiorly, that he said he could never again kill a man.

Why do you so often introduce a levitation scene into your films . . . a body rising up into the air?

Simply, because it is usually a scene (with) great potential. Some things happen to be more cinematographic, more photogenic than others. Water for instance, I consider very important: it lives, has depth, moves, changes, reflects as does a mirror; one can drown in it, drink it, wash in it, etc. not to mention the fact that it consists of one molecule which does not divide. It is a monad.

Likewise, when I imagine a man floating up into the air, it is something that pleases me . . . for me it is full of meaning. If an idiot asked me, why in my last film, people floated up into the air, I would answer: because one of them is a witch! If a more sensitive person, able to appreciate the poetry of the thing, were to ask me the same question, I would reply that for these two characters, Alexander and Maria, love is not the same thing that it is for the scriptwriter of *37°2 in the morning.*

For me, love is the supreme manifestation of mutual understanding, which the representation of the sexual act cannot express. If it could, why not go out into the fields and film the bulls mounting the cows? If 'love' is not explicit on the screen, everybody today thinks the film is censored. In actual fact, what is being portrayed is not love at all, but the sexual act. Now the genital expression of love is for each one, for each couple, a unique thing. When it is portrayed on the screen, it becomes the opposite.

In **The Sacrifice,** *Alexander's hesitation about going to Maria's house—which is a hesitation in his faith, and Maria's about sleeping with Alexander—which is a hesitation about love,—are they both the same hesitation?*

The only way to show the sincerity of these two characters, was to surmount the initial impossibility of establishing a relationship between them. To arrive at that, each was obliged to triumph over all differences.

In completing **The Sacrifice,** *how do you see the evolution of your artistic work?*

From the depth point of view; from that of my understanding of the world of modern man, I think I have succeeded between here than in my previous films. But from the artistic and poetic point of view, I would place *Nostalgia* above *The Sacrifice,* for *Nostalgia* does not rest upon an idea or a theme; its raison d'être is the poetic image and that alone, while *The Sacrifice* is based on classical drama. For this reason, I prefer *Nostalgia.* I have always admired Bresson for his spirit of continuity, for the logical relationship of one film to another. It is not an accident if this spirit of continuity appears in the emptying of the glass of water into the washbasin each morning, in discussion of the system etc. This is an element I consider very important. I hate leaving things to chance. Even the most poetic image, even the most innocent and gratuitous one, is never a thing of chance.

Stalker *would appear to be nearer to* **The Sacrifice?**

True. For me, *The Sacrifice* is the most sequential of my films. It is this spirit of integrity in one's own regard, right to the end, that can make a man insane. In this sense, *The Sacrifice* is completely different from my other films . . .

Why have you chosen St Antony as the subject of one of your future films?

Because I think it is very important today that we analyse a conflict which has always preoccupied the heart of man: what is holiness and what is sin? Is being a saint all that good? For in the Orthodox Church, communion with others is very important. For Orthodox Christians, the Church is a communion of persons united by the same sentiments and by the same faith. Now when the saint leaves everything to go off to the desert, we ask why? and the answer is: because he wishes to save his own soul. But what about the rest of mankind? I am very preoccupied with this question of the relationship between personal salvation, and participation in the life of the world.

But why choose Antony?

It could have been someone else . . . for me, the essential element is the price man must pay for his attempts to achieve an equilibrium between the material and the spiritual.

And why are you thinking of The Gospel According to Steiner as another possible subject for a film?

I did not choose Steiner myself. Everybody is asking me to make a film on him. To phrase it as 'The Gospel according to Steiner', is my way of reacting to such a proposition . . . but I'm not wholly convinced. What interests me much more, are those who are looking for a way out, for a solution . . . Those who say they have found one, well I'm afraid they are not telling the whole truth.

What about a film on E. T. A. Hoffmann?

Hoffmann! that's an old story. I'm very anxious to use this theme, in order to speak of romanticism in general, and be done with it. If you remember the story of the life and death of Kleist and his fiancée, you will know what I am talking about. Romantics are those who have always tried to imagine life different from what it was. What they dread most is routine, acquired habits, a relationship with life as with something predictable. Romantics are not fighters. When they perish, it is because of the impossible dreams they had thought up for themselves. I believe that romanticism—as a way of life—is very dangerous, for capital importance is given to personal talent . . . there are more important things in life than personal talent . . .

On the concrete level, what is your relationship to the Orthodox Church?

On the concrete level . . . difficult! I used to live in the U.S.S.R. I came to Italy, and now I'm in France, so unfortunately, I had no opportunity for a normal relationship. If I go to Mass in Florence, it is celebrated by a Greek, another time by an Italian, but never by a Russian. It is the Orthodox Church, of course, but Greek Orthodox, or something else. The one thing that deeply impressed me recently, was my meeting in London with Father Antony Bloom. Relationship with the Church means having a fairly settled life. I'm like someone under the débris after a bombing raid, so it is very difficult to expect me to have a normal relationship.

It has been said that Lounatcharski, writer and member of the Communist Party, referred to the religious character of the 1917 Revolution. Have you any comment to make?

Where did he say that? What nonsense! Perhaps he said it to justify his admiration for the Revolution. I don't think he did say that, but when it was necessary to court popularity, those belonging to NARKOM (Popular Education Committee), said and admitted everything!

You seem fascinated by the Apocalypse, *as though you wished to accelerate its coming!*

No, I'm simply looking at where we are today . . . and since the *Apocalypse* is about the Last things . . .

In his book Visionnaires, *Olivier Clément writes that Fedorov wished that the traditional, individual form of asceticism become collective, thus making radical changes in culture. What is your opinion?*

If asceticism and interior effort could change the world, what has gone wrong after four thousand years, to produce such catastrophic results? It took Golgotha, 2000 years ago, to place humanity on the right road. But it didn't even bother to follow. I know that it is a painful thought that it was in vain . . . even though in a certain sense, it did help, for man aspires to the heights! If Golgotha hadn't taken place, there really would be nothing.

Several times; I noticed that you were reading Berdiaev. Are you one of his followers?

Not at all! I don't share all his views. Sometimes he places himself about a problem, as though he had resolved it. I don't believe in such people, such as Steiner or Berdiaev. Otherwise we should have to believe that there exist men with infused knowledge, which is impossible!

Why do Christians sometimes say: 'Christ is the only answer'?

The only thing we really have is faith. When Voltaire said: 'If God did not exist, we should have to invent him', he did not say it because he did not believe, which he did. It's not that at all. Materialists and positivists gave a horrible twist to Voltaire's words. Faith is the only thing that can save man. That's my profound conviction. Otherwise, what could we do? It is the only thing which man possesses without any doubt. Everything else is non-reality.

How would you interpret Dostoïevski's words: 'Beauty will save the world'?

Many various meanings, some vulgar, have been given to this saying. Of course when Dostoïevski spoke of beauty, he meant spiritual integrity. In the context, he was referring to Prince Myshkin or to Rogojine, not to the physical beauty of Nastassia Philippovna, who in reality was common, a prostitute . . .

You said that man ought to create, after the image of his Creator . . .

It is important to do so, and at the same time it is not important . . . for me, it is like breathing fresh air . . .

Would you draw a distinction between the artist and the saint or the monk?

They are in fact, different ways. The saint, the monk, both refuse to create, because they are not directly involved in the world. The standard of the saint or of the monk is non-participation. This is a very oriental idea . . . sort of Buddhist mentality . . . but the artist . . . the poor unfortu-

nate artist . . . has to plod about in the mud, in the middle of all that is going on around him. We have the example of the French poet Rimbaud, who didn't wish to be a poet. There are many like that.

As regards the monk, I have a kind of compassion for him, for he is only half living, that is, with just part of himself. As for the artist, his tendency would be to disperse his faculties, to be deceived, to get involved in the mess . . . his soul is at risk.

At the same time, we cannot oppose the saint and the poet as an angel to a devil! It's simply a question of man finding himself in differing situation. The saint will find salvation, the artist perhaps will not! I believe here in grace that hits you from above like that! Hermann Hesse said: 'All my life I wanted to become a saint, but I am a sinner. I can only count on help from on high.' I cannot be sure that my actions will unfold as I plan them to do. That is its significance.

There are parallels between the saint and the artist, but also different problems to be faced. The most important thing is that man live in a just manner, either by trying to be like his Creator, or by endeavouring to save his soul. So it is a question of saving oneself or trying to create a more spiritually rich environment for the entire world. Who knows how much longer we have here below? We must live with the thought that tomorrow we may well have to render to God an account of our lives. The question you put to me is one to which geniuses have devoted their lifetime! There, would be matter for a film! When I tackle Saint Antony, I'd like to bring up the subject . . . to try and understand and explain this agonising question for man. In the last analysis, the problem is not whether we die or do not die, for we shall all die, either together, or one after the other. (pp. 339-43)

Andrei Tarkovsky and Charles-Henri de Brantes, in an interview in The Month, *Vol. CCLVIII, Nos. 1436 & 1437, August-September, 1987, pp. 339-43.*

John Gianvito (review date October 1987)

[*In the following review, Gianvito praises* Sculpting in Time *for its insight into Tarkovsky's work and its lack of abstract critical theories.*]

Amid voluminous writing consecrated to aesthetic theory and criticism, there exists a conspicuous, albeit understandable, scarcity of literary analysis carried out by artists themselves. The innermost workings of art are mysterious and the ability to be sufficiently removed from the creative process in order to contemplate these activities does not come easy. In fact, this kind of intellectual pursuit strikes many practitioners as a superfluous expenditure of energy, detracting from the meaning and import of the art itself. The difficulty of analyzing creativity is compounded when the art being discussed is visual or musical. As one of the youngest and, arguably, most complex of art forms, the cinema has, I believe, fallen greatest victim to inadequate "translation."

And so, the publication in the United States of the late Soviet film director Andrey Tarkovsky's *Sculpting in Time* is a cause for celebration.

In the course of making seven feature films, Andrey Tarkovsky established himself firmly as not only the foremost living film artist in the Soviet Union (a fact which nonetheless did not always allow for easy distribution of his work) but, in the words of Ingmar Bergman, as "the most important director of our time." In terms of artistic achievement, skill and subtlety of expression, and high-mindedness of purpose and theme, nothing in contemporary American cinema holds a candle to such masterpieces as *Andrei Roublev, The Mirror,* and *Stalker.* That Tarkovsky should also bestow upon us a theoretical and philosophic volume on his craft is in the tradition of great Russian film directors: Eisenstein, Pudovkin, Kuleshev, and Vertov.

However, that this book exists at all, Tarkovsky informs us in his introduction, is only as a consequence of a difficult and prolonged period of professional inactivity which he hints was behind his decision to defect from the Soviet Union in 1983.

Sculpting in Time, which first appeared last year in Germany and Great Britain, is in the author's words a book with "no secrets," an attempt to set down over a quarter-century's observations on the nature and technique of cinema, including thoughts on the overall meaning and purpose of artistic endeavor, and concluding with a commentary upon nothing less than "the meaning of our existence." Intertwined, in general chronological sequence, Tarkovsky examines the creative development of each of his film projects, with the inclusion in the Knopf edition of a new chapter devoted to his final film, *The Sacrifice,* notes dictated by the fifty-four year old Tarkovsky in the last months of 1986 as he lay dying of lung cancer in Paris.

As imposing as all this may sound, the theory in *Sculpting in Time* is a far cry from the structuralism and semiotics presently burdening university bookshelves. There is no obfuscating rhetoric, no private jargon. On the contrary. "The fairly widely held view of cinema as a system of signs," writes Tarkovsky, "seems to me profoundly and essentially mistaken." Whereas in literature "everything is expressed by means of language, by a system of signs, of hieroglyphics," cinema, he feels, in its truest expression, "like music, allows for an utterly direct, emotional, sensuous perception of the work." Clearly seeking to defend himself against the many writers, critics, and viewers who have sought to reduce the imagery of his films to precisely classifiable symbols (including surprisingly the copywriter for the book's jacket), Tarkovsky argues that film first makes its impact upon the viewers' emotions. Once awakened, the viewers' emotions will then impel thought. What's important here, Tarkovsky warns us, is the risk in our era that "we shall lose the means of perceiving art immediately and exactly with the whole of our being . . ."

Drawing support and comparison for his ideas from a wealth of sources ranging from the bible, through Da Vinci, to the films of Bergman, Buñuel, and Kurosawa, and to the great Russian literary tradition, especially Dostoievsky, the comparison Tarkovsky makes most

often is to Japanese haiku. In its exacting simplicity, full of associative, multidimensional meaning, haiku forms the perfect corollary to Tarkovsky's carefully approached definition of "the artistic image." The essence of the successful artistic image, he observes, lies in the capacity to be both "indivisible and elusive," and to reflect the universal through the particular, thereby enabling the viewer, in the same way as the reader of haiku, "to be absorbed into it as into nature, to plunge in, lose himself in its depth, as in the cosmos where there is no bottom and no top." The difficulty of using film to attain such perfection is not only in mastering a complicated array of components but also in appreciating that which is unique to the language of film, the full nature of which, Tarkovsky maintains, I believe rightly, is only just beginning to reveal itself.

In discussing the struggle to develop and define cinema's properties separate from the influences of literature and theater, Tarkovsky sets forth the notion of "sculpting in time" as the primary principle of film: its near-miraculous ability to fix and preserve blocks of time. No other medium in the history of art, notes Tarkovsky, has so compellingly encapsulated the real. With a depth of reasoning and wide-ranging analyses, Tarkovsky pursues how a director can achieve cinema's full potential by grasping the specific character of film and by remaining unswervingly faithful to the pursuit of a personal vision.

If *Sculpting in Time* falters, it is only from an occasionally abrupt transition of thought, the result no doubt from having been assembled over a number of years from a variety of sources. There is also a periodic redundancy of expression or idea although more often than not this serves to reinforce the particular concept being discussed. What is more apparent, and consistent with Tarkovsky's work as filmmaker, is the thorough attention to detail in the assembly and packaging of the book. Not only are the sumptuous stills from each of Tarkovsky's films perceptively chosen and laid out but, adding to the pleasure of this text, there are translations of several poems by Tarkovsky's father, the distinguished Russian poet, Arseniy Tarkovsky. The poems, many of which are quoted in the films, give an additional degree of richness in the moving way in which they indicate familial attachment to much the same themes. This affinity is particularly poignant if one knows that Tarkovsky's father left wife and children when Andrey was a child.

By the end, with a near total refrain from biographical or anecdotal material, there emerges a clear image of Tarkovsky, a man devoutly in love with his profession, burning with the integrity of his convictions, and certain of art's ability to redeem modern man from his "spiritual impotence." In one of the book's most beautiful statements, Tarkovsky writes, "The allotted function of art is not, as is often assumed, to put across ideas, to propagate thoughts, to serve as example. The aim of art is to prepare a person for death, to plough and harrow his soul, rendering it capable of turning to good." With Tarkovsky's passing, *Sculpting in Time,* perhaps ironically, stands as testament to this affirmation, permitting each of us a rare entry into the soul of an artist carving out his own path towards eternity.

John Gianvito, "The Language of Film," in Boston Review, *Vol. XII, No. 5, October, 1987, p. 14.*

Simonetta Salvestroni   (essay date November 1987)

[*In the following essay, Salvestroni examines the metaphorical and thematic affinities between Tarkovsky's science-fiction films* Solaris *and* Stalker *and fantastic elements in Russian and Soviet literature.*]

Andrei Tarkovsky's SF films, *Solaris* (1972) and *Stalker* (1980), have precise and creative affinities with the fantastic strain in Russian and Soviet literature. The metaphoric interactions, the bipolarities, the relationships with an Otherness at once external to and inside the characters, the anticipation of ambiguous miracles, and the sense of being on the "threshold," that we meet with in Bulgakov, Dostoyevsky, Gogol, and the Strugatskys we also encounter in Tarkovsky. There is, however, a difference. The "magical role" assumed by the word in Gogol's Petersburg tales or in Bulgakov's *The Master and Margarita,* say, Tarkovsky transfers to the image, which he endows with a power not inferior to that of the word. It is within the power of the image to surmount spatial, temporal, and biological barriers, materialize memories and psychic realities, and bring alien places near and humanize them to the point that they come to life and participate in an extra-verbal communicatory relationship.

In Tarkovsky's *Solaris,* the dialogue between humankind and the planet transpires exclusively through images, and so finally does that between the director and his public, along with the process whereby Harey—an adult alien but at the start devoid of consciousness—becomes humanized. The Soviet director's first film thus exemplifies, in an original and complex way, the manner in which the image communicates and contributes to the development of cognition.

Typifying all of Tarkovsky's films to date, from *The Childhood of Ivan* (1962) to *Nostalgia* (1983), is a binary spatial organization. Each sets a quotidian world, grey, monological, and violent, against an anti-world which is dynamic, malleable, and full of color, the dominion of possibility and of choice. In his 1962 film, the luminous dimension of the dream and of memory presents a stark antithesis to the tragic greyness of the war, which one of the characters defines as the suspension of the vital flux and of communication. A similar antinomy is implicit throughout Tarkovsky's next film, *Andrei Rublev* (1966). This immediately becomes evident to the viewer towards the end, when the black-and-white footage reserved for a Medieval Russia devastated by pillagings, acts of repression, and massacres gives way to the colors of the final frames dedicated to the vital force of art and of a nature uncontaminated by violence and by the obtuse mechanicalness which human beings, according to Tarkovsky, tend to be guilty of. After the scenes of ruinous incursions by enemies, of the tortures which the authorities inflict on the Russian people, and of the blinding and killing of artists at the behest of princes to prevent them from beautifying the palaces of rivals, there finally appear on the screen

images of another world: that of Rublev's icons and then of the living water of a rainfall and of a great river traversing grassy expanses where horses move in natural freedom. Relating the two spheres is a matter entrusted to the film's addressees or, in *The Childhood,* implicitly to Ivan, who contemporaneously inhabits both dimensions and whose point of view the spectator gathers from images culled from his thoughts and sense perceptions.

While repeating this binary structure, *Solaris* introduces a substantial element of difference. There the dialogue between world and anti-world undergoes a concrete materialization inasmuch as one of the direct, first-person interlocutors, thanks to its peculiarities, is the planet itself. It is here that the originality of Tarkovsky's spatial treatment of Lem's materials manifests itself: in the director's metamorphosing of an animate space—or rather, the living planet inhabiting it—as one of the protagonists of the cinematic text. The other partner to the dialogue is, of course, Kris Kelvin, who has been given the assignment of investigating certain strange happenings at the Solaris space station and of deciding on the basis of his findings whether to destroy the alien entity or try to establish contact with it.

As in *The Diary of a Madman* or *The Master and Margarita,* the film *Solaris* centers upon a problematic communicative relationship—one which, in its context, is perilously beyond normal bounds. No less than the fictive worlds of Gogol and Bulgakov, the terrestrial society of the future as Tarkovsky envisions it—which has similarities to what was actually his own—is characterized finally by its rigid organization. Founded on the premise that truth is univocal, this social order refuses to accept diversity, which it proceeds to destroy whenever it becomes too prominent to be ignored. This is exactly the parabolic meaning connected with the Earth in its relations with Solaris—an import first instanced in the dogmatic refusal of scientists to verify the testimony of the astronaut Berton, and then in the wish to bombard the planet once the goings on at the space station prove to be too disquieting.

It is significant that Tarkovsky decided to have his film begin on Earth, thereby departing from Lem's fiction, which from its opening page immediately situates the human actors in the vicinity of Solaris. While thus focussing on the social system of the future, however, the director offers information about it only indirectly. It is up to the viewer to infer its characteristics: from the inquest concerning Berton's declarations; from the uninterrupted file of automobiles that appear to whirl by endlessly, thus metaphorically representing the mechanical world which Burton returns to after his stay at the home of Kris's father; and from the posturings of Sartorius, that bureaucrat of science, who holds it a duty to annihilate whatever does not correspond to its objective laws, which admit of nothing beyond themselves. Revealing itself obliquely, the Earth of the future emerges from a singular process involving not only the future expressly imaged in the film but also Tarkovsky's own present, Soviet reality in the 1970s.

His *Solaris* begins and ends with the scene of the house which Kris's father has built, in opposition to the purely

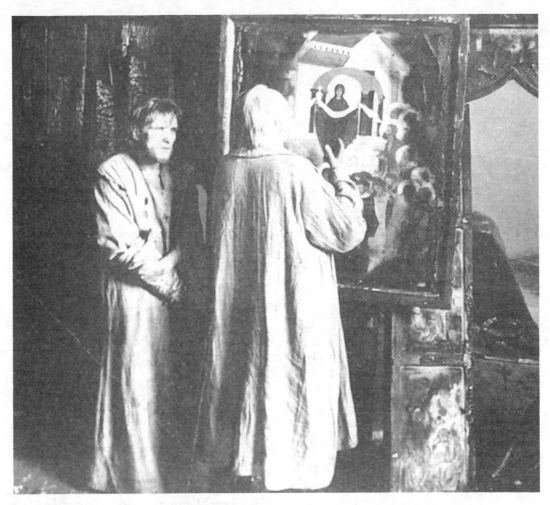

Andrei Rublev (Anatoliy Solonitsyn) with his teacher Theophanes in Andrei Rublev *(1966).*

technological developments of his time, to be in contact with a living and unmechanized nature. As the father himself underscores, he has designed the building so that its structure recreates that of his grandfather's house—a project that required research into his own roots on the land and in his familial past. Here the director also resorts to other images reinforcing that metaphoric significance: of a lake whose living waters exhibit a concentric movement complicated by a rainfall, and of a horse trotting freely in a manner reminiscent of the final frames of *Andrei Rublev.*

Old man Kelvin, then, lives an anomalous life with respect to the rest of the world; and by comparison with a son profoundly incapable of understanding him, he (along with Berton) vindicates Solaris's right to exist. (As he asserts, it should not be suppressed merely because it is different.) The father's dimension accordingly adds a third point of view to the dialogue between antinomial opposites which otherwise dominate this work of Tarkovsky's as they do his preceding films. Old Kelvin's point of view assumes a basically mediatory function, making fruitful on Earth young Kelvin's experience of two unknown dimensions: one cosmically distant and embodied in the ocean-planet;

the other, nearer but no less accessible, constituted by the depths of his psyche.

The anti-world of Solaris is disturbing to terrestrial minds because as a living entity, it invalidates the fixed laws and rules to which they are mechanically accustomed, standing at once outside and within the purview of such. This double valence, which scientists find logically unacceptable, has its correlative in their confrontations with the planet, in regard to which they are both hosts and guests. Their space station orbits above the waters of Solaris, but that thinking magmatic mass at the same time enters into them, insinuating itself into their minds as they sleep. From this position, the planet conducts its attempts to communicate with them, taking on a role analogous to, but more powerful than, that of the Unconscious. It does not limit itself to transmitting mental messages; it also succeeds in materializing them.

At this point it begins to become clear that the true center of the anti-world of limitless possibility which the three scientist-astronauts are exploring is not external, but instead lies inside them, in depths that terrestrial experience, confining as it is, has never allowed them to reach. The dialogue with the alien from here on transforms itself into an auto-communicative relationship, doubly parlous from the standpoint of any cultural code of earthly provenance. Indeed, it compels human beings to come to terms with a Difference which can neither be distanced nor evaded.

Tarkovsky and Lem, no doubt influenced by Freud, have endowed Solaris with a "symmetrical" logic, one capable of nullifying spatio-temporal distances along with the distinctions between life and death, part and whole, thinking and being. A homogeneous mass with the capacity for enveloping everything, the planet generates the monstrous midgets that populate Sartorius's Unconscious, for example, as well as reproducing the obsessive mental picture that Kris has of Harey, down to the mark of the injection she took to kill herself ten years earlier.

For this explosion from the Unconscious, which the monological and dogmatic Earth of the future would condemn to non-existence, the scientist-astronauts are quite unprepared; and that makes their dialogue with the Alien difficult, tense, even on the subjective level. In what is perhaps the most tragic case, the fear and shame that Gibarian discovers in himself are strong enough to drive him to suicide. On the other hand, the tendency towards violence that seizes the bureaucrat Sartorius seeks (though only apparently) an external outlet: the single means he determines on for getting free of and annihilating the most obscure and unsupportable part of himself is to destroy the planet. Nor does Kelvin, for all his specialist training in social psychology, prove to have brought totally adequate intellectual equipment from Earth. His first response, like that of his fellows, amounts to an act of rejection: he endeavors to do away with the new Harey, the disquieting material message which the planet has sent him; and he thus accomplishes the cruel deed for which in the past he was only indirectly responsible.

Even so, troubled as he is in his monological certainty about contact with the dimension his father inhabits, Kris is the one personage in the film capable of an evolution which concludes with the hard-won recovery of his human integrity. Towards that end, his alien companion takes on the same function that the anti-world has for the viewer: that of a model interaction with the primary field of investigation—in this instance, of the memory-object which was the terrestrial Harey—thereby assisting to bring to consciousness new realizations, new connections. Rendering this interaction productive is the fact that the model, though apparently identical to her original, lacks knowledge and memory—an adult just come into the world and therefore resembling an infant of extraordinary plasticity.

Traditional logic alone is of no use for comprehending the film and in particular Solaris's messages. Here the key to interpretation is the same principle of "symmetry" that governs the Unconscious, including dreams and emotions. With that idea in view, we can observe that Harey, Kris, and Solaris are autonomous beings, distinct from one another, *and* at the same time elements in which the part is identical to the whole. Thus Kelvin is a temporary visitor to a planet "out there" which is also his Unconscious, a part of himself. So, too, Harey, something external which he finds in his room upon awakening, at the same time is a part of him, a reproduction of the image stored in his mind, rather than a totally independent creature.

As a result of the collaboration between Kelvin and Solaris, Harey constitutes for them a point of encounter, of contact, a materialized message which man and planet alike participate in as senders and intended addressees. Thanks to its peculiarities, the "text" that they produce together can inform each of them about the partner. Harey brings together the human traits derived from Kris's memory of his woman and an Otherness she shares with Solaris (evinced by the fact that her cells are of a type unknown to Kelvin and his colleagues).

One of the most important moments of *Solaris*—the moment in which the potentialities and ductility of the language of images reach their apex—is when Harey, a materialized image and at the same time a message resulting from the iconic exchange between Kris and Solaris, in turn develops an interactive process, using images that she visually perceives.

Typical of Tarkovsky's films is an insistent use of quotations: verbal ones (of the sort which we shall consider in regard to his next work, *Stalker*), but also—and above all—visual ones. In *Solaris* there are the copies of famous paintings, hanging on the walls of the space station and repeatedly focussed on, and three film inserts: the one documenting the Berton inquest; the audio-visual message which Gibarian records before his suicide for Kelvin's benefit; and the short of Kris as a child filmed by his father. The interpolation of these three makes for an implicit and suggestive parallel between the magical operations of Solaris and the possibilities which the cinema holds out for human beings. Like the products of the Unconscious materialized by the planet, the three film sequences bring the remote near and cause the past and even the dead to return (Gibarian, Kris's mother, the dog Kris had as a child).

These iconic moments make for the kind of dialectical interaction which goes along with intertextuality. The situation of intertextuality, as Juri Lotman points out, carries with it an "awakening of the text" and "a sense of the multiplying of meanings."

In Tarkovsky's *Solaris,* the most important of these moments concerns the short dealing with Kris's childhood (the only sequence among the three mentioned filmed in color). It works on a double level. As we shall see, it initiates in Harey the process by which she moves towards knowledge and humanization. At the same time, it has an indirect effect on Kris, who, thanks to her progress, modifies his vision of reality, a vision which he discovers to be penurious and dogmatic.

The only moving images that Harey observes on the screen as the short is being shown are the leaping, warm, red flames of a fire around which Kris's family is gathered in a snow-covered winter landscape. It is after viewing this footage that she regards the reproduction of Pieter Bruegel's *Hunters in the Snow* with intense concentration. It has hitherto frequently figured in the confines of the space station; but, as she attends to it now for the first time, it assumes for her a polyvalent significance, which

Tarkovsky forcefully brings home through a synthesis of images.

Certain comments that Ludwig Wittgenstein makes about visual perceptions prove to be especially helpful in explaining this peculiar, indeed unique, operation which takes place in Tarkovsky's film. The peculiarity lies in the fact that the author of the operation is an extraterrestrial possessing the natural language and cognitive capacities of an adult, but devoid of worldly experiences. The Austrian philosopher writes: "I contemplate a face and suddenly notice its likeness to another. I *see* that it has not changed; and yet I see it differently. I call this experience 'noticing an aspect' " (*Philosophical Investigations*). And again: "I meet someone whom I have not seen in years. I see him clearly; but fail to know him. Suddenly I know him, I see the old face in the altered one. I believe that I should do a different portrait of him now if I could paint."

This process exactly applies to Harey's case in regard to *Hunters in the Snow*. She notices the element which the painting has in common with the short she has viewed—snow—and this triggers an associative process that permits her to see the Bruegel in a different aspect. Here she is in the same position as the viewer of Solaris confronted with the phenomenon constituted by the planet's magmatic mass: faced with an image novel to her, she isolates certain of its properties, associates them with other images, and at the same time synthetizes their shared details so that they clarify and illuminate one another. Through the eye of the camera, which follows Harey's line of vision, the viewer sees on the screen segmented images of Bruegel's painting and footage from the short about Kris's childhood.

Unlike the latter's iconic message, the Bruegel, with its grey tonalities and its icy greens and whites, transmits a sense of cold, of solitude, of incommunicability. We see on the screen hunters (and their dogs), lugubrious and dark, men for whom the violent impulse which killing presupposes has nothing to do with a will to live, is not dictated by the necessity for survival; rather, they seem enclosed in an armor of ice which prevents contact with or comprehension of the Other. This central subject of the painting thus has a connection to Harey's own case: it relates to her impending dissolution in Sartorius's annihilator as victim of a cold ferocity that she obscurely senses but does not understand.

It is in this way that the "quotation" of Bruegel brings home to the viewer certain secondary meanings not evident in the painting by itself. Even more important, however, is the function that the painting has for Harey. Not only does it offer her a means (as the short does as well) of approaching a world and a past not her own. The use of a model, in this case the short on Kris's childhood, also allows her to connect the painting's message with her situation as victim and prey. At the same time, it permits her to organize a series of impressions and intuitions hitherto left without a unifying center (e.g., Kris's tender attitude and Sartorius's fixed destructive resolve).

The result of this process—silent only in the sense that it is not verbalized—is the resolution expressed in her explo-

sive attack on the bureaucrat Sartorius. This is the desperate protest of a being who senses that day by day she is becoming more and more human, but, like the planet that sent her, sees her right to live about to be abrogated in the name of the kind of science which upholds its dogmatic stasis by destroying the Alien.

The birth and death of Harey form part of the message that the planet transmits for the exclusive benefit of Kelvin. She is the living model which causes him to become aware of the obtuse and mechanical cruelty dominant in the world from which he originates. Yet the "cruel miracle" he passively awaits after losing a being whom he loved despite her Difference is not her resurrection, possible though that would be in this dimension. Instead, it is the unexpected materialization of another mental image, equivalent to the Unconscious because transmitting, through displacement, an analogous message.

This second, and again imperfect, model which the planet sends—and which Kris is able to decipher immediately—brings the viewer back to the initial scene of the film. As we look at what seems to be the water of the lake of the opening frames (it exhibits the same concentric movement), the camera slowly draws distant so that we perceive that what we are now seeing is an aquatic island, enveloped in its turn by the waters of Solaris, and on the island, old Kelvin's house drenched inside and out. The subsequent embrace between men from two generations is an event occurring far from Earth, on the space station, as the materialization of Kris's mental image; and this signals his acceptance of an Otherness less fantastic than Harey or the planet, though one that would have been incomprehensible to Kris before his extraordinary double experience.

This synthetic and polysemous final image has not been understood by those who claim that it represents "a submission to authority and to traditional social institutions" or "the archetype of power, the father figure," "a dour entity wrapped up in his logic of conservatism." Instead, the image's meaning is twofold, oscillating between the necessity of entrusting oneself to reassuring superior entities capable of performing miracles and the opening of a new vision of the world, a vision which discovers the richness of a reality full of possibilities. This ambivalence, central to the work of Gogol, Dostoyevsky, Bulgakov, and the Strugatskys, is what Tarkovsky recaptures in his film. The Soviet director apparently recovers both poles, utilizing one to the advantage of the other. His protagonist, through the planet's "cruel miracles" and the temporary escape into a "symmetrical" way of seeing which releases him from his too confining existential condition, projects himself towards a dynamic future in which there are no static and absolute verities.

Thanks to the film's artistic multidimensionality, the voyage embracing at once the cosmos and psychic reality is open to different interpretations. If Solaris is both a thinking planet and Kelvin's Unconscious, and if his dialogue with it is thus also a self-communication, then he is at once the intended addressee of a miracle and the active protagonist of a search beginning in the depths of his being but finally, once the dialogue gets under way, leading also to the Other. In this regard, it is significant that Kelvin is able to attain the infinite and creative potential hidden in himself only with the help of a fantastic and miraculous entity beyond him which compels him to establish with it a contact which he was not prepared for in advance.

Compared to *Solaris,* Tarkovsky's next film, freely adapted from the Strugatskys' *Roadside Picnic,* appears decidedly pessimistic. Absent from it is the kind of autonomous development which the preceding film represents as difficult, but not impossible—witness, for example, the independence that Kris's father attains.

Fundamental to the 1980 film is a complex interaction which amounts to what might be called the "*Solaris*-ation" of *Picnic,* and whose operation begins at the level of the scenario composed by a Tarkovsky who is the active and creative recipient of both books (i.e., Lem's and the Strugatskys'). *Stalker* resembles the Soviet director's version of *Solaris* in proposing a voyage into an animate space at once external and internal to the protagonist and modifiable according to his state of mind. That enterprise in this instance is not, however, imposed upon the characters, forced willy-nilly to come to terms with themselves; rather, it is an adventure desperately sought, yet useless; for no contact is established with the Alien and the world remains "a prison" governed by "iron laws" which "cannot be violated."

In considering *Stalker,* we can distinguish various phases of the film's conception. In the first, the director has utilized Lem's *Solaris* as a "subsidiary subject" or as a filter through which to see his main subject: the Strugatskys' novel serving as his point of departure. Thanks to the process of intertextual connection that Tarkovsky as Lem's and the Strugatskys' addressee performs, the technological treasures which in *Picnic* were retrieved from the Zone do not figure in the film's scenario. Nor do the black market, Red's weight of guilt, or the episode wherein Pilman explains his vision of the world along with the extraterrestrial mysteries. Furthermore, the eight years of the novel Tarkovsky compresses into a single day, one which has a double and antinomial valence: as the brief and decisive moment of the miracle which is simultaneously one of daily mechanical routine. The 24 hours lived by the Stalker are not fundamentally different from countless others repeatedly spent waiting-searching for something which never will happen. Then, too, the film deviates from *Picnic* (and also from Lem's *Solaris*) in regard to the status of the Alien; for as Tarkovsky himself stresses, it cannot certainly be concluded from *Stalker* that something actually can happen in the Zone—i.e., that the protagonist does not imagine everything.

For all its departures from the Strugatskys' book, the film nevertheless centers upon and reorganizes the last episode of *Picnic,* the one wherein Red, desperate over his daughter's illness, goes in search of the legendary Golden Ball, which according to rumor can grant everyone's deepest wishes. The Zone conceived by the Strugatskys impels introspection, just as Solaris does; and it is on this point which the Polish and Russian stories have in common that Tarkovsky concentrates *Stalker* (after abandoning a version "more faithful to *Picnic*" because he found it unsatisfying).

In the second phase of the film's conception, Tarkovsky draws not only upon Lem and the Strugatskys but also on passages from Dostoyevsky, Tjutchev, Lao Tze, the Gospels, and the Book of Revelation, all of which act as filters or magnifying lenses capable of bringing out new meanings and discoveries. With reference to Max Black's suggestive metaphor, we can say that in *Stalker* it is as if "the night sky," or the field of reality, were observed by Tarkovsky—and through him by viewers of his film—not with the naked eye directly but "through a piece of heavily smoked glass on which certain lines have been left clear." Thereby one "shall see only the stars that can be made to lie on the lines previously prepared upon the screen, and the stars . . . [one] do[es] see will be seen as organized by the screen's structure." Everything else is immediately eliminated.

The Stalker of the film, thanks to an interactive process within the film itself, is transformed from the simple and weak character whom the Strugatskys portray as attracted to adventure and lucre into a "ridiculous man." In his desire to escape from his existential prison, he is akin to Gogol's Poprishchin, to certain of Dostoyevsky's male personages, and in some ways to Bulgakov's Master. As his wife, addressing herself to the camera and thence to the spectators, says of the Stalker:

> Probably you have already understood that he is not normal. Everybody laughed at him and he was so lost, the poor thing. . . . But what could I do? I was sure I would have been okay with him. I knew there would be some bitter moments, but a bitter happiness is better than . . . a grey, boring life. . . . And if there weren't any suffering in our life, it wouldn't be better; it would be worse. Because then there wouldn't be any happiness either, and there wouldn't be hope even. . . .
>
> (*Stalker*)

What *Stalker*'s protagonist has in common with the Russian tradition of the fantastic in its Gogol-Dostoyevskian strain is his location at the margin of a rigid and ossified system, in a no man's land susceptible to centrifugal violent forces. Here a strong pressure against automatization exerts itself on the Stalker, also in the person of his wife. By her reflections on suffering, she articulates that impulse of a dialectic of opposites towards breaking the monotony of a mechanical and grey existence, an impulse previously given voice by the devil who is Ivan Karamazov's alter ego and then by Bulgakov's Woland.

The apparent alternative that presents itself in the face of the Stalker's despair is between an escape into a thaumaturgic dimension wherein to await an unforeseen resolutive event and an act of faith in the human possibilities hidden in the depths of one's being. In *Stalker,* however, the weight of everyday life is so crushing as to preclude that alternative. The threshold of the room where the protagonist believes the most secret desires can be fulfilled will not be crossed, and will not because no one dares confront the double risk that crossing it involves. If the miracle does not transpire, there will be nothing to believe in or hope for any longer. If, on the other hand, entering the room means acceding to the darkest part of oneself, the peril is of not being able to bear the shame of what one discovers.

In contrast to the Stalker's attitude, the reactions of the two intellectuals for whom he is supposed to act as guide—uncreative bureaucrats of science and literature—recapitulate the behavior of certain characters in Tarkovsky's *Solaris.* Like the Sartorius of that film, the scientist in *Stalker* wants to bomb out of existence an Otherness which does not fit the laws of his system. The writer, instead—who is closer to Gibarian—draws back so as "not to pour on anyone's head the loathing he has within," whereupon he would have "to put his head in a noose" (*Stalker*).

The Stalker, meanwhile, deprived of the possibilities allowed Kris Kelvin, restricts himself to dreaming of the Apocalypse and of a regeneration for which he would be not the architect but the Christ-like mediator; yet he cannot find within himself the courage to believe in this dream completely.

Still, one possibility remains open in the film. Its indicator is a passage from Lao Tze on the plasticity and flexibility of children. As Tarkovsky cites it in the *Stalker* filmscript, that quotation runs as follows:

> People are born weak and flexible; they die strong and obdurate. A growing tree is delicate and flexible; it perishes dry and strong. Rigidity and strength are the companions of death; weakness and elasticity express the freshness of being; what is unrigid will not be vanquished.

That idea, occupying in *Stalker* a place similar to the thought of Pilman's inserted in the middle of *Picnic* and then picked up at the end from Red's point of view, is likewise similarly crucial to understanding—in this case, particularly of the final frames of the film.

There, in a movement whose circularity, though only apparent, is nonetheless reminiscent of *The Childhood of Ivan* and *Solaris,* Tarkovsky ends the film where it began. From the luminous and colorful world of the Zone, we are returned to the squalor of an everyday existence rendered in black-and-white footage shading into tones of brown. Yet if the filthy and bemired village, the stagnant waters of the lake, and the house of the Stalker are essentially the same we see at the outset, they are not exactly so. For now the color footage which Tarkovsky (significantly enough) reserves for the sequences taking place within the Zone, with exception made (equally significantly) only for those moments when the point of view switches from the adults to the Stalker's daughter, Martyška, again briefly comes into play. As the mute and mutant Martyška, deprived of the use of her legs, is carried home on her father's shoulders from the bar where she had been taken to wait for him, we are suddenly and temporarily allowed to see the quotidian world completely transformed through her eyes. The hitherto polluted and dead surface of the lake, shot from above and as the girl sees it, suddenly appears bright and colorful, like the Zone.

The connection made here between Martyška and the lake ties *Stalker* in with Tarkovsky's previous films. It instances once again the "intratextual" association recurrent in the Soviet director's œuvre between images of water and childhood. His conjoining of the two, moreover, has an analogical basis—as he himself hints in his quotation of Lao Tze—which also points to the privileged status of childhood as a sanctuary from the mechanical rigidity of adult life. Hence the expanses of water so insistently present in *The Childhood of Ivan* and *Andrei Rublev* and transforming themselves into an entire living planet in *Solaris* have a metaphoric meaning. They image the elasticness, the inarrestibility, the dynamism which human beings are born with—the potential, also for apprehending the new, which figures in *Stalker*'s last scene.

Following the intervention of black-and-white, the color stock Tarkovsky has employed to shoot the lake from Martyška's point of view reappears. By that medium, we finally witness the long-awaited miracle. It takes place not within the Zone but outside it, in the realization of a wish capable of subduing the "iron laws" that none of the adults has been able to violate. What makes the miracle possible is not a material transference to forbidden territory (viz., the Zone), but the momentary escape into the world of art achieved by Martyška, who though she is, like Harey, an alien, is also a child and hence possesses a child's "elasticity."

In the sequence immediately preceding her "escape"—one of the last in the film—she appears silently absorbed in a book while on the soundtrack a voice, objectivizing her interior monologue, recites a lyric (untitled) by Tyutchev:

> I love your eyes, my love,
> Their wonderful, passionate play
> When suddenly you raise them
> And boldly cast your glance,
> Like skyborn lightning, about you.
> But there is a mightier magic:
> Of eyes to earth cast down
> All through a fervent kiss,
> And through the lowered lashes
> The sullen faint flame of desire.

The miracle performed by Martyška's glance, her eyes turned downward like the woman's in the poem, was the realization, through a process of displacement, of a desire which this alien, deprived of the use of her legs, is never able to fulfill otherwise. What she accomplishes by the exertion of mental energy is alone, from the standpoint of the dead mechanical world in which she lives, a prodigious feat, even if the result is equivalent to the effect produced on a glass by the noisy vibrations of a train in an opening scene of the film.

The small miracle that Martyška performs solely for her own benefit makes it clear to the viewer that the Zone is not some magical territory to be physically attained by passing through barbed-wire barriers. Rather, it is something existing everywhere, outside us and within, though this is lost sight of by the adults in *Stalker,* who are prisoners of a shabbily and rigidly one-dimensional world.

The Strugatskys' novel and Tarkovsky's film, though they differ from one another in language and point of view, share the same nucleus. Both problematically address the need to break out of the rigidity and automatism produced by all-encompassing dogmatic certainties and by models pretending to fit all situations. While pointing in somewhat different directions, the two works are thus instructively complementary. *Picnic* projects its search outwards via the indications of a scientist (Pilman) who, rather than seeking unshakable certitudes, wants to construct dynamic hypotheses, ones which can be extended and modified to explain ever new phenomena. Tarkovsky, instead, directs his investigations towards the interior of the individual above all, seeking to discover those uncontainable and infinite possibilities of a "symmetrical" being without which scientific and artistic creativity, and cognitive advances generally, could not occur. (pp. 294-304)

> Simonetta Salvestroni, "The Science-Fiction Films of Andrei Tarkovsky," in Science-Fiction Studies, *Vol. 14, No. 3, November, 1987, pp. 294-306.*

Valerie Z. Nollan   (review date Summer 1989)

[*In the following review of* Sculpting in Time, *Nollan commends Tarkovsky's insight into filmmaking and creativity.*]

Reading Andrei Tarkovskii's *Sculpting in Time* is a humbling experience, for the encounter with the profundity of the eminent Soviet filmmaker's insights into the creative mind leads to the conviction that one has touched the pinnacle of film criticism. In professing his feelings of inadequacy and amazement before the challenges of his art, Tarkovskii nevertheless shines in his exquisite articulation of such timeless concerns as the meaning and purpose of art, the intimate relationship between the artist and his audience, and the psychological process by which the film director transforms his creative vision into truthful images that remain, paradoxically, both typical and unique. Tarkovskii's "clandestine aim" in writing this book appears at the end of chapter I: "my hope is that those readers whom I manage to convince . . . may become kindred spirits, if only in recognition of the fact that I have no secrets from them." His tragic death in December 1986 makes this appeal even more poignant.

Tarkovskii's discussion interweaves theoretical and practical sections, the latter forming a verbal retrospective of his films. He returns repeatedly to the problem of film as an independent art form possessing a language all its own as well as a characteristic that sets it apart from other art forms, namely: the ability to appropriate time, along with "that material reality to which it is indissolubly bound." Permeating his comments is the notion that "searching" and "experimentation" fail to produce true art if the artist lacks a primary guiding vision. Tarkovskii similarly attaches utmost importance to spirituality in art; he relates this quality to the artist's unwavering focus on such issues as conscience and the quest for spiritual perfection and to his belief in his own moral and aesthetic principles. He castigates modern art precisely for its lack of spirituality, maintaining that the avant-garde has abandoned "the search for the meaning of existence" in its glorification of

the individual. He cites the Japanese haiku as a model for the utter purity and keen observation he seeks in his acknowledged "poetic" style of linking images.

The closing paragraph of the book crystallizes Tarkovskii's extraordinarily honest relationship with his readers, as well as his reverence towards the uncompromising, sacrificial creative act. We read, "Finally, I would enjoin the reader—confiding in him utterly—to believe that the one thing mankind has ever created in a spirit of self-surrender is the artistic image. Perhaps the meaning of all human activity lies in artistic consciousness, in the pointless and selfless creative act."

Like a Tarkovskii film, the book is well structured, containing nine chapters that flow smoothly between an introduction and a conclusion (all penned by Tarkovskii). The numerous stills from the director's films and photographs of him at work with his actors appear in appropriate places throughout the text. Further information is provided in the translator's brief notes at the end, and finally in the original texts of the cited poems by Arsenii Tarkovskii, the director's father.

Flaws in this book are rendered virtually unnoticeable by Kitty Hunter-Blair's elegant and seamless sculpting of the original Russian. My quibbles with her word choice concern the rare, though mildly jarring, intrusion of slang ("the event is . . . put together *any old how*" [and] "his conception will . . . *heel over*") and unidiomatic English ("*infringing the rules* of 'normal' behavior") into an otherwise impeccably crafted text.

Tarkovskii's critical work will be read eagerly not only by his devotees, but by all others who have an abiding, passionate interest in aesthetics and the human condition. (pp. 348-49)

> Valerie Z. Nollan, in a review of "Sculpting in Time: Reflections on the Cinema," in Slavic Review, *Vol. 48, No. 2, Summer, 1989, pp. 348-49.*

Jonathan Rosenbaum   (essay date July-August 1990)

[*In the following essay, Rosenbaum discusses the science-fictional elements and spirituality of* Solaris.]

It's taken nearly two decades for *Solaris* (1972), Andrei Tarkovsky's mind-boggling Soviet "reply" to *2001: A Space Odyssey,* to open in this country in its original form; but whatever doubts one might have about this beautiful film, I don't think that anyone could accuse it of being dated. Speculative technology plays such a minimal role in Tarkovsky's cosmology that state-of-the-art hardware and special effects are virtually irrelevant to his vision. (One quaint example of the former is the videotapes employed in the film; they all have the shape and size of audiocassettes, but the images they project are in black and white and 'Scope, and the video screens are correspondingly rectangular.) A handsome widescreen spectacle set in a remote galaxy, the movie expresses plenty of awe and terror about imponderables, but what's fundamentally at issue is the state of man's soul, not the physical state of the universe.

Having seen *Solaris* four times over the past 18 years, but only in its complete, 167-minute form, I can't detail the differences between this version and its mutilated predecessors circulating in the U.S. since 1976. I know that the original U.S. distributor hacked away 35 minutes without consulting Tarkovsky, and that subsequent prints making the repertory-theater rounds—partially dubbed and partially subtitled, cobbled together out of separate versions—were even shorter. Given the film's difficulties in its complete subtitled version, I have no doubt that *Solaris* in its truncated form must have been pretty incomprehensible.

Based on a Polish science-fiction novel of the same title by Stanislaw Lem, Tarkovsky's provocative head-scratcher can't really be "explained" to anyone's satisfaction by using the original source material as guide. A staunch nonbeliever in film genres ("I do not believe that cinema has genres—the cinema is *itself* a genre," he noted in a 1981 interview), Tarkovsky ironically regarded *Solaris* as the least successful of his films for probably the same reason that most people want to see it—because of its associations with science fiction. "Unfortunately the science-fiction element in *Solaris* was too prominent and became a distraction," he wrote in his fascinating (if maddening) book *Sculpting in Time.* "The rockets and space stations—required by Lem's novel—were interesting to construct; but it seems to me now that the idea of the film would have stood out more vividly and boldly had we managed to dispense with these things altogether."

Although portions of Tarkovsky's film defy synopsis, it is certainly possible to describe the main outlines of the plot, such as it is, with a minimal amount of surmise to fill in the gaps.

The film opens at the idyllic, rural childhood home of Kris Kelvin, a psychologist, who is back to visit his aging father and the latter's second wife before leaving on a space mission. He arrives with his little girl, who will apparently stay in the country during his absence, and there is a hint that Kelvin is hoping to resolve a conflict of some sort with his father before he leaves—a hope that is unfulfilled. There have been unexplained occurrences on the planet Solaris, where a permanently orbiting space station was established many decades ago; Kelvin has been asked to travel there alone to investigate, with the idea of closing down the station after subjecting the planet's oceanic surface to a final, exploratory burst of radiation.

Before Kelvin leaves, he is visited by Burton, one of the original Solaris crew members, who arrives with his little boy. Burton had been sent to explore the planet's misty, swirling surface some 20 years ago in search of Fechner, an astronaut who disappeared and was never found. With Burton, his father, and his stepmother, Kelvin watches a videotape of Burton's report on the mission to a scientific committee in which he describes sighting a 13-foot-high naked male child in a garden on the planet's surface. At this point in the report, Burton shows his own film of what he saw; all that is visible is cloud formations, and the committee dismisses his account as a hallucination brought about by strain. After the visit, however, on his way back to the city with his son, Burton calls back to the country

house on a videophone to report that 20 years ago, following the committee meeting, he went to visit Fechner's family: Fechner's son, whom he saw for the first time, was the spitting image of the child he had glimpsed on Solaris.

When Kelvin arrives at the ramshackle Solaris space station, he finds it nearly deserted. The two remaining scientists, Snouth and Sartorius, mainly stay cooped up in their laboratories and are unresponsive to most of Kelvin's questions; a third scientist, Gibarian, has committed suicide and left behind an enigmatic videotape addressed to Kelvin, which Kelvin plays back. (Much of this portion of the film seems steeped in a haunted-house atmosphere: squeaks and other offscreen sounds, and barely perceptible movements at the edges of the frame, along with the slow and suspenseful camera movements, all conjure up a sense of the uncanny without spelling it out.)

Eventually, Kelvin discovers that the amorphous surface of Solaris is a living entity, but not one that communicates directly. Rather, it materializes human figures drawn from the guilt-ridden memories and fantasies of the astronauts on the space station, so that each of them is literally accompanied by his own demon—a process that began after the astronauts first exposed the planet's surface to radiation. The various demons are glimpsed so elliptically that we know next to nothing about them: Sartorius is companioned in his own lab by a male dwarf in pajamas; Gibarian on his videotape is seen briefly with a little girl (who is occasionally seen wandering about the station, although Gibarian's corpse is now in cold storage); Snouth's demon appears at times to be an adult figure, although we perceive this figure so obliquely that we can't even be sure of that.

Kelvin's own demon appears in his cabin while he sleeps. We see a great deal of her; it is his dead wife Hari, who committed suicide on Earth after the failure of their marriage. Initially he is so horrified by her reappearance that he sends her off in a rocket, but she materializes before him again. Later she attempts suicide again by drinking liquid oxygen, but within moments she comes back to life in a series of spastic jerks. These and other resurrections of Hari occupy most of the remainder of the film. During this time, it becomes clear that her double is beginning to have an independent existence and feelings of her own, and Kelvin, who is now determined to remain on the space station indefinitely, struggles to make amends for his former lack of commitment to her. Finally, however, while he sleeps, she succeeds in destroying herself for Kelvin's sake, leaving behind a letter for him which she gives to Snouth.

Kelvin begins to think again about returning to Earth, and Snouth notes that islands are beginning to form on Solaris' oceanic surface. On one of these, we see Kelvin back beside the pond near his country house. Greeted by his dog, he approaches the house and peers through the window, making eye contact with his elderly father; rain is inexplicably falling inside the house, splattering books and teacups—a scene that clearly rhymes with a sudden rainfall outside the house in the film's opening sequence—and mist rises from his father as the water falls. Kelvin meets his father at the back door of the house, kneels at his feet and embraces him. The camera cranes upward, higher and higher, until we see the house on an island in the midst of Solaris' vast ocean.

The fact that we see so much of Hari on the space station and so little of the demons associated with the other astronauts can probably be traced back to the fact that Lem's novel is a first-person narrative. In keeping with this subjective emphasis, the entire film focuses on Kelvin's conscience and consciousness, and the objective side of the plot—everything that might be said to constitute the ingredients of a science-fiction adventure—gradually comes to seem like nothing but a pretext for telling Kelvin's individual story. In the final analysis, whether we interpret the final scene as a dream sequence is irrelevant; by this time the objective and subjective plots have become indistinguishable. The same ambiguity applies to certain previous sequences (omitted in my synopsis) in which the living room of Kelvin's country house merges with various parts of the space station to form an indissoluble whole.

Bearing this ambiguity in mind, one might argue that Tarkovsky's *Solaris,* unlike the Lem novel, qualifies more as anti-science fiction than as science fiction. In this respect it bears a certain resemblance to stories in Ray Bradbury's *The Martian Chronicles,* in which explorers on Mars hallucinate scenes and characters from their long-lost childhoods. A less obvious yet equally pertinent comparison can be made between Tarkovsky's vision and a book I consider the greatest of all science-fiction novels, Olaf Stapleton's *Star Maker* (1937)—a work that, significantly, has been cited with admiration by both Lem and Jorge Luis Borges, although it has never received much sustained attention in hardcore SF circles.

A speculative account of the entire history and breadth of the cosmos, *Star Maker* has a canvas so vast that the two-billion-year span of mankind, the focus of Stapleton's previous *Last and First Men* (1930), figures here in the space of less than a paragraph—a mere drop in the bucket. The crucial paradox underlying the book's awesome sweep is that the entire plot is framed by the mundane marital discord experienced by the human narrator. A rustic Englishman leaves his home in the midst of a quarrel to stand on a nearby hillside and gaze at the stars; here he experiences the entire narrative of the book in the form of a vision, before returning to the modesty and mundaneness of his individual life and problems.

Just as importantly, Stapleton's modest and humdrum prose becomes the vehicle for his staggering sense of the cosmic. While the contradictory conceit of most science-fiction writers trafficking in related subjects is that man can somehow think beyond the limitation of man's consciousness in imagining the cosmos, Stapleton's point of departure is precisely the reverse. Accepting the frailty and inadequacy of his vantage point at the outset, Stapleton proceeds to scale the heights like no other SF writer before or since, precisely because he knows how to use his limitations as an integral part of his descriptive technique.

Stapleton had a pronounced influence on Arthur C. Clarke, as one can detect in both Clarke's novel *Childhood's End* and the Clarke-Stanley Kubrick film *2001: A Space Odyssey.* But *2001,* which utilizes its resources to imagine an intelligence greater than man's, ultimately loses sight of the everyday underpinnings essential to Stapleton's vision. Tarkovsky's view, on the other hand—which is ultimately a good deal more conservative and pessimistic than either Clarke's or Stapleton's—uses the everyday not as a springboard into the cosmic but as a sign of man's inability to attain such reaches.

The fact that the only universe man can truly explore exists inside his own head is a key to Stapleton's technique (which Clarke and Kubrick learned from), but not to his vision. In the case of Tarkovsky, it becomes the irreducible message. So it is perfectly logical that Tarkovsky came to regret the science-fiction furnishings of *Solaris,* as provided by Lem, as a vehicle for his vision. We should note that Lem's novel is set exclusively on the space station; the action of the film is principally (if misleadingly) set there only so that Tarkovsky can ponder the significance of Kelvin's country house and family.

Consequently, in place of interstellar space travel, we get very slow pans past underwater plants swaying to drifting currents in the pond near this country house, and a lengthy hypnotic sequence that follows a car speeding along a freeway, through several long tunnels, and into a city as night falls. (The city is sufficiently anonymous that it could be almost anywhere—Los Angeles, Moscow, Tokyo, Berlin; no fully legible street signs are visible on the freeway.) Later, inside the space station the camera drifts endlessly across various details in a reproduction of Bruegel's *Hunters in the Snow* that is hanging, along with four other Bruegels, in a stateroom.

None of these meditative moments is motivated conventionally in narrative terms, although the first two are linked to narrative moments: Kris Kelvin brooding by the pond in which the underwater plants sway, and Burton returning from the country to the city with his son in a driverless car. (The selective survey of the Bruegel painting is "placed" retrospectively by a shot that occurs at the end, from a home movie that apparently shows Kelvin as a child in the snow.) To say that these moments effectively "replace" interstellar travel in the film is to suggest that they provide poetic rather than narrative substitutes—moments of seemingly endless drift that temporarily suspend the narrative flow. All of these camera movements mystically imply a continuous progress towards revelation that never actually arrives at one—a kind of spiritual tease. As in *Stalker*—probably Tarkovsky's greatest film, another work adapted from a science-fiction novel that uses the genre's come-on, the notion and promise of infinity, only to frustrate this expectation with an insistence on man's finitude and the poverty of the human imagination—the external journey of the plot, which we see, proves to be secondary to the inner journey of the characters, which we don't see. Bits of electronic music figure effectively in Eduard Artemev's score, but the essential theme is Bach's F Minor Choral Prelude.

Another level of ambiguity is introduced by periodic shifts between color and black-and-white. As in most of the director's other features (apart from *Andrei Roublev,* which shifts to color only in its epilogue), few of these switches can be accounted for by any consistent thematic, formal, or atmospheric strategy. A joke used to circulate in Russia that Tarkovsky shifted from color to black-and-white whenever he ran out of money, and other Russian directors have, by their own admission, occasionally switched to black-and-white in midfilm when they ran out of color stock. In the case of *Solaris,* some of these transitions occur *in the middle of* individual shots, which rules out any economic motivation. Whether the reasons behind them are conceptual or arbitrary, the shifts have the overall effect of intensifying the private and esoteric aspects of Tarkovsky's style—aspects that are clearly related to his spirituality.

To me, at least, the notion of spirituality in film art has always had something more than a little suspect about it. Filmmakers as diverse as Robert Bresson, Carl Dreyer, Leo McCarey, Kenji Mizoguchi, Yasujiro Ozu, Jean Renoir, Roberto Rossellini, and Michael Snow are frequently praised for their allegedly "transcendental" styles when it seems more appropriate to value them for qualities that suggest the opposites of spirituality and transcendence: the brute materiality of the worlds of Mizoguchi and Renoir, the physicality of McCarey and Ozu, the carnal sense of flesh in Bresson and Dreyer, the skepticism of Rossellini, the relentless mechanisms of Snow. If "pure" transcendence is what one is after, I'm afraid that even the more bogus spirituality of Disney, DeMille, and Spielberg may come closer to the mark.

I'm not trying to argue that a filmmaker's religious beliefs are irrelevant to his or her art. But it does seem to me that none of the best filmmakers requires religious beliefs in order to be understood or appreciated. Bresson's Jansenism may play some role in the selection and shaping of his plots, but divine providence is evident in neither the sounds nor the images of *Au hasard Balthazar,* and both *Lancelot du lac* and *L'argent* can easily be read as atheistic. Conversely, Dreyer's *Ordet* and Rossellini's *Viaggio in Italia (Strangers)* may both conclude with religious miracles, but this doesn't mean that Dreyer or Rossellini necessarily believes in them *as* religious miracles; both filmmakers, in fact, have made statements that suggest the contrary. John Huston's remarkably precise film adaptation of Flannery O'Connor's novel *Wise Blood* is the work of a believer "translated" by a nonbeliever, and there is nothing in the film that suggests any obvious sort of betrayal.

But when we come to a spiritual filmmaker like Tarkovsky, the question of acceptance or rejection becomes more complicated. I have to confess that, as a thinker about spiritual and holy matters, Tarkovsky often strikes me as pretentious, egocentric, and downright offensive; his sexual politics (especially in *Nostalghia* and *The Sacrifice*) are Neanderthal, and his view of piety is generally neither attractive nor inspiring. Yet as a passionate, critical thinker about the world we live in, and as a poetic filmmaker whose images and sounds have the ring of truth, I find it impossible to dismiss him. Even when his films irritate or infuriate me, they teach me something in spite of my objections.

Several years ago, in *American Film,* J. Hoberman offered an intriguing three-way comparison of Tarkovsky, Stan Brakhage, and Hans-Jürgen Syberberg as conservative avant-gardists:

> All are seers who see their art—and all of Art— as a quasi-religious calling; all three tend toward the solipsistic, invoking their parents, mates, and offspring as talismanic elements in their films. All three are natural surrealists, seemingly innocent of official surrealism's radical social program. All three privilege childhood innocence . . . and all three are militantly provincial. Tarkovsky is as hopelessly Russian as Syberberg is terminally German and Brakhage totally American.

Hoberman's comparison is instructive, but I'd like to suggest another parallel figure for consideration whose formal originality and problematic ideology are equally relevant: David Lynch. This is not to suggest that the ideologies of Lynch and Tarkovsky are in any way equivalent: if *Solaris* can be considered as a "humanistic" response to *2001,* there is certainly nothing humanistic in the same way or to the same degree about *Eraserhead, Dune, Blue Velvet, Twin Peaks,* or even *The Elephant Man.* Yet virtually all of the attributes assigned by Hoberman to his trio—to which one might add the equally salient trait of male chauvinism—apply to Lynch as well.

I'm not claiming that Tarkovsky's films "transcend" their sexism or their arrogance; these qualities remain, along with the films' beauties and genuine profundities, and no theory can shake them loose. But they are serious in a way and to a degree that is rare in contemporary movies, and their shortcomings are never a matter of aesthetic compromise or philosophical floundering—both of which can be found in some of Lynch's commercial efforts.

It might be added that misogyny plays a less pronounced role in *Solaris* than in some of Tarkovsky's other features, in part because of the strength and impact of Natalya Bondarchuk's remarkably nuanced performance as Hari. Kelvin's conscience may be the film's subject, but it is Hari's character that provides the film with its own conscience. Next to her, all the male astronauts register as so many blocks of wood—even (or, perhaps, especially) when they are engaged in heated philosophical discussions, which is often.

Like HAL, the computer in *2001,* Hari doesn't qualify as "human" to the same degree as the other characters. But this doesn't prevent her repeated deaths and resurrections from being highly affecting—tragic, disturbing, appalling—much as HAL's death in *2001* winds up moving one more than any of the human deaths in that film. Hari may be, like HAL, nothing more than a human projection that has gained a certain lonely autonomy. But like HAL she winds up providing us with a powerful lesson about what it means to be human, and what it means to die. (pp. 57-8, 60, 62)

Jonathan Rosenbaum, "Inner Space," in Film Comment, *Vol. 26, No. 4, July-August, 1990, pp. 57-8, 60, 62.*

James Saynor (review date 21 July 1991)

[*In the following review, Saynor unfavorably appraises* Time within Time.]

Russia's Andrei Tarkovsky, the director of films such as *Mirror, Stalker* and *The Sacrifice,* was the ultimate 'high concept' movie-maker, but hardly in the way the expression is used to describe a film in Hollywood ('*Batman* meets *9½ Weeks*'). Tarkovsky's elevated notions took hold of cinema—that most clumsy and mechanistic-seeming of art-forms—and tried to catapult it into realms so rarefied it might make the angels dizzy.

It is better to see a film once than read about it ten times.

—Andrei Tarkovsky, in an interview with Nicholas Wapshott, in The Times *(London), 1981.*

To him, a film was not a story, a moving painting, a set of symbols or a carrier of ideology. It was nothing less than a hot-line to the meaning of life—to the infinite, the spiritually transcendent, the morally pure, the death-surmounting. To him, the poet-filmmaker was potentially a high priest of all understanding, drawing together the skeins of art, philosophy, religion, science, mysticism and psychology in order to share an ante-room with God and help 'create the world'. As an artist, Tarkovsky made no bones about going for the metaphysical grand slam.

Did he get anywhere near it? Were his films, with their imagistic, free-association meanderings, cinematic epiphanies or shamanistic evasions? Was Tarkovsky a selfless visionary or an indulgent monomaniac? After being marginalised by the authorities—though kept on the payroll—during the pre-Gorbachev era (he died in Paris, at 54, in 1986), Tarkovsky is now lionised in the USSR. Over here, where critics are suspicious of formally intimidating works and grandstanding maestros, his status is more uncertain. For this reviewer, his highly oxygenated movies, with their time-bends and chimerical passages of memory and reverie, never fail to recharge the aesthetic cells for all their baleful obscurities. But Tarkovsky's high-minded pontifications can be off-putting, and [*Time within Time: The Diaries of Andrey Tarkovsky*], covering the period 1970 to 1986, won't make him more palatable to the sceptics.

This hotch-potch of jottings reveals a psyche prone to terrifying mood-swings, 'God! How utterly wretched I feel! To the point of nausea, to the point of hanging myself,' he rails at one point. 'Everyone has betrayed me or will betray me.' A week later: 'In this world, everything is possible.' Two thirds of the material consists of bitterness or outright bile—against the nightmarish Moscow officialdom ('inveterate liars, time-servers, crooks'), against contemporary Soviet film-making ('a slough of vapid, boot-

licking muck'), even against his own film students ('a dim lot'). He's a dab hand at snappy philosophy-bites on the quest for the absolute ('Anyone who does not aspire to greatness of soul is worthless; as insignificant as a field mouse'), yet this moral grandeur cohabits with niggly misanthropy ('I can't bear seeing people express their feelings . . . ') He's got the Great Artist blues, with a vengeance.

The diaries are short on anecdotes and continuous narrative, long on epigrams and whingeing. They're hopelessly badly annotated, and full of massive lacunae—notably, the period from mid-1982 to mid-1984, as Tarkovsky shoots *Nostalgia* in Italy and prepares to quit the USSR for good. Like one of his films, this book will be dense and elliptical to the uninitiated; in fact, only Tarkovsky-buffs will be able to make head or tail of it. Neophytes would be best advised to start off with his inspiriting essays, *Sculpting in Time,* before even attempting this volume.

James Saynor, "Deep Blues for Buffs," in The Observer, *July 21, 1991, p. 54.*

Euan Cameron (review date 27 July 1991)

[*In the following review, Cameron commends* Time within Time *for the insight it provides into Tarkovsky's works.*]

In December 1975, in his last diary entry for that year, Andrey Tarkovsky quotes Stendhal: 'Life is very short, and it ought not to be spent crawling at the feet of miserable scoundrels.' Tarkovsky never crawled to anyone, but throughout [*Time within Time: The Diaries of Andrey Tarkovsky*], which begin in 1970 and end with his death at the age of 54 in 1986, the great Russian film director repeatedly records his impotent fury and frustration with the Soviet authorities who, at a time when juries in the West were awarding prizes to films such as *Andrey Roubliev* and *Solaris,* refused to allow him to work, considered his powerful autobiographical film, *Mirror,* 'subversive' and did their best to prevent it from being shown in public.

Tarkovsky's early optimism after the success of his early films had given way to a Chekhovian despair. He was deeply unhappy, forever in debt, worried about everything from his lack of recognition to the cost of furnishing his *dacha;* above all, he felt humiliated by the authorities' treatment of *Mirror.* The dejection was only lifted by thoughts of his baby son and by the relative peace of his *dacha* at Myasnoye. In many ways Tarkovsky saw himself as a 'martyr' to the stifling Soviet system (indeed the title to one of the diaries in Russian is 'Martyrolog', 'pretentious and false as a title', he later notes, 'but let it stay there as a reminder of my ineradicable, futile worthlessness'), and scarcely a month passes without his registering his bitterness towards the bureaucrats who infringe artistic freedom, who are 'frightened by real art', and who are destroying Russia and making life unbearable.

Tarkovsky's problems with the Goskino reach a crescendo towards the end of 1979. He is 'surrounded by hatred, stupidity, selfishness and destruction'. He writes, 'The year is finishing, full of unresolved anxieties, unrealised dreams, and plans which are leading no one knows where.' Some sort of escape—death or exile—seem the only course, and as we read these absorbing diaries we witness the pendulum of fate swinging inevitably towards a climax that culminated with the press conference in Milan in July 1984 at which he announced his defection, the filming of his last work, *Sacrifice* in Sweden, the agonised waiting for his 14-year-old son to be finally released, and his death in Paris at the end of 1986.

It is unlikely that these diaries were ever intended for publication by their author, and they have probably been considerably edited. They are at once a record of the working life of a film director many consider to be a genius and a commonplace book in which Tarkovsky jots down ideas and quotations that please him (e.g. from the Bible, Chaadayev, Chekhov, Hesse, Dostoievsky, Thoreau, Tolstoy). On a deeper level, however, this book records a quest for faith in which we recognise the essential motivation for all his work.

The appeal of Tarkovsky's films is perhaps a rarefied one, but it knows no frontiers of ideology or class. Tarkovsky's admirers came from all walks of life, as was obvious to anyone who attended the lectures he gave in London in 1984. He had about him the charisma of a guru, and for his acolytes his films, his book, *Sculpting in Time,* and his public utterances were crucially important simply because in a confused world they seemed to contain the essence of truth. The experience of watching a Tarkovsky film, obscure and 'difficult' for some, is for others a profound one. In the manner of all great art, the films are demanding and one does not expect to be entertained, but for his admirers they provide an intense emotional experience of an intellectual truth.

Many scenes in Tarkovsky's films are like snatches of dreams, and it is fascinating to read his detailed descriptions of dreams and nightmares that are haunting and remarkably vivid. Spiritual reflections apart, these diaries give us Tarkovsky's *aide-mémoires;* verbatim letters to the authorities; gossip about his friends and fierce remarks about others; his reading (Hesse, 'with whom I have so much in common', Mann, Shaw, Ibsen, Lorca); complimentary comments about his films (there was clearly a need for acclaim, which he was never given officially until after his death); the amounts earned from lectures; the state of his health (often delicate). He is a bit of a Jeremiah, constantly bemoaning the 'spiritual deficiency' of his homeland where he is surrounded by 'lies, cant and death', and even in England he notes a friend's comment that 'money and make-believe [are] replacing the life of the spirit'. With some satisfaction, one feels, he quotes Dostoievsky

> . . . the Paris Commune and Western socialism
> do not want the best people, they want equality,
> and would chop off the head of a Shakespeare or
> a Raphael,

and there is some disenchantment with the West where, he notes, 'anything is allowed, provided that "anything" can be sold.' And he has little time for any of his fellow filmmakers: Bondarchuk's *Waterloo* is 'embarrassing',

Bunuel's *Tristana,* 'vulgar', Bertolucci's *La Luna* 'cheap and vulgar', Fellini's 'last film is a disaster', while a film by Jancso is 'monstrous rubbish'. Only Bresson, who 'is afraid of nothing', escapes such condemnation.

In Italy the gloomy introspection lifts and his entries for 1980 record a busier life in which he is given the recognition that should always have been his due. He is making *Tempo di Viaggio,* working on the script of *Nostalghia,* and forming a close friendship with Tonino Guerra. Italy enchants and inspires him, as it does the hero of *Nostalghia,* but soon, like the character Gorchakov, who was based on the 18th-century composer Beryozovsky, and like many a Russian émigré before him, he becomes acutely homesick. In that film Gorchakov lights a candle as he walks towards his death. In this book Kitty Hunter-Blair's fluent translation brings us closer to Tarkovsky than one would have thought possible and ensures that the candle he lit will continue to burn brightly.

> *Euan Cameron, "Full of Woe," in* The Spectator, *Vol. 267, No. 8506, July 27, 1991, p. 34.*

FURTHER READING

Cameron, Euan. "Guardian of the Spirit." *The Spectator* 258, No. 8270 (10 January 1987): 28-9.
    Announces Tarkovsky's death and discusses his career and artistic outlook.

Dryansky, G. Y. "Tarkovsky's Seventh." *Connoisseur* (April 1986): 100-05.
    Biographical and critical overview of Tarkovsky's career through *The Sacrifice.*

"The Power of Providence and the Power of Films." *The Economist* 299, No. 7448 (31 May 1986): 95, 99.
    Discusses *Sculpting in Time* and provides a brief overview of Tarkovsky's films.

Fedorowskij, Natan. "Tarkovsky Reflects: Dreams and Reality of a Soviet Filmmaker." *World Press Review* 31, No. 5 (May 1984): 75.
    Brief introductory overview of Tarkovsky's career, excerpted from the *Frankfurter Allgemeine.*

Green, Peter. "The Nostalgia of the Stalker." *Sight and Sound* 54, No. 1 (Winter 1984-85): 50-4.
    Examines the theme of nostalgia, or longing for a desired place, in *Nostalghia* and *Stalker.*

———. "Andrei Tarkovsky (1932-1986)." *Sight and Sound* 56, No. 2 (Spring 1987): 108-09.
    Biographical and critical overview of Tarkovsky.

Johnson, Vida T., and Petrie, Graham. "Andrei Tarkovskii's Films." *Journal of European Studies* 20, No. 79 (September 1990): 265-77.
    Reviews seven books on Tarkovsky and discusses the critical reception of his works.

Kennedy, Harlan. "Tarkovsky: A Thought in Nine Parts." *Film Comment* 23, No. 3 (May-June 1987): 44-6.

Reflects on Tarkovsky's unconventional style of movie-making. Kennedy concludes: "[Most Western cinema today] is rerunning all its old movies under the guise of new movies. . . . Tarkovsky, and his peers and precursors in the pre-populist European cinema, suggested that life should be a struggle toward the uncomfortable light, never a surrender to the comforting dark (of womb or movie theater). He set an example we will surely eventually follow. Out of boredom, if not malnutrition, the movie world will eventually realize that man cannot live by popcorn alone."

Kennedy Op, Marie-Humbert. "The Art of Tarkovsky." *The Month* 21, Nos. 8-9 (August 1988): 836-39.

Review of *Sculpting in Time* that provides a brief overview of Tarkovsky's career.

Le Fanu, Mark. "Bresson, Tarkovsky, and Contemporary Pessimism." *The Cambridge Quarterly* XIV, No. 1 (1985): 51-9.

Discusses the pessimistic outlook of Robert Bresson's *L'Argent* and Tarkovsky's *Nostalghia.*

——. *The Cinema of Andrei Tarkovsky.* London: BFI Publishing, 1987, 156 p.

Comprehensive critical study of Tarkovsky. Le Fanu examines Tarkovsky's place in Russian cinema, his early life and student films, and each of his major works. Includes a filmography.

——. "Sitting on an Anthill." *The Observer,* No. 10,427 (18 August 1991): 51.

Review of the translated script of *Andrei Rublev.*

Leszczylowski, Michal. "A Year with Andrei." *Sight and Sound* 56, No. 4 (Autumn 1987): 282-84.

Reminisces about working with Tarkovsky during the production of *The Sacrifice.*

Malcolm, Derek. "Poet of World Cinema." *The Guardian* (30 December 1986): 10.

Obituary notice and brief overview of Tarkovsky's career.

Marshall, Herbert. "Andrei Tarkovsky's *The Mirror.*" *Sight and Sound* 45, No. 2 (Spring 1976): 92-5.

Discusses the style and subject matter of *The Mirror* and examines the film's critical reception in the Soviet Union.

Matusevich, Vladimir B. "Tarkovsky's Apocalypse." *Sight and Sound* 50, No. 1 (Winter 1980): 8-9.

Discusses *Stalker,* focusing on Tarkovsky's difficulties with Soviet cultural authorities.

Mitchell, Tony. "Tarkovsky in Italy." *Sight and Sound* 52, No. 1 (Winter 1982-83): 54-6.

Discusses the work in progress on *Nostalghia* and reprints comments Tarkovsky made at the 1982 Cinema

Thieves conference about the films that had made the greatest impression on him.

——. "Andrei Tarkovsky and *Nostalghia.*" *Film Criticism* XI, Nos. 1-2 (Fall 1987): 101-10.

Discusses Tarkovsky's career and explicates the themes and plot of *Nostalghia.*

Petric, Vlada. "Tarkovsky's Dream Imagery." *Film Quarterly* XLIII, No. 2 (Winter 1989-90): 28-34.

Examines the dream imagery of Tarkovsky's films, focusing primarily on *The Mirror* and *Stalker.*

Ratschewa, Maria. "The Messianic Power of Pictures: The Films of Andrei Tarkovsky." *Cineaste* XIII, No. 1 (1983): 27-9.

Brief introductory overview and assessment of Tarkovsky's career.

Robinson, David. "Andrei Tarkovsky: 'I Am Not Guilty'." *The Times* (London), No. 61,880 (11 July 1984): 14.

Focuses on Tarkovsky's decision to seek asylum in the West.

——. "Noble Obsession with the Waters of Sacrifice." *The Times* (London), No. 62,151 (30 May 1985): 8.

Discusses Tarkovsky's work on *The Sacrifice.*

——. "Sculptor in Time, Master of Spirit." *The Times* (London), No. 62,656 (3 January 1987): 16.

Notice of Tarkovsky's death, focusing on his artistic philosophies and contributions to Soviet filmmaking.

Shchepotinnik, Peter. "With *Perestroika,* without Tarkovsky." *New Orleans Review* 17, No. 1 (Spring 1990): 79-83.

Discussion of the current state of Soviet cinema by an editor at *Iskusstvo Kino,* a leading Soviet film journal. Shchepotinnik comments: "At the moment, not all is well with our film geniuses. We are still living with the gradually fading light following Tarkovsky's death. Until recently his unique presence set the standard of spirituality (a purely Russian notion!) toward which all our directors tended, for they had before their eyes an example of supreme craftsmanship, philosophic profundity, and artistic obsession. We now see only rare reflections of his style. . . ."

Strick, Philip. "Tarkovsky's Translations." *Sight and Sound* 50, No. 3 (Summer 1981): 152-53.

Report of an interview with Tarkovsky in which he clarifies several misconceptions about his films.

Wapshott, Nicholas. "Another Stunner from Moscow." *The Times* (London), No. 60,846 (7 February 1981): 14.

Announcement of the release of *Stalker,* including numerous quotes from Tarkovsky.

Additional coverage of Tarkovsky's life and career is contained in the following source published by Gale Research: *Contemporary Authors,* Vol. 127.

☐ Contemporary Literary Criticism

Indexes

Literary Criticism Series
Cumulative Author Index
Cumulative Nationality Index
Title Index, Volume 75

How to Use This Index

The main references

Calvino, Italo
1923-1985.....CLC 5, 8, 11, 22, 33, 39,
73; SSC 3

list all author entries in the following Gale Literary Criticism series:

CLC = *Contemporary Literary Criticism*
CLR = *Children's Literature Review*
CMLC = *Classical and Medieval Literature Criticism*
DC = *Drama Criticism*
LC = *Literature Criticism from 1400 to 1800*
NCLC = *Nineteenth-Century Literature Criticism*
PC = *Poetry Criticism*
SSC = *Short Story Criticism*
TCLC = *Twentieth-Century Literary Criticism*

The cross-references

See also CANR 23; CA 85-88;
obituary CA 116

list all author entries in the following Gale biographical and literary sources:

AAYA = *Authors & Artists for Young Adults*
AITN = *Authors in the News*
BLC = *Black Literature Criticism*
BW = *Black Writers*
CA = *Contemporary Authors*
CAAS = *Contemporary Authors Autobiography Series*
CABS = *Contemporary Authors Bibliographical Series*
CANR = *Contemporary Authors New Revision Series*
CAP = *Contemporary Authors Permanent Series*
CDALB = *Concise Dictionary of American Literary Biography*
CDBLB = *Concise Dictionary of British Literary Biography*
DLB = *Dictionary of Literary Biography*
DLBD = *Dictionary of Literary Biography Documentary Series*
DLBY = *Dictionary of Literary Biography Yearbook*
HW = *Hispanic Writers*
MAICYA = *Major Authors and Illustrators for Children and Young Adults*
MTCW = *Major 20th-Century Writers*
SAAS = *Something about the Author Autobiography Series*
SATA = *Something about the Author*
WLC = *World Literature Criticism, 1500 to the Present*
YABC = *Yesterday's Authors of Books for Children*

Literary Criticism Series
Cumulative Author Index

Appleton, Lawrence
See Lovecraft, H(oward) P(hillips)

Apuleius, (Lucius Madaurensis)
125(?)-175(?) . . . . **CMLC 1**

Aquin, Hubert 1929-1977 . . . . **CLC 15**
See also CA 105; DLB 53

Aragon, Louis 1897-1982 . . . . **CLC 3, 22**
See also CA 69-72; 108; CANR 28;
DLB 72; MTCW

Arany, Janos 1817-1882 . . . . **NCLC 34**

Arbuthnot, John 1667-1735 . . . . **LC 1**
See also DLB 101

Archer, Herbert Winslow
See Mencken, H(enry) L(ouis)

Archer, Jeffrey (Howard) 1940- . . . . **CLC 28**
See also BEST 89:3; CA 77-80; CANR 22

Archer, Jules 1915- . . . . **CLC 12**
See also CA 9-12R; CANR 6; SAAS 5;
SATA 4

Archer, Lee
See Ellison, Harlan

Arden, John 1930- . . . . **CLC 6, 13, 15**
See also CA 13-16R; CAAS 4; CANR 31;
DLB 13; MTCW

Arenas, Reinaldo 1943-1990 . . . . **CLC 41**
See also CA 124; 128; 133; HW

Arendt, Hannah 1906-1975 . . . . **CLC 66**
See also CA 17-20R; 61-64; CANR 26;
MTCW

Aretino, Pietro 1492-1556 . . . . **LC 12**

Arguedas, Jose Maria
1911-1969 . . . . **CLC 10, 18**
See also CA 89-92; DLB 113; HW

Argueta, Manlio 1936- . . . . **CLC 31**
See also CA 131; HW

Ariosto, Ludovico 1474-1533 . . . . **LC 6**

Aristides
See Epstein, Joseph

Aristophanes
450B.C.-385B.C. . . . . **CMLC 4; DC 2**

Arlt, Roberto (Godofredo Christophersen)
1900-1942 . . . . **TCLC 29**
See also CA 123; 131; HW

Armah, Ayi Kwei 1939- . . . . **CLC 5, 33**
See also BLC 1; BW; CA 61-64; CANR 21;
DLB 117; MTCW

Armatrading, Joan 1950- . . . . **CLC 17**
See also CA 114

Arnette, Robert
See Silverberg, Robert

Arnim, Achim von (Ludwig Joachim von
Arnim) 1781-1831 . . . . **NCLC 5**
See also DLB 90

Arnim, Bettina von 1785-1859 . . . . **NCLC 38**
See also DLB 90

Arnold, Matthew
1822-1888 . . . . **NCLC 6, 29; PC 5**
See also CDBLB 1832-1890; DLB 32, 57;
WLC

Arnold, Thomas 1795-1842 . . . . . . **NCLC 18**
See also DLB 55

Arnow, Harriette (Louisa) Simpson
1908-1986 . . . . **CLC 2, 7, 18**
See also CA 9-12R; 118; CANR 14; DLB 6;
MTCW; SATA 42, 47

Arp, Hans
See Arp, Jean

Arp, Jean 1887-1966 . . . . **CLC 5**
See also CA 81-84; 25-28R

Arrabal
See Arrabal, Fernando

Arrabal, Fernando
1932- . . . . **CLC 2, 9, 18, 58, 73**
See also CA 9-12R; CANR 15

Arrick, Fran . . . . **CLC 30**

Artaud, Antonin 1896-1948 . . . . . **TCLC 3, 36**
See also CA 104

Arthur, Ruth M(abel) 1905-1979 . . . . **CLC 12**
See also CA 9-12R; 85-88; CANR 4;
SATA 7, 26

Artsybashev, Mikhail (Petrovich)
1878-1927 . . . . **TCLC 31**

Arundel, Honor (Morfydd)
1919-1973 . . . . **CLC 17**
See also CA 21-22; 41-44R; CAP 2;
SATA 4, 24

Asch, Sholem 1880-1957 . . . . **TCLC 3**
See also CA 105

Ash, Shalom
See Asch, Sholem

Ashbery, John (Lawrence)
1927- . . . **CLC 2, 3, 4, 6, 9, 13, 15, 25, 41**
See also CA 5-8R; CANR 9, 37; DLB 5;
DLBY 81; MTCW

Ashdown, Clifford
See Freeman, R(ichard) Austin

Ashe, Gordon
See Creasey, John

Ashton-Warner, Sylvia (Constance)
1908-1984 . . . . **CLC 19**
See also CA 69-72; 112; CANR 29; MTCW

Asimov, Isaac
1920-1992 . . . . **CLC 1, 3, 9, 19, 26**
See also BEST 90:2; CA 1-4R; 137;
CANR 2, 19, 36; CLR 12; DLB 8;
MAICYA; MTCW; SATA 1, 26

Astley, Thea (Beatrice May)
1925- . . . . **CLC 41**
See also CA 65-68; CANR 11

Aston, James
See White, T(erence) H(anbury)

Asturias, Miguel Angel
1899-1974 . . . . **CLC 3, 8, 13**
See also CA 25-28; 49-52; CANR 32;
CAP 2; DLB 113; HW; MTCW

Atares, Carlos Saura
See Saura (Atares), Carlos

Atheling, William
See Pound, Ezra (Weston Loomis)

Atheling, William Jr.
See Blish, James (Benjamin)

Atherton, Gertrude (Franklin Horn)
1857-1948 . . . . **TCLC 2**
See also CA 104; DLB 9, 78

Atherton, Lucius
See Masters, Edgar Lee

Atkins, Jack
See Harris, Mark

Atticus
See Fleming, Ian (Lancaster)

Atwood, Margaret (Eleanor)
1939- . . . . **CLC 2, 3, 4, 8, 13, 15, 25, 44;**
SSC 2
See also BEST 89:2; CA 49-52; CANR 3,
24, 33; DLB 53; MTCW; SATA 50; WLC

Aubigny, Pierre d'
See Mencken, H(enry) L(ouis)

Aubin, Penelope 1685-1731(?) . . . . **LC 9**
See also DLB 39

Auchincloss, Louis (Stanton)
1917- . . . . **CLC 4, 6, 9, 18, 45**
See also CA 1-4R; CANR 6, 29; DLB 2;
DLBY 80; MTCW

Auden, W(ystan) H(ugh)
1907-1973 . . . . . **CLC 1, 2, 3, 4, 6, 9, 11,**
14, 43; PC 1
See also CA 9-12R; 45-48; CANR 5;
CDBLB 1914-1945; DLB 10, 20; MTCW;
WLC

Audiberti, Jacques 1900-1965 . . . . . . **CLC 38**
See also CA 25-28R

Auel, Jean M(arie) 1936- . . . . **CLC 31**
See also AAYA 7; BEST 90:4; CA 103;
CANR 21

Auerbach, Erich 1892-1957 . . . . **TCLC 43**
See also CA 118

Augier, Emile 1820-1889 . . . . **NCLC 31**

August, John
See De Voto, Bernard (Augustine)

Augustine, St. 354-430 . . . . **CMLC 6**

Aurelius
See Bourne, Randolph S(illiman)

Austen, Jane
1775-1817 . . . . **NCLC 1, 13, 19, 33**
See also CDBLB 1789-1832; DLB 116;
WLC

Auster, Paul 1947- . . . . **CLC 47**
See also CA 69-72; CANR 23

Austin, Mary (Hunter)
1868-1934 . . . . **TCLC 25**
See also CA 109; DLB 9, 78

Autran Dourado, Waldomiro
See Dourado, (Waldomiro Freitas) Autran

Averroes 1126-1198 . . . . **CMLC 7**
See also DLB 115

Avison, Margaret 1918- . . . . **CLC 2, 4**
See also CA 17-20R; DLB 53; MTCW

Ayckbourn, Alan
1939- . . . . **CLC 5, 8, 18, 33, 74**
See also CA 21-24R; CANR 31; DLB 13;
MTCW

Aydy, Catherine
See Tennant, Emma (Christina)

Ayme, Marcel (Andre) 1902-1967 . . . **CLC 11**
See also CA 89-92; CLR 25; DLB 72

Ayrton, Michael 1921-1975 . . . . **CLC 7**
See also CA 5-8R; 61-64; CANR 9, 21

Bart, Andre Schwarz
See Schwarz-Bart, Andre

Barth, John (Simmons)
1930- . . . . . . **CLC 1, 2, 3, 5, 7, 9, 10, 14,**
27, 51; SSC 10
See also AITN 1, 2; CA 1-4R; CABS 1;
CANR 5, 23; DLB 2; MTCW

Barthelme, Donald
1931-1989 . . . . . **CLC 1, 2, 3, 5, 6, 8, 13,**
23, 46, 59; SSC 2
See also CA 21-24R; 129; CANR 20;
DLB 2; DLBY 80, 89; MTCW; SATA 7,
62

Barthelme, Frederick 1943- . . . . **CLC 36**
See also CA 114; 122; DLBY 85

Barthes, Roland (Gerard)
1915-1980 . . . . **CLC 24**
See also CA 130; 97-100; MTCW

Barzun, Jacques (Martin) 1907- . . . . **CLC 51**
See also CA 61-64; CANR 22

Bashevis, Isaac
See Singer, Isaac Bashevis

Bashkirtseff, Marie 1859-1884 . . . **NCLC 27**

Basho
See Matsuo Basho

Bass, Kingsley B. Jr.
See Bullins, Ed

Bassani, Giorgio 1916- . . . . **CLC 9**
See also CA 65-68; CANR 33; MTCW

Bastos, Augusto (Antonio) Roa
See Roa Bastos, Augusto (Antonio)

Bataille, Georges 1897-1962 . . . . **CLC 29**
See also CA 101; 89-92

Bates, H(erbert) E(rnest)
1905-1974 . . . . **CLC 46; SSC 10**
See also CA 93-96; 45-48; CANR 34;
MTCW

Bauchart
See Camus, Albert

Baudelaire, Charles
1821-1867 . . . . **NCLC 6, 29; PC 1**
See also WLC

Baudrillard, Jean 1929- . . . . **CLC 60**

Baum, L(yman) Frank 1856-1919 . . . **TCLC 7**
See also CA 108; 133; CLR 15; DLB 22;
MAICYA; MTCW; SATA 18

Baum, Louis F.
See Baum, L(yman) Frank

Baumbach, Jonathan 1933- . . . . . . **CLC 6, 23**
See also CA 13-16R; CAAS 5; CANR 12;
DLBY 80; MTCW

Bausch, Richard (Carl) 1945- . . . . . . **CLC 51**
See also CA 101; CAAS 14

Baxter, Charles 1947- . . . . **CLC 45**
See also CA 57-60

Baxter, James K(eir) 1926-1972 . . . . **CLC 14**
See also CA 77-80

Baxter, John
See Hunt, E(verette) Howard Jr.

Bayer, Sylvia
See Glassco, John

Beagle, Peter S(oyer) 1939- . . . . **CLC 7**
See also CA 9-12R; CANR 4; DLBY 80;
SATA 60

Bean, Normal
See Burroughs, Edgar Rice

Beard, Charles A(ustin)
1874-1948 . . . . **TCLC 15**
See also CA 115; DLB 17; SATA 18

Beardsley, Aubrey 1872-1898 . . . . . **NCLC 6**

Beattie, Ann
1947- . . . . **CLC 8, 13, 18, 40, 63; SSC 11**
See also BEST 90:2; CA 81-84; DLBY 82;
MTCW

Beattie, James 1735-1803 . . . . **NCLC 25**
See also DLB 109

Beauchamp, Kathleen Mansfield 1888-1923
See Mansfield, Katherine
See also CA 104; 134

Beauvoir, Simone (Lucie Ernestine Marie
Bertrand) de
1908-1986 . . . **CLC 1, 2, 4, 8, 14, 31, 44,**
50, 71
See also CA 9-12R; 118; CANR 28;
DLB 72; DLBY 86; MTCW; WLC

Becker, Jurek 1937- . . . . **CLC 7, 19**
See also CA 85-88; DLB 75

Becker, Walter 1950- . . . . **CLC 26**

Beckett, Samuel (Barclay)
1906-1989 . . . . . **CLC 1, 2, 3, 4, 6, 9, 10,**
11, 14, 18, 29, 57, 59
See also CA 5-8R; 130; CANR 33;
CDBLB 1945-1960; DLB 13, 15;
DLBY 90; MTCW; WLC

Beckford, William 1760-1844 . . . . **NCLC 16**
See also DLB 39

Beckman, Gunnel 1910- . . . . **CLC 26**
See also CA 33-36R; CANR 15; CLR 25;
MAICYA; SAAS 9; SATA 6

Becque, Henri 1837-1899 . . . . **NCLC 3**

Beddoes, Thomas Lovell
1803-1849 . . . . **NCLC 3**
See also DLB 96

Bedford, Donald F.
See Fearing, Kenneth (Flexner)

Beecher, Catharine Esther
1800-1878 . . . . **NCLC 30**
See also DLB 1

Beecher, John 1904-1980 . . . . **CLC 6**
See also AITN 1; CA 5-8R; 105; CANR 8

Beer, Johann 1655-1700 . . . . **LC 5**

Beer, Patricia 1924- . . . . **CLC 58**
See also CA 61-64; CANR 13; DLB 40

Beerbohm, Henry Maximilian
1872-1956 . . . . **TCLC 1, 24**
See also CA 104; DLB 34, 100

Begiebing, Robert J(ohn) 1946- . . . . . **CLC 70**
See also CA 122

Behan, Brendan
1923-1964 . . . . **CLC 1, 8, 11, 15**
See also CA 73-76; CANR 33;
CDBLB 1945-1960; DLB 13; MTCW

Behn, Aphra 1640(?)-1689 . . . . **LC 1**
See also DLB 39, 80; WLC

Behrman, S(amuel) N(athaniel)
1893-1973 . . . . **CLC 40**
See also CA 13-16; 45-48; CAP 1; DLB 7,
44

Belasco, David 1853-1931 . . . . **TCLC 3**
See also CA 104; DLB 7

Belcheva, Elisaveta 1893- . . . . **CLC 10**

Beldone, Phil "Cheech"
See Ellison, Harlan

Beleno
See Azuela, Mariano

Belinski, Vissarion Grigoryevich
1811-1848 . . . . **NCLC 5**

Belitt, Ben 1911- . . . . **CLC 22**
See also CA 13-16R; CAAS 4; CANR 7;
DLB 5

Bell, James Madison 1826-1902 . . . **TCLC 43**
See also BLC 1; BW; CA 122; 124; DLB 50

Bell, Madison (Smartt) 1957- . . . . . . **CLC 41**
See also CA 111; CANR 28

Bell, Marvin (Hartley) 1937- . . . . . **CLC 8, 31**
See also CA 21-24R; CAAS 14; DLB 5;
MTCW

Bell, W. L. D.
See Mencken, H(enry) L(ouis)

Bellamy, Atwood C.
See Mencken, H(enry) L(ouis)

Bellamy, Edward 1850-1898 . . . . . . **NCLC 4**
See also DLB 12

Bellin, Edward J.
See Kuttner, Henry

Belloc, (Joseph) Hilaire (Pierre)
1870-1953 . . . . **TCLC 7, 18**
See also CA 106; DLB 19, 100; YABC 1

Belloc, Joseph Peter Rene Hilaire
See Belloc, (Joseph) Hilaire (Pierre)

Belloc, Joseph Pierre Hilaire
See Belloc, (Joseph) Hilaire (Pierre)

Belloc, M. A.
See Lowndes, Marie Adelaide (Belloc)

Bellow, Saul
1915- . . . . . **CLC 1, 2, 3, 6, 8, 10, 13, 15,**
25, 33, 34, 63
See also AITN 2; BEST 89:3; CA 5-8R;
CABS 1; CANR 29; CDALB 1941-1968;
DLB 2, 28; DLBD 3; DLBY 82; MTCW;
WLC

Belser, Reimond Karel Maria de
1929- . . . . **CLC 14**

Bely, Andrey . . . . **TCLC 7**
See also Bugayev, Boris Nikolayevich

Benary, Margot
See Benary-Isbert, Margot

Benary-Isbert, Margot 1889-1979 . . . **CLC 12**
See also CA 5-8R; 89-92; CANR 4;
CLR 12; MAICYA; SATA 2, 21

Benavente (y Martinez), Jacinto
1866-1954 . . . . **TCLC 3**
See also CA 106; 131; HW; MTCW

Benchley, Peter (Bradford)
1940- . . . . **CLC 4, 8**
See also AITN 2; CA 17-20R; CANR 12,
35; MTCW; SATA 3

Benchley, Robert (Charles)
1889-1945 . . . . **TCLC 1**
See also CA 105; DLB 11

Benedikt, Michael 1935- . . . . **CLC 4, 14**
See also CA 13-16R; CANR 7; DLB 5

Benet, Juan 1927-............... **CLC 28**

Benet, Stephen Vincent
1898-1943 .... **TCLC 7; SSC 10**
See also CA 104; DLB 4, 48, 102; YABC 1

Benet, William Rose 1886-1950 ... **TCLC 28**
See also CA 118; DLB 45

Benford, Gregory (Albert) 1941-.... **CLC 52**
See also CA 69-72; CANR 12, 24;
DLBY 82

Bengtsson, Frans (Gunnar)
1894-1954 .... **TCLC 48**

Benjamin, Lois
See Gould, Lois

Benjamin, Walter 1892-1940..... **TCLC 39**

Benn, Gottfried 1886-1956........ **TCLC 3**
See also CA 106; DLB 56

Bennett, Alan 1934-.............. **CLC 45**
See also CA 103; CANR 35; MTCW

Bennett, (Enoch) Arnold
1867-1931 .... **TCLC 5, 20**
See also CA 106; CDBLB 1890-1914;
DLB 10, 34, 98

Bennett, Elizabeth
See Mitchell, Margaret (Munnerlyn)

Bennett, George Harold 1930-
See Bennett, Hal
See also BW; CA 97-100

Bennett, Hal .... **CLC 5**
See also Bennett, George Harold
See also DLB 33

Bennett, Jay 1912-............... **CLC 35**
See also CA 69-72; CANR 11; SAAS 4;
SATA 27, 41

Bennett, Louise (Simone) 1919-..... **CLC 28**
See also BLC 1; DLB 117

Benson, E(dward) F(rederic)
1867-1940 .... **TCLC 27**
See also CA 114

Benson, Jackson J. 1930-......... **CLC 34**
See also CA 25-28R; DLB 111

Benson, Sally 1900-1972 .... **CLC 17**
See also CA 19-20; 37-40R; CAP 1;
SATA 1, 27, 35

Benson, Stella 1892-1933........ **TCLC 17**
See also CA 117; DLB 36

Bentham, Jeremy 1748-1832 ..... **NCLC 38**
See also DLB 107

Bentley, E(dmund) C(lerihew)
1875-1956 .... **TCLC 12**
See also CA 108; DLB 70

Bentley, Eric (Russell) 1916-....... **CLC 24**
See also CA 5-8R; CANR 6

Beranger, Pierre Jean de
1780-1857 .... **NCLC 34**

Berger, Colonel
See Malraux, (Georges-)Andre

Berger, John (Peter) 1926-...... **CLC 2, 19**
See also CA 81-84; DLB 14

Berger, Melvin H. 1927-.......... **CLC 12**
See also CA 5-8R; CANR 4; SAAS 2;
SATA 5

Berger, Thomas (Louis)
1924-.......... **CLC 3, 5, 8, 11, 18, 38**
See also CA 1-4R; CANR 5, 28; DLB 2;
DLBY 80; MTCW

Bergman, (Ernst) Ingmar
1918-.................... **CLC 16, 72**
See also CA 81-84; CANR 33

Bergson, Henri 1859-1941........ **TCLC 32**

Bergstein, Eleanor 1938-.......... **CLC 4**
See also CA 53-56; CANR 5

Berkoff, Steven 1937-............. **CLC 56**
See also CA 104

Bermant, Chaim (Icyk) 1929-...... **CLC 40**
See also CA 57-60; CANR 6, 31

Bernanos, (Paul Louis) Georges
1888-1948 .... **TCLC 3**
See also CA 104; 130; DLB 72

Bernard, April 1956- .... **CLC 59**
See also CA 131

Bernhard, Thomas
1931-1989 .... **CLC 3, 32, 61**
See also CA 85-88; 127; CANR 32;
DLB 85; MTCW

Berrigan, Daniel 1921-............. **CLC 4**
See also CA 33-36R; CAAS 1; CANR 11;
DLB 5

Berrigan, Edmund Joseph Michael Jr.
1934-1983
See Berrigan, Ted
See also CA 61-64; 110; CANR 14

Berrigan, Ted.................... **CLC 37**
See also Berrigan, Edmund Joseph Michael
Jr.
See also DLB 5

Berry, Charles Edward Anderson 1931-
See Berry, Chuck
See also CA 115

Berry, Chuck .... **CLC 17**
See also Berry, Charles Edward Anderson

Berry, Jonas
See Ashbery, John (Lawrence)

Berry, Wendell (Erdman)
1934- .... **CLC 4, 6, 8, 27, 46**
See also AITN 1; CA 73-76; DLB 5, 6

Berryman, John
1914-1972 ..... **CLC 1, 2, 3, 4, 6, 8, 10, 13, 25, 62**
See also CA 13-16; 33-36R; CABS 2;
CANR 35; CAP 1; CDALB 1941-1968;
DLB 48; MTCW

Bertolucci, Bernardo 1940-........ **CLC 16**
See also CA 106

Bertrand, Aloysius 1807-1841 .... **NCLC 31**

Bertran de Born c. 1140-1215..... **CMLC 5**

Besant, Annie (Wood) 1847-1933 ... **TCLC 9**
See also CA 105

Bessie, Alvah 1904-1985.......... **CLC 23**
See also CA 5-8R; 116; CANR 2; DLB 26

Bethlen, T. D.
See Silverberg, Robert

Beti, Mongo..................... **CLC 27**
See also Biyidi, Alexandre
See also BLC 1

Betjeman, John
1906-1984 .... **CLC 2, 6, 10, 34, 43**
See also CA 9-12R; 112; CANR 33;
CDBLB 1945-1960; DLB 20; DLBY 84;
MTCW

Betti, Ugo 1892-1953 .... **TCLC 5**
See also CA 104

Betts, Doris (Waugh) 1932-.... **CLC 3, 6, 28**
See also CA 13-16R; CANR 9; DLBY 82

Bevan, Alistair
See Roberts, Keith (John Kingston)

Beynon, John
See Harris, John (Wyndham Parkes Lucas)
Beynon

Bialik, Chaim Nachman
1873-1934 .... **TCLC 25**

Bickerstaff, Isaac
See Swift, Jonathan

Bidart, Frank 19(?)-.............. **CLC 33**

Bienek, Horst 1930-............. **CLC 7, 11**
See also CA 73-76; DLB 75

Bierce, Ambrose (Gwinett)
1842-1914(?) ..... **TCLC 1, 7, 44; SSC 9**
See also CA 104; CDALB 1865-1917;
DLB 11, 12, 23, 71, 74; WLC

Billings, Josh
See Shaw, Henry Wheeler

Billington, Rachel 1942-........... **CLC 43**
See also AITN 2; CA 33-36R

Binyon, T(imothy) J(ohn) 1936- .... **CLC 34**
See also CA 111; CANR 28

Bioy Casares, Adolfo 1914-.... **CLC 4, 8, 13**
See also CA 29-32R; CANR 19; DLB 113;
HW; MTCW

Bird, C.
See Ellison, Harlan

Bird, Cordwainer
See Ellison, Harlan

Bird, Robert Montgomery
1806-1854 .... **NCLC 1**

Birney, (Alfred) Earle
1904- .... **CLC 1, 4, 6, 11**
See also CA 1-4R; CANR 5, 20; DLB 88;
MTCW

Bishop, Elizabeth
1911-1979 ..... **CLC 1, 4, 9, 13, 15, 32; PC 3**
See also CA 5-8R; 89-92; CABS 2;
CANR 26; CDALB 1968-1988; DLB 5;
MTCW; SATA 24

Bishop, John 1935-............... **CLC 10**
See also CA 105

Bissett, Bill 1939-............... **CLC 18**
See also CA 69-72; CANR 15; DLB 53;
MTCW

Bitov, Andrei (Georgievich) 1937-... **CLC 57**

Biyidi, Alexandre 1932-
See Beti, Mongo
See also BW; CA 114; 124; MTCW

Bjarme, Brynjolf
See Ibsen, Henrik (Johan)

Bjornson, Bjornstjerne (Martinius)
1832-1910 .... **TCLC 7, 37**
See also CA 104

Black, Robert
See Holdstock, Robert P.

Blackburn, Paul 1926-1971 . . . . . . **CLC 9, 43**
See also CA 81-84; 33-36R; CANR 34;
DLB 16; DLBY 81

Black Elk 1863-1950 . . . . **TCLC 33**

Black Hobart
See Sanders, (James) Ed(ward)

Blacklin, Malcolm
See Chambers, Aidan

Blackmore, R(ichard) D(oddridge)
1825-1900 . . . . **TCLC 27**
See also CA 120; DLB 18

Blackmur, R(ichard) P(almer)
1904-1965 . . . . **CLC 2, 24**
See also CA 11-12; 25-28R; CAP 1; DLB 63

Black Tarantula, The
See Acker, Kathy

Blackwood, Algernon (Henry)
1869-1951 . . . . **TCLC 5**
See also CA 105

Blackwood, Caroline 1931- . . . . **CLC 6, 9**
See also CA 85-88; CANR 32; DLB 14;
MTCW

Blade, Alexander
See Hamilton, Edmond; Silverberg, Robert

Blaga, Lucian 1895-1961 . . . . **CLC 75**

Blair, Eric (Arthur) 1903-1950
See Orwell, George
See also CA 104; 132; MTCW; SATA 29

Blais, Marie-Claire
1939- . . . . **CLC 2, 4, 6, 13, 22**
See also CA 21-24R; CAAS 4; CANR 38;
DLB 53; MTCW

Blaise, Clark 1940- . . . . **CLC 29**
See also AITN 2; CA 53-56; CAAS 3;
CANR 5; DLB 53

Blake, Nicholas
See Day Lewis, C(ecil)
See also DLB 77

Blake, William 1757-1827 . . . . **NCLC 13**
See also CDBLB 1789-1832; DLB 93;
MAICYA; SATA 30; WLC

Blasco Ibanez, Vicente
1867-1928 . . . . **TCLC 12**
See also CA 110; 131; HW; MTCW

Blatty, William Peter 1928- . . . . **CLC 2**
See also CA 5-8R; CANR 9

Bleeck, Oliver
See Thomas, Ross (Elmore)

Blessing, Lee 1949- . . . . **CLC 54**

Blish, James (Benjamin)
1921-1975 . . . . **CLC 14**
See also CA 1-4R; 57-60; CANR 3; DLB 8;
MTCW; SATA 66

Bliss, Reginald
See Wells, H(erbert) G(eorge)

Blixen, Karen (Christentze Dinesen)
1885-1962
See Dinesen, Isak
See also CA 25-28; CANR 22; CAP 2;
MTCW; SATA 44

Bloch, Robert (Albert) 1917- . . . . **CLC 33**
See also CA 5-8R; CANR 5; DLB 44;
SATA 12

Blok, Alexander (Alexandrovich)
1880-1921 . . . . **TCLC 5**
See also CA 104

Blom, Jan
See Breytenbach, Breyten

Bloom, Harold 1930- . . . . **CLC 24**
See also CA 13-16R; CANR 39; DLB 67

Bloomfield, Aurelius
See Bourne, Randolph S(illiman)

Blount, Roy (Alton) Jr. 1941- . . . . . . **CLC 38**
See also CA 53-56; CANR 10, 28; MTCW

Bloy, Leon 1846-1917 . . . . **TCLC 22**
See also CA 121; DLB 123

Blume, Judy (Sussman) 1938- . . . **CLC 12, 30**
See also AAYA 3; CA 29-32R; CANR 13,
37; CLR 2, 15; DLB 52; MAICYA;
MTCW; SATA 2, 31

Blunden, Edmund (Charles)
1896-1974 . . . . **CLC 2, 56**
See also CA 17-18; 45-48; CAP 2; DLB 20,
100; MTCW

Bly, Robert (Elwood)
1926- . . . . **CLC 1, 2, 5, 10, 15, 38**
See also CA 5-8R; DLB 5; MTCW

Bobette
See Simenon, Georges (Jacques Christian)

Boccaccio, Giovanni 1313-1375
See also SSC 10

Bochco, Steven 1943- . . . . **CLC 35**
See also CA 124; 138

Bodenheim, Maxwell 1892-1954 . . . **TCLC 44**
See also CA 110; DLB 9, 45

Bodker, Cecil 1927- . . . . **CLC 21**
See also CA 73-76; CANR 13; CLR 23;
MAICYA; SATA 14

Boell, Heinrich (Theodor) 1917-1985
See Boll, Heinrich (Theodor)
See also CA 21-24R; 116; CANR 24;
DLB 69; DLBY 85; MTCW

Bogan, Louise 1897-1970 . . . . . **CLC 4, 39, 46**
See also CA 73-76; 25-28R; CANR 33;
DLB 45; MTCW

Bogarde, Dirk . . . . **CLC 19**
See also Van Den Bogarde, Derek Jules
Gaspard Ulric Niven
See also DLB 14

Bogosian, Eric 1953- . . . . **CLC 45**
See also CA 138

Bograd, Larry 1953- . . . . **CLC 35**
See also CA 93-96; SATA 33

Boiardo, Matteo Maria 1441-1494 . . . . **LC 6**

Boileau-Despreaux, Nicolas
1636-1711 . . . . **LC 3**

Boland, Eavan 1944- . . . . **CLC 40, 67**
See also DLB 40

Boll, Heinrich (Theodor)
1917-1985 . . . **CLC 2, 3, 6, 9, 11, 15, 27,**
　　　　　　　　　　　　　　　　　　39, 72
See also Boell, Heinrich (Theodor)
See also DLB 69; DLBY 85; WLC

Bolt, Robert (Oxton) 1924- . . . . **CLC 14**
See also CA 17-20R; CANR 35; DLB 13;
MTCW

Bomkauf
See Kaufman, Bob (Garnell)

Bonaventura . . . . **NCLC 35**
See also DLB 90

Bond, Edward 1934- . . . . **CLC 4, 6, 13, 23**
See also CA 25-28R; CANR 38; DLB 13;
MTCW

Bonham, Frank 1914-1989 . . . . **CLC 12**
See also AAYA 1; CA 9-12R; CANR 4, 36;
MAICYA; SAAS 3; SATA 1, 49, 62

Bonnefoy, Yves 1923- . . . . **CLC 9, 15, 58**
See also CA 85-88; CANR 33; MTCW

Bontemps, Arna(ud Wendell)
1902-1973 . . . . **CLC 1, 18**
See also BLC 1; BW; CA 1-4R; 41-44R;
CANR 4, 35; CLR 6; DLB 48, 51;
MAICYA; MTCW; SATA 2, 24, 44

Booth, Martin 1944- . . . . **CLC 13**
See also CA 93-96; CAAS 2

Booth, Philip 1925- . . . . **CLC 23**
See also CA 5-8R; CANR 5; DLBY 82

Booth, Wayne C(layson) 1921- . . . . . **CLC 24**
See also CA 1-4R; CAAS 5; CANR 3;
DLB 67

Borchert, Wolfgang 1921-1947 . . . . . **TCLC 5**
See also CA 104; DLB 69

Borges, Jorge Luis
1899-1986 . . . **CLC 1, 2, 3, 4, 6, 8, 9, 10,**
　　　　　　　　　　　13, 19, 44, 48; SSC 4
See also CA 21-24R; CANR 19, 33;
DLB 113; DLBY 86; HW; MTCW; WLC

Borowski, Tadeusz 1922-1951 . . . . . . **TCLC 9**
See also CA 106

Borrow, George (Henry)
1803-1881 . . . . **NCLC 9**
See also DLB 21, 55

Bosschere, Jean de 1878(?)-1953 . . . **TCLC 19**
See also CA 115

Boswell, James 1740-1795 . . . . **LC 4**
See also CDBLB 1660-1789; DLB 104;
WLC

Bottoms, David 1949- . . . . **CLC 53**
See also CA 105; CANR 22; DLB 120;
DLBY 83

Boucolon, Maryse 1937-
See Conde, Maryse
See also CA 110; CANR 30

Bourget, Paul (Charles Joseph)
1852-1935 . . . . **TCLC 12**
See also CA 107; DLB 123

Bourjaily, Vance (Nye) 1922- . . . . **CLC 8, 62**
See also CA 1-4R; CAAS 1; CANR 2;
DLB 2

Bourne, Randolph S(illiman)
1886-1918 . . . . **TCLC 16**
See also CA 117; DLB 63

Bova, Ben(jamin William) 1932- . . . . **CLC 45**
See also CA 5-8R; CANR 11; CLR 3;
DLBY 81; MAICYA; MTCW; SATA 6,
68

Brooke-Haven, P.
See Wodehouse, P(elham) G(renville)

Brooke-Rose, Christine 1926- ...... **CLC 40**
See also CA 13-16R; DLB 14

Brookner, Anita 1928- ...... **CLC 32, 34, 51**
See also CA 114; 120; CANR 37; DLBY 87;
MTCW

Brooks, Cleanth 1906- .... **CLC 24**
See also CA 17-20R; CANR 33, 35;
DLB 63; MTCW

Brooks, George
See Baum, L(yman) Frank

Brooks, Gwendolyn
1917- .... **CLC 1, 2, 4, 5, 15, 49**
See also AITN 1; BLC 1; BW; CA 1-4R;
CANR 1, 27; CDALB 1941-1968;
CLR 27; DLB 5, 76; MTCW; SATA 6;
WLC

Brooks, Mel .... **CLC 12**
See also Kaminsky, Melvin
See also DLB 26

Brooks, Peter 1938- .... **CLC 34**
See also CA 45-48; CANR 1

Brooks, Van Wyck 1886-1963 ...... **CLC 29**
See also CA 1-4R; CANR 6; DLB 45, 63,
103

Brophy, Brigid (Antonia)
1929- .... **CLC 6, 11, 29**
See also CA 5-8R; CAAS 4; CANR 25;
DLB 14; MTCW

Brosman, Catharine Savage 1934- .... **CLC 9**
See also CA 61-64; CANR 21

Brother Antoninus
See Everson, William (Oliver)

Broughton, T(homas) Alan 1936- ... **CLC 19**
See also CA 45-48; CANR 2, 23

Broumas, Olga 1949- .... **CLC 10, 73**
See also CA 85-88; CANR 20

Brown, Charles Brockden
1771-1810 .... **NCLC 22**
See also CDALB 1640-1865; DLB 37, 59,
73

Brown, Christy 1932-1981 .... **CLC 63**
See also CA 105; 104; DLB 14

Brown, Claude 1937- .... **CLC 30**
See also AAYA 7; BLC 1; BW; CA 73-76

Brown, Dee (Alexander) 1908- .. **CLC 18, 47**
See also CA 13-16R; CAAS 6; CANR 11;
DLBY 80; MTCW; SATA 5

Brown, George
See Wertmueller, Lina

Brown, George Douglas
1869-1902 .... **TCLC 28**

Brown, George Mackay 1921- .... **CLC 5, 48**
See also CA 21-24R; CAAS 6; CANR 12,
37; DLB 14, 27; MTCW; SATA 35

Brown, (William) Larry 1951- ...... **CLC 73**
See also CA 130; 134

Brown, Moses
See Barrett, William (Christopher)

Brown, Rita Mae 1944- .... **CLC 18, 43**
See also CA 45-48; CANR 2, 11, 35;
MTCW

Brown, Roderick (Langmere) Haig-
See Haig-Brown, Roderick (Langmere)

Brown, Rosellen 1939- .... **CLC 32**
See also CA 77-80; CAAS 10; CANR 14

Brown, Sterling Allen
1901-1989 .... **CLC 1, 23, 59**
See also BLC 1; BW; CA 85-88; 127;
CANR 26; DLB 48, 51, 63; MTCW

Brown, Will
See Ainsworth, William Harrison

Brown, William Wells
1813-1884 .... **NCLC 2; DC 1**
See also BLC 1; DLB 3, 50

Browne, (Clyde) Jackson 1948(?)- ... **CLC 21**
See also CA 120

Browning, Elizabeth Barrett
1806-1861 .... **NCLC 1, 16; PC 6**
See also CDBLB 1832-1890; DLB 32; WLC

Browning, Robert
1812-1889 .... **NCLC 19; PC 2**
See also CDBLB 1832-1890; DLB 32;
YABC 1

Browning, Tod 1882-1962 .... **CLC 16**
See also CA 117

Bruccoli, Matthew J(oseph) 1931- .. **CLC 34**
See also CA 9-12R; CANR 7; DLB 103

Bruce, Lenny .... **CLC 21**
See also Schneider, Leonard Alfred

Bruin, John
See Brutus, Dennis

Brulls, Christian
See Simenon, Georges (Jacques Christian)

Brunner, John (Kilian Houston)
1934- .... **CLC 8, 10**
See also CA 1-4R; CAAS 8; CANR 2, 37;
MTCW

Brutus, Dennis 1924- .... **CLC 43**
See also BLC 1; BW; CA 49-52; CAAS 14;
CANR 2, 27; DLB 117

Bryan, C(ourtlandt) D(ixon) B(arnes)
1936- .... **CLC 29**
See also CA 73-76; CANR 13

Bryan, Michael
See Moore, Brian

Bryant, William Cullen
1794-1878 .... **NCLC 6**
See also CDALB 1640-1865; DLB 3, 43, 59

Bryusov, Valery Yakovlevich
1873-1924 .... **TCLC 10**
See also CA 107

Buchan, John 1875-1940 .... **TCLC 41**
See also CA 108; DLB 34, 70; YABC 2

Buchanan, George 1506-1582 .... **LC 4**

Buchheim, Lothar-Guenther 1918- ... **CLC 6**
See also CA 85-88

Buchner, (Karl) Georg
1813-1837 .... **NCLC 26**

Buchwald, Art(hur) 1925- .... **CLC 33**
See also AITN 1; CA 5-8R; CANR 21;
MTCW; SATA 10

Buck, Pearl S(ydenstricker)
1892-1973 .... **CLC 7, 11, 18**
See also AITN 1; CA 1-4R; 41-44R;
CANR 1, 34; DLB 9, 102; MTCW;
SATA 1, 25

Buckler, Ernest 1908-1984 .... **CLC 13**
See also CA 11-12; 114; CAP 1; DLB 68;
SATA 47

Buckley, Vincent (Thomas)
1925-1988 .... **CLC 57**
See also CA 101

Buckley, William F(rank) Jr.
1925- .... **CLC 7, 18, 37**
See also AITN 1; CA 1-4R; CANR 1, 24;
DLBY 80; MTCW

Buechner, (Carl) Frederick
1926- .... **CLC 2, 4, 6, 9**
See also CA 13-16R; CANR 11, 39;
DLBY 80; MTCW

Buell, John (Edward) 1927- .... **CLC 10**
See also CA 1-4R; DLB 53

Buero Vallejo, Antonio 1916- ... **CLC 15, 46**
See also CA 106; CANR 24; HW; MTCW

Bufalino, Gesualdo 1920(?)- .... **CLC 74**

Bugayev, Boris Nikolayevich 1880-1934
See Bely, Andrey
See also CA 104

Bukowski, Charles 1920- .... **CLC 2, 5, 9, 41**
See also CA 17-20R; DLB 5; MTCW

Bulgakov, Mikhail (Afanas'evich)
1891-1940 .... **TCLC 2, 16**
See also CA 105

Bullins, Ed 1935- .... **CLC 1, 5, 7**
See also BLC 1; BW; CA 49-52; CAAS 16;
CANR 24; DLB 7, 38; MTCW

Bulwer-Lytton, Edward (George Earle Lytton)
1803-1873 .... **NCLC 1**
See also DLB 21

Bunin, Ivan Alexeyevich
1870-1953 .... **TCLC 6; SSC 5**
See also CA 104

Bunting, Basil 1900-1985 .... **CLC 10, 39, 47**
See also CA 53-56; 115; CANR 7; DLB 20

Bunuel, Luis 1900-1983 .... **CLC 16**
See also CA 101; 110; CANR 32; HW

Bunyan, John 1628-1688 .... **LC 4**
See also CDBLB 1660-1789; DLB 39; WLC

Burford, Eleanor
See Hibbert, Eleanor Burford

Burgess, Anthony
1917- ..... **CLC 1, 2, 4, 5, 8, 10, 13, 15,
22, 40, 62**
See also Wilson, John (Anthony) Burgess
See also AITN 1; CDBLB 1960 to Present;
DLB 14

Burke, Edmund 1729(?)-1797 .... **LC 7**
See also DLB 104; WLC

Burke, Kenneth (Duva) 1897- .... **CLC 2, 24**
See also CA 5-8R; CANR 39; DLB 45, 63;
MTCW

Burke, Leda
See Garnett, David

Burke, Ralph
See Silverberg, Robert

Carlyle, Thomas 1795-1881 ...... NCLC 22
See also CDBLB 1789-1832; DLB 55

Carman, (William) Bliss
1861-1929 .... TCLC 7
See also CA 104; DLB 92

Carossa, Hans 1878-1956........ TCLC 48
See also DLB 66

Carpenter, Don(ald Richard)
1931- .... CLC 41
See also CA 45-48; CANR 1

Carpentier (y Valmont), Alejo
1904-1980 .... CLC 8, 11, 38
See also CA 65-68; 97-100; CANR 11;
DLB 113; HW

Carr, Emily 1871-1945........... TCLC 32
See also DLB 68

Carr, John Dickson 1906-1977 ...... CLC 3
See also CA 49-52; 69-72; CANR 3, 33;
MTCW

Carr, Philippa
See Hibbert, Eleanor Burford

Carr, Virginia Spencer 1929-....... CLC 34
See also CA 61-64; DLB 111

Carrier, Roch 1937- .... CLC 13
See also CA 130; DLB 53

Carroll, James P. 1943(?)- .... CLC 38
See also CA 81-84

Carroll, Jim 1951- .... CLC 35
See also CA 45-48

Carroll, Lewis .... NCLC 2
See also Dodgson, Charles Lutwidge
See also CDBLB 1832-1890; CLR 2, 18;
DLB 18; WLC

Carroll, Paul Vincent 1900-1968.... CLC 10
See also CA 9-12R; 25-28R; DLB 10

Carruth, Hayden 1921- .... CLC 4, 7, 10, 18
See also CA 9-12R; CANR 4, 38; DLB 5;
MTCW; SATA 47

Carson, Rachel Louise 1907-1964... CLC 71
See also CA 77-80; CANR 35; MTCW;
SATA 23

Carter, Angela (Olive)
1940-1991 .... CLC 5, 41
See also CA 53-56; 136; CANR 12, 36;
DLB 14; MTCW; SATA 66; SATO 70

Carter, Nick
See Smith, Martin Cruz

Carver, Raymond
1938-1988 ... CLC 22, 36, 53, 55; SSC 8
See also CA 33-36R; 126; CANR 17, 34;
DLBY 84, 88; MTCW

Cary, (Arthur) Joyce (Lunel)
1888-1957 .... TCLC 1, 29
See also CA 104; CDBLB 1914-1945;
DLB 15, 100

Casanova de Seingalt, Giovanni Jacopo
1725-1798 .... LC 13

Casares, Adolfo Bioy
See Bioy Casares, Adolfo

Casely-Hayford, J(oseph) E(phraim)
1866-1930 .... TCLC 24
See also BLC 1; CA 123

Casey, John (Dudley) 1939-........ CLC 59
See also BEST 90:2; CA 69-72; CANR 23

Casey, Michael 1947-.............. CLC 2
See also CA 65-68; DLB 5

Casey, Patrick
See Thurman, Wallace (Henry)

Casey, Warren (Peter) 1935-1988 ... CLC 12
See also CA 101; 127

Casona, Alejandro................. CLC 49
See also Alvarez, Alejandro Rodriguez

Cassavetes, John 1929-1989....... CLC 20
See also CA 85-88; 127

Cassill, R(onald) V(erlin) 1919-... CLC 4, 23
See also CA 9-12R; CAAS 1; CANR 7;
DLB 6

Cassity, (Allen) Turner 1929- .... CLC 6, 42
See also CA 17-20R; CAAS 8; CANR 11;
DLB 105

Castaneda, Carlos 1931(?)-......... CLC 12
See also CA 25-28R; CANR 32; HW;
MTCW

Castedo, Elena 1937- .... CLC 65
See also CA 132

Castedo-Ellerman, Elena
See Castedo, Elena

Castellanos, Rosario 1925-1974..... CLC 66
See also CA 131; 53-56; DLB 113; HW

Castelvetro, Lodovico 1505-1571..... LC 12

Castiglione, Baldassare 1478-1529 ... LC 12

Castle, Robert
See Hamilton, Edmond

Castro, Guillen de 1569-1631....... LC 19

Castro, Rosalia de 1837-1885 ..... NCLC 3

Cather, Willa
See Cather, Willa Sibert

Cather, Willa Sibert
1873-1947 ...... TCLC 1, 11, 31; SSC 2
See also CA 104; 128; CDALB 1865-1917;
DLB 9, 54, 78; DLBD 1; MTCW;
SATA 30; WLC

Catton, (Charles) Bruce
1899-1978 .... CLC 35
See also AITN 1; CA 5-8R; 81-84;
CANR 7; DLB 17; SATA 2, 24

Cauldwell, Frank
See King, Francis (Henry)

Caunitz, William J. 1933- .... CLC 34
See also BEST 89:3; CA 125; 130

Causley, Charles (Stanley) 1917-..... CLC 7
See also CA 9-12R; CANR 5, 35; DLB 27;
MTCW; SATA 3, 66

Caute, David 1936-.............. CLC 29
See also CA 1-4R; CAAS 4; CANR 1, 33;
DLB 14

Cavafy, C(onstantine) P(eter)...... TCLC 2, 7
See also Kavafis, Konstantinos Petrou

Cavallo, Evelyn
See Spark, Muriel (Sarah)

Cavanna, Betty .... CLC 12
See also Harrison, Elizabeth Cavanna
See also MAICYA; SAAS 4; SATA 1, 30

Caxton, William 1421(?)-1491(?)..... LC 17

Cayrol, Jean 1911- .... CLC 11
See also CA 89-92; DLB 83

Cela, Camilo Jose 1916-...... CLC 4, 13, 59
See also BEST 90:2; CA 21-24R; CAAS 10;
CANR 21, 32; DLBY 89; HW; MTCW

Celan, Paul .... CLC 53
See also Antschel, Paul
See also DLB 69

Celine, Louis-Ferdinand
.... CLC 1, 3, 4, 7, 9, 15, 47
See also Destouches, Louis-Ferdinand
See also DLB 72

Cellini, Benvenuto 1500-1571 .... LC 7

Cendrars, Blaise
See Sauser-Hall, Frederic

Cernuda (y Bidon), Luis
1902-1963 .... CLC 54
See also CA 131; 89-92; HW

Cervantes (Saavedra), Miguel de
1547-1616 .... LC 6
See also WLC

Cesaire, Aime (Fernand) 1913- ... CLC 19, 32
See also BLC 1; BW; CA 65-68; CANR 24;
MTCW

Chabon, Michael 1965(?)- .... CLC 55

Chabrol, Claude 1930- .... CLC 16
See also CA 110

Challans, Mary 1905-1983
See Renault, Mary
See also CA 81-84; 111; SATA 23, 36

Chambers, Aidan 1934- .... CLC 35
See also CA 25-28R; CANR 12, 31;
MAICYA; SAAS 12; SATA 1, 69

Chambers, James 1948-
See Cliff, Jimmy
See also CA 124

Chambers, Jessie
See Lawrence, D(avid) H(erbert Richards)

Chambers, Robert W. 1865-1933... TCLC 41

Chandler, Raymond (Thornton)
1888-1959 .... TCLC 1, 7
See also CA 104; 129; CDALB 1929-1941;
DLBD 6; MTCW

Chang, Jung 1952-............... CLC 71

Channing, William Ellery
1780-1842 .... NCLC 17
See also DLB 1, 59

Chaplin, Charles Spencer
1889-1977 .... CLC 16
See also Chaplin, Charlie
See also CA 81-84; 73-76

Chaplin, Charlie
See Chaplin, Charles Spencer
See also DLB 44

Chapman, Graham 1941-1989 ...... CLC 21
See also Monty Python
See also CA 116; 129; CANR 35

Chapman, John Jay 1862-1933 ..... TCLC 7
See also CA 104

Chapman, Walker
See Silverberg, Robert

Chappell, Fred (Davis) 1936-....... CLC 40
See also CA 5-8R; CAAS 4; CANR 8, 33;
DLB 6, 105

Char, Rene(-Emile)
1907-1988 . . . . CLC 9, 11, 14, 55
See also CA 13-16R; 124; CANR 32;
MTCW

Charby, Jay
See Ellison, Harlan

Chardin, Pierre Teilhard de
See Teilhard de Chardin, (Marie Joseph)
Pierre

Charles I 1600-1649 . . . . LC 13

Charyn, Jerome 1937- . . . . CLC 5, 8, 18
See also CA 5-8R; CAAS 1; CANR 7;
DLBY 83; MTCW

Chase, Mary (Coyle) 1907-1981 . . . . . . DC 1
See also CA 77-80; 105; SATA 17, 29

Chase, Mary Ellen 1887-1973 . . . . CLC 2
See also CA 13-16; 41-44R; CAP 1;
SATA 10

Chase, Nicholas
See Hyde, Anthony

Chateaubriand, Francois Rene de
1768-1848 . . . . NCLC 3
See also DLB 119

Chatterje, Sarat Chandra 1876-1936(?)
See Chatterji, Saratchandra
See also CA 109

Chatterji, Bankim Chandra
1838-1894 . . . . NCLC 19

Chatterji, Saratchandra . . . . TCLC 13
See also Chatterje, Sarat Chandra

Chatterton, Thomas 1752-1770 . . . . LC 3
See also DLB 109

Chatwin, (Charles) Bruce
1940-1989 . . . . CLC 28, 57, 59
See also AAYA 4; BEST 90:1; CA 85-88;
127

Chaucer, Daniel
See Ford, Ford Madox

Chaucer, Geoffrey 1340(?)-1400 . . . . . LC 17
See also CDBLB Before 1660

Chaviaras, Strates 1935-
See Haviaras, Stratis
See also CA 105

Chayefsky, Paddy . . . . CLC 23
See also Chayefsky, Sidney
See also DLB 7, 44; DLBY 81

Chayefsky, Sidney 1923-1981
See Chayefsky, Paddy
See also CA 9-12R; 104; CANR 18

Chedid, Andree 1920- . . . . CLC 47

Cheever, John
1912-1982 . . . . . CLC 3, 7, 8, 11, 15, 25,
64; SSC 1
See also CA 5-8R; 106; CABS 1; CANR 5,
27; CDALB 1941-1968; DLB 2, 102;
DLBY 80, 82; MTCW; WLC

Cheever, Susan 1943- . . . . CLC 18, 48
See also CA 103; CANR 27; DLBY 82

Chekhonte, Antosha
See Chekhov, Anton (Pavlovich)

Chekhov, Anton (Pavlovich)
1860-1904 . . . . . . TCLC 3, 10, 31; SSC 2
See also CA 104; 124; WLC

Chernyshevsky, Nikolay Gavrilovich
1828-1889 . . . . NCLC 1

Cherry, Carolyn Janice 1942-
See Cherryh, C. J.
See also CA 65-68; CANR 10

Cherryh, C. J. . . . . CLC 35
See also Cherry, Carolyn Janice
See also DLBY 80

Chesnutt, Charles W(addell)
1858-1932 . . . . TCLC 5, 39; SSC 7
See also BLC 1; BW; CA 106; 125; DLB 12,
50, 78; MTCW

Chester, Alfred 1929(?)-1971 . . . . . . CLC 49
See also CA 33-36R

Chesterton, G(ilbert) K(eith)
1874-1936 . . . . TCLC 1, 6; SSC 1
See also CA 104; 132; CDBLB 1914-1945;
DLB 10, 19, 34, 70, 98; MTCW;
SATA 27

Chiang Pin-chin 1904-1986
See Ding Ling
See also CA 118

Ch'ien Chung-shu 1910- . . . . CLC 22
See also CA 130; MTCW

Child, L. Maria
See Child, Lydia Maria

Child, Lydia Maria 1802-1880 . . . . NCLC 6
See also DLB 1, 74; SATA 67

Child, Mrs.
See Child, Lydia Maria

Child, Philip 1898-1978 . . . . CLC 19, 68
See also CA 13-14; CAP 1; SATA 47

Childress, Alice 1920- . . . . CLC 12, 15
See also AAYA 8; BLC 1; BW; CA 45-48;
CANR 3, 27; CLR 14; DLB 7, 38;
MAICYA; MTCW; SATA 7, 48

Chislett, (Margaret) Anne 1943- . . . . CLC 34

Chitty, Thomas Willes 1926- . . . . CLC 11
See also Hinde, Thomas
See also CA 5-8R

Chomette, Rene Lucien 1898-1981 . . CLC 20
See also Clair, Rene
See also CA 103

Chopin, Kate . . . . TCLC 5, 14; SSC 8
See also Chopin, Katherine
See also CDALB 1865-1917; DLB 12, 78

Chopin, Katherine 1851-1904
See Chopin, Kate
See also CA 104; 122

Chretien de Troyes
c. 12th cent. - . . . . CMLC 10

Christie
See Ichikawa, Kon

Christie, Agatha (Mary Clarissa)
1890-1976 . . . . . . CLC 1, 6, 8, 12, 39, 48
See also AAYA 9; AITN 1, 2; CA 17-20R;
61-64; CANR 10, 37; CDBLB 1914-1945;
DLB 13, 77; MTCW; SATA 36

Christie, (Ann) Philippa
See Pearce, Philippa
See also CA 5-8R; CANR 4

Christine de Pizan 1365(?)-1431(?) . . . . LC 9

Chubb, Elmer
See Masters, Edgar Lee

Chulkov, Mikhail Dmitrievich
1743-1792 . . . . LC 2

Churchill, Caryl 1938- . . . . CLC 31, 55
See also CA 102; CANR 22; DLB 13;
MTCW

Churchill, Charles 1731-1764 . . . . LC 3
See also DLB 109

Chute, Carolyn 1947- . . . . CLC 39
See also CA 123

Ciardi, John (Anthony)
1916-1986 . . . . CLC 10, 40, 44
See also CA 5-8R; 118; CAAS 2; CANR 5,
33; CLR 19; DLB 5; DLBY 86;
MAICYA; MTCW; SATA 1, 46, 65

Cicero, Marcus Tullius
106B.C.-43B.C. . . . . CMLC 3

Cimino, Michael 1943- . . . . CLC 16
See also CA 105

Cioran, E(mil) M. 1911- . . . . CLC 64
See also CA 25-28R

Cisneros, Sandra 1954- . . . . CLC 69
See also AAYA 9; CA 131; DLB 122; HW

Clair, Rene . . . . CLC 20
See also Chomette, Rene Lucien

Clampitt, Amy 1920- . . . . CLC 32
See also CA 110; CANR 29; DLB 105

Clancy, Thomas L. Jr. 1947-
See Clancy, Tom
See also CA 125; 131; MTCW

Clancy, Tom. . . . . CLC 45
See also Clancy, Thomas L. Jr.
See also AAYA 9; BEST 89:1, 90:1

Clare, John 1793-1864 . . . . NCLC 9
See also DLB 55, 96

Clarin
See Alas (y Urena), Leopoldo (Enrique
Garcia)

Clark, (Robert) Brian 1932- . . . . CLC 29
See also CA 41-44R

Clark, Eleanor 1913- . . . . CLC 5, 19
See also CA 9-12R; DLB 6

Clark, J. P.
See Clark, John Pepper
See also DLB 117

Clark, John Pepper 1935- . . . . CLC 38
See also Clark, J. P.
See also BLC 1; BW; CA 65-68; CANR 16

Clark, M. R.
See Clark, Mavis Thorpe

Clark, Mavis Thorpe 1909- . . . . CLC 12
See also CA 57-60; CANR 8, 37; MAICYA;
SAAS 5; SATA 8

Clark, Walter Van Tilburg
1909-1971 . . . . CLC 28
See also CA 9-12R; 33-36R; DLB 9;
SATA 8

Clarke, Arthur C(harles)
1917- . . . . . . CLC 1, 4, 13, 18, 35; SSC 3
See also AAYA 4; CA 1-4R; CANR 2, 28;
MAICYA; MTCW; SATA 13, 70

Clarke, Austin C(hesterfield)
1934- . . . . CLC 8, 53
See also BLC 1; BW; CA 25-28R;
CAAS 16; CANR 14, 32; DLB 53

Clarke, Austin 1896-1974........ **CLC 6, 9**
See also CA 29-32; 49-52; CAP 2; DLB 10, 20

Clarke, Gillian 1937-............ **CLC 61**
See also CA 106; DLB 40

Clarke, Marcus (Andrew Hislop)
1846-1881 .... **NCLC 19**

Clarke, Shirley 1925-............ **CLC 16**

Clash, The...................... **CLC 30**
See also Headon, (Nicky) Topper; Jones, Mick; Simonon, Paul; Strummer, Joe

Claudel, Paul (Louis Charles Marie)
1868-1955 .... **TCLC 2, 10**
See also CA 104

Clavell, James (duMaresq)
1925-................ **CLC 6, 25**
See also CA 25-28R; CANR 26; MTCW

Cleaver, (Leroy) Eldridge 1935-.... **CLC 30**
See also BLC 1; BW; CA 21-24R;
CANR 16

Cleese, John (Marwood) 1939-..... **CLC 21**
See also Monty Python
See also CA 112; 116; CANR 35; MTCW

Cleishbotham, Jebediah
See Scott, Walter

Cleland, John 1710-1789 .... **LC 2**
See also DLB 39

Clemens, Samuel Langhorne 1835-1910
See Twain, Mark
See also CA 104; 135; CDALB 1865-1917;
DLB 11, 12, 23, 64, 74; MAICYA;
YABC 2

Clerihew, E.
See Bentley, E(dmund) C(lerihew)

Clerk, N. W.
See Lewis, C(live) S(taples)

Cliff, Jimmy...................... **CLC 21**
See also Chambers, James

Clifton, (Thelma) Lucille
1936-.................... **CLC 19, 66**
See also BLC 1; BW; CA 49-52; CANR 2,
24; CLR 5; DLB 5, 41; MAICYA;
MTCW; SATA 20, 69

Clinton, Dirk
See Silverberg, Robert

Clough, Arthur Hugh 1819-1861.. **NCLC 27**
See also DLB 32

Clutha, Janet Paterson Frame 1924-
See Frame, Janet
See also CA 1-4R; CANR 2, 36; MTCW

Clyne, Terence
See Blatty, William Peter

Cobalt, Martin
See Mayne, William (James Carter)

Coburn, D(onald) L(ee) 1938-...... **CLC 10**
See also CA 89-92

Cocteau, Jean (Maurice Eugene Clement)
1889-1963........ **CLC 1, 8, 15, 16, 43**
See also CA 25-28; CAP 2; DLB 65;
MTCW; WLC

Codrescu, Andrei 1946-........... **CLC 46**
See also CA 33-36R; CANR 13, 34

Coe, Max
See Bourne, Randolph S(illiman)

Coe, Tucker
See Westlake, Donald E(dwin)

Coetzee, J(ohn) M(ichael)
1940-................. **CLC 23, 33, 66**
See also CA 77-80; MTCW

Cohen, Arthur A(llen)
1928-1986 .... **CLC 7, 31**
See also CA 1-4R; 120; CANR 1, 17;
DLB 28

Cohen, Leonard (Norman)
1934-.................... **CLC 3, 38**
See also CA 21-24R; CANR 14; DLB 53;
MTCW

Cohen, Matt 1942-............... **CLC 19**
See also CA 61-64; DLB 53

Cohen-Solal, Annie 19(?)- .... **CLC 50**

Colegate, Isabel 1931-........... **CLC 36**
See also CA 17-20R; CANR 8, 22; DLB 14;
MTCW

Coleman, Emmett
See Reed, Ishmael

Coleridge, Samuel Taylor
1772-1834 .... **NCLC 9**
See also CDBLB 1789-1832; DLB 93, 107;
WLC

Coleridge, Sara 1802-1852....... **NCLC 31**

Coles, Don 1928-................ **CLC 46**
See also CA 115; CANR 38

Colette, (Sidonie-Gabrielle)
1873-1954 ...... **TCLC 1, 5, 16; SSC 10**
See also CA 104; 131; DLB 65; MTCW

Collett, (Jacobine) Camilla (Wergeland)
1813-1895 .... **NCLC 22**

Collier, Christopher 1930-......... **CLC 30**
See also CA 33-36R; CANR 13, 33;
MAICYA; SATA 16, 70

Collier, James L(incoln) 1928- ..... **CLC 30**
See also CA 9-12R; CANR 4, 33;
MAICYA; SATA 8, 70

Collier, Jeremy 1650-1726.......... **LC 6**

Collins, Hunt
See Hunter, Evan

Collins, Linda 1931-.............. **CLC 44**
See also CA 125

Collins, (William) Wilkie
1824-1889 .... **NCLC 1, 18**
See also CDBLB 1832-1890; DLB 18, 70

Collins, William 1721-1759 .... **LC 4**
See also DLB 109

Colman, George
See Glassco, John

Colt, Winchester Remington
See Hubbard, L(afayette) Ron(ald)

Colter, Cyrus 1910-.............. **CLC 58**
See also BW; CA 65-68; CANR 10; DLB 33

Colton, James
See Hansen, Joseph

Colum, Padraic 1881-1972........ **CLC 28**
See also CA 73-76; 33-36R; CANR 35;
MAICYA; MTCW; SATA 15

Colvin, James
See Moorcock, Michael (John)

Colwin, Laurie (E.)
1944-1992 .... **CLC 5, 13, 23**
See also CA 89-92; CANR 20; DLBY 80;
MTCW

Comfort, Alex(ander) 1920-........ **CLC 7**
See also CA 1-4R; CANR 1

Comfort, Montgomery
See Campbell, (John) Ramsey

Compton-Burnett, I(vy)
1884(?)-1969 ...... **CLC 1, 3, 10, 15, 34**
See also CA 1-4R; 25-28R; CANR 4;
DLB 36; MTCW

Comstock, Anthony 1844-1915 .... **TCLC 13**
See also CA 110

Conan Doyle, Arthur
See Doyle, Arthur Conan

Conde, Maryse .... **CLC 52**
See also Boucolon, Maryse

Condon, Richard (Thomas)
1915-............. **CLC 4, 6, 8, 10, 45**
See also BEST 90:3; CA 1-4R; CAAS 1;
CANR 2, 23; MTCW

Congreve, William
1670-1729 .... **LC 5, 21; DC 2**
See also CDBLB 1660-1789; DLB 39, 84;
WLC

Connell, Evan S(helby) Jr.
1924-.................. **CLC 4, 6, 45**
See also AAYA 7; CA 1-4R; CAAS 2;
CANR 2, 39; DLB 2; DLBY 81; MTCW

Connelly, Marc(us Cook)
1890-1980 .... **CLC 7**
See also CA 85-88; 102; CANR 30; DLB 7;
DLBY 80; SATA 25

Connor, Ralph................... **TCLC 31**
See also Gordon, Charles William
See also DLB 92

Conrad, Joseph
1857-1924 ...... **TCLC 1, 6, 13, 25, 43;**
SSC 9
See also CA 104; 131; CDBLB 1890-1914;
DLB 10, 34, 98; MTCW; SATA 27; WLC

Conrad, Robert Arnold
See Hart, Moss

Conroy, Pat 1945-............. **CLC 30, 74**
See also AAYA 8; AITN 1; CA 85-88;
CANR 24; DLB 6; MTCW

Constant (de Rebecque), (Henri) Benjamin
1767-1830 .... **NCLC 6**
See also DLB 119

Conybeare, Charles Augustus
See Eliot, T(homas) S(tearns)

Cook, Michael 1933-............. **CLC 58**
See also CA 93-96; DLB 53

Cook, Robin 1940-............... **CLC 14**
See also BEST 90:2; CA 108; 111

Cook, Roy
See Silverberg, Robert

Cooke, Elizabeth 1948-.......... **CLC 55**
See also CA 129

Cooke, John Esten 1830-1886..... **NCLC 5**
See also DLB 3

Cooke, John Estes
See Baum, L(yman) Frank

Crumarums
See Crumb, R(obert)

Crumb, R(obert) 1943- . . . . **CLC 17**
See also CA 106

Crumbum
See Crumb, R(obert)

Crumski
See Crumb, R(obert)

Crum the Bum
See Crumb, R(obert)

Crunk
See Crumb, R(obert)

Crustt
See Crumb, R(obert)

Cryer, Gretchen (Kiger) 1935- . . . . . . **CLC 21**
See also CA 114; 123

Csath, Geza 1887-1919 . . . . **TCLC 13**
See also CA 111

Cudlip, David 1933- . . . . **CLC 34**

Cullen, Countee 1903-1946 . . . . . **TCLC 4, 37**
See also BLC 1; BW; CA 108; 124;
CDALB 1917-1929; DLB 4, 48, 51;
MTCW; SATA 18

Cum, R.
See Crumb, R(obert)

Cummings, Bruce F(rederick) 1889-1919
See Barbellion, W. N. P.
See also CA 123

Cummings, E(dward) E(stlin)
1894-1962 . . . . . **CLC 1, 3, 8, 12, 15, 68;**
PC 5
See also CA 73-76; CANR 31;
CDALB 1929-1941; DLB 4, 48; MTCW;
WLC 2

Cunha, Euclides (Rodrigues Pimenta) da
1866-1909 . . . . **TCLC 24**
See also CA 123

Cunningham, E. V.
See Fast, Howard (Melvin)

Cunningham, J(ames) V(incent)
1911-1985 . . . . **CLC 3, 31**
See also CA 1-4R; 115; CANR 1; DLB 5

Cunningham, Julia (Woolfolk)
1916- . . . . **CLC 12**
See also CA 9-12R; CANR 4, 19, 36;
MAICYA; SAAS 2; SATA 1, 26

Cunningham, Michael 1952- . . . . **CLC 34**
See also CA 136

Cunninghame Graham, R(obert) B(ontine)
1852-1936 . . . . **TCLC 19**
See also Graham, R(obert) B(ontine)
Cunninghame
See also CA 119; DLB 98

Currie, Ellen 19(?)- . . . . **CLC 44**

Curtin, Philip
See Lowndes, Marie Adelaide (Belloc)

Curtis, Price
See Ellison, Harlan

Czaczkes, Shmuel Yosef
See Agnon, S(hmuel) Y(osef Halevi)

D. P.
See Wells, H(erbert) G(eorge)

Dabrowska, Maria (Szumska)
1889-1965 . . . . **CLC 15**
See also CA 106

Dabydeen, David 1955- . . . . **CLC 34**
See also BW; CA 125

Dacey, Philip 1939- . . . . **CLC 51**
See also CA 37-40R; CANR 14, 32;
DLB 105

Dagerman, Stig (Halvard)
1923-1954 . . . . **TCLC 17**
See also CA 117

Dahl, Roald 1916-1990 . . . . **CLC 1, 6, 18**
See also CA 1-4R; 133; CANR 6, 32, 37;
CLR 1, 7; MAICYA; MTCW; SATA 1,
26; SATO 65

Dahlberg, Edward 1900-1977 . . . **CLC 1, 7, 14**
See also CA 9-12R; 69-72; CANR 31;
DLB 48; MTCW

Dale, Colin . . . . **TCLC 18**
See also Lawrence, T(homas) E(dward)

Dale, George E.
See Asimov, Isaac

Daly, Elizabeth 1878-1967 . . . . **CLC 52**
See also CA 23-24; 25-28R; CAP 2

Daly, Maureen 1921- . . . . **CLC 17**
See also AAYA 5; CANR 37; MAICYA;
SAAS 1; SATA 2

Daniels, Brett
See Adler, Renata

Dannay, Frederic 1905-1982 . . . . **CLC 11**
See also Queen, Ellery
See also CA 1-4R; 107; CANR 1, 39;
MTCW

D'Annunzio, Gabriele
1863-1938 . . . . **TCLC 6, 40**
See also CA 104

d'Antibes, Germain
See Simenon, Georges (Jacques Christian)

Danvers, Dennis 1947- . . . . **CLC 70**

Danziger, Paula 1944- . . . . **CLC 21**
See also AAYA 4; CA 112; 115; CANR 37;
CLR 20; MAICYA; SATA 30, 36, 63

Dario, Ruben . . . . **TCLC 4**
See also Sarmiento, Felix Ruben Garcia

Darley, George 1795-1846 . . . . **NCLC 2**
See also DLB 96

Daryush, Elizabeth 1887-1977 . . . . **CLC 6, 19**
See also CA 49-52; CANR 3; DLB 20

Daudet, (Louis Marie) Alphonse
1840-1897 . . . . **NCLC 1**
See also DLB 123

Daumal, Rene 1908-1944 . . . . **TCLC 14**
See also CA 114

Davenport, Guy (Mattison Jr.)
1927- . . . . **CLC 6, 14, 38**
See also CA 33-36R; CANR 23

Davidson, Avram 1923-
See Queen, Ellery
See also CA 101; CANR 26; DLB 8

Davidson, Donald (Grady)
1893-1968 . . . . **CLC 2, 13, 19**
See also CA 5-8R; 25-28R; CANR 4;
DLB 45

Davidson, Hugh
See Hamilton, Edmond

Davidson, John 1857-1909 . . . . **TCLC 24**
See also CA 118; DLB 19

Davidson, Sara 1943- . . . . **CLC 9**
See also CA 81-84

Davie, Donald (Alfred)
1922- . . . . **CLC 5, 8, 10, 31**
See also CA 1-4R; CAAS 3; CANR 1;
DLB 27; MTCW

Davies, Ray(mond Douglas) 1944- . . **CLC 21**
See also CA 116

Davies, Rhys 1903-1978 . . . . **CLC 23**
See also CA 9-12R; 81-84; CANR 4

Davies, (William) Robertson
1913- . . . . **CLC 2, 7, 13, 25, 42, 75**
See also BEST 89:2; CA 33-36R; CANR 17;
DLB 68; MTCW; WLC

Davies, W(illiam) H(enry)
1871-1940 . . . . **TCLC 5**
See also CA 104; DLB 19

Davies, Walter C.
See Kornbluth, C(yril) M.

Davis, B. Lynch
See Bioy Casares, Adolfo; Borges, Jorge
Luis

Davis, Gordon
See Hunt, E(verette) Howard Jr.

Davis, Harold Lenoir 1896-1960 . . . . **CLC 49**
See also CA 89-92; DLB 9

Davis, Rebecca (Blaine) Harding
1831-1910 . . . . **TCLC 6**
See also CA 104; DLB 74

Davis, Richard Harding
1864-1916 . . . . **TCLC 24**
See also CA 114; DLB 12, 23, 78, 79

Davison, Frank Dalby 1893-1970 . . . **CLC 15**
See also CA 116

Davison, Lawrence H.
See Lawrence, D(avid) H(erbert Richards)

Davison, Peter 1928- . . . . **CLC 28**
See also CA 9-12R; CAAS 4; CANR 3;
DLB 5

Davys, Mary 1674-1732 . . . . **LC 1**
See also DLB 39

Dawson, Fielding 1930- . . . . **CLC 6**
See also CA 85-88

Day, Clarence (Shepard Jr.)
1874-1935 . . . . **TCLC 25**
See also CA 108; DLB 11

Day, Thomas 1748-1789 . . . . **LC 1**
See also DLB 39; YABC 1

Day Lewis, C(ecil)
1904-1972 . . . . **CLC 1, 6, 10**
See also Blake, Nicholas
See also CA 13-16; 33-36R; CANR 34;
CAP 1; DLB 15, 20; MTCW

Dazai, Osamu . . . . **TCLC 11**
See also Tsushima, Shuji

de Andrade, Carlos Drummond
See Drummond de Andrade, Carlos

Deane, Norman
See Creasey, John

Dickinson, Peter (Malcolm)
1927- .... **CLC 12, 35**
See also AAYA 9; CA 41-44R; CANR 31;
DLB 87; MAICYA; SATA 5, 62

Dickson, Carr
See Carr, John Dickson

Dickson, Carter
See Carr, John Dickson

Didion, Joan 1934- ..... **CLC 1, 3, 8, 14, 32**
See also AITN 1; CA 5-8R; CANR 14;
CDALB 1968-1988; DLB 2; DLBY 81,
86; MTCW

Dietrich, Robert
See Hunt, E(verette) Howard Jr.

Dillard, Annie 1945- .... **CLC 9, 60**
See also AAYA 6; CA 49-52; CANR 3;
DLBY 80; MTCW; SATA 10

Dillard, R(ichard) H(enry) W(ilde)
1937- .... **CLC 5**
See also CA 21-24R; CAAS 7; CANR 10;
DLB 5

Dillon, Eilis 1920- .... **CLC 17**
See also CA 9-12R; CAAS 3; CANR 4, 38;
CLR 26; MAICYA; SATA 2

Dimont, Penelope
See Mortimer, Penelope (Ruth)

Dinesen, Isak .... **CLC 10, 29; SSC 7**
See also Blixen, Karen (Christentze
Dinesen)

Ding Ling .... **CLC 68**
See also Chiang Pin-chin

Disch, Thomas M(ichael) 1940- ... **CLC 7, 36**
See also CA 21-24R; CAAS 4; CANR 17,
36; CLR 18; DLB 8; MAICYA; MTCW;
SAAS 15; SATA 54

Disch, Tom
See Disch, Thomas M(ichael)

d'Isly, Georges
See Simenon, Georges (Jacques Christian)

Disraeli, Benjamin 1804-1881 .. **NCLC 2, 39**
See also DLB 21, 55

Ditcum, Steve
See Crumb, R(obert)

Dixon, Paige
See Corcoran, Barbara

Dixon, Stephen 1936- .... **CLC 52**
See also CA 89-92; CANR 17

Doblin, Alfred .... **TCLC 13**
See also Doeblin, Alfred

Dobrolyubov, Nikolai Alexandrovich
1836-1861 .... **NCLC 5**

Dobyns, Stephen 1941- .... **CLC 37**
See also CA 45-48; CANR 2, 18

Doctorow, E(dgar) L(aurence)
1931- ..... **CLC 6, 11, 15, 18, 37, 44, 65**
See also AITN 2; BEST 89:3; CA 45-48;
CANR 2, 33; CDALB 1968-1988; DLB 2,
28; DLBY 80; MTCW

Dodgson, Charles Lutwidge 1832-1898
See Carroll, Lewis
See also CLR 2; MAICYA; YABC 2

Doeblin, Alfred 1878-1957 .... **TCLC 13**
See also Doblin, Alfred
See also CA 110; DLB 66

Doerr, Harriet 1910- .... **CLC 34**
See also CA 117; 122

Domecq, H(onorio) Bustos
See Bioy Casares, Adolfo; Borges, Jorge
Luis

Domini, Rey
See Lorde, Audre (Geraldine)

Dominique
See Proust,
(Valentin-Louis-George-Eugene-)Marcel

Don, A
See Stephen, Leslie

Donaldson, Stephen R. 1947- .... **CLC 46**
See also CA 89-92; CANR 13

Donleavy, J(ames) P(atrick)
1926- .... **CLC 1, 4, 6, 10, 45**
See also AITN 2; CA 9-12R; CANR 24;
DLB 6; MTCW

Donne, John 1572-1631 ...... **LC 10; PC 1**
See also CDBLB Before 1660; DLB 121;
WLC

Donnell, David 1939(?)- .... **CLC 34**

Donoso (Yanez), Jose
1924- .... **CLC 4, 8, 11, 32**
See also CA 81-84; CANR 32; DLB 113;
HW; MTCW

Donovan, John 1928-1992 .... **CLC 35**
See also CA 97-100; 137; CLR 3;
MAICYA; SATA 29

Don Roberto
See Cunninghame Graham, R(obert)
B(ontine)

Doolittle, Hilda
1886-1961 .... **CLC 3, 8, 14, 31, 34, 73;
PC 5**
See also H. D.
See also CA 97-100; CANR 35; DLB 4, 45;
MTCW; WLC

Dorfman, Ariel 1942- .... **CLC 48**
See also CA 124; 130; HW

Dorn, Edward (Merton) 1929- ... **CLC 10, 18**
See also CA 93-96; DLB 5

Dorsan, Luc
See Simenon, Georges (Jacques Christian)

Dorsange, Jean
See Simenon, Georges (Jacques Christian)

Dos Passos, John (Roderigo)
1896-1970 ... **CLC 1, 4, 8, 11, 15, 25, 34**
See also CA 1-4R; 29-32R; CANR 3;
CDALB 1929-1941; DLB 4, 9; DLBD 1;
MTCW; WLC

Dossage, Jean
See Simenon, Georges (Jacques Christian)

Dostoevsky, Fedor Mikhailovich
1821-1881 .... **NCLC 2, 7, 21, 33; SSC 2**
See also WLC

Doughty, Charles M(ontagu)
1843-1926 .... **TCLC 27**
See also CA 115; DLB 19, 57

Douglas, Ellen
See Haxton, Josephine Ayres

Douglas, Gavin 1475(?)-1522 .... **LC 20**

Douglas, Keith 1920-1944 .... **TCLC 40**
See also DLB 27

Douglas, Leonard
See Bradbury, Ray (Douglas)

Douglas, Michael
See Crichton, (John) Michael

Douglass, Frederick 1817(?)-1895 .. **NCLC 7**
See also BLC 1; CDALB 1640-1865;
DLB 1, 43, 50, 79; SATA 29; WLC

Dourado, (Waldomiro Freitas) Autran
1926- .... **CLC 23, 60**
See also CA 25-28R; CANR 34

Dourado, Waldomiro Autran
See Dourado, (Waldomiro Freitas) Autran

Dove, Rita (Frances) 1952- ... **CLC 50; PC 6**
See also BW; CA 109; CANR 27; DLB 120

Dowell, Coleman 1925-1985 .... **CLC 60**
See also CA 25-28R; 117; CANR 10

Dowson, Ernest Christopher
1867-1900 .... **TCLC 4**
See also CA 105; DLB 19

Doyle, A. Conan
See Doyle, Arthur Conan

Doyle, Arthur Conan 1859-1930 .... **TCLC 7**
See also CA 104; 122; CDBLB 1890-1914;
DLB 18, 70; MTCW; SATA 24; WLC

Doyle, Conan
See Doyle, Arthur Conan

Doyle, John
See Graves, Robert (von Ranke)

Doyle, Sir A. Conan
See Doyle, Arthur Conan

Doyle, Sir Arthur Conan
See Doyle, Arthur Conan

Dr. A
See Asimov, Isaac; Silverstein, Alvin

Drabble, Margaret
1939- .... **CLC 2, 3, 5, 8, 10, 22, 53**
See also CA 13-16R; CANR 18, 35;
CDBLB 1960 to Present; DLB 14;
MTCW; SATA 48

Drapier, M. B.
See Swift, Jonathan

Drayham, James
See Mencken, H(enry) L(ouis)

Drayton, Michael 1563-1631 .... **LC 8**

Dreadstone, Carl
See Campbell, (John) Ramsey

Dreiser, Theodore (Herman Albert)
1871-1945 .... **TCLC 10, 18, 35**
See also CA 106; 132; CDALB 1865-1917;
DLB 9, 12, 102; DLBD 1; MTCW; WLC

Drexler, Rosalyn 1926- .... **CLC 2, 6**
See also CA 81-84

Dreyer, Carl Theodor 1889-1968 .... **CLC 16**
See also CA 116

Drieu la Rochelle, Pierre(-Eugene)
1893-1945 .... **TCLC 21**
See also CA 117; DLB 72

Drop Shot
See Cable, George Washington

Droste-Hulshoff, Annette Freiin von
1797-1848 .... **NCLC 3**

Drummond, Walter
See Silverberg, Robert

Drummond, William Henry
 1854-1907 . . . . **TCLC 25**
 See also DLB 92

Drummond de Andrade, Carlos
 1902-1987 . . . . **CLC 18**
 See also Andrade, Carlos Drummond de
 See also CA 132; 123

Drury, Allen (Stuart) 1918- . . . . **CLC 37**
 See also CA 57-60; CANR 18

Dryden, John 1631-1700 . . . . **LC 3, 21; DC 3**
 See also CDBLB 1660-1789; DLB 80, 101;
 WLC

Duberman, Martin 1930- . . . . **CLC 8**
 See also CA 1-4R; CANR 2

Dubie, Norman (Evans) 1945- . . . . . . **CLC 36**
 See also CA 69-72; CANR 12; DLB 120

Du Bois, W(illiam) E(dward) B(urghardt)
 1868-1963 . . . . **CLC 1, 2, 13, 64**
 See also BLC 1; BW; CA 85-88; CANR 34;
 CDALB 1865-1917; DLB 47, 50, 91;
 MTCW; SATA 42; WLC

Dubus, Andre 1936- . . . . **CLC 13, 36**
 See also CA 21-24R; CANR 17

Duca Minimo
 See D'Annunzio, Gabriele

Ducharme, Rejean 1941- . . . . **CLC 74**
 See also DLB 60

Duclos, Charles Pinot 1704-1772 . . . . . **LC 1**

Dudek, Louis 1918- . . . . **CLC 11, 19**
 See also CA 45-48; CAAS 14; CANR 1;
 DLB 88

Duerrenmatt, Friedrich
 1921-1990 . . . . . . **CLC 1, 4, 8, 11, 15, 43**
 See also Durrenmatt, Friedrich
 See also CA 17-20R; CANR 33; DLB 69;
 MTCW

Duffy, Bruce (?)- . . . . **CLC 50**

Duffy, Maureen 1933- . . . . **CLC 37**
 See also CA 25-28R; CANR 33; DLB 14;
 MTCW

Dugan, Alan 1923- . . . . **CLC 2, 6**
 See also CA 81-84; DLB 5

du Gard, Roger Martin
 See Martin du Gard, Roger

Duhamel, Georges 1884-1966 . . . . **CLC 8**
 See also CA 81-84; 25-28R; CANR 35;
 DLB 65; MTCW

Dujardin, Edouard (Emile Louis)
 1861-1949 . . . . **TCLC 13**
 See also CA 109; DLB 123

Dumas, Alexandre (Davy de la Pailleterie)
 1802-1870 . . . . **NCLC 11**
 See also DLB 119; SATA 18; WLC

Dumas, Alexandre
 1824-1895 . . . . **NCLC 9; DC 1**

Dumas, Claudine
 See Malzberg, Barry N(athaniel)

Dumas, Henry L. 1934-1968 . . . . . **CLC 6, 62**
 See also BW; CA 85-88; DLB 41

du Maurier, Daphne
 1907-1989 . . . . **CLC 6, 11, 59**
 See also CA 5-8R; 128; CANR 6; MTCW;
 SATA 27, 60

Dunbar, Paul Laurence
 1872-1906 . . . . **TCLC 2, 12; PC 5; SSC 8**
 See also BLC 1; BW; CA 104; 124;
 CDALB 1865-1917; DLB 50, 54, 78;
 SATA 34; WLC

Dunbar, William 1460(?)-1530(?) . . . . **LC 20**

Duncan, Lois 1934- . . . . **CLC 26**
 See also AAYA 4; CA 1-4R; CANR 2, 23,
 36; MAICYA; SAAS 2; SATA 1, 36

Duncan, Robert (Edward)
 1919-1988 . . . **CLC 1, 2, 4, 7, 15, 41, 55;**
 PC 2
 See also CA 9-12R; 124; CANR 28; DLB 5,
 16; MTCW

Dunlap, William 1766-1839 . . . . **NCLC 2**
 See also DLB 30, 37, 59

Dunn, Douglas (Eaglesham)
 1942- . . . . **CLC 6, 40**
 See also CA 45-48; CANR 2, 33; DLB 40;
 MTCW

Dunn, Katherine (Karen) 1945- . . . . . **CLC 71**
 See also CA 33-36R

Dunn, Stephen 1939- . . . . **CLC 36**
 See also CA 33-36R; CANR 12; DLB 105

Dunne, Finley Peter 1867-1936. . . . **TCLC 28**
 See also CA 108; DLB 11, 23

Dunne, John Gregory 1932- . . . . **CLC 28**
 See also CA 25-28R; CANR 14; DLBY 80

Dunsany, Edward John Moreton Drax
 Plunkett 1878-1957
 See Dunsany, Lord; Lord Dunsany
 See also CA 104; DLB 10

Dunsany, Lord. . . . . **TCLC 2**
 See also Dunsany, Edward John Moreton
 Drax Plunkett
 See also DLB 77

du Perry, Jean
 See Simenon, Georges (Jacques Christian)

Durang, Christopher (Ferdinand)
 1949- . . . . **CLC 27, 38**
 See also CA 105

Duras, Marguerite
 1914- . . . . . . **CLC 3, 6, 11, 20, 34, 40, 68**
 See also CA 25-28R; DLB 83; MTCW

Durban, (Rosa) Pam 1947- . . . . **CLC 39**
 See also CA 123

Durcan, Paul 1944- . . . . **CLC 43, 70**
 See also CA 134

Durrell, Lawrence (George)
 1912-1990 . . . . **CLC 1, 4, 6, 8, 13, 27, 41**
 See also CA 9-12R; 132;
 CDBLB 1945-1960; DLB 15, 27;
 DLBY 90; MTCW

Durrenmatt, Friedrich
 . . . . **CLC 1, 4, 8, 11, 15, 43**
 See also Duerrenmatt, Friedrich
 See also DLB 69

Dutt, Toru 1856-1877. . . . . **NCLC 29**

Dwight, Timothy 1752-1817. . . . . . **NCLC 13**
 See also DLB 37

Dworkin, Andrea 1946- . . . . **CLC 43**
 See also CA 77-80; CANR 16, 39; MTCW

Dylan, Bob 1941- . . . . **CLC 3, 4, 6, 12**
 See also CA 41-44R; DLB 16

Eagleton, Terence (Francis) 1943-
 See Eagleton, Terry
 See also CA 57-60; CANR 7, 23; MTCW

Eagleton, Terry . . . . **CLC 63**
 See also Eagleton, Terence (Francis)

East, Michael
 See West, Morris L(anglo)

Eastaway, Edward
 See Thomas, (Philip) Edward

Eastlake, William (Derry) 1917- . . . . . **CLC 8**
 See also CA 5-8R; CAAS 1; CANR 5;
 DLB 6

Eberhart, Richard (Ghormley)
 1904- . . . . **CLC 3, 11, 19, 56**
 See also CA 1-4R; CANR 2;
 CDALB 1941-1968; DLB 48; MTCW

Eberstadt, Fernanda 1960- . . . . **CLC 39**
 See also CA 136

Echegaray (y Eizaguirre), Jose (Maria Waldo)
 1832-1916 . . . . **TCLC 4**
 See also CA 104; CANR 32; HW; MTCW

Echeverria, (Jose) Esteban (Antonino)
 1805-1851 . . . . **NCLC 18**

Echo
 See Proust,
 (Valentin-Louis-George-Eugene-)Marcel

Eckert, Allan W. 1931- . . . . **CLC 17**
 See also CA 13-16R; CANR 14; SATA 27,
 29

Eckhart, Meister 1260(?)-1328(?) . . **CMLC 9**
 See also DLB 115

Eckmar, F. R.
 See de Hartog, Jan

Eco, Umberto 1932- . . . . **CLC 28, 60**
 See also BEST 90:1; CA 77-80; CANR 12,
 33; MTCW

Eddison, E(ric) R(ucker)
 1882-1945 . . . . **TCLC 15**
 See also CA 109

Edel, (Joseph) Leon 1907- . . . . . . **CLC 29, 34**
 See also CA 1-4R; CANR 1, 22; DLB 103

Eden, Emily 1797-1869 . . . . **NCLC 10**

Edgar, David 1948- . . . . **CLC 42**
 See also CA 57-60; CANR 12; DLB 13;
 MTCW

Edgerton, Clyde (Carlyle) 1944- . . . . **CLC 39**
 See also CA 118; 134

Edgeworth, Maria 1767-1849 . . . . . . **NCLC 1**
 See also DLB 116; SATA 21

Edmonds, Paul
 See Kuttner, Henry

Edmonds, Walter D(umaux) 1903- . . **CLC 35**
 See also CA 5-8R; CANR 2; DLB 9;
 MAICYA; SAAS 4; SATA 1, 27

Edmondson, Wallace
 See Ellison, Harlan

Edson, Russell . . . . **CLC 13**
 See also CA 33-36R

Edwards, G(erald) B(asil)
 1899-1976 . . . . **CLC 25**
 See also CA 110

Edwards, Gus 1939- . . . . **CLC 43**
 See also CA 108

Esenin, Sergei (Alexandrovich)
1895-1925 .... **TCLC 4**
See also CA 104

Eshleman, Clayton 1935-.......... **CLC 7**
See also CA 33-36R; CAAS 6; DLB 5

Espriella, Don Manuel Alvarez
See Southey, Robert

Espriu, Salvador 1913-1985........ **CLC 9**
See also CA 115

Espronceda, Jose de 1808-1842... **NCLC 39**

Esse, James
See Stephens, James

Esterbrook, Tom
See Hubbard, L(afayette) Ron(ald)

Estleman, Loren D. 1952-........ **CLC 48**
See also CA 85-88; CANR 27; MTCW

Evans, Mary Ann
See Eliot, George

Evarts, Esther
See Benson, Sally

Everett, Percival
See Everett, Percival L.

Everett, Percival L. 1956-........ **CLC 57**
See also CA 129

Everson, R(onald) G(ilmour)
1903- .... **CLC 27**
See also CA 17-20R; DLB 88

Everson, William (Oliver)
1912- .... **CLC 1, 5, 14**
See also CA 9-12R; CANR 20; DLB 5, 16;
MTCW

Evtushenko, Evgenii Aleksandrovich
See Yevtushenko, Yevgeny (Alexandrovich)

Ewart, Gavin (Buchanan)
1916- .... **CLC 13, 46**
See also CA 89-92; CANR 17; DLB 40;
MTCW

Ewers, Hanns Heinz 1871-1943... **TCLC 12**
See also CA 109

Ewing, Frederick R.
See Sturgeon, Theodore (Hamilton)

Exley, Frederick (Earl) 1929-.... **CLC 6, 11**
See also AITN 2; CA 81-84; 138; DLBY 81

Eynhardt, Guillermo
See Quiroga, Horacio (Sylvestre)

Ezekiel, Nissim 1924-............ **CLC 61**
See also CA 61-64

Ezekiel, Tish O'Dowd 1943-....... **CLC 34**
See also CA 129

Fagen, Donald 1948-............. **CLC 26**

Fainzilberg, Ilya Arnoldovich 1897-1937
See Ilf, Ilya
See also CA 120

Fair, Ronald L. 1932-............ **CLC 18**
See also BW; CA 69-72; CANR 25; DLB 33

Fairbairns, Zoe (Ann) 1948- .... **CLC 32**
See also CA 103; CANR 21

Falco, Gian
See Papini, Giovanni

Falconer, James
See Kirkup, James

Falconer, Kenneth
See Kornbluth, C(yril) M.

Falkland, Samuel
See Heijermans, Herman

Fallaci, Oriana 1930-............. **CLC 11**
See also CA 77-80; CANR 15; MTCW

Faludy, George 1913-............. **CLC 42**
See also CA 21-24R

Faludy, Gyoergy
See Faludy, George

Fanon, Frantz 1925-1961......... **CLC 74**
See also BLC 2; BW; CA 116; 89-92

Fanshawe, Ann .... **LC 11**

Fante, John (Thomas) 1911-1983... **CLC 60**
See also CA 69-72; 109; CANR 23;
DLBY 83

Farah, Nuruddin 1945-............. **CLC 53**
See also BLC 2; CA 106

Fargue, Leon-Paul 1876(?)-1947... **TCLC 11**
See also CA 109

Farigoule, Louis
See Romains, Jules

Farina, Richard 1936(?)-1966 .... **CLC 9**
See also CA 81-84; 25-28R

Farley, Walter (Lorimer)
1915-1989 .... **CLC 17**
See also CA 17-20R; CANR 8, 29; DLB 22;
MAICYA; SATA 2, 43

Farmer, Philip Jose 1918-....... **CLC 1, 19**
See also CA 1-4R; CANR 4, 35; DLB 8;
MTCW

Farquhar, George 1677-1707....... **LC 21**
See also DLB 84

Farrell, J(ames) G(ordon)
1935-1979 .... **CLC 6**
See also CA 73-76; 89-92; CANR 36;
DLB 14; MTCW

Farrell, James T(homas)
1904-1979 .... **CLC 1, 4, 8, 11, 66**
See also CA 5-8R; 89-92; CANR 9; DLB 4,
9, 86; DLBD 2; MTCW

Farren, Richard J.
See Betjeman, John

Farren, Richard M.
See Betjeman, John

Fassbinder, Rainer Werner
1946-1982 .... **CLC 20**
See also CA 93-96; 106; CANR 31

Fast, Howard (Melvin) 1914- ...... **CLC 23**
See also CA 1-4R; CANR 1, 33; DLB 9;
SATA 7

Faulcon, Robert
See Holdstock, Robert P.

Faulkner, William (Cuthbert)
1897-1962 .... **CLC 1, 3, 6, 8, 9, 11, 14,**
18, 28, 52, 68; SSC 1
See also AAYA 7; CA 81-84; CANR 33;
CDALB 1929-1941; DLB 9, 11, 44, 102;
DLBD 2; DLBY 86; MTCW; WLC

Fauset, Jessie Redmon
1884(?)-1961 .... **CLC 19, 54**
See also BLC 2; BW; CA 109; DLB 51

Faust, Irvin 1924-................. **CLC 8**
See also CA 33-36R; CANR 28; DLB 2, 28;
DLBY 80

Fawkes, Guy
See Benchley, Robert (Charles)

Fearing, Kenneth (Flexner)
1902-1961 .... **CLC 51**
See also CA 93-96; DLB 9

Fecamps, Elise
See Creasey, John

Federman, Raymond 1928- ...... **CLC 6, 47**
See also CA 17-20R; CAAS 8; CANR 10;
DLBY 80

Federspiel, J(uerg) F. 1931-........ **CLC 42**

Feiffer, Jules (Ralph) 1929-.... **CLC 2, 8, 64**
See also AAYA 3; CA 17-20R; CANR 30;
DLB 7, 44; MTCW; SATA 8, 61

Feige, Hermann Albert Otto Maximilian
See Traven, B.

Fei-Kan, Li
See Li Fei-kan

Feinberg, David B. 1956-.......... **CLC 59**
See also CA 135

Feinstein, Elaine 1930-............ **CLC 36**
See also CA 69-72; CAAS 1; CANR 31;
DLB 14, 40; MTCW

Feldman, Irving (Mordecai) 1928-.... **CLC 7**
See also CA 1-4R; CANR 1

Fellini, Federico 1920-............ **CLC 16**
See also CA 65-68; CANR 33

Felsen, Henry Gregor 1916- .... **CLC 17**
See also CA 1-4R; CANR 1; SAAS 2;
SATA 1

Fenton, James Martin 1949-....... **CLC 32**
See also CA 102; DLB 40

Ferber, Edna 1887-1968........... **CLC 18**
See also AITN 1; CA 5-8R; 25-28R; DLB 9,
28, 86; MTCW; SATA 7

Ferguson, Helen
See Kavan, Anna

Ferguson, Samuel 1810-1886..... **NCLC 33**
See also DLB 32

Ferling, Lawrence
See Ferlinghetti, Lawrence (Monsanto)

Ferlinghetti, Lawrence (Monsanto)
1919(?)- .... **CLC 2, 6, 10, 27; PC 1**
See also CA 5-8R; CANR 3;
CDALB 1941-1968; DLB 5, 16; MTCW

Fernandez, Vicente Garcia Huidobro
See Huidobro Fernandez, Vicente Garcia

Ferrer, Gabriel (Francisco Victor) Miro
See Miro (Ferrer), Gabriel (Francisco
Victor)

Ferrier, Susan (Edmonstone)
1782-1854 .... **NCLC 8**
See also DLB 116

Ferrigno, Robert .... **CLC 65**

Feuchtwanger, Lion 1884-1958..... **TCLC 3**
See also CA 104; DLB 66

Feydeau, Georges (Leon Jules Marie)
1862-1921 .... **TCLC 22**
See also CA 113

Ficino, Marsilio 1433-1499........ **LC 12**

Fiedler, Leslie A(aron)
1917- .... **CLC 4, 13, 24**
See also CA 9-12R; CANR 7; DLB 28, 67;
MTCW

Field, Andrew 1938-.............. **CLC 44**
See also CA 97-100; CANR 25

Field, Eugene 1850-1895 .... **NCLC 3**
See also DLB 23, 42; MAICYA; SATA 16

Field, Gans T.
See Wellman, Manly Wade

Field, Michael .... **TCLC 43**

Field, Peter
See Hobson, Laura Z(ametkin)

Fielding, Henry 1707-1754 .... **LC 1**
See also CDBLB 1660-1789; DLB 39, 84,
101; WLC

Fielding, Sarah 1710-1768 .... **LC 1**
See also DLB 39

Fierstein, Harvey (Forbes) 1954- ... **CLC 33**
See also CA 123; 129

Figes, Eva 1932-................. **CLC 31**
See also CA 53-56; CANR 4; DLB 14

Finch, Robert (Duer Claydon)
1900-....................... **CLC 18**
See also CA 57-60; CANR 9, 24; DLB 88

Findley, Timothy 1930-........... **CLC 27**
See also CA 25-28R; CANR 12; DLB 53

Fink, William
See Mencken, H(enry) L(ouis)

Firbank, Louis 1942-
See Reed, Lou
See also CA 117

Firbank, (Arthur Annesley) Ronald
1886-1926 .... **TCLC 1**
See also CA 104; DLB 36

Fisher, Roy 1930-................ **CLC 25**
See also CA 81-84; CAAS 10; CANR 16;
DLB 40

Fisher, Rudolph 1897-1934 .... **TCLC 11**
See also BLC 2; BW; CA 107; 124; DLB 51,
102

Fisher, Vardis (Alvero) 1895-1968.... **CLC 7**
See also CA 5-8R; 25-28R; DLB 9

Fiske, Tarleton
See Bloch, Robert (Albert)

Fitch, Clarke
See Sinclair, Upton (Beall)

Fitch, John IV
See Cormier, Robert (Edmund)

Fitgerald, Penelope 1916- .... **CLC 61**

Fitzgerald, Captain Hugh
See Baum, L(yman) Frank

FitzGerald, Edward 1809-1883 .... **NCLC 9**
See also DLB 32

Fitzgerald, F(rancis) Scott (Key)
1896-1940 .... **TCLC 1, 6, 14, 28; SSC 6**
See also AITN 1; CA 110; 123;
CDALB 1917-1929; DLB 4, 9, 86;
DLBD 1; DLBY 81; MTCW; WLC

Fitzgerald, Penelope 1916-...... **CLC 19, 51**
See also CA 85-88; CAAS 10; DLB 14

FitzGerald, Robert D(avid)
1902-1987 .... **CLC 19**
See also CA 17-20R

Fitzgerald, Robert (Stuart)
1910-1985 .... **CLC 39**
See also CA 1-4R; 114; CANR 1; DLBY 80

Flanagan, Thomas (James Bonner)
1923-..................... **CLC 25, 52**
See also CA 108; DLBY 80; MTCW

Flaubert, Gustave
1821-1880 ..... **NCLC 2, 10, 19; SSC 11**
See also DLB 119; WLC

Flecker, (Herman) James Elroy
1884-1915 .... **TCLC 43**
See also CA 109; DLB 10, 19

Fleming, Ian (Lancaster)
1908-1964 .... **CLC 3, 30**
See also CA 5-8R; CDBLB 1945-1960;
DLB 87; MTCW; SATA 9

Fleming, Thomas (James) 1927- .... **CLC 37**
See also CA 5-8R; CANR 10; SATA 8

Fletcher, John Gould 1886-1950... **TCLC 35**
See also CA 107; DLB 4, 45

Fleur, Paul
See Pohl, Frederik

Flying Officer X
See Bates, H(erbert) E(rnest)

Fo, Dario 1926-................. **CLC 32**
See also CA 116; 128; MTCW

Fogarty, Jonathan Titulescu Esq.
See Farrell, James T(homas)

Folke, Will
See Bloch, Robert (Albert)

Follett, Ken(neth Martin) 1949- .... **CLC 18**
See also AAYA 6; BEST 89:4; CA 81-84;
CANR 13, 33; DLB 87; DLBY 81;
MTCW

Fontane, Theodor 1819-1898 ..... **NCLC 26**

Foote, Horton 1916-.............. **CLC 51**
See also CA 73-76; CANR 34; DLB 26

Foote, Shelby 1916-.............. **CLC 75**
See also CA 5-8R; CANR 3; DLB 2, 17

Forbes, Esther 1891-1967......... **CLC 12**
See also CA 13-14; 25-28R; CAP 1;
CLR 27; DLB 22; MAICYA; SATA 2

Forche, Carolyn (Louise) 1950-..... **CLC 25**
See also CA 109; 117; DLB 5

Ford, Elbur
See Hibbert, Eleanor Burford

Ford, Ford Madox
1873-1939 .... **TCLC 1, 15, 39**
See also CA 104; 132; CDBLB 1914-1945;
DLB 34, 98; MTCW

Ford, John 1895-1973............. **CLC 16**
See also CA 45-48

Ford, Richard 1944-.............. **CLC 46**
See also CA 69-72; CANR 11

Ford, Webster
See Masters, Edgar Lee

Foreman, Richard 1937-........... **CLC 50**
See also CA 65-68; CANR 32

Forester, C(ecil) S(cott)
1899-1966 .... **CLC 35**
See also CA 73-76; 25-28R; SATA 13

Forez
See Mauriac, Francois (Charles)

Forman, James Douglas 1932-...... **CLC 21**
See also CA 9-12R; CANR 4, 19;
MAICYA; SATA 8, 70

Fornes, Maria Irene 1930-...... **CLC 39, 61**
See also CA 25-28R; CANR 28; DLB 7;
HW; MTCW

Forrest, Leon 1937-.............. **CLC 4**
See also BW; CA 89-92; CAAS 7;
CANR 25; DLB 33

Forster, E(dward) M(organ)
1879-1970 .... **CLC 1, 2, 3, 4, 9, 10, 13,
15, 22, 45**
See also AAYA 2; CA 13-14; 25-28R;
CAP 1; CDBLB 1914-1945; DLB 34, 98;
DLBD 10; MTCW; SATA 57; WLC

Forster, John 1812-1876 .... **NCLC 11**

Forsyth, Frederick 1938-...... **CLC 2, 5, 36**
See also BEST 89:4; CA 85-88; CANR 38;
DLB 87; MTCW

Forten, Charlotte L. .... **TCLC 16**
See Grimke, Charlotte L(ottie) Forten
See also BLC 2; DLB 50

Foscolo, Ugo 1778-1827.......... **NCLC 8**

Fosse, Bob .... **CLC 20**
See also Fosse, Robert Louis

Fosse, Robert Louis 1927-1987
See Fosse, Bob
See also CA 110; 123

Foster, Stephen Collins
1826-1864 .... **NCLC 26**

Foucault, Michel
1926-1984 .... **CLC 31, 34, 69**
See also CA 105; 113; CANR 34; MTCW

Fouque, Friedrich (Heinrich Karl) de la Motte
1777-1843 .... **NCLC 2**
See also DLB 90

Fournier, Henri Alban 1886-1914
See Alain-Fournier
See also CA 104

Fournier, Pierre 1916-............ **CLC 11**
See also Gascar, Pierre
See also CA 89-92; CANR 16

Fowles, John
1926- .... **CLC 1, 2, 3, 4, 6, 9, 10, 15, 33**
See also CA 5-8R; CANR 25; CDBLB 1960
to Present; DLB 14; MTCW; SATA 22

Fox, Paula 1923-................. **CLC 2, 8**
See also AAYA 3; CA 73-76; CANR 20,
36; CLR 1; DLB 52; MAICYA; MTCW;
SATA 17, 60

Fox, William Price (Jr.) 1926- ..... **CLC 22**
See also CA 17-20R; CANR 11; DLB 2;
DLBY 81

Foxe, John 1516(?)-1587 .... **LC 14**

Frame, Janet .... **CLC 2, 3, 6, 22, 66**
See also Clutha, Janet Paterson Frame

France, Anatole.................. **TCLC 9**
See also Thibault, Jacques Anatole Francois
See also DLB 123

Francis, Claude 19(?)- .... **CLC 50**

Francis, Dick 1920- .... **CLC 2, 22, 42**
See also AAYA 5; BEST 89:3; CA 5-8R;
CANR 9; CDBLB 1960 to Present;
DLB 87; MTCW

Francis, Robert (Churchill)
1901-1987 .... **CLC 15**
See also CA 1-4R; 123; CANR 1

Frank, Anne(lies Marie)
1929-1945 . . . . TCLC 17
See also CA 113; 133; MTCW; SATA 42;
WLC

Frank, Elizabeth 1945- . . . . CLC 39
See also CA 121; 126

Franklin, Benjamin
See Hasek, Jaroslav (Matej Frantisek)

Franklin, (Stella Maraia Sarah) Miles
1879-1954 . . . . TCLC 7
See also CA 104

Fraser, Antonia (Pakenham)
1932- . . . . CLC 32
See also CA 85-88; MTCW; SATA 32

Fraser, George MacDonald 1925- . . . . CLC 7
See also CA 45-48; CANR 2

Fraser, Sylvia 1935- . . . . CLC 64
See also CA 45-48; CANR 1, 16

Frayn, Michael 1933- . . . . . . CLC 3, 7, 31, 47
See also CA 5-8R; CANR 30; DLB 13, 14;
MTCW

Fraze, Candida (Merrill) 1945- . . . . . CLC 50
See also CA 126

Frazer, J(ames) G(eorge)
1854-1941 . . . . TCLC 32
See also CA 118

Frazer, Robert Caine
See Creasey, John

Frazer, Sir James George
See Frazer, J(ames) G(eorge)

Frazier, Ian 1951- . . . . CLC 46
See also CA 130

Frederic, Harold 1856-1898 . . . . . . NCLC 10
See also DLB 12, 23

Frederick the Great 1712-1786 . . . . . . LC 14

Fredro, Aleksander 1793-1876 . . . . . NCLC 8

Freeling, Nicolas 1927- . . . . CLC 38
See also CA 49-52; CAAS 12; CANR 1, 17;
DLB 87

Freeman, Douglas Southall
1886-1953 . . . . TCLC 11
See also CA 109; DLB 17

Freeman, Judith 1946- . . . . CLC 55

Freeman, Mary Eleanor Wilkins
1852-1930 . . . . TCLC 9; SSC 1
See also CA 106; DLB 12, 78

Freeman, R(ichard) Austin
1862-1943 . . . . TCLC 21
See also CA 113; DLB 70

French, Marilyn 1929- . . . . . . CLC 10, 18, 60
See also CA 69-72; CANR 3, 31; MTCW

French, Paul
See Asimov, Isaac

Freneau, Philip Morin 1752-1832 . . NCLC 1
See also DLB 37, 43

Friedan, Betty (Naomi) 1921- . . . . . . CLC 74
See also CA 65-68; CANR 18; MTCW

Friedman, B(ernard) H(arper)
1926- . . . . CLC 7
See also CA 1-4R; CANR 3

Friedman, Bruce Jay 1930- . . . . CLC 3, 5, 56
See also CA 9-12R; CANR 25; DLB 2, 28

Friel, Brian 1929- . . . . CLC 5, 42, 59
See also CA 21-24R; CANR 33; DLB 13;
MTCW

Friis-Baastad, Babbis Ellinor
1921-1970 . . . . CLC 12
See also CA 17-20R; 134; SATA 7

Frisch, Max (Rudolf)
1911-1991 . . . . . CLC 3, 9, 14, 18, 32, 44
See also CA 85-88; 134; CANR 32;
DLB 69; MTCW

Fromentin, Eugene (Samuel Auguste)
1820-1876 . . . . NCLC 10
See also DLB 123

Frost, Robert (Lee)
1874-1963 . . . CLC 1, 3, 4, 9, 10, 13, 15,
26, 34, 44; PC 1
See also CA 89-92; CANR 33;
CDALB 1917-1929; DLB 54; DLBD 7;
MTCW; SATA 14; WLC

Froy, Herald
See Waterhouse, Keith (Spencer)

Fry, Christopher 1907- . . . . CLC 2, 10, 14
See also CA 17-20R; CANR 9, 30; DLB 13;
MTCW; SATA 66

Frye, (Herman) Northrop
1912-1991 . . . . CLC 24, 70
See also CA 5-8R; 133; CANR 8, 37;
DLB 67, 68; MTCW

Fuchs, Daniel 1909- . . . . CLC 8, 22
See also CA 81-84; CAAS 5; DLB 9, 26, 28

Fuchs, Daniel 1934- . . . . CLC 34
See also CA 37-40R; CANR 14

Fuentes, Carlos
1928- . . . . . . CLC 3, 8, 10, 13, 22, 41, 60
See also AAYA 4; AITN 2; CA 69-72;
CANR 10, 32; DLB 113; HW; MTCW;
WLC

Fuentes, Gregorio Lopez y
See Lopez y Fuentes, Gregorio

Fugard, (Harold) Athol
1932- . . . . CLC 5, 9, 14, 25, 40; DC 3
See also CA 85-88; CANR 32; MTCW

Fugard, Sheila 1932- . . . . CLC 48
See also CA 125

Fuller, Charles (H. Jr.)
1939- . . . . CLC 25; DC 1
See also BLC 2; BW; CA 108; 112; DLB 38;
MTCW

Fuller, John (Leopold) 1937- . . . . CLC 62
See also CA 21-24R; CANR 9; DLB 40

Fuller, Margaret . . . . NCLC 5
See also Ossoli, Sarah Margaret (Fuller
marchesa d')

Fuller, Roy (Broadbent)
1912-1991 . . . . CLC 4, 28
See also CA 5-8R; 135; CAAS 10; DLB 15,
20

Fulton, Alice 1952- . . . . CLC 52
See also CA 116

Furphy, Joseph 1843-1912 . . . . TCLC 25

Fussell, Paul 1924- . . . . CLC 74
See also BEST 90:1; CA 17-20R; CANR 8,
21, 35; MTCW

Futabatei, Shimei 1864-1909 . . . . . . TCLC 44

Futrelle, Jacques 1875-1912 . . . . . . TCLC 19
See also CA 113

G. B. S.
See Shaw, George Bernard

Gaboriau, Emile 1835-1873 . . . . . . NCLC 14

Gadda, Carlo Emilio 1893-1973 . . . . CLC 11
See also CA 89-92

Gaddis, William
1922- . . . . CLC 1, 3, 6, 8, 10, 19, 43
See also CA 17-20R; CANR 21; DLB 2;
MTCW

Gaines, Ernest J(ames)
1933- . . . . CLC 3, 11, 18
See also AITN 1; BLC 2; BW; CA 9-12R;
CANR 6, 24; CDALB 1968-1988; DLB 2,
33; DLBY 80; MTCW

Gaitskill, Mary 1954- . . . . CLC 69
See also CA 128

Galdos, Benito Perez
See Perez Galdos, Benito

Gale, Zona 1874-1938 . . . . TCLC 7
See also CA 105; DLB 9, 78

Galeano, Eduardo (Hughes) 1940- . . . CLC 72
See also CA 29-32R; CANR 13, 32; HW

Galiano, Juan Valera y Alcala
See Valera y Alcala-Galiano, Juan

Gallagher, Tess 1943- . . . . CLC 18, 63
See also CA 106; DLB 120

Gallant, Mavis
1922- . . . . CLC 7, 18, 38; SSC 5
See also CA 69-72; CANR 29; DLB 53;
MTCW

Gallant, Roy A(rthur) 1924- . . . . CLC 17
See also CA 5-8R; CANR 4, 29; MAICYA;
SATA 4, 68

Gallico, Paul (William) 1897-1976 . . . CLC 2
See also AITN 1; CA 5-8R; 69-72;
CANR 23; DLB 9; MAICYA; SATA 13

Gallup, Ralph
See Whitemore, Hugh (John)

Galsworthy, John 1867-1933 . . . . TCLC 1, 45
See also CA 104; CDBLB 1890-1914;
DLB 10, 34, 98; WLC 2

Galt, John 1779-1839 . . . . NCLC 1
See also DLB 99, 116

Galvin, James 1951- . . . . CLC 38
See also CA 108; CANR 26

Gamboa, Federico 1864-1939 . . . . . . TCLC 36

Gann, Ernest Kellogg 1910-1991 . . . . CLC 23
See also AITN 1; CA 1-4R; 136; CANR 1

Garcia Lorca, Federico
1898-1936 . . . . . TCLC 1, 7; DC 2; PC 3
See also CA 104; 131; DLB 108; HW;
MTCW; WLC

Garcia Marquez, Gabriel (Jose)
1928- . . . CLC 2, 3, 8, 10, 15, 27, 47, 55;
SSC 8
See also Marquez, Gabriel (Jose) Garcia
See also AAYA 3; BEST 89:1, 90:4;
CA 33-36R; CANR 10, 28; DLB 113;
HW; MTCW; WLC

Gard, Janice
See Latham, Jean Lee

Gard, Roger Martin du
See Martin du Gard, Roger

Gardam, Jane 1928- .... **CLC 43**
See also CA 49-52; CANR 2, 18, 33;
CLR 12; DLB 14; MAICYA; MTCW;
SAAS 9; SATA 28, 39

Gardner, Herb .... **CLC 44**

Gardner, John (Champlin) Jr.
1933-1982 .... **CLC 2, 3, 5, 7, 8, 10, 18,
28, 34; SSC 7**
See also AITN 1; CA 65-68; 107;
CANR 33; DLB 2; DLBY 82; MTCW;
SATA 31, 40

Gardner, John (Edmund) 1926-..... **CLC 30**
See also CA 103; CANR 15; MTCW

Gardner, Noel
See Kuttner, Henry

Gardons, S. S.
See Snodgrass, William D(e Witt)

Garfield, Leon 1921-.............. **CLC 12**
See also AAYA 8; CA 17-20R; CANR 38;
CLR 21; MAICYA; SATA 1, 32

Garland, (Hannibal) Hamlin
1860-1940 .... **TCLC 3**
See also CA 104; DLB 12, 71, 78

Garneau, (Hector de) Saint-Denys
1912-1943 .... **TCLC 13**
See also CA 111; DLB 88

Garner, Alan 1934-................ **CLC 17**
See also CA 73-76; CANR 15; CLR 20;
MAICYA; MTCW; SATA 18, 69

Garner, Hugh 1913-1979 .... **CLC 13**
See also CA 69-72; CANR 31; DLB 68

Garnett, David 1892-1981 .... **CLC 3**
See also CA 5-8R; 103; CANR 17; DLB 34

Garos, Stephanie
See Katz, Steve

Garrett, George (Palmer)
1929- .... **CLC 3, 11, 51**
See also CA 1-4R; CAAS 5; CANR 1;
DLB 2, 5; DLBY 83

Garrick, David 1717-1779 .... **LC 15**
See also DLB 84

Garrigue, Jean 1914-1972 .... **CLC 2, 8**
See also CA 5-8R; 37-40R; CANR 20

Garrison, Frederick
See Sinclair, Upton (Beall)

Garth, Will
See Hamilton, Edmond; Kuttner, Henry

Garvey, Marcus (Moziah Jr.)
1887-1940 .... **TCLC 41**
See also BLC 2; BW; CA 120; 124

Gary, Romain .... **CLC 25**
See also Kacew, Romain
See also DLB 83

Gascar, Pierre .... **CLC 11**
See also Fournier, Pierre

Gascoyne, David (Emery) 1916- .... **CLC 45**
See also CA 65-68; CANR 10, 28; DLB 20;
MTCW

Gaskell, Elizabeth Cleghorn
1810-1865 .... **NCLC 5**
See also CDBLB 1832-1890; DLB 21

Gass, William H(oward)
1924- .... **CLC 1, 2, 8, 11, 15, 39**
See also CA 17-20R; CANR 30; DLB 2;
MTCW

Gasset, Jose Ortega y
See Ortega y Gasset, Jose

Gautier, Theophile 1811-1872 ..... **NCLC 1**
See also DLB 119

Gawsworth, John
See Bates, H(erbert) E(rnest)

Gaye, Marvin (Penze) 1939-1984 ... **CLC 26**
See also CA 112

Gebler, Carlo (Ernest) 1954-....... **CLC 39**
See also CA 119; 133

Gee, Maggie (Mary) 1948-........ **CLC 57**
See also CA 130

Gee, Maurice (Gough) 1931-....... **CLC 29**
See also CA 97-100; SATA 46

Gelbart, Larry (Simon) 1923- ... **CLC 21, 61**
See also CA 73-76

Gelber, Jack 1932-........... **CLC 1, 6, 14**
See also CA 1-4R; CANR 2; DLB 7

Gellhorn, Martha Ellis 1908- ... **CLC 14, 60**
See also CA 77-80; DLBY 82

Genet, Jean
1910-1986 ... **CLC 1, 2, 5, 10, 14, 44, 46**
See also CA 13-16R; CANR 18; DLB 72;
DLBY 86; MTCW

Gent, Peter 1942-................. **CLC 29**
See also AITN 1; CA 89-92; DLBY 82

George, Jean Craighead 1919-..... **CLC 35**
See also AAYA 8; CA 5-8R; CANR 25;
CLR 1; DLB 52; MAICYA; SATA 2, 68

George, Stefan (Anton)
1868-1933 .... **TCLC 2, 14**
See also CA 104

Georges, Georges Martin
See Simenon, Georges (Jacques Christian)

Gerhardi, William Alexander
See Gerhardie, William Alexander

Gerhardie, William Alexander
1895-1977 .... **CLC 5**
See also CA 25-28R; 73-76; CANR 18;
DLB 36

Gerstler, Amy 1956-.............. **CLC 70**

Gertler, T. .... **CLC 34**
See also CA 116; 121

Ghalib 1797-1869 .... **NCLC 39**

Ghelderode, Michel de
1898-1962 .... **CLC 6, 11**
See also CA 85-88

Ghiselin, Brewster 1903-.......... **CLC 23**
See also CA 13-16R; CAAS 10; CANR 13

Ghose, Zulfikar 1935-............. **CLC 42**
See also CA 65-68

Ghosh, Amitav 1956- .... **CLC 44**

Giacosa, Giuseppe 1847-1906 ...... **TCLC 7**
See also CA 104

Gibb, Lee
See Waterhouse, Keith (Spencer)

Gibbon, Lewis Grassic .... **TCLC 4**
See also Mitchell, James Leslie

Gibbons, Kaye 1960- .... **CLC 50**

Gibran, Kahlil 1883-1931....... **TCLC 1, 9**
See also CA 104

Gibson, William (Ford) 1948- ... **CLC 39, 63**
See also CA 126; 133

Gibson, William 1914-............ **CLC 23**
See also CA 9-12R; CANR 9; DLB 7;
SATA 66

Gide, Andre (Paul Guillaume)
1869-1951 .... **TCLC 5, 12, 36**
See also CA 104; 124; DLB 65; MTCW;
WLC

Gifford, Barry (Colby) 1946-....... **CLC 34**
See also CA 65-68; CANR 9, 30

Gilbert, W(illiam) S(chwenck)
1836-1911 .... **TCLC 3**
See also CA 104; SATA 36

Gilbreth, Frank B. Jr. 1911-........ **CLC 17**
See also CA 9-12R; SATA 2

Gilchrist, Ellen 1935-.......... **CLC 34, 48**
See also CA 113; 116; MTCW

Giles, Molly 1942- .... **CLC 39**
See also CA 126

Gill, Patrick
See Creasey, John

Gilliam, Terry (Vance) 1940-....... **CLC 21**
See also Monty Python
See also CA 108; 113; CANR 35

Gillian, Jerry
See Gilliam, Terry (Vance)

Gilliatt, Penelope (Ann Douglass)
1932- .... **CLC 2, 10, 13, 53**
See also AITN 2; CA 13-16R; DLB 14

Gilman, Charlotte (Anna) Perkins (Stetson)
1860-1935 .... **TCLC 9, 37**
See also CA 106

Gilmour, David 1944-............. **CLC 35**
See also Pink Floyd
See also CA 138

Gilpin, William 1724-1804....... **NCLC 30**

Gilray, J. D.
See Mencken, H(enry) L(ouis)

Gilroy, Frank D(aniel) 1925-........ **CLC 2**
See also CA 81-84; CANR 32; DLB 7

Ginsberg, Allen
1926- ..... **CLC 1, 2, 3, 4, 6, 13, 36, 69;
PC 4**
See also AITN 1; CA 1-4R; CANR 2;
CDALB 1941-1968; DLB 5, 16; MTCW;
WLC 3

Ginzburg, Natalia
1916-1991 .... **CLC 5, 11, 54, 70**
See also CA 85-88; 135; CANR 33; MTCW

Giono, Jean 1895-1970......... **CLC 4, 11**
See also CA 45-48; 29-32R; CANR 2, 35;
DLB 72; MTCW

Giovanni, Nikki 1943- ..... **CLC 2, 4, 19, 64**
See also AITN 1; BLC 2; BW; CA 29-32R;
CAAS 6; CANR 18; CLR 6; DLB 5, 41;
MAICYA; MTCW; SATA 24

Giovene, Andrea 1904-............ **CLC 7**
See also CA 85-88

Gippius, Zinaida (Nikolayevna) 1869-1945
See Hippius, Zinaida
See also CA 106

Giraudoux, (Hippolyte) Jean
  1882-1944 .... TCLC 2, 7
  See also CA 104; DLB 65

Gironella, Jose Maria 1917- .... CLC 11
  See also CA 101

Gissing, George (Robert)
  1857-1903 .... TCLC 3, 24, 47
  See also CA 105; DLB 18

Giurlani, Aldo
  See Palazzeschi, Aldo

Gladkov, Fyodor (Vasilyevich)
  1883-1958 .... TCLC 27

Glanville, Brian (Lester) 1931- ...... CLC 6
  See also CA 5-8R; CAAS 9; CANR 3;
  DLB 15; SATA 42

Glasgow, Ellen (Anderson Gholson)
  1873(?)-1945 .... TCLC 2, 7
  See also CA 104; DLB 9, 12

Glassco, John 1909-1981 .... CLC 9
  See also CA 13-16R; 102; CANR 15;
  DLB 68

Glasscock, Amnesia
  See Steinbeck, John (Ernst)

Glasser, Ronald J. 1940(?)- .... CLC 37

Glassman, Joyce
  See Johnson, Joyce

Glendinning, Victoria 1937- .... CLC 50
  See also CA 120; 127

Glissant, Edouard 1928- .... CLC 10, 68

Gloag, Julian 1930- .... CLC 40
  See also AITN 1; CA 65-68; CANR 10

Gluck, Louise (Elisabeth)
  1943- .... CLC 7, 22, 44
  See also Glueck, Louise
  See also CA 33-36R; DLB 5

Glueck, Louise................... CLC 7, 22
  See also Gluck, Louise (Elisabeth)
  See also DLB 5

Gobineau, Joseph Arthur (Comte) de
  1816-1882 .... NCLC 17
  See also DLB 123

Godard, Jean-Luc 1930- .... CLC 20
  See also CA 93-96

Godden, (Margaret) Rumer 1907- ... CLC 53
  See also AAYA 6; CA 5-8R; CANR 4, 27,
  36; CLR 20; MAICYA; SAAS 12;
  SATA 3, 36

Godoy Alcayaga, Lucila 1889-1957
  See Mistral, Gabriela
  See also CA 104; 131; HW; MTCW

Godwin, Gail (Kathleen)
  1937- .... CLC 5, 8, 22, 31, 69
  See also CA 29-32R; CANR 15; DLB 6;
  MTCW

Godwin, William 1756-1836...... NCLC 14
  See also CDBLB 1789-1832; DLB 39, 104

Goethe, Johann Wolfgang von
  1749-1832 .... NCLC 4, 22, 34; PC 5
  See also DLB 94; WLC 3

Gogarty, Oliver St. John
  1878-1957 .... TCLC 15
  See also CA 109; DLB 15, 19

Gogol, Nikolai (Vasilyevich)
  1809-1852 .....   NCLC 5, 15, 31; DC 1;
                                    SSC 4
  See also WLC

Gold, Herbert 1924- .... CLC 4, 7, 14, 42
  See also CA 9-12R; CANR 17; DLB 2;
  DLBY 81

Goldbarth, Albert 1948- .... CLC 5, 38
  See also CA 53-56; CANR 6; DLB 120

Goldberg, Anatol 1910-1982 .... CLC 34
  See also CA 131; 117

Goldemberg, Isaac 1945- .... CLC 52
  See also CA 69-72; CAAS 12; CANR 11,
  32; HW

Golden Silver
  See Storm, Hyemeyohsts

Golding, William (Gerald)
  1911- ..... CLC 1, 2, 3, 8, 10, 17, 27, 58
  See also AAYA 5; CA 5-8R; CANR 13, 33;
  CDBLB 1945-1960; DLB 15, 100;
  MTCW; WLC

Goldman, Emma 1869-1940...... TCLC 13
  See also CA 110

Goldman, William (W.) 1931- .... CLC 1, 48
  See also CA 9-12R; CANR 29; DLB 44

Goldmann, Lucien 1913-1970 ...... CLC 24
  See also CA 25-28; CAP 2

Goldoni, Carlo 1707-1793 .... LC 4

Goldsberry, Steven 1949- .... CLC 34
  See also CA 131

Goldsmith, Oliver 1728(?)-1774....... LC 2

Goldsmith, Peter
  See Priestley, J(ohn) B(oynton)

Gombrowicz, Witold
  1904-1969 .... CLC 4, 7, 11, 49
  See also CA 19-20; 25-28R; CAP 2

Gomez de la Serna, Ramon
  1888-1963 .... CLC 9
  See also CA 116; HW

Goncharov, Ivan Alexandrovich
  1812-1891 .... NCLC 1

Goncourt, Edmond (Louis Antoine Huot) de
  1822-1896 .... NCLC 7
  See also DLB 123

Goncourt, Jules (Alfred Huot) de
  1830-1870 .... NCLC 7
  See also DLB 123

Gontier, Fernande 19(?)- .... CLC 50

Goodman, Paul 1911-1972.... CLC 1, 2, 4, 7
  See also CA 19-20; 37-40R; CANR 34;
  CAP 2; MTCW

Gordimer, Nadine
  1923- .... CLC 3, 5, 7, 10, 18, 33, 51, 70
  See also CA 5-8R; CANR 3, 28; MTCW

Gordon, Adam Lindsay
  1833-1870 .... NCLC 21

Gordon, Caroline
  1895-1981 .... CLC 6, 13, 29
  See also CA 11-12; 103; CANR 36; CAP 1;
  DLB 4, 9, 102; DLBY 81; MTCW

Gordon, Charles William 1860-1937
  See Connor, Ralph
  See also CA 109

Gordon, Mary (Catherine)
  1949- .... CLC 13, 22
  See also CA 102; DLB 6; DLBY 81;
  MTCW

Gordon, Sol 1923-................ CLC 26
  See also CA 53-56; CANR 4; SATA 11

Gordone, Charles 1925- .... CLC 1, 4
  See also BW; CA 93-96; DLB 7; MTCW

Gorenko, Anna Andreevna
  See Akhmatova, Anna

Gorky, Maxim................... TCLC 8
  See also Peshkov, Alexei Maximovich
  See also WLC

Goryan, Sirak
  See Saroyan, William

Gosse, Edmund (William)
  1849-1928 .... TCLC 28
  See also CA 117; DLB 57

Gotlieb, Phyllis Fay (Bloom)
  1926- .... CLC 18
  See also CA 13-16R; CANR 7; DLB 88

Gottesman, S. D.
  See Kornbluth, C(yril) M.; Pohl, Frederik

Gottfried von Strassburg
  fl. c. 1210- .... CMLC 10

Gottschalk, Laura Riding
  See Jackson, Laura (Riding)

Gould, Lois .... CLC 4, 10
  See also CA 77-80; CANR 29; MTCW

Gourmont, Remy de 1858-1915.... TCLC 17
  See also CA 109

Govier, Katherine 1948-........... CLC 51
  See also CA 101; CANR 18

Goyen, (Charles) William
  1915-1983 .... CLC 5, 8, 14, 40
  See also AITN 2; CA 5-8R; 110; CANR 6;
  DLB 2; DLBY 83

Goytisolo, Juan 1931- .... CLC 5, 10, 23
  See also CA 85-88; CANR 32; HW; MTCW

Gozzi, (Conte) Carlo 1720-1806 .. NCLC 23

Grabbe, Christian Dietrich
  1801-1836 .... NCLC 2

Grace, Patricia 1937-............. CLC 56

Gracian y Morales, Baltasar
  1601-1658 .... LC 15

Gracq, Julien................. CLC 11, 48
  See also Poirier, Louis
  See also DLB 83

Grade, Chaim 1910-1982 .... CLC 10
  See also CA 93-96; 107

Graduate of Oxford, A
  See Ruskin, John

Graham, John
  See Phillips, David Graham

Graham, Jorie 1951-............. CLC 48
  See also CA 111; DLB 120

Graham, R(obert) B(ontine) Cunninghame
  See Cunninghame Graham, R(obert)
  B(ontine)
  See also DLB 98

Graham, Robert
  See Haldeman, Joe (William)

Graham, Tom
See Lewis, (Harry) Sinclair

Graham, W(illiam) S(ydney)
1918-1986 .... CLC 29
See also CA 73-76; 118; DLB 20

Graham, Winston (Mawdsley)
1910- .... CLC 23
See also CA 49-52; CANR 2, 22; DLB 77

Granville-Barker, Harley
1877-1946 .... TCLC 2
See also Barker, Harley Granville
See also CA 104

Grass, Guenter (Wilhelm)
1927- .. CLC 1, 2, 4, 6, 11, 15, 22, 32, 49
See also CA 13-16R; CANR 20; DLB 75;
MTCW; WLC

Gratton, Thomas
See Hulme, T(homas) E(rnest)

Grau, Shirley Ann 1929- .... CLC 4, 9
See also CA 89-92; CANR 22; DLB 2;
MTCW

Gravel, Fern
See Hall, James Norman

Graver, Elizabeth 1964- .... CLC 70
See also CA 135

Graves, Richard Perceval 1945- .... CLC 44
See also CA 65-68; CANR 9, 26

Graves, Robert (von Ranke)
1895-1985 ..... CLC 1, 2, 6, 11, 39, 44,
45; PC 6
See also CA 5-8R; 117; CANR 5, 36;
CDBLB 1914-1945; DLB 20, 100;
DLBY 85; MTCW; SATA 45

Gray, Alasdair (James) 1934- ...... CLC 41
See also CA 126; MTCW

Gray, Amlin 1946- .... CLC 29
See also CA 138

Gray, Francine du Plessix 1930-.... CLC 22
See also BEST 90:3; CA 61-64; CAAS 2;
CANR 11, 33; MTCW

Gray, John (Henry) 1866-1934 .... TCLC 19
See also CA 119

Gray, Simon (James Holliday)
1936- .... CLC 9, 14, 36
See also AITN 1; CA 21-24R; CAAS 3;
CANR 32; DLB 13; MTCW

Gray, Spalding 1941- .... CLC 49
See also CA 128

Gray, Thomas 1716-1771 .... LC 4; PC 2
See also CDBLB 1660-1789; DLB 109;
WLC

Grayson, David
See Baker, Ray Stannard

Grayson, Richard (A.) 1951- .... CLC 38
See also CA 85-88; CANR 14, 31

Greeley, Andrew M(oran) 1928- .... CLC 28
See also CA 5-8R; CAAS 7; CANR 7;
MTCW

Green, Brian
See Card, Orson Scott

Green, Hannah .... CLC 3
See also CA 73-76

Green, Hannah
See Greenberg, Joanne (Goldenberg)

Green, Henry .... CLC 2, 13
See also Yorke, Henry Vincent
See also DLB 15

Green, Julian (Hartridge)
1900- .... CLC 3, 11
See also CA 21-24R; CANR 33; DLB 4, 72;
MTCW

Green, Julien 1900-
See Green, Julian (Hartridge)

Green, Paul (Eliot) 1894-1981...... CLC 25
See also AITN 1; CA 5-8R; 103; CANR 3;
DLB 7, 9; DLBY 81

Greenberg, Ivan 1908-1973
See Rahv, Philip
See also CA 85-88

Greenberg, Joanne (Goldenberg)
1932- .... CLC 7, 30
See also CA 5-8R; CANR 14, 32; SATA 25

Greenberg, Richard 1959(?)- .... CLC 57
See also CA 138

Greene, Bette 1934- .... CLC 30
See also AAYA 7; CA 53-56; CANR 4;
CLR 2; MAICYA; SATA 8

Greene, Gael .... CLC 8
See also CA 13-16R; CANR 10

Greene, Graham (Henry)
1904-1991 ... CLC 1, 3, 6, 9, 14, 18, 27,
37, 70, 72
See also AITN 2; CA 13-16R; 133;
CANR 35; CDBLB 1945-1960; DLB 13,
15, 77, 100; DLBY 91; MTCW;
SATA 20; WLC

Greer, Richard
See Silverberg, Robert

Greer, Richard
See Silverberg, Robert

Gregor, Arthur 1923- .... CLC 9
See also CA 25-28R; CAAS 10; CANR 11;
SATA 36

Gregor, Lee
See Pohl, Frederik

Gregory, Isabella Augusta (Persse)
1852-1932 .... TCLC 1
See also CA 104; DLB 10

Gregory, J. Dennis
See Williams, John A(lfred)

Grendon, Stephen
See Derleth, August (William)

Grenville, Kate 1950- .... CLC 61
See also CA 118

Grenville, Pelham
See Wodehouse, P(elham) G(renville)

Greve, Felix Paul (Berthold Friedrich)
1879-1948
See Grove, Frederick Philip
See also CA 104

Grey, Zane 1872-1939 .... TCLC 6
See also CA 104; 132; DLB 9; MTCW

Grieg, (Johan) Nordahl (Brun)
1902-1943 .... TCLC 10
See also CA 107

Grieve, C(hristopher) M(urray)
1892-1978 .... CLC 11, 19
See also MacDiarmid, Hugh
See also CA 5-8R; 85-88; CANR 33;
MTCW

Griffin, Gerald 1803-1840 .... NCLC 7

Griffin, John Howard 1920-1980.... CLC 68
See also AITN 1; CA 1-4R; 101; CANR 2

Griffin, Peter .... CLC 39

Griffiths, Trevor 1935-.......... CLC 13, 52
See also CA 97-100; DLB 13

Grigson, Geoffrey (Edward Harvey)
1905-1985 .... CLC 7, 39
See also CA 25-28R; 118; CANR 20, 33;
DLB 27; MTCW

Grillparzer, Franz 1791-1872...... NCLC 1

Grimble, Reverend Charles James
See Eliot, T(homas) S(tearns)

Grimke, Charlotte L(ottie) Forten
1837(?)-1914
See Forten, Charlotte L.
See also BW; CA 117; 124

Grimm, Jacob Ludwig Karl
1785-1863 .... NCLC 3
See also DLB 90; MAICYA; SATA 22

Grimm, Wilhelm Karl 1786-1859 .. NCLC 3
See also DLB 90; MAICYA; SATA 22

Grimmelshausen, Johann Jakob Christoffel
von 1621-1676 .... LC 6

Grindel, Eugene 1895-1952
See Eluard, Paul
See also CA 104

Grossman, David .... CLC 67
See also CA 138

Grossman, Vasily (Semenovich)
1905-1964 .... CLC 41
See also CA 124; 130; MTCW

Grove, Frederick Philip .... TCLC 4
See also Greve, Felix Paul (Berthold
Friedrich)
See also DLB 92

Grubb
See Crumb, R(obert)

Grumbach, Doris (Isaac)
1918- .... CLC 13, 22, 64
See also CA 5-8R; CAAS 2; CANR 9

Grundtvig, Nicolai Frederik Severin
1783-1872 .... NCLC 1

Grunge
See Crumb, R(obert)

Grunwald, Lisa 1959-............. CLC 44
See also CA 120

Guare, John 1938- .... CLC 8, 14, 29, 67
See also CA 73-76; CANR 21; DLB 7;
MTCW

Gudjonsson, Halldor Kiljan 1902-
See Laxness, Halldor
See also CA 103

Guenter, Erich
See Eich, Guenter

Guest, Barbara 1920-............. CLC 34
See also CA 25-28R; CANR 11; DLB 5

Guest, Judith (Ann) 1936- .... **CLC 8, 30**
See also AAYA 7; CA 77-80; CANR 15;
MTCW

Guild, Nicholas M. 1944- .... **CLC 33**
See also CA 93-96

Guillemin, Jacques
See Sartre, Jean-Paul

Guillen, Jorge 1893-1984 .... **CLC 11**
See also CA 89-92; 112; DLB 108; HW

Guillen (y Batista), Nicolas (Cristobal)
1902-1989 .... **CLC 48**
See also BLC 2; BW; CA 116; 125; 129;
HW

Guillevic, (Eugene) 1907- .... **CLC 33**
See also CA 93-96

Guillois
See Desnos, Robert

Guiney, Louise Imogen
1861-1920 .... **TCLC 41**
See also DLB 54

Guiraldes, Ricardo (Guillermo)
1886-1927 .... **TCLC 39**
See also CA 131; HW; MTCW

Gunn, Bill .... **CLC 5**
See also Gunn, William Harrison
See also DLB 38

Gunn, Thom(son William)
1929- .... **CLC 3, 6, 18, 32**
See also CA 17-20R; CANR 9, 33;
CDBLB 1960 to Present; DLB 27;
MTCW

Gunn, William Harrison 1934(?)-1989
See Gunn, Bill
See also AITN 1; BW; CA 13-16R; 128;
CANR 12, 25

Gunnars, Kristjana 1948- .... **CLC 69**
See also CA 113; DLB 60

Gurganus, Allan 1947- .... **CLC 70**
See also BEST 90:1; CA 135

Gurney, A(lbert) R(amsdell) Jr.
1930- .... **CLC 32, 50, 54**
See also CA 77-80; CANR 32

Gurney, Ivor (Bertie) 1890-1937 ... **TCLC 33**

Gurney, Peter
See Gurney, A(lbert) R(amsdell) Jr.

Gustafson, Ralph (Barker) 1909- .... **CLC 36**
See also CA 21-24R; CANR 8; DLB 88

Gut, Gom
See Simenon, Georges (Jacques Christian)

Guthrie, A(lfred) B(ertram) Jr.
1901-1991 .... **CLC 23**
See also CA 57-60; 134; CANR 24; DLB 6;
SATA 62; SATO 67

Guthrie, Isobel
See Grieve, C(hristopher) M(urray)

Guthrie, Woodrow Wilson 1912-1967
See Guthrie, Woody
See also CA 113; 93-96

Guthrie, Woody .... **CLC 35**
See also Guthrie, Woodrow Wilson

Guy, Rosa (Cuthbert) 1928- .... **CLC 26**
See also AAYA 4; BW; CA 17-20R;
CANR 14, 34; CLR 13; DLB 33;
MAICYA; SATA 14, 62

Gwendolyn
See Bennett, (Enoch) Arnold

H. D. .... **CLC 3, 8, 14, 31, 34, 73; PC 5**
See also Doolittle, Hilda

Haavikko, Paavo Juhani
1931- .... **CLC 18, 34**
See also CA 106

Habbema, Koos
See Heijermans, Herman

Hacker, Marilyn 1942- .... **CLC 5, 9, 23, 72**
See also CA 77-80; DLB 120

Haggard, H(enry) Rider
1856-1925 .... **TCLC 11**
See also CA 108; DLB 70; SATA 16

Haig, Fenil
See Ford, Ford Madox

Haig-Brown, Roderick (Langmere)
1908-1976 .... **CLC 21**
See also CA 5-8R; 69-72; CANR 4, 38;
DLB 88; MAICYA; SATA 12

Hailey, Arthur 1920- .... **CLC 5**
See also AITN 2; BEST 90:3; CA 1-4R;
CANR 2, 36; DLB 88; DLBY 82; MTCW

Hailey, Elizabeth Forsythe 1938- ... **CLC 40**
See also CA 93-96; CAAS 1; CANR 15

Haines, John (Meade) 1924- .... **CLC 58**
See also CA 17-20R; CANR 13, 34; DLB 5

Haldeman, Joe (William) 1943- ..... **CLC 61**
See also CA 53-56; CANR 6; DLB 8

Haley, Alex(ander Murray Palmer)
1921-1992 .... **CLC 8, 12**
See also BLC 2; BW; CA 77-80; 136;
DLB 38; MTCW

Haliburton, Thomas Chandler
1796-1865 .... **NCLC 15**
See also DLB 11, 99

Hall, Donald (Andrew Jr.)
1928- .... **CLC 1, 13, 37, 59**
See also CA 5-8R; CAAS 7; CANR 2;
DLB 5; SATA 23

Hall, Frederic Sauser
See Sauser-Hall, Frederic

Hall, James
See Kuttner, Henry

Hall, James Norman 1887-1951 ... **TCLC 23**
See also CA 123; SATA 21

Hall, (Marguerite) Radclyffe
1886(?)-1943 .... **TCLC 12**
See also CA 110

Hall, Rodney 1935- .... **CLC 51**
See also CA 109

Halliday, Michael
See Creasey, John

Halpern, Daniel 1945- .... **CLC 14**
See also CA 33-36R

Hamburger, Michael (Peter Leopold)
1924- .... **CLC 5, 14**
See also CA 5-8R; CAAS 4; CANR 2;
DLB 27

Hamill, Pete 1935- .... **CLC 10**
See also CA 25-28R; CANR 18

Hamilton, Clive
See Lewis, C(live) S(taples)

Hamilton, Edmond 1904-1977 .... **CLC 1**
See also CA 1-4R; CANR 3; DLB 8

Hamilton, Eugene (Jacob) Lee
See Lee-Hamilton, Eugene (Jacob)

Hamilton, Franklin
See Silverberg, Robert

Hamilton, Gail
See Corcoran, Barbara

Hamilton, Mollie
See Kaye, M(ary) M(argaret)

Hamilton, (Anthony Walter) Patrick
1904-1962 .... **CLC 51**
See also CA 113; DLB 10

Hamilton, Virginia 1936- .... **CLC 26**
See also AAYA 2; BW; CA 25-28R;
CANR 20, 37; CLR 1, 11; DLB 33, 52;
MAICYA; MTCW; SATA 4, 56

Hammett, (Samuel) Dashiell
1894-1961 .... **CLC 3, 5, 10, 19, 47**
See also AITN 1; CA 81-84;
CDALB 1929-1941; DLBD 6; MTCW

Hammon, Jupiter 1711(?)-1800(?) .. **NCLC 5**
See also BLC 2; DLB 31, 50

Hammond, Keith
See Kuttner, Henry

Hamner, Earl (Henry) Jr. 1923- .... **CLC 12**
See also AITN 2; CA 73-76; DLB 6

Hampton, Christopher (James)
1946- .... **CLC 4**
See also CA 25-28R; DLB 13; MTCW

Hamsun, Knut .... **TCLC 2, 14**
See also Pedersen, Knut

Handke, Peter 1942- .. **CLC 5, 8, 10, 15, 38**
See also CA 77-80; CANR 33; DLB 85;
MTCW

Hanley, James 1901-1985 ... **CLC 3, 5, 8, 13**
See also CA 73-76; 117; CANR 36; MTCW

Hannah, Barry 1942- .... **CLC 23, 38**
See also CA 108; 110; DLB 6; MTCW

Hannon, Ezra
See Hunter, Evan

Hansberry, Lorraine (Vivian)
1930-1965 .... **CLC 17, 62; DC 2**
See also BLC 2; BW; CA 109; 25-28R;
CABS 3; CDALB 1941-1968; DLB 7, 38;
MTCW

Hansen, Joseph 1923- .... **CLC 38**
See also CA 29-32R; CANR 16

Hansen, Martin A. 1909-1955 ..... **TCLC 32**

Hanson, Kenneth O(stlin) 1922- .... **CLC 13**
See also CA 53-56; CANR 7

Hardwick, Elizabeth 1916- .... **CLC 13**
See also CA 5-8R; CANR 3, 32; DLB 6;
MTCW

Hardy, Thomas
1840-1928 ..... **TCLC 4, 10, 18, 32, 48;**
SSC 2
See also CA 104; 123; CDBLB 1890-1914;
DLB 18, 19; MTCW; WLC

Hare, David 1947- .... **CLC 29, 58**
See also CA 97-100; CANR 39; DLB 13;
MTCW

Harford, Henry
See Hudson, W(illiam) H(enry)

Hargrave, Leonie
See Disch, Thomas M(ichael)

Harlan, Louis R(udolph) 1922- ..... **CLC 34**
See also CA 21-24R; CANR 25

Harling, Robert 1951(?)- .... **CLC 53**

Harmon, William (Ruth) 1938- ..... **CLC 38**
See also CA 33-36R; CANR 14, 32, 35;
SATA 65

Harper, F. E. W.
See Harper, Frances Ellen Watkins

Harper, Frances E. W.
See Harper, Frances Ellen Watkins

Harper, Frances E. Watkins
See Harper, Frances Ellen Watkins

Harper, Frances Ellen
See Harper, Frances Ellen Watkins

Harper, Frances Ellen Watkins
1825-1911 .... **TCLC 14**
See also BLC 2; BW; CA 111; 125; DLB 50

Harper, Michael S(teven) 1938- .. **CLC 7, 22**
See also BW; CA 33-36R; CANR 24;
DLB 41

Harper, Mrs. F. E. W.
See Harper, Frances Ellen Watkins

Harris, Christie (Lucy) Irwin
1907- .... **CLC 12**
See also CA 5-8R; CANR 6; DLB 88;
MAICYA; SAAS 10; SATA 6

Harris, Frank 1856(?)-1931 ...... **TCLC 24**
See also CA 109

Harris, George Washington
1814-1869 .... **NCLC 23**
See also DLB 3, 11

Harris, Joel Chandler 1848-1908 ... **TCLC 2**
See also CA 104; 137; DLB 11, 23, 42, 78,
91; MAICYA; YABC 1

Harris, John (Wyndham Parkes Lucas)
Beynon 1903-1969 .... **CLC 19**
See also CA 102; 89-92

Harris, MacDonald
See Heiney, Donald (William)

Harris, Mark 1922- .... **CLC 19**
See also CA 5-8R; CAAS 3; CANR 2;
DLB 2; DLBY 80

Harris, (Theodore) Wilson 1921-... **CLC 25**
See also BW; CA 65-68; CAAS 16;
CANR 11, 27; DLB 117; MTCW

Harrison, Elizabeth Cavanna 1909-
See Cavanna, Betty
See also CA 9-12R; CANR 6, 27

Harrison, Harry (Max) 1925- ...... **CLC 42**
See also CA 1-4R; CANR 5, 21; DLB 8;
SATA 4

Harrison, James (Thomas) 1937-
See Harrison, Jim
See also CA 13-16R; CANR 8

Harrison, Jim .... **CLC 6, 14, 33, 66**
See also Harrison, James (Thomas)
See also DLBY 82

Harrison, Kathryn 1961- .... **CLC 70**

Harrison, Tony 1937- .... **CLC 43**
See also CA 65-68; DLB 40; MTCW

Harriss, Will(ard Irvin) 1922- ...... **CLC 34**
See also CA 111

Harson, Sley
See Ellison, Harlan

Hart, Ellis
See Ellison, Harlan

Hart, Josephine 1942(?)- .... **CLC 70**
See also CA 138

Hart, Moss 1904-1961 .... **CLC 66**
See also CA 109; 89-92; DLB 7

Harte, (Francis) Bret(t)
1836(?)-1902 .... **TCLC 1, 25; SSC 8**
See also CA 104; CDALB 1865-1917;
DLB 12, 64, 74, 79; SATA 26; WLC

Hartley, L(eslie) P(oles)
1895-1972 .... **CLC 2, 22**
See also CA 45-48; 37-40R; CANR 33;
DLB 15; MTCW

Hartman, Geoffrey H. 1929- .... **CLC 27**
See also CA 117; 125; DLB 67

Haruf, Kent 19(?)- .... **CLC 34**

Harwood, Ronald 1934- .... **CLC 32**
See also CA 1-4R; CANR 4; DLB 13

Hasek, Jaroslav (Matej Frantisek)
1883-1923 .... **TCLC 4**
See also CA 104; 129; MTCW

Hass, Robert 1941- .... **CLC 18, 39**
See also CA 111; CANR 30; DLB 105

Hastings, Hudson
See Kuttner, Henry

Hastings, Selina .... **CLC 44**

Hatteras, Amelia
See Mencken, H(enry) L(ouis)

Hatteras, Owen
See Mencken, H(enry) L(ouis)

Hatteras, Owen .... **TCLC 18**
See also Nathan, George Jean

Hauptmann, Gerhart (Johann Robert)
1862-1946 .... **TCLC 4**
See also CA 104; DLB 66, 118

Havel, Vaclav 1936- .... **CLC 25, 58, 65**
See also CA 104; CANR 36; MTCW

Haviaras, Stratis .... **CLC 33**
See also Chaviaras, Strates

Hawes, Stephen 1475(?)-1523(?) ..... **LC 17**

Hawkes, John (Clendennin Burne Jr.)
1925- ...... **CLC 1, 2, 3, 4, 7, 9, 14, 15,
27, 49**
See also CA 1-4R; CANR 2; DLB 2, 7;
DLBY 80; MTCW

Hawking, S. W.
See Hawking, Stephen W(illiam)

Hawking, Stephen W(illiam)
1942- .... **CLC 63**
See also BEST 89:1; CA 126; 129

Hawthorne, Julian 1846-1934 ..... **TCLC 25**

Hawthorne, Nathaniel
1804-1864 .... **NCLC 39; SSC 3**
See also CDALB 1640-1865; DLB 1, 74;
WLC; YABC 2

Haxton, Josephine Ayres 1921- .... **CLC 73**
See also CA 115

Hayaseca y Eizaguirre, Jorge
See Echegaray (y Eizaguirre), Jose (Maria
Waldo)

Hayashi Fumiko 1904-1951 ...... **TCLC 27**

Haycraft, Anna
See Ellis, Alice Thomas
See also CA 122

Hayden, Robert E(arl)
1913-1980 ...... **CLC 5, 9, 14, 37; PC 6**
See also BLC 2; BW; CA 69-72; 97-100;
CABS 2; CANR 24; CDALB 1941-1968;
DLB 5, 76; MTCW; SATA 19, 26

Hayford, J(oseph) E(phraim) Casely
See Casely-Hayford, J(oseph) E(phraim)

Hayman, Ronald 1932- .... **CLC 44**
See also CA 25-28R; CANR 18

Haywood, Eliza (Fowler)
1693(?)-1756 .... **LC 1**

Hazlitt, William 1778-1830 ...... **NCLC 29**
See also DLB 110

Hazzard, Shirley 1931- .... **CLC 18**
See also CA 9-12R; CANR 4; DLBY 82;
MTCW

Head, Bessie 1937-1986 .... **CLC 25, 67**
See also BLC 2; BW; CA 29-32R; 119;
CANR 25; DLB 117; MTCW

Headon, (Nicky) Topper 1956(?)- ... **CLC 30**
See also The Clash

Heaney, Seamus (Justin)
1939- .... **CLC 5, 7, 14, 25, 37, 74**
See also CA 85-88; CANR 25;
CDBLB 1960 to Present; DLB 40;
MTCW

Hearn, (Patricio) Lafcadio (Tessima Carlos)
1850-1904 .... **TCLC 9**
See also CA 105; DLB 12, 78

Hearne, Vicki 1946- .... **CLC 56**

Hearon, Shelby 1931- .... **CLC 63**
See also AITN 2; CA 25-28R; CANR 18

Heat-Moon, William Least .... **CLC 29**
See also Trogdon, William (Lewis)
See also AAYA 9

Hebert, Anne 1916- .... **CLC 4, 13, 29**
See also CA 85-88; DLB 68; MTCW

Hecht, Anthony (Evan)
1923- .... **CLC 8, 13, 19**
See also CA 9-12R; CANR 6; DLB 5

Hecht, Ben 1894-1964 .... **CLC 8**
See also CA 85-88; DLB 7, 9, 25, 26, 28, 86

Hedayat, Sadeq 1903-1951 .... **TCLC 21**
See also CA 120

Heidegger, Martin 1889-1976 ...... **CLC 24**
See also CA 81-84; 65-68; CANR 34;
MTCW

Heidenstam, (Carl Gustaf) Verner von
1859-1940 .... **TCLC 5**
See also CA 104

Heifner, Jack 1946- .... **CLC 11**
See also CA 105

Heijermans, Herman 1864-1924 ... **TCLC 24**
See also CA 123

Heilbrun, Carolyn G(old) 1926- ..... **CLC 25**
See also CA 45-48; CANR 1, 28

Heine, Heinrich 1797-1856 .... **NCLC 4**
See also DLB 90

Heinemann, Larry (Curtiss) 1944- .. **CLC 50**
See also CA 110; CANR 31; DLBD 9

Hirsch, Edward 1950- . . . . **CLC 31, 50**
See also CA 104; CANR 20; DLB 120

Hitchcock, Alfred (Joseph)
1899-1980 . . . . **CLC 16**
See also CA 97-100; SATA 24, 27

Hoagland, Edward 1932- . . . . **CLC 28**
See also CA 1-4R; CANR 2, 31; DLB 6;
SATA 51

Hoban, Russell (Conwell) 1925- . . **CLC 7, 25**
See also CA 5-8R; CANR 23, 37; CLR 3;
DLB 52; MAICYA; MTCW; SATA 1, 40

Hobbs, Perry
See Blackmur, R(ichard) P(almer)

Hobson, Laura Z(ametkin)
1900-1986 . . . . **CLC 7, 25**
See also CA 17-20R; 118; DLB 28;
SATA 52

Hochhuth, Rolf 1931- . . . . **CLC 4, 11, 18**
See also CA 5-8R; CANR 33; MTCW

Hochman, Sandra 1936- . . . . **CLC 3, 8**
See also CA 5-8R; DLB 5

Hochwaelder, Fritz 1911-1986 . . . . . . **CLC 36**
See also Hochwalder, Fritz
See also CA 29-32R; 120; MTCW

Hochwalder, Fritz . . . . **CLC 36**
See also Hochwaelder, Fritz

Hocking, Mary (Eunice) 1921- . . . . . **CLC 13**
See also CA 101; CANR 18

Hodgins, Jack 1938- . . . . **CLC 23**
See also CA 93-96; DLB 60

Hodgson, William Hope
1877(?)-1918 . . . . **TCLC 13**
See also CA 111; DLB 70

Hoffman, Alice 1952- . . . . **CLC 51**
See also CA 77-80; CANR 34; MTCW

Hoffman, Daniel (Gerard)
1923- . . . . **CLC 6, 13, 23**
See also CA 1-4R; CANR 4; DLB 5

Hoffman, Stanley 1944- . . . . **CLC 5**
See also CA 77-80

Hoffman, William M(oses) 1939- . . . **CLC 40**
See also CA 57-60; CANR 11

Hoffmann, E(rnst) T(heodor) A(madeus)
1776-1822 . . . . **NCLC 2**
See also DLB 90; SATA 27

Hofmann, Gert 1931- . . . . **CLC 54**
See also CA 128

Hofmannsthal, Hugo von
1874-1929 . . . . **TCLC 11**
See also CA 106; DLB 81, 118

Hogan, Linda 1947- . . . . **CLC 73**
See also CA 120

Hogarth, Charles
See Creasey, John

Hogg, James 1770-1835 . . . . **NCLC 4**
See also DLB 93, 116

Holbach, Paul Henri Thiry Baron
1723-1789 . . . . **LC 14**

Holberg, Ludvig 1684-1754 . . . . **LC 6**

Holden, Ursula 1921- . . . . **CLC 18**
See also CA 101; CAAS 8; CANR 22

Holderlin, (Johann Christian) Friedrich
1770-1843 . . . . **NCLC 16; PC 4**

Holdstock, Robert
See Holdstock, Robert P.

Holdstock, Robert P. 1948- . . . . **CLC 39**
See also CA 131

Holland, Isabelle 1920- . . . . **CLC 21**
See also CA 21-24R; CANR 10, 25;
MAICYA; SATA 8, 70

Holland, Marcus
See Caldwell, (Janet Miriam) Taylor
(Holland)

Hollander, John 1929- . . . . . . **CLC 2, 5, 8, 14**
See also CA 1-4R; CANR 1; DLB 5;
SATA 13

Hollander, Paul
See Silverberg, Robert

Holleran, Andrew 1943(?)- . . . . **CLC 38**

Hollinghurst, Alan 1954- . . . . **CLC 55**
See also CA 114

Hollis, Jim
See Summers, Hollis (Spurgeon Jr.)

Holmes, John
See Souster, (Holmes) Raymond

Holmes, John Clellon 1926-1988 . . . . **CLC 56**
See also CA 9-12R; 125; CANR 4; DLB 16

Holmes, Oliver Wendell
1809-1894 . . . . **NCLC 14**
See also CDALB 1640-1865; DLB 1;
SATA 34

Holmes, Raymond
See Souster, (Holmes) Raymond

Holt, Victoria
See Hibbert, Eleanor Burford

Holub, Miroslav 1923- . . . . **CLC 4**
See also CA 21-24R; CANR 10

Homer c. 8th cent. B.C.- . . . . **CMLC 1**

Honig, Edwin 1919- . . . . **CLC 33**
See also CA 5-8R; CAAS 8; CANR 4;
DLB 5

Hood, Hugh (John Blagdon)
1928- . . . . **CLC 15, 28**
See also CA 49-52; CANR 1, 33; DLB 53

Hood, Thomas 1799-1845 . . . . **NCLC 16**
See also DLB 96

Hooker, (Peter) Jeremy 1941- . . . . . . **CLC 43**
See also CA 77-80; CANR 22; DLB 40

Hope, A(lec) D(erwent) 1907- . . . . **CLC 3, 51**
See also CA 21-24R; CANR 33; MTCW

Hope, Brian
See Creasey, John

Hope, Christopher (David Tully)
1944- . . . . **CLC 52**
See also CA 106; SATA 62

Hopkins, Gerard Manley
1844-1889 . . . . **NCLC 17**
See also CDBLB 1890-1914; DLB 35, 57;
WLC

Hopkins, John (Richard) 1931- . . . . . . **CLC 4**
See also CA 85-88

Hopkins, Pauline Elizabeth
1859-1930 . . . . **TCLC 28**
See also BLC 2; DLB 50

Horatio
See Proust,
(Valentin-Louis-George-Eugene-)Marcel

Horgan, Paul 1903- . . . . **CLC 9, 53**
See also CA 13-16R; CANR 9, 35;
DLB 102; DLBY 85; MTCW; SATA 13

Horn, Peter
See Kuttner, Henry

Horovitz, Israel 1939- . . . . **CLC 56**
See also CA 33-36R; DLB 7

Horvath, Odon von
See Horvath, Oedoen von
See also DLB 85

Horvath, Oedoen von 1901-1938 . . . **TCLC 45**
See also Horvath, Odon von
See also CA 118

Horwitz, Julius 1920-1986 . . . . **CLC 14**
See also CA 9-12R; 119; CANR 12

Hospital, Janette Turner 1942- . . . . . **CLC 42**
See also CA 108

Hostos, E. M. de
See Hostos (y Bonilla), Eugenio Maria de

Hostos, Eugenio M. de
See Hostos (y Bonilla), Eugenio Maria de

Hostos, Eugenio Maria
See Hostos (y Bonilla), Eugenio Maria de

Hostos (y Bonilla), Eugenio Maria de
1839-1903 . . . . **TCLC 24**
See also CA 123; 131; HW

Houdini
See Lovecraft, H(oward) P(hillips)

Hougan, Carolyn 19(?)- . . . . **CLC 34**

Household, Geoffrey (Edward West)
1900-1988 . . . . **CLC 11**
See also CA 77-80; 126; DLB 87; SATA 14,
59

Housman, A(lfred) E(dward)
1859-1936 . . . . **TCLC 1, 10; PC 2**
See also CA 104; 125; DLB 19; MTCW

Housman, Laurence 1865-1959 . . . . . **TCLC 7**
See also CA 106; DLB 10; SATA 25

Howard, Elizabeth Jane 1923- . . . **CLC 7, 29**
See also CA 5-8R; CANR 8

Howard, Maureen 1930- . . . . . **CLC 5, 14, 46**
See also CA 53-56; CANR 31; DLBY 83;
MTCW

Howard, Richard 1929- . . . . . . **CLC 7, 10, 47**
See also AITN 1; CA 85-88; CANR 25;
DLB 5

Howard, Robert Ervin 1906-1936 . . . **TCLC 8**
See also CA 105

Howard, Warren F.
See Pohl, Frederik

Howe, Fanny 1940- . . . . **CLC 47**
See also CA 117; SATA 52

Howe, Julia Ward 1819-1910 . . . . . **TCLC 21**
See also CA 117; DLB 1

Howe, Susan 1937- . . . . **CLC 72**
See also DLB 120

Howe, Tina 1937- . . . . **CLC 48**
See also CA 109

Howell, James 1594(?)-1666 . . . . **LC 13**

Howells, W. D.
See Howells, William Dean

Howells, William D.
See Howells, William Dean

Ishiguro, Kazuo 1954- ...... **CLC 27, 56, 59**
See also BEST 90:2; CA 120; MTCW

Ishikawa Takuboku
1886(?)-1912 .... **TCLC 15**
See also CA 113

Iskander, Fazil 1929- .... **CLC 47**
See also CA 102

Ivan IV 1530-1584 .... **LC 17**

Ivanov, Vyacheslav Ivanovich
1866-1949 .... **TCLC 33**
See also CA 122

Ivask, Ivar Vidrik 1927- .... **CLC 14**
See also CA 37-40R; CANR 24

Jackson, Daniel
See Wingrove, David (John)

Jackson, Jesse 1908-1983 .... **CLC 12**
See also BW; CA 25-28R; 109; CANR 27;
CLR 28; MAICYA; SATA 2, 29, 48

Jackson, Laura (Riding) 1901-1991 .. **CLC 7**
See also Riding, Laura
See also CA 65-68; 135; CANR 28; DLB 48

Jackson, Sam
See Trumbo, Dalton

Jackson, Sara
See Wingrove, David (John)

Jackson, Shirley
1919-1965 .... **CLC 11, 60; SSC 9**
See also AAYA 9; CA 1-4R; 25-28R;
CANR 4; CDALB 1941-1968; DLB 6;
SATA 2; WLC

Jacob, (Cyprien-)Max 1876-1944 ... **TCLC 6**
See also CA 104

Jacobs, Jim 1942- .... **CLC 12**
See also CA 97-100

Jacobs, W(illiam) W(ymark)
1863-1943 .... **TCLC 22**
See also CA 121

Jacobsen, Jens Peter 1847-1885 .. **NCLC 34**

Jacobsen, Josephine 1908- .... **CLC 48**
See also CA 33-36R; CANR 23

Jacobson, Dan 1929- .... **CLC 4, 14**
See also CA 1-4R; CANR 2, 25; DLB 14;
MTCW

Jacqueline
See Carpentier (y Valmont), Alejo

Jagger, Mick 1944- .... **CLC 17**

Jakes, John (William) 1932- .... **CLC 29**
See also BEST 89:4; CA 57-60; CANR 10;
DLBY 83; MTCW; SATA 62

James, Andrew
See Kirkup, James

James, C(yril) L(ionel) R(obert)
1901-1989 .... **CLC 33**
See also BW; CA 117; 125; 128; MTCW

James, Daniel (Lewis) 1911-1988
See Santiago, Danny
See also CA 125

James, Dynely
See Mayne, William (James Carter)

James, Henry
1843-1916 ..... **TCLC 2, 11, 24, 40, 47;**
SSC 8
See also CA 104; 132; CDALB 1865-1917;
DLB 12, 71, 74; MTCW; WLC

James, Montague (Rhodes)
1862-1936 .... **TCLC 6**
See also CA 104

James, P. D. .... **CLC 18, 46**
See also White, Phyllis Dorothy James
See also BEST 90:2; CDBLB 1960 to
Present; DLB 87

James, Philip
See Moorcock, Michael (John)

James, William 1842-1910 ..... **TCLC 15, 32**
See also CA 109

James I 1394-1437 .... **LC 20**

Jami, Nur al-Din 'Abd al-Rahman
1414-1492 .... **LC 9**

Jandl, Ernst 1925- .... **CLC 34**

Janowitz, Tama 1957- .... **CLC 43**
See also CA 106

Jarrell, Randall
1914-1965 ...... **CLC 1, 2, 6, 9, 13, 49**
See also CA 5-8R; 25-28R; CABS 2;
CANR 6, 34; CDALB 1941-1968; CLR 6;
DLB 48, 52; MAICYA; MTCW; SATA 7

Jarry, Alfred 1873-1907 .... **TCLC 2, 14**
See also CA 104

Jarvis, E. K.
See Bloch, Robert (Albert); Ellison, Harlan;
Silverberg, Robert

Jeake, Samuel Jr.
See Aiken, Conrad (Potter)

Jean Paul 1763-1825 .... **NCLC 7**

Jeffers, (John) Robinson
1887-1962 .... **CLC 2, 3, 11, 15, 54**
See also CA 85-88; CANR 35;
CDALB 1917-1929; DLB 45; MTCW;
WLC

Jefferson, Janet
See Mencken, H(enry) L(ouis)

Jefferson, Thomas 1743-1826 .... **NCLC 11**
See also CDALB 1640-1865; DLB 31

Jeffrey, Francis 1773-1850 .... **NCLC 33**
See also DLB 107

Jelakowitch, Ivan
See Heijermans, Herman

Jellicoe, (Patricia) Ann 1927- ...... **CLC 27**
See also CA 85-88; DLB 13

Jen, Gish .... **CLC 70**
See also Jen, Lillian

Jen, Lillian 1956(?)-
See Jen, Gish
See also CA 135

Jenkins, (John) Robin 1912- .... **CLC 52**
See also CA 1-4R; CANR 1; DLB 14

Jennings, Elizabeth (Joan)
1926- .... **CLC 5, 14**
See also CA 61-64; CAAS 5; CANR 8, 39;
DLB 27; MTCW; SATA 66

Jennings, Waylon 1937- .... **CLC 21**

Jensen, Johannes V. 1873-1950.... **TCLC 41**

Jensen, Laura (Linnea) 1948- ...... **CLC 37**
See also CA 103

Jerome, Jerome K(lapka)
1859-1927 .... **TCLC 23**
See also CA 119; DLB 10, 34

Jerrold, Douglas William
1803-1857 .... **NCLC 2**

Jewett, (Theodora) Sarah Orne
1849-1909 .... **TCLC 1, 22; SSC 6**
See also CA 108; 127; DLB 12, 74;
SATA 15

Jewsbury, Geraldine (Endsor)
1812-1880 .... **NCLC 22**
See also DLB 21

Jhabvala, Ruth Prawer
1927- .... **CLC 4, 8, 29**
See also CA 1-4R; CANR 2, 29; MTCW

Jiles, Paulette 1943- .... **CLC 13, 58**
See also CA 101

Jimenez (Mantecon), Juan Ramon
1881-1958 .... **TCLC 4**
See also CA 104; 131; HW; MTCW

Jimenez, Ramon
See Jimenez (Mantecon), Juan Ramon

Jimenez Mantecon, Juan
See Jimenez (Mantecon), Juan Ramon

Joel, Billy .... **CLC 26**
See also Joel, William Martin

Joel, William Martin 1949-
See Joel, Billy
See also CA 108

John of the Cross, St. 1542-1591 .... **LC 18**

Johnson, B(ryan) S(tanley William)
1933-1973 .... **CLC 6, 9**
See also CA 9-12R; 53-56; CANR 9;
DLB 14, 40

Johnson, Charles (Richard)
1948- .... **CLC 7, 51, 65**
See also BLC 2; BW; CA 116; DLB 33

Johnson, Denis 1949- .... **CLC 52**
See also CA 117; 121; DLB 120

Johnson, Diane (Lain)
1934- .... **CLC 5, 13, 48**
See also CA 41-44R; CANR 17; DLBY 80;
MTCW

Johnson, Eyvind (Olof Verner)
1900-1976 .... **CLC 14**
See also CA 73-76; 69-72; CANR 34

Johnson, J. R.
See James, C(yril) L(ionel) R(obert)

Johnson, James Weldon
1871-1938 .... **TCLC 3, 19**
See also BLC 2; BW; CA 104; 125;
CDALB 1917-1929; DLB 51; MTCW;
SATA 31

Johnson, Joyce 1935- .... **CLC 58**
See also CA 125; 129

Johnson, Lionel (Pigot)
1867-1902 .... **TCLC 19**
See also CA 117; DLB 19

Johnson, Mel
See Malzberg, Barry N(athaniel)

Johnson, Pamela Hansford
1912-1981 .... **CLC 1, 7, 27**
See also CA 1-4R; 104; CANR 2, 28;
DLB 15; MTCW

Johnson, Samuel 1709-1784........ **LC 15**
See also CDBLB 1660-1789; DLB 39, 95,
104; WLC

Johnson, Uwe
1934-1984 .... CLC 5, 10, 15, 40
See also CA 1-4R; 112; CANR 1, 39;
DLB 75; MTCW

Johnston, George (Benson) 1913- ... CLC 51
See also CA 1-4R; CANR 5, 20; DLB 88

Johnston, Jennifer 1930- .... CLC 7
See also CA 85-88; DLB 14

Jolley, (Monica) Elizabeth 1923- ... CLC 46
See also CA 127; CAAS 13

Jones, Arthur Llewellyn 1863-1947
See Machen, Arthur
See also CA 104

Jones, D(ouglas) G(ordon) 1929-.... CLC 10
See also CA 29-32R; CANR 13; DLB 53

Jones, David (Michael)
1895-1974 .... CLC 2, 4, 7, 13, 42
See also CA 9-12R; 53-56; CANR 28;
CDBLB 1945-1960; DLB 20, 100; MTCW

Jones, David Robert 1947-
See Bowie, David
See also CA 103

Jones, Diana Wynne 1934- .... CLC 26
See also CA 49-52; CANR 4, 26; CLR 23;
MAICYA; SAAS 7; SATA 9, 70

Jones, Gayl 1949- .... CLC 6, 9
See also BLC 2; BW; CA 77-80; CANR 27;
DLB 33; MTCW

Jones, James 1921-1977.... CLC 1, 3, 10, 39
See also AITN 1, 2; CA 1-4R; 69-72;
CANR 6; DLB 2; MTCW

Jones, John J.
See Lovecraft, H(oward) P(hillips)

Jones, LeRoi .... CLC 1, 2, 3, 5, 10, 14
See also Baraka, Amiri

Jones, Louis B. .... CLC 65

Jones, Madison (Percy Jr.) 1925-.... CLC 4
See also CA 13-16R; CAAS 11; CANR 7

Jones, Mervyn 1922- .... CLC 10, 52
See also CA 45-48; CAAS 5; CANR 1;
MTCW

Jones, Mick 1956(?)- .... CLC 30
See also The Clash

Jones, Nettie (Pearl) 1941- .... CLC 34
See also CA 137

Jones, Preston 1936-1979 .... CLC 10
See also CA 73-76; 89-92; DLB 7

Jones, Robert F(rancis) 1934-....... CLC 7
See also CA 49-52; CANR 2

Jones, Rod 1953- .... CLC 50
See also CA 128

Jones, Terence Graham Parry
1942- .... CLC 21
See also Jones, Terry; Monty Python
See also CA 112; 116; CANR 35; SATA 51

Jones, Terry
See Jones, Terence Graham Parry
See also SATA 67

Jong, Erica 1942-.......... CLC 4, 6, 8, 18
See also AITN 1; BEST 90:2; CA 73-76;
CANR 26; DLB 2, 5, 28; MTCW

Jonson, Ben(jamin) 1572(?)-1637...... LC 6
See also CDBLB Before 1660; DLB 62, 121;
WLC

Jordan, June 1936-......... CLC 5, 11, 23
See also AAYA 2; BW; CA 33-36R;
CANR 25; CLR 10; DLB 38; MAICYA;
MTCW; SATA 4

Jordan, Pat(rick M.) 1941- .... CLC 37
See also CA 33-36R

Jorgensen, Ivar
See Ellison, Harlan

Jorgenson, Ivar
See Silverberg, Robert

Josipovici, Gabriel 1940-........ CLC 6, 43
See also CA 37-40R; CAAS 8; DLB 14

Joubert, Joseph 1754-1824 .... NCLC 9

Jouve, Pierre Jean 1887-1976...... CLC 47
See also CA 65-68

Joyce, James (Augustine Aloysius)
1882-1941 .... TCLC 3, 8, 16, 35; SSC 3
See also CA 104; 126; CDBLB 1914-1945;
DLB 10, 19, 36; MTCW; WLC

Jozsef, Attila 1905-1937......... TCLC 22
See also CA 116

Juana Ines de la Cruz 1651(?)-1695 ... LC 5

Judd, Cyril
See Kornbluth, C(yril) M.; Pohl, Frederik

Julian of Norwich 1342(?)-1416(?) .... LC 6

Just, Ward (Swift) 1935- .... CLC 4, 27
See also CA 25-28R; CANR 32

Justice, Donald (Rodney) 1925- .. CLC 6, 19
See also CA 5-8R; CANR 26; DLBY 83

Juvenal c. 55-c. 127 .... CMLC 8

Juvenis
See Bourne, Randolph S(illiman)

Kacew, Romain 1914-1980
See Gary, Romain
See also CA 108; 102

Kadare, Ismail 1936- .... CLC 52

Kadohata, Cynthia................. CLC 59

Kafka, Franz
1883-1924 ...... TCLC 2, 6, 13, 29, 47;
SSC 5
See also CA 105; 126; DLB 81; MTCW;
WLC

Kahn, Roger 1927-............... CLC 30
See also CA 25-28R; SATA 37

Kain, Saul
See Sassoon, Siegfried (Lorraine)

Kaiser, Georg 1878-1945 .... TCLC 9
See also CA 106

Kaletski, Alexander 1946-......... CLC 39
See also CA 118

Kalidasa fl. c. 400- .... CMLC 9

Kallman, Chester (Simon)
1921-1975 .... CLC 2
See also CA 45-48; 53-56; CANR 3

Kaminsky, Melvin 1926-
See Brooks, Mel
See also CA 65-68; CANR 16

Kaminsky, Stuart M(elvin) 1934- ... CLC 59
See also CA 73-76; CANR 29

Kane, Paul
See Simon, Paul

Kane, Wilson
See Bloch, Robert (Albert)

Kanin, Garson 1912-.............. CLC 22
See also AITN 1; CA 5-8R; CANR 7;
DLB 7

Kaniuk, Yoram 1930-............. CLC 19
See also CA 134

Kant, Immanuel 1724-1804 ...... NCLC 27
See also DLB 94

Kantor, MacKinlay 1904-1977 ...... CLC 7
See also CA 61-64; 73-76; DLB 9, 102

Kaplan, David Michael 1946- ...... CLC 50

Kaplan, James 1951- .... CLC 59
See also CA 135

Karageorge, Michael
See Anderson, Poul (William)

Karamzin, Nikolai Mikhailovich
1766-1826 .... NCLC 3

Karapanou, Margarita 1946-...... CLC 13
See also CA 101

Karinthy, Frigyes 1887-1938...... TCLC 47

Karl, Frederick R(obert) 1927-..... CLC 34
See also CA 5-8R; CANR 3

Kastel, Warren
See Silverberg, Robert

Kataev, Evgeny Petrovich 1903-1942
See Petrov, Evgeny
See also CA 120

Kataphusin
See Ruskin, John

Katz, Steve 1935-................ CLC 47
See also CA 25-28R; CAAS 14; CANR 12;
DLBY 83

Kauffman, Janet 1945-............ CLC 42
See also CA 117; DLBY 86

Kaufman, Bob (Garnell)
1925-1986 .... CLC 49
See also BW; CA 41-44R; 118; CANR 22;
DLB 16, 41

Kaufman, George S. 1889-1961..... CLC 38
See also CA 108; 93-96; DLB 7

Kaufman, Sue .... CLC 3, 8
See also Barondess, Sue K(aufman)

Kavafis, Konstantinos Petrou 1863-1933
See Cavafy, C(onstantine) P(eter)
See also CA 104

Kavan, Anna 1901-1968......... CLC 5, 13
See also CA 5-8R; CANR 6; MTCW

Kavanagh, Dan
See Barnes, Julian

Kavanagh, Patrick (Joseph)
1904-1967 .... CLC 22
See also CA 123; 25-28R; DLB 15, 20;
MTCW

Kawabata, Yasunari
1899-1972 .... CLC 2, 5, 9, 18
See also CA 93-96; 33-36R

Kaye, M(ary) M(argaret) 1909-..... CLC 28
See also CA 89-92; CANR 24; MTCW;
SATA 62

Kaye, Mollie
See Kaye, M(ary) M(argaret)

Kaye-Smith, Sheila 1887-1956..... TCLC 20
See also CA 118; DLB 36

Kaymor, Patrice Maguilene
See Senghor, Leopold Sedar

Kazan, Elia 1909- . . . . **CLC 6, 16, 63**
See also CA 21-24R; CANR 32

Kazantzakis, Nikos
1883(?)-1957 . . . . **TCLC 2, 5, 33**
See also CA 105; 132; MTCW

Kazin, Alfred 1915- . . . . **CLC 34, 38**
See also CA 1-4R; CAAS 7; CANR 1;
DLB 67

Keane, Mary Nesta (Skrine) 1904-
See Keane, Molly
See also CA 108; 114

Keane, Molly . . . . **CLC 31**
See also Keane, Mary Nesta (Skrine)

Keates, Jonathan 19(?)- . . . . **CLC 34**

Keaton, Buster 1895-1966 . . . . **CLC 20**

Keats, John 1795-1821 . . . . . . **NCLC 8; PC 1**
See also CDBLB 1789-1832; DLB 96, 110;
WLC

Keene, Donald 1922- . . . . **CLC 34**
See also CA 1-4R; CANR 5

Keillor, Garrison . . . . **CLC 40**
See also Keillor, Gary (Edward)
See also AAYA 2; BEST 89:3; DLBY 87;
SATA 58

Keillor, Gary (Edward) 1942-
See Keillor, Garrison
See also CA 111; 117; CANR 36; MTCW

Keith, Michael
See Hubbard, L(afayette) Ron(ald)

Kell, Joseph
See Wilson, John (Anthony) Burgess

Keller, Gottfried 1819-1890 . . . . . . **NCLC 2**

Kellerman, Jonathan 1949- . . . . **CLC 44**
See also BEST 90:1; CA 106; CANR 29

Kelley, William Melvin 1937- . . . . . . **CLC 22**
See also BW; CA 77-80; CANR 27; DLB 33

Kellogg, Marjorie 1922- . . . . **CLC 2**
See also CA 81-84

Kellow, Kathleen
See Hibbert, Eleanor Burford

Kelly, M(ilton) T(erry) 1947- . . . . **CLC 55**
See also CA 97-100; CANR 19

Kelman, James 1946- . . . . **CLC 58**

Kemal, Yashar 1923- . . . . **CLC 14, 29**
See also CA 89-92

Kemble, Fanny 1809-1893 . . . . **NCLC 18**
See also DLB 32

Kemelman, Harry 1908- . . . . **CLC 2**
See also AITN 1; CA 9-12R; CANR 6;
DLB 28

Kempe, Margery 1373(?)-1440(?) . . . . . **LC 6**

Kempis, Thomas a 1380-1471 . . . . **LC 11**

Kendall, Henry 1839-1882 . . . . **NCLC 12**

Keneally, Thomas (Michael)
1935- . . . . . . **CLC 5, 8, 10, 14, 19, 27, 43**
See also CA 85-88; CANR 10; MTCW

Kennedy, Adrienne (Lita) 1931- . . . . **CLC 66**
See also BLC 2; BW; CA 103; CABS 3;
CANR 26; DLB 38

Kennedy, John Pendleton
1795-1870 . . . . **NCLC 2**
See also DLB 3

Kennedy, Joseph Charles 1929- . . . . . . **CLC 8**
See also Kennedy, X. J.
See also CA 1-4R; CANR 4, 30; SATA 14

Kennedy, William 1928- . . **CLC 6, 28, 34, 53**
See also AAYA 1; CA 85-88; CANR 14,
31; DLBY 85; MTCW; SATA 57

Kennedy, X. J. . . . . **CLC 42**
See also Kennedy, Joseph Charles
See also CAAS 9; CLR 27; DLB 5

Kent, Kelvin
See Kuttner, Henry

Kenton, Maxwell
See Southern, Terry

Kenyon, Robert O.
See Kuttner, Henry

Kerouac, Jack . . . . . **CLC 1, 2, 3, 5, 14, 29, 61**
See also Kerouac, Jean-Louis Lebris de
See also CDALB 1941-1968; DLB 2, 16;
DLBD 3

Kerouac, Jean-Louis Lebris de 1922-1969
See Kerouac, Jack
See also AITN 1; CA 5-8R; 25-28R;
CANR 26; MTCW; WLC

Kerr, Jean 1923- . . . . **CLC 22**
See also CA 5-8R; CANR 7

Kerr, M. E. . . . . **CLC 12, 35**
See also Meaker, Marijane (Agnes)
See also AAYA 2; SAAS 1

Kerr, Robert . . . . **CLC 55**

Kerrigan, (Thomas) Anthony
1918- . . . . **CLC 4, 6**
See also CA 49-52; CAAS 11; CANR 4

Kerry, Lois
See Duncan, Lois

Kesey, Ken (Elton)
1935- . . . . **CLC 1, 3, 6, 11, 46, 64**
See also CA 1-4R; CANR 22, 38;
CDALB 1968-1988; DLB 2, 16; MTCW;
SATA 66; WLC

Kesselring, Joseph (Otto)
1902-1967 . . . . **CLC 45**

Kessler, Jascha (Frederick) 1929- . . . . **CLC 4**
See also CA 17-20R; CANR 8

Kettelkamp, Larry (Dale) 1933- . . . . . **CLC 12**
See also CA 29-32R; CANR 16; SAAS 3;
SATA 2

Kherdian, David 1931- . . . . **CLC 6, 9**
See also CA 21-24R; CAAS 2; CANR 39;
CLR 24; MAICYA; SATA 16

Khlebnikov, Velimir . . . . **TCLC 20**
See also Khlebnikov, Viktor Vladimirovich

Khlebnikov, Viktor Vladimirovich 1885-1922
See Khlebnikov, Velimir
See also CA 117

Khodasevich, Vladislav (Felitsianovich)
1886-1939 . . . . **TCLC 15**
See also CA 115

Kielland, Alexander Lange
1849-1906 . . . . **TCLC 5**
See also CA 104

Kiely, Benedict 1919- . . . . **CLC 23, 43**
See also CA 1-4R; CANR 2; DLB 15

Kienzle, William X(avier) 1928- . . . . **CLC 25**
See also CA 93-96; CAAS 1; CANR 9, 31;
MTCW

Kierkegaard, Soeren 1813-1855 . . . **NCLC 34**

Kierkegaard, Soren 1813-1855 . . . . **NCLC 34**

Killens, John Oliver 1916-1987 . . . . . **CLC 10**
See also BW; CA 77-80; 123; CAAS 2;
CANR 26; DLB 33

Killigrew, Anne 1660-1685 . . . . **LC 4**

Kim
See Simenon, Georges (Jacques Christian)

Kincaid, Jamaica 1949- . . . . **CLC 43, 68**
See also BLC 2; BW; CA 125

King, Francis (Henry) 1923- . . . . . **CLC 8, 53**
See also CA 1-4R; CANR 1, 33; DLB 15;
MTCW

King, Stephen (Edwin)
1947- . . . . **CLC 12, 26, 37, 61**
See also AAYA 1; BEST 90:1; CA 61-64;
CANR 1, 30; DLBY 80; MTCW;
SATA 9, 55

King, Steve
See King, Stephen (Edwin)

Kingman, Lee . . . . **CLC 17**
See also Natti, (Mary) Lee
See also SAAS 3; SATA 1, 67

Kingsley, Charles 1819-1875 . . . . . **NCLC 35**
See also DLB 21, 32; YABC 2

Kingsley, Sidney 1906- . . . . **CLC 44**
See also CA 85-88; DLB 7

Kingsolver, Barbara 1955- . . . . **CLC 55**
See also CA 129; 134

Kingston, Maxine (Ting Ting) Hong
1940- . . . . **CLC 12, 19, 58**
See also AAYA 8; CA 69-72; CANR 13,
38; DLBY 80; MTCW; SATA 53

Kinnell, Galway
1927- . . . . **CLC 1, 2, 3, 5, 13, 29**
See also CA 9-12R; CANR 10, 34; DLB 5;
DLBY 87; MTCW

Kinsella, Thomas 1928- . . . . **CLC 4, 19**
See also CA 17-20R; CANR 15; DLB 27;
MTCW

Kinsella, W(illiam) P(atrick)
1935- . . . . **CLC 27, 43**
See also AAYA 7; CA 97-100; CAAS 7;
CANR 21, 35; MTCW

Kipling, (Joseph) Rudyard
1865-1936 . . . . **TCLC 8, 17; PC 3; SSC 5**
See also CA 105; 120; CANR 33;
CDBLB 1890-1914; DLB 19, 34;
MAICYA; MTCW; WLC; YABC 2

Kirkup, James 1918- . . . . **CLC 1**
See also CA 1-4R; CAAS 4; CANR 2;
DLB 27; SATA 12

Kirkwood, James 1930(?)-1989 . . . . . . **CLC 9**
See also AITN 2; CA 1-4R; 128; CANR 6

Kis, Danilo 1935-1989 . . . . **CLC 57**
See also CA 109; 118; 129; MTCW

Kivi, Aleksis 1834-1872 . . . . **NCLC 30**

Kizer, Carolyn (Ashley) 1925- . . . **CLC 15, 39**
See also CA 65-68; CAAS 5; CANR 24;
DLB 5

Lacan, Jacques (Marie Emile)
1901-1981 . . . . **CLC 75**
See also CA 121; 104

**Laclos, Pierre Ambroise Francois Choderlos
de** 1741-1803 . . . . **NCLC 4**

La Colere, Francois
See Aragon, Louis

Lacolere, Francois
See Aragon, Louis

La Deshabilleuse
See Simenon, Georges (Jacques Christian)

Lady Gregory
See Gregory, Isabella Augusta (Persse)

Lady of Quality, A
See Bagnold, Enid

**La Fayette, Marie (Madelaine Pioche de la
Vergne Comtes** 1634-1693 . . . . . . **LC 2**

Lafayette, Rene
See Hubbard, L(afayette) Ron(ald)

Laforgue, Jules 1860-1887 . . . . **NCLC 5**

Lagerkvist, Paer (Fabian)
1891-1974 . . . . **CLC 7, 10, 13, 54**
See also CA 85-88; 49-52; MTCW

Lagerkvist, Par
See Lagerkvist, Paer (Fabian)

Lagerloef, Selma (Ottiliana Lovisa)
1858-1940 . . . . **TCLC 4, 36**
See also Lagerlof, Selma (Ottiliana Lovisa)
See also CA 108; CLR 7; SATA 15

Lagerlof, Selma (Ottiliana Lovisa)
See Lagerloef, Selma (Ottiliana Lovisa)
See also CLR 7; SATA 15

La Guma, (Justin) Alex(ander)
1925-1985 . . . . **CLC 19**
See also BW; CA 49-52; 118; CANR 25;
DLB 117; MTCW

Laidlaw, A. K.
See Grieve, C(hristopher) M(urray)

Lainez, Manuel Mujica
See Mujica Lainez, Manuel
See also HW

Lamartine, Alphonse (Marie Louis Prat) de
1790-1869 . . . . **NCLC 11**

Lamb, Charles 1775-1834 . . . . **NCLC 10**
See also CDBLB 1789-1832; DLB 93, 107;
SATA 17; WLC

Lamb, Lady Caroline 1785-1828 . . **NCLC 38**
See also DLB 116

Lamming, George (William)
1927- . . . . **CLC 2, 4, 66**
See also BLC 2; BW; CA 85-88; CANR 26;
MTCW

L'Amour, Louis (Dearborn)
1908-1988 . . . . **CLC 25, 55**
See also AITN 2; BEST 89:2; CA 1-4R;
125; CANR 3, 25; DLBY 80; MTCW

Lampedusa, Giuseppe (Tomasi) di . . . **TCLC 13**
See also Tomasi di Lampedusa, Giuseppe

Lampman, Archibald 1861-1899 . . **NCLC 25**
See also DLB 92

Lancaster, Bruce 1896-1963 . . . . **CLC 36**
See also CA 9-10; CAP 1; SATA 9

Landau, Mark Alexandrovich
See Aldanov, Mark (Alexandrovich)

Landau-Aldanov, Mark Alexandrovich
See Aldanov, Mark (Alexandrovich)

Landis, John 1950- . . . . **CLC 26**
See also CA 112; 122

Landolfi, Tommaso 1908-1979 . . . **CLC 11, 49**
See also CA 127; 117

Landon, Letitia Elizabeth
1802-1838 . . . . **NCLC 15**
See also DLB 96

Landor, Walter Savage
1775-1864 . . . . **NCLC 14**
See also DLB 93, 107

Landwirth, Heinz 1927-
See Lind, Jakov
See also CA 9-12R; CANR 7

Lane, Patrick 1939- . . . . **CLC 25**
See also CA 97-100; DLB 53

Lang, Andrew 1844-1912 . . . . **TCLC 16**
See also CA 114; 137; DLB 98; MAICYA;
SATA 16

Lang, Fritz 1890-1976 . . . . **CLC 20**
See also CA 77-80; 69-72; CANR 30

Lange, John
See Crichton, (John) Michael

Langer, Elinor 1939- . . . . **CLC 34**
See also CA 121

Langland, William 1330(?)-1400(?) . . . **LC 19**

Langstaff, Launcelot
See Irving, Washington

Lanier, Sidney 1842-1881 . . . . **NCLC 6**
See also DLB 64; MAICYA; SATA 18

Lanyer, Aemilia 1569-1645 . . . . **LC 10**

Lao Tzu . . . . **CMLC 7**

Lapine, James (Elliot) 1949- . . . . **CLC 39**
See also CA 123; 130

Larbaud, Valery (Nicolas)
1881-1957 . . . . **TCLC 9**
See also CA 106

Lardner, Ring
See Lardner, Ring(gold) W(ilmer)

Lardner, Ring W. Jr.
See Lardner, Ring(gold) W(ilmer)

Lardner, Ring(gold) W(ilmer)
1885-1933 . . . . **TCLC 2, 14**
See also CA 104; 131; CDALB 1917-1929;
DLB 11, 25, 86; MTCW

Laredo, Betty
See Codrescu, Andrei

Larkin, Maia
See Wojciechowska, Maia (Teresa)

Larkin, Philip (Arthur)
1922-1985 . . . **CLC 3, 5, 8, 9, 13, 18, 33,
39, 64**
See also CA 5-8R; 117; CANR 24;
CDBLB 1960 to Present; DLB 27;
MTCW

Larra (y Sanchez de Castro), Mariano Jose de
1809-1837 . . . . **NCLC 17**

Larsen, Eric 1941- . . . . **CLC 55**
See also CA 132

Larsen, Nella 1891-1964 . . . . **CLC 37**
See also BLC 2; BW; CA 125; DLB 51

Larson, Charles R(aymond) 1938- . . . **CLC 31**
See also CA 53-56; CANR 4

Latham, Jean Lee 1902- . . . . **CLC 12**
See also AITN 1; CA 5-8R; CANR 7;
MAICYA; SATA 2, 68

Latham, Mavis
See Clark, Mavis Thorpe

Lathen, Emma . . . . **CLC 2**
See also Hennissart, Martha; Latsis, Mary
J(ane)

Lathrop, Francis
See Leiber, Fritz (Reuter Jr.)

Latsis, Mary J(ane)
See Lathen, Emma
See also CA 85-88

Lattimore, Richmond (Alexander)
1906-1984 . . . . **CLC 3**
See also CA 1-4R; 112; CANR 1

Laughlin, James 1914- . . . . **CLC 49**
See also CA 21-24R; CANR 9; DLB 48

Laurence, (Jean) Margaret (Wemyss)
1926-1987 . . **CLC 3, 6, 13, 50, 62; SSC 7**
See also CA 5-8R; 121; CANR 33; DLB 53;
MTCW; SATA 50

Laurent, Antoine 1952- . . . . **CLC 50**

Lauscher, Hermann
See Hesse, Hermann

Lautreamont, Comte de
1846-1870 . . . . **NCLC 12**

Laverty, Donald
See Blish, James (Benjamin)

Lavin, Mary 1912- . . . . . . **CLC 4, 18; SSC 4**
See also CA 9-12R; CANR 33; DLB 15;
MTCW

Lavond, Paul Dennis
See Kornbluth, C(yril) M.; Pohl, Frederik

Lawler, Raymond Evenor 1922- . . . . **CLC 58**
See also CA 103

Lawrence, D(avid) H(erbert Richards)
1885-1930 . . . . . . **TCLC 2, 9, 16, 33, 48;
SSC 4**
See also CA 104; 121; CDBLB 1914-1945;
DLB 10, 19, 36, 98; MTCW; WLC

Lawrence, T(homas) E(dward)
1888-1935 . . . . **TCLC 18**
See also Dale, Colin
See also CA 115

Lawrence Of Arabia
See Lawrence, T(homas) E(dward)

Lawson, Henry (Archibald Hertzberg)
1867-1922 . . . . **TCLC 27**
See also CA 120

Laxness, Halldor . . . . **CLC 25**
See also Gudjonsson, Halldor Kiljan

Layamon fl. c. 1200- . . . . **CMLC 10**

Laye, Camara 1928-1980 . . . . **CLC 4, 38**
See also BLC 2; BW; CA 85-88; 97-100;
CANR 25; MTCW

Layton, Irving (Peter) 1912- . . . . . **CLC 2, 15**
See also CA 1-4R; CANR 2, 33; DLB 88;
MTCW

Lazarus, Emma 1849-1887 . . . . **NCLC 8**

Lazarus, Felix
See Cable, George Washington

Lea, Joan
See Neufeld, John (Arthur)

Leacock, Stephen (Butler)
1869-1944 .... TCLC 2
See also CA 104; DLB 92

Lear, Edward 1812-1888 .... NCLC 3
See also CLR 1; DLB 32; MAICYA;
SATA 18

Lear, Norman (Milton) 1922- ...... CLC 12
See also CA 73-76

Leavis, F(rank) R(aymond)
1895-1978 .... CLC 24
See also CA 21-24R; 77-80; MTCW

Leavitt, David 1961-.............. CLC 34
See also CA 116; 122

Lebowitz, Fran(ces Ann)
1951(?)-.................. CLC 11, 36
See also CA 81-84; CANR 14; MTCW

le Carre, John .... CLC 3, 5, 9, 15, 28
See also Cornwell, David (John Moore)
See also BEST 89:4; CDBLB 1960 to
Present; DLB 87

Le Clezio, J(ean) M(arie) G(ustave)
1940- .... CLC 31
See also CA 116; 128; DLB 83

Leconte de Lisle, Charles-Marie-Rene
1818-1894 .... NCLC 29

Le Coq, Monsieur
See Simenon, Georges (Jacques Christian)

Leduc, Violette 1907-1972......... CLC 22
See also CA 13-14; 33-36R; CAP 1

Ledwidge, Francis 1887(?)-1917 ... TCLC 23
See also CA 123; DLB 20

Lee, Andrea 1953- .... CLC 36
See also BLC 2; BW; CA 125

Lee, Andrew
See Auchincloss, Louis (Stanton)

Lee, Don L. .... CLC 2
See also Madhubuti, Haki R.

Lee, George W(ashington)
1894-1976 .... CLC 52
See also BLC 2; BW; CA 125; DLB 51

Lee, (Nelle) Harper 1926- ...... CLC 12, 60
See also CA 13-16R; CDALB 1941-1968;
DLB 6; MTCW; SATA 11; WLC

Lee, Julian
See Latham, Jean Lee

Lee, Lawrence 1903- .... CLC 34
See also CA 25-28R

Lee, Manfred B(ennington)
1905-1971 .... CLC 11
See also Queen, Ellery
See also CA 1-4R; 29-32R; CANR 2

Lee, Stan 1922-.................. CLC 17
See also AAYA 5; CA 108; 111

Lee, Tanith 1947-................ CLC 46
See also CA 37-40R; SATA 8

Lee, Vernon..................... TCLC 5
See also Paget, Violet
See also DLB 57

Lee, William
See Burroughs, William S(eward)

Lee, Willy
See Burroughs, William S(eward)

Lee-Hamilton, Eugene (Jacob)
1845-1907 .... TCLC 22
See also CA 117

Leet, Judith 1935- .... CLC 11

Le Fanu, Joseph Sheridan
1814-1873 .... NCLC 9
See also DLB 21, 70

Leffland, Ella 1931- .... CLC 19
See also CA 29-32R; CANR 35; DLBY 84;
SATA 65

Leger, (Marie-Rene) Alexis Saint-Leger
1887-1975 .... CLC 11
See also Perse, St.-John
See also CA 13-16R; 61-64; MTCW

Leger, Saintleger
See Leger, (Marie-Rene) Alexis Saint-Leger

Le Guin, Ursula K(roeber)
1929- .... CLC 8, 13, 22, 45, 71
See also AAYA 9; AITN 1; CA 21-24R;
CANR 9, 32; CDALB 1968-1988; CLR 3,
28; DLB 8, 52; MAICYA; MTCW;
SATA 4, 52

Lehmann, Rosamond (Nina)
1901-1990 .... CLC 5
See also CA 77-80; 131; CANR 8; DLB 15

Leiber, Fritz (Reuter Jr.) 1910- .... CLC 25
See also CA 45-48; CANR 2; DLB 8;
MTCW; SATA 45

Leimbach, Martha 1963-
See Leimbach, Marti
See also CA 130

Leimbach, Marti .... CLC 65
See also Leimbach, Martha

Leino, Eino .... TCLC 24
See also Loennbohm, Armas Eino Leopold

Leiris, Michel (Julien) 1901-1990... CLC 61
See also CA 119; 128; 132

Leithauser, Brad 1953-............ CLC 27
See also CA 107; CANR 27; DLB 120

Lelchuk, Alan 1938-.............. CLC 5
See also CA 45-48; CANR 1

Lem, Stanislaw 1921-........ CLC 8, 15, 40
See also CA 105; CAAS 1; CANR 32;
MTCW

Lemann, Nancy 1956-............. CLC 39
See also CA 118; 136

Lemonnier, (Antoine Louis) Camille
1844-1913 .... TCLC 22
See also CA 121

Lenau, Nikolaus 1802-1850 ...... NCLC 16

L'Engle, Madeleine (Camp Franklin)
1918- .... CLC 12
See also AAYA 1; AITN 2; CA 1-4R;
CANR 3, 21, 39; CLR 1, 14; DLB 52;
MAICYA; MTCW; SAAS 15; SATA 1,
27

Lengyel, Jozsef 1896-1975.......... CLC 7
See also CA 85-88; 57-60

Lennon, John (Ono)
1940-1980 .... CLC 12, 35
See also CA 102

Lennox, Charlotte Ramsay
1729(?)-1804 .... NCLC 23
See also DLB 39

Lentricchia, Frank (Jr.) 1940-...... CLC 34
See also CA 25-28R; CANR 19

Lenz, Siegfried 1926-............. CLC 27
See also CA 89-92; DLB 75

Leonard, Elmore (John Jr.)
1925- .... CLC 28, 34, 71
See also AITN 1; BEST 89:1, 90:4;
CA 81-84; CANR 12, 28; MTCW

Leonard, Hugh
See Byrne, John Keyes
See also DLB 13

Leopardi, (Conte) Giacomo (Talegardo
Francesco di Sales Save
1798-1837 .... NCLC 22

Le Reveler
See Artaud, Antonin

Lerman, Eleanor 1952-............. CLC 9
See also CA 85-88

Lerman, Rhoda 1936-............. CLC 56
See also CA 49-52

Lermontov, Mikhail Yuryevich
1814-1841 .... NCLC 5

Leroux, Gaston 1868-1927....... TCLC 25
See also CA 108; 136; SATA 65

Lesage, Alain-Rene 1668-1747....... LC 2

Leskov, Nikolai (Semyonovich)
1831-1895 .... NCLC 25

Lessing, Doris (May)
1919- .... CLC 1, 2, 3, 6, 10, 15, 22, 40;
SSC 6
See also CA 9-12R; CAAS 14; CANR 33;
CDBLB 1960 to Present; DLB 15;
DLBY 85; MTCW

Lessing, Gotthold Ephraim
1729-1781 .... LC 8
See also DLB 97

Lester, Richard 1932-............. CLC 20

Lever, Charles (James)
1806-1872 .... NCLC 23
See also DLB 21

Leverson, Ada 1865(?)-1936(?) .... TCLC 18
See also Elaine
See also CA 117

Levertov, Denise
1923- ...... CLC 1, 2, 3, 5, 8, 15, 28, 66
See also CA 1-4R; CANR 3, 29; DLB 5;
MTCW

Levi, Peter (Chad Tigar) 1931-..... CLC 41
See also CA 5-8R; CANR 34; DLB 40

Levi, Primo 1919-1987........ CLC 37, 50
See also CA 13-16R; 122; CANR 12, 33;
MTCW

Levin, Ira 1929- .... CLC 3, 6
See also CA 21-24R; CANR 17; MTCW;
SATA 66

Levin, Meyer 1905-1981 .... CLC 7
See also AITN 1; CA 9-12R; 104;
CANR 15; DLB 9, 28; DLBY 81;
SATA 21, 27

Levine, Norman 1924-............ CLC 54
See also CA 73-76; CANR 14; DLB 88

Levine, Philip 1928-... CLC 2, 4, 5, 9, 14, 33
See also CA 9-12R; CANR 9, 37; DLB 5

Lord Byron
See Byron, George Gordon (Noel)

Lord Dunsany .... TCLC 2
See also Dunsany, Edward John Moreton
Drax Plunkett

Lorde, Audre (Geraldine)
1934- .... CLC 18, 71
See also BLC 2; BW; CA 25-28R;
CANR 16, 26; DLB 41; MTCW

Lord Jeffrey
See Jeffrey, Francis

Lorenzo, Heberto Padilla
See Padilla (Lorenzo), Heberto

Loris
See Hofmannsthal, Hugo von

Loti, Pierre .... TCLC 11
See also Viaud, (Louis Marie) Julien
See also DLB 123

Louie, David Wong 1954- .... CLC 70

Louis, Father M.
See Merton, Thomas

Lovecraft, H(oward) P(hillips)
1890-1937 .... TCLC 4, 22; SSC 3
See also CA 104; 133; MTCW

Lovelace, Earl 1935- .... CLC 51
See also CA 77-80; MTCW

Lowell, Amy 1874-1925 .... TCLC 1, 8
See also CA 104; DLB 54

Lowell, James Russell 1819-1891 .. NCLC 2
See also CDALB 1640-1865; DLB 1, 11, 64,
79

Lowell, Robert (Traill Spence Jr.)
1917-1977 ... CLC 1, 2, 3, 4, 5, 8, 9, 11,
15, 37; PC 3
See also CA 9-12R; 73-76; CABS 2;
CANR 26; DLB 5; MTCW; WLC

Lowndes, Marie Adelaide (Belloc)
1868-1947 .... TCLC 12
See also CA 107; DLB 70

Lowry, (Clarence) Malcolm
1909-1957 .... TCLC 6, 40
See also CA 105; 131; CDBLB 1945-1960;
DLB 15; MTCW

Lowry, Mina Gertrude 1882-1966
See Loy, Mina
See also CA 113

Loxsmith, John
See Brunner, John (Kilian Houston)

Loy, Mina .... CLC 28
See also Lowry, Mina Gertrude
See also DLB 4, 54

Loyson-Bridet
See Schwob, (Mayer Andre) Marcel

Lucas, Craig 1951- .... CLC 64
See also CA 137

Lucas, George 1944- .... CLC 16
See also AAYA 1; CA 77-80; CANR 30;
SATA 56

Lucas, Hans
See Godard, Jean-Luc

Lucas, Victoria
See Plath, Sylvia

Ludlam, Charles 1943-1987 ..... CLC 46, 50
See also CA 85-88; 122

Ludlum, Robert 1927- .... CLC 22, 43
See also BEST 89:1, 90:3; CA 33-36R;
CANR 25; DLBY 82; MTCW

Ludwig, Ken .... CLC 60

Ludwig, Otto 1813-1865 .... NCLC 4

Lugones, Leopoldo 1874-1938 ..... TCLC 15
See also CA 116; 131; HW

Lu Hsun 1881-1936 .... TCLC 3

Lukacs, George .... CLC 24
See also Lukacs, Gyorgy (Szegeny von)

Lukacs, Gyorgy (Szegeny von) 1885-1971
See Lukacs, George
See also CA 101; 29-32R

Luke, Peter (Ambrose Cyprian)
1919- .... CLC 38
See also CA 81-84; DLB 13

Lunar, Dennis
See Mungo, Raymond

Lurie, Alison 1926- .... CLC 4, 5, 18, 39
See also CA 1-4R; CANR 2, 17; DLB 2;
MTCW; SATA 46

Lustig, Arnost 1926- .... CLC 56
See also AAYA 3; CA 69-72; SATA 56

Luther, Martin 1483-1546 .... LC 9

Luzi, Mario 1914- .... CLC 13
See also CA 61-64; CANR 9

Lynch, B. Suarez
See Bioy Casares, Adolfo; Borges, Jorge
Luis

Lynch, David (K.) 1946- .... CLC 66
See also CA 124; 129

Lynch, James
See Andreyev, Leonid (Nikolaevich)

Lynch Davis, B.
See Bioy Casares, Adolfo; Borges, Jorge
Luis

Lyndsay, Sir David 1490-1555 .... LC 20

Lynn, Kenneth S(chuyler) 1923- .... CLC 50
See also CA 1-4R; CANR 3, 27

Lynx
See West, Rebecca

Lyons, Marcus
See Blish, James (Benjamin)

Lyre, Pinchbeck
See Sassoon, Siegfried (Lorraine)

Lytle, Andrew (Nelson) 1902- ...... CLC 22
See also CA 9-12R; DLB 6

Lyttelton, George 1709-1773 .... LC 10

Maas, Peter 1929- .... CLC 29
See also CA 93-96

Macaulay, Rose 1881-1958 ..... TCLC 7, 44
See also CA 104; DLB 36

MacBeth, George (Mann)
1932-1992 .... CLC 2, 5, 9
See also CA 25-28R; 136; DLB 40; MTCW;
SATA 4; SATO 70

MacCaig, Norman (Alexander)
1910- .... CLC 36
See also CA 9-12R; CANR 3, 34; DLB 27

MacCarthy, (Sir Charles Otto) Desmond
1877-1952 .... TCLC 36

MacDiarmid, Hugh ..... CLC 2, 4, 11, 19, 63
See also Grieve, C(hristopher) M(urray)
See also CDBLB 1945-1960; DLB 20

MacDonald, Anson
See Heinlein, Robert A(nson)

Macdonald, Cynthia 1928- ...... CLC 13, 19
See also CA 49-52; CANR 4; DLB 105

MacDonald, George 1824-1905 ..... TCLC 9
See also CA 106; 137; DLB 18; MAICYA;
SATA 33

Macdonald, John
See Millar, Kenneth

MacDonald, John D(ann)
1916-1986 .... CLC 3, 27, 44
See also CA 1-4R; 121; CANR 1, 19;
DLB 8; DLBY 86; MTCW

Macdonald, John Ross
See Millar, Kenneth

Macdonald, Ross ..... CLC 1, 2, 3, 14, 34, 41
See also Millar, Kenneth
See also DLBD 6

MacDougal, John
See Blish, James (Benjamin)

MacEwen, Gwendolyn (Margaret)
1941-1987 .... CLC 13, 55
See also CA 9-12R; 124; CANR 7, 22;
DLB 53; SATA 50, 55

Machado (y Ruiz), Antonio
1875-1939 .... TCLC 3
See also CA 104; DLB 108

Machado de Assis, Joaquim Maria
1839-1908 .... TCLC 10
See also BLC 2; CA 107

Machen, Arthur .... TCLC 4
See also Jones, Arthur Llewellyn
See also DLB 36

Machiavelli, Niccolo 1469-1527 ...... LC 8

MacInnes, Colin 1914-1976 ...... CLC 4, 23
See also CA 69-72; 65-68; CANR 21;
DLB 14; MTCW

MacInnes, Helen (Clark)
1907-1985 .... CLC 27, 39
See also CA 1-4R; 117; CANR 1, 28;
DLB 87; MTCW; SATA 22, 44

Mackenzie, Compton (Edward Montague)
1883-1972 .... CLC 18
See also CA 21-22; 37-40R; CAP 2;
DLB 34, 100

Mackintosh, Elizabeth 1896(?)-1952
See Tey, Josephine
See also CA 110

MacLaren, James
See Grieve, C(hristopher) M(urray)

Mac Laverty, Bernard 1942- .... CLC 31
See also CA 116; 118

MacLean, Alistair (Stuart)
1922-1987 .... CLC 3, 13, 50, 63
See also CA 57-60; 121; CANR 28; MTCW;
SATA 23, 50

MacLeish, Archibald
1892-1982 .... CLC 3, 8, 14, 68
See also CA 9-12R; 106; CANR 33; DLB 4,
7, 45; DLBY 82; MTCW

MacLennan, (John) Hugh
1907- .... **CLC 2, 14**
See also CA 5-8R; CANR 33; DLB 68;
MTCW

MacLeod, Alistair 1936- .... **CLC 56**
See also CA 123; DLB 60

MacNeice, (Frederick) Louis
1907-1963 .... **CLC 1, 4, 10, 53**
See also CA 85-88; DLB 10, 20; MTCW

MacNeill, Dand
See Fraser, George MacDonald

Macpherson, (Jean) Jay 1931- ...... **CLC 14**
See also CA 5-8R; DLB 53

MacShane, Frank 1927- .... **CLC 39**
See also CA 9-12R; CANR 3, 33; DLB 111

Macumber, Mari
See Sandoz, Mari(e Susette)

Madach, Imre 1823-1864 .... **NCLC 19**

Madden, (Jerry) David 1933- .... **CLC 5, 15**
See also CA 1-4R; CAAS 3; CANR 4;
DLB 6; MTCW

Maddern, Al(an)
See Ellison, Harlan

Madhubuti, Haki R.
1942- .... **CLC 6, 73; PC 5**
See also Lee, Don L.
See also BLC 2; BW; CA 73-76; CANR 24;
DLB 5, 41; DLBD 8

Madow, Pauline (Reichberg) .... **CLC 1**
See also CA 9-12R

Maepenn, Hugh
See Kuttner, Henry

Maepenn, K. H.
See Kuttner, Henry

Maeterlinck, Maurice 1862-1949 ... **TCLC 3**
See also CA 104; 136; SATA 66

Maginn, William 1794-1842 ...... **NCLC 8**
See also DLB 110

Mahapatra, Jayanta 1928- .... **CLC 33**
See also CA 73-76; CAAS 9; CANR 15, 33

Mahfouz, Naguib (Abdel Aziz Al-Sabilgi)
1911(?)-
See Mahfuz, Najib
See also BEST 89:2; CA 128; MTCW

Mahfuz, Najib .... **CLC 52, 55**
See also Mahfouz, Naguib (Abdel Aziz
Al-Sabilgi)
See also DLBY 88

Mahon, Derek 1941- .... **CLC 27**
See also CA 113; 128; DLB 40

Mailer, Norman
1923- ...... **CLC 1, 2, 3, 4, 5, 8, 11, 14,
28, 39, 74**
See also AITN 2; CA 9-12R; CABS 1;
CANR 28; CDALB 1968-1988; DLB 2,
16, 28; DLBD 3; DLBY 80, 83; MTCW

Maillet, Antonine 1929- .... **CLC 54**
See also CA 115; 120; DLB 60

Mais, Roger 1905-1955 .... **TCLC 8**
See also BW; CA 105; 124; MTCW

Maitland, Sara (Louise) 1950- ...... **CLC 49**
See also CA 69-72; CANR 13

Major, Clarence 1936- .... **CLC 3, 19, 48**
See also BLC 2; BW; CA 21-24R; CAAS 6;
CANR 13, 25; DLB 33

Major, Kevin (Gerald) 1949- .... **CLC 26**
See also CA 97-100; CANR 21, 38;
CLR 11; DLB 60; MAICYA; SATA 32

Maki, James
See Ozu, Yasujiro

Malabaila, Damiano
See Levi, Primo

Malamud, Bernard
1914-1986 ..... **CLC 1, 2, 3, 5, 8, 9, 11,
18, 27, 44**
See also CA 5-8R; 118; CABS 1; CANR 28;
CDALB 1941-1968; DLB 2, 28;
DLBY 80, 86; MTCW; WLC

Malcolm, Dan
See Silverberg, Robert

Malherbe, Francois de 1555-1628 ..... **LC 5**

Mallarme, Stephane
1842-1898 .... **NCLC 4; PC 4**

Mallet-Joris, Francoise 1930- ...... **CLC 11**
See also CA 65-68; CANR 17; DLB 83

Malley, Ern
See McAuley, James Phillip

Mallowan, Agatha Christie
See Christie, Agatha (Mary Clarissa)

Maloff, Saul 1922- .... **CLC 5**
See also CA 33-36R

Malone, Louis
See MacNeice, (Frederick) Louis

Malone, Michael (Christopher)
1942- .... **CLC 43**
See also CA 77-80; CANR 14, 32

Malory, (Sir) Thomas
1410(?)-1471(?) .... **LC 11**
See also CDBLB Before 1660; SATA 33, 59

Malouf, (George Joseph) David
1934- .... **CLC 28**
See also CA 124

Malraux, (Georges-)Andre
1901-1976 ...... **CLC 1, 4, 9, 13, 15, 57**
See also CA 21-22; 69-72; CANR 34;
CAP 2; DLB 72; MTCW

Malzberg, Barry N(athaniel) 1939- ... **CLC 7**
See also CA 61-64; CAAS 4; CANR 16;
DLB 8

Mamet, David (Alan)
1947- .... **CLC 9, 15, 34, 46**
See also AAYA 3; CA 81-84; CABS 3;
CANR 15; DLB 7; MTCW

Mamoulian, Rouben (Zachary)
1897-1987 .... **CLC 16**
See also CA 25-28R; 124

Mandelstam, Osip (Emilievich)
1891(?)-1938(?) .... **TCLC 2, 6**
See also CA 104

Mander, (Mary) Jane 1877-1949 ... **TCLC 31**

Mandiargues, Andre Pieyre de .... **CLC 41**
See also Pieyre de Mandiargues, Andre
See also DLB 83

Mandrake, Ethel Belle
See Thurman, Wallace (Henry)

Mangan, James Clarence
1803-1849 .... **NCLC 27**

Maniere, J.-E.
See Giraudoux, (Hippolyte) Jean

Manley, (Mary) Delariviere
1672(?)-1724 .... **LC 1**
See also DLB 39, 80

Mann, Abel
See Creasey, John

Mann, (Luiz) Heinrich 1871-1950... **TCLC 9**
See also CA 106; DLB 66

Mann, (Paul) Thomas
1875-1955 ... **TCLC 2, 8, 14, 21, 35, 44;
SSC 5**
See also CA 104; 128; DLB 66; MTCW;
WLC

Manning, Frederic 1887(?)-1935 ... **TCLC 25**
See also CA 124

Manning, Olivia 1915-1980 ...... **CLC 5, 19**
See also CA 5-8R; 101; CANR 29; MTCW

Mano, D. Keith 1942- .... **CLC 2, 10**
See also CA 25-28R; CAAS 6; CANR 26;
DLB 6

Mansfield, Katherine... **TCLC 2, 8, 39; SSC 9**
See also Beauchamp, Kathleen Mansfield
See also WLC

Manso, Peter 1940- .... **CLC 39**
See also CA 29-32R

Mantecon, Juan Jimenez
See Jimenez (Mantecon), Juan Ramon

Manton, Peter
See Creasey, John

Man Without a Spleen, A
See Chekhov, Anton (Pavlovich)

Manzoni, Alessandro 1785-1873 .. **NCLC 29**

Mapu, Abraham (ben Jekutiel)
1808-1867 .... **NCLC 18**

Mara, Sally
See Queneau, Raymond

Marat, Jean Paul 1743-1793 .... **LC 10**

Marcel, Gabriel Honore
1889-1973 .... **CLC 15**
See also CA 102; 45-48; MTCW

Marchbanks, Samuel
See Davies, (William) Robertson

Marchi, Giacomo
See Bassani, Giorgio

Marie de France c. 12th cent. -.... **CMLC 8**

Marie de l'Incarnation 1599-1672.... **LC 10**

Mariner, Scott
See Pohl, Frederik

Marinetti, Filippo Tommaso
1876-1944 .... **TCLC 10**
See also CA 107; DLB 114

Marivaux, Pierre Carlet de Chamblain de
1688-1763 .... **LC 4**

Markandaya, Kamala .... **CLC 8, 38**
See also Taylor, Kamala (Purnaiya)

Markfield, Wallace 1926- .... **CLC 8**
See also CA 69-72; CAAS 3; DLB 2, 28

Markham, Edwin 1852-1940 ...... **TCLC 47**
See also DLB 54

Markham, Robert
See Amis, Kingsley (William)

Marks, J
See Highwater, Jamake (Mamake)

Marks-Highwater, J
See Highwater, Jamake (Mamake)

Markson, David M(errill) 1927- .... **CLC 67**
See also CA 49-52; CANR 1

Marley, Bob. .... **CLC 17**
See also Marley, Robert Nesta

Marley, Robert Nesta 1945-1981
See Marley, Bob
See also CA 107; 103

Marlowe, Christopher 1564-1593 ..... **DC 1**
See also CDBLB Before 1660; DLB 62;
WLC

Marmontel, Jean-Francois
1723-1799 .... **LC 2**

Marquand, John P(hillips)
1893-1960 .... **CLC 2, 10**
See also CA 85-88; DLB 9, 102

Marquez, Gabriel (Jose) Garcia. ...... **CLC 68**
See also Garcia Marquez, Gabriel (Jose)

Marquis, Don(ald Robert Perry)
1878-1937 .... **TCLC 7**
See also CA 104; DLB 11, 25

Marric, J. J.
See Creasey, John

Marrow, Bernard
See Moore, Brian

Marryat, Frederick 1792-1848 .... **NCLC 3**
See also DLB 21

Marsden, James
See Creasey, John

Marsh, (Edith) Ngaio
1899-1982 .... **CLC 7, 53**
See also CA 9-12R; CANR 6; DLB 77;
MTCW

Marshall, Garry 1934- .... **CLC 17**
See also AAYA 3; CA 111; SATA 60

Marshall, Paule 1929- .. **CLC 27, 72; SSC 3**
See also BLC 3; BW; CA 77-80; CANR 25;
DLB 33; MTCW

Marsten, Richard
See Hunter, Evan

Martha, Henry
See Harris, Mark

Martin, Ken
See Hubbard, L(afayette) Ron(ald)

Martin, Richard
See Creasey, John

Martin, Steve 1945- .... **CLC 30**
See also CA 97-100; CANR 30; MTCW

Martin, Webber
See Silverberg, Robert

Martin du Gard, Roger
1881-1958 .... **TCLC 24**
See also CA 118; DLB 65

Martineau, Harriet 1802-1876.... **NCLC 26**
See also DLB 21, 55; YABC 2

Martines, Julia
See O'Faolain, Julia

Martinez, Jacinto Benavente y
See Benavente (y Martinez), Jacinto

Martinez Ruiz, Jose 1873-1967
See Azorin; Ruiz, Jose Martinez
See also CA 93-96; HW

Martinez Sierra, Gregorio
1881-1947 .... **TCLC 6**
See also CA 115

Martinez Sierra, Maria (de la O'LeJarraga)
1874-1974 .... **TCLC 6**
See also CA 115

Martinsen, Martin
See Follett, Ken(neth Martin)

Martinson, Harry (Edmund)
1904-1978 .... **CLC 14**
See also CA 77-80; CANR 34

Marut, Ret
See Traven, B.

Marut, Robert
See Traven, B.

Marvell, Andrew 1621-1678......... **LC 4**
See also CDBLB 1660-1789; WLC

Marx, Karl (Heinrich)
1818-1883 .... **NCLC 17**

Masaoka Shiki. .... **TCLC 18**
See also Masaoka Tsunenori

Masaoka Tsunenori 1867-1902
See Masaoka Shiki
See also CA 117

Masefield, John (Edward)
1878-1967 .... **CLC 11, 47**
See also CA 19-20; 25-28R; CANR 33;
CAP 2; CDBLB 1890-1914; DLB 10;
MTCW; SATA 19

Maso, Carole 19(?)- .... **CLC 44**

Mason, Bobbie Ann
1940- .... **CLC 28, 43; SSC 4**
See also AAYA 5; CA 53-56; CANR 11,
31; DLBY 87; MTCW

Mason, Ernst
See Pohl, Frederik

Mason, Lee W.
See Malzberg, Barry N(athaniel)

Mason, Nick 1945-............... **CLC 35**
See also Pink Floyd

Mason, Tally
See Derleth, August (William)

Mass, William
See Gibson, William

Masters, Edgar Lee
1868-1950 .... **TCLC 2, 25; PC 1**
See also CA 104; 133; CDALB 1865-1917;
DLB 54; MTCW

Masters, Hilary 1928- .... **CLC 48**
See also CA 25-28R; CANR 13

Mastrosimone, William 19(?)-...... **CLC 36**

Mathe, Albert
See Camus, Albert

Matheson, Richard Burton 1926- ... **CLC 37**
See also CA 97-100; DLB 8, 44

Mathews, Harry 1930-.......... **CLC 6, 52**
See also CA 21-24R; CAAS 6; CANR 18

Mathias, Roland (Glyn) 1915-...... **CLC 45**
See also CA 97-100; CANR 19; DLB 27

Matsuo Basho 1644-1694........... **PC 3**

Mattheson, Rodney
See Creasey, John

Matthews, Greg 1949- .... **CLC 45**
See also CA 135

Matthews, William 1942-......... **CLC 40**
See also CA 29-32R; CANR 12; DLB 5

Matthias, John (Edward) 1941-...... **CLC 9**
See also CA 33-36R

Matthiessen, Peter
1927- .... **CLC 5, 7, 11, 32, 64**
See also AAYA 6; BEST 90:4; CA 9-12R;
CANR 21; DLB 6; MTCW; SATA 27

Maturin, Charles Robert
1780(?)-1824 .... **NCLC 6**

Matute (Ausejo), Ana Maria
1925- .... **CLC 11**
See also CA 89-92; MTCW

Maugham, W. S.
See Maugham, W(illiam) Somerset

Maugham, W(illiam) Somerset
1874-1965 .... **CLC 1, 11, 15, 67; SSC 8**
See also CA 5-8R; 25-28R;
CDBLB 1914-1945; DLB 10, 36, 77, 100;
MTCW; SATA 54; WLC

Maugham, William Somerset
See Maugham, W(illiam) Somerset

Maupassant, (Henri Rene Albert) Guy de
1850-1893 .... **NCLC 1; SSC 1**
See also DLB 123; WLC

Maurhut, Richard
See Traven, B.

Mauriac, Claude 1914-............. **CLC 9**
See also CA 89-92; DLB 83

Mauriac, Francois (Charles)
1885-1970 .... **CLC 4, 9, 56**
See also CA 25-28; CAP 2; DLB 65;
MTCW

Mavor, Osborne Henry 1888-1951
See Bridie, James
See also CA 104

Maxwell, William (Keepers Jr.)
1908- .... **CLC 19**
See also CA 93-96; DLBY 80

May, Elaine 1932- .... **CLC 16**
See also CA 124; DLB 44

Mayakovski, Vladimir (Vladimirovich)
1893-1930 .... **TCLC 4, 18**
See also CA 104

Mayhew, Henry 1812-1887 ...... **NCLC 31**
See also DLB 18, 55

Maynard, Joyce 1953-............ **CLC 23**
See also CA 111; 129

Mayne, William (James Carter)
1928- .... **CLC 12**
See also CA 9-12R; CANR 37; CLR 25;
MAICYA; SAAS 11; SATA 6, 68

Mayo, Jim
See L'Amour, Louis (Dearborn)

Maysles, Albert 1926- .... **CLC 16**
See also CA 29-32R

Maysles, David 1932-............ **CLC 16**

Mazer, Norma Fox 1931- .... **CLC 26**
See also AAYA 5; CA 69-72; CANR 12, 32; CLR 23; MAICYA; SAAS 1; SATA 24, 67

Mazzini, Guiseppe 1805-1872 .... **NCLC 34**

McAuley, James Phillip 1917-1976 .... **CLC 45**
See also CA 97-100

McBain, Ed
See Hunter, Evan

McBrien, William Augustine 1930- .... **CLC 44**
See also CA 107

McCaffrey, Anne (Inez) 1926- ...... **CLC 17**
See also AAYA 6; AITN 2; BEST 89:2; CA 25-28R; CANR 15, 35; DLB 8; MAICYA; MTCW; SAAS 11; SATA 8, 70

McCann, Arthur
See Campbell, John W(ood Jr.)

McCann, Edson
See Pohl, Frederik

McCarthy, Cormac 1933- .... **CLC 4, 57**
See also CA 13-16R; CANR 10; DLB 6

McCarthy, Mary (Therese) 1912-1989 ... **CLC 1, 3, 5, 14, 24, 39, 59**
See also CA 5-8R; 129; CANR 16; DLB 2; DLBY 81; MTCW

McCartney, (James) Paul 1942- .... **CLC 12, 35**

McCauley, Stephen 19(?)- .... **CLC 50**

McClure, Michael (Thomas) 1932- .... **CLC 6, 10**
See also CA 21-24R; CANR 17; DLB 16

McCorkle, Jill (Collins) 1958- ...... **CLC 51**
See also CA 121; DLBY 87

McCourt, James 1941- .... **CLC 5**
See also CA 57-60

McCoy, Horace (Stanley) 1897-1955 .... **TCLC 28**
See also CA 108; DLB 9

McCrae, John 1872-1918........ **TCLC 12**
See also CA 109; DLB 92

McCreigh, James
See Pohl, Frederik

McCullers, (Lula) Carson (Smith) 1917-1967 .. **CLC 1, 4, 10, 12, 48; SSC 9**
See also CA 5-8R; 25-28R; CABS 1, 3; CANR 18; CDALB 1941-1968; DLB 2, 7; MTCW; SATA 27; WLC

McCulloch, John Tyler
See Burroughs, Edgar Rice

McCullough, Colleen 1938(?)- ...... **CLC 27**
See also CA 81-84; CANR 17; MTCW

McElroy, Joseph 1930- .... **CLC 5, 47**
See also CA 17-20R

McEwan, Ian (Russell) 1948- ... **CLC 13, 66**
See also BEST 90:4; CA 61-64; CANR 14; DLB 14; MTCW

McFadden, David 1940- .... **CLC 48**
See also CA 104; DLB 60

McFarland, Dennis 1950- .... **CLC 65**

McGahern, John 1934-....... **CLC 5, 9, 48**
See also CA 17-20R; CANR 29; DLB 14; MTCW

McGinley, Patrick (Anthony) 1937- .... **CLC 41**
See also CA 120; 127

McGinley, Phyllis 1905-1978 ...... **CLC 14**
See also CA 9-12R; 77-80; CANR 19; DLB 11, 48; SATA 2, 24, 44

McGinniss, Joe 1942-............. **CLC 32**
See also AITN 2; BEST 89:2; CA 25-28R; CANR 26

McGivern, Maureen Daly
See Daly, Maureen

McGrath, Patrick 1950-........... **CLC 55**
See also CA 136

McGrath, Thomas (Matthew) 1916-1990 .... **CLC 28, 59**
See also CA 9-12R; 132; CANR 6, 33; MTCW; SATA 41; SATO 66

McGuane, Thomas (Francis III) 1939- .... **CLC 3, 7, 18, 45**
See also AITN 2; CA 49-52; CANR 5, 24; DLB 2; DLBY 80; MTCW

McGuckian, Medbh 1950-........ **CLC 48**
See also DLB 40

McHale, Tom 1942(?)-1982....... **CLC 3, 5**
See also AITN 1; CA 77-80; 106

McIlvanney, William 1936-....... **CLC 42**
See also CA 25-28R; DLB 14

McIlwraith, Maureen Mollie Hunter
See Hunter, Mollie
See also SATA 2

McInerney, Jay 1955- .... **CLC 34**
See also CA 116; 123

McIntyre, Vonda N(eel) 1948- ..... **CLC 18**
See also CA 81-84; CANR 17, 34; MTCW

McKay, Claude .... **TCLC 7, 41; PC 2**
See also McKay, Festus Claudius
See also BLC 3; DLB 4, 45, 51, 117

McKay, Festus Claudius 1889-1948
See McKay, Claude
See also BW; CA 104; 124; MTCW; WLC

McKuen, Rod 1933-............. **CLC 1, 3**
See also AITN 1; CA 41-44R

McLoughlin, R. B.
See Mencken, H(enry) L(ouis)

McLuhan, (Herbert) Marshall 1911-1980 .... **CLC 37**
See also CA 9-12R; 102; CANR 12, 34; DLB 88; MTCW

McMillan, Terry 1951- .... **CLC 50, 61**

McMurtry, Larry (Jeff) 1936- .... **CLC 2, 3, 7, 11, 27, 44**
See also AITN 2; BEST 89:2; CA 5-8R; CANR 19; CDALB 1968-1988; DLB 2; DLBY 80, 87; MTCW

McNally, Terrence 1939-...... **CLC 4, 7, 41**
See also CA 45-48; CANR 2; DLB 7

McNamer, Deirdre 1950-......... **CLC 70**

McNeile, Herman Cyril 1888-1937
See Sapper
See also DLB 77

McPhee, John (Angus) 1931- ...... **CLC 36**
See also BEST 90:1; CA 65-68; CANR 20; MTCW

McPherson, James Alan 1943-..... **CLC 19**
See also BW; CA 25-28R; CANR 24; DLB 38; MTCW

McPherson, William (Alexander) 1933- .... **CLC 34**
See also CA 69-72; CANR 28

McSweeney, Kerry .... **CLC 34**

Mead, Margaret 1901-1978........ **CLC 37**
See also AITN 1; CA 1-4R; 81-84; CANR 4; MTCW; SATA 20

Meaker, Marijane (Agnes) 1927-
See Kerr, M. E.
See also CA 107; CANR 37; MAICYA; MTCW; SATA 20, 61

Medoff, Mark (Howard) 1940- ... **CLC 6, 23**
See also AITN 1; CA 53-56; CANR 5; DLB 7

Meged, Aharon
See Megged, Aharon

Meged, Aron
See Megged, Aharon

Megged, Aharon 1920-.............. **CLC 9**
See also CA 49-52; CAAS 13; CANR 1

Mehta, Ved (Parkash) 1934-....... **CLC 37**
See also CA 1-4R; CANR 2, 23; MTCW

Melanter
See Blackmore, R(ichard) D(oddridge)

Melikow, Loris
See Hofmannsthal, Hugo von

Melmoth, Sebastian
See Wilde, Oscar (Fingal O'Flahertie Wills)

Meltzer, Milton 1915-............. **CLC 26**
See also AAYA 8; CA 13-16R; CANR 38; CLR 13; DLB 61; MAICYA; SAAS 1; SATA 1, 50

Melville, Herman 1819-1891 ...... **NCLC 3, 12, 29; SSC 1**
See also CDALB 1640-1865; DLB 3, 74; SATA 59; WLC

Menander
c. 342B.C.-c. 292B.C.... **CMLC 9; DC 3**

Mencken, H(enry) L(ouis) 1880-1956 .... **TCLC 13**
See also CA 105; 125; CDALB 1917-1929; DLB 11, 29, 63; MTCW

Mercer, David 1928-1980........... **CLC 5**
See also CA 9-12R; 102; CANR 23; DLB 13; MTCW

Merchant, Paul
See Ellison, Harlan

Meredith, George 1828-1909 ... **TCLC 17, 43**
See also CA 117; CDBLB 1832-1890; DLB 18, 35, 57

Meredith, William (Morris) 1919-................. **CLC 4, 13, 22, 55**
See also CA 9-12R; CAAS 14; CANR 6; DLB 5

Merezhkovsky, Dmitry Sergeyevich 1865-1941 .... **TCLC 29**

Merimee, Prosper 1803-1870 .... **NCLC 6; SSC 7**
See also DLB 119

Mukherjee, Bharati 1940- .... **CLC 53**
See also BEST 89:2; CA 107; DLB 60;
MTCW

Muldoon, Paul 1951- .... **CLC 32, 72**
See also CA 113; 129; DLB 40

Mulisch, Harry 1927-............. **CLC 42**
See also CA 9-12R; CANR 6, 26

Mull, Martin 1943-.............. **CLC 17**
See also CA 105

Mulock, Dinah Maria
See Craik, Dinah Maria (Mulock)

Munford, Robert 1737(?)-1783 .... **LC 5**
See also DLB 31

Mungo, Raymond 1946-.......... **CLC 72**
See also CA 49-52; CANR 2

Munro, Alice
1931- .... **CLC 6, 10, 19, 50; SSC 3**
See also AITN 2; CA 33-36R; CANR 33;
DLB 53; MTCW; SATA 29

Munro, H(ector) H(ugh) 1870-1916
See Saki
See also CA 104; 130; CDBLB 1890-1914;
DLB 34; MTCW; WLC

Murasaki, Lady................. **CMLC 1**

Murdoch, (Jean) Iris
1919- ...... **CLC 1, 2, 3, 4, 6, 8, 11, 15,**
22, 31, 51
See also CA 13-16R; CANR 8;
CDBLB 1960 to Present; DLB 14;
MTCW

Murphy, Richard 1927-........... **CLC 41**
See also CA 29-32R; DLB 40

Murphy, Sylvia 1937-............. **CLC 34**
See also CA 121

Murphy, Thomas (Bernard) 1935-... **CLC 51**
See also CA 101

Murray, Albert L. 1916- .... **CLC 73**
See also BW; CA 49-52; CANR 26; DLB 38

Murray, Les(lie) A(llan) 1938- ..... **CLC 40**
See also CA 21-24R; CANR 11, 27

Murry, J. Middleton
See Murry, John Middleton

Murry, John Middleton
1889-1957 .... **TCLC 16**
See also CA 118

Musgrave, Susan 1951- .... **CLC 13, 54**
See also CA 69-72

Musil, Robert (Edler von)
1880-1942 .... **TCLC 12**
See also CA 109; DLB 81

Musset, (Louis Charles) Alfred de
1810-1857 .... **NCLC 7**

My Brother's Brother
See Chekhov, Anton (Pavlovich)

Myers, Walter Dean 1937- .... **CLC 35**
See also AAYA 4; BLC 3; BW; CA 33-36R;
CANR 20; CLR 4, 16; DLB 33;
MAICYA; SAAS 2; SATA 27, 41, 70, 71

Myers, Walter M.
See Myers, Walter Dean

Myles, Symon
See Follett, Ken(neth Martin)

Nabokov, Vladimir (Vladimirovich)
1899-1977 .... **CLC 1, 2, 3, 6, 8, 11, 15,**
23, 44, 46, 64; SSC 11
See also CA 5-8R; 69-72; CANR 20;
CDALB 1941-1968; DLB 2; DLBD 3;
DLBY 80, 91; MTCW; WLC

Nagy, Laszlo 1925-1978........... **CLC 7**
See also CA 129; 112

Naipaul, Shiva(dhar Srinivasa)
1945-1985 .... **CLC 32, 39**
See also CA 110; 112; 116; CANR 33;
DLBY 85; MTCW

Naipaul, V(idiadhar) S(urajprasad)
1932- .... **CLC 4, 7, 9, 13, 18, 37**
See also CA 1-4R; CANR 1, 33;
CDBLB 1960 to Present; DLBY 85;
MTCW

Nakos, Lilika 1899(?)-............ **CLC 29**

Narayan, R(asipuram) K(rishnaswami)
1906- .... **CLC 7, 28, 47**
See also CA 81-84; CANR 33; MTCW;
SATA 62

Nash, (Frediric) Ogden 1902-1971 .. **CLC 23**
See also CA 13-14; 29-32R; CANR 34;
CAP 1; DLB 11; MAICYA; MTCW;
SATA 2, 46

Nathan, Daniel
See Dannay, Frederic

Nathan, George Jean 1882-1958 ... **TCLC 18**
See also Hatteras, Owen
See also CA 114

Natsume, Kinnosuke 1867-1916
See Natsume, Soseki
See also CA 104

Natsume, Soseki .... **TCLC 2, 10**
See also Natsume, Kinnosuke

Natti, (Mary) Lee 1919-
See Kingman, Lee
See also CA 5-8R; CANR 2

Naylor, Gloria 1950- .... **CLC 28, 52**
See also AAYA 6; BLC 3; BW; CA 107;
CANR 27; MTCW

Neihardt, John Gneisenau
1881-1973 .... **CLC 32**
See also CA 13-14; CAP 1; DLB 9, 54

Nekrasov, Nikolai Alekseevich
1821-1878 .... **NCLC 11**

Nelligan, Emile 1879-1941....... **TCLC 14**
See also CA 114; DLB 92

Nelson, Willie 1933-.............. **CLC 17**
See also CA 107

Nemerov, Howard (Stanley)
1920-1991 ....**CLC 2, 6, 9, 36**
See also CA 1-4R; 134; CABS 2; CANR 1,
27; DLB 6; DLBY 83; MTCW

Neruda, Pablo
1904-1973 .... **CLC 1, 2, 5, 7, 9, 28, 62;**
PC 4
See also CA 19-20; 45-48; CAP 2; HW;
MTCW; WLC

Nerval, Gerard de 1808-1855...... **NCLC 1**

Nervo, (Jose) Amado (Ruiz de)
1870-1919 .... **TCLC 11**
See also CA 109; 131; HW

Nessi, Pio Baroja y
See Baroja (y Nessi), Pio

Neufeld, John (Arthur) 1938- ...... **CLC 17**
See also CA 25-28R; CANR 11, 37;
MAICYA; SAAS 3; SATA 6

Neville, Emily Cheney 1919-....... **CLC 12**
See also CA 5-8R; CANR 3, 37; MAICYA;
SAAS 2; SATA 1

Newbound, Bernard Slade 1930-
See Slade, Bernard
See also CA 81-84

Newby, P(ercy) H(oward)
1918-.....................**CLC 2, 13**
See also CA 5-8R; CANR 32; DLB 15;
MTCW

Newlove, Donald 1928- .... **CLC 6**
See also CA 29-32R; CANR 25

Newlove, John (Herbert) 1938-..... **CLC 14**
See also CA 21-24R; CANR 9, 25

Newman, Charles 1938-.......... **CLC 2, 8**
See also CA 21-24R

Newman, Edwin (Harold) 1919- .... **CLC 14**
See also AITN 1; CA 69-72; CANR 5

Newman, John Henry
1801-1890 .... **NCLC 38**
See also DLB 18, 32, 55

Newton, Suzanne 1936-........... **CLC 35**
See also CA 41-44R; CANR 14; SATA 5

Nexo, Martin Andersen
1869-1954 .... **TCLC 43**

Nezval, Vitezslav 1900-1958 ...... **TCLC 44**
See also CA 123

Ngema, Mbongeni 1955- .... **CLC 57**

Ngugi, James T(hiong'o)........ **CLC 3, 7, 13**
See also Ngugi wa Thiong'o

Ngugi wa Thiong'o 1938-.......... **CLC 36**
See also Ngugi, James T(hiong'o)
See also BLC 3; BW; CA 81-84; CANR 27;
MTCW

Nichol, B(arrie) P(hillip)
1944-1988 .... **CLC 18**
See also CA 53-56; DLB 53; SATA 66

Nichols, John (Treadwell) 1940-.... **CLC 38**
See also CA 9-12R; CAAS 2; CANR 6;
DLBY 82

Nichols, Peter (Richard)
1927-.................. **CLC 5, 36, 65**
See also CA 104; CANR 33; DLB 13;
MTCW

Nicolas, F. R. E.
See Freeling, Nicolas

Niedecker, Lorine 1903-1970.... **CLC 10, 42**
See also CA 25-28; CAP 2; DLB 48

Nietzsche, Friedrich (Wilhelm)
1844-1900 .... **TCLC 10, 18**
See also CA 107; 121

Nievo, Ippolito 1831-1861 .... **NCLC 22**

Nightingale, Anne Redmon 1943-
See Redmon, Anne
See also CA 103

Nik.T.O.
See Annensky, Innokenty Fyodorovich

Author Index

Nin, Anais
1903-1977 ..... **CLC 1, 4, 8, 11, 14, 60; SSC 10**
See also AITN 2; CA 13-16R; 69-72;
CANR 22; DLB 2, 4; MTCW

Nissenson, Hugh 1933- .... **CLC 4, 9**
See also CA 17-20R; CANR 27; DLB 28

Niven, Larry .... **CLC 8**
See also Niven, Laurence Van Cott
See also DLB 8

Niven, Laurence Van Cott 1938-
See Niven, Larry
See also CA 21-24R; CAAS 12; CANR 14;
MTCW

Nixon, Agnes Eckhardt 1927- ...... **CLC 21**
See also CA 110

Nizan, Paul 1905-1940 .... **TCLC 40**
See also DLB 72

Nkosi, Lewis 1936- .... **CLC 45**
See also BLC 3; BW; CA 65-68; CANR 27

Nodier, (Jean) Charles (Emmanuel)
1780-1844 .... **NCLC 19**
See also DLB 119

Nolan, Christopher 1965- .... **CLC 58**
See also CA 111

Norden, Charles
See Durrell, Lawrence (George)

Nordhoff, Charles (Bernard)
1887-1947 .... **TCLC 23**
See also CA 108; DLB 9; SATA 23

Norman, Marsha 1947- .... **CLC 28**
See also CA 105; CABS 3; DLBY 84

Norris, Benjamin Franklin Jr.
1870-1902 .... **TCLC 24**
See also Norris, Frank
See also CA 110

Norris, Frank
See Norris, Benjamin Franklin Jr.
See also CDALB 1865-1917; DLB 12, 71

Norris, Leslie 1921- .... **CLC 14**
See also CA 11-12; CANR 14; CAP 1;
DLB 27

North, Andrew
See Norton, Andre

North, Captain George
See Stevenson, Robert Louis (Balfour)

North, Milou
See Erdrich, Louise

Northrup, B. A.
See Hubbard, L(afayette) Ron(ald)

North Staffs
See Hulme, T(homas) E(rnest)

Norton, Alice Mary
See Norton, Andre
See also MAICYA; SATA 1, 43

Norton, Andre 1912- .... **CLC 12**
See also Norton, Alice Mary
See also CA 1-4R; CANR 2, 31; DLB 8, 52;
MTCW

Norway, Nevil Shute 1899-1960
See Shute, Nevil
See also CA 102; 93-96

Norwid, Cyprian Kamil
1821-1883 .... **NCLC 17**

Nosille, Nabrah
See Ellison, Harlan

Nossack, Hans Erich 1901-1978 ..... **CLC 6**
See also CA 93-96; 85-88; DLB 69

Nosu, Chuji
See Ozu, Yasujiro

Nova, Craig 1945- .... **CLC 7, 31**
See also CA 45-48; CANR 2

Novak, Joseph
See Kosinski, Jerzy (Nikodem)

Novalis 1772-1801 .... **NCLC 13**
See also DLB 90

Nowlan, Alden (Albert) 1933-1983 .. **CLC 15**
See also CA 9-12R; CANR 5; DLB 53

Noyes, Alfred 1880-1958 .... **TCLC 7**
See also CA 104; DLB 20

Nunn, Kem 19(?)- .... **CLC 34**

Nye, Robert 1939- .... **CLC 13, 42**
See also CA 33-36R; CANR 29; DLB 14;
MTCW; SATA 6

Nyro, Laura 1947- .... **CLC 17**

Oates, Joyce Carol
1938- ..... **CLC 1, 2, 3, 6, 9, 11, 15, 19, 33, 52; SSC 6**
See also AITN 1; BEST 89:2; CA 5-8R;
CANR 25; CDALB 1968-1988; DLB 2, 5;
DLBY 81; MTCW; WLC

O'Brien, E. G.
See Clarke, Arthur C(harles)

O'Brien, Edna
1936- ... **CLC 3, 5, 8, 13, 36, 65; SSC 10**
See also CA 1-4R; CANR 6; CDBLB 1960
to Present; DLB 14; MTCW

O'Brien, Fitz-James 1828-1862 ... **NCLC 21**
See also DLB 74

O'Brien, Flann .... **CLC 1, 4, 5, 7, 10, 47**
See also O Nuallain, Brian

O'Brien, Richard 1942- .... **CLC 17**
See also CA 124

O'Brien, Tim 1946- .... **CLC 7, 19, 40**
See also CA 85-88; DLBD 9; DLBY 80

Obstfelder, Sigbjoern 1866-1900 ... **TCLC 23**
See also CA 123

O'Casey, Sean
1880-1964 .... **CLC 1, 5, 9, 11, 15**
See also CA 89-92; CDBLB 1914-1945;
DLB 10; MTCW

O'Cathasaigh, Sean
See O'Casey, Sean

Ochs, Phil 1940-1976 .... **CLC 17**
See also CA 65-68

O'Connor, Edwin (Greene)
1918-1968 .... **CLC 14**
See also CA 93-96; 25-28R

O'Connor, (Mary) Flannery
1925-1964 ... **CLC 1, 2, 3, 6, 10, 13, 15, 21, 66; SSC 1**
See also AAYA 7; CA 1-4R; CANR 3;
CDALB 1941-1968; DLB 2; DLBY 80;
MTCW; WLC

O'Connor, Frank .... **CLC 23; SSC 5**
See also O'Donovan, Michael John

O'Dell, Scott 1898-1989 .... **CLC 30**
See also AAYA 3; CA 61-64; 129;
CANR 12, 30; CLR 1, 16; DLB 52;
MAICYA; SATA 12, 60

Odets, Clifford 1906-1963 .... **CLC 2, 28**
See also CA 85-88; DLB 7, 26; MTCW

O'Donnell, K. M.
See Malzberg, Barry N(athaniel)

O'Donnell, Lawrence
See Kuttner, Henry

O'Donovan, Michael John
1903-1966 .... **CLC 14**
See also O'Connor, Frank
See also CA 93-96

Oe, Kenzaburo 1935- .... **CLC 10, 36**
See also CA 97-100; CANR 36; MTCW

O'Faolain, Julia 1932- .... **CLC 6, 19, 47**
See also CA 81-84; CAAS 2; CANR 12;
DLB 14; MTCW

O'Faolain, Sean
1900-1991 .... **CLC 1, 7, 14, 32, 70**
See also CA 61-64; 134; CANR 12;
DLB 15; MTCW

O'Flaherty, Liam
1896-1984 .... **CLC 5, 34; SSC 6**
See also CA 101; 113; CANR 35; DLB 36;
DLBY 84; MTCW

Ogilvy, Gavin
See Barrie, J(ames) M(atthew)

O'Grady, Standish James
1846-1928 .... **TCLC 5**
See also CA 104

O'Grady, Timothy 1951- .... **CLC 59**
See also CA 138

O'Hara, Frank 1926-1966 ..... **CLC 2, 5, 13**
See also CA 9-12R; 25-28R; CANR 33;
DLB 5, 16; MTCW

O'Hara, John (Henry)
1905-1970 .... **CLC 1, 2, 3, 6, 11, 42**
See also CA 5-8R; 25-28R; CANR 31;
CDALB 1929-1941; DLB 9, 86; DLBD 2;
MTCW

O Hehir, Diana 1922- .... **CLC 41**
See also CA 93-96

Okigbo, Christopher (Ifenayichukwu)
1932-1967 .... **CLC 25**
See also BLC 3; BW; CA 77-80; MTCW

Olds, Sharon 1942- .... **CLC 32, 39**
See also CA 101; CANR 18; DLB 120

Oldstyle, Jonathan
See Irving, Washington

Olesha, Yuri (Karlovich)
1899-1960 .... **CLC 8**
See also CA 85-88

Oliphant, Margaret (Oliphant Wilson)
1828-1897 .... **NCLC 11**
See also DLB 18

Oliver, Mary 1935- .... **CLC 19, 34**
See also CA 21-24R; CANR 9; DLB 5

Olivier, Laurence (Kerr)
1907-1989 .... **CLC 20**
See also CA 111; 129

Olsen, Tillie 1913- ..... **CLC 4, 13; SSC 11**
See also CA 1-4R; CANR 1; DLB 28;
DLBY 80; MTCW

Olson, Charles (John)
1910-1970 . . . . . CLC 1, 2, 5, 6, 9, 11, 29
See also CA 13-16; 25-28R; CABS 2;
CANR 35; CAP 1; DLB 5, 16; MTCW

Olson, Toby 1937- . . . . CLC 28
See also CA 65-68; CANR 9, 31

Olyesha, Yuri
See Olesha, Yuri (Karlovich)

Ondaatje, Michael 1943- . . . . CLC 14, 29, 51
See also CA 77-80; DLB 60

Oneal, Elizabeth 1934-
See Oneal, Zibby
See also CA 106; CANR 28; MAICYA;
SATA 30

Oneal, Zibby . . . . CLC 30
See also Oneal, Elizabeth
See also AAYA 5; CLR 13

O'Neill, Eugene (Gladstone)
1888-1953 . . . . TCLC 1, 6, 27
See also AITN 1; CA 110; 132;
CDALB 1929-1941; DLB 7; MTCW;
WLC

Onetti, Juan Carlos 1909- . . . . CLC 7, 10
See also CA 85-88; CANR 32; DLB 113;
HW; MTCW

O Nuallain, Brian 1911-1966
See O'Brien, Flann
See also CA 21-22; 25-28R; CAP 2

Oppen, George 1908-1984 . . . . CLC 7, 13, 34
See also CA 13-16R; 113; CANR 8; DLB 5

Oppenheim, E(dward) Phillips
1866-1946 . . . . TCLC 45
See also CA 111; DLB 70

Orlovitz, Gil 1918-1973 . . . . CLC 22
See also CA 77-80; 45-48; DLB 2, 5

Orris
See Ingelow, Jean

Ortega y Gasset, Jose 1883-1955 . . . TCLC 9
See also CA 106; 130; HW; MTCW

Ortiz, Simon J(oseph) 1941- . . . . CLC 45
See also CA 134; DLB 120

Orton, Joe . . . . CLC 4, 13, 43; DC 3
See also Orton, John Kingsley
See also CDBLB 1960 to Present; DLB 13

Orton, John Kingsley 1933-1967
See Orton, Joe
See also CA 85-88; CANR 35; MTCW

Orwell, George . . . . TCLC 2, 6, 15, 31
See also Blair, Eric (Arthur)
See also CDBLB 1945-1960; DLB 15, 98;
WLC

Osborne, David
See Silverberg, Robert

Osborne, George
See Silverberg, Robert

Osborne, John (James)
1929- . . . . CLC 1, 2, 5, 11, 45
See also CA 13-16R; CANR 21;
CDBLB 1945-1960; DLB 13; MTCW;
WLC

Osborne, Lawrence 1958- . . . . CLC 50

Oshima, Nagisa 1932- . . . . CLC 20
See also CA 116; 121

Oskison, John M(ilton)
1874-1947 . . . . TCLC 35

Ossoli, Sarah Margaret (Fuller marchesa d')
1810-1850
See Fuller, Margaret
See also SATA 25

Ostrovsky, Alexander
1823-1886 . . . . NCLC 30

Otero, Blas de 1916- . . . . CLC 11
See also CA 89-92

Otto, Whitney 1955- . . . . CLC 70

Ouida . . . . TCLC 43
See also De La Ramee, (Marie) Louise
See also DLB 18

Ousmane, Sembene 1923- . . . . CLC 66
See also BLC 3; BW; CA 117; 125; MTCW

Ovid 43B.C.-18th cent. (?) . . . CMLC 7; PC 2

Owen, Wilfred 1893-1918 . . . . . . TCLC 5, 27
See also CA 104; CDBLB 1914-1945;
DLB 20; WLC

Owens, Rochelle 1936- . . . . CLC 8
See also CA 17-20R; CAAS 2; CANR 39

Oz, Amos 1939- . . . CLC 5, 8, 11, 27, 33, 54
See also CA 53-56; CANR 27; MTCW

Ozick, Cynthia 1928- . . . . . . CLC 3, 7, 28, 62
See also BEST 90:1; CA 17-20R; CANR 23;
DLB 28; DLBY 82; MTCW

Ozu, Yasujiro 1903-1963 . . . . CLC 16
See also CA 112

Pacheco, C.
See Pessoa, Fernando (Antonio Nogueira)

Pa Chin
See Li Fei-kan

Pack, Robert 1929- . . . . CLC 13
See also CA 1-4R; CANR 3; DLB 5

Padgett, Lewis
See Kuttner, Henry

Padilla (Lorenzo), Heberto 1932- . . . CLC 38
See also AITN 1; CA 123; 131; HW

Page, Jimmy 1944- . . . . CLC 12

Page, Louise 1955- . . . . CLC 40

Page, P(atricia) K(athleen)
1916- . . . . CLC 7, 18
See also CA 53-56; CANR 4, 22; DLB 68;
MTCW

Paget, Violet 1856-1935
See Lee, Vernon
See also CA 104

Paget-Lowe, Henry
See Lovecraft, H(oward) P(hillips)

Paglia, Camille 1947- . . . . CLC 68

Pakenham, Antonia
See Fraser, Antonia (Pakenham)

Palamas, Kostes 1859-1943 . . . . TCLC 5
See also CA 105

Palazzeschi, Aldo 1885-1974 . . . . CLC 11
See also CA 89-92; 53-56; DLB 114

Paley, Grace 1922- . . . . CLC 4, 6, 37; SSC 8
See also CA 25-28R; CANR 13; DLB 28;
MTCW

Palin, Michael (Edward) 1943- . . . . . CLC 21
See also Monty Python
See also CA 107; CANR 35; SATA 67

Palliser, Charles 1947- . . . . CLC 65
See also CA 136

Palma, Ricardo 1833-1919 . . . . TCLC 29

Pancake, Breece Dexter 1952-1979
See Pancake, Breece D'J
See also CA 123; 109

Pancake, Breece D'J . . . . CLC 29
See also Pancake, Breece Dexter

Papadiamantis, Alexandros
1851-1911 . . . . TCLC 29

Papadiamantopoulos, Johannes 1856-1910
See Moreas, Jean
See also CA 117

Papini, Giovanni 1881-1956 . . . . TCLC 22
See also CA 121

Paracelsus 1493-1541 . . . . LC 14

Parasol, Peter
See Stevens, Wallace

Parfenie, Maria
See Codrescu, Andrei

Parini, Jay (Lee) 1948- . . . . CLC 54
See also CA 97-100; CAAS 16; CANR 32

Park, Jordan
See Kornbluth, C(yril) M.; Pohl, Frederik

Parker, Bert
See Ellison, Harlan

Parker, Dorothy (Rothschild)
1893-1967 . . . . CLC 15, 68; SSC 2
See also CA 19-20; 25-28R; CAP 2;
DLB 11, 45, 86; MTCW

Parker, Robert B(rown) 1932- . . . . . . CLC 27
See also BEST 89:4; CA 49-52; CANR 1,
26; MTCW

Parkes, Lucas
See Harris, John (Wyndham Parkes Lucas)
Beynon

Parkin, Frank 1940- . . . . CLC 43

Parkman, Francis Jr. 1823-1893 . . NCLC 12
See also DLB 1, 30

Parks, Gordon (Alexander Buchanan)
1912- . . . . CLC 1, 16
See also AITN 2; BLC 3; BW; CA 41-44R;
CANR 26; DLB 33; SATA 8

Parnell, Thomas 1679-1718 . . . . LC 3
See also DLB 94

Parra, Nicanor 1914- . . . . CLC 2
See also CA 85-88; CANR 32; HW; MTCW

Parson Lot
See Kingsley, Charles

Partridge, Anthony
See Oppenheim, E(dward) Phillips

Pascoli, Giovanni 1855-1912 . . . . . . TCLC 45

Pasolini, Pier Paolo
1922-1975 . . . . CLC 20, 37
See also CA 93-96; 61-64; MTCW

Pasquini
See Silone, Ignazio

Pastan, Linda (Olenik) 1932- . . . . . . CLC 27
See also CA 61-64; CANR 18; DLB 5

Pasternak, Boris (Leonidovich)
1890-1960 . . . . . CLC 7, 10, 18, 63; PC 6
See also CA 127; 116; MTCW; WLC

Patchen, Kenneth 1911-1972 . . . CLC 1, 2, 18
See also CA 1-4R; 33-36R; CANR 3, 35;
DLB 16, 48; MTCW

Pater, Walter (Horatio)
1839-1894 .... **NCLC 7**
See also CDBLB 1832-1890; DLB 57

Paterson, A(ndrew) B(arton)
1864-1941 .... **TCLC 32**

Paterson, Katherine (Womeldorf)
1932- .... **CLC 12, 30**
See also AAYA 1; CA 21-24R; CANR 28;
CLR 7; DLB 52; MAICYA; MTCW;
SATA 13, 53

Patmore, Coventry Kersey Dighton
1823-1896 .... **NCLC 9**
See also DLB 35, 98

Paton, Alan (Stewart)
1903-1988 .... **CLC 4, 10, 25, 55**
See also CA 13-16; 125; CANR 22; CAP 1;
MTCW; SATA 11, 56; WLC

Paton Walsh, Gillian   1939-
See Walsh, Jill Paton
See also CANR 38; MAICYA; SAAS 3;
SATA 4

Paulding, James Kirke   1778-1860.. **NCLC 2**
See also DLB 3, 59, 74

Paulin, Thomas Neilson   1949-
See Paulin, Tom
See also CA 123; 128

Paulin, Tom .... **CLC 37**
See also Paulin, Thomas Neilson
See also DLB 40

Paustovsky, Konstantin (Georgievich)
1892-1968 .... **CLC 40**
See also CA 93-96; 25-28R

Pavese, Cesare   1908-1950 .... **TCLC 3**
See also CA 104

Pavic, Milorad   1929- .... **CLC 60**
See also CA 136

Payne, Alan
See Jakes, John (William)

Paz, Gil
See Lugones, Leopoldo

Paz, Octavio
1914- ...... **CLC 3, 4, 6, 10, 19, 51, 65;**
                                                PC 1
See also CA 73-76; CANR 32; DLBY 90;
HW; MTCW; WLC

Peacock, Molly   1947-............. **CLC 60**
See also CA 103; DLB 120

Peacock, Thomas Love
1785-1866 .... **NCLC 22**
See also DLB 96, 116

Peake, Mervyn   1911-1968 .... **CLC 7, 54**
See also CA 5-8R; 25-28R; CANR 3;
DLB 15; MTCW; SATA 23

Pearce, Philippa .... **CLC 21**
See also Christie, (Ann) Philippa
See also CLR 9; MAICYA; SATA 1, 67

Pearl, Eric
See Elman, Richard

Pearson, T(homas) R(eid)   1956- .... **CLC 39**
See also CA 120; 130

Peck, John   1941- .... **CLC 3**
See also CA 49-52; CANR 3

Peck, Richard (Wayne)   1934- ...... **CLC 21**
See also AAYA 1; CA 85-88; CANR 19,
38; MAICYA; SAAS 2; SATA 18, 55

Peck, Robert Newton   1928-........ **CLC 17**
See also AAYA 3; CA 81-84; CANR 31;
MAICYA; SAAS 1; SATA 21, 62

Peckinpah, (David) Sam(uel)
1925-1984 .... **CLC 20**
See also CA 109; 114

Pedersen, Knut   1859-1952
See Hamsun, Knut
See also CA 104; 119; MTCW

Peeslake, Gaffer
See Durrell, Lawrence (George)

Peguy, Charles Pierre
1873-1914 .... **TCLC 10**
See also CA 107

Pena, Ramon del Valle y
See Valle-Inclan, Ramon (Maria) del

Pendennis, Arthur Esquir
See Thackeray, William Makepeace

Pepys, Samuel   1633-1703.......... **LC 11**
See also CDBLB 1660-1789; DLB 101;
WLC

Percy, Walker
1916-1990 ... **CLC 2, 3, 6, 8, 14, 18, 47,**
                                                          65
See also CA 1-4R; 131; CANR 1, 23;
DLB 2; DLBY 80, 90; MTCW

Perec, Georges   1936-1982 .... **CLC 56**
See also DLB 83

Pereda (y Sanchez de Porrua), Jose Maria de
1833-1906 .... **TCLC 16**
See also CA 117

Pereda y Porrua, Jose Maria de
See Pereda (y Sanchez de Porrua), Jose
Maria de

Peregoy, George Weems
See Mencken, H(enry) L(ouis)

Perelman, S(idney) J(oseph)
1904-1979 ... **CLC 3, 5, 9, 15, 23, 44, 49**
See also AITN 1, 2; CA 73-76; 89-92;
CANR 18; DLB 11, 44; MTCW

Peret, Benjamin   1899-1959 .... **TCLC 20**
See also CA 117

Peretz, Isaac Loeb   1851(?)-1915... **TCLC 16**
See also CA 109

Peretz, Yitzhok Leibush
See Peretz, Isaac Loeb

Perez Galdos, Benito   1843-1920 ... **TCLC 27**
See also CA 125; HW

Perrault, Charles   1628-1703 .... **LC 2**
See also MAICYA; SATA 25

Perry, Brighton
See Sherwood, Robert E(mmet)

Perse, Saint-John
See Leger, (Marie-Rene) Alexis Saint-Leger

Perse, St.-John .... **CLC 4, 11, 46**
See also Leger, (Marie-Rene) Alexis
Saint-Leger

Peseenz, Tulio F.
See Lopez y Fuentes, Gregorio

Pesetsky, Bette   1932-............. **CLC 28**
See also CA 133

Peshkov, Alexei Maximovich   1868-1936
See Gorky, Maxim
See also CA 105

Pessoa, Fernando (Antonio Nogueira)
1888-1935 .... **TCLC 27**
See also CA 125

Peterkin, Julia Mood   1880-1961.... **CLC 31**
See also CA 102; DLB 9

Peters, Joan K.   1945-............. **CLC 39**

Peters, Robert L(ouis)   1924-........ **CLC 7**
See also CA 13-16R; CAAS 8; DLB 105

Petofi, Sandor   1823-1849........ **NCLC 21**

Petrakis, Harry Mark   1923-........ **CLC 3**
See also CA 9-12R; CANR 4, 30

Petrov, Evgeny .... **TCLC 21**
See also Kataev, Evgeny Petrovich

Petry, Ann (Lane)   1908- ...... **CLC 1, 7, 18**
See also BW; CA 5-8R; CAAS 6; CANR 4;
CLR 12; DLB 76; MAICYA; MTCW;
SATA 5

Petursson, Halligrimur   1614-1674 .... **LC 8**

Philipson, Morris H.   1926- .... **CLC 53**
See also CA 1-4R; CANR 4

Phillips, David Graham
1867-1911 .... **TCLC 44**
See also CA 108; DLB 9, 12

Phillips, Jack
See Sandburg, Carl (August)

Phillips, Jayne Anne   1952- ..... **CLC 15, 33**
See also CA 101; CANR 24; DLBY 80;
MTCW

Phillips, Richard
See Dick, Philip K(indred)

Phillips, Robert (Schaeffer)   1938-... **CLC 28**
See also CA 17-20R; CAAS 13; CANR 8;
DLB 105

Phillips, Ward
See Lovecraft, H(oward) P(hillips)

Piccolo, Lucio   1901-1969.......... **CLC 13**
See also CA 97-100; DLB 114

Pickthall, Marjorie L(owry) C(hristie)
1883-1922 .... **TCLC 21**
See also CA 107; DLB 92

Pico della Mirandola, Giovanni
1463-1494 .... **LC 15**

Piercy, Marge
1936- .... **CLC 3, 6, 14, 18, 27, 62**
See also CA 21-24R; CAAS 1; CANR 13;
DLB 120; MTCW

Piers, Robert
See Anthony, Piers

Pieyre de Mandiargues, Andre   1909-1991
See Mandiargues, Andre Pieyre de
See also CA 103; 136; CANR 22

Pilnyak, Boris .... **TCLC 23**
See also Vogau, Boris Andreyevich

Pincherle, Alberto   1907-1990 ... **CLC 11, 18**
See also Moravia, Alberto
See also CA 25-28R; 132; CANR 33;
MTCW

Pineda, Cecile   1942-............. **CLC 39**
See also CA 118

Pinero, Arthur Wing   1855-1934 ... **TCLC 32**
See also CA 110; DLB 10

Pinero, Miguel (Antonio Gomez)
1946-1988 .... **CLC 4, 55**
See also CA 61-64; 125; CANR 29; HW

Priestley, J(ohn) B(oynton)
1894-1984 . . . . **CLC 2, 5, 9, 34**
See also CA 9-12R; 113; CANR 33;
CDBLB 1914-1945; DLB 10, 34, 77, 100;
DLBY 84; MTCW

Prince, F(rank) T(empleton) 1912- . . **CLC 22**
See also CA 101; DLB 20

Prince 1958(?)- . . . . **CLC 35**

Prince Kropotkin
See Kropotkin, Peter (Aleksieevich)

Prior, Matthew 1664-1721 . . . . **LC 4**
See also DLB 95

Pritchard, William H(arrison)
1932- . . . . **CLC 34**
See also CA 65-68; CANR 23; DLB 111

Pritchett, V(ictor) S(awdon)
1900- . . . . **CLC 5, 13, 15, 41**
See also CA 61-64; CANR 31; DLB 15;
MTCW

Private 19022
See Manning, Frederic

Probst, Mark 1925- . . . . **CLC 59**
See also CA 130

Prokosch, Frederic 1908-1989 . . . . **CLC 4, 48**
See also CA 73-76; 128; DLB 48

Prophet, The
See Dreiser, Theodore (Herman Albert)

Prose, Francine 1947- . . . . **CLC 45**
See also CA 109; 112

Proudhon
See Cunha, Euclides (Rodrigues Pimenta) da

Proust,
(Valentin-Louis-George-Eugene-)Marcel
1871-1922 . . . . **TCLC 7, 13, 33**
See also CA 104; 120; DLB 65; MTCW;
WLC

Prowler, Harley
See Masters, Edgar Lee

Prus, Boleslaw . . . . **TCLC 48**
See also Glowacki, Aleksander

Pryor, Richard (Franklin Lenox Thomas)
1940- . . . . **CLC 26**
See also CA 122

Przybyszewski, Stanislaw
1868-1927 . . . . **TCLC 36**
See also DLB 66

Pteleon
See Grieve, C(hristopher) M(urray)

Puckett, Lute
See Masters, Edgar Lee

Puig, Manuel
1932-1990 . . . . **CLC 3, 5, 10, 28, 65**
See also CA 45-48; CANR 2, 32; DLB 113;
HW; MTCW

Purdy, A(lfred) W(ellington)
1918- . . . . **CLC 3, 6, 14, 50**
See also Purdy, Al
See also CA 81-84

Purdy, Al
See Purdy, A(lfred) W(ellington)
See also DLB 88

Purdy, James (Amos)
1923- . . . . **CLC 2, 4, 10, 28, 52**
See also CA 33-36R; CAAS 1; CANR 19;
DLB 2; MTCW

Pure, Simon
See Swinnerton, Frank Arthur

Pushkin, Alexander (Sergeyevich)
1799-1837 . . . . **NCLC 3, 27**
See also SATA 61; WLC

P'u Sung-ling 1640-1715 . . . . **LC 3**

Putnam, Arthur Lee
See Alger, Horatio Jr.

Puzo, Mario 1920- . . . . **CLC 1, 2, 6, 36**
See also CA 65-68; CANR 4; DLB 6;
MTCW

Pym, Barbara (Mary Crampton)
1913-1980 . . . . **CLC 13, 19, 37**
See also CA 13-14; 97-100; CANR 13, 34;
CAP 1; DLB 14; DLBY 87; MTCW

Pynchon, Thomas (Ruggles Jr.)
1937- . . **CLC 2, 3, 6, 9, 11, 18, 33, 62, 72**
See also BEST 90:2; CA 17-20R; CANR 22;
DLB 2; MTCW; WLC

Qian Zhongshu
See Ch'ien Chung-shu

Qroll
See Dagerman, Stig (Halvard)

Quarrington, Paul (Lewis) 1953- . . . . **CLC 65**
See also CA 129

Quasimodo, Salvatore 1901-1968 . . . **CLC 10**
See also CA 13-16; 25-28R; CAP 1;
DLB 114; MTCW

Queen, Ellery . . . . **CLC 3, 11**
See also Dannay, Frederic; Davidson,
Avram; Lee, Manfred B(ennington);
Sturgeon, Theodore (Hamilton); Vance,
John Holbrook

Queen, Ellery Jr.
See Dannay, Frederic; Lee, Manfred
B(ennington)

Queneau, Raymond
1903-1976 . . . . **CLC 2, 5, 10, 42**
See also CA 77-80; 69-72; CANR 32;
DLB 72; MTCW

Quin, Ann (Marie) 1936-1973 . . . . **CLC 6**
See also CA 9-12R; 45-48; DLB 14

Quinn, Martin
See Smith, Martin Cruz

Quinn, Simon
See Smith, Martin Cruz

Quiroga, Horacio (Sylvestre)
1878-1937 . . . . **TCLC 20**
See also CA 117; 131; HW; MTCW

Quoirez, Francoise 1935- . . . . **CLC 9**
See also Sagan, Francoise
See also CA 49-52; CANR 6, 39; MTCW

Raabe, Wilhelm 1831-1910 . . . . **TCLC 45**

Rabe, David (William) 1940- . . . **CLC 4, 8, 33**
See also CA 85-88; CABS 3; DLB 7

Rabelais, Francois 1483-1553 . . . . **LC 5**
See also WLC

Rabinovitch, Sholem 1859-1916
See Aleichem, Sholom
See also CA 104

Radcliffe, Ann (Ward) 1764-1823 . . **NCLC 6**
See also DLB 39

Radiguet, Raymond 1903-1923 . . . . **TCLC 29**
See also DLB 65

Radnoti, Miklos 1909-1944 . . . . **TCLC 16**
See also CA 118

Rado, James 1939- . . . . **CLC 17**
See also CA 105

Radvanyi, Netty 1900-1983
See Seghers, Anna
See also CA 85-88; 110

Raeburn, John (Hay) 1941- . . . . **CLC 34**
See also CA 57-60

Ragni, Gerome 1942-1991 . . . . **CLC 17**
See also CA 105; 134

Rahv, Philip . . . . **CLC 24**
See also Greenberg, Ivan

Raine, Craig 1944- . . . . **CLC 32**
See also CA 108; CANR 29; DLB 40

Raine, Kathleen (Jessie) 1908- . . . **CLC 7, 45**
See also CA 85-88; DLB 20; MTCW

Rainis, Janis 1865-1929 . . . . **TCLC 29**

Rakosi, Carl . . . . **CLC 47**
See also Rawley, Callman
See also CAAS 5

Raleigh, Richard
See Lovecraft, H(oward) P(hillips)

Rallentando, H. P.
See Sayers, Dorothy L(eigh)

Ramal, Walter
See de la Mare, Walter (John)

Ramon, Juan
See Jimenez (Mantecon), Juan Ramon

Ramos, Graciliano 1892-1953 . . . . . **TCLC 32**

Rampersad, Arnold 1941- . . . . **CLC 44**
See also CA 127; 133; DLB 111

Rampling, Anne
See Rice, Anne

Ramuz, Charles-Ferdinand
1878-1947 . . . . **TCLC 33**

Rand, Ayn 1905-1982 . . . . **CLC 3, 30, 44**
See also CA 13-16R; 105; CANR 27;
MTCW; WLC

Randall, Dudley (Felker) 1914- . . . . . . **CLC 1**
See also BLC 3; BW; CA 25-28R;
CANR 23; DLB 41

Randall, Robert
See Silverberg, Robert

Ranger, Ken
See Creasey, John

Ransom, John Crowe
1888-1974 . . . . **CLC 2, 4, 5, 11, 24**
See also CA 5-8R; 49-52; CANR 6, 34;
DLB 45, 63; MTCW

Rao, Raja 1909- . . . . **CLC 25, 56**
See also CA 73-76; MTCW

Raphael, Frederic (Michael)
1931- . . . . **CLC 2, 14**
See also CA 1-4R; CANR 1; DLB 14

Ratcliffe, James P.
See Mencken, H(enry) L(ouis)

Rathbone, Julian 1935- . . . . **CLC 41**
See also CA 101; CANR 34

Rattigan, Terence (Mervyn)
1911-1977 . . . . **CLC 7**
See also CA 85-88; 73-76;
CDBLB 1945-1960; DLB 13; MTCW

Ratushinskaya, Irina 1954-........ CLC 54
Scc also CA 129

Raven, Simon (Arthur Noel)
    1927-...................... CLC 14
See also CA 81-84

Rawley, Callman 1903-
See Rakosi, Carl
See also CA 21-24R; CANR 12, 32

Rawlings, Marjorie Kinnan
    1896-1953 .... TCLC 4
See also CA 104; 137; DLB 9, 22, 102;
MAICYA; YABC 1

Ray, Satyajit 1921-.............. CLC 16
See also CA 114; 137

Read, Herbert Edward 1893-1968.... CLC 4
See also CA 85-88; 25-28R; DLB 20

Read, Piers Paul 1941-...... CLC 4, 10, 25
See also CA 21-24R; CANR 38; DLB 14;
SATA 21

Reade, Charles 1814-1884 .... NCLC 2
See also DLB 21

Reade, Hamish
See Gray, Simon (James Holliday)

Reading, Peter 1946-............. CLC 47
See also CA 103; DLB 40

Reaney, James 1926-............. CLC 13
See also CA 41-44R; CAAS 15; DLB 68;
SATA 43

Rebreanu, Liviu 1885-1944 .... TCLC 28

Rechy, John (Francisco)
    1934-............... CLC 1, 7, 14, 18
See also CA 5-8R; CAAS 4; CANR 6, 32;
DLB 122; DLBY 82; HW

Redcam, Tom 1870-1933 .... TCLC 25

Reddin, Keith.................... CLC 67

Redgrove, Peter (William)
    1932-..................... CLC 6, 41
See also CA 1-4R; CANR 3, 39; DLB 40

Redmon, Anne.................... CLC 22
See also Nightingale, Anne Redmon
See also DLBY 86

Reed, Eliot
See Ambler, Eric

Reed, Ishmael
    1938-........ CLC 2, 3, 5, 6, 13, 32, 60
See also BLC 3; BW; CA 21-24R;
CANR 25; DLB 2, 5, 33; DLBD 8;
MTCW

Reed, John (Silas) 1887-1920 ...... TCLC 9
See also CA 106

Reed, Lou....................... CLC 21
See also Firbank, Louis

Reeve, Clara 1729-1807 .... NCLC 19
See also DLB 39

Reid, Christopher 1949-........... CLC 33
See also DLB 40

Reid, Desmond
See Moorcock, Michael (John)

Reid Banks, Lynne 1929-
See Banks, Lynne Reid
See also CA 1-4R; CANR 6, 22, 38;
CLR 24; MAICYA; SATA 22

Reilly, William K.
See Creasey, John

Reiner, Max
See Caldwell, (Janet Miriam) Taylor
(Holland)

Reis, Ricardo
See Pessoa, Fernando (Antonio Nogueira)

Remarque, Erich Maria
    1898-1970 .... CLC 21
See also CA 77-80; 29-32R; DLB 56;
MTCW

Remizov, A.
See Remizov, Aleksei (Mikhailovich)

Remizov, A. M.
See Remizov, Aleksei (Mikhailovich)

Remizov, Aleksei (Mikhailovich)
    1877-1957 .... TCLC 27
See also CA 125; 133

Renan, Joseph Ernest
    1823-1892 .... NCLC 26

Renard, Jules 1864-1910 .... TCLC 17
See also CA 117

Renault, Mary.............. CLC 3, 11, 17
See also Challans, Mary
See also DLBY 83

Rendell, Ruth (Barbara) 1930- .. CLC 28, 48
See also Vine, Barbara
See also CA 109; CANR 32; DLB 87;
MTCW

Renoir, Jean 1894-1979 .... CLC 20
See also CA 129; 85-88

Resnais, Alain 1922-.............. CLC 16

Reverdy, Pierre 1889-1960 .... CLC 53
See also CA 97-100; 89-92

Rexroth, Kenneth
    1905-1982 ...... CLC 1, 2, 6, 11, 22, 49
See also CA 5-8R; 107; CANR 14, 34;
CDALB 1941-1968; DLB 16, 48;
DLBY 82; MTCW

Reyes, Alfonso 1889-1959 .... TCLC 33
See also CA 131; HW

Reyes y Basoalto, Ricardo Eliecer Neftali
See Neruda, Pablo

Reymont, Wladyslaw (Stanislaw)
    1868(?)-1925 .... TCLC 5
See also CA 104

Reynolds, Jonathan 1942-....... CLC 6, 38
See also CA 65-68; CANR 28

Reynolds, Joshua 1723-1792 .... LC 15
See also DLB 104

Reynolds, Michael Shane 1937- .... CLC 44
See also CA 65-68; CANR 9

Reznikoff, Charles 1894-1976 .... CLC 9
See also CA 33-36; 61-64; CAP 2; DLB 28,
45

Rezzori (d'Arezzo), Gregor von
    1914-..................... CLC 25
See also CA 122; 136

Rhine, Richard
See Silverstein, Alvin

Rhys, Jean
    1890(?)-1979 .... CLC 2, 4, 6, 14, 19, 51
See also CA 25-28R; 85-88; CANR 35;
CDBLB 1945-1960; DLB 36, 117; MTCW

Ribeiro, Darcy 1922-............. CLC 34
See also CA 33-36R

Ribeiro, Joao Ubaldo (Osorio Pimentel)
    1941-.................... CLC 10, 67
See also CA 81-84

Ribman, Ronald (Burt) 1932-....... CLC 7
See also CA 21-24R

Ricci, Nino 1959-................ CLC 70
See also CA 137

Rice, Anne 1941-................ CLC 41
See also AAYA 9; BEST 89:2; CA 65-68;
CANR 12, 36

Rice, Elmer (Leopold)
    1892-1967 .... CLC 7, 49
See also CA 21-22; 25-28R; CAP 2; DLB 4,
7; MTCW

Rice, Tim 1944-................. CLC 21
See also CA 103

Rich, Adrienne (Cecile)
    1929-...... CLC 3, 6, 7, 11, 18, 36, 73;
                                          PC 5
See also CA 9-12R; CANR 20; DLB 5, 67;
MTCW

Rich, Barbara
See Graves, Robert (von Ranke)

Rich, Robert
See Trumbo, Dalton

Richards, David Adams 1950-...... CLC 59
See also CA 93-96; DLB 53

Richards, I(vor) A(rmstrong)
    1893-1979 .... CLC 14, 24
See also CA 41-44R; 89-92; CANR 34;
DLB 27

Richardson, Anne
See Roiphe, Anne Richardson

Richardson, Dorothy Miller
    1873-1957 .... TCLC 3
See also CA 104; DLB 36

Richardson, Ethel Florence (Lindesay)
    1870-1946
See Richardson, Henry Handel
See also CA 105

Richardson, Henry Handel......... TCLC 4
See also Richardson, Ethel Florence
(Lindesay)

Richardson, Samuel 1689-1761 ...... LC 1
See also CDBLB 1660-1789; DLB 39; WLC

Richler, Mordecai
    1931-....... CLC 3, 5, 9, 13, 18, 46, 70
See also AITN 1; CA 65-68; CANR 31;
CLR 17; DLB 53; MAICYA; MTCW;
SATA 27, 44

Richter, Conrad (Michael)
    1890-1968 .... CLC 30
See also CA 5-8R; 25-28R; CANR 23;
DLB 9; MTCW; SATA 3

Riddell, J. H. 1832-1906 .... TCLC 40

Riding, Laura.................... CLC 3, 7
See also Jackson, Laura (Riding)

Riefenstahl, Berta Helene Amalia 1902-
See Riefenstahl, Leni
See also CA 108

Riefenstahl, Leni................. CLC 16
See also Riefenstahl, Berta Helene Amalia

Riffe, Ernest
See Bergman, (Ernst) Ingmar

Riley, Tex
See Creasey, John

Rilke, Rainer Maria
1875-1926 . . . . **TCLC 1, 6, 19; PC 2**
See also CA 104; 132; DLB 81; MTCW

Rimbaud, (Jean Nicolas) Arthur
1854-1891 . . . . **NCLC 4, 35; PC 3**
See also WLC

Ringmaster, The
See Mencken, H(enry) L(ouis)

Ringwood, Gwen(dolyn Margaret) Pharis
1910-1984 . . . . **CLC 48**
See also CA 112; DLB 88

Rio, Michel 19(?)- . . . . **CLC 43**

Ritsos, Giannes
See Ritsos, Yannis

Ritsos, Yannis 1909-1990 . . . . . **CLC 6, 13, 31**
See also CA 77-80; 133; CANR 39; MTCW

Ritter, Erika 1948(?)- . . . . **CLC 52**

Rivera, Jose Eustasio 1889-1928 . . . **TCLC 35**
See also HW

Rivers, Conrad Kent 1933-1968 . . . . . . **CLC 1**
See also BW; CA 85-88; DLB 41

Rivers, Elfrida
See Bradley, Marion Zimmer

Riverside, John
See Heinlein, Robert A(nson)

Rizal, Jose 1861-1896 . . . . **NCLC 27**

Roa Bastos, Augusto (Antonio)
1917- . . . . **CLC 45**
See also CA 131; DLB 113; HW

Robbe-Grillet, Alain
1922- . . . . . . **CLC 1, 2, 4, 6, 8, 10, 14, 43**
See also CA 9-12R; CANR 33; DLB 83;
MTCW

Robbins, Harold 1916- . . . . **CLC 5**
See also CA 73-76; CANR 26; MTCW

Robbins, Thomas Eugene 1936-
See Robbins, Tom
See also CA 81-84; CANR 29; MTCW

Robbins, Tom . . . . **CLC 9, 32, 64**
See also Robbins, Thomas Eugene
See also BEST 90:3; DLBY 80

Robbins, Trina 1938- . . . . **CLC 21**
See also CA 128

Roberts, Charles G(eorge) D(ouglas)
1860-1943 . . . . **TCLC 8**
See also CA 105; DLB 92; SATA 29

Roberts, Kate 1891-1985 . . . . **CLC 15**
See also CA 107; 116

Roberts, Keith (John Kingston)
1935- . . . . **CLC 14**
See also CA 25-28R

Roberts, Kenneth (Lewis)
1885-1957 . . . . **TCLC 23**
See also CA 109; DLB 9

Roberts, Michele (B.) 1949- . . . . **CLC 48**
See also CA 115

Robertson, Ellis
See Ellison, Harlan; Silverberg, Robert

Robertson, Thomas William
1829-1871 . . . . **NCLC 35**

Robinson, Edwin Arlington
1869-1935 . . . . **TCLC 5; PC 1**
See also CA 104; 133; CDALB 1865-1917;
DLB 54; MTCW

Robinson, Henry Crabb
1775-1867 . . . . **NCLC 15**
See also DLB 107

Robinson, Jill 1936- . . . . **CLC 10**
See also CA 102

Robinson, Kim Stanley 1952- . . . . . . **CLC 34**
See also CA 126

Robinson, Lloyd
See Silverberg, Robert

Robinson, Marilynne 1944- . . . . **CLC 25**
See also CA 116

Robinson, Smokey . . . . **CLC 21**
See also Robinson, William Jr.

Robinson, William Jr. 1940-
See Robinson, Smokey
See also CA 116

Robison, Mary 1949- . . . . **CLC 42**
See also CA 113; 116

Roddenberry, Eugene Wesley 1921-1991
See Roddenberry, Gene
See also CA 110; 135; CANR 37; SATA 45

Roddenberry, Gene . . . . **CLC 17**
See also Roddenberry, Eugene Wesley
See also AAYA 5; SATO 69

Rodgers, Mary 1931- . . . . **CLC 12**
See also CA 49-52; CANR 8; CLR 20;
MAICYA; SATA 8

Rodgers, W(illiam) R(obert)
1909-1969 . . . . **CLC 7**
See also CA 85-88; DLB 20

Rodman, Eric
See Silverberg, Robert

Rodman, Howard 1920(?)-1985 . . . . . **CLC 65**
See also CA 118

Rodman, Maia
See Wojciechowska, Maia (Teresa)

Rodriguez, Claudio 1934- . . . . **CLC 10**

Roelvaag, O(le) E(dvart)
1876-1931 . . . . **TCLC 17**
See also CA 117; DLB 9

Roethke, Theodore (Huebner)
1908-1963 . . . . . . **CLC 1, 3, 8, 11, 19, 46**
See also CA 81-84; CABS 2;
CDALB 1941-1968; DLB 5; MTCW

Rogers, Thomas Hunton 1927- . . . . . **CLC 57**
See also CA 89-92

Rogers, Will(iam Penn Adair)
1879-1935 . . . . **TCLC 8**
See also CA 105; DLB 11

Rogin, Gilbert 1929- . . . . **CLC 18**
See also CA 65-68; CANR 15

Rohan, Koda . . . . **TCLC 22**
See also Koda Shigeyuki

Rohmer, Eric . . . . **CLC 16**
See also Scherer, Jean-Marie Maurice

Rohmer, Sax . . . . **TCLC 28**
See also Ward, Arthur Henry Sarsfield
See also DLB 70

Roiphe, Anne Richardson 1935- . . . **CLC 3, 9**
See also CA 89-92; DLBY 80

Rolfe, Frederick (William Serafino Austin
Lewis Mary) 1860-1913 . . . . . . **TCLC 12**
See also CA 107; DLB 34

Rolland, Romain 1866-1944 . . . . **TCLC 23**
See also CA 118; DLB 65

Rolvaag, O(le) E(dvart)
See Roelvaag, O(le) E(dvart)

Romain Arnaud, Saint
See Aragon, Louis

Romains, Jules 1885-1972 . . . . **CLC 7**
See also CA 85-88; CANR 34; DLB 65;
MTCW

Romero, Jose Ruben 1890-1952 . . . **TCLC 14**
See also CA 114; 131; HW

Ronsard, Pierre de 1524-1585 . . . . **LC 6**

Rooke, Leon 1934- . . . . **CLC 25, 34**
See also CA 25-28R; CANR 23

Roper, William 1498-1578 . . . . **LC 10**

Roquelaure, A. N.
See Rice, Anne

Rosa, Joao Guimaraes 1908-1967 . . . **CLC 23**
See also CA 89-92; DLB 113

Rosen, Richard (Dean) 1949- . . . . **CLC 39**
See also CA 77-80

Rosenberg, Isaac 1890-1918 . . . . **TCLC 12**
See also CA 107; DLB 20

Rosenblatt, Joe . . . . **CLC 15**
See also Rosenblatt, Joseph

Rosenblatt, Joseph 1933-
See Rosenblatt, Joe
See also CA 89-92

Rosenfeld, Samuel 1896-1963
See Tzara, Tristan
See also CA 89-92

Rosenthal, M(acha) L(ouis) 1917- . . . **CLC 28**
See also CA 1-4R; CAAS 6; CANR 4;
DLB 5; SATA 59

Ross, Barnaby
See Dannay, Frederic

Ross, Bernard L.
See Follett, Ken(neth Martin)

Ross, J. H.
See Lawrence, T(homas) E(dward)

Ross, (James) Sinclair 1908- . . . . **CLC 13**
See also CA 73-76; DLB 88

Rossetti, Christina (Georgina)
1830-1894 . . . . **NCLC 2**
See also DLB 35; MAICYA; SATA 20;
WLC

Rossetti, Dante Gabriel
1828-1882 . . . . **NCLC 4**
See also CDBLB 1832-1890; DLB 35; WLC

Rossner, Judith (Perelman)
1935- . . . . **CLC 6, 9, 29**
See also AITN 2; BEST 90:3; CA 17-20R;
CANR 18; DLB 6; MTCW

Rostand, Edmond (Eugene Alexis)
1868-1918 . . . . **TCLC 6, 37**
See also CA 104; 126; MTCW

Roth, Henry 1906- . . . . **CLC 2, 6, 11**
See also CA 11-12; CANR 38; CAP 1;
DLB 28; MTCW

Roth, Joseph 1894-1939 . . . . **TCLC 33**
See also DLB 85

Roth, Philip (Milton)
1933- ...... **CLC 1, 2, 3, 4, 6, 9, 15, 22,
31, 47, 66**
See also BEST 90:3; CA 1-4R; CANR 1, 22,
36; CDALB 1968-1988; DLB 2, 28;
DLBY 82; MTCW; WLC

Rothenberg, Jerome 1931- .... **CLC 6, 57**
See also CA 45-48; CANR 1; DLB 5

Roumain, Jacques (Jean Baptiste)
1907-1944 .... **TCLC 19**
See also BLC 3; BW; CA 117; 125

Rourke, Constance (Mayfield)
1885-1941 .... **TCLC 12**
See also CA 107; YABC 1

Rousseau, Jean-Baptiste 1671-1741 ... **LC 9**

Rousseau, Jean-Jacques 1712-1778... **LC 14**
See also WLC

Roussel, Raymond 1877-1933 ..... **TCLC 20**
See also CA 117

Rovit, Earl (Herbert) 1927- .... **CLC 7**
See also CA 5-8R; CANR 12

Rowe, Nicholas 1674-1718 .... **LC 8**
See also DLB 84

Rowley, Ames Dorrance
See Lovecraft, H(oward) P(hillips)

Rowson, Susanna Haswell
1762(?)-1824 .... **NCLC 5**
See also DLB 37

Roy, Gabrielle 1909-1983 ...... **CLC 10, 14**
See also CA 53-56; 110; CANR 5; DLB 68;
MTCW

Rozewicz, Tadeusz 1921- .... **CLC 9, 23**
See also CA 108; CANR 36; MTCW

Ruark, Gibbons 1941- .... **CLC 3**
See also CA 33-36R; CANR 14, 31;
DLB 120

Rubens, Bernice (Ruth) 1923- ... **CLC 19, 31**
See also CA 25-28R; CANR 33; DLB 14;
MTCW

Rudkin, (James) David 1936- ...... **CLC 14**
See also CA 89-92; DLB 13

Rudnik, Raphael 1933- .... **CLC 7**
See also CA 29-32R

Ruffian, M.
See Hasek, Jaroslav (Matej Frantisek)

Ruiz, Jose Martinez .... **CLC 11**
See also Martinez Ruiz, Jose

Rukeyser, Muriel
1913-1980 .... **CLC 6, 10, 15, 27**
See also CA 5-8R; 93-96; CANR 26;
DLB 48; MTCW; SATA 22

Rule, Jane (Vance) 1931- .... **CLC 27**
See also CA 25-28R; CANR 12; DLB 60

Rulfo, Juan 1918-1986 .... **CLC 8**
See also CA 85-88; 118; CANR 26;
DLB 113; HW; MTCW

Runyon, (Alfred) Damon
1884(?)-1946 .... **TCLC 10**
See also CA 107; DLB 11, 86

Rush, Norman 1933- .... **CLC 44**
See also CA 121; 126

Rushdie, (Ahmed) Salman
1947- .... **CLC 23, 31, 55**
See also BEST 89:3; CA 108; 111;
CANR 33; MTCW

Rushforth, Peter (Scott) 1945- ..... **CLC 19**
See also CA 101

Ruskin, John 1819-1900 .... **TCLC 20**
See also CA 114; 129; CDBLB 1832-1890;
DLB 55; SATA 24

Russ, Joanna 1937- .... **CLC 15**
See also CA 25-28R; CANR 11, 31; DLB 8;
MTCW

Russell, George William 1867-1935
See A. E.
See also CA 104; CDBLB 1890-1914

Russell, (Henry) Ken(neth Alfred)
1927- .... **CLC 16**
See also CA 105

Russell, Willy 1947- .... **CLC 60**

Rutherford, Mark .... **TCLC 25**
See also White, William Hale
See also DLB 18

Ruyslinck, Ward
See Belser, Reimond Karel Maria de

Ryan, Cornelius (John) 1920-1974 ... **CLC 7**
See also CA 69-72; 53-56; CANR 38

Ryan, Michael 1946- .... **CLC 65**
See also CA 49-52; DLBY 82

Rybakov, Anatoli (Naumovich)
1911- .... **CLC 23, 53**
See also CA 126; 135

Ryder, Jonathan
See Ludlum, Robert

Ryga, George 1932-1987 .... **CLC 14**
See also CA 101; 124; DLB 60

S. S.
See Sassoon, Siegfried (Lorraine)

Saba, Umberto 1883-1957 .... **TCLC 33**
See also DLB 114

Sabatini, Rafael 1875-1950 .... **TCLC 47**

Sabato, Ernesto (R.) 1911- ...... **CLC 10, 23**
See also CA 97-100; CANR 32; HW;
MTCW

Sacastru, Martin
See Bioy Casares, Adolfo

Sacher-Masoch, Leopold von
1836(?)-1895 .... **NCLC 31**

Sachs, Marilyn (Stickle) 1927- ..... **CLC 35**
See also AAYA 2; CA 17-20R; CANR 13;
CLR 2; MAICYA; SAAS 2; SATA 3, 68

Sachs, Nelly 1891-1970 .... **CLC 14**
See also CA 17-18; 25-28R; CAP 2

Sackler, Howard (Oliver)
1929-1982 .... **CLC 14**
See also CA 61-64; 108; CANR 30; DLB 7

Sacks, Oliver (Wolf) 1933- .... **CLC 67**
See also CA 53-56; CANR 28; MTCW

Sade, Donatien Alphonse Francois Comte
1740-1814 .... **NCLC 3**

Sadoff, Ira 1945- .... **CLC 9**
See also CA 53-56; CANR 5, 21; DLB 120

Saetone
See Camus, Albert

Safire, William 1929- .... **CLC 10**
See also CA 17-20R; CANR 31

Sagan, Carl (Edward) 1934- .... **CLC 30**
See also AAYA 2; CA 25-28R; CANR 11,
36; MTCW; SATA 58

Sagan, Francoise .... **CLC 3, 6, 9, 17, 36**
See also Quoirez, Francoise
See also DLB 83

Sahgal, Nayantara (Pandit) 1927- ... **CLC 41**
See also CA 9-12R; CANR 11

Saint, H(arry) F. 1941- .... **CLC 50**
See also CA 127

St. Aubin de Teran, Lisa 1953-
See Teran, Lisa St. Aubin de
See also CA 118; 126

Sainte-Beuve, Charles Augustin
1804-1869 .... **NCLC 5**

**Saint-Exupery, Antoine (Jean Baptiste Marie
Roger) de** 1900-1944 .... **TCLC 2**
See also CA 108; 132; CLR 10; DLB 72;
MAICYA; MTCW; SATA 20; WLC

St. John, David
See Hunt, E(verette) Howard Jr.

Saint-John Perse
See Leger, (Marie-Rene) Alexis Saint-Leger

Saintsbury, George (Edward Bateman)
1845-1933 .... **TCLC 31**
See also DLB 57

Sait Faik .... **TCLC 23**
See also Abasiyanik, Sait Faik

Saki .... **TCLC 3**
See also Munro, H(ector) H(ugh)

Salama, Hannu 1936- .... **CLC 18**

Salamanca, J(ack) R(ichard)
1922- .... **CLC 4, 15**
See also CA 25-28R

Sale, J. Kirkpatrick
See Sale, Kirkpatrick

Sale, Kirkpatrick 1937- .... **CLC 68**
See also CA 13-16R; CANR 10

Salinas (y Serrano), Pedro
1891(?)-1951 .... **TCLC 17**
See also CA 117

Salinger, J(erome) D(avid)
1919- .... **CLC 1, 3, 8, 12, 55, 56; SSC 2**
See also AAYA 2; CA 5-8R; CANR 39;
CDALB 1941-1968; CLR 18; DLB 2, 102;
MAICYA; MTCW; SATA 67; WLC

Salisbury, John
See Caute, David

Salter, James 1925- .... **CLC 7, 52, 59**
See also CA 73-76

Saltus, Edgar (Everton)
1855-1921 .... **TCLC 8**
See also CA 105

Saltykov, Mikhail Evgrafovich
1826-1889 .... **NCLC 16**

Samarakis, Antonis 1919- .... **CLC 5**
See also CA 25-28R; CAAS 16; CANR 36

Sanchez, Florencio 1875-1910 .... **TCLC 37**
See also HW

Sanchez, Luis Rafael 1936- .... **CLC 23**
See also CA 128; HW

Sanchez, Sonia 1934- .... **CLC 5**
See also BLC 3; BW; CA 33-36R;
CANR 24; CLR 18; DLB 41; DLBD 8;
MAICYA; MTCW; SATA 22

Sand, George 1804-1876......... **NCLC 2**
See also DLB 119; WLC

Sandburg, Carl (August)
1878-1967 ... **CLC 1, 4, 10, 15, 35; PC 2**
See also CA 5-8R; 25-28R; CANR 35;
CDALB 1865-1917; DLB 17, 54;
MAICYA; MTCW; SATA 8; WLC

Sandburg, Charles
See Sandburg, Carl (August)

Sandburg, Charles A.
See Sandburg, Carl (August)

Sanders, (James) Ed(ward) 1939- ... **CLC 53**
See also CA 13-16R; CANR 13; DLB 16

Sanders, Lawrence 1920-.......... **CLC 41**
See also BEST 89:4; CA 81-84; CANR 33;
MTCW

Sanders, Noah
See Blount, Roy (Alton) Jr.

Sanders, Winston P.
See Anderson, Poul (William)

Sandoz, Mari(e Susette)
1896-1966 .... **CLC 28**
See also CA 1-4R; 25-28R; CANR 17;
DLB 9; MTCW; SATA 5

Saner, Reg(inald Anthony) 1931- .... **CLC 9**
See also CA 65-68

Sannazaro, Jacopo 1456(?)-1530...... **LC 8**

Sansom, William 1912-1976....... **CLC 2, 6**
See also CA 5-8R; 65-68; MTCW

Santayana, George 1863-1952..... **TCLC 40**
See also CA 115; DLB 54, 71

Santiago, Danny .... **CLC 33**
See also James, Daniel (Lewis); James,
Daniel (Lewis)
See also DLB 122

Santmyer, Helen Hooven
1895-1986 .... **CLC 33**
See also CA 1-4R; 118; CANR 15, 33;
DLBY 84; MTCW

Santos, Bienvenido N(uqui) 1911-... **CLC 22**
See also CA 101; CANR 19

Sapper .... **TCLC 44**
See also McNeile, Herman Cyril

Sappho fl. 6th cent. B.C.-.... **CMLC 3; PC 5**

Sarduy, Severo 1937-.............. **CLC 6**
See also CA 89-92; DLB 113; HW

Sargeson, Frank 1903-1982 .... **CLC 31**
See also CA 25-28R; 106; CANR 38

Sarmiento, Felix Ruben Garcia 1867-1916
See Dario, Ruben
See also CA 104

Saroyan, William
1908-1981 ..... **CLC 1, 8, 10, 29, 34, 56**
See also CA 5-8R; 103; CANR 30; DLB 7,
9, 86; DLBY 81; MTCW; SATA 23, 24;
WLC

Sarraute, Nathalie
1900- .... **CLC 1, 2, 4, 8, 10, 31**
See also CA 9-12R; CANR 23; DLB 83;
MTCW

Sarton, (Eleanor) May
1912- .... **CLC 4, 14, 49**
See also CA 1-4R; CANR 1, 34; DLB 48;
DLBY 81; MTCW; SATA 36

Sartre, Jean-Paul
1905-1980 ... **CLC 1, 4, 7, 9, 13, 18, 24,
44, 50, 52; DC 3**
See also CA 9-12R; 97-100; CANR 21;
DLB 72; MTCW; WLC

Sassoon, Siegfried (Lorraine)
1886-1967 .... **CLC 36**
See also CA 104; 25-28R; CANR 36;
DLB 20; MTCW

Satterfield, Charles
See Pohl, Frederik

Saul, John (W. III) 1942- .... **CLC 46**
See also BEST 90:4; CA 81-84; CANR 16

Saunders, Caleb
See Heinlein, Robert A(nson)

Saura (Atares), Carlos 1932-....... **CLC 20**
See also CA 114; 131; HW

Sauser-Hall, Frederic 1887-1961.... **CLC 18**
See also CA 102; 93-96; CANR 36; MTCW

Savage, Catharine
See Brosman, Catharine Savage

Savage, Thomas 1915- .... **CLC 40**
See also CA 126; 132; CAAS 15

Savan, Glenn .... **CLC 50**

Saven, Glenn 19(?)- .... **CLC 50**

Sayers, Dorothy L(eigh)
1893-1957 ....TCLC 2, 15
See also CA 104; 119; CDBLB 1914-1945;
DLB 10, 36, 77, 100; MTCW

Sayers, Valerie 1952-............. **CLC 50**
See also CA 134

Sayles, John Thomas 1950-... **CLC 7, 10, 14**
See also CA 57-60; DLB 44

Scammell, Michael .... **CLC 34**

Scannell, Vernon 1922- .... **CLC 49**
See also CA 5-8R; CANR 8, 24; DLB 27;
SATA 59

Scarlett, Susan
See Streatfeild, (Mary) Noel

Schaeffer, Susan Fromberg
1941- ....CLC 6, 11, 22
See also CA 49-52; CANR 18; DLB 28;
MTCW; SATA 22

Schary, Jill
See Robinson, Jill

Schell, Jonathan 1943-............ **CLC 35**
See also CA 73-76; CANR 12

Schelling, Friedrich Wilhelm Joseph von
1775-1854 .... **NCLC 30**
See also DLB 90

Scherer, Jean-Marie Maurice 1920-
See Rohmer, Eric
See also CA 110

Schevill, James (Erwin) 1920-....... **CLC 7**
See also CA 5-8R; CAAS 12

Schiller, Friedrich 1759-1805 .... **NCLC 39**
See also DLB 94

Schisgal, Murray (Joseph) 1926-..... **CLC 6**
See also CA 21-24R

Schlee, Ann 1934-................ **CLC 35**
See also CA 101; CANR 29; SATA 36, 44

Schlegel, August Wilhelm von
1767-1845 .... **NCLC 15**
See also DLB 94

Schlegel, Johann Elias (von)
1719(?)-1749 .... **LC 5**

Schmidt, Arno (Otto) 1914-1979.... **CLC 56**
See also CA 128; 109; DLB 69

Schmitz, Aron Hector 1861-1928
See Svevo, Italo
See also CA 104; 122; MTCW

Schnackenberg, Gjertrud 1953-..... **CLC 40**
See also CA 116; DLB 120

Schneider, Leonard Alfred 1925-1966
See Bruce, Lenny
See also CA 89-92

Schnitzler, Arthur 1862-1931 ...... **TCLC 4**
See also CA 104; DLB 81, 118

Schor, Sandra (M.) 1932(?)-1990 ... **CLC 65**
See also CA 132

Schorer, Mark 1908-1977 .... **CLC 9**
See also CA 5-8R; 73-76; CANR 7;
DLB 103

Schrader, Paul Joseph 1946-....... **CLC 26**
See also CA 37-40R; DLB 44

Schreiner, Olive (Emilie Albertina)
1855-1920 .... **TCLC 9**
See also CA 105; DLB 18

Schulberg, Budd (Wilson)
1914- .... **CLC 7, 48**
See also CA 25-28R; CANR 19; DLB 6, 26,
28; DLBY 81

Schulz, Bruno 1892-1942.......... **TCLC 5**
See also CA 115; 123

Schulz, Charles M(onroe) 1922- .... **CLC 12**
See also CA 9-12R; CANR 6; SATA 10

Schuyler, James Marcus
1923-1991 .... **CLC 5, 23**
See also CA 101; 134; DLB 5

Schwartz, Delmore (David)
1913-1966 ....CLC 2, 4, 10, 45
See also CA 17-18; 25-28R; CANR 35;
CAP 2; DLB 28, 48; MTCW

Schwartz, Ernst
See Ozu, Yasujiro

Schwartz, John Burnham 1965- .... **CLC 59**
See also CA 132

Schwartz, Lynne Sharon 1939-..... **CLC 31**
See also CA 103

Schwartz, Muriel A.
See Eliot, T(homas) S(tearns)

Schwarz-Bart, Andre 1928-....... **CLC 2, 4**
See also CA 89-92

Schwarz-Bart, Simone 1938-........ **CLC 7**
See also CA 97-100

Schwob, (Mayer Andre) Marcel
1867-1905 .... **TCLC 20**
See also CA 117; DLB 123

Sciascia, Leonardo
1921-1989 .... **CLC 8, 9, 41**
See also CA 85-88; 130; CANR 35; MTCW

Scoppettone, Sandra 1936-........ **CLC 26**
See also CA 5-8R; SATA 9

Sheldon, Alice Hastings Bradley
1915(?)-1987
See Tiptree, James Jr.
See also CA 108; 122; CANR 34; MTCW

Sheldon, John
See Bloch, Robert (Albert)

Shelley, Mary Wollstonecraft (Godwin)
1797-1851 . . . . **NCLC 14**
See also CDBLB 1789-1832; DLB 110, 116;
SATA 29; WLC

Shelley, Percy Bysshe
1792-1822 . . . . **NCLC 18**
See also CDBLB 1789-1832; DLB 96, 110;
WLC

Shepard, Jim 1956- . . . . **CLC 36**
See also CA 137

Shepard, Lucius 19(?)- . . . . **CLC 34**
See also CA 128

Shepard, Sam
1943- . . . . **CLC 4, 6, 17, 34, 41, 44**
See also AAYA 1; CA 69-72; CABS 3;
CANR 22; DLB 7; MTCW

Shepherd, Michael
See Ludlum, Robert

Sherburne, Zoa (Morin) 1912- . . . . . . **CLC 30**
See also CA 1-4R; CANR 3, 37; MAICYA;
SATA 3

Sheridan, Frances 1724-1766 . . . . **LC 7**
See also DLB 39, 84

Sheridan, Richard Brinsley
1751-1816 . . . . **NCLC 5; DC 1**
See also CDBLB 1660-1789; DLB 89; WLC

Sherman, Jonathan Marc . . . . **CLC 55**

Sherman, Martin 1941(?)- . . . . **CLC 19**
See also CA 116; 123

Sherwin, Judith Johnson 1936- . . . **CLC 7, 15**
See also CA 25-28R; CANR 34

Sherwood, Robert E(mmet)
1896-1955 . . . . **TCLC 3**
See also CA 104; DLB 7, 26

Shiel, M(atthew) P(hipps)
1865-1947 . . . . **TCLC 8**
See also CA 106

Shiga, Naoya 1883-1971 . . . . **CLC 33**
See also CA 101; 33-36R

Shimazaki Haruki 1872-1943
See Shimazaki Toson
See also CA 105; 134

Shimazaki Toson . . . . **TCLC 5**
See also Shimazaki Haruki

Sholokhov, Mikhail (Aleksandrovich)
1905-1984 . . . . **CLC 7, 15**
See also CA 101; 112; MTCW; SATA 36

Shone, Patric
See Hanley, James

Shreve, Susan Richards 1939- . . . . . . **CLC 23**
See also CA 49-52; CAAS 5; CANR 5, 38;
MAICYA; SATA 41, 46

Shue, Larry 1946-1985 . . . . **CLC 52**
See also CA 117

Shu-Jen, Chou 1881-1936
See Hsun, Lu
See also CA 104

Shulman, Alix Kates 1932- . . . . . . **CLC 2, 10**
See also CA 29-32R; SATA 7

Shuster, Joe 1914- . . . . **CLC 21**

Shute, Nevil . . . . **CLC 30**
See also Norway, Nevil Shute

Shuttle, Penelope (Diane) 1947- . . . . . **CLC 7**
See also CA 93-96; CANR 39; DLB 14, 40

Sidney, Mary 1561-1621 . . . . **LC 19**

Sidney, Sir Philip 1554-1586 . . . . **LC 19**
See also CDBLB Before 1660

Siegel, Jerome 1914- . . . . **CLC 21**
See also CA 116

Siegel, Jerry
See Siegel, Jerome

Sienkiewicz, Henryk (Adam Alexander Pius)
1846-1916 . . . . **TCLC 3**
See also CA 104; 134

Sierra, Gregorio Martinez
See Martinez Sierra, Gregorio

Sierra, Maria (de la O'LeJarraga) Martinez
See Martinez Sierra, Maria (de la
O'LeJarraga)

Sigal, Clancy 1926- . . . . **CLC 7**
See also CA 1-4R

Sigourney, Lydia Howard (Huntley)
1791-1865 . . . . **NCLC 21**
See also DLB 1, 42, 73

Siguenza y Gongora, Carlos de
1645-1700 . . . . **LC 8**

Sigurjonsson, Johann 1880-1919 . . . **TCLC 27**

Sikelianos, Angelos 1884-1951 . . . . **TCLC 39**

Silkin, Jon 1930- . . . . **CLC 2, 6, 43**
See also CA 5-8R; CAAS 5; DLB 27

Silko, Leslie Marmon 1948- . . . . **CLC 23, 74**
See also CA 115; 122

Sillanpaa, Frans Eemil 1888-1964 . . . **CLC 19**
See also CA 129; 93-96; MTCW

Sillitoe, Alan
1928- . . . . **CLC 1, 3, 6, 10, 19, 57**
See also AITN 1; CA 9-12R; CAAS 2;
CANR 8, 26; CDBLB 1960 to Present;
DLB 14; MTCW; SATA 61

Silone, Ignazio 1900-1978 . . . . **CLC 4**
See also CA 25-28; 81-84; CANR 34;
CAP 2; MTCW

Silver, Joan Micklin 1935- . . . . **CLC 20**
See also CA 114; 121

Silverberg, Robert 1935- . . . . **CLC 7**
See also CA 1-4R; CAAS 3; CANR 1, 20,
36; DLB 8; MAICYA; MTCW; SATA 13

Silverstein, Alvin 1933- . . . . **CLC 17**
See also CA 49-52; CANR 2; CLR 25;
MAICYA; SATA 8, 69

Silverstein, Virginia B(arbara Opshelor)
1937- . . . . **CLC 17**
See also CA 49-52; CANR 2; CLR 25;
MAICYA; SATA 8, 69

Sim, Georges
See Simenon, Georges (Jacques Christian)

Simak, Clifford D(onald)
1904-1988 . . . . **CLC 1, 55**
See also CA 1-4R; 125; CANR 1, 35;
DLB 8; MTCW; SATA 56

Simenon, Georges (Jacques Christian)
1903-1989 . . . . **CLC 1, 2, 3, 8, 18, 47**
See also CA 85-88; 129; CANR 35;
DLB 72; DLBY 89; MTCW

Simic, Charles 1938- . . . **CLC 6, 9, 22, 49, 68**
See also CA 29-32R; CAAS 4; CANR 12,
33; DLB 105

Simmons, Charles (Paul) 1924- . . . . . **CLC 57**
See also CA 89-92

Simmons, Dan 1948- . . . . **CLC 44**
See also CA 138

Simmons, James (Stewart Alexander)
1933- . . . . **CLC 43**
See also CA 105; DLB 40

Simms, William Gilmore
1806-1870 . . . . **NCLC 3**
See also DLB 3, 30, 59, 73

Simon, Carly 1945- . . . . **CLC 26**
See also CA 105

Simon, Claude 1913- . . . . **CLC 4, 9, 15, 39**
See also CA 89-92; CANR 33; DLB 83;
MTCW

Simon, (Marvin) Neil
1927- . . . . **CLC 6, 11, 31, 39, 70**
See also AITN 1; CA 21-24R; CANR 26;
DLB 7; MTCW

Simon, Paul 1942(?)- . . . . **CLC 17**
See also CA 116

Simonon, Paul 1956(?)- . . . . **CLC 30**
See also The Clash

Simpson, Harriette
See Arnow, Harriette (Louisa) Simpson

Simpson, Louis (Aston Marantz)
1923- . . . . **CLC 4, 7, 9, 32**
See also CA 1-4R; CAAS 4; CANR 1;
DLB 5; MTCW

Simpson, Mona (Elizabeth) 1957- . . . **CLC 44**
See also CA 122; 135

Simpson, N(orman) F(rederick)
1919- . . . . **CLC 29**
See also CA 13-16R; DLB 13

Sinclair, Andrew (Annandale)
1935- . . . . **CLC 2, 14**
See also CA 9-12R; CAAS 5; CANR 14, 38;
DLB 14; MTCW

Sinclair, Emil
See Hesse, Hermann

Sinclair, Mary Amelia St. Clair 1865(?)-1946
See Sinclair, May
See also CA 104

Sinclair, May . . . . **TCLC 3, 11**
See also Sinclair, Mary Amelia St. Clair
See also DLB 36

Sinclair, Upton (Beall)
1878-1968 . . . . **CLC 1, 11, 15, 63**
See also CA 5-8R; 25-28R; CANR 7;
CDALB 1929-1941; DLB 9; MTCW;
SATA 9; WLC

Singer, Isaac
See Singer, Isaac Bashevis

Southern, Terry 1926- . . . . **CLC 7**
See also CA 1-4R; CANR 1; DLB 2

Southey, Robert 1774-1843 . . . . **NCLC 8**
See also DLB 93, 107; SATA 54

Southworth, Emma Dorothy Eliza Nevitte
1819-1899 . . . . **NCLC 26**

Souza, Ernest
See Scott, Evelyn

Soyinka, Wole
1934- . . . . **CLC 3, 5, 14, 36, 44; DC 2**
See also BLC 3; BW; CA 13-16R;
CANR 27, 39; MTCW; WLC

Spackman, W(illiam) M(ode)
1905-1990 . . . . **CLC 46**
See also CA 81-84; 132

Spacks, Barry 1931- . . . . **CLC 14**
See also CA 29-32R; CANR 33; DLB 105

Spanidou, Irini 1946- . . . . **CLC 44**

Spark, Muriel (Sarah)
1918- . . . . **CLC 2, 3, 5, 8, 13, 18, 40;**
SSC 10
See also CA 5-8R; CANR 12, 36;
CDBLB 1945-1960; DLB 15; MTCW

Spaulding, Douglas
See Bradbury, Ray (Douglas)

Spaulding, Leonard
See Bradbury, Ray (Douglas)

Spence, J. A. D.
See Eliot, T(homas) S(tearns)

Spencer, Elizabeth 1921- . . . . **CLC 22**
See also CA 13-16R; CANR 32; DLB 6;
MTCW; SATA 14

Spencer, Leonard G.
See Silverberg, Robert

Spencer, Scott 1945- . . . . **CLC 30**
See also CA 113; DLBY 86

Spender, Stephen (Harold)
1909- . . . . **CLC 1, 2, 5, 10, 41**
See also CA 9-12R; CANR 31;
CDBLB 1945-1960; DLB 20; MTCW

Spengler, Oswald (Arnold Gottfried)
1880-1936 . . . . **TCLC 25**
See also CA 118

Spenser, Edmund 1552(?)-1599 . . . . **LC 5**
See also CDBLB Before 1660; WLC

Spicer, Jack 1925-1965 . . . . . . **CLC 8, 18, 72**
See also CA 85-88; DLB 5, 16

Spielberg, Peter 1929- . . . . **CLC 6**
See also CA 5-8R; CANR 4; DLBY 81

Spielberg, Steven 1947- . . . . **CLC 20**
See also AAYA 8; CA 77-80; CANR 32;
SATA 32

Spillane, Frank Morrison 1918-
See Spillane, Mickey
See also CA 25-28R; CANR 28; MTCW;
SATA 66

Spillane, Mickey . . . . **CLC 3, 13**
See also Spillane, Frank Morrison

Spinoza, Benedictus de 1632-1677 . . . . **LC 9**

Spinrad, Norman (Richard) 1940- . . . **CLC 46**
See also CA 37-40R; CANR 20; DLB 8

Spitteler, Carl (Friedrich Georg)
1845-1924 . . . . **TCLC 12**
See also CA 109

Spivack, Kathleen (Romola Drucker)
1938- . . . . **CLC 6**
See also CA 49-52

Spoto, Donald 1941- . . . . **CLC 39**
See also CA 65-68; CANR 11

Springsteen, Bruce (F.) 1949- . . . . . . **CLC 17**
See also CA 111

Spurling, Hilary 1940- . . . . **CLC 34**
See also CA 104; CANR 25

Squires, Radcliffe 1917- . . . . **CLC 51**
See also CA 1-4R; CANR 6, 21

Srivastava, Dhanpat Rai 1880(?)-1936
See Premchand
See also CA 118

Stacy, Donald
See Pohl, Frederik

Stael, Germaine de
See Stael-Holstein, Anne Louise Germaine
Necker Baronn
See also DLB 119

Stael-Holstein, Anne Louise Germaine Necker
Baronn 1766-1817 . . . . **NCLC 3**
See also Stael, Germaine de

Stafford, Jean 1915-1979 . . . **CLC 4, 7, 19, 68**
See also CA 1-4R; 85-88; CANR 3; DLB 2;
MTCW; SATA 22

Stafford, William (Edgar)
1914- . . . . **CLC 4, 7, 29**
See also CA 5-8R; CAAS 3; CANR 5, 22;
DLB 5

Staines, Trevor
See Brunner, John (Kilian Houston)

Stairs, Gordon
See Austin, Mary (Hunter)

Stannard, Martin . . . . **CLC 44**

Stanton, Maura 1946- . . . . **CLC 9**
See also CA 89-92; CANR 15; DLB 120

Stanton, Schuyler
See Baum, L(yman) Frank

Stapledon, (William) Olaf
1886-1950 . . . . **TCLC 22**
See also CA 111; DLB 15

Starbuck, George (Edwin) 1931- . . . . **CLC 53**
See also CA 21-24R; CANR 23

Stark, Richard
See Westlake, Donald E(dwin)

Staunton, Schuyler
See Baum, L(yman) Frank

Stead, Christina (Ellen)
1902-1983 . . . . **CLC 2, 5, 8, 32**
See also CA 13-16R; 109; CANR 33;
MTCW

Stead, William Thomas
1849-1912 . . . . **TCLC 48**

Steele, Richard 1672-1729 . . . . **LC 18**
See also CDBLB 1660-1789; DLB 84, 101

Steele, Timothy (Reid) 1948- . . . . **CLC 45**
See also CA 93-96; CANR 16; DLB 120

Steffens, (Joseph) Lincoln
1866-1936 . . . . **TCLC 20**
See also CA 117

Stegner, Wallace (Earle) 1909- . . . **CLC 9, 49**
See also AITN 1; BEST 90:3; CA 1-4R;
CAAS 9; CANR 1, 21; DLB 9; MTCW

Stein, Gertrude
1874-1946 . . . . **TCLC 1, 6, 28, 48**
See also CA 104; 132; CDALB 1917-1929;
DLB 4, 54, 86; MTCW; WLC

Steinbeck, John (Ernst)
1902-1968 . . . . . **CLC 1, 5, 9, 13, 21, 34,**
45, 75; SSC 11
See also CA 1-4R; 25-28R; CANR 1, 35;
CDALB 1929-1941; DLB 7, 9; DLBD 2;
MTCW; SATA 9; WLC

Steinem, Gloria 1934- . . . . **CLC 63**
See also CA 53-56; CANR 28; MTCW

Steiner, George 1929- . . . . **CLC 24**
See also CA 73-76; CANR 31; DLB 67;
MTCW; SATA 62

Steiner, Rudolf 1861-1925 . . . . **TCLC 13**
See also CA 107

Stendhal 1783-1842 . . . . **NCLC 23**
See also DLB 119; WLC

Stephen, Leslie 1832-1904 . . . . **TCLC 23**
See also CA 123; DLB 57

Stephen, Sir Leslie
See Stephen, Leslie

Stephen, Virginia
See Woolf, (Adeline) Virginia

Stephens, James 1882(?)-1950 . . . . . . **TCLC 4**
See also CA 104; DLB 19

Stephens, Reed
See Donaldson, Stephen R.

Steptoe, Lydia
See Barnes, Djuna

Sterchi, Beat 1949- . . . . **CLC 65**

Sterling, Brett
See Bradbury, Ray (Douglas); Hamilton,
Edmond

Sterling, Bruce 1954- . . . . **CLC 72**
See also CA 119

Sterling, George 1869-1926 . . . . **TCLC 20**
See also CA 117; DLB 54

Stern, Gerald 1925- . . . . **CLC 40**
See also CA 81-84; CANR 28; DLB 105

Stern, Richard (Gustave) 1928- . . . **CLC 4, 39**
See also CA 1-4R; CANR 1, 25; DLBY 87

Sternberg, Josef von 1894-1969 . . . . . **CLC 20**
See also CA 81-84

Sterne, Laurence 1713-1768 . . . . **LC 2**
See also CDBLB 1660-1789; DLB 39; WLC

Sternheim, (William Adolf) Carl
1878-1942 . . . . **TCLC 8**
See also CA 105; DLB 56, 118

Stevens, Mark 1951- . . . . **CLC 34**
See also CA 122

Stevens, Wallace
1879-1955 . . . . **TCLC 3, 12, 45; PC 6**
See also CA 104; 124; CDALB 1929-1941;
DLB 54; MTCW; WLC

Stevenson, Anne (Katharine)
1933- . . . . **CLC 7, 33**
See also CA 17-20R; CAAS 9; CANR 9, 33;
DLB 40; MTCW

Stevenson, Robert Louis (Balfour)
1850-1894 . . . . **NCLC 5, 14; SSC 11**
See also CDBLB 1890-1914; CLR 10, 11;
DLB 18, 57; MAICYA; WLC; YABC 2

Swift, Jonathan   1667-1745. . . . .   **LC 1**
See also CDBLB 1660-1789; DLB 39, 95,
101; SATA 19; WLC

Swinburne, Algernon Charles
1837-1909 . . . .   **TCLC 8, 36**
See also CA 105; CDBLB 1832-1890;
DLB 35, 57; WLC

Swinfen, Ann. . . . .   **CLC 34**

Swinnerton, Frank Arthur
1884-1982 . . . .   **CLC 31**
See also CA 108; DLB 34

Swithen, John
See King, Stephen (Edwin)

Sylvia
See Ashton-Warner, Sylvia (Constance)

Symmes, Robert Edward
See Duncan, Robert (Edward)

Symonds, John Addington
1840-1893 . . . .   **NCLC 34**
See also DLB 57

Symons, Arthur   1865-1945 . . . .   **TCLC 11**
See also CA 107; DLB 19, 57

Symons, Julian (Gustave)
1912- . . . .   **CLC 2, 14, 32**
See also CA 49-52; CAAS 3; CANR 3, 33;
DLB 87; MTCW

Synge, (Edmund) J(ohn) M(illington)
1871-1909 . . . .   **TCLC 6, 37; DC 2**
See also CA 104; CDBLB 1890-1914;
DLB 10, 19

Syruc, J.
See Milosz, Czeslaw

Szirtes, George   1948-. . . . .   **CLC 46**
See also CA 109; CANR 27

Tabori, George   1914-. . . . .   **CLC 19**
See also CA 49-52; CANR 4

Tagore, Rabindranath   1861-1941. . . .   **TCLC 3**
See also CA 104; 120; MTCW

Taine, Hippolyte Adolphe
1828-1893 . . . .   **NCLC 15**

Talese, Gay   1932-. . . . .   **CLC 37**
See also AITN 1; CA 1-4R; CANR 9;
MTCW

Tallent, Elizabeth (Ann)   1954- . . . . .   **CLC 45**
See also CA 117

Tally, Ted   1952-. . . . .   **CLC 42**
See also CA 120; 124

Tamayo y Baus, Manuel
1829-1898 . . . .   **NCLC 1**

Tammsaare, A(nton) H(ansen)
1878-1940 . . . .   **TCLC 27**

Tan, Amy   1952- . . . .   **CLC 59**
See also AAYA 9; BEST 89:3; CA 136

Tandem, Felix
See Spitteler, Carl (Friedrich Georg)

Tanizaki, Jun'ichiro
1886-1965 . . . .   **CLC 8, 14, 28**
See also CA 93-96; 25-28R

Tanner, William
See Amis, Kingsley (William)

Tao Lao
See Storni, Alfonsina

Tarassoff, Lev
See Troyat, Henri

Tarbell, Ida M(inerva)
1857-1944 . . . .   **TCLC 40**
See also CA 122; DLB 47

Tarkington, (Newton) Booth
1869-1946 . . . .   **TCLC 9**
See also CA 110; DLB 9, 102; SATA 17

Tarkovsky, Andrei (Arsenyevich)
1932-1986 . . . .   **CLC 75**
See also CA 127

Tasso, Torquato   1544-1595 . . . .   **LC 5**

Tate, (John Orley) Allen
1899-1979 . . . .   **CLC 2, 4, 6, 9, 11, 14, 24**
See also CA 5-8R; 85-88; CANR 32;
DLB 4, 45, 63; MTCW

Tate, Ellalice
See Hibbert, Eleanor Burford

Tate, James (Vincent)   1943-. . .   **CLC 2, 6, 25**
See also CA 21-24R; CANR 29; DLB 5

Tavel, Ronald   1940-. . . . .   **CLC 6**
See also CA 21-24R; CANR 33

Taylor, Cecil Philip   1929-1981 . . . . .   **CLC 27**
See also CA 25-28R; 105

Taylor, Edward   1642(?)-1729. . . . . . .   **LC 11**
See also DLB 24

Taylor, Eleanor Ross   1920-. . . . .   **CLC 5**
See also CA 81-84

Taylor, Elizabeth   1912-1975 . . .   **CLC 2, 4, 29**
See also CA 13-16R; CANR 9; MTCW;
SATA 13

Taylor, Henry (Splawn)   1942-. . . . . .   **CLC 44**
See also CA 33-36R; CAAS 7; CANR 31;
DLB 5

Taylor, Kamala (Purnaiya)   1924-
See Markandaya, Kamala
See also CA 77-80

Taylor, Mildred D.. . . . .   **CLC 21**
See also BW; CA 85-88; CANR 25; CLR 9;
DLB 52; MAICYA; SAAS 5; SATA 15,
70

Taylor, Peter (Hillsman)
1917- . . . . .   **CLC 1, 4, 18, 37, 44, 50, 71;
SSC 10**
See also CA 13-16R; CANR 9; DLBY 81;
MTCW

Taylor, Robert Lewis   1912-. . . . .   **CLC 14**
See also CA 1-4R; CANR 3; SATA 10

Tchekhov, Anton
See Chekhov, Anton (Pavlovich)

Teasdale, Sara   1884-1933. . . . .   **TCLC 4**
See also CA 104; DLB 45; SATA 32

Tegner, Esaias   1782-1846. . . . .   **NCLC 2**

Teilhard de Chardin, (Marie Joseph) Pierre
1881-1955 . . . .   **TCLC 9**
See also CA 105

Temple, Ann
See Mortimer, Penelope (Ruth)

Tennant, Emma (Christina)
1937- . . . .   **CLC 13, 52**
See also CA 65-68; CAAS 9; CANR 10, 38;
DLB 14

Tenneshaw, S. M.
See Silverberg, Robert

Tennyson, Alfred
1809-1892 . . . .   **NCLC 30; PC 6**
See also CDBLB 1832-1890; DLB 32; WLC

Teran, Lisa St. Aubin de . . . .   **CLC 36**
See also St. Aubin de Teran, Lisa

Teresa de Jesus, St.   1515-1582. . . . . .   **LC 18**

Terkel, Louis   1912-
See Terkel, Studs
See also CA 57-60; CANR 18; MTCW

Terkel, Studs.   **CLC 38**
See also Terkel, Louis
See also AITN 1

Terry, C. V.
See Slaughter, Frank G(ill)

Terry, Megan   1932-. . . . .   **CLC 19**
See also CA 77-80; CABS 3; DLB 7

Tertz, Abram
See Sinyavsky, Andrei (Donatevich)

Tesich, Steve   1943(?)-. . . . .   **CLC 40, 69**
See also CA 105; DLBY 83

Teternikov, Fyodor Kuzmich   1863-1927
See Sologub, Fyodor
See also CA 104

Tevis, Walter   1928-1984 . . . .   **CLC 42**
See also CA 113

Tey, Josephine. . . . .   **TCLC 14**
See also Mackintosh, Elizabeth
See also DLB 77

Thackeray, William Makepeace
1811-1863 . . . .   **NCLC 5, 14, 22**
See also CDBLB 1832-1890; DLB 21, 55;
SATA 23; WLC

Thakura, Ravindranatha
See Tagore, Rabindranath

Tharoor, Shashi   1956-. . . . .   **CLC 70**

Thelwell, Michael Miles   1939- . . . . .   **CLC 22**
See also CA 101

Theobald, Lewis Jr.
See Lovecraft, H(oward) P(hillips)

The Prophet
See Dreiser, Theodore (Herman Albert)

Theroux, Alexander (Louis)
1939-.   **CLC 2, 25**
See also CA 85-88; CANR 20

Theroux, Paul (Edward)
1941-. . . . .   **CLC 5, 8, 11, 15, 28, 46**
See also BEST 89:4; CA 33-36R; CANR 20;
DLB 2; MTCW; SATA 44

Thesen, Sharon   1946-. . . . .   **CLC 56**

Thevenin, Denis
See Duhamel, Georges

Thibault, Jacques Anatole Francois
1844-1924
See France, Anatole
See also CA 106; 127; MTCW

Thiele, Colin (Milton)   1920-. . . . . . .   **CLC 17**
See also CA 29-32R; CANR 12, 28;
CLR 27; MAICYA; SAAS 2; SATA 14

Thomas, Audrey (Callahan)
1935-. . . . .   **CLC 7, 13, 37**
See also AITN 2; CA 21-24R; CANR 36;
DLB 60; MTCW

Thomas, D(onald) M(ichael)
1935- . . . . CLC 13, 22, 31
See also CA 61-64; CAAS 11; CANR 17;
CDBLB 1960 to Present; DLB 40;
MTCW

Thomas, Dylan (Marlais)
1914-1953 . . . . . . TCLC 1, 8, 45; PC 2;
SSC 3
See also CA 104; 120; CDBLB 1945-1960;
DLB 13, 20; MTCW; SATA 60; WLC

Thomas, (Philip) Edward
1878-1917 . . . . TCLC 10
See also CA 106; DLB 19

Thomas, Joyce Carol   1938- . . . . CLC 35
See also BW; CA 113; 116; CLR 19;
DLB 33; MAICYA; MTCW; SAAS 7;
SATA 40

Thomas, Lewis   1913- . . . . CLC 35
See also CA 85-88; CANR 38; MTCW

Thomas, Paul
See Mann, (Paul) Thomas

Thomas, Piri   1928- . . . . CLC 17
See also CA 73-76; HW

Thomas, R(onald) S(tuart)
1913- . . . . CLC 6, 13, 48
See also CA 89-92; CAAS 4; CANR 30;
CDBLB 1960 to Present; DLB 27;
MTCW

Thomas, Ross (Elmore)   1926- . . . . . . CLC 39
See also CA 33-36R; CANR 22

Thompson, Francis Clegg
See Mencken, H(enry) L(ouis)

Thompson, Francis Joseph
1859-1907 . . . . TCLC 4
See also CA 104; CDBLB 1890-1914;
DLB 19

Thompson, Hunter S(tockton)
1939- . . . . CLC 9, 17, 40
See also BEST 89:1; CA 17-20R; CANR 23;
MTCW

Thompson, Jim   1906-1976 . . . . CLC 69

Thompson, Judith . . . . CLC 39

Thomson, James   1700-1748 . . . . LC 16

Thomson, James   1834-1882 . . . . . NCLC 18

Thoreau, Henry David
1817-1862 . . . . NCLC 7, 21
See also CDALB 1640-1865; DLB 1; WLC

Thornton, Hall
See Silverberg, Robert

Thurber, James (Grover)
1894-1961 . . . . CLC 5, 11, 25; SSC 1
See also CA 73-76; CANR 17, 39;
CDALB 1929-1941; DLB 4, 11, 22, 102;
MAICYA; MTCW; SATA 13

Thurman, Wallace (Henry)
1902-1934 . . . . TCLC 6
See also BLC 3; BW; CA 104; 124; DLB 51

Ticheburn, Cheviot
See Ainsworth, William Harrison

Tieck, (Johann) Ludwig
1773-1853 . . . . NCLC 5
See also DLB 90

Tiger, Derry
See Ellison, Harlan

Tilghman, Christopher   1948(?)- . . . . . CLC 65

Tillinghast, Richard (Williford)
1940- . . . . CLC 29
See also CA 29-32R; CANR 26

Timrod, Henry   1828-1867 . . . . . . NCLC 25
See also DLB 3

Tindall, Gillian   1938- . . . . CLC 7
See also CA 21-24R; CANR 11

Tiptree, James Jr. . . . . CLC 48, 50
See also Sheldon, Alice Hastings Bradley
See also DLB 8

Titmarsh, Michael Angelo
See Thackeray, William Makepeace

Tocqueville, Alexis (Charles Henri Maurice
Clerel Comte)   1805-1859 . . . . . NCLC 7

Tolkien, J(ohn) R(onald) R(euel)
1892-1973 . . . . CLC 1, 2, 3, 8, 12, 38
See also AITN 1; CA 17-18; 45-48;
CANR 36; CAP 2; CDBLB 1914-1945;
DLB 15; MAICYA; MTCW; SATA 2,
24, 32; WLC

Toller, Ernst   1893-1939 . . . . TCLC 10
See also CA 107

Tolson, M. B.
See Tolson, Melvin B(eaunorus)

Tolson, Melvin B(eaunorus)
1898(?)-1966 . . . . CLC 36
See also BLC 3; BW; CA 124; 89-92;
DLB 48, 76

Tolstoi, Aleksei Nikolaevich
See Tolstoy, Alexey Nikolaevich

Tolstoy, Alexey Nikolaevich
1882-1945 . . . . TCLC 18
See also CA 107

Tolstoy, Count Leo
See Tolstoy, Leo (Nikolaevich)

Tolstoy, Leo (Nikolaevich)
1828-1910 . . . . . TCLC 4, 11, 17, 28, 44;
SSC 9
See also CA 104; 123; SATA 26; WLC

Tomasi di Lampedusa, Giuseppe   1896-1957
See Lampedusa, Giuseppe (Tomasi) di
See also CA 111

Tomlin, Lily . . . . CLC 17
See also Tomlin, Mary Jean

Tomlin, Mary Jean   1939(?)-
See Tomlin, Lily
See also CA 117

Tomlinson, (Alfred) Charles
1927- . . . . CLC 2, 4, 6, 13, 45
See also CA 5-8R; CANR 33; DLB 40

Tonson, Jacob
See Bennett, (Enoch) Arnold

Toole, John Kennedy
1937-1969 . . . . CLC 19, 64
See also CA 104; DLBY 81

Toomer, Jean
1894-1967 . . . . . CLC 1, 4, 13, 22; SSC 1
See also BLC 3; BW; CA 85-88;
CDALB 1917-1929; DLB 45, 51; MTCW

Torley, Luke
See Blish, James (Benjamin)

Tornimparte, Alessandra
See Ginzburg, Natalia

Torre, Raoul della
See Mencken, H(enry) L(ouis)

Torrey, E(dwin) Fuller   1937- . . . . . . CLC 34
See also CA 119

Torsvan, Ben Traven
See Traven, B.

Torsvan, Benno Traven
See Traven, B.

Torsvan, Berick Traven
See Traven, B.

Torsvan, Berwick Traven
See Traven, B.

Torsvan, Bruno Traven
See Traven, B.

Torsvan, Traven
See Traven, B.

Tournier, Michel (Edouard)
1924- . . . . CLC 6, 23, 36
See also CA 49-52; CANR 3, 36; DLB 83;
MTCW; SATA 23

Tournimparte, Alessandra
See Ginzburg, Natalia

Towers, Ivar
See Kornbluth, C(yril) M.

Townsend, Sue   1946- . . . . CLC 61
See also CA 119; 127; MTCW; SATA 48,
55

Townshend, Peter (Dennis Blandford)
1945- . . . . CLC 17, 42
See also CA 107

Tozzi, Federigo   1883-1920 . . . . TCLC 31

Traill, Catharine Parr
1802-1899 . . . . NCLC 31
See also DLB 99

Trakl, Georg   1887-1914 . . . . TCLC 5
See also CA 104

Transtroemer, Tomas (Goesta)
1931- . . . . CLC 52, 65
See also CA 117; 129

Transtromer, Tomas Gosta
See Transtroemer, Tomas (Goesta)

Traven, B.   (?)-1969 . . . . CLC 8, 11
See also CA 19-20; 25-28R; CAP 2; DLB 9,
56; MTCW

Treitel, Jonathan   1959- . . . . CLC 70

Tremain, Rose   1943-. . . . . CLC 42
See also CA 97-100; DLB 14

Tremblay, Michel   1942-. . . . . CLC 29
See also CA 116; 128; DLB 60; MTCW

Trevanian (a pseudonym)   1930(?)-. . . CLC 29
See also CA 108

Trevor, Glen
See Hilton, James

Trevor, William
1928- . . . . CLC 7, 9, 14, 25, 71
See also Cox, William Trevor
See also DLB 14

Trifonov, Yuri (Valentinovich)
1925-1981 . . . . CLC 45
See also CA 126; 103; MTCW

Trilling, Lionel   1905-1975 . . . . CLC 9, 11, 24
See also CA 9-12R; 61-64; CANR 10;
DLB 28, 63; MTCW

Trimball, W. H.
See Mencken, H(enry) L(ouis)

Tristan
See Gomez de la Serna, Ramon

Tristram
See Housman, A(lfred) E(dward)

Trogdon, William (Lewis) 1939-
See Heat-Moon, William Least
See also CA 115; 119

Trollope, Anthony 1815-1882 .. **NCLC 6, 33**
See also CDBLB 1832-1890; DLB 21, 57;
SATA 22; WLC

Trollope, Frances 1779-1863 ..... **NCLC 30**
See also DLB 21

Trotsky, Leon 1879-1940........ **TCLC 22**
See also CA 118

Trotter (Cockburn), Catharine
1679-1749 .... **LC 8**
See also DLB 84

Trout, Kilgore
See Farmer, Philip Jose

Trow, George W. S. 1943-........ **CLC 52**
See also CA 126

Troyat, Henri 1911-.............. **CLC 23**
See also CA 45-48; CANR 2, 33; MTCW

Trudeau, G(arretson) B(eekman) 1948-
See Trudeau, Garry B.
See also CA 81-84; CANR 31; SATA 35

Trudeau, Garry B.................. **CLC 12**
See also Trudeau, G(arretson) B(eekman)
See also AITN 2

Truffaut, Francois 1932-1984....... **CLC 20**
See also CA 81-84; 113; CANR 34

Trumbo, Dalton 1905-1976 .... **CLC 19**
See also CA 21-24R; 69-72; CANR 10;
DLB 26

Trumbull, John 1750-1831....... **NCLC 30**
See also DLB 31

Trundlett, Helen B.
See Eliot, T(homas) S(tearns)

Tryon, Thomas 1926-1991 .... **CLC 3, 11**
See also AITN 1; CA 29-32R; 135;
CANR 32; MTCW

Tryon, Tom
See Tryon, Thomas

Ts'ao Hsueh-ch'in 1715(?)-1763....... **LC 1**

Tsushima, Shuji 1909-1948
See Dazai, Osamu
See also CA 107

Tsvetaeva (Efron), Marina (Ivanovna)
1892-1941 .... **TCLC 7, 35**
See also CA 104; 128; MTCW

Tuck, Lily 1938-................. **CLC 70**

Tunis, John R(oberts) 1889-1975 ... **CLC 12**
See also CA 61-64; DLB 22; MAICYA;
SATA 30, 37

Tuohy, Frank.................... **CLC 37**
See also Tuohy, John Francis
See also DLB 14

Tuohy, John Francis 1925-
See Tuohy, Frank
See also CA 5-8R; CANR 3

Turco, Lewis (Putnam) 1934- ... **CLC 11, 63**
See also CA 13-16R; CANR 24; DLBY 84

Turgenev, Ivan
1818-1883 .... **NCLC 21; SSC 7**
See also WLC

Turner, Frederick 1943-........... **CLC 48**
See also CA 73-76; CAAS 10; CANR 12,
30; DLB 40

Tusan, Stan 1936-................ **CLC 22**
See also CA 105

Tutuola, Amos 1920- .... **CLC 5, 14, 29**
See also BLC 3; BW; CA 9-12R; CANR 27;
MTCW

Twain, Mark
.... **TCLC 6, 12, 19, 36, 48; SSC 6**
See also Clemens, Samuel Langhorne
See also DLB 11, 12, 23, 64, 74; WLC

Tyler, Anne
1941- .... **CLC 7, 11, 18, 28, 44, 59**
See also BEST 89:1; CA 9-12R; CANR 11,
33; DLB 6; DLBY 82; MTCW; SATA 7

Tyler, Royall 1757-1826.......... **NCLC 3**
See also DLB 37

Tynan, Katharine 1861-1931 .... **TCLC 3**
See also CA 104

Tytell, John 1939- .... **CLC 50**
See also CA 29-32R

Tyutchev, Fyodor 1803-1873..... **NCLC 34**

Tzara, Tristan .... **CLC 47**
See also Rosenfeld, Samuel

Uhry, Alfred 1936-.............. **CLC 55**
See also CA 127; 133

Ulf, Haerved
See Strindberg, (Johan) August

Ulf, Harved
See Strindberg, (Johan) August

Unamuno (y Jugo), Miguel de
1864-1936 .... **TCLC 2, 9; SSC 11**
See also CA 104; 131; DLB 108; HW;
MTCW

Undercliffe, Errol
See Campbell, (John) Ramsey

Underwood, Miles
See Glassco, John

Undset, Sigrid 1882-1949.......... **TCLC 3**
See also CA 104; 129; MTCW; WLC

Ungaretti, Giuseppe
1888-1970 .... **CLC 7, 11, 15**
See also CA 19-20; 25-28R; CAP 2;
DLB 114

Unger, Douglas 1952-............. **CLC 34**
See also CA 130

Updike, John (Hoyer)
1932- ...... **CLC 1, 2, 3, 5, 7, 9, 13, 15,
23, 34, 43, 70**
See also CA 1-4R; CABS 1; CANR 4, 33;
CDALB 1968-1988; DLB 2, 5; DLBD 3;
DLBY 80, 82; MTCW; WLC

Upshaw, Margaret Mitchell
See Mitchell, Margaret (Munnerlyn)

Upton, Mark
See Sanders, Lawrence

Urdang, Constance (Henriette)
1922- .... **CLC 47**
See also CA 21-24R; CANR 9, 24

Uris, Leon (Marcus) 1924-........ **CLC 7, 32**
See also AITN 1, 2; BEST 89:2; CA 1-4R;
CANR 1; MTCW; SATA 49

Urmuz
See Codrescu, Andrei

Ustinov, Peter (Alexander) 1921- .... **CLC 1**
See also AITN 1; CA 13-16R; CANR 25;
DLB 13

V
See Chekhov, Anton (Pavlovich)

Vaculik, Ludvik 1926- .... **CLC 7**
See also CA 53-56

Valenzuela, Luisa 1938-........... **CLC 31**
See also CA 101; CANR 32; DLB 113; HW

Valera y Alcala-Galiano, Juan
1824-1905 .... **TCLC 10**
See also CA 106

Valery, (Ambroise) Paul (Toussaint Jules)
1871-1945 .... **TCLC 4, 15**
See also CA 104; 122; MTCW

Valle-Inclan, Ramon (Maria) del
1866-1936 .... **TCLC 5**
See also CA 106

Vallejo, Antonio Buero
See Buero Vallejo, Antonio

Vallejo, Cesar (Abraham)
1892-1938 .... **TCLC 3**
See also CA 105; HW

Valle Y Pena, Ramon del
See Valle-Inclan, Ramon (Maria) del

Van Ash, Cay 1918-.............. **CLC 34**

Vanbrugh, Sir John 1664-1726 ...... **LC 21**
See also DLB 80

Van Campen, Karl
See Campbell, John W(ood Jr.)

Vance, Gerald
See Silverberg, Robert

Vance, Jack...................... **CLC 35**
See also Vance, John Holbrook
See also DLB 8

Vance, John Holbrook 1916-
See Queen, Ellery; Vance, Jack
See also CA 29-32R; CANR 17; MTCW

**Van Den Bogarde, Derek Jules Gaspard Ulric
Niven** 1921-
See Bogarde, Dirk
See also CA 77-80

Vandenburgh, Jane .... **CLC 59**

Vanderhaeghe, Guy 1951- .... **CLC 41**
See also CA 113

van der Post, Laurens (Jan) 1906- ... **CLC 5**
See also CA 5-8R; CANR 35

van de Wetering, Janwillem 1931- .. **CLC 47**
See also CA 49-52; CANR 4

Van Dine, S. S. .... **TCLC 23**
See also Wright, Willard Huntington

Van Doren, Carl (Clinton)
1885-1950 .... **TCLC 18**
See also CA 111

Van Doren, Mark 1894-1972..... **CLC 6, 10**
See also CA 1-4R; 37-40R; CANR 3;
DLB 45; MTCW

Wakoski, Diane
        1937- . . . . **CLC 2, 4, 7, 9, 11, 40**
    See also CA 13-16R; CAAS 1; CANR 9;
    DLB 5

Wakoski-Sherbell, Diane
    See Wakoski, Diane

Walcott, Derek (Alton)
        1930- . . . . **CLC 2, 4, 9, 14, 25, 42, 67**
    See also BLC 3; BW; CA 89-92; CANR 26;
    DLB 117; DLBY 81; MTCW

Waldman, Anne   1945- . . . . **CLC 7**
    See also CA 37-40R; CANR 34; DLB 16

Waldo, E. Hunter
    See Sturgeon, Theodore (Hamilton)

Waldo, Edward Hamilton
    See Sturgeon, Theodore (Hamilton)

Walker, Alice (Malsenior)
        1944- . . . . . . **CLC 5, 6, 9, 19, 27, 46, 58;
                                                            SSC 5**
    See also AAYA 3; BEST 89:4; BLC 3; BW;
    CA 37-40R; CANR 9, 27;
    CDALB 1968-1988; DLB 6, 33; MTCW;
    SATA 31

Walker, David Harry   1911-1992. . . . **CLC 14**
    See also CA 1-4R; 137; CANR 1; SATA 8;
    SATO 71

Walker, Edward Joseph   1934-
    See Walker, Ted
    See also CA 21-24R; CANR 12, 28

Walker, George F.   1947- . . . . **CLC 44, 61**
    See also CA 103; CANR 21; DLB 60

Walker, Joseph A.   1935- . . . . **CLC 19**
    See also BW; CA 89-92; CANR 26; DLB 38

Walker, Margaret (Abigail)
        1915- . . . . **CLC 1, 6**
    See also BLC 3; BW; CA 73-76; CANR 26;
    DLB 76; MTCW

Walker, Ted. . . . . **CLC 13**
    See also Walker, Edward Joseph
    See also DLB 40

Wallace, David Foster   1962- . . . . **CLC 50**
    See also CA 132

Wallace, Dexter
    See Masters, Edgar Lee

Wallace, Irving   1916-1990 . . . . . . **CLC 7, 13**
    See also AITN 1; CA 1-4R; 132; CAAS 1;
    CANR 1, 27; MTCW

Wallant, Edward Lewis
        1926-1962 . . . . **CLC 5, 10**
    See also CA 1-4R; CANR 22; DLB 2, 28;
    MTCW

Walpole, Horace   1717-1797. . . . . **LC 2**
    See also DLB 39, 104

Walpole, Hugh (Seymour)
        1884-1941 . . . . **TCLC 5**
    See also CA 104; DLB 34

Walser, Martin   1927- . . . . **CLC 27**
    See also CA 57-60; CANR 8; DLB 75

Walser, Robert   1878-1956 . . . . **TCLC 18**
    See also CA 118; DLB 66

Walsh, Jill Paton. . . . . **CLC 35**
    See also Paton Walsh, Gillian
    See also CLR 2; SAAS 3

Walter, Villiam Christian
    See Andersen, Hans Christian

Wambaugh, Joseph (Aloysius Jr.)
        1937- . . . . **CLC 3, 18**
    See also AITN 1; BEST 89:3; CA 33-36R;
    DLB 6; DLBY 83; MTCW

Ward, Arthur Henry Sarsfield   1883-1959
    See Rohmer, Sax
    See also CA 108

Ward, Douglas Turner   1930- . . . . . . **CLC 19**
    See also BW; CA 81-84; CANR 27; DLB 7,
    38

Warhol, Andy   1928(?)-1987. . . . . **CLC 20**
    See also BEST 89:4; CA 89-92; 121;
    CANR 34

Warner, Francis (Robert le Plastrier)
        1937- . . . . **CLC 14**
    See also CA 53-56; CANR 11

Warner, Marina   1946- . . . . **CLC 59**
    See also CA 65-68; CANR 21

Warner, Rex (Ernest)   1905-1986. . . . **CLC 45**
    See also CA 89-92; 119; DLB 15

Warner, Susan (Bogert)
        1819-1885 . . . . **NCLC 31**
    See also DLB 3, 42

Warner, Sylvia (Constance) Ashton
    See Ashton-Warner, Sylvia (Constance)

Warner, Sylvia Townsend
        1893-1978 . . . . **CLC 7, 19**
    See also CA 61-64; 77-80; CANR 16;
    DLB 34; MTCW

Warren, Mercy Otis   1728-1814. . . **NCLC 13**
    See also DLB 31

Warren, Robert Penn
        1905-1989 . . . **CLC 1, 4, 6, 8, 10, 13, 18,
                                                    39, 53, 59; SSC 4**
    See also AITN 1; CA 13-16R; 129;
    CANR 10; CDALB 1968-1988; DLB 2,
    48; DLBY 80, 89; MTCW; SATA 46, 63;
    WLC

Warshofsky, Isaac
    See Singer, Isaac Bashevis

Warton, Thomas   1728-1790. . . . . **LC 15**
    See also DLB 104, 109

Waruk, Kona
    See Harris, (Theodore) Wilson

Warung, Price   1855-1911. . . . . **TCLC 45**

Warwick, Jarvis
    See Garner, Hugh

Washington, Alex
    See Harris, Mark

Washington, Booker T(aliaferro)
        1856-1915 . . . . **TCLC 10**
    See also BLC 3; BW; CA 114; 125;
    SATA 28

Wassermann, (Karl) Jakob
        1873-1934 . . . . **TCLC 6**
    See also CA 104; DLB 66

Wasserstein, Wendy   1950- . . . . . . **CLC 32, 59**
    See also CA 121; 129; CABS 3

Waterhouse, Keith (Spencer)
        1929- . . . . **CLC 47**
    See also CA 5-8R; CANR 38; DLB 13, 15;
    MTCW

Waters, Roger   1944-. . . . . **CLC 35**
    See also Pink Floyd

Watkins, Frances Ellen
    See Harper, Frances Ellen Watkins

Watkins, Gerrold
    See Malzberg, Barry N(athaniel)

Watkins, Paul   1964-. . . . . **CLC 55**
    See also CA 132

Watkins, Vernon Phillips
        1906-1967 . . . . **CLC 43**
    See also CA 9-10; 25-28R; CAP 1; DLB 20

Watson, Irving S.
    See Mencken, H(enry) L(ouis)

Watson, John H.
    See Farmer, Philip Jose

Watson, Richard F.
    See Silverberg, Robert

Waugh, Auberon (Alexander)   1939- . . **CLC 7**
    See also CA 45-48; CANR 6, 22; DLB 14

Waugh, Evelyn (Arthur St. John)
        1903-1966 . . . **CLC 1, 3, 8, 13, 19, 27, 44**
    See also CA 85-88; 25-28R; CANR 22;
    CDBLB 1914-1945; DLB 15; MTCW;
    WLC

Waugh, Harriet   1944- . . . . **CLC 6**
    See also CA 85-88; CANR 22

Ways, C. R.
    See Blount, Roy (Alton) Jr.

Waystaff, Simon
    See Swift, Jonathan

Webb, (Martha) Beatrice (Potter)
        1858-1943 . . . . **TCLC 22**
    See also Potter, Beatrice
    See also CA 117

Webb, Charles (Richard)   1939- . . . . . . **CLC 7**
    See also CA 25-28R

Webb, James H(enry) Jr.   1946- . . . . **CLC 22**
    See also CA 81-84

Webb, Mary (Gladys Meredith)
        1881-1927 . . . . **TCLC 24**
    See also CA 123; DLB 34

Webb, Mrs. Sidney
    See Webb, (Martha) Beatrice (Potter)

Webb, Phyllis   1927-. . . . . **CLC 18**
    See also CA 104; CANR 23; DLB 53

Webb, Sidney (James)
        1859-1947 . . . . **TCLC 22**
    See also CA 117

Webber, Andrew Lloyd. . . . . **CLC 21**
    See also Lloyd Webber, Andrew

Weber, Lenora Mattingly
        1895-1971 . . . . **CLC 12**
    See also CA 19-20; 29-32R; CAP 1;
    SATA 2, 26

Webster, John   1579(?)-1634(?) . . . . **DC 2**
    See also CDBLB Before 1660; DLB 58;
    WLC

Webster, Noah   1758-1843 . . . . **NCLC 30**

Wedekind, (Benjamin) Frank(lin)
        1864-1918 . . . . **TCLC 7**
    See also CA 104; DLB 118

Weidman, Jerome   1913-. . . . . **CLC 7**
    See also AITN 2; CA 1-4R; CANR 1;
    DLB 28

Weil, Simone (Adolphine)
1909-1943 . . . . **TCLC 23**
See also CA 117

Weinstein, Nathan
See West, Nathanael

Weinstein, Nathan von Wallenstein
See West, Nathanael

Weir, Peter (Lindsay) 1944- . . . . **CLC 20**
See also CA 113; 123

Weiss, Peter (Ulrich)
1916-1982 . . . . **CLC 3, 15, 51**
See also CA 45-48; 106; CANR 3; DLB 69

Weiss, Theodore (Russell)
1916- . . . . **CLC 3, 8, 14**
See also CA 9-12R; CAAS 2; DLB 5

Welch, (Maurice) Denton
1915-1948 . . . . **TCLC 22**
See also CA 121

Welch, James 1940- . . . . **CLC 6, 14, 52**
See also CA 85-88

Weldon, Fay
1933(?)- . . . . **CLC 6, 9, 11, 19, 36, 59**
See also CA 21-24R; CANR 16;
CDBLB 1960 to Present; DLB 14;
MTCW

Wellek, Rene 1903- . . . . **CLC 28**
See also CA 5-8R; CAAS 7; CANR 8;
DLB 63

Weller, Michael 1942- . . . . **CLC 10, 53**
See also CA 85-88

Weller, Paul 1958- . . . . **CLC 26**

Wellershoff, Dieter 1925- . . . . **CLC 46**
See also CA 89-92; CANR 16, 37

Welles, (George) Orson
1915-1985 . . . . **CLC 20**
See also CA 93-96; 117

Wellman, Mac 1945- . . . . **CLC 65**

Wellman, Manly Wade 1903-1986 . . **CLC 49**
See also CA 1-4R; 118; CANR 6, 16;
SATA 6, 47

Wells, Carolyn 1869(?)-1942 . . . . . . **TCLC 35**
See also CA 113; DLB 11

Wells, H(erbert) G(eorge)
1866-1946 . . . . . . **TCLC 6, 12, 19; SSC 6**
See also CA 110; 121; CDBLB 1914-1945;
DLB 34, 70; MTCW; SATA 20; WLC

Wells, Rosemary 1943- . . . . **CLC 12**
See also CA 85-88; CLR 16; MAICYA;
SAAS 1; SATA 18, 69

Welty, Eudora
1909- . . . . **CLC 1, 2, 5, 14, 22, 33; SSC 1**
See also CA 9-12R; CABS 1; CANR 32;
CDALB 1941-1968; DLB 2, 102;
DLBY 87; MTCW; WLC

Wen I-to 1899-1946 . . . . **TCLC 28**

Wentworth, Robert
See Hamilton, Edmond

Werfel, Franz (V.) 1890-1945 . . . . . . **TCLC 8**
See also CA 104; DLB 81

Wergeland, Henrik Arnold
1808-1845 . . . . **NCLC 5**

Wersba, Barbara 1932- . . . . **CLC 30**
See also AAYA 2; CA 29-32R; CANR 16,
38; CLR 3; DLB 52; MAICYA; SAAS 2;
SATA 1, 58

Wertmueller, Lina 1928- . . . . **CLC 16**
See also CA 97-100; CANR 39

Wescott, Glenway 1901-1987 . . . . **CLC 13**
See also CA 13-16R; 121; CANR 23;
DLB 4, 9, 102

Wesker, Arnold 1932- . . . . **CLC 3, 5, 42**
See also CA 1-4R; CAAS 7; CANR 1, 33;
CDBLB 1960 to Present; DLB 13;
MTCW

Wesley, Richard (Errol) 1945- . . . . **CLC 7**
See also BW; CA 57-60; DLB 38

Wessel, Johan Herman 1742-1785 . . . . **LC 7**

West, Anthony (Panther)
1914-1987 . . . . **CLC 50**
See also CA 45-48; 124; CANR 3, 19;
DLB 15

West, C. P.
See Wodehouse, P(elham) G(renville)

West, (Mary) Jessamyn
1902-1984 . . . . **CLC 7, 17**
See also CA 9-12R; 112; CANR 27; DLB 6;
DLBY 84; MTCW; SATA 37

West, Morris L(anglo) 1916- . . . . . **CLC 6, 33**
See also CA 5-8R; CANR 24; MTCW

West, Nathanael
1903-1940 . . . . **TCLC 1, 14, 44**
See also CA 104; 125; CDALB 1929-1941;
DLB 4, 9, 28; MTCW

West, Paul 1930- . . . . **CLC 7, 14**
See also CA 13-16R; CAAS 7; CANR 22;
DLB 14

West, Rebecca 1892-1983 . . **CLC 7, 9, 31, 50**
See also CA 5-8R; 109; CANR 19; DLB 36;
DLBY 83; MTCW

Westall, Robert (Atkinson) 1929- . . . **CLC 17**
See also CA 69-72; CANR 18; CLR 13;
MAICYA; SAAS 2; SATA 23, 69

Westlake, Donald E(dwin)
1933- . . . . **CLC 7, 33**
See also CA 17-20R; CAAS 13; CANR 16

Westmacott, Mary
See Christie, Agatha (Mary Clarissa)

Weston, Allen
See Norton, Andre

Wetcheek, J. L.
See Feuchtwanger, Lion

Wetering, Janwillem van de
See van de Wetering, Janwillem

Wetherell, Elizabeth
See Warner, Susan (Bogert)

Whalen, Philip 1923- . . . . **CLC 6, 29**
See also CA 9-12R; CANR 5, 39; DLB 16

Wharton, Edith (Newbold Jones)
1862-1937 . . . . **TCLC 3, 9, 27; SSC 6**
See also CA 104; 132; CDALB 1865-1917;
DLB 4, 9, 12, 78; MTCW; WLC

Wharton, James
See Mencken, H(enry) L(ouis)

Wharton, William (a pseudonym)
. . . . **CLC 18, 37**
See also CA 93-96; DLBY 80

Wheatley (Peters), Phillis
1754(?)-1784 . . . . **LC 3; PC 3**
See also BLC 3; CDALB 1640-1865;
DLB 31, 50; WLC

Wheelock, John Hall 1886-1978 . . . . **CLC 14**
See also CA 13-16R; 77-80; CANR 14;
DLB 45

White, E(lwyn) B(rooks)
1899-1985 . . . . **CLC 10, 34, 39**
See also AITN 2; CA 13-16R; 116;
CANR 16, 37; CLR 1, 21; DLB 11, 22;
MAICYA; MTCW; SATA 2, 29, 44

White, Edmund (Valentine III)
1940- . . . . **CLC 27**
See also AAYA 7; CA 45-48; CANR 3, 19,
36; MTCW

White, Patrick (Victor Martindale)
1912-1990 . . **CLC 3, 4, 5, 7, 9, 18, 65, 69**
See also CA 81-84; 132; MTCW

White, Phyllis Dorothy James 1920-
See James, P. D.
See also CA 21-24R; CANR 17; MTCW

White, T(erence) H(anbury)
1906-1964 . . . . **CLC 30**
See also CA 73-76; CANR 37; MAICYA;
SATA 12

White, Terence de Vere 1912- . . . . . . **CLC 49**
See also CA 49-52; CANR 3

White, Walter
See White, Walter F(rancis)
See also BLC 3

White, Walter F(rancis)
1893-1955 . . . . **TCLC 15**
See also White, Walter
See also CA 115; 124; DLB 51

White, William Hale 1831-1913
See Rutherford, Mark
See also CA 121

Whitehead, E(dward) A(nthony)
1933- . . . . **CLC 5**
See also CA 65-68

Whitemore, Hugh (John) 1936- . . . . . **CLC 37**
See also CA 132

Whitman, Sarah Helen (Power)
1803-1878 . . . . **NCLC 19**
See also DLB 1

Whitman, Walt(er)
1819-1892 . . . . **NCLC 4, 31; PC 3**
See also CDALB 1640-1865; DLB 3, 64;
SATA 20; WLC

Whitney, Phyllis A(yame) 1903- . . . . **CLC 42**
See also AITN 2; BEST 90:3; CA 1-4R;
CANR 3, 25, 38; MAICYA; SATA 1, 30

Whittemore, (Edward) Reed (Jr.)
1919- . . . . **CLC 4**
See also CA 9-12R; CAAS 8; CANR 4;
DLB 5

Whittier, John Greenleaf
1807-1892 . . . . **NCLC 8**
See also CDALB 1640-1865; DLB 1

Whittlebot, Hernia
See Coward, Noel (Peirce)

Wicker, Thomas Grey 1926-
See Wicker, Tom
See also CA 65-68; CANR 21

Wicker, Tom . . . . CLC 7
See also Wicker, Thomas Grey

Wideman, John Edgar
1941- . . . . CLC 5, 34, 36, 67
See also BLC 3; BW; CA 85-88; CANR 14;
DLB 33

Wiebe, Rudy (H.)   1934- . . . . . . CLC 6, 11, 14
See also CA 37-40R; DLB 60

Wieland, Christoph Martin
1733-1813 . . . . NCLC 17
See also DLB 97

Wieners, John   1934- . . . . CLC 7
See also CA 13-16R; DLB 16

Wiesel, Elie(zer)   1928- . . . . CLC 3, 5, 11, 37
See also AAYA 7; AITN 1; CA 5-8R;
CAAS 4; CANR 8; DLB 83; DLBY 87;
MTCW; SATA 56

Wiggins, Marianne   1947- . . . . CLC 57
See also BEST 89:3; CA 130

Wight, James Alfred   1916-
See Herriot, James
See also CA 77-80; SATA 44, 55

Wilbur, Richard (Purdy)
1921- . . . . CLC 3, 6, 9, 14, 53
See also CA 1-4R; CABS 2; CANR 2, 29;
DLB 5; MTCW; SATA 9

Wild, Peter   1940- . . . . CLC 14
See also CA 37-40R; DLB 5

Wilde, Oscar (Fingal O'Flahertie Wills)
1854(?)-1900 . . . . TCLC 1, 8, 23, 41;
SSC 11
See also CA 104; 119; CDBLB 1890-1914;
DLB 10, 19, 34, 57; SATA 24; WLC

Wilder, Billy . . . . CLC 20
See also Wilder, Samuel
See also DLB 26

Wilder, Samuel   1906-
See Wilder, Billy
See also CA 89-92

Wilder, Thornton (Niven)
1897-1975 . . . . . CLC 1, 5, 6, 10, 15, 35;
DC 1
See also AITN 2; CA 13-16R; 61-64;
DLB 4, 7, 9; MTCW; WLC

Wilding, Michael   1942- . . . . CLC 73
See also CA 104; CANR 24

Wiley, Richard   1944- . . . . CLC 44
See also CA 121; 129

Wilhelm, Kate . . . . CLC 7
See also Wilhelm, Katie Gertrude
See also CAAS 5; DLB 8

Wilhelm, Katie Gertrude   1928-
See Wilhelm, Kate
See also CA 37-40R; CANR 17, 36; MTCW

Wilkins, Mary
See Freeman, Mary Eleanor Wilkins

Willard, Nancy   1936- . . . . CLC 7, 37
See also CA 89-92; CANR 10, 39; CLR 5;
DLB 5, 52; MAICYA; MTCW;
SATA 30, 37, 71

Williams, C(harles) K(enneth)
1936- . . . . CLC 33, 56
See also CA 37-40R; DLB 5

Williams, Charles
See Collier, James L(incoln)

Williams, Charles (Walter Stansby)
1886-1945 . . . . TCLC 1, 11
See also CA 104; DLB 100

Williams, (George) Emlyn
1905-1987 . . . . CLC 15
See also CA 104; 123; CANR 36; DLB 10,
77; MTCW

Williams, Hugo   1942- . . . . CLC 42
See also CA 17-20R; DLB 40

Williams, J. Walker
See Wodehouse, P(elham) G(renville)

Williams, John A(lfred)   1925- . . . . CLC 5, 13
See also BLC 3; BW; CA 53-56; CAAS 3;
CANR 6, 26; DLB 2, 33

Williams, Jonathan (Chamberlain)
1929- . . . . CLC 13
See also CA 9-12R; CAAS 12; CANR 8;
DLB 5

Williams, Joy   1944- . . . . CLC 31
See also CA 41-44R; CANR 22

Williams, Norman   1952- . . . . CLC 39
See also CA 118

Williams, Tennessee
1911-1983 . . . . CLC 1, 2, 5, 7, 8, 11, 15,
19, 30, 39, 45, 71
See also AITN 1, 2; CA 5-8R; 108;
CABS 3; CANR 31; CDALB 1941-1968;
DLB 7; DLBD 4; DLBY 83; MTCW;
WLC

Williams, Thomas (Alonzo)
1926-1990 . . . . CLC 14
See also CA 1-4R; 132; CANR 2

Williams, William C.
See Williams, William Carlos

Williams, William Carlos
1883-1963 . . . CLC 1, 2, 5, 9, 13, 22, 42,
67
See also CA 89-92; CANR 34;
CDALB 1917-1929; DLB 4, 16, 54, 86;
MTCW

Williamson, David Keith   1942- . . . . . CLC 56
See also CA 103

Williamson, Jack . . . . CLC 29
See also Williamson, John Stewart
See also CAAS 8; DLB 8

Williamson, John Stewart   1908-
See Williamson, Jack
See also CA 17-20R; CANR 23

Willie, Frederick
See Lovecraft, H(oward) P(hillips)

Willingham, Calder (Baynard Jr.)
1922- . . . . CLC 5, 51
See also CA 5-8R; CANR 3; DLB 2, 44;
MTCW

Willis, Charles
See Clarke, Arthur C(harles)

Willy
See Colette, (Sidonie-Gabrielle)

Willy, Colette
See Colette, (Sidonie-Gabrielle)

Wilson, A(ndrew) N(orman)   1950- . . CLC 33
See also CA 112; 122; DLB 14

Wilson, Angus (Frank Johnstone)
1913-1991 . . . . CLC 2, 3, 5, 25, 34
See also CA 5-8R; 134; CANR 21; DLB 15;
MTCW

Wilson, August
1945- . . . . CLC 39, 50, 63; DC 2
See also BLC 3; BW; CA 115; 122; MTCW

Wilson, Brian   1942- . . . . CLC 12

Wilson, Colin   1931- . . . . CLC 3, 14
See also CA 1-4R; CAAS 5; CANR 1, 22,
33; DLB 14; MTCW

Wilson, Dirk
See Pohl, Frederik

Wilson, Edmund
1895-1972 . . . . CLC 1, 2, 3, 8, 24
See also CA 1-4R; 37-40R; CANR 1;
DLB 63; MTCW

Wilson, Ethel Davis (Bryant)
1888(?)-1980 . . . . CLC 13
See also CA 102; DLB 68; MTCW

Wilson, John (Anthony) Burgess
1917- . . . . CLC 8, 10, 13
See also Burgess, Anthony
See also CA 1-4R; CANR 2; MTCW

Wilson, John   1785-1854 . . . . NCLC 5

Wilson, Lanford   1937- . . . . CLC 7, 14, 36
See also CA 17-20R; CABS 3; DLB 7

Wilson, Robert M.   1944- . . . . CLC 7, 9
See also CA 49-52; CANR 2; MTCW

Wilson, Robert McLiam   1964- . . . . . CLC 59
See also CA 132

Wilson, Sloan   1920- . . . . CLC 32
See also CA 1-4R; CANR 1

Wilson, Snoo   1948- . . . . CLC 33
See also CA 69-72

Wilson, William S(mith)   1932- . . . . . CLC 49
See also CA 81-84

Winchilsea, Anne (Kingsmill) Finch Counte
1661-1720 . . . . LC 3

Windham, Basil
See Wodehouse, P(elham) G(renville)

Wingrove, David (John)   1954- . . . . . . CLC 68
See also CA 133

Winters, Janet Lewis . . . . CLC 41
See also Lewis, Janet
See also DLBY 87

Winters, (Arthur) Yvor
1900-1968 . . . . CLC 4, 8, 32
See also CA 11-12; 25-28R; CAP 1;
DLB 48; MTCW

Winterson, Jeanette   1959- . . . . CLC 64
See also CA 136

Wiseman, Frederick   1930- . . . . CLC 20

Wister, Owen   1860-1938 . . . . TCLC 21
See also CA 108; DLB 9, 78; SATA 62

Witkacy
See Witkiewicz, Stanislaw Ignacy

Witkiewicz, Stanislaw Ignacy
1885-1939 . . . . TCLC 8
See also CA 105

Wittig, Monique   1935(?)- . . . . CLC 22
See also CA 116; 135; DLB 83

Wittlin, Jozef   1896-1976 . . . . CLC 25
See also CA 49-52; 65-68; CANR 3

Zangwill, Israel 1864-1926........ **TCLC 16**
 See also CA 109; DLB 10

Zappa, Francis Vincent Jr. 1940-
 See Zappa, Frank
 See also CA 108

Zappa, Frank..................... **CLC 17**
 See also Zappa, Francis Vincent Jr.

Zaturenska, Marya 1902-1982.... **CLC 6, 11**
 See also CA 13-16R; 105; CANR 22

Zelazny, Roger (Joseph) 1937-..... **CLC 21**
 See also AAYA 7; CA 21-24R; CANR 26;
  DLB 8; MTCW; SATA 39, 57

Zhdanov, Andrei A(lexandrovich)
 1896-1948 .... **TCLC 18**
 See also CA 117

Zhukovsky, Vasily 1783-1852.... **NCLC 35**

Ziegenhagen, Eric .... **CLC 55**

Zimmer, Jill Schary
 See Robinson, Jill

Zimmerman, Robert
 See Dylan, Bob

Zindel, Paul 1936- .... **CLC 6, 26**
 See also AAYA 2; CA 73-76; CANR 31;
  CLR 3; DLB 7, 52; MAICYA; MTCW;
  SATA 16, 58

Zinov'Ev, A. A.
 See Zinoviev, Alexander (Aleksandrovich)

Zinoviev, Alexander (Aleksandrovich)
 1922- .... **CLC 19**
 See also CA 116; 133; CAAS 10

Zoilus
 See Lovecraft, H(oward) P(hillips)

Zola, Emile (Edouard Charles Antoine)
 1840-1902 .... **TCLC 1, 6, 21, 41**
 See also CA 104; 138; DLB 123; WLC

Zoline, Pamela 1941-............. **CLC 62**

Zorrilla y Moral, Jose 1817-1893.. **NCLC 6**

Zoshchenko, Mikhail (Mikhailovich)
 1895-1958 .... **TCLC 15**
 See also CA 115

Zuckmayer, Carl 1896-1977........ **CLC 18**
 See also CA 69-72; DLB 56

Zuk, Georges
 See Skelton, Robin

Zukofsky, Louis
 1904-1978 .... **CLC 1, 2, 4, 7, 11, 18**
 See also CA 9-12R; 77-80; CANR 39;
  DLB 5; MTCW

Zweig, Paul 1935-1984......... **CLC 34, 42**
 See also CA 85-88; 113

Zweig, Stefan 1881-1942 .... **TCLC 17**
 See also CA 112; DLB 81, 118

CLC Cumulative Nationality Index

Nationality Index

Nationality Index

Nationality Index

CLC-75 Title Index

ISBN 0-8103-4981-7

90000

9 780810 349810